HTML:
The Complete Reference

HTML: The Complete Reference

Reference

Thomas A. Powell

Osborne **McGraw-Hill**

Berkeley New York St. Louis San Francisco
Auckland Bogotá Hamburg London Madrid
Mexico City Milan Montreal New Delhi Panama City
Paris São Paulo Singapore Sydney
Tokyo Toronto

Osborne/**McGraw-Hill**
2600 Tenth Street
Berkeley, California 94710
U.S.A.

For information on translations or book distributors outside the U.S.A., or to arrange bulk purchase discounts for sales promotions, premiums, or fund-raisers, please contact Osborne/**McGraw-Hill** at the above address.

HTML: The Complete Reference

234567890 AGM AGM 901987654321098

ISBN 0-07-882397-8

Publisher
Brandon A. Nordin

Editor-in-Chief
Scott Rogers

Acquisitions Editor
Megg Bonar

Project Editor
Emily Rader

Editorial Assistant
Stephane Thomas

Technical Editor
MegaZone

Copy Editor
Kimberly Torgerson

Proofreaders
Linda Medoff
Paul Medoff
Roberta Rieger

Indexer
David Heiret

Computer Designer
Sue Albert

Illustrator
Arlette Crosland

About the Author...

Thomas Powell has long been involved in the Internet community, first with network support at UCLA's PICnet, followed by several years at CERFnet. After leaving CERFnet in 1994 he founded Powell Internet Consulting, LLC (www.pint.com), a firm specializing in Web research and development and site construction for high-technology companies. His articles about the Web have been published in *NetGuide*, *Internet Week* (formerly called *Communications Week*), and other magazines. His Web technology column, "The Web Mechanic," appeared in the print and online versions of *Interactive Age* throughout 1996. He has also edited numerous books about the Internet for Prentice-Hall and teaches Web publishing classes at the University of California, San Diego Extension, where he serves as the senior instructor and faculty advisor in the Information Technologies program. Mr. Powell holds a Bachelor of Science from UCLA and a Master's degree in Computer Science from UCSD.

Contents at a Glance

Contents

Acknowledgments

Writing a comprehensive book about a topic as large as HTML is a daunting task. As my business partner Jimmy Tam is fond of saying, "Don't let anybody tell you that HTML is easy." This is more true than any of us would like to admit. Even though I have taught HTML at UCSD, written numerous articles on the subject, and been involved in the construction of dozens of corporate sites, I am just as guilty as anybody else of underestimating the true details and complexities of the language when you get beyond layout. The specifications aren't perfect, documentation varies among browser vendors, and there is a great deal of misconception and oral history floating around the Web. Worst of all, it's a continuously moving target. The new HTML 4.0 specification represents a significant change in the flavor of HTML. I and many others tried as hard as we could to clarify everything to our understanding; I would like to thank those who made the extra effort to make this more than just another HTML book.

First I would like to thank all the staff members at PINT who put up with their over-committed, grumpy boss and his big book project. Dan Whitworth did a great job fixing what I thought were complete sentences, as well as putting everything else together. Dominique Cutts and David Jones provided indispensable help with editing, research, and the gigantic reference section. Jimmy Tam provided research for the server-side chapter. Rob McFarlane produced quality illustrations on demand. Tyde Richards was especially helpful in providing hard-to-find information and insight into XML and other emerging technologies; he deserves much of the credit for Chapter 16.

Megg Bonar at Osborne McGraw-Hill, who graciously allowed me to write this book, provided the appropriate heat to keep this project running. I did get scorched a few times, but Megg, Emily Rader, Gordon Hurd, and Stephane Thomas made sure that things were in and edited properly. My technical editor, MegaZone from Livingston Enterprises, Inc., kept me on track and provided a voice of reason, as well as an attention to detail that is rare in this field. Don't let the name fool you; he is a real HTML expert in his own right. Thanks also to Microsoft's Christine Chang, who provided assistance in dealing with Microsoft technology ambiguities.

My family and friends, particularly my sister Diana Powell and her friend Michael Collins, provided moral support and the essential junk food deliveries (chili dogs and soda) that ensured the eventual completion of this project. Special thanks to my good friends at Datanet in Mexico City, particularly Tony Rihan, who have always shown support and friendship when I have needed it. Apologies to neglected friends, especially George and Penny, for missing their wedding in Hawaii. I thought I would be finished in time. I am sure you'll be very happy together.

Tim Sears and Troy Snyder at ConnectNet deserve thanks for offering to host the www.htmlref.com Web site. Last, the staff at UCSD Extension, particularly Pete Rossi, has provided me with the opportunity to teach Web publishing over the past three years. The students there have provided great feedback on much of the content included in this book.

Thomas A. Powell

Preface

Times change. Web pages and HTML are not what they used to be. HTML 4.0 is nearly finished, Dynamic HTML is taking off, and style sheets are now well supported by Netscape and Microsoft's Internet Explorer. The Web is getting even more complex. Vestigial elements of the past, like <ISINDEX>, are rapidly disappearing. Despite this rapid change, many people still believe the future of HTML is dire. Some pundits even predict that the need for intimate knowledge of HTML may go away in a year or two. This doesn't seem ridiculous when you consider WYSIWYG editors like Microsoft's FrontPage. These tools provide the illusion that we are a mere drag-and-drop away from a "killer Web site." We will eventually get there, but for the moment things remain complex. WYSIWYG tools provide an illusion of simplicity, but the instability of HTML and the lack of control over layout still make custom coding a necessity. If anything, authoring Web pages is becoming *more* complex.

HTML is the heart and soul of Web pages. It is still an important technology and probably will be for at least for the next few years. Eventually, the tools will catch up. For now, learning the basics of HTML isn't hard. If you arm yourself with a tool, you can produce decent HTML code relatively quickly. As a teacher of Web publishing classes at UCSD, I know that students can produce very nice Web pages after only a few classes. On the other hand, mastering HTML can be a daunting task. Errors creep into pages, particularly across browsers, and new elements are invented all the time. Coding techniques are becoming more important. Furthermore, the latest version of HTML represents a serious increase in the number of attributes available to modify HTML elements. This book attempts to bring the ideas of HTML 4.0, Netscape, Microsoft, and even WebTV together with new technologies that affect HTML, like Cascading Style Sheets (CSS) and Dynamic HTML (DHTML). Don't forget that there is more to making Web pages than HTML; I'll hint at this where I can. But rather than try to talk about everything related to Web design, I want to do one thing the best I can: cover HTML. This isn't just meant to be a book about learning HTML, either. I want this to be a book you can come back to if you forget an element's syntax or just want to look something up. I want to be current and cover Netscape, Microsoft, WebTV, and any other important HTML viewing platform, as well as show the relationship of HTML to emerging technologies such as style sheets and present the open issues facing HTML. I would even like to stimulate your thought about your authoring techniques. If I've done a good job, this book will be true to its name—a complete reference.

Thomas A. Powell
tpowell@pint.com
December 1997

How This Book Is Organized

The first half of this book provides information that can help you learn HTML from scratch, brush up on the basics, and learn about some of the new aspects of HTML 4.0 and related technologies. HTML beginners will want to read the book in order. Experienced HTML coders will probably want to skim the first six chapters and begin reading carefully around Chapter 7, paying particular attention to the chapters about tables, forms, style sheets, and programming facilities, as these areas are undergoing changes.

- **Chapters 1–3** provide an introduction to the ideas of HTML, the Web, and the Web publishing process.
- **Chapters 4–9** cover core HTML issues.
- **Chapter 10** discusses style sheets.
- **Chapters 11–14** address programming and HTML.
- **Chapter 15** explains how to deliver a Web site.
- **Chapters 16–17** inform you about advanced technologies and trends, including XML.
- **Appendixes A–F** provide a wealth of reference information about HTML, including a complete element reference, a style sheet rule guide, a list of character entities, information on how to read document type definitions, and a variety of other useful charts.

Updates on the Web

Errata, HTML examples, and updates are available on the Web at www.htmlref.com, as well as linked from Osborne/McGraw-Hill's Web site (www.osborne.com). For definitive HTML information, be sure to frequent the World Wide Web Consortium's site at www.w3.org.

The Complete Reference

HTML

Chapter 1

Introduction to HTML

W hat exactly is Hypertext Markup Language (HTML)? HTML is the text markup language currently used on the World Wide Web. If you have ever written a school report or business memo, you are undoubtedly familiar with text markup. Your documents probably came back to you covered in red ink, courtesy of your teacher or boss; and the special symbols and acronyms used in those editorial markups suggested changes for you to interpret or implement (see Figure 1-1). In that scenario, markup was separate from the actual content of your document. When you create a document with a word processing program like Microsoft Word or WordPerfect, the program uses markup language to indicate the structure and formatting of that electronic document. What you see on your screen looks like a page of formatted text; the rest is done out of sight. HTML is the not-so-behind-the-scenes markup language that you use to tell Web browsers how to display Web pages.

Basic HTML Concepts

The behind-the-scenes markup used in word processing programs is similar to the HTML markup used to create Web pages. In the case of HTML, markup commands directed to your Web-based content tell the browser software the structure of the document, and where possible, how you want it to be displayed. If you wished to display a section of text in boldface, you would surround the corresponding text with the boldface markup tags **<B>** and **</B>**, as shown here:

```
<B>This is important text</B>
```

When the browser reads a document that has HTML markup in it, it determines how to render it onscreen by considering the HTML elements embedded within the

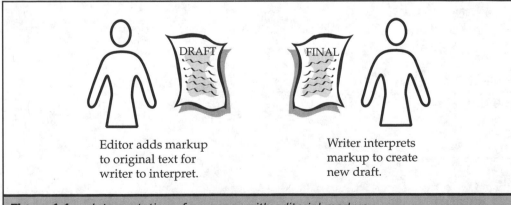

Editor adds markup to original text for writer to interpret.

Writer interprets markup to create new draft.

Figure 1-1.   *Interpretation of an essay with editorial markup*

document (see Figure 1-2). Be aware, however, that browsers don't always render things the way you think they will. This is due in part to the design of HTML and in part to the nature of the Web, as discussed in Chapters 3 and 4.

An HTML document is simply a text file that contains the information you want to publish. It also contains embedded instructions, called *elements*, that indicate how a Web browser should structure or present the document. In Figure 1-3, the HTML elements are highlighted in a bold font. These are explained in greater detail later in this chapter.

By looking at Figure 1-3, you should be able to tell that HTML elements generally consist of a pair of angle-bracketed tags surrounding some text. The *end tag* (**</TAG>**) is just like the *start tag* (**<TAG>**), except that it has a slash (*/*) in it, as shown here:

```
<TAG>  ←——— Start tag

    . . .
    Text that the tags affect
    . . .
</TAG>  ←——— End tag
```

HTML elements indicate the "markup" on the surrounded text. They may indicate the meaning of the enclosed information (for example, a citation) or how it should be rendered (for example, in bold). HTML elements normally consist of a pair of tags called *container* tags, because content goes between them. However, some elements, such as the horizontal rule tag **<HR>**, do not have a corresponding end tag. These are

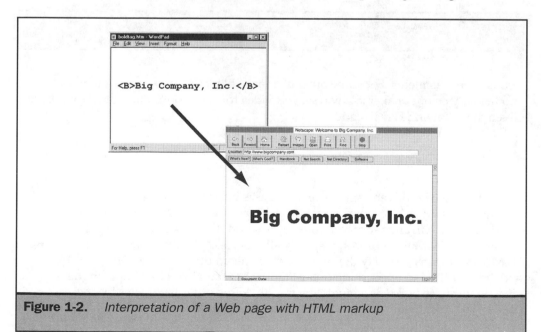

Figure 1-2.   *Interpretation of a Web page with HTML markup*

```
<!DOCTYPE HTML PUBLIC "-//W3C//DTD HTML 3.2 Final//EN">
<HTML>
<HEAD>
<TITLE>The Big Company's Big Home Page</TITLE>
</HEAD>
<BODY>
<H1 ALIGN="CENTER">Big Company, Inc.</H1>
<HR>
<IMG SRC="logo.gif" ALIGN="LEFT">
<P>Welcome to Big Company, Inc.--your best source
 for widgets and cogs. We do widgets right!</P>
<BR><BR>
<UL>
<LI><A HREF="new.htm">What's New</A>
<LI><A HREF="services.htm">Products</A>
<LI><A HREF="staff.htm">Staff</A>
<LI><A HREF="contact.htm">Contact</A>
</UL>
<HR>
<ADDRESS>webmaster@bigcompany.com</ADDRESS>
</BODY>
</HTML>
```

Figure 1-3.   *Sample HTML document*

termed *empty* elements. For some other elements, like the paragraph element **<P>**, the end tag may be optional. It is always a good idea to use the end tag if one is available. Given the following HTML code,

```
<B>This is important</B>
```

a Web browser should render the phrase "This is important" in a bold typeface.

The World Wide Web Consortium (W3C) is an organization that attempts to standardize HTML and other technologies used on the Web. In order to provide a standard, the W3C must carefully specify all aspects of the technology. In the case of HTML, this means precisely defining the elements in the language. The W3C has defined HTML as an application of the Standard Generalized Markup Language (SGML). In short, SGML is a language used to define other languages by specifying the allowed document structure in the form of a *document type definition (DTD),* a document that indicates the syntax that can be used for elements. To indicate the particular DTD an HTML file conforms to, all HTML files should begin with a **<!DOCTYPE>** indicator. Unfortunately, DOCTYPE is rarely used, and HTML's relationship to SGML is not well understood by many HTML writers. Most browsers don't seem to care if a document type is indicated or not. The ideas behind SGML and the benefits of using the **<!DOCTYPE>** statement are discussed in Chapter 2. An HTML file usually begins with the **<HTML>** element, which indicates that the contents of the file include markup. The file should end with that element's end tag, **</HTML>**. The rest of a typical HTML file is composed of the head and the body.

The head, which is enclosed within the **<HEAD>** element (consisting of the **<HEAD>** and **</HEAD>** tags), includes supplementary information about the document, such as the title of the document, which most browsers display in a title bar at the top of the browser window. The title is indicated between the **<TITLE>** and **</TITLE>** tags. The document title is required under the current HTML specification. While some browsers may not require the inclusion of the **<TITLE>** element, it should always be included for correctness, book marking, and the sake of good HTML style.

Because the information in the heading contains information about information—in this case information about the document itself—it is generally referred to as *meta-information*. This is a very important and often overlooked aspect of HTML documents. Search engines like Lycos use meta-information to index Web pages. Besides meta-information, the head of a document can also include author contact information, scripts, style sheets, or comments.

The body, which is enclosed between **<BODY>** and **</BODY>** tags, contains the actual content and appropriate markup tags needed to render the page. A basic HTML template is shown in Figure 1-4.

```
<!DOCTYPE HTML PUBLIC "-//W3C//DTD HTML 3.2 Final//EN">
<HTML>
<HEAD>
<TITLE>Document Title</TITLE>
 ...Other supplementary information goes here...
</HEAD>
<BODY>

 ...Marked-up text goes here...

</BODY>
</HTML>
```

Figure 1-4.   *HTML document template*

Note   *In the template in Figure 1-4, an HTML 3.2 document type indicator is used. This is an example of a document type. Other HTML standard conformance indicators are also possible, as discussed in Chapter 2.*

Now that you have a template, take a look at an example HTML document, as shown in Figure 1-5, that uses four elements. These are some of the most common elements used in HTML documents:

- The **<TITLE>** and **</TITLE>** tag pair specify the title of the document.
- The **<H1>** and **</H1>** header tag pair create a headline.
- The **<P>** and **</P>** paragraph tag pair indicate paragraphs of text.
- The **<HR>** element, which has no end tag, inserts a horizontal rule, or bar, across the screen.

If you are using a word processing program, you can type the example in and save it with a filename like first.htm or first.html. Your file must end in either the .htm or .html extension in order for a browser to read it properly. If you do not save your file with the appropriate extension, the browser will not attempt to interpret the HTML markup. When this happens, the codes appear in the browser window as shown in Figure 1-6.

```
<!DOCTYPE HTML PUBLIC "-//W3C//DTD HTML 3.2 Final//EN">
<HTML>
<HEAD>
<TITLE>HTML First Example</TITLE>
</HEAD>
<BODY>
<H1>Welcome to HTML</H1>
<HR>
<P>This really isn't so hard!</P>
<P>You can put in lots of text if you want to.
In fact, you could keep on typing and make up
more sentences and continue on and on and on.</P>
</BODY>
</HTML>
```

Figure 1-5.   *Example HTML document*

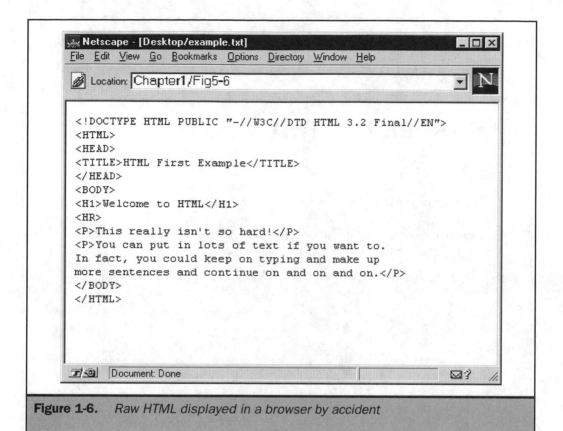

```
Netscape - [Desktop/example.txt]
File  Edit  View  Go  Bookmarks  Options  Directory  Window  Help

Location: Chapter1/Fig5-6

<!DOCTYPE HTML PUBLIC "-//W3C//DTD HTML 3.2 Final//EN">
<HTML>
<HEAD>
<TITLE>HTML First Example</TITLE>
</HEAD>
<BODY>
<H1>Welcome to HTML</H1>
<HR>
<P>This really isn't so hard!</P>
<P>You can put in lots of text if you want to.
In fact, you could keep on typing and make up
more sentences and continue on and on and on.</P>
</BODY>
</HTML>

Document: Done
```

Figure 1-6.   *Raw HTML displayed in a browser by accident*

Tip   *For this quick example, use a simple text editing tool like Notepad in Windows 95/NT, SimpleText on the Macintosh, or vi in UNIX. While such simple programs may not give you all the features you want, you'll avoid accidentally saving the file in the wrong format, possibly with a .txt extension, or even saving it in a proprietary word processing format that the browser cannot read.*

After saving the example file on your system, use your browser to open it by using the Open or Open File command. Once it reads the file, your browser should render a page like the one shown in Figure 1-7.

If your page does not display properly, go back to your file and make sure you typed it in correctly. If you find a mistake and make a change to the file, simply save it, go back to your browser, and click the Reload button. Keeping the browser and the text editor open at the same time is a good idea, in order to avoid constantly reopening one or the other. Once you get the hang of it, you'll see that HTML design at this raw level is like the edit, compile, and run cycle so familiar to programmers. This manual process is probably not the way you want to develop Web pages since it can

Figure 1-7. *Example HTML Web page in a browser*

be tedious, error prone, and not helpful when thinking of visual design. For illustrative purposes, however, it works fine.

Given this simple example, you might guess that learning HTML is merely a matter of learning the multitude of markup tags like **<B>**, which specify the format and structure of documents to browsers. While in some sense that is true, it would be like trying to learn print publishing by understanding only the various commands available in Microsoft Word, while disregarding paper types, document structure, and issues of style. You also need to consider the intent of HTML, its purpose, and the medium in which HTML is used, the World Wide Web.

Overview of HTML

A markup language like HTML is simply a collection of codes—*elements* in this case—that are used to indicate the structure and format of a document. The codes have meaning that is interpreted by a formatting program, often a Web browser, which renders the document. Elements in HTML consist of alphanumeric tags within angle brackets. They usually come in pairs, but there are exceptions to these rules. The following table shows a few HTML elements:

Start Tag	End Tag	Description
<H1>	</H1>	The largest headline
<B>	</B>	Bold text
<CITE>	</CITE>	A citation
<P>	</P> (optional)	A paragraph of text
<HR>	None	A horizontal rule

The alphanumeric tags themselves are case insensitive. As far as Web browsers are concerned, **<H1>** is equivalent to **<h1>**, and **<cite>** is equivalent to **<CiTe>**. For stylistic reasons, however, case should be kept consistent.

Tip   *Using all uppercase elements makes it easier to distinguish markup from document content. Many HTML editing tools provide tag-coloring features to make it easier to maintain documents with complex tagging structures.*

HTML elements often have attributes that affect the rendering of the element's content by modifying the function of the element. Attributes are very common with complex elements such as **<IMG>**, which specifies an image to load into a Web page. The name and location of the image in question are set via the **SRC** attribute, which indicates the "source" of the image file. **<IMG SRC="logo.gif">** tells the browser to display the file called logo.gif. An element may have many attributes with quoted values that are separated by one space, as shown here:

```
<IMG SRC="logo.gif" ALT="Big Company Logo" HEIGHT="100" WIDTH="200">
```

Note   *Attribute values should be enclosed within double quotes. Many browsers allow you to use single quotes or no quotes at all, particularly for values that consist of a single word. There are also situations in which single quotes may be used within attribute values. This occurs when JavaScript is used, or when the value of the attribute includes special characters like spaces or punctuation. Attributes are discussed in more detail in Chapter 4.*

While HTML elements like **<IMG>** are not case sensitive, the contents of attributes usually are. **<IMG SRC="logo.gif">** is not necessarily equivalent to **<IMG SRC="LOGO.GIF">** since the **SRC** value follows casing rules specific to the attribute. In the case of the filename, some operating systems are case sensitive, so LOGO.GIF would not necessarily specify the same file as logo.gif.

HTML files are not generally sensitive to spacing. Browsers tend to collapse multiple spaces or tabs into a single space. For example,

```
<B>This is a test</B>
```

displays the same way in a browser as does the following:

```
<B>This     is       a
         test</B>
```

Spaces, tabs, and returns collapse when HTML files are displayed in a browser, unless they are included within elements such as the preformatted element **<PRE>**. Because HTML allows judicious spacing, you should space out content with white space for easy reading of the source document, particularly by separating markup from content. Additional spacing does not affect the browser's rendering of the document.

Note   *In the future, when tools generate the majority of HTML, spacing and tagging styles may not be as big of an issue; but until people stop editing HTML files directly, it would be wise to format documents for human reading.*

Another aspect of HTML elements is the idea of *nesting,* which means that HTML elements can surround each other. If you have some text that you want to make bold and italic, you can apply both the **<B>** and the **<I>** elements to the text, as shown in the following illustration. In this example the tags are nested and do not cross.

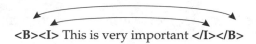

<B><I> This is very important </I></B>

The idea of crossing tags is shown here:

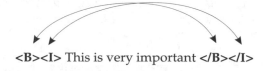

<B><I> This is very important </B></I>

You can always tell when tags cross by connecting arcs from start tag to end tag and seeing if the arcs cross each other.

While the nesting rule agrees with the formal definition of HTML, most browsers do not have a problem with crossed tags or tags used outside their normal context. Nevertheless, just because browsers are lax in enforcing HTML's "rules" is not an excuse to abuse HTML or sloppily code a page. This reveals a very interesting problem with HTML. Standards impose a specific structure requirement on documents. Unfortunately, many document authors are unfamiliar with standards, and most browsers do not strictly enforce them. It may be that authors do not pay attention to the structure because they do not understand the philosophy of HTML; they may think of HTML as a physical page description language like PostScript rather than a logical, structure-oriented markup language. Browsers do nothing to discourage this view and may even encourage the physical view. As the Web gets more complicated, however, things may go wrong if the rules are not followed at least in spirit.

Logical and Physical Elements

Many of the complaints people have with HTML result from the fact that it is not a physical page description language. Most people are already very familiar with physical or specific markup because they normally use WYSIWYG ("what you see is what you get") text editors like Microsoft Word. When they want to make something bold in Word, they simply select the appropriate button and the item is made bold. In HTML, it would seem that you could make something bold just by enclosing it within the **<B>** and **</B>** tags, as shown here:

```
<B>This is important</B>
```

While this is true, the language as a whole is not as precise as people would like. Markup languages do allow for formatting by using specific instructions for a desired format. However, with the proliferation of PostScript laser printers—which allow the specification of font names such as Britannic Bold, font point sizes such as 28, and even margins of 1.5 inches—many have come to expect a greater degree of control over electronic documents than HTML allows.

For example, onscreen, users might desire a precise pixel-level control of 15 pixels from the top and 100 pixels from the left. New proprietary HTML elements like **<SPACER>**, which moves things around, or **<FONT FACE="Arial">**, which lets users specify the font they want to use (in this case, Arial), seem downright necessary. However, other technologies like style sheets may provide a better solution for formatting text than a slew of inconsistently supported elements.

According to some, HTML was not designed to provide most of the document layout features that people have come to expect. (Historically, it is unclear whether HTML was designed this way or if the rigorous structural concepts of SGML were applied to HTML after the fact.) Many people are interested in HTML as a logical, or generalized, markup language that defines a document's structure, not its appearance.

For example, instead of defining the introduction of a document with a particular margin, font, and size, HTML just labels it as an introduction section and lets another system determine the appropriate presentation. In the case of HTML, the browser or a style sheet has the final say on how a document looks.

HTML already contains many logical elements. An example of a logical element is **<STRONG>**, which indicates something of importance, as shown here:

```
<STRONG>This is important</STRONG>
```

The **<STRONG>** element says nothing about how the phrase "This is important" will actually appear, although it will probably be rendered in bold.

The benefits of logical elements may not be obvious to those comfortable with physical markup. To understand the benefits, it's important to realize that on the Web, many browsers render things differently. In addition, it's difficult to predict what the viewing environment will be. What browser does the user have? What is his or her monitor's screen resolution? Does the user even have a screen? Going to the extreme of no screen at all, how would a speaking browser render the **<BOLD>** element? What about the **<STRONG>** elements? Text tagged with **<STRONG>** might be read in a firm voice, but boldfaced text doesn't have a meaning outside the visual realm.

There are many realistic examples of the power of logical elements. Think about the multinational or multilingual aspects of the Web. In some countries, the date is written with the day first, followed by the month and the year. In the United States, it is generally written with the month first, and then the day and year. A **<DATE>** element, if it existed, could tag the information and let the browser localize it for the appropriate viewing environment. Another example is the problem of screen sizes, which could, theoretically, be reduced by logical structuring concepts. For example, logical elements could allow for different renderings based on the screen size of the computer running the browser. This would allow the creation of documents that look good on laptop screens as well as large workstation monitors.

Whether you subscribe to the physical (specific) or logical (general) viewpoint, HTML as it stands is not purely a physical *or* logical language. In other words, when you look at current HTML elements, you will find that they come in both flavors: physical and logical. Elements that specify fonts, type sizes, type styles, and so on are physical. Elements that specify content or importance, like **<CITE>** and **<H1>**, and let the browser decide how to do things are logical. A quick look at Web pages across the Internet suggests that logical elements often go unused because Web developers want more layout control than HTML provides. They abuse elements like **<TABLE>** and **<FRAME>**, use nonstandard elements like **<SPACER>**, and even use tricks to implement layouts the way they want them. This is the struggle that exists today between what people want out of HTML and what HTML actually provides.

What HTML Is Not

HTML is a powerful technology, but there are many misconceptions about it. Many people have a basic notion of what HTML is, but few seriously consider what it isn't.

HTML Is Not a Programming Language

Many people think that making pages is like programming. However, HTML is unlike programming in that it does not specify logic. It specifies only the layout and structure of a document. Because of spacing rules and the fact that a browser interprets HTML markup similarly to the way in which a compiler reads source code, people often view it as a programming language. HTML is a structured language; but unlike a programming language, in which the rules are enforced by the compiler, HTML rules (such as nesting, for example) are not strictly enforced by browsers. The language does not provide any sort of execution order like programming languages do. The introduction of scripting languages like dynamic HTML, which allows elements and their content to be manipulated after the page has been loaded, and JavaScript are beginning to blur the lines between HTML as a layout language and HTML as a programming environment.

HTML Is Not Truly Standardized

While the World Wide Web Consortium defines the HTML specification, in practical terms browser vendors and users often define their own de facto standards. While this may sound like heresy, it is true. When a new browser comes out supporting a new feature, many companies and individuals rush to use it, whether or not it is included in the W3C HTML standard. Why? Because in the competitive environment of the Web, there is a need to be first. Don't misread the last few sentences as an anti-W3C statement: The behind-the-scenes markup used in word processing programs is similar to the HTML markup used to create Web pages. In this kind of environment, there is more of a need for a standards body than ever. The W3C serves an important role in today's wild, wild Web by serving as a forum to foster agreement among browser vendors and codify what should be supported, particularly technologies that are in the long-term interest of the Web. Nevertheless, the browsers themselves are the final arbiters of the meaning of HTML elements as far as end users are concerned. In this sense, HTML resembles English. New elements and technologies are the slang of HTML. They may not be correct, but eventually many slang terms become an accepted part of the language. There are many ways to "speak" HTML, but the key issue is whether the browser understands the code, just as the key issue in English is whether one person understands another person's slang.

HTML Is Not a WYSIWYG Design Language

HTML is not a specific, screen- or printer-precise formatting language like PostScript or troff. Many people struggle against the technology on a daily basis trying to create perfect layouts by using HTML elements inappropriately, or using images to make up for HTML's lack of screen- and font-handling features.

HTML Is Not Complete

HTML is not finished. The language does not provide all the facilities it should. If HTML is meant to be a physical design language, it still does not provide font or pixel-level control, which is very important. But should it? If the language is to be a logical structuring language, it needs to be integrated appropriately with a technology that provides formatting features like style sheets. Either way, HTML is far from complete.

HTML Is Not Extensible

Some people feel that it is easy to change HTML as long as the language is simple enough for browser vendors and standards groups to easily determine new elements. A long battle has been waged to implement features correctly. The proliferation of elements and features like frames, which are inconsistently supported across browsers, shows that it is difficult to add features to the language. Truly extensible markup environments such as SGML and Extended Markup Language (XML), in conjunction with style sheets, allow users to invent elements and renderings for those elements without compromising the experience for other users. This is currently impossible with HTML.

HTML Is Not All You Need to Know to Create Good Web Pages

While HTML is the basis for Web pages, you need to know a lot more in order to build useful Web pages unless the page is very simple. Document design, graphic design, and even programming are often necessary to create sophisticated Web pages. HTML serves as the foundation environment for all these tasks, and a complete understanding of HTML technology can only aid document authors.

The features that HTML does not support lead to a general problem with how people use the language. Much of the tension surrounding HTML and its abuse stems from the "logical versus physical markup" debate (discussed previously under "Logical and Physical Elements") and from the desire for absolute positioning of text and graphics within Web pages. These themes recur throughout this book.

Summary

HTML is not a programming language nor a physical page description language. It is a markup language that combines physical and logical structuring ideas. Elements in the form of tags like <B> and </B> are embedded within text documents to indicate to browsers how to render pages. The rules for HTML are fairly simple but are not fully enforced. Browsers are the final arbiters of page layout. The rapid development of the HTML language and the looseness of its use in markup have created a great deal of misunderstanding about how to use the language. This is due in part to the chaotic nature of the Web publishing environment and in part to HTML's failure to address all the needs of its users. As it stands today, HTML does not provide all the features necessary to build modern Web pages. The big question is not whether HTML is or isn't being used properly or if it is designed properly. Rather than argue the correctness of HTML, or the lack of understanding of the end developer, people should agree that they all want the same thing—a great deal of control and flexibility in their documents. So the real question is what approach should be taken with HTML in order to meet these needs, and that is a difficult one to answer. Should the language be enhanced with new elements to provide the features users require, such as absolute positioning for document layout, or should it be reduced to its core functionality while other technologies like style sheets handle its shortcomings? Current trends in browser features suggest that the latter is going to be the answer. Combining style sheets with the use of HTML as a logical structure language has many benefits, but there is still an open question as to whether or not this will take. In the market, this is largely a matter of opinion.

Chapter 2 takes a look at the role of HTML on the World Wide Web and why HTML was designed the way it was.

Chapter 2

HTML and the World Wide Web

A
s defined in Chapter 1, HTML is a text markup language used to author Web pages. This isn't the whole picture, however. There's more to the Web than HTML. Even document authors with perfect HTML skills who can write Standard Generalized Markup Language (SGML) document type definitions (DTDs) in their spare time might not be able to produce functional Web pages. To produce high-quality pages that work on the Web, you also need an understanding of the environment in which HTML is used and what the technology is designed to do. This chapter focuses on the medium of the Web—the Internet, hypertext, servers, and other areas that shape this chaotic publishing medium. Although this discussion offers a good starting perspective, you may also wish to look into other books that discuss these topics in greater depth.

HTML Is a Tool for Disseminating Information

Creating and publishing HTML documents on the Web or on an intranet allows information to be disseminated. This information can be any message you wish to communicate to another individual and is not limited to text forms. It can be expressed as images, sound, movies, and just about any other form you can imagine. This information is distributed through a networked environment called the World Wide Web. It is useful to examine this environment before focusing on the HTML markup tags used to build Web pages, so that you can understand that HTML is just a tool for use toward the overall goal of publishing and disseminating information electronically via the Internet or an intranet. An intranet is simply a private Web, such as one a company would put together for its employees. While an intranet uses HTML documents and a browser like Netscape or Internet Explorer, because it is on a private LAN it is not accessible to the Web at large.

The medium over which this communication occurs is a network (see Figure 2-1): the Internet, if you are discussing the World Wide Web, or a local area network, if you are discussing an intranet. It's important to understand the ramifications of this medium, particularly the Internet at large, because it tends to be a less-than-ideal environment for communication. Some of these problems stem from the recent wild growth of the Internet; others are due to the nature of networks themselves. It's important to understand networks, since they affect the Web every day.

Types of Networks and How They Operate

Networks usually take the form of a small office network, or *local area network (LAN)*. A LAN is shown in Figure 2-2. Networks that cover a city or some other large physical distance can be called *metropolitan area networks (MANs)* or, more generally, *wide area networks (WANs)*.

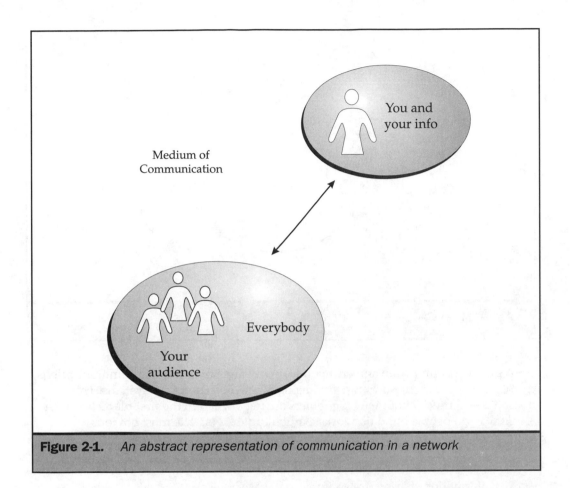

Figure 2-1. *An abstract representation of communication in a network*

Definition A network *is a collection of computers linked together using some medium (for example, wires or radio) so that data can be transmitted between computers, or nodes on the network.*

In a sense, computers on a network "talk" to each other. This "conversation" is accomplished using a network protocol.

Definition A network protocol *is the set of rules, or a "language," that computers on a network use to communicate. Common network protocols include Novell Internet Packet Exchange (IPX), Apple AppleTalk, and Transmission Control Protocol/Internet Protocol (TCP/IP). The Internet utilizes TCP/IP.*

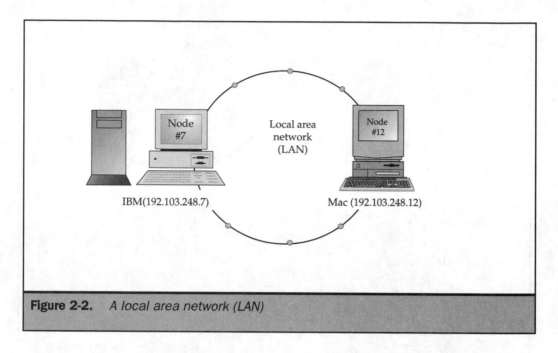

Figure 2-2.   *A local area network (LAN)*

A protocol is simply an agreed-upon way of doing something. In communications, a protocol is a set of rules for transmitting data between computer systems. This doesn't reveal much about why computers are networked in the first place, however.

So why do people build networks, particularly LANs? The most obvious reasons include

- Communication (for example, e-mail)
- Information sharing (for example, database access)
- Resource sharing (for example, networked printers)

If you are a manager or a pragmatic person, you might look further. Typically, networks are created in the hopes of saving money and increasing efficiency. Buying a laser printer for every computer in a large office, for example, would be cost prohibitive. A single laser printer shared across a network can save money and improve productivity.

Moving beyond a small office network to a large network, things get more complicated. Suppose a company has two LANs, one on the first floor of the building and one on the second, that need to be joined together. This can be done by drilling a hole in the floor, setting up some network equipment, and wiring the two networks. The resulting combination of networks has a special name—an *internetwork,* or internet for short. A diagram of an internetwork is shown in Figure 2-3.

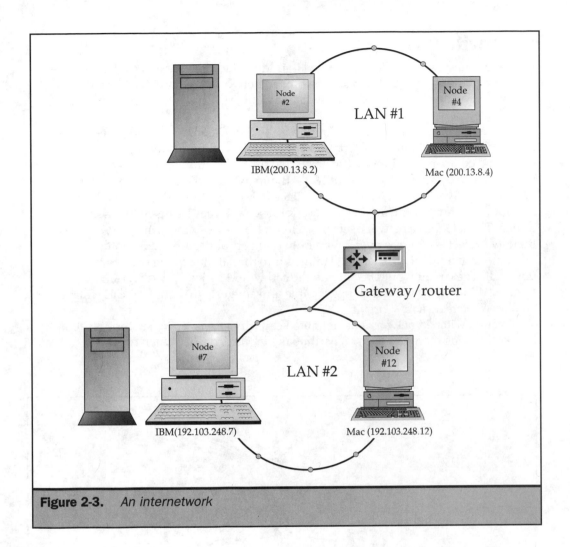

Figure 2-3. *An internetwork*

> **Definition**
>
> *An* internetwork, *or* internet *(note the lowercase, generic use of the word "internet" here), is a collection of two or more distinct networks joined together, typically using a router, to form a larger "network of networks."*

That's *an* internet. So what is *the* Internet? The Internet is simply a particular internetwork—a large public internetwork that shares a common network protocol. The key to understanding this definition is TCP/IP.

> **Definition**
>
> *The* Internet *is the name given to the worldwide collection of data networks (an internetwork) that "speak" the TCP/IP network protocol.*

Circuit Switching

Before learning about TCP/IP, you need to understand the idea of a packet-switched network; and to understand a packet-switched network, you first need to consider another type of network: the circuit-switched network. This is the type of network used for telephone systems.

If you make a phone call from your house in San Diego to a friend who lives in Mexico City, the call follows a certain path. First, the call routes through a local telephone company, such as Pacific Bell. Then the call is routed through a long-distance company—let's say AT&T—that may send the call to Mexico through land lines or over a satellite connection. Once in Mexico, the call is routed through a Mexican telephone company, in this case Telmex, and finally rings your friend's phone. The telephone network sets up a circuit from one point to another, so you can literally project your voice over a wire from one part of the world to another. Consider what might happen if an asteroid slammed into the satellite being used to complete your call. The circuit would be cut and the call would be lost. The diagram in Figure 2-4 illustrates the foregoing example and suggests that another call will have to be placed to create a new circuit.

Circuit-switched networks have limited capacity and are very susceptible to link breaks. Imagine there has been an earthquake in Mexico City. When everyone calls at

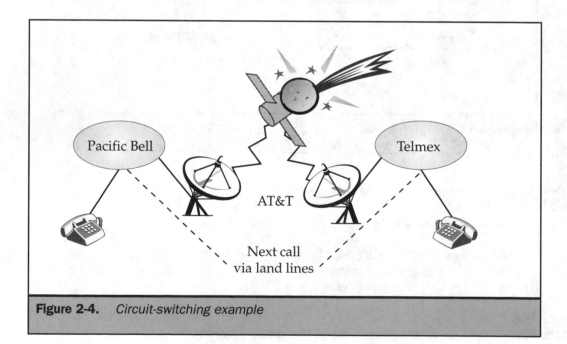

Figure 2-4. *Circuit-switching example*

once to see if their friends are all right, they might hear a message like, "All circuits are busy." There are only so many wires for people to place calls over. The up side is that if you can get a wire to make your call, nobody else affects your communication. A network that is more robust than a circuit-switched network might be preferable, but such a network would probably sacrifice performance.

Packet Switching

Packet switching breaks up the data to be transmitted on a network. This produces a number of individual packets, or datagrams, that are delivered separately across the network. When they reach the other end, the packets are reassembled in the proper order to create the complete message. In theory, packets are routed appropriately and may take the best route or bypass congestion. Furthermore, a packet-switched network can scale very large. More packets mean a slower network, not a busy signal or an "all circuits are busy" message.

The best way to illustrate the idea of packet-switching networks is by using a short analogy that highlights some of the potential problems with this technique. Imagine you're vacationing in Paris. You want to communicate with a friend back home, but since you're a starving student, you are limited to a bunch of postcards you bought at the Eiffel Tower. To make matters worse, between the printing on the card, the bar code, the stamp and your poor handwriting, there is room for only one word on each postcard. So you write one word on each card ("THIS," "IS," "A," and "TEST"), address each card to your friend, and drop them in the mailbox. If you have ever used the European postal system, you'll know that things often operate in mysterious ways. The first postcard you send takes six months to arrive. The last postcard arrives in one day. The second post card gets lost, while the third card takes a week. Your friend gets the postcards out of order and has no idea what the message was. This analogy is shown in Figure 2-5.

What can be done to improve the postcard idea so the message is transmitted properly? You could number the cards so your friend can reorder them, regardless of when then arrive. This doesn't solve the entire problem. What about the card that got lost? You could send the postcards by certified mail and wait to receive an acknowledgment that they got through. You could stipulate that the acknowledgment include some indication that your friend understands the word on each postcard. If you don't receive any acknowledgment after a few weeks, you can assume that the cards didn't get through and send them again (and again) until you receive a reply. Put together, these ideas form a viable, acceptable means of communication.

The postcards analogy illustrates how data is transmitted over a packet-switched network. In a packet-switched environment, there is much overhead in the numbering and reordering of the packets, as well as waiting for acknowledgments. Such an environment does not guarantee delivery time of data; however, it is very robust, scales well, and is very cost-effective. Why is this important? The answer is simple: because the Internet is a packet-switched network.

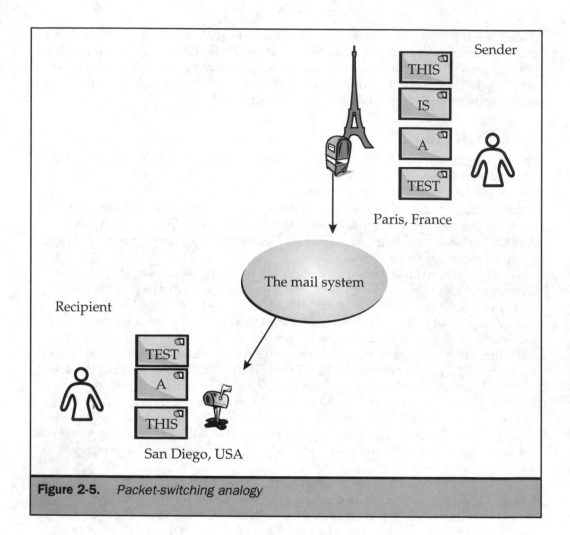

Figure 2-5. *Packet-switching analogy*

TCP/IP

Because the Internet is a packet-switched network, data can arrive out of order, get lost, and so on. The TCP/IP network protocol deals with these problems. TCP/IP is actually a suite of protocols that includes two main protocols: TCP (Transmission Control Protocol) and IP (Internet Protocol). TCP does exactly what its name indicates: it controls the transmission of data. In the postcards analogy, TCP would be responsible for reassembling the message, sending replies, and resending data. In the postcards analogy, the IP protocol, which handles the addressing scheme on the Internet, would be the address on the postcard; this would be read so that the data packet could be routed to the appropriate destination.

There is a lot one could say about TCP/IP, but because this book is not about networking, the discussion winds down here. A little knowledge of the protocol can pay off down the line, however. Since a packet-switched network in conjunction with TCP/IP doesn't guarantee delivery time, sending time-sensitive information like real-time voice or video over the Internet is less than ideal. This may come as a shock to people who expect the Internet to be as straightforward as a circuit-switched network.

Another interesting fact of TCP/IP on Web pages is the slow-start mechanism. Many people are very concerned about optimizing images to the smallest size, but anyone who has used the Internet to download large files has seen download rates start slowly and increase to a maximum speed. This is TCP/IP in action. Does a page with one big image load faster than a page with ten small images when the byte count is the same, or even slightly smaller, for the ten small images? The large image beats the ten small ones without trouble. Once you have mastered HTML and other aspects of Web publishing, consider studying networks a little. Even a casual understanding of how networks work will save you the trouble of going against the nature of the Internet.

What Is the Internet?

When most people talk about the Internet, they don't usually think about protocols and wires. That would be like defining television as the cables and satellites that allow the broadcast of television shows. Most people focus on what they can do with the Internet, so a more appropriate definition of the Internet follows.

  The Internet *is the name given to the worldwide collection of data networks (an internetwork) that speak the TCP/IP network protocol, and to the facilities (e-mail, the Web, etc.) that are provided or available using it.*

Going beyond this definition, consider the social ramifications of the Internet, each of its facilities like the Web, and the underlying technologies that tend to be used. If you think about television, this complexity issue seems obvious. What is television? People don't tend to talk about the sets, the broadcast systems, or the protocols used. They focus on the content—the television programs, the advertisements, and the experience. Since experience may be influenced greatly by the environment, it is important to understand the environment of the Internet, as well as how it works.

Basic Uses of the Internet

Networks tend to be used for communication, information sharing, and resource sharing. In this sense, the Internet is no different than any other network. The typical individual doesn't use the Internet for resource sharing. Sharing a printer on a local area network is resource sharing, one of the most common motivations for building a network. On the Internet, you might imagine sharing a supercomputer. One of the main motivations for building the National Science Foundation network (NSFnet), which became the backbone for the Internet between 1986 and 1995, was to share supercomputing resources among scientists. Internet users usually encounter resource sharing when they use telnet to access a remote database or use a timesharing system to do some work remotely. While this is not necessarily the main use of the Internet, as with all networks, resource sharing is a very important factor.

The most basic use—some say the most important use—of the Internet is communication in the form of electronic mail, or e-mail. With millions of users online and a fixed cost structure, e-mail is a prime motivation for many firms to connect to the Internet. Other types of Internet-based communication include mailing lists, USENET News, text chat, graphical chat, and voice or videoconferencing.

> **Note**   *The distinction between communication in the form of an e-mail message and a person reading a Web page is becoming less and less obvious. Pages can now be generated specifically for individual users. In fact, pages can even provide multiuser chatting facilities.*

There are millions of people using the Internet—and almost as many connected computers. Each one of these computers may have disk drives filled with information ready to be served out to other Internet users. This motivates the third and most important aspect of the Internet at this point: information sharing. Many tools can be used to access information over the Internet, but most people tend to characterize information on the Internet by the World Wide Web. The Web is relatively new, however, so looking at previous generations of information sharing on the Internet can be very helpful.

Information Search and Retrieval on the Internet

All the files on all the computers on the Internet comprise an amorphous body—a *document space*—of electronic information that you may want to access. How do you find the information you're looking for and then retrieve it? Normally, on the Internet you would use a tool or service to look for, and eventually retrieve, information from some remote system.

If you use a tool to retrieve information, it typically resides on your local computer and is termed a *client*. In order to retrieve information, the client software communicates to a remote system called a *server*. The client program requests a document from the remote server, which returns the document to the client program for display. This relationship between client and server programs is known, aptly enough, as client/server-based computing. This is the basis of most, if not all, Internet-based communications. An example of client/server computing is shown in Figure 2-6.

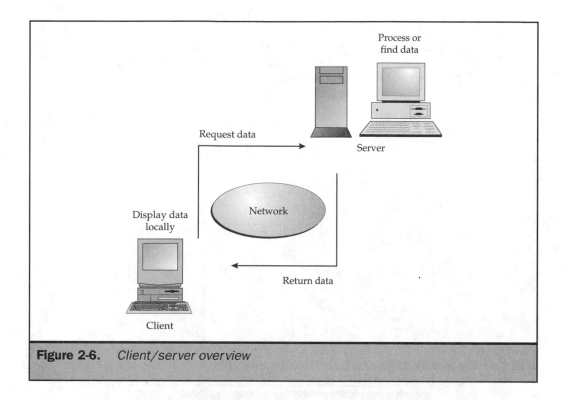

Figure 2-6.   *Client/server overview*

The advantage to the client/server architecture is that it separates the computing workload between the client machine—typically your local computer—and the remote server. This separation is important because it allows one server to talk to many different types of clients. For example, a Windows server could easily give out information to a Macintosh client (and vice versa). Furthermore, the client/server architecture scales very well since users don't have to be dependent on one monolithic system. (Previous computing models, such as the host model, involved many terminals tied into a mainframe.) These ideas will be covered in this book as we discuss the Web more specifically.

Over the years, there have been a variety of Internet-based information retrieval schemes, and you'll find out about some of them in the next section.

First Generation: FTP

Initially, information retrieval on the Internet was characterized by a program (and protocol) known as the File Transfer Protocol (FTP). FTP allows a user to connect to a remote system and to send and receive files from that system. While FTP is very efficient, it initially required users to know what file they were looking for, as it did not facilitate browsing. Over time, better FTP clients with easy-to-use graphical interfaces were built, but the protocol still did not facilitate information browsing.

Because FTP did not allow people to find what they were looking for with ease, a service called Archie was developed to allow keyword searching of the files available for FTP. The theoretical collection of all files available to be downloaded with FTP is known as *ftpspace*. Two examples of FTP client software interfaces are shown in Figure 2-7.

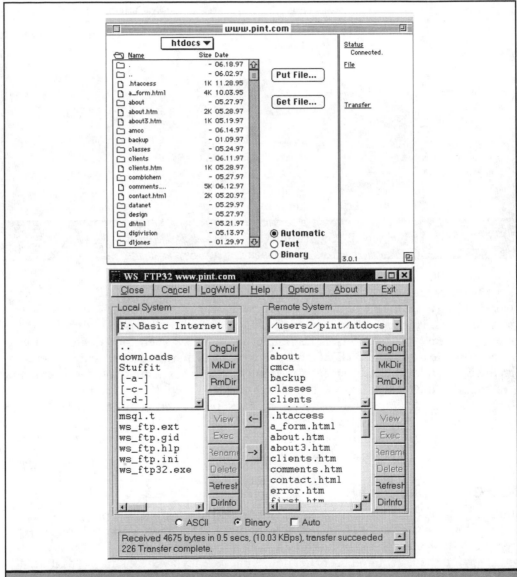

Figure 2-7. *Two FTP client interfaces*

Because of its efficiency in transferring files, FTP is still used, particularly for file downloading. Chapter 5 discusses the uniform resource locator (URL) and how it made arbitrary distinctions between information spaces unnecessary.

Second Generation: Gopher

The second generation of information search and retrieval service on the Internet was characterized by a menu-style information browsing system called Gopher. Developed at the University of Minnesota as a campuswide information system, Gopher was named after the school's mascot. After development, the Gopher client/server software was made available freely on the Internet and flourished between 1991 and 1993. Gopher provides a menu-driven interface to large amounts of primarily textual information. Three examples of Gopher client interfaces are shown in Figure 2-8. Moving about in *gopherspace,* the space of all Gopher documents, is easy, requiring only a menu selection.

Gopher overcame many of FTP's shortcomings by facilitating browsing of large bodies of content. As content increased, however, menu navigation became burdensome. A search facility for Gopher was developed and called Veronica, as a play—known to readers of comics—on the existing Archie service. Veronica allowed searching for Gopher-based documents by keyword and title. Veronica is tightly coupled with Gopher. It is simply a service available via a Gopher menu selection, as compared to Archie, which is generally a separate service from FTP. Because Gopher sites can grow to enormous sizes, a local search service called Jughead, which continues the joke, was later developed. Gopher's simple linear nature and its lack of sufficient support for multimedia doomed it to a relatively short life span.

 While a large amount of Gopher-based information still exists on the Internet, much of it appears trapped. It has only slowly migrated to the Web, despite the ability to link its content via Gopher URLs (see Chapter 5).

Third Generation: Web

The Web, which was proposed at about the same time as Gopher, presented a method to organize information on the Internet as a collection of linked documents called hypertext, or, in the case of the Web, hypermedia. Using a Web browser like Mosaic or Netscape Navigator, Internet users could navigate large bodies of hypertext and other forms of Internet information in a nonlinear fashion. The Web and its browser interface provided greater ease of use and richness of expression. The Web took off like wildfire. Unlike FTP and Gopher, the Web features many search and directory facilities. These include Lycos, HotBot, AltaVista, Yahoo!, and dozens of others. So what makes the Web so different from other Internet-based information systems? The answer is hypermedia.

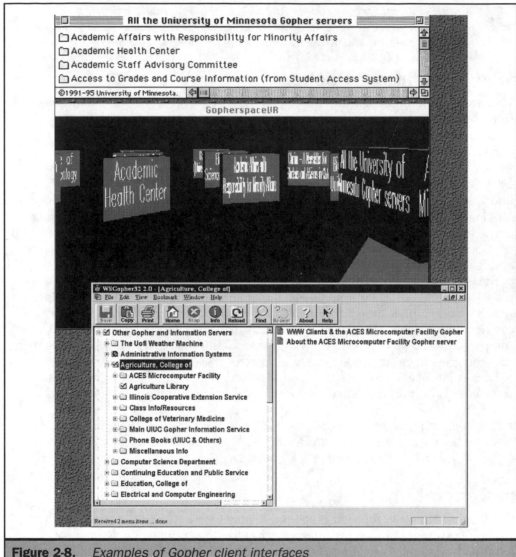

Figure 2-8.   *Examples of Gopher client interfaces*

Hypertext and Hypermedia

Traditional text in the form of a book is typically defined as sequential or linear because there is an order in which the text must be read—page two follows page one, and so on. There are many advantages to this method of presenting information. It provides a logical sense of order. It can, however, be an inefficient way to access large bodies of information. (Imagine reading an entire 20-volume encyclopedia page by page to find a single relevant bit of information.)

A variety of mechanisms can speed a user's search for information within documents. For example, a book such as this one uses an index, table of contents, and section headings to speed access to various bits of information. The index provides a mapping from an idea to a particular page in the document containing this information. References or footnotes within the information can provide links to related pieces of information. Nonsequential ways to access information such as footnotes, references, and indexes are useful ways to deal with navigating and organizing large bodies of related information. With the amount of information available for consumption, exploring an alternative to sequential access seems appropriate. This is where the idea of hypertext comes in.

A hypertext document is an electronic document that contains links to related pieces of information. It could be characterized as providing generalized footnotes. For example, a hypertext document about cows may feature a link from the word "milk," which, when followed, sends the reader to other documents about the types of milk, as shown in Figure 2-9. Hypertext is a nonlinear way to access information. Many people find it similar to the way they think about problems.

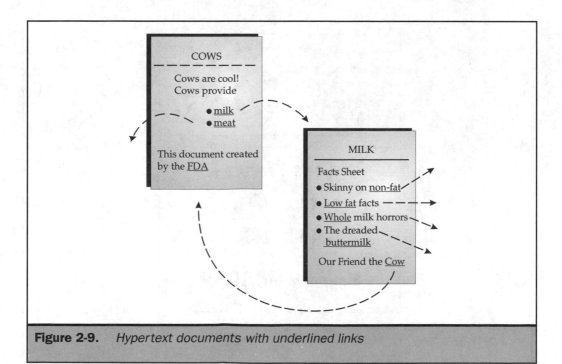

Figure 2-9.   *Hypertext documents with underlined links*

Note *Although hypertext and hypermedia are relatively new technologies, the idea of hypertext is nearly 50 years old. Most people credit Vannevar Bush with the core idea. Serious research in hypertext theory has been done for nearly 35 years. The term "hypertext" was coined in the mid-sixties by Ted Nelson. The first major public introduction to hypertext wasn't until 1987, when Apple introduced HyperCard. The Web, which followed soon after, was greatly influenced by past research.*

Hypermedia is similar to hypertext, but it extends the concept to include multimedia capabilities such as sound and graphics. A hypermedia document about cows might include pictures of cows, buttons that produce cow sounds, and general hyperlinks that take readers to other documents about cows (see Figure 2-10).

Most people have encountered hypermedia on CD-ROMs such as digital encyclopedias. While CD-ROMs exhibit many of the same hypermedia characteristics as the Web, they are not dynamic. In other words, you cannot typically link from a CD-ROM, although this is changing with the use of hybrid CD-ROMs. When jumping from one document to another in a hypertext CD-ROM environment, the user is simply moving from one part of the disc to another, as shown in Figure 2-11. The user is trapped on the CD-ROM, stuck in an information cul-de-sac.

Figure 2-10.   *Example of a hypermedia document*

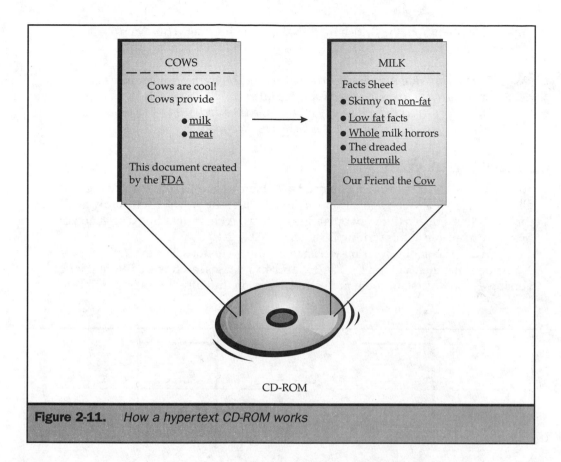

Figure 2-11.   *How a hypertext CD-ROM works*

Note   *Hybrid CD-ROMs that access the Internet to download new information are now possible, as are fill-in templates from the CD. By leveraging the benefits of pre-cached CD information with the dynamic nature of the Internet, users can experience a visually lush experience without heavy bandwidth requirements.*

The Web provides a significant benefit over CD-ROM–based hypermedia: the content presented is nearly boundless because it can be added to at will.

What Is the World Wide Web?

The *World Wide Web,* or simply the *Web,* for short, is the name given to the collection of hypermedia documents spread out on machines all over the Internet. The links in these documents transcend the machine where the document is located. In the cow example presented earlier, this would mean that the general COWS document might reside on a machine in the United States, while the MILK document might reside on a machine in England. When a user clicks the "milk" hyperlink, he or she fetches the milk information from the British machine over the Internet. This example is illustrated in Figure 2-12.

 The World Wide Web *is a collection of hypertext/hypermedia documents that reside on Web servers located all over the Internet. The documents found on these Web servers contain pointers that connect the documents. The collection of all these documents creates what is known as* Webspace.

Accessing the Web

To access the World Wide Web, you need a Web browser—the client software that allows you to view Web pages. There are many different browsers currently available, for more than a dozen different operating systems. A chart detailing a selection of browsers available at this writing is shown in Table 2-1.

Even a particular browser may exist in multiple versions. For example, for Netscape alone there are the 1.x, 2.x, 3.x, and 4.x releases, each with different language versions, a Gold version, and a professional version. Initially, it was impossible to

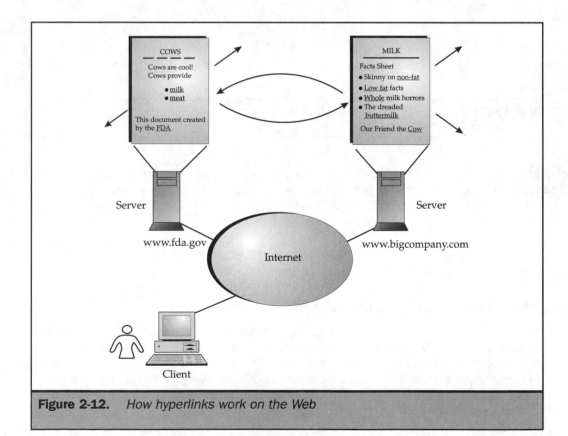

Figure 2-12. *How hyperlinks work on the Web*

Browser	URL	Windows	Mac	Solaris/ Sun OS	Other UNIX	Other
Accent Multilingual Mosaic	http://www. accentsoft.com/	3.x and 95				
Amaya	http://www. w3.org/ pub/WWW/ Amaya/	95 (planned)		Yes	Linux, Irix, AIX, and OSF	
ArcWeb	http://louis. ecs.soton.ac.uk/ ~snb94r/ arcweb.html					Acorn RISC OS
Arena	http://www. yggdrasil.com/ Products/Arena/				Linux and Unix	
Aweb	http://www. amitrix.com/ aweb.html					Amiga
Booklink/ AOL	http://www. booklink.com/	3.x and 95	Yes			
Cello	http://www. law.cornell.edu/ cello/cellotop.html	3.x				
Chimera	http://www. unlv.edu/ chimera/				With X Window	
Cyberdog	http://cyberdog. apple.com/		Yes			
Galahad	http://www. mcs.com/ ~jvwater/main. html	3.x, 95, and NT				OS/2

Table 2-1.   *Partial List of Browsers*

Browser	URL	Windows	Mac	Solaris/ Sun OS	Other UNIX	Other
Emacs-W3	http://www. cs.indiana. edu/elisp/ w3/docs.html	3.x, 95, and NT	Yes	Yes	With X Window	Amiga, OS/2, and VMS
MMM	http://pauillac. inria.fr/~rouaix/ mmm/			Yes	Linux, Irix, AIX, and OSF	ELF
HotJava	http://java.sun. com:80/ products/hotjava/ index.html	95 and NT		Yes		
I-Comm	http://www. best.com/ ~icomm/icomm/ index.html	3.x, 95, and NT				OS/2
InterGo	http://www. teachersoft.com	3.x and 95				
Internet WorkHorse	http://mkn.co. uk/help/system/ horse	3.x and 95				
LIKSE	http://www. faico.net/likse/ index.html	3.x and 95				
Lynx	http://www. crl.com/~subir/ lynx.html	3.x and 95	Yes	Yes	Linux, Irix, AIX, and others	Amiga and VMS
Microsoft Internet Explorer	http://www. microsoft.com/ ie/	3.x, 95, and NT	Yes		Planned	

Table 2-1. *Partial List of Browsers* (continued)

Browser	URL	Windows	Mac	Solaris/ Sun OS	Other UNIX	Other
NCSA Mosaic	http://www. ncsa.uiuc.edu/ SDG/Software/ Mosaic/ NCSAMosaic Home.html	3.x, 95, and NT	Yes	Yes	With X Window	Amiga, OS/2, and VMS
NetCruiser	http://www. netcom.com/ netcom/ netcrz.html	3.x, 95, and NT				
Netscape Navigator	http://www. netscape.com/ comprod/ products/ navigator/	3.x, 95, and NT	Yes	Yes	Linux, Irix, Digital Unix, AIX, HP-UX, and BSD/OS	OS/2 and VMS
Netsurfer	http://www. netsurfer.com/					NEXT-STEP
OmniWeb 2	http://www. omnigroup.com/ Software/ OmniWeb/					NEXT-STEP
Opera	http://traviata. nta.no/opera.htm	3.x and 95				OS/2
pwWebSpeak	http://www. prodworks.com/	3.x and 95				
Slipknot	http://www. users.interport. net/~pbrooks/ slipknot.html	3.x, 95, and NT	Yes			

Table 2-1.   *Partial List of Browsers* (continued)

Browser	URL	Windows	Mac	Solaris/ Sun OS	Other UNIX	Other
Softerm	http://www. softronics.com/	3.x and 95				
Tango	http://www. alis.com/internet_ products/ browser/ browser.en.html	3.x and 95				
tkWWW	http://uu-gna.mit. edu:8001/tk-www/ help/overview. html					System with tk Inter- preter
UdiWWW	http://www. uni-ulm.de/ ~richter/ udiwww/ index.htm	3.x, 95, and NT				
WebExplorer	http://www. networking.ibm. com/WebExplorer/					OS/2
Web-On-Call	http://www. netphonic.com/ product/woc/ wocprod.htm					Tele- phone
WebTV	http://www. webtv.com/					WebTV box

Table 2-1.   *Partial List of Browsers* (continued)

access the Web in a very appealing manner because it was mostly restricted to text style interfaces. In fact, the Lynx browser is still very popular in text-only environments. Unfortunately, when using a text browser you cannot view any of the multimedia aspects that make the Web so popular. Like it or not, graphical browsers and graphics started the Web boom. With the introduction of Mosaic, the first easy-to-use browser with inline graphic viewing, the Web exploded in popularity. Later on, Netscape introduced a browser, as did Microsoft. While there are many browsers available these days, Microsoft's Internet Explorer and Netscape's Navigator/Communicator dominate the market.

While, statistically speaking, the Web is a two-browser world, statistics can be deceiving. Ignoring other browsers may be foolish in certain situations. Depending on your audience, you may find that WebTV or Lynx is more important to you. Another factor to consider is magnitude. Even though a particular browser might only account for a two to five percent market share, that percentage could mean a considerable number of people. As the Web explodes, even a browser with less than a ten percent market share might represent a viable platform. Remember: The Web is not a popularity contest. It is a communications medium. Browsers are software packages, not religions. The browser landscape changes daily. If you are interested in keeping up with the latest in browsers, visit BrowserWatch (www.browserwatch.com) or BROWSERS.COM (www.browsers.com).

Overview of Web Use

The process of a Web browser or other user agent, such as a Web indexing robot or spider requesting a document, is simple. Remember the client/server relationship discussed earlier in the chapter. The Web browser is the client application that resides on the user's local system. The Web server is the system that responds to requests from the client to deliver various pages of information. A diagram of how this relationship works is shown in Figure 2-13.

As shown in Figure 2-13, the first step is for a user to request a document from a Web server by entering the document's address in the form of a uniform resource locator, or URL. A *URL* is the address of an object; it specifies where and how to retrieve or activate that object. Users should already be familiar with URLs like http://www.toyota.com/, as they are bombarded by them on a daily basis in advertisements on the Web. More discussion of URLs can be found in Chapter 5. Once the document to retrieve has been specified, the location of that document must be determined, which involves the browser looking up the domain name.

Every computer on the Internet is addressed by a unique numeric address called an IP address. An example IP address is 192.102.249.3, which corresponds to an important machine located at a large Internet service provider based in San Diego. The IP address identifies the machine so that information can be routed to it. While computers and network devices like routers can handle numeric values like IP addresses, remembering these values is difficult for people. Because of this, computers are generally referenced by their alphanumeric, or *domain name*. A domain name is something like www.ucsd.edu. Domain names are easier to remember than IP addresses, and provide some meaning. For example: www is the name of a machine that provides Web services, UCSD is a university in San Diego, and edu indicates that it is an educational organization. Because there is a mapping from a name to a numeric value, or from a numeric value to a name, the address must be translated.

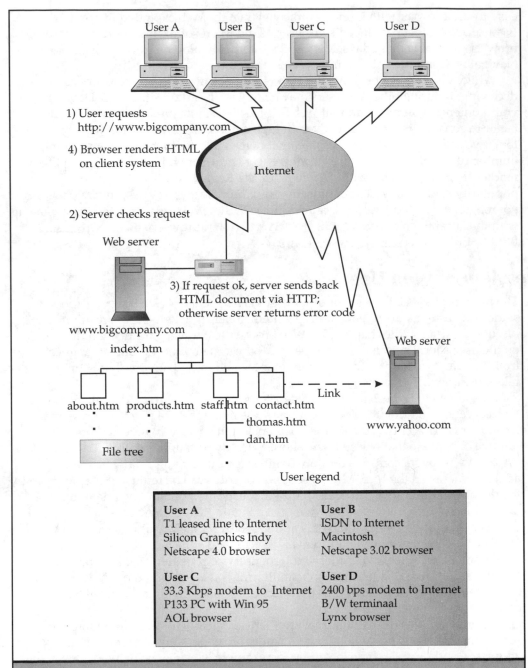

1) User requests
   http://www.bigcompany.com

4) Browser renders HTML
   on client system

2) Server checks request

Web server

3) If request ok, server sends back
   HTML document via HTTP;
   otherwise server returns error code

www.bigcompany.com

index.htm

about.htm   products.htm   staff.htm   contact.htm

Link

thomas.htm

dan.htm

File tree

Web server

www.yahoo.com

User legend

User A	**User B**
T1 leased line to Internet	ISDN to Internet
Silicon Graphics Indy	Macintosh
Netscape 4.0 browser	Netscape 3.02 browser
User C	**User D**
33.3 Kbps modem to Internet	2400 bps modem to Internet
P133 PC with Win 95	B/W terminaal
AOL browser	Lynx browser

Figure 2-13.   *Relationship between a browser and a Web server*

When addresses are typed in a browser, a domain name server is responsible for resolving the name into a numeric value. This name resolution process may take some time. It may even fail because the machine is unavailable, the lookup service is down, or an error was made in the address. If all works well, the machine will be found so that a request for a document can be made. More discussion about domain names can be found in Chapter 5, which discusses URLs.

Once the machine has been located, a request can be sent to the server. The discussion between the Web browser and the server is handled by the HTTP protocol. The Hypertext Transfer Protocol defines the language the user agent uses when talking to a server, as well as the format of the responses to be made by the server. It is not really much of a transport protocol. The actual transportation of data across a network is handled by an underlying protocol like TCP/IP, not by an application-level protocol like HTTP. This is a very important distinction. HTTP is a very simple protocol. A request for http://www.ucsd.edu/ would result in an HTTP request like "GET /HTTP/1.0." This request simply says, "get the root-level document, using HTTP version 1.0." This will produce the default document at that location; if the location in question is the top level of the site, the request will return the "home page" of the site.

Note   *The expression "Web server" is often used to describe both the physical hardware that works as a server, as well as the HTTP server software that runs on the hardware. The expression "home page" is also difficult to pin down, since it may indicate a personal home page about an individual, the first page that loads in a browser when it is started (start page), or the entry page to a Web site. "Personal home page" and "start page" are more appropriate for the first two instances, while "home page" or "entry page" is useful to describe the root level document for a Web site.*

Once an HTTP request is transmitted to the Web server, the Web server attempts to process it. If the server is working, it looks at the request and determines if it is valid. There may be some restrictions. Is the browser from a safe address that is "allowed" to talk to this server? Is the request well formed? Is the file being requested even there? If something goes wrong, the server responds with an error announcement like the infamous "404: Not Found" message. If the request is valid, the server attempts to fulfill the request by finding the file (or executing a program) and sends back the result with the appropriate header information to indicate the nature of the data. What the server sends back to the browser is not only the information requested. It also includes such extra information as the status of the request, the time it was performed, the data returned, and so on. The most important part of this supplementary information is the header information, which comes in the form of a MIME header that indicates the type of data in the document. For example, when a Web server sends back HTML data, it sends it back with a MIME content-type of text/html. Regardless of how the file is named, if the browser sees a MIME heading of this sort, it treats the data received as HTML. The browser looks at the MIME type of incoming data it receives and determines what to do with it by looking in an internal table that maps MIME types to actions. A portion of this table under Netscape 3 is shown in Figure 2-14.

In the case of a Web page consisting of HTML tags, the browser normally reads the information sent and renders the page in the browser window. Other data, like video, might launch a helper application or a plug-in to view the information. Completely unknown MIME types might cause the browser to prompt the user to save the data, display it in some helper application, or delete it. This type of browser request is shown here:

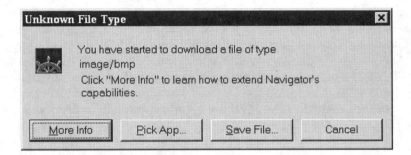

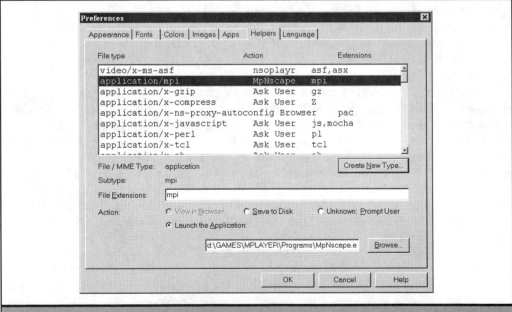

Figure 2-14. *An example of browser MIME-type mappings*

As the browser reads data, it may find that there is more information, such as images, to request from a Web server. If this is the case, the process is repeated, though the early steps may be much more rapid since the location of the server has already been established.

In summary, the Web uses a client/server model. The browser (client) requests pages from a Web server over a network like the Internet. The discussion is handled by the HTTP protocol. The actual transmission of data is handled by TCP/IP. The addressing of data objects to request takes the form of a Uniform Resource Locator (URL), which relies heavily on domain name services. Once a request is processed, the resulting information is transmitted with a MIME content-type indicator so a browser can interpret it. Most pages are created using the HTML markup language as discussed in Chapter 1, but MIME allows other technologies to be included as well.

HTML's Role in the Web

It should be obvious by now that HTML is just one part of an overall system used to deliver Web pages. The Web really includes the pages themselves built with technologies like HTML, the software and hardware that serve up the pages, the Internet and its connectivity issues, and the browsers that render the pages. When you get right down to it, the document author has very little control over anything other than the structure of the page. How quickly it gets to an end user, and what it looks like on the end user's browser, can vary over time and from browser to browser. This is a very aggravating aspect of publishing on the Web. The Web also allows open access to any platform, which is what makes it so powerful. It is interesting to look at the Web as a community and try to understand why HTML is used the way it is. Looking back at the history of the Web so far reveals the fundamental aspects of HTML's role on the Web and the issues facing the technology.

Historical Roots of HTML

When thinking about why HTML is the way it is, ask a simple question. Do you know for sure what kind of computer, screen, or browser type that the person viewing your Web page has? The answer is no. There are so many different screen sizes, operating systems, color palettes, and other factors that creating software on all systems would be a nightmare.

Imagine, then, the problem faced by Tim Berners-Lee, a researcher at the Conseil Europeen pour Recherche Nucleaire (CERN) laboratory in Geneva, Switzerland. Berners-Lee had to create a hypertext delivery environment that would be used as an interface to scientific information. This environment would render information equally well on Macintosh systems with small screens, NeXT Workstations, IBM PCs, and a variety of other platforms. Rather than give up because of the variation in screen support, Berners-Lee opted to develop the first versions of HTML to concentrate on providing the content and structure first and worry about the presentation later. This made sense, since the group of people he was serving were scientists looking at technical information—hardly a group looking for the latest in fonts and graphic design techniques. The presentation would be left up to the browser. The HTML language eventually was defined as an application of Standard Generalized Markup Language (SGML), which serves as a base for defining markup languages. Much of the flavor of HTML as a structured language (instead of a presentation language) comes from this relationship with SGML.

> **Note**   *There is nothing to indicate that the original design of the Web didn't care about presentation. There's plenty of evidence to suggest that it did. It was just that the project was to evolve over time. Fundamental issues like linking, structure, and network delivery needed to be resolved first.*

Deployed by late 1991, the Web grew slowly at first. In its infancy, it was characterized by a textual interface that was unattractive and somewhat difficult to use. However, much of the infrastructure necessary to make the Web work—including basic HTML, HTTP, and MIME—were already in place long before the Web took off.

Mosaic: The Web Community Changes

While the division of structure and style suggested by HTML was a good design decision, it has proved to be a huge point of contention in the Web community. At first, the Web community was a homogenous bunch of folks, mostly researchers and academics. As the Web matured, there was a call to make it easier to use and provide multimedia facilities. In 1993, Marc Andreessen, an undergraduate working for the National Center for Supercomputing Applications (NCSA) in Illinois, was involved, with others, in developing a graphical browser for the Web. This graphical browser, called Mosaic, made the Web much easier to use. The most influential aspect of the Mosaic browser was its introduction of inline images, making the Web a visual experience. Mosaic took the Internet world by storm. The number of Web servers exploded into the hundreds, and then thousands, within months of the browser's release. Soon the Web landscape was dominated by media, marketing, entertainment, and commercial Web sites of all shapes and sizes. In a matter of a few years, the Web community changed significantly to encompass many groups with fewer academic interests.

Commercial and entertainment professionals can agree on one important point: presentation matters. In these arenas, how something looks is nearly as important as what it is. "Perception is reality" is a common expression in the business community. As originally designed, the Web did not fit well with this motto. The first-generation Web provided relatively stark pages with gray backgrounds and left alignment. In first-generation (Mosaic) pages, it was impossible to even center text. Figure 2-15 shows an abstract view of a Web page generated in Mosaic.

Figure 2-15.   *Mosaic-generation Web page*

The Rise of Netscape

By the spring of 1994, Andreessen and many of his colleagues left NCSA and joined Dr. James Clark, the founder of Silicon Graphics, to form a company originally called Mosaic Communications Corporation. The firm, which later changed its name to Netscape due to legal problems with NCSA, released a preliminary version of its next-generation browser in the fall of 1994. The program, later to be called Netscape Navigator, was nicknamed Mozilla (after Mosaic and Godzilla) because it was destined to be the monster browser that would kill Mosaic—and so it did. By early 1995, Netscape was well entrenched in the marketplace. The reason Netscape dominated the market so easily was that it made significant enhancements to its browser and HTML to improve the performance and look of the Web. For example, Netscape introduced background colors and limited font sizing. It introduced improved page layout with text flowing around images, centering, and the much-maligned and nearly universally despised **<BLINK>** element. An early Netscape-style page is shown in Figure 2-16.

Many longtime Web professionals complained of Netscape's general disregard for HTML standards and argued in favor of the process they felt should be used to expand the Web. The market, largely oblivious to such concerns, responded well to the improvements. According to most estimates, Netscape was used by nearly 80 percent of the Internet market in 1995. The tags it introduced were used on many Web sites.

Figure 2-16. *Early Netscape-style Web page*

The Market Matures: Microsoft Enters

The Web underwent other significant changes during 1995. Larger content producers, including media conglomerates like Time Warner and Hollywood, embraced the Web. Advertising dollars soon followed. The phenomenal growth of the content on the Web led to the development of such services as Yahoo!, which could provide directories or search facilities to navigate the flood of incoming data. Many new browsers were developed in 1995, but none except Microsoft's Internet Explorer posed a serious threat to Netscape's dominance of the market. Microsoft initially introduced its own features and HTML tags like **<MARQUEE>** in an attempt to extend the presentation of the Web and gain market share. This worked to some degree, but Microsoft later decided to return to its normal approach of "embrace and extend," taking World Wide Web Consortium ideas like style sheets and implementing them first.

By 1996, the Web world had turned into a two-party system with mostly Microsoft and Netscape browsers in use. Still, many other browsers were in use by limited numbers of people. Designers faced with supporting a variety of standards often gave up on cross-platform compatibility and focused on making pages look good under one browser or another. This was an unfortunate turn of events. To this day, many sites lock users out with requests to download one browser or another in order to view proprietary HTML tags on a page. To further complicate the Web, print designers started to force HTML to render pages the way they wanted. Pixel-level control was the graphic designer's goal, and with tables and graphics layout tricks (discussed in Chapter 8), they almost had it, at times. Of course, pages became increasingly complicated. The HTML used became more confusing and proprietary. Even now, the Web continues to change.

From Pages to Programs

Many people view the Web simply as a way to deliver documents, or as a digital print distribution system. This is a very narrow view, however. People want to order things online, play, and communicate through the Web. The Web can do these things, but it means thinking about the Web not as a collection of documents but as a software system. The page view of the Web world is quickly being replaced with a program view of Web sites. Common Gateway Interface (CGI) programs were introduced at the dawn of the Web and are still widely in use. Plug-ins, Java, JavaScript, and ActiveX controls have helped the Web become more and more programmed.

Why have a button on a page to click for a Netscape version or a Microsoft version of the site, when a program can sense the browser type and build the appropriate page? Why design around 640 × 480 screen displays as a minimum, when the resolution can be sensed and the appropriate graphics provided? This is the idea of programmed sites with pages that are dynamically generated from database information. Pages are no longer just collections of words. They are collections of media objects glued together with programming logic in sophisticated, windowed user interfaces. An example of this style of page is shown in Figure 2-17.

The programmed page introduces new issues for HTML; however, while many people still focus on graphic design problems affecting the Web, these problems are being worked out. The ramifications of proprietary HTML tags are better understood. People are starting to understand the benefits of the separation of style and structure. Style sheets and other improvements may help provide designers with the control they desire without completely sacrificing the purity of HTML. However, new problems arise with programmed pages. For example, how will HTML and scripting be mixed? Just as design and content were separated, shouldn't the logic be separated out too? Time will tell.

Issues Facing HTML and the Web

Looking at HTML, the common issue always seems to be one of structure and style. HTML can be used to structure documents, but it does not yet provide all the features necessary for making them look the way the author wants. This is one of the inherent compromises of the Web, but it isn't the only issue facing HTML and the Web. There are many others.

The Web and HTML are still relatively new. In the commercial sense the Web is only a few years old. Many things remain to be worked out. Users expect perfect presentation and CD-ROM–like interfaces. HTML doesn't provide these features, but

Figure 2-17.   *Programmed-style page*

extensions, style sheets, or binary formats will. However, with an increasing arena of different browsing options, compatibility across platforms may be an issue for a long time to come. Second, while a Web browser is easy to use, finding things is not so simple. The Web needs more organization. Web search facilities, linking features, and addressing need to be improved. Third, the Web needs to be more responsive. This isn't so much an issue with HTML or Web servers, but with the medium of delivery. The protocols and the network have to be improved so that people are satisfied with the responsiveness of Web sites. The introduction of multimedia elements and CD-ROM–like interfaces only worsens the hunger for bandwidth. Last, the Web has to be useful. Programmed pages do something. Ordering tickets, playing games, communicating, and finding information is what the Web is all about. HTML will have to support programming technologies so that pages are more dynamic and sites that interact with the user become easier to build.

Summary

The Web has had an interesting history so far. Though many people are surprised by the phenomenal growth of the Web, that growth makes sense when you consider that the technology behind the Web is both powerful and easy to use. Despite these benefits, however, there are serious issues facing the Web. These include organization, presentation, and programming facilities. Some of these issues apply to networked hypertext, while others are unique to the rapidly expanding Internet. HTML is only one part of the overall medium of the Web. Developing a Web site is more than just understanding the HTML tags involved; there are many other technologies and issues to consider.

The next chapter discusses Web publishing. Undoubtedly, HTML will continue to be a very important part of Web pages, but new questions arise about the role HTML will play as we move to a more programmed and visual Web.

Chapter 3

Web Publishing

One of the problems with discussing the creation of Web pages is that mastery of HTML is often confused with understanding the process of Web design and publishing. Web design describes the process of creating appealing and usable Web sites. Graphic design is only part of the process of Web design. HTML and more programming-oriented technologies are also part of the process. Web publishing is a more appropriate term to describe the overall process of planning and putting together a Web site, particularly when some degree of forethought, skill, and artistry is employed. Knowledge of HTML alone does not provide all the facilities required to make appealing, usable Web sites. It is important to understand the Web process and how HTML works in that process, before getting too caught up in the details of markup tags.

The Goals of Web Design

So what, exactly, is good Web page design? Some discuss what it is not (www.webpagesthatsuck.com), but this really doesn't demonstrate how to create good Web sites. Others like to discuss aesthetics and layout (www.highfive.com). This may be appropriate on a superficial level, but beauty is in the eye of the beholder. Looks aren't everything. Function is important. Some like to answer the good Web design question with pure function. If it's not usable (www.useit.com), it isn't reasonable—but function without motivating form is boring. Some talk too much about success, citing large numbers of visitors as validation of a site's design. This assumes that the Web is primarily about popularity. Who cares how many visitors come to a page unless there is some benefit to it? Think about quality and success. If serving the most burgers says anything about making good hamburgers, then McDonald's makes the world's best hamburger. This kind of logic gets people in trouble on the Web all the time. Think about whether or not economically successful or even trendy Web pages are well designed. Characterizing good Web design is not easy, especially since it depends largely on your target audience.

Most Web discussions lose sight of the big picture. They place too much emphasis on how pages look, and not on their content, purpose, functionality, or the user's experience. Web design is not just graphic design. True, Web design includes graphic design. Artistic style, color theory, typography, and other visual concerns are an important part of the Web design process. There's more to it than that, however. Web design also includes information design, which specifies how information should be organized and linked. In this sense, hypertext theory is also a part of Web design. To some extent, so is technical writing. Web design might also include system design. Web pages aren't always static pages, but programs that do something. Programming is a part of Web design, as are network and server design. Business issues and project management also might be considered realities of Web design. It is obvious that many talents are part of Web design. At the top of the list is knowing the site's ultimate purpose.

The goal of a Web designer is to come up with a usable and appealing visual design for a software system in the form of a Web site that helps a user fulfill some goal. In other words, the goal is to develop a site that can be delivered to the user in a satisfactory manner, be interpreted correctly by the user, and induce the desired outcome. Web design should be concerned not only with the aesthetic qualities of a Web site, but with the overall user's experience in the context of a specific task or problem. The focus is on how something can be done, not just on how it looks.

It is easy to throw out expressions like "perception is reality" or "content is king" as arguments for or against focus on the visual nature of the Web. However, the reality is a balance between these extreme points of view. Compare a user interacting with or consuming the information at your Web site with a person eating at a restaurant. If a person eats the finest cuisine in surroundings like a death row jail cell, that person's experience of the food is dramatically affected. If the surroundings are wonderful with impeccable décor, but the meal consists of stale junk food, the surroundings don't help the taste at all. The best approach in this analogy is a holistic one, where the food fits the surroundings. Any restaurant owner will tell you that. Similarly, amusement parks aren't just about the rides, but the whole experience.

While both of these analogies involve places where people go and do something, Web sites really are, in a sense, places. Do people talk about reading a Web page, or do they *visit* it? Navigating around a Web site is like moving around a place—back to home, on to the next section, and so on. Going to a Web site is about accomplishing something in a pleasing or effective manner. This requires balancing function and aesthetics.

So how can we make something visually appealing that works without exceeding the constraints of the Internet and Web technologies? Focusing on the technology and then decorating a Web page leads to the dreaded "Christmas Tree" design shown in Figure 3-1. Putting a page together with HTML and then sprucing it up with a few colored balls, a rainbow color bar, and animated clip art doesn't help. The page looks slapped together, and the graphics provide little more than extra eye-catching glitz. The background also interferes with the user's ability to read the text.

On the other hand, focusing too much on the visual leads to online brochures with slow downloading, full-screen images. Everything is created with graphic composition tools like PhotoShop. While layout control is nearly absolute, the resulting files are huge. Text on a page can't be changed without a graphic designer, let alone indexed by a Web search engine. This also excludes those who surf with images off, use a text browser, or the disabled who simply cannot see your images. The full-screen image design style, shown in Figure 3-2, may produce nice-looking pages, but it tends to relegate Web sites to nice digital brochures. Many large sites fall into this trap because they never test their pages over a dial-in link. A page that seems to work well over the local ethernet network may take ages to load over a 28.8 Kbps modem connection. The typical modem user is still connecting at that speed, or lower, and most are not willing to wait forever for your page to load before giving up and moving on to greener pastures.

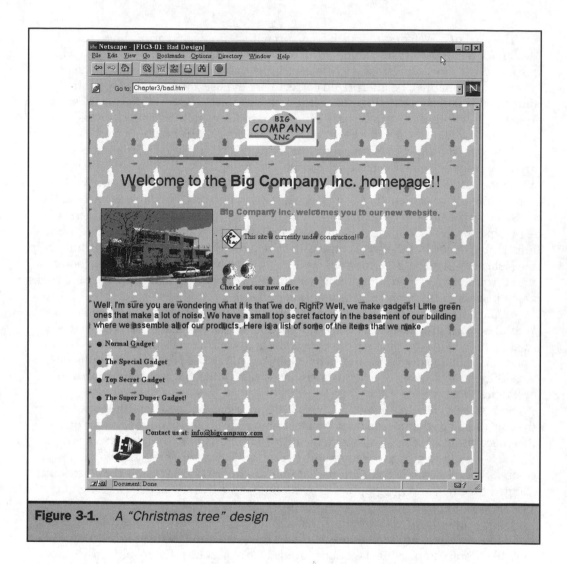

Figure 3-1.   *A "Christmas tree" design*

Again, balance is the issue. Sometimes, stark pages are okay. Other times, full-screen images make sense. And you can optimize your images to use a small palette, or contain less detail, to reduce the file size. The form of a site depends on its goals. Start with the purpose, determine the information design, and then work on visuals and technical implementation. Once the simplicity of HTML is revealed, many authors are eager to quickly mark up pages and then try to improve them by adding graphics. Designers can ruin the site just by thinking more about the user interface than about what is actually delivered. There is a process to the creation of Web sites, not an ad hoc decision to focus more on visuals or more on content.

Figure 3-2. *A full-screen image design*

The Process of Web Publishing

Planning, organizing, and visualizing Web sites and pages may be more important than knowing HTML. Unfortunately, these are very difficult things to teach, and tend to be learned only by experience. The biggest mistake in Web development is not having a clear goal for a Web site. Even if the site is launched on time and under budget, how can you understand whether you did a good job if there was no goal in the first place? Most of the time, goals are vague. Initially, many corporate Web site projects were fueled by "FUD"—fear, uncertainty, and doubt. With the hype surrounding the Web, it was important to get on before the competition. If the competition was already online, a Web site appeared even more crucial to corporate success. This is a dangerous situation to be in. Even if budget is not an issue, the benefit of the site will eventually be questioned. Web professionals may find their jobs on the line. Thus, the first step in the Web publishing process is defining the purpose of a site. Remember the old adage: "If you don't have time to do it right, when will you have time to do it over?"

Determining Purpose

Finding a purpose for a Web site isn't necessarily very hard. The Web can be very useful, and there are many common reasons to put up a site. A few common purposes for Web sites are listed here:

Business-to-business communication
Commerce
Entertainment
Information
Marketing
Personal home pages
Presence
Processing
Promotion
Research and education
Retail sales
Technical support

One problem with Web sites is that they may have multiple purposes. A corporate Web site may include demands for marketing, public relations, investor relations, technical support, commerce, and human resource services such as job recruiting. Trying to meet all these needs while thinking about the Web site as one entity can be difficult. Just like a large scale software system with many functions, a site with many different goals probably should be broken into modules or subprojects that make up part of a larger whole. This leads to the idea of a *microsite*—a very specific subsite that is part of a larger site and may be built separately. Microsites have the advantage of allowing the focus, look, or technology of a portion of a site to change without having to change the site as a whole. Determining a purpose usually isn't hard, but as will be discussed later, a purpose must be well defined. Otherwise, it becomes difficult to understand the viability of a Web project.

When using the concept of microsites, it is still important to establish a consistent look and feel for the site as a whole. People should feel comfortable as they move from your support pages to your marketing pages to your employment pages. A consistent user interface breeds familiarity and generates a united front. The user need not know that the site is constructed in modules, and a changing interface can lead to a user becoming lost and confused while exploring. It helps to have one person designated as the overall Webmaster for the project, to coordinate the efforts of the various subgroups. The Webmaster's role is basically the same as a project manager on a large software project.

Who Is the Audience?

Of course, just having a purpose for a site isn't enough; you need to consider a site's audience. Are the users coming from within your organization, or from outside? Is it young or old? What language do they speak? When do they visit the site? What technologies do they support? What browsers do they use? Figuring out an audience doesn't have to be that hard, but don't assume that your audience is too large. People from South America or the Sudan can visit your Web page—but do they? Should they? It is important to be realistic about the audience of the Web. There may be millions of users on the Web, but they aren't all going to visit a particular Web site. If they did, things would probably not work well. When the idea of a site's audience is discussed, do not think in terms of a nameless, faceless John Q. Cybercitizen with a modem and an America Online account.

If the site is about selling magnetic components and the primary buyers of those components are engineers at large electronics firms, are they likely to access the site from a personal AOL account? Not really—so why build the site around the requirements of AOL's Web browser? The key to understanding audiences is to get specific, perhaps even talk to the intended users of the site. Far too often, sites are designed around the needs or beliefs of their authors, not around the needs and beliefs of the actual users of the sites. This is a sure way to limit the success of the site.

If you have a site up now, see if you can obtain access to your server logs. These logs can tell you quite a bit about your user base. Depending on the server and its configuration, you can learn the time of day you get the most hits, the pages visited the most, the browsers and versions being used, the domains your visitors come from, and even the pages that referred them to your site—as well as more technical data such as the protocol version and requesting method.

If you do not have a server running yet, begin with your best estimates of the kinds of visitors you expect. Once the site is running, check the logs against your estimates—you may find that your audience is different than you expected. An important point in Web design is that you must be willing to revise your designs, even going as far as throwing away your favorite ideas, if they do not fit with your actual audience.

Who Will Pay for It?

Sites cost money to produce, so they generally have to produce some benefit in order to continue. While people do put up sites for personal enjoyment, there is a limit even to this type of site in terms of an individual's investment of time and money. It is very important to understand the business model of the site. Only a year or two ago, many corporate Web budgets were not always the first concern due to the novelty of the technology. Today, however, Web sites often have to prove that they're "worth it." The money has to come from somewhere.

A site's creator could pay for everything, but that probably isn't reasonable unless the Web site is for pure enjoyment or nonprofit. Typically, some funds have to be collected, probably indirectly, to support the site. A promotional site for a movie may not directly collect revenues, but hopefully the site will influence the audience and have some impact on the success or failure of the film. What's interesting is that many Web sites are nearly as indirect as a movie promotion site. It can be very difficult to measure the direct benefit of having such sites. More directly measurable sites are those where leads are collected or goods are sold. Some value can be put on these transactions, and an understanding of the benefit of the site can be determined.

Another possible business model for a Web site would be to have the viewer pay, as in a subscription model. The problem with this model is that there must be a reason for the viewer to pay for the information or service available at the Web site. Making a Web site valuable to a user is tricky, especially considering that value often is both psychological and real. When looking at the value of the information available in an encyclopedia, think about its form. If the encyclopedia's information is in book form, the cost might be as high as $1,000. Put the same information on a CD-ROM, and see if the information can be sold for the same cost. What if the same information is on a Web site? On a CD-ROM, the information probably can be sold for $50–$100. On a Web site, it goes for even less, particularly if the user only wants to buy a specific piece of information. Users often place more value on the delivery of a good or service than on the good itself. Consider software, where the design and production of packaging often costs more than reproducing the software itself. The bottom line is that packaging does count. It is no wonder that users often mistakenly overvalue the graphic aspect of a site.

> **Note**　*As information services become more pervasive, consumers will probably begin to value content on the Internet despite its lack of tangibility.*

Another business model involves getting someone besides the owner or the intended audience of the site to pay. This model typically comes in the form of an advertising-driven site. However, what is interesting about advertising is that there is actually a good being sold—the audience. Advertisers are interested in reaching a particular audience and are willing to pay for an advertisement based on the effectiveness of that ad reaching the intended audience. The question is how can an audience be attracted, measured, and then sold to the advertisers? The obvious approach is to provide some reason that an audience will want to come to a Web site and identify themselves. This is very difficult. Furthermore, the audience must be accurately measured so the advertiser has a way to compare the size of audience from one site to the next and knows how to spend his or her advertising dollars. People often discuss the number of visitors to their site as an indication of value to an advertiser. The advertisers, however, may not care about the number of visitors unless those visitors are in their target audience. Furthermore, the number of visitors doesn't mean much of anything as far as price is concerned unless it can be compared against other advertising venues—even those beyond the Web. Planning a business model around advertising is less than straightforward. Parties interested in funding their ventures in this manner would be well advised to study traditional advertising-based media, like magazines, to understand the pros and cons of this approach.

Whoever is paying for the site, there must be some understanding of the costs and the benefits of the site. How much does each visitor actually cost, and what benefit does he or she produce? Understand that the number of visitors doesn't count, even when using the advertising model. The value of the site transcends this figure and addresses the effectiveness of the visitation. In other words, many visits don't necessarily mean success. Having many visitors to an online store who nonetheless make few purchases may mean huge losses, particularly if it costs more to reach each visitor. Even the form of the Web site may change the cost. Since the amount of data delivered from a Web site is generally related directly to the site's variable costs, sending video would cost more than sending regular HTML text. High costs aren't a bad thing if there is a big payoff. This is why a goal must be set.

Defining Goals

A goal for a site is not the same as its purpose. A purpose gives a general idea of what the site is for, while a goal is very specific. A goal can help define how much should be spent, but goals must be measurable. What is a measurable goal of the site? Selling x dollars worth of product directly via the Web site is a measurable goal, as is selling x dollars of product or service indirectly through leads. Reaching a certain usage level per day, week, or month can be a goal. So is lowering the number of incoming technical support phone calls. There are many ways to measure the success or failure of a Web project, but measurements generally come in two categories: soft and hard. Hard measurements are those that are easily measured, such as the number of visitors per day. Soft measurements are a little less clear. For example, with a promotional site for a movie, it might be difficult to understand if the site had any effect on the box office sales.

Why are measurements so important? From a manager's perspective, measurements can be used to determine how much to spend. If a Web site's goal is to produce $10,000 of new sales, then spending $500,000 on the site is not acceptable unless the site has some other nonmeasurable value that can make up the other $490,000. While this seems like common sense, a clear return on investment or cost benefit is seldom determined for corporate Web sites. Soft measurements can make things difficult, since it is not clear what effect the Web site may have. In the advertising industry, certain rules of thumb apply, like spending ten percent of overall sales on advertising. A percentage of that would obviously go toward a Web site. Due to the hype surrounding the Web, very little business sense is exhibited toward Web development. Even if sites were considered as little more than online brochures, it is obvious that the more brochures printed on paper, the more expensive. The more pages, the more expensive. The more complicated, the more expensive. Web sites are the same way.

> **Note** *Both on paper and on the Web, economies of scale do reduce the per-unit cost, but there is still a point of diminishing returns. Web sites often have diminishing returns that are ignored. For example, the expense of making a site engineered perfectly for every situation and every browser provides only a little more benefit than one engineered for most users, from a financial point of view. It is interesting that Web experts tend to get somewhat religious on the point of how a site should be. In the face of managerial and financial realities, things can't always be done perfectly.*

It takes little effort to ensure basic interoperability, such as including the **ALT** attribute on **<IMG>** elements (to be introduced in Chapter 4), providing text link alternatives to image maps, and so on. Many users of graphic browsers turn image loading off to speed up their surfing over modem links. In the design community, the number of stories of complaints from such users are countless—yet designers continue to make the same mistakes. The point is to find a good balance for *your* audience. This is another reason to monitor your server logs. Many designers have been surprised at the number of users hitting their sites with "outdated" browser versions. Never depend on users having the latest and greatest. A general rule of thumb is to wait six months before relying on a new technology, and even then it is good design to allow for graceful degradation of the pages so they can display coherently in older browsers that do not support the new technology.

Setting the Scope

Scope equals money. The more that is put into a Web site, the more it costs. Because of the flexible nature of the Web, many developers want to add as much as possible to the Web site. However, more isn't always better. The more that is added to the site, the more it costs. Furthermore, having too much information makes it difficult to find essential information. To think about scope, return to one of the first steps in the process. What is the main purpose of the site? Shouldn't the information of the site reflect this purpose? Looking at the Web, this doesn't seem to always be the case. Have you ever gone to a site and not understood its point?

Finding the essentials of a Web site might not be easy, particularly if there are many purposes or many parties involved in its development. One approach is to have a brainstorming session where users provide ideas. Each idea is then written down on a 3 x 5 card. After all the cards have been created, ask the users to sort the cards into piles. First, sort the cards into like piles to see how things are related. Next, sort the piles in order of importance. What is important can eventually be distilled out of the cards. Remember to cut down the number of cards to make people focus on what is truly important.

Instead of coming up with ideas of what should go into a site to meet a particular goal or goals, you may be tempted to take existing materials such as marketing pieces and convert them to the Web. Unfortunately, creating the content of the site based solely on all the text of all manuals, brochures, and other support materials rarely works. Migrating text from print to the Web is troublesome because the media are so different. Reading onscreen has been shown to be 25 percent slower than reading from paper. In practice, people do not tend to read information online carefully. They tend to scan it quickly and then print out what they need. In this sense, writing for paper tends to go against screen reading. Think about newspaper or TV news stories: the main point is said first and then discussed. This goes against the slow buildup of many paper documents, which carefully spell out a point. With visitors skimming the site, key bullet points get read while detailed information might get skipped. The main thing is to keep the point obvious and simple. Even if information is presented well, organization can ruin all the hard work in preparing the information. If a viewer can't find the information, who cares how great it looks or how well it reads?

Organization of Information

Organizing the information at a Web site is often just as important as the information itself. If visitors to a Web site can't find what they are looking for, they may get frustrated and leave. Organizing information is a matter of grouping similar items in the same place. The card-sorting discussion in the previous section helps define what items should go together. Site designers often use a tree structure for a site, as shown in Figure 3-3.

While the tree structure seems the most appropriate choice for Web sites, there is an issue of how many choices should be at the top level and how wide the tree is versus how deep it is. If there are too many choices at the top level, the structure is flat and may be confusing. Forcing people farther down the tree can be frustrating, as it requires them to keep moving level by level to find the appropriate information. The depth versus breadth issue is illustrated in Figure 3-4.

From the initial studies on hypertext, there are three "golden rules":

- Hypertext is a body of information organized into numerous fragments. By definition, most Web sites—unless they are a single page—should fit this rule.

- These fragments relate to each other somehow. If the site doesn't have a clear goal, the relationship between pages might not be obvious.

- The user needs only a small fraction of the information presented at any time.

Sites that are too flat and provide all choices all the time confuse the user by presenting too many choices. How many choices are okay? Studies suggest that between six and eight choices are optimal, because users can retain the choices in short-term memory fairly easily. Too many choices will make the selection process suboptimal, and the user may focus on extremes like first item, last item, or item in the center. Too few choices may indicate that you are creating a needless layer; a long

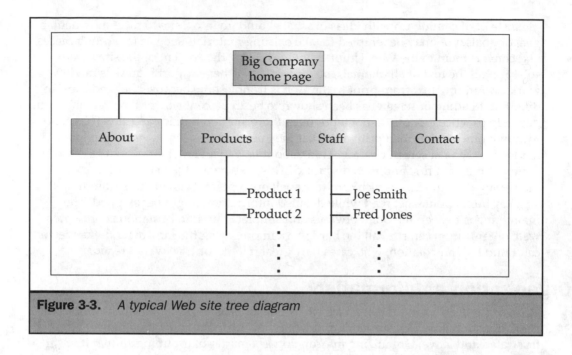

Figure 3-3.   *A typical Web site tree diagram*

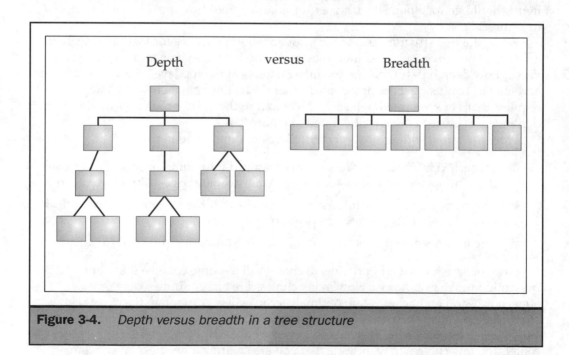

Figure 3-4.   *Depth versus breadth in a tree structure*

sequence of pages with only two choices on each may simply slow things down. It might be better to combine some of those choices on fewer pages. Structuring the site appropriately may help improve a user's interaction with information. Unfortunately, sometimes the tree is considered the only structure for a Web site.

Web-based information doesn't necessarily have to be structured in the form of a tree. Sometimes a pure linear organization with one page after another makes sense. A slide show, tour, or presentation probably should be in the form of a linear progression. Of course, because of the browser back button, at one level Web sites are always bi-directional linear. The basic idea of a linear structure is shown in Figure 3-5.

Another approach might be a linear progression with alternatives, a series of yes and no questions that eventually lead to the next question in the sequence. This application would make sense for the "linear with alternatives" structure. An effective application of the linear with alternatives structure came in the form of an AIDS awareness site that discussed risk factors in a yes and no fashion but eventually lead to the next risk category regardless of the choice. This gave the site a false sense of interactivity, which engaged the viewer more than a pure linear structure. The linear form with alternatives is shown in Figure 3-6.

Another form of organization is the linear style with options structure. This structure, shown in Figure 3-7, is good for a set of information that is sometimes optional. For example, in many surveys the taker is asked to skip a set of questions depending on his or her answer. A Web form of such a survey would be a perfect candidate for linear with options, as it would allow the reader to skip ahead over questions that were not relevant while still preserving the general path of the information.

The linear with side trips structure is perfect for a body of information that may have useful supplementary information. For example, a linear Web presentation about flowers may lead to a side trip about beekeeping that the user can view, but later return to the main discussion as shown in Figure 3-8. This form of a site provides diversion while still preserving path. Linear with side trips is a form of a tree—just turn the structure on its side. When used with linear content, it warrants its own discussion.

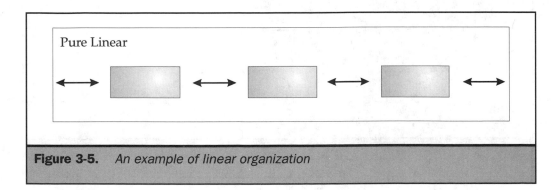

Figure 3-5.   *An example of linear organization*

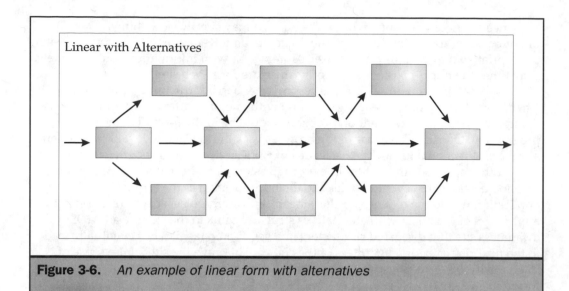

Figure 3-6. *An example of linear form with alternatives*

One uncommon form of structuring information, at least on the Web, is the grid style. The grid style has a great degree of spatial organization, as do many of the linear forms. In the grid, there is a sense of up, down, left, and right. Because of its regular structure, the grid form is good for related items and organization, such as what might be found in a catalog. Imagine the columns of the grid being associated with a particular product line and the nodes representing the products in that particular product line. Moving across columns might be like moving among equivalent products between product lines. The basic idea of the grid is shown in Figure 3-9.

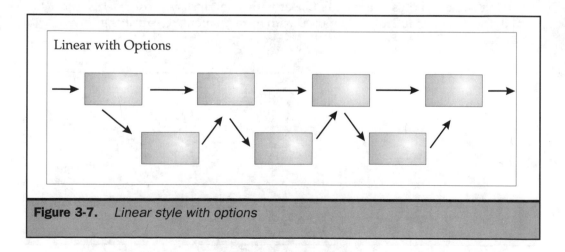

Figure 3-7. *Linear style with options*

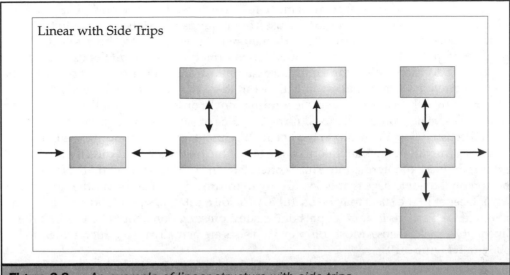

Figure 3-8. *An example of linear structure with side trips*

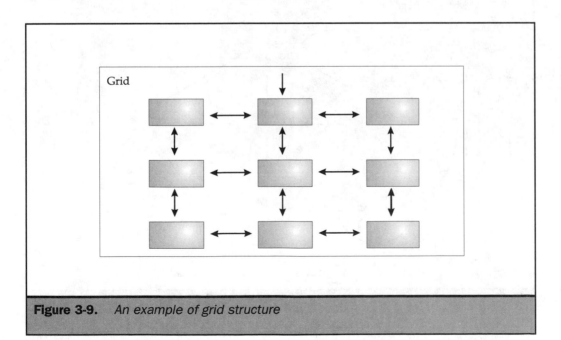

Figure 3-9. *An example of grid structure*

The tree structure or hierarchy is much less structured than the grid. A narrow hierarchy provides few choices for the user, but requires many clicks to get to the destination. On the other hand, the wide hierarchy provides many choices so it requires fewer clicks to get to the destination information, assuming the user makes the correct decision. This is the same discussion illustrated in Figure 3-4. Both forms of the tree provide some spatial organization, but there is a question of how much. The wider the tree, the less structured the information. In order to balance the problems of hierarchies, many consider a mixed form. The idea of skips ahead or alternatives has been discussed in relationship to the linear structure. How about adding a skip ahead to a tree structure? A special link from the top of the tree could lead directly to an important piece of information. This is often seen in Web sites where there is a special button on the home page that links directly to the free download or another important item. Deeper in the site it may be useful to provide a catalog, so the grid structure may make sense. Perhaps in another part of the site a presentation should be used, so the linear style makes sense. Most complex Web sites are actually mixed hierarchies, as shown in Figure 3-10.

The problem with the mixed hierarchy is that it can easily degrade into the pure Web form, which is a tangled mess of links where the organization is unclear. All sense

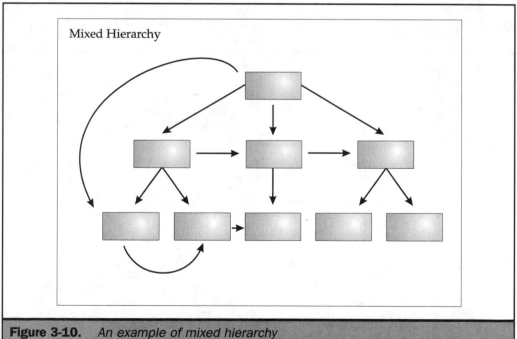

Figure 3-10.   *An example of mixed hierarchy*

of spatiality is lost in the pure Web form. The only navigational sense is "signpost based," where the viewer recognizes landmarks in the site like the home page. The benefit of the pure Web form is obvious if the user is familiar with the data, since it is easy to navigate among items that are fully connected. However, the organization may be so unclear that the confusion factor drives users away. An example of a pure Web structure is shown in Figure 3-11.

When organizing information, the aim is to achieve a balance between predictability and expressiveness. Although the Web form may be very expressive, it may be completely unpredictable as far as the user is concerned. On the other hand, the linear form is very predictable but not terribly expressive. The balance of these forms is shown in Figure 3-12. There is a temptation to add links anywhere one *can*. This was commonly seen in early Web sites, when any word that referred to a different topic became a hyperlink. Resist this temptation. When you are adding a link, ask yourself "Does this link add value to the audience?" If the answer is "No," then the link is inappropriate. Every link is an invitation for the user to break away from the content on that page.

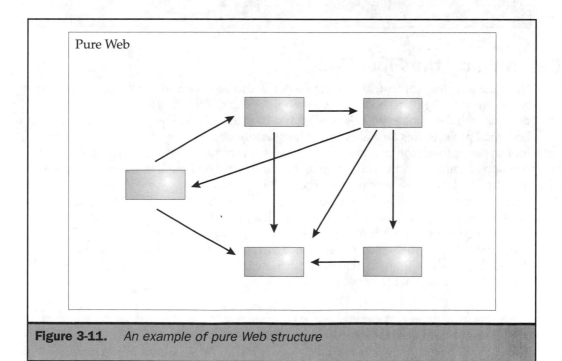

Figure 3-11.   *An example of pure Web structure*

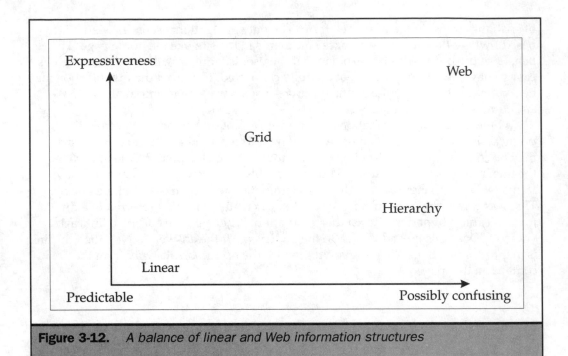

Figure 3-12. *A balance of linear and Web information structures*

Determining the Final Plan

Once the purpose, content, and structure of the site have been determined, a plan can be developed. The plan should consist of a flow chart of the site, a time line, and a document that describes what is needed and how the site will be put together. For small projects, this formality might be overkill. On larger projects, however, it is foolish to approach the task without a sense of where the project is going. If the site is developed commercially, such planning is mandatory. Without a sense of what goes into the site, how can a vendor price the site? People often ask Web developers how much a site costs, but this depends on the size, scope, and technology that goes into the site, among other factors. A company with a comprehensive site plan can send the project out for bid. Without a plan, comparing proposals from competing firms provides little information of value. Notice that, up until this point, no specific discussion of what the site will look like or how it works has been addressed. These tasks are part of the implementation phase.

Implementation

Readers might assume that the implementation phase of the Web publishing process is the most difficult, but depending on how well the site was planned it may be very straightforward. With a clear plan in hand, a site can be built very quickly. When the various parts of the site are well defined, many people can work on the site simultaneously. Even so, there are potential problems with the implementation phase of a Web project.

Creating the Content

One of the first signs of trouble is when content is not ready for the Web, or there is too much content. When planning a Web site, people often provide ideas for things that would be nice to put in, with no consideration of the cost. Information can be formatted quickly—but if the information doesn't exist, formatting can't take place. While this sounds like simple common sense, it is probably the second most common problem on the Web beyond purpose.

Just ask yourself what "under construction" means. Why do so many sites have many choices, but 90 percent of the pages are under construction? Wouldn't the site be better if only the working areas were available? This is the problem of not having the content ready. The cost of developing the content often outweighs the cost of preparing it for the Web. A good plan pares the site down to what it should do and considers the cost of creating the content. Without content, the site goes nowhere. Buttons to navigate around, and yellow and black animated pictures of men digging up a road, do not make a good site. Commercial Web design projects are often late more because the client was unable to produce content on time than because the firm was unable to finish the technology or graphics.

While we're on the subject, do not place "Under Construction" images on your pages. All Web sites are either under construction or stagnant. If an area of the site is not yet ready for visitors, simply do not place the links to that area online yet. If users don't know an area doesn't exist, they won't be disappointed when it isn't ready. It is frustrating to find a link to something you need, only to discover it is "under construction."

Visual Design

Once content is in hand, visual design may be produced. Why can't visual design come before content generation? One simple reason: the visual style of the site should reflect the content of the site. Until the content is close to being finished, any developed visual style can only provide decoration. It won't add any real value to the content. Think about the idea of product literature on a Web site. What happens if the visual design is developed first in a very corporate style, but the copy is written in a sarcastic, unprofessional tone? The site won't make much sense. Visuals should be discussed early to set the tone of the site, but the specifics of exactly what shade of red to use, or what size an image should be, must wait until the implementation phase. The visual design phase generally requires that paper designs first be explored. Then image composites can be created using a tool like Adobe PhotoShop. The choice of a particular look and feel is dependent on the purpose of the site, the look and feel of related materials, technological considerations such as download time, and personal taste.

Graphic designers are often the best people to approach to make a good-looking site. Unfortunately, designers often attempt to directly imitate existing print materials. This doesn't always work well. Subtle textures will be lost onscreen, complex gradients will translate into large byte-sized images, and bleeds generally won't work. Often the best approach is to keep the spirit of existing materials and fit them to suit the needs of the Web. This doesn't give the Web designer license to reinvent the corporate look and feel, but rather to modify an approach so that it creates a visually stimulating page that downloads quickly. This balance between visual appeal and download speed, combined with the imprecise layout afforded by HTML and unpredictable viewing environments, is what makes Web design so challenging. The best Web designers know enough about Web technology to work within its constraints. Web designers with graphics backgrounds occasionally undervalue the sense of organization that may have been applied to a site, and want to move sections around. On the other hand, some HTML or organization gurus don't respect the difficulty of design. Both content and visuals are equally important to the overall success of a site.

Technology Design

Far too many Web sites are viewed as glorified brochures. A page is just a bunch of words and pictures marked up with HTML. If this is true, then all books are just a bunch of words and pictures marked up with their own formatting language. They, too, should be easy to produce—but the reality is far more complicated. Maybe the real issues are novelty and complexity. Print designers don't charge the same rates as interactive designers, and many question why. One reason is the newness of the technology. Today, relatively few people know how to design Web pages well. Looking beyond this situation, however, there is a much different answer. Many Web sites are not brochures. Some sites let the user purchase something, others provide searching features, and some even let the user play games. Very advanced sites automatically configure themselves depending on the visitor's preferences or browser type.

If you extend these ideas to a Web site, it becomes a lot more than a brochure. By adding technology—such as a database, interactive forms, or programmed objects like Java applets—to the mixture, the Web becomes more like software and less like print media. In this sense, some effort must be made to select the appropriate technology for the job, and to properly integrate the look and content. As sites become more complex, look will still be important, but much of the effort will go into the technology. The shift away from a page paradigm of Web sites to a program paradigm is fast becoming a reality. How programming ideas relate to HTML, which is the core Web technology, will be discussed in depth starting in Chapter 12.

HTML

The heart of nearly every modern Web page is HTML. While it is possible with an embedded media type to have a complex Web page that consists of one HTML element alone like **<EMBED SRC="bigbinary.dcr" HEIGHT="200" WIDTH="500">**, HTML is still required. In the strict sense, all Web pages must contain some HTML, whether or not the focus and content is in an embedded binary object. As discussed in Chapter 1, HTML is a text markup language that is used to describe the structure of a page. Until recently, HTML was also used to describe the appearance of the page. This is not the preferred way to do things. Presentation should be left to style sheets, as discussed in Chapter 10, but this is not how most pages are now created. HTML often serves as the bridge between the content of a page and the interactive objects like scripts and programmed objects that may also be part of the Web site.

In many ways, HTML provides the framework on which a Web page is built. The images, text content, and programming are equally important, but HTML is necessary to bring it all together. Because of this, some people view putting a Web site together like putting a puzzle together—just assemble the pieces. This analogy would be appropriate if the puzzle had to be designed and the pieces created, broken apart, and then put back together. Given the pieces of a site, how can HTML be used to create the pages?

The creation of an HTML document for publishing on the Web is as simple as using the text editor of your choice (vi, Microsoft Word, Notepad, and so on) to insert the markup tags indicating format and links into the text. It is also possible to use a conversion program that converts files into HTML automatically. For example, it is possible to quickly convert Word 97 files or Rich Text Format (RTF) documents to HTML. The translation program preserves paragraphs, character formatting, and so on. However, the translated file may have to be checked and cleaned up. Furthermore, the translation program may not add links and other items necessary for Web publishing if they were not indicated in the original document.

Today, HTML editors are commonplace. Some editors for Windows, such as HotMetal Pro (www.softquad.com), HomeSite (www.allaire.com), and Hot Dog (www.sausage.com), show the insertion of the actual HTML tags into the document directly. Some of these tools are very simple tag insertion programs, while others are similar to programmers' editing tools, as shown by the screen snapshot of Allaire's HomeSite in Figure 3-13.

Other editing environments allow WYSIWYG ("what you see is what you get") style editing of pages, which keeps the HTML tags hidden behind the scenes. These include Netscape Navigator Gold, now called Composer (www.netscape.com), Adobe PageMill (www.adobe.com), and Microsoft FrontPage (www.microsoft.com/frontpage). Traditional WYSIWYG desktop publishing tools like Pagemaker, QuarkXPress, and Microsoft Word also now support automatic HTML output.

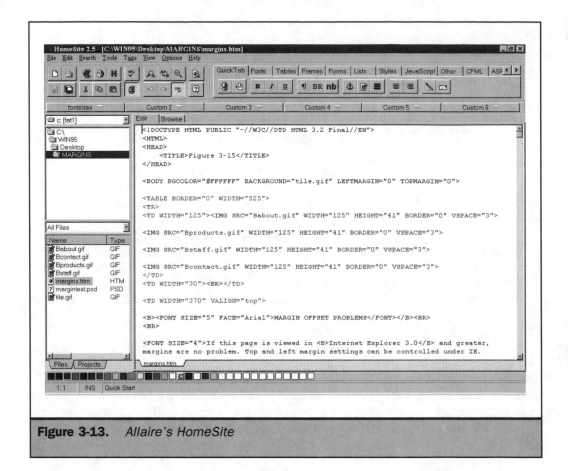

Figure 3-13. *Allaire's HomeSite*

The concept of WYSIWYG Web page design is somewhat flawed. As stated in Chapter 1, the browser is the final decision-maker for how a page will look. If a page is composed in one program and rendered under its internal display engine, there is no guarantee that it will come out the same way under another browser's rendering engine. This idea is illustrated in Figure 3-14.

Choosing the right Web tool for the job is not easy. In many cases, HTML tools are only useful to get a first cut of an HTML document. Manual editing of a Web document may still be necessary to create superior hypermedia documents using the latest HTML features. Furthermore, HTML tools tend to take a "one-page-at-a-time" view of the world. In the case of large-scale sites, it might be better to create a template

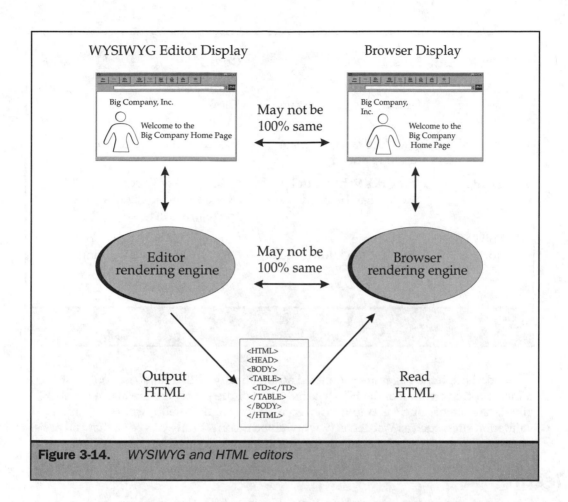

Figure 3-14.   *WYSIWYG and HTML editors*

of a standard page and flow content into it directly. Table 3-1 compares the pros and cons of using particular methods to create Web pages.

The tool you use to compose your HTML is a matter of both taste and applicability. In some cases, a WYSIWYG editor provides a good enough solution, particularly considering the ease in which the page can be created. In situations where tight control is demanded, a tagging editor may be in order. If a quick change is all that is needed to fix a typo, then a text editor works just fine. A large volume of files might warrant a translation tool. In practicality, no one tool will fit all jobs. Don't dismiss WYSIWYG tools for editors because they are easy. Many large Web firms still generate Web pages

Method	Pros	Cons
By hand	*Allows strict control *Allows use of latest tags	*Error prone *Slow *Requires knowledge of HTML
Translator	*Provides fast conversion of existing documents	*Requires manual editing
Tag editor	*Provides tight control *Faster than by hand	*Requires knowledge of HTML *Makes previsualization of the page difficult
WYSIWYG editor	*Easy to use *Requires no knowledge of HTML	*Often behind in tag support *May make manual editing of generated files difficult *Not really WYSIWYG

Table 3-1.   HTML Creation Issues

by hand, though the pages are populated automatically with a database tool. Just remember that creation of the HTML is only part of the job. There are also a number of validation tools, such as Weblint (www.cre.canon.co.uk/~neilb/weblint/), or validation sites, such as WebTechs (www.webtechs.com/html-val-svc/), that can assist authors who work by hand or need to polish the work done by a translating program.

Testing

Once a site or page has been created, it must be tested. Testing in the basic sense requires that the page be checked to see if it looks proper under a particular set of browsers. Unfortunately, Web page authors often mistakenly assume that if a page looks fine under their browser, it will look fine under others. The same page under WebTV and Netscape might appear very different. So which browsers should the site look perfect under? This gets back to an issue of audience. If the primary audience is AOL users, then obviously the site should be heavily tested under such conditions. The idea is not to lock people out.

Unfortunately, some HTML pundits take the idea of audience to an extreme. "The site should be available to everyone" is their rallying cry. While this is true in theory, a marketing person funding a site won't allocate a budget for a site that makes them look bad for the sake of 100 percent browser compatibility. The sad fact is that the Web isn't nearly as open as people like to think. Many sites don't work well under certain browsers, particularly more esoteric browsers or those made for users, such as blind users, with accessibility issues.

A little effort can go a long way to improve a site, such as the use of alternative text for browsers that can't render images. However, there is a point of diminishing returns where the facts of budget and practicality come in. One problem is testing a site under every browser. HTML theory says that if a page conforms to standard HTML, it works. However, browsers don't always work properly, and don't always conform to HTML standards. Even among the same form of browser, "slight problems" creep in, that can cause huge problems. For example, under Netscape 3.0, each platform (Macintosh, Windows, and Unix) has a different margin offset. For designers attempting to lay an image on a background, these differences are infuriating, as shown in Figure 3-15.

Testing is a big issue, particularly as the paradigm moves to a programming one. No longer will a page look strange, a link break, or an image be colored strangely. Now with sloppy coding and little testing, a user's system may crash. Making sure

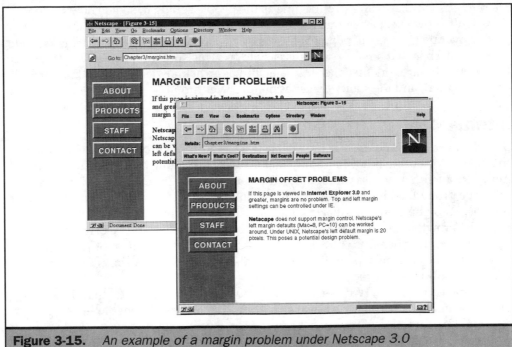

Figure 3-15.   *An example of a margin problem under Netscape 3.0*

that a complex page works under all situations can be very difficult. Even if the world only consisted of two browsers, how many permutations are there? In the Netscape camp, there is the 1.x generation, 2.x generation, 3.x generation, and 4.x generation, each on three major platforms (Mac, Unix, and Windows), as well as numerous beta versions. This also doesn't take into account a "professional" or Gold edition, the numerous other ports like to OS/2, or even foreign-language versions. All may have subtle differences. Now add in Internet Explorer with 2.x, 3.x, and 4.x generations on Mac, Windows, and soon even Unix, and there are literally dozens of test possibilities. While in most cases things aren't so bad, there are some real lessons to learn from browser testing. A simple JavaScript program works fine on Netscape 3.0 under Windows but crashes the Macintosh every time. The Unix version doesn't even support the calls used, while Internet Explorer 3.0 works fine, but under a new beta exhibits strange behavior. These are real problems.

Browser and system testing isn't the end of testing. User testing is probably the most important part of testing a site. Do the users know what to do? Do they like the site? Getting some users to evaluate a site and make suggestions for improvements is probably the single most important thing a site developer can do. A site may seem okay to its developers, but they are too close to it to know what's wrong. Customers are rarely as familiar with a product line as the people selling it, so it is no wonder they don't know that part number XG57-6 is the "Super Widget." Having the site looked over by a variety of people removes many embarrassing gaffes. The good thing about the Web is that, unlike print, it is easy to fix. This shouldn't be used as an excuse to put up sub-par work first and fix it later, but as an acknowledgment of the flexibility of the medium, and the reality that sites mature over time.

Maintenance

Sites are born, live, and die. Far too often, sites are born full grown and slowly die due to neglect. A Web site is not a building that is rarely expanded once it's finished. It's more like a tree. Most sites continually grow and change. Occasionally, whole sections might be pruned, while other sections grow out of control like a sucker at the trunk of the tree. Many times the original creators of a site don't think about the future, and stunt the growth of a site by not designing with room to expand. The original creators may move on to other sites or get bored of the task and assign it to another person. Sometimes the new owners rip the site up and start afresh. Other times they take the site in a whole new direction.

For the long life of a Web site, there must be a realization early on that the site is always under construction and always growing. The original budget to develop a site might be a fraction of the overall cost to keep the site running even if little new material is added. As the site continues, needs change. The purpose of the site may have to be re-evaluated. Maybe phase two of the Web site suggests a whole new look or a section to sell goods online. This suggests that the whole process needs to start over with planning, implementation, and all the other steps.

The Phases of Web Site Development

In summary, there are four basic phases to a Web project: planning, implementation, testing, and maintenance. Professionals versed in software engineering should note the basic similarity to the well known, but not always followed, "rules" of software development. The phases of Web site development are listed here:

- **Planning** Setting goals, specifying content, organizing content, and setting the user interface to navigate content

- **Implementing** Creating content, implementing navigation and the user interface, and coding the site, which may include HTML, programming, and database development

- **Testing** User, browser, and system testing

- **Maintenance** Maintaining and updating the site, questioning old goals, and returning to the planning stage

Each phase listed above has distinct subphases that could be expanded to provide more detail. For example, planning could include determining an audience, setting a budget, and performing other project-oriented tasks. Following the software engineering comparison inevitably leads to a discussion of CASE (Computer Aided Software Engineering) tools, which in many ways are similar to emerging tools for Web development such as Macromedia Backstage, NetObjects Fusion, or Microsoft FrontPage. HTML tools alone provide only small help in a much larger process.

Summary

The process of creating a large Web site is more than just putting together some text with images and HTML. While a simple site with a few pages might not take a great deal of forethought, a little planning can go a long way even for a small site. What is the site supposed to do? How should it look? What should it say? What is its goal? Who is the target audience? What is the site's value? Setting a goal can help ensure the future success of the site, particularly if the value of the site can be measured. Determining what the site should do, given a particular goal, might be hard, particularly with many competing purposes. Isolating the core essence of the site is possible using some known techniques. Once content and purpose are determined, the shape and structure of the site can be set. At this point, the Web page author has a blueprint to explore building the site by gathering the raw materials that make it up (images, text, and other content). The content and navigation can then be assembled using Web technologies like HTML.

Once built, the site must be thoroughly tested, since it is created for the benefit of users, not authors. Web sites are not static—they evolve. The mission of the site may change over time. Its look and technology may become dated. The process of Web publishing is an endless loop. HTML plays only a small role in the overall development of a site, but an important one. At the core of every Web page is HTML. Understanding the language, its syntax, and its purpose is integral to Web mastery. Chapter 4 provides an overview of commonly used aspects of HTML.

The Complete Reference

HTML

Chapter 4

Introduction to Common HTML

79

This chapter is a detailed introduction to common HTML. Common HTML is the form of HTML used in most Web pages, and although it is not perfectly correct according to the "rules," it is also not poorly formed. In fact, it could even be called "well-formed HTML." Common HTML is like a spoken language. For example, very few people speak like a grammar book, but they can still be understood. In the same way, very few HTML authors strictly follow formal HTML specifications, but their documents can still be understood by most Web browsers. HTML 3.2 and its predecessor, HTML 2.0, are the starting point for this chapter, which discusses their specifications and official rules. How the rules are often broken is also discussed, particularly when the workarounds are useful, although, as you will see, authors are encouraged to avoid breaking the rules. As new Web technologies appear with increasing regularity, however, workarounds may no longer be necessary. This chapter is at the introductory level, but it does not provide "cookbook" HTML. Seasoned HTML authors might want to read on, as the inline notes and some of the explanations might present previously unknown nuances of the elements.

HTML Overview

As mentioned in Chapter 1, Hypertext Markup Language (HTML) is a structured markup language used to create Web pages. A markup language like HTML is simply a collection of codes, called elements, that are used to indicate the structure and format of a document. A user agent, usually a Web browser that renders the document, interprets the meaning of these codes. Elements in HTML consist of alphanumeric tokens within angle brackets, like **<B>**, **<HTML>**, **<IMG>**, and **<HR>**.

Most elements consist of paired tags: a start tag and an end tag. The start tag is simply a mnemonic symbol for the element surrounded by angle brackets. For example, the symbol for bold text is **B** and its start tag is **<B>**. An end tag is identical to a start tag except that the symbol is preceded by a forward slash: **</B>**. An element's instruction applies to whatever content is contained between its start and end tags:

```
<B>This text is bold</B> but this text is not
```

While most tags come in pairs, there are exceptions. Some elements do not require an end tag because they do not enclose content. One example is the break element **
, which indicates a line break. Other elements do not require an end tag because the end of the content they affect can always be inferred from surrounding elements. An example is the list item element **<HR>, which indicates a horizontal rule that occupies a line all its own. Finally, for some elements like the paragraph element **<P>**, an end tag is optional.

HTML specifications define the type of content an element can enclose. This is known as an element's *content model*. The content options include other elements, text, a mixture of elements and text, or nothing at all. For example, the **<HEAD>** element provides general information about an HTML document. Its content model only allows it to contain a small number of related elements such as **<TITLE>** and **<META>**. The content model for the bold element **<B>** allows it to enclose text and some elements, such as the one for italic **<I>**, but not others like **<HEAD>**. The content model of the break element **
** is said to be *empty* because it encloses no content. Content models define the relationships possible between elements and content in valid HTML documents.

An HTML start tag can sometimes contain attributes that modify the element's meaning. Attributes within a tag's brackets must be separated from the element's name by at least one space. Some attributes indicate an effect simply by their name. An example is adding the **COMPACT** attribute to the ordered list element: **<OL COMPACT>**. Other attributes indicate an effect by assigning values to their names. For example, **<OL TYPE="I">** assigns the bullet type of an ordered list to uppercase roman numerals. An element may contain multiple attributes if those attributes are separated by at least one space, as in **<OL COMPACT TYPE="I">**.

A complete HTML element is defined by a start tag, an end tag (where applicable), possible attributes, and a content model. Figure 4-1 shows an overview of the syntax of a typical HTML element.

HTML Rules

As discussed in Chapter 1, there are some rules to remember when writing HTML. These are briefly reviewed here.

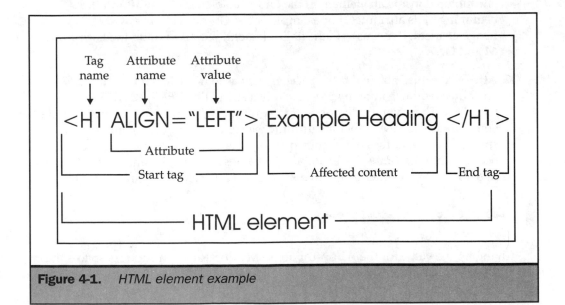

Figure 4-1. *HTML element example*

- **HTML documents are structured documents.** As mentioned in Chapter 2, the HTML 3.2 document type definition uses the SGML convention to formally define the structure of HTML documents. It defines what elements a document can contain, their possible relationships to one another inside a document, and their possible attributes and values. If the elements in an actual HTML document agree with this formal definition, the document is said to be valid.

- **Element names are not case sensitive.** An element like **<hTml>** is equivalent to **<html>** or **<HTML>**. Element case does not matter to a browser. However, writing elements consistently in upper- or lowercase makes HTML documents easier to understand and maintain. Convention suggests that uppercase is the preferred practice.

- **Attribute names are not case sensitive.** Just as **<hr>** is equivalent to **<HR>**, **<HR NOSHADE>** is equivalent to **<HR noshade>** or **<HR NoShade>**. As with elements, consistent use of case improves legibility, and uppercase is preferred.

- **Attribute values may be case sensitive.** The value of an attribute may be case sensitive, especially if it refers to a file. The filename in **<IMG SRC="filename.gif">** may not be the same as the filename in **<IMG SRC="FILENAME.GIF">**; it depends on whether or not case matters to the operating system of the server containing the file. For best results, always specify a filename exactly as it has been saved.

- **Element names cannot contain spaces.** Browsers treat the first space encountered inside an element as the end of an element's name and the beginning of its attributes. For example, **<I M G>** does not mean **<IMG>**, the image element. It means **<I>**, the italic element, with two undefined attributes **M** and **G**.

- **Attribute values may contain spaces if the value is enclosed by quotes.** Some attributes require a known value, usually a string like **LEFT**, **RIGHT**, or **CENTER**. These values do not require surrounding quotes unless they contain embedded spaces. Whether an attribute is user defined or can contain only a specified value, it does not require quotes unless spaces or special characters occur within the value. For example, the values for the **SRC** and **ALT** attributes in the following element contain no spaces and therefore require no quotes.

```
<IMG SRC=dog.gif ALT=Rover>
```

Changing the value for the **ALT** attribute to My dog Rover introduces spaces into the value and quotes must be added.

```
<IMG SRC=dog.gif ALT="My dog Rover">
```

Omitting quotes in the previous example assigns My to the **ALT** attribute and causes dog and Rover to be treated as two undefined attributes. Surrounding a value with quotes has no negative consequences if they are not required. HTML authors are well advised to quote attribute values if there is any concern of misinterpretation. For stylistic reasons, it is better to quote everything in case values change. Values that contain any characters other than alphanumeric characters [a–z, A–Z. 0–9], dash [-], or period [.] must be quoted. Be careful with so-called "special characters."

- **Browsers collapse and ignore space characters in HTML content.** Browsers collapse any sequence of spaces, tabs, and returns in an HTML document into a single space character. These characters convey no formatting information unless they occur inside a special preformatting element like **<PRE>**, which preserves their meaning. Extra spacing can be used liberally within an HTML document to make it more legible to HTML authors.

- **HTML documents may contain comments.** HTML supports comments that are not displayed within a browser window. Comments are denoted by a start value of **<!** and an end value of **-->**. Comments can be many lines long. For example,

```
<!--

        Document Name: My HTML Document
        Creation Date: 1/5/97

        © 1997 Big Company, Inc.

-->
```

is a valid comment. Be careful not to put spaces between the dashes or exclamation point in the comment. Comments may also include HTML elements. Older browsers may have problems with commented markup. For more information about comments, see Appendix A, the "HTML Element Reference."

- **An element that encloses the start tag of another element must also enclose its end tag, if one exists.** Elements often contain other elements inside the document section they enclose. Any element that starts within a section enclosed by another must also end there. In other words, an element's tag pairs should be nested within one another and their end tags should not cross. To make some text bold and italic, use **<B><I>**Correct**</I></B>** and not **<B><I>**Not correct**</B></I>**.

This is primarily a stylistic issue, since no major browsers at this time have a problem with this. Authors are still advised to nest tags rather than cross them. Incorrect nesting may result in incompatibilities with emerging technologies, and may cause rendering problems in some esoteric browsers.

■ **Browsers ignore unknown elements.** Browsers ignore elements they do not understand. They do attempt to interpret any content enclosed by an unknown element. If a browser does not understand the **<STORY>** element in **<STORY>**A Tale of Two Cities**</STORY>**, it ignores it. It does, however, render the words "A Tale of Two Cities" as normal text.

■ **Browsers ignore unknown attributes.** As with elements, browsers ignore any attributes they do not understand. Technically, the imaginary **CLOWN** attribute in the following example is well-formed HTML. Unless a browser happens to understand it, however, it is ignored.

```
<IMG CLOWN="BOZO" SRC="bozo.gif">
```

In a pragmatic sense, the final arbiter of an HTML document's correctness is the browser used to view it. Browsers rarely enforce formally defined HTML. Instead, most browsers liberally interpret what they treat as acceptable. They make heuristic guesses about unusual constructs and attempt to render whatever they receive. Few authors understand the rules for composing HTML according to a document type definition. Unfortunately, permissive browsers provide little incentive to learn. This is an important lesson for HTML authors. As permissiveness varies from browser to browser, and even between different versions of the same browser, simply testing pages in a browser does not ensure portability of documents. Authoring HTML to a recognized DTD and using a program called a *validator*, which checks that written code meets the specification, may ensure that documents are open to the widest possible audience. Most end users, however, do not concern themselves with such specifics, but draw their beliefs about appropriate code from how their browsers render that code. Even if a validator states a document is correct, things may not work in a browser due to bugs in the software. It is always a good idea to test documents under an assortment of browsers, including Microsoft Internet Explorer, Netscape, WebTV, and even Lynx. They should also be tested on multiple platforms like Windows and Macintosh, when available. Even rigorous testing may not ensure that things work out—that is the challenge of the Web.

Note *Permissive HTML interpretation by browsers serves a practical purpose. Imagine if browsers treated HTML errors like syntax errors in a programming language. If this were the case, a document could not be successfully viewed unless it was absolutely correct. If browsers had followed this model, the World Wide Web would not have gotten very far. Few complex documents on the Web today would pass extremely strict validation.*

Understanding and following a formal HTML definition takes time and practice. However, the benefits to cross-platform rendering and document maintenance make it worthwhile. This is essential for large corporations with many documents. Fortunately, the path toward writing well-formed HTML documents does not require an initial understanding of the language's nuances. Well-formed documents share a common, easily comprehended document structure. Like peeling an onion, understanding this makes it easier to understand the nuances of HTML later, all the way down to the character level.

The Structure of HTML Documents

Regardless of document content, all well-written HTML documents share a common structure. Figure 4-2 provides a template for this.

An HTML document begins with a **<!DOCTYPE>** declaration indicating the version of HTML used by the document. Following this, the **<HTML>** element encloses the actual document. It contains two primary sections: the head and the body, enclosed respectively by the **<HEAD>** and **<BODY>** elements. The *head* contains identifying and other meta-information about the document. It always contains the document's title, enclosed by the **<TITLE>** element. The *body* contains the actual document content.

```
<!DOCTYPE HTML PUBLIC "html version">
<HTML>
<HEAD>
<TITLE>Document Title</TITLE>
   ...Other supplementary information goes here...
</HEAD>
<BODY>
   ...Marked-up text goes here...
</BODY>
</HTML>
```

Figure 4-2.   *HTML document template*

Document Types

HTML follows the SGML notation for defining structured documents. From SGML, HTML inherits the requirement that all documents begin with a **<!DOCTYPE>** declaration. In an HTML context, this identifies the HTML "dialect" used in a document by referring to an external *document type definition,* or *DTD.* A DTD defines the actual elements, attributes, and element relationships that are valid in the document. The **<!DOCTYPE>** declaration allows validation software to identify the HTML DTD being followed in a document and verify that the document is syntactically correct. Technically, any HTML construct not defined in the document's DTD should not occur. Some common **<!DOCTYPE>** declarations are shown here:

- Document containing HTML 2.0 as standardized by the Internet Engineering Task Force:

  ```
  <!DOCTYPE HTML PUBLIC "-//IETF//DTD HTML//EN">
  ```

  Document containing HTML 3.2 as defined by the World Wide Web Consortium (W3C):

  ```
  <!DOCTYPE HTML PUBLIC "-//W3C//DTD HTML 3.2 Final//EN">
  ```

- Document containing HTML 2.0 with Netscape extensions as defined by a third party:

  ```
  <!DOCTYPE HTML PUBLIC "-//WebTechs//DTD Mozilla HTML 2.0//EN">
  ```

- Document containing Internet Explorer 3.0 HTML as defined by Microsoft Corporation:

  ```
  <!DOCTYPE HTML PUBLIC "-//Microsoft//DTD Internet Explorer 3.0 HTML//EN">
  ```

The HTML document template suggests always using a **<!DOCTYPE>** declaration. In some cases this may not be practical. Including a DTD declaration conveys the intention to follow it. Unfortunately, not every HTML dialect has a DTD. Unlike the W3C, browser vendors have historically favored innovation over standardization. For an HTML author, it is better to omit a **<!DOCTYPE>** declaration than to include one that will not be followed. Misuse is pervasive.

Some HTML authoring tools automatically insert a **<!DOCTYPE>** declaration while also encouraging the use of elements not found in the related DTD. Several mass media Web sites support advanced features like frames in documents declared according to the conservative HTML 2.0 specification.

Note   *At the time of this book's writing, Netscape did not provide document type definitions. Many interested third parties have written document type definitions that address Netscape extensions in case an author would like to validate a Netscape document.*

The HTML Element

The <HTML> element delimits the beginning and the end of an HTML document. It contains only the <HEAD> element and the <BODY> element. The HTML document template shown in Figure 4-2 shows its typical use in a document as a container for all other elements. The <HEAD> element is optional. The HTML 3.2 DTD does not require its use, nor do popular browsers. Including it, however, makes a document more legible.

The Head Element

The <HEAD> element encloses a document section that contains identification and supplementary information about the document. Browsers do not display this information. Including the <HEAD> element in a document is not technically necessary because its boundaries can always be inferred. Nevertheless, it should always be included for document style and legibility. In the HTML 3.2 DTD, the elements allowed within the <HEAD> element include <BASE>, <ISINDEX>, <LINK>, <META>, <SCRIPT>, <STYLE>, and <TITLE>. The <TITLE> element must always occur. A brief discussion of these elements follows. Complete information is available in the cross-referenced chapters and reference section.

The <BASE> element specifies an absolute URL address used to provide server and directory information for partially specified URL addresses used within the document. Known as *relative links*, they are discussed in Chapter 5, which covers linking.

The <ISINDEX> element indicates that the document contains a searchable index. It causes the browser to display a query prompt and a field for entering a query. Usually used with simple site searching mechanisms, this element is rarely used today, having been mostly replaced by forms. It is discussed with forms in Chapter 11.

The <LINK> element specifies a special relationship between the current document and another document. One use concerns hypertext navigational relationships. This is discussed in Chapter 5. Another use, which concerns linking to a document style sheet, is discussed in Chapter 10.

The <META> element uses name/value pairs to provide meta-information about a document. The <META> element often provides descriptive information targeted by Web indexing services. In a very different use, the <META> element can define an HTTP request header that causes one page to automatically load another after a specified time interval. This use is discussed in Chapter 5.

Note

A document's head section contains all the descriptive information about the document. Traditionally this section was much smaller than the document's body and could be retrieved independently from a Web server. Because of this, Web indexing robots often place special emphasis on the document head. Authors often provide various forms of "spider bait" to increase indexing relevance. With the introduction of the <SCRIPT> and <STYLE> elements, the amount of information in the head has exploded. It is unclear what impact this may have on strategies for automatic document indexing.

The **<SCRIPT>** element allows programs written in a scripting language to be directly embedded in a Web page. The two most popular scripting languages are JavaScript and VBScript, a form of Visual Basic. This approach to making Web pages more interactive is known as client-side scripting. The **<SCRIPT>** element and associated usage is discussed in Chapter 14.

The **<STYLE>** element encloses style specifications covering fonts, colors, positioning, and other aspects of content presentation. These styles can be associated with document elements. Use of **<STYLE>** is discussed in Chapter 10.

Note

Comments may occur anywhere in an HTML document. They are especially valuable in the head section to assist document maintenance. Useful head comments include the document's purpose, authorship, required resources, and modification history. The form of HTML comments was discussed earlier in the chapter.

The **<TITLE>** element, discussed next, is the only element that is absolutely required in the head of a document.

Title Elements

The **<TITLE>** element must be used in every HTML document. It gives an HTML document a title by which it is known to browsers and indexing robots. Browsers display the document title while it is being viewed, and they also use the title in bookmark lists.

Note

Most browsers attempt to deduce a title for a document missing the <TITLE> element. The browser often uses the URL of the document being viewed, which may indicate nothing about the document's content. However, this behavior is not guaranteed. For example, WebTV simply lists the document as "untitled document." Figure 4-3 shows an example of an untitled document rendered in a browser.

A document title may contain standard text as well as character entities (for example, ©), which are discussed later in the chapter. A title of Big Company Home Page is just as valid as Big Company ©1997. However, HTML markup is not

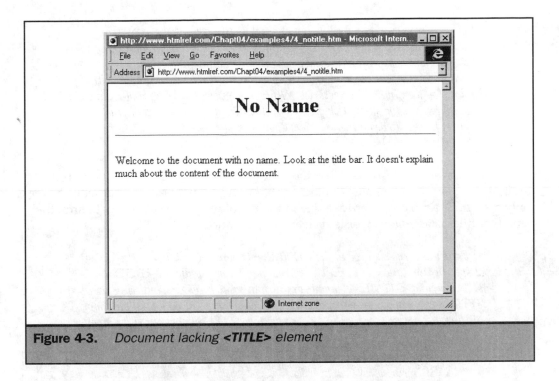

Figure 4-3.   *Document lacking <TITLE> element*

permitted in a title element and does not produce the expected result. According to the rules of the **<TITLE>** element,

```
<TITLE><B>Home Page</B></TITLE>
```

is not valid while

```
<TITLE>Big Company &copy;<TITLE>
```

is valid. A well-formed title is not necessarily a meaningful title. Remember that a user sees a title in his or her bookmark list if the page is bookmarked. Robots and spiders that index the Web often place special meaning on the contents of the **<TITLE>** element when determining what a page is about. Because of this, a title should indicate the contents of a page without ambiguity. Titles like "My Page" or "Home Page" don't make sense; "John Smith's Page" and "Big Company" do. A well-formed title can actually add navigational value to a site by showing an implicit hierarchy among a group of pages. While "Widget X-103 Datasheet" seems to be a reasonable title, "Big Company: Products: Widget X-103 Datasheet" is a better title. It not only indicates the company the product is related to, but implies a hierarchy in the site.

Note

Initially, there were issues with using characters like colon (:), slash (/), or backslash (\) in titles. An operating system may have a problem with these titles if the document is saved to the local system. For example, the colon is not allowed within Macintosh filenames. Slashes generally are not allowed within filenames as they indicate directories. While this appears to be a problem, most browsers remove the suspect characters and reduce them to spaces during the save process. To be on the safe side, dashes can be used to delimit sections in the title.

While titles should be descriptive, they should also be concise. Authors should limit title length to a reasonable number of characters. Netscape and Internet Explorer only display 20 to 30 characters of a title in their bookmark lists. One way to limit the length of titles is to remove words such as "a," "an," and "the."

Tip

Browsers are very sensitive to the <TITLE> element. According to the HTML 3.2 specification, the <TITLE> element is mandatory, while the <BODY>, <HEAD>, and <HTML> elements are not. In some browsers, omitting the <TITLE> element causes a document not to display. So, if you get a bunch of junk on your screen (see Figure 4-4), check the <TITLE> element right away.

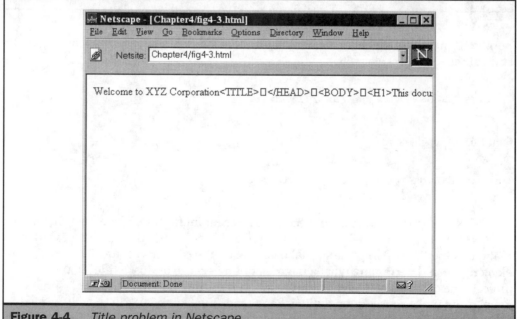

Figure 4-4.   *Title problem in Netscape*

According to the HTML 3.2 specification, there should only be one <TITLE> element in every document. The title should appear in the head of the document. Until Netscape 1.1 was released, multiple <TITLE> elements were often used within documents to create an animated title. This was a bug, not a Netscape innovation. More recent browsers do not support this capability, and it should not be used.

If you do have multiple instances of the <TITLE> element in your document, HTML does not define what will happen, so different browsers handle them differently. Internet Explorer uses the last <TITLE> defined; Netscape uses the first. This may change with version numbers and platform types and should never be assumed.

The Body

As shown in the HTML document template of Figure 4-2, the body of a document is delimited by <BODY> and </BODY>. Under the HTML 3.2 specification and most browsers, the <BODY> element is optional, but should be included. There can be only one <BODY> element per document.

Note *Under an older version of Netscape the browser read multiple <BODY> elements within a document. In combination with the BGCOLOR attribute of the <BODY> element, HTML authors were able to exploit this bug to produce a document that loaded after flipping through a variety of colors. Often this hack was used to create a fade-in or fade-out effect for a page. This bug has been fixed, so multiple <BODY> elements do not provide any benefit. If multiple <BODY> elements are encountered in a file, typically the browser either pays attention to the first or last <BODY> element encountered.*

Common attributes for the <BODY> element affect the colors for a document's text, background, and links. These attributes include **TEXT** for text color, **BGCOLOR** for background color, **ALINK** for active link color, **VLINK** for visited link color, and **LINK** for nonvisited link color. These and other browser-specific attributes of the <BODY> element are discussed in Chapter 8.

The <BODY> element may contain many other HTML elements. The rest of the chapter introduces the basic HTML elements common to nearly every browser as defined by the HTML 3.2 specification. These fall into three distinct groups: block-level elements, text-level elements, and character entities. The elements are presented from top to bottom, from larger block-oriented structures like paragraphs to smaller units like the actual character entities.

Block-Level Elements

Block-level elements define structural content blocks like paragraphs or lists. If a document is written carefully in a block style, it may be possible to improve its machine readability. The basic idea of a document following a block structure is shown in Figure 4-5.

Headings

The heading elements are used to create "headlines" in documents. There are six different levels of headings: **<H1>**, **<H2>**, **<H3>**, **<H4>**, **<H5>**, and **<H6>**. These range in importance from **<H1>**, the most important, to **<H6>**, the least. Most browsers display headings in larger and/or bolder font than normal text. This causes many HTML authors to think erroneously of heading elements as formatting that makes text

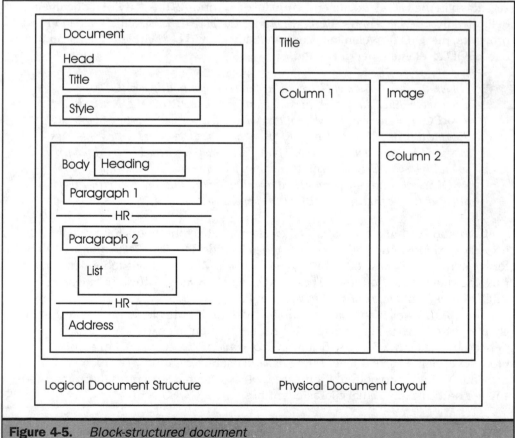

Figure 4-5. *Block-structured document*

bigger or bolder. Actually, heading elements, like headings themselves, convey logical meaning about a document's structure. Sizing and weight are relative to the importance of the heading, so **<H1>** level headings are larger than **<H3>** headings. As headings, text included is displayed in an alternative style (bigger and/or bold) and on a line of its own. In addition, an extra line is generally inserted after the heading. The example in Figure 4-6 shows the heading elements.

*The Lynx text browser renders headings very differently than commercial graphical browsers. Lynx can't display larger fonts, so it may attempt to bold them or align them. **<H1>** headings are aligned in the center, while each lower-level heading is indented more than the next highest level.*

Sample renderings of the HTML code in Figure 4-6 are shown in Figure 4-7.

It is possible to add an attribute to the heading elements that aligns the text left, right, or center. This more recent HTML feature was not supported by HTML 2.0. By default, headings are usually left-aligned, but by setting the **ALIGN** attribute of the various heading elements, the text may be aligned to the right, left, or center of the screen. The example in Figure 4-8 and the result in Figure 4-9 show the usage and rendering of the **ALIGN** attribute.

HTML authors often use headings to make text large. As with all HTML elements, size is a relative, not an absolute, concept. The actual size of the heading depends on

```
<!DOCTYPE HTML PUBLIC "-//W3C//DTD HTML 3.2 Final//EN">
<HTML>
<HEAD>
<TITLE>Heading Example</TITLE>
</HEAD>
<BODY>
        <H1>Heading 1</H1>
        <H2>Heading 2</H2>
        <H3>Heading 3</H3>
        <H4>Heading 4</H4>
        <H5>Heading 5</H5>
        <H6>Heading 6</H6>
</BODY>
</HTML>
```

Figure 4-6.   *Heading style examples*

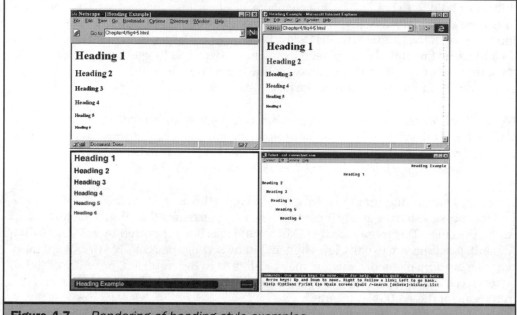

Figure 4-7. *Rendering of heading style examples*

the browser, the browser's setting, and the platform on which it is running. An **<H1>** header under Netscape on a UNIX system appears a different size than the same **<H1>** header on a Windows 3.1 machine running Internet Explorer. The headlines are relatively bigger, but the exact size is unknown, making consistent layout difficult.

```
<!DOCTYPE HTML PUBLIC "-//W3C//DTD HTML 3.2 Final//EN">
<HTML>
<HEAD>
<TITLE>Heading Alignment Example</TITLE>
</HEAD>
<BODY>
<H1 ALIGN="LEFT">Aligned Left</H1>
<H1 ALIGN="CENTER">Aligned Center</H1>
<H1 ALIGN="RIGHT">Aligned Right</H1>
</BODY>
</HTML>
```

Figure 4-8. *Heading alignment example*

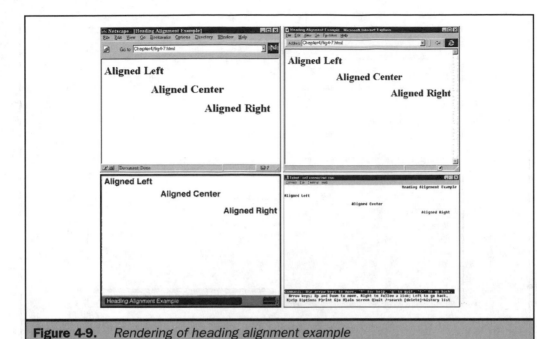

Figure 4-9.   *Rendering of heading alignment example*

Furthermore, headlines have an implied logical meaning and typically do more than simply make something big. Working under the assumption that headings only enlarge text, novice HTML authors might attempt to use a headline to simulate a drop cap. This does not work, as shown in Figure 4-10; renderings appear in Figure 4-11.

```
<!DOCTYPE HTML PUBLIC "-//W3C//DTD HTML 3.2 Final//EN">
<HTML>
<HEAD>
<TITLE>Heading Misused for Sizing Example</TITLE>
</HEAD>
<BODY>
<H1 ALIGN=LEFT>D</H1>
don't think about using headings as sizing devices for
things like drop caps.
</BODY>
</HTML>
```

Figure 4-10.   *Heading misused for sizing*

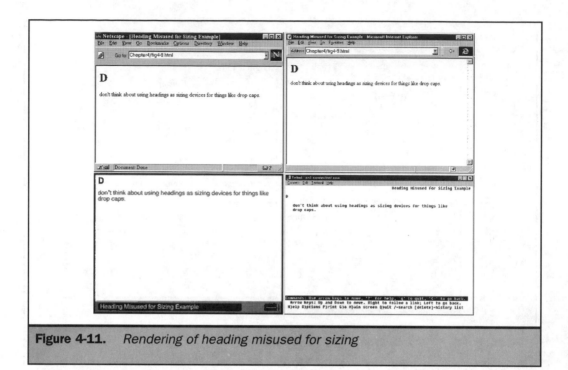

Figure 4-11.   *Rendering of heading misused for sizing*

Headings actually have a logical meaning. While HTML does not enforce the use of headings in a hierarchical, ordered way, some people feel that this use is implied. It is suggested that documents order the use of headlines so that **<H3>** doesn't appear before **<H1>** and that less important headings are nested within more important ones or occur after. Given the logical use of headings, a page may support indexing features or allow for navigation schemes not currently available in browsers. For example, a browser might allow a user to view an outline of a Web document by showing the headings and then expand relevant headings (as shown in Figure 4-12). While an outline view is not built into most browsers, it is possible to create this type of navigation using programming facilities such as Java or Dynamic HTML. More information about this is presented in Chapter 14.

Note   *A quick survey of heading use on the Web should reveal that headings beyond* ***<H3>*** *are rarely used. Why? This is partially because people use headings in a visual fashion. The effects of* ***<H4>***, ***<H5>***, *and* ***<H6>*** *can be achieved with other elements. Finally, it is unusual for documents to have sections nested more than three levels deep.*

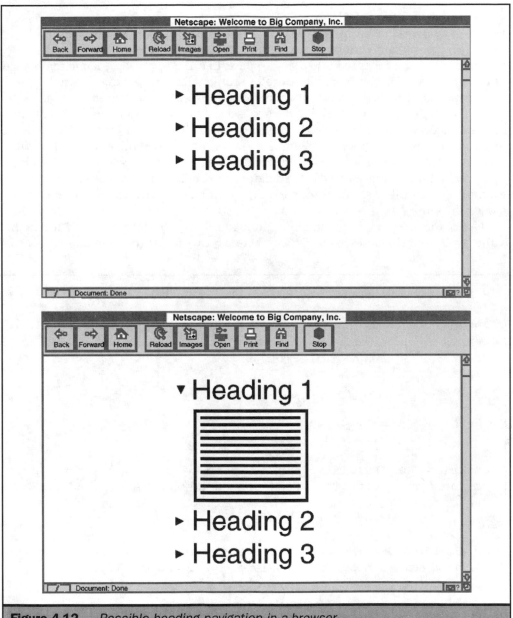

Figure 4-12.   *Possible heading navigation in a browser*

Paragraphs and Breaks

Unlike documents in word processors, HTML documents ignore spaces, tabs, and carriage returns. Word wrapping can occur at any point in your source file, and multiple spaces are collapsed into a single space. In order to preserve some semblance of text formatting, elements are introduced to sectionalize the document. One of the most important structuring elements is the paragraph element. Surrounding text with the **<P>** and **</P>** tags indicates that the text is a logical paragraph unit. Normally the browser places a blank line or two before the paragraph, but the exact rendering of the text depends on the browser. Text within the **<P>** is normally rendered flush left with a ragged right margin. The **ALIGN** attribute makes it possible to specify a left, right, or center alignment. Since **LEFT** is the default value, it is usually not seen. The example in Figure 4-13 shows three paragraphs with alignment. The rendering is shown in Figure 4-14.

Notice that the paragraph renderings in Figure 4-13 do not necessarily wrap in the same place. Font size and screen size vary across browsers, so trying to use

```
<!DOCTYPE HTML PUBLIC "-//W3C//DTD HTML 3.2 Final//EN">

<HTML>
<HEAD>
<TITLE>Paragraph Example</TITLE>
</HEAD>
<BODY>

<P>This is the first paragraph in the example about the P
tag. There really isn't too much to say here.</P>

<P ALIGN="CENTER">This is the second paragraph.  Again, more
of the same stuff. This time the paragraph is aligned in
the center. This might not be such a good idea as it makes
text hard to read.</P>

<P ALIGN="RIGHT">Here things are aligned to the right. Right
aligned text can also be troublesome to read. Otherwise
there is very little to say about the P tag.</P>

</BODY>
</HTML>
```

Figure 4-13.   *Paragraph examples with **ALIGN** attribute*

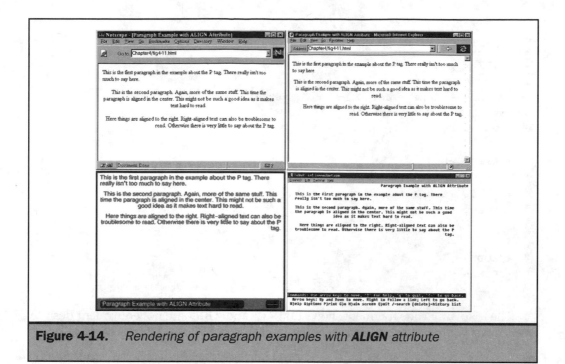

Figure 4-14.   *Rendering of paragraph examples with **ALIGN** attribute*

paragraphs to get a sense of screen layout is not possible. If a browser resizes, even to an extremely unlikely size, its content will reflow to accommodate the new dimensions. That's the beauty and the challenge of HTML layout design.

Because the **<P>** element generally causes a blank line, some HTML authors attempt to insert blank lines into a document by using multiple **<P>** elements. This rarely results in the desired outcome. The browser collapses empty **<P>** elements since they represent logical text units, not physical formatting. To actually insert a return the **
** element must be used. The **
** element is a text-level element that inserts a single carriage return or break into a document. It contains no content and has no end tag. The one common attribute used with **
** is **CLEAR**. This attribute allows **
** to affect how text flows around images or embedded objects. The use of **
** in this fashion is discussed in Chapter 6. Because of its relationship with the **<P>** element, it is important to discuss the basic use of **
** here. The following code fragment shows how **
** might be used both within and outside of paragraphs. Screen renderings are shown in Figure 4-15.

```
<!DOCTYPE HTML PUBLIC "-//W3C//DTD HTML 3.2 Final//EN">
<HTML>
<HEAD>
<TITLE>Break Example</TITLE>
```

```
</HEAD>
<BODY>

<P>This is the first paragraph.<BR>
Not much to say here.
</P>

<BR><BR><BR>

<P>This is the second paragraph. Notice all the extra space
between these paragraphs. That's from the BR tags.</P>


</BODY>
</HTML>
```

The following code fragment shows that **<P>** and **
** are not equivalent despite their physical rendering similarities; screen renderings appear in Figure 4-16.

```
<!DOCTYPE HTML PUBLIC "-//W3C//DTD HTML 3.2 Final//EN">
<HTML>
<HEAD>
<TITLE>Break Example</TITLE>
</HEAD>
<BODY>

<P>This is the first paragraph.<BR>
Not much to say here, either.
</P>

<P><P><P>

<P>This is the second paragraph. Notice that the three P
tags are treated as empty paragraphs and ignored. </P>

</BODY>
</HTML>
```

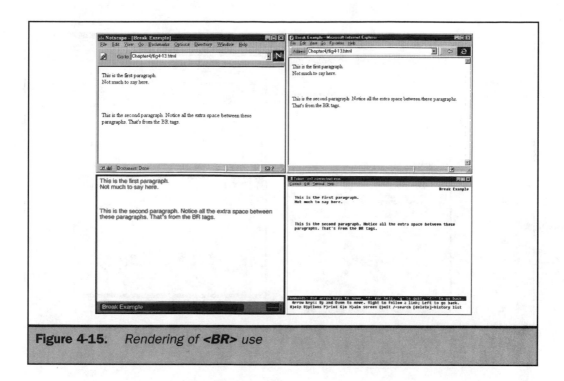

Figure 4-15.   *Rendering of <BR> use*

> **Tip**   *Users looking for blank lines have to insert multiple <BR> elements into their document. A single <BR> element merely goes to the next line rather than inserting a blank line.*

Center as a Block Element

In the original HTML 2.0-based browsers, centering text was impossible. One of the major additions introduced by Netscape was the <CENTER> element. HTML 3.2 adopted this element because of its widespread use. To center text or embedded objects like images, simply enclose the content within <CENTER> and </CENTER>. In this sense it appears that <CENTER> is a text formatting style element, but under the HTML 3.2 specification and beyond it has been defined as a block-level structuring element. Under the HTML 3.2 DTD, <CENTER> is simply an alias for <DIV ALIGN=CENTER> and is treated exactly the same way. It is unlikely that the <"CENTER"> element will go away, considering its simplicity and widespread use.

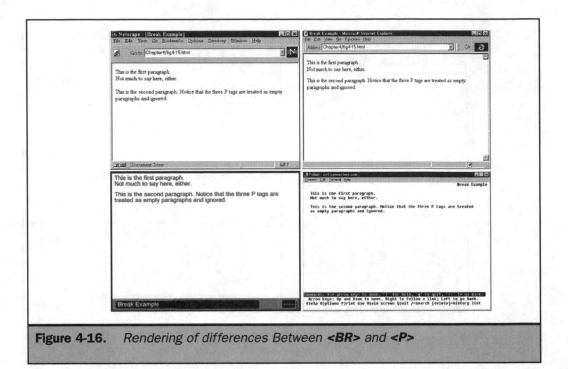

Figure 4-16.   *Rendering of differences Between <BR> and <P>*

But according to specifications, there are two preferred ways to center content: the <DIV> element with a center alignment attribute, or the **ALIGN** attribute used in conjunction with some elements.

Divisions

The **<DIV>** element is used to structure HTML documents into unique sections or divisions. Adding the ALIGN attribute makes it possible to align a portion of the document to the left, right, or center. By default, content within the **<DIV>** element is left-aligned. Divisions are also useful when used in conjunction with style sheets (see Chapter 10). The example in Figure 4-17 shows the use of **<CENTER>** and **<DIV>**. Figure 4-18 shows their screen renderings.

Block Quotes

You may sometimes wish to quote a large body of text to make it stand out from the rest. The **<BLOCKQUOTE>** element provides a facility to enclose large block

```
<!DOCTYPE HTML PUBLIC "-//W3C//DTD HTML 3.2 Final//EN">
<HTML>
<HEAD>
<TITLE>Center and Division Example</TITLE>
</HEAD>
<BODY>

<CENTER>
<H1>Sample CENTER Use</H1>
<P>This paragraph is also centered by using the CENTER tag</P>
</CENTER>

<DIV ALIGN="RIGHT">
<H1>Sample DIV Use</H1>
<P>Many paragraphs and other block elements can be affected
by a DIV at once</P>
<P> Notice that all the paragraphs are right aligned</P>
</DIV>

</BODY>
</HTML>
```

Figure 4-17.   *Center and division example*

quotations from other works within a document. Though the element is logical in nature, enclosing text within **<BLOCKQUOTE>** and **</BLOCKQUOTE>** usually indents the blocked information. Like a paragraph element, text within beginning and ending **<BLOCKQUOTE>** elements ignores all spacing, tabs, and returns and requires the use of **
** or other elements to modify line wrapping and spacing. Figures 4-19 and 4-20 show an example of **<BLOCKQUOTE>** and its renderings, respectively.

Note   *The first HTML 2.0-compliant browsers did not provide any indentation or tab facility in regular text. Many HTML authors use **<BLOCKQUOTE>** to provide indentation. Text within **<BLOCKQUOTE>** may be indented on both sides of a page. It may render in an alternative style (for example, italics). For this reason, the list elements, particularly the unordered list, are common workarounds to provide indentation for HTML 2.0–level browsers. In fact many HTML editors insert these elements to create indentation. Until style sheets become more common, these workarounds will continue.*

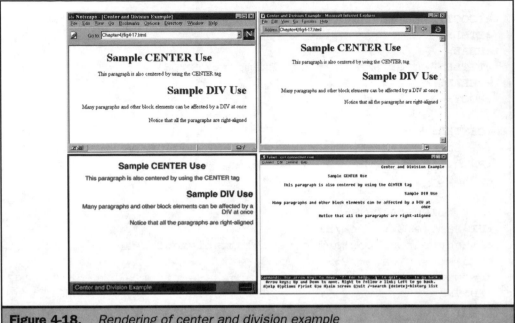

Figure 4-18. *Rendering of center and division example*

Preformatted Text

There are occasions where spacing, tabs, and returns are so important in text that HTML's default disregard for them would ruin the text's meaning. In these cases you may want to preserve the given formatting by specifying the text to be preformatted. Imagine that source code of the poetry of e. e. cummings is to be inserted into a Web page. This will require a directive that indicates the preservation of format. The **<PRE>** and **</PRE>** tags can be used to surround text that should not be formatted by the browser. The text enclosed within the **<PRE>** tags retains all its spacing and returns, and does not reflow when the browser is resized. Scroll bars and horizontal scrolling are required if the lines are longer than the width of the window. The browser generally renders the preformatted text in a monospaced font, usually Courier. Some text formatting, like bold, italics or links, can be used within the **<PRE>** tags. A sample using the **<PRE>** element and comparing it to regular paragraph text is shown in Figure 4-21. The rendering of the preformatted text example is shown in Figure 4-22.

```
<!DOCTYPE HTML PUBLIC "-//W3C//DTD HTML 3.2 Final//EN">
<HTML>
<HEAD>
<TITLE>Blockquote Example</TITLE>
</HEAD>
<BODY>

<H1 ALIGN="CENTER">
Excerpt from HTML: The Complete Reference 2nd Edition</H1>

<P>
The second edition of the epic story of HTML will soon reach a
store near you. Follow the adventures of our faithful but somewhat
naive hero Wilbur as he journeys on a quest to destroy the
dangerous Mozilla and rescue the Princess Public from the clutches
of the Redmond Wizard.   In the excerpt below Wilbur wonders about
his quest after recovering from a Cougar attack. </P>

<BLOCKQUOTE>
"To be or not to be a specific or general markup language: that
is the question. Whether it is more important to appease the
structuralists or appease the stylists, we may never know. . .
though if everybody eventually gets what they want, then maybe
all's well that ends well."
</BLOCKQUOTE>

<P>
Join us next time as Wilbur is framed for a mysterious
navigation crime.
</P>

</BODY>
</HTML>
```

Figure 4-19.   *Example of* *<BLOCKQUOTE>*

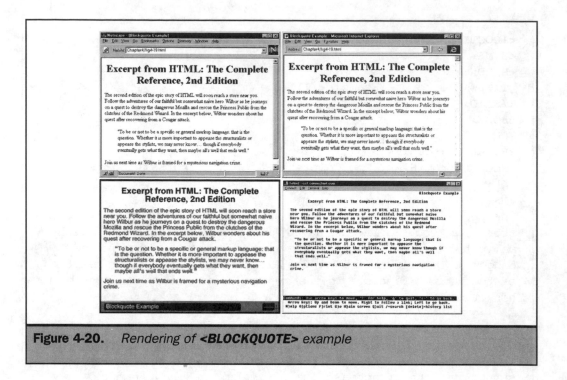

Figure 4-20. *Rendering of* **<BLOCKQUOTE>** *example*

According to the HTML 3.2 specification, other block elements, images, and elements that change font size are allowed within the **<PRE>** *element. Most browsers allow any elements, even those beyond the stated specification, to appear within the* **<PRE>** *elements and renders these as expected. Authors should not, however, rely on this.*

Authors should be careful about using the **<PRE>** element to create simple tables or preserve spacing. Unpredictable differences in browser window sizes may introduce horizontal scrolling for wide preformatted content. In these cases, other elements may provide better formatting control.

Lists

There are three basic forms of lists in modern HTML: ordered lists (**<OL>**), unordered lists (**<UL>**), and definition lists (**<DL>**). Two other rarely used list elements, **<MENU>** and **<DIR>** are sparsely supported and are usually treated as an unordered list. Lists are block formatting elements that define a block structure. They can be nested, and can contain other block-level structures like paragraphs.

```
<!DOCTYPE HTML PUBLIC "-//W3C//DTD HTML 3.2 Final//EN">
<HTML>
<HEAD>
<TITLE>PRE Example</TITLE>
</HEAD>
<BODY>
<PRE>
  This is P R E F O R M A T E D

    T
      E
        X
          T

  SPACES    are ok!  So are
          RETURNS!
</PRE>
<BR><BR>
<P>

  This is N O T  P R E F O R M A T E D

    T
      E
        X
          T

  SPACES    and RETURNS
          are lost.
</P>
</BODY>
</HTML>
```

Figure 4-21.   *Comparison of **<PRE>** element and regular text*

ORDERED LISTS   An ordered list, as enclosed by <OL> and </OL>, defines a list where order should matter. Ordering is typically rendered by a numbering scheme using Arabic numbers, letters, or Roman numerals. Ordered lists are suitable for

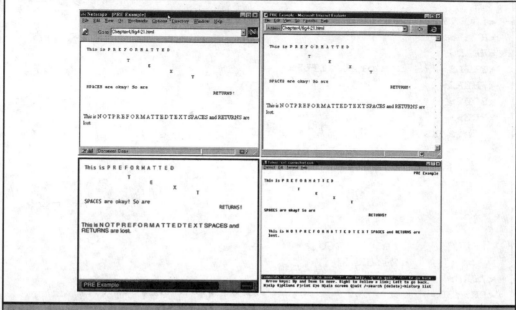

Figure 4-22. *Typical rendering of preformatted and regular text*

creating simple outlines or step-by-step instructions because the list items are numbered automatically by the browser. List items in ordered and other lists are defined using the list item element **<LI>**. The **<LI>** element does not require an end tag. List items are usually indented by the browser. Numbering starts from 1. A generic ordered list looks like this:

```
<OL>
<LI>Item 1
<LI>Item 2
. . .
<LI>Item n
</OL>
```

*In many browsers, the **<LI>** element has some meaning outside a list. It often renders as a nonindented bullet. Some books recommend using **<LI>** in this way, but it is not correct practice. While many browsers assume an unordered bullet list, the meaning of this use of **<LI>** is undefined in the HTML specification. This hack should not be used.*

The **<OL>** element itself has three basic attributes, none of which are required: **COMPACT**, **START**, and **TYPE**. The **COMPACT** attribute requires no value. It simply suggests that the browser attempt to compact the list to use less space onscreen. In reality, most browsers ignore the **COMPACT** attribute.

The **TYPE** attribute of **<OL>** can be set to **a** for lowercase letters, **A** for uppercase letters, **i** for lowercase roman numerals, **I** for uppercase Roman numerals, or **1** for regular numerals. The numeral **1** is the default value. Remember that the **TYPE** attribute within the **<OL>** element sets the numbering scheme for the whole list unless it is overridden by a **TYPE** value in an **<LI>** element. Each **<LI>** element may have a local **TYPE** attribute set to **a**, **A**, **i**, **I**, or **1**. Once an **<LI>** element is set with a new type, it overrides the numbering style for the rest of the list unless another **<LI>** sets the **TYPE** attribute.

The **<OL>** element also has a **START** attribute that takes a numeric value to begin the list numbering. Whether the **TYPE** attribute is a letter or a numeral, the **START** value must be a number. To start ordering from the letter "j," **<OL TYPE="a" START="10">** would be used since "j" is the tenth letter. An **<LI>** element within an ordered list can override the current numbering with the **VALUE** attribute, which is also set to a numeric value. Numbering of the list should continue from the value set.

The uses of ordered lists and their attributes are shown in Figure 4-23. Rendered lists are shown in Figure 4-24.

Note   *When dealing with extremes, numbering should be used with caution. Negative values or very large values produce unpredictable results. While Netscape ignores negative numbers, Internet Explorer numbers up toward zero, as expected. Browsers may allocate a fixed width to the left of a list item to display its number. Under Netscape, a list not embedded in another block structure can only accommodate about four digits; larger numbers may overwrite list elements. A list indented by nesting in another block structure may have more space. Numbering in both Netscape and Internet Explorer loses meaning with large integer values around 10 to 100 billion, most likely due to limitations with the operating environment.*

UNORDERED LISTS   An unordered list as signified by **<UL>** and **</UL>** is used for lists of items where the ordering is not specific. This might be useful in a list of features and benefits for a product. A browser typically adds a bullet of some sort (a filled circle, a square, or an empty circle) for each item and indents the list.

Unordered lists can be nested. Each level of nesting indents the list further, and the bullet changes accordingly. Generally, a filled circle or solid round bullet is used on the first level of lists. An empty circle is used for the second-level list. Third-level nested lists use a square. These renderings for bullets are common to browsers, but should not be counted on. Starting with Netscape 1.x–level browsers, it became possible to set the bullet type with the **TYPE** attribute; this was later added to the HTML

```
<!DOCTYPE HTML PUBLIC "-//W3C//DTD HTML 3.2 Final//EN">
<HTML>
<HEAD>
<TITLE>Ordered List Modifications</TITLE>
</HEAD>

<BODY>

<P>Ordered lists can be very simple</P>

<OL>
<LI>Item 1
<LI>Item 2
<LI>Item 3
</OL>

<P>Ordered lists can have a variety of types</P>

<OL>
<LI TYPE="a">Lowercase letters
<LI TYPE="A">Uppercase letters
<LI TYPE="i">Lowerroman numerals
<LI TYPE="I">Upperroman numerals
<LI TYPE="1">Plainnumerals
</OL>

<P>Ordered lists can start at different values
 and with different types.</P>
<OL START="10" TYPE="a">
<LI>This should be j
<LI>This should be k
  <OL>
    <LI>Lists can be nested
      <OL>
        <LI>to an arbitrary depth
      </OL>
  </OL>
</OL>

</BODY>
</HTML>
```

Figure 4-23.   *Ordered lists example*

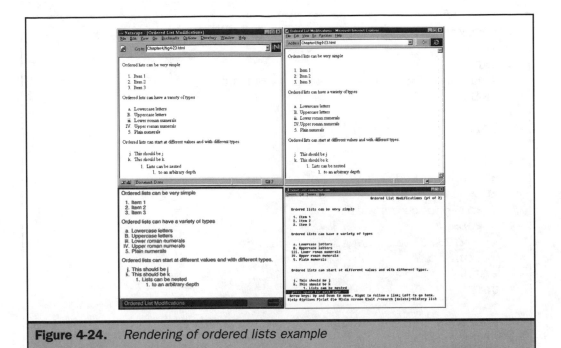

Figure 4-24. *Rendering of ordered lists example*

specification. The **TYPE** attribute may appear within the <UL> element and set the type for the whole list, or it may appear within each <LI>. A **TYPE** specification in an <LI> element overrides the value for the rest of the list unless it is overridden by another **TYPE** specification. The allowed values for **TYPE**, as suggested by the default actions, are **disc**, **circle**, or **square**. This change is not consistently supported across browsers. In the case of WebTV, a triangle bullet type is also available. For the greatest level of cross-browser compatibility, authors are encouraged to only set the bullet type for the list as a whole.

Internet Explorer 3.0–level browsers under Windows do not render TYPE settings for unordered lists. This has been fixed under Internet Explorer 4.

An example of unordered lists is shown in Figure 4-25. Various renderings of the example are shown in Figure 4-26.

```
<!DOCTYPE HTML PUBLIC "-//W3C//DTD HTML 3.2 Final//EN">
<HTML>
<HEAD>
<TITLE>Unordered Lists Example</TITLE>
</HEAD>

<BODY>

<UL>
  <LI>Unordered lists
  <UL>
    <LI>can be nested
    <UL>
      <LI>Bullet shapes will change
    </UL>
  </UL>
</UL>

<P>Bullets can be controlled with the TYPE
attribute</P>

<UL TYPE="square">
<LI>Type can be set for
<LI>the list as a whole or
<LI>item by item.
<LI TYPE="disc">Disc item
<LI TYPE="circle">Circle item
<LI TYPE="square">Square item
</UL>

</BODY>
</HTML>
```

Figure 4-25.   *Unordered lists example*

DEFINITION LIST   A definition list is a list of terms paired with associated definitions—in other words, a glossary. Definition lists are enclosed within **<DL>** and **</DL>**. Each term being defined is indicated by a **<DT>** element, for "definition term." Each definition itself is defined by **<DD>**. Both the **<DT>** and **<DD>** elements do not

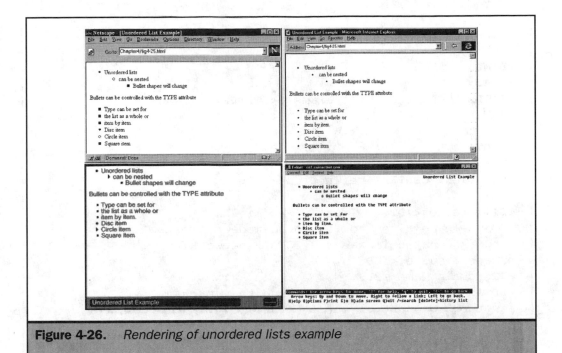

Figure 4-26.   *Rendering of unordered lists example*

require a close tag, but for long definitions, it may be helpful. A basic example using **<DL>** is shown in Figure 4-27. The renderings are shown in Figure 4-28.

Because definition lists do not add numbering or bullets, many earlier HTML writers used this element to indent text. While functionally this is the most appropriate way to achieve some rudimentary indentation, the unordered list is often used instead. Looking at the use of **<UL>** and the output of HTML tools suggests that the use of **<UL>** instead of **<DL>** to quickly indent text is very common. The reason for the preference for **<UL>** is that it requires fewer elements to achieve indentation. Remember that lists can be nested, so a varying degree of indentation can be achieved. Users desiring a fine degree of control should avoid using lists to move things around. How far something is moved away from the left is not precise, and may depend on the font size of the browser. A simple example of indenting with lists is shown in Figure 4-29, with renderings shown in Figure 4-30.

```
<!DOCTYPE HTML PUBLIC "-//W3C//DTD HTML 3.2 Final//EN">

<HTML>
<HEAD>
<TITLE>Definition List Example</TITLE>
</HEAD>

<BODY>

<H1 ALIGN="CENTER">Definitions</H1>
<DL>
<DT>Internet</DT>
<DD>The name given to the world wide network of
networks that utilizes the TCP/IP networking
protocol suite.</DD>
<DT>Domain Name</DT>
<DD>An alphanumeric moniker used to represent
a network or host on the Internet (e.g. apple.com,
nic.cerf.net).</DD>
</DL>

</BODY>
</HTML>
```

Figure 4-27. *Definition list example*

Note *Some HTML purists are offended by the use of **<UL>** to indent. HTML authors might consider using the definition list, or tables, if possible, to indent text. However, with tools spitting out **<UL>** elements in mass numbers, this may be more of a fine point than a real issue. The rise of style sheets and other technologies should, in time, put an end to this issue.*

UNCOMMON LISTS: DIR AND MENU   Beyond basic ordered, unordered, and definition lists, there are two other lists specified in HTML: menu and directory. These rarely used elements generally appear as unordered lists in most browsers. These elements are presented for completeness. Authors are warned not to use them, as future versions of HTML will probably phase them out.

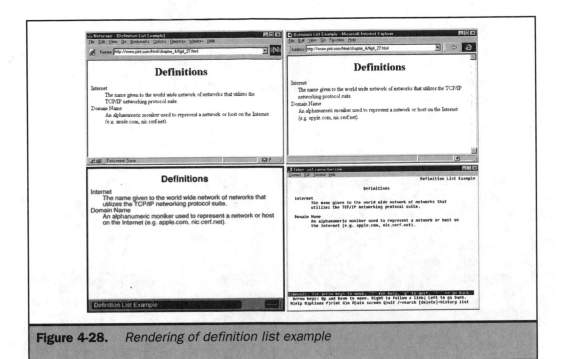

Figure 4-28.   *Rendering of definition list example*

Using the **<DIR>** element, it supposedly is possible to create listings for directory elements. Imagine a DOS listing that is displayed wide across the screen. Elements are specified using **<LI>** just like in the unordered list. In reality, most browsers do not render **<DIR>** lists any differently than unordered lists.

The **<MENU>** element can be used to create a "short" list of items. Most browsers just interpret this as a plain old unordered list. Theoretically, you can get multiple columns and no bullets in some special browsers. An example using these uncommon list types is shown in Figure 4-31. Their rendering in common browsers appears in Figure 4-32.

 *Despite the similarity between **<DIR>**, **<MENU>**, and **<UL>**, the **<DIR>** and **<MENU>** elements do not support any attributes other than **COMPACT**, which is typically implied anyway.*

Horizontal Rules

As sections are added to an HTML document, it is often desirable to break the document up into visually distinct regions. A horizontal rule, indicated by the **<HR>**

```
<!DOCTYPE HTML PUBLIC "-//W3C//DTD HTML 3.2 Final//EN">
<HTML>
<HEAD>
<TITLE>Indenting with Lists Example</TITLE>
</HEAD>

<BODY>

<DL>
<DT><DD><P>This paragraph is indented.  Watch out for
the left edge. Get too close and you hurt yourself!</P>
</DL>

<BR><BR>

<UL><UL>
<P>This paragraph is even further indented.  Most HTML
tools and authors tend to use this style to indent
because it takes fewer tags. </P>
</UL></UL>

</BODY>
</HTML>
```

Figure 4-29.   *Example of indentation with lists*

element, is a block-level element that serves this purpose. Under HTML 2.0, horizontal rules generally were rendered as an etched bar or line across a browser window. With HTML 3.2, more control over the horizontal rule's look and size was added. The exact look of the line is still left to the browser rendering the page.

Note   *Though it looks like a physical element, **<HR>** can have some logical meaning as a section break. For example, under an alternative browser like a speech-based browser, a horizontal rule might theoretically be interpreted as a pause. A hand-held browser with limited resolution might use it as a device to limit the text until scrolled to on the page.*

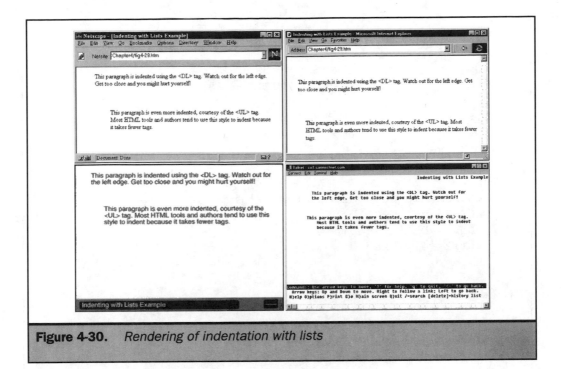

Figure 4-30. *Rendering of indentation with lists*

The **<HR>** element is an empty element in that it has no close tag and encloses no data. Just adding an **<HR>** element between two paragraphs provides a simple way of putting a horizontal rule between two sections.

Netscape and later Internet Explorer added several attributes to the **<HR>** element. **SIZE** sets the bar's thickness (height). **WIDTH** sets the bar's width. **ALIGN** sets its vertical alignment. **NOSHADE** renders the bar without a surrounding shadow. The HTML 3.2 specification supports these basic attributes. Additional, browser-specific attributes such as **COLOR** are described in the element reference. Table 4-1 describes the common attributes for **<HR>**.

Examples of horizontal rules and their basic attributes are shown in Figure 4-33, with renderings in Figure 4-34.

Address

The **<ADDRESS>** element is used to surround information such as the signature of the person who created the page or the address of the organization the page is about. Upon first observation, the **<ADDRESS>** element appears like a logical formatting element since it results, typically, in italicized text. The 3.2 specification treats

```
<!DOCTYPE HTML PUBLIC "-//W3C//DTD HTML 3.2 Final//EN">
<HTML>
<HEAD>
<TITLE>DIR and MENU Example</TITLE>
</HEAD>
<BODY>

<H2>DIR Example</H2>

<DIR>
    <LI>Should be a directory listing
    <LI>Supposed to be compact
    <LI>Maybe in columns
    <LI>Rarely used
</DIR>

<H2>MENU Example</H2>

<MENU>
    <LI>A short list of items
    <LI>Really compact
    <LI>Rarely used
</MENU>

</BODY>
</HTML>
```

Figure 4-31. *Example of <DIR> and <MENU>*

<ADDRESS> as an idiosyncratic block-level element. According to the specification, it is a special element of its own. Like other block-level elements, it inserts a blank before and after the block. It may enclose many lines of text, formatting elements to change the font characteristics, and even images. According to the specification, it is not

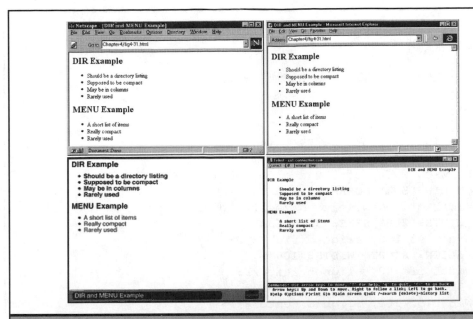

Figure 4-32.   *Rendering of <DIR> and <MENU>*

Attribute	Description	Acceptable Values	Example
ALIGN	Aligns the rule to the left, right, or center of the screen or a table	LEFT, RIGHT, or CENTER (default)	<HR ALIGN="LEFT" WIDTH="50%">
NOSHADE	Draws the horizontal rule without a shading effect	N/A	<HR NOSHADE>
SIZE	Sets the vertical size of the rules in pixels	Pixels (reasonable value*)	<HR SIZE="10">
WIDTH	Sets the width of the rule relative to the screen in pixels or percentage	Pixels or percentage value	<HR WIDTH="50%"> <HR WIDTH="200">

* Reasonable value indicates that while a SIZE of 10,000 may be possible, the browser may not render it. Under Netscape 3.02 on Windows, the maximum size for a horizontal rule is around a few hundred pixels. Under Internet Explorer such a limit is not as obvious, but the limit is probably the maximum integer size on the system.

Table 4-1.   *Standard <HR> Attributes*

```
<!DOCTYPE HTML PUBLIC "-//W3C//DTD HTML 3.2 Final//EN">
<HTML>
<HEAD>
<TITLE>Horizontal Rules Example</TITLE>
</HEAD>
<BODY>

<P>HR with size of 10</P>
<HR SIZE="10">
<P>HR with width of 50% and no shading</P>
<HR WIDTH="50%" NOSHADE>
<P>Width of 200 pixels, size of 3 pixels, and no shade</P>
<HR WIDTH="200" SIZE="3" NOSHADE>
<P>Width of 100, aligned right</P>
<HR ALIGN="RIGHT" WIDTH="100">
<P>Width of 100, aligned left</P>
<HR ALIGN="LEFT" WIDTH="100">
<P>Width of 100, aligned center</P>
<HR ALIGN="CENTER" WIDTH="100">

</BODY>
</HTML>
```

Figure 4-33.   *Examples of horizontal rules*

supposed to enclose other block-level elements like **<UL>**. Browsers generally allow this, particularly with the paragraph element.

An example of **<ADDRESS>** use is shown in Figure 4-35. The rendering appears in Figure 4-36.

Other Block-Level Elements

There are many other block-level elements in HTML, most notably tables and forms. Under Netscape and Internet Explorer there are many other elements, including frames, layers, and a variety of other formatting and structure features. These ideas could be introduced in this chapter, but because of their complexity, it makes sense to

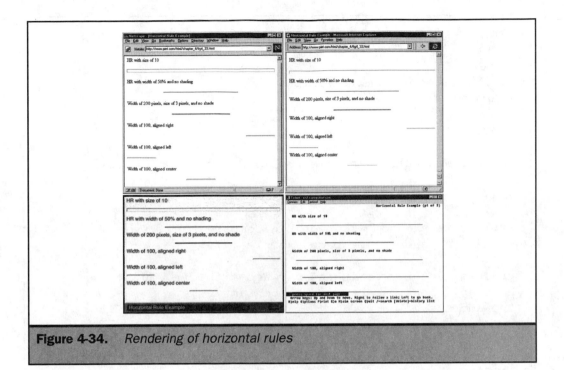

Figure 4-34.   *Rendering of horizontal rules*

discuss these topics later. Tables are discussed in depth in Chapter 8, and forms are discussed in Chapter 11. Beyond block-level elements, there are also text-level elements, as well as many miscellaneous elements that are difficult to categorize.

Text-Level Elements

Text elements in HTML come in two basic flavors: physical and logical. Physical elements, like **<B>** for bold and **<I>** for italic, are used to specify how text should be rendered. Logical elements such as **<STRONG>** and **<EM>** indicate what text is, but not necessarily how it should look. While there are common renderings for logical text elements, the ambiguity of these elements and the limited knowledge of this type of document structuring have minimized their use. However, the rise of style sheets and the growing diversity of user agents mean that it makes more sense than ever to use logical elements.

```
<!DOCTYPE HTML PUBLIC "-//W3C//DTD HTML 3.2 Final//EN">
<HTML>
<HEAD>
<TITLE>Address Example</TITLE>
</HEAD>

<BODY>

<H1 ALIGN="CENTER">Welcome to Big Company, Inc.</H1>

<HR>

<P>This is the home page of Big Company, Inc., the
leader in generic Web page examples.</P>

<P>Thank you for coming to our Web site. If you
have any questions be sure to contact us at
the address below.</P>

<HR>

<ADDRESS>
Big Company, Inc.<BR>
1122 Big Company Court<BR>
San Diego, CA 92109<BR>
619.555.2086<BR>
info@bigcompany.com
</ADDRESS>

</BODY>
</HTML>
```

Figure 4-35.   *Example of* **<ADDRESS>**

Physical Character Format Elements

It may sometimes be desirable to use bold, italics, or other font attributes to set off
certain text, such as computer code. Common HTML supports a number of elements
that can be used to influence physical formatting. The elements have no meaning
other than to make text render a particular way. Any other meaning is assigned by the
reader. The common physical elements are listed in Table 4-2.

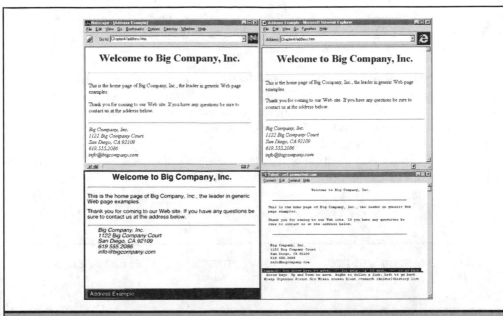

Figure 4-36. *Rendering of <ADDRESS>*

Element	Element Type
<I> ... </I>	Italics
<B> ... </B>	Bold
<TT> ... </TT>	Typewriter (Monospaced)
<U> ... </U>	Underline
<STRIKE> ... </STRIKE>	Strikethrough
<S> ... </S>	Alternative element form of strikethrough
_{...}	Subscript
^{...}	Superscript
<BIG> ... </BIG>	Bigger font (one font size bigger)
<SMALL> ... </SMALL>	Smaller font (one font size smaller)

Table 4-2. *Table of Common Physical Text Formatting Elements*

The <S> form of strikethrough is not an official element under HTML 3.2. It is, however, generally supported by browsers like Internet Explorer and Netscape. It may be included in future standards.

The example code in Figure 4-37 shows the basic use of the physical formatting elements. These elements can be combined in arbitrary ways. Just because text *can* be made monospaced, bold, italic, and superscript doesn't mean that various types of formatting should be applied to it. Figure 4-38 shows the rendering of the physical text elements under popular browsers.

Several physical text formatting elements—<U>, <STRIKE>, <S>, <BIG>, and <SMALL>—present certain problems that warrant extra discussion.

```
<!DOCTYPE HTML PUBLIC "-//W3C//DTD HTML 3.2 Final//EN">
<HTML>
<HEAD>
<TITLE>Physical Text Elements</TITLE>
</HEAD>
<BODY>
<H1 ALIGN="CENTER">Physical Text Elements</H1>
<HR>

This is <B>Bold</B>                        <BR>
This is <I>Italic</I>                      <BR>
This is <TT>Monospaced</TT>                <BR>
This is <U>Underline</U>                    <BR>
This is <STRIKE>Strike-through</STRIKE>    <BR>
This is also <S>Strike-through</S>         <BR>
This is <BIG>Bigger</BIG>                   <BR>
This is <SMALL>Smaller</SMALL>             <BR>
This is <SUB>Subscript</SUB> Text          <BR>
This is <SUP>Superscript</SUP> Text        <BR>

</BODY>
</HTML>
```

Figure 4-37. *Physical text formatting elements*

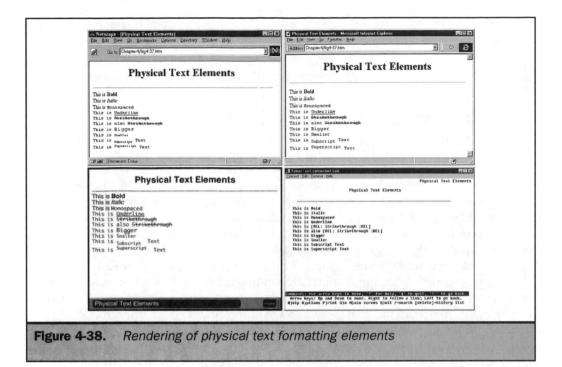

Figure 4-38. *Rendering of physical text formatting elements*

CONFUSION CAUSED BY UNDERLINING   Most browsers support the **<U>** element, which underlines text. It was not initially defined under HTML 2.0, and for good reason. The meaning of underlined text can be unclear to people who use the Web. In most graphical browsers, clickable hypertext links are represented as blue underlined text. (Link color may vary.) Users instinctively think of underlined text as something that can be clicked. Some feel that link color sufficiently distinguishes links from text underlined purely for stylistic purposes. This does not take into consideration monochrome monitors or people who are colorblind. Because the underline element may introduce more trouble than it is worth, it should be avoided.

TWO FORMS OF STRIKETHROUGH   Of the common HTML text formatting elements, only one has two forms—strikethrough. These elements draw a horizontal line through the middle of enclosed text. Netscape introduced the **<STRIKE>** element. The never-adopted HTML 3.0 specification proposed **<S>**, but changed to **<STRIKE>** in HTML 3.2. Both forms are common. Authors worried about platform support for

<S> and **<STRIKE>** can resort to a simple trick. Because browsers disregard unknown elements, the following covers the union of browsers supporting either element.

```
<S><STRIKE>THIS WILL BE STRUCK IF EITHER ELEMENT IS SUPPORTED</STRIKE></S>
```

USING <BIG> AND <SMALL>   What do the **<BIG>** and **<SMALL>** elements actually do? On the face of it, putting the **<BIG>** element around something makes it bigger. Putting the **<SMALL>** element around something makes it smaller. What about when multiple **<BIG>** and **<SMALL>** elements are nested? In HTML, there are relative fonts ranging from size 1 to size 7. Size 7 is very large, and size 1 is very small. Every application of **<BIG>** generally bumps the font up one notch to the next level. The default font for a document is usually relative size 3, so two applications of **<BIG>** would raise the font size to 5. Multiple occurrences of **<SMALL>** do the opposite—they make things one notch smaller.

What happens when the maximum or minimum size is reached? Ideally, the browser just ignores extra applications. Depending on the browser, however, this may or may not happen. Some Web browser versions, notably Internet Explorer 3.0, handle multiple occurrences of the **<BIG>** and **<SMALL>** elements in an unpredictable manner. While this has been fixed under Internet Explorer 4.0, HTML authors are warned to think of using only one **<BIG>** or **<SMALL>** element at a time. Other font sizing changes should be handled with the **<FONT>** element to be discussed in Chapter 8.

Logical Elements

Logical elements indicate the type of content they enclose. The browser is relatively free to determine the presentation of that content, although there are expected renderings for these elements that are followed by nearly all browsers. While this conforms to the design of HTML, there are issues about perception. Will a designer think strong or bold? As mentioned previously, HTML pundits push for strong, since a browser for the blind could read strong text properly. For the majority of people coding Web pages, however, HTML is used as a visual language, despite its design intentions. Seasoned experts know the beauty and intentions behind logical elements, and with style sheets, they may catch on more. For now, a quick survey of sites will show that logical text elements are relatively rare. In fact, many HTML editors make it downright difficult to add logical elements to a page, which only furthers why most logical elements are rarely used. When style sheets become more commonplace, HTML authors should re-examine their use of these elements. Table 4-3 illustrates the logical text formatting elements generally supported by browsers.

The example in Figure 4-39 uses all the logical elements in a test document. Figure 4-40 shows the rendering of the logical elements under common browsers. Note the subtle differences in rendering. For example, **<VAR>** results in monospaced text under Internet Explorer 3.0 but italicized text under Netscape 3.0. Under Internet

Element	Element Type
<ABBR> ... </ABBR>	Abbreviation
<CITE> ... </CITE>	Citation
<CODE> ... </CODE>	Source code
<DFN> ... </DFN>	Definition
<EM> ... <EM>	Emphasis
<KBD> ... </KBD>	Keystrokes
<SAMP> ... </SAMP>	Sample (example information)
<STRONG> ... </STRONG>	Strong emphasis
<VAR> ... </VAR>	Programming variable

Table 4-3.   *Table of Logical Text Formatting Elements*

```
<!DOCTYPE HTML PUBLIC "-//W3C//DTD HTML 3.2 Final//EN">
<HTML>
<HEAD>
<TITLE>Logical Text Elements</TITLE>
</HEAD>
<BODY>
<H1 ALIGN="CENTER">Logical Text Elements</H1>
<HR>
This is <EM>Emphasis</EM>          <BR>
This is <STRONG>Strong</STRONG>          <BR>
This is <CITE>Citation</CITE>          <BR>
This is <CODE>Code</CODE>          <BR>
This is <DFN>Definition</DFN>          <BR>
This is <KBD>Keyboard</KBD>          <BR>
This is <SAMP>Sample</SAMP>          <BR>
This is <VAR>Variable</VAR>          <BR>
</BODY>
</HTML>
```

Figure 4-39.   *Logical text formatting elements*

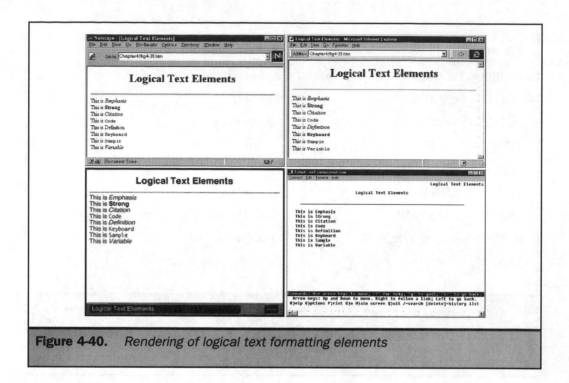

Figure 4-40. *Rendering of logical text formatting elements*

Explorer 4.0, **<VAR>** produces italicized text. There is no guarantee of rendering, and older versions of browsers may vary on other logical elements including even **<EM>**.

Probably the biggest question HTML authors have about logical elements is where to use them. This is really a philosophical question. Does the author want to strictly define content presentation, or let the browser decide on a presentation appropriate for the element's logical meaning? Advocates of logical document structuring note that if a browser doesn't support bolding, the **<B>** element has no effect. Instead, the logical **<STRONG>** element, usually rendered as bold, would be rendered in some appropriate alternative. It is an open question whether or not this type of reasoning justifies logical structure. With the proliferation of Web-browsing devices such as cellular phones, personal digital assistants, WebTV, and popular browsers like Netscape and Internet Explorer, logical document structuring may yet catch on. In conjunction with style sheets (discussed in Chapter 10), this approach to structure may become commonplace, as it allows different presentations for different situations. A cellular phone browser might require a different style than Netscape on a PC with a high-resolution monitor. While this may happen, an inspection of published pages shows that few people currently use logical text elements. From a presentation perspective, why use the ambiguous **<STRONG>** element when you can use the precise **<B>** element? In addition, many HTML development tools make it difficult to insert logically oriented HTML.

Character Entities

After covering the basic text formatting elements, there would appear to be nothing left to talk about—but there is still one more level to HTML documents: the characters themselves.

Sometimes it is necessary to put special characters within a document. These include accented letters, copyright symbols, or even the angle brackets used to enclose HTML elements. To use such characters in an HTML document, they must be "escaped" using a special code. All character codes take the form **&*code*;** where code is a word or numeric code indicating the actual character you want to put on the screen. Some of the more commonly used characters are shown in Table 4-4.

Note
The character entity ™ may not always be acceptable as trademark. On many UNIX platforms, and potentially on Macs or Windows systems using various "other" character sets, this entity does not render as trademark. Because &153; may be undefined, HTML authors should try to avoid it even though it tends to coincide with ™ on the default Windows platform and some character sets. Trademarks are important legally, so they are often needed. There is likely to be a trademark element under future versions of HTML, but for now the commonly used workaround is to use ^{<SMALL>TM</SMALL>}. This code creates a superscript trademark symbol (™) in a slightly smaller font. As standard HTML, it works on nearly every platform.

Figure 4-41 shows an example of HTML code containing character entities. Figure 4-42 shows how the HTML renders in different common browsers.

Numeric Value	Named Value	Symbol	Description
&#034;	&quot;	"	Quotation mark
&#038;	&amp;	&	Ampersand
&#060;	&lt;	<	Less than
&#062;	&gt;	>	Greater than
&#153;	N/A	™	Trademark
			Nonbreaking space
&#169;	&copy;	©	Copyright symbol
&#174;	&reg;	®	Registered trademark

Table 4-4.   *A Few Common Character Entities*

```
<!DOCTYPE HTML PUBLIC "-//W3C//DTD HTML 3.2 Final//EN">

<HTML>
<HEAD>
<TITLE>Character Entities Example</TITLE>
</HEAD>
<BODY>

<H1 ALIGN="CENTER">Big Company Inc.'s Tagging Products</H1>
<HR>
<P>
Character entites like &amp;copy; allow users
to insert special characters like &copy;.<BR><BR>

One entity is often abused: the nonbreaking
space.<BR>

Inserting spaces is easy with   <BR>

Look:   S       P      
A       C      
E       S.<BR>

</P>
<HR>
<ADDRESS>
Contents of this page
&copy; 1997 Big Company, Inc.<BR>
The <B>Wonder Tag</B> &lt;P&gt; &#153;,
a registered trademark of  Big Company, Inc.
</ADDRESS>

</BODY>
</HTML>
```

Figure 4-41.   *Example of HTML containing character entities*

> **Note**   *The use of the nonbreaking space to push text or elements around the screen is an overused crutch. Many HTML editors overuse this technique in an attempt to preserve look and feel. This entity is discussed further in Chapter 8.*

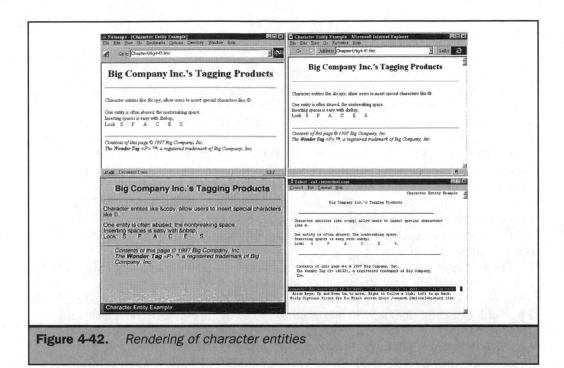

Figure 4-42.   *Rendering of character entities*

Excessive use of character entities can make HTML source documents difficult to read if they are not well spaced.

The character set currently supported by HTML is the ISO Latin-1 character set. Many of its characters, like accents and special symbols, cannot be typed on all keyboards. They must be entered into HTML documents using the appropriate code. Even if the character in question is supported on the keyboard (for example, the copyright symbol), simply typing in the symbol probably will not produce the correct encoding. Of course, many HTML editors make the appropriate insertion. A complete list of the character entities is presented in Appendix D.

HTML is capable of representing the standard ASCII characters and all the extended characters as defined by the ISO Latin-1 character set. However, for non-Western characters such as Japanese, Russian, or Arabic alphabets, special encoding and a special browser are needed.

Summary

Common HTML is a synthesis of the HTML 3.2 specification and the way authors actually use the available elements. Ideally, HTML is a formally defined, structured language with rules governing correct element usage. Pragmatically, however, browsers determine correct HTML usage by the HTML constructs they successfully render. Browsers are lax in their interpretation of HTML rules, which encourages some authors to break those rules frequently. Well-written HTML documents begin with a <!DOCTYPE> declaration followed by an <HTML> element. This encloses the document and divides it into a <HEAD> section followed by a <BODY> section. The <HEAD> element contains descriptive information and must contain one <TITLE> element. The <BODY> element contains the document's displayed content. It may be structured using block-level elements, text-level elements, and special character entities. Some text-level elements assign content a logical purpose. Others assign a physical presentation.

The elements presented so far are common across nearly all systems. Whether or not they are used, they are simple and widely understood. Yet despite their simplicity, many of these basic elements, particularly the list structures, are still abused to achieve a particular document look, which continues the struggle between the logical and physical nature of HTML. Despite some manipulation, these elements are generally used in a reasonable manner. More-complex formatting elements and programming elements are introduced in later chapters. The simplicity of this chapter should provide you with some assurance that HTML rests on a stable core.

A great number of elements have been left out of this discussion. There was no mention of browser-specific elements like Microsoft's <MARQUEE> or Netscape's <LAYER>. Graphics have been completely avoided. These topics and others are covered in upcoming chapters. Chapter 5 discusses the "H" in HTML, namely hypertext, and presents the concept of linking documents and objects.

Chapter 5

Links and Addressing

Previous chapters have shown how HTML can be used as a document formatting and structuring language, but little has been said about the hypertext aspect of the language. HTML makes it possible to define hyperlinks to other information items located all over the world, thus allowing documents to join the global information space known as the Web. Linking is possible because every document on the Web has a unique address known as a uniform resource locator (URL). The explosive growth of documents on the Web has created a tangled mess, even when document locations are named consistently. The disorganized nature of the Web often leaves users lost in cyberspace. Finding information online can feel like trying to find the proverbial needle in a worldwide haystack. Things don't have to be this way. Application of logical structure to sites, new ideas like uniform resource names (URNs), and uniform resource characteristics (URCs) in the form of meta-data like PICS (Platform for Internet Content Selection) labels may eventually lead to a more understandable and organized Web.

Linking Basics

In HTML, the main way to define hyperlinks is with the anchor element: **<A>**. A link is simply a unidirectional pointer from the source document that contains the link to some destination. In hypertext, the end points of a link are typically called anchors, thus the use of the anchor nomenclature in HTML documentation.

For linking purposes, the **<A>** element requires one attribute: **HREF**. The **HREF** attribute is set to the URL of the target resource, which is basically the address of the document to link to, such as http://www.yahoo.com. The text enclosed by the anchor elements specifies a "hot spot" to activate the hyperlink. Anchor content may include text, images, or a mixture of the two. A general link takes the form **<A HREF="URL">**Visit our site**</A>**. The text "Visit our site" is the link. The URL specified by the **HREF** attribute is the destination if the link is activated. An example of simple anchor element usage is shown in Figure 5-1. In the example, the text "Yahoo!" is the first link.

When the example in Figure 5-1 is loaded in a Web browser, the links are generally indicated by underlined text, typically in a different color—usually blue or purple, depending on whether the link object has been viewed before. Status information in the browser may change when a mouse is positioned over the link. The pointer may also change, as well as other indicators showing that the information is a link. Examples of this feedback are shown in Figure 5-2. Note that the cursor over the HotBot link in the upper left corner now looks like a pointing finger, and the URL for the HotBot home page appears in the status area in the lower left corner of the browser frame.

The actual rendering of links depends on the browser or other user agent. If you are using HTML style sheets, the links you create may have different decoration. For example, a color may change for a link that has been visited previously.

```
<!DOCTYPE HTML PUBLIC "-//W3C//DTD HTML 3.2 Final//EN">
<HTML>
<HEAD>
<TITLE>Simple Link Example</TITLE>
</HEAD>
<BODY>

<H1 ALIGN="CENTER">Lots of Links</H1>
<HR>
<UL>
    <LI>Visit <A HREF="http://www.yahoo.com">Yahoo!</A>
    <LI>Conduct powerful searches with
<A HREF="http://www.hotbot.com">HotBot</A>
    <LI>Go to the <A HREF="http://www.w3.org">W3C</A>
</UL>
</BODY>
</HTML>
```

Figure 5-1.   *Simple HTML link example*

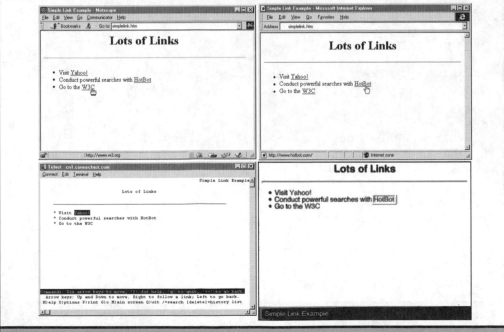

Figure 5-2.   *Renderings of links with feedback*

> **Note**   *It is possible to underline any text in an HTML document by tagging it with the underline element* **<U>**. *This practice may lead to confusion between hyperlinks and text underlined for stylistic purposes. This is particularly evident if the link is viewed in a black-and-white environment or by a color-blind individual. Therefore, use the* **<U>** *element for nonlinked items with caution.*

In the simplest example, all the anchor elements refer to an address that only contains an external server address in the form of a URL. In many cases, however, links are made within a Web site. In this situation a shortened URL, called a *relative URL*, that only includes the filename or directory structure, is used. The document in Figure 5-3 links to several other documents: a document in the same directory called "specs.htm," a document in the "extras" subdirectory called "access.htm," and a link back to a home page.

```
<!DOCTYPE HTML PUBLIC "-//W3C//DTD HTML 3.2 Final//EN">
<HTML>
<HEAD>
<TITLE>Simple Link Example 2</TITLE>
</HEAD>
<BODY>

<H1 ALIGN="CENTER">Green Gadgets</H1>

<HR>

<P ALIGN="CENTER">Information about the mysterious Green
Gadget--the wonder tool of the millennium.</P>

<UL>
   <LI><A HREF="specs.htm">Specifications</A>
   <LI><A HREF="extras/access.htm">Accessories</A>
</UL>

<P ALIGN=CENTER>
<A HREF="../index.htm">Back to Big Company Home Page</A>
</P>

</BODY>
</HTML>
```

Figure 5-3.   *Another simple link example*

These basic examples show that the use of links, at least within text, is simple. Specifying the destination URL may not be so obvious. HTML authors are often tempted to use only very simple relative URLs, like a filename, or fully qualified URLs without a sense of what URLs really can provide. Later in this chapter, the discussion returns to the HTML syntax for forming links. Before continuing, let's take a closer look, as it is important to thoroughly understand URLs.

What Are URLs?

A URL is a standard, or, more appropriately, a uniform way to refer to objects and services on the Internet. Even novice users should be familiar with typing a URL, such as http://www.yahoo.com/, in a browser dialog in order to get to a Web site. Users supply URLs in order to invoke other Internet services, such as transferring files via FTP or sending electronic mail. HTML authors also use URLs in their documents to define hyperlinks to other Web documents. Despite its potentially confusing collection of slashes and colons, the URL syntax was designed to provide a clear, simple notation that people could easily understand. The designers intended URLs to be useful as information for books, business cards, and even the backs of paper napkins, not just computers. The following concepts will help in understanding the major components of a URL address.

Note   *Many people call URLs* universal resource locators. *Except for a historical reference to universal resource identifiers in documentation from a few years ago, the current official wording is* uniform resource locator.

Basic Concepts

What is necessary for finding any arbitrary object on the Internet? First, it is necessary to locate and access the machine on the Internet (or intranet) where the object resides. Locating the site might be a matter of specifying its domain name or IP address, while accessing the machine might be a matter of providing a user name and password. On the distant machine, where is the file located? This is generally indicated by the name of the appropriate directory. What is the name of the file desired, and how will the file be retrieved? What protocol will be used to fetch the information or access the object? Given this basic sense of things, the URL simply describes where something is and how it will be retrieved. The "how" is specified by the protocol, for example, HTTP. The "where" is specified by a machine name, directory name, and filename. Slashes and other characters are used to separate the parts of the address into machine-parseable pieces. The basic structure of the URL is shown here:

```
protocol://site address/directory/file name
```

Taking a look at the individual pieces of a URL shows that there is significant detail to consider.

Site Address

Any Web document exists on a server computer somewhere on the global Internet or within a private intranet. The first step in finding a document is to identify its server. The most convenient way to do this on a TCP/IP-based network is with a symbolic name, called a *domain name*. On the Internet at large, a fully qualified domain name typically consists of a machine name followed by a domain name. For example, www.microsoft.com specifies a machine named *www* in the microsoft.com domain. On an intranet, however, things may be a little different, in that you can avoid using a domain name. For example, the machine name "hr-server" may be all that is necessary to access the human resources server.

> **Note** *A machine name can be just about any name. A machine name indicates the local, intra-organizational name for the actual server. There are no mandated rules for these names. Conventions exist, however, for identifying servers that provide common Internet resources. Servers for Web documents usually begin with the www prefix. However, many local machines have names like the user's own name (for example, jsmith), his or her favorite cartoon character (for example, homer), or even an esoteric machine name (for example, dell-p6-200-a12). Machine naming conventions are important because they allow users to form URLs without explicitly spelling them out. A user who understands domain names and machine naming conventions should be able to guess that Toyota's Web server is http://www.toyota.com/.*

The other part of most site addresses, the domain name, is fairly regular. Within the United States, a domain name consists of the actual domain or organization name followed by a period and then a domain type. An example would be sun.com. The domain itself is "sun," which represents Sun Microsystems. The "sun" domain exists within the commercial zone because of Sun's corporate status, so it ends with the domain type of *com*. In the United States, most domain identifiers currently use a three-character code that indicates the type of organization that owns the server. The most common codes are *com* for commercial, *gov* for government, *org* for nonprofit organization, *edu* for educational institution, *net* for network, and *mil* for military. Recently, there has been some debate as to the extent of the domain name space. Soon there may be a variety of new domain endings like *firm*, *web*, and *nom*. See Table 5-1 for a basic listing of U.S. domain types.

Domain Type	Domain Description	Example
com	Commercial entities and individuals	apple.com
net	Networks and network providers	cerf.net
org	Nonprofits and other organizations	greenpeace.org
edu	Four-year colleges and universities	ucla.edu
gov	United States Federal government agencies	whitehouse.gov
mil	United States Federal government military entities	nosc.mil
us	Used for a variety of organizations and individuals including K–12 education, libraries, and city and county governments	co.san-diego.ca.us

Table 5-1.   *Domain Types in the United States circa Spring 1997*

Domain space beyond the United States is somewhat more complicated. A fully qualified domain name, including a country code, is generally written as

```
machine name. domain name . domain type . country code
```

Zone identifiers outside the United States use a two-character code to indicate the country hosting the server. These include *ca* for Canada, *mx* for Mexico, and *jp* for Japan. Within each country, the local naming authorities may create domain types at their own discretion. These may not correspond to American extensions. For example, www.sony.co.jp specifies a Web server for Sony in the *co* zone of Japan. In this case, *co*, rather than *com*, indicates a commercial venture. In the United Kingdom, educational domain space has a different name, *ac*. Oxford University's Web server is www.ox.ac.uk, where *ac* indicates academic rather than the U.S. *edu* extension. Despite a flattening of geographical name use for large multinational companies like Sony, regional naming differences are very much alive. Web page authors linking to non-native domains are encouraged to understand the naming conventions of those environments. One special top-level domain, *int*, is reserved for organizations established by international treaties between governments, such as the European Union (eu.int). Top-level domains like *com*, *net*, and the upcoming new domains like *nom* should be considered similar to *int* in that they do not necessarily correspond to a particular geographic area.

Symbolic names make it convenient for people to refer to Internet servers. A server's real address is its Internet Protocol (IP) numeric address. Every accessible server on the Internet has a unique IP address by which it can be located using the TCP/IP protocol. An IP address is a numeric string made up of four numbers between 0 and 255 separated by periods (for example, 213.6.17.34). A server's symbolic name must be translated or resolved into an IP address before it can be used to locate a server. An Internet service known as Domain Name System (DNS) automatically performs this translation. You can use an IP address instead of a symbolic name to specify an Internet server. Doing this gives up mnemonic convenience. In some cases, it may be necessary, because while every server has an IP address, not all have symbolic names.

Investigating all aspects of the domain name structure is beyond the scope of this book. However, domain name problems and the robustness of the domain name service are very critical to the operation of the Web. If the domain name server is unavailable, it will be impossible to access a Web server. To learn more about machine and domain names, explore the following Web sites: http://rs.internic.net/rs-internic.html, http://www.isi.edu/div7/iana/, or http://www.iahc.org/.

NOTE: Domain names are not case sensitive. Addresses may be written as www.BigCompany.com or www.BIGCOMPANY.com. A browser should handle both properly. Case is typically changed for marketing or branding purposes. Directory values following the domain name may be case sensitive, depending on the operating system the Web server is running on. For example, Unix systems are case sensitive, while Windows machines are not. Trouble can arise if casing is used randomly. As a rule of thumb, keep everything in lowercase, or consistently uppercase just the first letters in directory or filenames.

Once the machine has been specified, either by its domain name or its IP address, it may be necessary to specify the particular directory on the machine in question.

Directory

Servers may contain hundreds, if not thousands, of files. For practical use, files need to be organized into manageable units analogous to the manila folders traditionally used to organize paper documents. This unit is known as a *file directory*. Once you know what server a document resides on, the next step toward identifying its location is to specify the directory that contains the file. Just as one manila folder can contain other folders, directories can contain other directories. Directories contain other directories in a nested, hierarchical structure that resembles the branches of a tree. The directory that contains all others is known as the *root directory*. Taken together, all the directories and files form a file tree, or *file system*. A file is located in a file system by specifying its *directory path*. This is the nested list of all directories that contain the file from the most general, the root directory, to the most specific. Similar to the Unix operating system, directories hosted on Web servers are separated by forward slashes (/) rather than backslashes as in DOS (\). Figure 5-4 shows a sample file tree for a Web site.

Figure 5-4 shows how directories are organized within (or above and below) one another. For example, the directory called "special" is within the "products" directory, which is within the root directory as indicated by the forward slash (/). The full path should be written as "/products/special/" to indicate that "special" is an actual directory, not a file in the "products" directory. When linking to other files, it may be necessary to refer to a directory above the current directory or the current directory itself. In the scheme presented, ./ means the current directory while ../ means one directory up in the hierarchy. A document in the "special" directory with a link path of ../ will link up to the "products" directory.

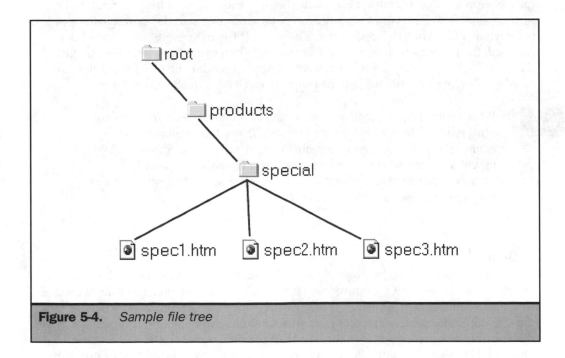

Figure 5-4.   *Sample file tree*

> **Note** *Directory names may follow conventions specific to an operating system, including being case sensitive. Authors are cautioned to take a careful look at directory casing. Furthermore, directories may follow popular usage conventions (for example, tmp), or they may be arbitrary. Usually they reflect aspects of media types, subject matter, or access privileges of their content. For example, a directory called* images *might be the name of a directory containing images.*

Filename

Having specified the server and directory path for a document, the next step toward locating it is to specify its filename. This step typically has two parts, a filename followed by a standard file extension. Filenames can be any names that are applicable under the server's operating system. Special characters like spaces, colons, and slashes might play havoc if used in names of Web-available files. A file named test:1.htm would present problems on a Macintosh system, while test/1.htm might be legal on a Macintosh and problematic on a PC or Unix machine. A dot separates the filename and the extension, which is a code, usually three letters, that identifies the type of information contained in the file. For example, HTML source files have an *htm* or *html* extension. JPEG images have a *jpg* extension. A file's extension is critically important for Web applications because it is usually the only indication of the information type a file contains. A Web server reads a file extension and uses it to determine what headers to attach to a file when delivering it to a browser. If file extensions are omitted or misused, the file may be interpreted incorrectly. When browsers read files directly, they also look at file extensions to determine how to render the file. If the extension is missing or incorrect, a file will not be properly displayed in a Web browser.

> **Note** *While many operating systems support four or more letters for file extensions, using a three-letter extension (.htm) versus a four-letter extension (.html) ensures that cross-platform incompatibilities are minimized. Spaces, uppercasing, and special characters should also be avoided to provide the greatest flexibility. Authors and users should particularly be aware of case sensitivity in filenames and directory names.*

Protocol

In may seem that nothing more is needed to locate a document than its server, directory, and filename. One component is missing—the protocol. The Internet supports a standard set of resources, each with its own associated protocol. A *protocol* is a structured discussion that computers follow to negotiate resource-specific services. For example, the protocol that makes the Web possible is the Hypertext Transfer Protocol (HTTP). When you click on a hyperlink in a Web document, your browser uses the HTTP protocol to contact a Web server and retrieve the appropriate document.

While HTTP stands for Hypertext Transfer Protocol, it does not specify how a file is transported from a server to a browser, only how the discussion between the server and browser will take place in order to get the file. The actual transport of files is usually up to a lower-layer network protocol like TCP. This subtle transport misconception is common in the case of the protocol aspect of a URL.

While less frequently used, other protocols are important to HTML authors because they can be invoked by hyperlinks. Here are some examples:

file	Enables a hyperlink to access a file on the local file system
File Transfer Protocol (FTP)	Enables a hyperlink to download files from remote systems
gopher	Enables a hyperlink to access a gopher server
mailto	Calls SMTP (Simple Mail Transport Protocol), the Internet mail protocol, and enables a hyperlink to send an addressed e-mail message
Network News Transport Protocol (NNTP)	Enables a hyperlink to access a USENET news article
news	Enables a hyperlink to access a USENET newsgroup
telnet	Enables a hyperlink to open a telnet session on a remote host

These are the common protocols, but a variety of new protocols and URL forms are being debated all the time. Someday, things like *ldap* (Lightweight Directory Access Protocol), *irc* (Internet Relay Chat), *phone*, *fax*, and even *tv* might be used to reference how data should be accessed. More about the future of URLs and other naming ideas will be discussed toward the end of this chapter.

Beyond the protocol, server address, directory, and filename, URLs often include a user name and password, port number, and sometimes a fragment identifier. Some URLs, such as mailto, might even contain a different form of information altogether, like an e-mail address rather than a server or filename.

User and Password

FTP and telnet are protocols for *authenticated services*. Authenticated services may assume access by authorized users, and the protocols may require a user name and password as parameters. A user name and password precedes a server name and looks like this: *username:password@server-address*. The password may be optional or unspecified in the URL, making the form simply *username@server-address*.

HTML authors are warned not to include password information in URLs, because the information will be readily viewable in a Web page or within the browser's URL box.

Port

Although the situation is rare, it is possible to specify the communication port in a URL. Browsers speaking a particular protocol communicate with servers through entry points, known as *ports*, that are generally identified by numeric addresses. Associated with each protocol is a default port number. For example, an HTTP request defaults to port number 80. A server administrator can configure a server to handle protocol requests at ports other than the default numbers. Usually this occurs for experimental or secure applications. In these cases, the intended port must be explicitly addressed in a URL. To specify a port number, place it after the server address separated by a colon: for example, site-address:90. Web administrators are forewarned not to arbitrarily change port numbers. This will confuse users and may result in people having difficulty accessing a site, particularly if access comes from behind a firewall (a security feature) via a proxy server. Such systems may not be set up to allow traffic on nonstandard port numbers.

Fragment

Another area to discuss is the fragment identifier. After a file has been specified, a user may desire to go directly to a particular point in the file. Because it is possible to set up named links under HTML, there must be a way to link directly to that point. To jump to a particular named link, the URL must include the link name preceded by a hash symbol (#), indicating that the value is a fragment identifier. To specify a point called *contents* in a file called *test.htm*, use *test.htm#contents*.

Encoding

When writing the components of a URL, take care that they are written using only the displayable characters in the US-ASCII character set. Even when using characters within this basic keyboard character range, you will find certain unsafe characters or reserved characters that may have special meaning within the context of a URL or the operating system the resource is found on. If any unsafe, reserved, or nonprintable characters occur in a URL, they must be encoded in a special form. Failure to encode these charatcers may lead to errors.

The form of encoding consists of a percent sign and two hexadecimal digits corresponding to the value of the character in the ASCII character set. Within many intranet environments, filenames often include user-friendly names like "first quarter earnings 1997.doc." Such names contain unsafe characters. If this file were to live on a departmental Web server, it would have a URL with a file portion of "first%20quarter%20earnings%201997.doc." Notice how the spaces have been mapped to **%20** values—the hex value of the space character in ASCII. Other characters that will be troublesome in URLs include the slash character (/), which encodes as **%2F**, the question mark, which maps to **%3F**, and the percent itself, which encodes as **%25**. Only alphanumeric values and some special characters ($ - _ . + ! * '), including parentheses, may be used in a URL. Other characters should be encoded. In general, special characters such as accents, spaces, and some punctuation marks will have to be encoded. HTML authors are encouraged to name files with encoding in mind so that encoding can be avoided whenever possible. Table 5-2 shows the reserved and potentially dangerous characters for URLs.

Character	Encoding
Space	%20
/	%2F
?	%3F
:	%3A
;	%3B
&	%26
@	%40
=	%3D
#	%23
%	%25
>	%3E
<	%3C
{	%7B
}	%7D
[	%5B
]	%5D
"	%22
'	%27
`	%60
^	%5E

Table 5-2.   *Common Character Encoding Values*

Character	Encoding
~	%7E
\	%5C
		%7C

Table 5-2. *Common Character Encoding Values* (continued)

Many of the characters in Table 5-2 don't have to be encoded. There is never a problem if a character is encoded, so when in doubt, encode it.

With this brief discussion of all the various components coming to a close, let's look at a formula for creating URLs and some examples.

Formula for a URL

All URLs share the same basic syntax: a protocol name followed by a colon, followed by a protocol-specific resource description.

```
<protocol_name>:<resource_description>
```

Beyond this, enough variation exists between protocol specifics for each to merit a separate discussion.

HTTP

A minimal HTTP URL simply gives a server name. It provides no directory or file information. A minimal HTTP formula commonly occurs for corporate addresses used in advertising.

```
Formula:   http://<server>/
Example:   http://www.company.com/
```

A minimal HTTP URL implicitly requests the home directory of a Web site. Even when a trailing slash is not used, it is assumed and added either by the user agent or the Web server, making an address like http://www.company.com become http://www.company.com/. By default, requesting a directory often results in the server returning a default file from the directory, termed the *index file*. Usually index files are named index.htm or default.htm (or index.html and default.html), depending on the server software being used. This is only convention; Web administrators are free to name default index files whatever they like. It is interesting to note that many people put special importance on the minimal HTTP URL form, when, like all other file-retrieval URLs, this form simply specifies a particular directory or default index file to return, though this is not always explicitly written out.

Making the HTTP URL example slightly more complex, a formula is presented to retrieve a specific HTML file assumed to exist in the default directory for the server.

```
Formula:  http://<server>/<file>
Example:  http://www.company.com/hello.htm
```

An alternate incremental extension adds directory information without specifying a file. While the final slash should be provided, servers will imply its existence if it is omitted and look for a "home" document in the given directory. In practice, the final slash is optional, but recommended.

```
Formula: http://<server>/<directory>/
Example: http://www.company.com/products/
```

An HTTP URL can specify both a directory and file.

```
Formula: http://<server>/<directory>/<file>
Example: http://www.company.com/products/greeting.htm
```

On some systems, there may be special shorthand conventions for directory use. For example, a Unix-based Web server may support many directories, each owned by a specific user. Rather than spelling out the full path to a user's root directory, the user directory can be abbreviated by using the tilde character (~), followed by the user's account, followed by a slash. Any directory or file information that follows this point will be relative to the user's root directory.

```
Formula: http://<server>/~<user>/
Example: http://www.company.com/~jsmith/
```

User directories indicated by the tilde are somewhat similar to the convention used on the Unix operating system, though other Web servers on different operating systems may provide similar shortcut support.

A URL can refer to a named location inside an HTML document. This can be called a *marker*, or *named link*. How markers are created will be discussed later in the chapter, but for now, to refer to a document marker, follow the target document's filename with the pound character, (#), and then with the marker name.

```
Formula: http://<server>/<directory>/<file>#marker.
Example: http://www.company.com/profile.htm#introduction
```

In addition to referring to HTML documents, an HTTP URL can request any type of file. For example, http://www.company.com/images/logo.gif would retrieve a GIF image from a server rather than an HTML file. Authors should be aware that the flexibility of Web servers and URLs is often overlooked because of the common belief that all Web-based documents must be in the HTML format in order to be linked to. An HTTP URL can even reference and execute a server program. These server-side programs are typically termed CGI (Common Gateway Interface) programs, after the interface standard that describes how to pass data in and out of a program. Quite often, server-side programs are used to access databases and then generate HTML documents in response to user-entered queries. Parameters for such programs can be directly included in a URL by appending a question mark followed by the actual parameter string. Because the user may type in special characters in a query, characters normally not allowed within a URL are encoded. Remember that the formula for special-character encoding is a percent sign followed by two hex numbers representing the character's ASCII value. For example, a blank character can be represented by **%20**.

```
Formula: http://<server>/<directory>/<file>?<parameters>
Example: http://www.company.com/products/search.cgi?cost=400.00
```

Forming complex URLs with encoding and query strings looks very difficult. In reality, this is rarely done manually. Typically, the browser generates such a string on the fly based upon data provided via a file form. A more detailed discussion of HTML interaction with programming facilities appears in Chapters 11 through 15.

Finally, any HTTP request can be directed to a port other than the default port value of 80 by following the server identification with a colon and the intended port number.

```
Formula: http://<server>:<port>/<directory>/<file>
Example: http://www.bigcompany.com:8080/products/greetings.htm
```

In the preceding example, the URL references a Web server running on port 8080. While any unreserved port number is valid, using nonstandard port numbers on servers is not good practice. To access the address in the example, a user would need to include the port number in the URL. If it is omitted, it will be impossible to access www.bigcompany.com.

There is one case of HTTP that is, in a sense, a different protocol: secured Web transactions using the Secure Sockets Layer (SSL). In this case the protocol will be referenced as https, and the port value will be assumed to be 443. An example formula for Secure HTTP is shown here; other than the cosmetic difference of the "s" and the different port value, it is identical to other HTTP URLs.

```
Formula: https://server:<port>/<directory>/<file>
Example: https://www.wellsfargo.com/
```

An HTTP URL for a Web page is probably the most common URL, but users may find file or similar types of URLs growing in popularity due to the rise of intranets and serverless-style access.

file

The file protocol specifies a file residing somewhere on a computer or locally accessible computer network. It does not specify an access protocol and has limited value except for one important case. It allows a browser to access files residing on a user's local computer, an important capability for Web page development. In this usage, the server name is omitted or replaced by the keyword *localhost*. Following this is the local directory and file specification.

```
Formula: file://<server>/<directory>/<file>
Example: file:///dev/web/testpage.html
```

In some environments, the actual drive name and path to the file is specified. On a Macintosh, a URL might be file:///Macintosh %20HD/Desktop%20Folder/Bookmarks.html. On a PC. there may be a file URL like file://\\pc1\C\Netlog.txt to access a file on the C drive of a PC on the local network pc1. Depending on browser complexity, file URLs might not be required, as with Internet Explorer 4.0, where the operating system is tightly coupled with the user agent. It is interesting to note that in the case of intranets, many drives may be mapped or file systems mounted so that no server is required to deliver files. In this "Web serverless" environment, it may be possible to access network drives with a file URL. This idea demonstrates how simple a Web server is. In fact, to some people, a Web server is merely a very inefficient, though open, file server. With this said, it is no great leap to see that alternative file delivery systems like those that use the Network File System (NFS) protocol might be possible or preferable to HTTP-based servers. Already, work is being done on WebNFS and other alternative Web-oriented remote file access technologies. This realization of file transfer leads immediately to the idea of the FTP URL.

FTP

The File Transfer Protocol (FTP), which predates the browser-oriented HTTP protocol, transfers files from a server. It is generally not geared toward transferring files to be immediately viewed, but rather to be locally stored. A browser may allow files to be viewed immediately. Today FTP is most commonly used to download large files, such as complete applications, because of its efficiency. These URLs share with HTTP the formula for indicating a server, port, directory, and file.

> Formula: `ftp://<server>:<port>/<directory>/<file>`

A minimal FTP URL specifies a server and then lists the following directory: ftp://ftp.company.com. Generally, however, ftp URLs are used to access a particular file in an archive by name and directory, as shown in this formula:

> Formula: `ftp://<server>/<directory path><file>`
> Example: `ftp://ftp.company.com/info/somefile.exe`

The File Transfer Protocol is an authenticated protocol. Every valid FTP request requires a defined user account on the server downloading files. In practice, many FTP resources are intended for general access, and it would be impractical to define a unique account for every potential user. An FTP convention known as *anonymous FTP* handles this common situation. The user name "anonymous" or "ftp" allows general access to any public FTP resource supported by a server. As in the previous example, the anonymous user account is implicit in any FTP URL that does not explicitly provide account information.

An FTP URL can specify the name and password for a user account. If included, they precede the server declaration according to the following formula. It is not wise to mention an account password in a public document such as an HTML file. If you omit the password, generally the user agent prompts you to enter one if a password is required.

> Formula: `ftp://<user>:<password>@<server>/<directory>/<file>`
> Example: `ftp://jsmith:harmony@ftp.company.com/products/list`

This formula shows the password embedded within the URL, a dangerous proposition because it is transmitted in plain text and viewable both in the HTML source and browser address bar. Only public passwords should be embedded in any URL for an authenticated service. It is more appropriate to provide a link to the service and require user and password to be entered or just provide the user ID and have the user agent prompt for a password as would happen in the next example.

```
Formula: ftp://<user>@<server>/<directory>/<file>
Example: ftp://jsmith@ftp.company.com/products/sales
```

The FTP protocol assumes that a downloaded file contains binary information. You can override this default assumption by appending a type code to an FTP URL. There are three common values. An **a** code indicates the file is an ASCII text file. The **i** code, which is also the default, indicates the file is an image/binary file. A **d** code causes the URL to return a directory listing of the specified path instead of a file. An example formula is presented here for completeness.

```
Formula: ftp://<server>/<directory>/<file>;type=<code>
Example: ftp://ftp.compay.com/products;type=d
```

In reality, the type codes are rarely encountered, because the binary transfer format generally does not harm text files and the user agent is usually smart enough to handle FTP URLs without type codes. Like many other URLs, the port accessed can be changed to something besides the default port of 21, but this is not recommended.

Gopher

The Gopher system, the first popular document-based technology on the Internet, arose in the early 1990s as client/server architecture appropriate for campus information systems. It provided a way to hierarchically organize and navigate documents. Gopher servers continue today, but with much of their original purpose overshadowed by the more popular HTML-based Web content. For backward compatibility, you may find it important to link via a Web page to Gopher-based information using a Gopher URL.

A Gopher URL follows the same formula used by other protocols to specify a server and optional port address. However, compared to HTTP or FTP, Gopher URLs differ in the way they specify resources on a server. This specification begins with a single-digit code indicating the resource type referred to. The default code is 1, which indicates a directory list. Following this is a "selector string," which corresponds to a directory and file specification found in other URL formulas. If the resource type supports an appended query, a tab character, with an ASCII value of **%09**, separates the selector string from the query string.

Code	Resource Type
0	Text file
1	Directory listing
2	CSO phone book server

Code	Resource Type
3	Error
4	Macintosh binhex file
5	DOS binary file
6	Unix-unencoded file
7	Full-text index search
8	telnet session
9	Binary file

```
Formula:
gopher://<server>:<port>/<type><selector>%09<query>%09<gopher+>
Example: gopher://gopher.company.com/4mac/somefile.hxq
```

Because of the encoding and the use of the file type numbers, a Gopher URL can look extremely complex. In the preceding example, the 4 indicated a Macintosh binhex file. Normally, users will see 00 or 0 for files and 1 or 11 for directories. The numbers are often repeated because some Gopher strings begin with a copy of the content type. Readers may wonder why Web pages do not use such numeric codes to indicate content type. MIME types provide a far better solution (see Chapter 2). Beyond the file types and encoded characters, Gopher is very similar to other file retrieval URLs. Gopher may also include electronic forms for searching that, like HTTP, add a query string after a question mark. For example, gopher://mudhoney.micro.umn.edu: 4326/7?Mexico. Notice the use of the 7 code to indicate the type of data is a full-text index search. Also notice in this example that like many other protocols, Gopher may run on another port than its standard port of 70. This may be specified in the URL. As noted earlier, this is not recommended.

mailto

Atypically, this protocol does not locate and retrieve an Internet resource. Instead, it opens a window for editing and sending a mail message to a particular user address.

```
Formula: mailto:<user>@<server>
Example: mailto:president@whitehouse.gov
```

This rather simple formula shows standard Internet mail addressing; other more complex addresses may be just as valid. Using mailto URLs is very popular in Web sites for providing a basic feedback mechanism. Note that if a user agent has not been set up properly to send e-mail, this type of URL may produce error messages when used in a link, prompting the user to set up mailing preferences.

> **Note**
>
> *Some browsers have introduced proprietary extensions to the mailto element, such as the '?subject' extension. These extensions are not standard as of this writing and will cause other browsers to be unable to send e-mail using the link. There is work underway on standardizing extensions to the mailto element, but for now use of the proprietary extensions is discouraged.*

news

A news URL invokes a news browser that allows access to USENET news groups. It can take one of two alternate approaches, each with limitations. In the first approach, a news URL requests a named news group. Like the mailto URL, in this form the URL does not specify which news server to use in order to fulfill the request. A default news server address is usually set as a Web browser preference. Unfortunately, not all news servers may carry the same groups. News archives are large, and tend to be distributed across multiple servers. If the requested news group does not exist on the default news server, it will not be found.

In the second approach, a news URL requests a message on a particular news server using a server-specific message identifier such as 13c65a7a. Because messages generally have an expiration date, this approach has limited value. In addition, the message identifier obviously varies from server to server so it is not easily transferable.

```
Formula: news:<newsgroup>
Example: news:microsoft.public
Formula: news:<message>@<server>
Example: news:13c65a7a@news.company.com
```

Both the second form of the news URL and the NNTP URL (to be discussed next) show the limitations of URLs when dealing with time-sensitive information. There is very little way to deal with data that changes as rapidly as USENET news. News URLs are generally used simply to access a group rather than a particular message.

NNTP

The Network News Transport Protocol (NNTP) allows the retrieval of individual USENET articles qualified by server, news group, and article number. Like many protocols, an optional port value can be specified to direct a user agent to a specific server port. The NNTP URL has a limitation in that a particular article number is referenced. Article numbers will vary from server to server so this URL is not transportable. Furthermore, articles generally expire rather quickly so fully specified NNTP URLs are of somewhat limited value.

```
Formula: nntp://<server>:<port>/<newsgroup>/<article-number>
Example: nntp://news.company.com/microsoft.public/118
```

The default port value of nntp is 118, but another port value may be set in the URL. A special version of NNTP that adds security runs on port 563. The form of the URL is nntps://secnews.company.com/microsoft.public/118.

In general, the news URL appears to be more commonly used on the Web.

telnet

The telnet protocol allows a user to open an interactive terminal session on a remote host computer. A minimal telnet URL simply gives the remote system's name. Once a connection is made, the system prompts for an account name and password.

```
Formula: telnet://<server>
Example: telnet://company.com
```

As an authenticated protocol, telnet generally requires a defined user account on the remote system. When this is unspecified, the user agent or helper application handling telnet will prompt for such information. Like FTP, a telnet URL can also contain an account name and password as parameters. As with FTP URLs, be careful about including passwords in public access documents like HTML files on the Web. Because of this, the password is optional in the formula.

```
Formula: telnet://<user>:<password>@<server>
Example: telnet://jsmith:harmony@company.com
Example: telnet://jsmith@company.com
```

Finally, any telnet URL can direct a request to a specific port by appending the port address to the server name.

```
Formula: telnet://<server>:<port>
Example: telnet://company.com:94
```

Some telnet information sources may be configured to run on a particular port besides port 23, the standard telnet port. Consequently, use of the port within a telnet URL is more common than other URLs.

Other Protocols

There are a wide variety of other protocols that can be used. However, a browser may not support many of these URL forms. Some protocols, like the wais protocol, have historical interest. There is little evidence that people actually use this protocol much on the Web, despite its presence in books only one or two years old. Beyond old protocols like wais, there are operating-biased protocols like finger, and esoteric protocols for things like VEMMI video text services. New protocols are being added all the time. In fact, there are dozens of proposed or even implemented protocols that can be referenced with some form of nonstandard URL. If you are interested in other URL forms, visit http://www.w3.org/pub/WWW/Addressing/schemes or http://www.ics.uci.edu/pub/ietf/uri/ for more information.

Relative URLs

Up until this point, the discussion has focused on a specific form of URL, typically termed an absolute URL. Absolute URLs completely spell out the protocol, host, directory, and filename. Providing such detail can be tedious and unnecessary. This is where a shortened form of URL, termed a *relative URL*, comes in. With relative URLs, the various parts of the address—the site, directory, and protocol—might be inferred by the URL of the current document, or via the **<BASE>** element. The best way to illustrate the idea of relative URLs is by example.

If a Web site has an address of www.bigcompany.com, a user may access the home page with a URL like http://www.bigcompany.com/. A link to this page from an outside system would also contain the address http://www.bigcompany.com/. Once at the site, however, there is no reason to continue spelling out the full address of the site. A fully qualified link from the home page to a staff page in the root directory called staff.html would be http://www.bigcompany.com/staff.html. The protocol, address, and directory name can be inferred, so all that is needed is the address staff.html. This relative scheme works because http://www.bigcompany.com/ is inferred as the base of all future links, thus allowing for the shorthand relative notation. The relative notation can be used with filename and directories as shown by the examples in Table 5-3.

When relative URLs are used within a Web site, the site becomes transportable. By not spelling out the server name in every link, you can develop a Web site on one server and move it to another. If you used absolute URLs, all links would have to be changed if a server changed names or the files were moved to another site. Of course, there is a potential downside to relative URLs: they can become confusing in a large site, particularly if there are centralized directories for things like images. Imagine having URLs like ../../../images/logo.gif in files deep in a site structure. Some users might be tempted to simply copy files to avoid such problems, but then there are

Current Page Address	Destination Address	Relative URL
http://www.bigcompany.com/index.htm	http://www.bigcompany.com/staff.htm	staff.htm
http://www.bigcompany.com/index.htm	http://www.bigcompany.com/products/gadget1.htm	products/gadget1.htm
http://www.bigcompany.com/products/gadget1.htm	http://www.bigcompany.com/index.htm	../index.htm

Table 5-3.   *Relative URL Formation Examples*

issues of updating and caching. One solution is to use the **<BASE>** element. Another would be the use of symbolic links on the Web server to reference one copy of the file from multiple locations. However, because HTML is the subject here, let's focus on the former solution.

The **<BASE>** element defines the base for all relative URLs within a document. Setting the **HREF** attribute of this element to a fully qualified URL allows all other relative references to use the defined base. For example, **<BASE HREF="http://www.bigcompany.com/">** sets all the anchors later on that are not fully qualified to prefix http:// www.bigcompany.com / to the destination URL. The **<BASE>** element may occur only once in a document. It is only allowed within the head of an HTML document, so it is impossible to create sections of a document with different base URL values. It is possible to imagine that such a feature might be added to the **<DIV>** element or similar sectioning element, but until then HTML authors will have to deal with shorthand notation being useful in some places and not in others.

Linking in HTML

Up until this point, the discussion has focused solely on the forms of URLs. Little has been said about how to link objects together on the Web. Later in this chapter, the discussion returns to URLs and their counterparts, URIs, URCs, and URNs.

The Anchor Element

Using a URL makes it possible to specify the location of many types of information resources, both on the Internet and within a local area network. But how, exactly, is HTML used to specify a hyperlink that links one document to another? The most common way to define hyperlinks is with the anchor element: **<A>**. In its most basic form, this element needs two pieces of information: the URL of the target resource, and the document content needed to activate the hyperlink. Assigning a URL value to an anchor element's **HREF** attribute specifies the target resource. Most defined hyperlinks will probably use an HTTP URL to link one HTML document to another. Remember, however, that URLs to other information resources are also possible.

The anchor element's content specifies a document hot spot for activating the hyperlink. Anchor content may include text, images, or a mixture of the two. By enclosing some text or other content with the **<A>** and **</A>**, you make the item into a link that, when selected, requests a new object to be accessed. In the following code fragment, the text "Linked content" will load the URL referenced by the **HREF** attribute when it's selected.

```
<A HREF="URL">Linked content</A>
```

 An anchor element may not enclose another anchor element. The code <A HREF="URL1">Linked<A HREF="URL2">More linked</A></A> makes no sense.

The simplest hyperlink combines an anchor element with a URL that only contains a Web server address. Implicitly, the referenced document is the server's home page, which is the default document returned from the Web server's root directory. Many more complex examples of links are also possible. A variety of HTTP links are shown here:

EXAMPLE

```
<A HREF="http://www.whitehouse.gov/">Visit the President</A>
```

DESCRIPTION   Here is a link to the home page of a Web site with a basic HTTP URL.

EXAMPLE

```
<A HREF="http://www.microsoft.com/gallery/">MS Web Gallery</A>
```

DESCRIPTION   Adding a directory path to the URL references the default document in a specific directory.

EXAMPLE

```
<A HREF="http://www.pint.com/staff/thomas.htm">Thomas Bio</A>
```

DESCRIPTION   Adding a filename to a URL fully describes the document location.

EXAMPLE

```
<A HREF="http://www.bigcompany.com/spec.htm#top">Go to top</A>
```

DESCRIPTION   Adding a fragment to a filename describes a particular location within a document.

EXAMPLE

```
<A HREF="staff/index.htm">Staff</A>
```

DESCRIPTION   Anchors may use relative URLs.

EXAMPLE

```
<A HREF="../../index.htm">Back to home</A>
```

DESCRIPTION   Relative URLs may be complex.

EXAMPLE

```
<A HREF="ftp://ftp.cdrom.com">Access FTP archive</A>
```

DESCRIPTION   Anchors are not limited to HTTP URLs.

EXAMPLE

```
<A HREF="mailto:info@pint.com">More information?</A>
```

DESCRIPTION   Beyond retrieving files, anchors may trigger e-mail or even run programs.

Figure 5-5 shows a complete example of relative and absolute URLs and their use within an HTML document.

Various renderings of the example in Figure 5-5 are shown in Figure 5-6.

```
<!DOCTYPE HTML PUBLIC "-//W3C//DTD HTML 3.2 Final//EN">
<HTML>
<HEAD>
<TITLE>Link Example 3</TITLE>
</HEAD>
<BODY>
<H1 ALIGN="CENTER">Green Gadgets</H1>

<HR>
<P ALIGN="CENTER">Information about the mysterious Green
   Gadget--the wonder tool of the millenium.</P>

<UL>

<LI><A HREF="specs.htm">Specifications</A>

<LI><A HREF="extras/access.htm">Accessories</A>

<LI><A HREF="http://www.bigcompany.com">Distributors</A>

<LI><A HREF="ftp://ftp. bigcompany.com/order.pdf">Download
order form</A>

</UL>

<P ALIGN="CENTER">

<A HREF="../index.htm">Back to Big Company Home Page</A>

</P>

<HR>

<ADDRESS>
Questions?
<A HREF="mailto:info@gadget.com">info@bigcompany.com</A>
</ADDRESS>
</BODY>
</HTML>
```

Figure 5-5. *Link example 3 (relative and absolute URLs)*

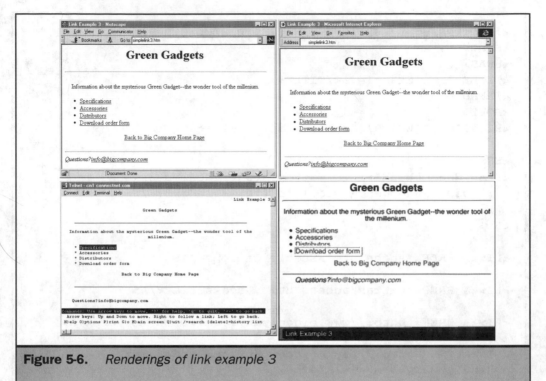

Figure 5-6. Renderings of link example 3

Link Renderings

In most browsers, text links are indicated by underlined text. Coloring the text—blue if the destination has never been visited, purple if it has been visited—is another common convention. If a link includes an image, the border of the image will also be blue or purple, unless the border attribute has been set to zero. HTML authors can override these default link colors with changes to the **LINK**, **ALINK**, and **VLINK** attributes of the **<BODY>** element. The **LINK** attribute changes the color of all unvisited links; the **VLINK** attribute changes all visited links. The **ALINK** attribute changes the color of the "active link," which is the brief flash that appears when a link is pressed. Using an HTML style sheet, authors can also change the decoration of links to turn off underlining, or even display links in another fashion. These two changes are shown in Figure 5-7. More information on the body attributes can be found in the element reference, and in Chapter 8, which covers layout facilities in HTML.

Aesthetically and logically, changing link colors or removing underlining makes sense. It may also confuse readers who have come to expect a standard color scheme for links. On occasion, authors may try to encourage return visits by setting visited links to remain blue, or may reverse colors for layout consistency. Such changes can significantly impair the usability of the site by thwarting user expectations.

```
<!DOCTYPE HTML PUBLIC "-//W3C//DTD HTML 3.2 Final//EN">
<HTML>
<HEAD>
<TITLE>Link Style Changes</TITLE>
<STYLE TYPE="text/css">

<!--
A          {text-decoration: none} /* avoid underlining links */
-->
</STYLE>
</HEAD>
<BODY LINK="blue" ALINK="red" VLINK="red">
<A HREF="http://www.yahoo.com">Test Link to Yahoo!</A>
</BODY>
</HTML>
```

Figure 5-7.   *Changing link appearance example*

Note   *Under WebTV, the **NOCOLOR** attribute is also supported. This attribute, when added to the **<A>** element, will prevent the text of a link from being drawn in the link color specified in the **<BODY>** element. This is a proprietary extension, but may be useful under television viewing conditions.*

Like it or not, the standard Web experience has taught users to click underlined text that is blue or purple. Such user habits suggest that underlining for emphasis be used sparingly, if at all, in HTML documents. Furthermore, HTML text should probably not be colored blue or purple unless it is obvious that the text is not a link. Controlling link colors is very important, but it is only one of many aspects of anchors that can be controlled.

Anchor Attributes

There are many possible attributes for the anchor element that are specific to the element besides **HREF**, as shown in Table 5-4. The more important attributes are discussed in the sections to follow, along with the concepts of binding scripts to anchors, using anchors with images, and creating a special type of image link called an image map. Refer to the element reference (Appendix A) to see a complete listing of all possible attributes for the anchor element.

Attribute Name	Possible Value	Description
HREF	URL	Sets the URL of the destination object for the anchor
NAME	Text	Names the anchor so that it may be a target of another anchor
ID	Text	Identifies the anchor for target by another anchor, style sheet access, and scripting exposure
TARGET	A frame name	Defines the frame destination of the link
TITLE	Text	Sets the hint text for the link
ACCESSKEY	A character	Sets the key for keyboard access to the link
TABINDEX	A numeric value	Sets the order in the tabbing index for using the TAB key to move through links in a page
REL	Text	Defines the relationship of the object being linked to
REV	Text	Defines the relationship of the current object to the object being linked to

Table 5-4. *Common Anchor Attributes*

Note *In proposed versions of HTML, the **<A>** element may also support the **SHAPE** and **COORDS** attribute. This can be used with the **<OBJECT>** element to create a generalized form of image maps. These extensions to **<A>** are discussed in the element reference in Appendix A, as well as in Chapter 6, which discusses the **<OBJECT>** element in relation to images. Today, however, this attribute of **<A>** is not widely supported. HTML authors are encouraged to use client-side image maps, which are discussed later in this chapter.*

Using the NAME Attribute

The anchor element usually defines a hyperlink source location: where the link goes, and what you click on to go there. One possible destination for a hyperlink is a named location inside an HTML document. The anchor element is also used to define these locations in a special usage known as setting a fragment, though the term "marker" might make more sense. To set a marker, the **NAME** attribute replaces the **HREF** attribute. The value of the **NAME** attribute is an arbitrary symbolic name for the marker location that must be unique within the document. Wherever the marker is placed within an HTML document becomes a named candidate destination for hyperlinks. For example, the HTML markup **<A NAME="marker">This is a marker</A>** sets the text "This is a marker" to be associated with the fragment **#marker**.

 Unlike hyperlink anchors, a marker location is not underlined or in anyway visually distinguished.

In practice, when an anchor element is used solely as a marker, it often does not enclose any text, though this does not suggest that the close tag should be left off, as it often is. Setting a marker like **<A NAME="top">** is accepted by most browsers, but **<A NAME="top"></A>** is the valid form.

It is possible for an anchor element to serve both as a destination and a link at the same time, For example,

```
<A NAME="yahoo link" HREF="http://www.yahoo.com/">Yahoo!</A>
```

creates a link to a site as well as naming the anchor so it may be referenced by other links. There may be some confusion with the dual use of the anchor element, but it is valid HTML.

 *Under current HTML practices, the **ID** attribute is also available for nearly every element. It can also be used to set a marker. The example given could have been written **<A ID="yahoo link" HREF="http://www.yahoo.com">Yahoo!</A>**, thus exposing the anchor for targeted linking, style sheets, and dynamic manipulation via a scripting language. For backward compatibility, the **NAME** attribute could also be used.*

The need for named anchors is not always obvious. Thanks to the unidirectional nature of links on the Web, they can be used to navigate to locations within the same document. This is especially useful in lengthy reference works. Such link usage can be accomplished by using markers to define named locations and anchors that refer to them. Remember that the URL formula to refer to a location within the current document is simply the pound symbol (#), followed by a marker name. Thus, code like **<A HREF="#top">Top of the document</A>** could be used if a marker called "top" was set at the start of the document. Be careful to always use the # symbol with marker names. Otherwise, the user agent will probably interpret the link as referencing a file rather than a marker.

In the more general case, a marked location in any HTML document can be referenced by placing the pound sign and a marker name after its normal URL. For example,

```
<A HREF="http://www.bigcompany.com/products.htm#spec">Specification
Section</A>
```

will link to a named marker called "spec" in the "products.htm" file. A complete example of linking within a file and to markers outside the file is shown in Figure 5-8.

```
<!DOCTYPE HTML PUBLIC "-//W3C//DTD HTML 3.2 Final//EN">
<HTML>
<HEAD>
<TITLE>Name Attribute Example</TITLE>
</HEAD>
<BODY>
<A NAME="top"></A>
Go to the <A HREF="#bottom">bottom</A> of this document.<BR>
Link right to a <A HREF="document1.htm#marker1">marker</A>
in another document.

<P>To make this work we need to simulate the document
being very long by using many breaks.</P>

<BR><BR><BR><BR><BR><BR><BR><BR><BR>
<BR><BR><BR><BR><BR><BR><BR><BR><BR>
<STRONG ID=MIDDLE>The Middle</STRONG>
<BR><BR><BR><BR><BR><BR><BR><BR><BR>
<BR><BR><BR><BR><BR><BR><BR><BR><BR>

<HR>
<A NAME="bottom" HREF="#top">Return to Top</A>
<A HREF="#middle">Go to middle</A>
</BODY>
</HTML>
```

Figure 5-8. Name attribute example

*Named values must be unique, whether they are set using the **NAME** attribute or the **ID** attribute.*

TITLE Attributes for Anchors

Normally, the **TITLE** attribute is not terribly helpful to a user, because it only provides basic advisory information about the use of a particular element. In the case of anchors, however, **TITLE** is very useful, since it can be used to provide tool tip information or help balloons for the link. In browsers like Internet Explorer, if a user holds the mouse over the link long enough, a tool tip showing the information specified by the **TITLE** attribute will be displayed. The following code fragment provides some helpful information for the link:

```
<A HREF="staff/index.htm" TITLE="Resumes and information about
our staff">Staff</A>
```

If the **TITLE** attribute is not used, the destination URL will generally be displayed. Figure 5-9 shows a tool tip for a link under Internet Explorer 4.0.

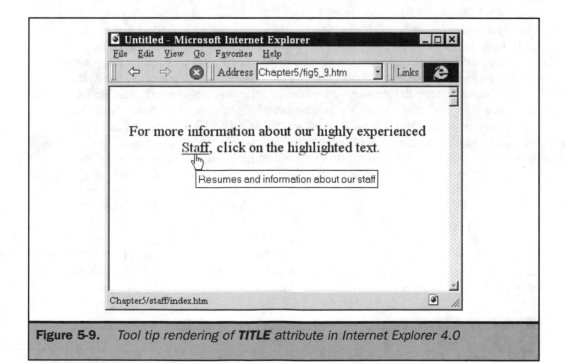

Figure 5-9. *Tool tip rendering of **TITLE** attribute in Internet Explorer 4.0*

*While the **TITLE** attribute is usable in nearly every HTML element under Internet Explorer, it makes sense mainly for links, images, binary objects, and forms.*

The **TITLE** attribute serves another purpose: it provides the title information for a bookmark when a link is bookmarked before the destination page is visited. If the page is visited, the information enclosed within the **<TITLE>** element of the destination page will be used in the bookmark instead of the information in the **TITLE** attribute of the anchor that loaded the page. (Note that the **TITLE** attribute and the **<TITLE>** element are two entirely different things.)

Accelerator Keys

The HTML 4.0 proposed specification adds the **ACCESSKEY** to the **<A>** element, as well as to various form elements. This is currently supported only by Internet Explorer 4.0. With this attribute, it is possible to set a key to invoke an anchor without requiring a pointing device to select the link. The link is activated with the combination of the accelerator key, usually ALT, and the key specified by the attribute. So

```
<A HREF="http://www.yahoo.com/" ACCESSKEY="Y">Yahoo!</A>
```

makes a link to Yahoo!, which can be activated by pressing ALT+Y. So far, however, only Internet Explorer appears to be supporting this upgrade to link access.

While adding keyboard access to a Web page would seem a dramatic improvement, HTML authors are cautioned to be aware of access key bindings in the browsing environment. Under the prerelease version of Internet Explorer 4.0, **ACCESSKEY** was implemented. Eight keys were already reserved for browser functions. Netscape's Communicator does not currently support the **ACCESSKEY** attribute, but differs in one accelerator key. Assuming that both browsers will support this function, authors would be cautioned to stay away from accelerators using the keys in Table 5-5.

One other problem with accelerator keys is how to show them in the page. In most software, underlining indicates the letter of the accelerator key. Links are generally underlined in browsers, so this approach is not feasible. It is possible to use style sheets to change link direction so underlining the first letter is possible, but then the user may be disoriented, expecting links to be fully underlined. Another approach to indicating the accelerator key might be to set the access key letter of a text link in bold or slightly larger size. Authors are encouraged to adopt whatever notation becomes standard on Web pages.

TABINDEX Attribute

Proposed for HTML 4.0, but not implemented by any browser to date, the **TABINDEX** attribute of the **<A>** element defines the order in which links will be tabbed through in

Key	Mapping	Notes
F	File menu	
E	Edit menu	
C	Communicator menu	Netscape Communicator only
V	View menu	
G	Go menu	
A	Favorites menu	Internet Explorer only
H	Help	
LEFT ARROW	Back in history	
RIGHT ARROW	Forward in history	

Table 5-5. *Reserved Browser Key Bindings*

a browser that supports keyboard navigation. The value of **TABINDEX** is usually a positive number. A browser will tab through links with increasing **TABINDEX** values, but will generally skip over those with negative values. So **<A HREF="about.htm" TABINDEX="1">** sets this anchor to be the first thing tabbed to. If the **TABINDEX** attribute is undefined, the browser tends to tab though links in the order in which they are found within an HTML document.

*WebTV supports a usability improvement similar to **TABINDEX**: the **SELECTED** attribute. When you add the word **SELECTED** as an attribute to an anchor, the WebTV browser will preselect the anchor with the yellow highlight rectangle. If two or more anchors are selected in a page, the last one appearing in the document will be selected. While it seems that the browser would scroll to the first item selected if it did not appear in the first screen, in practice the WebTV browser does not do this.*

TARGET Attribute

The **TARGET** attribute is used in conjunction with frames first introduced by Netscape. The attribute is also part of the HTML 4.0 proposal. In order to target a link so that the result loads in a particular frame, the **TARGET** attribute was added to the **<A>** element. Generally a frame has a name, so setting the **TARGET** equal to the frame name will result in the link loading in the frame named in the attribute. For example, a link like **<A HREF="http://www.yahoo.com/" TARGET="display_frame">** will, when selected, load the object referenced by the URL into the frame named

"display_frame" . If the TARGET attribute is left out, the current window or frame the document is in will be used. Besides author-named frames, there are reserved names for frames that, when used with the **TARGET** attribute, have special meaning: **_blank**, **_self**, **_parent**, and **_top**. For more information about frames and how the **<A>** element is used with frames and the various reserved frame names, refer to the element reference (Appendix A) and Chapter 9.

Anchors and Link Relationships

The anchor element has two attributes, **REL** and **REV**, whose meanings are often misunderstood. They are not widely supported by browsers. The **REL** attribute is used to describe the relationship played by the object referenced by the anchor's **HREF** attribute. For example, if the destination of the link specified the glossary associated with a document, the anchor might read **<A HREF="words.htm" REL="glossary">**. The **REV** attribute defines the reverse relationship, in this case what the relationship is from the destination document's perspective. An example might be in the case of a linear set of documents where the **REL** attribute was set to **"next"** and the **REV** attribute set to **"prev"** as shown in the following code fragment.

```
<A HREF="page2.htm" REL="next" REV="prev">Page 2</A>
```

While the **REL** and **REV** attributes might seem very useful, few, if any, browsers support them. Currently the only major use of these attributes is for documenting the relationship of links with the anchor elements themselves. The **<LINK>** element discussed later in this chapter, which has semantic link purposes similar to the **REL** and **REV** attributes, is actually supported in a limited manner by some browsers. A list of many of the proposed values for the **REL** and **REV** attribute can be found in this chapter's upcoming section about link relationships.

Scripting and Anchors

Adding logic to anchors is possible through the use of client-side scripting languages like JavaScript or VBScript. Proposed extensions to the anchor element include the use of the **onClick**, **onMouseOver**, and **onMouseOut** attributes, which can be bound to scripting events. These events correspond to an anchor being clicked, a pointer being positioned on a link, and a pointer leaving a link. One obvious use of such events could be to animate links so that when a mouse passes over the link the text changes color and when the link is clicked the system issues a click sound. Generically, this is the idea of a rollover. Besides the basic events that might be useful to create rollover links, event models from Microsoft and Netscape may include a variety of other events like the help button being pressed or a key being clicked. HTML authors interested in scripting anchor activities should consult Chapter 14. Combined with images, anchor scripting additions can be used to create very persuasive Web pages.

Images and Anchors

As mentioned earlier, anchor elements may enclose text and other content, including images. When an anchor encloses an image, the image becomes *hot*. A hot image can activate the link and provide a basic mechanism for a graphic button. Normally, a browser shows an image to be part of an anchor by putting a colored border around the image; generally the same color as the colored link text, either blue or purple. The browser may also indicate the image is a link by changing the pointer to a different shape, like a finger, when the pointer is positioned over an image link. If combined with scripting, the anchor may also modify the size or content of the image, creating a form of animated button. The HTML markup code in Figure 5-10 shows how an anchor can be combined with the **<IMG>** element, as discussed in Chapter 6, to create a pressable button. Notice how the **BORDER** attribute is set to **"0"** to turn off the image's border.

```
<!DOCTYPE HTML PUBLIC "-//W3C//DTD HTML 3.2 Final//EN">
<HTML>
<HEAD>
<TITLE>Anchors and Images</TITLE>
</HEAD>

<BODY>
<B>Button with a border</B><BR>
<A HREF="about.htm">
<IMG SRC="about.gif" ALT="About Button" HEIGHT="55" WIDTH="55">
</A>

<BR><BR>

<B>Same button without a border</B><BR>

<A HREF="about.htm">
<IMG SRC="about.gif" ALT="About Button" BORDER="0" HEIGHT="55"
WIDTH="55">
</A>

</BODY>
</HTML>
```

Figure 5-10.   *Anchors and images example*

Note that Figure 5-10 contains a small but significant error. When there is a space between the close of an image element and the closing **</A>** element, a small blue or purple line, or "tick," may occur as shown in Figure 5-11. To remove a tick, make certain there is no space between the image element and the closing **</A>** element.

While ticks aren't the worst offense on the Web, they indicate a lack of attention to detail in Web page coding. In print literature, spelling errors or small nicks or ticks on an image would be cause for serious alarm. Eventually, the same level of standards will be applied to Web pages, so HTML authors should begin to look for such small mistakes.

All the examples given so far show images with only one destination. Wherever a user clicks on the image link, the destination remains the same. In another class of image links, called *image maps*, different regions of the image can be made hot links for different destinations.

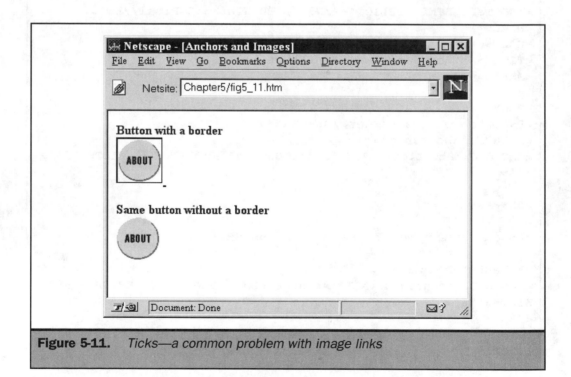

Figure 5-11. *Ticks—a common problem with image links*

Image Maps

An *image map* is an image that contains numerous hot spots that may result in a different URL being loaded, depending on where the user clicks. There are two basic types of image maps: *server-side image maps* and *client-side image maps*. In the server-side image map, the following process is followed:

1. The user clicks somewhere within the image.

2. The browser sends a request to the Web server, asking for the URL of the document associated with the area clicked. The coordinates clicked on are sent to a program on the server, usually called image map, which decodes the information.

3. After consulting a file that shows which coordinates map to which URL, the server sends back the information requested.

4. After receiving the response, the browser now requests the new URL.

There are some major downsides to the server-side image map idea. First of all, users really don't have a sense, URL-wise, where a particular click will take them. All the users see as they run a mouse over the image is a set of coordinates showing the current x, y value. The second major, and more significant, problem is that the server must be consulted in order to go on to the next page. This can be a major bottleneck that slows down the process of moving between pages. The slow speed of decoding, combined with the possibility that a user can click on a hot spot that is not mapped and have nothing happen, makes client-side image maps preferable to server-side maps.

With client-side image maps, all of the map information—which regions map to which URLs—can be specified in the same HTML file that contains the image. Including the map data with the image and letting the browser decode it has several advantages, including

■ There is no need to visit a server to determine the destination, so links are resolved faster.

■ Destination URLs can be shown as the user's pointer moves over the image.

■ Image maps can be created and tested locally, without requiring a server or system administration support.

While this discussion makes it obvious that client-side image maps are far superior to their server-side cousins, older browsers may not support this feature. This does not have to be a problem, however, because it is possible to include support for both types of image maps at once.

Server-Side Image Maps

To specify a server-side image map, you use the **<A>** element to enclose a specially marked **<IMG>** element. The **<A>** element **HREF** attribute should be set to the URL of a program or map file to decode the image map. The **<IMG>** element must contain the attribute **ISMAP** so that the browser can decode the image appropriately.

> **Note** *Depending on the Web server being used, support for server-side image maps may or may not be built in. If image maps are supported directly, the **<A>** element must simply point to the URL of the .map file directly and it will be decoded. This is shown in the example in Figure 5-12. On some older servers, however, the anchor may have to point to an image map program in that server's cgi-bin directory.*

As with all linked images, it may be desirable to turn the image borders off by setting the **<IMG>** element's **BORDER** attribute equal to 0. A simple example showing the syntax of a server-side image map is shown in Figure 5-12.

As mentioned before, server-side image maps do not provide adequate feedback to the user and may incur performance penalties. HTML authors are encouraged to prefer client-side image maps, in addition to using the server-side image map as needed.

Client-Side Image Maps

The key to using a client-side map is to add the **USEMAP** attribute to the **<IMG>** element and have it reference a **<MAP>** element that defines the image map's active areas. An example of the **<IMG>** element syntax is **<IMG SRC="controlbar.gif" USEMAP="#controlmap">**. Note that, like server-side image maps, the image will be indicated as a link regardless of the lack of the **<A>** element surrounding the **<IMG>**. The **BORDER** attribute should be set to zero if necessary.

The **<MAP>** element generally occurs within the same document, though there may be support for it outside of the current document. This is similar, in a sense, to the way server-side maps work. The **<MAP>** element may occur anywhere within the body of an HTML document, though it is usually found at the end of HTML documents.

> **Note** *Theoretically, a client-side map file may exist within another file, but most browsers do not yet support such a feature.*

The **<MAP>** element has one attribute, **NAME**, which is used to specify the identifier associated with the map. The map name is then referenced within the **<IMG>** element using the **USEMAP** attribute and the associated fragment identifier. The **<MAP>** element must have a closing **</MAP>** tag. Within the **<MAP>** and **</MAP>** element are defined shapes that are mapped onto an image and define the hot spots for the image map. Shapes are defined by the **<AREA>** element, which is

```
<!DOCTYPE HTML PUBLIC "-//W3C//DTD HTML 3.2 Final//EN">
<HTML>
<HEAD>
<TITLE>Server-side Image Map Example</TITLE>
</HEAD>
<BODY>

<H1 ALIGN="CENTER">Server-side Imagemap Test</H1>

<DIV ALIGN="CENTER">
<A HREF="shapes.map">
<IMG SRC="shapes.gif" ISMAP BORDER="0" WIDTH="400"
HEIGHT="200"></A>
</DIV>

</BODY>
</HTML>
```

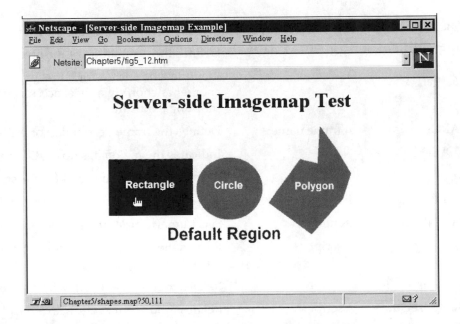

Figure 5-12. *Server-side image map example*

found only within the **<MAP>** element. The **<AREA>** element requires no closing element and has a variety of attributes, as shown in Table 5-6.

The most important attributes of an **<AREA>** entity are **HREF**, **SHAPE**, and **COORDS**. The **HREF** attribute defines the destination URL for the browser if that particular region of the image is selected. The **SHAPE** and **COORDS** attributes define the particular region in question. When the **SHAPE** attribute is set to **RECT**, it defines a rectangular region, and the coordinates should be set to provide the top left and bottom right coordinates of the image. If the **SHAPE** attribute is set to **CIRCLE**, the **COORDS** attribute must provide the x, y coordinates of the center of the circle, followed by its radius. If the shape is set to **POLY**, it indicates that the area defined is an irregular polygon; each coordinate makes up a point in the polygon, with lines between each successive point, and the last point connected to the first.

Attribute Name	Possible Values	Description
SHAPE	RECT, CIRCLE, and POLY	Sets the type of shape
COORDS	x, y coordinate pairs	Sets the points that define the shape
HREF	URL	Defines the destination of the link
ID	Text	Identifies the anchor for target by another anchor, style sheet access, and scripting exposure
TARGET	A frame name	Defines the frame destination of the link
NOHREF	N/A	Indicates the region has no destination
ALT	Text	Defines the alternative text for the shape
TITLE	Text	Sets the hint text for a shape
TABINDEX	A number	Sets numeric order in tabbing sequence
OnClick	A script	Relates the click event of a link with a script
OnMouseOver	A script	Relates mouse over event with a script
OnMouseOut	A script	Relates mouse out event with a script

Table 5-6. Attributes for **<AREA>**

*If the **SHAPE** attribute is not set or omitted, **RECT** is assumed.*

Table 5-7 summarizes the possibilities for the **AREA** element, and provides examples.

*Under many browsers, the **SHAPE** attribute also supports **RECTANGLE**, **CIRC**, and **POLYGON**. HTML authors are encouraged to use only **RECT**, **CIRCLE**, and **POLY**, as they are defined by the standard.*

The various x and y coordinates are measured in pixels from the top left corner (0,0) of the mapped image. It is also possible to use percentage values of the image's height and width. For example, **<AREA SHAPE=RECT COORDS="0,0,50%,50%">** would define a rectangular region from the upper left corner to a point halfway up and down and halfway across. While percentage style notation might allow the image to resize, it is generally not useful for all but the most basic image maps. The biggest difficulty with image maps is how to determine the coordinates for the individual shapes within the image. Rather than measuring these values by hand, HTML authors are encouraged to use an image mapping tool. Many HTML editing systems include image-mapping facilities. Mapedit (www.boutell.com/mapedit), for Windows and Unix; and WebMap, for Macintosh also provide rudimentary mapping facilities.

*It is not recommended to use any **HEIGHT** and **WIDTH** values besides the actual sizes for a mapped image. Once it has been mapped, resizing will ruin the map.*

Shape	Coordinate Format	Example
RECT	left-x, top-y, right-x, bottom-y	<AREA SHAPE="RECT" COORDS="0,0,100,50" HREF="about.htm">
CIRCLE	center-x, center-y, radius	<AREA SHAPE="CIRCLE" COORDS="25,25,10" HREF="products.htm">
POLY	$x1, y1, x2, y2, x3, y3, \ldots$	<AREA SHAPE="POLY" COORDS="255,122,306,53,334,62,255,122" HREF="contact.htm">

Table 5-7. *Shape Format and Examples*

An example using a client-side image map is shown in Figure 5-13.

It is possible to combine support for both server-side and client-side image maps into one file. The browser typically overrides the server-side support with the improved client-side style. This approach guarantees backward compatibility with older browsers. To support both, use the **ISMAP** and **USEMAP** attributes in

```
<!DOCTYPE HTML PUBLIC "-//W3C//DTD HTML 3.2 Final//EN">
<HTML>
<HEAD>
<TITLE>Client-side Image Map Example</TITLE>
</HEAD>
<BODY>

<H1 ALIGN="CENTER">Client-side Imagemap Test</H1>

<DIV ALIGN="CENTER">
<IMG SRC="shapes.gif" USEMAP="#shapes" BORDER="0" WIDTH="400"
HEIGHT="200">
</DIV>

<!-- Start of Client Side Image Map  -->

<MAP NAME="shapes">
<AREA SHAPE="RECT" COORDS="6,50,140,143" HREF="rectangle.htm"
ALT="Rectangle">
<AREA SHAPE="CIRCLE" COORDS="195,100,50" HREF="circle.htm"
ALT="Circle">
<AREA SHAPE="POLY"
COORDS="255,122,306,53,334,62,338,0,388,77,374,116,323,171,
255,122" HREF="polygon.htm" ALT="Polygon">
<AREA SHAPE="default" HREF="defaultreg.htm">
</MAP>

</BODY>
</HTML>
```

Figure 5-13.   *Client-side image map*

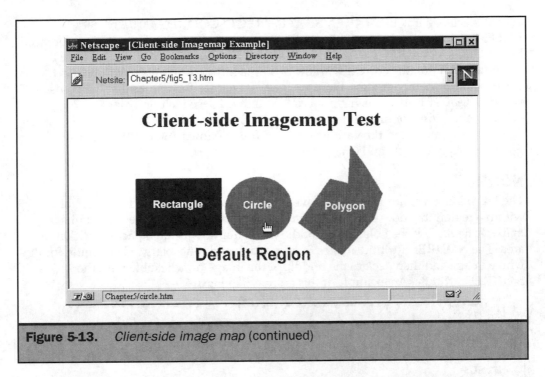

Figure 5-13.   *Client-side image map* (continued)

conjunction with an embedded map and a remote map, as shown by the following code fragment:

```
<A HREF="shapes.map">
<IMG SRC="shapes.gif" USEMAP="#shapes" BORDER="0" ISMAP WIDTH="400"
HEIGHT="200"></A>
```

Image Map Attributes

Client-side image maps have a variety of attributes that can be used with the **<AREA>** element. Server-side image maps have no attributes other than those normally associated with the **<IMG>** element, such as **BORDER**. The important attributes supported in HTML 3.2 and upcoming versions of HTML are discussed here, as well as the issues of adding scripting facilities to image maps.

TARGET

Like the addition to the **<A>** element itself, the **<AREA>** element for client-side image maps has been extended to support a **TARGET** attribute. The **TARGET** value should be set to the name of a frame or window. Generally a frame has a name, so setting **TARGET** to the frame name will result in the link loading in the frame named in the attribute.

When selected, a link like **<AREA SHAPE="RECT" COORDS="0,0,50%, 50%"
HREF="http://www.yahoo.com" TARGET="display_frame">** loads the page referenced
by the URL set by **HREF** into the frame named **"display_frame"**. If the **TARGET**
attribute is left out, the current window or frame the document is in will be used.
Besides author-named frames, there are reserved names for frames that, when used
with the **TARGET** attribute, have special meaning. These include **_blank**, **_self**,
_parent, and **_top**. For more information about frames and how the **<AREA>** element
is used with frames and the various reserved frame names, refer to the element
reference (Appendix A) and Chapter 9.

NOHREF

The **NOHREF** attribute appears to have little use, but it can be used to cut a hole
within a region that does nothing. An image of a donut might make a great image
map, particularly if the hole in the middle of the donut was not an active, clickable
area. The **NOHREF** attribute makes this simple. Just define a large click region for the
whole image and then declare the middle of the image nonclickable with the
NOHREF attribute. An example of this is shown in Figure 5-14.

```
<!DOCTYPE HTML PUBLIC "-//W3C//DTD HTML 3.2 Final//EN">
<HTML>
<HEAD>
<TITLE>NOHREF Example</TITLE>
</HEAD>
<BODY>

<IMG SRC="donut.gif" WIDTH="300" HEIGHT="300" BORDER="0"
ALT="Donut Widget" usemap="#donut">

<MAP NAME="donut">
<AREA SHAPE="circle" COORDS="147,149,72" ALT="Donut Hole"
NOHREF>
<AREA SHAPE="circle" ALT="Donut Widget" COORDS="149,150,143"
HREF="donutspec.htm">
<AREA SHAPE="default" NOHREF>
</MAP>

</BODY>
</HTML>
```

Figure 5-14.   *Use of NOHREF*

Given that **NOHREF** creates an inactive region that sits on top of another, what happens when one region overlaps another? According to the specification, if two or more regions overlap, the region defined first within the **<MAP>** element takes precedence over subsequent regions. This rule implies that **AREA** elements with the **NOHREF** attribute should be placed before **AREA** elements that are active, in that they actually go to a new URL when selected.

ALT and TITLE

Image maps have some major drawbacks, even in their client-side aspect, when it comes to text-based browsers. The **ALT** attribute can be used, as shown in the previous examples, and tends to provide text labels that are displayed in the status line when the pointer passes over the hot spots. While **TITLE** can be added to all elements and can provide a function similar to **ALT** in graphical browsers, in practice browsers seem to pick up **ALT** before **TITLE**. To be on the safe side, you can use both attributes simultaneously. One unfortunate problem with the **ALT** attribute and client-side image maps is that nongraphical browsers do not always pick up the **ALT** attributes and build meaningful renderings. Instead of a set of links, the viewer might only see a cryptic message, as shown in Figure 5-15.

HTML authors are encouraged to provide secondary navigation that mirrors the choices available in the image map. These should be text links located below the image. This will make the site accessible for nongraphical user agents and may improve the site's usability. Users on slow connections may opt to select text links before the image is completely downloaded. An example of text links in conjunction with an image map is shown in Figure 5-16. Also, when using server-side image maps, you may make the default choice to be a new page that is a text menu of the choices provided via the image map. In this way, a user who selects the ISMAP provided by an older browser will receive the menu, not the map.

Discussion of the design and navigation issues surrounding image maps is left to books that focus on site design. Where possible, HTML authors should avoid relying too heavily on single-image style image maps for navigation purposes.

TABINDEX

Under the HTML 4.0 proposed specification, it is possible to use the **TABINDEX** attribute of the **<AREA>** element to define the order in which hot spots in a client-side image map are tabbed through in a browser that supports keyboard navigation. The value of **TABINDEX** is typically a positive number. A browser will tab through links with increasing **TABINDEX** values, but will generally skip over those with negative values. So, the following line sets this anchor to be the first thing tabbed to:

```
<AREA SHAPE="RECT" COORDS="0,0,50%,50%" HREF="http://www.yahoo.com/"
TABINDEX="1">
```

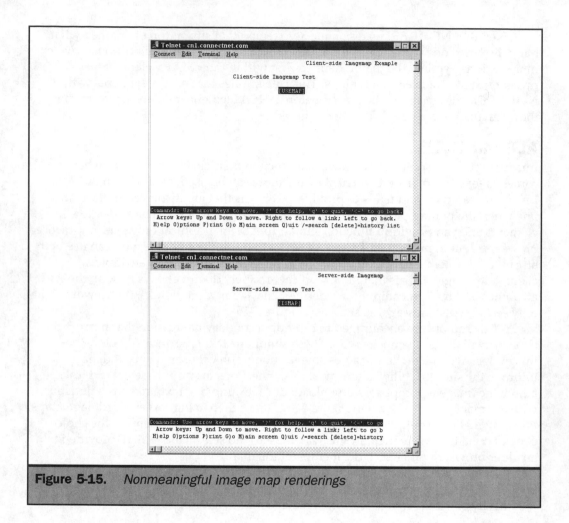

Figure 5-15. *Nonmeaningful image map renderings*

If the **TABINDEX** attribute is undefined, the browser will tend to tab though links in the order in which they are found within an HTML document. Currently, Internet Explorer and Netscape do not support **TABINDEX** within image maps.

SCRIPTING

As already noted, it is possible to add logic to image maps with client-side scripting languages like JavaScript or VBScript. Three extensions to the **<AREA>** element—**onClick**, **onMouseOver**, and **onMouseOut**—can be bound to scripting events that provide feedback when a mouse passes over a link. This is the rollover idea discussed earlier. However, the **<AREA>** element is less flexible than using anchors in conjunction with single images, since it is impossible to replace only a

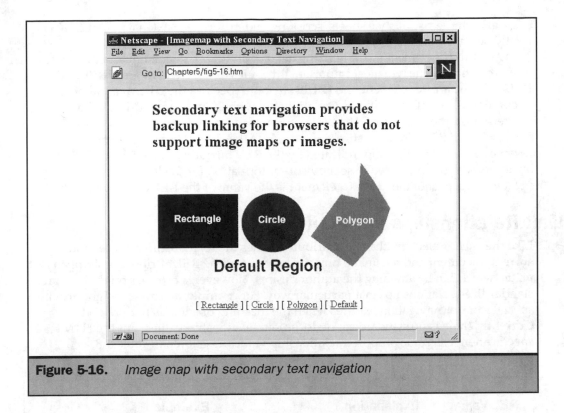

Figure 5-16.   *Image map with secondary text navigation*

portion of the image on the fly. Most rollover-style Web interfaces do not use image maps, but rely instead on images cut up and pieced together to resemble an image map. HTML authors interested in scripting image maps should consult Chapter 14.

Semantic Linking with the <LINK> Element

Syntactically, a link to another document created by an anchor says nothing about the relationship between the current document and the object being pointed to. While it is possible to use the **TITLE** attribute to provide a hint or advisory information about the link, used as written it is just a link and nothing more. The viewer of a page tends to associate meaning with a link, but in HTML itself, links lack any semantic meaning. The **<LINK>** element, however, does provide a way to define the relationship between documents. The concept of the **<LINK>** element is that a document may have predefined relationships that can be specified, and that some of these relationships might be useful to a browser when offering navigation choices, rendering a page, or preparing a page to be printed. While **<LINK>** has been around for a number of years, until recently few browsers have supported **<LINK>** to any degree. With the rise of style sheets, scripting and proprietary extensions, **<LINK>** is finally being supported by browsers, at least in a limited manner.

The **<LINK>** element is found in the head of an HTML document and may occur numerous times. The two most important attributes of the element are **HREF** and **REL**. Like the anchor element, the **HREF** attribute specifies the URL of another document, while **REL** specifies the relationship with that document. The value of **REL** is often called the "link type." The basic syntax of the **<LINK>** element is **<LINK HREF="URL" REL="relationship">**. Under HTML 3.2, **<LINK>** also supports a reverse semantic relationship indicated by the **REV** attribute, as well as the **TITLE** attribute, which can be used to set advisory information for the link. The most mysterious aspect of the **<LINK>** element is the value of the **REL** and **REV** attributes.

Link Relationships in Detail

Like the anchor element, the **REL** attribute defines the relationship between the current document and the linked object. The value of the **REL** attribute is simply a text value, which can be anything the author desires. However, a browser might interpret standardized relationships in a particular way. For example, a browser might provide special icons or navigation features when the meaning of a link is understood. Currently, there is no standard set of document relationship values, but the HTML 3.2 specification lists some proposed relationship values, as shown in Table 5-8.

REL Value	Explanation	Example
TOP	The link references the top of a hierarchy. This could be the first page of a collection of documents or the home page of a site.	<LINK HREF="../index.htm" REL="TOP">
CONTENTS	The link references a document that serves as a table of contents most likely for the site, though it might be for the document. The meaning is unclear.	<LINK HREF="toc.htm" REL="CONTENTS">
INDEX	The link references a page that provides an index for the current document.	<LINK HREF="docindex.htm" REL="INDEX">

Table 5-8.   *REL* Values Proposed by HTML 3.2

REL Value	Explanation	Example
GLOSSARY	The link references a document that provides a glossary of terms for the current document.	`<LINK HREF="glossary.htm" REL="GLOSSARY">`
COPYRIGHT	The link references a page that contains a copyright statement for the current document.	`<LINK HREF="copyright.htm" REL="COPYRIGHT">`
NEXT	The link references the next document to visit in a linear collection of documents. It can be used, for example, to "prefetch" the next page as in the WebTV browsers.	`<LINK HREF="page2.htm" REL="NEXT">`
PREVIOUS	The link references the previous document in a linear collection of documents.	`<LINK HREF="page1.htm" REL="PREVIOUS">`
HELP	The link references a help document for the current document or site.	`<LINK HREF="help.tm" REL="HELP">`
SEARCH	The link references a page for searching a collection of pages.	`<LINK HREF="cgi-bin/search.pl" REL="SEARCH">`

Table 5-8.   *REL Values Proposed by HTML 3.2 (continued)*

Beyond the HTML 3.2 proposed relationships, there are a variety of other relationships being discussed. In fact, HTML authors can make up their own relationships if they desire, but should be careful to avoid **BACK**, **FORWARD**, and **HOME** as **REL** or **REV** values since they tend to hold special meaning for browsers. Table 5-9 shows some proposed **REL** values.

The most interesting of the proposed relationships are those that are actually supported by a browser. Otherwise, they serve as little more than comments to a reader of the document about the meaning of a link.

REL Value	Explanation	Example
NAVIGATE	The target document contains information, such as an image map, that will help users to gain a sense of how to navigate the site.	`<LINK HREF="navbar.gif" REL="NAVIGATE">`
CHILD	Many Web sites have a hierarchical or tree structure. The child relationship identifies a subordinate or subdocument in the hierarchy. Any document may have multiple CHILD documents within the same hierarchy.	`<LINK HREF="subpage.htm" REL="CHILD">`
PARENT	The opposite of the child relationship, the parent relationship identifies the superior or container node in a hierarchical environment. Some might prefer "up."	`<LINK HREF="index.htm" REL="PARENT">`
SIBLING	Another hierarchical relationship, sibling identifies a sibling in the current hierarchy. Any document may have multiple SIBLING documents within the same hierarchy.	`<LINK HREF="product2.htm" REL="SIBLING">`
BEGIN or FIRST	The BEGIN or FIRST relationship identifies the start of a sequence of documents of which the current document is part. The obvious meaning of this relationship is to reference the first document in a linear sequence.	`<LINK HREF="page1.htm" REL="BEGIN">`
END or LAST	The END or LAST relationship identifies the end of a sequence of documents of which the current document is a part. The obvious meaning of this relationship is to reference the last document in a linear sequence.	`<LINK REL="END" HREF="conclusion.htm">`

Table 5-9. *Some Proposed **REL** Values*

REL Value	Explanation	Example
BIBLIOENTRY	The BIBLIOENTRY relationship identifies a bibliographic entry.	`<LINK HREF="biblio.htm#doc1" REL="BIBLIOENTRY">`
BIBLIOGRAPHY	The BIBLIOGRAPHY relationship identifies a bibliography.	`<A HREF="biblio.htm" REL="BIBLIOGRAPHY">…</A>`
CITATION	The CITATION relationship identifies a bibliographic citation. Typically, this is used with anchors rather than the `<LINK>` element, and possibly in conjunction with the `<CITE>` element.	`<A REL="CITATION" HREF="#Sources"> Smith [1] </A>`
DEFINITION	The DEFINITION relationship identifies a definition of a term. The meaning of the term may be found in the document referenced by the GLOSSARY relationship.	`<A REL="DEFINITION" HREF="glossary.htm#widget"> Widget</A>`
FOOTNOTE	The FOOTNOTE relationship identifies a footnote. This relationship is generally used with the `<A>` element. Theoretically, a browser may open a small pop-up window to display the footnote.	`<A REL="FOOTNOTE" HREF="note1.htm">Extra info</A>`
MADE	The MADE relationship has been used to identify the author or "maker" of an HTML document. The maker might include a tool if this is used with the `<LINK>` element.	`<A REV="MADE" HREF="mailto:webmaster@bigcompany.com"> Webmaster</A>`
AUTHOR	The AUTHOR relationship identifies a link to information about the author of the current document, or a method to contact the author.	`<LINK REL="AUTHOR" HREF="author.htm">`

Table 5-9. *Some Proposed* **REL** *Values* (continued)

REL Value	Explanation	Example
EDITOR	The EDITOR relationship identifies a hypertext link to an editor. It may include a mailto URL or a link to an editor's personal home page.	`<LINK REL="EDITOR" HREF="mailto:editor@bigcompany.com">`
PUBLISHER	The PUBLISHER relationship identifies a link to information about a document's publisher or a way to contact the publisher via a mailto URL.	`<LINK REL="PUBLISHER" HREF="http://www.osborne.com">`
DISCLAIMER	The DISCLAIMER relationship identifies a link to a legal disclaimer applying to the document.	`<LINK REL="DISCLAIMER" HREF="legal.htm">`
TRADEMARK	The TRADEMARK relationship identifies a link to a trademark notice concerning the current document.	`<LINK REL="TRADEMARK" HREF="trademark.htm">`
META	The META relationship identifies a link to a document containing meta-information (information about information) related to the current document. This is a very general relationship. The information linked to could be just about anything.	`<LINK REL="META" HREF="descript.htm">`
TRANSLATION	The TRANSLATION relationship specifies a link to a document with a translation to another language.	`<LINK REL="TRANSLATION" HREF="japanese.htm">`
STYLESHEET	The STYLESHEET relationship identifies a style sheet for the current document.	`<LINK REL="STYLESHEET" HREF="corporate.css">`

Table 5-9. *Some Proposed **REL** Values (continued)*

WebTV Support for <LINK>

As defined by HTML 3.2, the only fairly common browser to support **<LINK>** is WebTV. In the WebTV environment, **<LINK>** is used to improve performance. If the

REL attribute is set with the value of **next** and an HREF is specified, the browser will "prefetch" the page in question. If the content of the next page is stored in a memory cache, the page will load much faster than if the page had to be requested from the server. If a WebTV user were being presented a brief set of pages in a linear fashion, like a slide-show or tour, the next page could be preloaded with the <LINK> element. For example, **<LINK REL="next" HREF="second.htm">** would load the next page, called second.htm, in advance. This technique assumes that the user is going to a predictable next page. This may not be easy to determine for all possible Web site organizations.

> **Note**
> *HTML authors not using WebTV who are interested in "prefetching" pages can use Microsoft's preloader ActiveX control. It is also possible to prefetch images by setting both their **HEIGHT** and **WIDTH** attributes to 1: **<IMG SRC="image_on_nextpage.gif" HEIGHT="1" WIDTH="1">**. This technique will load an image into the page, but it won't be seen as more than a barely perceptible dot. Then, when the next page loads, the image will have been precached by the browser. Combined with a scripting language, the loading of images could be handled after the current page has loaded by using the onLoad event for the document.*

<LINK> and Style Sheets

Beyond the HTML 3.2 specification, a variety of new attributes have been added to the <LINK> element. These include **TYPE**, **MEDIA**, and **TARGET**. These new attributes are already being supported in browsers like Internet Explorer and Netscape for handling style sheets. The <LINK> element allows a style sheet for a document to be referenced from a separate file. If the markup code **<LINK REL="stylesheet" HREF="corpstyle.css">** were to be inserted in the head of an HTML document it would associate the style sheet corpstyle.css with the current document. The **REL** value of **STYLESHEET** indicates the relationship.

The **ALTERNATE STYLESHEET** relationship, which would allow users to pick from a variety of styles, has also been suggested. To define several alternative styles, the **TITLE** attribute must be set to group elements belonging to the same style. All members of the same style **must** have exactly the same value for **TITLE**. For example, the following fragment defines a standard style called "basestyle.css" while two alternative styles titled "640by480" and "1024by768" have been added; these refer to style sheets to improve layout at various screen resolutions.

```
<LINK REL="alternate stylesheet" TITLE="640by480"
HREF="small-1.css">
<LINK REL="alternate stylesheet" TITLE="640by480"
HREF="small-2.css">
<LINK REL="alternate stylesheet" TITLE="1024by768" HREF="big.css">
<LINK REL=stylesheet HREF="basestyle.css">
```

A Web browser should provide a method for users to view and pick from the list of alternative styles where the **TITLE** attribute might be used to name each choice. Currently, this alternative choice for style sheets is not supported.

Because there are potentially many different kinds of linked objects, the **TYPE** attribute was added to the **<LINK>** element to indicate the data type of the related object. Because there are so many style sheet technologies today, **TYPE** can be especially helpful when used to indicate the type of style sheet being used. **TYPE** is used by browsers to indicate the type of the linked style, as in this example: **<LINK REL="STYLESHEET" HREF="corpstyle.css" TYPE="text/css">**. In the case of style sheets, **TYPE** usually takes a MIME type, which indicates the format of the style sheet being linked to.

The **MEDIA** attribute is another new attribute for the **<LINK>** element, but is not widely supported. In the case of style sheets, this attribute would indicate what type of media the style sheet should be used with. This would allow a different style for printing versus screen. The browser is then responsible for filtering out those style sheets that are not appropriate for the current environment. The following code fragment shows an example of this idea.

```
<LINK REL="STYLESHEET" MEDIA="PRINT" HREF="corp-print.css">
<LINK REL="STYLESHEET" MEDIA="SCREEN" HREF="corp-screen.css">
```

There are a variety of proposed values for the **MEDIA** attribute, including **PRINT**, **PROJECTION**, **SCREEN**, **BRAILLE**, **AURAL**, and **ALL**. When not specified, **ALL** would be the default type, suggesting that the style be used in all output environments.

Meta-Information

Meta-information is simply "information about information." Information on the Web often involves many pieces of associated descriptive information that is not always explicitly represented in the resource itself. Examples of meta-information include the creator of a document, the document's subject, the publisher, the creation date, and even the title. When used properly, descriptive meta-information has many benefits. It can make information easier to locate by providing search tools like HotBot with more detailed indexing information, rate information to protect minors from viewing certain content, and a variety of other things. As already discussed, meta-information is related to linking in that it helps provide meaning for a document's role in a global or local information space. It can also provide room for miscellaneous information related to the document. HTML's primary support for meta-information is through the **<META>** element, which allows authors to add arbitrary forms of meta-data.

<META> and the NAME Attribute

A **<META>** element that uses the **NAME** attribute is the easiest to understand. The **NAME** attribute specifies the type of information. The **CONTENT** attribute is set to the content of the meta-information itself. For example, **<META NAME="Favorite Sandwich" CONTENT="Turkey and Swiss">** defines meta-information indicating the document author's favorite lunch. While meta-data can be inserted into a document and list characteristics limited only by an author's imagination, there are some well-understood values that have meaning for Web search tools like AltaVista, HotBot, or Infoseek. Many search robots understand the **AUTHOR**, **DESCRIPTION**, and **KEYWORDS** values for the **NAME** attribute. By setting the **NAME** and **CONTENT** attributes, HTML authors can add meta-information to the head of their documents and improve the indexing of their pages by Web search robots. The code shown in Figure 5-17 sets the description of a Web page for a fictitious company that makes Green Gadgets.

As shown in Figure 5-17, all HTML authors have to do to improve the indexing of their pages is provide the appropriate keywords in the correct **<META>** element format and alert the search robot to the site's existence. In many cases, the site may already be indexed without submission. Authors who do not want search robots indexing their sites can put a file called "robots.txt," which provides information on which directories or files not to index, in their Web server's root directory. All well-behaved Web robots should request the robots.txt file first before deciding what to index on a site. If a site is known as http://www.bigcompany.com/, a well-behaved robot will begin by requesting http://www.bigcompany.com/robots.txt and analyzing the file. After analyzing the file, the robot will index part, all, or none of the

```
<HTML>
<HEAD>
<TITLE>Big Company, Inc. Home Page</TITLE>
<META NAME="AUTHOR" CONTENT="Big Company, Inc.">
<META NAME="DESCRIPTION" CONTENT="#1 vendor of Green
Gadgets.">
<META NAME="KEYWORDS" CONTENT="Big, Company, Gadgets, Green,
San Diego">
</HEAD>
<BODY>
. . .
</BODY>
</HTML>
```

Figure 5-17. *Meta-information example*

site. The format of the robots.txt file is relatively simple. It includes a field for specifying a user agent, followed by a Disallow field indicating what is disallowed. For example, if a robots.txt file contained

```
User-agent: *
Disallow: /
```

then every robot would be barred from indexing anything from the root directory on down. In other words, the whole site would be skipped. There is only one User-agent field in a robots.txt file. Wildcards like * may be used, or particular agents can be named directly. There may be multiple Disallow fields that specify the relative URL that is not to be visited. For example, "Disallow: /staff" bars robots from a file named "staff," as well as any information in the subdirectory called "staff."

The robots.txt file must reside in the root directory of the Web server and must be named in lowercase. Blank lines are not permitted in the file. Errors in the file may result in the file being ignored.

It is also possible to put a **<META NAME="ROBOT" CONTENT="NOINDEX, NOFOLLOW">** element in the head of nonindexed documents, but this is not as widely supported as using a robots.txt file. The robot version of the **<META>** element allows **CONTENT** values of **ALL**, **INDEX**, **NOINDEX**, and **NOFOLLOW**.

While many Web-searching services like HotBot freely publish their formats for indexing, others do not. The reason for this secrecy of indexing rules is that many HTML authors will attempt to attract traffic to their site by putting an excessive amount of "spider bait" and **<META>** elements in their pages in hopes of getting higher rankings in search results. Loading up a **<META>** element with excessive keywords may backfire, however, and result in the page being dropped from the search engines. Most search engines take a few dozen words, approximately 1,024 characters at most.

Even without people trying to defeat search engine indexing algorithms, the current approach to cataloging the Web is far from sufficient. Most search engines return far too much, and there is no sense to the value, quality, or decency of links returned. Many groups are already working on standard sets of meta-data for Web documents. When more standardized meta-information is established, the organization of the Web should significantly improve, and browsers should provide better decisions about content appropriateness.

META and HTTP-EQUIV

The other form of the **<META>** element uses the **HTTP-EQUIV** attribute, which directly allows the document author to insert HTTP header information. The browser can access this information during read time. The server may also access it when the document is sent, but this is rare. The **HTTP-EQUIV** attribute is set to a particular HTTP header type, while the **CONTENT** value is set to the value associated with the header. For example, **<META HTTP-EQUIV="Expires" CONTENT="Wed, 04 Jun 1998 22:34:07 GMT">** placed in the head of a document sets the expiration date to be June 4, 1998. A variety of HTTP headers can be placed in the **<META>** element. The most useful are those for two concepts, known as client-pull and site filtering.

Client-Pull

Beginning with Netscape, an extension was made that allows a page to be automatically loaded after a certain period of time. This concept is called *client-pull*. For example, it is possible to build an entry page, or *splash page,* that welcomes visitors to a site and then automatically follows with a second page after a certain period of time. The example **<META>** element, shown next, loads a page called secondpage.htm ten seconds after the first page loads.

```
<META HTTP-EQUIV="REFRESH" CONTENT="10;URL=secondpage.htm">
```

Using the client-pull form of the **<META>** element is easy. Just set the content equal to the desired number of seconds, followed by a semicolon and the URL (full or relative) of the page to load. Note, however, that not all browsers support this form of meta-refresh.

 The client-pull concept is often discussed with a partner idea called server-push. Server-push was primarily used to create simple animations. Today there is no reason to even address server-push animation or other tricks, since they are more easily accomplished using animated GIF images or Java scripting.

The **<META>** element is very open-ended. The W3C is already developing more sophisticated approaches for representing meta-data. The most interesting is probably PICS, which provides a standard for site filtering.

Site Filtering

One major use of meta-information for links and pages is *site filtering.* At its base level, a filter can be used to restrict access to certain files or types of information. As a technology, this sounds rather innocuous, but when extended, site filtering can lead quickly to censorship. Whether or not it is right or wrong to filter the information on the Internet is an area of great debate. Obviously, parents and educators are extremely concerned with the availability of pornographic, violent, or other "inappropriate" types of information on the Internet. Deciding what is inappropriate is the key to the censorship problem, since definitions of what should be allowed vary from person to person. Regardless of how it is defined, there is no arguing that information that is considered inappropriate by just about everyone does exist on the Internet. The perceived extent of this information tends to be directly related to a person's belief system. The W3C has proposed the Platform for Internet Content Selection, or PICS (www.w3.org/pub/WWW/PICS/), as a way to address the problem of content filtering on the Web.

The idea behind PICS is relatively simple. A rated page or site will include a **<META>** element within the head of an HTML document. This **<META>** element indicates the rating of the particular item in question. A rating service, which can be any group, organization, or company that provides content ratings, assigns the rating. Rating services range from independent nonprofit groups like the Recreational Software Advisory Council (RSAC) (www.rsac.org), which already implements a rating system for video games, to software vendors such as Net Sheperd (www.netshepherd.com), which sells rating services and software. The rating label used by a particular rating service must be based on a well-defined set of rules that describes the criteria for rating, the scale of values for each aspect of the rating, and a description of the criteria used in setting a value. Usually the specification of a rating is found in a .rat file that can be accessed by browser or filtering software. Figure 5-18 shows a .rat file for the violence category of RSAC-based (RSACi) PICS ratings. Other categories not shown include sex, nudity, and language.

```
((PICS-version 1.0)
(rating-system "http://www.rsac.org/Ratings/Description/")
(rating-service "http://www.rsac.org/ratingsv01.html")
(name "RSACi")
(description "The Recreational Software Advisory Council
rating service for the Internet. Based on the work of Dr.
Donald F. Roberts of Stanford University, who has studied
the effects of media for nearly 20 years.")

(category
(transmit-as "v")
(name "Violence")
(label
(name "Level 0: No violence")
(description "No aggressive violence; No natural or
accidental violence.")
(value 0) )
(label
```

Figure 5-18. *RSACi rating system .rat file*

```
(name "Level 1: Fighting")
(description "Creatures injured or killed; damage to realistic
objects.")
(value 1) )
(label
(name "Level 2: Killing")
(description "Humans or creatures injured or killed. Rewards
injuring non-threatening creatures.")
(value 2) )
(label
(name "Level 3: Killing with blood and gore")
(description "Humans injured or killed.")
(value 3) )
(label
(name "Level 4: Wanton and gratuitous violence")
(description "Wanton and gratuitous violence.")
(value 4) ))
```

Figure 5-18.   *RSACi rating system .rat file* (continued)

To add rating information to a site or document, a PICS label in the form of a META element must be added to the head of an HTML file. This META element must include the URL of the rating service that produced the rating, some information about the rating itself (such as its version, submitter, or date of creation), and the rating itself. Many rating services such as RSACi, the Internet rating system from RSAC, allow free self-rating. Filling out a form and answering a few questions about a site's content is all that is required to generate an RSACi PICS label, as shown in Figure 5-19.

Once the questionnaire is Figure 5-19 is filled out and submitted, you will receive an e-mail containing the appropriate meta-information, which can then be placed in the head of your HTML documents. An example of a PICS label using the RSACi rating is shown in Figure 5-20. Under the RSACi rating system, information is rated on nudity, sex, violence, and language on a five-category scale from 0 to 4. In this case, the rating is for a typical corporate site, which generally has little "inappropriate" information concerning sex and violence but may use slang or jargon that could be misconstrued out of context.

*The **<META>** element with PICS information must occur within the head of the document. Otherwise, it will not be recognized. It is possible to include more than one **<META>** element within the head, so multiple rating services can be used simultaneously.*

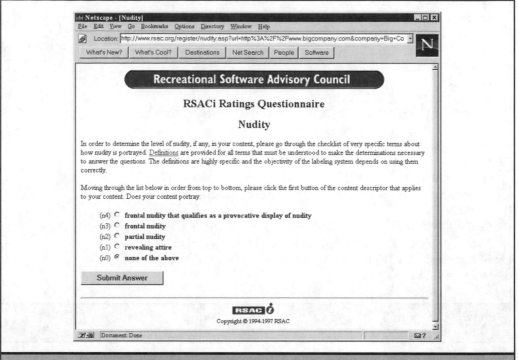

Figure 5-19.   *Rating form*

```
<!DOCTYPE HTML PUBLIC "-//W3C//DTD HTML 3.2 Final//EN">
<HTML>
<HEAD>
<TITLE>PICS Meta Tag Example</TITLE>

<META http-equiv="PICS-Label"
  content='(PICS-1.1 "http://www.rsac.org/ratingsv01.html"
  l gen true comment "RSACi North America Server"
  by "webmaster@bigcompany.com" for
  "http://www.bigcompany.com" on
  "1997.05.26T13:05-0500" r (n 0 s 0 v 0 l 1))'>

</HEAD>
<BODY>
```

Figure 5-20.   *Example use of PICS meta-information*

```
<H1 ALIGN=CENTER>Big Company, Inc.</H1>
<HR>

There's nothing offensive at this site.

</BODY>
</HTML>
```

Figure 5-20.   *Example use of PICS meta-information* (continued)

When filtering software reads a file that contains a rating, it will determine if the information should be allowed or denied. Very strict filtering environments may deny all sites that have no rating, so sites with a broad audience are encouraged to use ratings to avoid restricting readership.

Filtering technology that supports PICS is beginning to achieve widespread acceptance and use. Internet Explorer 3.0 and 4.0 already include PICS-based rating filtering, as shown in Figure 5-21.

SurfWatch (www.surfwatch.com) software is extremely popular. Of course, the technology itself isn't always the problem. Trust in a particular ratings system is a major stumbling block in adoption of the filtering idea. Even when trust is gained, if the rating system seems confusing or arbitrary its value is lowered. In the "real world," Hollywood's MPAA movie rating system has a single value of G, PG, PG-13, R, or NC-17. The assignment of a particular movie rating is based on many factors that often seem arbitrary to casual observers. Parents may wonder how scenes of a dinosaur ripping a man to pieces or a priest pulling a beating heart out of a person's chest merits a PG or PG-13 rating, while the use of certain four-letter words indicates an R. Because of the imprecise nature of ratings, the topic is a loaded one.

Beyond simple content rating, there are some potential benefits of PICS that aren't obvious. With PICS-based environments, employers could limit employee access to Web sites that are used for day-to-day business. The idea of PICS can be extended not just to deny or to allow information, but to prefer it. Imagine a filtering service for search engines that could return sites that have a particular quality of content or level of accuracy. In the general sense, labels are important in that they allow documents to move beyond a mere description of where the document *is* to what the document is *about*.

Linking Issues

One of the biggest problems with linking documents together with <A>, <AREA>, or <LINK> is that the link often breaks. Authors and users alike are already familiar with links to outside sites that change, resulting in the annoying "404 Not Found" messages

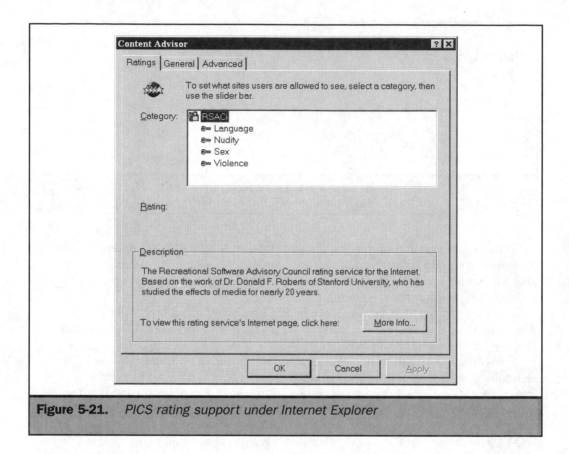

Figure 5-21.   *PICS rating support under Internet Explorer*

so common on the Web. Unfortunately, documents do move around. Some have a very limited lifetime. Even if a link is good, intermittent problems on the Internet can make outside links temporarily stall or break. Clicking on a link only to have the browser slowly attempt to resolve the host can be a frustrating interruption for a user. As you'll see next, document authors can do a great deal to ensure that outside linking and broken link problems are the exception rather than the norm.

While it is impossible to keep other sites from changing addresses, it is possible to be a good network citizen and not move linked files around carelessly. Most Web servers are equipped to provide referrer information that indicates the URL of a linking document. If a document must move, it is possible to alert the Webmasters of the referring URLs to the move and have them update their links. Even better would be to not remove documents but to forward them to a new location. Web servers can be set up to redirect users to new sites or directories if things must be moved around. In some cases, however, a user may eventually click on a broken link into the site no matter what precautions are taken. Rather than providing a vague error message, it would be worthwhile to create a custom message that can help the user locate the document in question. For example, a "404 Not Found" message could be returned with a link to a site map, table of contents, or search engine that the user can access to search for the document in question. An example of a customized server error message is shown in Figure 5-22.

The other aspect of linking that can be troublesome often occurs when a user moves from a site to an outside link. Because of conditions on the Internet or at the end server, outside sites might not always respond right away—if at all. To warn users that they are leaving the site and accessing an outside server, a small icon can be placed next to a link, such as the one Microsoft uses with great success, shown here:

Because of the chaotic nature of the Internet, links will break and documents will move. Unfortunately, URLs themselves provide very little infrastructure to alleviate

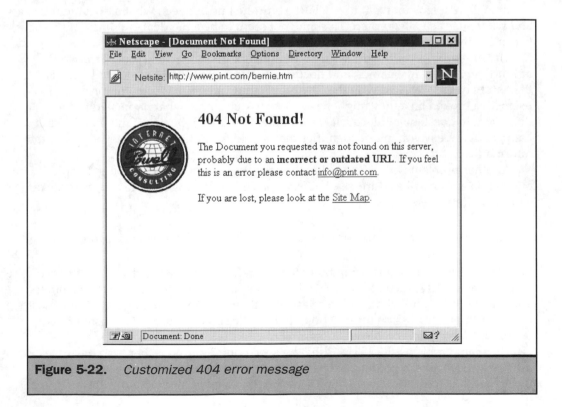

Figure 5-22.   *Customized 404 error message*

these problems. New ideas, like universal resource names (URNs), might help improve this situation.

Beyond Location

An amazing wealth of information is available on the Web. While many people complain of information overload, the real problem isn't volume. It's relevance. How can a particular piece of information be located quickly and easily? If the Web were ideal, it would be like the computer on *Star Trek*, which always delivers any information a user requests in a matter of seconds. On the Internet, a request to a search tool often yields an overwhelming list of 20,000 entries. Some of these entries may be outdated, the document may have been moved, or the server may be unreachable. While the Web isn't science fiction, many of the ideas presented are valid goals. The key problem with building a more organized Web is URL-based addressing.

Problems with URLs

The primary problem with URLs is that they define location rather than meaning. URLs specify where something is on the Web, not what it is or anything about it. URLs specify where to go, not what to get. URLs blur the line between what a document is and where it is actually located. This may not seem to be a big deal, but it is. This issue becomes obvious when the problems with URLs are enumerated.

The first problem with URLs is that they are not persistent. Documents move around, servers change names, and documents might eventually be deleted. This is the nature of the Web, and why the "404 Not Found" message is so common. When users hit a broken link, they might be at a loss to determine what happened to the document in question and locate its new home. Wouldn't it be nice if, no matter what happened, there was a unique identifier that would indicate where to get a copy of the information?

Another problem with URLs is that they tend to be long and confusing. People often have to transcribe addresses. For example, the following is quite a lot to write on a piece of literature:

http://www.bigcompany.com/products/supergadget/specsheets/prod1.htm

Marketing firms are already scrambling for short domain names and site structures that use short URLs, such as http://www.bigcompany.com/prod1. Advertisers often assume the "http," the colon, and the slashes in their promotional material. While most browsers fill in the missing information, this practice could cause problems with older browsers that require complete URLs.

The main problem with URLs is that by specifying location rather than meaning they create an artificial bottleneck and extreme reliance on DNS services. For example, the text of the HTML 3.2 specification is a useful document and certainly has an address at the W3C Web site. But does it live other places on the Internet? It is probably mirrored in a variety of locations. But what happens if the W3C server is unreachable, or DNS services fail to resolve the host? In this case, the resource is unreachable. URLs create a point source for information. Rather than trying to find a particular document wherever it might be on the Internet, we try to go to a particular location. Rather than talking about where something is, we should try to talk about *what* it is.

URNs, URCs, and URIs

Talking about what a document is rather than where it is makes sense when thinking about how information is organized outside the Internet. Nobody talks about which library carries a particular book, or what shelf it is on. The relevant information is the title of the book, its author, and maybe even some other information. But what happens if there are two or more books with the same title, or two authors with the same name? This is actually quite common. At the bottom of everything there is a way to sort things out. Generally, a book should have a unique identifier, such as an ISBN number, that, when combined with other descriptive information like the author, publisher, and publication date, uniquely describes the book. This naming scheme allows people to specify a particular book and then hunt down where it might live.

The Web, however, is not as ordered as a library. On the Web, people name their documents whatever they like, and search robots organize their indexes however they like. Categorizing things is difficult. The only unique item for documents is the URL, which simply says where the document lives. But how many URLs does the HTML 3.2 specification have? There could be many places where this document lives. Even worse than a document with multiple locations, what happens when the content at the location changes? Perhaps a particular URL address points to information about dogs one day and cats the next. This is how the Web really is. However, a great deal of research is being done to address some of the shortcomings of the Web and its addressing schemes.

URN

A new set of addressing ideas, including URNs, URCs, and URIs, are emerging to remedy some of the Web's shortcomings. A *uniform resource name (URN)* can locate a resource by giving it a unique symbolic name rather than a unique address. Network services analogous to the current DNS services will transparently translate a URN into the URL (server *ip* address, directory path, and filename) needed to actually locate a resource. This translation could be used to select the closest server in order to improve document delivery speed, or to try various backup servers in case a server is unavailable. The benefit of the abstraction provided by URNs should be obvious from this simple idea alone.

To better understand the idea behind URNs, think about the idea of domain names themselves, like www.xyz.com. These names are already translated into numeric IP addresses like 192.102.249.3 all the time. This mapping provides the ability to change a machine's numeric address or location without seriously disrupting access to it, since the name stays the same. Furthermore, numeric addresses provide no meaning to a user, while domain names provide some indication of the entity in question. It seems obvious that the level of abstraction provided by a system like DNS would logically make sense on the Web. Rather than typing in some unwieldy URL, a URN would be issued that would be translated to an underlying URL. Some experts worry that using a resolving system to translate URNs to URLs is inherently flawed and will not scale well. As the DNS system is fairly fragile, there may be some truth behind this concern. Another problem with this idea is that, in reality, URNs will probably not be easy to remember like urn: booktitle and be something more like urn:isbn: 0-12-518408-5.

URC

A *uniform resource characteristic (URC)*, also known as a uniform resource *citation*, describes a set of attribute/value pairs that define some aspect of an information resource. URCs are somewhat like the **<META>** data items or the PICS labels associated with a Web document. The form of a URC is still under discussion, but it is obvious that many of the ideas of URCs are already in use.

Taken all together, a URL, URN, and a collection of URCs describe an information resource. For example, the document "Big Company Corporate Summary" might have a unique URN like urn://corpid:55127.

 The syntax of the URN above is fictional. It simply shows that URNs probably won't have easily remembered names and that there might be many naming schemes like ISBN numbers or corporate IDs.

The "Big Company Corporate Summary" would also have a set of URCs that describe the rating of the file, the author, the publisher, and so on. In addition, the document would have a location or locations on the Web where the document lived. For example, these could be http://www.bigcompany.com/about/corp.htm or http://www.bigcompany.com.jp/about/corp.htm.

URI

Taken all together, a particular information resource has been identified. The collection of information, which is used to specifically identify this document, is termed a *uniform resource identifier (URI)*.

 Occasionally, URI is used interchangeably with URL. While this is acceptable, research into the theories behind the names suggests that URI is more generic than URLs and serves to encompass the ideal of an information resource. At the moment, a URL is the only common way to identify an information resource on the Internet. Although technically a URL could be considered a URI, this confuses the issue and obscures the ultimate goal of trying to talk about information more generally than a network location.

While many of the ideas covered here are still being discussed, some systems, like Persistent URLs or Purls (www.purl.org) and Handles (www.handle.net), already implement many of the features of URNs and URCs. They are not, however, widely implemented.These could be thought of as true URIs when compared to the URLs used today. However, URLs are likely to remain the most common way to describe information on the Web for the near future. Because of this, the system will have to be extended to deal with new types of information and access methods.

New URL Forms

URLs are here to stay, but as new ideas are added to the Internet, URLs will evolve into new forms. For example, as telephone and television are joined with desktop computers and the Internet, addressing schemes for telephone numbers and TV channels will become necessary. WebTV, Sega Saturn Netlink, and cellular phone browsers already demonstrate that the Web is reaching users beyond the personal computer or workstation. On these devices, some of the URL schemes described early in the chapter are inappropriate. Many of these devices lack local storage, so the "file" scheme is of little use. On the other hand, many of these devices usually have access to other sources of information such as television channels and telephone services. A television channel URL form might look like tv://*channel*, where *channel* was either an alpha-numeric name like nbc or nbc7-39, or a numeric channel number. Similar to the news URL form, there would be no need to differentiate between nbc in one area and another as the system would be configured to get the information locally. Similarly, a phone URL might look like phone://*phone-number*, with a numeric value for the phone number and any extra digit information required, like country code or calling card information. For example, phone://+1-619-270-2086 might dial a phone number in the United States. An instruction to send a fax could be written in a similar way except with fax://*phone-number*.

New content types and URL schemes bring new challenges, particularly in the way links and fragment identifiers are used within HTML documents. For example, how will a particular scene in a video stream be addressed? Random access to large audio and video files is very useful, particularly considering the download requirements for such data. Subsections or "clips" of a data stream must be addressable via URLs that describe a time range. How can a URL describe the idea of accessing an audio file called "nirvana.audio" and playing a ten-second clip starting at time 2:05? Once into clips, particularly video clips, there will have to be some mechanism to link from the data stream to other data streams or objects on the Web. Some experimental systems already show video with hot spots that work like image maps. The leads to the conclusion that URL schemes are far from complete. Many new schemes are being proposed all the time. There are already a variety of esoteric schemes out there. If you are interested in new URL schemes, take a look at the W3 area on addressing (www.w3.org/Addressing/) for more information.

Summary

Linking documents on the Web requires a consistent naming scheme. URLs provide the basic information necessary to locate an object on the Internet by including the host name, directory, filename, and access protocol. URLs are written in a regular format, so it is possible to write an address for any object. A common shorthand notation, relative URLs, is particularly useful when creating links within a Web site. If a document's URL can be determined, whether it's relative or fully spelled out, it can be specified in the **<A>** element to create an anchor from one document to another. Links within HTML documents can be made with text or with images. A special type of clickable image, called an *image map*, allows areas of an image to be defined as "hot."

Simply linking documents together is the most basic form of hypertext. Using the **<LINK>** element as well as the **REL** and **REV** attributes of the anchor element, it is possible to create relationships between documents. Once documents are linked together, providing extra information about the document can be very useful. HTML provides such a facility through the use of the **<META>** element. But even if Web authors master all aspects of linking, there is a bigger picture to worry about. The Web is a chaotic environment, and navigating among documents and linking documents presents serious challenges to the HTML author. In the future, some of these problems may be solved by the URNs, URCs, and improved URLs, which, taken together, make up the uniform resource identifier (URI). However, until URN and similar technologies are more readily available, HTML authors should be cautious about linking and consistently check links in their sites.

Chapter 6

HTML and Images

Until recently, HTML (Hypertext Markup Language) has been true to its name. However, text alone wasn't what made the Web popular. While the Web dates from the early '90s, the environment didn't take off until Mosaic appeared with support for inline images using the **<IMG>** element. Today, images and other binary objects are everywhere on the Web. The modern Web is more about hypermedia than plain hypertext, but it is unlikely that the language will be renamed HMML any time soon. While images have played an important role in the success of the Web, they must be used carefully. Images should not be used just for decoration. They should provide benefit, but at what cost? When used carelessly, Web visuals may require the user to wait a long time for a page to render. Images can improve the message delivered, but when abused, they may confuse or hide a message as easily as they improve it. While this is not a book about design and image use, the intersection of HTML and images is important enough to warrant some discussion.

The Role of Images on the Web

When Mosaic first came out, the ability to view an image within the browser window was a huge improvement. Gopher, the popular information system at the time, was primarily textual. It didn't support multimedia and navigation to the same degree as the Web. At first, images often were used to show the logo of the company or present a graph. Today, however, some sites seem to be more about the images than the information. So what are images on the Web good for?

Web images can be used to illustrate an idea, show strictly visual information, provide navigation, and serve as decoration. It can be said that a picture is worth a thousand words. When illustrating an idea, this is very true. Images can be used to show procedures, product applications, design styles, and a variety of other concepts. Think about a Web site that teaches people to dance. While it might be possible to explain the various dance steps in writing, a diagram is far easier to understand. People may complain about byte count and download time, but in the communication sense, a picture is worth a thousand bytes.

Beyond illustrating ideas, there are some topics that require visuals. If a photographer puts up a Web site, how can she illustrate what she does without pictures? For things that are intrinsically visual in nature, pictures are mandatory. Images can also be used for navigation. Visual cues can help make it easier for users to find their way around the tangled Web. Even a unique home page image can serve as a consistent beacon, helping the user find his way back to a familiar point of reference. Last but not least, images can provide decoration for a site. Pictures make things more interesting, even if they just break up the monotony of page after page of text. A splash of color and a few images can be pleasing. Too much decoration, however, can turn a page into the online equivalent of an over-decorated Christmas tree complete with pink snow flocking.

The basic problem with images on the Web relates to confusion about their value. Far too often, the quality of a Web site is judged solely on its look and feel—but what are sites really for? While perception and experience are important, ultimately the user will not focus solely on the interface. The site must provide information or some other beneficial function. In this sense, sites become like software. In a traditional software product, what is most important: the look, the functionality, or both? The answer is both, but over time, the functionality far outweighs the look. The user interface is important. A good-looking, logical user interface improves a site; a poorly designed user interface negatively affects the best content. Navigation is important and should look graphically appropriate, but the logic behind it is what really matters. While textured backgrounds, beveled buttons, and full-screen image maps may look great, they don't ensure that a site is logically organized. Pleasing graphics that reflect well-thought-out site architecture can facilitate navigation throughout the site. Confusing graphical navigation, on the other hand, may actually bring a site down.

In the long run, purely decorative images are not terribly valuable. Rainbow bars and multicolored bullets may make the site appear more exciting initially, but over time they may irritate the user by hindering speedy navigation of the site. The first time a "What's New" animated GIF runs, the action may catch the user's eye. But what about the twentieth time? Decorating the page just for the sake of having images is not a good reason.

Images are most important when they enhance the content of the Web site. An image that provides more information than would be conveyed with plain text is truly valuable. Even if the image significantly increases the download time of the page, the supplementary information provided may be well worth it. What better way to describe the body style of a car than with a visual? A text description of a low-profile car with smooth curves doesn't sell nearly as many cars as an actual picture. Maps, diagrams, specifications, product pictures, portraits, and other visual content—this is what Web images are for. About the only people who should be adding pictures for the sake of pictures to the Web site are those people who create them for a living—graphic artists, photographers, and so on. Even then, what the image presents is still important.

Note   *Software products or Web sites that are entertainment driven may have different perspectives on presentation because the presentation may actually be the content.*

Image Preliminaries

Before discussing image use on the Web, consider how images are represented in a computer. Images on a computer screen are made up of thousands of *pixels* (shorthand for picture elements). A pixel is a tiny dot, the smallest unit of measure on a screen. The number of pixels that can be displayed on a screen is termed the *screen resolution*. Screen resolution equals the number of pixels across by the number of pixels down.

The more pixels on screen or in an image, the greater the detail or resolution of the image. Some common screen resolutions are listed next:

640×480
800×600
1024×768
1200×1600

The number of pixels is only one part of a digital image. Images also have color. Every monitor supports a certain number of colors that can be displayed at once. The more colors used, the more realistic the image will look. Color support is measured by the number of bits used to store the color information for each pixel. Common color resolutions are listed here:

Standard VGA: 4 bits per pixel=16 colors
Super VGA: 8 bits per pixel=256 colors
High Resolution: 16 bits per pixel=thousands of colors
"True Color": 24 bits per pixel=millions of colors

Computer-based images come in two basic flavors: *vector images* and *bitmapped images*. Figure 6-1 illustrates the basic idea behind vector and bitmap images.

A vector image is described mathematically as a set of curves. When a computer reads a vector image, it evaluates the mathematical information and draws the resulting information on the screen. Because the image is defined mathematically, it is very compact. For example, a vector image of a red circle might be described simply as a circle with a radius of 50 pixels filled with red. While vector images are very useful to describe shapes, lines, and other forms of illustration, photographic and similar imagery is better described by a bitmap. A bitmap image is specified as a collection of pixels of different color values. Because of the large number of pixels that may be in an image, as well as the color information that must be described, bitmaps can be very large. For example, an uncompressed bitmap image at 640×480 pixels—the typical screen size—with 24 bits of color information would take up a staggering 930MB. Bitmaps are the most common image formats. They include images made up of a collection of dots or pixels, such as photographs and television pictures.

The main problem with bitmaps is that the file size can be very large. Their excessive size makes it impractical to store bitmaps on disk or transmit them across a network like the Internet. One approach to dealing with the size problem is to compress the images. In general, there are two forms of image compression: *lossless* and *lossy*. Lossless image compression means that the compressed image is identical to the uncompressed image. Because all the data in the image must be preserved, the degree of compression, and the corresponding savings, is relatively minor. Lossy

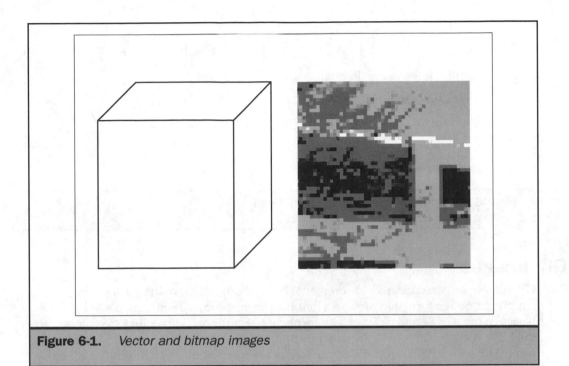

Figure 6-1.   *Vector and bitmap images*

compression, on the other hand, does not preserve the image exactly, but does provide a much higher degree of compression. With lossy compression, the image quality is compromised for a smaller byte count. Because the human eye may barely notice the loss, the tradeoff may be acceptable.

Image compression depends on the image file format. There are a variety of image formats in the computer world, including vector image formats like Encapsulated PostScript (EPS) and bitmap formats like GIF, TIFF, and JPEG. While the HTML standard says nothing about what image formats can be used on the Web, the browser vendors tend to support the same image types. On the Web, the primary image formats are GIF (Graphic Interchange Format) and JPEG (Joint Photographic Experts Group). A new format called PNG (Portable Network Graphics), which should also eventually become a Web image standard, is being heavily endorsed by the World Wide Web Consortium (W3C). Given the historical association between Unix and the Internet, the X image formats—XBM (X Bitmaps) and XPM (X Pixelmaps)—are often supported natively by browsers. Table 6-1 provides an overview of basic file types.

Note   *Internet Explorer also supports the bitmap (BMP) file type popular with Windows users. This format has not been adopted widely on the Web.*

File Type	File Extension
GIF (Graphics Interchange Format)	.gif
JPEG (Joint Photographic Experts Group)	.jpg or .jpeg
XBM (X Bitmaps)	.xbm
XPM (X Pixelmaps)	.xpm
PNG (Portable Network Graphics)	.png

Table 6-1.   *Selected Internet Image File Types*

GIF Images

GIF images are used extensively on the Web. They are probably the most widely supported image format in browsers that handle graphics. GIF images come in two basic flavors: *GIF87* and *GIF89a*. Both forms of GIF support 8-bit color (256 colors), use the LZW (Lempel-Ziv-Welch) lossless compression scheme, and generally have the file extension .gif. GIF 89a supports transparency and animation, both of which will be discussed in this section.

Note   *There is some concern about the use of GIF images due to the patent on the LZW algorithm held by Unisys that would require payment for use of the proprietary scheme. This concern is unsubstantiated. Nevertheless, the PNG format described in this chapter has been positioned as a substitute for the GIF format.*

The run-length encoding compression scheme used by GIF works well with large areas of continuous color, so GIF is very efficient in compression of flat-style illustration. Figure 6-2 shows the GIF compression scheme in practice. Notice in the figure how the images with large horizontal continuous areas of color compress highly, while those with variation do not. Simply taking a box filled with lines and rotating it shows how dramatic the compression effect can be.

As mentioned earlier, GIF images support 8-bit color for a maximum of 256 colors in the image. Consequently, some degree of loss is inevitable when representing true-color images such as photographs. Typically, when an image is remapped from a large number of colors to a smaller color palette, *dithering* occurs. Dithering attempts to imitate colors by placing similar colors near each other. Dithering also produces a speckling or banding effect that may cause images to appear rough or fuzzy. Web authors should be careful to use GIF images appropriately. Netscape and Microsoft

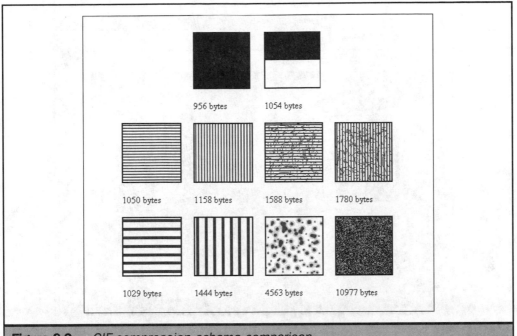

Figure 6-2. *GIF compression scheme comparison*

currently use a so-called "browser safe" color palette of 216 colors that are common across systems like the Macintosh or Windows. If a GIF image using a color outside this color palette is displayed on an 8-bit system, dithering will occur. Authors looking to avoid image problems such as dithering are invited to visit the Web site http://www.lynda.com/dwg/.

Note *According to the GIF specification, the idea of layering can be used to create a GIF image that supports more than 256 colors. However, not all browsers support this little-known feature. Layering also allows for an interesting form of color interlacing, which can bring in one set of colors before another.*

GIF images also support a concept called *transparency*. One bit of transparency is allowed, which means that one color can be set to be transparent. Transparency allows the background that an image is placed upon to show through, making a variety of complex effects possible. Transparency is illustrated in Figure 6-3.

GIF transparency is far from ideal, as it can result in a halo effect in certain situations. For example, in order to smooth images, a technique called *anti-aliasing* is used. Anti-aliased images appear smooth because the image is progressively made

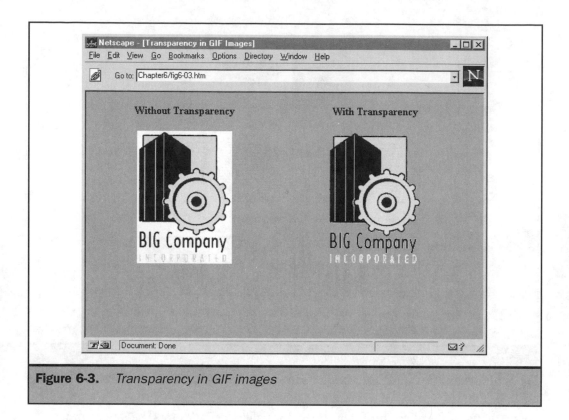

Figure 6-3.   *Transparency in GIF images*

light to fade into the background. However, because only one color of transparency can be set in an image, the anti-aliasing colors may show up as a halo or residue around the image. The idea of anti-aliasing is shown in Figure 6-4.

GIF images also support a feature called *interlacing*. Interlacing allows an image to load in a venetian-blind fashion rather than from top to bottom a line at a time. The interlacing effect allows a user to get an idea of what an image looks like before the entire image has downloaded. The idea of interlacing is shown in Figure 6-5. Only 26 percent of this 163K image is loaded, producing an indistinct, highly pixelated image. Once the image is completely loaded, it will present a clear image of an office building; at this point in its progress, however, it already gives the user a good idea of what is being downloaded. The previsualization benefit of interlacing is very useful on the Web, where download speed is often an issue. While interlacing a GIF image is generally a good idea, occasionally it comes with a downside. First, interlaced images may be slightly larger than noninterlaced images. Second, an interlaced image may

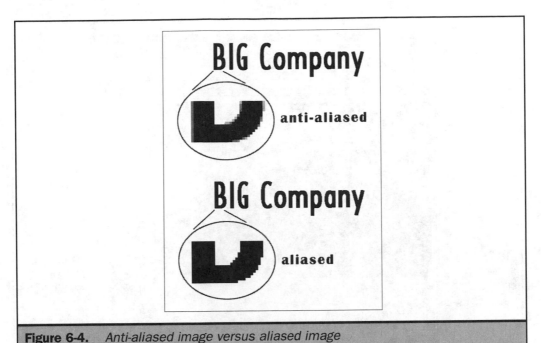

Figure 6-4.   *Anti-aliased image versus aliased image*

not always provide its intended previsualization benefit. For example, if the GIF image is of graphic text, the text will probably not be readable until the image is fully loaded.

Starting with the GIF89a format, which was supported first by Netscape 2.0, animation has been possible on the Web. The GIF89a format supports a series of GIF images that act as the individual frames of animation. The animation can be set up so one image is displayed after another, similar to a little flipbook. The animation extension also allows timing and looping information to be added to the image. Today, animated GIFs are one of the most popular ways to add simple animation to a Web page because nearly every browser supports them. Browsers that do not support the animated GIF format generally display the first frame of the animation in its place. Even though plug-ins or other browser facilities are not required, authors should not rush out to use animation on their pages. Excessive animation can be distracting as well as inefficient to download, particularly when frames are not used efficiently. One approach to combat file bloat is to replace only the moving parts of an individual animation frame. This may result in a dramatic saving of file size, as shown in Figure 6-6.

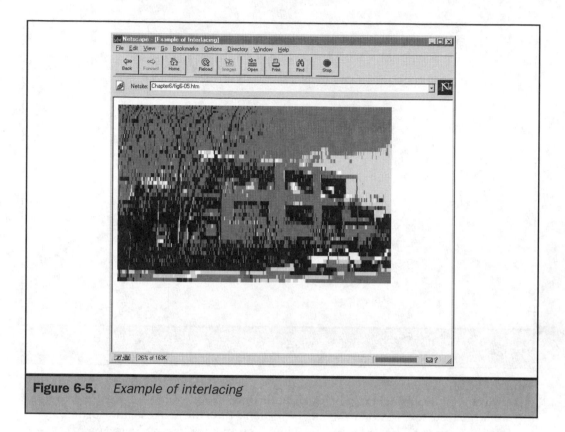

Figure 6-5.   *Example of interlacing*

In summary, because of their compression scheme and support for 8-bit color, GIF images tend to be best suited for illustrations. GIF images do support interlacing, which may provide previsualization for Web-based imagery. Because of the nature of their image compression, GIF images may not be suitable for photographic-style imagery, which is probably better left to the JPEG format discussed in the next section. In their favor, GIF images are the most widely supported image format, and do have advanced features such as transparency and animation. Probably the only controversial aspect of the image format, besides its compression issues, is its pronunciation with either a hard "g" or a "j" sound. The author prefers the hard "g" as the other pronunciation sounds like a popular brand of peanut butter, but this sticky issue will probably never be settled.

JPEG Images

The other common Web image format is JPEG, which usually is indicated by a file name ending with .jpg or .jpeg. JPEG, which stands for the Joint Photographic Experts Group—the name of the committee that wrote the standard—is a lossy image format

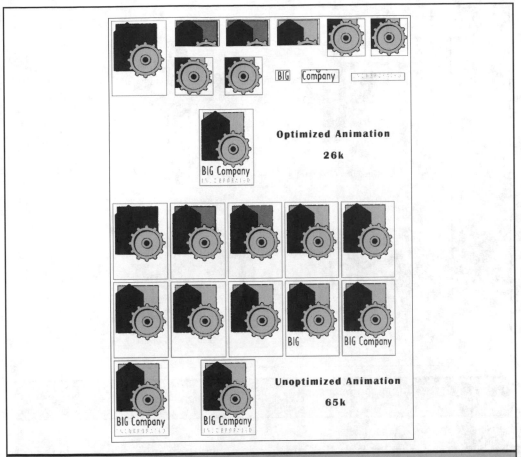

Figure 6-6. *GIF animation frame optimization*

designed for compressing photographic images that may contain thousands, or even millions, of colors or shades of gray. Because JPEG is a lossy image format, there is some trade-off between image quality and file size. However, the JPEG format stores high-quality 24-bit color images in a significantly smaller amount of space than GIF, thus saving precious disk space or download time on the Web. The degree of compression in JPEG images is shown in Figure 6-7.

While the JPEG format may compress photographic images well, it is not well suited to line drawings or text. When such images are saved in JPEG format, they may acquire extraneous information, often in the form of unwanted dots or other residue. Because JPEG is so well suited to photographs and GIF to illustrations, it is no wonder

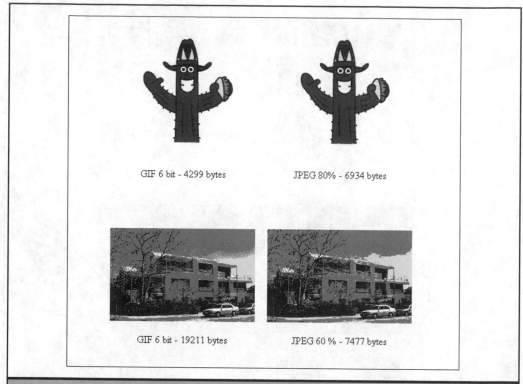

GIF 6 bit - 4299 bytes   JPEG 80% - 6934 bytes

GIF 6 bit - 19211 bytes   JPEG 60 % - 7477 bytes

Figure 6-7.   *Comparison between GIF and JPEG formats*

that both are used on the Web. JPEG images do not support animation, nor do they support any form of transparency. Web designers needing such effects must turn to another image format, such as GIF. JPEG images do support a form of interlacing in a format called progressive JPEG. Progressive JPEGs fade in from a low resolution to a high resolution, going from fuzzy to clear. Like interlaced GIFs, progressive JPEG images are slightly larger than their nonprogressive counterparts. One problem with progressive JPEGs is that older browsers, particularly those before Netscape 2.0, do not support them.

PNG Images

The Portable Network Graphics (PNG) format has all of the features of GIF89a in addition to several other features. Notable features include greater color depth support, color and gamma correction, and 8-bit transparency. In addition, the compression algorithm for PNG is nonproprietary, making PNG a likely successor of GIF. Though Internet Explorer 4.0 supports inline PNG images, Netscape Communicator requires a plug-in.

Other Useful Image Formats

There are many image formats beyond GIF, JPEG, and PNG that may be used on the Web. These include vector formats like Illustrator and Flash (with the file extension .swf), compressed Freehand files, AutoCAD files (often used for architecture sites), and images that require heavy compression, such as fractals. Most of the less-common image formats may require a helper application or plug-in to the browser to allow the image to be displayed. Unless you have a specific need, you should probably avoid special image types requiring browser add-ons; users may become frustrated by the work involved in obtaining the extra software.

Image Download Issues

One major criticism of using images on a Web page is the time they take to download and the frustration that this may cause the user. The speed of the Web has prompted some to dub it the World Wide Wait. The bottom line is that it takes time to transmit data across the Internet. The amount of data that can be transmitted across a link in a certain period of time is termed *bandwidth* and is often measured in bits (bps), kilobits (Kbps), or megabits per second (Mbps). The higher the bandwidth, the more data can be transmitted quickly. Unfortunately, users accessing the Internet via a modem often have very limited bandwidth available. Some common speeds and the approximate time it takes to transmit 1MB of data are shown in Table 6-2. As you can see, the faster the data connection, the faster the Web will appear to load. Currently, ISDN is the fastest connection available to most home users. However, several reports indicate that the average modem speed today is still between 14.4Kbps and 28.8Kbps, primarily due to the very large number of users still using 14.4Kbps modems. Designers who design for such audiences might want to keep this in mind.

Modem Speed	Download Time
14.4Kbps	10 minutes
28.8Kbps	5 minutes
33.6Kbps	4 minutes
56Kbps	2.5 minutes
1B ISDN (64Kbps)	2 minutes
2B ISDN (128Kbps)	1 minute
T1	5 seconds

Table 6-2. *Bandwidth and Download Time Comparison for 1MB of Data*

Given that users have only so much bandwidth available, one way to reduce wait time is to reduce the amount of data that must be sent. In a typical Web page, the majority of the data transmitted tends to be binary, particularly in the form of images. Given this observation, one approach to improving Web page accessibility is to reduce the file size of the images in your Web page.

The size of a graphic file is determined first by its physical pixel size and then by the color information. The larger the physical image, the larger it tends to be byte-wise. Also, the more bits used to represent color information for a particular image, the larger the file size. One approach to reduce file size would be to reduce the physical size of an image file, possibly by creating thumbnail images that could be clicked to download the full-sized image. Another approach to reduce file size is to reduce the number of colors in the image. Often times, particularly with GIF images, there are far more bits used to represent color information than there are actual colors in the image. For example, reducing the bit depth from 8 bits (256 colors) to 5 bits (32 colors) can result in significant byte savings.

Another approach to reducing the byte count in an image is through compression. As discussed previously, image compression is handled by the image file format, so choosing the correct format for a particular image is integral to reducing byte count. A basic rule of thumb is to use GIF images for illustrations and JPEGs for photographs. Also, by setting the degree of compression when using a JPEG image, you can reduce file size, at a small sacrifice in image quality. Because the human eye can't often perceive the difference between an image of high quality and one of medium quality, at least on the Web, tuning the image can often result in significant file size savings without penalty.

While image size is certainly important to improving the loading time of Web pages, designers shouldn't get carried away with optimizing images without consideration for the rest of the Web process. For example, while a designer may compress images to their minimum size, the user may still perceive the Web page to be slow. This occurs because there are many aspects to the delivery of a Web page, including the Web server, the links traveled on the Internet, the traffic on the Internet, the protocols, the software being used, and even the processing speed of the computer at the other end. All of these factors affect the user's experience. There is little reason to optimize images for a Web site that will be hosted on a slow or poorly connected server?

Obtaining Images

One of the first problems many novice Web designers face is where to get images for their Web pages. This shouldn't be any more difficult than getting images for a different type of project. One way to obtain images is simply to make them. There are a variety of vector drawing programs, such as Adobe Illustrator, and bitmap editing or paint programs, such as Adobe Photoshop. With such tools, you can create images directly in the computer and then save them to the appropriate Web image format, such as GIF or JPEG. Images do not have to be made within the computer, however.

You could scan drawings with a flatbed scanner, or take pictures with a traditional camera and scan them with a flatbed scanner, slide scanner, or even a drum scanner. Digital cameras are also very useful for capturing imagery and avoiding the scanning process altogether.

Another approach to obtaining images to use on the Web is to buy them. You may be aware of the many clip art CD-ROMs available for sale. High-quality images also can be licensed from traditional stock photography companies, such as Comstock (www.comstock.com). Some page authors who believe that clip art is not of high enough quality prefer to piece together images. Outlets such as ImageClub (www.imageclub.com) license professional-grade imagery. CD-ROMs with 100,000 images for $100 dollars aren't always the best deal considering the quality of the imagery and the fact that you might only need one image. You truly get what you pay for with image clip art.

Note *Not all stock photography houses understand the Web. A few still charge exorbitant prices for imagery if it will be used online. Given the popularity of the Web, this situation will probably change as they lose business to their more open-minded competitors.*

The expense of licensing images and the ease with which images can be copied have convinced many people that they can simply appropriate whatever images they need. Unfortunately, this is stealing the work of others. True, there are stiff penalties for copyright infringement, but it can be difficult to enforce these laws. Also, some page designers tend to bend the rules thanks to the legal concept called *fair use*, which allows the use of someone else's copyrighted work under certain circumstances.

There are four basic questions used to define the fair-use concept.

First, is the work in question being appropriated for a nonprofit or profit use? The fair use defense is less likely to stand up if the "borrowed" work has been used to make money for someone other than its copyright holder.

Second, is the work creative (for example, a speculative essay on the impact of a recent congressional debate) or factual (a straightforward description of the debate without commentary)? "Fair use" would cover use of the factual work more than use of the creative one.

Third, how much of the copyrighted work has been used? It is possible to use someone else's images if the image is changed substantially from the original image. The problem is determining what constitutes enough change in the image to make it a new work. Simply using a photo-editing tool to flip an image or change its colors is not enough. There is a fine line between using portions of another person's work and outright stealing. Even if you don't plan on using noncleared images, be careful of using images from free Internet clip art libraries. These so-called free images may have been submitted with the belief that they are free, but some of them may have been appropriated from a commercial clip art library somewhere down the line. Be particularly careful with high-quality images of famous individuals and commercial products. While such groups may often appreciate people using their images, the usage is generally limited to noncommercial purposes.

The third fair use question leads to the fourth. What impact does the image have on the economic value of the work? While unauthorized use of a single *Star Trek*–related image might not substantially affect the money earned by Paramount Pictures in a given fiscal year, Paramount's lawyers take a dim view of such use. They have even taken steps to make it very difficult for Web page designers to use such images. The Fox Network is equally defensive of images relating to *The X-Files* and other popular television shows.

One could, perhaps, even add a fifth question to the list: who owns the original work, and how vigorously will the owner defend it? This whole discussion begs many legal questions that are far beyond the scope of this book. The bottom line is that in the long run, it's always safer to create original work, license images, or use material that lies in the public domain. Just because many Web designers skirt the law doesn't mean you should.

HTML Image Basics

To insert an image into a Web page, use the **<IMG>** element and set the **SRC** attribute of the element equal to the URL of the image. As discussed in Chapter 5, the form of the URL may be either an absolute URL or a relative URL. Most likely, the image element will use a relative URL to an image found locally. To insert a GIF image called logo.gif residing in the same directory as the current document, use

```
<IMG SRC="logo.gif">
```

Of course, an absolute URL could also be used to reference an image on another server, for example

```
<IMG SRC="http://www.bigcompany.com/images/logo.gif">
```

Using an external URL is not advised since images may move and cause the page to load at an uneven pace.

Note *The SRC attribute must be included. Otherwise, browsers that support images may display a placeholder or broken image icon.*

A short example of using **<IMG>** (from Chapter 4) is shown in Figure 6-8. The rendering of the code in Figure 6-8 is shown in Figure 6-9.

```
<!DOCTYPE HTML PUBLIC "-//W3C//DTD HTML 3.2 Final//EN">
<HTML>
<HEAD>
<TITLE>Rendering of Image Example</TITLE>
</HEAD>
<BODY>

<IMG SRC="images/photo.gif" WIDTH="234" HEIGHT="150" BORDER="0">

</BODY>
</HTML>
```

Figure 6-8.   *Simple <IMG> example*

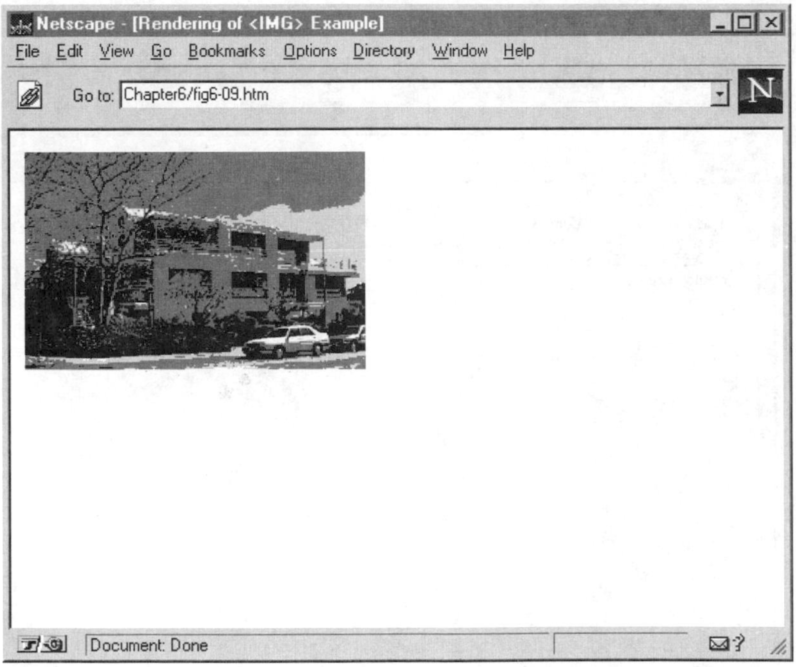

Figure 6-9.   *Rendering of <IMG> example*

Under HTML 2.0, besides **SRC**, there were only three other attributes to the <IMG> element: **ISMAP**, **ALIGN**, and **ALT**. Later on, Netscape and Microsoft added numerous attributes, many of which have been incorporated into the HTML 4.0 specification that is currently in progress. The next few sections will cover the basic attributes. A more complete rundown of the image options available will follow.

ALT Attribute

The **ALT** attribute was set to provide alternative text for user agents that did not display images, or for graphical browsers where the user has turned image rendering off. The **ALT** attribute's value may display in place of the image or be used as a tool tip or placeholder information in image-based browsers. The **ALT** attribute's value is typically enclosed in double quotes and may include spaces and other characters. However, any HTML markup found in the **ALT** element will be rendered as plain text. If the option to display images is turned off, the browser will display the alternative text, as shown in Figure 6-10.

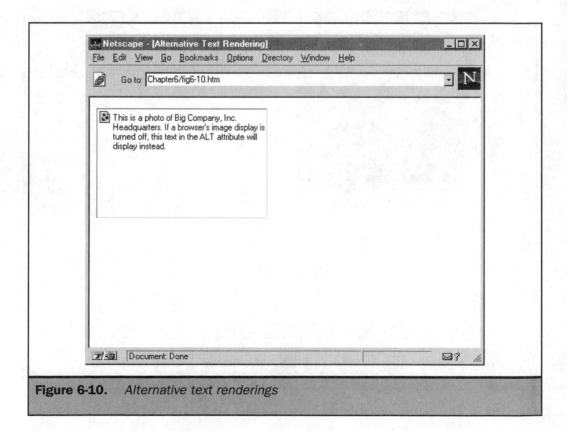

Figure 6-10.   *Alternative text renderings*

Many modern graphical browsers will also display the **ALT** text as the tool tip for the image once the pointer is positioned over the image for a period of time, as shown in Figure 6-11.

While some sources suggest that **ALT** text be limited to 1,024 characters, there is no limit to the text that may theoretically be used. However, anything more than a few hundred characters may become unwieldy. Furthermore, the current version of Netscape (at the time of this writing 4.0) does not handle long tool tips properly, as it does not wrap the text.

The Importance of ALT

It is easy to forget that many different types of browsers can be used to access the Web. While much of the world may access a page via Netscape or Microsoft products, what about the rest of the people out there? There are many people who have access to the Web from a text-only environment. Figure 6-12 shows the same page two ways: under Netscape with the image turned on and as rendered under Lynx.

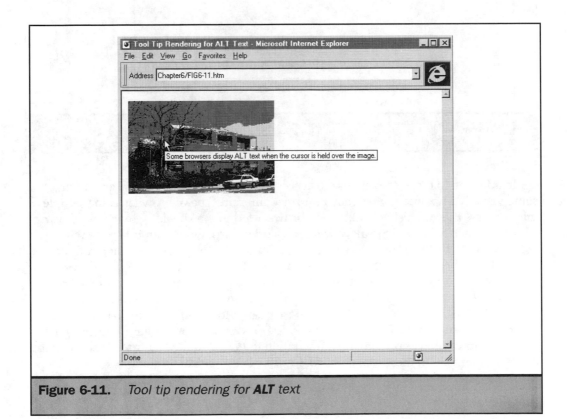

Figure 6-11.   *Tool tip rendering for **ALT** text*

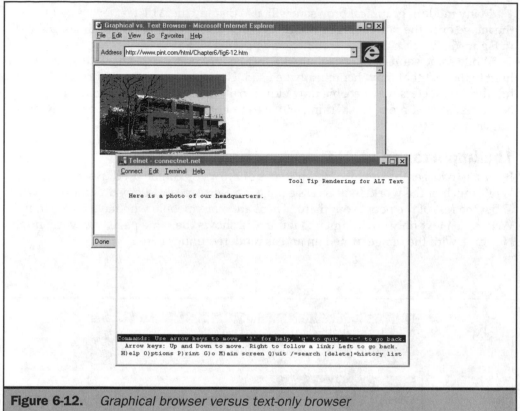

Figure 6-12.   *Graphical browser versus text-only browser*

In addition to those who choose to access the Web via a text-only environment, some visually impaired people may require a different type of browser. Blind people might access the Web using a text mode browser fed into a speaking machine or using a browser such as pwWebSpeak (www.prodworks.com), which can integrate with a voice synthesizer. Other users may access the Web via a telephone or other automated system just for ease of use or quick information. Already, systems like the Web-on-Call Voice Browser (www.netphonic.com) can be used to provide automated phone access to Web sites. Imagine a situation where an automated telephone system to access the Web read, "Press 1 for corporate information, press 2 for product information." Last, what about robots that come through and index a Web site for relevant information? The contents of images provide no information to index. In the last three cases, images don't mean much. In these cases, the **ALT** attribute can be very valuable.

Setting the **ALT** attribute to provide alternative information for an image can solve many accessibility problems, but simply setting alternative text is not adequate. The biggest problem with alternative text is that it often does not really provide any benefit. Imagine a company logo on a page for a company called Big Company. Should the **ALT** text be set to something like "Logo of Big Company, Inc.?" Imagine a person hearing this read out loud. Does just "Big Company, Inc." make more sense?

ALT text for pictures of things may prove even more cryptic. A picture of the corporate office with **ALT** text set to read "Picture of Corporate Office" is not terribly explanatory. A more detailed description such as "A picture of the exterior of the Big Company Corporate office—a three-story building with beach-flavored architecture surrounded by large trees" is much more useful. In this case, there is some added value even for the sighted user. A general rule is that if an image conveys information, the **ALT** text should convey the same information, and if an image is simply decoration, you can set the **ALT** text to nothing: **ALT=" "**.

Last is the famous case of the bullet item. Many users add small red or blue circles or bullets to their pages. In many cases, the **ALT** text for these objects is set to be "bullet." Now think about the aggravation of seeing the word "bullet" over and over again on a page, not to mention hearing it read aloud. Maybe putting an asterisk would be more appropriate for **ALT** text in this instance.

While a lot of people might argue that the Web wasn't popular until graphics were integrated or that the Web is inherently a visual medium, the value of textual content on the Web is indisputable. Consequently, it should be made as accessible as possible. There is no arguing that a picture may be worth a thousand words; but if that is the case, why not provide a few words in exchange?

Image Alignment

Probably the first thing that a user wants to do after he is able to put an image in a Web page is to figure out how to position it on the page. Under the HTML 2.0 standard, there was very little that allowed the user to format image layout on a page. Initially, the **ALIGN** attribute could be set to a value of **TOP**, **BOTTOM**, or **MIDDLE**. When an image was included within a block structure of text, the next line of text would be aligned either to the top, middle, or bottom of the image depending on the value of the **ALIGN** attribute. If the attribute wasn't set, it would default to the bottom. The example in Figure 6-13 shows how image alignment works under HTML 2.0. The rendering of the image alignment example is shown in Figure 6-14.

One of the problems with initial image alignment in early HTML was that the text really didn't flow around the image. In fact, only one line of text was aligned next to the image, which meant the inline images had to be very small or the layout looked somewhat strange, as shown in Figure 6-15.

```
<!DOCTYPE HTML PUBLIC "-//W3C//DTD HTML 3.2 Final//EN">
<HTML>
<HEAD>
<TITLE>Image Alignment Rendering</TITLE>
</HEAD>
<BODY>

<P><IMG SRC="images/aligntest1.gif" ALIGN="TOP" BORDER="1">
This text should be aligned to the top of the image.</P>

<P><IMG SRC="images/aligntest1.gif" ALIGN="MIDDLE" BORDER="1">
This text should be aligned to the middle of the image.</P>

<P><IMG SRC="images/aligntest1.gif" ALIGN="BOTTOM" BORDER="1">
This text should be aligned to the bottom of the image.

</BODY>
</HTML>
```

Figure 6-13. *Basic image alignment*

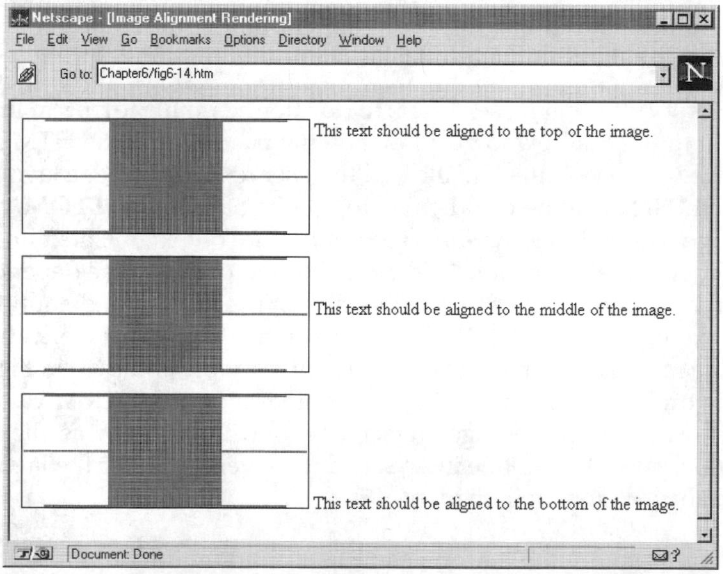

Figure 6-14. *Image alignment rendering*

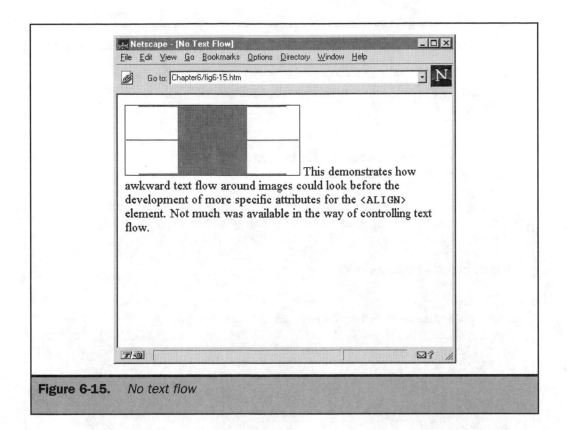

Figure 6-15.   *No text flow*

Netscape introduced the **LEFT** and **RIGHT** values for **ALIGN**, which allowed text to flow around the image. When setting an image element like **<IMG SRC="logo.gif" ALIGN="LEFT">**, the image is aligned to the left and the text flows around to the right. Correspondingly, when you are using markup like **<IMG SRC="logo.gif" ALIGN="RIGHT">** the image is aligned to the right and the text flows around to the left. It is even possible to flow the text between two objects if things are done carefully. The HTML in Figure 6-16 shows how the **ALIGN** attribute would be used to flow text around images. The rendering of this last example is shown in Figure 6-17.

Notice in the example markup in Figure 6-16 that there is a special attribute to the **
** element. This is necessary to force the text to flow properly and will be discussed shortly. However, there are still some aspects of the **ALIGN** attribute that should be discussed. There is some confusion regarding the use of the value **CENTER** with the **ALIGN** attribute for the **<IMG>** element. Typically, this attribute value acts the same as the **MIDDLE** value and should be avoided. To actually center an image in the middle of the screen requires enclosing the image within **<P ALIGN="CENTER">**, **<DIV ALIGN="CENTER">**, or a plain **<CENTER>** element.

Netscape and Microsoft also support four other values for **ALIGN: TEXTOP, BASELINE, ABSMIDDLE,** and **ABSBOTTOM.** All these attributes should be

```
<!DOCTYPE HTML PUBLIC "-//W3C//DTD HTML 3.2 Final//EN">
<HTML>
<HEAD>
<TITLE>Text Flow Rendering</TITLE>
</HEAD>
<BODY>

<IMG SRC="images/redsquare.gif" ALIGN="left">
The top image has its ALIGN attribute set to "left," so the
text flows around it to the right. The top image has its ALIGN
attribute set to "left," so the text flows around it to the
right. The top image has its ALIGN attribute set to "left,"
so the text flows around it to the right.

<BR CLEAR=left><BR><BR>

<IMG SRC="images/redsquare.gif" ALIGN="right">
The top image has its ALIGN attribute set to "right," so the
text flows around it to the left. The top image has its ALIGN
attribute set to "right," so the text flows around it to the
left. The top image has its ALIGN attribute set to "right,"
so the text flows around it to the left.

</BODY>
</HTML>
```

Figure 6-16.   *Text flow image alignment*

avoided in most cases, since they may not be supported identically across browsers and are not yet part of any standards. Positioning is handled more precisely by technologies like style sheets, to be discussed in Chapter 10. The basic meaning of these attribute values is discussed here.

Setting the **ALIGN** attribute to **TEXTTOP** aligns the top of an image with the top of the tallest character in the current line; this attribute works erratically under various browsers. The **BASELINE** value aligns the bottom of an image with the baseline of the text in the current line. (The baseline is the unseen line that all the characters sit on.) **ABSMIDDLE** aligns the middle of an image with the middle of the text in the current

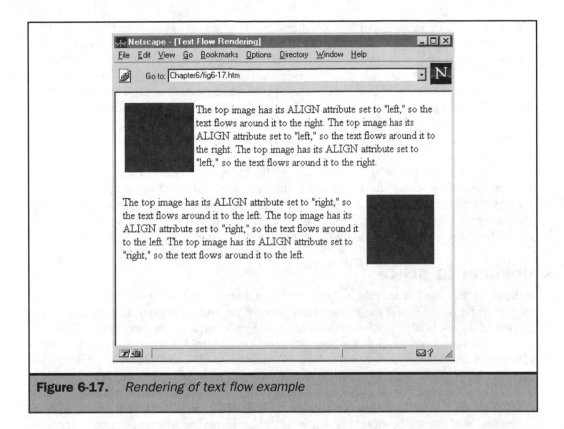

Figure 6-17.   *Rendering of text flow example*

line, which means in the actual middle of the characters themselves. The **ABSBOTTOM** value aligns the bottom of an image with the bottom of the lowest item in the current line of text, including descender characters, such as lowercase "y" and "g," that go below the baseline. Unlike **ABSBOTTOM, BASELINE** does not include the descenders in a character. For example, in a lowercase "g," the lower half of the letter will sit below the baseline.

HSPACE and VSPACE

Just floating an image and allowing text to wrap around it may not be adequate. There is also the issue of how to position the image more precisely with the text and make sure that text breaks where it ought to. Initially introduced by Netscape and made official in HTML 3.2, the **HSPACE** and **VSPACE** attributes can be used to introduce "run around" or buffer space around an inland image. The **HSPACE** attribute is used to insert a buffer of horizontal space on the left and right of an image, while the

VSPACE attribute is used to insert a buffer of vertical space in between the top and bottom of the image and other objects. The value of both attributes should be a positive number of pixels. While under some browsers it may be possible to set the attribute values to percentage values, this is inadvisable, as very high values may produce strange results. However, the most problematic aspect of the **HSPACE** and **VSPACE** attributes is the amount of buffer space that occurs on both sides of the image. Take a look at the HTML markup in Figure 6-18 to see how **HSPACE** and **VSPACE** work. Figure 6-19 displays a possible browser rendering of the code in Figure 6-18.

It turns out that in the future, by using style sheets (discussed in Chapter 10), it may be possible to avoid these somewhat imprecise layout features altogether. The **HSPACE** and **VSPACE** attributes have been very useful, albeit occasionally abused by Web designers. How these attributes can be used in conjunction with the so-called invisible *pixel gif* to force layouts will be discussed in Chapter 8.

Extensions to

In flowing text around an image, there may be a situation where the designer wants to clear the text flow around the image. For example, creating a caption like the one shown in Figure 6-20 might be somewhat problematic because the text may reflow.

To deal with such problems, a new attribute called **CLEAR** was added to the **
** element; this extension is now part of the HTML standard. The **CLEAR** attribute can be set to **LEFT**, **RIGHT**, **ALL**, or **NONE** and will clear the gutter around an inline object like an image. For example, imagine the fragment **<IMG SRC="photo. gif" ALIGN="LEFT">** with text wrapping around it. If **<BR CLEAR="LEFT">** is included in the text and the wrapped text is still wrapping around the image, the text will be cleared to pass the image. The **CLEAR="RIGHT"** attribute to **
** works for text flowing around right-aligned images. Of course, setting the attribute to **NONE** makes the element act as it normally would and is implied when using the **
** by itself. An example of the use of this attribute is found in Figure 6-21.

HEIGHT and WIDTH

The **HEIGHT** and **WIDTH** attributes to the **<IMG>** element, introduced in HTML 3.2, are used to set the dimensions of an image. The value for these attributes is either a positive pixel value or a percentage value from 1 to 100 percent. While an image can be stretched or shrunk with this attribute, the main purpose is actually to reserve space for images that are being downloaded. As pages are requested by a browser, each individual image is requested separately. However, the browser can't lay out parts of the page, including text, until the space that the image takes up is determined. This may mean waiting for the image to download completely. By telling the browser

```
<!DOCTYPE HTML PUBLIC "-//W3C//DTD HTML 3.2 Final//EN">
<HTML>
<HEAD>
<TITLE>HSPACE and VSPACE Example Rendering</TITLE>
</HEAD>

<FONT SIZE="4">
<P>
The image below has its <FONT FACE="Courier"><B>&lt;HSPACE&gt;</B>
</FONT> and <FONT FACE="Courier"><B>&lt;VSPACE&gt;</B></FONT>
attributes set to 50 pixels, so the text will flow around it at
a distance of 50 pixels. The rest of this text is dummy text.
If it said anything interesting you would certainly be the
first to know.

<IMG SRC="images/redsquare.gif" ALIGN=LEFT HSPACE="50"
VSPACE="50">

This is dummy text. If it said anything interesting you would
certainly be the first to know. There's really no point in
reading the rest of it. This is dummy text. If it said anything
interesting you would certainly be the first to know. There's
really no point in reading the rest of it. This is dummy text.
If it said anything interesting you would certainly be the first
to know. There's really no point in reading the rest of it. This
is dummy text. If it said anything interesting you would certainly
be the first to know. There's really no point in reading the rest
of it. This is dummy text. If it said anything interesting you
would certainly be the first to know. There's really no point in
reading the rest of it. This is dummy text. If it said anything
interesting you would certainly be the first to know. There's
really no point in reading the rest of it.</P></FONT>

</BODY>
</HTML>
```

Figure 6-18.   *HSPACE and VSPACE example*

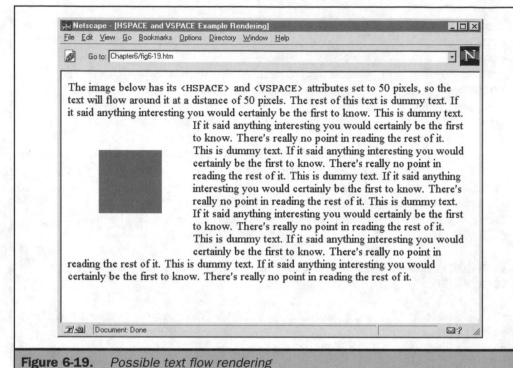

Figure 6-19. Possible text flow rendering

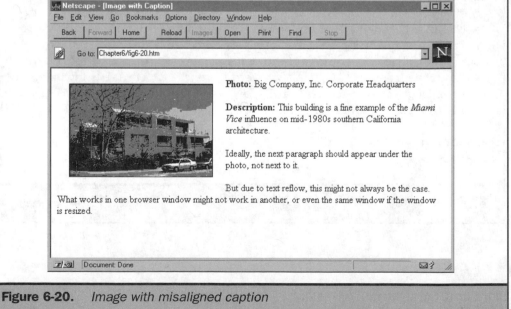

Figure 6-20. Image with misaligned caption

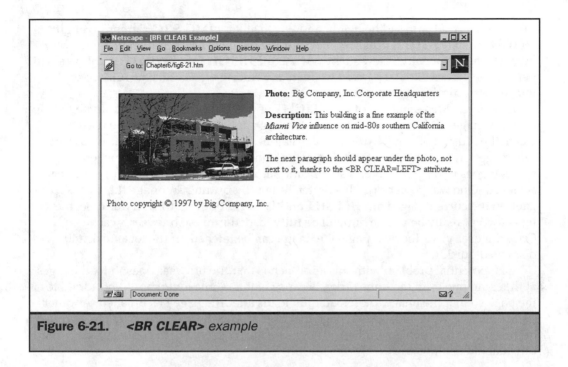

Figure 6-21. *<BR CLEAR> example*

the height and width of the image, the browser can go ahead and reserve space with a bounding box into which the image will load. Setting the height and width thus allows a browser to download and lay out text quickly while the images are still loading. For an image called test.gif that has a height of 10 and width of 150, use **<IMG SRC="test.gif" HEIGHT="10" WIDTH="150">**. The usability improvement of using **HEIGHT** and **WIDTH** attributes for images is significant, and they should always be included.

Note *Many people wonder what the measurements of a particular image are. Using Netscape, it is possible to view the dimensions quite easily. First, load the image into the browser by itself without any accompanying HTML. Now look at the title bar of the browser, which should display the dimensions. Also, using the option to view document information for the image within the browser should reveal the dimensions.*

Beyond the prelayout advantages, the **HEIGHT** and **WIDTH** attributes can also be used to size images. This is rarely a good idea, as the image may end up being distorted. One way to avoid distortion is to shrink images in a proportional manner. However, if the image is to be made smaller, it is a better idea to size the image appropriately in a graphics program. Shrinking the image with the **HEIGHT** and **WIDTH** attributes does not affect the file size, while resizing the image beforehand will shrink the file, and hence reduce the download time. Another use of **HEIGHT** and **WIDTH** sizing might be to grow a flat image. For example, imagine an image of a single green pixel, and set the height and width alike: **<IMG SRC="greenpixel.gif" HEIGHT="100" WIDTH="100">**. The resulting image is a large green box with very little download penalty. A few sites even use the **HEIGHT** and **WIDTH** attributes with percentage values like 100 percent to create interesting effects such as full-screen images or vertical or horizontal color bars.

One other interesting use of the **HEIGHT** and **WIDTH** attributes would be to help preload images. With the desire for fast-loading pages, preloading can be used to create the illusion of a quick download. Imagine that during the idle time on a page, the images on the next page are being downloaded so that they are precached when the user goes to the next page. A significant perceived performance improvement is achieved. One way to perform this prefetching is by putting an image that will appear later on the current page with **HEIGHT** and **WIDTH** both set to **1**. In this case, the image won't really be visible but will be fully loaded into the browser's cache. Once the user visits the next page, the image can be fetched off the local disk and displayed quickly.

One potential problem with this approach is that the browser doesn't load images at the same rate or in the same order. Because of this, some logic should be added to the page so that the image to preload only loads after the page has finished. Another issue occurs if the user chooses a page that doesn't use the prefetched image. Because of these potential problems, a linear order of pages is probably the only structure than can benefit from this trick.

 The possibilities for preloading are significant. Already, Microsoft has made a preloading control available that loads not only images, but whole pages, in advance. WebTV also supports similar preloading functionality in another manner.

LOWSRC

Another potential speed improvement introduced by Netscape, not currently part of the HTML 4.0 standard, is the **LOWSRC** attribute. The **LOWSRC** attribute should be set to the URL of an image to load in first, before the so-called high source image indicated by the **SRC** attribute. In this sense, the attribute can be set to the address of a low-resolution or black-and-white file, which can be downloaded first and then followed by a high-resolution file. For example,

```
<IMG SRC="hi-res-photo.gif" LOWSRC="bw-photo.gif" HEIGHT="100"
WIDTH="100" ALT="Outside of building photograph">
```

The **LOWSRC** attribute can provide significant usability improvement when large full-screen images must be used.

One interesting aspect of the **LOWSRC** attribute is that the browser tends to use the image dimensions of the **LOWSRC** file to reserve space within the Web page if the **HEIGHT** and **WIDTH** attributes are not set. Because of this, some strange distortion could happen if the high-resolution image is not the same size as the low-resolution image. This problem actually occurs under versions of Netscape.

Another interesting aspect of the **LOWSRC** attribute is the possibility for simple animation. For example, the **LOWSRC** attribute could be set to a picture of a closed book and the regular **SRC** attribute set to a picture of an open book. When loaded, it appears as a small two-frame animation. However, this method of animation is very simplistic and lacks timing; so while it might look good on a relatively slow connection, the effect may be lost over a T1 connection where the images load rapidly. For animation, an animated GIF should be used as discussed earlier in the chapter. Animated GIFs require no special syntax and may be used for either **SRC** or **LOWSRC**. If more complex animation is required, using an **<EMBED>** or **<OBJECT>** element to reference a Shockwave file might be in order, as discussed in Chapter 7.

These are only the most basic attributes for the **<IMG>** element. A more complete listing of **<IMG>** element attributes can be found in the element reference, as well as the section "Full Syntax of Image" later in this chapter, which discusses other image attributes.

Images as Buttons

One of the most important aspects of images, as previously discussed in Chapter 5, is how they can be combined with the **<A>** element to create buttons. To make an image "pressable," simply enclose it within an anchor.

```
<A HREF="http://www.bigcompany.com"><IMG SRC="logo.gif"></A>
```

When the page is rendered in the browser, clicking on the image will take the user to the anchor destination specified. Generally, to indicate that an image is pressable, the browser will put a border around the image, as well as provide some feedback to the user when the cursor or pointing device is over the hot area, such as turning the pointer to a finger or highlighting the text. For some basic feedback types, note the example in Figure 6-22, which shows a border, finger pointer, and URL destination all indicating that the image is pressable.

One issue that may be troublesome for page designers is the border that appears around the image when it is made pressable. As of HTML 3.2, it is possible to turn this border off by setting the **BORDER** attribute of the image equal to **0**. For example,

```
<A HREF="http://www.bigcompany.com"><IMG SRC="logo.gif" BORDER="0"></A>
```

Figure 6-22.   *Image button feedback*

Of course, without the border it might be difficult to determine which images on a page are links and which are not. This can cause users to play a little game of finding the active click region by running their mouse all over the screen. One way to avoid such usability problems is to provide visual cues in images that are made pressable. These might include embossing, beveling, or drop shadows. Examples of such buttons are shown in Figure 6-23.

While from a design perspective some of the effects, particularly drop shadows, are a little overblown, there are tangible benefits to adding feedback information to button graphics. Another approach to providing feedback about what images are clickable is to animate the buttons. Using a very simple piece of JavaScript, it is possible to animate a button so that when a mouse passes over an image it comes alive. A brief discussion about how HTML pages can be made more dynamic using a scripting language like JavaScript can be found in Chapter 14.

One nonbutton-oriented use of the **BORDER** attribute is to put a simple stroke around an image. Many times people will use a graphics tool to create a frame on an image, but the **BORDER** attribute is a bandwidth-cheap way to get much of the same effect. Try setting the **BORDER** attribute equal to a positive value on a nonclickable

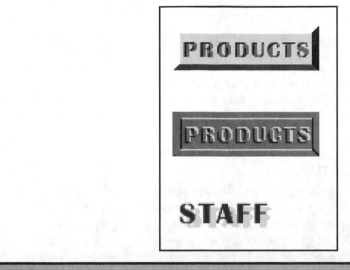

Figure 6-23.   *Button styles for usability*

image, for example **<IMG SRC="portrait.gif" BORDER="5">**. This little change provides an easy way to frame an image and might even lend itself to interesting design ideas.

Image Maps

Another form of clickable images, discussed previously in Chapter 5, is the idea of an image map. An image map is a large image that contains numerous hot spots that can be selected, sending the user to a different anchor destination. There are two basic forms of image maps: *server side* and *client side*. In the server-side image map, the user clicks on an image but the server must decode where the user clicked before the destination page (if any) is loaded. With client-side image maps, all of the map information—which regions map to which URLs—can be specified in the same HTML file that contains the image. Including the map data with the image and letting the browser decode it has several advantages, including:

1. There is no need to visit a server to determine the destination so links are resolved faster.

2. Destination URLs can be shown in the status box as the user's pointer moves over the image.

3. Image maps can be created and tested locally, without requiring a server or system administration support.

4. Client-side image maps can be created so that they present an alternate text menu to users of text-only browsers.

While this discussion makes it obvious that client-side image maps are far superior to their server-side cousins, older browsers may not support this feature. This does not have to be a problem, since it is possible to include support for both types of image maps at once.

Server-Side Image Maps

To specify a server-side image map, the **<A>** element is used to enclose a specially marked **<IMG>** element. The **<A>** element's **HREF** attribute should be set to the URL of the program or map file to decode the image map. The **<IMG>** element must contain the attribute **ISMAP** so the browser can decode the image appropriately. As with all linked images, it may be desirable to turn the image borders off by setting the **<IMG>** element's **BORDER** attribute equal to **0**. As mentioned in Chapter 5, server-side image maps do not provide adequate feedback to the user because they show coordinates, and may incur performance penalties. HTML authors are encouraged to use client-side image maps.

Client-Side Image Maps

The key to using a client-side map is to add the **USEMAP** attribute to the **<IMG>** element and have it reference a **<MAP>** element that defines the image map's active areas. An example of the **<IMG>** element syntax is **<IMG SRC="controlbar.gif" USEMAP="#controlmap">**. Note that, like server-side image maps, the image will be indicated as a link regardless of the lack of the **<A>** element surrounding the **<IMG>**. The **BORDER** attribute should be set to **0** if necessary.

The **<MAP>** element generally occurs within the same document, though support for it outside of the current document is sparse at best. This is similar, in a sense, to the way server-side maps work. The **<MAP>** element may occur anywhere within the body of an HTML document, though it is usually found at the end of HTML documents.

The **<MAP>** element has one attribute, **NAME**, which is used to specify the identifier associated with the map. The map name is then referenced within the **<IMG>** element using the **USEMAP** attribute and the associated fragment identifier. The **<MAP>** element must have a closing **</MAP>** element. Within the **<MAP>** and **</MAP>** tags are defined "shapes" that are mapped onto an image and define the hot spots for the image map. Shapes are defined by the **<AREA>** element, which is found only within the **<MAP>** element. The format of the mapping tags is discussed in Chapter 5. However, memorizing or creating client- or server-side image maps by hand is not advised. Page designers should be able to find tools to automate the creation of image hot spots.

It is possible to combine support for both server-side and client-side image maps into one file. The browser will typically override the server-side support with the improved client-side style. This approach will guarantee backward compatibility with older browsers. To support both, use the **ISMAP** and **USEMAP** attributes in conjunction with an embedded map and a remote map as shown in the following code fragment:

```
<A HREF="shapes.map">
<IMG SRC="shapes.gif" USEMAP="#shapes" BORDER="0" ISMAP WIDTH="400"
HEIGHT="200"></A>
```

Client-side image maps have a variety of attributes that can be used with the **<AREA>** element. Server-side image maps really have no attributes other than those normally associated with the <IMG> element, such as **BORDER**. The important attributes supported in HTML 3.2 and 4.0 are discussed in Chapter 5.

Full Syntax of Image

The previous discussion has only touched on the most common uses of the <IMG> element and how it works in the case of buttons and image maps. There are numerous other attributes to the element, however, some of which are proprietary to particular browsers. A fairly complete extended syntax for the <IMG> element is presented in Table 6-3.

Attribute Name	Possible Value(s)	Description
SRC	URL	References the source (URL) of an image file (GIF or JPG)
ALIGN	ABSBOTTOM, ABSMIDDLE, BASELINE, BOTTOM, LEFT, and MIDDLE	Sets alignment for the image within the page relative to text
ALT	"*Alternative text description*"	Provides a text alternative to the image

Table 6-3.   *Complete Syntax of <IMG>*

Attribute Name	Possible Value(s)	Description
BORDER	*Number (pixels)*	Sets the thickness of the border for an image; 0 "turns off" the border
CLASS	*Class name*	Indicates the class for the style sheet reference
CONTROLS	N/A	Displays controls under a video clip (Internet Explorer)
DATAFLD	*Data column*	Identifies the column name in a database or file identified by DATASRC (Internet Explorer)
DATASRC	*Data source*	Identifies database or file to provide information for this element or its attributes, such as SRC (Internet Explorer)
DIR	LTR and RTL	Determines text direction for the ALT attribute
DYNSRC	*"URL of movie"*	Specifies the URL of a video clip (Internet Explorer)
HEIGHT	*Number (pixels or percentage)*	Sets the height of an image
HSPACE	*Number (pixels)*	Creates a margin around the horizontal sides of an image
ID	*Unique identifier*	Defines a document-wide identifier
ISMAP	N/A	Defines an image as a server-side image map
LANGUAGE	JAVASCRIPT, JSCRIPT, VBS, and VBSCRIPT	Determines the scripting language for any bound events
LONGDESC	*URL of long description*	Links to a page that provides a longer description of an image, similar to ALT

Table 6-3.   *Complete Syntax of <IMG>* (continued)

Attribute Name	Possible Value(s)	Description
LOOP	*Positive number*, INFINITE, and -1	Sets the number of times a sound or video will loop (Internet Explorer)
LOWSRC	*"URL of low source image"*	References a low-source image to load in before a high-source image
RELOAD	*Number*	Determines the frequency of image reloading (WebTV)
SELECTED	*Coordinates (x, y)*	Determines the area to be selected in an image map (WebTV)
START	FILEOPEN and MOUSEOVER	Defines when a video clip will start playing (Internet Explorer)
STYLE	*Style information*	Identifies an inline style sheet for the <IMG> element
TITLE	*Text*	Provides advisory information for rating of Web pages
TRANSPARENCY	0 to 100	Determines relative transparency of an image (0=no transparency; 100=complete transparency) (WebTV)
USEMAP	*"URL of map file"*	Defines an image as a client-side image map; names the MAP to be used
VSPACE	*Number (pixels)*	Creates a margin around the vertical sides of an image, in pixels
WIDTH	*Number (pixels or percentage)*	Sets the height of an image

Table 6-3.   *Complete Syntax of **<IMG>*** (continued)

Attribute Name	Possible Value(s)	Description
Events: onclick, ondblclick, onmousedown, onmouseup, onmouseover, onmousemove, onmouseout, onkeypress, onkeydown, onkeyup	*Script handler*	Binds an image event to a script

Table 6-3. *Complete Syntax of <IMG>* (continued)

Most of these attributes have been discussed previously; however, a few of the ones that have not will be pointed out here.

Dynamic Data Attributes

Microsoft's Internet Explorer supports a dynamic image source attribute called **DYNSRC** that allows the page author to specify the address of a video clip or VRML world to display in the window. Typically, this is used for displaying AVI movie files in the windows as introduced in Internet Explorer 2.0. The **LOOP**, **CONTROL**, and **START** attributes are extensions that are used in conjunction with the **DYNSRC** attribute to control the looping and the dynamic content. A more detailed discussion and example of adding a movie to a Web page with this attribute, as well as with other elements, can be found in Chapter 7.

Another aspect of Microsoft additions is the idea of dynamically bound data. Using the **DATAFLD** and **DATASRC** attributes, it is possible to bind an <IMG> element. The **DATASRC** attribute is used to specify the data source from which to pull data, which is quite often a database. The **DATAFLD** attribute is used to specify the column within that data source. While these attributes make a great deal of sense in relation to tables, their meaning with regard to images is less than clear. At this point, it is best to leave the discussion of how dynamic data can be added to a page to the discussion of databinding in Chapter 8.

WebTV Specifics

WebTV has several attribute extensions to the <IMG> element. For example, the **ANI** attribute can be set to the URL of an animation file. Other related attributes allow the page designer to position the animation as well as control it, so the animation begins only when selected by the user or loops continuously. Page authors are cautioned to avoid using these attributes as WebTV has indicated that they may be depreciated in favor of animation forms like Macromedia Flash.

Another attribute specific to WebTV is the **LOOP** attribute, which indicates how often an image should be reloaded. By default, there is no image reloading, but it can be set to any positive number to reload the image a certain number of times. This could be used to create an updating page if the contents of the image were dynamically changed on the server side.

The **SELECTED** attribute can be used in conjunction with an image map so that an initial spot or selection is selected on the image. The value of the **SELECTED** attribute is either the x, y coordinate if the image is a server-side map or an index of the area within the map file.

Probably the most interesting attribute with the **<IMG>** element under WebTV is **TRANSPARENCY**. In the WebTV browser, setting the **TRANSPARENCY** attribute of an image allows the background to show through. A value of **0** indicates the image is fully opaque, while a value of **100** indicates the image is fully transparent. WebTV will probably introduce a number of other extensions to HTML that take into consideration the less than optimal viewing environment. Interested readers should visit the WebTV site at www.webtv.net for the most current information on authoring for the device.

Scripting and Style Considerations for Images

Because an image may be referenced by a style sheet or by a scripting environment, it may be very important to provide a name or identifier for it. The **CLASS**, **ID**, and **NAME** attributes can be used to provide names for images so they can be referenced and manipulated by scripting or style information that is usually found in the head of the document. Names should be unique and in the proper HTML form. The **TITLE** attribute may also be set to provide advisory text about what the image is. While with other elements a browser may render the **TITLE** information as a tool tip, most browsers appear to use the **ALT** attribute instead, as shown earlier in this chapter.

It is possible to include inline scripting or style information directly with an image. For example, setting the **STYLE** attribute allows an inline style to bind to the particular **<IMG>** element. Style sheets are discussed in Chapter 10. Furthermore, it is possible to have images bound to a particular event using an event attribute such as **onmouseover** and tying it to a script. There are many events defined under the preliminary HTML 4.0 specification, and some browsers like Microsoft Internet Explorer 4.0 and above have an even richer event model. Table 6-4 lists the events for the **<IMG>** element in all cases and marks those that are currently Microsoft specific.

Events can be used like attributes within the **<IMG>** element itself and set to call script code or even have it included inline. A very simple but motivating use of the dynamic event model with images is to have the image change state depending on the

onabort (Microsoft)	onafterupdate (Microsoft)
onbeforeupdate (Microsoft)	onblur (Microsoft)
onclick	ondblclick
onerror (Microsoft)	onfocus (Microsoft)
onhelp (Microsoft)	onkeydown
onkeypress	onkeyup
onload (Microsoft)	onmousedown
onmousemove	onmouseout
onmouseover	onmouseup
onreadystatechange (Microsoft)	

Table 6-4.   *Image Events (Microsoft-Specific and Non-Microsoft-Specific)*

user's action. The most basic use would be to create animated buttons or buttons that make a sound when clicked, but the possibilities are endless. A more detailed discussion and examples of how to bind JavaScript to an image event are presented in Chapter 14.

Image and Color Attributes for <BODY>

The **<BODY>** element has numerous attributes that can be used to affect the display of content in the body of the document. These include background colors, the color of the text and links in the document, and background images. Some attributes, like the ones that set margin values and the properties of background images, only work in Internet Explorer. With the rise of style sheets, most of the attributes for presentation used in the body have been depreciated in the HTML 4.0 specification, though it is doubtful that their use will diminish for some time.

Color-Based <BODY>Attributes: BGCOLOR, TEXT, and the LINK Family

One of the most commonly used **<BODY>** element attributes, **BGCOLOR** defines the document's background color. This was a distinct improvement over the default gray (or white under Macintosh) of Mosaic, although it and the other **<BODY>** attributes have led to a multitude of sins. Employed wisely, they can enhance a page's appearance; misused, they have been known to induce migraines. Hexadecimal RGB values and color names can be used with **BGCOLOR** and the four attributes to follow. To create a white background, the attribute could be set to **BGCOLOR="#FFFFFF"** (hexadecimal) or simply **BGCOLOR="white"**. Most browsers will recognize words such as "white," "red," or "black" and render the background accordingly. Determining the HTML hexadecimal value for a particular color isn't difficult when following the basic formula of *#RRGGBB*, where *RR* equals the hex value for red, *GG* for green, and *BB* for blue. If the hex value for all "off", or zero, is **00**, and the hex value for all "on" is **FF**, then the color **#FF0000** is red. All the red in the image is turned on in this case. A value of **#000000** would be black, **#0000FF** would be blue. and so on. According to the HTML 4.0 specification, there are 16 widely known color names that correspond to the standard VGA colors. These names and their values are shown in Table 6-5.

There are many other color names that are referenced by browser vendors; these are listed in Appendix E. The problem with using browser vendor-defined colors is that they don't always do what they are supposed to do. Under Netscape 4.0, the color "aliceblue" doesn't look very close to the Internet Explorer color. Even worse, you can invent your own colors. Try setting the following and viewing it under Netscape and Microsoft Internet Explorer:

```
<BODY BGCOLOR="HTML COLOR NAMES ARE TROUBLESOME">
```

This color name is totally invalid, but it still results in a shade of green that is very distinct in each browser. It is possible to make up colors like "chilidog brown" or "stale beer yellow," but this is no more recommended than using the Netscape-defined color of "Dodgerblue."

Black=#000000	Green=#008000
Silver=#C0C0C0	Lime=#00FF00
Gray=#808080	Olive=#808000
White=#FFFFFF	Yellow=#FFFF00
Maroon=#800000	Navy=#000080
Red=#FF0000	Blue=#0000FF
Purple=#800080	Teal=#008080
Fuchsia= #FF00FF	Aqua=#00FFFF

Table 6-5. *Common HTML Color Names*

The **TEXT** attribute of the **<BODY>** element defines the color of text in the entire document. The attribute takes a color in the form of either a hex code or color name. Note that the text color can be overridden in the text by applying the **<FONT>** element to selected text with its **COLOR** attribute, as discussed in Chapter 8. Page authors must be extremely careful when setting text and background colors so that readability is preserved. Page designers are often tempted to use light colors on light backgrounds or dark colors on dark backgrounds. For example, a gray text on a black background might look cool, but will it look cool on every person's monitor? If the gamma value of some other person's monitor is much different than your monitor, it will be unreadable. White and black always make a good pairing and red is certainly useful. The best combination, in terms of contrast, is actually yellow and black, but imagine the headache from reading a page that looks like a road sign. Despite the high contrast, designers should be careful of white text on a black background when font sizes are very small, particularly on poor-resolution monitors.

 Gamma *is a term used to describe the relationship between the input and output for a particular image device. Different monitors have inherently different gamma settings. As a result, the same image on two different monitors may appear significantly different. While the gamma of a monitor cannot be changed by the user, monitor settings such as contrast, brightness, and color can be adjusted.*

Besides the body text, it is also possible to define the colors of links by setting the **<BODY>** element attributes: **LINK**, **ALINK**, and **VLINK**.

LINK defines the color of unvisited links in a document. For example, if you've set your background color to black, it might be more useful to use a light link color instead of the standard blue. **ALINK** defines the color of the link as it is being clicked. This is often too quick to be noticed, but can create a flash effect, if desired. For a more subdued Web experience, it might be better to set the **ALINK** attribute to match either the **LINK** attribute or the next one, **VLINK**. **VLINK** defines the color of a link after it has been visited, which under many user agents is purple. Many authors wish to set the value of the **VLINK** attribute to red, which makes sense given standard color interpretation.

Users should be forewarned not to choose link colors that might confuse the viewers. For example, reversing link colors so that visited links are blue and nonvisited links are red could confuse a user. While it is unlikely that a page author would do such a thing, it has been seen more than once—particularly in situations where the look and feel is the driving force of the site. Other common problems with link color changes include the idea of setting all link values to blue with the belief that users will revisit sections thinking they haven't been there before. While this may make sense from a marketing standpoint, the frustration factor due to the lost navigation cues may override any potential benefit from extra visits.

Creating Background Effects with Image Files

Besides setting background colors, you can also change the appearance of a Web page by setting a background image using the **BACKGROUND** attribute. The value of **BACKGROUND** is the URL for a GIF or JPEG file, usually one in the image directory of the Web site in question: **BACKGROUND="images/tile.gif"**. The value could just as easily include a complete URL to access an image at another site, but this would be a rather unwieldy approach to the task at hand. Images accessed in this fashion repeat, or *tile*, in the background of a Web page. This can make or break a Web page. Imagine someone who used the **BACKGROUND** attribute to place a 200 × 300 pixel JPEG of a favorite dog on his or her home page. The dog's image would repeat, both vertically and horizontally, in the background of the page. This would make the dog's owner very happy—and make the page very difficult to read. Figure 6-24 shows an example of a bothersome repeating background.

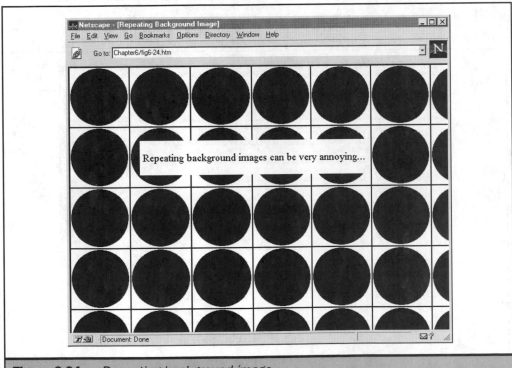

Figure 6-24.   *Repeating background image*

In general, complex background images tend to be a poor design decision. Taking the subtle approach can backfire as well. Some users attempt to create a light background like a texture or watermark thinking that, like paper, it will create a classy effect. The problem with this is that under many monitors, the image may be difficult to make out at all, or the texture may even blur the text on top of it slightly. Just like setting background colors, the most important consideration is the degree of contrast. Always attempt to keep the foreground and background at a high level of contrast so that users can read the information. What good is an impressive layout if nobody can read it?

If a background is desired, image manipulation programs such as Photoshop can be used to create seamless background tiles that are more pleasing to the eye and show no seam; but this, too, can be abused. Figure 6-25 demonstrates the idea of a repeating background tile.

Background images, or tiles, can also be used to create other effects. A single GIF 5 pixels high and 1,200 pixels wide could be used to create a useful page layout. The first 200 horizontal pixels of the GIF could be black, while the rest could be white. Assuming 1,200 pixels as the maximum width of a browser, this tile would only repeat

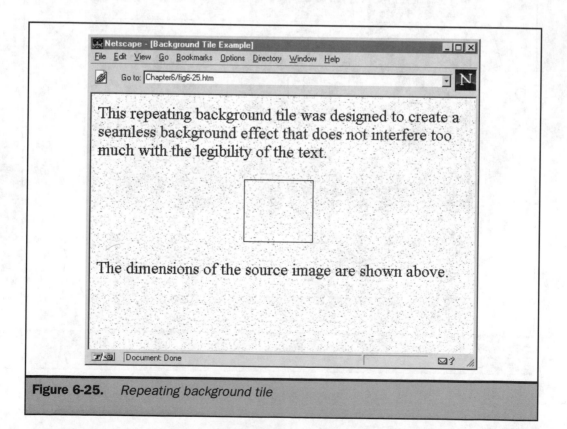

Figure 6-25. *Repeating background tile*

vertically, thus creating the illusion of a two-tone background. This has become a very common concept on the Web. Many sites use the left-hand color for navigation buttons, while the remaining area is used for text, as shown in Figure 6-26. Some designers try to minimize file size and download time by making such background images a single pixel tall, but this can be overkill; if the image is too narrow, it will take longer for the browser to draw it in. A background image can be 5 pixels or taller, depending on how many colors are used. If colors are kept to a minimum, there is no harm in making the image 20 or 30 pixels high.

Creating more than two areas with the background image can be overcomplicated. Another method is to use a vertical image in order to create horizontal areas (Figure 6-27).

On the down side, such backgrounds will still repeat if viewed on a monitor with a particularly large screen resolution, such as 1,600 × 1,200. Advanced layouts that look great on Mac or Windows machines often have serious problems when viewed on a Unix machine. There are other practical limitations to this approach. Generally speaking, it is necessary to choose between vertical and horizontal background tile effects. A long, narrow two-color GIF file of 5 to 10K offers an economical approach to backgrounds. A huge background that tries to juggle both dimensions will probably

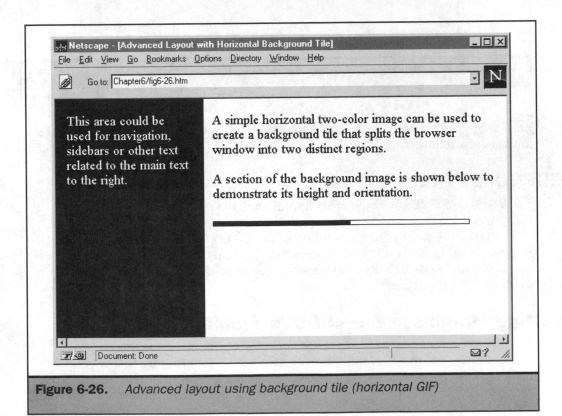

Figure 6-26.   *Advanced layout using background tile (horizontal GIF)*

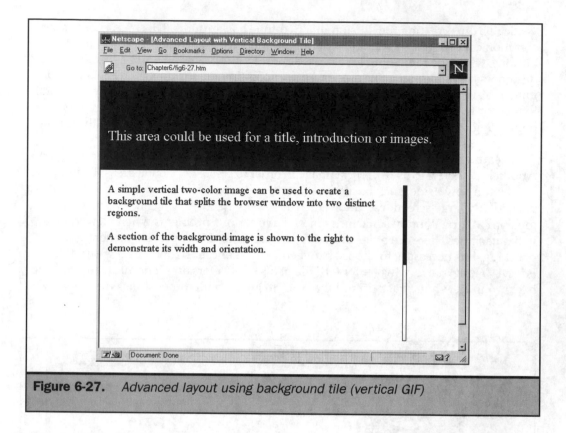

Figure 6-27. *Advanced layout using background tile (vertical GIF)*

need to be 1,200 or more pixels in both directions, with a resulting increase in file size and download time.

BGPROPERTIES

The **BGPROPERTIES** attribute offers a solution to the problem of scrolling background images. At present, however, it is only supported by Internet Explorer. The **<BODY>** element's attribute and value **BGPROPERTIES="fixed"** will, under Internet Explorer, allow text and images to scroll while the background image accessed with the **BACKGROUND** attribute remains in place. The only value for this attribute is **"fixed"**.

Setting Margins in the <BODY> Element

The **<BODY>** element also allows the setting of margins, but so far this is only realized under Internet Explorer. There are two **<BODY>** attributes that affect margins: **LEFTMARGIN** and **TOPMARGIN**. Each is set with a number value. For example, **LEFTMARGIN="25"** will create a margin of 25 pixels between the left edge of the browser window and its content; **TOPMARGIN="15"** will create a 15-pixel margin between the top of the browser window and its content, as well as at the bottom if the content extends that far. Figure 6-28 shows an example of margins with these values under Internet Explorer.

WebTV <BODY> Settings

WebTV supports a variety of attributes to the **<BODY>** element that are useful for controlling background images and content including **NOHTILEBG, NOVTLEBG, HSPACE, VSPACE, XSPEED,** and **YSPEED.** The **NOVTILEBG** prevents a background image from tiling vertically. This attribute takes no value and when found in the **<BODY>** element it will allow a background image to repeat horizontally but not vertically. The color that may have been set by the **BGCOLOR** attribute will then show through in any area below the one horizontal tiling. Note that when the **NOVTILEBG** attribute is set, the background image that is found at the top of the page won't scroll along with the page. The **NOHTILEBIG** attribute prevents an image from tiling horizontally so the background is only tiled once vertically. In the case of color sidebars, this is a nice addition as it prevents the bars from reappearing on a very

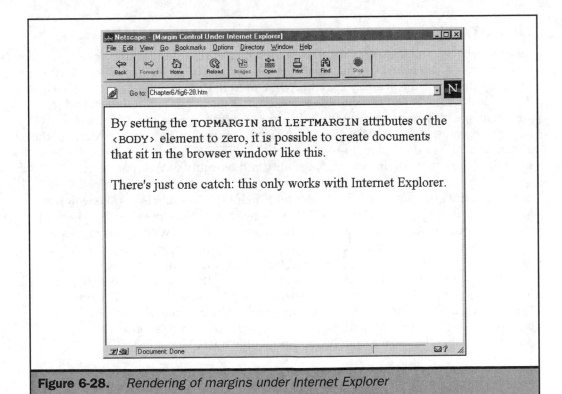

Figure 6-28.   *Rendering of margins under Internet Explorer*

wide monitor. As with **NOVTILEBG**, any space not taken up by the background image will default to the **BGCOLOR** setting. The **HSPACE** and **VSPACE** attributes for the **<BODY>** element under WebTV allow the page author to specify horizontal and vertical buffers between the edge of the screen and the content of the page. The default values for **VSPACE** and **HSPACE** are 6 and 8 pixels, respectively. On some pages, such as full-screen splash images, setting the **HSPACE** and **VSPACE** to **0** might allow for an interesting full-screen bleed effect. The **XSPEED** and **YSPEED** attributes control the speed in which a background image scrolls horizontally and vertically, respectively. Note that under WebTV, the Web page content remains in place while the background image moves. The value for both **XSPEED** and **YSPEED** is in pixels per second. By default, the value for both is **0**, but values of **1** (slow scroll) to **4** (fast scroll) are responsible settings for the attribute. Despite their proprietary nature, many of these extensions are useful given the viewing environment for WebTV.

While many of the body properties discussed in the last few sections are useful to set the color and image attributes of a page, many of them are browser specific or are depreciated under HTML 4.0. It is too soon to tell if users will embrace image layout via style sheets or continue to use the elements previously discussed. For backward compatibility, it may be required to use both layout forms for another year or two.

Summary

Like them or not, inline images are what helped popularize the Web. However, just because images can be used to improve the look and feel of a Web page doesn't mean that they should be the primary content. While presentation is important to the Web, it is still fundamentally about the communication of information, some of which does well in image form and some of which does not. Adding images to a Web page is accomplished using the **<IMG>** element, which has numerous attributes. Many of the attributes of the **<IMG>** element—including **ALT**, **HEIGHT**, **WIDTH**, and **LOWSRC**—are useful to improve accessibility and usability of Web pages.

As always, the eternal struggle between nice-looking pages and download time continues, and knowledge of HTML features is helpful to combat excessive wait time. Many of the other attributes for the **<IMG>** element were developed with layout in mind, particularly **ALIGN**. Images can be used in conjunction with colors to create motivating layouts, including tiled backgrounds. In the future, style sheets may take over the duties of many of these attributes; but for the moment, their use is very important. The next chapter discusses the inclusion of other forms of media objects like movies or sounds. However, once programming is discussed, it will be obvious that a generalized solution for inserting any form of object is the best way to deal with both programming elements and media types like images. In this sense, the syntax presented in this chapter may not be relevant within a few years.

The Complete Reference

Chapter 7

HTML and Other Media Types

Adding images to a Web page is just the tip of the iceberg. Web pages can support a variety of media forms, including animation, sound, video, virtual reality, and other binary forms. Browser vendors have introduced special extensions to handle these new media types, but the long-term solution is to handle all media types in a similar fashion, as plain binary objects. Once programming elements and true interactivity are mixed, things may become even more complicated. This chapter will tie up some loose ends regarding binary object support and miscellaneous vendor-specific elements. It also previews many of the issues that will arise during the discussion of interactivity on the Web.

HTML and Binary Objects

As discussed in Chapter 6, images are not directly part of HTML. Images are binary objects that are included, or pulled into, a Web page. Other objects such as videos, animations, sound files, and programs can be also pulled into Web pages. Initially, since there was no way to insert an object like a video into a Web page inline, the only option was to link to it. By creating a link to a movie file, for example **<A HREF= "trailer.avi">**View Movie Trailer**</A>**, the viewer could click on the link and launch a helper application to view the movie. Combining linked data with helper applications is certainly an easy approach, similar to the way images were supported on the Web before Mosaic introduced support for inline images. So how can objects be inserted and supported inline?

Plug-ins and <EMBED>

First-generation browsers displayed static HTML pages and offered the ability to launch helper applications to view different media and file types. Helper applications still run in separate windows from the browser, providing a nonintegrated experience. In contrast, plug-ins enable users to experience content such as Shockwave files or QuickTime movies directly within a Web page. The plug-in architecture developed by Netscape is also supported by Internet Explorer 3.0.

There are drawbacks to the plug-in approach of extending a browser's features. Users must locate and download plug-ins, install them, and restart their browsers. Many users find this rather complicated. Netscape 4.0 may offer some installation relief with so-called self-installing plug-ins and other features, but for now, plug-ins remain troublesome. Furthermore, plug-ins are not available on every machine; a plug-in binary must be compiled for each particular operating system. Because of this machine-specific approach, many plug-ins only work on Windows-95 and Windows NT. A decreasing number of plug-ins work on Windows 3.1, Macintosh, or UNIX operating systems. Finally, each plug-in installed on a system is a persistent extension to the browser that only needs to be downloaded once, and takes up memory and disk space. More plug-ins equals increased memory requirements. A Macintosh running ten common plug-ins may need 20MB of RAM to operate. Plug-ins are a so-called *fat-client approach*: the more functionality desired, the fatter the client application.

On the upside, Netscape already bundles audio, video, and VRML (Virtual Reality Modeling Language) plug-ins in the browser. Other widely used plug-ins include Macromedia's Shockwave and Adobe's Acrobat format. Adding support for binary objects (sounds, videos, or multimedia files) is a matter of learning the appropriate syntax for the **<EMBED>** element. In general, the **<EMBED>** element takes an **SRC** attribute to specify the URL of the included binary object. **HEIGHT** and **WIDTH** attributes often are used to indicate the pixel dimensions of the included object, if it is visible. To embed a short AVI (Audio-Video Interleave) format movie called "welcome.avi" that could be viewed by the Netscape LiveVideo plug-in, use the following HTML fragment:

```
<EMBED SRC="welcome.avi" HEIGHT="100" WIDTH="100">
```

Beyond this simple example, things get a little more problematic. Beyond **HEIGHT** and **WIDTH**, common attributes include **ALIGN**, **HIDDEN**, **ID**, **HSPACE**, **PALETTE**, **PLUGINSPAGE**, **TITLE**, and **VSPACE**. Some of these attributes, like **ALIGN**, **HSPACE**, and **VSPACE**, work just like those for the **<IMG>** element. These elements may not be supported by all plug-ins. Many other vendor-defined attributes may also be very important. Plug-in vendors are free to define their own attributes, which makes dealing with plug-ins difficult from a developer's point of view. This chapter will discuss built-in Netscape plug-ins and similar Microsoft features. A more generalized discussion of plug-ins, how they work and how to deal with them will be presented in Chapter 14.

<NOEMBED>

One important aspect of plug-ins is the **<NOEMBED>** element. Some browsers do not understand Netscape's plug-in architecture or understand the **<EMBED>** element. Rather than lock these browsers out of a Web page, the **<NOEMBED>** element allows you to provide some alternative text or marked up content. In the short example presented here, an AVI video is embedded in the page. The **<NOEMBED>** element contains an image, which in turn has an alternative text reading set with the **ALT** attribute. Note how the example degrades from a very sophisticated setting all the way down to a text-only environment.

```
<EMBED SRC="welcome.avi" HEIGHT="100" WIDTH="100">
<NOEMBED>
<IMG SRC="welcome.gif" ALT="Welcome to Big Company, Inc.">
</NOEMBED>
```

One big problem with the **<NOEMBED>** approach occurs when a browser supports plug-ins but lacks the specific plug-in to deal with the included binary object. In this case, the user will be presented with a broken puzzle-piece or similar icon, and may be directed to a page to download the missing plug-in. This level of user interaction is inappropriate for novice users who do not understand how to download plug-ins. A better approach is for the page author to attempt to provide pages that do not require setup. More information on the accessibility aspects of plug-ins is presented in Chapter 14.

ActiveX Controls and <OBJECT>

Microsoft's ActiveX technology is another approach to inserting binary objects, such as movie and audio players, into a Web page. ActiveX controls are small binary components that are downloaded to a user's system and may be accessed from within the Web page. Compared to plug-ins, installation is fairly straightforward for the user. It may even be automatic. However, this technology has some security issues that can be very problematic. Because of security and design, the ActiveX control is very different from plug-ins, or Java, though the basic way to access Microsoft's form of binaries is similar as far as HTML is concerned. Microsoft uses the **<OBJECT>** element to insert an ActiveX control in a page. The **<OBJECT>** element acts like the **<EMBED>** element in that it has attributes like **ALIGN**, **HEIGHT**, and **WIDTH**. Beyond this, the two elements are very different. Using **<OBJECT>** with an ActiveX control requires the page author to specify the **CLASSID** value that corresponds to the object to insert. This unique code might be something like **CLSID:99B42120-6EC7-11CF-A6C7-00AA00A47DD2**—not exactly something that is easy to remember. Furthermore, a variety of data items must be passed to the ActiveX control via the **<PARAM>** element, which is included numerous times within the **<OBJECT>** element. The **<PARAM>** element usually has an attribute called **NAME** (used to set the name of the parameter) and a **VALUE** parameter (which sets the value of the particular argument to the control). For example, look at the code fragment shown here, which is used to insert a simple graphical label, and notice how the **FontName** is set to "Arial" using the **<PARAM>** element.

```
<OBJECT ID="IeLabel1" WIDTH="122" HEIGHT="57"
  CLASSID="CLSID:99B42120-6EC7-11CF-A6C7-00AA00A47DD2">
  <PARAM NAME="_ExtentX" VALUE="2582">
  <PARAM NAME="_ExtentY" VALUE="1207">
  <PARAM NAME="Caption" VALUE="Test Label">
  <PARAM NAME="Angle" VALUE="0">
  <PARAM NAME="Alignment" VALUE="4">
  <PARAM NAME="Mode" VALUE="1">
  <PARAM NAME="FillStyle" VALUE="0">
  <PARAM NAME="FillStyle" VALUE="0">
  <PARAM NAME="ForeColor" VALUE="#000000">
  <PARAM NAME="BackColor" VALUE="#C0C0C0">
  <PARAM NAME="FontName" VALUE="Arial">
```

```
<PARAM NAME="FontSize" VALUE="12">
<PARAM NAME="FontItalic" VALUE="0">
<PARAM NAME="FontBold" VALUE="0">
<PARAM NAME="FontUnderline" VALUE="0">
<PARAM NAME="FontStrikeout" VALUE="0">
<PARAM NAME="TopPoints" VALUE="0">
<PARAM NAME="BotPoints" VALUE="0">
</OBJECT>
```

As you can see here, using the **<OBJECT>** element is less than straightforward. Depending on the object being inserted, the parameters may vary wildly. Because of this, Microsoft has provided a variety of tools such as the ControlPad (www.microsoft. com/sitebuilder) that can be used to insert ActiveX controls into a page and set their parameters.

While ActiveX controls were initially the first binary forms to use the **<OBJECT>** element, in the future all binary objects, including images, will probably use this form. The W3C is attempting to standardize included binary data by adopting a generalized approach to binary data using the **<OBJECT>** element. This will be discussed in depth in Chapter 14. For the rest of this discussion, simply note that the syntax of the **<OBJECT>** element, when used in this manner, is best generated by tools, since it is so variable even in the case of included Microsoft controls.

Java Applets

It is also possible to insert new media forms into a Web page using Sun Microsystems' Java. Java technology (http://www.javasoft.com) is an attractive, revolutionary approach to cross-platform, Internet-based development. It promises a platform-neutral development language that allows programs to be written once and deployed on any machine, browser, or operating system that supports the Java virtual machine. It uses small Java programs, called *applets*, that were introduced by Sun's HotJava browser. Today many popular browsers, including Navigator and Internet Explorer, support Java. When applets are referenced in a Web page using the **<APPLET>** element, they are downloaded and run directly within a browser to provide new functionality or media forms like animation or video.

Applets are written in the Java language and compiled to a machine-independent byte code that is downloaded automatically to the Java-capable browser and run within the browser environment. But even with a fast processor, the end system runs the byte code slowly compared to a natively compiled application. This is because the virtual Java machine must interpret the byte code. Even with recent JIT (Just-In-Time) compilers in newer browsers, Java can't deliver ideal performance. Even if compilation weren't an issue, Java applets are not currently persistent; they must be downloaded for each use. Java browsers act like thin-client applications: they only add code when they need it.

Security in Java has been a serious concern from the outset. Because programs are downloaded and run automatically, a malicious program could be downloaded and run without the user being able to stop it. Java applets actually have little access to resources outside the browser's environment. Within Web pages, applets can't write to local disks or perform other harmful functions. This framework has been referred to as the "Java Sandbox." Developers wishing to provide Java functions outside of the sandbox must write Java applications, which run as separate applications from browsers. Other Internet programming technologies (plug-ins, ActiveX) provide little or no safety from damaging programs. Oddly, Java developers often want to add just these types of unsecure features, as well as powerful features like persistence and inter-object communication. Most of the features are already far along in development, and should soon become commonplace.

As far as HTML is concerned, a Java applet is yet another object to insert into a Web page. Rather than using the **<EMBED>** or **<OBJECT>** element, there is a special **<APPLET>** element that is used to insert a Java applet. Like the **<EMBED>** element, **<APPLET>** will most likely be replaced by the **<OBJECT>** element. It is important to know how this works in case Java media objects need to be inserted, particularly for Netscape support. The **<APPLET>** element specifies the Java applet to run in the form a URL to a class file containing the Java byte code. To set the applet to run, set the **CODE** attribute equal to the URL of the Java class. The **CODEBASE** attribute can also be used to set a base URL reference for the **CODE** attribute. Other basic attributes to the **<APPLET>** element include similar ones to **<IMG>** such as **ALIGN**, **HEIGHT**, **WIDTH**, **HSPACE**, **VSPACE**, and **ALT**. Within the **<APPLET>** and **</APPLET>** elements, the user may specify parameters or arguments to the applet using the **<PARAM>** element in a similar fashion to how data is passed to ActiveX controls. Plain text may also appear between the **<APPLET>** and **</APPLET>** elements. Such text can be used to provide alternative text in situations where the element is not understood at all. A small example of how **<APPLET>** might be used is shown here:

```
<APPLET CODE="http://www.bigcompany.com/java/test.class"
     ALIGN="LEFT"
     HEIGHT="100"
     WIDTH="100"
     HSPACE="10"
     VSPACE="10">
<PARAM NAME="caption" value="Hello World">
</APPLET>
```

Depending on the Java applet being accessed, there may be many different parameters that can be passed to it. A general discussion of Java applets and how they can be used will be presented in Chapter 14. The discussion here is only meant to show that there are many forms of binary formats that may be included in Web pages.

The three elements that are useful for inserting nonimage binary objects are **<APPLET>**, **<EMBED>**, and **<OBJECT>**. In most cases, it is too tedious to spell out all the aspects of the **<APPLET>** and **<OBJECT>** elements since there are so many variations. As far as plug-ins are concerned, however, a few are commonly available within browsers to support media types such as audio, video, and VRML. Furthermore, some media forms, such as Acrobat and Shockwave, are so common as to deserve a brief discussion regarding how they are handled within HTML. The rest of the chapter will review common plug-ins and controls for dealing with audio, video, multimedia, VRML, and Acrobat. Before that, however, let's look closer at an element that defies classification—the **<MARQUEE>** element.

Object-Like Element: <MARQUEE>

One approach to adding new support for objects is by adding new elements and building in support to the browser for the object. One particular element, **<MARQUEE>,** defies much description. Although it isn't an embedded binary object, it tends to act like one in its support for **HSPACE**, **VSPACE**, **HEIGHT**, and **WIDTH** attributes. In the proprietary HTML extension wars, Microsoft is the culprit for introducing the dreaded **<MARQUEE>** element, which is certainly as annoying as **<BLINK>**. Thanks to **<MARQUEE>**, it is now possible to create messages that scroll and slide across a viewer's screen in a variety of different ways. Like Netscape's **<BLINK>** element, **<MARQUEE>** degrades fairly well and can be used by HTML authors who understand the ramifications of using such proprietary tags. However, the bottom line is that this author in good conscience cannot recommend more than a very occasional use of this element.

Internet Explorer, as well as WebTV, supports the **<MARQUEE>** element. The element requires a closing tag **</MARQUEE>**. The included text is transformed into a scrolling ticker tape similar to the one found at Times Square. A very simple continuous marquee could be set with the following HTML fragment:

```
<MARQUEE>
    Welcome to Big Company, Inc. -- the biggest fake company in the world!
</MARQUEE>
```

Under Microsoft Internet Explorer and other browsers that support the **<MARQUEE>** element, the enclosed text would scroll from right to left over and over again. Under browsers that do not support **<MARQUEE>**, the text would be displayed simply as plain text.

The **<MARQUEE>** element has a variety of attributes that can control the speed, direction, and form of the scrolling message. Numerous other attributes are also available for programming and layout support. The full syntax for the **<MARQUEE>** element is

```
<MARQUEE ALIGN=ABSBOTTOM | ABSMIDDLE | BASELINE | BOTTOM |
                LEFT | MIDDLE | RIGHT| TEXTOP | TOP
     BEHAVIOR=ALTERNATE | SCROLL | SLIDE
     BGCOLOR=color value
     DIRECTION=DOWN | LEFT | RIGHT | UP
     HEIGHT=pixels
     HSPACE=pixels
     ID=unique identifying string
     LOOP=integer | INFINITE
     SCROLLAMOUNT=pixels
     SCROLLDELAY=milliseconds
     STYLE=style sheet information
     TITLE=advisory information
     VSPACE=pixels
     WIDTH=pixels >
Text to scroll
</MARQUEE>
```

Like the **<IMG>** element, the **ALIGN** attribute is used to set how the **<MARQUEE>** element is treated as an object so that text may flow around it. The values are the same as **<IMG> ALIGN** attribute vales and produce the same results.

The **BEHAVIOR** attribute may be set to **ALTERNATE**, **SCROLL**, or **SLIDE**. This attribute determines how the scrolling text will behave. By default, a marquee will scroll text from left to right unless the **DIRECTION** is set. The scrolled text, if it is looped, must first disappear before reappearing on the other side. When the attribute is set to **ALTERNATE**, the text will bounce across the scroll region. When the attribute is set to **SLIDE**, it will slide into position based on direction and stay put once on screen.

The **BGCOLOR** attribute can be set to a color value to set the background color of the marquee scroll region. The color value may be in either a hex format like #FF0000 or a color name like purple.

The **DIRECTION** attribute is used to set the direction in which the scrolled text will move. The allowed values for this attribute are **DOWN**, **LEFT**, **RIGHT**, and **UP**. Using Dynamic HTML features, it may be possible to create interesting effects with **<MARQUEE>** by modifying this attribute.

As with the **<IMG>** element, the **HEIGHT** attribute is used to set the height of the marquee scroll region either in pixels or in a percentage value of the screen.

The **HSPACE** attribute takes a pixel value to set the horizontal buffer region for the marquee.

The **ID** attribute is used to name an occurrence of **<MARQUEE>** so that it can be manipulated by a style sheet or scripting language. The **ID** should be unique within the document.

The **LOOP** attribute is used to set the number of times the message will loop in the scroll region. By default, unless the **BEHAVIOR** is set to **SLIDE**, a marquee will scroll forever. The value of the **LOOP** attribute should be a positive integer.

Setting **SCROLLAMOUNT** to a particular number of pixels allows the smoothness of the scroll to be controlled. The value of the **SCROLLAMOUNT** attribute is set to the number of pixels between each drawing of the scrolled message in the display area. The larger the value in pixels, the jerkier the scroll.

SCROLLDELAY is used to set the number of milliseconds between each rendering of the scrolled message. A higher value for this attribute will slow down the scrolling. A reasonable value for this attribute is 50 or greater. Lower values for **SCROLLDELAY** tend to produce marquees that are very difficult to read.

The **STYLE** attribute is used to specify an inline style for the marquee object. With a style sheet, the look of the scrolled text can be controlled, including font size, font family, and a variety of other things. See Chapter 10 for more information about how style sheets may be used with elements such as **<MARQUEE>**.

TITLE can be set to a string that is used as advisory information. Under many browsers, the advisory information will show as tool tip information when the mouse is positioned over the marquee for a short period of time.

The **VSPACE** attribute is used to set the vertical buffer space between the marquee object and other objects laid out on the page.

The **WIDTH** attribute is used to set the width of the marquee object in pixels or as a percentage value of the available screen.

*WebTV supports a special **TRANSPARENCY** attribute for <MARQUEE> that can be set to a value from 0 to 100 where 0 is fully opaque and 100 is a fully transparent background. The value of 50 for this attribute will render very fast under the Web appliance's browser.*

Besides these attributes to **<MARQUEE>**, the element supports a complete set of event attributes for control by a scripting language like JavaScript as well as some attributes like **DATAFLD**, **DATAFORMATS**, and **DATASRC** that may be useful to pull the scrolling information out of a database. A brief discussion about attributes like these will be handled in Chapter 14. A complete example showing a very basic use of the **<MARQUEE>** element is shown in Figure 7-1. The rendering for Figure 7-1 is shown in Figure 7-2.

The **<MARQUEE>** element is certainly interesting, but as a simple form of animated text it doesn't hold a candle to more persuasive media forms like sound or video.

```
<!DOCTYPE HTML PUBLIC "-//W3C//DTD HTML 4.0 Final//EN">
<HTML>
<HEAD>
<TITLE>Marquee Example</TITLE>
</HEAD>
<BODY>
<DIV ALIGN="CENTER">
<MARQUEE BGCOLOR="YELLOW"
         BEHAVIOR="ALTERNATE"
         DIRECTION="RIGHT"
         LOOP="6"
         SCROLLAMOUNT="1"
         SCROLLDELAY="40"
         TITLE="Silly tags aren't just for Netscape anymore."
         WIDTH="80%">
   Welcome to Big Company, the biggest fake company of them all!
</MARQUEE>
</DIV>
</BODY>
</HTML>
```

Figure 7-1. *<MARQUEE>* example

Audio Support in Browsers

Few things are as persuasive as sound. Just try watching television with the volume turned all the way down. It's not terribly interesting. Sound is a vital element of true multimedia Web pages—but how should sound be used? What Web audio technology is appropriate for the job? Just adding a MIDI file to a site to provide continuous background sound may turn your page into the online equivalent of an in-store electronic organ demonstration. The latest audio technologies on the Internet cover a lot of ground, from to traditional download-and-play systems in a variety of formats to *streaming audio*, which plays in close to real time. Surprisingly, the most advanced technologies, and the most popular, may not be the best solution.

Digital Sound Basics

This section will provide a very brief overview of digital sound in general. Digital sound is measured by the frequency of sampling, or how many times the sound is digitized during a given time period. Sampling frequencies are specified in kilohertz (kHz), which indicate the sound sampling rate per second. CD-quality sound is

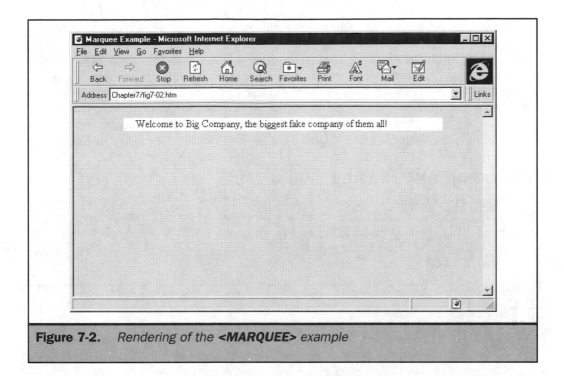

Figure 7-2.   *Rendering of the **<MARQUEE>** example*

approximately 44.1 kHz, or 44,100 samples every second. For stereo, two channels are required, each at 8 bits. At 16 bits per sample, that yields 705,600 bits of data for each second of CD-quality sound. In theory, the bits of data on a CD could be delivered over the Internet, creating high-quality music at the end user's demand. In reality, transmitting this amount of data would take nearly half a T1 network's bandwidth. Obviously, this type of bandwidth is not available to the average Web user. Another approach must be taken.

One approach is to lower the sampling rate when creating digital sound for Web delivery. A sampling rate of 8 kHz in mono might produce acceptable playback results for simple applications such as speech, particularly considering that playback hardware often consists of a simple sound card and small speaker combination. Low-quality audio requires a mere 64,000 bits of data per second, but the end user still has to wait to download the sound. For modem users, even in the best of conditions, each second of low-quality sound takes a few seconds to be delivered, making continuous sound unrealistic.

Audio File Formats and Compression

Like graphics files, audio files can be compressed to reduce the amount of data being sent. The software on the serving side compresses the data, which is decompressed and played back on the receiving end. The compression/decompression software is known together as a *codec*. Just like image formats, audio compression methods are either lossy or lossless. Lossy data compression doesn't perfectly represent what was compressed, but it's close enough, given the size savings. Since lossless compression techniques guarantee that what goes in one end comes out on the other, most cannot compress files to any significant degree. Compression always involves a trade-off between sound quality and file size; larger file sizes mean longer download times.

When dealing with sounds, you don't really select different forms of compression. You select file formats. There are many standard file formats available, as shown in Table 7-1.

Downloading and Playing Audio

Early approaches to delivering sound via the Internet followed the "download and play" model. In this scenario, users must download sounds completely before they can play them. This takes up valuable hard drive space, even if they only want to hear the

File Format	Description
WAV	Waveform or simply *wave* files are the most common format of sound on Windows platforms. It is also possible to play back WAVs on Macs and other systems with player software.
AU	Sparc-audio, or u-law format is one of the oldest Internet sound formats. There is a player for nearly every platform available.
AIFF	The Audio Interchange File Format is very common on Macs. Widely used in multimedia applications, it is not very common on the Web.
MIDI	The Musical Instrument Digital Interface format is not a digitized audio format. It represents notes and other information so that music can be synthesized. MIDI is well supported and files are very small, but it is useful for only certain applications due to its sound quality when reproduced on PC hardware.
MPEG	MPEG format is a standard format that has significant compression capabilities. It is not as standardized as many people might think: it lacks widespread playing and encoding acceptance despite its quality.

Table 7-1.   *Standard Internet Sound Formats*

first few seconds of a file. Sounds must be degraded significantly in this situation, which may not be acceptable for content that requires flawless playback. Even at very low sampling rates, these sounds must be fairly short in order to spare impatient users the agony of prolonged download times. Download time can be reduced by creating smaller audio files, which only accentuates the drawbacks of this method.

Using HTML, the simplest way to support the download-and-play approach is by linking to a sound file and letting another application like a helper or plug-in deal with it. If none is configured, the user will be prompted to deal with the sound. For example, to link to an audio file in WAV format, insert a link like this:

```
<A HREF="starspangled.wav">Star Spangled Banner (6 second WAV - 900K)</A>
```

A good idea with the download-and-play approach is to put the decision to download the file in the hands of users. Warn them about the file format and size, so that the user has some indication of how long it will take to download. Another helpful bit of information might be how long the sound is going to be.

For download-and-play delivery, WAV and AU are the safest formats for low-quality music or speech. MPEG is the only choice for high-quality playback. Download-and-play-based audio delivery is recommended where a quick bit of sound, like an entrance gong, is required. AU and WAV files are supported via helper applications and plug-ins. They are even supported natively by some recent Web browsers, including Netscape with its LiveAudio plug-in and Microsoft Internet Explorer with its proprietary **<BGSOUND>** tag. Both browsers also support MIDI sound files. However, MIDI files played back via PC sound cards like the SoundBlaster often sound like cheap synthesized music, which is more a reflection of the playback hardware than the protocol itself.

LiveAudio

Starting with Netscape 3.0, the LiveAudio plug-in was included with the Netscape browser. The LiveAudio plug-in supports AU, AIFF, WAV, and MIDI sound files in the download-and-play fashion. Adding support for audio with LiveAudio simply requires using the appropriate form of the **<EMBED>** element to access the LiveAudio plug-in. For example, to set LiveAudio to include a sound called "test.wav" and a panel to control the sound, use the following HTML fragment:

```
<EMBED SRC="test.wav" HEIGHT="60" WIDTH="144">
```

It is important to include the **HEIGHT** and **WIDTH** values. Otherwise, the browser may clip the console. The default size for the LiveAudio control is 60 pixels high and 144 pixels across. Other control styles have different default sizes.

The LiveAudio plug-in has a variety of features that can be controlled with **ATTRIBUTE** settings for the **<EMBED>** element. The syntax for the LiveAudio plug-in is shown here:

```
<EMBED SRC=URL of sound file to play
       ALIGN=top | bottom | center | baseline | left | right |
              texttop | middle | absmiddle | absbottom
       AUTOSTART=true | false
       CONTROLS=console | smallconsole | playbutton | pausebutton |
              stopbutton | volumelever
       ENDTIME=minutes:seconds
       HEIGHT=pixels or precentage
       HIDDEN=true | false
       MASTERSOUND
       NAME=unique name
       LOOP=true | false | positive integer
       STARTTIME=minutes:seconds
       VOLUME=number from 0 to 100
       WIDTH=pixels or percentage
>
```

Like the **<IMG>** element, the LiveAudio plug-in must have an **SRC** attribute setting. The **SRC** value is a URL to a sound file supported by the plug-in. Remember to take the same precautions for using a complete URL to an outside file compared to using a locally referenced file with a relative URL.

The **AUTOSTART** attributes can take one of two values, **true** or **false**. When set to **true**, the sound file will begin playing as soon as it is downloaded. By default, if unspecified, **AUTOSTART** is set to **false**.

The **LOOP** attribute can take one of three values, **true**, **false**, or a positive integer. Setting the value to **true** will loop the sound continuously until the stop button is pressed. When combined with the **AUTOSTART** attribute, infinite looping could become very annoying, particularly if the stop button is unavailable. By default, the value of **LOOP** is set to **false**. The **LOOP** attribute can also be set to a positive integer that will play the sound a specified number of times or until the stop button is pressed.

The **STARTTIME** attribute can be set to a time value within a sound file to determine from where to begin playback. For example, to start playback 2 seconds into the sound, the attribute could be set to **00:02**.

The **ENDTTIME** attribute is similar to the **STARTTIME** attribute, but determines the time value to end playback and is written in the same way.

> **Note**
>
> *STARTTIME and ENDTTIME provide little benefit without using scripting technology since the whole sound must be downloaded regardless. It is curious why a user wouldn't simply edit a sound to avoid the idea of starting and stopping at a certain time index. If the controls in the LiveAudio plug-in supported a fast-forward and reverse feature, these attributes would be far more useful.*

The **VOLUME** attribute can be set to an integer between 0 and 100 where **0** is the sound completely off and **100** at maximum volume. Values outside this range generally default to the extreme, so a value of **200** would set the volume to maximum. When combined with the **MASTERVOLUME** setting for the **NAME** attribute, it is possible to set volume for other sounds. The default volume level is the current system volume or typically a value of **50**.

The **WIDTH** attribute sets the width in pixels for the audio controls. The page author should set this value unless the **HIDDEN** attribute is used. The width for the default console is 144 pixels and should be set explicitly. When the **CONTROLS** attribute is set to **SMALLCONSOLE**, the **WIDTH** attribute should also be set to 144 pixels. If the **CONTROLS** attribute is set to **VOLUMELEVER**, the **WIDTH** attribute should be set to 74 and when it is set to any of the buttons like **PLAYBUTTON**, the width should be set to 37 pixels. The values for the **WIDTH** attribute are summarized in Table 7-2.

The **HEIGHT** attribute is used to set the height in pixels for the audio controls. The page author should also make sure to set this value as well as the **WIDTH** attribute unless the **HIDDEN** attribute is used. The height for the default console is 60 pixels, while the small console is only 15 pixels high. Each button, such as the play button, is 22 pixels up and down, and the volume lever has a height of 22 pixels. All the suggested height values are summarized in Table 7-2.

The **ALIGN** attribute acts just like the **ALIGN** attribute for the <IMG> element.

The **CONTROLS** attribute sets the type of control objects to include for the sound file. By default, the value of the **CONTROLS** attribute is set to **CONSOLE**, which includes a volume lever, play button, and stop button. If space is an issue, the **CONTROLS** value can be set to **SMALLCONSOLE**, which provides the same functionality in much less space. Each button—including the **PLAYBUTTON**, **PAUSEBUTTON**, and **STOPBUTTON**—can be set independently as can the **VOLUMELEVER**. The various controls are shown in Figure 7-3.

The **HIDDEN** value can be set to **true** if the page author wants the audio file to act as a background sound. The user will not be able to control the sound if this attribute is set to the true value. When **HIDDEN** is set, **HEIGHT** and **WIDTH** attributes are unnecessary. By default, the **HIDDEN** attribute is set to **false**.

CONTROL Setting	Suggested WIDTH Value	Suggested HEIGHT Value
CONSOLE (Default)	144	60
SMALLCONSOLE	144	15
VOLUMELEVER	74	20
PLAYBUTTON	37	22
PAUSEBUTTON	37	22
STOPBUTTON	37	22

Table 7-2.   *Suggested **HEIGHT** and **WIDTH** Values for LiveAudio*

The **NAME** attribute is used to group a set of individual controls together that control one sound. The attribute value must be a unique identifier for all the controls. For example, the group could be called SoundGroup1. All the **<EMBED>** elements that reference the same sound should then have their **NAME** attribute value set to

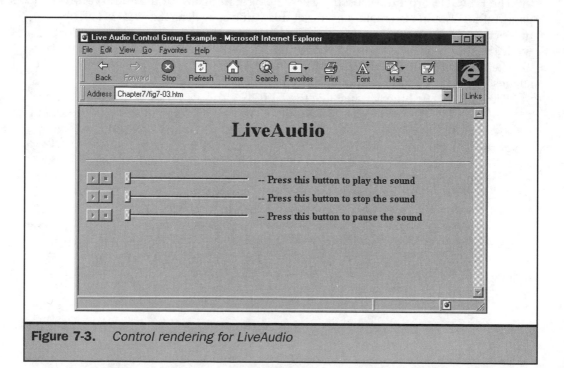

Figure 7-3.   *Control rendering for LiveAudio*

SoundGroup1. One particular **<EMBED>** occurrence must be set to be the "master sound" by setting an attribute **MASTERSOUND**, which requires no value. The master sound must point to a real sound file. However, the other occurrences of the **<EMBED>** element with the group need only to point to a dummy sound file called a "stub file" in the Netscape documentation. The stub file is simply a file that is named appropriately to look like a sound file, for example stub1.wav. The file itself need contain no information and may be a blank text file just with the appropriate name. This is somewhat of a hack and is required since the LiveAudio plug-in must see a value for the **SRC** attribute in order to work. While it is not obvious what use the **NAME** and **MASTERSOUND** attributes might have, the HTML example in Figure 7-4 shows how a small page could be built that uses three buttons separately to control the same sound.

As shown in the example in Figure 7-4, it is important not to point all the **SRC** attributes for the stub files to the same dummy file. The stubs must be unique file names and must all exist though they may have a zero length.

By dividing up the controls, the page author has more possibilities for integrating the audio control into the page without resorting to programming. However, the real power with the **NAME** attribute comes with the introduction of LiveConnect and other forms of Dynamic HTML. With JavaScript, it is possible to create new buttons to control sound playing, defer sounds to play later, and to create buttons that play sound when clicked.

While Netscape's LiveAudio is not an official standard by any means, it is common enough that it could be used carefully within a Netscape environment. In a most basic form, it is also possible to support both Netscape and Microsoft browsers with LiveAudio itself or with Microsoft-specific elements such as **<BGSOUND>**, discussed next.

Microsoft's <BGSOUND>

Microsoft's Internet Explorer 2.0 and up supports WAV and MIDI files with the **<BGSOUND>** element, which will play a sound in the background once it is loaded. The user has no control over the volume or the playback of the sound, which may be annoying. The element takes an **SRC** attribute that is set to the URL of the sound file to play. A **LOOP** attribute, which can be set to an integer value indicating how many times the sound should play, is also available. The **LOOP** attribute can also be set to the value infinite to keep playing over and over. A simple example to play a sound called test.wav two times under Internet Explorer could be written as **<BGSOUND SRC="test.wav" LOOP="2">**.

The **<BGSOUND>** element also supports other attributes such as **TITLE**, but currently the support of programming for the **<BGSOUND>** element under Dynamic HTML is not well developed. While this element is in fairly heavy use, other approaches are suggested, particularly with Microsoft taking a more standards-oriented approach. Microsoft also supports the ActiveMovie format that can be used to insert sound-only movies. See the section "Microsoft's ActiveMovie" later in this chapter.

```
<!DOCTYPE HTML PUBLIC "-//W3C//DTD HTML 4.0 Final//EN">
<HTML>
<HEAD>
<TITLE>LiveAudio Control Group Example</TITLE>
</HEAD>
<BODY>
<H1 ALIGN="CENTER">LiveAudio</H1>
<HR>
<EMBED SRC="test.wav"
 CONTROLS="PLAYBUTTON"
 HEIGHT="22"
    WIDTH="37"
    NAME="SoundGroup1"
    MASTERSOUND
    ALIGN="MIDDLE">

<B> -- Press this button to play the sound</B><BR>
<EMBED SRC="stub1.wav"
 CONTROLS="STOPBUTTON"
 HEIGHT="22"
 WIDTH="37"
 NAME="SoundGroup1"
 ALIGN="MIDDLE">

<B> -- Press this button to stop the sound</B><BR>
<EMBED SRC="stub2.wav"
CONTROLS="PAUSEBUTTON"
HEIGHT="22"
WIDTH="37"
NAME="SoundGroup1"
ALIGN="MIDDLE">
<B> -- Press this button to pause the sound</B><BR>
</BODY>
</HTML>
```

Figure 7-4. *LiveAudio console group example*

Note   *It is possible to include both the **<BGSOUND>** and Netscape LiveAudio syntax in one page, but it is advised to use JavaScript to control which form is inserted into the document. With both forms of sound support enabled, there can be conflicts and page authors are advised to test their documents thoroughly.*

Proprietary Audio Formats

There are many proprietary audio formats, including RealAudio, ToolVox, TrueSpeech, and others. Of these, RealAudio is by far the most popular. But why use RealAudio if audio is built into the browser? Proprietary audio formats offer one thing that many "standard" digital audio formats lack: the possibility of streaming data. As a rule of thumb, a 14.4Kbps modem user receives approximately 1K of data per second. If 1 second of sound could be represented in 1K, and the data could get to the end user at a rate of 1K every second, then the data would effectively *stream*, or play real time. Streaming seems to make a whole lot of sense. Why wait for an hour-long speech to download before playing when you only care about the current second of data being listened to? Streamed data doesn't take up hard drive space, and it opens up random access to any position in an audio file. However, there are a few potential serious drawbacks to streaming audio. First, to compress audio far enough for streaming, you have to sacrifice a certain degree of sound quality. Second, the Internet protocols themselves do not readily support the requirements of streaming.

Why the Internet and Streaming Don't Mix

As mentioned in Chapter 2, the Internet uses the TCP/IP protocol, and the network is subject to bursts and traffic delays. Here are a couple of key points to remember. The TCP/IP protocols used on the Internet were designed for robustness and scalability. The Internet is a packet-switched network that breaks data up into little chunks and sends them separately, to be reassembled at the other end. Because these packets may be lost along their journey or arrive out of order, the Transmission Control Protocol, or TCP, guarantees the integrity of the data. This way, many users can share a fixed circuit that allows for economies of scale. However, packet-switched networks have one serious problem—they cannot guarantee delivery time without special modifications. This makes streamed audio, video, and other "real time" applications on packet-switched networks very difficult.

Packet-switched networks can be augmented with protocols such as RTP (Real Time Transport Protocol) and RSVP (Resource Reservation Setup Protocol), which help guarantee delivery times by making a bandwidth reservation when needed. These protocols can improve real-time data delivery, but they are not widely supported yet. They also raise the question of how to limit reservations, since a user would always want maximum bandwidth. Some experts argue that once these protocols are in place, fee structures based on bandwidth will become commonplace. For the moment, this is pure speculation as the various real-time protocols are still very much in development. Another solution to real-time data on the Internet is necessary.

One potential solution to real time data on the Internet is really just an assumption—you hope the end user has the end-to-end bandwidth to receive the file in real time. (Remember the 1 kilobyte per second rule for 14.4Kbps modems.) If audio compression can get 1 second of data to fit within those ranges, real time data can be served to 14.4Kbps users—when the assumption holds. When the assumption doesn't hold, a glitch will occur in the audio stream called a *drop-out*. If there is too much drop-out, the user turns off the audio stream. One way to avoid drop-out is to buffer data. This process gives you a head start by preloading a certain amount of data in a buffer so that rough spots can be overcome. An initial buffering delay of 10 or 15 seconds is acceptable for long audio clips; buffering short sounds is counterproductive. Many Internet audio solutions use a combination of intensive compression, buffering, and some level of bandwidth assumption to achieve streaming. More complex audio solutions use servers to control the process. Both approaches to streaming audio have their pros and cons.

RealAudio

The first and still most popular approach to streaming audio was developed by Progressive Networks. RealAudio (www.realaudio.com) uses a special server to send continuous audio data to a browser helper application, Netscape plug-in, Shockwave Xtra, or ActiveX control. With players available for all major platforms, RealAudio is the most common streaming audio format on the Internet. Putting data in RealAudio format is fairly easy if the files exist in WAV or other common audio formats. Simply use the RealAudio encoder available from Progressive, and it's ready to publish. But despite RealAudio's wide support, it has certain drawbacks that mostly revolve around the use of a special server.

Servers can provide a higher degree of control. For example, they can limit or control the number of audio streams delivered and allow for easy access to specified points in an audio stream. With simpler "serverless" audio-streaming solutions, the virtual fast forward button provided by random access is sacrificed. Some sophisticated servers could potentially upgrade data quality as bandwidth becomes available. Less complex systems give the same quality of data regardless of the end-to-end access speed. Server-based systems are expensive and require computing resources beyond the basic Web server. RealAudio-based streaming audio servers have a per stream cost that keeps many small users from adopting this solution. This price does buy quality, however, and many services are starting to provide RealAudio for their customers.

Note   *One technical issue of RealAudio that bothers many users is that the server sends audio data using the User Datagram Protocol (UDP) protocol rather than the more common and reliable TCP protocol used for standard Internet data transmission. UDP is fast and helps provide data to the end user quickly, but lost packets are much more common with UDP. To get around lost packets, RealAudio data is delivered in an interleaved fashion so that single drop-outs are not noticeable. While UDP may help avoid link use problems surrounding TCP, when mixed with a firewall, RealAudio's UDP link becomes a liability. Most firewalls filter out UDP, so people accessing the Internet through a firewall may find it difficult, if not impossible, to access a UDP-based service like RealAudio.*

From an HTML point of view, using RealAudio is really no different from using LiveAudio or any other plug-in. Similar to LiveAudio, the **SRC** attribute can be set as well as controls and a variety of other attributes. A portion of the RealAudio syntax is shown here:

```
<EMBED SRC=URL of Real Audio stream or file
    AUTOSTART=true | false
    CONTROLS=ALL | ControlPanel | InfoVolumePanel | InfoPanel |
            StatusBar | PlayButton | StopButton | VolumeSlider |
            PositionSlider | PositionField | StatusField
    HEIGHT=pixels or percentage
    NAME=identifier for sound file
    WIDTH=pixels or percentage>
```

The **SRC** attribute is used to set the source of the RealAudio clip. The **SRC** should be set to a URL which may be of the form of a full URL using the pnm:, file:, or http: protocol or it may be a relative URL to the appropriate file type. This attribute is required.

The **CONTROLS** attribute sets the visible control components of the player in a similar manner to LiveAudio. The default value is **ALL**, but the attribute also individually controls the aspects **ControlPanel**, **InfoVolumePanel**, **InfoPanel**, **StatusBar**, **PlayButton**, **StopButton**, **VolumeSlider**, **PositionSlider**, **PositionField**, and **StatusField**.

The **NAME** attribute is used to specify the identifier associated with the RealAudio plug-in and clip. This value can then be used to reference and control the clip from Java, JavaScript or other programming technologies.

The **HEIGHT** attribute is used to set the height in pixels of the control panel used.

The **WIDTH** attribute can set the width in pixels of the control panel used.

The **AUTOSTART** attribute is used to set whether or not the RealAudio Plug-in will automatically start playing once the source data is available. Valid values for this attribute are **true** and **false**.

Given that the user has access to the appropriate audio stream, using a proprietary audio technology like RealAudio is no more difficult than using LiveAudio. For more specific information about how to use RealAudio technology, please see Progressive's Web site (www.real.com).

Sound Conclusions

The future of audio on the Internet ultimately lies in integration. People will resist downloading dozens of plug-ins for numerous data formats. They prefer single technologies that integrate into one whole presentation, like animation or video with sound since the uses of background music on the Internet are limited. While more advanced technologies such as RealAudio allow simple embedding of URLs and other forms of synchronization, a controlled environment is required. With programming technologies such as JavaScript and Macromedia's Shockwave, which have streaming audio support, full integration is available.

Adding sound to a Web site should not be an infuriating experience for the Web master or the Web user. Using a simple download-and-play sound format built into a browser might be better than streaming data that requires special encoding or download of a special plug-in. If streaming is required, RealAudio is probably the best bet (if it's affordable). For a complete Web page solution requiring tight integration between technologies, Shockwave with streaming audio is the only choice beyond some custom integration using programming technologies such as JavaScript. Regardless of how sound is included, don't expect CD quality for Internet-based audio. And remember: a little sound can go a long way.

Video Support

The holy grail of Internet multimedia is certainly high-quality, 30 frames-per-second real-time video. Many companies are working towards the idea of television on the Web, but most of their solutions just don't work well within the bandwidth limitations faced by the average Internet user. Sooner or later, video will be used extensively on Web pages—but what Web video technology, if any, is appropriate for the job and how can video be accessed via HTML? The latest net video technologies range from low-quality streaming audio with an occasional picture to traditional download-and-play systems for a variety of file formats. As with audio, the most popular technologies—and the most advanced—may not offer the best solutions for simple Web video needs.

Digital Video Basics

Digital video is measured by the number of frames per second of video, and by the size and resolution of these frames. The total size requirement for video is huge, particularly if you want NTSC (TV quality) video. A 640 × 480 image with 24-bits of data representation for color and a frame rate of 30 frames per second takes up a staggering 27MB per second—and that's without sound. Add CD quality audio (705,600 bits of data for each second of data) and the file size increases proportionately. In theory, the bits of data necessary to deliver TV-quality video could be transmitted over the Internet, creating the long sought-after interactive TV. In the real world, transmitting this amount of data is generally not feasible, even after compression.

One approach to video on the Internet is breathtakingly simple: just don't do it. A simple frame of movement every once in a while or a static picture with continuous audio can provide the illusion required for simple "talking head" applications. It is possible to reduce frame rates and image size enough to make download sizes seem plausible, but even a simple slide show with audio narration is nearly impossible to do real time without compression.

Video File Formats and Compression

Like audio files, video files can be compressed to reduce the amount of data being sent. Because of the degree of compression required by video, most video codecs uses a lossy approach that involves a trade-off between picture/sound quality and file size, with larger file sizes obviously resulting in longer download times.

There are three standardized video file formats used on the Web: AVI, QuickTime, and MPEG as summarized in Table 7-3. The file format usually determines which compression technique will be used. However some file formats, such as QuickTime, allow different codecs to be selected. In some ways, this makes QuickTime the most flexible video format.

Video Format	Description
AVI	Audio Video Interleaved. The Video for Windows file format for digital video and audio is very common and easy to specify. A growing number of video files in AVI format are being used on the Internet, but file size of AVI is significant. Both Netscape and Internet Explorer are capable of dealing with AVIs easily.
MOV (QuickTime)	MOV is the extension that indicates the use of Apple QuickTime format. Probably the most common digital video format, it continues its popularity on the Internet, QuickTime has a strong following in the multimedia development community. Various codecs and technology enhancements make QuickTime a strong digital video solution that may work in conjunction with MPEG.
MPEG	The Motion Picture Experts Group video format is the supposed standard format for digital video. While compression and image quality of MPEG files is impressive, it can be expensive and difficult to work with this format.

Table 7-3.   *Standard Internet Video Formats*

For download-and-play delivery, AVI and QuickTime are the safest formats for short video clips. Regardless of length, MPEG is typically the only choice for high-quality playback. AVI and QuickTime files are commonly supported via helper applications. They're even supported natively by many modern Web browsers in a download-and-play style.

Waiting for Video

As with audio, many online video delivery systems follow the download-and-play model, where users must download video clips completely before they can play them. Some Web video solutions allow the user to see the video as it comes down despite the slow speed; this allows users to cancel the download before it ends. Shortening video clips and reducing frame rates helps keep users from giving up during download time, but this may not be acceptable for content that requires flawless playback. Even at very low frame rates with no audio, video clips more than a few seconds long tend to exceed the patience of the average user. With download-and-play video, you should stick to common formats like AVI, Quicktime, or MPEG, unless the proprietary format has a wide degree of industry acceptance or provides a really motivating feature such as compression high enough to allow streaming.

LiveVideo

Netscape's LiveVideo plug-in, which was introduced with Netscape 3.0, supports AVI on Windows. The plug-in is rather simplistic and does not even include controls to show, pause, or rewind a video, let alone any sort of volume control. The user must click on the embedded video to start it unless the video has an auto-play feature enabled. The basic syntax for the **<EMBED>** element as related to LiveVideo is shown here:

```
<EMBED SRC=URL of video file
    ALIGN=top | bottom | center | baseline | left | right | texttop
        |middle | absmiddle | absbottom
    AUTOSTART=true | false
    HEIGHT=pixels or percentage
    HSPACE=pixels
    LOOP=true | false
    VSPACE=pixels
    WIDTH=pixels or percentage>
```

The **SRC** attribute must be set to the URL of a valid AVI file.

The **ALIGN** attribute acts similarly to the same attribute for the **<IMG>** element and accepts the same values.

The **AUTOSTART** attribute may be set to **true** to begin play immediately after the entire AVI file has been downloaded. The default for this attribute is "false" and thus requires the user to click on the video in order to begin its play.

The **HEIGHT** attribute specifies the pixel height of the video. This attribute also takes a percentage value.

The **HSPACE** attribute creates a horizontal buffer region around an image of the specified number of pixels.

The **LOOP** attribute can be set to true to loop the video continuously. There is currently no way to set the plug-in to loop the video a particular number of times, which seems a likely modification to this attribute. The **LOOP** attribute has a default value of **false**.

The **VSPACE** attribute can be set to a pixel value to create a vertical buffer area above and below the embedded media.

The **WIDTH** attribute is set to either a pixel value or a screen percentage to specify the width of the embedded AVI file.

A brief example of how LiveVideo would be used to include an AVI video in a page is shown in Figure 7-5. A rendering of the example in Figure 7-5 is shown in Figure 7-6.

Beyond this simple discussion, it is also possible to use Java or JavaScript to control the functionality of the LiveVideo plug-in, particularly playing, stopping, rewinding, and seeking a particular frame in the video. Some discussion of this idea with plug-ins in general will be presented in Chapter 14.

```
<!DOCTYPE HTML PUBLIC "-//W3C//DTD HTML 3.2 Final//EN">
<HTML>
<HEAD>
<TITLE>LiveVideo Rendering Under Netscape</TITLE>
<BODY>

<EMBED SRC="critterloop.avi" LOOP="TRUE" AUTOSTART="TRUE"
HEIGHT="90" WIDTH="120" ALIGN="LEFT" HSPACE="15" VSPACE="15">

</BODY>
</HTML>
```

Figure 7-5.   *LiveVideo Example HTML*

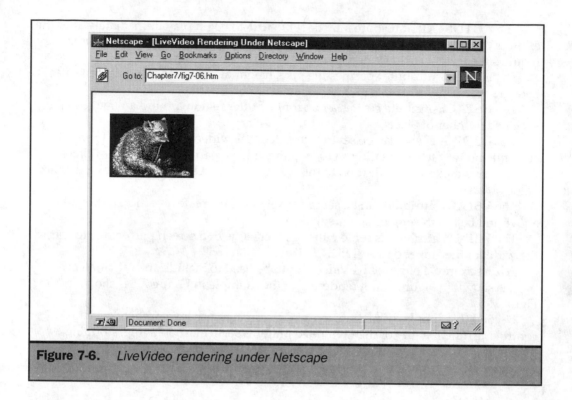

Figure 7-6. *LiveVideo rendering under Netscape*

QuickTime

QuickTime videos offer a lot more benefits than just the fact that they tend to be smaller than AVI files. QuickTime is designed to provide the framework for the synchronization of time-based data in a variety of formats, including video, sound, MIDI, and even text. An interesting aspect of QuickTime is that it can work with different video compression codecs such as Cinepack, Indeo, MPEG, and even exotic fractal compression codecs. By itself, QuickTime with standard Cinepack encoding lacks the small file size of MPEG or proprietary video files, but the quality of QuickTime files is high. Creating or editing QuickTime files is also relatively easy when using tools such as the popular Adobe Premiere package.

Starting with Netscape 3.0, QuickTime was supported in Macintosh and Windows versions of Netscape. Although the plug-in is available on both systems, Windows users are required to install QuickTime services for their operating system. The way to include QuickTime media into a Web page is similar to LiveVideo support. Keep in mind, however, that QuickTime provides support for many forms of media and is really more of a generic media architecture than AVI.

The basic syntax for the **<EMBED>** statement for the Netscape QuickTime plug-in is shown here:

```
<EMBED SRC=URL of QuickTime object
       ALIGN=top | bottom | center | baseline | left | right
       | texttop | middle | absmiddle | absbottom
       AUTOPLAY=true | false
       CACHE=true | false
       CONTROLLER=true | false
       CORRECTION=none | partial | full    (QuickTime VR Only)
       FOV=5.0 to 85.0                      (QuickTime VR Only)
       HEIGHT=pixels or percentage
       HIDDEN
       HOTSPOT hotspot-id="URL of page to load"
       HREF="URL of page to load"
       HSPACE=pixels
       LOOP=true | false | palindrome
       NODE=node number                     (QuickTime VR Only)
       PAN=0.0 to 360.0                      (QuickTime VR Only)
       PLUGINSPAGE="URL of page with plug-in information"
       PLAYEVERYFRAME=true | false
       TARGET=valid frame name
       TILT=-42.5 to 42.5                    (QuickTime VR Only)
       VOLUME=0 - 256
       VSPACE=pixels
       WIDTH=pixels or percentage>
```

The **SRC** attribute is required and should be set to the URL of a valid QuickTime file.

The **ALIGN** attribute acts similarly to the same attribute for the **<IMG>** element and accepts the same values.

The **AUTOPLAY** attribute can be set to **true** or **false** and indicates if the movie should be played as soon as it is possible. The default value for this attribute is **false**. This attribute has no meaning when embedding a QuickTime VR (Virtual Reality) file.

The **CACHE** attribute can be set to true or false. Providing the attribute by itself implies a true value. Under Netscape 3.0 and beyond, a **CACHE** value of **true** will cause the browser to treat the information just like other information and keep it in a local disk cache so it does not need to be downloaded again. When set to **false**, the movie must be downloaded again.

The **CONTROLLER** attribute may be set to **true** or **false** and determines if the movie controller is visible. The controller provides standard stop, play, pause, rewind, frame selection, and volume controls. The controller is 24 pixels high so the **HEIGHT** value should be set to account for this. By default, the value of **CONTROLLER** is generally set to **true** unless a QuickTime VR file is being embedded. The QuickTime VR object does not use the same style of controls.

The **CORRECTION** attribute may be set to **NONE, PARTIAL** or **FULL** and is used to set the display correction for a QuickTime VR object. If no value is set, the default value is **FULL**. This attribute has no meaning beyond a QuickTime VR scene.

The **FOV** attribute is used to specify the initial field of view angle for a QuickTime movie. Typical values for this attribute range from 5.0 to 85.0 degrees. This attribute has no meaning outside of QuickTime VR objects.

The **HEIGHT** attribute is set like the **WIDTH** attribute, with a pixel value or percentage. The value specifies the **HEIGHT** of the object and will be cropped or expanded in the same method as **WIDTH**. For example, if a supplied height is greater than the height of the movie, the movie is centered within this height. If the value is smaller, the object is cropped. Be careful to avoid values of **0** or **1** for the **HEIGHT** attribute since it may cause unpredictable results. Also be aware that the controls for the movie are 24 pixels high so this must be added to the **HEIGHT** value for the object to display properly.

The **HIDDEN** attribute takes no parameters and its presence determines if the movie should be visible. By default, the **HIDDEN** value is **off**. In most cases, such as embedding a QuickTime video or QuickTime VR object, this is not an appropriate attribute to use. However in the case where a sound-only movie is being inserted, this can provide a background sound-like function assuming that **AUTOPLAY** has been set to true. The **HIDDEN** attribute typically will set the **CONTROLLER** attribute to **false**, but to make sure, the attribute can be set directly by the page author.

The **HOTSPOT** attribute comes in a strange format. By setting the hotspot identifier to a URL, it is possible to link the hotspot to a Web object. Hotspots in a movie can be defined using a QuickTime VR authoring tool. This attribute makes sense only within a QuickTime panorama.

The **HREF** attribute may be set to indicate the URL of a page to load when the movie is clicked. The meaning of this attribute is somewhat troublesome if the **CONTROLLER** attribute is set to **false**. The problem revolves around the click having two meanings, one to start the movie and the other to go to the page. Page authors should either use the autoplay feature or provide controls when using this attribute. This attribute is not appropriate when using QuickTime VR objects that may have included their own hot links.

The **HSPACE** attribute is used to set the horizontal pixel buffer for the plug-in and acts the same way as the **HSPACE** attribute for the **<IMG>** element.

The **LOOP** attribute is used to indicate if the movie should play in a looped fashion. By default, the value of **LOOP** is **false**. Setting the attribute to **true** loops the movie until the user stops it. When the **LOOP** value is set to **PALINDROME**, the movie will loop back and forth. Setting this value produces interesting effects with movies and even reverses the soundtrack. This parameter is not appropriate for QuickTime VR objects as they have no distinct time order.

The **NODE** attribute is an optional attribute that has meaning to a multinode QuickTime VR movie. In many QuickTime VR situations, setting multiple areas or viewpoints called *nodes* is desirable. Setting the **NODE** attribute to the integer value of a node in the scene will load the movie at the particular scene. This attribute has no meaning for non-QuickTime VR objects.

The **PAN** attribute is an optional attribute for QuickTime VR objects and allows the author to specify the initial pan angle in degrees. The range for the **PAN** attribute is between 0 and 360 degrees. This attribute has no meaning for other forms of QuickTime objects.

The **PLAYEVERYFRAME** attribute may be set to either **true** or **false**. When set to true, this attribute indicates to the plug-in to play every frame even if it requires the movie to play at a slower rate. In some sense this is appropriate in the case that the processor drops frames that may be valuable. Note that setting this value to **true** is not advisable for movies with audio tracks; it has the side-effect of turning the sound off. Furthermore, this attribute should not be used when embedding QuickTime VR objects.

The **PLUGINSPAGE** is used to set the URL of the page that contains information about the required plug-in and how it can be downloaded and installed if it is not currently installed. This feature is supported by Netscape; it is also documented to work under Internet Explorer. Be careful when using this attribute. It generally should be set to http://quicktime.apple.com unless there is special instructions beyond standard QuickTime information.

The **SCALE** attribute takes a value of **TOFIT**, **ASPECT**, or a number corresponding to the desired scaling factor, for example 1.5. The default **SCALE** value is **1**, which is a normally scaled movie. Setting the attribute to **ASPECT** scales the movie to fit the bounding box set by the **HEIGHT** and **WIDTH** attributes. A value of **TOFIT** scales the movie to fit the **HEIGHT** and **WIDTH** attribute with no regard to aspect ratio. Be careful when scaling movies, as it may degrade the playback performance and image quality.

The **TARGET** can be used in conjunction with the **HREF** attribute to set the name of a frame into which to load the page indicated by the **HREF** attribute. The normal reserved frame names such as _blank as well as explicitly named frames are available as valid targets. More information on frames can be found in Chapter 9.

The **TILT** attribute can be set when using QuickTime VR objects to specify the initial tilt angle (either up or down) for the scene. The value of the attribute is specified in degrees and typically ranges from around -42.5 to 42.5 degrees. The parameter has no meaning outside of QuickTime VR objects.

The **VOLUME** attribute may be set to a value from 0 to 256. The higher the value, the louder the audio track on the QuickTime movie. A value of **0** effectively mutes the soundtrack while **256** sets the volume at the maximum level. If the attribute is not set, the default is **256**. This option does not have meaning with QuickTime VR. This is a newer attribute and will not be supported under older versions of the QuickTime plug-in.

The **VSPACE** attribute should be set to the number of vertical pixels to buffer between the embedded object and surrounding content. This attribute is used in the same way as the corresponding attribute for the **<IMG>** element.

The **WIDTH** attribute is set to a pixel value or percentage. Be aware that the plug-in may not necessarily stretch the video image to take up the space. As mentioned previously, setting the **SCALE** attribute to **ASPECT** scales the movie to fit the bounding box set by the **HEIGHT** and **WIDTH** attributes. If the value supplied for the object width is smaller than the object's true width, it will be cropped to fit the dimensions provided. The **WIDTH** value must be set unless the **HIDDEN** attribute is used. Be careful when using small widths such as 0 and 1 pixels, as this can cause problems.

The QuickTime plug-in for Netscape is quite complex. The example shown in Figure 7-7 only illustrates the most basic use of the plug-in. The rendering of the QuickTime example is shown in Figure 7-8.

Interested readers are directed to Apple's QuickTime site (www.quicktime.apple.com) for more information about using QuickTime and QuickTime VR on the Web.

Microsoft's ActiveMovie

Microsoft's media technology comes under many guises but the main effort is called ActiveMovie. ActiveMovie provides services for the playback of multimedia streams from local files or network-based servers. Specifically, ActiveMovie allows playback of video and audio content, compressed in various formats. ActiveMovie supports the following formats:

MPEG-1 and MPEG-2 (.mpg, .mpeg, .mpv, .mp2, .mpa)
Audio-Video Interleaved (.avi)
Nonproprietary QuickTime files (.mov)
Wave (.wav)
AU (.au, .snd)
AIFF (.aif, .aiff)

```
<!DOCTYPE HTML PUBLIC "-//W3C//DTD HTML 3.2 Final//EN">
<HTML>
<TITLE>QuickTime Support Under Netscape</TITLE>
<BODY>

<FONT SIZE="4">This example shows a frame from a promotional
clip for QuickTime, as viewed in a Netscape browser.</FONT>

<EMBED SRC="quicktime.mov" WIDTH="136" HEIGHT="178"
AUTOPLAY="TRUE" ALIGN="LEFT" HSPACE="12" VSPACE="20">

</BODY>
</HTML>
```

Figure 7-7.   *Simple QuickTime plug-in example*

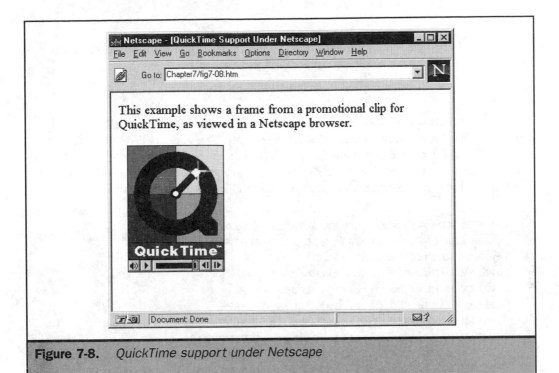

Figure 7-8.   *QuickTime support under Netscape*

Note   *If QuickTime is already available on a system, ActiveMovie will keep existing relationships. This is particularly useful since ActiveMovie does not support proprietary QuickTime features such as QuickTime VR.*

ActiveMovie-supported files can be played in one of two ways, either embedded within a Web page, or externally in a window displayed separately. External support of active content is handled through use of a linked object with the **<A>** element, as discussed earlier in the chapter. However, there are three HTML elements that you can use to embed ActiveMovie content. These elements are

```
<OBJECT>
<EMBED>
<IMG DYNSRC="movie.avi">
```

ACTIVEMOVIE WITH THE OBJECT ELEMENT   Using the **<OBJECT>** element, the **CLASSID** attribute must be set to the appropriate ActiveMovie class identifier (**CLSID**) so that a control to be used for playback is specified. The short code fragment sets this control explicitly and uses the **<PARAM>** element to specify the address of the file to play.

```
<OBJECT CLASSID="CLSID:05589FA1-C356-11CE-BF01-00AA0055595A">
<PARAM NAME="FileName" VALUE="test.avi">
</OBJECT>
```

The **CLASSID** value should not be entered by hand unless absolutely necessary. This may change someday, though it is very unlikely. The various **PARAM** values that can be set for the **<OBJECT>** element are too numerous to discuss. As discussed earlier in the chapter, a tool such as Microsoft's ControlPad should be used to set the **PARAM** values. To illustrate, some sample parameter values are shown here:

```
<OBJECT ID="TestMovie " HEIGHT="200" WIDTH="200"
 CLASSID="CLSID:05589FA1-C356-11CE-BF01-00AA0055595A">
<PARAM NAME="Version" VALUE="1">
<PARAM NAME="EnableContextMenu" VALUE="-1">
<PARAM NAME="ShowDisplay" VALUE="-1">
<PARAM NAME="ShowControls" VALUE="-1">
<PARAM NAME="ShowPositionControls" VALUE="0">
<PARAM NAME="ShowSelectionControls" VALUE="0">
<PARAM NAME="EnablePositionControls" VALUE="-1">
<PARAM NAME="EnableSelectionControls" VALUE="-1">
<PARAM NAME="ShowTracker" VALUE="-1">
<PARAM NAME="EnableTracker" VALUE="-1">
<PARAM NAME="AllowHideDisplay" VALUE="-1">
<PARAM NAME="AllowHideControls" VALUE="-1">
<PARAM NAME="MovieWindowSize" VALUE="0">
<PARAM NAME="FullScreenMode" VALUE="0">
<PARAM NAME="MovieWindowWidth" VALUE="200">
<PARAM NAME="MovieWindowHeight" VALUE="200">
<PARAM NAME="AutoStart" VALUE="0">
<PARAM NAME="AutoRewind" VALUE="-1">
<PARAM NAME="PlayCount" VALUE="1">
<PARAM NAME="Appearance" VALUE="1">
<PARAM NAME="BorderStyle" VALUE="1">
<PARAM NAME="FileName"
VALUE="http://www.bigcompany.com/movies/test.mpg">
<PARAM NAME="DisplayMode" VALUE="0">
<PARAM NAME="AllowChangeDisplayMode" VALUE="-1">
<PARAM NAME="DisplayForeColor" VALUE="16777215">
<PARAM NAME="DisplayBackColor" VALUE="0">
</OBJECT>
```

USING THE EMBED ELEMENT   It is also possible to insert an ActiveMovie file using the Netscape style **<EMBED>** syntax. The **<EMBED>** element works identically to the **<OBJECT>** element when used with Internet Explorer 3.0 or greater because the browser simply figures out what the content is and launches the ActiveMovie control with the appropriate parameters. An example of using ActiveMovie would be

```
<EMBED SRC="test.avi"
       AUTOSTART="FALSE"
       LOOP="FALSE"
       HEIGHT="100"
       WIDTH="100">
```

If ActiveMovie is available, this HTML fragment will work both under Netscape and Internet Explorer. Microsoft pushes the **<OBJECT>** element, and the HTML 4.0 specification favors this syntax. Nevertheless, for the time being, to guarantee support across browsers, enclosing an **EMBED** element inside of the **<OBJECT>** element, to allow for fallback, may be desirable.

USING THE <IMG> ELEMENT WITH THE DYNSRC=ATTRIBUTE   The DYNSRC attribute for the **<IMG>** element originated in Internet Explorer 2.0 and allowed AVI files to be played within a Web page. Although the syntax is currently maintained for backward compatibility, it is preferable to use the **<OBJECT>** or **<EMBED>** elements. Originally the **DYNSRC** attribute supported only AVI files, but testing shows that any ActiveMovie-supported data can be included with this syntax. The basic attributes for **<IMG>** are all valid; however the following additions are also available:

```
DYNSRC=URL of Active content
```

This attribute should be set to the URL, either relative or absolute, of the content to play.

```
CONTROLS
```

If this attribute is present, controls are presented below the content if possible. The attribute does not need a value.

```
LOOP=value
```

This attribute is used to set the number of times to loop the included content. When set to a positive integer, the content loops the specified number of times. When set to **-1** or the keyword **INFINITE**, the content loops continuously.

 START=FILEOPEN | MOUSEOVER

This attribute to the **<IMG>** element is used with **DYNSRC** to specify how the content should be played. Setting the value to **FILEOPEN** plays the content as soon as the data file has finished opening. Setting the value equal to **MOUSEOVER** delays playing the content until the mouse is positioned over it. The default action for active content is **FILEOPEN**.

An example of using the **DYNSRC** attribute with the image element for an AVI movie is shown in Figure 7-9.

Figure 7-10 shows a rendering of an example using the **DYNSRC** attribute under Internet Explorer.

In terms of browser support, it is difficult to come up with a best bet for simple Web video. Netscape 3.0 and Internet Explorer both support AVI in their Windows incarnations, but Macintosh users don't even get a consolation prize. For QuickTime,

```
<!DOCTYPE HTML PUBLIC "-//W3C//DTD HTML 3.2 Final//EN">
<HTML>
<HEAD>
<TITLE>DYNSRC Viewed Under Internet Explorer</TITLE>
</HEAD>

<BODY>

<FONT SIZE="4">
This example shows use of the DYNSRC element, with the CONTROL
attribute, as viewed in an Internet Explorer browser.
</FONT>

<IMG SRC="critter.gif" DYNSRC="critter.avi" CONTROLS
ALIGN="left" VSPACE="20">

</BODY>
</HTML>
```

Figure 7-9.   *DYNSRC HTML example*

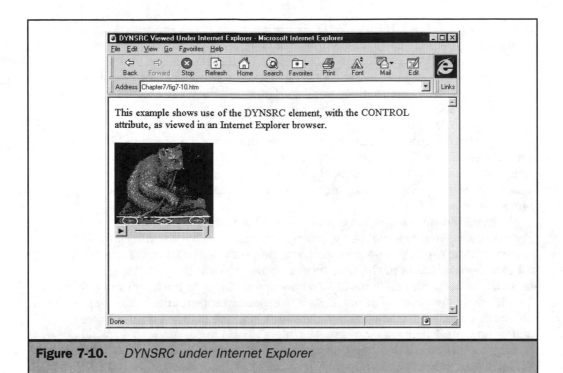

Figure 7-10.   *DYNSRC under Internet Explorer*

Internet Explorer and Netscape for Windows users without QuickTime installed on their operating system are left out in the cold. It seems that AVI might be less of a problem, but the size and synchronization quality of AVI video files makes the format far from ideal.

Other Video Formats

Like their audio compatriots, proprietary video formats offer one thing that many "standard" digital video formats lack: the possibility of truly streaming data. Remember, a 14.4Kbps modem user receives approximately 1K of data per second. If we could represent 1 second of video and sound in 1K and get that data to the end user in time to play it, we could effectively "stream" the video over the Internet. Still, there are a few potential drawbacks to streaming audio. First, to compress video far enough for streaming, you have to sacrifice a certain degree of quality. Second, the Internet protocols themselves do not readily support the requirements of streaming as discussed in the section about audio earlier in the chapter.

The main video formats include Progressive's RealVideo (www.real.com), VivoActive (www.vivo.com), Vosaic (www.vosaic.com), and VDOLive (www.vdo.net). Each of these technologies uses different attributes with the **<EMBED>** and **<OBJECT>** elements to support their own protocols. While most share common attributes such as **HEIGHT** and **WIDTH**, make sure to check the appropriate site for information about the particular syntax to support a proprietary video format. While proprietary formats may offer many benefits as far as streaming or image quality may be concerned, page authors should carefully consider the lack of built-in support before rushing out to use a new technology. Choosing the wrong technology could limit the audience that could view the content in the page.

Like audio, the future of video on the Internet ultimately lies in integration. People will resist downloading dozens of plug-ins for numerous data formats. They prefer single technologies that integrate into one whole presentation and QuickTime and ActiveMovie show how this can be done. Furthermore, Macromedia supports a variety of extras for Shockwave, and video should be possible to integrate into a presentation as well.

Even with better integration of video into a Web page, compression and performance guarantees will be the key points unless the bandwidth problem is resolved. More exotic compression technologies, such as fractal or wavelet video compression, will certainly become more commonplace as people struggle to stream users the smallest files and provide the closest semblance to the holy grail of Web TV. The Internet, however, is a difficult place to broadcast information. With single sites as video stream sources, latency will make streaming to distant users impossible no matter how much compression is used. Unless a wide range of video and audio mirror services are deployed, allowing European users the same access to video clips as users in North America or Asia, real-time broadcasting of video on the Internet will remain restricted to a select few.

Other Binary Formats

Besides audio and video, there are many other data objects that may be inserted into a Web page. The most common binary object besides those discussed in this chapter are Adobe Acrobat files, which are cross-platform documents, and Macromedia Shockwave complex multimedia files. Both of these technologies can be included in a Web page either using the **<EMBED>** syntax popularized by Netscape or the **<OBJECT>** syntax to reference an ActiveX control. The **<EMBED>** syntax is the safest until **<OBJECT>** is finally cleared up as the standard way to include a file. Of course, the **<OBJECT>** element syntax allows authors to include an **<EMBED>** element to allow for fallback on browsers that do not yet support **<OBJECT>**.

Shockwave

One of the most popular plug-ins on the Internet is Macromedia's Shockwave for Director plug-in (www.macromedia.com). This program also comes in an ActiveX control version for use with Microsoft's Internet Explorer. Because of compatibility issues, the **<EMBED>** syntax will be used.

Macromedia's Director authoring tool has a long history in the development of multimedia, including games and educational reference CD-ROMs. The program may be somewhat difficult to learn, but it's powerful enough to create any time-based animation an author could imagine, as shown by the example in Figure 7-11.

The biggest problem with Director-built animations is that they tend to be very large. Most are built to be delivered by CD-ROM. A technology called Shockwave compresses Director files (as well as other media types like Authorware and Freehand) for speedy delivery over the Internet. Shockwave also adds features to support interaction and playback over the Internet. To assemble a Director-based animation, a designer must create animation cells in a graphics program, put them together with Director, compress the result with a tool called Afterburner or by saving the file appropriately, and finally place it into a Web page with an **<EMBED>** element. End users with the Shockwave plug-in installed can then download and view the Director file.

The real advantage to using Director files for animation is the complexity of what can be done. As its name suggests, the program directs the flow of a program or animation. With Director, sound effects can be synchronized with animation, buttons can be activated, and games and interactive comic strips can be created. This requires mastering a fairly difficult program, and begs the question: is Director more than what's needed for simple animation? Despite the wonders of Shockwave, Director-based animations on the Web can still range from 50K to multiple megabytes

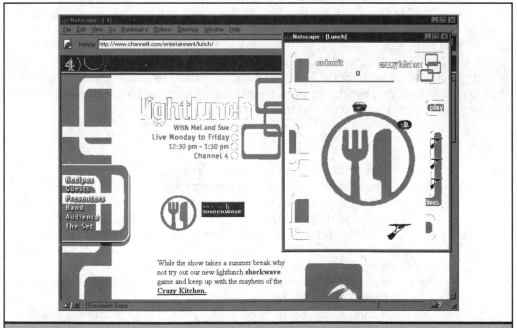

Figure 7-11.   *Example Shockwave page*

of data. Many users are not prepared to wait minutes to download a file that only plays for 10 or 15 seconds. Animation and multimedia applications must be delivered continuously or streamed if reasonable usability is to be achieved. One exciting technology that suggests the possibilities of streaming multimedia applications is the Enliven plug-in (www.narrative.com). Macromedia also has begun to support streaming Shockwave.

Shockwave files require a very simple **<EMBED>** statement with no extra attributes in most cases. For example, to embed a Shockwave filed called filename.dcr, use a code fragment similar to the one shown here:

```
<EMBED SRC="filename.dcr"
    ALIGN="LEFT"
    HEIGHT="100"
    WIDTH="400"
    HSPACE="10"
    VSPACE="10">
```

The dimensions of the Shockwave file are important but otherwise its syntax is really almost identical to a basic image insertion. Just be careful to avoid using **HEIGHT** and **WIDTH** values like **0** or **1**. For simple animation on a page that doesn't have complex timing requirements or interactivity, Shockwave is probably overkill; the animated GIF is probably a better idea. As discussed in the previous chapter, most modern browsers support animation in the form of GIF89a images, otherwise known as animated GIFs. There are no special features in HTML for animated GIFs. Simply set the **SRC** attribute for the **<IMG>** element to the image to insert. Remember that it is also possible to create a simple two-frame animation under browsers that support the **LOWSRC** attribute, but this approach lacks the timing and looping possibilities of an animated GIF and is not recommended.

Acrobat

Adobe's Acrobat technology is one approach to the distribution of electronic documentation. Originally proposed to help implement the mythical ideal of the "paperless office," Acrobat has now matured into a product with uses both on and off the Web. Adobe Acrobat provides the capability to deliver an electronic document to an end user without requiring the reader to have the authoring environment to open the file. Visually, it preserves the exact look and feel of the document, both on-screen and in print. For design-oriented Web publishers, Acrobat provides a highly motivating alternative to HTML that easily surpasses HTML's relatively simplistic and imprecise layout features as shown in Figure 7-12.

Acrobat files are created using a combination of traditional text authoring tools (word processors and desktop publishing software) and special Acrobat authoring software (Adobe Exchange or Distiller). They are then saved in a file format aptly

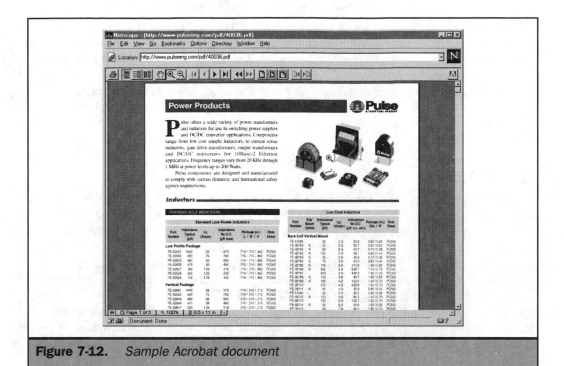

Figure 7-12.   *Sample Acrobat document*

named portable document format, or PDF. PDF files are small, self-contained documents that can be transported in a variety of ways: via diskette, CD-ROM, or network. The end user then reads the files using special Adobe Acrobat Reader software. Thus, by its very nature, Acrobat reader technology must be cross-platform. Acrobat Reader software is currently available for the following operating systems: Microsoft Windows3.1, Windows 95, and Windows NT; Macintosh; Linux; Sun Microsystems' Sun SPARC Solaris and Sun SPARC SunOS; Hewlett-Packard's HP-UX; Silicon Graphic's IRIX; IBM's AIX and OS/2; and Digital's VMS.

As far as HTML is concerned, inserting an Acrobat file in a page is a choice between linking to the document with the **<A>** element or using the **<EMBED>** or **<OBJECT>** element to insert the document inline. The format of the **<EMBED>** element is very straightforward as shown by the following HTML fragment:

```
<EMBED SRC="spec.pdf"
       ALIGN="LEFT
       HSPACE="20"
       HEIGHT="300"
       VSPACE="20"
       WIDTH="480">
```

The only thing to worry about is how the **HEIGHT** and **WIDTH** attributes are handled with the Acrobat Reader. Be careful not to use widths smaller than around 480 pixels, otherwise some of the controls on the reader will be chopped off. It seems like the controls should be settable with attributes or even eliminated, but any support for that appears to be undocumented. For more information about Acrobat and more details on how Acrobat might be included in a Web page, visit Adobe's Web site (www.adobe.com).

Summary

There are many different binary objects that may be inserted into a Web page. Most all these objects use either the **<EMBED>**, **<APPLET>**, or **<OBJECT>** element. There are a few instances in some proprietary browsers where special elements or attributes have been invented to deal with new media types. A prime example is the **DYNSRC** attribute to the **<IMG>** element as introduced by Microsoft. While the specific attributes vary from one media type to another, most of these elements share common attributes such as **HEIGHT**, **WIDTH**, **ALIGN**, **HSPACE**, **VSPACE**, and so on. For the most common media types such as audio and video, there is often built-in browser support either with a plug-in or a control. The syntax for these common forms was discussed in detail. A brief mention was also made of other important media types such as Shockwave and Acrobat. For the moment, the syntax is in a state of flux. However, the W3C is actively moving all included binary objects to a common object format using the **<OBJECT>** element.

Chapter 8

Introduction to Layout: Text Alignment, Tables, and Fonts

Web page designers strive to create attractive Web pages, but until recently, it hasn't been easy. HTML was not created with design features in mind. Even a simple layout technique like centering text has only been possible for a few years. Browser vendors have added many HTML attributes and elements in order to provide page developers with more control over the look and feel of their pages. Standardized elements such as **<TABLE>** were pressed into service as structuring and layout tools. New font facilities have also provided more design capabilities in HTML. Despite all these advances, tricks and workarounds are still occasionally required to create visually appealing pages. While it's best to avoid these nonstandard techniques, they often are a reality of page design—at least until technologies such as style sheets become more widely deployed and understood.

Design Requirements

In the best of all possible Web worlds, what would the designer want? The Web was created for a cross-platform environment with little support for screen presentation, but today's Web requires better positioning control. The ability to design for every platform is the ideal situation, but the reality of designing for a particular audience is becoming more accepted. By understanding a user's environment, the designer has more control over presentation. Designers also want more control over font use. Initially, there was no way to specify what font to use in a document, whether or not the user actually had the font. Other complex layout features common to electronic composition, such as more complex color control and layers, might also be desirable. At the very least, pixel-level control and font selection are necessary to bring the Web closer to a level equal with print design.

Simply providing features to allow pixel-level placement of objects and text on the screen doesn't make Web design a straightforward process, any more than font selection does. It is still difficult to understand exactly what kind of display environment the end user has. Web displays range from small liquid crystal screens on cellular phones and pocket organizers to 20-inch monitors, or larger. Each display may have different types of color support, ranging from four shades of gray on a typical handheld Windows-CE machine to millions of colors on a high-end graphic designer's system. There may not even be a screen at all, as in the case of voice-based browsers. If a guess is made about what screen configuration the user might have, or some programming facilities are provided to determine the same, a better layout could be provided.

The challenges of designing for the Web are significant. In the past they have only been exacerbated by the lack of technology and tools, not to mention problems associated with bandwidth or usability.

HTML Approach to Web Design

While HTML was not designed with layout in mind, it has been abused and extended to support layout as best it can. Today, there are many elements, both standard and nonstandard, that can provide layout control. These include the various **ALIGN** values for elements, new proprietary elements like **<SPACER>** and <MULTICOL>, and tables. This section covers some of the basic HTML elements used to control text and screen layout.

Alignment Choices

The first thing to consider in the HTML approach to layout is all the elements and attributes used to position text and objects on a page. Web page designers have long tended to abuse elements like **<UL>** to indent text. Many HTML page development tools still use this approach to move things around the screen. Layout problems didn't end with the inability to control text positioning. In early HTML, it was impossible to control text flow around images. Netscape eventually introduced a few elements and attribute changes useful for positioning, including the **<CENTER>** element.

The **<CENTER>** element can enclose any form of content, which is then centered in the browser window. In early HTML, a headline could be centered using the following code:

```
<CENTER><H1>Welcome to Big Company</H1></CENTER>
```

<CENTER> can be used around an arbitrary amount of content in many different forms, including images and text. Use of the **<CENTER>** element is common on the Web, and it has been included in the HTML 4.0 standard. However, the element is shorthand for **<DIV ALIGN="CENTER">**. Later, the **ALIGN** attribute (discussed in the next few paragraphs) was added to many elements.

  <CENTER> is a block element. As such, it may cause a line break, just as using the <DIV> element does.

Text Alignment

Beyond **<CENTER>**, there are many elements under HTML 3.2 and 4.0 that support the **ALIGN** attribute. The **<DIV>** element, which is used to create a division in a document, may have the **ALIGN** attribute set to **LEFT**, **CENTER**, **RIGHT**, or, under 4.0, **JUSTIFY**. If the **ALIGN** attribute is not set, text generally is aligned to the left when language direction is set to **ltr** (left to right) and to the right when the language direction is set to **rtl** (right to left). Up until recently, the **JUSTIFY** attribute did not work in most browsers; now it is supported by the latest versions of the two major browsers. The **<P>** paragraph element; the **<TABLE>** element; and the headings **<H1>**, **<H2>**, **<H3>**, **<H4>**, **<H5>**, and **<H6>** also support the **ALIGN** attribute, with the same basic values and meaning. Note that, as discussed in Chapter 6, the **ALIGN** attribute on the **<IMG>** element serves a different purpose.

Word Hinting

Under many current browsers, it is possible to control text layout beyond simple alignment. Because font size and browser widths may be different, word wrapping may occur in strange ways. Microsoft and Netscape, as well as many other browsers, support the **<NOBR>** and **<WBR>** elements as a way to provide browser hints for text layout.

The **<NOBR>** element makes sure that a line of text does not wrap to the next line, regardless of browser width. This element is useful for words or phrases that must be kept together on one line. If the line of text is long, it may extend beyond the browser window, obliging the user to scroll in order to view the unbroken text. A simple example of using the **<NOBR>** element is shown here:

```
<NOBR> This is a very important long line of text, so it should
not be allowed to break across two lines. </NOBR>
```

The <NOBR> Element

It is possible to use the **<NOBR>** element in conjunction with images, but the images may need to be scrolled in order to be seen. In some cases, the browser may attempt to rescale the images in order to fit them all on one line. In the case of WebTV, the browser will scale down to 80 percent of the image's original size before moving the image to the next line. **<NOBR>** acts different under WebTV because WebTV does not allow for any horizontal scrolling.

The **<NOBR>** element has no major attributes beyond those common to most HTML elements, such as **CLASS**, **ID**, **STYLE**, and **TITLE**.

The <WBR> Element

In contrast to the **<NOBR>** element, which is quite firm in its word wrapping, the **<WBR>** element allows the page designer to suggest a soft break within text enclosed by the **<NOBR>** element. (**<WBR>** is not part of the HTML standard, but many browsers support it.) In essence, the **<WBR>** element marks a spot where a line break can take place. The element is an advisory one, unlike **
** and **<NOBR>**, which force layout. Depending on the situation, the browser may choose to ignore the **<WBR>** element because there is no need for it. The **<WBR>** element is an empty element that does not require a closing tag. Here's a simple example showing how **<WBR>** works:

```
<NOBR>This is a very important long line of text that should not
break across two lines. If the line must be split, it should
happen here <WBR> and nowhere else.</NOBR>
```

The **<WBR>** element should only exist within a **<NOBR>** element, although it may work outside of it. This element does not have any major attributes, though **CLASS**, **ID**, **STYLE**, and **TITLE** are typically specified as being allowed in the element. It is unlikely that any attribute but **ID** would be used; applying a style to a **<WBR>** element would have no effect, since it encloses no text. The **ID** attribute could be used to manipulate the element, perhaps to remove it using a scripting language. The basic point, and a very useful one, of this element, is simply to suggest a line break point.

Other Word Hinting Techniques

The last techniques for word hinting really aren't hinting at all, but very strict techniques to force spacing. The first idea is to use the **<PRE>** element, as discussed in Chapter 4. Any text enclosed by **<PRE>** preserves returns, tabs, and spaces. Using **<PRE>**, it is possible to force text to lay out the way the page author requires, even forcing the browser to scroll to the right to read text. Generally speaking, the browser changes the typeface of any preformatted text to a fixed-width font such as Courier. This font change may not be desired. How can spaces be inserted to improve text layout without a font change? Using the character entity ** ** or **&160;** should insert a nonbreaking space that will not be collapsed by the browser. To enter three spaces between words, use **   **. While use of this entity is somewhat a crutch, it is interesting to note how many of these character entities will be entered into a document when using a so-called WYSIWYG page editor.

Alignment with Images

As discussed in Chapter 6, under HTML 2.0 the **<IMG>** element specified the **ALIGN** attribute with allowed values of **TOP**, **BOTTOM**, or **MIDDLE**. When an image was included within a block structure of text, the next line of text would be aligned to the top, middle, or bottom of the image, depending on the value of the **ALIGN** attribute. If the attribute were not set, it would default to the bottom.

One problem with image alignment in early HTML was that the text didn't flow around the image. Only one line of text was aligned next to the image. Netscape introduced the **LEFT** and **RIGHT** values for **ALIGN**, which allowed text to flow around the image. When setting an image element like **<IMG SRC="logo.gif"**

ALIGN="LEFT">, the image is aligned to the left and the text flows around to the right. Correspondingly, when using code such as **<IMG SRC="logo.gif" ALIGN="RIGHT">**, the image is aligned to the right and the text flows around to the left.

Netscape and Microsoft also support four other values for **ALIGN**: **TEXTOP**, **BASELINE**, **ABSMIDDLE**, and **ABSBOTTOM**. Avoid these attributes in most cases, since they may not be supported identically across browsers, and are not yet part of any standards. For more information on these attributes, see Chapter 6 as well as the element reference (Appendix A).

Because text may flow in undesirable ways around images, extensions to the **
** element were developed. The **
** element now takes a **CLEAR** attribute, which can be set to **LEFT**, **RIGHT**, **ALL**, or **NONE**. By default, the **CLEAR** attribute is set to **NONE**, which makes the element produce a carriage return. When an image is aligned to the **LEFT**, it may be useful to return past the image to start a new section of text. Placing another object using **<BR CLEAR="LEFT">** causes the browser to go clear down a column until the left side of the window is clear. **<BR CLEAR="RIGHT">** does the same thing in regard to right-aligned images. When trying to pass multiple images that may be aligned both on the **LEFT** and **RIGHT**, use **<BR CLEAR="ALL">**.

While the **ALIGN** attribute and the extensions to **
** provide some degree of page layout control (to be discussed in Chapter 10), technologies such as style sheets handle positioning with greater precision. Until style sheets become more common, there are certain instances where the **<IMG>** element and its attributes (including **HSPACE**, **VSPACE**, and **ALIGN**) can be used to create interesting page layouts.

Invisible Images and Layout

Another way to push text around in a layout is by using an image. This approach is well known to users of the desktop publishing program QuarkXPress. With this program, users can create invisible regions and run text around them to achieve specific layout effects. This can be done under HTML by using an invisible image in combination with the **ALIGN**, **HSPACE**, and **VSPACE** attributes. Given a clear 1-pixel image, the designer can perform a variety of interesting tricks. For example, take a clear pixel and set the **HSPACE** value to **5**. Now put this at the front of a paragraph, as shown here:

```
<P><IMG SRC="pixel.gif" HSPACE=5>This is the start of the
paragraph.</P>
```

Given this fragment, the first line of the paragraph is indented 11 pixels (5 pixels on either side of the one-pixel image). Imagine doing the same thing between lines using the **VSPACE** attribute. By setting the **VSPACE** attribute and using hard carriage returns, the designer could achieve arbitrary line spacing. Taken to an extreme, a design like the one in Figure 8-1 is possible using this so-called invisible pixel trick.

Imagine creating a much larger region with an invisible pixel by setting the **HEIGHT** and **WIDTH** attributes of the **<IMG>** element and using **ALIGN** to flow text around the invisible region. For example, **<IMG SRC="pixel.gif" HEIGHT="100" WIDTH="50" ALIGN="LEFT">** could create a large invisible block to run text around.

The pixel trick can be a useful workaround. In certain situations, however, the pixel trick has its failings. One potential use for the invisible pixel trick is to force line space between lines. For example, the code **<IMG SRC="pixel.gif" VSPACE="10">** could allow the designer to create line spacing. But what happens when the page is viewed with the images turned off, or the stop button is pressed early? The resulting page might look like the one in Figure 8-2.

Despite its problems, image layout tricks are still very common on the Web. They are considered so useful that Netscape introduced a special element called **<SPACER>** that mimics much of the functionality of invisible images.

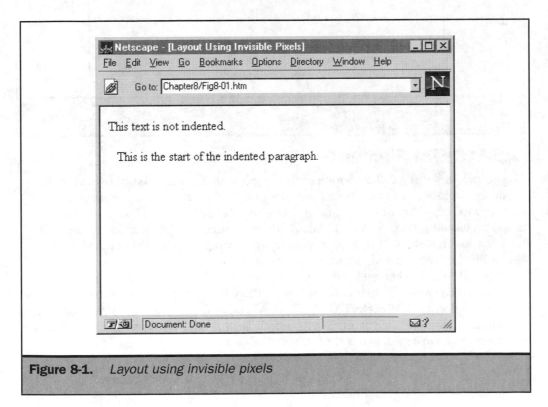

Figure 8-1.   *Layout using invisible pixels*

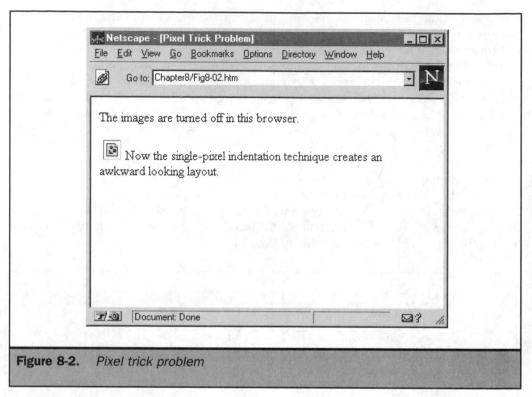

Figure 8-2.   Pixel trick problem

The <SPACER> Element

The proprietary **<SPACER>** element, introduced with Netscape 3.0, allows users to create invisible regions to push text and other objects around the browser screen. In many ways, this element is a response to the invisible single-pixel GIF trick discussed in the previous section. While **<SPACER>** does an adequate job of reproducing this hack for screen design, its lack of cross-platform support suggests that using the single-pixel image or a style sheet is more appropriate.

The **<SPACER>** element is an empty element and is used to insert an invisible region to force layout. Its main attribute is **TYPE**, which specifies the form of the invisible region as **HORIZONTAL**, **VERTICAL**, or **BLOCK**. The other attributes are used to set the size of the spacer. Example code to create a horizontal space of 75 pixels between words in a sentence is shown here:

```
This is the start of the sentence <SPACER TYPE="HORIZONTAL"
SIZE="75"> and this is the end.
```

As with invisible pixels, it is possible to push lines apart. In the next example, the **<SPACER>** element is set to create a vertical region of 15 pixels to give the appearance of double spacing. Notice how the vertical spacer induces line breaks.

```
This is line one.
 <SPACER TYPE="VERTICAL" SIZE="15">
 This is line two
```

The **<SPACER>** element can only be one type at a time. It is not possible to have a vertical and horizontal spacer. If such functionality is required, use the **BLOCK** type. The **<SPACER>** element can also be used to flow text around invisible blocks. The following HTML code creates an invisible runaround region 150 pixels high and 100 pixels across.

```
... text...
<SPACER TYPE="BLOCK" HEIGHT="150" WIDTH="100" ALIGN="LEFT">
... text...
```

Notice how the **ALIGN** attribute is used just as it would be with an image, with a default alignment value of **BOTTOM** and so on. The element could also be combined with **<BR CLEAR=LEFT>** to avoid the spacing element affecting text that may follow.

<SPACER> Syntax

The complete syntax for **<SPACER>** under Netscape 3.0 is shown here:

```
<SPACER>
     ALIGN=LEFT|RIGHT|TOP|ABSMIDDLE|ABSBOTTOM|
     TEXTTOP|MIDDLE|BASELINE|BOTTOM       (Use with BLOCK)
     HEIGHT=pixels      (Use with BLOCK)
     SIZE=pixels        (Use with HORIZONTAL and VERTICAL)
     TYPE=HORIZONTAL|VERTICAL|BLOCK
     WIDTH=pixels       (Use with BLOCK)>
```

Be careful not to make layouts rely on **<SPACER>**, as it is a somewhat all or nothing element, that is completely unsupported beyond Netscape browsers. If it is just hinting, or providing browser tips, page layout such as line spacing can be used and will safely be ignored by other browsers. Invisible images, on the other hand, may show up under text-only browsers if you do not set the **ALT** text to no value. When using block forms to create runaround space, the invisible pixel trick may still provide a better workaround than **<SPACER>**, because it will be picked up by most graphical browsers.

The <MULTICOL> Element

Like **<SPACER>**, the <MULTICOL> element is unique to Netscape browsers starting with Navigator 3.0. This element allows page designers to specify text in multiple columns, which are rendered with equal width. The element is not supported in previous versions of Netscape or Internet Explorer; it will not degrade gracefully if layout depends on it.

The most important attribute of the **<MULTICOL>** element is **COLS**, which is set to the number of text columns to display. The browser should attempt to flow the text evenly across columns and make the columns the same height, except for the last column, which may be shorter depending on the amount of text in the columns. The element also supports the attribute **GUTTER**, which is used to specify the gutter space between columns in pixels. By default, the gutter width (if unspecified) is 10 pixels. The last attribute supported by **<MULTICOL>** is **WIDTH**, which specifies the width of each column in pixels. All columns are the same width; there is no way to directly adjust a particular column's width. If the **WIDTH** attribute is not set, its value is determined by subtracting from the display width the number of pixels that constitute the gutter and then dividing by the number of columns set in the **COLS** attribute. The syntax is summarized here:

```
<MULTICOL
    COLS=number of columns
    GUTTER=gutter width in pixels or percentage
    WIDTH=column width in pixels or percentage>

Text to put in column form

</MULTICOL>
```

An example showing how **<MULTICOL>** can be used is shown in Figure 8-3. The rendering of the last example is shown in Figure 8-4. Notice how the layout is not preserved in Internet Explorer.

```
<!DOCTYPE HTML PUBLIC "-//W3C//DTD HTML 3.2 Final//EN">
<HTML>
<HEAD>
<TITLE>MULTICOL Example</TITLE>
</HEAD>
<BODY>

<MULTICOL COLS="2" GUTTER="50" WIDTH="80%">
The rain in Spain falls mainly on the plain. Now is the time
for all good men to come to the aid of the country. There's no
business like show business. The rain in Spain falls mainly on
the plain.  Now is the time for all good men to come to the aid
of the country. There's no business like show business. The rain
in Spain falls mainly on the plain.  Now is the time for all good
men to come to the aid of the country. There's no business like show
business. The rain in Spain falls mainly on the plain. Now is the
time for all good men to come to the aid of the country. There's no
business like show business. The rain in Spain falls mainly on the
plain. The rain in Spain falls mainly on the plain.
</MULTICOL>

</BODY>
</HTML>
```

Figure 8-3.   *<MULTICOL> example*

When including other objects within the **<MULTICOL>** element, particularly tables and images with alignment information, the element will be unpredictable, as shown in Figure 8-5.

Because browsers are generally unable to set hyphenation, page authors may need to manually insert **<WBR>** elements between words that may overrun column size. A further problem with **<MULTICOL>** is that it will degrade when too many columns are set, so try to keep the value for **COLS** around six or less. An example showing how the problem of too many columns and how **<WBR>** can help is shown in Figure 8-6.

Use the **<MULTICOL>** element only in an all-Netscape environment. This element is only a somewhat more flexible shorthand notation for what can be accomplished with tables, except for text reflow.

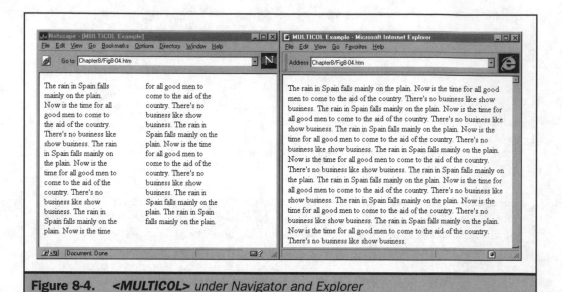

Figure 8-4. **<MULTICOL>** under Navigator and Explorer

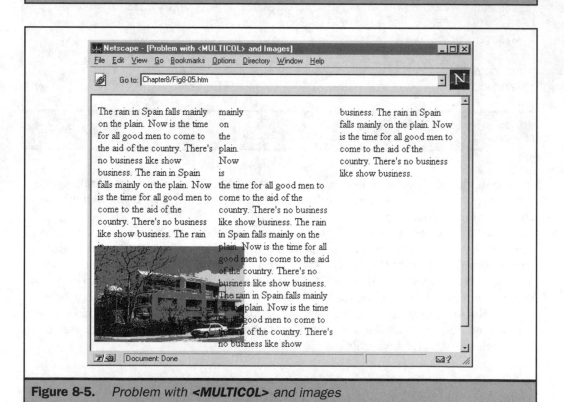

Figure 8-5. Problem with **<MULTICOL>** and images

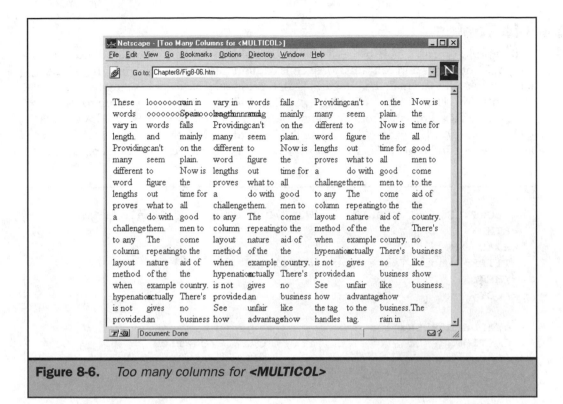

Figure 8-6. *Too many columns for* **<MULTICOL>**

Introduction to Tables

A table represents information in a tabular way, like a spreadsheet: distributed across a grid of rows and columns. In printed documents, tables commonly serve a subordinate function, illustrating some point described by an accompanying text. Tables still perform this illustrative function in HTML documents. Because many HTML documents rely less on text than their printed equivalents, Web-based tables have become an important way to structure documents. Unlike printed tables, HTML tables can contain information that is *dynamic,* or interactive. This capability often leads to HTML tables being used to perform a function not commonly associated with them: document layout and design. Tables are also the natural way to represent the results of a database query. To address this use, the databinding feature allows an HTML table template to be directly connected with a database source. A table is dynamically generated using the template and the results of a particular database query. Taken together, these capabilities make tables one of HTML's most useful and sophisticated resources.

Simple Tables

In its simplest form, a table places information inside the cells formed by dividing a rectangle into rows and columns. Most cells contain data. Some cells, usually on the table's top or side, contain headings. HTML represents a basic table using four elements. In HTML, a table, **<TABLE>** … **</TABLE>**, contains one or more rows, **<TR>** … **</TR>**. Each row contains cells holding a heading, **<TH>** … **</TH>**, or data, **<TD>** … **</TD>**. The example in Figure 8-7 illustrates a basic table. Note that the only attribute used in Figure 8-7 is **BORDER**, which is used to specify a 1-pixel border so it

```
<!DOCTYPE HTML PUBLIC "-//W3C//DTD HTML 3.2 Final//EN">
<HTML>
<HEAD>
<TITLE>Simple Table Example</TITLE>
</HEAD>
<BODY>

 <TABLE BORDER="1">
<CAPTION>Basic Fruit Comparison Chart</CAPTION>
    <TR>
        <TH>Fruit</TH>
        <TH>Color</TH>
    </TR>
    <TR>
        <TD>Apple</TD>
        <TD>Red</TD>
    </TR>
    <TR>
        <TD>Avocado</TD>
        <TD>Green</TD>
    </TR>
    <TR>
        <TD>Watermelon</TD>
        <TD>Pink</TD>
    </TR>
 </TABLE>
</BODY>
</HTML>
```

Figure 8-7.   *Simple table example*

is clear what the table looks like. The rendering for the simple table under various browsers is shown in Figure 8-8.

This simple table example shows the use of the most basic table elements: headings, rows, and data cells.

Again, a table is made up of rows enclosed within **<TR>** . . . **</TR>**. The number of rows in the table is determined by the number of occurrences of the **<TR>** element. What about columns? Generally, the number of columns in a table is determined by the maximum number of data cells indicated by **<TD>** . . . **</TD>**, or headings indicated by **<TH>** . . . **</TH>** within the table. It may be useful to hint to the browser at the number of columns in the table by setting the **COLS** attribute, introduced in HTML 4.0, for the **<TABLE>** element equal to the number of columns in the table (for example, **<TABLE BORDER="1" COLS="2">**, as in the last example).

The headings for the table are set using the **<TH>** element. Generally the browser renders the style of headings differently, possibly centering the contents of the heading and placing the text in bold style. The actual cells of the table are indicated by the **<TD>** element. Both the **<TD>** and **<TH>** elements may enclose an arbitrary amount

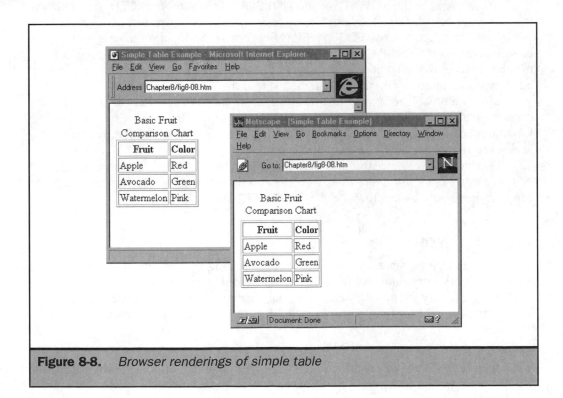

Figure 8-8.   *Browser renderings of simple table*

of data of just about any type. In the previous example, a full paragraph of text could be enclosed in a table cell along with an image, lists, and links. Last, the table may have a caption enclosed within **<CAPTION>** ... **</CAPTION>**, whose contents are generally rendered above or below the table indicating what the table contains.

Because tables may get very complex, the close tags for the **<TR>**, **<TH>**, and **<TD>** tags are optional and can be omitted. This may make for a cleaner-looking table. Some of the examples in this chapter forego the use of close tags. HTML writers are still encouraged to use the close tags, as well as indentation, so that table cells and rows are clearly defined, particularly for nested tables.

ROWSPAN and COLSPAN

While the previous example shows that it is possible to create a simple table with a simple structure, what about when the table cells need to be larger or smaller? The HTML code in Figure 8-9 creates tables that are somewhat more complicated. By adding the **ROWSPAN** and **COLSPAN** attributes to the table elements, it is possible to create data cells that span a given number of rows or columns. The rendering of this idea appears in Figure 8-10.

The basic idea of the **ROWSPAN** and **COLSPAN** attributes for **<TD>** and **<TH>** is to extend the size of the cells across two or more rows or columns respectively. To set a cell to span three rows, use **<TD ROWSPAN="3">**; to set a heading to span two columns, use **<TH COLSPAN="2">**. Setting the value of **ROWSPAN** to more than the number of rows in the table does not extend the size of the table. Browsers should not add rows or columns when attributes suggest that there are more.

Besides being able to span rows and columns, the **<TABLE>** element, as well as its enclosed elements **<TD>**, **<TH>**, and **<CAPTION>**, supports a variety of attributes for alignment, sizing, and layout. The example in Figure 8-11 shows a more complex table example.

The last example shows that it is possible to place any form of content in a cell, as well as control the individual size of the cells and the table itself. The logical step is to control page layout by creating a grid with the **<TABLE>** element.

Tables for Layout

In and of themselves, tables do not seem that interesting to many people. They are, however, a very important tool for HTML page layout. The foundation of graphic design is the ability to spatially arrange visual elements in relation to each other. Tables can be used to define a layout grid for just this purpose. Prior to the advent of

```
<!DOCTYPE HTML PUBLIC "-//W3C//DTD HTML 3.2 Final//EN">
<HTML>
<HEAD>
<TITLE>ROWSPAN and COLSPAN Example</TITLE>
</HEAD>
<BODY>

 <TABLE BORDER="1">
<CAPTION>ROWSPAN Example</CAPTION>
   <TR>
       <TD ROWSPAN=2>Element 1</TD>
       <TD>Element 2</TD>
   </TR>
   <TR>
       <TD>Element 3</TD>
   </TR>
 </TABLE>

  <BR><BR>

 <TABLE BORDER="1">
<CAPTION>COLSPAN Example</CAPTION>
   <TR>
       <TD COLSPAN="3">Element 1</TD>
   </TR>
   <TR>
       <TD>Element 2</TD>
       <TD>Element 3</TD>
       <TD>Element 4</TD>
   </TR>
 </TABLE>
</BODY>
</HTML>
```

Figure 8-9.   ***ROWSPAN*** *and* ***COLSPAN*** *example*

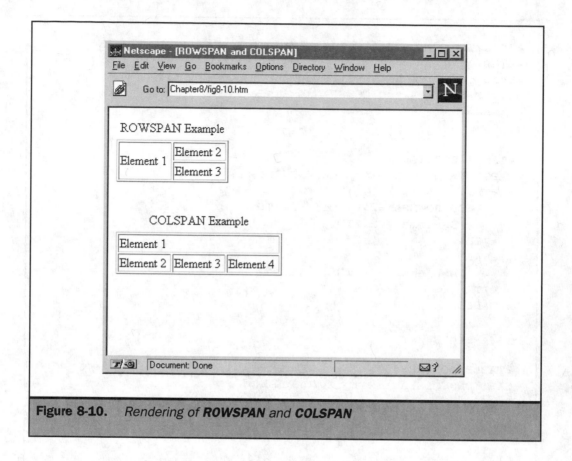

Figure 8-10. *Rendering of **ROWSPAN** and **COLSPAN***

style sheets supporting positioning, tables were the only reliable way to accomplish this. They remain the most commonly used technique.

The key to using a table in order to create a precise page grid is the use of the **WIDTH** attribute. The **WIDTH** attribute for the **<TABLE>** element specifies the width of a table in pixels, or as percentage value, such as 80 percent. It is also possible to set the individual pixel widths of each cell within the table, using a **WIDTH** attribute for the **<TD>** or **<TH>** element. Imagine trying to create a 400-pixel column of text down the page with a buffer of 50 pixels on the left and 100 pixels on the right. With older HTML, this would be literally impossible without making the text a giant image. With a table, it is easy, as shown by the markup code in Figure 8-12.

```html
<!DOCTYPE HTML PUBLIC "-//W3C//DTD HTML 4.0 Final//EN">
<HTML>
<HEAD>
<TITLE>Complex Table Example</TITLE>
</HEAD>
<BODY>

 <P>Notice how the text of a paragraph
 <TABLE ALIGN="LEFT" BORDER="1" WIDTH="300">
<CAPTION ALIGN="BOTTOM">The Super Widget</CAPTION>
   <TR>
      <TD ROWSPAN="2"><IMG SRC="widget.gif" ALT="Super Widget"
      WIDTH="100" HEIGHT="120"></TD>
   <TH BGCOLOR=LIGHTGREEN>Specifications</TH>
   </TR>
   <TR>
      <TD>
         <UL>
            <LI>Diameter: 10 cm
            <LI>Composition: Kryptonite
            <LI>Color: Green
         </UL>
      </TD>
   </TR>
 </TABLE>
can flow around a table just as it would any other
embedded object form. Notice how the text of a paragraph
can flow around a table just as it would any other
embedded object form. Notice how the text of a paragraph
can flow around a table just as it would any other
embedded object form.</P>

</BODY>
</HTML>
```

Figure 8-11.   *Complex table example*

```
<!DOCTYPE HTML PUBLIC "-//W3C//DTD HTML 3.2 Final//EN">
<HTML>
<HEAD>
<TITLE>Table Layout</TITLE>
</HEAD>
<BODY>
 <TABLE BORDER=0>
   <TR>
      <TD WIDTH="50"><BR></TD>
      <TD WIDTH="400">
  <H1 ALIGN="CENTER">Layout is here!</H1>
      <HR>
<P>This is a very simple layout that would
have been nearly impossible to do without tables.</P>
      </TD>
      <TD WIDTH="100"><BR></TD>
   </TR>
 </TABLE>
</BODY>
</HTML>
```

Figure 8-12.   *Simple layout with table*

In Figure 8-12, **the BORDER** value is set to zero. This attribute isn't necessary; if the browser does not see a **BORDER** attribute in the **<TABLE>** element, it won't draw a border. It may be convenient to keep the attribute in, but set to zero, so the border can be turned on and off to check to see what is going on with a particular layout. When creating empty table cells, it is a good idea to put a line break **
** or a nonbreaking space (** **) into the cell so it doesn't collapse vertically.

Tables might also be used to provide more precise layout in relation to a background. One popular design concept employs a vertical strip of colored background on the left of the page, that contains navigation controls; the rest of the document contains the main text. Without tables, it is difficult to keep body content from going on top of the background image. An example of the HTML markup code to create a two-column design that works on top of a 100-pixel-wide color background is shown in Figure 8-13.

The rendering of this layout appears in Figure 8-14. Note how the foreground content (the **<BODY>** content) is aligned over the **BACKGROUND** image. Another way to achieve such effects is to set the **BGCOLOR** attribute for the table cells. **BGCOLOR** was introduced in Netscape Navigator 3.0 and is also supported in

```html
<!DOCTYPE HTML PUBLIC "-//W3C//DTD HTML 3.2 Final//EN">
<HTML>
<HEAD>
<TITLE>Table Layout with Background</TITLE>
</HEAD>

<BODY BACKGROUND="yellowtile.gif">

 <TABLE WIDTH="550">
   <TR>
      <TD WIDTH="100">
<A HREF="about.htm">About</A><BR><BR>
<A HREF="prodcuts.htm">Products</A><BR><BR>
<A HREF="staff.htm">Staff</A><BR><BR>
<A HREF="contact.htm">Contact</A><BR><BR>
      </TD>
      <TD WIDTH="450">
<H1 ALIGN=CENTER>Welcome to Big Company, Inc.</H1>
  <HR>
<P>This text is positioned over a white background;
the navigation links are over a colored background.
This layout combines a table with background images.
</P>
      </TD>
   </TR>
 </TABLE>
</BODY>
</HTML>
```

Figure 8-13.   *Tables to integrate foreground and background*

Internet Explorer. Background shading can also be controlled via style sheets, as discussed in Chapter 10. While such techniques would appear to help get rid of the headaches of aligning foreground and background elements, there is an issue of backward compatibility.

In HTML documents, tables have many nontraditional uses for graphic design and layout. These extend beyond creating grids; even single-cell tables can be put to many uses. As a simple example, consider using a table to define a pastel-colored "sticky" note. These can be inserted throughout HTML documents to draw attention to

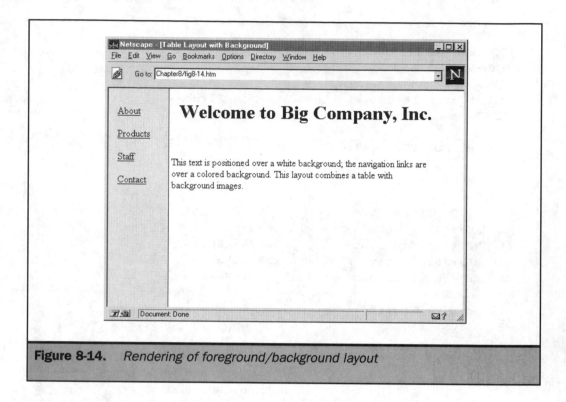

Figure 8-14. Rendering of foreground/background layout

important ideas. An example HTML fragment to insert a single-cell, colored table is shown here:

```
<TABLE ALIGN=LEFT BGCOLOR="#FFFFCC" CELLPADDING="20" HSPACE="15"
VSPACE="15">
 <TR><TD>This is an important point!</TD></TR>
 </TABLE>
```

Notice that this example contains only a single data item—certainly unusual for a conventional table. It also demonstrates two more **<TABLE>** attributes. The **BGCOLOR** attribute sets the background color for a table using either a standard color name or hexadecimal RGB value. The given value indicates a light pastel yellow. The **CELLPADDING** attribute sets the distance in pixels between a table cell's outer border and the point at which content begins. Besides "sticky" notes and other forms of colored tables to draw out information, there are various uses for single-cell tables. When combined with width, this might just be a good way to constrain the text within a page.

Tables in HTML 4.0

So far, the discussion of tables has mentioned five elements: **<TABLE>**, **<CAPTION>**, **<TR>**, **<TH>**, and **<TD>**. These are the most commonly used elements. HTML 4.0 introduces several new elements that provide increased control over table formatting: **<COL>**, **<COLGROUP>**, **<THEAD>**, **<TFOOT>**, and **<TBODY>**. An HTML table as defined by the HTML 4.0 specification has the following structure:

- An opening **<TABLE>** element.
- An optional caption specified by **<CAPTION>** . . . **</CAPTION>**.
- One or more groups of rows. These may consist of a header section specified by **<THEAD>**, a footer section specified by **<TFOOT>**, and a body section specified by **<TBODY>**. While all these elements are optional, the table must at least contain a series of rows specified by **<TR>**. The rows themselves must contain at least one header or data cell, specified by **<TH>** and **<TD>**, respectively.
- One or more groups of columns specified by **<COLGROUP>** with individual columns within the group indicated by **<COL>**.
- A closing **</TABLE>** element.

The main difference between HTML 4.0 tables and the more basic table form is that rows and columns may be grouped together. The advantage to grouping is that it conveys structural information about the table that may be useful for rendering the table more quickly, or keeping it together when displaying on the screen. For example, specifying the **<THEAD>** or **<TFOOT>** may allow a consistent header or footer to be used across larger tables when they span many screens (or sheets of paper when printed). The use of these elements is mandatory when using dynamically populated tables that use the idea of databinding as introduced by Microsoft and discussed later in this chapter.

The example in Figure 8-15 explains the use of the new HTML 4.0 table elements.

The first thing to notice in Figure 8-15 is the use of the **FRAME** and **RULES** attributes for the **<TABLE>** element. The **FRAME** attribute specifies which sides of the frame that surrounds the table will be visible. In Figure 8-15, the value is set to **BOX**, which means that the frame around the outside of the table is on. Other values for this attribute include **ABOVE**, **BELOW**, **HSIDES**, **VSIDES**, **LHS**, **RHS**, **VOID**, and **BORDER**. The meaning of all these values is discussed in the table syntax sections that follow.

Do not confuse the idea of the **FRAME** attribute with that of **RULES**. The **RULES** attribute defines the rules that may appear between the actual cells in the table. In Figure 8-15, the value of **RULES** is set to **GROUPS**; this displays lines between the row or column groupings of the table. The **RULES** attribute also takes a value of **NONE**, **GROUPS**, **ROWS**, **COLS**, and **ALL**.

```
<!DOCTYPE HTML PUBLIC "-//W3C//DTD HTML 4.0 Final//EN"
<HTML>
<HEAD>
<TITLE>HTML 4.0 Tables</TITLE>
</HEAD>
<BODY>
 <TABLE BORDER="1" FRAME="BOX" RULES="GROUPS">
<CAPTION>Fun with Food</CAPTION>
<COLGROUP>
    <COL>
</COLGROUP>
<COLGROUP>
    <COL ALIGN="CENTER">
    <COL ALIGN="CHAR" CHAR=".">
</COLGROUP>
<THEAD>
    <TR>
        <TH BGCOLOR="YELLOW">Fruit</TH>
        <TH BGCOLOR="YELLOW">Color<TH>
        <TH BGCOLOR="YELLOW">Cost per pound<TH>
    </TR>
</THEAD>
<TBODY>
    <TR>
        <TD>Grapes</TD>
        <TD>Purple</TD>
        <TD>$1.25</TD>
    </TR>
    <TR>
        <TD>Cherries</TD>
        <TD>Red</TD>
        <TD>$1.79</TD>
    </TR>
    <TR>
        <TD>Kiwi</TD>
        <TD>Brown</TD>
        <TD>$10.50</TD>
    </TR>
</TBODY>
```

Figure 8-15.   *HTML 4.0 table example*

```
<TFOOT>
    <TR>
        <TH COLSPAN="3">This has been another fine table
        example.</TH>
    </TR>
</TFOOT>
</TABLE>

</BODY>
</HTML>
```

Figure 8-15. *HTML 4.0 table example* (continued)

The other major difference in the table shown in Figure 8-15 is the inclusion of the **<THEAD>** and **<TBODY>** elements. **<THEAD>** contains the rows (**<TR>**), headings (**<TH>**), and cells (**<TD>**) that make up the head of the table. Beyond organization and the application of styles, the advantage of grouping these items is that it may be possible to repeat the elements over multiple pages (under certain browsers). Imagine printing out a large table and having the headers for the rows appear on every page of the printout. This is what **<THEAD>** may be able to provide. Similarly, the **<TFOOT>** element creates a footer to use in the table, which may also run over multiple pages. Last, the **<TBODY>** indicates the body of the table, which contains the rows and columns that make up the inner part of a table. While there should be only one occurrence of **<THEAD>** and **<TFOOT>**, there may be multiple occurrences of **<TBODY>**. Multiple bodies in a document may seem confusing, but these elements are more for grouping purposes than anything else. When a table is specified without **<THEAD>**, **<TFOOT>**, or **<TBODY>** it is assumed to have one body by default.

While tables are becoming more difficult to code, you can take heart from the variety of tools that can be used to create tables. Most HTML editing tools can easily add the elements needed to make tables. This is good, since the combination of HTML 4.0's new table elements with various proprietary extensions introduced by Microsoft, Netscape, and WebTV results in a dizzying array of elements, and attributes for the individual table elements. The next few sections specify a complete syntax for the various table elements.

<TABLE> Syntax

Every table is defined by the **<TABLE>** element, which must have a corresponding **</TABLE>** element. These elements indicate that the contained content is organized into a table with rows and columns as specified by the **<TR>**, **<TD>**, and **<TH>** elements. It is also possible to use the **<CAPTION>**, **<COL>**, **<COLGROUP>**,

<THEAD>, <TBODY>, <TFOOT>, and **<THEAD>** elements to organize a table and apply attributes to numerous columns, rows, and data cells at once. A complete syntax for the **<TABLE>** element, including proprietary extensions, is shown here. The attributes introduced by the HTML 4.0 specification are noted to show the extent to which the table syntax has expanded under the new specification.

```
<TABLE
    ALIGN=LEFT|RIGHT|CENTER
    BACKGROUND=URL of image     (IE and N4)
    BGCOLOR=color        (4.0)
    BORDER=pixels
    BORDERCOLOR=color         (Netscape and IE)
    BORDERCOLORDARK=color        (IE)
    BORDERCOLORLIGHT=color        (IE)
    CELLBORDER=pixels        (WebTV)
    CELLPADDING=pixels
    CELLSPACING=pixels
    CLASS=name for style sheet access   (4.0)
    COLS=number of columns       (4.0)
    DATAPAGESIZE=n         (IE)
    DATASRC=#ID         (IE)
    DIR=text direction        (4.0)
    FRAME=ABOVE|BELOW|BORDER|BOX|INSIDES|LHS|RHS|VOID|VSIDES   (4.0)
    HEIGHT=pixel or percentage value   (Netscape and IE)
    HREF= Destination URL        (WebTV)
    ID=unique value        (4.0)
    LANG=ISO language abbreviation   (4.0)
    LANGUAGE=JAVASCRIPT|JSCRIPT|VBSCRIPT|VBS   (IE)
    RULES=ALL|COLS|GROUPS|NONE|ROWS   (4.0)
    STYLE=style sheet properties       (4.0)
    TITLE=advisory text        (4.0)
    TRANSPARENCY=0 to 100      (WebTV)
    WIDTH=pixels or percentage value
    event=script         (4.0)>

Table elements

</TABLE>
```

The **ALIGN** attribute may be set to **LEFT, RIGHT,** or **CENTER.** It defines how the table should align with respect to the document. The table is considered a block element; it is possible to flow content around it.

The **BACKGROUND** attribute can be set to the URL of an image to use as a background picture for a cell. Like a background for the document itself, it may be tiled. Under Internet Explorer 4.0, the image is placed behind the entire table, while under Netscape 4.0 the **BACKGROUND** attribute sets the image under all cells and seems to be a shorthand for setting the background for each **<TD>** element.

The **BGCOLOR** attribute is used to set the background color for the entire table. The value may be either in the form of an RGB hexadecimal triplet (such as **#FF0000**) or a color name (such as red). The color set in the **<TABLE>** element may be overridden within the cells or rows.

The **BORDER** attribute indicates the thickness of the border on the table. The value of the element should be **0** or some realistic positive integer value. Realistic means that while 100,000 might be valid, the browser will probably not render the table with such a border. Use the **BORDER** attribute to set numeric values, but look to **FRAME** and **RULES** to provide more control over the lines in a table. By default, the **BORDER** value for a table is **0**.

The **BORDERCOLOR** attribute is used to set the color of the borders of the table and should be set to a valid color name. Note that the **BORDERCOLOR** must be used with a positive value for **BORDER**; otherwise, it has no effect. **BORDERCOLOR** is not part of the HTML 4.0 standard, but it is supported by the two major browser vendors.

The **BORDERCOLORDARK** attribute is used under Internet Explorer to set one of the two colors used to draw the 3-D border around the table. The value of **BORDERCOLORDARK** is a valid color value, either as a hexadecimal triplet (such as **#FF0000**) or color name. The **BORDERCOLORDARK** attribute should specify the shading of the right and bottom borders of the table. The **BORDER** attribute (or **FRAME**) must be set for this attribute to have any meaning.

The **BORDERCOLORLIGHT** attribute is used under Internet Explorer to set one of the two colors used to draw the 3-D border around the table, as compared to **BORDERCOLORDARK**. The value of **BORDERCOLORLIGHT** is a valid color value, either as a hexadecimal triplet or color name, and should be lighter than the **BORDERCOLORDARK** value. The **BORDERCOLORLIGHT** should specify the shading of the top and left borders of the table. The **BORDER** attribute (or **FRAME**) must be set for this attribute to have any meaning.

The **CELLBORDER** attribute is used to set the width of the table cell borders in pixels. By default, the width of these borders is the same as that of the table.

The **CELLPADDING** attribute is used to set the amount of space, in pixels, between the border of a table cell and the actual contents of the cell. To force the contents of a cell to jut up next to a table cell, set the value of this attribute to **0**.

The **CELLSPACING** attribute is used to set the amount of space in pixels between the cells in the table. When used to lay out graphics on screen, it may be helpful to set both **CELLSPACING** and **CELLPADDING** to **0**.

The **CLASS** attribute is used to specify the table's class name. This allows the table to be accessed as a subclass from a style sheet, as discussed in Chapter 10.

The **COLS** attribute is used to indicate the number of columns in the table. This value is not enforced; it is simply used by browsers to render tables much more quickly. In general, to take advantage of improved table layout performance, page designers also must specify the width of all the cells, and avoid nested tables.

The **DATAPAGESIZE=***n* attribute sets the number of records displayed in a databound repeated table. *Databinding* is discussed later in this chapter under "Databinding: Tables Generated from a Data Source."

The **DATASRC=#***ID* attribute indicates the ID of the data source object that supplies the data that is bound to this element.

The **DIR** attribute sets the text direction for the table to **rtl** (right to left) or **ltr** (left to right).

The **FRAME** attribute is used to indicate which sides of the table frame should be displayed. The frame of the table is the outside borders of the table. Possible values for the **FRAME** attribute and their meanings are shown in Table 8-1.

The **HEIGHT** attribute indicates the height of the table in pixels, or as a percentage value of the browser window. If the value for **HEIGHT** is less than the possible height of the table with contents, the attribute has no effect. The WebTV browser may ignore the **HEIGHT** attribute.

The **HREF** attribute is unique to WebTV. It specifies the destination address when the table is selected. With this attribute, it is possible to make the whole table a giant clickable, button link.

The **ID** attribute sets a unique identifier for the table to use as a target for hypertext links, or to name the table for access via a style sheet or manipulation by a scripting language.

The **LANG** attribute specifies the language the table is written in. The language is specified by the ISO standard language abbreviation.

Value	Meaning
ABOVE	Displays a border on the top side of the table frame
BELOW	Displays a border on the bottom side of the table frame
BORDER	Displays a border on all sides of the table frame
BOX	Displays a border on all sides of the table frame
HSIDES	Displays a border on the top and bottom sides of the table frame
LHS	Displays a border on the left-hand side of the table frame
RHS	Displays a border on the right-hand side of the table frame
VOID	Removes all outside table borders
VSIDES	Displays a border on the left and right sides of the table frame

Table 8-1. *FRAME* Values

The **LANGUAGE** attribute specifies the language that any script bound to the table is written in. Possible values for this attribute include **JavaScript**, **JSCRIPT**, **VBS**, and **VBSCRIPT**. Without using an event attribute within the **<TABLE>** element, this attribute has little meaning.

The **RULES** specifies the dividing lines within a table. Do not confuse this with **FRAME**, which indicates the lines around the table. The possible values for the **RULES** attribute are indicated in Table 8-2.

The **STYLE** attribute specifies an inline style for the table as a collection of Cascading Style Sheet (CSS) properties. Style sheets are discussed in depth in Chapter 10.

The **TITLE** attribute is used to set advisory information for the table. In many browsers, when the mouse is over the table, the value of **<TITLE>** displays as a tool tip.

The **TRANSPARENCY** attribute is specific to WebTV. It sets the transparency of the table background to the background of the page as a whole. The value for the transparency attribute can range from **0** (fully opaque) to **100** (fully transparent). The WebTV browser renders a transparency value of **50** faster than other values. The default value for **TRANSPARENCY** is **0**.

The **WIDTH** attribute sets the width of the table, either in absolute pixels or as a percentage of the screen. Setting the value of the table width to an absolute pixel is useful when creating precise screen layouts.

A variety of events can be specified as attributes to be bound to script code. HTML 4.0 defines **onclick**, **ondblclick**, **onmousedown**, **onmouseup**, **onmouseover**, **onmousemove**, **onmouseout**, **onkeypress**, **onkeydown**, and **onkeyup**. Microsoft Internet Explorer also supports **onafterupdate**, **onbeforeupdate**, **onblur**, **ondragstart**,

Value	Meaning
ALL	Displays a border on all rows and columns. Same as old form of BORDER attribute
GROUPS	Displays horizontal borders between all table groups specified by <THEAD>, <TBODY>, and <TFOOT>
COLS	Displays vertical borders between all table columns
NONE	Removes all interior table borders (DEFAULT)
ROWS	Displays horizontal borders between all table rows

Table 8-2. *RULES* Values

onfocus, onhelp, onresize, onrowenter, onrowexit, onscroll, and **onselectstart**. Some of the more esoteric events for the **<TABLE>** element have to do with the possibility for the table to change contents dynamically through databinding, a topic discussed later in the chapter.

<CAPTION> Syntax

The **<CAPTION>** element specifies a caption for the table. The **<CAPTION>** element generally appears as the first element within a table, but it may occur anywhere within the **<TABLE>** element. The **<CAPTION>** element encloses the text that is used as the caption for the table; it must include both a start tag and a close tag. The major attributes to be aware of include **ALIGN** and **VALIGN**. **ALIGN** specifies where the caption will be positioned relative to the table. Acceptable values for **ALIGN** under HTML 4.0 include **TOP**, **BOTTOM**, **LEFT**, or **RIGHT**. Internet Explorer also supports **CENTER**. By default in popular browsers, the caption is centered at the top of the table. It may also be positioned below the table, as well as to the left or right, by setting the appropriate value for the **ALIGN** attribute.

According to the HTML 4.0 specification, it is impossible to set the caption to the bottom left of the table. However, Internet Explorer supports the **VALIGN** attribute, which can be used to position the caption below (**VALIGN=BOTTOM**) and then combined with **ALIGN=LEFT** to achieve the desired layout. The complete syntax for the **<CAPTION>** element is shown here:

```
<CAPTION
    ALIGN=BOTTOM | LEFT | RIGHT | TOP | CENTER*    (*=IE)
    CLASS=name for style sheet access
    DIR=text direction
    ID=unique identifier
    LANG=ISO language abbreviation
    LANGUAGE=JAVASCRIPT | JSCRIPT | VBS | VBSCRIPT    (IE)
    STYLE=style sheet information
    TITLE=advisory information
    VALIGN=BOTTOM | TOP             (IE)
    event=script>

Caption text

</CAPTION>
```

Note that the event model for the **<CAPTION>** element is quite rich. HTML 4.0 specifies **onclick, ondblclick, onmousedown, onmouseup, onmouseover, onmousemove, onmouseout, onkeypress, onkeydown**, and **onkeyup** attributes, while Internet Explorer also allows **onafterupdate, onbeforeupdate, onblur, ondragstart, onfocus, onhelp, onresize, onrowenter, onrowexit, onscroll**, and **onselectstart**. More discussion about how to interact with the event model of Dynamic HTML is presented in Chapter 13.

<COLGROUP> Syntax

The <COLGROUP> element defines a logical grouping of columns for formatting purposes. The start tag of this element is required, but the end tag is optional. Implicitly, every table contains a single column group if none are explicitly declared. The number of columns included in a group is determined by the **SPAN** attribute, which is set to an integer value. If no **SPAN** attribute or enclosed <COL> element is found, the default number of columns is a single column. A column group can contain one or more <COL> tags to control the formatting of individual columns it contains. The other important attributes for this element include **ALIGN** and **WIDTH**. The **ALIGN** attribute sets the alignment for the columns within the column group. One interesting value for **ALIGN** is **CHAR**, which can be used to align the contents of the column group based on a particular character in a column, such as a period or comma. The **CHAROFF** attribute defines the offset distance, in characters, of contents aligned to the character defined by **CHAR**.

> **Note** At the time of this writing, most browsers did not support CHAROFF style alignment.

The **WIDTH** attribute is also useful, since it sets the width for the columns in the column group in pixels. The value of **0*** for this attribute indicates that the browser should set columns to their minimum width, which is typically the default action of a browser.

The complete syntax for the <COLGROUP> element is shown here:

```
<COLGROUP
      ALIGN=CENTER | LEFT | RIGHT | CHAR | JUSTIFY
      CHAR=character to set alignment from
      CHAROFF=offset from CHAR value
      CLASS=name for style sheet sub-classing
      DIR=text direction value
      ID=unique identifier
      LANG=ISO language abbreviation
      LANGUAGE=JAVASCRIPT | JSCRIPT | VBS | VBSCRIPT      (IE)
      SPAN=integer number of columns in group
      STYLE=style sheet information for columns
      TITLE=advisory text
      VALIGN=BASELINE | BOTTOM | MIDDLE | TOP
      WIDTH=string
      Event=script>
```

The event model for the <COLGROUP> includes the following attributes: **onclick**, **ondblclick**, **onmousedown**, **onmouseup**, **onmouseover**, **onmousemove**, **onmouseout**, **onkeypress**, **onkeydown**, and **onkeyup**. Currently, Microsoft does not document any events for **<COLGROUP>**, but it may eventually accept many of the same events as the **<TABLE>** element.

<COL> Syntax

The **<COL>** element is somewhat of a convenience feature used to associate a set of attribute settings with one or more table columns. It is an empty element that does not enclose any content and does not require a close tag. Like the **<COLGROUP>** tag, it uses the **WIDTH** attribute to specify column width and the **SPAN** attribute to specify the number of columns to which it applies. It is also possible to assign alignment and style information for column contents with this element. The syntax for the **<COL>** element is shown here:

```
<COL
     ALIGN=CENTER | LEFT | RIGHT | CHAR | JUSTIFY
     CHAR=character to set alignment from
     CHAROFF=offset from CHAR
     CLASS=name for style sheet subclassing
     DIR=text direction
     ID=unique identifier
     LANG=ISO language abbreviation
     LANGUAGE=JAVASCRIPT | JSCRIPT | VBS | VBSCRIPT     (IE)
     SPAN=number of columns to span
     STYLE=inline style sheet information
     TITLE=advisory text
     VALIGN=BASELINE | BOTTOM | MIDDLE | TOP
     WIDTH=string
     Event=script>
```

The event model for the **<COL>** element includes the following attributes: **onclick**, **ondblclick**, **onmousedown**, **onmouseup**, **onmouseover**, **onmousemove**, **onmouseout**, **onkeypress**, **onkeydown**, and **onkeyup**. Microsoft does not currently document any events for **<COL>**, but it will probably accept many of the same events as the **<TABLE>** element in the future.

<TBODY>, <THEAD>, and <TFOOT> Syntax

The **<THEAD>** element contains one or more rows used to define a table heading. The close tag for the **<THEAD>** element is optional. Likewise, the **<TFOOT>** element contains one or more rows used to define a table footer. The close tag for **<TFOOT>** is also optional. And the **<TBODY>** element contains one or more rows used to define a table body. The close tag for **<TBODY>** is also optional. These elements may someday assist in printing common header and footer information for tables that extend over several pages. A special case of formatting with **<TBODY>** occurs when the **<TABLE>** element contains a **RULES="GROUPS"** declaration. This causes horizontal rules to only be drawn where a **<TBODY>** element occurs, rather than after every row. This functionality is not supported in browsers released at the time of this writing. The only major difference between **<THEAD>**, **<TFOOT>**, and **<TBODY>** syntactically is that there should only be one **<THEAD>** and **<TFOOT>** per table, but there may be many occurrences of **<TBODY>**.

All three elements can be used to group items together to allow scripting, style sheets, or formatting to be applied to a group of cells. One particularly useful possibility might be to set the alignment for a group of cells, rather than each cell. The complete syntax for **<TBODY>**, **<THEAD>**, and **<TFOOT>** follows. Note that the syntax is the same for all three elements; just substitute **THEAD** or **TFOOT** for **TBODY** in the example shown here:

```
<TBODY
     ALIGN=CENTER | LEFT | RIGHT | JUSTIFY | CHAR
     BGCOLOR=color                  (IE)
     CHAR=character to set alignment from
     CHAROFF =offset from CHAR
     CLASS=name for style sheet sub-classing
     DIR=text direction
     ID=unique identifier
     LANG=ISO language abbreviation
     LANGUAGE =JAVASCRIPT | JSCRIPT | VBS | VBSCRIPT    (IE)
     STYLE=inline style sheet properties
     TITLE=advisory text
     VALIGN=BASELINE | BOTTOM | MIDDLE | TOP
     event=script>

Table elements

</TBODY>
```

The event model for the **<TBODY>**, **<THEAD>**, and **<TFOOT>** elements under HTML 4.0 specifies the following attributes: **onclick, ondblclick, onmousedown, onmouseup, onmouseover, onmousemove, onmouseout, onkeypress, onkeydown,** and **onkeyup.** Microsoft also supports **onhelp** and **onselectstart** events, and attributes for **<TBODY>**, **<THEAD>**, and **<TFOOT>**.

<TR> Syntax

The **<TR>** element is used to create a row within a table. The **<TR>** element should occur within the **<TABLE>**, **<TBODY>**, **<THEAD>**, or **<TFOOT>** elements. The element does not require a close tag, but its use is encouraged in order to make the end of each table row more obvious in the HTML document. The element should not be empty, and should contain one or more occurrences of either **<TH>** or **<TD>** to set table headings or data elements, respectively.

The attributes of the element set the alignment, background, color, script, and style information for the whole group of cells defined by the row. This element's most important attributes are **ALIGN**, which sets the alignment of the cells in the row to **LEFT**, **RIGHT**, or **CENTER**; and **VALIGN**, which aligns the cell contents in the row vertically. The alignment, as well as background and other attributes, may be overridden by similar attributes in the **<TD>** or **<TH>** elements enclosed within the particular row. Otherwise, the attributes are similar to those of the **<TABLE>** element. A complete syntax of the **<TR>** element is shown here for reference. Like the **<TABLE>** element, the additions since 3.2 are noted to show how much the syntax has changed and so that designers can consider backward compatibility.

```
<TR
    ALIGN=CENTER | LEFT | RIGHT | CHAR* | JUSTIFY*  (*=4.0)
    BGCOLOR=color          (4.0)
    BORDERCOLOR=color         (IE or Netscape)
    BORDERCOLORDARK=color        (IE)
    BORDERCOLORLIGHT=color        (IE)
    CHAR=character to set alignment from    (4.0)
    CHAROFF=offset from CHAR       (4.0)
    CLASS=name for style sheet sub-classing     (4.0)
    DIR=text direction        (4.0)
    ID=unique identifier        (4.0)
    LANG=ISO language abbreviation       (4.0)
    LANGUAGE =JAVASCRIPT | JSCRIPT | VBS | VBSCRIPT  (IE)
    STYLE=inline style sheet properties     (4.0)
    TITLE=advisory text        (4.0)
    TRANSPARENCY=0 to 100       (WebTV)
    VALIGN=BASELINE* | BOTTOM | MIDDLE* | CENTER** | TOP   (*=4.0 ** = IE)
    event=script>

Table cells

</TR>
```

The event model for **<TR>** under HTML 4.0 specifies the following attributes: **onclick, ondblclick, onmousedown, onmouseup, onmouseover, onmousemove, onmouseout, onkeypress, onkeydown,** and **onkeyup.** Microsoft also supports **onafterupdate, onbeforeupdate, onblur, ondragstart, onfocus, onhelp, onresize, onrowenter, onrowexit,** and **onselectstart** events and attributes for the element.

<TH> and <TD> Syntax

The final elements necessary to create a table in HTML are the table heading <TH> and table data <TD> elements. These elements must be contained within a <TR> element, and may occur in any combination. From a logical view, however, a row will usually be dominated by table data or table heading elements. The main difference between the two elements is that table headings tend to be rendered in a different style. Under the two major browsers, <TH> enclosed content is centered, and often rendered in bold. Other browsers may have different formatting. If you wish to use tables solely for page layout purposes, stick to the <TD> element to avoid unforeseen layout changes. Otherwise, the <TH> element is helpful for creating row and column headings. The syntax for the <TH> and <TD> element is identical and is detailed here with indications of the changes from the HTML 3.2 to the 4.0 specification.

```
<TD
     ABSHEIGHT=pixels or percentage     (WebTV)
     ABSWIDTH=pixels or percentage    (WebTV)
     ALIGN=CENTER | LEFT | RIGHT | CHAR | JUSTIFY*      (*=4.0)
     AXIS=name of cell or heading         (4.0)
     AXES=list of related cells or headings     (4.0)
     BACKGROUND=URL of background image for cell  (Netscape and IE)
     BGCOLOR=color          (4.0)
     BORDERCOLOR=color         (Netscape and IE)
     BORDERCOLORDARK=color         (IE)
     BORDERCOLORLIGHT=color        (IE)
     CHAR=Character to set alignment from  (4.0)
     CHAROFF=offset from CHAR         (4.0)
     CLASS=name for style sheet sub-classing     (4.0)
     COLSPAN=integer number of columns
     DIR=language direction         (4.0)
     HEIGHT=pixels or percentage
        (Netscape and IE. Removed in W3C 4.0)
     ID=unique string         (4.0)
     LANG=ISO language abbreviation       (4.0)
     LANGUAGE =JAVASCRIPT | JSCRIPT | VBS | VBSCRIPT      (IE)
     MAXLINES=positive number       (WebTV)
     NOWRAP
     ROWSPAN=integer number of rows
     STYLE=inline style sheet properties     (4.0)
     TITLE=advisory text         (4.0)
     TRANSPARENCY=0 to 100       (WebTV)
     VALIGN=BASELINE* | BOTTOM | MIDDLE | CENTER** | TOP
     (* =4.0, **=IE)
```

```
WIDTH=pixels or percentage value
    (Netscape and IE. Removed in W3C 4.0)
event=script            (4.0)>
```

Cell contents

```
</TD>
```

Note *Under HTML 4.0, the **HEIGHT** and **WIDTH** attributes for the table cell are missing. The two major browsers both support these attributes, however. It is unclear if the W3C style will be adopted by page designers any time soon.*

The attributes that are unique to the **<TH>** and **<TH>** elements, or warrant further consideration, are discussed here.

The **ABSHEIGHT** attribute is unique to WebTV, and is used to set the absolute height of a cell. If the enclosed content does not fit in the cell, it is not visible. There is no default value for **ABSHEIGHT**.

Similar to **ABSHEIGHT**, **ABSWIDTH** is used to set the absolute width of the cell. Like **ABSHEIGHT**, content that doesn't fit within the cell is clipped. There is no default value for **ABSWIDTH**.

The **AXES** attribute should be set to a comma-delimited list of **AXIS** names. This list specifies the row and column headings that apply to the particular cell. In general, the browser should be able to infer this information from the structure of the table. This attribute is new in HTML 4.0 and is currently unsupported by the major browsers.

The **AXIS** attribute is used to create a name to associate with a header cell. The attribute is defined for both **<TD>** and **<TH>**, but it makes more sense for **<TH>** elements. The name set with **AXIS** can provide a shorthand notation for a row or column heading in the **AXES** attribute. When this is not set, the browser tends to use the content of the cell to name the cell for later access. This attribute is new in HTML 4.0 and is currently unsupported by the major browsers.

The **COLSPAN** attribute specifies the number of columns the current cell should span. The default value is **1**. A value of **0** indicates that the cell should span all columns until reaching the last column of the table. Use of this attribute is best illustrated by the example shown in Figure 8-9.

The **MAXLINES** attribute supported by WebTV sets the maximum number of lines to display in the cell. Content is not displayed if it does not fit within the lines specified. There is no default value for this attribute.

The **NOWRAP** attribute requires no value. The presence of this value tells a graphical browser to disable text wrapping in the cell. When used improperly, this attribute may result in wide table cells. This attribute has been depreciated under HTML 4.0, and its use is not suggested.

The **ROWSPAN** attribute specifies the number of rows the current cell should span. The default value is **1**. A value of **0** indicates that the cell should span all rows to the bottom of the table. Use of this attribute is best illustrated by the example shown in Figure 8-9.

The **TRANSPARENCY** attribute is a WebTV-specific attribute that sets the transparency of the table cell background so the background of the page can be shown. The value for the transparency attribute can range from **0** (fully opaque) to **100** (fully transparent). The WebTV browser renders a transparency value of **50** faster than other values. The default value for transparency is **0**.

The event model for **<TD>** and **<TH>** under HTML 4.0 specifies the following attributes: **onclick, ondblclick, onmousedown, onmouseup, onmouseover, onmousemove, onmouseout, onkeypress, onkeydown,** and **onkeyup**. Microsoft also supports **onafterupdate, onbeforeupdate, onblur, ondragstart, onfocus, onhelp, onresize, onrowenter, onrowexit,** and **onselectstart** events and attributes for the element.

Databinding: Tables Generated from a Data Source

Tables often contain row after row of identically formatted data that originates in a database. There are two basic methods to create these data-dependent tables. Neither one is ideal:

- If the table data is relatively static, it is common to build a long table by hand or with a tool, individually coding each data cell.

- If the table data is dynamic, it is common to generate the entire page containing the table using a server-side CGI (Common Gateway Interface) technology.

The first approach is difficult for an HTML author. The second, which does not really qualify as HTML authoring, usually requires programming. *Databinding* is a technology recently introduced by Microsoft to dynamically bind HTML elements to data coming from an external source. While not technically restricted to HTML tables, it does represent a simpler, more powerful approach for generating large data-dependent tables.

In HTML databinding, a data source that provides information is associated with a data consumer that presents it. The data source is a control with some means to access external information that is embedded in an HTML document using the **<OBJECT>** element. This element, briefly introduced in Chapter 7, is further explained in Chapter 14. For now, it will be useful to understand that **<OBJECT>** adds a small program to the page that can be used to access an external data source. The document also contains a data consumer, an HTML element that uses special attributes to ask the ActiveX control for data that the element subsequently displays. Data consumers come in two sorts: those that present single data values, and those that present tabular data. Tables fall into the latter category.

Creating an HTML table using databinding is a very simple process. It is only necessary to define one table row. The rest are generated automatically according to the template defined by the first row. Think of each row in a tabular data set as corresponding to a database record, and each column as corresponding to a database field. A template table row is defined in HTML that associates **<TD>** or **<TH>** elements with field names in the data set. A table will subsequently be generated with one row for each record in the data set, and with cell values filled in from the appropriate record fields. The data source control may support processing capabilities such as sorting or filtering the data set. If so, the table can be dynamically regenerated on the client side in response to update information from the data source.

For example, a data source may contain a tabular data set for product price information. One field may contain the name of the product, another its price. By default, a table could present this information sorted alphabetically by product name. In response to a button on an HTML page, the data source could sort the data set by price. The table that displays the information would be dynamically regenerated. The following is a simple databinding example.

An external data file contains two or more columns of comma-delimited data. The first line contains the names of the data set fields corresponding to the columns. The following lines contain the actual data for the appropriate fields. A sample file called alphabet.txt is shown in Figure 8-16.

To access the data, an HTML document references an object for a data source control and a related table definition. An example of how this would be accomplished is shown in Figure 8-17.

This HTML code generates a table from the file alphabet.txt in which each table row contains a letter of the alphabet and the name of a thing that can remind the reader of that letter. The rendering of this example under Internet Explorer 4.0 is shown in Figure 8-18.

```
Letter, Thing
A, Apple
B, Boy
C, Cat
D, Dog
E, Elephant
F, Fox
G, Girl
H, Hat
```

Figure 8-16.   *Contents of alphabet.txt*

```
<!DOCTYPE HTML PUBLIC "-//W3C//DTD HTML 4.0 Final//EN">
<HTML>
<HEAD>
<TITLE>Data Binding Example</TITLE>
</HEAD>
<BODY>

<OBJECT ID=alphabet
CLASSID="clsid:333C7BC4-460F-11D0-BC04-0080C7055A83">
    <PARAM NAME="DataURL" VALUE="alphabet.txt">
    <PARAM NAME="UseHeader" VALUE="True">
</OBJECT>

<TABLE DATASRC="#alphabet" BORDER=1>
<THEAD>
   <TR BGCOLOR="YELLOW">
      <TH>Letter</TH>
      <TH>Reminder</TH>
   </TR></THEAD>
<TBODY>
   <TR ALIGN="CENTER">
      <TD><SPAN DATAFLD="Letter"></SPAN> </TD>
      <TD><SPAN DATAFLD="Thing"></SPAN></TD>
   </TR>
</TBODY>
</TABLE>
</BODY>
</HTML>
```

Figure 8-17.   *Databinding example*

Examine the pieces needed to make this databinding example work a little more closely. First, the data source. This example uses the Tabular Data Control (TDC) object: an ActiveX control provided by Microsoft and identified by the lengthy class identifier. This particular control locates and manipulates text data files in a tabular format. Other controls supporting databinding could have been used instead. These might support different data access capabilities such as access to remote relational databases. The Microsoft ActiveX Data Objects control (ADO), however, is a representative example. The TDC supports several parameters of which two are used in this example. The **"DataURL"** parameter tells the TDC the name and location of the

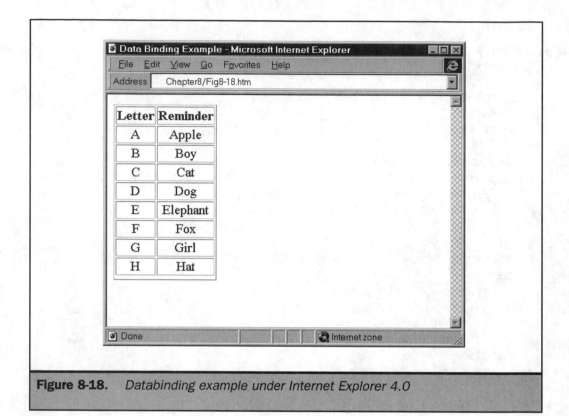

Figure 8-18. Databinding example under Internet Explorer 4.0

data file it is to use. In this case, since only a filename is provided, the TDC looks in the same directory containing the Web page. By default, the TDC treats every line in a data file as data. The **"UseHeader"** parameter tells the TDC that the first line in the data file does not contain data but rather the names of data fields.

As a data consumer, the **<TABLE>** element uses its **DATASRC** attribute to connect to a data source. Note in the example how this attribute is set to the name of the **<OBJECT>** tag invoking the data source control. The name must be preceded by the **#** symbol. The **<OBJECT>** element must declare a name using the **ID** attribute in order to be accessed by a data consumer. In summary, the **DATASRC** attribute identifies a data source to be used in generating a table.

The next step is to associate cells in the template table row with particular fields in the data set. This is done using the **DATAFLD** attribute of appropriate elements. It contains the name of the field in the data set that its element is to be bound to. If data set-specific names are not defined, then fields can be identified using default positional names: "Column1", "Column2", and so fourth. The **<TD>** tag, commonly used for cell data, does not support the **DATAFLD** attribute. To bind a field to a table cell, the **<TD>** tag needs to contain one of the elements that do support **DATAFLD**. The elements that make the most sense in the context of a table are **<SPAN>**, **<DIV>**,

<OBJECT>, and **<IMG>**. The latter two tags illustrate that databinding is not confined to textual data. For example, a column of images can be created by using a tag declaration such as **<IMG DATAFLD="Picture">** inside a table cell. Note that the usual **SRC** attribute is not required. Instead, the **DATAFLD** attribute identifies a field inside the data set that contains a valid image filename, such as mypict.gif, and binds the image to that value.

If a table does not explicitly declare header or footer section elements, then implicitly all table content is in the body section. In static tables, this does not usually have visual consequences, but it does in tables generated by databinding. All body rows are included in the template for table row generation, not just the rows containing databound fields. To prevent header or footer information from being repeated for every row in the table, it is necessary to enclose it with the **<THEAD>** or **<TFOOT>** element. The **<TBODY>** element can then be used to signal the beginning of the template to be databound.

Such a brief example scratches the surface of databinding and merely shows the importance of tables in relation to dynamic data. For more information on databinding, visit Microsoft Sitebuilder, at www.microsoft.com/sitebuilder, and the Advanced Data Connector site, at www.microsoft.com/adc.

Fonts

Tables provide a great deal of control over page layout. Besides better support for layout, Web page designers have long desired to be able to specify fonts in their documents. HTML 2.0 only supported two fonts, a proportional font and a fixed-width font. Under browsers such as Netscape and Internet Explorer, the proportional font was usually Times or Times New Roman, while the fixed width font was Courier. To set text into Courier, page authors would use an element like **<TT>**. Otherwise, all text on the page was generally in the proportional font unless it was preformatted with the **<PRE>** element. There was also little control over the size of the font, even in relative terms. The font size of the browser was generally 12 point for the variable-width font and 10 point for the fixed-width font, but end users were free to change font size as they pleased.

There wasn't much control over typography in early browsers. In fact, the only way to use a new font or control the precise layout of text was to make it a graphic. To this day, many page designers still embed a great deal of text as graphics in order to precisely control spacing and to use fonts that the user may not have. Because of download and accessibility issues, this should not be the *de facto* approach to dealing with fonts.

With Netscape Navigator 1.1, it became possible to control fonts a little more. Netscape introduced the **<FONT>** element, which was used to specify the size and, starting with Navigator 2.0, color of text using the **SIZE** and **COLOR** attributes. Microsoft later added an attribute called **FACE** to indicate which font type should be used. Both **SIZE** and **COLOR** were introduced to the standard in HTML 3.2. Today all of these attributes are considered part of the HTML 4.0 standard.

Under HTML 4.0, it is possible to color a certain portion of text a particular color by enclosing it within the **<FONT>** element and setting the **COLOR** attribute equal to a valid color name or RGB value. The code

```
<FONT COLOR="#FF0000">This is important</FONT>
```

sets the text "This is important" in red. The **<FONT>** element can contain a great deal of text or very little, so it is possible to control the colors of individual letters, though such resulting rainbow effects might be hard on the eyes.

It is also possible to set the relative size of type by setting the **SIZE** attribute of the **<FONT>** element. In a Web page, there are seven relative sizes for text numbered from **1** to **7**, where **1** is the smallest text in a document and **7** is the largest. To set some text into the largest size, use **<FONT SIZE="7">This is big</FONT>**. By default, the typical size of text is **3**; this can be overridden with the **<BASEFONT>** element discussed later in this chapter. If the font size is not known but the text should just be made one size bigger, the author can use an alternative sizing value such as **<FONT SIZE="+1">** instead of specifying the size directly. The **+** and **-** nomenclature makes it possible to bring the font size up or down a specified number of settings. The values for this form of the **SIZE** attribute should range from **+1** to **+6** and **-1** to **-6**. It is not possible to specify **<FONT SIZE="+10">** because there are only seven sizes. If the increase or decrease goes beyond acceptable sizes, the font defaults at the largest or smallest size, respectively.

Microsoft introduced the **FACE** attribute to the **<FONT>** element that has come to be supported by nearly all browsers, as well as the HTML 4.0 specification. The **FACE** attribute can be set to the name of the font to render the text. So, a page designer who wants to render a particular phrase in Britannic Bold could use the following code:

```
<FONT FACE="Britannic Bold">This is important</FONT>
```

The browser would then read this HTML fragment and render the text in the different font—but only for users who have the font installed on their systems. This raises an interesting problem: what happens if a user doesn't have the font specified? Using the **FACE** attribute, it is possible to specify a comma-delimited list of fonts to try one by one before defaulting to the normal proportional or fixed-width font. The fragment shown here would try first Arial, then Helvetica, and finally Sans Serif before giving up and using whatever the current browser font is.

```
<FONT FACE="Arial, Helvetica, Sans Serif">This should be in a
different font</FONT>
```

While it is impossible to know what fonts users may have on their systems, the previous example shows how a little guesswork can be applied to take advantage of the **FACE** attribute. Most Macintosh, Windows, and Unix users have a standard set of fonts. If equivalent fonts are specified, it may be possible to provide similar page renderings across platforms. Table 8-3 shows some of the fonts that can be found on Macintosh, Windows, and Unix systems. The table does not attempt to cross-reference the fonts. In fact, while Windows does not always have Helvetica, Arial is fairly similar.

Most users may have many other fonts beyond the ones shown in the table. Users of Microsoft's Office will probably also have access to fonts like Algerian, Book Antiqua, Bookman Old Style, Britannic Bold, Desdemona, Garamond, Century Gothic, Haettenschweiller, and many others. The various browsers are also trying to make new fonts available. Under Internet Explorer 4.0, Microsoft has introduced a new font called WebDings, which provides many common icons for use on the page. Some of these icons would be useful for navigation, like arrows, while others look like audio or video symbols that could provide indication of link contents before selection. Just using font sizing, colors, and simple layout, it is possible to make interesting layouts with WebDings as shown in Figure 8-19.

Windows	**Macintosh**	**Unix***
Arial	Chicago	Charter
Comic Sans MS	Courier	Clean
Courier New	Geneva	Courier
Impact	Helvetica	Fixed
Times New Roman	Monaco	Helvetica
Symbol	New York	Lucida
Verdana	Palatino	Sans Serif
Wingding	Symbol	Serif
	Times	Symbol
		Times
		Utopia

*Unix fonts vary; this is just meant to show most of the common fonts under a standard X Window environment.

Table 8-3.   *Sample Default Fonts by Platform Type*

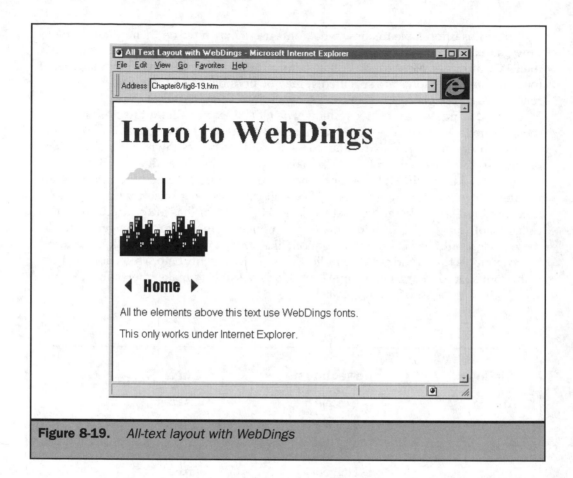

Figure 8-19. *All-text layout with WebDings*

A common set of icons for the Web is actually not a new idea. The W3C has a working draft covering a predefined set of icon-like symbols. The Microsoft font actually includes many of these symbols, but does not use the same naming convention. It may eventually be possible to include **&audio;** to add an audio icon to a Web page, but for now setting the WebDings value or inserting a GIF is the best choice.

Downloadable Fonts

While the Microsoft solution to type on the Web attempts to promote a common set of faces, it isn't a very flexible approach outside the Windows world. While many Windows, Macintosh, and Unix systems have similar fonts, what about the situation where the page author wants to use a customized font? In this case, the page author is forced to create a static image of the font. This could take a great deal of time to download, and gives up the ability to easily index the text, let alone copy and paste it.

The best solution for fonts on the Web would be to come up with some cross-platform form of font that could be downloaded to the browser on the fly. While this sounds easy enough, the problem with downloadable fonts is that they must be highly compact. Page viewers must not be able to steal the font from the page and install it on their own machines. Both of the major browser vendors have been working on downloadable fonts. Microsoft's solution for Web type is called OpenType (www.microsoft.com/opentype). Netscape's solution, called Dynamic Fonts, is based on TrueDoc (www.bitstream.com/world). Currently, only Netscape 4.0 and Internet Explorer 4.0 support downloadable fonts, but they can be used in an obtrusive way already to provide enhanced screen layout.

Netscape's Dynamic Fonts

To use a dynamic font under Netscape, the page author simply uses the **FACE** attribute of the **<FONT>** element, or a style sheet attribute as discussed in Chapter 10, to set the font face. If the user does not have the font installed on the system, a downloadable font linked to the page can be fetched and used to render the page. To include a link to a Netscape font definition file in Portable Font Resource (PFR) format, use the **<LINK>** element by setting the **REL** attribute to **fontdef** and the **SRC** attribute equal to the URL where the font definition file resides. The **<LINK>** element must be found within the **<HEAD>** of the document. An example of how this element would be used is shown here:

```
<LINK REL=fontdef SRC="http://www.bigcompany.com/fonts/customfonts.pfr">
```

Note that there may be many fonts in the same font definition file. There is no limit to how many fonts can be used on a page. Once the font is accessed, it is used just as if it were installed on a user's system. Two attributes available under Netscape 4.0 are useful when dealing with dynamic fonts. The first extension to the **<FONT>** element is **POINT-SIZE**, which can be set to the point size of the font. The other extension to **<FONT>** is the **WEIGHT** attribute, which can be set to a value between **100** and **900** in increments of **100**. The value of the **WEIGHT** attribute determines the weight or "boldness" of the font. A value of **100** is the lightest weight, while **900** indicates to make the font as bold as it can be. If the **<B>** element is used, the **WEIGHT** attribute is equivalent to **900**. If dynamic fonts are to be used, it is more likely that style sheets will be the preferred way to interact with them, rather than these proprietary extensions. The only obstacle to using dynamic fonts is that the .pfr file describing the font must be created. Otherwise, they are no more troublesome than attempting to guess the font on the end user's system or rasterizing the font into a GIF image.

Microsoft's Dynamic Fonts

Microsoft also provides a way to embed fonts in a Web page. To include a font, you must first build the page using the **<FONT>** element, or style sheet rules that set fonts, as discussed in Chapter 10. When creating your page, don't worry about whether or not the end user has the font installed; it will be downloaded. Next, use the Web Embedding Fonts Tool or a similar facility to analyze the font usage on the page. The program should create an .eot file that contains the embedded fonts. The font use information will then be added to the page in the form of CSS (Cascading Style Sheets) style rules, as shown here:

```
<STYLE TYPE="text/css">
<!--

  @font-face {
    font-family: Britannic Bold;
    font-style:  normal;
    font-weight: normal;
    src: url(http://www.bigcompany.com/BRITANN0.eot);
  }
-->
</STYLE>
```

The use of the **@font-face** acts as a pseudo element that allows you to bring any number of fonts into a page. The form of the font embedding supported by Microsoft conforms to the initial W3C specification for font embedding. For more information on embedded fonts under Internet Explorer, and links to font file creation tools like WEFR, see the Microsoft Typography site (www.microsoft.com/opentype).

Document-Wide Fonts

In some cases, it may be appropriate to change the font size, color, or face document wide. To do this, use the **<BASEFONT>** element in the **<HEAD>** of the document. The **<BASEFONT>** should only occur once in the document and has major attributes **COLOR, FACE,** and **SIZE.** Like the **<FONT>** element, **COLOR** should be set to an RGB value or color name. **FACE** should be set to a font name or comma-delimited list of fonts. **SIZE** should be set to a size value between **1** and **7.** Relative sizing for the **SIZE** attribute does not generally make any sense. To set the font of the document in red Arial or Helvetica with a relative size of 6 use **<BASEFONT COLOR="RED" FACE="Arial, Helvetica" SIZE="6">** within the **<HEAD>** element of the document.

<FONT> Syntax

The complete syntax for the **<FONT>** element, including extensions from Microsoft, Netscape, and WebTV, is shown here:

```
<FONT
    CLASS=classname              (IE)
```

```
      COLOR=color
      EFFECT=EMBOSS | RELIEF | SHADOW      (WebTV)
      FACE=font
      ID=value              (IE)
      LANG=language           (IE)
      POINTSIZE=points         (Netscape)
      SIZE=1-7, +n, -n
      STYLE=style information      (IE)
      TRANSPARENCY=0 - 100        (WebTV)
      TITLE=advisory text        (IE)
      WEIGHT=100 - 900          (Netscape)
      event=script           (IE)>
</FONT>
```

Note   *Under the HTML 4.0 specification, the* **<FONT>** *element does not even support many of the core attributes for events, naming (**ID**), and style (**STYLE**). This may simply be an oversight or a way to push the item toward its depreciated status. Nevertheless, these attributes have been documented by Microsoft and hinted at by Netscape.*

The **CLASS** attribute is used to specify the class of the element to be used so that it can be associated with a style sheet. It is unlikely that the **CLASS** attribute would be used with the **<FONT>** element, as style sheets generally preclude most of the use of this element.

The **COLOR** attribute is used to set the color of the font either by specifying its RGB value in the form of a hexadecimal triplet (such as **#FF0000**) or as a reserved name (such as purple).

The **EFFECT** attribute is proprietary to WebTV and is used to create an effect on the enclosed text. The value of the attribute is **EMBOSS, RELIEF**, or **SHADOW**. A value of **RELIEF** draws text so that it seems raised from the surface of the page. A value of **EMBOSS** draws the text so that it seems pressed into the surface of the page. Finally, the attribute value **SHADOW** draws the text with a shadow cast down and to the right of the text. If the effect attribute is not specified, the text is plain.

The **FONT** attribute is used to specify the name of the current font typeface. The value of the attribute may be a single font name or a comma-delimited collection of font names that are tried in order. If no font is found in the list, the browser should default to whatever the current browser font is.

The **ID** attribute is used to set an identifier so that the element may be the target of a link or manipulated by a script or style sheet.

The **LANG** attribute should be set to the ISO standard language abbreviation for the language being used for the enclosed text. This value should probably be set document-wide rather than within a particular **<FONT>** element.

The Netscape 4.0–specific **POINTSIZE** attribute may specify an exact point size, for example 18 or 36. There is no need to specify measurement with this attribute; it is always in points.

The **SIZE** attribute is used to specify the relative size of the font face, which ranges between **1** (the smallest) and **7** (the largest). It is also possible to increase or decrease the current font size using the *+n* or *-n* nomenclature, for example, **<FONT SIZE="+3">**.

The **STYLE** attribute is used to specify an inline style for the **<FONT>** tag. Style sheets are discussed in depth in Chapter 10.

The **TITLE** attribute is used to provide advisory information. The contents of the **TITLE** attribute may be displayed as a tool tip during the **onmouseover** event.

The **TRANSPARENCY** attribute is a WebTV extension, which is used to set the transparency of the text. With the value of this attribute set, the background may be able to show through text. The transparency of the text can range from a value of **0** (fully opaque) to **100** (fully transparent). The default value for **TRANSPARENCY** under WebTV is **0**, and a value of **50** is recommended.

The Netscape 4.0–specific attribute **WEIGHT** is used to set the "boldness" of a font. The value for the font is between **100** and **900** in increments of **100**. The value of **100** indicates the lightest value for the font and **900** the boldest. When the **<B>** element is used, the maximum boldness is always used.

Under browsers that support scripting, it is possible to use an event attribute to bind an event to a script action. Internet Explorer supports a rich event model, including **onclick, ondblclick, onhelp, onkeydown, onkeypress, onmousedown, onmousemove, onmouseout, onmouseover, onmouseup**, and **onselectstart**, which can be set. Other browsers may support a much different set of events.

Summary

While HTML does not provide a great deal of support for layout, it really wasn't meant to. While it is easy to say that people shouldn't use HTML to lay out pages, the fact of the matter is they wanted and needed to. Designers desperately want pixel-level layout control of Web pages and support for fonts. The need for improved page design gave rise to the occasional abuse of HTML elements, "cheats" like the invisible pixel GIF trick, and the rise of proprietary elements such as **<SPACER>**. The development of tables made it possible to create effective layouts with HTML. Designers should remember, however, that tables have great use beyond grid-style layouts.

Despite the improvement in layout capabilities, fonts are still an open issue in HTML; but with some assumptions regarding the use of downloadable font technology, font use is becoming a reality on the Web. Later chapters will reveal that many of the problems raised in this chapter will cease once style sheets become more prevalent. Then tables can go back to being used as tables, and other more proprietary tags may eventually be eliminated.

The Complete Reference

Chapter 9

Advanced Layout:

Frames and Layers

Tables and the other HTML techniques introduced in Chapter 8 provide a significant improvement in Web page layout, especially compared to what was available under HTML 2.0. Many designers want even more design facilities, including multiple windows and layers. Such expectations aren't unreasonable, because these features are common in design programs and computer interfaces. Such power comes at a price, however. Frames and layers may provide significant layout flexibility, but when misused these structures can confuse users—or even lock them out completely.

Frames

A framed document divides a browser window into multiple panes, or smaller window frames. Each frame may contain a different document. The benefits of this approach are obvious. Users can view information in one frame while keeping another frame open for reference, instead of moving back and forth between pages. The contents of one frame can be manipulated, or linked to the contents of another. This allows designers to build sophisticated interfaces. For example, one frame can contain links that produce a result in another frame. An example of such an interface is shown in Figure 9-1.

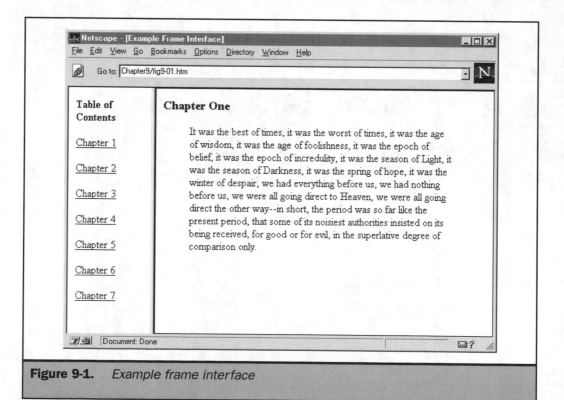

Figure 9-1.   *Example frame interface*

Frames offer many possibilities. They can contain tables of contents, site indexes, and lists of links. Frames offer fixed-screen navigation—where certain information is always at the forefront—and other options not found in the single-window approach. However, framed documents could be difficult to deal with. When Netscape 2.0 introduced the concept of frames, many users were very confused by framed Web sites. Frames couldn't be printed, sites were hard to bookmark, and the back button of browsers didn't work as expected. Regardless, many site designers, excited by a new approach, rushed to develop framed pages. Then they removed them just as quickly due to navigation problems and user complaints.

Today, many of the problems associated with frames have been fixed at the browser level, and users have become more comfortable in understanding and working with frames. Used properly in the right situation, as you'll learn about in this chapter, frames are an important tool in the Web designer's toolbox. No longer considered proprietary browser extensions, frames are included in the HTML 4.0 standard.

Overview of Frames

A frame is an independent scrolling region, or window, of a Web page. Every Web page may be divided up into many individual frames, which can even be nested within other frames. Fixed screen sizes limit how many frames can realistically be used at once. Each frame in a window may be separated from the others with a border; in this way, a framed document may resemble a table. Frames, however, are not a fancy form of tables. Each separate frame may contain a different document indicated by a unique URL. Because the documents included in a framed region may be much larger than the room available on the screen, each frame may provide a scroll bar or other controls to manipulate the size of the frame. Last, the individual frames are usually named so that they may be referenced through links or scripting, allowing the contents of one frame to affect the contents of another. This referencing capability is a major difference between tables and frames. Frames provide layout facilities *and*, potentially, navigation. Figure 9-2 provides a visual overview of the components of a framed document.

Simple Frame Example

The first point to remember is that a framed document is composed of several documents. To illustrate, a page with two frames will actually involve three files:

- The framing document that defines the framing relationship
- The file that contains the contents of frame one
- The file that contains the contents of frame two

Let's consider the simple two-frame document shown in Figure 9-3. The first frame, on the left, takes up around 20 percent of the screen and contains a table of contents. The larger column on the right, which takes up the other 80 percent of the

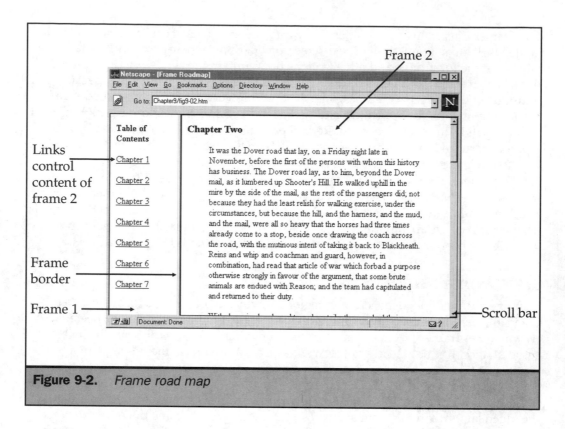

Figure 9-2. Frame road map

screen, displays the actual contents. For the purposes of this example, the left frame is named Controls, and the right frame is named Display.

To specify the framing document, you need to create a file that uses the **<FRAMESET>** element instead of the **<BODY>** element. The **<FRAMESET>** element defines the set of frames that make up the document. The major attributes for this element are the **ROWS** or **COLS** attributes. In this case, there are two columns that take up set percentages of the screen, so the code reads **<FRAMESET COLS="20%, 80%">**. It would be just as easy to set up something like **<FRAMESET ROWS="10%, 80%, 10%">**, which would set up three rows across the screen.

The **ROWS** and **COLS** attributes can also be set to pixel values, so **<FRAMESET COLS="200,400">** would define a column 200 pixels wide followed by a column 400 pixels wide. Since determining the exact size of the screen is difficult, setting these attributes to exact values might be dangerous. If absolute pixels are used and the screen is larger than the area specified, there will be an empty space in the browser window. If the screen is smaller than the specified frame values, scrolling may be required. Because of this, use absolute pixel values only when they make sense.

If you know that the Controls frame contains a graphic that is 150 pixels across, you might consider setting the size of the first frame to 175 pixels, to fit the graphic

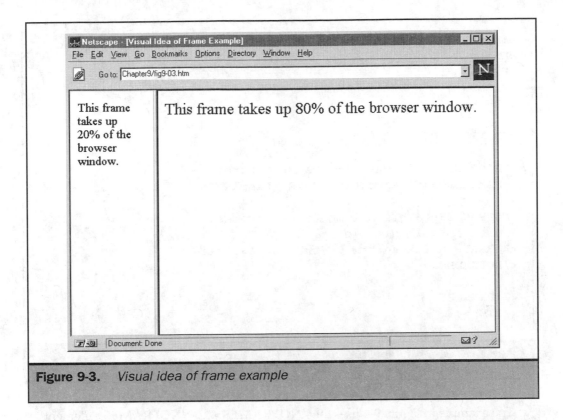

Figure 9-3.   *Visual idea of frame example*

plus some white space. If the frame were any smaller than this size, the graphic would be clipped, so using an absolute pixel value makes sense. But what should the size of the other frame be? To simply take up the rest of the screen with whatever is left over after 175 pixels, you could easily use the wildcard (*) to specify use the rest of the screen. The code for such a frame set would be <FRAMESET COLS="175,*">.

In summary, the **ROWS** and **COLS** attributes may be set to pixels, percentage, or a wildcard value. There may be multiple occurrences of wildcards, and things may be mixed and matched. It is recommended to stick with all percentages or all pixels, and use wildcards where needed.

Once the frame layout is specified with the **<FRAMESET>** element, the contents of each frame must be specified using the **<FRAME>** element in the order that the frames were defined in the **ROW** or **COL** attribute. In the case of **<FRAMESET COLS="175, 100, *">**, the contents of the first **<FRAME>** element encountered is loaded in the 175-pixel column, the contents of the second **<FRAME>** element in the 100-pixel column, and so on. The primary attribute of the **<FRAME>** element is **SRC**, which is set to the URL of the document to load into the frame. The **NAME** attribute should also be set to some name. Naming of frames is important, as it allows each frame to be targeted by links and manipulated by scripting languages. A very simple example of a framing document is shown in Figure 9-4.

```
<!DOCTYPE HTML PUBLIC "-//W3C//DTD HTML 4.0 Final//EN">
<HTML>
<HEAD>
<TITLE>Simple Frame Example</TITLE>
</HEAD>

<FRAMESET COLS="250,*">

<FRAME SRC="fileone.htm" NAME="Controls">
<FRAME SRC="filetwo.htm" NAME="Display">

<NOFRAMES><P>This document uses frames.
Please follow this link to a
<A HREF="noframes.htm">noframes</A>version.
</NOFRAMES>

</FRAMESET
</HTML>
```

Figure 9-4.   *Simple frame example*

The example in Figure 9-4 uses the **<NOFRAMES>** ... **</NOFRAMES>** element within the frame set. This element provides information to be displayed in browsers that do not support frames. Although this approach seems like a good idea, the page author may need to maintain both a frame and no frame version of a site in order to accommodate different browsers. A rendering of the last example is shown in Figure 9-5.

Frame Targeting

When using frames, you may often find it desirable to make the links in one frame target another frame. This way, when a user presses a button or activates a link in one framed document, the requested page loads in another frame. In Figure 9-4, the desire might be to have the frame named Controls target the frame named Display. The first part of link targeting is to ensure frame naming by setting the **NAME** attribute in the **<FRAME>** element to a unique name. The next part of linking is to use the **TARGET** attribute in the **<A>** element to set the target for the anchor. For example, a link like **<A HREF="http://www.yahoo.com" TARGET="Display">** would load the site specified by the **HREF** into the window called Display, if there is such a frame. If the target specified by the name does not exist, the link loads over the window it is in. Some particular values for the **TARGET** attribute have special meaning; these are summarized in Table 9-1.

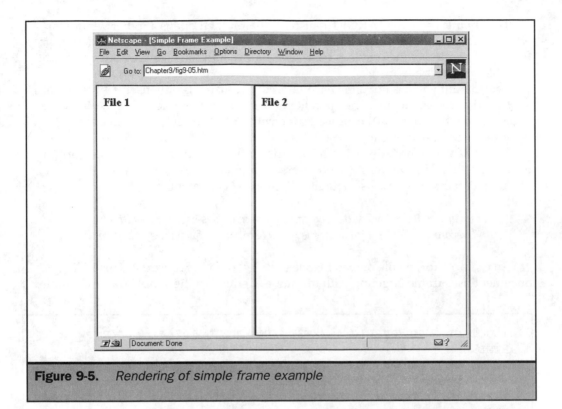

Figure 9-5. *Rendering of simple frame example*

The **_top** value for the **TARGET** attribute may be useful for "frame busting." Many page authors do not want their sites to be viewed under a framed environment. Setting the **TARGET** attribute of the links within a site to **_top** ensures that any frames being used will be removed once a link is followed.

Value	Meaning
_blank	Load the page into a new, generally unnamed, window.
_self	Load the page over the current frame.
_parent	Load the link over the parent frame.
_top	Load the link over all the frames in the window.

Table 9-1. *Reserved **TARGET** Values*

The **_blank** value for **TARGET** is also useful in that it opens another window in which to display the link. The only problem with this action is that the window may tile directly on top of the previous browser window, and the user may not know that multiple windows are open.

The **_parent** value is not often encountered, because it is only useful when frames are nested to a great degree. The **_parent** value makes it possible to overwrite the parent frame that contains the nested frame without destroying any frames that the parent may be nested within.

The **_self** value for **TARGET**, which loads a page over its current frame, duplicates the typical default action for most browsers. It might be useful, however, to accommodate browsers whose default actions are set differently.

 According to the HTML 4.0 specification, frame names beginning with an underscore are discouraged since they may be reserved for values like _top.

An example for the file named fileone.htm is shown in Figure 9-6. This HTML document uses frame targeting with the names defined in the simple frame example.

```
<!DOCTYPE HTML PUBLIC "-//W3C//DTD HTML 3.2 Final//EN">
<HTML>
<HEAD>
<TITLE>Framed Document One</TITLE>
</HEAD>
<BODY>

<H1>Framed Document One</H1>
<HR>
<H2 ALIGN="CENTER">Test Links</H2>
<UL>
    <LI><A HREF="http://www.yahoo.com" TARGET="Display">
        Yahoo in Display frame</A>
    <LI><A HREF="http://www.hotbot.com" TARGET="_new">
        HotBot in new window</A>
    <LI><A HREF="http://www.infoseek.com" TARGET="_self">
        Infoseek in this frame</A>
    <LI><A HREF="http://www.excite.com" TARGET="_top">
        Excite over whole window</A>
</UL>
</BODY>
</HTML>
```

Figure 9-6.   *File using frame-targeting links*

<FRAMESET> Syntax

The **<FRAMESET>** element encloses the **<FRAME>** element and defines the structure of the framed document. The **<FRAMESET>** element must have a **</FRAMESET>** close tag. A **<FRAMESET>** may be nested within other **<FRAMESET>** elements to create a nested frame structure. The **<FRAMESET>** element should be used in place of the **<BODY>** element in the document that defines the frame relationships. It is, however, possible to provide a **<BODY>** element after the **<FRAMESET>** in place of the **<NOFRAMES>** element as an alternative way to provide information for browsers that do not support frames. The syntax of **<FRAMESET>**, as defined by the HTML 4.0 specification, is rather simple. It defines only the **ROWS** or **COLS** attributes, as previously discussed. However, browser vendors, particularly Microsoft, have provided a variety of attributes that can be set for the tag. A listing of the extended **<FRAMESET>** syntax follows with explanations of each attribute.

```
<FRAMESET
    BORDER=pixels    (IE and Netscape)
    BORDERCOLOR=color    (IE and Netscape)
    CLASS=name of class    (IE)
    COLS=column widths
    FRAMEBORDER=NO | YES | 0 | 1    (IE and Netscape)
    FRAMESPACING=pixels    (IE)
    ID=unique identifier
    LANG=ISO language code    (IE)
    LANGUAGE=JAVASCRIPT | JSCRIPT | VBSCRIPT | VBS    (IE)
    ROWS=row heights
    TITLE=advisory text
    Event=Script code>

</FRAME> ... </FRAME>

</FRAMESET>
```

The **BORDER** attribute defines the size of the border in pixels. The border determines the space between the various frames. If the elements are nested, the **BORDER** value should only be defined for the top level **<FRAMESET>** element.

The **BORDERCOLOR** attribute can be set to a valid color value: a name (such as red) or a hexadecimal format (such as #FF0000). **BORDERCOLOR** is used to color the **BORDER** if that value is set. The **BORDERCOLOR** attribute of **<FRAMESET>** affects all included frames, but may be overridden by an attribute within an individual **<FRAME>** element or within a nested **<FRAMESET>**.

The **CLASS** attribute defines a class for the frames so that a style sheet can be applied to their contents.

The **COLS** attribute is a standard attribute that defines the frames to define in a column format. The widths of the columns must be specified separated by commas. The width of a frame can be defined in a percentage width of the screen, such as 20 percent; a pixel value, such as 300; or with the * wildcard, which will determine size automatically.

The **FRAMEBORDER** attribute determines whether or not to display a border for the frames enclosed within the **<FRAMESET>** element. The attribute may be set to **NO (0)** or **YES (1)**. A value of **NO** or **0** "turns off" the border, overriding any value set with the **BORDER** attribute. The value of the **FRAMEBORDER** attribute can be overridden by a similar attribute within the **<FRAME>** element. While an author may define frame borders as off (**NO** or **0**) for a document, a particular frame may turn its borders on.

The **FRAMESPACING** attribute creates a space between frames. The value of this attribute is set in pixels. Setting the **BORDER** value to "off" has the same effect as using this attribute by itself. If **BORDERCOLOR** is applied to the spacing set up by this attribute, this simply creates an invisible border. This attribute is currently only supported by Internet Explorer.

The **<FRAMESET>** element may have an **ID** attribute that can be set to a unique identifier. This is particularly useful in conjunction with style sheets. While in many tags **ID** may have some use as an anchor destination, that meaning is unclear, and should be avoided.

The **LANG** attribute defines the language the framed documents are written in. The value of this attribute is in the form of the ISO standard abbreviation for languages—**en** for English, **fr** for French, and so on.

The **LANGUAGE** attribute indicates the scripting language used in case there is a script bound to an event associated with the **<FRAMESET>** element. The standard values for this attribute include **JAVASCRIPT**, **JSCRIPT**, **VBS**, and **VBSCRIPT**. By default, this value is **JAVASCRIPT**.

Like the **COLS** attribute, the **ROWS** attribute defines the frames in the **<FRAMESET>** by row heights. The value of this attribute is a comma-delimited list of frame sizes specified in pixels, percentage values, or with the * wildcard.

The **TITLE** attribute provides advisory information to the user in the form of a tool tip or simply as a note to future readers of the document. A browser may render the **TITLE** attribute value when the pointer is positioned over the **<FRAMESET>** border. It is possible to bind scripts to events to the **<FRAMESET>** element. The HTML 4.0 specification defines two basic events, **onload** and **onunload**, which define the event of finishing frame loading and unloading. Netscape also supports **onblur** and **onfocus**. Other browsers may define other events, but **onload** and **onunload** events are probably the most important.

<FRAME> Syntax

The **<FRAME>** element must occur within the **<FRAMESET>** element. The primary attributes, as discussed previously, are the **SRC** attribute, which indicates the URL of the frame content, and the **NAME** attribute, which sets a name for the frame for linking and scripting purposes. The HTML 4.0 specification also defines the **FRAMEBORDER, MARGINWIDTH, MARGINHEIGHT, NORESIZE,** and **SCROLLING** attributes, which control the basic presentation of the specified frame. Browser vendors have also specified numerous additions to the **<FRAME>** element to control its presentation and provide hooks to style sheets and scripting languages. The complete syntax for the **<FRAME>** element and a discussion of its attributes are shown here:

```
<FRAME
    BORDERCOLOR=color value    (IE and Netscape)
    CLASS=class name           (IE and Netscape)
    DATAFLD=column name        (IE)
    DATASRC=#ID                (IE)
    FRAMEBORDER=NO | YES | 0 | 1
    ID=unique identifier
    LANG=ISO language code              (IE)
    LANGUAGE=JAVASCRIPT | JSCRIPT | VBSCRIPT | VBS      (IE)
    MARGINHEIGHT=pixels
    MARGINWIDTH=pixels
    NAME=frame name
    NORESIZE
    SCROLLING=AUTO | NO | YES
    SRC=URL of frame contents
    TITLE=advisory text
    event=script code       (IE)>
```

The **BORDERCOLOR** attribute sets the border color of the frame. The value of the attribute may be a color name or a hexadecimal color value. The **BORDERCOLOR** attribute should be set when the **BORDER** attribute is set; otherwise, there will be no effect.

 *Be careful when setting the **BORDERCOLOR** of adjacent frames to different values, as the meaning is unclear.*

The **CLASS** attribute specifies the class name of the frame to provide a name for a style sheet application.

The **DATAFLD** attribute is a Microsoft extension first made available under Internet Explorer 4.0. This attribute indicates the column name of a bound data source to pull information from. In the case of frames, it is possible to dynamically set the **SRC** attribute from an external data source such as a database. (See Chapter 8 for a discussion of databinding.)

The **DATASRC** attribute indicates the **ID** of the data source object that supplies the data bound to the SRC value of the frame element.

The **FRAMEBORDER** attribute specifies whether to display a border for the frame. A value of **YES** or **1** indicates that a border should be drawn, while a value of **NO** or **0** indicates it should not. The **FRAMEBORDER** value for a particular frame overrides the value of the same attribute specified for the entire frame set. The HTML 4.0 defines **0** and **1** as the standard values, though Microsoft and Netscape both support a **YES** or **NO** value as well.

The attribute **ID** can be set to a unique identifier to be used for linking, style sheet binding, or scripting. Page authors should be careful with the **ID** attribute since it specifies the name of the frame for link targeting, just like the **NAME** attribute. This brings up a potential problem: which attribute should be used to set the name of the frame? If only **ID** is used, older browsers may not work properly. Using **NAME** alone doesn't embrace the latest standard. Page developers may be tempted to use both and set them to the same value. While most browsers will probably target frames with names defined both with **ID** and **NAME**, the standard suggests this is illegal. Page developers should probably stick with **NAME** as the sole way to identify frames for the moment.

The **LANG** attribute defines the language the framed documents are written in. The value of this attribute is in the form of the ISO standard abbreviation for languages, such as **en** for English, **fr** for French, and so on.

The **LANGUAGE** attribute indicates the scripting language used in case there is a script bound to an event associated with the **<FRAMESET>** element. The standard values for this attribute include **JAVASCRIPT**, **JSCRIPT**, **VBS**, and **VBSCRIPT**. By default, this value is **JAVASCRIPT**.

The **MARGINHEIGHT** attribute indicates the amount of pixels between the top and bottom of a frame and the internal contents of a frame. It is possible to set the value equal to **0** to pull content right next to the frame border.

The **MARGINWIDTH** attribute sets the amount of pixels the right and left margins should be set to before displaying the text in a frame. Like **MARGINHEIGHT**, **MARGINWIDTH** is set to a pixel value that indicates the size in pixels of the left and right margins. The left and right margins provide a buffer between the frame border and the enclosed content.

The **NAME** attribute specifies the name of the frame to be used by the **TARGET** attribute of the anchor element or to reference via a scripting language. Be careful not to specify names that begin with an underscore, particularly **_blank**, **_parent**, **_self**, or **_top**, which are reserved names with special meanings.

The **NORESIZE** attribute indicates that a frame may not be resized. The attribute does not require a value, but setting it to **RESIZE** or **NORESIZE** may have meaning under some browsers. This is not recommended, however, as all browsers recognize the occurrence of the **NORESIZE** attribute as an indication not to allow user resizing. If this attribute does not occur, the default action is to allow the user to resize the frame.

The **SCROLLING** attribute indicates whether a frame can be scrolled using a scroll bar or similar device. The default action for frames is to automatically provide a scroll bar if the content within the frame is too large to fit within the region defined. However, it is possible to override the automatic scroll bar setting and turn scroll bars off by setting this attribute to **NO** or turn scroll bars on by setting the attribute to **YES**. Be careful not to use this attribute with the **NORESIZE** attribute unless you are absolutely certain the content will fit within the framed region. Leaving it to the default, **AUTO**, is generally the best course of action, because scroll bars will only be present if they are required to see all of the content in the frame. Forcing them on when not needed only wastes real estate, and forcing them off when required is extremely frustrating to the user.

The **SRC** attribute specifies the URL of the document to load into the given frame. It is not allowed to use a local target, such as **#area1** and point to a location within a document. The URL should be a relative or complete URL to an outside document.

The **TITLE** attribute, as defined by Microsoft, sets text that provides advisory information about the frame. In some browsers, when the user positions the mouse over the frame, a tool tip showing the **TITLE** value may appear. Otherwise, the information may simply serve as a comment to a future reader of the HTML document.

It may be possible to set an event handler using an event attribute. Internet Explorer defines the event **onreadystatechange**, which fires whenever the **readystate** for the object has changed. According to Microsoft documentation, when an element changes to the loaded state, this event fires immediately before the firing of the load event. The value of the attribute should be set to script code in the language defined by the **LANG** attribute or JavaScript by default.

A more complex example using frames that illustrates many of the attributes described is shown in Figure 9-7.

<NOFRAMES> Syntax

The **<NOFRAMES>** attribute is used to enclose the HTML and text to be displayed when a browser does not support frames. The **<NOFRAMES>** element should only be found within the **<FRAMESET>** element. Nevertheless, **<NOFRAMES>** is often found directly outside the **<FRAMESET>** element. Because of the permissive nature of browsers, this tends to be interpreted correctly. By default, there are no special

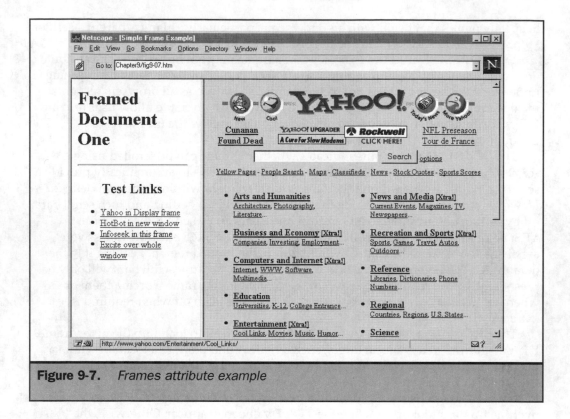

Figure 9-7. *Frames attribute example*

attributes for the **<NOFRAMES>** element, although Microsoft also indicates that **ID**, **STYLE**, and **TITLE** attributes are supported. The syntax for **<NOFRAMES>** is shown here:

```
<NOFRAMES
   CLASS=class name(s)
   DIR=LTR   | RTL
   ID=unique alphanumeric identifier
   LANG=ISO language code
   STYLE=inline style information
   TITLE=advisory text
   event=script code
   Non-framed content
   ID=unique identifier    (IE)
   STYLE=inline style information    (IE)
   TITLE=advisory text>    (IE)
```

```
   Nonframed content

</NOFRAMES>
```

It is difficult to see the use of many of these attributes. For example, how would the **TITLE** attribute be used to provide advisory information? It is unlikely that a browser that doesn't support frames will support tool tip style information, which is the common rendering of the **TITLE** attribute value, but the attribute may still serve a function to provide a note to a future reader of the HTML markup code. Regardless of obvious meaning, like most elements under HTML 4.0, **<NOFRAMES>** supports a wealth of attributes.

Floating Frames

Up until this point, all the frames shown have been attached to the sides of the browser (left, right, top, or bottom). Another form of frame, called a *floating frame*, was introduced by Microsoft and the idea has been incorporated into the HTML 4.0 standard. The idea of the floating frame is to create an inline framed region or window that acts similarly to any other embedded object, in that text can be flowed around it. An inline frame is defined by the **<IFRAME>** element and may occur anywhere within the **<BODY>** of an HTML document. Compare this to the **<FRAME>** element that should only occur within the **<FRAMESET>** element, which should preclude the body.

The major attributes to set for the **<IFRAME>** element include **SRC**, **HEIGHT**, and **WIDTH**. The **SRC** is set to the URL of the file to load, while the **HEIGHT** and **WIDTH** are set to the pixel or percentage value of the screen that the floating frame region should consume. Like an **<IMG>** element, floating frames should support **ALIGN**, **HSPACE**, and **VSPACE** attributes for basic positioning within the flow of text. Note that, unlike the **<FRAME>** element, the **<IFRAME>** element comes with a close tag. **<IFRAME>** and **</IFRAME>** should contain any HTML markup code and text that should be displayed in browsers that do not support floating frames. A simple example of floating frames is shown in Figure 9-8.

The rendering of the example code in Figure 9-8 is shown in Figure 9-9. Note how the Netscape browser does not support the **<IFRAME>** element but renders the enclosed text instead.

<IFRAME> Syntax

The complete syntax for **<IFRAME>** is strikingly similar to the **<IMG>** element, as well as to other elements such as **<OBJECT>** that are used to insert other forms of content inline. The **<IFRAME>** element, defined under HTML 4.0, includes many of the attributes that would be expected. The most important attributes are **SRC**, which

```
<!DOCTYPE HTML PUBLIC "-//W3C//DTD HTML 4.0 Draft//EN">
<HTML>
<HEAD>
<TITLE>Floating Frame Example</TITLE>
</HEAD>
<BODY>

<H1 ALIGN=CENTER>Floating Frame Example</H1>

<IFRAME NAME="float1" SRC="fileone.htm" WIDTH="350"
        HEIGHT="200" ALIGN="LEFT">

There would be an floating frame here if your browser
supported it.

</IFRAME>

<P>
This is a simple example of how floating frames are used.
Notice that in many ways the floating frame acts very
similar to an inline image. Floating frames act like
embedded objects in many ways.</P>

</BODY>
</HTML>
```

Figure 9-8. *Simple floating frame example*

defines the content of the floating frame, and **NAME**, which is used for link targeting. As a frame itself, floating frames also support the **FRAMEBORDER**, **MARGINWIDTH, MARGINHEIGHT,** and **SCROLLING** attributes. Because the floating frame is an inlined object, it also supports the **ALIGN, HEIGHT,** and **WIDTH** attributes, which can be useful for content layout. Microsoft also supports other

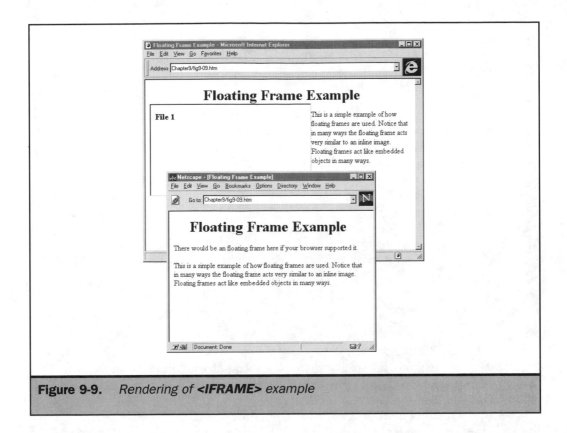

Figure 9-9.   *Rendering of <IFRAME> example*

attributes to define the look of the floating frame as well as provide hooks into scripting technologies. The complete syntax of the **<IFRAME>** element is provided here:

```
<IFRAME
   ALIGN=ABSBOTTOM* | ABSMIDDLE* | BASELINE* | BOTTOM |
      LEFT | MIDDLE | RIGHT |    TEXTTOP* | TOP    (*IE)
   BORDER=pixels   (IE)
   BORDERCOLOR=color   (IE)
   CLASS=class name   (IE)
   DATAFLD-column name    (IE)
   DATASRC=Data source   (IE)
   FRAMEBORDER=0 | NO | YES | 1
```

```
HEIGHT=pixels or percentage
HSPACE=pixels  (IE)
ID=unique identifier
LANG=language  (IE)
LANGUAGE=JAVASCRIPT | JSCRIPT | VBSCRIPT | VBS  (IE)
MARGINHEIGHT=pixels
MARGINWIDTH=pixels
NAME=frame name
NORESIZE  (IE)
SCROLLING=AUTO | NO | YES
SRC=URL of frame contents
STYLE=inlined style information  (IE)
TITLE=advisory text
VSPACE=pixels  (IE)
WIDTH=pixels or percentage
Event=script>

</IFRAME>
```

Most of the attributes are similar to those associated with other frame values, discussed earlier in this chapter. Those that differ or may have qualities unique to **<IFRAME>** are discussed here.

Because a floating frame is really a form of inline object, the **ALIGN** attribute may be very important. Under HTML 4.0, the **ALIGN** attribute does not support special values like **ABSBOTTOM**, **ABSMIDDLE**, **TEXTTOP**, and **BASELINE**. However, browsers may support these values. Review the **<IMG>** attribute to understand the meaning of the **ALIGN** values.

The **FRAMEBORDER** attribute for the **<IFRAME>** element can be set to display a border for the floating frame. A value of **1** or **YES** turns the border on and **0** or **NO** turns it off. Under Internet Explorer 4.0, by default there is a slight border around all floating frames, but there is no sense of being able to set a border in any other fashion.

As with the **<IMG>** element, it is possible to specify the height of the floating frame in pixels or as a percentage value of the **HEIGHT** attribute. The **WIDTH** attribute, which specifies the width of the floating frame, takes a similar value.

The **HSPACE** and **VSPACE** attributes can be set in pixels to specify the margins for the floating frame to allow text flow around the image.

The **NORESIZE** attribute can be used to indicate that the frame is not resizable by the user. Floating frames as implemented under Internet Explorer 4.0 do not recognize this attribute, and the user is never capable of resizing the frame. Because resizing is never possible, the **SCROLLING** attribute should never be set to **NO**.

Using Frames

One of the biggest problems with frames is that, initially, they were used just because they existed. Framed documents can provide considerable benefit, but at a price. A potential benefit of frames is that frames allow content to be fixed on the screen. In previous examples, it has been mentioned that one frame may contain a table of contents, while the other frame contains the actual information. Keeping the table of contents on the screen provides a convenient way to navigate the body of information. Furthermore, if one frame has fixed navigation, the user may perceive the Web interface to be more responsive, since only part of the screen needs to update between selections. The primary benefit of frames is to present two or more things at once, but this extra window of information has its costs, as you'll see in the next section.

Frame Problems

Many usability experts, such as Jakob Nielsen (www.useit.com), are extremely critical of frames. Given the current implementation of frames and designers who don't understand the potential drawbacks of framed documents, there is some truth to the statement that frames can give designers more rope to hang themselves with. However, browser vendors are addressing many of the problems of frames. With any luck, designers will be aware enough to use frames only when they provide added benefit.

The problems with frames are numerous. They include design issues, navigation confusion, bookmarking problems, loss of URL context, and printing issues. Designers may not like frames because they often come with borders, which can look strange in a design. However, modern frame implementations allow the designer to turn frame borders off, so this really isn't an issue anymore. The only potential design issue is the possibility that a framed document may give up valuable screen real estate because of scroll bars, which could pose trouble for people with lower-resolution monitors. The only way to get around this problem is to limit the number of frames used on a page.

Navigation confusion is still a big issue with frames. Under Netscape 2.0, the first browser to implement frames, the browser back button did not go back in the frame history but instead went back in a page history. Because Netscape 2.0 and subsequent versions of the browser do things differently, there may be some lingering confusion about what back means in a framed environment. Another problem involves the sense of what happens when a link is clicked. Unless the framing is kept very simple, it may not be obvious what frames will change when the user clicks on a link. In some sites, numerous frames are updated at once. This may cause users to lose their sense of navigation. Even worse, if the user wants to bookmark the current page, she is actually bookmarking the top-level entry frame rather than the deeper level she progressed to. If the user bookmarks the actual frame content, she may lose any navigation necessary to navigate the site when they return.

Additional navigational problems include loss of context, since the URL of the document tends not to change. This accounts for why bookmarking doesn't work as expected. Many people use URLs as a way to orient themselves at a site; frames give up this clue to location.

Up until the release of Internet Explorer 4.0, it has been difficult to print frames. While it may be possible to print the contents of individual frames, it was generally impossible to print an entire document that consists of many frames.

While none of the problems with frames, except possibly navigation and bookmarking, are insurmountable, designers should approach the technology with caution and not just use it to show off their technical prowess.

Layers

Netscape introduced the **<LAYER>** element starting with the Communicator (Netscape 4.0) release of its browser. The layer function allows the page designer to define precisely positioned, overlapping layers of transparent or opaque content in a page. Besides being able to stack layers on top of each other to create complex layouts, authors can bind the layers to code that can move them around or change the order of overlap. Scripting combined with absolute positioning can truly make pages more dynamic. While the **<LAYER>** element does sound very useful, page authors should look to positioning with style sheets (discussed in the next chapter) as the way to absolutely control page layout.

Layers are too Netscape-specific at this point to recommend their use. The W3C is no longer considering layers for potential inclusion in forthcoming versions of HTML. While this may change, for the moment it's best to approach using layers (as defined with this proprietary HTML element) with extreme caution. It may be helpful to know more about layering, however.

The basic idea of a layer is similar to the idea of a frame, except that layers may overlap. They generally are defined in the same document, unlike frames, which require multiple documents. A layer defines a region or portion of the browser window that can be manipulated and may overlap other layers. Layers come in two basic forms: *positioned layers* defined by the **<LAYER>** element and *inflow layers* defined by the **<ILAYER>** element. This discussion focuses first on positioned layers, which are slightly easier to understand.

Positioned Layers

To define a section of a document as a layer to position, enclose it within **<LAYER>** and **</LAYER>**. The layer should be named, just as a frame is named, so that it can be manipulated later. To name a layer, set the **ID** attribute of the element to a unique identifier. For a positioned layer, specify the upper corner of the layer by setting the **TOP** and **LEFT** attributes to the pixel coordinate of the upper-left corner of the layer relative to the browser window. It may also be desirable to set the **WIDTH** and **HEIGHT** attributes of the layer. These take pixel values, so the actual size of the layer can be controlled regardless of its content. A simple example showing how absolutely positioned layers work is presented in Figure 9-10.

Note that the **BGCOLOR** attribute is used with the layers to show how the layers clip each other. The rendering of the layer example is shown in Figure 9-11. To see how this code looks on a browser that does not support layers, see Figure 9-12.

Because the position of layers is defined absolutely, there is no need to define how they fall on a page; but it would make sense to define layers in a logical order based upon a left-to-right, top-to-bottom flow of the page.

For browsers that do not support layers, the **<NOLAYER>** tag may be useful. Content placed within **<NOLAYER>** and **</NOLAYER>** elements is ignored by a browser like Netscape 4.0, which understands layers, but renders normally on all

```
<HTML>
<HEAD>
<TITLE>Layer Example</TITLE>
</HEAD>
<BODY>
<H1 ALIGN=CENTER>Simple Layer Example</H1>
<LAYER ID="Layer1" TOP="100" LEFT="50" BGCOLOR="LIGHTGREEN">
   <H2>This is a layer</H2>
<UL>
   <LI>This layer is positioned at 100,150
</UL>
</LAYER>
<LAYER ID="Layer2" TOP="180" LEFT="250" BGCOLOR="ORANGE">
   <H2>This is another layer</H2>
<UL>
   <LI>Position of this layer is 180,250
</UL>
</LAYER>
</BODY>
</HTML>
```

Figure 9-10.   *Simple layer example*

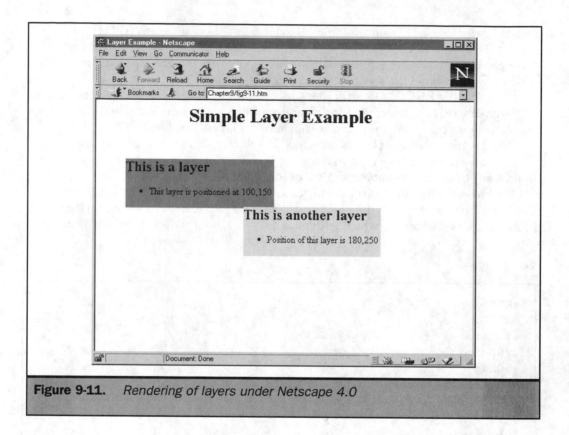

Figure 9-11. *Rendering of layers under Netscape 4.0*

others. This could allow extra information to be added into the page in the case that a nonlayering browser was being used. Since the contents of the **<LAYER>** element are rendered onscreen by browsers that do not understand the element, it is best to use the **SRC** attribute to include the contents of the layer from another file, as shown here:

```
<LAYER ID="Layer1" SRC="layercontents.htm" TOP="100" LEFT="100">
</LAYER>
<NOLAYER>
. . . normal HTML . . .
</NOLAYER>
```

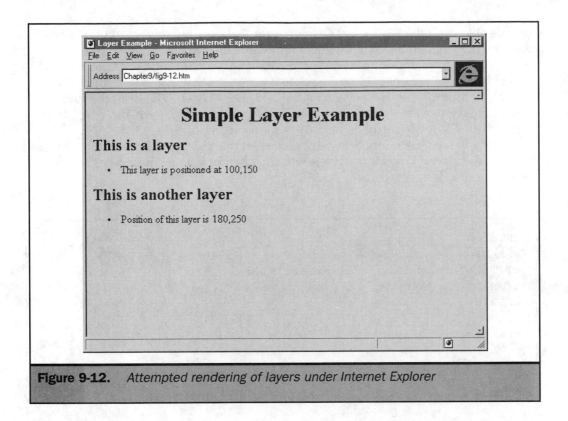

Figure 9-12. *Attempted rendering of layers under Internet Explorer*

Using this technique, you can use layers without ruining the layout for other browsers. As with frames, this may require keeping two separate forms of the site, which may be unreasonable.

Inflow Layers

Inflow layers are different than positioned layers in that they fall naturally within the flow of a document, much as an inlined object like an image is positioned. To indicate that content is part of an inflow layer, enclose it within **<ILAYER>** and **</ILAYER>** elements. Unlike positioned layers, where the inflow layer is defined matters, and affects where the content ends up on the page. Similar to the **<LAYER>** element, a name is probably required for the layer, and should be set using the **ID** attribute. It is also possible to set the **LEFT** and **TOP** values for the layer, but this positions the layer relative to the content the layer is within, not within the upper-left corner of the browser window or enclosing layer. This positioning may be useful to move content around by a certain number of pixels, relative to text in the document. A simple example of inflow layers is shown in Figure 9-13. The **BGCOLOR** attribute is used again, so that when the example is rendered the location of the layers can be determined. The rendering of Figure 9-13 is shown in Figure 9-14.

Note how the second inflow layer clips the text that follows it. Page authors must be very careful with layers, since layers will clip other objects on the screen. This is their nature by design.

```
<HTML>
<HEAD>
<TITLE>Inflow Layer Example</TITLE>
</HEAD>
<BODY>

<P>An inflow layer can be found

<ILAYER ID="Layer1" BGCOLOR="YELLOW">
within the flow
</ILAYER> of text</P>

<P>This <ILAYER ID="Layer2" BGCOLOR="YELLOW" LEFT="25">
is positioned 25 pixels from the left
</ILAYER>
of the current flow of the content.</P>

<P>This <ILAYER ID="Layer3" BGCOLOR="YELLOW" TOP="15">
is positioned 15 pixels below
</ILAYER> the current flow of content.</P>

</BODY>
</HTML>
```

Figure 9-13.   *Inflow layer example*

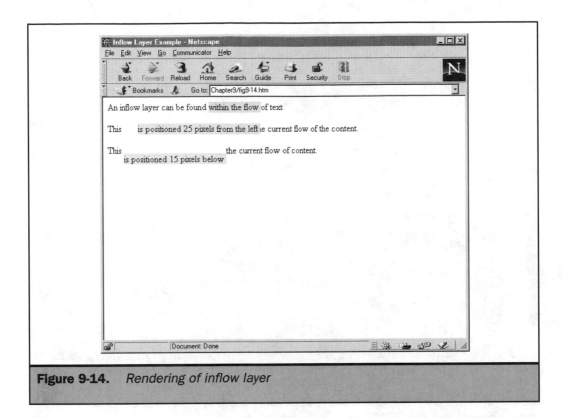

Figure 9-14.   *Rendering of inflow layer*

Layer Syntax

The syntax for both the **<LAYER>** and **<ILAYER>** elements is pretty much the same, but the attributes may have slightly different meanings under each element. The syntax for both **<ILAYER>** and **<LAYER>** is shown here. Simply substitute **ILAYER** for **LAYER** in the start tag and end tag.

```
<LAYER
   ABOVE=layer id
   BACKGROUND=URL of background image to load
   BELOW=layer id
   BGCOLOR=color
   CLASS=class name
   CLIP=left, top, right, bottom
```

```
HEIGHT=pixels or percentage value
ID=unique identifier
LEFT=pixel
NAME=unique identifier (Use ID instead)
PAGEX=pixel
PAGEY=pixel
SRC=URL of content to load into layer
STYLE=inline style information
TOP=pixel
VISIBILITY=SHOW | HIDDEN | INHERIT
WIDTH=pixelor percentage value
Z-INDEX=positive integer
Event=script code>

Layer contents

</LAYER>
```

The **ABOVE** attribute specifies the name, set by the **ID** attribute, of the layer that is immediately above the currently defined layer specified by the **<LAYER>** or **<ILAYER>** element. The element containing this attribute is created just below the layer named by the **ABOVE** attribute. The **ABOVE** attribute cannot be used in the same element with the **Z-INDEX** or **BELOW** attributes.

The **BACKGROUND** attribute can be set to the URL of an image to use as the background of a layer. The rendering of the background should be similar to the **BACKGROUND** attribute of the **<BODY>** element. This may include tiling or clipping of the background image, depending on the size of the layer. By default, a layer shows through to any layers it stacks on top of, assuming that the background image is transparent or not used.

The **BELOW** attribute specifies the name, set by the **ID** attribute, of the layer that is directly below the current layer defined. The **<LAYER>** or **<ILAYER>** element containing this attribute will be on top of the layer defined by the **BELOW** attribute. The **BELOW** attribute cannot be used in the same element with the **Z-INDEX** or **ABOVE** attributes.

The **BGCOLOR** attribute specifies the background color of the layer. It can be set to either a color name or hexadecimal value similar to how the **BGCOLOR** for the **<BODY>** element is used.

The **CLASS** attribute specifies a class name for access via a style sheet.

The **CLIP** attribute specifies the clipping region, or viewable area, of the layer. The size of the clipping region can be less than the actual size of the layer. To specify the clipping region for a layer, specify the left, top, right, and bottom edge coordinates of the visible region. For example: **<LAYER CLIP="10,10, 50,20">** sets the region to be 10 pixels from the left of the enclosing region, 10 pixels down from the top, 50 pixels in from the right, and 20 pixels up from the bottom. It is also possible to provide only two coordinate values for the attribute. In this case, the browser should assume the left and top edges of the clipping region to both be **0**: **<LAYER CLIP="50,20">** is equal to **<LAYER CLIP="0,0,50,20>**. The area in the layer outside the clipping region should be transparent and allow any covered content to show through. While it may not make sense why **CLIP** would be used when a layer could just be defined smaller, consider that the value can be changed dynamically using JavaScript. By changing the clipping region, it is possible to create wipes, an effect that is demonstrated in the next section. When the **CLIP** attribute is omitted, the clipping region of a layer is the entire layer, which is determined by the values of the **HEIGHT** and **WIDTH** attributes.

The **HEIGHT** attribute specifies the height of a layer. It may be set as a pixel or a percentage value. Like the **WIDTH** attribute, a percentage value is a percentage of the containing layer, or of the browser window if the layer is the top layer. If the contents of the layer do not fit in the specified size, the layer expands to contain its content.

The **ID** attribute specifies a unique name for a layer so that it can be referenced via JavaScript or other layers.

> **Note** *The **ID** attribute was called **NAME** in early versions of the element. The NAME attribute still works, but its use is discouraged. The **ID** attribute can be used both by the **<LAYER>** element and cascading style sheet syntax discussed in the next chapter. By default a layer has no name or identifier set.*

The **LEFT** attribute is set to a pixel value that indicates the horizontal position of an absolutely positioned layer from the left-hand side of the browser, or the layer in which the current layer is contained. When the **LEFT** attribute is set for an inflow layer, the value in pixels is relative to the content containing the layer. When setting the value of the **LEFT** attribute with an inflow layer, be aware that nearby content can be clipped.

The **PAGEX** attribute specifies the horizontal position of the layer relative to the browser window. This may be useful when layers are nested, since it specifies position relative to the browser window, not the enclosing layer's coordinate system.

The **PAGEY** attribute specifies the vertical position of the layer relative to the browser window rather than any enclosing layer.

The **SRC** attribute sets the URL of a file that contains the content to load into the layer. Depending on how a page is structured, it may be possible to use the **SRC** attribute to include a small portion of a file into a complex layout, as shown here:

```
<P>Static content here</P>
<LAYER SRC="changingcontent.htm"></LAYER>
<P>Static content here</P>
```

This code allows an included file like changingccontent.htm to be pulled into the page, thus allowing this second file to be updated with no knowledge of the layout of the page.

The **STYLE** attribute specifies an inline style for the layer. It is interesting that an author would consider using a style sheet with a layer, as style sheets can provide the same functionality as layers. Even so, this attribute is available.

The **TOP** attribute is set to a pixel value that indicates the vertical position of an absolutely positioned layer from the top of the browser. When the **TOP** attribute is set for an inflow layer, the pixel value is relative to the content that the layer is embedded within. When using this attribute with **<ILAYER>**, be careful not to clip nearby content.

The **VISIBILITY** attribute determines whether a layer is visible or not. The attribute may be set to **SHOW**, **HIDDEN**, or **INHERIT**. If the attribute is set to **SHOW**, it is visible. When set to **HIDDEN**, it is not. The normal default action is **INHERIT**, which means that the layer's visibility is determined by its enclosing layer. For top-level layers (layers not enclosed by other layers) the default is **SHOW**. The **VISIBILITY** value of a layer does not address whether or not the layer can be seen onscreen, as it may be clipped or behind an opaque layer.

The **WIDTH** attribute specifies the width, in pixels or percentage, of the layer. When using a percentage value for **WIDTH**, note that the value is relative to the enclosing layer and not necessarily the screen width. The width of the layer determines where content wraps in a layer. When using content that may not wrap, like images, note that the layer may resize to the point that the content fits.

The **Z-INDEX** attribute sets a z-order (layering order) in layering. All layers may have a z-order value specified in terms of an integer. Layers with higher **Z-INDEX** values are stacked on top of those with lower **Z-INDEX** values. Positive values for **Z-INDEX** are suggested. The **Z-INDEX** attribute should not be used with either the **ABOVE** or **BELOW** attribute.

There are several event handler attributes that can be set for a layer: **onmouseover**, **onmouseout**, **onfocus**, **onblur**, and **onload**. Using the mouse handlers, it is possible to bind a script action to the event of a mouse entering or leaving a layer's region. The **onfocus** and **onblur** events are used to signal when a keyboard event or a click into the region gives the layer focus, or when the focus is lost (blur). The last event currently available is the **onload** event, which can trigger bound script code after the layer has been loaded. A small example of using an event will be presented in the next section.

A more complex example illustrating many of the uses of the **<LAYER>** element is shown in Figure 9-15. A rendering of the example in Figure 9-15 is shown in Figure 9-16.

```
<HTML>
<HEAD>
<TITLE>Layer Attribute Example</TITLE>
</HEAD>
<BODY>

<LAYER ID="Layer1" TOP="50" LEFT="100" BGCOLOR="LIGHTGREEN"
      HEIGHT="60%" WIDTH="400">

<H1>This is layer 1</H1>

<LAYER ID="Layer2" TOP="100" LEFT="100" BGCOLOR="YELLOW"
      STYLE="font-family: Impact" WIDTH="10%">
<BR><BR>This is layer 2 inside layer 1.
</LAYER>

</LAYER>

<LAYER ID="Layer3" ABOVE="Layer2" BGCOLOR="WHITE"
      Z-INDEX="3" TOP="165" LEFT="125">
This layer is layer 3 on top of Layer 1 and 2.
</LAYER>
</BODY>
</HTML>
```

Figure 9-15.   *Layer example showing attribute usage*

While it is obvious that layers are powerful as far as positioning, let's next look at what can be done with them.

Interesting Layer Uses

Although they are very proprietary, layers can be used to create a variety of interesting effects. The next chapter will show that it is possible to create similar effects using style sheets, which is the preferred way of doing things. One major aspect of layers to

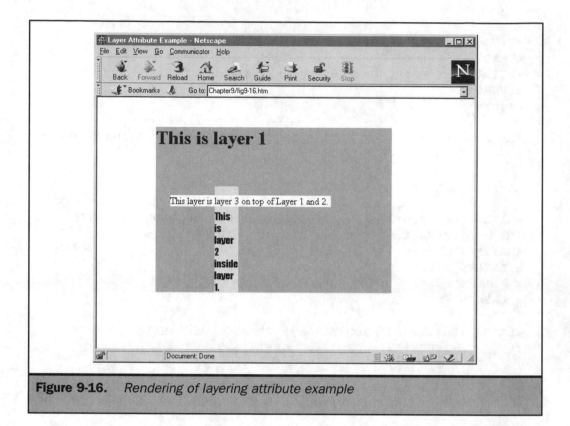

Figure 9-16. *Rendering of layering attribute example*

note is that they are, by default, transparent unless the content in the layer covers the layer entirely, as might happen in the case of a background image to a layer. Because layers are normally transparent, it is possible to overlay text on top of images. Before layers evolved, this was difficult to do. (While background images and table cells offered some degree of control, it was very limited; the positioning of text on top of the image was far from precise.) The example in Figure 9-17 shows how text may be positioned over an image. In case you are skeptical of this newfound ability, a rendering of the example under Netscape 4.0 is shown in Figure 9-18.

Programming Layers

Layers become very interesting when they are combined with JavaScript. The clipping region of a layer can be changed incrementally so that, at first, none of the layer shows, only to gradually appear in a matter of seconds. This effect is known as a *wipe*. This simple transition effect is an example of Dynamic HTML (DHTML). The original direction of Netscape's DHTML focused heavily on layers, but now the preferred

```
<HTML>
<HEAD>
<TITLE>Text Over Image</TITLE>
</HEAD>
<BODY>

<LAYER TOP="100" LEFT="100">
<IMG SRC="bclogonotext.gif" WIDTH="141" HEIGHT="197" BORDER="0">
</LAYER>

<LAYER TOP="200" LEFT="40">
<FONT COLOR="RED">
<H2>Big Company, Inc</H2>
</FONT>
</LAYER>

</BODY>
</HTML>
```

Figure 9-17.   *Simple text over image example*

method is to use style sheets, discussed in the next chapter. For old time's sake, a layer example that creates a simple wipe is shown here:

```
<HTML>
<HEAD>
<TITLE>Curtain Layers</TITLE>

<SCRIPT LANGUAGE="JavaScript">

function wipe(alayer,xinc,inctime,stopwidth)
  {
alayer.clip.left += -(xinc/2)
alayer.clip.right += (xinc/2)
if (alayer.clip.width < 0) {lyr.clip.width = 0}
if (((xinc < 0) && (alayer.clip.width > stopwidth)) ||
  ((xinc > 0) && (alayer.clip.width < stopwidth)))
  {
  setTimeout('wipe(document.layers["'+alayer.name+'"],
```

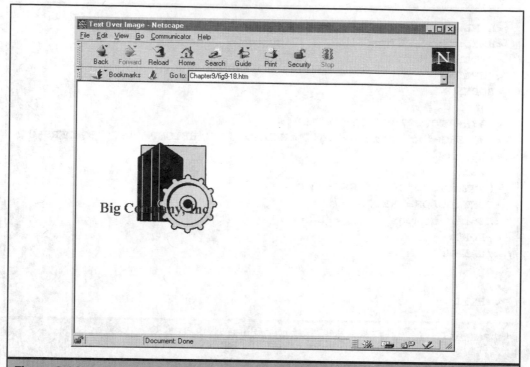

Figure 9-18. *Rendering of text over image example*

```
    '+xinc+','+inctime+','+stopwidth+')',inctime)
  }
}
</SCRIPT>
</HEAD>

<BODY BGCOLOR="WHITE"
 onLoad="wipe(document.layers['lasthurrah'],-2,10,0)">

<LAYER NAME="lasthurrah" TOP="100" LEFT="100" BGCOLOR="YELLOW">
<H1>Goodbye, cruel world. I am the last layer!</H1>
</LAYER>

</BODY>
</HTML>
```

Be careful with this example. It only works in Netscape 4.0 and above. The line that reads setTimeout belongs on one line regardless of any wrapping in the print.

Summary

Layout using HTML tags is not appropriate, but until recently that was all that was available. Frames are often used as a layout tool, and while the **<FRAME>** element can afford great power in making sophisticated layouts, it comes with a great price. Navigation confusion, printing, and design problems may all result from misuse of frames, but when used properly (providing fixed index pages), frames are a valuable addition to the page designer's arsenal. Because of their power and popularity, frames have finally been included in the HTML specification, so there should be no worry about their future use. However, more advanced page layout tags proprietary to Netscape browsers, such as the **<LAYER>** and **<ILAYER>** elements, should be approached with caution. These tags are very proprietary. While they can be used to create impressive, even dynamic layouts, it is possible to create similar effects using standardized technology—particularly style sheets—which are discussed in the next chapter.

Chapter 10

Style Sheets

HTML is a poor language for page formatting, but this isn't a failing of the technology. As mentioned throughout this book, HTML elements are not supposed to be used to represent layout. Even so, people often use HTML as a visual design environment. They tend to think visually, rather than organizationally, when building Web pages. Why? Well, there weren't very many choices in the past. Everybody wanted the same thing—a high degree of control over the layout of their Web pages. Until recently, this control required using tables, HTML tricks, and images for layout, or embedding a binary form like Acrobat in a page. These solutions were generally unsatisfactory, however.

A better solution is emerging. Finally, style sheets, in the form of Cascading Style Sheets (CSS1), are finally available in the major browsers. Style sheets offer what designers have been clamoring for over the years: more control over layout. Arguably, style sheets are the best approach for creating attractive pages. Although they are still relatively new, and only recently have the major browsers started to support them consistently, it is likely that style sheets will soon become the dominant way to format Web pages. As you'll see in this chapter, designers should begin transitioning away from HTML layout, which relies heavily on tables, and move toward using style sheets.

The Rise of Style

Basically, style sheets separate the structure of a document from its presentation. Dividing layout and presentation has many theoretical benefits; it can provide for flexible documents that display equally well across many types of output devices. In general, Web-based style sheets contain information that describes how documents are presented, whether on screens, in print, or perhaps even pronounced by a speech-based system for the visually impaired. While in some ways this doesn't sound different from how many people think about HTML, it is fundamentally different than the intended nature of HTML.

As early as 1993, people have been interested in adding more layout control to HTML. Many approaches have been discussed and continue to be used. As mentioned earlier, they include misuse of HTML tags and embedded binary object formats like Adobe's Acrobat. Because of their theoretical benefits, style sheets have been the favorite solution of the standards bodies. However, it wasn't until 1995 when Bert Bos of the World Wide Web Consortium (W3C) wrote a charter to work on the introduction of a style sheet standard for the Web. Eventually, Håkon Lie, also of the W3C, introduced a proposal for cascading style sheets; in December 1996, this proposal became the W3C's recommendation of Cascading Style Sheets Level 1 (CSS1). The cascading idea of the W3C style sheet approach allows a chain of precedence, so that local style may override global style, or a document creator's style might even override reader styles.

But the most interesting aspect of CSS1 is not the cascade. These newly introduced style rules allow us to move closer to device independence, and reduce reliance on proprietary HTML elements and tricks to force layout. As previously discussed, many of these HTML layout tags and tricks are not supported across the multitude of browsers. The motivation of style sheets to divide the semantic meaning of a page from its physical presentation may seem a bit grandiose, but they are gaining acceptance rapidly. The main reason that Web developers may start to use style sheets is that they provide a greater degree of layout control than has been previously possible. For example, style sheets can be used to create a paragraph with a .5-inch margin, 100 pixels between lines, and text rendered in 48-point green Impact font. Try doing that in HTML.

While style sheets might sound wonderful, the fact of the matter is that they are still not widely supported. To further complicate matters, there is more than one type of style sheet. Internet Explorer 3.0, Netscape 4.0, and Internet Explorer 4.0 all support CSS1-based style sheets to some degree, but no widely used browser supports all aspects of the W3C cascading style sheet definition. (A few browsers are getting close.) Furthermore, many industry pundits support a type of sheet known as DSSSL (Document Style Semantics and Specification Language), which was developed by the SGML community. The most recent addition is XSL, for eXtensible Style Language. XSL is an industry proposal based on DSSSL and uses XML (Extensible Markup Language) syntax. XSL allows for more complex style manipulation, but is more complex than CSS1 to use. Only time will tell if XSL achieves industry acceptance. Yet despite industry confusion and the browser vendors' historical slow adoption of style sheets, it is possible to take advantage of what style sheets have to offer today without causing problems for browsers that are not "style aware."

Style Sheet Basics

CSS1 style sheets rely on an underlying markup structure, such as HTML. They are not a replacement for HTML. Without a binding to an element, a style really doesn't mean anything. The purpose of a style sheet is to create a presentation for a particular element or set of elements. Binding an element to a style specification is very simple; it consists of an element followed by its associated style information within curly braces:

```
element    {style specification}
```

Imagine that you want to bind a style rule to the **<H1>** element so that a 28-point Impact font is always used. The following rule would result in the desired display:

```
H1    {font-family: Impact;
      font-size:    28pt}
```

In general, a style specification or style sheet is simply a collection of *rules*. These rules include an HTML element, class, or id, more generally called a *selector*, which is bound to a style *property* such as **font-family**, followed by a colon and the value(s) for that style property. Multiple style rules may be included in a style specification by separating them with semicolons. There are also many shorthand notations and grouping rules that can be used, as discussed in "Advanced Style Rules: Contextual Selection, Grouping, and Inheritance," later in this chapter. Currently, there are more than 50 properties specified under CSS1 that affect the presentation of an HTML document. Unfortunately, not all of them are supported consistently across the major browsers. Style sheets alone do nothing; first you must bind the rule to a tag(s) or class of HTML objects. The full CSS1 specification can be found at the following address: http://www.w3.org/TR/REC-CSS1.

> **Note** *The style sheet information itself is not HTML. While style information may be included within an HTML document, or outside it, it is not necessarily subject to the same rules as HTML pages. Many of the basic ideas do apply. Like HTML, style sheet rules are case insensitive except for the aspects of the rule that are outside the control of the style sheet language; these aspects include font family names (such as Britannic Bold) and URLs (such as http://www.bigcompany.com/Staff/thomas.htm), both of which may be case sensitive.*

Adding Style to a Document

There are three basic ways to include style information in an HTML document. The first is to use an outside style sheet, either by importing it or linking to it. The second is to embed a document-wide style in the **<HEAD>** element of the document. The third is to provide an inline style right where style needs to be applied. Each of these style sheet approaches has its own pros and cons, and they are listed in Table 10-1.

Linking to a Style Sheet

An external style sheet is simply a plain text file containing the style specifications for HTML tags or classes. The common extensions indicating that the provided information is a style sheet are .css for CSS1 style sheets and .jss for Netscape's JavaScript style sheets (JSSS). Page designers are encouraged to avoid the .jss style because it is not common across browsers.

The CSS1 style rules shown here might be found in a file called corpstyle.css, which defines a corporate style sheet for a large Web site.

```
BODY        {font: 10pt;
             font-family: Serif;
             color: black;
             background: white}

H1          {font: 24pt;
             font-family: Sans-Serif;
             color: black}

H2          {font: 16pt;
```

```
                    font-family: Sans-Serif;
                    color: black}

P              {text-indent: 0.5in;
                margin-left: 50px;
                margin-right: 50px}

A:link:        {color: blue;
                text-decoration: none}

A:visited:     {color: red;
                text-decoration: none}

A:active:      {color:red;
                text-decoration: none}

.important     {background: yellow;
                font-weight: extra-bold}

#note          {background: orange}
```

	External Style Sheets	Document-Wide Style	Inline Style
PROS	*Can set style for many documents with one style sheet	*Can control style for document in one place *No additional download time for style information	*Can control style to a single character instance *Overrides any external or document styles
CONS	*Require extra download time for style sheet, which may delay page rendering	*Need to reapply style information for other documents	*Need to reapply style information throughout the document and outside documents *Bound too closely to HTML—difficult to update

Table 10-1.   *Comparison of Style Sheet Approaches*

An HTML file that uses this style sheet could reference it using the **<LINK>** tag within the **<HEAD>** element of the document. Remember from Chapter 5 that the **<LINK>** element is not exclusive to style sheets and has a variety of possible relationship settings that can be set with the **REL** attribute. An example of how style sheet linking is used is shown here:

```
<HTML>
<HEAD>
<TITLE>Style Sheet Linking Example</TITLE>
<LINK REL="STYLESHEET" HREF="corpstyle.css" MEDIA="screen"
TYPE="text/css">
</HEAD>
<BODY>

. . .content affected by style sheet. . .

</BODY>
</HTML>
```

In this example, the relationship for the **<LINK>** element as indicated by the **REL** attribute is set to be **STYLESHEET**; then the **HREF** attribute is used to indicate the URL of the style sheet to use. In this case, the style sheet resides in the same directory as the referencing file and is known as **corpstyle.css**. However, there is no reason that a remote style sheet couldn't be referenced using a URL such as the following one: http://www.bigcompany.com/styles/test-style1.css. Note that linking to an external style sheet has the same problems as linking to an external object in that the object may no longer be available, or the speed of acquiring that object may inhibit performance of the page.

The **MEDIA** attribute is used to provide an indication of what media the style sheet should apply to. This attribute allows the page designer to define one style for computer screens, one for print, and perhaps one for personal digital assistants. For example, there could be two links in the document, one for screen and one for print, as shown here:

```
<LINK REL="STYLESHEET" HREF="screenstyle.css" MEDIA="screen"
TYPE="text/css">

<LINK REL="STYLESHEET" HREF="printstyle.css" MEDIA="print"
TYPE="text/css">
```

It is also possible to set multiple values for the attribute. These should be separated by commas to show that the style may apply to many media forms; for example, **MEDIA="screen,print"**. Currently, the **MEDIA** attribute isn't widely understood by browsers. Some possible values for this attribute include **screen**, **print**, **projection**, **braille**, **aural**, and **all**.

The last thing to note in the linked style sheet example is the use of the **TYPE** attribute in the **<LINK>** element, which is set to the MIME type **"text/css"**. This value indicates that the linked style sheet is a cascading style sheet, but it is certainly possible that another form of style sheet could be linked. It is possible to define a style sheet type both inline as well as document-wide. To avoid having to use the **TYPE** attribute, it may be desirable to set a default style sheet language in the **<HEAD>** element of the document using the **<META>** element as shown here:

```
<META HTTP-EQUIV="Content-Style-Type" Content="text/css">
```

As it stands, by default most browsers will assume that CSS1 is being used; the **TYPE** setting may have little effect no matter how it is applied.

Embedding and Importing Style Sheets

The second way to include an external style sheet is to embed it. When you embed a style sheet, you write the style rules directly within the HTML document. It is possible to separate the style rules into another file and then import these rules, much as an *include* file is used in a programming language like C. However, imported style sheets are not supported consistently by browsers and are merely shorthand for pulling in all the style information without typing it in directly.

Document-wide style is a very easy way to begin using style sheets. It involves the use of the **<STYLE>** element found within the **<HEAD>** element of an HTML document. Enclose the style rules within the **<STYLE>** and **</STYLE>** tag pair and place these within the head section of the HTML document. Since there may be multiple forms of style sheets beyond the standard cascading style sheet format, you should still include the type attribute to indicate what format of style sheet you are using regardless of the browser's support for other style sheet technologies. It is possible to have multiple occurrences of the **<STYLE>** element within the head of the document, including importing some styles, linking to some style rules, and specifying some directly. Dividing style information into multiple sections and forms may be very useful, but there must be a way to determine which style rules apply. This is the idea of the cascade, which will be discussed in more detail later in this chapter.

One thing to worry about with style sheets included within an HTML document is that not all browsers understand style information. To avoid problems, comment out the style information using an HTML comment like **<!-- -->** so that it is not displayed on the screen or misinterpreted by older browsers. A complete example of a document-wide style sheet, including hiding rules from older browsers, is shown here:

```
<HTML>
<HEAD>
<TITLE>Document-Wide Style Sheets</TITLE>
```

```
<STYLE TYPE="text/css" MEDIA="PRINT">
<!--
BODY    {background: white;
         margin-left: 1in;
         margin-right: 1.5in}

H1      {font-size: 24pt;
         font-family: sans-serif;
         color: red;
         text-align: center}

P       {font-size: 12pt;
         font-family: Serif;
         text-indent: 0.5in;
         color: black}
-->
</STYLE>
</HEAD>
<BODY>
. . . content affected by style sheet . . .
</BODY>
</HTML>
```

Another way to use a document-wide style rather than providing it directly is to import it into the document. The idea here is similar to linking. An external style sheet is referenced, but in this case is similar to a macro expansion inline. The syntax for the rule for importing a style sheet is **@import** and the URL of the style sheet to include. This rule must be included within the **<STYLE>** element; it has no meaning outside that element, as compared to the linked style sheet. An example of how to import a style sheet as well is shown here:

```
<!DOCTYPE HTML PUBLIC "-//W3C//DTD HTML 4.0 Final//EN">
<HTML>
<HEAD>
<TITLE>Imported Style Sheets</TITLE>
<STYLE TYPE="text/css">
<!--
@import "@import

http://www.bigcompany.com/styles/corpstyle.css";
@import "docstyle.css";
```

```
H1    {font-size: 24pt;
       color: red;
       text-align: center} /* local rules
       that may override import */
-->
</STYLE>
</HEAD>
<BODY>
. . . content affected by style sheet . . .
</BODY>
</HTML>
```

While imported style sheets may seem to provide a great advantage for organizing style information, at the time of this writing their use is limited by the fact that none of the browsers support this form of style sheet access. Page designers should stick to the <LINK> form of accessing external style sheets until this form has more support.

Using Inline Style

Beyond using a style sheet for the whole document, it is possible to add style information right down to the single element. The simplest way to add style information, but not necessarily the best, is to add style rules to the particular HTML element in question. Here's how it works. Let's say you want to set one particular <H1> tag to render in 48-point, green, Arial font. You could apply that style to all <H1> elements or to a class of them (discussed in the next section) by applying a document-wide style. On the other hand, you could apply the style to only the tag in question; this is done with the **STYLE** attribute, which can be used within nearly any HTML element. For example, see how style rules could be applied to a particular <H1> element as shown here:

```
<H1 STYLE="font-size: 48pt; font-family: Arial; color:
green">CSS1 Test</H1>
```

There is no need to hide this sort of style information from a browser that is not style-sheet-aware, since browsers ignore any attributes they don't understand.

Using the idea of inline style, it is easy to apply a style to a certain section or division of a document using the <DIV> element. Setting a two-paragraph portion of a document to have a yellow background with bold black text on top of it is fairly simple, as shown here:

```
<DIV STYLE="background: yellow; font-weight: bold; color: black">

<P>Style sheets separate the structure of a document from its
presentation. Dividing layout and presentation has many theoretical
benefits and can provide for flexible documents that display
equally well on large graphically rich systems and palmtop
computers.</P>

<P>This is another paragraph describing the wonderful benefits of
style sheets</P>

</DIV>
```

If you want to provide style information solely for a few words or even letters, the best approach is to use the **<SPAN>** element. As a block element, the **<DIV>** element will work surrounding other block elements like paragraphs; but when setting a localized style within a paragraph, the correct element to bind style information is **<SPAN>**. For example, notice how **<SPAN>** is used here to call attention to a particular section of text:

```
<P>Calling out <SPAN STYLE="background: yellow; font-weight: bold;
color: black">special sections of text</SPAN> isn't hard with
SPAN</P>
```

While it may seem that putting style inline with the elements is the best way to get started with style sheets, it isn't. It is possible to add style to a particular set of elements, or even a single unique occurrence of a **<P>** element.

Using Classes and IDs

In the previous examples, the style rules were bound to a particular element or included directly within the tag in the form of an attribute. While inlining style seems easy, it gives up much of the benefit of dividing the structure of the document from the style. But without inline styles, how can a particular style be applied to one occurrence of the **<H1>** element, or only to a few particular **<H1>** elements? The solutions to these problems are the **CLASS** and **ID** attributes.

As discussed in Chapter 5, it was possible to name a particular tag with the **ID** attribute so it could be made a destination for a link. For example,

```
<H1 ID="FirstHeading">Welcome to Big Company, Inc.</H1>
```

assigns a name of "**FirstHeading**" to the **<H1>** element so that it can be referenced from an anchor element:

```
<A HREF="#FirstHeading">Go to Heading 1</A>
```

The **ID** attribute is common to nearly all HTML elements. **ID** and **CLASS** should be available to most HTML elements, except for a few like **<HTML>**, **<HEAD>**, and **<BODY>**. Style sheets can also use **ID** values as selectors for the style rules, making it possible to affect a particular element with a rule without creating an inline style for it. The following markup shows how a green background is applied to the paragraph element with the **ID** value of **"SecondParagraph"** while no style is applied to the other paragraph.

```
<HTML>
<HEAD>
<TITLE>ID Style Sheet Example</TITLE>
<STYLE TYPE="text/css">
 #SecondParagraph    {background: green}
</STYLE>
</HEAD>
<BODY>
<P>This is the first paragraph.</P>
<P ID="SecondParagraph">This is the  second paragraph</P>
<P>This is the third paragraph. </P>
</BODY>
</HTML>
```

Because almost every element can have an **ID** attribute, it isn't necessary to put the style information within the tag. To write a style rule for an **ID** value, simply include a rule with the name of the **ID** preceded by a hash mark as the selector for the rule. For example, to create a simple rule for an element with an **ID** value of **FirstHeading** use the following syntax:

```
#FirstHeading    {color: blue}
```

The only worry that a page designer might have with the **ID** attribute is the idea of naming, since every **ID** value must be unique. So how can a style be applied to some occurrence of an element, but not to others? In the markup shown above, how can the same style be applied to the first and third **<P>** elements but not the second? The answer is simple: use a class rule.

Another attribute that has been found throughout the book when discussing the syntax of various elements is the **CLASS** attribute. The **CLASS** attribute defines the name of the class to which that particular element belongs. **CLASS** values do not have to be unique. Many elements can be members of the same class; in fact, elements don't even have to be of the same type to be in a common class. The idea of using **CLASS** is illustrated here:

```
<HTML>
<HEAD>
<TITLE>ID Style Sheet Example</TITLE>
<STYLE TYPE="text/css">
 .important      {background: yellow}
</STYLE>
</HEAD>
<BODY>
<H1 CLASS="important">Example</H1>
<P CLASS="important">This is the first paragraph.</P>
<P>This is the second paragraph</P>
<P CLASS="important">This is the third paragraph.</P>
</BODY>
</HTML>
```

This example has three elements whose **CLASS** attribute is set to **important**. According to the style sheet information, all members of the important class, as indicated by the period, have a yellow background color. Writing rules for classes is easy: just specify the class name with a period before it as the selector.

```
.main-item {font-size: 150%}
```

Other variations on class rules are possible. Setting all **<H1>** elements of the class important to have a background of orange could be written like this:

```
H1.important {background: orange}
```

Classes can be used to significantly reduce the number of style rules necessary in a document. There are more forms, such as contextual selection, grouping, and inheritance, that might also be useful in certain situations.

Advanced Style Rules: Contextual Selection, Grouping, and Inheritance

While the **CLASS** and **ID** attributes provide a great deal of flexibility for creating style rules, there are many other types of rules of equal value. For example, it might be useful to be able to say that all **<STRONG>** elements that occur within a **<P>** element get treated a certain way, as compared to the same elements occurring elsewhere within the document. To create such a rule, the idea of contextual selection must be used. Contextual selectors are created by showing the order in which the attributes must be nested for the rule to be applied:

```
P STRONG {background: yellow}
```

This rule would set all occurrences of the **<STRONG>** element within a **<P>** element to have a yellow background. Other occurrences of **<STRONG>** might not necessarily have the yellow background, because there are potential issues of inheritance that may creep in.

There is an implicit structure to HTML documents. They all have an **<HTML>** element. Within this element lies the **<HEAD>** and **<BODY>** elements, which might contain the **<TITLE>** and **<P>** elements, respectively. The structure of the document looks somewhat like a family tree. For example, the document shown here would have a parse tree, as shown in Figure 10-1.

```
<HTML>
<HEAD>
<TITLE>Test File</TITLE>
</HEAD>
<BODY>
<H1>Test</H1>
<P>This is a <B>Test</B></P>
</BODY>
</HTML>
```

In the example parse tree, note how the **<B>** element is enclosed within the **<P>** element, which is in the **<BODY>**, which is in the **<HTML>** element. What happens if you set a style rule to the **<P>** element?

Wouldn't this rule also apply to the **<B>** element? Sometimes it would; this is the idea of inheritance. Not all items inherit, so be careful when making any assumptions about this idea.

In some cases, it may be useful to apply similar rules to several different elements rather than rewrite the rule for each separate element or create a special grouping

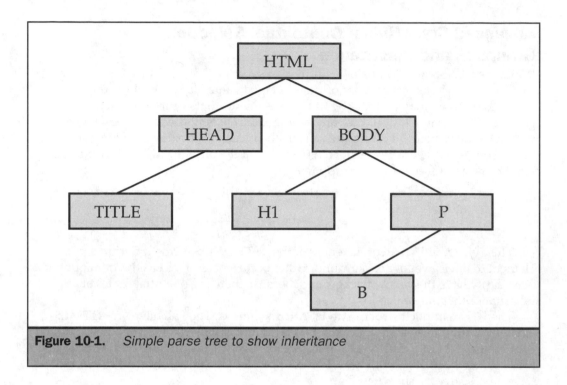

Figure 10-1. *Simple parse tree to show inheritance*

class. It is possible to provide a shorthand notation known as *element grouping*. If you wanted **<H1>**, **<H2>**, and **<H3>** to have the same basic background and color, you could apply the following rule.

```
H1, H2, H3   {background: yellow; color: black}
```

Now it may turn out that each particular heading should have a different size, so how can that be represented? Other rules can also be added:

```
H1    {font-size: 200%}
H2    {font-size: 150%}
H3    {font-size: 125%}
```

When the grouping rule and the other rules are encountered, they are combined. The resulting rules create the whole style. But what happens in the following situation?

```
H1, H2, H3    {background: yellow; color: black}
H1        {background: green}
```

What's the background color for the <H1> element supposed to be? Is it green or yellow? Some might say green because it is second. But what happens if the rules are swapped? This idea, called the *cascade*, is the key to powerful style sheet rules.

The general idea of the cascade, in effect, is that it there may be many style sheets in a given document, and there has to be a way to sort out what rules will be applied. For example, there may be a linked style sheet, embedded style definition, and inline style information for a given element. There may even be a special style definition assigned by the user in his or her browser. With all these different style rules in the document, one rule, perhaps a compound rule, will eventually take precedence. The basic idea is that the browser's style is the least important, then the user's style, and finally the specified style from the designer. From a designer's point of view, this seems appropriate. Beyond this basic priority scheme, within the document itself, inline styles such as those set with a **STYLE** attribute will take precedence over document styles, which take precedence over linked or included styles. The closer to the element, the more priority the style has.

The cascade idea, along with the idea of inheritance, makes style sheets very flexible. Imagine setting a corporate-wide style in one document and linking it to every file in a Web site. Unfortunately, for one particular document there are some special changes. Why redo the corporate style when a local style can be added to take precedence over the global style? It really isn't too important to get theoretical about the idea of the cascade. Simply using style sheets will reveal all that a page designer will need to know.

Style Sheet Example

Before describing all the various properties that can be applied via a style sheet, consider a simple example. The example shown in Figure 10-2 uses three forms of style: linked, document-wide, and inline. The example also illustrates the use of the **CLASS** and **ID** attributes. Most of the properties should make sense, particularly after seeing the rendering. If you don't get it, don't worry; basic cascading style sheet properties and examples will be covered later in the chapter. Figure 10-3 shows how the cascading style sheet example is rendered by Internet Explorer 4.0.

Style Sheet Properties

The basic idea of how rules are formed in style sheets was discussed earlier in this chapter (see "Style Sheet Basics"), but what are the various properties that can be set? CSS1 defines more than 50 different properties and values, and the browser vendors are busy inventing new ones all the time. This section covers the standard CSS1 properties, which should work in all browsers. Although they *should* work, some properties may not work in your browser. While cascading style sheets promise a lot more flexibility than HTML, there is still the issue of support across browsers, as well as minor rendering differences.

```
<!DOCTYPE HTML PUBLIC "-//W3C//DTD HTML 4.0 Final//EN">
<HTML>
<HEAD>
<TITLE>Simple CSS Example</TITLE>

<STYLE TYPE="text/css">
<!--

BODY    {background: black}

DIV.PAGE   {background: #FFD040;
            color: black;
            margin: 50px 10px 50px 10px;
            padding: 10px 10px;
            width: 100%;
            height: 100%}

H1         {font-size: 24pt;
            font-family: Comic Sans Ms, Cursive;
            text-align: center}

           .black {color: black; background: white}
           .white {color: white; background: black}

P          {font-family: Arial, Sans-serif;
            font-size: 16pt;
            line-height: 200%;
            text-align: justify;
            text-indent: 20px;}

.style     {color: blue; font-family: Arial; font-style: oblique}
.size      {font-size: x-large}
#letterspace    {letter-spacing: 15pt}


-->
</STYLE>
</HEAD>
<BODY>
```

Figure 10-2.   *Cascading style sheet example*

```
<DIV CLASS=PAGE>

<H1><SPAN CLASS="black">CSS</SPAN> <SPAN CLASS="white">Fun</SPAN></H1>

<HR>

<P>
With style sheets, you will be able to control the presentation
of Web pages with greater precision. Style sheets can be used to
set everything from <SPAN CLASS="style">font styles</SPAN>
and <SPAN CLASS="size">sizes</SPAN> to <SPAN ID="letterspace">letter
spacing</SPAN> and line heights.
</P>

</DIV>

</BODY>
</HTML>
```

Figure 10-2. *Cascading style sheet example* (continued)

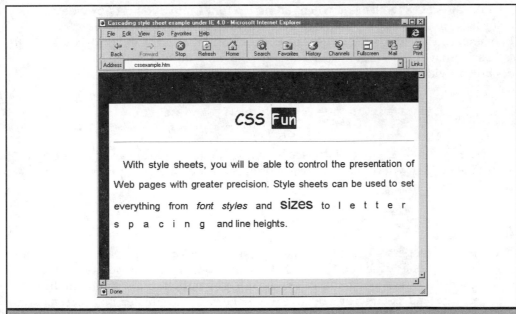

Figure 10-3. *Cascading style sheet example under Internet Explorer 4.0*

Font Properties

CSS1 provides a great deal of font-oriented properties to set the family, style, size, and variations of the font used within a Web page. Beyond font properties, you will also see it is possible to combine these rules with color, background, margin, and spacing rules to create a variety of interesting typographic effects.

font-family

This property is used to set the font family used to render text. The **font-family** property may be set to a specific font like Arial or a generic family like sans serif. You will need to quote any font family names that contain white space, like "Britannic Bold," and you may have to capitalize font values for a match.

According to the CSS1 specification, the generic families listed here should be available on all browsers that support cascading style sheets:

```
Serif        (e.g., Times)
Sans-serif   (e.g., Helvetica)
Cursive      (e.g., Zapf-Chancery)
Fantasy      (e.g., Western)
Monospace    (e.g., Courier)
```

Like the **<FONT>** element, when setting the **font-family** you can provide a prioritized list of names separated by commas that will be checked in order. Remember to always provide a generic font family at the end of the **font-family** list to fall back on in case the user does not support the fonts suggested. To set a document-wide font, use a rule like

```
BODY    {font-family: Arial, Helvetica, Sans-serif}
```

The end of this chapter discusses how downloadable fonts are handled with style sheets. You will find a discussion of other important font properties and a complete example.

font-size

The **font-size** property is used to set the relative or physical size of the font used. The value for the property may be a value that is mapped to a physical point size or a relative word. Physical point-size values include **xx-small**, **x-small**, **small**, **medium**, **large**, **x-large**, and **xx-large**, or a relative word like larger or smaller. Physical sizes also may include examples such as 48 pt, 2 cm, or .25 in. Percentage values like 150 percent are also valid for relative sizing; negative percentage or point sizes are not allowed. A few examples rules are shown here:

```
P        {font-size: 18pt}
STRONG   {font-size: larger}
H1       {font-size: 200%}
```

One suggestion with the **font-size** property is to avoid setting point sizes where possible. The problem is that users who can't see well may have a hard time adjusting size. On certain monitors, a 10-point font might look fine; on others, it might be microscopic. If exact point size is to be used, remember that large is often better as far as readability is concerned.

font-style

The **font-style** property is used to specify **normal**, **italic**, or **oblique** font style for the font being used. A few examples are shown here:

```
H1       {font-style: oblique}
.first   {font-style: italic}
.plain   {font-style: normal}
```

Don't try to override HTML elements with this property. Setting a rule where the **<B>** element has an italic rendering may not work. When it does, it makes for confusing markup.

font-weight

The **font-weight** property selects the weight or darkness of the font. Values for the property range from 100 to 900 in increments of 100. Keywords are also supported; these include **bold**, **bolder**, and **lighter** to set relative weights. Some browsers may also provide keywords such as **extra-light**, **light**, **demi-light**, **medium**, **demi-bold**, **bold**, and **extra-bold**, which correspond to the 100 to 900 values. Because font families also include bold values, and the meaning within them varies, the numeric scheme is preferred. A few examples are shown here:

```
STRONG    {font-weight:   bolder}
H1        {font-weight:   900}
.special  {font-weight:   extra-bold}
```

Typically, the value **bold** is the same as 700, while the **normal** font value is 400.

font-variant

The **font-variant** property is used to select a variation of the specified (or default) font family. The only current variants supported with this property are **small-caps**, which displays as small uppercase letters, and **normal**, which doesn't do anything. A simple rule is shown here:

```
EM    {font-variant: small-caps}
```

font

The **font** property provides a concise way to specify all the font properties with one style rule. One attribute that is also included within **font** is **line-height**, which specifies the distance between two lines of text. Each font attribute can be indicated on the line separated by spaces, except for line height; that is used with **font-size** and separated by a slash. As few or as many font rules can be used in this shorthand notation, as desired. The general form of the font rule is shown here:

```
font: font-style font-variant font-weight font-size/line-height
font-family
```

One example of using a compact font rule would be

```
P {font:italic small-caps 600 18pt/24pt "Arial, Helvetica"}
```

The shorthand notation does not require all the properties, so the next example is just as valid as the complete notation.

```
P    {font: italic 18pt/24pt}
```

Two other properties, **text-transform** and **text-decoration**, also affect type, so they will be discussed here before presenting a complete example.

text-decoration

The **text-decoration** property is used to define an effect on text. The standard values for this property include **blink**, **line-through**, **overline**, **underline**, and **none**. The meaning of these values is obvious, except for **overline**, which creates a line above text. The following examples show possible uses for this property:

```
.struck         {text-decoration: line-through}
SPAN.special    {text-decoration: blink}
H1            {text-decoration: overline}
A             {text-decoration: none}
#author         {text-decoration: underline}
```

As shown in one of the examples preceding, this property is often used with the
<A> element and its associated pseudoclasses. The pseudoclasses are **A:link, A:active,**
and **A:visited**. Make sure to note the colon in the pseudoclass. The following example
sets nonselected links to be underlined, turns the underlining off during the click, and
puts a line through already visited links:

```
A:link        {text-decoration: underline}
A:active      {text-decoration: none}
A:visited     {text-decoration: line-through}
```

Using grouping or just applying the rule to the **<A>** element itself might be more
appropriate if the same style is to be applied to all states of a link. For example,

```
A:link, A:active, A:visited    {text-decoration: underline}
```

text-transform

This property determines the capitalization of the text it affects. The possible values
for this property are **capitalize, uppercase, lowercase,** and **none**. Note that the value
capitalize may result in capitalizing every word.

```
P          {text-transform: capitalize}
.upper     {text-transform: uppercase}
.lower     {text-transform: lower}
```

A complete style sheet example using all the font rules, as well as **text-transform**
and **text-decoration**, is shown in Figure 10-4. The rendering of the font and text
example is shown in Figure 10-5. Note that there are still small differences between
Netscape and Microsoft style sheet implementations.

```
<HTML>
<HEAD>
<TITLE>CSS Font Attributes Example</TITLE>
<STYLE TYPE="text/css">
<!--

BODY           {font-size: 14pt}

.serif         {font-family: serif}
.sans-serif    {font-family: sans-serif}
.cursive       {font-family: cursive}
.fantasy       {font-family: fantasy}
.comic         {font-family: Comic Sans MS}

.xx-small      {font-size: xx-small}
.x-small       {font-size: x-small}
.small         {font-size: small}
.medium        {font-size: medium}
.large         {font-size: large}
.x-large       {font-size: x-large}
.xx-large      {font-size: xx-large}
.smaller       {font-size: smaller}
.larger        {font-size: larger}
.points        {font-size: 18pt}
.percentage    {font-size: 200%}

.italic        {font-style: italic}
.oblique       {font-style: oblique}
.weight        {font-weight: 900}
.smallcaps     {font-variant: small-caps}

.uppercase     {text-transform: uppercase}
.lowercase     {text-transform: lowercase}
.capitalize    {text-transform: capitalize}

.underline     {text-decoration: underline}
.blink         {text-decoration: blink}
.line-through  {text-decoration: line-through}
.overline      {text-decoration: overline}
```

Figure 10-4.   *Font rules example*

```
-->
</STYLE>
</HEAD>
<BODY>

<H2>Font Family</H2>

This text is in <SPAN CLASS="serif">Serif.</SPAN><BR>
This text is in <SPAN CLASS="sans-serif">Sans-Serif.</SPAN><BR>
This text is in <SPAN CLASS="cursive">Cursive.</SPAN><BR>
This text is in <SPAN CLASS="fantasy">Fantasy.</SPAN><BR>
Actual fonts can be specified like <SPAN CLASS=comic>
Comic Sans MS</SPAN><BR>


<H2>Font Sizing</H2>

This is <SPAN CLASS="xx-small">xx-small text.</SPAN><BR>
This is <SPAN CLASS="x-small">x-small text.</SPAN><BR>
This is <SPAN CLASS="small">small text.</SPAN><BR>
This is <SPAN CLASS="medium">medium text.</SPAN><BR>
This is <SPAN CLASS="large">large text.</SPAN><BR>
This is <SPAN CLASS="x-large">xx-large text.</SPAN><BR>
This is <SPAN CLASS="xx-large">xx-large text.</SPAN><BR>
This is <SPAN CLASS="smaller">smaller text</SPAN>than the rest.<BR>
This is <SPAN CLASS="larger">larger text</SPAN>than the rest.<BR>
This is <SPAN CLASS="points">exactly 18 point text.</SPAN><BR>
This is <SPAN CLASS="percentage">200% larger text.</SPAN><BR>

<H2>Font Style, Weight, and Variant</H2>

This text is <SPAN CLASS="italic">italic.</SPAN><BR>
This text is <SPAN CLASS="oblique">oblique.</SPAN><BR>
This text is <SPAN CLASS="weight">bold.</SPAN><BR>
This text is in <SPAN CLASS="smallcaps">smallcaps.</SPAN><BR>

<H2>Text Transformation</H2>

The next bit of text is transformed <SPAN CLASS="uppercase">to all
uppercase.</SPAN><BR>
```

Figure 10-4.   *Font rules example* (continued)

```
The next bit of text is transformed <SPAN CLASS="lowercase">to
all lowercase.</SPAN><BR>
<SPAN CLASS="capitalize">This text is all capitalized. It doesn't do
what you think, does it?</SPAN><BR>

<H2>Text Decoration</H2>

This text should <SPAN CLASS="blink">blink under Netscape.</SPAN>
<BR><BR>
This text should be <SPAN CLASS="underline">underlined.</SPAN>
<BR><BR>
This text should be <SPAN CLASS="line-through">struck.</SPAN>
<BR><BR>
This text should be <SPAN CLASS="overline">overline.</SPAN><BR><BR>

</BODY>
</HTML>
```

Figure 10-4.   *Font rules example* (continued)

Downloadable fonts and other changes to font support under style sheets are discussed later in this chapter. The next section covers colors and backgrounds.

Color and Background Properties

CSS1 supports a variety of properties that can be used to control the colors and backgrounds in a document. With style sheets, you can create arbitrary regions with different background colors and images. In the past, such designs were difficult to accomplish without turning to tables or proprietary HTML extensions.

CSS1 style sheets support three basic forms of color specifications: color names, hex values in three- or six-digit format, and RGB values. The suggested keyword colors supported by browsers are a set of 16 color names taken from the Windows VGA palette. The colors include **Aqua**, **Black**, **Blue**, **Fuchsia**, **Gray**, **Green**, **Lime**, **Maroon**, **Navy**, **Olive**, **Purple**, **Red**, **Silver**, **Teal**, **White**, and **Yellow**. Notice that these are the same predefined colors from the HTML specification. Besides predefined color names, hexadecimal values in the standard color form #*RRGGBB* as used with the <FONT> and <BODY> elements are supported. A shortened three-digit color form, where R, G, and B are hex digits, is also supported under CSS, but this is currently an uncommon form of color specification and is not suggested. A third form in the RGB format is also specified in the form *rgb (R, B, G)*, where the values for R, G, and B range from 0 to 255. This format should be very familiar to users of Adobe Photoshop.

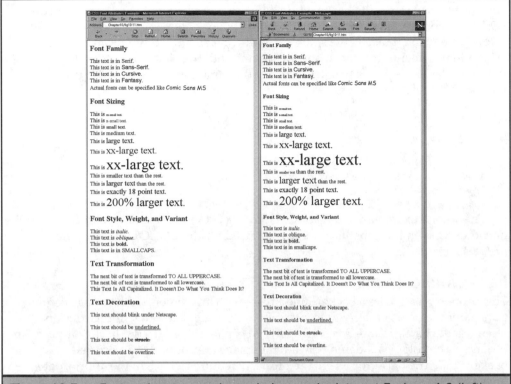

Figure 10-5. *Font and text example renderings under Internet Explorer 4.0 (left)
and Netscape Communicator (right)*

Currently, most browsers do not support the *rgb (R,G,B)* color format, so use it
with caution.

color

CSS supports the **color** property, which is used to set the text color. Its use is illustrated
in the following examples:

```
BODY    {color: green}
H1   {color: #FF0088}
.fun    {color: #0f0}
#test    {color: rgb(0,255,0)}
```

background-color

This property sets an element's background color. The default value is **none**, which
allows any underlying content to show through. This state is also specified by the

keyword **transparent**. The **background-color** property is often used in conjunction with the color property that sets text color. With block elements, **background-color** colors content and *padding,* the space between an element's contents and its margins. With inline elements, it colors a box that wraps with the element if it occurs over multiple lines. This property takes colors in the same format as the **color** property. A few example rules are shown here:

```
P     {background-color: yellow}
BODY    {background-color: #0000FF}
.fun    {background-color: #F00}
#test   {background-color: rgb(0,0,0)}
```

The second example is interesting in that it sets the background color for the entire document. Given this capability, there is no need for the **BGCOLOR** attribute of the **<BODY>** element.

background-image

This property associates a background image with an element. If the image contains transparent regions, underlying content shows through. To prevent this, designers often use the **background-image** property in conjunction with the **background-color** property. The color is rendered beneath the image and provides an opaque background. The **background-image** property requires a URL to the appropriate image to use as a background. Images that can be used as backgrounds are whatever the browser supports for **BACKGROUND** attribute for the **<BODY>** element, typically GIF and JPEG. A few examples are shown here, including some that work in conjunction with the **background-color** property:

```
B     {background-image: url(donut-tile.gif); background-color:
white}
BODY    {background-image: url(funtile.gif)}
.brick    {background-image: url(brick.gif)}
#prison    {background-image: url(bars.gif)}
```

Notice how it is possible to set a background for a small element like **<B>**, just as easily as for the whole document, by applying the rule to the **<BODY>** element.

background-repeat

The **background-repeat** property determines how background images tile in cases where they are smaller than the canvas space used by their associated elements. The default value is **repeat**, which causes the image to tile in the horizontal and vertical dimensions. A value of **repeat-x** for the property limits tiling to the horizontal dimension. The **repeat-y** value behaves similarly for the vertical dimension. The **no-repeat** value prevents the image from tiling.

```
P       {background-image: url(donut-tile.gif); background-repeat:
repeat-x}
BODY    {background-image: url(donut-tile.gif); background-repeat:
no-repeat}
```

In the second example, there may be an issue of what happens when the user scrolls the screen: should the background be fixed or scroll off screen? It turns out this behavior is specified by the next property, **background-attachment**.

background-attachment

This property determines whether a background image should scroll as the element content it is associated with scrolls, or whether the image should stay fixed on the screen. The default value is **scroll**. The alternate value, **fixed**, can implement a watermark effect similar to the proprietary attribute **BGPROPERTIES** to the **<BODY>** element introduced by Microsoft. An example of how this might be used is shown here:

```
BODY    {background-image:url(logo.gif);background-attachment: fixed}
```

background-position

This property specifies how a background image, not a color, is positioned within the canvas space used by its element. There are three ways to specify a position. First, the top left corner of the image can be specified as an absolute distance. Second, the position can be specified as a percentage along the horizontal and vertical dimensions. Third, the position can be specified with keywords to describe the horizontal and vertical dimensions. The keywords for the horizontal dimension are **left**, **center**, and **right**. The keywords for the vertical dimension are **top**, **center**, and **bottom**. When keywords are used, the default for an unspecified dimension is assumed to be **center**. The first example shows how to specify the top left corner of the background using an absolute distance.

```
P   {background-image:url(picture.gif);background-position: 10px 10px}
```

Remember that this distance is relative to the element and not to the document as a whole, unless of course the property is being set for the **<BODY>** element.

The next example shows how to specify a background image position using percentage values along the horizontal and vertical dimensions.

```
P   {background-image:url(picture.gif);background-position: 20% 40%}
```

If you forget to specify one percentage value, the other value is assumed to be 50 percent.

Specifying an image position using keywords is an easy way to do simple placement of an image. When setting a value, remember that the keywords in pairs have the meanings shown here:

TOP LEFT	0%	0%
TOP CENTER	50%	0%
TOP RIGHT	100%	0%
CENTER LEFT	0%	50%
CENTER CENTER	50%	50%
CENTER RIGHT	100%	50%
BOTTOM LEFT	0%	100%
BOTTOM CENTER	50%	100%
BOTTOM RIGHT	100%	100%

An example of using keywords to position a background image is shown here:

```
BODY    {background-image: url(picture.gif); background-position:
center center}
```

Remember that if only one keyword is set, the second one defaults to **center**. In the last example, the keyword center was only needed once.

background

The **background** property is a comprehensive property that allows any or all of the specific background properties to be set at once, not unlike the shorthand **font** property. Property order does not matter. Any property not specified uses the default value. A few examples are shown here:

```
P       {background: white url(picture.gif) repeat-y center}
BODY    {background: url(tile.jpg) top center fixed}
.bricks   {background: repeat-y top top url(bricks.gif)}
```

A complete example of all the background properties is shown in Figure 10-6. Notice how it is possible to include multiple background types with a variety of elements. A similar layout would be possible under pure HTML but the required

```
<HTML>
<HEAD>
<TITLE>CSS Background Attributes Example</TITLE>
<STYLE TYPE="text/css">
<!--

P    {background: yellow url(logo.gif) repeat-y }
-->
</STYLE>
</HEAD>
<BODY>

<P>This is a paragraph of text. It will probably be very
hard to read this text because it is on top of an image,
but don't worry this is just an example and not a real Web
page. Notice that the area not covered by the background image
is filled with the background color. This is more text just to
illustrate the idea. This is even more text. This is more text
just to illustrate the idea. This is even more text. This is
more text just to illustrate the idea. This is even more text.
This is more text just to illustrate the idea. This is even more
text. This is more text just to illustrate the idea. This is
even more text.
</P>
</BODY>
</HTML>
```

Figure 10-6.   *Example showing use of background properties in cascading style sheets*

<TABLE> element would have been somewhat complicated. A rendering of the background style sheet example is shown in Figure 10-7.

Text Properties

Text properties are used to affect the spacing and layout of text inline, namely, the text within block elements such as paragraphs. The basic properties allow the page designer to set indentation, word spacing, letter spacing, spacing between lines, and horizontal and vertical text alignment. While these would seem to be very useful properties, they are not well supported at this time in browsers.

When manipulating text and other objects with a style sheet, a length or size must often be specified. Cascading style sheets support a variety of measurement forms. For

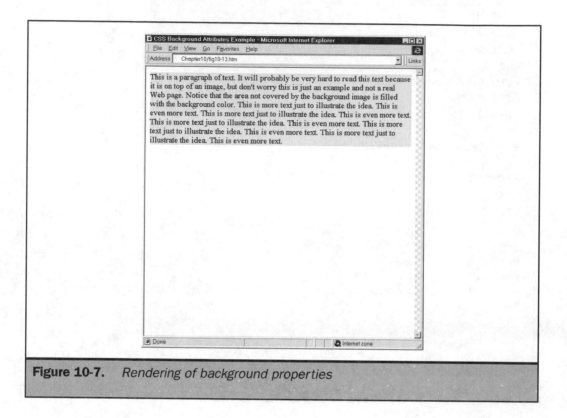

Figure 10-7.   *Rendering of background properties*

fonts, the most familiar form of measurement is probably points (pt). The CSS1 specification also supports measurements like inches (in), centimeters (cm), and millimeters (mm), as well as picas (pc), the em measurement (em), the ex unit (x-height) and, under certain measurement situations, pixels (px). In other cases, it may be possible to specify relative measurements such as 150 percent. Page designers used to electronic layout tools will probably stick to the measurements most familiar to them, like points or pixels.

 At the time of this writing, the major browsers had only limited support, if any, for measurements using em or x-height.

word-spacing

This property specifies the amount of space between words. The default value, **normal**, uses the browser's word-spacing default. Designers are free to specify the distance between words in a variety of measurements including inches (in), centimeters (cm), millimeters (mm), points (pt), picas (pc), the em (em) measurement, and pixels (px). A few examples are shown here.

```
P      {word-spacing: 1em}
BODY   {word-spacing: 10pt}
```

At the time of this writing, neither of the major browsers supported the **word-spacing** property. Page designers should check to make sure this property works in their target audience's browser before relying on this property.

letter-spacing

This property specifies the amount of space between letters. The default value, **normal**, uses the browser's letter spacing default. Like the **word-spacing** property, it is possible to use a variety of measurements to set word spacing from pixels to em values. A few examples of this property are shown here.

```
P    {letter-spacing: 0.2em}
BODY   {letter-spacing: 2px}
.wide   {letter-spacing: 10pt}
#Fun   {letter-spacing: 2cm}
```

vertical-align

This property controls the vertical positioning of text and images with respect to the baseline currently in effect. The possible values for the vertical-align property include **baseline, sub, super, top, text-top, middle, bottom, text-bottom**, and percentage values. Compare these values with the **ALIGN** attribute for the <IMG> element, as well as alignment options for table cells, and things should begin to make sense. The flexibility of style sheets makes it possible to set element values on individual characters. When not specified, the default value of **vertical-align** is **baseline**. A few examples are shown here:

```
P           {vertical-align: text-top}
.superscript   {vertical-align: super; font-size: smaller}
.subscript   {vertical-align: sub; font-size: 75%}
```

Notice in the example how **vertical-align** can be used with other properties to create an interesting contextual class, like **.superscript**.

text-align

This property determines how text in a block-level element such as the paragraph element is horizontally aligned. The allowed values for this property are **left, right,**

center, and **justify**. The default value for the property is **left**. This property should act similar to most of the **ALIGN** attributes, which are available on certain block-level elements in HTML. Be aware that justification of a block element may be very noticeable when the font is very large, and may show the added spaces. A few examples are shown here:

```
P        {text-align: justify}
DIV         {text-align: center}
.goright    {text-align: right}
```

text-indent

This property sets the indentation for text in the first line of a block-level element. Its value can be given either as a length value (.5 cm, 15 px, 12 pt, and so on) or as a percentage of the width of the block, like 10 percent. The default value for the property is **0**, which indicates no indentation. A few examples of how text-indent might be used are shown here:

```
P         {text-indent: 2em}
P.heavy    {text-indent: 50px}
```

One interesting effect is the use of negative values to create a hanging indent where the text within the block element expands outside of the block. The following rule creates a paragraph with a yellow background where the first line of text starts left of the text.

```
P    {text-indent: -10px; background: yellow}
```

Combining the hanging indent with a large first letter for the paragraph could create an interesting effect.

line-height

The **line-height** property sets the height between lines in a block-level element like a paragraph. The basic idea is to set the line spacing, known more appropriately as *leading*. The value of the attribute may be specified as the number of lines (1.4), a length (14 pt), or as a percentage of the line height (200 percent). So double spacing could be written as

```
P.double    {line-height: 2}
```

as well as

```
P.double2      {line-height: 200%}
```

Other examples of using **line-height** are shown here:

```
P        {font-size: 12pt; line-height: 18pt}
P.carson    {font-size: 24pt;    line-height: 6pt}
```

Notice in the second example how the **line-height** property is much smaller than the **font-size** property. A browser should generally render the text on top of the other text, creating a hard-to-read, but potentially "cool" effect.

A complete example showing all the text properties is shown in Figure 10-8. The rendering of the text properties example is shown in Figure 10-9.

Box Properties

Block style elements such as the **<P>** element can be thought of as occupying rectangular boxes on the screen. Three aspects of these boxes can be controlled with style properties. The box properties that can be controlled include margins, borders, padding, height, width, and positioning. The margin properties determine the distance between edges of an element's box and the edges of adjacent elements. The border properties determine the visual characteristics of a border surrounding an element's edges. The padding properties determine the distance inside an element between its edges and its actual content. Height, width, and positioning properties determine the size and position of the box that the element creates. The box properties are equivalent to the attributes like **BORDER**, **HEIGHT**, and **WIDTH** with block elements like **<IMG>**, but provide even more power than has been available under standard HTML.

Margin Properties

There are four margin properties to individually set each of an element's four margins. A fifth margin property allows all of them to be set together. Individual margins for a block element can be set using **margin-top**, **margin-right**, **margin-bottom**, or **margin-left** properties. The values for the margins should be a length like 15 pt or 2 em, a percentage value of the block element's width like 20 percent, or the value **auto**, which attempts to figure out the appropriate margin automatically.

```
BODY    {margin-top: 20px; margin-bottom: 20px; margin-left: 30px;
margin-left: 50px}
P        {margin-bottom: 20mm}
DIV.fun    {margin-left: 1.5cm; margin-right: 1.5cm}
```

```
<HTML>
<HEAD>
<TITLE>CSS Text Attributes Example</TITLE>
<STYLE TYPE="text/css">
<!--

.letterspaced    {letter-spacing: 10pt}
.sub             {vertical-align: sub}
.super           {vertical-align: super}
.right           {text-align: right}
.left            {text-align: left}
.center          {text-align: center}

P.indent         {text-indent: 20px;
                  line-height: 200%}

P.negindent      {text-indent: -10px;
                  background: yellow}

#BIGCHAR         {background: red;
                  color: white;
                  font-size: 28pt;
                  font-family: Impact;
                  }

P.carson         {font-size: 12pt;
                  font-family: Courrier;
                  letter-spacing: 4pt;
                  line-height: 5pt}
-->
</STYLE>
</HEAD>
<BODY>

<H2>Letter Spacing and Vertical Alignment</H2>

<P>This is a paragraph of text.
<SPAN CLASS="letterspaced">Spacing letters is possible
but word spacing is not.</SPAN>
Vertical alignment can be used to make <SPAN CLASS="sub">Subscript
```

Figure 10-8.   *HTML and cascading style sheet markup for text properties*

```
</SPAN> and <SPAN CLASS="super">Superscript</SPAN> text, but the
real use of the property is when aligning text next to images
and objects.</P>

<H2>Alignment</H2>

<P CLASS="LEFT">
It is possible to set paragraphs to align left
</P>

<P CLASS="RIGHT">
It is possible to align paragraphs to the right.
</P>
<SPAN CLASS="CENTER">Even lines can be set to center.</SPAN>

<H2>Indentation and Line Height</H2>

<P CLASS="indent">
With style sheets it is possible to set indentation as well as
line height. Now double spacing is a reality. This is just dummy
text to show the effects of the indentation and spacing. This is
just dummy text to show the effects of the indentation
and spacing.</P>

<P CLASS="negindent"><SPAN ID="BIGCHAR">T</SPAN>his is another
paragraph which has negative indenting. Notice how you can pull
a character outside the paragraph for interesting effects. This
is just dummy text to show the effect of the indent. This is
just dummy text to show the effect of the indent.</P>

<H2>Surf Gun</H2>

<P CLASS="carson">Don't get carried away with your new found
powers. You may be tempted to show how cool you can be using
text on top of other text. While this may be good for certain
situations, it may also confuse the viewer.</P>

</BODY>
</HTML>
```

Figure 10-8.   *HTML and cascading style sheet markup for text
properties (continued)*

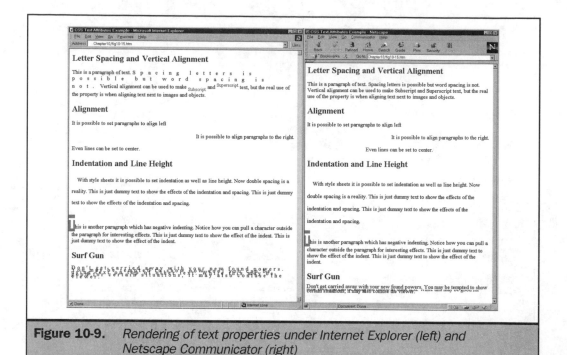

Figure 10-9. *Rendering of text properties under Internet Explorer (left) and Netscape Communicator (right)*

One interesting use of margin properties is to set negative margin values. Of course, negative margins may clip the content of the block element in the browser window if you aren't careful. Try an example like

```
P    {margin-left: -2cm; background: green}
```

to get the idea of how negative margins work.

The last few examples show that it is possible to set one or many margins. There is a shorthand notation that lets the page designer set all the margins at once. Using the **margin** property, one to four values can be assigned to affect the block element margins. If a single value is specified, it is applied to all four margins. For example,

```
P    {margin: 1.5cm}
```

sets all the margins equal to 1.5 cm. If multiple values are specified, they are applied in a clockwise order: first the top margin, then right, then bottom, then left. For example,

```
P      {margin: 10px, 5px, 15px, 5px}
```

sets the top margin at 10 pixels, the right at 5 pixels, the bottom at 15 pixels and the
left at 5 pixels. If only two or three values are specified in the rule, the missing values
are determined from the opposite sides. For example,

```
P      {margin: 10px, 5px}
```

would set the top margin at 10 pixels and the right margin at 5 pixels. The opposites
are then set accordingly, making the bottom margin 10 pixels and the left 5 pixels.

A complete example using the margin properties is shown in Figure 10-10. Notice
that the example uses negative margins. The background color makes it easier to see
the effect, as shown in Figure 10-11 under Internet Explorer 4.0.

Border Properties

Elements may be completely or partially surrounded by borders placed between their
margins and their padding. The border properties control the edges of block elements
by setting whether they should have a border, what the borders look like, their width,
their color, and so on. Borders are supposed to work with both block-level and inline
elements; you may, however, see browsers automatically convert elements with
borders to block elements by adding preceding and following carriage returns.

BORDER-STYLE   The **border-style** property is used to set the appearance of the
borders. The default value for the property is **none**, so no border will be drawn
regardless of any other setting. The values for **border-style** include **dotted**, **dashed**,
solid, **double**, **groove**, **ridge**, **inset**, and **outset**. The value **dotted** creates a dotted
border for the object, **dashed** a dashed-line border, and **solid** the normal solid-line
border. The value **double** specifies a double-line border. A value of **groove** creates an
etched border, while **ridge** creates an extruded border. A value of **inset** makes the
object look like it is set into the page, while **outset** puts a bevel on the border making
the object look raised. A few examples of **border-style** rules are shown here:

```
H1        {border-style: solid}
P.boxed   {border-style: double}
.button   {border-style: outset}
```

```
<HTML>
<HEAD>
<TITLE>CSS Margin Example</TITLE>
<STYLE TYPE="text/css">
<!--

P.ONE      {background: yellow;
            margin: 1cm 1cm;
           }

P.TWO      {background: orange;
            margin-top: 1cm;
            margin-bottom: 1cm;
            margin-right: .5cm;
            margin-left: -10px;
           }

#BIGCHAR   {background: red;
            color: white;
            font-size: 28pt;
            font-family: Impact;
           }
-->
</STYLE>
</HEAD>
<BODY>

<P CLASS="ONE">This is a paragraph of text which has
margins set for all sides to 1 cm. This is just dummy
text to show the effects of the margins. This is just
dummy text to show the effects of the margins.</P>

<P CLASS="TWO"><SPAN ID="BIGCHAR">T</SPAN>his is another
paragraph which has negative margins on one side. Be
careful not to clip things with negative margins. This
is just dummy text to show the effect of the margins.
This is just dummy text to show the effect of the margin.</P>

</BODY>
</HTML>
```

Figure 10-10.   *Cascading style sheet margin example*

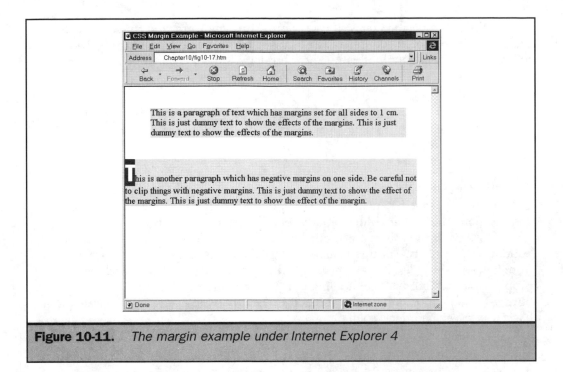

Figure 10-11. *The margin example under Internet Explorer 4*

This property sets the borders for each of the sides of the element. It is possible to control the individual border styles with **border-top-style**, **border-bottom-style**, **border-left-style**, and **border-right-style**. The **border-style** property can also act as a shorthand notation and may take up to four values starting from top, right, bottom, and then left. Like the **margin** property, when less than four values are set the opposite sides are set automatically. To set double borders on the top and bottom, use either of the following rules.

```
P      {border-style: double none}
P.one      {border-style: double none double none}
P.two      {border-top-style: double; border-bottom-style: double;
  border-left-style: none; border-right-style: none}
```

BORDER-WIDTH   There are numerous properties that set the width of borders. Four properties set the width for specific borders: **border-top-width**, **border-right-width**, **border-bottom-width**, and **border-left-width**. Similar to the **border-style** property, the **border-width** property sets all four borders at once and takes from one to four values. Multiple values are applied to borders in a clockwise order: top, right, bottom, left. If only two or three values are used, the missing values are determined from the opposite sides just as margins and border styles are.

Width can be specified using the keywords **thin, medium**, and **thick** as a value indicating the size of the border as an absolute measurement like 10 pixels. The following examples should illustrate how border widths can be set:

```
P          {border-style: solid; border-width: 10px}
P.double        {border-style: double; border-width: thick}
P.thickandthin   {border-style: solid; border-width: thick thin}
.fun       {border-style: double none; border-width: thick}
```

BORDER-COLOR   Borders may be assigned a color using the **border-color** property. Color values are specified using either a supported color name or a numeric RGB specification. The **border-color** property sets all four borders and takes from one to four values. Multiple values are applied to borders in a clockwise order: top, right, bottom, left. If only two or three values are used, the missing values are determined from the opposite sides. As with border widths and styles, it is also possible to use a property for each border's color **using border-top-color**, **border-right-color**, **border-bottom-color**, and **border-left-color**. The following examples illustrate the basic way to set a border's colors:

```
P   {border-style: solid; border-color: green}
P.all   {border-style: solid; border-top-color: green;
 border-right-color: #FF0000; border-bottom-color: yellow;
 border-left-color: blue}
```

BORDER SHORTHAND   Several border properties allow any combination of width, color, and style information to be set in a single property. The **border-top**, **border-right**, **border-bottom**, and **border-left** properties support this for their respective borders. To set the top border or paragraph elements to be red, double-line style, and 20 pixels thick, use

```
P   {border-top: double 20px red}
```

The order of the property values to set the style, width, and color is arbitrary, but according to the specification, designers should probably set the style, then width, followed by color. It would be possible to combine multiple properties in one rule to set the borders differently, as shown in the following example:

```
#RainbowBox { background: yellow;
border-top: solid 20px red;
border-right: double 10px blue;
```

```
border-bottom: solid 20px green;
border-left: dashed 10px orange}
```

Besides a shorthand notation for each individual border side, it is possible to use a shorthand notation for all sides using the **border** property. For example, to set all borders of a paragraph to be red, double-line style, and 20 pixels thick, use

```
P    {border: double 20px red}
```

Note that it is impossible to set the individual border sides with this shorthand notation. The actual properties to set the various borders such as **border-top** or even, more specifically, **border-top-style** must be used.

A brief example showing all the border properties used so far is shown in Figure 10-12. Notice that both compact and explicit notations are used in the example.

```
<HTML>
<HEAD>
<TITLE>CSS Border Example</TITLE>
<STYLE TYPE="text/css">
<!--

DIV.OUTER {background: orange;
           border-style: solid;
           border-width: 5px;
           padding: 10px 10px}

P.ONE      {background: yellow;
            border-style: double;
            border-width: medium;
           }

P.TWO      {background: yellow;
            border-style: double solid;
            border-color: red green purple blue;
            border-width: thin medium thick .25cm;
           }
```

Figure 10-12.   *Cascading style sheets border properties example*

```
-->
</STYLE>
</HEAD>
<BODY>

<DIV CLASS=OUTER>

<P CLASS=ONE>This is a paragraph of text which has a
red double border around it. Notice how the text
creeps up on the edges. Padding values will help you
avoid this problem.</P>

<P CLASS=TWO>This is another paragraph which has its
borders set in a very bizarre way!</P>

Notice that the paragraph blocks can be within a large
boxed block structure.

</DIV>

</BODY>
</HTML>
```

Figure 10-12. *Cascading style sheets border properties example (continued)*

The rendering of the border property example under Internet Explorer 4.0 is shown in Figure 10-13.

Padding Properties

The space between an element's border and its content can be specified using the padding properties. An element's four padding regions can be set using the **padding-top**, **padding-right**, **padding-bottom**, and **padding-left** properties. As with borders and margins, it is also possible to use a shorthand notation property called simply **padding** to set the padding for all sides at once. This example illustrates some basic uses of padding properties:

```
DIV    {padding-top: 1cm}
P      {border-style: solid; padding-left: 20mm; padding-right: 50mm}
```

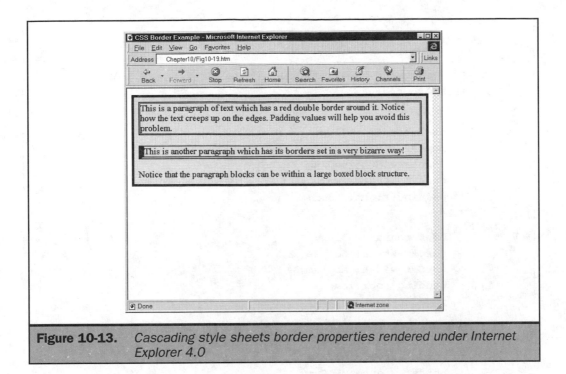

Figure 10-13.   *Cascading style sheets border properties rendered under Internet Explorer 4.0*

The shorthand notation property called **padding** allows a single property assignment to specify all four padding regions. It can take from 1 to 4 values. A single value is applied to all four padding areas. Multiple values are applied to padding regions in a clockwise order: top, right, bottom, left. If only two or three values are used, the missing values are determined from the opposite sides. So,

```
DIV    {border-style: solid; padding: 1cm}
```

sets a region with a solid border but with contents padded 1 cm from the border on all sides, while the following sets padding on the top and bottom 2 mm and the right and left 4 mm for all paragraphs:

```
P    {padding: 2mm 4mm}
```

An example showing padding and border to make the padding values clear is shown in Figure 10-14. The rendering of the padding example is shown in Figure 10-15.

```
<HTML>
<HEAD>
<TITLE>CSS Padding Example</TITLE>
<STYLE TYPE="text/css">
<!--

P.ONE      {background: yellow;
            border-style: double;
            border-width: medium;
            padding-left: 1cm;
            padding-right: .5cm;
            }

P.TWO      {background: yellow;
            border-style: double;
            border-width: medium;
            padding-top: 1cm;
            padding-bottom: 1cm;
            }

P.THREE    {background: yellow;
            border-style: double;
            border-width: medium;
            padding: 1cm 1cm;
            margin: .5cm 4cm;
            }
-->
</STYLE>
</HEAD>
<BODY>

<P CLASS=ONE>This paragraph of text has padding on the
left and right, but not on the top and bottom.</P>

<P CLASS=TWO>This paragraph has padding, but this time
only on the top and bottom.</P>

<P CLASS=THREE>Be careful when using margins. They
don't necessarily apply to the text within the box,
but to the box itself.</P>

</BODY>
</HTML>
```

Figure 10-14.   *Cascading style sheet padding example markup*

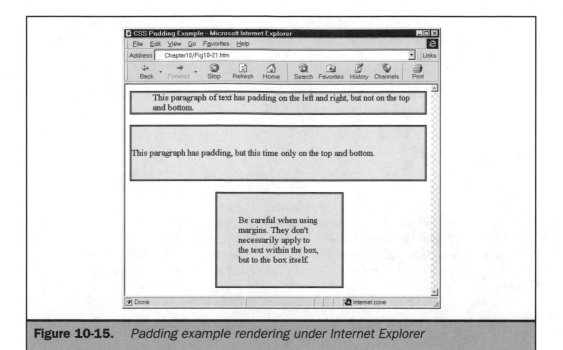

Figure 10-15.   *Padding example rendering under Internet Explorer*

Width and Height

The **width** property sets the width of an element's content region (the width of the area actually filled with content as opposed to its padding, border, or margin). The following example sets a paragraph with a width of 300 pixels:

```
P    {width: 300px;
      padding: 10px;
      border: solid 5px;
      background: yellow;
      color: black}
```

It is also possible to use percentage values for the width. With the **width** property, it seems as if tables are not necessary under cascading style sheets. This is true, but given current support for these style sheets, it is probably a good idea not to rely on this feature for layout.

Similar to **width**, the **height** property sets the height of an element's content region. When thinking about elements in Web pages, except images, it might seem unusual to set the **height** property. In most cases, it is probably best to leave it alone so the default value, **auto**, is used. The most legitimate use of this property is to set the height for objects like images. An absolute value or a percentage is supported for the **height** property, just like **width**. The following examples show how these properties might be used:

```
IMG     {height: 10cm; width: 10%}
P       {width: 300px; height: 100px}
```

float and clear

The **float** property influences the horizontal alignment of elements. It causes them to "float" toward either the left or right margins of their containing element. This is especially useful for placing embedded media objects like images and similar support into a Web page. Similar floating capabilities under vanilla HTML can be found with the **ALIGN** attribute settings. As with HTML, the values available for the **float** property include **left**, **right**, or **none**. The value of **none** is the default. To imitate the HTML code **<IMG SRC="logo.gif" ALIGN=RIGHT>**, apply a style sheet rule like this to the element:

```
IMG.LOGO { float: right }
```

The previous example might raise a few questions. How can the **HSPACE** and **VSPACE** of the item be set? You have a great deal of control over the border, margin, padding, height, and width of any object, so it shouldn't be difficult to achieve the desired layout. One thing, which may not be obvious, is how to clear the content that may flow around an object.

The use of floating elements creates a need to vertically position those elements that immediately follow them in an HTML document. Should the content flow continue at the floating elements side or after its bottom? If floating elements are defined on the right and left margins of the page, should content flow continue between them, after the bottom of the left element, the right element, or whichever is larger? The **clear** property allows this to be specified. A value of **left** for the property clears floating objects to the left, a value of **right** clears floating objects to the right, and the **both** value clears whichever is larger. The default value is **none**. Notice that this is extremely similar to the use of the **CLEAR** attribute with the **
** element in HTML. The example in Figure 10-16 demonstrates the use of the **clear** and **float** properties. Figure 10-17 shows a rendering of the code in Figure 10-16.

Classification Properties

Cascading style sheets contain several classification properties that determine an element's kind of displayed entity. Is it a block-level element or an inline element? Does it preserve or collapse white space characters? Is it a list element? If so, what list

```
<!DOCTYPE HTML PUBLIC "//W3C//DTD HTML 4.0 Final//EN">
<HTML>
<HEAD>
<TITLE>Image and Layout Control under CSS</TITLE>

<STYLE TYPE="text/css">
<!--
 IMG.aligned-right {width: 150; height: 150; float:right}
 BR.clear-text {clear:both}
-->
</STYLE>
</HEAD>
<BODY>

<P>This is some dummy text.
<IMG CLASS="aligned-right" SRC="bluecircle.gif">
This is some dummy text. This is some dummy text.
This is some dummy text. This is some dummy text.
This dummy text should stop flowing here.
<BR CLASS="clear-text">
This text should appear after the picture.
</P>

</BODY>
</HTML>
```

Figure 10-16.   *Image alignment and text flow under cascading style sheets*

style does is use? The following attributes are some of the miscellaneous items in cascading style sheets..

display

The cascading style sheet model recognizes three types of displayed elements: block elements, inline elements, and lists. The **display** property allows an element's display type to be changed. There are four values: **block**, **inline**, **list-item**, and **none**. The **none** value causes an element not to display or use canvas space. This differs from the property setting **visibility**, to be discussed in the next section, which also prevents an element from displaying but may reserve canvas space. To turn off a paragraph, try a rule like

```
P.remove    {display:none}
```

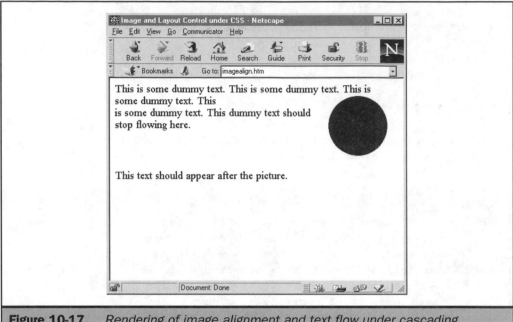

Figure 10-17.   *Rendering of image alignment and text flow under cascading style sheets*

Besides turning off elements, the browser should be able to turn a block element like a paragraph into an inline element, thus keeping it from adding a new line. For example, the following would change the form of all paragraphs in the document. Overriding the known action of the element is not suggested:

```
P    {display:inline}
```

Browsers may be able to turn an inline element into a block:

```
EM    {display:block}
```

It is also possible to coerce an element to act somewhat like a list by casting it with the display property, as shown here:

```
B    {display: list-item}
```

In very few cases, other than setting display to **none**, will type overriding make sense. While you might be able to dream up interesting uses for element form changing, it upsets the improved simplicity of HTML files provided by cascading style sheets.

white-space

The **white-space** property controls how spaces, tabs, and newline characters are handled in an element. The default value, **normal**, collapses white space characters into a single space and automatically wraps lines just as normal HTML. When a value of **pre** is used for the property, white space formatting is preserved, similar to how the **<PRE>** element works in HTML. The **nowrap** value prevents lines from wrapping if they exceed the element's content width. This short example shows how the **white-space** property would be used to simulate the **<PRE>** element:

```
<HTML>
<HEAD>
  <STYLE TYPE="text/css">
  P.pre {white-space:pre}
  </STYLE>
  <BODY>
  <P CLASS=pre> This      will      be      preformatted</P>
</BODY>
</HTML>
```

Like many of the display attributes already discussed, the **nowrap** and **pre** values are not well supported in browsers at the time of this writing.

List Properties

As discussed in Chapter 4, HTML supports three major forms of lists: ordered lists, unordered lists, and definition lists. HTML also has supported other forms of lists that were more compact or formatted differently, but browser support has been spotty. Cascading style sheets provide some list manipulation, including three style properties that can be set for lists: **list-style-type**, **list-style-image**, and **list-style-position**. A general property, **list-style**, provides a shorthand notation to set all three properties at once.

LIST-STYLE-TYPE   The items in ordered or unordered lists are labeled with a numeric value or a bullet, depending on the list form. These list labels can be set in cascading style sheets using the **list-style-type** property. Six values are appropriate for

ordered lists: **decimal, lower-roman, upper-roman, lower-alpha,** and **upper-alpha.**
Three values are appropriate for unordered lists: **disc, circle,** and **square.** The value
none prevents a label from displaying. These values are similar to the **TYPE** attribute
for the list elements in HTML. Setting the following

```
OL    {list-style-type: upper-roman}
```

is equivalent to **<OL TYPE="I">,** while the following is equivalent to
<UL TYPE="square">:

```
UL    {list-style: square}
```

Nested lists can be controlled using context selection rules. For example, to set an
outer order list to upper roman numerals, an inner list to lower roman numerals, and
a further embedded list to lowercase letters, use the following rules:

```
OL    {list-style-type:upper-roman}
OL OL    {list-style-type:lower-roman}
OL OL OL {list-style-type:lower-alpha}
```

It is also possible to associate the **list-style-type** property with the **<LI>** element,
but be aware that setting individual list elements to a particular style might require the
use of the **ID** attribute, or even inline styles.

LIST-STYLE-IMAGE   The **list-style-type** property provides little different
functionality from HTML lists, but the **list-style-image** property can assign a graphic
image to a list label; this is awkward to do under plain HTML. The value of the
property is either the URL of the image to use as a bullet or the keyword **none.** So to
use the lovely red 3-D balls with your list, use a rule like this:

```
UL    {list-style-image: url(ball.gif)}
```

While it may be possible to set the **list-style-image** for an ordered list, be careful,
since the meaning of the list is then lost.

LIST-STYLE-POSITION   Display elements in cascading style sheets are treated as
existing inside a rectangular box. Unlike other elements, the labels for list items can
exit outside and to the left of the list element's box. The **list-style-position** property
controls where a list item's label is displayed in relation to the element's box. The
values allowed for this property are **inside** or **outside,** which is the default. The

following example would tighten up a list by bringing the bullets inside the box for the list:

```
UL.COMPACT   {list-style-position: inside}
```

LIST-STYLE   Like margin, padding, and other shorthand notation, the **list-style** property allows a list's type, image, or position properties to all be set by a single property. The properties may appear in any order and are determined by value. An example of the shorthand notation that sets an unordered list with a bullet image that appears within the list block is shown here:

```
UL.special {list-style: inside url("bullet.gif")}
```

Up until this point, we have discussed the basic CSS1 standard, but there are still a few things missing. Already new style sheet properties are being introduced. One extension in particular, positioning, bears closer inspection.

Positioning Under CSS1

At the start of this chapter, a big point was made about the inadequacies of HTML as a formatting language. While CSS1 has certainly provided a fair number of improvements, it doesn't meet all possible needs. What about absolute pixel-level control for layout, or downloadable font control? Many of these features are already in the works. Positioning is already well supported by the major browser vendors with the position property available in cascading style sheets. When combined with elements like **<DIV>**, the functionality of proprietary elements like **<LAYER>** can be achieved with style sheets.

Positioning and Sizing of Regions

The first property to discuss for layout is the position property. This property has three values: **static**, **absolute**, and **relative**. Static positioning places elements according to the natural order they occur in a document, and is the default. An element whose position is **absolute** becomes a visual container for any elements enclosed in its content. It defines a coordinate system independent from the usual block and inline element placement common in HTML documents. If it is repositioned, all the elements defined inside it move with it. If any of those contained elements are assigned coordinates outside their parent's dimensions, they disappear. Setting the value of **position** to **relative** means making it relative to the element's natural position in document flow. This can be confusing so most designers tend to use absolute values.

After specifying how the region will be positioned (absolute or relative), the actual location of positioned elements should be specified using their top left corner. The position will be set with the left and top style properties. The coordinate system for positioned elements uses the upper-left corner as the origin point, namely, 0,0. Values for the x coordinate increase to the right; y values increase going down from the origin. A value like 10,100 would be 10 units to the right and 100 units down from the origin. Values may be specified as a length in a valid cascading style sheet measurement (like pixels) or as a percentage of the containing object's (parent's) dimension. You may find that elements contain other elements, so 0,0 isn't always the upper-left corner of the browser.

Once the region has been positioned, it may be desirable to set its size. By default, the **height** and **width** of the positioned region are set to fit the enclosed content, but the **height** and **width** properties as discussed early in the chapter can be used to specify the region's size.

An example using an inline style to set a **<DIV>** element to be 120 pixels from the left and 50 pixels down from the top left corner of the browser is shown here:

```
<DIV STYLE="{position:absolute;
    left: 120px;  top: 50px;
    height: 100px; width: 150px;
    background: yellow}">
At last absolute positioning!
</DIV>
```

While using the inline style form isn't the best way to do things, it serves its purpose here.

Before rushing off and positioning elements all over the screen, be aware of the nuances of nested items. For example, look at the markup in Figure 10-18. The rendering of this example is shown in Figure 10-19. Notice how the second area is relative to the first, position wise. If you read the coordinate values numerically, the inner area should be positioned to the left and above where it shows onscreen. Remember, the coordinates are relative to the containing box.

Clipping Regions

For elements whose position type is absolute, a clipping rectangle defines the subset of the content rectangle that will actually be shown. The property **clip** can be used to set the coordinates of the clipping rectangle that houses the content. The form of the property is

```
clip: rect( top right bottom left)
```

```
<HTML>
<HEAD>
<TITLE>Positioning Nested Items</TITLE>

<STYLE TYPE="text/css">
<!--
#outer    {position:absolute;
           left: 100px;
           top: 50px;
           height: 100px;
           width: 150px;
           background: yellow}

#inner    {position:absolute;
           left: 75px;
           top: 50px;
           height: 30px;
           width: 40px;
           background: orange}

-->
</STYLE>
</HEAD>
<BODY>

<DIV ID="outer">

This is the outer part of the nest.

<P ID="inner">This is the inner part of the nest</P>

</DIV>

</BODY>
</HTML>
```

Figure 10-18.   *Positioning nested items*

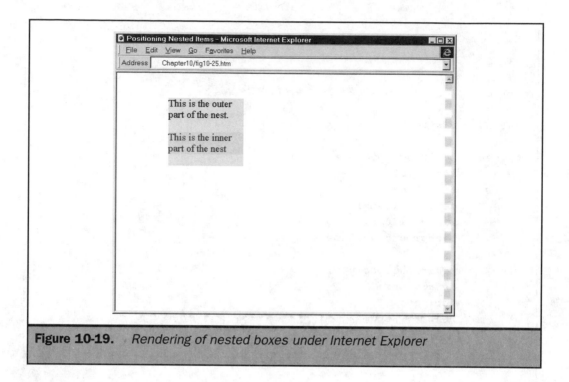

Figure 10-19. Rendering of nested boxes under Internet Explorer

where **top**, **right**, **bottom**, and **left** are the coordinate values that set the clipping region:

```
<DIV STYLE="{position:absolute;
left:20; top:20;
width:100; height:100;
clip: rect(10 90 90 10)}">
This<BR>is<BR>a<BR>case<BR>of<BR>
lines<BR>going<BR>outside<BR>the<BR>box
and may be clipped.
</DIV>
```

overflow

Sometimes an element's content is greater than the space allocated for it. Most browsers will allocate space for content unless size is set explicitly or a clipping region is set. The **overflow** property determines how an element should handle the situation when content doesn't fit. A value of **clip** for the property clips content to the size defined for the container. The **scroll** value allows content to scroll using a browser-dependent mechanism, maybe scroll bars. The default value is **none**, which does nothing and may clip the content. The following example, which mimics the functionality of a floating frame, creates a positioned region that will allow scrolling if content goes beyond its defined size:

```
<DIV STYLE="{position:absolute;
left:20; top:20;
width:100; height:100;
clip: rect(10 90 90 10);
overflow: scroll}">
This<BR>is<BR>a<BR>case<BR>of<BR>
lines<BR>going<BR>outside<BR>the<BR>box
and may be clipped.
</DIV>
```

z-index

Absolute and relative positioning allow element content to overlap. By default, overlapping elements stack in the order in which they are defined in an HTML document. The most recent elements go on top. This default order can be redefined using an element's **z-index** property. Absolute or relative positioned elements define a **z-index** context for the elements they contain. The containing element has an index of 0; the index increases with higher numbers stacked on top of lower numbers. The example shown in Figure 10-20 forces all images inside a container to overlap and uses the top class to position one image on top. The rendering of the example in Figure 10-20 is shown in Figure 10-21. Notice how the elements stack in the specified order rather than as defined.

visibility

The **visibility** property determines if an element is visible or not. The values for the property are **hidden**, **visible**, or **inherit**. The **inherit** value means that a property inherits its visibility state from the element that contains it. If an element is **hidden**, it still occupies the full canvas space but is rendered as transparent. This simple example shows how the item is made invisible, but is not removed:

```
<P>This is a <EM STYLE="visibility: hidden">test</EM> of the
visibility property
```

The rendering in Figure 10-22 shows how the word "test" still takes up space but is not visible.

```
<HTML>
<HEAD>
<TITLE>Z-order Example</TITLE>
<STYLE TYPE="text/css">
<!--
DIV.one       {position:absolute;
               top:20;left:20;
               height: 50; width: 50;
               background-color:blue;
               z-index: 2}

DIV.two       {position:absolute;
               top:30;left:30;
               height: 25; width: 100;
               background-color:orange;
               z-index: 1}

DIV.three     {position:absolute;
               top:40;left:40;
               height: 25; width: 25;
               background-color:yellow;
               z-index: 3}
-->
</STYLE>
</HEAD>
<BODY>
<DIV CLASS="one">
This is section one
</DIV>
<DIV CLASS="two">
This is section two
</DIV>
<DIV CLASS="three">
This is section three
</DIV>
</BODY>
</HTML>
```

Figure 10-20.   *Z-order example*

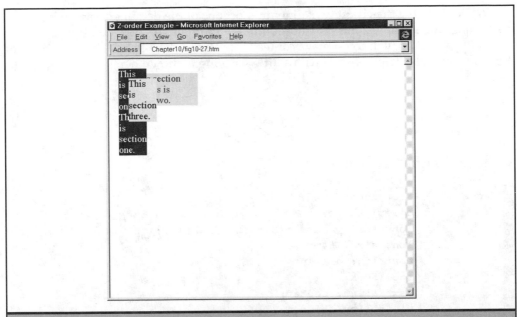

Figure 10-21.   *Rendering of z-order example*

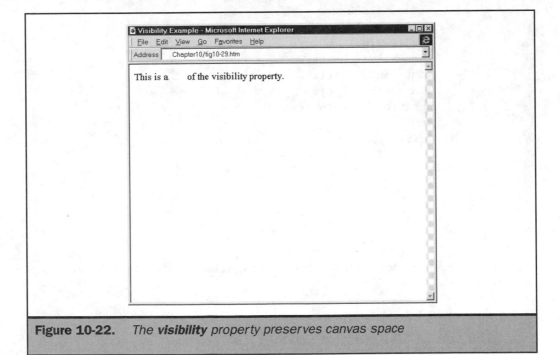

Figure 10-22.   *The **visibility** property preserves canvas space*

While changing the visibility of different portions of the document may not seem that important, imagine if the visibility could be controlled. If you could turn the visibility on and off, you could make content appear and disappear. A brief example of how this might be accomplished with a little scripting is shown here:

```
<HTML>
<HEAD>
<TITLE>Visibility and Scripting</TITLE>

<STYLE TYPE="text/css">
<!--
#peek       {background: red;
             color: white;
             font-family: Comic Sans Ms, Fantasy;
             font-size: 64pt;
             position: absolute;
             top: 50px;
             text-align: center;
             visibility: hidden
             }

#button     {background: yellow;
             color: black;
             border-style: outset;
             border-width: thin;
             text-align: center;
             font-family: Arial, Sans-serif;
             font-size: 12pt;
             position: absolute;
             top: 10px;
             left: 10px;
             }
-->
</STYLE>
</HEAD>

<BODY>

<DIV ID=button onClick="peek.style.visibility='visible'">
Press me!
</DIV>
```

```
<SPAN ID=peek>
Gotcha!
</SPAN>

</BODY>
</HTML>
```

While the discussion goes beyond this brief introduction to style sheets, note that it is possible to manipulate style values on the fly. By changing the look and feel of items depending on a user action, a variety of effects are possible. Look at the small code fragment here:

```
<A HREF="http://www.yahoo.com" onMouseover="this.style.color='red'"
onMouseout="this.style.color='black'">
```

The markup for the link is modified so that the color of the item is changed to red and back to black as a user passes their mouse over it.

The are many possibilities with dynamic styles. Both Netscape and Microsoft support access to style sheets from a scripting language, though in different ways and to a different degree. Beyond modifiable style sheets, Microsoft has added a variety of new features available in cascading style sheets; these warrant a short discussion.

Microsoft-Specific Style Sheet Properties

Browser vendors are already making new additions to cascading style sheets. Microsoft has added a variety of multimedia filters and transitions that can be accessed via a style sheet. Under Internet Explorer, it is also possible to change the cursor of an object, control the printing of a document to a limited degree, and even use downloadable fonts. Undoubtedly, these additions are just the beginning of a slew of new proprietary changes introduced into style sheets. For definitive information on the latest style sheet extensions, check the browser vendor's developer information.

Filters

Microsoft initially supported a variety of multimedia filters, such as ActiveX controls, that were included with the Internet Explorer browser. Use of these multimedia effects was somewhat limited due to the proprietary nature of ActiveX, as well as the public's lack of familiarity with the technology. Instead of using controls directly, Microsoft has taken an approach to make these multimedia effects available via style sheets. What is interesting about this approach is that they did it in a very generalized manner, thus showing how other filters might be added by other vendors. The basic form of a filter rule is shown here:

```
Filter: filtername(filtervalue1, filtervalue2, ...)
```

Each of the possible values for *filtername* is shown in Table 10-2. Note that each filter may have many values that must be set in order to make it work properly. See the Microsoft documentation available at http://www.microsoft.com/sitebuilder/ for a complete discussion of the possible values for the various filters.

An example that illustrates how the filters may be used with some text is shown in Figure 10-23. Playing with the values for the various filter properties may change the effects dramatically. A rendering of the text filters from the last example is shown in Figure 10-24.

Filter Name	Description
Alpha	Sets a uniform transparency level
Blur	Creates the impression of moving at high speed
Chroma	Makes a specific color transparent
DropShadow	Creates a solid silhouette of the object
FlipH	Creates a horizontal mirror image
FlipV	Creates a vertical mirror image
Glow	Adds radiance around the outside edges of the object
Grayscale	Drops color information from the image
Invert	Reverses the hue, saturation, and brightness values
Light	Projects a light source onto an object
Mask	Creates a transparent mask from an object
Shadow	Creates an offset solid silhouette
Wave	Creates a sine wave distortion along the X axis
Xray	Shows just the edges of the object

Table 10-2. *Filter Names Supported in Internet Explorer 4.0*

```
<HTML>
<HEAD>
<TITLE>Microsoft Filter Test</TITLE>
<STYLE TYPE="text/css">
<!--
.glow   {height: 10; width: 400;
         filter: Glow(Color=#00FF00, Strength=4)}

.blur    {height: 10; width: 400;
        filter: Blur(Add = 1, Direction = 90, Strength = 10);}

.dropshadow   {height: 10; width: 400;
    filter:DropShadow(Color=#FF0000, OffX=2, OffY=2,
Positive=1)}
  .fliph   {height: 10; width: 400; filter: fliph()}
  .flipv   {height: 10; width: 400; filter: flipv()}
  .shadow {height: 10; width: 400;
filter: Shadow(color=#00FF00)}
.wave    {height: 10; width: 400;
    filter: Wave(Add=1, Freq=4, LightStrength=50, Phase=50,
Strength=10)}

-->
</STYLE>
</HEAD>
<BODY>
<H1 ALIGN="CENTER">Microsoft Multimedia Filters</H1>

<DIV CLASS="blur">This is the blur filter</DIV>
<DIV CLASS="dropshadow">This is the dropshadow filter</DIV>
<DIV CLASS="fliph">This is the flip horizontal filter</DIV>
<DIV CLASS="flipv">This is the flip vertical filter</DIV>
<DIV CLASS="glow">This is the glow filter</DIV>
<DIV CLASS="shadow">This is the shadow filter</DIV>
<DIV CLASS="wave">This is the wave filter</DIV>

</BODY>
</HTML>
```

Figure 10-23.   *Filter example for Internet Explorer only*

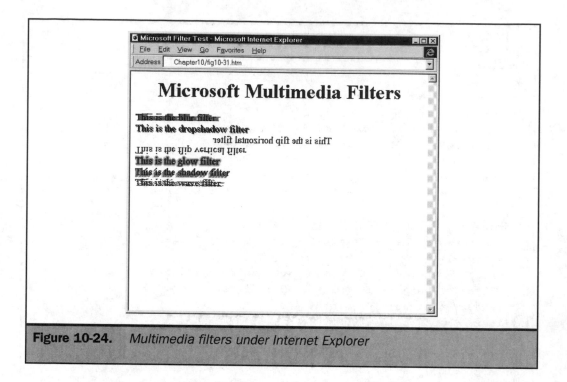

Figure 10-24. *Multimedia filters under Internet Explorer*

Remember that a visual filter can be applied to any visible element on the HTML page that supports the filter property, ranging from a single spanned character to the entire body of the document. It is even possible to apply a visual filter to a **<DIV>** tag to utilize a single set of filter effects on all the visual objects in that region and even stack up effects on enclosed objects.

Reveal Transition Filter

The reveal transition filter allows objects to be revealed using a variety of transitions like box-ins or wipes. These transitions are similar to those found in presentation programs like Microsoft's PowerPoint. The form of the filter property for **revealtrans** is shown here:

```
filter: revealtrans(duration=duration, transition=transition#)
```

The value of **duration** is the time it should take to reveal or hide the object in seconds.milliseconds. The transition number is a numeric value from zero to 24, which corresponds to one of the predefined patterns to reveal objects. The following table shows the values and their corresponding meanings:

Value	Meaning
0	Box in
1	Box out
2	Circle in
3	Circle out
4	Wipe up
5	Wipe down
6	Wipe right
7	Wipe left
8	Vertical blinds
9	Horizontal blinds
10	Checkerboard across
11	Checkerboard down
12	Random dissolve
13	Split vertical in
14	Split vertical out
15	Split horizontal in
16	Split horizontal out
17	Strips left down
18	Strips left up
19	Strips right down
20	Strips right up
21	Random bars horizontal
22	Random bars vertical
23	Random

A rule such as the following would set all paragraph elements of the class intro to reveal themselves by using an expanding circle:

```
P.intro   { filter: revealtrans(duration=4.0, transition=3)}
```

It may be required to trigger the transition with script code, so don't just throw a bunch of transitions on the page and hope it starts animating. These transitions might be of little use on a set page, but what about between pages?

Interpage Transitions

Interpage transitions make it possible to provide multimedia effects as a Web page is loaded or exited. They are not handled with style sheets but by using the **<META>** element within the **<HEAD>** section of a Web page. However, since the syntax of the transitions is the same as the reveal transition, it seems appropriate to cover it here.

The syntax for transitions consists of three parts: specifying when the event should be played, the duration of the transition, and what kind of transition effect to use. The following two examples show how to set transitions upon entry and exit of a page. To make a checkerboard entrance that lasts three seconds, use a **<META>** element like the following:

```
<META http-equiv="Page-Enter"
   CONTENT="RevealTrans(Duration=3.0,Transition=10)">
```

To make a big exit, you could set a wipe effect that lasts two seconds:

```
<META http-equiv="Page-Exit"
    CONTENT="RevealTrans(Duration=2.0,Transition=7)>
```

Of course, leaving the page would require a link from the page to another destination.

Experiment with all the different transition effects by setting the transition number anywhere from 0 to 23. While transitions seem pretty interesting, don't get carried away. They can be even more annoying than **<BLINK>**.

Setting the Cursor

Starting with Internet Explorer 4.0, Microsoft has added the capability to set the form of the cursor when it is placed over an object. Because everything on the page can be made pressable, resetting the cursor is certainly very useful. To set the cursor, create a rule like this:

```
P    {cursor: hand}
```

Now whenever the user places the mouse over a paragraph element, the cursor will show up as a hand.

The possible values for the **cursor** property are **crosshair**, **default**, **hand**, **move**, **e-resize**, **ne-resize**, **nw-resize**, **n-resize**, **se-resize**, **sw-resize**, **s-resize**, **w-resize**, **text**, **wait**, and **help**. The default value of **auto** sets the cursor to whatever it should be, based on the element it is over.

Setting Page Breaks

While in the future style sheets will certainly be extended to support more printing capabilities, Microsoft has already provided the **page-break-before** property and **page-break-after** property under Internet Explorer 4.0. These can be used to set a page break on the printer. Using these properties, it is possible to set the printer to go to a new page before or after a particular element. The default value for either of the properties is **auto**. Other possible values include **always**, **left**, and **right**. Most likely, the value **always** will be used to tell the printer to always insert a page break. Imagine a rule like this:

```
BR.newpage    {page-break-after: always}
```

Adding this rule would always cause a page break wherever it was inserted into a document.

If there is an issue of the newline showing on the screen, a nonbreaking element like <SPAN> could be used to set the page break. Ongoing work for standardized CSS Printing Extensions is documented at the following Web site: http://www.w3.org/TR/WD-print.

Downloadable Fonts

As with the font technology discussed in Chapter 9, it is possible to embed fonts in a Web page using style sheet syntax. To embed fonts in a Web document under Microsoft Internet Explorer, use the **@font-face** property. This property allows the designer to specify fonts in the document that might not be available on the viewer's system.

To embed a font, first specify the **font-family** property. Then specify the **src** property and set it equal to the URL of an embedded OpenType file, which should have an .eot or .ote extension. When the file is downloaded, it is converted to a TrueType font and then displayed on the screen. By putting a rule such as the following in the style sheet, the font named GhostTown can be used elsewhere on the page using the **font-family** property:

```
@font-face {font-family:GhostTown;

        src:url(http://www.bigcompany.com/fonts/ghost.eot);}
```

One big question is, how can a special embedded font file be created? The designer has to run the font through a tool to create the font definition file and then place that file on the Web server. There may also be an issue of making changes to the Web server in order for the file to be delivered correctly. See the Microsoft OpenType Web site at http://www.microsoft.com/opentype/ for information about the font creation tool and other deployment issues.

To embed fonts by the Netscape definition, use the **@fontdef** rule in a style sheet to indicate the downloadable font. To bring in GhostTown, use

```
@fontdef url(http://www.bigcompany.com/fonts/ghosttown.pfr);
```

or, as discussed in Chapter 9, a **<LINK>** element could also be used in the **<HEAD>** of the document as shown here:

```
<LINK REL="FONTDEF"
SRC="http://www.bigcompany.com/fonts/ghosttown.pfr">
```

These style sheet and HTML font solutions work for Netscape. The Microsoft style of adding an **SRC** rule for **@font-face** is the proposed solution from the World Wide Web Consortium and should eventually be supported by Netscape. More information about Netscape's current font and style sheet syntax can be found at http://developer.netscape.com.

Summary

Cascading style sheets provide better control over the look and feel of Web pages. Style sheets aren't just useful for making attractive pages. By dividing structure and style, they make documents simpler, and easier to manipulate. While style sheets provide a great deal of flexibility in creating pages, they are not fully implemented yet in today's browsers. Some inconsistencies exist between implementations. When used in a nonobtrusive manner, style sheets are a great way to improve the layout of pages without locking into a proprietary solution.

Despite the open nature of style sheets, extensions are already being made by browser vendors, so this open nature of the technology might not be quite what it has been built up to be. Pixel-level layout control and downloadable fonts are almost here, but the innovations don't stop. Why just strive for a print style layout, when fully programmed pages are possible? Chapter 11 starts the transition from static Web pages to programmed pages, beginning with forms.

Chapter 11

Basic Interactivity and HTML:

Forms

One of the Web's most interesting possibilities is the creation of interactivity. Up to this point, the discussion has focused on the Web as a static publishing environment. Adding a way for the end viewer to submit information makes the Web more powerful than traditional media. At the lowest level you could create a link with a mailto URL, covered in Chapter 5, and have visitors send in e-mail comments. There are other times when creating a fill-out form would make more sense. With fill-out forms and the appropriate programs to handle the submitted information, it is possible to create an interactive environment ranging from an order entry system to a dynamically created Web site.

How Are Forms Used?

There are many uses for forms on the Web. The most common ones include comment response forms, order entry forms, subscription forms, registration forms, and customization forms:

- A comment response is generally used as a way to collect comments from Web site viewers and have people suggest improvements.

- Order entry forms, which are now common on the Web, provide a way for viewers to order goods from online stores. Order entry forms typically require the user to provide an address, credit card number, and other information necessary to facilitate online commerce. (People worry about the interception of credit card numbers when they are generally sending them to firms they may know very little about. There are facilities to encrypt data transmitted between Web browser and server, but users should be very cautious about who is at the other end of the connection. A little common sense can remove much of the fear around sensitive data transmission.)

- Many sites are adopting a subscriber model, particularly those that attempt to generate revenue through direct subscriptions or by selling advertising space.

- Registration forms are used to collect information about a user and often are tied to an authentication system, which limits access to the site.

Some sites allow the user to select the look and feel for the site itself, literally creating a custom site for each visitor. A customization form might allow users to specify what topics they are interested in within an online magazine. When tied to an authentication system, a user accessing the site views a version set according to his or her tastes.

There are many other examples of how forms might be used on the Web. The point here is to illustrate the kind of interactivity provided by forms.

Form Preliminaries

Making forms is easy. Just add the **<FORM>** element to the document and associated fields, as you'll learn more about in the next section But how can the contents of a form be processed once the user submits the information? After a form is filled in, it is sent somewhere (as specified by a URL); generally, a program on a remote Web server will then parse the submitted information and do something with it. The programs that handle the incoming form data are usually Common Gateway Interface (CGI) programs. They can also be more complex NSAPI (Netscape Server API) programs or ISAPI (Internet Information Server API) filters. A basic overview of how the relationship works is shown in Figure 11-1.

The point here isn't to get into the complications of how to make a CGI program or other programs to handle form submitted data, just to understand that the form itself is only part of the equation. There still must be some way to make the form do something, but this may not be your responsibility. CGI can get complicated, since it usually involves real programming in languages like C, Perl, or even Applescript. It may be beyond the skill set of the page designer. It is possible to use off-the-shelf CGI programs in many cases.

But why worry about these issues? Does the person who creates the IRS tax form know how the program that calculates things works? Why should you worry about how the CGI for the database query form you created is written? This division of labor is far too often missing in Web projects. The people who build the back-end of the Web site that the form interacts with probably aren't the best ones to code the form. The person who codes the form isn't necessarily always the best person to write the back-end CGI program. Think about how the form works in the grand scheme of things, but worry mostly about making your end of the site work.

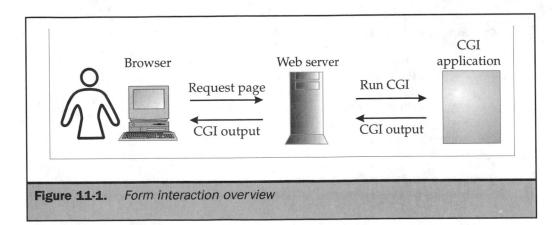

Figure 11-1.   *Form interaction overview*

The <FORM> Element

A form in HTML is enclosed with the **<FORM>** and **</FORM>** tags. The form itself contains regular text, other HTML elements such as tables, and form elements such as check boxes, pull-down menus, and text fields. The W3C specification calls these form elements *controls*. This is somewhat confusing, because Microsoft also refers to ActiveX objects as controls. This book talks about form controls or form elements, not just controls. The form controls are set by a user to indicate the contents of the form. Once the user has finished filling out the form, it must be submitted for processing. Completed forms are generally passed to a remote program that handles the data. The contents may even be mailed to a user for further inspection. To make the form work, you must specify three things: the address of the program that will handle the form contents (**ACTION**), the method in which the form data will be passed (**METHOD**), and potentially how the form data will be encoded (**ENCTYPE**).

ACTION Attribute

How an HTML form is to be handled is set using the **ACTION** attribute for the form element. The **ACTION** attribute is usually set to a URL of the program that will handle the form data. This URL will usually point to a CGI script to decode the form results. For example, the code

```
<FORM ACTION="http://www.bigcompany.com/cgi-bin/post-query"
METHOD="POST">
```

would be for a script called post-query in the cgi-bin directory on the server www.bigcompany.com. It is also possible to use a relative URL for the **ACTION** attribute if the form is delivered by the same server that houses the form handling program:

```
<FORM ACTION="../cgi-bin/post-query" METHOD="POST">
```

Setting the **ACTION** immediately begs this question: what program should the data be passed to? This depends on who writes the program. There may be canned programs to handle the contents of the form. But what happens if there is no way to use a remote program? It is possible to create a "poor man's" form using the mailto URL. Remember that the **ACTION** attribute is set to a URL. Thus, in some cases a form element like

```
<FORM ACTION="mailto:formtest@bigcompany.com" METHOD="POST"
ENCTYPE="text/plain">
```

will work. It is even possible to use an extended form of mailto URL, which is supported by Netscape browsers. For example:

```
<FORM ACTION="mailto:formtest@bigcompany.com?
Subect=Comment%20Form%20Result">
```

Although the mailto form seems the best way to do things, not all browsers support this style; and there are also potential security issues. Even if the browser supports the mailto style, the data should be passed using the **POST** method. It may be useful to encode the data differently by setting it to use text/plain encoding rather than the default style, which is a cryptic encoding style similar to how URLs look. The next section will discuss the methods and the encoding type.

METHOD Attribute

It is also necessary to specify how the form will be submitted to the address specified by the **ACTION** attribute. How data will be submitted is handled by the **METHOD** attribute. There are two acceptable values for the **METHOD** attribute: **GET** and **POST**. If this remains unspecified, most browsers will default to the **GET** method. While much of the following discussion is more applicable to the people writing the programs that handle form data, it is important to understand the basic idea of each method.

GET Method

The **GET** method is generally the default method for browsers to submit information. In fact, HTML documents are generally retrieved by requesting a single URL from a Web server using the **GET** method, which is part of the HTTP protocol. When you type a URL like http://www.bigcompany.com/staff/thomas.htm into your Web browser, it is translated into a valid HTTP **GET** request like this:

```
GET /staff/thomas.htm HTTP/1.0
```

This request is then sent to the server www.bigcompany.com. What this request says, essentially, is "Get me the file thomas.htm in the staff directory. I am speaking the 1.0 dialect of HTTP." How does this relate to forms? You really aren't getting a file *per se* when you submit a form, are you? In reality, you are running a program to handle the form data. For example, the **ACTION** value might specify a URL like http://www.bigcompany.com/cgi-bin/comment.exe, which is the address of a program that can parse your comment form. So wouldn't the HTTP request be something like the one shown here?

```
GET /cgi-bin/comment.exe HTTP/1.0
```

Not quite. You need to pass the form data along with the name of the program to run. To do this, all the information from the form is appended onto the end of the URL being requested. This produces a hundred-character URL with the actual data in it, as shown here:

```
http://www.bigompany.com/cgi-bin/comments.exe?
Name=Al+Smith&Age=30&Sex=male
```

The **GET** method isn't a very secure method, since the data input appears in the URL. Furthermore, there is a limitation to just how much data can be passed with the **GET** method. It would be impossible to append a 10,000-word essay to the end of a URL, as most browsers limit a URL to several thousand characters. Further problems with **GET** become obvious when dealing with foreign language environments. Would it be possible to deal with Japanese Kanji characters in the URL using the GET method? Maybe not. Under the HTML 4.0 specification, the **GET** method has been depreciated. Despite the fact that **GET** is not recommended, it is still the default method when the **METHOD** attribute is not specified.

With all these problems, why use **GET**? First, **GET** is easy to deal with. An example URL like the following should make it obvious that the Name field is set to "Al Smith," the Age is "30," and the "Sex" is male:

```
http://www.bigompany.com/cgi-bin/comments.exe?Name=Al+Smith&Age=30&S
ex=male
```

Form field names are set to values that are generally encoded with plus signs instead of spaces. Non-alphanumeric characters are replaced by "%*nn*" where *nn* is the hexadecimal ASCII code for the character, similar to the URL encoding, as described in Chapter 5. The individual form field values are separated by ampersands. It would be trivial to write a parsing program to recover data out of this form.

The other method, **POST**, is just as easy, so this is not a motivating reason to use **GET**. Perhaps the best reason to use **GET** is that it comes in a form of a URL, so it can be set as a **LINK** or bookmarked. **GET** is used well in search engines. When a user submits a query to a search engine, the engine runs the query and then returns page upon page of result. It is possible to bookmark the query results and rerun the query later. It is also possible to create anchors that fire off canned CGI programs. This is particularly useful in certain varieties of dynamic Web sites. For example, the link shown next fires off a CGI program written in the Cold Fusion Markup language (CFM) and passes it a value setting—setting the ExecutiveID to 1.

```
<A HREF="displayexec.cfm?ExecutiveId=1">John Kowalski</A>
```

The query is built into the link; when the link is clicked, the CGI program will access the appropiate database of executives and bring up information about John Kowalski.

While the **GET** method is far from perfect, there are certain situations where it makes a great deal of sense. It is unlikely that **GET** will be truly depreciated for quite some time.

POST Method

In situations where a large amount of information must be passed back, the **POST** method is more appropriate than **GET**. The **POST** method transmits all form input information immediately after the requested URL. In other words, once the server has received a request from a form using **POST**, it knows to continue "listening" for the rest of the information. In some sense, this method requires two contacts to make to the Web server. The **GET** method only requires one, because the method comes with the data to use right in the request. The encoding of the form data is handled in the same general way as the **GET** method by default; spaces become plus signs and other characters are encoded in the URL fashion. A sample form might send data that would look like

```
Name=Al+Smith&Age=30&Sex=male
```

The data will still have to be broken up to be used by the handling program. The benefit of using the **POST** method is that a large amount of data can be submitted this way because the form contents are not in the URL. It is even possible to send the contents of files using this method. In the case of the **POST** example, the encoding of the form data is the same as **GET**. It is possible to change the encoding method using the **ENCTYPE** attribute.

ENCTYPE

When data is passed from a form to a Web server, it is typically encoded just like a URL. In this encoding, spaces are replaced by the "+" symbol and non-alphanumeric characters are replaced by "%*nn*" where *nn* is the hexadecimal ASCII code for the character. The form of this is described the special MIME file format *application/x-www-form-urlencoded*. By default, all form data is submitted in this form. It is possible, however, to set the encoding method for form data by setting the **ENCTYPE** attribute. When using a mailto URL in the **ACTION** attribute, the encoding type of *text/plain* might be more desirable. The result would look like the example shown here:

```
First Name=Joe
Last Name=Smith
Sex=Male
Submit=Send it
```

Each form field is on a line of its own. Even with this encoding form,
non-alphanumeric characters may be encoded in the hexadecimal form.

Another form of encoding is also important: **multiform/form-data**. When passing
files back via a form, it is important to designate where each file begins and ends. A
value of **multipart/form-data** for the **ENCTYPE** is used to indicate this style. In this
encoding, spaces and non-alphanumeric characters are preserved; data elements are
separated by special delimiter lines. The following file fragment shows the submission
of a form with **multipart/form-data** encoding, including the contents of the attached
files:

```
Content-type: multipart/form-data;
boundary=--------------------------2988412654262
Content-Length: 5289
---------------------------2988412654262
Content-Disposition: form-data; name="firstname"
David
---------------------------2988412654262
Content-Disposition: form-data; name="lastname"
Jones
---------------------------2988412654262
Content-Disposition: form-data; name="myfile";
filename="C:\WINNT\PROFILES\ADMINISTRATOR\DESKTOP\TEST.HTM"
Content-Type: text/html
<html><head><title>Test File</title></head><BODY ><BR>
<center>Test File</center><hr></BODY></html>
-----------------------------------------
8/12/97 4:47:45 PM--SF_NOTIFY_PREPROC_HEADERS
URL=/clients/postit.cfm?
-----------------------------------------
8/12/97 4:47:45 PM--SF_NOTIFY_URL_MAP
URL=/clients/postit.cfm
Physical Path=C:\InetPub\wwwroot\clients\postit.cfm
-----------------------------------------
```

Simple Form Syntax

Given that we have a destination for the form contents as specified by the **ACTION** attribute and possibly a **METHOD**, either **GET** or **POST**, and maybe an encoding form, we can write a simple stub example for a form as shown here:

```
<!DOCTYPE HTML PUBLIC "-//W3C//DTD HTML 3.2 Final//EN">
<HTML>
<HEAD>
<TITLE>Form Stub</TITLE>
</HEAD>
<BODY>
<FORM ACTION="/cgi-bin/post-query" METHOD="POST">
Form field controls and standard HTML markup
</FORM>
</BODY>
</HTML>
```

While this syntax is adequate to build the form framework in most cases, there are other attributes for the form element that may be useful for frame targeting, scripting, and style sheets. Before discussing the individual form controls, let's review the complete syntax for the **<FORM>** element.

Complete Form Syntax

The **<FORM>** element is a block-level structure used to define a fill-in form. Form contents are enclosed within the **<FORM>** and **</FORM>** tag, both of which are mandatory. The **<FORM>** element has a variety of attributes shown here:

```
<FORM
     ACCEPT-CHARSET=list of supported characters sets
     ACTION=URL
     CLASS=class name(s)
     DIR=LTR | RTL
     ENCTYPE=MIME Type
     ID=unique alphanumeric identifier
     LANG=language code
     LANGUAGE=JAVASCRIPT | JSCRIPT | VBSCRIPT | VBS....IE 4
     METHOD=GET | POST
     NAME=unique alphanumeric identifier........IE 4 and N 4
     STYLE=style information
     TARGET=frame name
```

```
TITLE=advisory text

Eventhandler="script">

. . . Form controls and HTML markup . . .

</FORM>
```

The **<FORM>** element has a variety of attributes. Most of these are common to the HTML 4.0 standard or the major browsers.

The **ACTION** attribute specifies the address of where to send the form contents. This is usually the URL of a server-side program that handles the form content. It may also be a mailto URL. The **ACTION** value is required for working forms, though on some browsers a value similar to the base URL of the document will be assumed if the **ACTION** is left out.

The **CLASS** attribute is used to specify the class name for the form so that it can be used as a subclass from a style sheet, as discussed in Chapter 10.

The **ENCTYPE** attribute is used to specify the encoding form of the form data. By default, the encoding value is **application/x-www-form-urlencoded**, where spaces are translated to plus signs and other non-alphanumeric values are translated into hexadecimal values just as URLs are encoded. As discussed earlier, other possible values for this attribute include plain/text, which is useful when mailing form contents to people, and multipart/form-data, which is used to upload files via forms.

The **ID** attribute is used to specify a unique name for the **<FORM>** element. It can also serve as the destination of a link, or be manipulated by a style sheet. The **ID** value also makes the form available for scripting; for backward compatibility, for the moment you may want to stick to specifying only the **NAME** attribute as older browsers will recognize this attribute.

The **LANG** attribute is used to specify the language being used in the form. The language is specified by setting the attribute to the ISO standard language abbreviation form.

The **LANGUAGE** attribute is used to specify the language of the script associated with the form element. In particular, this attribute applies to the script handlers bound to the various events handled in the **<FORM>** element itself. This attribute has no bearing on the language of scripts called by form controls or the functions that may be called via the event handlers. The value for the **LANGUAGE** attribute by default is JavaScript, but **JSCRIPT**, **VBS**, and **VBSCRIPT** are also possible.

The **METHOD** attribute indicates how the form data should be sent to the address specified by the **ACTION** attribute. The possible values for this attribute are **GET** and **POST**. **GET** sends the information within the URL of the request, while **POST** sends it following the request. Under HTML 4.0 the **GET** element is considered depreciated;

however, it is still the default value when this method is unspecified. When using a mailto **ACTION** value, be sure to set the **METHOD** to **POST**.

The **NAME** attribute is used to provide a name for the form for manipulation from a scripting language. While the HTML 4.0 specification may prefer the **ID** attribute, browsers, including Netscape 2.0 and 3.0, depend on the occurrence of **NAME** to provide access to the form. Page authors looking to use **ID** instead should consider setting **NAME** and **ID** to the same value. However, note that while many browsers will handle this just fine, it is not allowed according to the specification, since the **NAME** and **ID** attributes share namespace. This example is again one of these specification-versus-practice problems so common on the Web.

The **STYLE** attribute is used to specify an inline style rule for the **<FORM>** element.

The **TARGET** attribute is used to set the window or frame that should display any results returned by the form action. As with all frames-oriented extensions, values of **_blank**, **_parent**, **_self**, and **_top** have special meaning. When the value is not specified, the form loads over itself.

The **TITLE** attribute is used to set advisory text for the form. The contents of the **TITLE** attribute might be rendered on screen as a tool tip when the user's mouse hovers over the form, or may simply act as a note to readers of the HTML text. **TITLE** will also benefit users of speech browsers or other alternative access media. The use of the **TITLE** attribute generally makes more sense for the individual form controls than the form itself.

A variety of events can be associated with the form. HTML 4.0 defines **onsubmit** and **onreset** as the primary events that correspond to the submission of the form and the resetting of the form's fields to their defaults respectively. Other events defined include **onclick**, **ondblcick**, **onmousedown**, **onmouseup**, **onmouseover**, **onmouseover**, **onmouseout**, **onkeypress**, **onkeydown**, and **onkeyup**. Microsoft Internet Explorer 4.0 also supports **onhelp** and **onselectstart** as events for a form. A more detailed discussion of how events are used with forms is presented later in the section "Forms and Events."

Form Controls

A form is made up of fields or controls, as well as the markup necessary to structure the form and control its presentation. The controls are the items filled in or manipulated by the user to indicate the state of the form. Form controls include text fields, password fields, multiple line text fields, pop-up menus, scrolled lists, radio buttons, check boxes, and buttons. Hidden form controls are also possible. The most common element used to specify a form control is the **<INPUT>** element. However, **<SELECT>** in conjunction with the **<OPTION>** element and the **<TEXTAREA>** element are also common in forms. Rather than discuss the syntax of the particular elements, let's first approach learning forms by exploring the form controls, then the complete syntax for the elements. This discussion only covers basic form controls.

Newer form items as represented by **<BUTTON>**, **<LABEL>**, **<FIELDSET>**, and **<LEGEND>** will be discussed in the section "New and Emerging Form Elements".

Text Controls

Text controls are form fields, generally one line long, that take text input like a person's name, address, and other information. These fields are specified with the **<INPUT>** element, but it is possible to specify a multiple line text field using the **<TEXTAREA>** element.

Simple Text Entry

The simplest type of form control is the text entry type. To set a text entry control, use the **<INPUT>** element and set the **TYPE** attribute equal to **TEXT**:

```
<INPUT TYPE="TEXT" NAME="CustName">
```

All form elements should be named. **NAME="CustName"** is used to create a text field to collect a customer's name on an order form.

This example creates a one-line text entry field that will be associated with the name **CustName**:

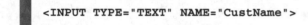

Remember to pick a name that makes sense and is unique to the form. The name will be used when the form is submitted as well as for manipulation by scripting languages.

The last example does not specify the size of the field or the maximum number of characters that can be entered into the field. By default, unless specified this field generally will be a width of 20 characters. To set the size of the field in characters, use the **SIZE** attribute. For example,

```
<INPUT TYPE="TEXT" NAME="CustName" SIZE="40">
```

The value of the **SIZE** field for an **<INPUT>** element is the number of characters to be displayed. It is possible for the user to type more characters than this value. The text will just scroll by. If you want to limit the size of the field, you need to set the value of the **MAXLENGTH** attribute to the maximum number of characters allowed in the field. The browser will deny the user from typing more than the number of characters specified. Browser feedback may include beeping or may just overstrike the last character. To set a text field that shows 30 characters but has a maximum of 60 characters that can be entered, use something like

```
<INPUT TYPE="TEXT" NAME="CustName" SIZE="30" MAXLENGTH="60">
```

The last attribute that is useful to set with a text entry field is the **VALUE** attribute. With this attribute, you can specify the default text you want to appear in the field when the form is first loaded. For example, in the following code fragment, a value of **"Enter your name here"** is provided as a prompt to the user to fill in the field properly:

```
<INPUT TYPE="TEXT" NAME="CustName" SIZE="30" MAXLENGTH="60"
       VALUE="Enter your name here">
```

A very simple example of the basic text field type is shown here:

```
<!DOCTYPE HTML PUBLIC "-//W3C//DTD HTML 4.0 Final//EN">
<HTML>
<HEAD>
<TITLE>Text Field Example</TITLE>
</HEAD>
<BODY>
<H1 ALIGN=CENTER>Gadget Order Form</H1>
<HR>
<FORM ACTION="http://www.bigcompany.com/cgi-bin/post-query"
METHOD="POST">

<B>Customer Name:</B>
<INPUT TYPE="text"
    NAME="Cust_name"
    SIZE="25"
```

```
            MAXLENGTH="35">

</FORM>
<HR>
</BODY>
</HTML>
```

Password Fields

The password style of form control is the same as the simple text entry field, except that the input to the field is not revealed. In many cases, the browser may render each character as an asterisk or dot to avoid people seeing the password being entered, as shown here:

Not echoing the password on screen is appropriate. It discourages the idea of "shoulder surfing" where an unscrupulous user looks on your screen to see what secret data you input. To set a password form control, use the **<INPUT>** element but set the **TYPE** attribute equal to **PASSWORD**. As with the text entry field, it is possible to specify the size of the field in characters with **SIZE**, the maximum entry with **MAXLENGTH** in characters. In the case of the password control, it is probably wise to limit the length of the field so users don't become confused about how many characters they have entered.

The password form is very similar to the single-line text entry field. However, setting a default value for the password field with the **VALUE** attribute doesn't make much sense since the user can see it by viewing the HTML source of the document. A complete example of the password field's use within the form is shown here:

```
<!DOCTYPE HTML PUBLIC "-//W3C//DTD HTML 4.0 Final//EN">
<HTML>
<HEAD>
```

```
<TITLE>Password Field Example</TITLE>
</HEAD>
<BODY>
<H1 ALIGN=CENTER>Gadget Order Form</H1>
<HR>
<FORM ACTION="http://www.bigcompany.com/cgi-bin/post-query"
METHOD="POST">

<B>Customer Name:</B>
<INPUT TYPE="text"
       NAME="Cust_name"
       SIZE="25"
       MAXLENGTH="35">
<BR>

<B>Customer ID:</B>
<INPUT TYPE="PASSWORD"
       NAME="Cust_ID"
       SIZE="10"
       MAXLENGTH="10">

</FORM>
<HR>
</BODY>
</HTML>
```

Multiple Line Text Input

When it is necessary to enter more than one line of text in a form field, the **<INPUT>** element must be abandoned in favor of the **<TEXTAREA>** element. Like the text input field, there are similar attributes to control the size of the data entry area as well as the default value and the name of the control. For example, to set the number of rows in the text entry area, set the **ROWS** attribute equal to the number of rows desired. To set the number of characters per line, set the **COLS** attribute. So to define a text area of five rows of 80 characters each, use the following:

```
TEXTAREA ROWS="5" COLS="80" NAME="CommentBox">
/TEXTAREA>
```

Because there may be many lines of text within the **<TEXTAREA>** element, it is not possible to set the default text for the area using the **VALUE** attribute. Instead, place the default text between the **<TEXTAREA>** and **</TEXTAREA>** tags:

```
<TEXTAREA ROWS=5 COLS=80 NAME="CommentBox">
Please fill in your comments here.
</TEXTAREA>
```

The information enclosed within the **<TEXTAREA>** element must be plain text and should not include any HTML markup. In fact, the contents of the element act like the **<PRE>** element by preserving spaces, returns, and other characters. HTML elements entered within the form control will not be interpreted. A complete example of a multiline text field is shown in Figure 11-2. A rendering of the text area example is shown in Figure 11-3.

Netscape supports a special **WRAP** attribute for the **<TEXTAREA>** element. The values for this attribute are **OFF**, **HARD**, and **SOFT**. A value of **OFF** disables word wrapping in the form control. Any text the user enters is displayed exactly as is, though the user may insert hard returns of their own. A value of **HARD** allows word

```
<!DOCTYPE HTML PUBLIC "-//W3C//DTD HTML 4.0 Final//EN">
<HTML>
<HEAD>
<TITLE>Multiline Text Field Example</TITLE>
</HEAD>
<BODY>
<H1 ALIGN=CENTER>Gadget Order Form</H1>
<HR>
<FORM ACTION="http://www.bigcompany.com/cgi-bin/post-query"
METHOD="POST">

<B>Special Instructions:</B><BR>

<TEXTAREA ROWS="10" COLS="40" NAME="Instructions">
Enter any special gadget ordering
instructions in this space.
</TEXTAREA>

</FORM>
<HR>
</BODY>
</HTML>
```

Figure 11-2.   *Multiline text input example*

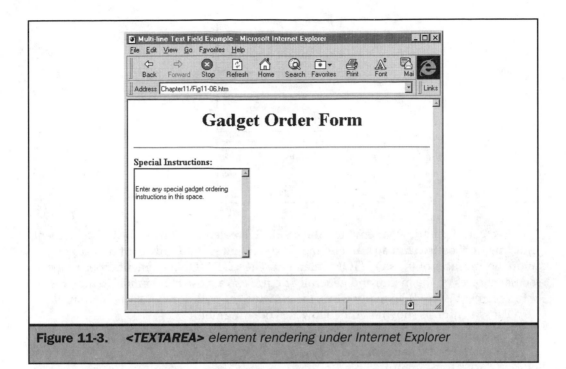

Figure 11-3.   *<TEXTAREA> element rendering under Internet Explorer*

wrapping and the actual break points are included when the form is submitted. A value of **SOFT** allows word wrapping in the form control but the line breaks are not sent with the forms contents. A value of **SOFT** is the default, and this mimics how other browsers deal with the <TEXTAREA> element. These are the only unique attributes for <TEXTAREA>, but like most elements under HTML 4.0, <TEXTAREA> also supports **ID, CLASS, STYLE, TITLE, LANG, DIR**, and a multitude of event handler attributes like **onclick**. See Appendix A for more information about these. The <TEXTAREA> element has three important accessibility attributes, **DISABLED, TABINDEX**, and **READONLY**, which are described beginning in "Form Accessibility Enhancements" later in this chapter.

Pull-Down Menus

HTML form controls include pull-down menus. A pull-down menu lets the user select one choice out of many possible choices. One nice aspect of pull-down menus is that all choices do not have to be seen on the screen and are normally hidden. The following illustration shows the rendering of a pull-down menu under different browsers:

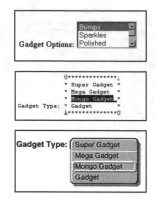

To create a pull-down menu, use the **<SELECT>** element. The **<SELECT>** element must include both a start and an end tag. The element should only contain zero or more occurrences of the **<OPTION>** element. The **<OPTION>** elements specify the actual choices on the menu, and generally do not use a close tag (similar to how the **<LI>** element is used). In many ways, the structure of pull-down menu looks similar to a list structure, as shown in the following code fragment:

```
<SELECT NAME="GadgetType">
    <OPTION>Super Gadget
    <OPTION>Mega Gadget
    <OPTION>Mongo Gadget
    <OPTION>Plain Gadget
</SELECT>
```

As shown in the code fragment, like all form controls the **<SELECT>** element has a **NAME** attribute that is used to set a unique name for the control for purposes of decoding the user selection. It is also possible to set attributes for the **<OPTION>** element. An occurrence of the attribute **SELECTED** in the **<OPTION>** element sets the form control to select this item by default. If no value is selected, typically the field remains undefined. Some user agents may preselect the first item specified with the **<OPTION>** element. Normally, the value submitted when the form is sent is the value enclosed by the **<OPTION>** element. However, it is possible to set the **VALUE** attribute for the element that will be returned instead. This might be important when the user has a different name for items than "official names." A complete example of a simple pull-down menu is shown here:

```
<!DOCTYPE HTML PUBLIC "-//W3C//DTD HTML 4.0 Final//EN">
<HTML>
<HEAD>
```

```
<TITLE>Pull-down Menu Example</TITLE>
</HEAD>
<BODY>
<H1 ALIGN=CENTER>Gadget Order Form</H1>
<HR>
<FORM ACTION="mailto:test@bigcompany.com" METHOD="POST">

<B>Gadget Type:</B>
<SELECT NAME="GadgetType">
        <OPTION VALUE="SG-01">Super Gadget
        <OPTION VALUE="MEG-G5">Mega Gadget
        <OPTION VALUE="MO-45">Mongo Gadget
        <OPTION SELECTED>Gadget
</SELECT>

</FORM>
<HR>
</BODY>
</HTML>
```

Scrolled Lists

The <SELECT> element also may contain the **SIZE** attribute, which is used to specify
the number of items showing on the screen at once. The default value for this attribute
is 1, which specifies a normal pull-down menu. Setting a positive number creates a list
in a window of the specified number of rows, as shown here:

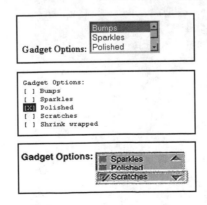

In many cases, scrolled lists act just like pull-down menus. However, if the <SELECT> element contains the attribute **MULTIPLE**, it becomes possible to select more than one entry. How multiple items are selected depends on the browser, but generally, it requires holding down some modifier key such as ALT, COMMAND, or SHIFT and selecting the appropriate items with the mouse.

Note
Many novice users have a hard time with the scrolled list control and multiple entries. Depending on your target audience, it might be wise to provide instructions near the control to assist the user.

Because it is possible to select more than one entry in a scrolled list when the multiple option is applied, it is then possible to use the **SELECTED** attribute multiple times in the enclosed <OPTION> elements. A complete example illustrating how the scrolled list is used is shown here:

```
<!DOCTYPE HTML PUBLIC "-//W3C//DTD HTM  4.0 Final//EN">
<HTML>
<HEAD>
<TITLE>Scrolled List Example</TITLE>
</HEAD>
<BODY>
<H1 ALIGN=CENTER>Gadget Order Form</H1>
<HR>
<FORM ACTION="mailto:order@bigcompany.com" METHOD="POST">

<B>Gadget Options:</B>
<SELECT NAME="GadgetOptions" MULTIPLE SIZE=3>
    <OPTION VALUE="Hit with hammer" SELECTED>Bumps
    <OPTION VALUE="Add glitter">Sparkles
    <OPTION VALUE="Buff it">Polished
    <OPTION SELECTED>Scratches
    <OPTION>Shrink wrapped
</SELECT>

</FORM>
<HR>
</BODY>
</HTML>
```

Check Boxes

With the scrolled list, it is possible to select many items out of a large group of items. Unfortunately, not all the items are presented at once for the user to choose. If there are a few options to select from which are not mutually exclusive, it is probably better to use a group of check boxes that the user can check off. Check boxes are best used to toggle choices on and off. While it is possible to have multiple numbers of check boxes and let the user select as many as he or she wants, if there are too many it may be difficult to deal with. Don't forget about scrolled lists.

To create a check box, use the **<INPUT>** element and set the **TYPE** attribute equal to **CHECKBOX**. The check box should also be named by setting the **NAME** attribute. For example, to create a check box asking if a user wants cheese, use some markup like

```
Cheese: <INPUT TYPE="CHECKBOX"  NAME="Cheese">
```

In this example, the label to the left is arbitrary. It could be the right as well. The label could say "Put cheese on it," but there will be no indication to the receiving program of this label. In this simple example, if the check box is selected, a value of **Cheese=on** will be transmitted to the server. Setting a value for the check box might make more sense. Values to be transmitted instead of the default value can be set with the **VALUE** attribute. The code

```
Cheese: <INPUT TYPE="Checkbox" NAME="Extras" VALUE="Cheese">
```

would send a response like **Extras=Cheese** to the server. It is also possible to have multiple check box controls with the same name. The code

```
Cheese: <INPUT TYPE="CHECKBOX"  NAME="Extras" VALUE="Cheese">
Pickles: <INPUT TYPE="CHECKBOX"  NAME="Extras" VALUE="Pickles">
```

would send multiple entries like the following to the server when both extras were selected:

```
Extras=Cheese&Extras=Pickels
```

It is possible to set a check box to be selected by default by using the **CHECKED** attribute within the **<INPUT>** element. The **CHECKED** attribute requires no value. A complete example using check box controls is shown here:

```
<!DOCTYPE HTML PUBLIC "-//W3C//DTD HTML 4.0 Final//EN">
<HTML>
<HEAD>
<TITLE>Check Box Example</TITLE>
</HEAD>
<BODY>
<H1 ALIGN="CENTER">Gadget Order Form</H1>
<HR>
<FORM ACTION="mailto:order@bigcompany.com" METHOD="POST">

<B>Gadget Bonus Options:</B>
<BR>
Super-magneto: <INPUT TYPE="CHECKBOX" NAME="BONUS"
VALUE="Magnetize">
<BR>
Kryptonite Coating: <INPUT TYPE="CHECKBOX" NAME="BONUS"
VALUE="Anti-Superman" CHECKED><BR>
Anti-gravity: <INPUT TYPE="CHECKBOX" NAME="BONUS"
VALUE="Anti-gravity">
<BR>

</FORM>
<HR>
</BODY>
</HTML>
```

Radio Buttons

Radio buttons use a similar notation to check boxes, but only one option may be chosen among many. This is an especially good option for choices that don't make sense when selected together. In this sense, radio buttons are like pull-down menus that allow only one choice. The main difference is that all options are shown at once with radio buttons.

Just like check boxes, this form control uses the standard **<INPUT TYPE=" ">** format. In this case, set **TYPE** equal to **RADIO**. Setting the **NAME** field is very important in the case of radio buttons because it groups together controls that share the radio functionality. The radio functionality says that when an item is selected it deselects the previously pressed item. If the names are different for each radio button, the functionality becomes that of a check box, only with a different shape. Possible renderings of the radio button form control are shown here:

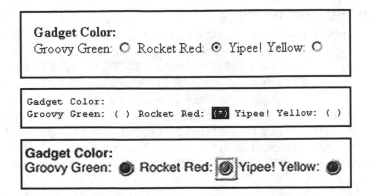

Another important attribute is **VALUE**. It is important to set each individual radio button to a different value entry. Otherwise, it will be impossible to decipher which button was selected. Like check boxes, the occurrence of the **SELECTED** attribute in the **<INPUT>** element will preselect the item. Only one item may be selected as a default out of a radio group. If the **SELECTED** attribute does not occur, the browser will typically not display any items as selected. A complete example using radio buttons is shown here:

```
<!DOCTYPE HTML PUBLIC "-//W3C//DTD HTML 4.0 Final//EN">
<HTML>
<HEAD>
<TITLE>Radio Button Example</TITLE>
</HEAD>
<BODY>
<H1 ALIGN="CENTER">Gadget Order Form</H1>
<HR>
<FORM ACTION="mailto:order@bigcompany.com" METHOD="POST">

<B>Gadget Color:</B><BR>
Groovy Green: <INPUT TYPE="RADIO" NAME="Color" VALUE="Green">
Rocket Red: <INPUT TYPE="RADIO" NAME="Color" VALUE="Red" CHECKED>
Yipee! Yellow: <INPUT TYPE="RADIO" NAME="Color" VALUE="Yellow">

</FORM>
<HR>
</BODY>
</HTML>
```

Reset and Submit Buttons

Once a form has been filled in, there must be a way to send it on its way, whether it is submitted to a program for processing or simply mailed to an e-mail address. The <INPUT> element has two values, **RESET** and **SUBMIT**, for the **TYPE** attribute; these can create common buttons that are useful for just about any form. Setting the **TYPE** attribute for the <INPUT> element to **RESET** creates a button that allows the user to clear or set to default all the form controls at once. Setting the **TYPE** attribute for <INPUT> to **SUBMIT** creates a button that triggers the browser to send the contents of the form to the address specified in the **ACTION** attribute of the <FORM> element. Common renderings of the **SUBMIT** and **RESET** form controls are shown here:

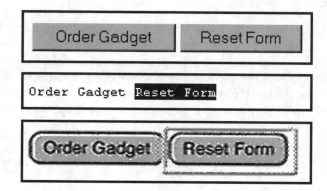

The buttons themselves take two basic attributes: **NAME** and **VALUE**. The **VALUE** attribute sets both the value of the button when pressed as well as the wording of the button. The **NAME** value associates an identifier with the form control. A complete example showing a small form with submit and reset buttons is shown here:

```
<!DOCTYPE HTML PUBLIC "-//W3C//DTD HTML 4.0 Final//EN">
<HTML>
<HEAD>
<TITLE>Complete Form Example</TITLE>
</HEAD>
<BODY>
<H1 ALIGN="CENTER">Gadget Order Form</H1>
<HR>
<FORM ACTION="mailto:order@bigcompany.com"
      METHOD="POST" ENCTYPE="text/plain">

<B>Customer Name:</B>
<INPUT TYPE="TEXT"
```

```
            NAME="Cust_name"
            SIZE="25"
            MAXLENGTH="35">

<BR><BR>

<B>Customer ID:</B>
<INPUT TYPE="PASSWORD"
       NAME="Cust_ID"
       SIZE="10"
       MAXLENGTH="10">

<BR><BR>

<B>Gadget Type:</B>
<SELECT NAME="GadgetType">
    <OPTION VALUE="SG-01">Super Gadget
    <OPTION VALUE="MEG-G5">Mega Gadget
    <OPTION VALUE="MO-45">Mongo Gadget
    <OPTION SELECTED>Gadget
</SELECT>

<BR><BR>

<INPUT TYPE="SUBMIT" VALUE="Order Gadget" NAME="SubmitButton">
<INPUT TYPE="RESET" VALUE="Reset Form" NAME="ResetButton">

</FORM>
<HR>
</BODY>
</HTML>
```

Because the submit and reset buttons cause an action, either form submission or field reset, it would not seem obvious why the **VALUE** or **NAME** field might be useful. While having multiple reset buttons might not be useful, multiple submit buttons are useful because the value of the button is sent to the address specified in the **<FORM>** element's **ACTION** attribute. One possible use might be to have three submit buttons: one for add, one for delete, and one for update.

```
<INPUT TYPE="SUBMIT" VALUE="Place Order" NAME="Add">
<INPUT TYPE="SUBMIT" VALUE="Delete Order" NAME="Delete">
<INPUT TYPE="SUBMIT" VALUE="Update Order" NAME="Update">
<INPUT TYPE="RESET"  VALUE="Reset Form" NAME="ResetButton">
```

When the form is submitted, the value of the button is sent to the form handling program, which will decide what to do with the submitted data based upon its contents. This use of a submit button hints at a more generalized form of button, which will be discussed in the next section.

Additional <INPUT> Types

There are a few forms of the **<INPUT>** element that have not been discussed. These form elements hint at the potential complexity of using forms. Some of these elements, particularly the file selection form element, are not supported in older browsers.

Hidden Text and Its Uses

The usefulness of this form control is not always obvious to the new user. By setting the **TYPE** attribute of the **<INPUT>** element to a value of **HIDDEN**, it is possible to transmit default or previously specified text that is hidden from the user to the handling program. If there were many versions of the same form all over a Web site, then the hidden text could be used to specify where the form came from, as shown below.

```
<INPUT TYPE="HIDDEN" NAME="SubmittingFormName"  VALUE="Form1">
```

Because this field is not shown on the page, it is impossible for the user to modify it. Thus, it must have its **VALUE** attribute set. While this last example seems rather contrived, there is actually a very important use for hidden form controls.

When filling in forms, there is often an issue of remembering information from one form to the next. Imagine a form where the user fills in his or her personal information on one page and the ordering information on the next page. How will the two pages be related to each other? This presents the state-loss problem. The protocols of the Web, primarily, HTTP do not support a "memory." In other words, they don't preserve state. One way to get around this is to use hidden text. Imagine that, in the last example, the personal information is passed to the next page by dynamically embedding it in the ordering page as hidden text. Then state has been preserved—or has it? When users are finished ordering, they submit the whole form at once as a complete transaction. This idea of using hidden text to get around the state-loss problem is illustrated in Figure 11-4.

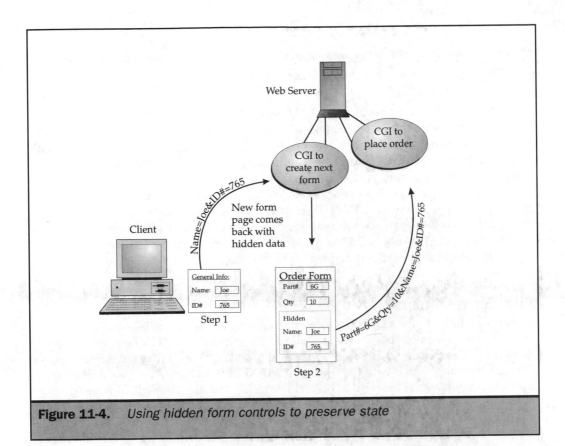

Figure 11-4.   *Using hidden form controls to preserve state*

There are other approaches to saving state, including extended path information and cookies. These ideas will be briefly discussed in Chapter 12 and Chapter 15.

Image Type

One form of the <INPUT> element which is somewhat strange is the image type, as specified by setting **TYPE=IMAGE**. This form of <INPUT> creates a graphical version of the submit button, which not only submits the form but transmits coordinate information about where the user clicked in the image. The image is specified by the **SRC** attribute. Many of the attributes used for the <IMG> element may be valid for this form of <INPUT> as well. The specification defines **ALT** and **ALIGN**. Other attributes like **BORDER**, **HSPACE**, or **VSPACE** may or may not be supported by browsers. Like all other forms of <INPUT>, the **NAME** attribute is a very important part of how the coordinate information is transmitted. The example use of <INPUT> shown next could be used to insert a map of the United States, allowing users to click on the regional office where they want to submit their order form.

```
<INPUT TYPE=IMAGE SRC="usamap.gif" NAME="Sales" ALT="Sales Region
Map">
```

When clicked, the form values would be submitted, along with two extra values, **Sales.x** and **Sales.y**. **Sales.x** and **Sales.y** would be set equal to the x and y coordinates of where the image was clicked. The x and y coordinates are relative to the image with an origin in the upper left-hand corner of the image. You may notice a similarity to image maps. Indeed, much of the functionality of this form control could be imitated with a client-side image map in conjunction with some scripting code. A future extension to this form of the **<INPUT>** element would be to make it less server-side dependent, possibly even allowing the page author set a map name to decode coordinates or set function. Except for specialized needs, page designers should probably look to provide the functionality of the image form control in some other way.

File Form Control

A recent addition to the **<INPUT>** element that is now part of the HTML 4.0 specification is the possibility of setting the **TYPE** attribute to **FILE**. This form control is used for file uploading. The field generally consists of a text entry box for a filename that can be manipulated with the **SIZE** and **MAXLENGTH** attributes, as well as a button immediately to the right of the field, which is usually labeled "Browse...". Pressing the browse button allows the user to browse the local system to find a file to specify for upload. The logistics of how a file is selected depends on the user agent.

An example of the syntax of the file form control is shown in Figure 11-5. In this example, the **ENCTYPE** value has been set to **multipart/form-data** to allow the file to be attached to the uploaded form. A rendering of the file upload example showing the browsing mechanism is shown in Figure 11-6.

While it is possible to set the **SIZE** and **MAXLENGTH** values of the file entry box, this is not suggested, since the path name may larger than the size specified. (This depends on how the user has set up his or her system.) The file form control is not supported by all browsers. HTML 4.0 also specified the **ACCEPT** attribute for the **<INPUT TYPE="FILE">** element, which can be used specify a comma-separated list of MIME types that the server receiving the contents of the form will know how to handle properly. Browsers could use this attribute to keep users from uploading files to a server which are unacceptable, for example executable files. It is not known if browsers actually pay any attention to this attribute.

Generalized Buttons

One last form of the **<INPUT>** element, hinted at earlier, is the generalized button. By using **<INPUT TYPE="BUTTON">**, it is possible to create a button in the style of the

```
<!DOCTYPE HTML PUBLIC "-//W3C//DTD HTML 4.0 Final//EN">
<HTML>
<HEAD>
<TITLE>File Upload Test</TITLE>
</HEAD>
<BODY>

<H1 ALIGN="CENTER">File Upload System</H1>
<HR>

<FORM ACTION="http://www.bigcompany.com/cgi-bin/uploadfile.pl"
           METHOD=POST ENCTYPE="mutipart/form-data">

<B>File Description:</B><BR>
<INPUT TYPE="TEXT" NAME="Description" SIZE="50" MAXLENGTH="100"><BR>
<B>Specify File to Post:</B><BR>
<INPUT TYPE="FILE" NAME="FileName">

<BR><BR>
<HR>

<DIV ALIGN="CENTER">
<INPUT TYPE="SUBMIT" NAME="Submit" Value="Send it">
</DIV>

</FORM>

</BODY>
</HTML>
```

Figure 11-5.   *File upload example*

submit or reset buttons, but which has no predetermined actions. Inserting something like the following doesn't really do much:

```
<INPUT TYPE="BUTTON" VALUE="Press Me!" NAME="Abutton">
```

If you click the rendering of this button, no action is triggered, and no value will be submitted. So what's the point? By using a scripting language, it is possible to tie an event to the button and create an action. At the end of this chapter, as well as in

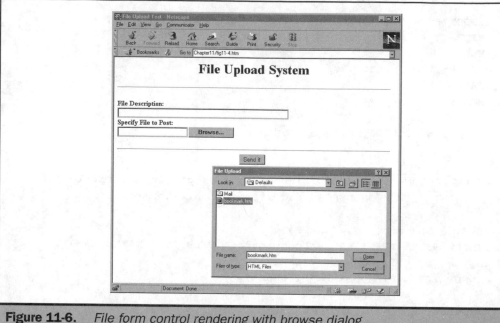

Figure 11-6. *File form control rendering with browse dialog*

Chapter 13, you'll see how forms can be tied to scripting languages to create powerful interactive documents.

New and Emerging Form Elements

At the time of this writing, the W3C has proposed adding several form-related tags and attributes to the next version of HTML. These are intended to address limitations in the current forms and to make them more interactive. Microsoft has already implemented several of these proposed extensions in Internet Explorer 4.0.

<BUTTON> Element

This element provides a way to add generic buttons to forms. The text enclosed by the tag is the button's label. In its simplest usage, the **<BUTTON>** element is functionally equivalent to **<INPUT TYPE="BUTTON">**, which is not supported by the official HTML 3.2 definition. In newer browsers like Internet Explorer 4 that support both button forms, the following two statements render identically.

```
<INPUT TYPE=BUTTON VALUE="Press Me">
<BUTTON>Press Me</BUTTON>
```

The **<BUTTON>** usage is more versatile because its content can include most inline and block-level elements. The following example illustrates a button element containing text, an embedded image, and using a cascading style sheet rule to change the background and text color.

```
<BUTTON Name="HomePage" VALUE="Test Button"
    STYLE="{background-color:blue; color:yellow}">
    <IMG SRC="images/logonotext.gif" WIDTH=141 HEIGHT=197>
    <BR>BigCompany Home Page
</BUTTON>
```

What is interesting about this element is that the browser should render the button in a relief style and even present a pushing effect, just like a submit or reset button, so it is not quite the same as **<INPUT TYPE="IMAGE">**. Another key difference between the image button previously described and the new **<BUTTON>** element is that the new element does not submit any coordinate information, nor is it strictly a submit button. In fact, it is possible to tie this style of button to a general action using the **TYPE** attribute. Allowed values for this attribute are **BUTTON** (default), **SUBMIT**, and **RESET**. The HTML 4.0 documentation suggests that **SUBMIT** is the default value, but this does not make sense, nor is it supported by the browsers that understand the **<BUTTON>** element.

Note *It is incorrect to associate an image map with any image enclosed by a <BUTTON> element.*

While the **<BUTTON>** element seems a more generalized way to deal with images as form buttons, it is not widely supported yet—only by Internet Explorer 4.0. Older browsers may require an alternative approach.

Labels

Another new form element introduced in HTML 4.0 and supported by advanced browsers is the **<LABEL>** element. One motivation for this tag is to better support speech-based browsers that can read descriptions next to form fields. However, a more common use of the **<LABEL>** element is to associate the labeling text of form controls with the actual controls they describe.

The **<LABEL>** element can be associated with a form control by enclosing it as shown here:

```
<LABEL>First Name:
    <INPUT TYPE="TEXT" NAME="FirstName" SIZE="20" MAXLENGTH="30">
</LABEL>
```

A **<LABEL>** element can also be associated with a control by referring to the control's **ID** with the **FOR** attribute. In this usage, the label does not need to enclose the control. This allows labels to be positioned in tables with their own cells. It is common to use tables to make better looking forms. Far too often, form elements snake down a page and are not aligned very well. The following code fragment illustrates how the **<LABEL>** element with the **FOR** attribute would be used.

```
<TABLE>
<TR>
<TD ALIGN="RIGHT">
<LABEL FOR="CustName">Customer Name : </LABEL>
<TD ALIGN="LEFT">
<INPUT TYPE="TEXT" ID="CustName" SIZE="25" MAXLENGTH="35">
</TR>
</TABLE>
```

The **<LABEL>** element also supports the **ID, CLASS, STYLE, TITLE, LANG,** and **DIR** attributes as well as numerous event handlers. These are used in the same way as on any other HTML element. The **DISABLED** and **ACCESSKEY** are also supported attributes for this element and are discussed further in the section on form accessibility enhancements later on in the chapter.

<FIELDSET>

This proposed element groups related form elements analogous to the way the **<DIV>** element groups general body content. Like **<DIV>**, the **<FIELDSET>** element can be nested; it can also have an associated **<LEGEND>** element to describe the enclosed items. The **<FIELDSET>** element itself has no special attributes besides those common to all elements, like **ID, CLASS, LANG, DIR, TITLE, STYLE,** and event handlers. However, the **<LEGEND>** attribute does support the **ALIGN** attribute, which can be set to **TOP** (the default value), **BOTTOM, LEFT,** or **RIGHT,** and is used to specify where the description will be rendered in relation to the group of form items as well as the common attributes to most elements under HTML 4.0, **ID, CLASS, STYLE, TITLE, LANG, DIR,** and the numerous event handlers. See the element reference for more information about these. The example in Figure 11-7 illustrates how the **<FIELDSET>** and **<LEGEND>** elements are used.

The W3C proposal recommends that a **<FIELDSET>** be enclosed by a box. This rendering is supported by Internet Explorer 4.0, as shown by the rendering in Figure 11-8.

```
!DOCTYPE HTML PUBLIC "-//W3C//DTD HTML 4.0 Final//EN">
<HTML>
<HEAD>
<TITLE>Fieldset and Legend Example</TITLE>
</HEAD>

<BODY>
<FORM ACTION="mailto:order@bigcompany.com" METHOD=POST>

<FIELDSET>
   <LEGEND>Customer Identification</LEGEND>
       <BR>
   <LABEL>Customer Name:
   <INPUT TYPE="TEXT" ID="CustName" SIZE="25">
   </LABEL>
           <BR><BR>
   <LABEL>Customer ID:
   <INPUT TYPE="PASSWORD" ID="CustID" SIZE="8" MAXLENGTH="8">
    </LABEL>

       <BR>
</FIELDSET>

</FORM>
</BODY>
</HTML>
```

Figure 11-7.   *<FIELDSET> example*

Form Accessibility Enhancements

One of the most important changes made to forms under HTML 4.0 is the improved
support for accessibility. HTML 4.0 defines the **ACCESSKEY** attribute for the
<LABEL>, **<INPUT>**, **<BUTTON>**, and **<LEGEND>** elements. Setting the value of
the key to a character creates an accelerator key that can activate the form control
associated with the element. Generally, the key must be pressed in combination with
the CONTROL, ALT, or OPTION key in order to activate the field. An example of how this
attribute might be used is shown in the following code example:

```
<LABEL ACCESSKEY="N">Customer <U>N</U>ame:
<INPUT TYPE="TEXT" ID="CustName" SIZE="25">
</LABEL>
```

Notice how the **<U>** element is used to highlight the letter that will activate the field. This is the common practice to indicate accelerator keys in a Windows GUI. According to the HTML 4.0 specification, browsers should provide their own form of highlighting for an access key, but in practice this isn't very common.

The HTML 4.0 standard defines the **ACCESSKEY** attribute for the **<LABEL>**, **<INPUT>**, **<LEGEND>** and **<BUTTON>** elements, though it leaves off support for **<SELECT>** and **<TEXTAREA>**. Microsoft supports this attribute for the **<SELECT>**, and **<TEXTAREA>** elements. It seems likely that this will eventually be rolled into the final HTML 4.0 specification.

While the **ACCESSKEY** attribute can improve a form by making it more keyboard access friendly, there are certain letters to avoid because they map to browser functions in the two major browsers, as shown in Table 11-1.

Another accessibility improvement introduced in HTML 4.0 is the use of the **TABINDEX** attribute for the **<INPUT>**, **<SELECT>**, **<TEXTAREA>**, and **<BUTTON>**

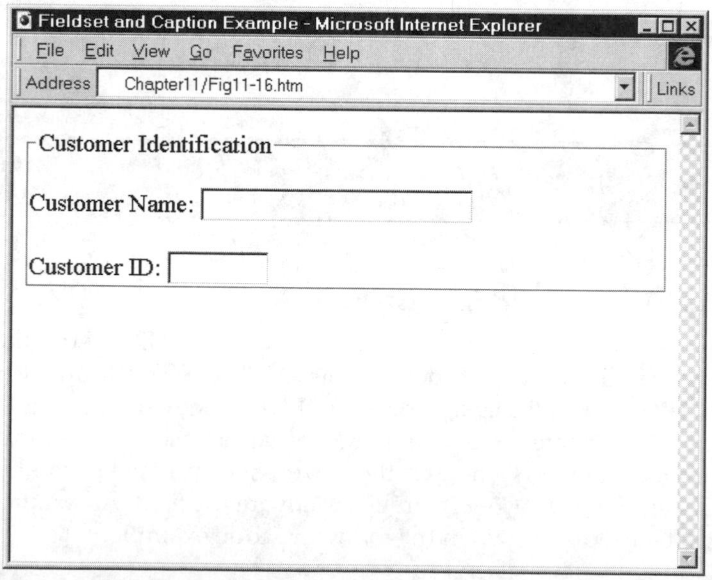

Figure 11-8.   **<FIELDSET>** and **<LEGEND>** rendering under Internet Explorer 4.0

Key	Mapping	Notes
F	File menu	
E	Edit menu	
C	Communicator menu	Netscape Communicator Only
V	View menu	
G	Go menu	
A	Favorites menu	Internet Explorer Only
H	Help	
LEFT ARROW	Back in history	
RIGHT ARROW	Forward in history	

Table 11-1.   *Reserved Browser Key Bindings*

elements. This attribute allows the tab order between fields to be defined. In the Microsoft implementation, elements with **TABINDEX** values greater than zero are selected in increasing order. Generally if a browser supports tabbing through form fields it is by the order in which they are defined. However, with the **TABINDEX** set the tabbing order goes from the lowest positive **TABINDEX** value to the highest. Any elements with a **TABINDEX** of **0** are selected in the order they are encountered after the rest of the tabbing controls have been exhausted. Fields with negative **TABINDEX** values should be left out of the tabbing order. So, in the next fragment, the last field gets selected first, then the first, and then the second field is completely skipped over.

```
<INPUT TYPE="TEXT" NAME="First Name" TABINDEX="2">
<INPUT TYPE="TEXT" NAME="Middle Name" TABINDEX="-1">
<INPUT TYPE="TEXT" NAME="Last Name" TABINDEX="1">
```

Be careful when setting the **TABINDEX** value with radio buttons, as the browser may use arrow keys to move among a group of radio buttons rather than the TAB key.

Page designers are encouraged to set **ACCESSKEY** and **TABINDEX** attributes to their documents immediately as they will have no harmful side-effects in older browsers and will simply be ignored.

Miscellaneous HTML 4.0 Form Attributes

The HTML 4.0 specification also adds two other attributes to certain form controls: **DISABLED** and **READONLY**. When the **DISABLED** attribute is present in a form control element, it turns off the field. Disabled elements will not be submitted nor may they receive any focus from the keyboard or mouse. The browser may also gray out the disabled form. The point of the **DISABLED** attribute might not be obvious, but imagine being able to disable the form submission button until the appropriate fields had been filled in. Of course, being able to dynamically turn the **DISABLED** attribute for a form control on or off implies scripting support that not all browsers have.

When the **READONLY** attribute is present in a form control element, it prevents the control's value from being changed. A form control set to **READONLY** can be selected by the user but cannot be changed. Selection may even include the inclusion of the form control in the tabbing order. Unlike disabled controls, the values of read-only controls are submitted with the form. In some sense, a read-only form control can be thought of as a visible for of **<INPUT TYPE="HIDDEN">**. According to the HTML 4.0 specification the **READONLY** attribute is defined for the **<INPUT TYPE="TEXT">**, **<INPUT TYPE="PASSWORD">** and **<TEXTAREA>** elements but some browser vendors may also support the **<SELECT>** element or even check boxes. Like a disabled form control, read-only controls can only be changed through the use of a script.

Form Presentation

Up to this point, most of the form elements in the HTML 4.0 specification, as well as those supported by the major browsers, have been presented. Some special considerations for the WebTV environment will be considered in a moment. However, let's first turn our attention to making forms more presentable. Unfortunately, on the Web, little attention seems to be paid to making logical or even presentable looking forms. For example, take a look at the form in Figure 11-9. Notice its ragginess: nothing is grouped or lined up.

Form designers are reminded that other HTML markup elements can be used within forms, so there is no excuse in having a poorly laid out form. For example, a form can be vastly improved by using a table as shown in Figure 11-10. The markup for the form using a table in Figure 11-10 is shown here:

```
<!DOCTYPE HTML PUBLIC "-//W3C//DTD HTML 4.0 Final//EN">
<HTML>
<HEAD>
<TITLE>
Table and Form Example</TITLE>
</HEAD>
<BODY>
```

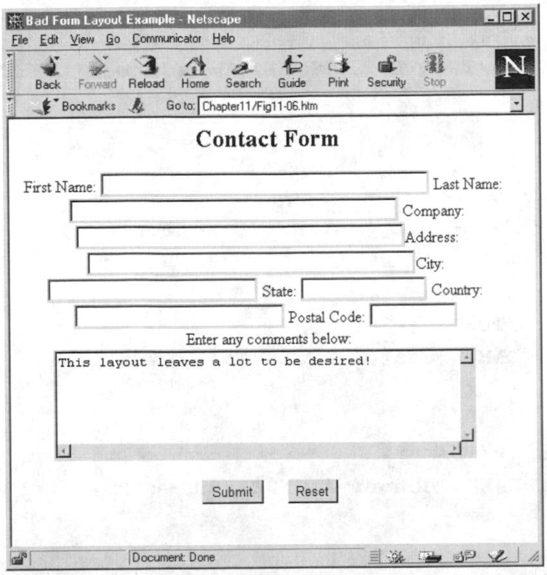

Figure 11-9.   *Example of a poorly laid out form*

```
<DIV ALIGN=CENTER>

<H2>Contact Form</H2>

<FORM ACTION="mailto: info@bigcompany.com" METHOD=POST>
<TABLE BORDER="1">
<TR>
    <TD>First Name:</TD>
    <TD><INPUT NAME="firstname" SIZE="40"></TD>
</TR>
<TR>
    <TD>Last Name:</TD>
    <TD><INPUT NAME="lastname" SIZE="40"></TD>
</TR>
<TR>
    <TD>Company:</TD>
<TD><INPUT NAME="company" SIZE="40"></TD>
</TR>
```

```
<TR>
    <TD>Address:</TD><TD><INPUT NAME="address" SIZE="40"></TD>
</TR>

<TR>
    <TD>City:</TD>
    <TD><INPUT NAME="city" SIZE="25"></TD>
</TR>
<TR>
    <TD>State:</TD>
    <TD><INPUT NAME="state" SIZE="15"></TD>
</TR>
<TR>
    <TD>Country:</TD>
    <TD><INPUT NAME="country" SIZE="25"></TD>
</TR>
<TR>

    <TD>Postal Code:</TD>
    <TD><INPUT NAME="zip" SIZE="10"></TD>
</TR>
<TR>
    <TD COLSPAN="2"><BR>Enter any comments below:<BR>
    <TEXTAREA NAME="text" ROWS="5" COLS="50"></TEXTAREA></TD>
</TR>
<TR>
    <TD COLSPAN="2"><CENTER><BR>
    <INPUT TYPE="submit"
VALUE="Submit">     
    <INPUT TYPE="reset"><BR><BR></CENTER></TD>
</TR>
</TABLE>
</FORM>

</DIV>

</BODY>
</HTML>
```

Besides laying out a table with tables, it might be nice to use the **<FIELDSET>** element to group and box form controls. However, until this element is widely supported it should not be relied on. Tables should be used instead. Coloring the

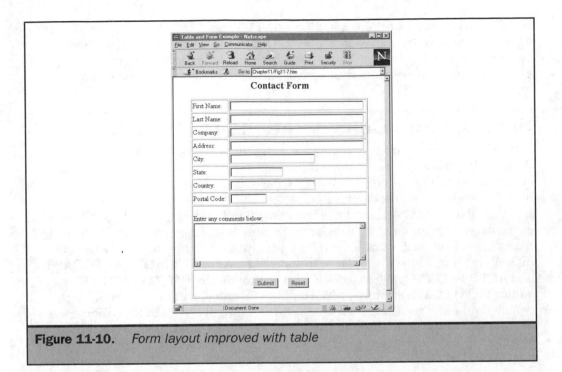

Figure 11-10.   *Form layout improved with table*

different sections of the table with a light background color could help improve the organization of the form as well.

Page authors might wonder if it is possible to improve the look and feel of forms using style sheets. Under the HTML 4.0 specification, both the **<FORM>** element and the form control elements support the **CLASS**, **ID**, and **STYLE** attributes to allow access from style sheets. For backward compatibility, particularly with scripting environments, they also support the **NAME** attribute. One interesting aspect about forms and style sheets is that style rules applied to the **<FORM>** element do not seem to be inherited by controls inside the form. This is contrary to the normal case, in which style specifications are inherited by contained elements. In other words, the text inside **<INPUT>** control in the following example will appear as black, not red, when viewed in a browser.

```
<FORM STYLE="{color:red}">
This text is red
<INPUT TYPE="TEXT" VALUE="but this text is black">
</FORM>
```

In theory, style sheets should be well supported in forms. In practice, support varies widely from browser to browser. Under Internet Explorer 4.0, the **CLASS**, **ID**, and **STYLE** attributes work for **<FORM>**, **<INPUT>** and **<SELECT>**. Under Netscape 4.0, style specifications only work for the **<FORM>** tag. Many of these problems may be bugs or oversights, but until these issues are cleared up page authors should explore the use of style sheets with form elements carefully before using them.

Special Form Considerations for WebTV

The WebTV browser introduces many attributes to form elements specifically designed to enhance TV-based interaction. This section covers some of these actions. For the latest extensions, visit the WebTV developer's site at http://www.webtv.net/primetime.

While the **<FORM>** element itself is not modified under WebTV, the **<INPUT>** element has many proprietary extensions. Because it is difficult to fill in forms using the onscreen keyboard, WebTV provides a variety of attributes that can be used to make form input a little easier. These include **ALLCAPS**, **NUMBERS**, **AUTOCAPS**, and **AUTOACTIVATE**. When using a form control of **<INPUT TYPE="TEXT">**, adding the **ALLCAPS** attribute, which requires no value, will make "caps lock" the default for the onscreen keyboard. On the other hand, the **NUMBERS** attribute sets the onscreen keyboard to start with numbers. Inserting the **AUTOCAPS** attribute in a text input element uppercases the first letter of individual words. Occurrences of **AUTOACTIVATE** inserts into a text field as shown as the user selects it. Because it may be difficult to see the text on screen, you can set the background color (**BGCOLOR**) as well as the cursor color (**CURSOR**) for individual **<INPUT TYPE="TEXT">** elements. WebTV has introduced many other form extensions. The purpose here is only to illustrate that forms may present issues unique to the viewing environment. This makes extensions worthwhile. However, for the future such presentational controls are better suited to style sheet developments. Perhaps "tv" will become a valid media type for style sheets.

Forms and Events

As presented here, forms really don't finish the job. It is easy to create a form that asks a users for their name and the number of gadgets they want to order. It is also easy to write a CGI program (assuming you're a programmer) that can take submitted form data and do something with it. However, it is not easy to make sure that the submitted data is correct. Why should you let the user enter a quantity of –10 (negative ten) gadgets in the form and submit it when that is obviously wrong? Sure, the CGI could catch this, but the best idea is to try to catch this at the browser level before submitting the form for processing. This is one of the main reasons for client-side scripting.

Starting with Netscape 2.0 and continuing until today, it has been possible to use a scripting language like JavaScript to associate scripts with user-generated events in a browser. The way to handle events for a form control is by setting an event handler using an attribute that corresponds to the name of the event. If you want to trigger a script when a button is pressed, you could insert some script code associated with the event attribute as shown in the following dummy form:

```
<FORM>
<INPUT TYPE="BUTTON" VALUE="Don't Press Me!"
       onClick="alert('Danger! Danger!');">
</FORM>
```

Events are added to form controls using attribute declarations such as **onclick**, **onsubmit**, **onreset** and so on. The number of events has grown significantly and now applies to elements outside forms. In fact, under Dynamic HTML the trend is for every displayed HTML element to have events associated with it. Let's look at a short example of how forms may be validated using a small amount of scripting code and follow with an overview of the form related events supported in current HTML dialects. Chapter 12 and 13 will provide more details on scripting in general.

Already you have learned that one possible use of form events is to validate form data before it is sent in. In the following example, a form collects a customer name, a customer identification value, and the quantity of gadgets requested. In this example, all values should be entered and a positive number of gadgets ordered. To perform this check, create a simple validation script that looks at the fields and prompts the user to fix any errors. The validation is triggered by the click of a generalized button. When everything checks out, the browser submits the form.

```
<!DOCTYPE HTML PUBLIC "-//W3C//DTD HTML 4.0 Final//EN">
<HTML>
<HEAD>
<TITLE>Basic Form Validation</TITLE>
<SCRIPT LANGUAGE="JavaScript">
<!--
function validate ()
{
    if (document.forms.order.CustName.value == "") {
        alert("Please enter your name.")
        return;
    }

    if (document.forms.order.CustID.value == "") {
        alert("Please enter your Customer ID.")
        return;
    }
```

```
        if (document.forms.order.Qty.value <= 0) {
            alert("Please enter a positive number of gadgets.")
            return;
        }

        document.forms.order.submit();
        alert ("Your order has been submitted");
}
// -->
</SCRIPT>
</HEAD>
<BODY>
<H1 ALIGN="CENTER">Gadget Order Form</H1>
<HR>
<FORM NAME="order" METHOD="POST"
ACTION="mailto:order@bigcompany.com">
<B>Customer Name: </B>
<INPUT TYPE="TEXT"
  NAME="CustName"
  SIZE="25"
  MAXLENGTH="35">
<BR><BR>

<B>Customer ID:</B>
<INPUT TYPE="PASSWORD"
  NAME="CustID"
  SIZE="8"
  MAXLENGTH="9">

<BR><BR>
<B>Quantity of Gadgets:</B>
<INPUT TYPE="TEXT"
  NAME="Qty"
  SIZE="2"
  MAXLENGTH="2">

<HR>
<INPUT TYPE="BUTTON"
  VALUE="Order"
  onclick="validate()">
```

```
<INPUT TYPE="RESET" VALUE="Reset">

</FORM>

</BODY>
</HTML>
```

There are a few things to point out in this example. First, the form has been assigned a name. Giving the form a name allows the form to be referred to by name in the validation script. Another thing to notice is the use of the **onclick** event attribute. This connects an event the button can respond to with a script to handle the event.

```
<INPUT TYPE="BUTTON" VALUE="Order" onclick="validate()">
```

The value for the **onclick** attribute is the name of the JavaScript function, defined elsewhere, that validates the form. The validation function is declared in the document head inside the **<SCRIPT>** element. Don't worry if the scripting issues, particularly the events, don't make complete sense. They will be covered in great detail in Chapter 13.

Summary

HTML forms provide a basic interface for adding interactivity to a Web site. HTML supports traditional graphical user interface controls like check boxes, radio buttons, pull-down menus, scrolled lists, multi- and single-line text areas, and buttons. These controls can be used to build a form that can be submitted via e-mail to a server-side program for processing. While making a rudimentary form isn't terribly difficult, laying out the form is often overlooked. Using tables and improved grouping elements like **<LABEL>**, **<FIELDSET>**, and **<LEGEND>** can improve a form dramatically. Other features new to HTML 4.0, such as accelerator keys and tabbing order specification, can also improve how a form may be used. Yet even if a nice form can be developed, it is missing the spark that makes it go. The logic of the form needs to be added either by a server-side program, or through a client-side technology like JavaScript. Until then, forms only provide a simple way to collect information.

Chapter 12

Introduction to Programmed Web Pages

The last chapter hinted at the move from static Web pages to a more dynamic paradigm. The Web is undergoing a shift from a page-oriented view of the world to a more program-oriented view. Although there is increased focus on the programmed elements of a Web page, this doesn't mean that HTML is going away any time soon. Knowing how to author well-formed HTML documents may become more important than ever with the rise of Dynamic HTML. Yet, even before the rise of client-side technologies, HTML has intersected with programming ideas. Server-side computing on the Web has often had an HTML flavor to it, particularly when server-side includes and parsed HTML solutions like Microsoft's Active Server Pages (ASP) or Allaire's Cold Fusion are involved. These technologies blur the lines between HTML and programming because they appear in the form of special markup tags that include information or perform programming tasks. These topics may not seem to be part of HTML and are not official in the standards sense, but they do illustrate how programming and HTML interact (see Chapter 13).

This chapter will examine the general concept of the programmed Web site, and some of the technologies that can be used on the server side to add interactivity to Web pages. The next two chapters will continue the discussion, but with a focus on client-side scripting technologies and object technologies, respectively.

Overview of Client/Server Programming on the Web

When it comes right down to it, the Web is just a form of client/server interaction. Web browsers make requests of Web servers to do some processing, or to return a file that is sent back and displayed in the browser. The basic idea of this is shown in Figure 12-1.

In this basic printed page idea of the Web, a Web server acts as a file server that delivers HTML files to a Web browser. As shown in the last chapter, thinking about the Web as a digital paper medium is somewhat limiting and does not take advantage of the potential of interactivity.

The most basic form of interactivity on the Web, beyond link selection, is using fill-out forms that are handled by programs, typically Common Gateway Interface (CGI) applications, running on a Web server. The way a user interacts with a CGI-based Web site is easy to describe. First, the user requests a dynamic page or fills out a form to perform a task like ordering a product. The request is sent to the Web server, which runs the CGI program, which then outputs information to return to the Web browser as shown in Figure 12-2.

In the last sense, the Web can be used to run programs on a remote server, which then returns a result. When described this way, the Web begins to look more and more like a client/server application environment.

The last diagram suggests a question: where should the computing happen? And with what technology? On the early Web, the browser tended to do very little computing. It was solely responsible for rendering pages on the screen. Now, with the

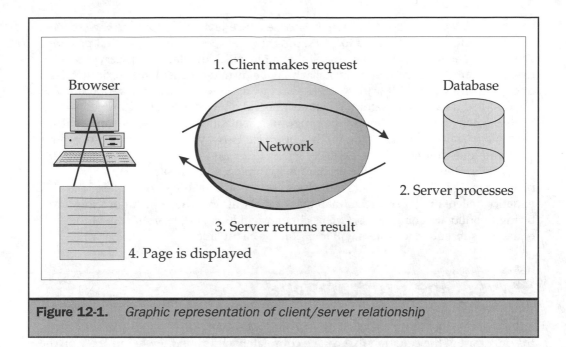

Figure 12-1.   *Graphic representation of client/server relationship*

rise of client-side technologies like Java, ActiveX, and JavaScript, it is possible to perform a great deal of computation from within the browser. Put all the pressure on the server, and it might bog down, or the user might get frustrated with poor responsiveness. Doing most of the computing on the client might cause problems with compatibility, since it's difficult to know what kind of clients are out there. Security may also be a problem. The best solution is a mixture: some things are better suited for the client; some are better suited for the server.

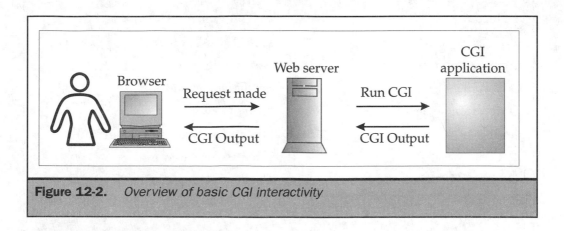

Figure 12-2.   *Overview of basic CGI interactivity*

As discussed in Chapter 11, it makes sense to use JavaScript to check the contents of a form before it is submitted to a CGI program, rather than have the CGI program check the data. However, you would still want to check the data at the server side for users who are running older clients or who have turned off client-side scripting. And, of course, you would still want to check whether a malicious user has deliberately sent the CGI bad data. A developer who wants to build a Web-based application must choose where to host the logic of the program (client side or server side) and which technology should be used to do it. The choice isn't always obvious, as illustrated by the numerous choices in Table 12-1.

What's interesting about the numerous technologies available for Web programming is that developers often focus solely on one tool or one side of the equation (client or server) rather than thinking about how the applications they are trying to build are going to work. This chapter will look at the server side of the equation; subsequent chapters will focus on the client side.

Server-Side Programming

When adding interactivity to a Web page, it often makes sense to add all functionality on the server side. There are two basic reasons for doing this. First, the server side is the only part of the equation that can be completely controlled. If we only rely on the browser to render HTML pages, life is simple. If we assume users have JavaScript, Java, or a particular plug-in, things become less predictable. Why is this, given that most modern browsers come with many of these technologies? There are too many variables and too many bugs. Users often turn off support for Java, JavaScript, or ActiveX due to fear of security breaches. Even when turned on, these technologies are

Client Side	Server Side
Helpers	CGI programs
Plug-ins	NSAPI/ISAPI programs
Active-X controls	Server-side scripting
Java applets	Server-side include
Scripting languages	Active Server pages
JavaScript	Server-side JavaScript (LiveWire)
VBScript	Database middleware
Dynamic HTML	Cold Fusion

Table 12-1. *Web Programming Technology Choices*

often far from robust. For example, JavaScript comes in two basic flavors (Microsoft and Netscape) and has three versions running on at least four major operating systems (Mac; Windows 3.1, 95/NT; and Unix). Each of these implementations has some subtle differences. These "differences" include lack of features and crashes. It is no wonder we would want to move computation to the server, where these issues are more controllable.

The second reason that server-side computation makes sense is that this is where much of the data that is required actually "lives." Consider a database. A common requirement of the Web is to act as a front-end to access a database. Imagine a Web site where the user wants to query a system to see if a particular product is available. A form could be developed for the user to submit the query. The contents of the form could be passed to a program on a Web server, which would parse the form data and form a database query. Such a program is called *middleware*, since it will sit between the back-end database server and the client-accessible Web server. A CGI program could be thought of as middleware, but there are other approaches. After the database completes the query, the result is passed back to the middleware, which formats the result as an HTML page and passes the result back to the browser. The Web server acts as the coordinator for this whole process, including interacting with and possibly even starting the middleware. The previous discussion is illustrated in Figure 12-3.

One potential downside to adding interactivity via server-side programs should be mentioned: too much reliance on the server. In the last examples, the browser was relatively simple in the sense that the computation took place almost entirely on the server side. The client browser was only responsible for rendering the entry form and the resulting pages. Choosing the appropriate approach to deal with a problem like database access is beyond the scope of this book, but remember that there can be disadvantages to putting all the computing responsibility on the server, namely, speed and scalability. For now, the discussion turns to the approaches to server-based interactivity and how it intersects with HTML.

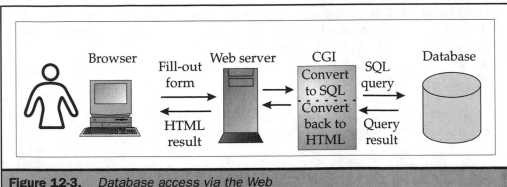

Figure 12-3. *Database access via the Web*

Common Gateway Interface (CGI)

Probably the most common way to add interactivity to a Web page is through a CGI program. Common Gateway Interface (CGI) is a protocol standard that specifies how information can be passed from a Web page via a Web server, to a program, and back from the program to a browser in the proper format. Many people confuse the program that does something for the idea of CGI. In reality, the program is just a program. It just happens to be a CGI program since it was written to pass information back and forth using the CGI specification.

How CGI interacts with a form is summarized by the following steps:

1. The user submits a form.

2. The form is sent to the server and eventually to the CGI program.

3. The CGI program processes the data and responds back to the server.

4. The Web server passes the CGI response back to the client.

Step 2 can be expanded to the following steps:

2.1. The server determines if the request is a document or program request by examining execution settings and path.

2.2. The server locates the program (in the cgi-bin directory on the server or elsewhere) and determines if the program can be executed.

2.3. The server starts the program and prepares the data to be sent to the program from the form fields and any extra information from the environment.

2.4. The program runs.

2.5. The server waits for the program to produce output (optional) and then passes back the properly formatted result to the client or, potentially, an error message.

 Server launching of the program (Step 2.3) is operating system–dependent and may require starting a new process.

It is possible to create anything, including games, with CGI, but complex tasks are often limited by the state problem. The common uses of CGI include

Form processing
Database access
Counters
Custom document generation

Browser-specific page delivery
Server push animation
Guest book and authentication
Threaded discussion
Games

Understanding how CGI works requires an understanding of how the HTTP protocol works. The only magic of CGI is understanding how to read data in and write data out to talk to a Web browser. Writing out data is the easiest. The key to writing out data for Web browsers is understanding the headers so the browser knows what it is getting, namely, MIME types. (MIME stands for Multipurpose Internet Mail Extensions. The MIME content type of a file tells a browser how to process it.).

The following example shows one way of "talking" to a Web browser.

To access a Web server directly, you can use a telnet program and literally "log in" to the TCP service port for HTTP. To do this, use a telnet program to access a Web server and set the port number to 80. Under Unix, you might type

```
telnet www.bigcompany.com 80
```

This could also be performed via telnet, which is built in to Windows 95/NT. Just make sure to set the port value to 80.

Once connected to the Web server, type in the proper HTTP request. A simple request would be

```
GET / HTTP/1.0
```

Then press RETURN twice to send a blank line. Without this blank line, things won't work.

Once the server processes the request, the result should be something like what is shown here:

```
HTTP/1.0 200 OK
Date:     Monday, 01-January-99 09:00:00 GMT
Server:   NCSA/1.3.1
MIME-version: 1.0
Content-type: text/html
Content-length: 1200

<HTML>
<HEAD>
<TITLE>Sample HTML Document</TITLE>
```

```
</HEAD>
<BODY>

. . . content. . .

</BODY>
```

If a Web browser were reading this data stream, it would read the Content-type line. The browser would then determine what to do with the data. Browsers have a mapping that takes a MIME type and then determines what to do with it. Figure 12-4 shows the mapping file from Netscape Navigator 3.0's helper application.

Notice in the preceding code how the type text/html has an action of browser, which would render the HTML within the browser window. Remember that Web servers can serve just about any type of data and pass that data to a plug-in or helper, or query the user to save the file.

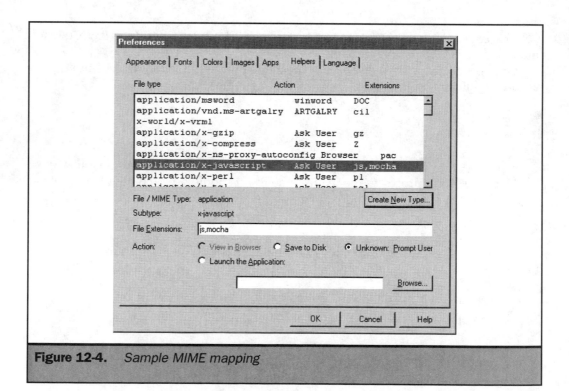

Figure 12-4.   Sample MIME mapping

CGI Output

Now, given that you have seen the manual execution of an HTTP request, what is important to the Web browser? The simple answer is the MIME type and its associated data. In most cases, the pages being delivered are HTML based, so the MIME type should be text/html and any HTML you want on your screen. With this idea in mind, it should be easy to write a CGI program that fakes an HTML page. To do this you need to print things out, most importantly, the MIME type indication "Content-type: text/html" followed by a series of HTML codes. The following small Perl program shows how this might be done. Any language including C, Pascal, or BASIC, could also be used to make such an example.

```perl
#!/usr/bin/perl# Note the path to perl may vary.
# Really simple CGI program
#
print "Content-type: text/html\n\n"

print "<HTML>\n<HEAD><TITLE>First CGI</TITLE></HEAD>\n"

print "<BODY>\n<H1>I was created by a CGI
program!</H1>\n</BODY>\n</HTML>"
```

If this example were typed and set to run on a Perl-capable Web server, it could be accessed directly by a user to print out the simple page shown in Figure 12-5. To see the program in action, try the URL http://www.htmlref.com/cgi-bin/firstcgi.pl.

In summary: to create a document on the fly, you have to print a group of headers. Make sure to do this in the correct format. Otherwise, the rest of the program is up to you. This only covers getting information from the server, which is only one half of the CGI equation. How do you get information to your program?

Passing Information to a CGI Program: Environment Variables

In order to get information into a CGI program, you generally need to use a form. The CGI program itself can actually read some information from the HTTP request and the local environment. This information can be used in conjunction with form data to understand the environment the program is running. Environment variables are actually very valuable. They can be used to help the CGI program decide what kind of pages to prepare. A list of most of the common CGI environment variables is provided in Table 12-2.

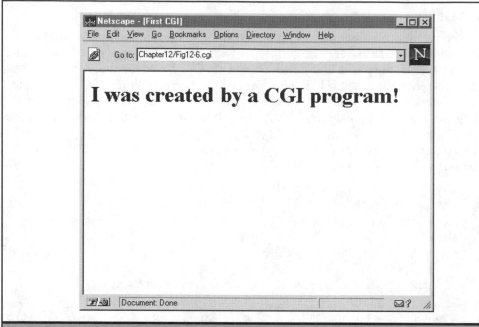

Figure 12-5. *Output of simple CGI program*

Variable Name	Description
GATEWAY_INTERFACE	The version number of CGI supported by the server; for example, CGI/1.1.
SERVER_NAME	The domain name or IP address of the Web server running the CGI program.
SERVER_SOFTWARE	Information about the Web server, typically the name and version number of the software; for example, Netscape-Commerce/1.12.
SERVER_PROTOCOL	The version number of the HTTP protocol being used in the request; for example, HTTP/1.1.
SERVER_PORT	The port on which the Web server is running, typically 80.

Table 12-2. *Common CGI Variables*

Variable Name	Description
REQUEST_METHOD	The method by which the information is being passed, in either GET or POST.
CONTENT_TYPE	For queries that have attached information because they use the POST or PUT method; contains the content type in MIME format of the passed data.
CONTENT_LENGTH	The length of any passed content (POST or PUT) as given by the client, typically as length in bytes.
PATH_INFO	Any extra path information passed in with the file request. This would usually be associated with the GET request.
SCRIPT_NAME	The relative path to the script that is running
QUERY_STRING	Query information passed to the program.
DOCUMENT_ROOT	The document root of the Web server
REMOTE_USER	If the server supports user authentication and the script is protected, this variable holds the user name that the user has authenticated.
AUTH_TYPE	This variable is set to the authentication method used to validate the user if the script being run is protected.
REMOTE_IDENT	If the Web server supports RFC 931–based identification, then this variable will be set to the remote user name retrieved from the server. This is rarely used.
REMOTE_HOST	The remote host name (for example, sun1.bigcompany.com) of the browser passing information to the server.
REMOTE_ADDR	The IP address of the browser making the request.
HTTP_ACCEPT	A list of MIME types the browser can accept.
HTTP_USER_AGENT	A code indicating the type of browser making the request.
HTTP_REFERER	The URL of the document that linked to the CGI being run, in other words the linking document. If the user typed in the address of the program directly, the HTTP_REFERER value will be unset.

Table 12-2.   *Common CGI Variables* (continued)

Figure 12-6 shows the results of a CGI program that prints out the environment information. Try to execute the program at http://www.htmlref.com/cgi-bin/printenv.cgi to see if the results are different.

Depending on the Web server and browser, there may be other useful environment variables. These include **HTTPS**, which is used to indicate if Secure Sockets Layer (SSL) security is on; **HTTP_CONNECTION**, which is used to indicate to keep a connection open for improved performance; and **HTTP_ACCEPT_LANGUAGE**, which is used to indicate what language the server accepts data in. There are other potential values available, so be certain to check the Web server programming documentation.

The Perl code for the result shown in Figure 12-6 is shown next. Notice how the code is written to make printing the appropriate headers, start of the HTML file, results, and close of the file more straightforward. Code libraries to do much of the work of CGI are commonly available.

```perl
#!/usr/bin/perl

&print_HTTP_header;
&print_head;
&print_body;
&print_tail;

# print the HTTP Content-type header

sub print_HTTP_header {
    print "Content-type: text/html\n\n";
}

#Print the start of the HTML file

sub print_head {
    print <<END;
<HTML>
<HEAD>
<TITLE>CGI Environment Variables</TITLE>
</HEAD>
<BODY>
<H1 ALIGN=CENTER>Environment Variables</H1>
<HR>
END
}

#Loop through the environment variable
```

```
#associative array and print out its values.

sub print_body {
    foreach $variable (sort keys %ENV) {
        print "<B>$variable:</B> $ENV{$variable}<BR>\n";
    }


}

#Print the close of the HTML file

sub print_tail {
        print <<END;
</BODY>
</HTML>
END
}
```

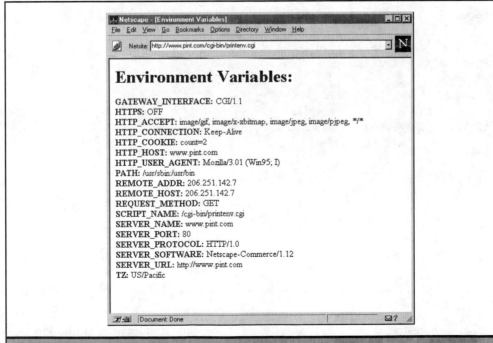

Figure 12-6.   *CGI environment variables example*

Browser Sensing with CGI

At first glance, the environment variables might not seem very useful. When used properly, however, they are indispensable. One of the most important uses of CGI is to sense the browser being used so that customized pages can be delivered for different browser types. Using a small program, it would be possible to sense a user's browser type and redirect him or her automatically to another page.

> **Note** *The server may have to be configured to run the CGI program automatically to make browser sensing work. This may just mean putting a file called index.cgi in the root directory, or some similar renaming.*

Here is how browser sensing works. The CGI environment variable **HTTP_USER_AGENT** is read in by the CGI program using a simple call available from a Perl CGI library. Once the value is set, a set of conditions determines which page to send, depending on the browser accessing the page. In the following example,, the file netscapehome.htm is sent if the browser is Netscape 3 or better. If the browser is Microsoft Internet Explorer 3 or better, the file mshome.htm is sent. Otherwise, the file home.htm is sent.

```perl
#!/usr/local/bin/perl

require '/usr/local/ns-home/cgi-bin/cgi-lib.pl';

# pulls in special library for easy reading of
# environment variables
&ReadParse;
$agent = $ENV{'HTTP_USER_AGENT'};

if ($agent =~ /Mozilla\/3.0|Mozilla\/4.0/i) {
    $file = "netscapehome.htm";
}
if ($agent =~ /MSIE 3.0|MSIE 4.0/i) {
    $file = "mshome.htm";
}

else {
    $file = "home.htm";
}
print "Location: http://www.bigcompany.com/$file", "\n\n";
```

What's interesting is that this file was used to sort out what form of animation could be used. The people who received the mshome.htm file could read Macromedia

Flash files. The Netscape 3.0 and 4.0 users could use JavaScript roll-over animations, and everyone who could do neither just received a static page. When a site is done well, there isn't an entrance page that says, "Click here for Netscape" and "Click here for other browsers." Things just work. Of course, one huge problem with this idea is having to keep different files for the same page. Parsed HTML, as discussed later in the chapter, may offer a better solution to browser-aware pages.

Passing Information to a CGI Program: Form Data

Forms are a good way to collect user input such as a survey result or a comment. They can also start database queries or launch programs. Creating HTML forms was discussed in Chapter 11. For a quick refresher on how HTML forms are used, take a look at the following example:

```
<!DOCTYPE HTML PUBLIC "-//W3C//DTD HTML 4.0 Final//EN">
<HTML>
<HEAD>
<TITLE>Meet and Greet</TITLE>
</HEAD>
<BODY>
<H1 ALIGN="CENTER">Welcome to CGI!</H1>
<HR>
<FORM METHOD="POST"
ACTION="http://www.pint.com/cgi-bin/helloworld.pl">

<B>What's your name?</B>
<INPUT TYPE="TEXT" NAME="user_name" SIZE="25">
<BR><BR>
<INPUT TYPE="SUBMIT" VALUE="Hi I am... ">
<INPUT TYPE="RESET" VALUE="RESET">

</FORM>
</BODY>
</HTML>
```

If this example is typed and run, it will greet the user by whatever name he or she types in. The **<FORM>** element is the key to this example, as it has an action to perform (as indicated by the **ACTION** attribute when the form is submitted). The action is to launch a CGI program indicated by the URL value of the **ACTION** attribute. The **<FORM>** element also has an attribute, **METHOD**, which indicates how information will be passed to the receiving CGI program. There are two basic methods to pass in data via a form: **GET** and **POST**. **GET** appends information on the end of the submitting URL, so the URL accessed in the previous example might be something like

```
http://www.pint.com/cgi-bin/hello.pl?user_name=Joe+Smith
```

The data sent will be encoded. Long strings may have **+** or **%***nn* hex-encoded values. Name/value pairs will be separated by ampersands. (The format of URL-encoded data was discussed in Chapter 11.) The problem with the **GET** method is that, besides being ugly, it is limited to the amount of data that can be easily sent in. **GET** does have two advantages: it is easy to understand, and provides the possibility for canned queries. The more common approach for larger forms is to use the **POST** method, which sends the form data as a separate data stream—in other words, a file—to the server. The data stream (essentially a file) consists of many lines such as **name=Joe%20Smith**. These lines can be parsed by the receiving program. Given how data is encoded, a skilled programmer could easily determine how to parse data and access the values. The following simple helloworld.pl example shows how this might be done in a brute force manner that does no error checking:

```perl
#! /usr/bin/perl

# Print the HTTP headers

print "Content-type: text/html\n";
print "\n";

read (STDIN, $GN_QUERY, $ENV{CONTENT_LENGTH});

# This statement will split data into different fields

@QUERY_LIST = split( /&/, $GN_QUERY);

foreach $item (@QUERY_LIST) {

    # First convert plus signs into spaces

    $item =~ s/\+/ /g;

    # Now convert $nn encoded data to characters

    $item =~ s/%(..)/pack("c",hex($1))/ge;
```

```
    # Now put the result into the QueryArray

    $loc=index($item,"=");
    $param=substr($item, 0, $loc);
    $value=substr($item, $loc+1);
    $QUERY_ARRAY{$param} .= $value;
}

# Now get the users name

$name = "$QUERY_ARRAY{user_name}";

# Print Return HTML
print "<HTML><HEAD><TITLE>Hello</TITLE></HEAD>\n<BODY>\n";
print "<H1>Hello $name. Welcome to CGI!</H1>\n";
print "</BODY></HTML>";
```

Writing CGI Programs

The previous examples might seem to suggest that writing CGI programs is trivial. This is true if data is only to be read in and written out. In fact, this part of CGI is so mechanical that page designers are encouraged not to attempt to parse the data themselves. There are many scripting libraries available for Perl. These include cgic (www.boutell.com/cgic/) for ANSI programs, libcgi++ (www.ncsa.uiuc.edu/People/daman/cgi++/) for C++, and CGI.pm (www-genome.wi.mit.edu/ftp/pub/software/WWW/cgi_docs.html) for Perl 5. These libraries, and others available on the Internet, make the reading of environment variables and parsing of encoded form data a simple process.

The difficult part of CGI isn't the input and output of data. It is logic of the code itself. Given that the CGI program can be written in nearly any language, Web programmers might wonder what language to use. Performance, Web suitability, and string handling are important criteria for selecting a language for CGI authoring. Performance-wise, compiled CGI programs typically will have better performance than interpreted programs written in a scripting language like Perl. However, it is probably easier to write a simple CGI in a scripting language like Perl or AppleScript than using C or C++.

Some programming languages may have better interfaces to Web servers and HTTP than others may. For example, Perl has a great number of CGI libraries and operating system facilities readily available. Because much of CGI is about reading and writing text data, ease of string handling may be a big consideration in selecting the language. The bottom line is that scripting language choice mainly depends on the server the script must run on, and the programmer's preference. It is even possible to use an old version of FORTRAN or some obscure language to write a CGI program. It would be easier to pick a language that works well with the Web server and use it to access some other program. CGI lives up to its name as a gateway.

Table 12-3 lists the common languages for CGI coding based on the Web server's operating system. Notice that Perl is common to most of the platforms due to its ease of use and long use on the Web.

Don't rush around and get ready to code your own form handlers. Consider how many other people in the world need to access a database or e-mail a form. Given these common needs, it may be better to borrow or buy a canned CGI solution than build a new one.

Buying or Borrowing CGI Programs

Most CGI programs are similar to one another. There is a great deal of shareware, freeware, or commercial packages available to do most of the common Web tasks. Matt's Script Archive (www.worldwidemart.com/scripts) is a good place to start looking for these. There are many scripts for form parsing, bulletin boards, counters, and countless other things available free on the Internet. There are also commercial programs, such as O'Reilly's Polyform (software.ora.com), that are compiled CGI programs made to perform a particular task. Site developers are urged to consider the cost of developing custom solutions versus buying a premade solution, particularly when time is an important consideration in building the site.

NSAPI/ISAPI

One serious problem with CGI programs is that they can be slow. There are two reasons for this. The first reason is that the launch of the CGI program by the Web server can be slow. Second, once launched, the program may run relatively slow because it is written in an interpreted language like Perl. Solving the second problem is easy: simply rewrite the program in a compiled language like C. Performance should quickly improve. What about the launch problem? One approach would be to

Web Server Operating System	Common CGI Languages
Unix	Perl, C, C++, Java, Shell script languages (csh, ksh, sh), Python
Windows	Visual Basic, C, C++, Perl
Macintosh	AppleScript, Perl, C, C++

Table 12-3.   *Common CGI Language Choices*

prelaunch the CGI program and have it running all the time. While this would help, the server still must communicate with an external program. This may be time consuming. If speed is of the essence, migrating the functionality of the CGI program into the server is required. This is the idea behind Netscape Server Application Programming Interface (NSAPI), and the Internet Server Application Programming Interface (ISAPI). Refer to Figure 12-3 for a refresher on the migration of middleware toward the server.

In short, NSAPI and ISAPI programs are like plug-ins for a server. A program, typically written in C or C++, that conforms to the NSAPI/ISAPI can be plugged into the server to add functionality to the system. Obviously, writing such a solution is much more difficult than writing a simple CGI program. There are other drawbacks as well. For example, a misbehaving server ISAPI/NSAPI program may bring a whole server down. Developers who write an Application Programming Interface (API)–based solution may also be stuck using a particular server platform, while CGI programs are generally portable from server to server. Regardless of their drawbacks, NSAPI/ISAPI programs have the advantage of speed and the ability to share data across sessions and users very easily. With this power, many third-party developers have created server extensions to allow fast and easy database access, threaded discussion capability, and many other features. While most developers are about as likely to use NSAPI or ISAPI programs as they are to write browser plug-ins, the technology has enabled the creation of server-side parsing technology, which is useful to almost every Web page developer.

Parsed HTML Solutions: Server-Side Scripting

CGI and NSAPI/ISAPI programs are often beyond the technical understanding of Web page developers. However, adding interactivity to a site does not always have to be difficult. Another form of server-based programming, generically termed *parsed HTML*, provides much of the sophistication of general CGI with the ease of HTML. The idea of parsed HTML is simple. First, code a page using standard HTML. Then add special new elements or directives to indicate what to do in particular cases. Imagine if you wanted to print out different HTML headings for Netscape users, Microsoft Internet Explorer, and other browser users. For illustration, using parsed HTML, you might put statements in a parsed HTML language like this in your file:

```
$if browser = Netscape
     <H1><BLINK>Hey Netscape User!</BLINK></H1>
$else if browser = IE
      <MARQUEE>Hey Microsoft User!</MARQUEE>
$else
      <H1>Hey User!</H1>
$endif
```

To indicate that the file is a special parsed HTML file, end its name with the extension .phtml. Next, configure the server to parse and execute the special statements you have added to the file. In this case, the server will then output only the HTML, depending on the particular browser being used. The general idea of parsed HTML solutions is shown in Figure 12-7.

While parsed HTML solutions are very easy for people to deal with, they can put an excessive load on the server. Use them wisely. The next few sections describe three common parsed HTML technologies used on the Web: server-side includes (SSI), Cold Fusion, and ASP.

Server-Side Includes (SSI)

Server-side includes are the simplest form of parsed HTML. The idea of SSI is to embed short directives in an HTML document indicating files to be read and included in the final output. This might be useful if the designer wanted to make one file with footer information like address and copyright and then append it to all pages dynamically. To do this, create a file called footer.htm and then include it dynamically using SSI.

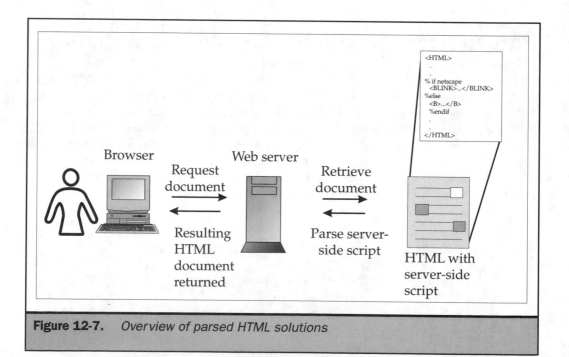

Figure 12-7.   *Overview of parsed HTML solutions*

The contents of footer.htm might look something like this:

```
<HR NOSHADE>
 <CENTER>
 <FONT SIZE="-1">
Copyright 1997 Big Company<BR>
   2105 Garnet Ave, Suite E, San Diego, CA 92109
 </FONT>
```

To include this file in another file, you would have to include an SSI directive like

```
<!--#include file="footer.htm" -->
```

Notice that this is just a special form of an HTML comment with a command **#include** and a parameter file, which is set to the file you want to include. To indicate to the server that the page contains SSI commands, use the .shtml extension. If the server is properly configured, it should pick up the file and execute it before sending the result. Besides including external files, SSI can also be used to show the results of programs, including CGI programs. In this sense, it can provide a way to query databases, make a page counter, and many other things. The simple example that follows shows how the echo SSI command can be used to access the environment variables that CGI programs have access to.

```
<HTML>
<HEAD>
<BODY>
<H2 ALIGN="CENTER">Welcome <!--#echo var="REMOTE_HOST" -->
to my server <!--#echo var="SERVER_NAME" --></H2>
<HR>
You are using <!--#echo var="HTTP_USER_AGENT" -->.
</BODY>
</HTML>
```

One possible result of this example is shown in Figure 12-8. Remember that your result will be different since the page is dynamically generated.

The environment variables that are accessible from SSI are similar to those that can be accessed by any CGI program. They also include the variables listed in Table 12-4.

Besides inserting CGI environment variable values, it is also possible to use SSI to embed the results of a CGI program into an HTML document by using the EXEC CGI command. For example, it would be possible to add a simple page counter to an HTML document by using an SSI command to execute the counter program and display its results in the page. Assuming there were a program called counter.cgi in the cgi-bin directory on the server, you could use a simple SSI statement like the following to add the page count:

```
<!--#exec cgi="cgi-bin/counter.cgi"-->
```

In general, SSI consists of a special comment form that indicates the SSI command, as well as any parameters to modify the command in the general format, as follows:

```
<!-- #command parameter=value -->
```

Table 12-5 lists some of the common SSI commands and their associated parameters.

Depending on the server, there may be more SSI statements, including **ODBC** and **EMAIL**, which are used to access a database and send e-mail respectively. The commands listed in Table 12-5 are the ones most common across most SSI capable servers.

While SSI looks appealing, it has two potential problems: security and performance. The security problem of SSI is mainly due to the EXEC command, which can be used to execute a program on the server. With this command, there is a possibility for a security breach. For example, it might be possible to insert a command to launch a

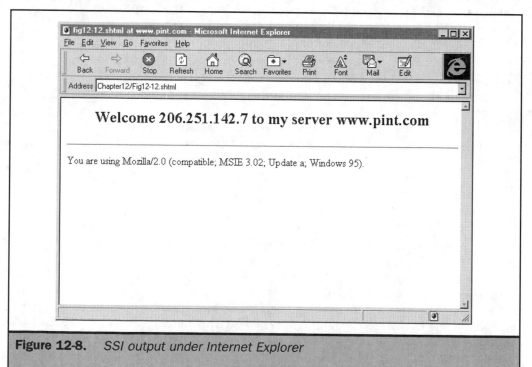

Figure 12-8.   *SSI output under Internet Explorer*

Variable Name	Description
DATE_GMT	This value references the current server local date, same as DATE_LOCAL, but in Greenwich mean time. This variable is subject to formatting from the CONFIG SSI command.
DATE_LOCAL	The current date, local time zone. Subject to formatting from the CONFIG SSI command.
DOCUMENT_NAME	The variable holds the current filename.
DOCUMENT_URI	The variable contains the virtual path to the current document, for example, /about/bigcompany/contact.shtml.
LAST_MODIFIED	The last modification date of the current document. This variable is subject to the date formatting set by the CONFIG SSI command.
QUERY_STRING_UNESCAPED	This variable contains the "unescaped" version of any search query (GET) sent by the browser. Any special characters are escaped using the \ character.

Table 12-4.   *SSI-Available Variables Potentially Outside the CGI Set*

remote session. Even if security isn't a big issue, depending on how SSI and the Web server are configured the executing command may have a great deal of permissions and be able to remove values. Web administrators are advised to limit use of this SSI command.

The other problem with SSI, performance, is not unique to this technology. Because all SSI files have to be parsed, they may cause a performance hit. This is typical with

Command	Parameters	Description	Example
ECHO	VAR	Used to insert the values of special SSI variables and environment variables into the page.	<!--#ECHO VAR="REMOTE_HOST"-->

Table 12-5.   *SSI Command Summary*

Command	Parameters	Description	Example
INCLUDE	FILE VIRTUAL	Used to insert the contents of a document into the current file. This pathname of the file can be either relative or virtual. Relative files paths are relative to the current directory, while virtual file names may access other directories using the ../ directory style or an absolute path.	`<!--#INCLUDE FILE="footer.htm" -->` `<!--#INCLUDE VIRTUAL="../templates/ footer.htm" -->`
FSIZE	FILE	Inserts the size of a given file.	`<!--#FSIZE FILE="index.htm"-->`
FLASTMOD	FILE	Inserts the last modification date of a given file.	`<!--#FLASTMOD FILE="index.htm"-->`
EXEC	CMD CGI	Allows you to execute external programs, either an application on the host or a CGI program.	`<!--#EXEC CMD="/usr/bin/ls"-->` `<!--#EXEC CGIi="cgi-bin/counter.cgi "-->`

CONFIG	ERRMSG=
	string
	SIZEFMT=
	bytes | abbrev
	TIMEFMT=
	format string
		Allows you to configure SSI output options for error output, file size output, and data output. The value for the ERRMSG is simply a string value for the error message. The SIZEFMT may be set to bytes or abbrev, while the TIMEFMT can be set to a Unix date format string in the form compatible with the strftime library.	`<!--#config errmsg="[SSI Statement Failed!]"-->`
			`<!--#CONFIG SIZEFMT="bytes"-->`
			`<!--#CONFIG TIMEFM="%A %b %d %j"-->`

Table 12-5. *SSI Command Summary (continued)*

any parsed HTML solution. If a site has serious performance requirements, parsed HTML solutions may be inappropriate. Fortunately, it is possible to limit parsed HTML or mix it with standard HTML by having only certain files, for example those ending in .shtml, parsed by the server. When used in a limited fashion, SSI can provide powerful features that are within the technical ability of any HTML writer. However, SSI is limited. Page designers may find other parsed HTML solutions like Cold Fusion or ASP more appropriate.

Cold Fusion

One of the most popular server-parsed HTML solutions is Allaire's Cold Fusion (www.allaire.com). Cold Fusion is a complete Web application development tool that allows developers to create dynamic database-driven Web site applications with an easy-to-use, server-side markup language similar to HTML. Getting started with Cold Fusion requires learning a few new markup tags that look like HTML, but make up what is called Cold Fusion Markup Language (CFML). Since one of its primary functions is database access, Cold Fusion uses the Open Database Connectivity (ODBC) standard to connect to popular database servers like Microsoft SQL Server, Access, Sybase, Oracle, and others. Cold Fusion is not dependent on a particular database or Web server, and works well on a variety of Windows NT–based servers. While Cold Fusion is not by any means a standard, it is widely used. It is presented here to illustrate an example of parsed HTML, and to show how HTML might be used to interact with a database.

Web applications built with Cold Fusion use dynamic pages composed of a mixture of CFML and HTML markup. When the page is requested, the Cold Fusion application running on the server preprocesses the page, interacts with a database or other server-side technologies, and returns a dynamically generated HTML page. It is probably better to refer to Cold Fusion–enabled pages as templates since the actual page output varies.

Using CFML

Here is how to use CFML to select and output data in a dynamic Web page. This section will show how to use a number of CFML tags to query data from a database, take the results of the query, and populate a Web page.

Database Overview

A database is simply a collection of data that is organized in a regular fashion, typically in the form of a table. Imagine you want to create a Web site to post the various job openings in your company. The first thing you need to do is to decide what information is relevant: position number, job title, location, brief description, hiring manager, and posting date. This information could be organized in the form of a database table, called Positions, as shown in Table 12-6.

The example is populated with some simple data, but how can the data be retrieved to be displayed in a Web page automatically?

Selecting the Data

The first step is to define a database query using Structured Query Language (SQL). SQL is the language used to retrieve or modify data from the tables in a database. The language is relatively simple, at least as far as mastering the basics. If you were interested in making a query to the database table called Positions, you would use a SQL statement like

```
SELECT * FROM Positions
```

This query simply says to select all items indicated by the wildcard (*) in the table called Positions. If you just want to list all the positions in Austin, you could qualify the query by adding a **WHERE** modifier indicating you only want entries where the location is Austin.

```
SELECT * FROM Positions WHERE Location="Austin"
```

Using the **WHERE** modifier, it is possible to create complex queries. For example, you could query all jobs in Austin, or in Los Angeles, where the position is Game Tester.

```
SELECT *
    FROM Positions
    WHERE ((Location="Austin" OR
        (Location="Los Angeles") AND
        (Position="Game Tester"))
```

This brief discussion should reveal the basic flavor of SQL. While the basic language is simple, queries can be more complicated. A full discussion of SQL is well beyond the scope of this book. For sake of this discussion, only simple queries are used in the examples.

In order to pull data out of the database, write a SQL query, and then place it within a **<CFQUERY>** element. The following example illustrates the use of **<CFQUERY>**. A select SQL query called **ListJobs**, as specified by the **NAME** attribute, will query a database and retrieve all the records in the Positions table. The syntax for this example is shown here.

```
<CFQUERY NAME="ListJobs"
        DATASOURCE="CompanyDataBase">
        SELECT * FROM Positions
</CFQUERY>
```

Notice that the **DATASOURCE** attribute is set equal to CompanyDataBase, which is the ODBC data source that contains a database called Company, which contains the Positions table data is pulled from.

Position-Num	JobTitle	Location	Description	Hiring Manager	Post Date
343	Gadget Sales	Austin	This position requires an aggressive sales person to sell gadgets to guys and gals.	M. Spacely	01/20/98
525	Office Manager	San Jose	Responsible for running the entire office single-handedly	P. Mohta	01/24/98
2585	President	San Diego	Figurehead position requires daily golf games and nightly poker parties	T. Powell	01/30/98
3950	Grounds-keeper	San Diego	Must like outdoor work and long hours in the sun with no sunscreen	J. Tam	01/30/98
1275	HTML Hacker	Seattle	Must be able to recite HTML specifications by heart and code HTML by hand. Long hours, low pay.	B. Gates	01/27/98
2015	Game Tester	Los Angeles	Must be able to play games all day long, including Russian card games.	Z. Ooki	01/18/98

Table 12-6. *Simple Database Table Called Positions*

Note ODBC, which stands for Open Database Connectivity, is a standardized way to access data from a variety of different databases. ODBC provides a layer of abstraction that protects the developer from having to learn the particulars of a specific database system. The database connected to in order to query the Positions table might be a simple Microsoft Access database, or a powerful Oracle system. In order to access a database, a developer needs to set up an ODBC data source. This requires that developer to select an ODBC driver, name the data source, and configure any specific settings for the database. A complete discussion of how to set up ODBC drivers and configure data sources can be found in the documentation for Cold Fusion.

Besides **NAME** and **DATASOURCE**, the <CFQUERY> element has a variety of attributes, as described in Table 12-7.

Outputing the Data

Using the <CFOUTPUT> element, it is possible to display the data retrieved from a previously defined <CFQUERY> element. For example, in order to output the query called ListJobs, you would use a code fragment as shown next.

```
<CFOUPUT QUERY="ListJobs">

    <HR NOSHADE><BR>
    Position Number: #PostionNum#<BR><BR>
    Title: #JobTitle#<BR><BR>
    Location: #Location#<BR><BR>
    Description: #Description#

</CFOUPUT>
```

Attribute	Description
NAME	Required. This attribute is used to assign a name to the SQL query. The name is used later in the template to reference the query results.
DATASOURCE	Required. This attribute is used to specify the name of the ODBC data source that will be used to access the database.

Table 12-7.   *<CFQUERY> Attribute Summary*

Attribute	Description
MAXROWS	Optional. This attribute is used to specify the maximum number of rows as a positive integer number that should be returned by the query. More output rows beyond this value will be dropped.
USERNAME	Optional. Since many databases have login features, this attribute is used to set the user name to access the data source. This attribute overrides the default settings in the Cold Fusion Administrator.
PASSWORD	Optional. This attribute is used to set the password associated for the user name that will access the database. This value overrides the default settings in the Cold Fusion Administrator.
TIMEOUT	Optional. This attribute can be set to a time, in milliseconds, for a query to successfully execute. Queries that take longer than this value will fail.
DEBUG	Optional. When present, this attribute turns on the tracing and debugging features for the file.

Table 12-7.   *<CFQUERY> Attribute Summary* (continued)

Notice the use of the # symbols throughout this code fragment. These values are used to delimit the areas in which you wish to place the data from the database. For example, #PositionNum# will be populated with data from the column PositionNum, while #JobTitle# will get the values for the JobTitle column in the database. Notice also that normal HTML markup can be used within the query.

The primary attribute for the **<CFOUTPUT>** element is **QUERY**, but there are numerous other attributes, as shown in Table 12-8.

By putting both the **<CFQUERY>** and the **<CFOUTPUT>** elements together in a complete CFML template file, which you could call example1.cfm, and putting this on a server that understands Cold Fusion, you could create a dynamically generated page. A complete listing showing the two primary Cold Fusion elements is shown in Figure 12-9.

Figure 12-10 shows a Cold Fusion dynamically generated page under Netscape. Note that there are no browser-side requirements for Cold Fusion. In other words, this application would work equally well under Internet Explorer, Lynx, WebTV, or any other browser.

Attribute	Description
QUERY	Required. This is set to the name of the <CFQUERY> that will be used to query the database.
MAXROWS	Optional. This attribute is used to specify the maximum number of rows in the query, a positive integer, that should be displayed.
GROUP	Optional. This attribute is used to group output and is useful for nested reporting.
STARTROW	Optional. This attribute is used to specify an integer row to start output from. For example, setting this attribute to 5 would start the output with the fifth row returned by the query.

Table 12-8.   *<CFOUTPUT> Attribute Summary*

Conditional Statements

When creating dynamic pages, things don't always work out as expected. What happens, for example, if there are no jobs in the database to print out? Should the user get a blank page, or one that says "Sorry, no jobs available?" Cold Fusion provides a number of facilities to take care of just such problems. Using the **<CFIF>** element, simple comparison conditions can be added to the page and simple applications can be built. The basic syntax for the **<CFIF>** element is shown here.

```
<CFIF expression>
HTML and CFML tags
<CFELSE>
HTML and FML tags
</CFIF>
```

An expression is a comparison condition. For example, **IS NOT " "** would be an expression to see if something is not set. So

```
<CFIF ListJobs.PostionNum IS NOT "">

    print the query here

</CFIF>
```

would only do the section "print the query here" if the PostionNum field was not empty. Note that, as shown in this example, the **<CFELSE>** element is optional.

The expression used in the **<CFIF>** element can be complex and may consist of one or many of the operators shown in Table 12-9.

```
<!DOCTYPE HTML PUBLIC "-//W3C//DTD HTML 3.2 Final//EN">
<!-- SQL statement to select jobs
     available from the database-->

<CFQUERY NAME="ListJobs" DATASOURCE="CompanyDataBase">
     SELECT * from Positions
</CFQUERY>


<HTML>
<HEAD>
<TITLE>Big Company Job Listings</TITLE>
</HEAD>
<BODY>


<H2 ALIGN="CENTER">Big Company Job Listings</H2>
<HR>
<CFOUPUT QUERY="ListJobs">
  <HR NOSHADE><BR>
   Position Number: #PositionNum#<BR><BR>
   Title: #JobTitle#<BR><BR>
   Location: #Location#<BR><BR>
   Description: #Description#
</CFOUPUT>


<HR>
<ADDRESS>
Big Company, Inc.
</ADDRESS>

</BODY>
</HTML>
```

Figure 12-9. *Simple Cold Fusion example*

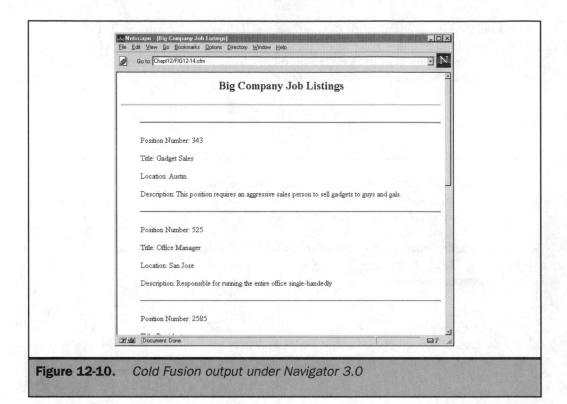

Figure 12-10. Cold Fusion output under Navigator 3.0

Using the conditional capabilities provided by the **<CFIF>** element, it is possible to create an improved example that checks whether the table has open positions. If not, it prints out a statement indicating no jobs are available, as shown here:

```
<!-- SQL statement to select jobs available from the database-->

<CFQUERY NAME="ListJobs" DATASOURCE="CompanyDataBase">
     SELECT * FROM Positions
</CFQUERY>

<CFIF ListJobs.PositionNumber IS NOT "">

<HTML>
<HEAD>
<TITLE>Big Company Job Listings</TITLE>
</HEAD>
<BODY>
```

```
<H2 ALIGN="CENTER">Big Company Job Listings</H2>

<HR>

<CFOUTPUT QUERY="ListJobs">
   <UL>
      <HR NOSHADE><BR>
      Position Number: #PositionNum#<BR><BR>
      Title: #JobTitle#<BR><BR>
      Location: #Location#<BR><BR>
      Description: #Description#
   </UL>
</CFOUPUT>

<HR>
<ADDRESS>
Big Company, Inc.
</ADDRESS>

</BODY>
</HTML>

<CFELSE>
   <CFLOCATION URL="nojobs.htm">
</CFIF>
```

The **<CFIF>** statement in this example checks to see if the PositionNum field is empty in the database. If the field is not empty, then it proceeds to populate the Web page. If the field is empty, it redirects to a page called nojobs.htm that indicates that there are no positions currently available at the company.

CFML Summary

It should be obvious from the examples presented that Cold Fusion can be used to create dynamic Web pages. When using conditional operators, as well as other CFML elements that can be used to loop or set variables, it is even possible to create full-fledged applications with Cold Fusion. What's great about Cold Fusion and other HTML-like, server-parsed languages is that they are relatively easy to get started with. There are fewer than two dozen CFML elements to learn. Some of these provide very powerful features like file upload, cookie manipulation, file inclusion, automatic HTML table creation, and mailing. A brief summary of the CFML elements available in Cold Fusion 3.0 is presented in Table 12-10.

Operator	Description
IS	Performs a case-insensitive comparison of two values and returns TRUE if the values are identical.
IS NOT *or* NEQ	Performs the opposite function as the IS operator returning TRUE only if the values are not equal.
CONTAINS	Performs a check to determine if the value on the left of the operator is contained in the value on the right of the operator and returns TRUE if it is.
DOES NOT CONTAIN	Opposite of the CONTAINS operator.
GREATER THAN *or* GT	Checks whether the value on the left is greater than the value on the right and returns TRUE if it is.
LESS THAN *or* LT	Checks whether the value on the left is less than the value on the right and returns TRUE if it is.
GREATER THAN OR EQUAL TO *or* GTE	Checks whether the value on the left is greater than or equal to the value on the right and returns TRUE if it is.
LESS THAN OR EQUAL TO *or* LTE	Checks whether the value on the left is less than or equal to the value on the right and returns TRUE if it is.

Table 12-9. *<CFIF> Operators Summary*

The previous discussion is just a sample of what Cold Fusion can do. It is only meant to illustrate what a server-side HTML language might do. For more detailed information on the syntax of Cold Fusion, as well as examples of its use, see the Cold Fusion Language Reference at Allaire's Web Site (www.allaire.com). While Cold

Element	Description
<CFABORT>	Aborts the processing of the CFML application or template at the specified location.
<CFAPPLICATION>	Defines the CFML application name and activates the client variables.

Table 12-10. *CFML Language Summary*

Element	Description
<CFCOL>	Used to define a table column header including setting width and alignment of the column.
<CFCONTENT>	Used to define the content type and the name of the file to be uploaded from the application.
<CFCOOKIE>	Defines and sets a cookie, which can be used to preserve state information.
<CFERROR>	Used to customize HTML error pages when things don't work out.
<CFFILE>	Allows the developer to define file-handling tasks within the CFML application.
<CFHEADER>	Used to generate HTTP headers in the application, which may be useful for avoiding the page being cached.
<CFIF>	Creates a conditional expression that is useful for catching error conditions or setting up more output logic.
<CFINCLUDE>	Used to include a Cold Fusion template file in the application. Useful for keeping routines in separate files.
<CFINSERT>	Used to insert records into an ODBC database.
<CFLOCATION>	Opens a Cold Fusion Template or HTML file. Most often used for redirection of output.
<CFLOOP>	Used to "loop" or repeat a set of instructions or display conditional output.
<CFMAIL>	Used to send SMTP e-mail from the CFML application.
<CFOUTPUT>	Displays the results of a database query as specified by the <CFQUERY> element.
<CFPARAM>	Used to assign a parameter an initial value.
<CFQUERY>	Used to pass a SQL statement, typically a query to an ODBC-connected database.
<CFREPORT>	Used to embed a report from Crystal Reports into the page.
<CFSET>	Used to define a variable within the CFML application that can be accessed later using a <CFIF> or similar construct.

Table 12-10. *CFML Language Summary (continued)*

Element	Description
<CFTABLE>	Used to build a quick HTML table to hold the output of a query.
<CFUPDATE>	Used to update records in an ODBC data source.

Table 12-10.   *CFML Language Summary* (continued)

Fusion is somewhat specific to database access, there are other server-side parsed HTML solutions, such as Microsoft's ASP, which may provide more general functionality.

Active Server Pages (ASP)

Microsoft's ASP is a server-side scripting environment primarily for the Microsoft Internet Information Server (IIS) Web server, although third-party vendors have recently ported ASP to other Web servers, such as the Netscape Enterprise server. Using ASP, it is possible to combine HTML, scripting code, and server-side ActiveX components to create dynamic Web applications. The ability to write scripts in standard scripting languages such as VBScript, JavaScript, or other scripting languages such as Perl enables developers to create applications with almost any type of functionality. This makes the ASP approach to server-side scripting very generalized for a broad range of applications. Server-side scripts can also access server-side objects in the form of ActiveX controls for a variety of functions, such as database access via ODBC. Like other parsed HTML solutions, an ASP-enabled page is parsed by the Web server to generate the dynamic HTML that is sent to the Web browser. This means that ASP-enabled pages work equally well on every browser.

Creating ASP Pages

To get started using ASP, the developer needs to have a working knowledge of HTML, as well as knowledge of a scripting language like VBScript or JavaScript. Files created for ASP have an .asp file extension associated with them. When an ASP-enabled server sees a file with such an extension, it will execute it before delivering it to the user. For example, the simple VBScript embedded into the file shown here is used to display the current date on a Web page dynamically:

```
<SCRIPT LANGUAGE=VBScript RUNAT=Server>
</SCRIPT>
<HTML>
<HEAD>
<TITLE>ASP Display Date Example</TITLE>
<HEAD>
<BODY>
<H1>Welcome to News of the Day</H1>
<% = date %>
<P>
Today the stock of a major software company<BR>
reached an all time high, making the company's CEO<BR>
the world's first and only trillionaire.<BR>
</BODY>
</HTML>
```

The **<SCRIPT>** element is used to indicate the primary scripting language being employed. This element also tells the Web server to execute the script code on the server rather than the client with the **RUNAT** attribute. This can be abbreviated as **<@ LANGUAGE = *ScriptLanguage*>**. Notice how the **<% %>** is used to delimit the script code that is run. ASP is a generalized technology. It can be used to do whatever a user dreams up. Since people commonly want to do things on the Web like access a database, it has been enhanced to do this well.

Database Access in ASP   In the following discussion, ASP will be used to access the job positions database described previously in the chapter. While this could probably be done more easily using Cold Fusion, the point here is to introduce the idea of object access from ASP. The first step in this example is to create an instance of the database component by adding the following line to an ASP file, which might be named example.asp.:

```
<OBJECT RUNAT=Server ID=Conn PROGID="ADODB.Connection"></OBJECT>
```

This statement creates an instance of a database access object called Conn that can be used with a server-side script.

Later on, the file will open a connection to the database and execute a SQL command to select job positions and return a set of records. The small code fragment shown next does this. The code is enclosed within **<%** and **%>** so that the server knows to execute this rather than display it on the screen.

```
<%
Conn.Open Session("ConnectionString")
SQL = "SELECT * FROM Positions"
Set RS = Conn.Execute(SQL)
Do While Not RS.EOF
%>
```

The code between the **<% %>** statements is VBScript, which is interpreted by the Web server when this page is requested. The Do While statement is a standard VBScript looping statement, which is used here to loop through the record set until an end of file (EOF) marker is reached, signifying the end of the records. While looping through each record, the output is displayed in the context of regular HTML code, such as displaying the Job Department field in a table cell:

```
<TD>
<%= RS("JobDepartment")%>
</TD>
```

Putting this all together in a file called example.asp provides a complete ASP database access example, as shown here:

```
<!DOCTYPE HTML PUBLIC "-//W3C//DTD HTML 3.2 Final//EN">
<OBJECT RUNAT=Server ID=Conn PROGID="ADODB.Connection"></OBJECT>
<%@ LANGUAGE = VBScript %>
<HTML>
<HEAD>
<TITLE>Open Positions</TITLE>
</HEAD>
<BODY>

<H2 ALIGN="CENTER">Open Positions</H2>
<BR><BR>
<TABLE WIDTH="100%" BORDER="1" CELLSPACING="0" CELLPADDING="4">
<TR>
    <TH>Position Number</TH>
    <TH>Location</TH>
    <TH>Description</TH>
    <TH>Hiring Manager</TH>
    <TH>Data Posted</TH>
```

```
</TR>


<!-- Open Database Connection
        Execute SQL query statement
        Set RS variable to store results of query
        Loop through records while still records to process
-->
<%
Conn.Open Session("ConnectionString")
SQL = "SELECT JobTitle, Location, Description, HiringManager,
PostDate FROM Positions"
Set RS = Conn.Execute(SQL)
Do While Not RS.EOF
%>


<!--  Display database fields in table cells -->
<TR>
  <TD>
    <%= RS("JobTitle") %>
  </TD>
  <TD>
    <%= RS("Location")%>
  </TD>
  <TD>
     <%= RS("Description")%>
  </TD>
  <TD>
      <%= RS("HiringManager")%>
  </TD>
  <TD>
      <%= RS("PostDate") d%>
  </TD>
</TR>


<!--  Move to next record and continue loop -->

<%
RS.MoveNext
Loop
%>
```

```
</TABLE>
</BODY>
</HTML>
```

From this example, you can see the advantages of ASP for generating dynamic pages. The actual data to be displayed is a database that the server can access with an ASP script using a database access object. The dynamically created page is built from a combination of VBScript that uses a small amount of programming and HTML. The result can be served to different browsers without any client-side compatibility problems, because the pages are generated on the server. While the previous example showed a more complicated way to access data from a database, it hints at the generalized power of ASP. Active Server Pages are useful for creating applications rather than just dynamic pages. With ASP, it is possible to determine the user's browser, keep track of the user's progress through a set of pages, and manage all the data that is passed back and forth from the user (including cookies and form fields). The key to this power is the server-side objects provided with ASP.

Built-In ASP Objects

What makes ASP so powerful is that the technology includes five built-in objects for global use:

Application
Request
Response
Server
Session

The application object is used to share common information within an application. An example would be a page counter. You can store the number of times a page has been accessed and use this object to display it on the page. The application object supports locking, since multiple users may be using the Web application at the same time, and could possibly corrupt data.

The request object is used to get information from the user, including form data, cookies, or standard HTTP request variables such as browser type (user agent). The request object contains collections of information that can be used in scripts. The request object supports the following collections:

- **ClientCertificate** The values of fields stored in the client certificate that is sent in the HTTP request

- **Cookies** The values of cookies sent in the HTTP request

- **Form** The values of the fields sent from a form submission

- **QueryString**   The values of the variables sent in an HTTP query string
- **ServerVariables**   HTTP server information like server name, type, version, and so on

The response object is used to send information to the user. It could be used to set the type of content to be sent to a browser such as HTML, Word files, or other formats such as graphics. It could also send and retrieve cookie values to a client to determine user preferences for creating customized pages.

The server object provides access to server methods and properties, including setting how long a script should run, and asking for server-side objects like database objects.

The session object, one of the most useful objects, is used to store information for a particular user session. This means that information is maintained as the user jumps from page to page, thus preserving state. The basic property for this object sets an ID for the session while the events deal with the start or end of a session.

A generalized language like VBScript or JavaScript, combined with server-side objects to do common tasks like maintaining user state, makes complex server-side applications possible. Many other technologies, like Netscape's LiveWire with its server-side JavaScript, take a similar approach.

This discussion introduces ASP and is by no means complete. It illustrates a much generalized method of parsed HTML that utilizes the power of popular scripting languages and access to server-side objects with common and powerful functions, such as database access and session tracking. Complete information on ASP can be found on the Microsoft Internet Information Server Web site (www.microsoft.com/iis/) or in the ASP Roadmap documentation that is included when ASP is installed on a Web server.

Summary

Server-side programming is one way to add interactivity to a Web page. CGI is the traditional way to do this. Writing a CGI program doesn't have to be difficult using libraries, but the price to pay for ease is often speed. Because so many CGI programs are very similar, some are rewritten as faster server-side plug-ins called NSAPI or ISAPI programs. While these types of server modules tend to be beyond most developers, it is easy to buy one to solve a common problem like database access. Some server engines now support a form of server-side scripting known generically as parsed HTML. Parsed HTML solutions such as SSIs, Cold Fusion, and ASP provide an easy way for HTML authors to add functionality to Web pages. While server-side technologies provide a great deal of power for the Web developer, they are only half the picture. It is also possible to add interactivity using a client-side technology like JavaScript or Java. The next chapters discuss these technologies and their intersection with HTML.

Chapter 13

Client-Side Scripting and HTML

A dding interactivity to a Web site is not limited to server-side programs. The client side of the Web, the browser, can generally execute code in the form of scripting or embedded programmed objects. For HTML writers, the easiest way to begin adding dynamic aspects to a Web page is through client-side scripting, using JavaScript or VBScript. This chapter will discuss the intersection between scripting and HTML, but will not attempt to teach scripting techniques. The idea of scripting requires the page designer to think more carefully about how the user will interact with the page. If scripting is not used carefully, errors may creep in and cause problems for the viewer.

As it stands now, scripting languages like JavaScript are often relegated to small embellishments like the ubiquitous rollover button. However, Dynamic HTML and the idea of the Document Object Model show how the idea of a page may change forever because of client-side scripting. Scripting has a major role to play on a Web page. While HTML may provide the structure, scripting may act as the glue, providing a link between static content and user actions, and between various embedded objects (to be discussed in Chapter 14).

Purpose of Scripting

How do Web scripting languages relate to full-fledged Web programming languages like Java? In general, scripting languages are used in small doses, for specific tasks. Scripting has a very limited domain. Some people use scripting languages for tasks such as loan calculators. Such simple tasks illustrate basic features of the scripting language. The basic uses of scripting include

Form validation
Page embellishment
Dynamic page generation
Inter-object communication "glue"

HTML developers tend to be comfortable with scripting languages because they can simply enter script commands into the HTML file along with the text markup. In fact, some developers simply cut and paste scripts to add scrolling marquees, dialog boxes, and other customized features to their pages. This form of quick embellishment comes at a cost. If testing is not rigorous, serious problems—even crashes—may creep in. With the rise of so many scripting languages such as JavaScript 1.0, 1.1, 1.2, and various versions of JScript, bugs are becoming more common. Furthermore, there are occasionally some security problems with scripting. Some more cautious users may even turn off script interpretation in their browsers, potentially causing the page to render improperly. If scripting makes sense for your site, you must choose between JavaScript and VBScript.

JavaScript

JavaScript is a scripting language developed by Netscape. Microsoft also supports JavaScript in the form of JScript, a clone language used in Internet Explorer. The language was turned over to the international standards body ECMA (European Computer Manufacturers Association), which announced during the summer of 1997 the approval of ECMA-262, or ECMAScript, as a cross-platform Internet standard for scripting. Browser vendors will comply with the specification, but will still use the commonly recognized JavaScript name.

As a scripting language, JavaScript is meant to be easy to use, noncompiled (interpreted), and useful in small chunks. This sets it apart from Java and other languages that might be used on the Internet, which tend to be compiled and relatively hard to master for the nonprogrammer. The syntax of JavaScript is somewhat like C or Java with Perl-style regular expression handling, and the language has basic object-oriented capabilities. It is not, however, a true object-oriented programming language, and retains features, like weak typing, common to simple scripting languages.

JavaScript is useful for small jobs such as checking form data, adding small bits of HTML code to a page on the fly, and performing browser-, time-, and user-specific computation. JavaScript is also a powerful means of controlling events in browsers and accessing the Document Object Model for programming Dynamic HTML. An important potential function of JavaScript is to act as the glue between different technologies such as plug-ins, Java applets, and HTML pages. An example of JavaScript code being used to perform form validation by checking the contents of a form before it is sent to a server-side program is shown in Figure 13-1. Figure 13-2 shows a rendering of the JavaScript prompting the user to enter the appropriate information for the form before submission.

JavaScript has undergone many changes. Not all browsers support it to the same degree, if at all. There are a few major dialects of JavaScript, including JavaScript 1.0 (=Netscape 2.X), JavaScript 1.1 (=Netscape 3.X) and JavaScript 1.2 (=Netscape 4.X). JScript in Internet Explorer 3.0 is approximately equivalent to JavaScript 1.0; it does not support JavaScript 1.1 features such as dynamic image replacement. Internet Explorer 4.0 appears to support JavaScript 1.1, but with a richer object model. Finally, there is the ECMAScript standard.

Table 13-1 shows the JavaScript versions supported by different browsers.

```
<HTML>
<HEAD>
<TITLE>JavaScript Example</TITLE>
<SCRIPT TYPE="JavaScript">
<!--
function validate()
{

 if (regform.name.value == "")
 {
 alert("You must enter your name");
 return;
 }
 else
 regform.submit()

}
//-->
</SCRIPT>
</HEAD>

<BODY>
<H1 ALIGN="CENTER">Registration Form</H1>
<HR>
<FORM ACTION="mailto: info@bigcompany.com" METHOD="POST" NAME="reg-
form">

Name: <INPUT NAME="name" TYPE="TEXT" SIZE="20" MAXLENGTH="40">
<BR><BR>

<INPUT TYPE="BUTTON" VALUE="Register" onClick="validate()">

</FORM>

</BODY>
</HTML>
```

Figure 13-1. *JavaScript example*

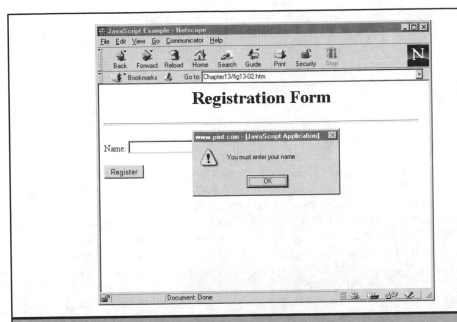

Figure 13-2. *JavaScript form validation rendering*

Browser	JavaScript Support
Netscape Navigator 2.X	JavaScript 1.0
Netscape Navigator 3.X	JavaScript 1.1
Netscape Navigator 4.X	JavaScript 1.2
Internet Explorer 2.X	None
Internet Explorer 3.X	JScript (JavaScript 1.0)
Internet Explorer 4.X	JScript (JavaScript 1.1), ECMAScript compliant

Table 13-1. *JavaScript Support by Browser Release*

For more information on JavaScript, visit Netscape's developer site (http://developer.netscape.com/). Information about Microsoft's implementation of JavaScript called JScript can be found at (http://www.microsoft.com/jscript/).

VBScript

Visual Basic Scripting Edition, generally called VBScript, is a subset of the popular Visual Basic language. Because of its Visual Basic heritage, VBScript is somewhat more defined and stable than JavaScript. VBScript is less prevalent than JavaScript on the Internet, largely because it is only fully supported in Internet Explorer 3.0 and later browsers. The language can be used to provide the same functionality as JavaScript, and is just as capable as accessing the various objects that compose a Web page (termed a browser's Document Object Model). As a cross-platform scripting solution, VBScript should be avoided. Used with ActiveX controls in a more controllable environment such as an intranet, VBScript might just be what the Microsoft-oriented developer needs. When dealing with ActiveX controls, as discussed in the next chapter, VBScript may provide more functionality. Following is a sample of VBScript to give a flavor of its syntax. (This example has the same functionality as the JavaScript example in Figure 13-1.)

```
<HTML>
<HEAD>
<TITLE>VBSscript Example</TITLE>
<SCRIPT LANGUAGE="VBScript">
<!--
Sub Reg_OnClick
Dim TheForm
Set TheForm = Document.regform

  If (TheForm.name.Value) = "" Then
     MsgBox "You must enter your name"
  Else
     TheForm.submit
  End If

End Sub
-->
</SCRIPT>
</HEAD>
<BODY>
<H1 ALIGN="CENTER">Registration Form</H1>
<HR>
```

```
<FORM ACTION="mailto:info@bigcompany.com" METHOD=POST NAME="regform">


Name: <INPUT NAME="name" TYPE="TEXT" SIZE="20" MAXLENGTH="40">
<BR><BR>

<INPUT TYPE="BUTTON" VALUE="Register" NAME="Reg">

</FORM>
</BODY>
</HTML>
```

Readers interested in more information about the syntax of VBScript are directed to Microsoft's VBScript site (http://www.microsoft.com/vbscript/).

Including Scripts in an HTML Document

As suggested by the last two examples, the main way to include scripts written in any language into a Web page is primarily with the **<SCRIPT>** element. The **<SCRIPT>** element is used to delimit the script code; anything that is found is treated as a script and not HTML by the browser. This is an important statement for HTML writers to ponder. Script code tends to be sensitive to returns and capitalization, while HTML is not. The HTML rules you know and love may not be valid once you are within the **<SCRIPT>** element.

While the contents of the **<SCRIPT>** element may be very complex, the syntax of the element is relatively simple. There are only three major attributes for **<SCRIPT>**, as shown in Table 13-2.

The actual script to execute should be placed between the **<SCRIPT>** and **</SCRIPT>** tags, as shown here:

```
<SCRIPT LANGUAGE="JavaScript">
Script goes here
</SCRIPT>
```

Remember that what is between these tags is script, not HTML markup. There may be a very different syntax involved, depending on the scripting language used.

The **<SCRIPT>** element can be used multiple times in the **<HEAD>** as well as the **<BODY>** element. Since HTML pages are read sequentially, a great deal of scripting code may appear in the head section of a document. Much of this script code could be termed deferred script, since it may be read but not executed until later. This script

Attribute Name	Possible Value(s)	Description
LANGUAGE	JavaScript, JScript, VBS, VBScript	The value of this attribute is used to specify the scripting language being used. There are two major possibilities: JavaScript or VBScript.
SRC	URL	This attribute is used to indicate the URL of a file which contains an external script to load.
TYPE	Application/x-javascript*, text/javascript, text/vbscript	Indicates the MIME type of the script to run.

* The TYPE value of application/x-javascript is not encouraged, though it is common for older browsers that support JavaScript.

Table 13-2. *Element Attributes*

code can be called later by immediate scripts or user-action scripts within the body of the HTML document. The type of script that tends to go into the **<HEAD>** element is similar to a function or procedure definition, as shown in the following example:

```
<HTML>
<HEAD>
<SCRIPT LANGUAGE="JavaScript">
<!--
function AlertTest( ){
 alert("Danger! Danger!");
 }
// -->
</SCRIPT>
</HEAD>
<BODY>
    HTML tags which eventually may trigger JavaScript
    code in head
</BODY>
```

The **<SCRIPT>** element may also occur in the body. It is generally used to create immediate scripts that are executed as soon as the browser reads them. For example, the following markup includes JavaScript code that adds the document modification time automatically to the end of the document.

```
<HTML>
<HEAD>
<TITLE>Immediate Script</TITLE>
</HEAD>
<BODY>
<H1 ALIGN="CENTER">Big Company, Inc.</H1>
<HR>
<P>Interesting text goes here.</P>
<HR>
<SCRIPT LANGUAGE="JavaScript">
<!--
 document.write("Last updated on: "+document.lastModified);
//-->
</SCRIPT>
</BODY>
</HTML>
```

Besides using the **<SCRIPT>** element, it is also possible to embed script code directly into HTML tags. Typically, scripts for handling user-triggered events are the common way that scripts are added outside the **<SCRIPT>** element. The HTML element will generally have a special attribute called a *script handler* for a particular user event. For example, to handle a click event to a button there is a special **onclick** attribute. While HTML attributes tend to be written in uppercase, event handlers are often written in mixed case or lowercase to distinguish the fact that the handler is concerned with scripting, as shown in the following example:

```
<FORM>
<INPUT TYPE="BUTTON" NAME="TestButton" VALUE="Don't push me!"
onclick="AlertTest()">
</FORM>
```

By combining deferred scripts with user-triggered events, it is possible to make dynamic documents. The following example presents a button that, when pressed, opens a small alert dialog using JavaScript.

```
<HTML>
<HEAD>
```

```
<SCRIPT LANGUAGE="JavaScript">
<!--
function AlertTest( ) {
 alert("Danger JavaScript ahead! ");
 }
// -->
</SCRIPT>
</HEAD>
<BODY>
<DIV ALIGN="CENTER">
<FORM>
<INPUT TYPE="BUTTON" NAME="TestButton"
 VALUE="Don't push me!" onClick="AlertTest()">
</FORM>
</DIV>
</BODY>
</HTML>
```

There are two more ways to add JavaScript code to an HTML document. The first way involves a URL scripting pseudo-protocol. Netscape browsers introduced the use of a new URL style in the form of **javascript:** which can be used with links. For example,

```
<A HREF='javascript:alert("Danger JavaScript ahead!")'>Script me!</A>
```

creates a link which, when pressed, executes the specified JavaScript code. Microsoft Internet Explorer also supports this style. Last, a very uncommon way to add JavaScript code to a Web page is with a character entity. (Remember that using **©** would include a copyright symbol.) It turns out that JavaScript code can be inserted inside of a special entity of the form **&{javascript code};**. The JavaScript code must be included within braces; it may even call functions or perform numerous statements. This entity form can only be used as an attribute value. This style could be used as a form of macro in Netscape 4.0 or Internet Explorer 4.0 pages. Imagine setting a bunch of identifiers for colors and font style in the **head** of the document, and then referencing them by name later, as shown in the following example:

```
<HTML>
<HEAD>
<TITLE>Entity Script</TITLE>
<SCRIPT LANGUAGE="JavaScript">
```

```
<!--
   textColor='green';
//-->
</SCRIPT>
</HEAD>
<BODY>
<FONT COLOR=&{textColor;};>This should be green</FONT>
</BODY>
</HTML>
```

This last example would probably have been better handled by a style sheet, but it is presented solely to show how the entity script style works. The entity and pseudo-URL style for adding JavaScript is specific to this particular scripting language. As more scripting languages are used online, other ways to add script to a page may very well arise. For now, the two standard ways are in the form of the **<SCRIPT>** element and the attribute event handlers for individual elements, such as **onclick**, which will be discussed in greater detail later in the chapter (see "Script Events and HTML").

Specifying the Scripting Language

By default, most browsers will assume that the script language being used is JavaScript. The **LANGUAGE** attribute can be used to specify other languages, including VBScript and many others. The HTML 4.0 specification depreciates the **LANGUAGE** attribute in favor of the **TYPE** attribute. The **TYPE** attribute is used to indicate the MIME type of the script to run; for example, text/javascript. This indication of scripting dialect is not often used; it may not provide the flexibility provided by **LANGUAGE**.

Not all versions of JavaScript support the same features. The object that animated buttons rely on was not available until JavaScript 1.1; it will cause errors in older browsers if it is not accounted for. It is possible to indicate the version of JavaScript being used with the **LANGUAGE** attribute. The attribute can be set to "JavaScript1.1" or "JavaScript1.2" rather than just simply "JavaScript." Only browsers that understand the particular dialect of JavaScript will execute the enclosed script code. With this idea, you can make a fall-through situation with multiple versions of similar code, as shown here:

```
<SCRIPT LANGUAGE="JavaScript">
   Simple version
</SCRIPT>
<SCRIPT LANGUAGE="JavaScript1.1">
   Netscape 3.0 version
```

```
</SCRIPT>
<SCRIPT LANGUAGE="JavaScript1.2">
 Netscape 4.0 version
</SCRIPT>
```

There is one final way to indicate a scripting language: using the **<META>** element in the **<HEAD>**. For example,

```
<META http-equivv="Content-Script-Type" content="text/javascript">
```

sets the default scripting language for the whole document to JavaScript unless overridden by a local occurrence of the **LANGUAGE** attribute. A Web server may also be configured to issue such a header.

External Scripts

It is also possible to place the script code in a separate file and specify that file using the **SRC** attribute that specifies the URL of the script to include. For example,

```
<SCRIPT SRC="http://www.bigcompany.com/scripts/myscript.js"></SCRIPT>
```

loads a script called myscript.js, specified by the URL for the **SRC** attribute.

When including an external script in a page by setting the **SRC** attribute, the **LANGUAGE** attribute may not be used. While JavaScript will be assumed anyway, the file extension of the file will be used by the Web server to specify the scripting language. The Web server should map the extension to the appropriate MIME type, in this case application/x-javascript, so that the browser receiving the file knows what to do with it. Older servers may have to have a MIME type configured to allow remote inclusion of script files.

Scripting and Nonscript-Aware Browsers

One advantage to the referencing of external script files is that it provides compatibility for older non-JavaScript-aware browsers. A browser will simply ignore any tags it does not understand, so nothing will happen when an older browser reads a **<SCRIPT>** element that uses a **SRC** attribute. If the script is used inline, as shown here, older browsers which don't understand JavaScript display the statement "alert ("I am a Script");" right on the screen rather than execute it.

```
<SCRIPT LANGUAGE="JavaScript">
alert("I am a Script");
</SCRIPT>
```

To improve compatibility with non-JavaScript-aware browsers, scripting code should be commented out. In JavaScript, this would be accomplished as shown here:

```
<SCRIPT LANGUAGE="JavaScript">
<!--
alert("I am a Script");
//-->
</SCRIPT>
```

Notice how the HTML comment starts the exclusion of JavaScript, but **//-->** is used to close the comment. This is because JavaScript will interpret lines with **//** as comments and not attempt to run a command **-->** as a command.

Commenting out VBScript code is similar, requiring only a simple comment, as shown here:

```
<SCRIPT LANGUAGE="VBScript">
<!--
    MsgBox "Hello World!", 0, ""
' -->
</SCRIPT>
```

Other languages may have different commenting styles in order to hide the script code from the nonscript-language-aware browser.

<NOSCRIPT>

Like other extensions to HTML, the **<SCRIPT>** element supports a special element to deal with browsers that don't execute a script. The **<NOSCRIPT>** element is used to enclose alternative text and markup for browsers that don't interpret a script. It is possible for a user to turn off support for a scripting language in his or her browser. The **<NOSCRIPT>** content will render on the screen if the user has turned off scripting support, or are using a browser that doesn't understand JavaScript. For example,

```
<HTML>
<HEAD>
<TITLE>JavaScript and NOSCRIPT</TITLE>
</HEAD>
<BODY>
<SCRIPT LANGUAGE="JavaScript">
<!--
```

```
  document.write('<H1 ALIGN="CENTER">JavaScript is ON</H1>');
//-->
</SCRIPT>
<NOSCRIPT>
<B>Please turn on JavaScript if you have it and reload page!</B>
</NOSCRIPT>
</BODY>
</HTML>
```

While the last example works, there is currently some confusion between the specification and current browser actions in relation to **<NOSCRIPT>** when the language is not understood. According to the HTML 4.0 specification, browsers should evaluate the content in **<NOSCRIPT>** when the scripting language used earlier in the **<SCRIPT>** statement is not understood. In the case of the new language named BozoScript, the browser should evaluate the content in **<NOSCRIPT>** in the markup here.

```
<SCRIPT LANGUAGE="BozoScript">
This is bozo language
</SCRIPT>
<NOSCRIPT>
I don't understand BozoScript.
</NOSCRIPT>
```

Unfortunately, this not how the major browsers act. In fact, the browsers will ignore the **<NOSCRIPT>** statement in this case. Furthermore, there is a major problem with **<NOSCRIPT>** when considering that multiple occurrences of the **<SCRIPT>** element can occur in a document. A big question arises when thinking about which **<NOSCRIPT>** occurrence matches which **<SCRIPT>**. The assumption would be the first element following the **<SCRIPT>** element in question, but is this, or should this, be the way things work?

Script Events and HTML

In the section "Including Scripts in an HTML Document" earlier in this chaper, it was mentioned that script code could be added to HTML documents through special attributes called *event handlers*. What are events? Events occur as the result of a user action, or potentially an external event such as a page loading. An example of an event is a user clicking a button, pressing a key, moving a window, or even simply moving the mouse around the screen. HTML provides a way to bind a script to the occurrence of a particular event through an event handler attribute. This is the name of the event prefixed by the word on, for example **onclick**. The following code shows how the **onclick** event handler attribute is used to bind some script to a button click occurrence.

```
<FORM>
<BUTTON onclick='alert("Hey this is JavaScript")' VALUE="Press Me">
</FORM>
```

Under HTML 4.0, event handler attributes can be added to quite a number of HTML elements. In practice, event handler attributes are most commonly associated with form controls specified by the **<INPUT>**, **<SELECT>**, **<TEXTAREA>**, and **<BUTTON>** elements, though this is changing with the rise of Dynamic HTML. As Table 13-3 shows, HTML 4.0 defines a wide range of events for nearly all the elements.

Event Attribute	Event Description	Allowed Elements under HTML 4.0
onblur	A blur event occurs when a form element loses focus, meaning that the user has entered into another form field either typically by clicking the mouse on it or tabbing to it.	<A>, <AREA>, <BUTTON>, <INPUT>, <LABEL>, <SELECT>, <TEXTAREA>
onchange	A change event signals that both the form control has lost user focus and its value has been modified during its last access.	<INPUT>, <SELECT>, <TEXTAREA>
onclick	Indicates that the element has been clicked.	Most elements
ondblclick	Indicates that the element has been double clicked which is two clicks quickly.	Most elements
onfocus	The focus event describes when a form control has received focus, namely it has been selected for manipulation or data entry.	<A>, <AREA>, <BUTTON>, <INPUT>, <LABEL>, <SELECT>, <TEXTAREA>

Table 13-3. *HTML 4.0 Event Attributes for Elements*

Event Attribute	Event Description	Allowed Elements under HTML 4.0
onkeydown	Indicates that a key is being pressed down.	Most elements
onkeypress	Describes the event of a key being pressed and released.	Most elements
onkeyup	Indicates that a key is being released.	Most elements
onload	Indicates the event of a window or set of frame finishing loading a document.	<BODY>, <FRAMESET>
onmousedown	Indicates the press of a mouse button.	Most elements
onmousemove	Indicates that the mouse has moved.	Most elements
onmouseout	Indicates that the mouse has moved away from an element.	Most elements
onmouseover	Indicates that the mouse has moved over an element.	Most elements
onmouseup	Indicates the release of a mouse button.	Most elements
onreset	Indicates that the form is being reset possibly by the press of a reset button.	<FORM>
onselect	Indicates the selection of text by the user, typically by high-lighting the desired text.	<INPUT>, <TEXTAREA>
onsubmit	Indicates a form submission, generally by pressing a submit button.	<FORM>
onunload	Indicates that browser is leaving the current document and unloading it from the window or frame.	<BODY>, <FRAMESET>

Table 13-3. *HTML 4.0 Event Attributes for Elements* (continued)

The core event model according to HTML 4.0 includes **onclick**, **ondblclick**, **onkeydown**, **onkeypress**, **onkeyup**, **onmousedown**, **onmousemove**, **onmouseout**, **onmouseover**, and **onmouseup**. These core events are defined for nearly all HTML elements where the element is displayed on screen. As noted in Table 13-3 the expression "most elements" is meant to include

<A>	<FORM>	<P>
<ACRONYMN>	<H1>	<PRE>
<ADDRESS>	<H2>	<Q>
<AREA>	<H3>	<S>
<B>	<H4>	<SAMP>
<BIG>	<H5>	<SELECT>
<BLOCKQUOTE>	<H6>	<SMALL>
<BODY>	<HR>	<SPAN>
<BUTTON>	<I>	<STRIKE>
<CAPTION>	<IMG>	<STRONG>
<CENTER>	<INPUT>	<SUB>
<CITE>	<INS>	<SUP>
<CODE>	<KBD>	<TABLE>
<COL>	<LABEL>	<TBODY>
<COLGROUP>	<LEGEND>	<TD>
<DD>	<LI>	<TEXTAREA>
<DEL>	<LINK>	<TFOOT>
<DFN>	<MAP>	<TH>
<DIR>	<MENU>	<THEAD>
<DIV>	<NOFRAMES>	<TR>
<DL>	<NOSCRIPT>	<TT>
<DT>	<OBJECT>	<U>
<EM>	<OL>	<UL>
<FIELDSET>	<OPTION>	<VAR>

Obviously, certain structuring or miscellaneous elements do not make any sense for events. Under the HTML 4.0 specification, these elements include

<APPLET>	<HTML>
<BASE>	<IFRAME>
<BASEFONT>	<ISINDEX>
<BDO>	<META>
 	<PARAM>
<FONT>	<SCRIPT>
<FRAME>	<STYLE>
<FRAMESET>	<TITLE>
<HEAD>	

Note that the HTML 4.0 specification indicates that **<APPLET>** and **<FONT>** do not take the core events. However, some browsers do define events for them.

Certain elements under HTML 4.0 have their own special events outside this core event model. For example, the **<BODY>** and **<FRAMESET>** elements have an event for loading and unloading pages, so both elements also have the **onload** and **onunload** event attributes. In the case of the **<FRAMESET>** element, the load and unload events don't fire until all the frames have been loaded or unloaded respectively. The **<FORM>** element itself also has two special events that are typically triggered when the user presses the submit or reset button. These events are **onsubmit** and **onreset**. Of course, with scripting these events may fire for other reasons. Last, the primary form element types under HTML 4.0 are **<BUTTON>**, **<INPUT>**, **<LABEL>**, **<SELECT>**, and **<TEXTAREA>**. For text fields set with the **<INPUT>** element, it is possible to catch the focus and blur events with **onfocus** and **onblur**. These events fire when the user accesses the field and moves on to another one. It is also possible to watch for the select event with **onselect**, which is triggered when a user selects some text, as well as the change event (**onchange**), which is triggered when a field's value changes and loses focus.

The following markup illustrates simple use of the HTML 4.0 event attributes with form elements and links.

```
<HTML>
<HEAD>
<TITLE>HTML 4.0 Events</TITLE>
</HEAD>

<BODY onload='alert("Event demo loaded")'
      onunload='alert("Leaving demo")'>

<H1 ALIGN="CENTER">HTML 4.0 Events</H1>

<FORM onreset='alert("Form reset")'
onsubmit='alert("Form submit");return false;'>

<UL>

<LI>onblur: <INPUT TYPE=TEXT VALUE="Click into field and then
leave" SIZE="40" onblur='alert("Lost focus")'><BR><BR>

<LI>onclick: <INPUT TYPE=BUTTON VALUE="Click Me"
onClick='alert("Button click")'><BR><BR>
```

```
<LI>onchange: <INPUT TYPE=TEXT VALUE="Change this text then leave"
SIZE=40 onchange='alert("Changed")'><BR><BR>

<LI>ondblclick: <INPUT TYPE=BUTTON VALUE="Double-click Me"
ondblclick='alert("Button double-clicked")'><BR><BR>

<LI>onfocus: <INPUT TYPE=TEXT VALUE="Click into field"
onfocus='alert("Gained focus")'><BR><BR>

<LI>onkeydown: <INPUT TYPE=TEXT VALUE="Press key and release
slowly here" SIZE=40 onkeydown='alert("Key down")'><BR><BR>

<LI>onkeypress: <INPUT TYPE=TEXT VALUE="Type here" SIZE=40
onkeypress='alert("Key pressed")'><BR><BR>

<LI>onkeyup: <INPUT TYPE=TEXT VALUE="Type and release" SIZE=40
onkeyup='alert("Key up")'><BR><BR>

<LI>onload:    Alert presented on initial document load.<BR><BR>

<LI>onmousedown: <INPUT TYPE=BUTTON VALUE="Click and hold"
onmousedown='alert("Mouse down")'><BR><BR>

<LI>onmousemove: Move mouse over this <A HREF=""
onmousemove='alert("Mouse moved")'>link</A><BR><BR>

<LI>onmouseout: Postion mouse <A HREF=""
onmouseout='alert("Mouse out")'>here</A> and now leave.<BR><BR>

<LI>onmouseover: Position mouse over this <A HREF=""
onmouseover='alert("Mouse over")'>link</A><BR><BR>

<LI>onmouseup: <INPUT TYPE="BUTTON" VALUE="Click and release"
onmouseup='alert("Mouse up")'><BR><BR>

<LI>onreset: <INPUT TYPE="RESET" VALUE="Reset Demo"><BR><BR>

<LI>onselect: <INPUT TYPE=TEXT VALUE="Select this text" SIZE=40
onselect='alert("Selected")'><BR><BR>
```

```
<LI>onsubmit: <INPUT TYPE="Submit" VALUE="Test Submit"><BR><BR>

<LI>onunload: Try to leave document by following this
<A HREF="http://www.yahoo.com">link</A>.<BR><BR>

</UL>

</FORM>

</BODY>
</HTML>
```

While the example events should work equally well under Internet Explorer 4.0 and Netscape 4.0 browsers, the extent to which the events can be used in various elements varies from browser to browser. For example, the **onclick** handler is defined for nearly all elements, including **<B>**, **<SPAN>**, and even **<HR>**. However, only Internet Explorer 4.0 currently supports markup like

```
<B onclick='alert("You clicked the bold text")'>Click here</B>
```

As of the time of this writing, Netscape does not provide as rich of an event or object model as the HTML 4.0 specification defines. Furthermore, both the browsers support other events not in the current specification.

Extended Event Models

While HTML 4.0 specifies numerous events, Netscape and Internet Explorer support many more events. Some of the events, such as **onabort**, have been around since Netscape 3.0 and are well understood. The **onabort** handler fires when a download of an image is not completed.

```
<IMG SRC="reallybigimportantimage.gif" onabort='alert("Please
reload page")'>
```

Other events, such as the numerous data binding events, are not nearly as well understood, and are supported only in Internet Explorer 4.0. Table 13-4 lists these extended events as well as their compatibility.

Event Attribute	Description	Associated Elements	Compatibility
onabort	Event triggered by user aborting image load with stop button or similar effect.	<IMG>	Netscape 3.0 Netscape 4.0, Internet Explorer 4.0
onafterupdate	Event fired after the transfer of data from the element to a data provider, namely a data update.	<APPLET>, <BODY>, <BUTTON>, <CAPTION>, <DIV>, <EMBED>, <IMG>, <INPUT>, <MARQUEE>, <OBJECT>, <SELECT>, <TABLE>, <TD>, <TEXTAREA>, <TR>	Internet Explorer 4.0
onbeforeunload	Event fired just prior to a document being unloaded from a window.	<BODY>	Internet Explorer 4.0
onbeforeupdate	Event triggered before the transfer of data from the element to the data provider. Event may be triggered explicitly or by loss of focus or page unload forcing data update.	<APPLET>, <BODY>, <BUTTON>, <CAPTION>, <DIV>, <EMBED>, <HR>, <IMG>, <INPUT>, <OBJECT>, <SELECT>, <TABLE>, <TD>, <TEXTAREA>, <TR>	Internet Explorer 4.0

Table 13-4.   *Extended Event Model*

Event Attribute	Description	Associated Elements	Compatibility
onbounce	Event triggered when bouncing contents of a marquee touch one side or another.	<MARQUEE>	Internet Explorer 4.0
ondataavailable	Event fired when data arrives from data sources that transmit information asynchronously.	<APPLET>, <OBJECT>	Internet Explorer 4.0
ondatasetchanged	Event triggered when the initial data is made available from data source or when the data changes.	<APPLET>, <OBJECT>	Internet Explorer 4.0
ondatasetcomplete	Event indicating that all the data is available from the data source.	<APPLET>, <OBJECT>	Internet Explorer 4.0
ondragstart	Event fired when a user begins to drag a highlighted selection.	<A>, <APPLET>, <AREA>, <BODY>, <BUTTON>, <DIV>, <EMBED>, <HR>, <IMG>, <INPUT>, <MARQUEE>, <OBJECT>, <SELECT>, <TABLE>, <TD>, <TEXTAREA>, <TR>	Internet Explorer 4.0

Table 13-4.   *Extended Event Model* (continued)

Event Attribute	Description	Associated Elements	Compatibility
ondragdrop	Event triggered when a user drags an object onto the browser window to attempt to load it.	<BODY> (window)	Netscape 4.0
onerror	Event fired when the loading of a document, particularly the execution of a script, causes an error. Used to trap syntax errors.	<BODY> (window)	Netscape 3.0 Netscape 4.0 Internet Explorer 4.0
onerrorupdate	Event fired if a data transfer has been canceled by the onbeforeupdate event handler.	<A>, <APPLET>, <OBJECT>, <SELECT>, <TEXTAREA>	Internet Explorer 4.0
onfilterchange	Event fired when a page filter changes state or finishes.	Nearly all elements	Internet Explorer 4.0
onfinish	Event triggered when a looping marquee finishes.	<MARQUEE>	Internet Explorer 4.0
onhelp	Event triggered when user presses F1 key or similar help button in user agent.	Nearly all elements	Internet Explorer 4.0
onmove	Event triggered when user moves a window.	<BODY>	Netscape 4.0

Table 13-4. *Extended Event Model (continued)*

Event Attribute	Description	Associated Elements	Compatibility
onreadystatechange	Similar to onload; fires whenever the ready state for an object has changed.	<APPLET>, <BODY>, <EMBED>, <FRAME>, <FRAMESET>, <IMG>, <LINK>, <OBJECT>, <SCRIPT>, <STYLE>	Internet Explorer 4.0
onresize	Event triggered whenever an object is resized. This event can only be bound to the window under Netscape as set via the <BODY> element.	<BODY>*, <APPLET>, <BUTTON>, <CAPTION>, <DIV>, <EMBED>, <HR>, <IMG>, <MARQUEE>, <OBJECT>, <SELECT>, <TABLE>, <TD>, <TEXTAREA>, <TR>	Netscape 4.0*, Internet Explorer 4.0
onrowenter	Event indicating that a bound data row has changed and new data values are available.	<APPLET>, <BODY>, <BUTTON>, <CAPTION>, <DIV>, <EMBED>, <HR>, <IMG>, <MARQUEE>, <OBJECT>, <SELECT>, <TABLE>, <TD>, <TEXTAREA>, <TR>	Internet Explorer 4.0

Table 13-4.   *Extended Event Model* (continued)

Event Attribute	Description	Associated Elements	Compatibility
onrowexit	Event fired just before a bound data source control changes the current row.	<APPLET>, <BODY>, <BUTTON>, <CAPTION>, <DIV>, <EMBED>, <HR>, <IMG>, <MARQUEE>, <OBJECT>, <SELECT>, <TABLE>, <TD>, <TEXTAREA>, <TR>	Internet Explorer 4.0
onscroll	Event fired when a scrolling element is repositioned.	<BODY>, <DIV>, <FIELDSET>, <IMG>, <MARQUEE>, <SPAN>, <TEXTAREA>	Internet Explorer 4.0
onselectstart	Event fired when user begins to select information by highlighting.	Nearly all elements	Internet Explorer 4.0
onstart	Event fired when a looped marquee begins or starts over.	<MARQUEE>	Internet Explorer 4.0

Table 13-4.   *Extended Event Model* (continued)

The following markup demonstrates a few of the extended events for Netscape 4.0 and Internet Explorer 4.0.

```
<HTML>
<HEAD>
<TITLE>Extended Events</TITLE>
</HEAD>
<BODY onhelp='alert("Going to help now")'
```

```
        ondragdrop='alert("Drag and drop.")'
        onmove='alert("Moving")'
        onresize='alert("Resizing")'>

<H1 ALIGN="CENTER">Extended Events Example</H1>


<UL>
  <LI>onbounce, onfinish, onstart:
      Watch marquee events fire (IE4 Only)<BR>
        <MARQUEE BEHAVIOR="ALTERNATE"
        BGCOLOR="yellow" LOOP="2" WIDTH="400"
        onstart='alert("Marquee start!")'
        onbounce='alert("Bounced!")'
        onfinish='alert("Marquee done!")'>
          Bouncing message
        </MARQUEE>
      <BR><BR>

  <LI>ondragdrop: Try dragging a file onto the browser window
  (N4 Only)

  <LI>ondragstart: Try selecting text and dragging (IE4 Only)<BR>
    <FORM>
    <TEXTAREA ROWS="1" COLS="80"
              ondragstart='alert("Going to drag")'>
    Select this text and attempt to drag
    </TEXTAREA>
    </FORM><BR>

  <LI>onhelp: Click in window and hit F1 key for help. (IE4 Only)

  <LI>onmove: Try moving the browser window.  (N4 Only)

  <LI>onresize: Try resizing the window.

  <LI>onscroll: Scroll the textarea (IE4 Only)<BR>

    <FORM>
    <TEXTAREA ROWS="1" COLS="80" onscroll='alert("Scrolled")'>
    Type some text in here and scroll this
    </TEXTAREA>
```

```
      </FORM><BR>

  <LI>onselectstart:
    <SPAN onselectstart='alert("Select starting")'>Try
     selecting this text</SPAN> (IE4 Only)

</UL>

</BODY>
</HTML>
```

As shown here, events currently vary from browser to browser. How these events can be captured also varies. Netscape current supports a concept called event capturing, while Microsoft supports event bubbling. The basic idea of event bubbling is that an event "bubbles up" through the document structure starting from where it occurred. If a user clicks on a **<B>** element, it may be passed up to an enclosing **<P>** element, then to the **<BODY>** element, and then disappear. Netscape takes the opposite approach, offering the event first to the highest-level structure and then on down. Such differences make coding cross-platform scripts somewhat difficult. Furthermore, the extent of elements that support particular events is changing rapidly. Only some elements under Netscape can respond to events, but this will probably change quickly. To guarantee compatibility, page authors should consider staying with events associated with form controls, as defined in the HTML 4.0 specification.

Error Handlers

One interesting event handler that warrants special consideration is **onerror**. An **onerror** event handler executes scripting code when an error (typically a scripting error) occurs while loading a document. The benefit to the **onerror** handler is that you can use it to turn off the annoying and often numerous error messages that may pester a user when reading a misbehaving script. When used properly, you might even provide the user with a simple feedback message instructing the user what to do to rectify the problem, or even how to report the bug. To display the entire error message in JavaScript and replace it, set window.onerror to the name of your special error handler. Make sure to return true to suppress any normal scripting alerts. The following example shows this idea in use:

```
<HTML>
<HEAD>
<TITLE>Error Handler</TITLE>
```

```
<SCRIPT Language="JavaScript">
<!--
 window.onerror=displaySorry

 function displaySorry(message, url, line)
{
   var msg="There has been a scripting error.\n"
   msg +="Please contact bugs@bigcompany.com\n";
   msg +="Reference file: " + url

   alert(msg);
   return true;
}
//-->
</SCRIPT>
</HEAD>

<BODY>

<SCRIPT>
 bad script code;
</SCRIPT>

</BODY>
</HTML>
```

The "bad script code" above will invoke a dialog, as shown here:

Many sites would benefit from adding such facilities to their pages to suppress and help clean up the numerous scripting errors that occur.

Microsoft Event Handling Extensions

Typically, event handlers are specified as attributes for the particular element the event is associated with. For example:

```
<INPUT TYPE=BUTTON onclick='script'>
```

However, Microsoft also supports a different form of event handler, first in the form of an extension to the **<SCRIPT>** element, and second as a naming convention for VBScript. Under Internet Explorer, the **<SCRIPT>** element also has an **EVENT** and a **FOR** attribute. The **EVENT** attribute is used to define a particular event that should be reacted to, and the **FOR** attribute is used to define the name or ID of the element that the event is tied to. Notice in the following example how the **FOR** attribute is associated with the particular button named myButton, and the **EVENT** attribute is used to specify the event to respond to, in this case **onclick**.

```
<HTML>
<HEAD>
<TITLE>Microsoft Alternate Event Form</TITLE>
<SCRIPT FOR="myButton" EVENT="onclick" LANGUAGE="JavaScript">
<!--
  alert("I've been clicked!");
//-->
</SCRIPT>
</HEAD>
<BODY>

<FORM>
<INPUT TYPE="BUTTON" NAME="myButton" VALUE="Click me">
</FORM>
</BODY>
</HTML>
```

This form of **<SCRIPT>** handler is specific to Microsoft and will cause errors with Netscape browsers. Using VBScript, this style is very common. VBScript also supports a naming convention style for event handling:

```
<HTML>
<HEAD>
<TITLE>Microsoft Alternate Event Form</TITLE>
```

```
<SCRIPT LANGUAGE="VBScript">
<!--
Sub myButton_OnClick
 msgBox "I've been clicked!"
End Sub
-->
</SCRIPT>
</HEAD>
<BODY>


<FORM>
<INPUT TYPE="BUTTON" NAME="myButton" VALUE="Click me">
</FORM>
</BODY>
</HTML>
```

Notice that the name of the subroutine has the event handler name in it, and requires no hooks into HTML. In some sense, this is the cleanest way to integrate scripts with HTML, but JavaScript does not support this style of event handling. The extensions introduced by Microsoft for event handling should be avoided except when using trying to access ActiveX controls, which tend to require the FOR/EVENT style for JScript or the VBScript naming idea.

Dynamic HTML and the Document Object Model

Dynamic HTML (DHTML) is not about new tags or attributes that can animate pages. Dynamic HTML actually extends the current set of HTML elements, and a few other things like style sheet properties, by allowing them to be accessed and modified by a scripting language like JavaScript or VBScript. Dynamic facilities can be added by exposing tags to a scripting language; this allows pages to come alive with movement and interactivity. The tags in a page are accessed through the Document Object Model (DOM).

Every Web document is made up of a variety of elements like **<B>**, **<IMG>**, and **<FORM>**. Browsers read pages in a regular fashion because they understand the extent of the objects that are possible in a page. A page might be composed of three image elements, two paragraphs, an unordered list, and the text within these elements. The DOM describes each document as a collection of individual objects like images, paragraphs, and forms, all the way down to the individual characters. Each particular object may have properties associated with it, typically in the form of HTML attributes. For example, the paragraph element has an alignment attribute that may be set to left, right, or center. In the object model, this attribute is called a property of the object. An object may have methods that are associated with it, and events that may occur and affect it. An image tag may have an **onmouseover** event that is triggered when a user places the cursor over the image. A form may have a submit method that can be used to trigger the submission of the form and its contents to a server-based CGI program. See Figure 13-3 for an overview of these ideas.

The DOM can be complex, but what it can do is impressive—and it doesn't always require a great deal of work, either. Developers may use the object model to find an image on a page and replace it with another image when a user rolls a cursor over it. Such rollovers, or animated buttons, are already common on the Web. In conjunction with scripting, the DOM can also animate a page by moving objects around, create an expanding tree structure to navigate a site, or create a complex application like a game or database front-end. To seasoned JavaScript programmers, many of these ideas might not sound so new. They've been around in a limited form since Netscape 2.0. Beginning with Netscape 2.0, JavaScript provided an object model that allowed access to many parts of a Web page, including anchors, form elements, and images. True Dynamic HTML, however, takes the idea much further. It gets right down to the actual text, styles, tags, and scripts within a page, making the whole page modifiable.

The DOM is the core component of both browser vendors' idea of Dynamic HTML. As defined by the World Wide Web Consortium (W3C), (http://www.w3.org/pub/WWW/MarkUp/DOM/), DOM is a "platform- and language-neutral interface that will allow programs and scripts to dynamically access and update the content, structure, and style of documents." The Web standards body has already released a preliminary version of a requirements document that details what a DOM should do. Work is underway to create a base-level standard documenting the object model already available under Netscape 3.0 and Internet Explorer 3.0; this is considered the Level 0 implementation. This will be followed by a Level 1 description of the new DOM, which also includes the syntax for accessing page elements. A Level 2 specification, which will detail the event model and user interaction issues, will follow later.

The definition of Dynamic HTML as a DOM isn't precisely what is meant by DHTML in the commercial arena. In the commercial environment, DHTML can include style sheets, absolute positioning, multimedia effects, database access facilities, dynamic fonts, and potentially any other thing that can make a page dynamic. This is where the confusion about Dynamic HTML arises. Netscape and Microsoft have the same basic idea about theDOM, and both companies are working jointly with the W3C to develop a standard. But when it comes down to specific details, DHTML varies, often significantly, between the two leading browser vendors. This can cause trouble for designers looking to create cross-platform dynamic pages.

Object Models

Since Netscape 2.0, the browser, window, document, and document contents—forms, images, links and so on—have been modeled as a collection of objects. This is

Given a standard HTML 4.0:

```
<HTML>
<HEAD>
<TITLE>Big Company</TITLE>
</HEAD>
<BODY BGCOLOR="WHITE">
<H1 ALIGN="CENTER">Big Company</H1>
<HR>
<P ID="para1">This is a paragraph of text.</P>
<UL>
      <LI><A HREF="about.htm">About</A>
      <LI><A HREF="products.htm">Products</A>
</UL>
</BODY>
</HTML>
```

This is how the document is modeled:

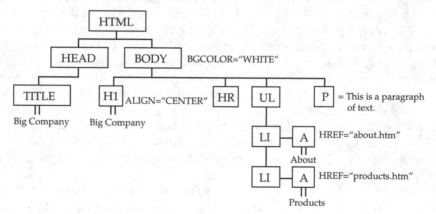

This is how scripting works within the document:

Scripting has access to the elements either directly by binding script code, as follows:

```
<A HREF="products.htm" onmouseover="this.style.color=red"
onmouseout="this.style.color=blue">Products Section</A>
```

or by referencing items by names or collections, as shown here:

```
para1.style.color=green
```

Events like **onclick** and **onmouseover** are used to bind script code to user actions.

Figure 13-3.   *Overview of the Document Object Model (DOM) and scripting*

generically referred to as the DOM Both of the major browsers support the DOM idea, but each has different naming conventions and a different degree of exposure. For example, under Netscape 3.0, only particular items—form elements—are accessible for scripting. Figure 13-4 illustrates the object model for Netscape 3.0 and Internet Explorer 3.0.

Notice that objects in the Netscape 3.0 object hierarchy provide access not only to page elements like links, anchors, frames, and forms but to things like the browser's name, history, plug-ins, and Java classes associated with the current window. When the W3C introduces the Level 0 DOM, it will bear some resemblance to this model, though it may be missing items that are not supported by Internet Explorer 3.0 like the **Images[]** collection, which is an array that exposes the images in a page to scripts.

With the introduction of Netscape 4.0, more elements, such as layers, are accessible. Under Internet Explorer 4.0, all page elements are scriptable, and it is obvious that Netscape will soon follow suit, making the entire page modifiable. Figure 13-5 shows an expanded object model. Note that many of the items in this model are available only under one browser or another.

Once the objects that make up a page are accessible, there are certain changes that must be made to HTML documents, particularly concerning correct markup and naming of elements.

HTML and Scripting Access

While the DOM specifies a model for all the objects and HTML elements that make a Web page, things need to be named properly to allow scripting languages to easily read and manipulate things. The basic way to attach a unique identifier to an HTML element under HTML 4.0 is by using the **ID** attribute. The **ID** attribute is associated with nearly every element, as shown in Table 13-5.

The point of the **ID** attribute is to bind a unique identifier to the element. To name a particular enclosed piece of text "SuperImportant," you could use the markup shown here:

```
<B ID="SuperImportant">This is very important</B>
```

Naming is very important. Authors are encouraged to adopt a consistent naming style and to avoid using potential confusing names that include the names of HTML elements themselves. For example, "button" does not make a very good name, and may interfere with scripting language access. To insure uniqueness in names, you may want to use an underscore in the name, as in, for example, _myButton.

NAME Attribute

Before HTML 4.0, the **NAME** attribute was often used to expose items to scripting. For backward compatibility, the **NAME** attribute is commonly defined for <A>, <APPLET>, <BUTTON>, <EMBED>, <FORM>, <FRAME>, <IFRAME>, <IMG>,

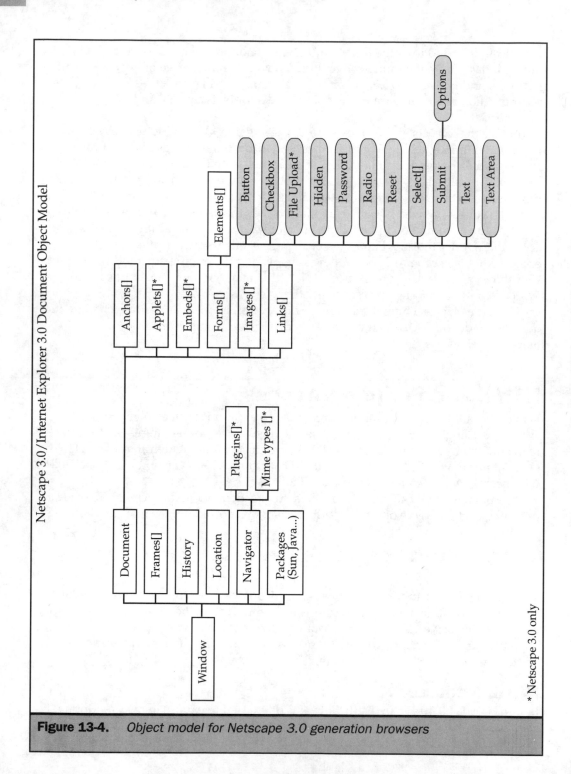

Figure 13-4. Object model for Netscape 3.0 generation browsers

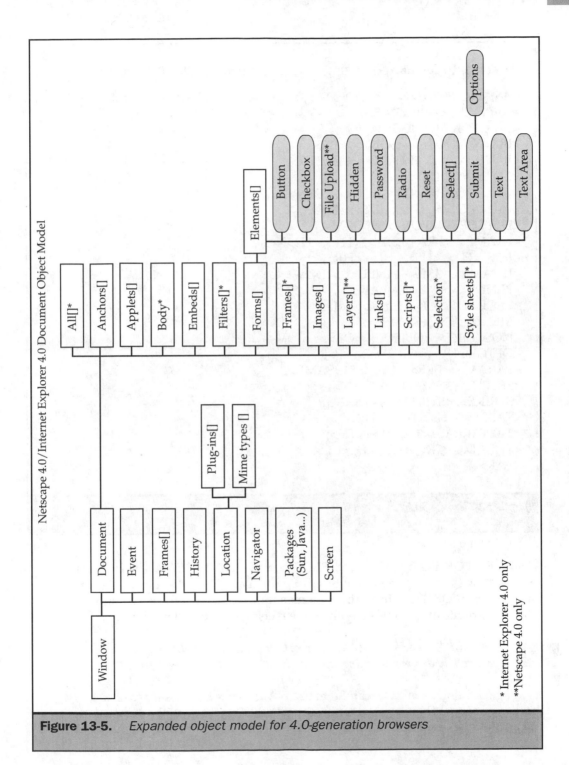

Figure 13-5.   *Expanded object model for 4.0-generation browsers*

ID Attribute Supported

<A>, <ACRONYMN>, <ADDRESS>,
<APPLET>, <AREA>, <B>,
<BASEFONT>, <BDO>, <BIG>,
<BLOCKQUOTE>, <BODY>, <BR>,
<BUTTON>, <CAPTION>, <CENTER>,
<CITE>, <CODE>, <COL>,
<COLGROUP>, <DD>, <DEL>, <DFN>,
<DIR>, <DIV>, <DL>, <DT>, <EM>,
<FIELDSET>, <FONT>, <FORM>,
<FRAME>, <FRAMESET>, <H1>, <H2>,
<H3>, <H4>, <H5>, <H6>, <HR>, <I>,
<IFRAME>, <IMG>, <INPUT>, <INS>,
<ISINDEX>, <KBD>, <LABEL>,
<LEGEND>, <LI>, <LINK>, <MAP>,
<MENU>, <NOFRAMES>,
<NOSCRIPT>, <OBJECT>, <OL>,
<OPTGROUP>, <OPTION>, <P>,
<PARAM>, <PRE>, <Q>, <S>, <SAMP>,
<SELECT>, <SMALL>, <SPAN>,
<STRIKE>, <STRONG>, <D, <SUP>,
<TABLE>, <TBODY>, <TD>,
<TEXTAREA>, <TFOOT>, <TH>,
<THEAD>, <TR>, <TT>, <D, <UL>,
<VAR>

ID Attribute Not Supported

<BASE>, <HEAD>, <HTML>, <META>,
<SCRIPT>, <STYLE>, <TITLE>

Table 13-5.   ID *Support for HTML 4.0 Elements*

<INPUT>, **<OBJECT>**, **<MAP>**, **<SELECT>**, and **<TEXTAREA>**. The HTML 4.0
specification does not support all these. In particular, **<FORM>** and **<IMG>** are
missing, and **<OBJECT>** has a different meaning. Notice that the occurrence of the
NAME attribute corresponds closely to the Netscape 3.0 object model.

Note   *Both* **<META>** *and* **<PARAM>** *support attributes called* **NAME**, *but these
have totally different meanings than script access.*

Page developers must be careful to use **NAME** where necessary to ensure
backward compatibility with older browser. Earlier browsers will not recognize the
ID attribute, so use **NAME** as well. However, as **NAME** and **ID** share the same

namespace, you must not use the same value for both. As **ID** is not case sensitive, values differentiated only by case are not allowed. For example **<A NAME="link1" ID="LINK1">** is not legal. If the names clash, what happens remains unclear; some browsers may ignore the second occurrence, while others may disable script access.

Another consideration when adding scripting to a page is whether the HTML is well formed. Simple things such as crossed elements, like

```
<B><I>Test</B></I>
```

may cause a problem with a scripting language. This has to do with the manipulation of the text within the elements. Page authors should consider it dangerous to manipulate malformed markup with scripts; according to the HTML 4.0 specification, the results are unpredictable.

When HTML documents are well formed, scripting languages like JavaScript and VBScript can be used to read and manipulate the various objects in a page. DOM defines a special set of reserved names that use this notation to allow scripting languages like JavaScript to refer to entities in the browser and the document, including form elements. The basic notation uses a series of object and property names separated by dots. To access the form defined by

```
<FORM NAME="myform" ID="myform">
<INPUT TYPE="TEXT" NAME="username">
</FORM>
```

with a scripting language, use either window.document.myform or simply document.myform. The field and its value can be accessed in a similar fashion. To access the text field, use document.myform.username. To access the actual value of the username field, access the value property using document.myform.username.value. This simple naming style can be used to access the properties of the various objects that make up the document. The following example shows how a form can be accessed and its contents displayed in a dialog box.

```
<HTML>
<HEAD>
<TITLE>Meet and Greet</TITLE>

<SCRIPT LANGUAGE="JavaScript">
<!--
function sayHello()
{
   theirname=document.myform.username.value;
```

```
  if (theirname !="")
   alert("Hello "+theirname+"!");
  else
   alert("Don't be shy.");
}
// -->
</SCRIPT>
</HEAD>
<BODY>
<FORM ACTION="mailto: info@bigcompany.com"
      METHOD="POST" NAME="myform">
<B>What's your name?</B>
<INPUT TYPE="TEXT" NAME="username" SIZE=20> <BR><BR>

<INPUT TYPE="BUTTON" VALUE="Greet" onclick='sayHello()'>

</BODY>
</HTML>
```

One potential difficult problem to overcome with naming document objects is the **NAME** and **ID** namespace conflict. Older browsers only understand **NAME** while the specification encourages **ID**. A likely approach would be simply to set the **NAME** and **ID** attributes to be the same values as those shown here:

```
<INPUT TYPE="TEXT" NAME="username" ID="username">
```

Unfortunately, this approach is not supposed to work since **NAME** and **ID** share the namespace, so this is a conflict. In practice browsers don't seem to care. Scripting could be used to deal with different names for the same object but that introduces needless complexity. The simple solution is to use **NAME** on all elements that support it and **ID** on the new elements.

Besides accessing the properties of various document objects, it is also occasionally possible to trigger actions called *methods*. An example of a method would be to submit a form. In the last example, **document.myform.submit()** would submit the form to the address specified by the **ACTION** attribute for the **<FORM>** element.

The last example only scratches the surface of the DOM. It is possible to refer to forms and form elements without assigning them a name using an array notation. Forms can be referred to by a forms array with the numbers beginning at 0. Elements within a form can be referred to by an elements array that also begins at 0. The last example contains only one form and one field, so the syntax **document.forms[0].elements[0].value** is the same as document.myform.username.value. Note that it is better to name elements rather than to access them via their position in a page, since any additions or movement of the HTML elements within the page may potentially break the script.

It is also possible, in some cases, to update the contents of certain elements such as form fields. The following example code shows how this might be done:

```
<HTML>
<HEAD>
<TITLE>Meet and Greet 2</TITLE>

<SCRIPT LANGUAGE="JavaScript">
<!--
function sayHello()
{
   theirname = document.myform.username.value;

   if (theirname != "")
    document.myform.response.value="Hello "+theirname+"!";
   else
     document.myform.response.value="Don't be shy.";
}
// -->
</SCRIPT>
</HEAD>
<BODY>
<FORM ID="myform">
<B>What's your name?</B>
<INPUT TYPE="TEXT" ID="username" SIZE="20"> <BR><BR>
<B>Greeting:</B>
<INPUT TYPE="TEXT" ID="response" SIZE="40"> <BR><BR>

<INPUT TYPE="BUTTON" VALUE="Greet" onclick='sayHello()'>

</BODY>
</HTML>
```

Under Netscape 3.0, 4.0, and Internet Explorer 3.0, only some objects in a page are changeable, notably form elements. Starting with Internet Explorer 4.0, everything in a page can be modified right down to the very text and markup itself. This is the real idea of Dynamic HTML. Look at the following markup:

```
<HTML>
<HEAD>
<TITLE>Simple DHTML for IE4</TITLE>
</HEAD>
<BODY>

<B ID="bold1" onclick='this.innerText="The text has
changed"'>Click me</B>
<BR><BR><BR>
<SPAN onclick="bold1.innerText='Click me'">Change text back</SPAN>

</BODY>
</HTML>
```

Notice that the **<B>** element is named bold1. This is later referenced by the **<SPAN>** element. Furthermore, notice that the actual text is changed when the user clicks on the text regions. It is obvious that this form of DHTML is very powerful, particularly when you consider that it can also be used to control style sheets.

Script Interaction with Style Sheets

Both Netscape and Microsoft support scripting access for style sheets. Netscape initially put a great deal of emphasis on JavaScript-accessible style sheets (JASS). With JASS, it was possible to script the initial creation of style sheets with JavaScript style syntax. However, once the page was rendered, the styles were fixed. Microsoft has shown how style sheets can be manipulated via scripting language. For example, the following code fragment shows how events can be tied with style changes to make text that changes to red when the mouse is over it.

```
<SPAN onmouseover='this.style.color="#FF0000"'
 onmouseout='this.style.color="#000000"'>Colored Button</SPAN>
```

The special scripting keyword "this" is a shortcut reference to the current element, but the **ID** attribute could be used just as well, as shown here:

```
<SPAN ID="testtext"
 onmouseover='testtext.style.color="#FF0000";
testtext.style.fontSize="larger"'
```

```
onmouseout='testtext.style.color="#000000";
testtext.style.fontSize="smaller"'>
Colored Button</SPAN>
```

It is also possible to use multiple style sheet rules, as presented in Chapter 10. In the last example, the size and color of the text are changed when the mouse rolls over it. Using positioning, style sheets and scripting, it is possible to make some very dynamic pages with little effort, as shown by the example in Figure 13-6. A sample rendering of this example under Internet Explorer showing the rollover text is shown in Figure 13-7.

Currently, Microsoft and Netscape differ on how style sheets can be accessed and the degree to which they can be manipulated. For example, under Netscape 4.0 the only style sheet properties that can be changed after the document has loaded are the absolute positioning properties left, top, z-index, and visibility.

Ramifications of Scripting

Scripting pages comes with a cost. Page developers must be extremely careful when scripting pages that are supposed to work under many different browsers. Subtle bugs exist in JavaScript that can ruin a page. For example, page developers might find using a variable called **name** troublesome under Netscape 3.0, but fine under Netscape 2, 4, and Internet Explorer. You should expect trouble, since **name** is a bad variable choice given its use as an attribute, but the example indicates the subtle nature of JavaScript. Other problems arise with the use of particular document objects, which may not be defined under older browsers. For example, using the screen object it is easy to query for the user's screen resolution and color depth. However, under Netscape 2.0 and 3.0, this object is not defined.

Even if you are extremely careful in coding your pages, bugs will still creep in. The browsers have bugs of their own, particularly in their scripting implementations. Without careful testing, it will be difficult to understand if script code will work under all browsers. Just how many systems would you have to test under? There are three major versions of JavaScript and two versions of JScript. Try to test under Macintosh, Windows 95/NT, and Windows 3.1, and UNIX where the browser is available and you have nearly twenty different testing platforms. Even if you test for all these situations, you can never assume anything. What happens if users turn off their JavaScript support and the page relies on it? Defensive programming techniques that account for error conditions and unusual situations should always be adopted. Pages should be developed with rigorous standards, just as any program would be developed. Last but not least, consider that the real point is to get something accomplished; client-side scripting is only one tool in your programming arsenal. For example, moving

```
<HTML>
<HEAD>
<TITLE>DHTML Example</TITLE>
</HEAD>

<STYLE TYPE="text/css">
<!--
BODY        {font-family: Impact; font-size: 18pt; text-indent: 20;
             line-height: 200%; background: black; color: white;}
H1          {font-size: 32pt; color: green;}
.over       {font-size: 20pt; color: red}
-->
</STYLE>

<BODY>

<H1 ALIGN="CENTER">Big Company, Inc.</H1>

<DIV onMouseOver="this.className='over';
Description.innerText='Information about Big Company, Inc.'"
onMouseOut="this.className=''; Description.innerText=' '">About
</DIV>

<DIV onMouseOver="this.className='over';
Description.innerText='Information about our Super Gadgets'"
onMouseOut="this.className=''; Description.innerText=''">Products
</DIV>

<DIV onMouseOver="this.className='over'; Description.innerText=
'How to contact us'" onMouseOut="this.className='';
Description.innerText=''">Contact</DIV>

<DIV ALIGN="RIGHT" ID="Description">  </DIV>

</BODY>
</HTML>
```

Figure 13-6.   *Dynamic HTML example*

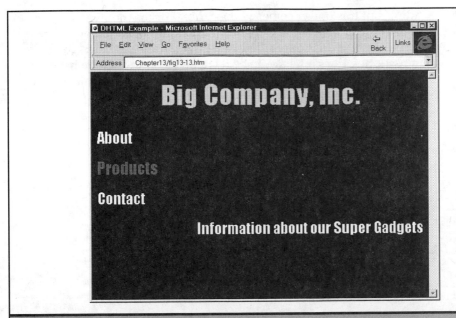

Figure 13-7.   *Rendering of DHTML example under Internet Explorer 4.0*

application logic to the server may be a good way to reduce headache potential, since the server will be under your control.

Summary

Client-side technologies have their place in a Web site. The evolution of scripting technologies has offloaded some of the processing that traditionally occurred on the server. For example, validating form field entries using JavaScript or VBScript on the client makes more sense than relegating this processing to the server. Integrating scripts into a Web page comes in two major forms: within the **<SCRIPT>** element and as event handlers. Script code can be used to modify elements within a page by accessing the Document Object Model (DOM), particularly when the HTML is well formed and named using the **ID** attribute. Modeling the document as a collection of objects has been around since Netscape 2.0, but under the idea of DHTML it has been taken to a new extreme. Now browsers like Internet Explorer 4.0 can be used to manipulate anything on a Web page from simple text elements like **<B>**, to style sheets, to even the very text of the page itself. DHTML shows where client-side computing is heading, but this power comes with a price. For the moment, there is no standard for DOM, so defensive programming techniques and major amounts of testing are required when building script-filled Web pages. If the page designer takes proper steps, client scripting does not have to be relegated to simple embellishments. It should be considered the "glue" that is used to tie elements of a Web page together, including embedded binary objects.

Chapter 14

Client-Side Programming and HTML

The last chapter discussed how scripting elements can be added to HTML pages. Scripts can manipulate a variety of form elements, and, in the case of Dynamic HTML, the page elements themselves. Scripts are also used to access embedded binary objects. As discussed in Chapter 7, embedded objects can be used to bring new media types like sounds and movies to the Web. They can also be used to add small executable programs to a page. Binary objects come in many forms, including Netscape plug-ins, Java applets, and ActiveX controls. Each of these requires special HTML elements. In the future all included media types will eventually be added with the **<OBJECT>** element. Until objects are standardized, however, it will be useful to understand each individual technology and how it might intersect with HTML.

Scripting, Programming, and Objects

You might wonder why this chapter is separate from the last. With both scripts and embedded objects, the interactivity takes place on the client side. What's the difference? Why distinguish between scripting and objects? Remember the point of Web client-side scripting—small bits of interpreted code used to add a bit of functionality to a page or fill the gaps in an application. Scripting is *not* necessarily as complex or general as programming, though it often seems like it. Programming is more generalized than scripting; it makes it possible to create just about anything you can imagine, though it tends to take longer than scripting. Think about checking the data fields of a form. A few lines of code to make sure the fields are filled in is all you need. Now think about trying to create something sophisticated like a Web-based resume handling system that can sort through thousands of submissions a day. This will take more than a few lines of code, and should probably be programmed in a language like Java, C/C++, or Visual Basic.

Scripting generally isn't powerful enough to build full applications, but it can be useful in tying things together. As you build your Web application, you may decide to build the logic entirely on the server, in the form of a Common Gateway Interface (CGI) program, or you may use a client-side technology (Java applets or ActiveX controls). If you choose a client-side technology, you'll probably build the Web pages with a combination of HTML, scripting, and embedded programming objects such as ActiveX controls, Netscape plug-ins or Java applets. Building objects is not trivial. It can require significant knowledge of programming. It may be possible to use premade objects, generically called *components*, and string these together using HTML and JavaScript or VBScript. For most casual Web page designers, putting together a custom object will probably not be necessary. This chapter will discuss each of the object technologies, as well as how such objects can be inserted into a Web page.

Plug-ins

Plug-ins were introduced by Netscape in Navigator 2.0 and later supported by Internet Explorer 3.0. They address the communication and integration issues that plagued helper applications. *Plug-ins* are small helper programs (components) that run within the context of the browser itself. There are drawbacks to the plug-in approach of extending a browser's features. Users must locate and download plug-ins, install them, and even restart their browsers. Many users find this rather complicated. Netscape 4.0 may offer some installation relief with somewhat self-installing plug-ins and other features, but plug-ins remain troublesome. Even worse than installation problems, plug-ins are not available on every machine; an executable program, or *binary*, must be created for each particular operating system. Because of this machine specific approach, many plug-ins only work on Windows-95/NT. A decreasing number of them work on Windows 3.1, Macintosh or UNIX. Finally, each plug-in installed on a system is a persistent extension to the browser, and takes up memory and disk space.

The benefit of plug-ins is that they can be well integrated into Web pages. They may be included using the HTML elements **<EMBED>** or **<OBJECT>**. Typically, the **<EMBED>** syntax is used, but over time the **<OBJECT>** form is the preferred method. In general, the **<EMBED>** element takes an **SRC** attribute to specify the URL of the included binary object. **HEIGHT** and **WIDTH** attributes often are used to indicate the pixel dimensions of the included object, if it is visible. To embed a short Audio Visual Interleaved (AVI) format movie called welcome.avi that could be viewed by the Netscape LiveVideo plug-in (built into Netscape 3.x and 4.x generation browsers), use the following HTML fragment:

```
<EMBED SRC="welcome.avi" HEIGHT="100" WIDTH="100">
```

The **<EMBED>** element displays the plug-in, in this case a movie, as part of the HTML document in a rectangular area of the page (shown in Figure 14-1).

While plug-ins can appear anywhere in a Web page, there are special limitations on plug-ins within a **<LAYER>** element. Plug-ins use the main window, and will usually appear on top of all other content.

A browser may have many plug-ins installed. To check which plug-ins are installed in Netscape, the user may enter a strange URL like **about:plugins** or look under the Help menu of the browser for an entry that reads "About Plug-ins." The browser will show a list of plug-ins that are installed, the associated MIME type that

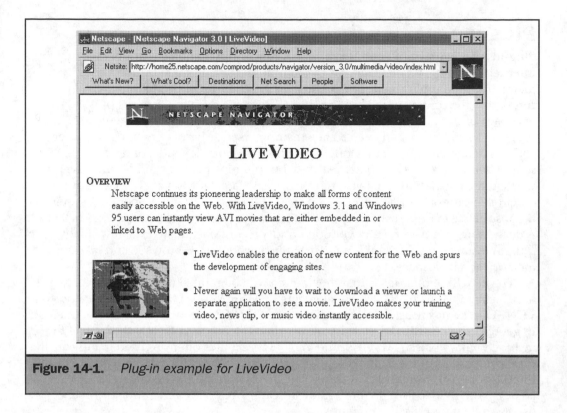

Figure 14-1. Plug-in example for LiveVideo

will invoke each plug-in, and information as to whether that plug-in is enabled. Figure 14-2 shows an example of the plug-in information page.

<EMBED> Syntax

The primary way to load plug-ins for Netscape 2.x, 3.x, and Internet Explorer 3.x browsers is to use the HTML element **<EMBED>**. The **<EMBED>** element is not part of the HTML 4.0 specification, but the **<OBJECT>** element is only available under Microsoft Internet Explorer 3.0 and beyond and Netscape 4.0 and beyond. For backward compatibility, both forms may have to be used, as shown later in this chapter. The general syntax of the **<EMBED>** element is shown here:

```
<EMBED
     SRC=URL of embedded data
     ALIGN=LEFT | RIGHT | TOP | BOTTOM | MIDDLE
     BORDER=pixels
     HEIGHT=pixels or percentage
     HIDDEN=TRUE | FALSE (default)
```

```
HSPACE=pixels
NAME=identifier
PALETTE=FOREGROUND | BACKGROUND
PLUGINSPAGE=URL
PLUGINURL=URL
TYPE=MIME Type
UNITS=PIXELS | EN
VSPACE=pixels
WIDTH=pixels or percentage>
```

The most important attribute for the **<EMBED>** element is probably **SRC**, which is set to the URL of the data object to pass to the plug-in and embed in the page. The browser generally determines the MIME type of the file, and thus the plug-in to pass the data to, by the filename suffix. For example, a file like test1.dcr would be mapped to a MIME type of application/x-director and passed to a Shockwave for Director plug-in. In some cases, however, the plug-in to use with a particular **<EMBED>** tag is not obvious. In some cases, the plug-in may not need to use an **SRC** attribute if it

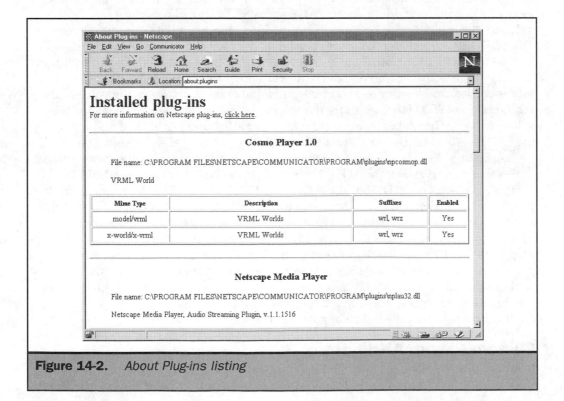

Figure 14-2.   *About Plug-ins listing*

reads all its data at run-time or doesn't need any external data. If there is no **SRC** attribute, how is the proper plug-in determined? The best way to indicate the plug-in is to use the **TYPE** attribute and set it to the MIME type, which then uses the appropriate plug-in. Don't use the **TYPE** attribute to override a MIME type or avoid using file extensions. In the following markup fragment, the file named mysteryfile has no filename suffix.

```
<EMBED SRC="mysteryfile" TYPE="application/x-director">
```

Although a **TYPE** attribute is used, this won't work because the server will send the file with a content type indication of plain/text or application/octet-stream and the browser will attempt to handle it accordingly. Instead, the file should be named correctly. In general, you should not need the **TYPE** attribute if the **SRC** attribute can be used to infer the type. The use of **TYPE** is mandatory if the **SRC** is not set.

Since plug-ins are rectangular embedded objects similar to images, the **<EMBED>** element has many of the same attributes as the **<IMG>** element: **ALIGN**, **BORDER**, **HEIGHT**, **WIDTH**, **HSPACE**, and **VSPACE**. Remember that the **ALIGN** attribute is used to align the object in relation to the page and allow text to flow text around the object. To achieve the desired text layout, you may have to use the **
** element with the **CLEAR** attribute. Setting the **HSPACE** and **VSPACE** attributes to a pixel value indicates the buffer region between the embedded object and the surrounding text. The **BORDER** attribute is used to set a border for the plug-in in pixels. As with images, it may be useful to set this attribute to zero when using the embedded object as a link.

As with the **<IMG>** element, the **HEIGHT** and **WIDTH** attributes can be used to set the vertical and horizontal size of the embedded object. Typically, the values for **HEIGHT** and **WIDTH** are in pixels, though they may be expressed as percentage values as well. The unit of measurement for these attributes can also be defined using the **UNITS** attribute. The default for this attribute is a pixel value, though a value of **EN** can be used to indicate that half the point size should be used as the measurement unit. Values for **HEIGHT** and **WIDTH** should always be set unless the **HIDDEN** attribute is used. The **HIDDEN** attribute set to **TRUE** in the **<EMBED>** causes the plug-in to be hidden and overrides any setting of **HEIGHT** and **WIDTH**, as well as any effect the object may have on layout. Another interesting attribute for the **<EMBED>** element is **PALETTE**. This attribute indicates the color palette for the plug-in to use. By default, the plug-in will use the background palette, but it is also possible to use the foreground color palette by setting the attribute to **FOREGROUND**. Setting this value properly may avoid the annoying color shifting that goes on under Windows environments with limited color support when switching between applications that use different color palettes.

Custom Plug-In Attributes

In addition to the standard attributes for the **<EMBED>** element, plug-ins may have custom attributes to communicate specialized information between the HTML page and the plug-in code. A movie-playing plug-in may have a **LOOP** attribute to indicate how many times to loop the movie. Remember that under HTML, the browser ignores all nonstandard attributes when parsing the HTML. All other attributes are passed to the plug-in, allowing the plug-in to examine the list for any custom attributes that could modify its behavior. There is no way to enumerate all the possible custom attributes there may be. Each particular plug-in used may have a variety of custom attributes. You should be certain to look at the documentation for whatever plug-in you are going to use.

Attributes for Installation of Plug-ins

Users often have a difficult time installing plug-ins. Under Netscape 2.0, plug-ins often had to be found and installed manually. Users could visit the Plug-in Plaza at Browserwatch (www.browserwatch.com) and install the plug-ins that interested them. These plug-ins often came with installation scripts; a few required the user to manually copy the plug-in to the appropriate directories. The directory, usually found in the same directory as the browser application itself, was named "plug-ins." On the Unix system, however, the directory could be set using the environment variable NPX_PLUGIN_PATH, which defaulted to /usr/local/netscape/plugins, ~/netscape/plugins. This path could be different than where the browser application was installed.

Having users figure out which plug-in to install manually by themselves isn't the best solution. It is possible to set the **PLUGINSPACE** attribute equal to a URL that indicates the instructions for installing the plug-in. This way, if the browser encounters an **<EMBED>** element it can't handle, it will visit the specified page and provide information on how to download and install the plug-in. Starting with Netscape 4.0, however, this attribute automatically points to a special Netscape plug-in finder page. Netscape's 4.0 browser release also simplifies the plug-in installation process by introducing the JAR Installation Manager (JIM), which is used to install Java Archive Files, or JAR files for short. JAR files are a collection of files, including plug-ins, that can be automatically downloaded and installed. Set the **PLUGINURL** attribute for the **<EMBED>** element to the URL of a JAR file containing the plug-in needed. If the user does not have the appropriate plug-in already installed, the browser will invoke JIM with the specified JAR file and begin the download and installation process. The user has control over this process. The downloaded objects may be signed—a type of authentication—in order to help users avoid downloading malicious code. Figure 14-3 shows a sample JIM window under Netscape 4.0.

In Netscape 4.0 or greater, the **PLUGINURL** attribute takes precedence over **PLUGINSPAGE**. It is recommended that you use **PLUGINURL** rather than **PLUGINSPAGE**, particularly since the Netscape browser will default to a plug-in finder page without the **PLUGINSPAGE** attribute. While the JIM provides a great deal of help in dealing with plug-ins, it is very specific to Netscape. Microsoft's Internet Explorer does support the **<EMBED>** element, and so any benefits of the JIM will not be experienced by Internet Explorer users.

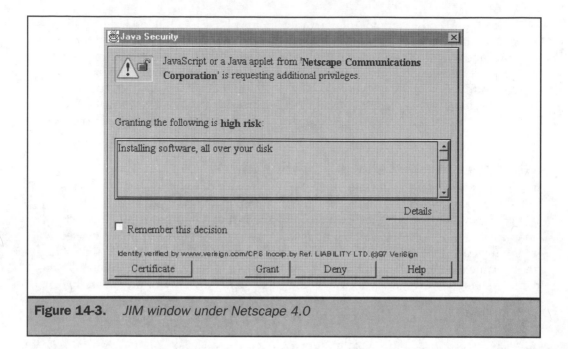

Figure 14-3. *JIM window under Netscape 4.0*

<NOEMBED>

One important aspect of plug-ins is the idea of **<NOEMBED>**. Some browsers do not understand Netscape's plug-in architecture, or even the **<EMBED>** element. Rather than lock these browsers out of a Web page, the **<NOEMBED>** element allows you to provide some alternative text or marked up content. In the short example presented below, an AVI video is embedded in the page. The **<NOEMBED>** element contains an image, which in turn has an alternative text reading set with the **ALT** attribute. Note how the example degrades from a very sophisticated setting all the way down to a text-only environment:

```
<EMBED SRC="welcome.avi" HEIGHT=100 WIDTH=100>
<NOEMBED>
   <IMG SRC="welcome.gif" ALT="Welcome to Big Company, Inc.">
</NOEMBED>
```

One potential problem with the **<NOEMBED>** approach occurs when a browser supports plug-ins but lacks the specific plug-in to deal with the included binary object. In this case, the user will be presented with a broken puzzle-piece or similar icon, and then be directed to a page to download the missing plug-in. The **PLUGINURL** or **PLUGSINPAGE** attribute should be set in order to start the user on the process of getting the plug-in to view the content.

<OBJECT> Syntax for Plug-ins

Starting with Netscape 4.0, it is possible to use the **<OBJECT>** element to include a variety of object types in a Web page, including Netscape plug-ins. Like the **<EMBED>** element, the **<OBJECT>** element's attributes determine the type of object to include as well as the type and location of the plug-in. The **<OBJECT>** element supports alternate representations if the browser is not capable of supporting the object. The **<EMBED>** element currently used for plug-ins does not handle this well, though it does provide the **<NOEMBED>** syntax. The syntax of **<OBJECT>** as it relates to the **<EMBED>** element is shown here. A more generalized discussion of the **<OBJECT>** element will be presented the upcoming section about ActiveX controls.

```
<OBJECT
    DATA=URL of Object's Data
    ALIGN==LEFT | RIGHT | TOP | BOTTOM | MIDDLE
    CODEBASE=URL
    CLASSID=URL of plug-in to download
    HEIGHT=pixels
    ID=Unique Identifier
    TYPE=MIME Type
    WIDTH=pixels>

  Alternative HTML representation here
</OBJECT>
```

The **DATA** attribute represents the URL of the object's data and is equivalent to the **SRC** attribute of **EMBED**. Like the **<EMBED>** element, the **TYPE** attribute represents the MIME type of the object's data. This may sometimes be inferred from the value of the **DATA** attributed. The **CODEBASE** attribute represents the URL of the plug-in. The **CODEBASE** attribute is similar to the **PLUGINSPAGE** attribute. The **CLASSID** attribute is used to specify the URL to be used to install the plug-in using the JIM. If there is no **CLASSID** attribute specified and the object can't be handled, the object is ignored, and any nested HTML is displayed. The **ID** attribute is used to set the name of the object for scripting. If the browser cannot handle the type, or cannot determine the type, it cannot embed the object. Subsequent HTML is parsed as normal. An example of using the LiveAudio plug-in under Netscape 4.0 with the **<OBJECT>** syntax is shown here:

```
<OBJECT DATA="click.wav" TYPE="audio/wav" HEIGHT=60 WIDTH=144
        AUTOSTART=FALSE>
   <B>Sorry, no LiveAudio installed...</B>
</OBJECT>
```

Page authors should be careful with this **<OBJECT>** element and referencing plug-ins, since compatibility issues with Microsoft Internet Explorer may arise.

Scripting and Plug-ins

It is possible to access plug-ins from a scripting language. Each plug-in in a document can be referenced by Netscape's version of JavaScript as an element of the **embeds[]** collection, which is part of the document object. The **NAME** attribute should be set to a unique identifier so the plug-in can be accessed easily by name from a scripting language. Internet Explorer and Netscape 4.0 prefer the use of the **ID** attribute; the plug-in may not work well with the **NAME** attribute. For backward compatibility with Netscape 3.x generation browsers, the **NAME** attribute should be used whenever possible. An example of how a plug-in is named is shown here:

```
<EMBED SRC="welcome.avi" NAME="WelcomeMovie" HEIGHT=100 WIDTH=100>
```

This example gives the LiveVideo plug-in the name WelcomeMovie. Once named, the plug-in can be accessed from JavaScript as **document.WelcomeMovie**. If it is the second plug-in in the page, it could also be referenced as **document.embeds[1]**. Why not index 2? Arrays in JavaScript, which is how collections are implemented, start numbering at zero, so **document.embeds[0]** references the first plug-in and **document.embeds[1]** references the second plug-in and so on.

Under Netscape 3.0, 4.0, and Internet Explorer 4.0, it is possible to determine which plug-ins are available in the browser by using the **plugins[]** collection, which is part of the navigator object in JavaScript. The following markup displays the plug-ins that are installed on the system:

```
<HTML>
<HEAD>
<TITLE>Print Plug-ins</TITLE>
</HEAD>
<BODY>

<H2 ALIGN="CENTER">Plug-ins Installed</H2>
<HR>

<SCRIPT LANGUAGE="JavaScript">

if (navigator.appName = "Microsoft Internet Explorer")
 document.write("Plug-ins[] collection not supported under IE");
else
 {
```

```
   num_plugins = navigator.plugins.length;
   for (count=0; count < num_plugins; count++)
   document.write(navigator.plugins[count].name + "<BR>");
 }

</SCRIPT>

</BODY>
</HTML>
```

Note that this example will not display the plug-ins under Internet Explorer, since that browser does not support the same **plugins[]** collection. Under Netscape, however, it would be possible to use some simple if-then logic to determine what HTML to use if a particular plug-in is loaded in the browser.

Once an occurrence of a plug-in is named in a page, it may be possible to manipulate the plug-in's actions even after the page has been loaded. Netscape browsers starting with the 3.x generation include a technology called LiveConnect that makes it possible for JavaScript to communicate with Java applets and plug-ins. Not all plug-ins can be manipulated using LiveConnect, only those written to support LiveConnect. Netscape's LiveAudio, as presented in Chapter 7, does support LiveConnect. Using LiveAudio in conjunction with LiveConnect, it would be possible to create audio-enhanced buttons. The next simple example shows how the link could play a short sound when the mouse passes over it. It would be easy to extend this example to create animated buttons with synchronized sounds using LiveConnect.

```
<HTML>
<HEAD>
<TITLE>Audio Link</TITLE>
</HEAD>
<BODY>
  <EMBED SRC="click.wav" ID="ClickSound" HIDDEN="TRUE"
         AUTOSTART="FALSE">
  <A HREF="http://www.yahoo.com"
     onMouseOver="document.embeds[0].play(false)">Yahoo!</A>
</BODY>
</HTML>
```

Note   *For LiveConnect to work, both Java and JavaScript must be enabled on the browser. Under Communicator, the **ID** attribute had to be used, and the sound referenced by numeric index rather than name. There are still some bugs in LiveConnect.*

Tying together plug-ins using a scripting language in conjunction with LiveConnect hints at the power of such component models as Netscape's plug-ins. However, Netscape plug-ins are often passed over in favor of Java or ActiveX for general programming tasks and are often regulated for handling new media forms.

Java Applets

Sun Microsystems' Java technology (www.javasoft.com) is an attractive, revolutionary approach to cross-platform, Internet-based development. It promises a platform-neutral development language that allows programs to be written once and deployed on any machine, browser, or operating system that supports the Java virtual machine. It uses small Java programs, called *applets*, that were first introduced by Sun's HotJava browser. Also used by Netscape, Microsoft and others, applets are downloaded and run directly within a browser to provide new functionality.

Applets are written in the Java language and compiled to a machine-independent byte-code, which is downloaded automatically to the Java capable browser and run within the browser environment. But even with a fast processor, the end system runs the byte-code slowly compared to a natively compiled application because the byte code must be interpreted by the virtual Java machine. Even with recent JIT (Just-In-Time) compilers in newer browsers, Java often does not deliver performance equal to natively compiled applications. Even if compilation weren't an issue, current Java applets are not generally persistent; they may have to be downloaded again in the future. Java-enabled browsers act like thin-client applications because they only add code when they need it. In this sense, the browser does not become bloated with added features but expands and contracts upon use.

Security in Java has been a serious concern from the outset. Because programs are downloaded and run automatically, a malicious program could be downloaded and run without the user being able to stop it. Under the first implementation of the technology, Java applets had little access to resources outside the browser's environment. Within Web pages, applets can't write to local disks or perform other harmful functions. This framework has been referred to as the *Java sandbox*. Developers wishing to provide Java functions outside of the sandbox must write Java applications, which run as separate applications from browsers. Other Internet programming technologies (plug-ins, ActiveX) provide little or no safety from damaging programs. Oddly, Java developers often want to add just these types of insecure features, as well as powerful features like persistence and inter-object communication. In fact, under new browsers it is possible to get extended access for signed Java applets. (Signed applets allow users to determine who authored the code in question and to accept or reject it accordingly.) Java applets can securely request limited disk access, limited disk access and network usage, limited disk read access and unlimited disk write access, and unrestricted access. Users downloading an applet requesting any enhanced privileges will be presented with a dialog box outlining the requested access and presenting the applet's credentials in the form of its digital signature. The user can then approve or reject the applet's request. If the user does not approve the request, the applet may continue to run but cannot perform the denied actions.

Java looks very much like C++. The following code fragment shows a simple example of a Java applet.

```
import java.applet.Applet;
import java.awt.Graphics;

public class helloworld extends Applet {

    public void paint(Graphics g)
      {
         g.drawString("Hello World", 50, 25);
      }

}
```

Sending this code through a Java compiler like javac should produce a class file called helloworld.class, which can be used on a Web page to display the phrase "hello world." To add a Java applet to a Web page you can use the **<APPLET>** element. As with the **<EMBED>** element, you must indicate the object to add. In this case, use the **CODE** attribute to indicate the URL of the Java class file to load. since this is an included object, the **HEIGHT** and **WIDTH** attribute should also be set. The example shown in Figure 14-4 includes the HelloWorld applet in a Web page. Figure 14-5 shows the rendering of the Java example under Netscape 4.0 with Java on. Figure 14-6 shows the same example rendered with Java off.

Notice in the code example in Figure 14-4 that between **<APPLET>** and **</APPLET>** is an alternative rendering for browsers that do not support Java or the **<APPLET>** element, or that have Java support disabled.

<APPLET> Syntax

Since Java applets are included objects just like Netscape plug-ins, the syntax for the **<APPLET>** element is similar to the **<EMBED>** element, particularly for things like alignment and sizing.

```
<HTML>
<HEAD>
<TITLE>Java Hello World</TITLE>
</HEAD>
<BODY>
<H1 ALIGN="CENTER">Java Applet Demo</H1>
<HR>
<APPLET CODE="helloworld.class"
        HEIGHT="50"
        WIDTH="175">
<H1>Hello World for you non-Java-aware browsers</H1>
</APPLET>
</BODY>
</HTML>
```

Figure 14-4.   *HTML example including HelloWorld applet*

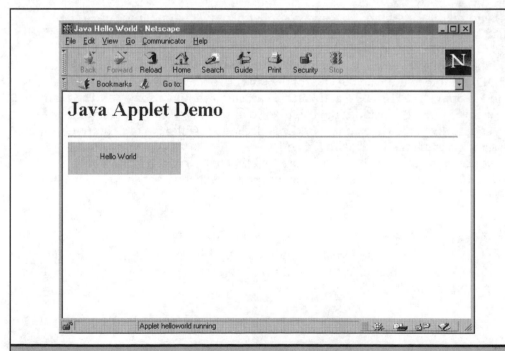

Figure 14-5.   *Java example under Netscape 4.0 with Java on*

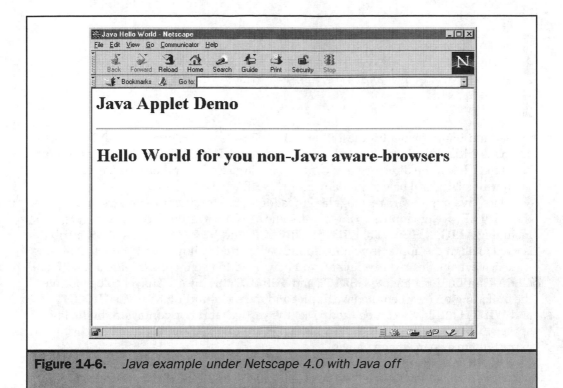

Figure 14-6.   *Java example under Netscape 4.0 with Java off*

The general syntax for **<APPLET>** is shown here:

```
<APPLET
       CODE=URL for Applet Class file
       ALIGN=LEFT | RIGHT | TOP | ABSMIDDLE* | ABSBOTTOM* |
             TEXTTOP* | MIDDLE | BASELINE* | BOTTOM  (*IE, *Netscape)
       ALT=Alternative text
       ARCHIVE=Archive file
       CLASS=Class name(s)
       CODEBASE=URL Base for loading class files
       HEIGHT=pixels
       HSPACE=pixels
       ID=unique alphanumeric identifier
       MAYSCRIPT    (Netscape)
       NAME=Unique identifier
       OBJECT=Serialized applet file
       STYLE=Style sheet rules
       TITLE=advisory text
       VSPACE=pixels
```

```
    WIDTH=pixels>

Passed parameters and alternative HTML text goes here
</APPLET>
```

The most important attribute for the **<APPLET>** element is probably **CODE**, which is set to the URL of the Java class to load into the page. The **CODEBASE** attribute can be set to the URL of the directory that contains the Java classes; otherwise, the current document's URL will be used for any relative URLs.

Since Java applets are rectangular embedded objects similar to images or plug-ins, the **<APPLET>** element has many of the same attributes as these other elements, including **ALIGN**, **HEIGHT**, **WIDTH**, **HSPACE**, and **VSPACE**. The **ALIGN** attribute is used to align the applet in relation to the page, and to allow text to flow text around it. To achieve the desired text layout, you may need to use the **
** element with the **CLEAR** attribute. Setting the **HSPACE** and **VSPACE** attributes to a pixel value indicates the buffer region between the Java applet and the surrounding text. The **HEIGHT** and **WIDTH** attributes can be used to set the vertical and horizontal size of the Java applets. The values for **HEIGHT** and **WIDTH** are in pixels. It may also be possible to express them as percentage values.

The **ARCHIVE** attribute can be used to include many classes into a single archive file, which can be downloaded to the local disk. The file specified by the **ARCHIVE** attribute may be a compressed PKZIP file (.zip) or a Java Archive (.jar) which can be made with a JAR packaging utility. For example,

```
<APPLET ARCHIVE="bunchofclasses.zip"
        CODE="sampleApp.class"
        WIDTH=560
        HEIGHT=270>
</APPLET>
```

would download all the classes in bunchofclasses.zip. After the file is downloaded, the **CODE** attribute is examined and the archive is checked to see if sampleApp.class exists there. If not, it is fetched from the network. Because of the expense of fetching many class files using HTTP, it is ideal to attempt to archive all potentially used classes and send them down at once. There may also be some caching benefit to using the **ARCHIVE** attribute, which will keep class files in the user's cache or a temporary directory. According to the HTML 4.0 specification, the **ARCHIVE** attribute may take a comma-separated list of archive files. So far, however, no browsers support more than one archive file per **<APPLET>** occurrence. The **ARCHIVE** attribute is currently only supported by Netscape 3.0 and later browsers.

According to the HTML 4.0 specification, "the **OBJECT** attribute is used to give the name of the resource that contains a serialized representation of an applet. The applet will be deserialized. The **init()** method will not be invoked, but its **start()** method will. Attributes valid when the original object was serialized are not restored. Any attributes passed to this applet instance will be available to the applet." At this point may be wondering what a serialized applet is. Starting with Java 1.1, there is the possibility to create serialized objects. The **OBJECT** attribute is used to specify the name of the class file that contains a serialized representation of an applet. Serialization supports the encoding of objects into a stream of bytes and the reconstruction of objects from the stream. The main point of serialization is that it can be used to implement lightweight persistence and communication between objects on a network.

Passing Data to Java Applets

Unlike plug-ins, Java applets do not use special attributes to pass data. Instead, they use a different element called **<PARAM>**, which is enclosed within the **<APPLET>** element as the way to pass information in. You could extend the HelloWorld applet to allow the message output to be modified by using **<PARAM>** elements to pass in a message, as shown here:

```
<APPLET CODE="helloworld.class"
        WIDTH="50"
        HEIGHT="175">
        <PARAM NAME="Message" VALUE="Hello World in Java!">
<H1>Hello World for you non-Java-aware browsers</H1>

</APPLET>
```

The HTML 4.0 syntax for **<PARAM>** is shown here. It is the same for Java applets and ActiveX controls.

```
<PARAM NAME=Object property name
       VALUE=Value to pass in with object name
       VALUETYPE=DATA | REF | OBJECT
       TYPE=MIME Type
       ID=document-wide unique id>
```

The **NAME** attribute for **<PARAM>** is used to specify the name of the object property that is being set; in the previous example, this was "Message." If you are using a premade Java applet, the various property names should be specified in the documentation for the applet. The actual value to be assigned to the property is set by the **VALUE** attribute. The **VALUETYPE** attribute specifies the meaning of the **VALUE** attribute. The typical meaning for data passed to an attribute is just as a string. Setting the **VALUETYPE** attribute to **DATA** results in the default action. Setting **VALUETYPE** to **REF** indicates that the data assigned to the **VALUE** attribute is a URL that references an external file to load for the attribute. The last value for **VALUETYPE** is **OBJECT**, which indicates that **VALUE** is set to the name of an applet or object somewhere else within the document to reference for data which allows objects to "talk" to each other.

The **<PARAM>** elements for a particular Java applet occur with the **<APPLET>** tag; there may be many of them. There may also be regular HTML markup enclosed by the **<APPLET>** element to provide an alternative rendering for non-Java capable browsers. When alternative content is found within the **<APPLET>** element, the **<PARAM>** elements should be placed before the other content. It is also possible to set the **ALT** attribute for the **<APPLET>** element to provide a short description. User-agents that support **<APPLET>** could allow users to leave them off by default and present the **ALT** text with a way for the user to load the applet if they so desire. Authors should use the text contained within the element as the alternative text, and not the **ALT** attribute.

Java and Scripting

Java applets may control scripts in a Web page. Inclusion of the **MAYSCRIPT** attribute in the **<APPLET>** element permits the applet to access JavaScript. When dealing with applets retrieved from other sources, you can use this attribute to keep the applet from accessing JavaScript without the user's knowledge. If an applet attempts to access JavaScript when this attribute has not been specified, a run-time exception should occur.

Probably more interesting for page designers is the fact that scripts can control or even modify Java applets embedded in a page. In order to be accessed, the applet should be named using the **NAME** attribute for the **<APPLET>** element. Microsoft also supports the **ID** attribute, which has the same functionality as **NAME**. For compatibility purposes, **NAME** should be used.

Providing a unique name for the applet allows scripts to access the applet and its public interfaces, as well as other applets, to potentially communicate with each other. JavaScript in Netscape 3.0 and beyond, as well as Internet Explorer 4.0 and later, allows access to the applets in a page via the **applets[]** collection, which is a property of the document object. When an applet is named, it can be accessed via JavaScript as **document.***appletname* (**document.myApplet**) or **document.applets["myApplet"]**. If the Java applet has exposed public properties, they can be modified from a script in a Web page. The simple Java code shown here takes the Hello World example from earlier in the chapter and expands it with a **setMessage** method, which can be used to change the message displayed in the applet:

```
import java.applet.Applet;
import java.awt.Graphics;
```

```
public class newhelloworld extends Applet {

    String theMessage;

    public void init()
      {
        theMessage = new String("Hello World");
      }
    public void paint(Graphics g)
      {
         g.drawString(theMessage, 50, 25);
      }
    public void setMessage(String message)
      {
        theMessage = message;
        repaint();
      }
}
```

If this Java code is compiled into a class file, it can be included into a Web page and accessed via JavaScript, as shown next. The following example markup shows how a form could be used to collect data from the user and update the applet in real time.

```
<HTML>
<HEAD>
<TITLE>LiveConnect Java Hello World</TITLE>
</HEAD>
<BODY>
<H1 ALIGN="CENTER">LiveConnect Java Applet Demo</H1>
<HR>
<APPLET CODE="newhelloworld.class"
        NAME="NewHello"
        HEIGHT="50"
        WIDTH="175">
<H1>Hello World for you non-Java-aware browsers</H1>
</APPLET>

<FORM NAME="TestForm">
<INPUT TYPE="TEXT" SIZE="15" MAXLENGTH="15" NAME="NewMessage">

<INPUT TYPE=BUTTON VALUE="Set Message"
```

```
onClick="document.NewHello.setMessage(NewMessage.value)">

</BODY>
</HTML>
```

Netscape initially called this technology LiveConnect. It is similar to how you may communicate with plug-ins embedded in a Web page. Microsoft also supports the same form of applet access under Internet Explorer, so it is unclear if the idea of JavaScript being used to communicate with Java applets will continue to be known as LiveConnect. The bottom line is that this technology is not unique to Netscape.

<OBJECT> Syntax for Java Applets

The HTML 4.0 specification indicates that the **<APPLET>** element has been depreciated and that **<OBJECT>** should be used instead. While this may be the decree, there are some serious problems with using **<OBJECT>** for Java applets. The simple syntax for inserting an object like a Java applet under HTML 4.0 is as follows:

```
<OBJECT CLASSID=URL of Object to include
        HEIGHT=pixels
        WIDTH=pixels>
Parameters and alternative text
</OBJECT>
```

Notice that the **CLASSID** attribute is used to specify the URL of the object to include. In the case of Java applets, you should use **java:**. For ActiveX controls, use **clsid:**. To rewrite a simple Java example, use the following code:

```
<OBJECT CLASSID="java:Blink.class"  WIDTH="300" HEIGHT="100">
<PARAM NAME="LBL" VALUE="Java, is, fun, exciting, and new.">
<PARAM NAME="SPEED" VALUE="2">
This will display in non-Java-aware or non-Java-enabled browsers.
</OBJECT>
```

Using Java Without Programming

The broad functionality of Java can cost both time and money. Java programming assumes familiarity with an advanced programming language as well as object-oriented design. Web professionals lacking programming skills or budgets will find many free premade applets available for reuse or sale at directories like Gamelan (www.gamelan.com). Commercial vendors actively sell a variety of premade Java applets, as well as Java components called *JavaBeans*, which can be used to create powerful Web applications. JavaBeans is a portable, platform-independent component model written in Java. Like other components such as ActiveX controls, JavaBeans components (called Beans for short) are reusable software components that can be strung together to form complex applications. In one sense, Beans are just a special form of applets written so that tools can inspect and manipulate the Beans and the Beans can communicate together in a predictable manner. Beans are generally self-contained, and have persistence. You could think of components such as Beans as bricks that form larger structures like buildings. Tools such as Netscape's Visual JavaScript (See Figure 14-7) already provide some basic drag-and-drop programming capabilities by using JavaBeans components and tying them together with JavaScript code.

While Java provides a relatively secure and powerful cross-platform development environment, it does so at the expense of speed and local operating system integration. Because of this, many Web developers, particularly those building intranet applications, have looked into using ActiveX controls as Web page components.

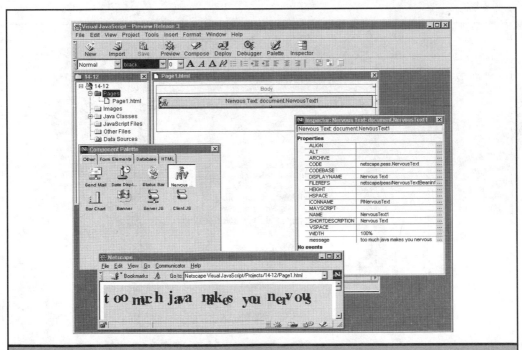

Figure 14-7.   *Netscape's Visual JavaScript uses Beans*

ActiveX Controls

ActiveX (www.microsoft.com/activex) is Microsoft's component technology for creating small components or controls within a Web page. ActiveX is intended to distribute these controls via the Internet to add new functionality to browsers like Internet Explorer. Microsoft maintains that ActiveX controls are more like generalized components than plug-ins: they can reside beyond the browser, within container programs like Microsoft Office. ActiveX controls are like Netscape plug-ins in that they are persistent and machine specific. While this makes resource use a problem, installation is not an issue: the components download and install automatically.

Security is a big concern for ActiveX controls. Because these small pieces of code could potentially have full access to a user's system, they could cause serious damage. This capability, combined with automatic installation, creates a serious problem with ActiveX. End users will be quick to click a button to install new functionality, only to accidentally get their hard drives erased. This unlimited functionality of ActiveX controls creates a gaping security hole. To address this problem, Microsoft provides authentication information to indicate who wrote a control in the form of code signed by a certificate as shown in Figure 14-8.

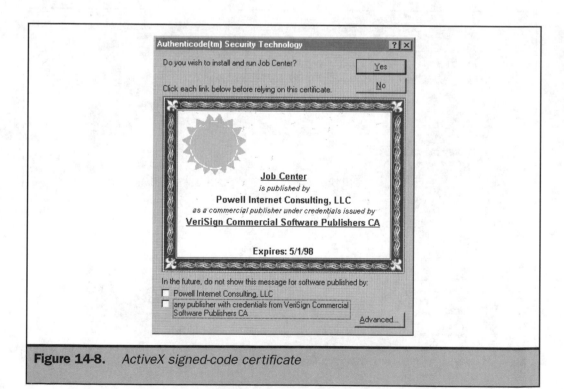

Figure 14-8.   *ActiveX signed-code certificate*

Certificates only provide some indication that the control creator is reputable, but does nothing to actually prevent a control from doing something malicious. Safe Web browsing should be practiced by accepting controls only from reputable sources.

Adding Controls to Web Pages

Adding an ActiveX control to a Web page requires the use of the **<OBJECT>** element. The basic form of the **<OBJECT>** element for an ActiveX control is as follows:

```
<OBJECT CLASSID=CLSID:class-identifier
        HEIGHT=pixels
        WIDTH=pixels
        ID=unique identifier>

Parameters and alternative text rendering
</OBJECT>
```

The most important attribute for the **<OBJECT>** element when inserting ActiveX controls is **CLASSID**. The value of this attribute identifies the object to include. Each ActiveX control has a class identifier of the form "CLSID: class-identifier" where the value for class-identifier is a complex string such as the following, which uniquely identifies the control:

99B42120-6EC7-11CF-A6C7-00AA00A47DD2

This is the identifier for the ActiveX label control.) The other important attributes for the basic form of **<OBJECT>** when used with ActiveX controls include **HEIGHT** and **WIDTH**, which are set to the pixel dimensions of the included control, and **ID**, which associates a unique identifier with the control for scripting purposes. Between the **<OBJECT>** and **</OBJECT>** tags are various **<PARAM>** elements that specify information to pass to the control, and alternative HTML markup to display in non-ActiveX-aware browsers. A complete example using the **<OBJECT>** element to insert an ActiveX control into a Web page is shown in Figure 14-9. The markup shown specifies a simple label control. Figure 14-10 shows the rendering of the control under Internet Explorer 4.0 and Netscape 4.0.

After looking at the "ActiveX Label Test" code in Figure 14-9, you may have questions about how to determine the **CLASSID** value for the control and the associated **<PARAM>** values that can be set. There is no need to provide a chart for all the controls and their associated identifiers. Many Web page tools, including Microsoft Control Pad (www.microsoft.com/workshop/author/cpad), support the automated insertion of controls into a page as well as configuration of the various control properties. Figure 14-11 shows an example of the Control Pad and the configuration of controls.

```
<HTML>
<HEAD>
<TITLE>ActiveX Label Test</TITLE>
</HEAD>
<BODY>

<H1 ALIGN="CENTER">ActiveX Demo</H1>
<HR>

<OBJECT CLASSID="CLSID:99B42120-6EC7-11CF-A6C7-00AA00A47DD2"
   ID="IeLabel1" HEIGHT="65" WIDTH="325">
     <PARAM NAME="_ExtentX" VALUE="6879">
     <PARAM NAME="_ExtentY" VALUE="1376">
     <PARAM NAME="Caption" VALUE="Hello World">
     <PARAM NAME="Alignment" VALUE="4">
     <PARAM NAME="Mode" VALUE="1">
     <PARAM NAME="ForeColor" VALUE="#FF0000">
     <PARAM NAME="FontName" VALUE="Arial">
     <PARAM NAME="FontSize" VALUE="36">
      <B>Hello World for you non-ActiveX users!</B>
</OBJECT>


</BODY>
</HTML>
```

Figure 14-9.   *<OBJECT> example for ActiveX control insertion*

<OBJECT> Syntax

The **<OBJECT>** element is the catch-all inclusion element specified in HTML 4.0.
Browsers do not yet support this element properly for plug-ins, Java applets, and
images, so it is primarily relegated for use with ActiveX controls. The discussion here
will present the syntax as specified by the World Wide Web Consortium (W3C) as well
as Microsoft extensions. The complete syntax for the **<OBJECT>** element is shown here:

```
<OBJECT
   ACCESSKEY=key                           (IE 4.0)
   ALIGN=ABSBOTTOM* | ABSMIDDLE* | BASELINE* | BOTTOM |
        LEFT | MIDDLE | RIGHT | TEXTTOP* | TOP (* IE 4.0)
   ARCHIVE=URL of archive file
```

```
    BORDER=Pixels
    CLASS=Class name for CSS use
    CLASSID=Object identifier
    CODE=Applet URL   (IE 3.0)
    CODEBASE=URL of code to download
    CODETYPE=MIME type for CLASSID
    DATA=URL of associated data
    DATAFLD=Column name for binding (IE 4.0)
    DATASRC=#ID for data binding (IE 4.0)
    DECLARE
    DIR=LTR | RTL
    EXPORT
    HEIGHT=Pixels or Percentage
    HSPACE=Pixels
    ID=Unique identifier
    LANG=ISO Language Code
    LANGUAGE=JAVASCRIPT | JSCRIPT | VBSCRIPT | VBS     (IE 4.0)
    NAME=Unique identifier
    SHAPES
    STANDBY=Loading message
    STYLE=Inline CSS Properties
    TABINDEX=Integer indicating tab order
    TITLE=Advisory text
    TYPE=MIME-type for DATA attribute
    USEMAP=URL to client side image map declaration
    VSPACE=Pixels
    WIDTH=Pixels or Percentage

    Event handlers>

Zero or more occurrences of <PARAM> elements followed by
alternative text to display


</OBJECT>
```

The specification defines **EXPORT, SHAPES,** and **USEMAP,** and provides a different meaning of **NAME** as related to Web-based forms. These will not be discussed in the context of inserting programming objects into a Web page.

The main purpose of **<OBJECT>** is to insert objects (images, applets, ActiveX controls, or documents) into a Web page. As rectangular objects, ActiveX controls generally require the **HEIGHT, WIDTH, HSPACE, VSPACE, BORDER,** and **ALIGN**

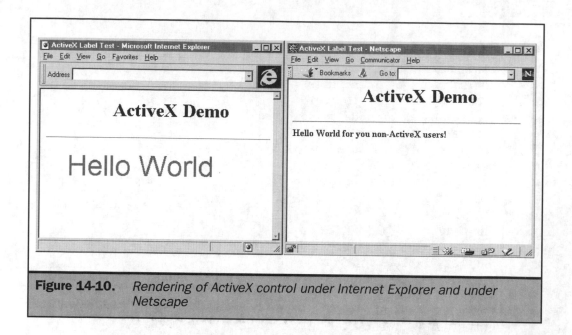

Figure 14-10. Rendering of ActiveX control under Internet Explorer and under Netscape

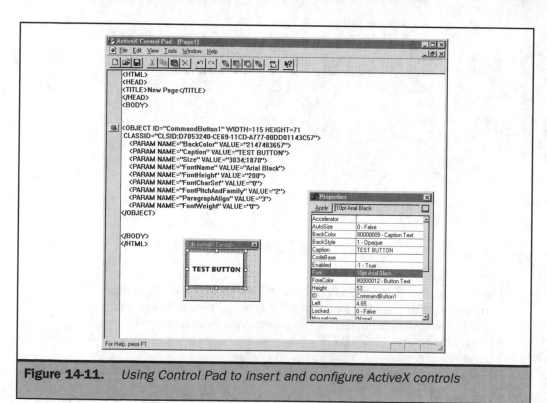

Figure 14-11. Using Control Pad to insert and configure ActiveX controls

attributes, which act the same as they do for the <IMG>, <EMBED>, and <APPLET> elements. The HTML 4.0 specification also defines the attributes **ID**, **CLASS**, **LANG**, **DIR**, **TITLE**, **STYLE**, and **TABINDEX**. **ID** is used for naming the included object for access from style sheets and scripting languages. **CLASS** is used to subclass the object for style sheet access. **STYLE** is used to inline Cascading Style Sheets (CSS) style rules directly. **LANG** is used to indicate the language used by the object. **DIR** indicates the text direction of that language. The **TITLE** attribute provides advisory information that may be rendered as a tool tip by some browsers. **TABINDEX** is used to indicate the object's place in the tabbing order. Microsoft also defines the **ACCESSKEY** attribute, which can be used to set an accelerator key to activate the object. The use of **ACCESSKEY** is exactly the same as when used with form controls. Page authors are warned to avoid using keys that are predefined by the browser. See Chapter 11 for more information about **ACCESSKEY** and its use.

Installing ActiveX Controls

As mentioned earlier in "Adding Controls to Web Pages," the most important attribute in the <OBJECT> syntax is probably **CLASSID**, which is used to identify the particular object to include. For example, the syntax is "CLSID:class-identifier" is for registered ActiveX controls. In a generalized sense, however, when the <OBJECT> element supports other included items well, this might be set to other forms like "java: Blink.class," as shown earlier in the chapter in "<OBJECT> Syntax for Java Applets." Microsoft also allows the use of the **CODE** attribute for the <OBJECT> element. This is used to set the URL of the Java class file to include.

ActiveX and plug-ins are similar in the sense that both are persistent platform-specific components. ActiveX controls, however, are easily downloaded and installed. This installation or running of ActiveX controls can be described as a series of steps. First, the browser loads an HTML page that references an ActiveX control with the <OBJECT> element and associated **CLASSID** attribute. The browser checks the system registry to see if the control specified by the **CLASSID** value is installed; this control takes the form the form of "CLSID: some-id-number." If it is installed, it compares the **CODEBASE** version attribute stored in the registry against the **CODEBASE** version attribute in the HTML page. If a newer version is specified in the page, a newer control will be needed. Similarly, if the control is not installed, the value of the **CODEBASE** attribute is used to determine the location of the control to download. The **CODETYPE** attribute might also be used to set the MIME type of the object to download. Most inclusions of ActiveX controls avoid this, since it tends to default to the MIME type application/octet-stream.

For security reasons, the browser checks to see if the code is signed before the download and installation begins. If the code is not signed, the user will be warned of this. If the code is signed, an Authenticode certificate bearing the identity of the author of the control will be presented to the user. Based on these criteria, the user can allow or deny the installation of the control on his or her system. If the user accepts the control, it is automatically downloaded, installed, and invoked in the page for its specific function. Finally, it is persistently stored on the client machine for further invocation. This process may be avoided when the **DECLARE** attribute is present. The **DELCARE** attribute is used to indicate if the **<OBJECT>** is being defined only and not actually instantiated until later **<OBJECT>** occurrences, which will start the installation process.

*The W3C HTML 4.0 specification also indicates the use of the **STANDBY** attribute which can be used to specify a message to display as the object is being downloaded. This is not currently supported by any browsers.*

Passing Data to ActiveX Controls

Like Java applets, ActiveX controls do not use special attributes to pass data. Instead they use a different element, called **<PARAM>**, which is enclosed within the **<OBJECT>** element. You can pass parameters to the label control using the **<PARAM>** elements, as shown here:

```
<OBJECT CLASSID="CLSID:99B42120-6EC7-11CF-A6C7-00AA00A47DD2"
    ID="IeLabel1" HEIGHT="65" WIDTH="325">
   <PARAM NAME="Caption" VALUE="Hello World">
   <PARAM NAME="FontName" VALUE="Arial">
   <PARAM NAME="FontSize" VALUE="36">
   <B>Hello World for you non-ActiveX users!</B>
</OBJECT>
```

In this case, the parameter Caption is set to Hello World, the parameter FontName is set to Arial and the FontSize parameter is set to 36 points. Recall the HTML 4.0 syntax for **<PARAM>**, which is shown again here. It is the same for Java applets and ActiveX controls.

```
<PARAM   NAME=Object property name
         VALUE=Value to pass in with object name
         VALUETYPE=DATA | REF | OBJECT
         TYPE=MIME Type
         ID=unique alphanumeric identifier
```

The meaning of these attributes can be found in the "Java Applets" section earlier in the chapter, as well as in the element reference appendix. There are a few changes as introduced by Microsoft for data binding. Microsoft Internet Explorer 4.0 and later supports the ability to dynamically bind data from a database or text file. With data binding it would be possible to set the parameters for an ActiveX control using an external file or database entry. The attributes that provide this functionality include **DATAFLD**, **DATASRC** and **DATAFORMATS**. **DATAFLD** sets the column name to use for the **<PARAM>** element. **DATASRC** is bound to the identifier, which indicates the data to bind to. **DATAFORMATS** is set to either **HTML** or **TEXT**, indicating whether the bound data is HTML or plain text. For more information on how to use data binding, see the Microsoft SiteBuilder Network (www.microsoft.com/sitebuilder).

Another way to pass data to ActiveX controls or other embedded objects is by using the **DATA** attribute. The **DATA** attribute should be set to a URL that references a data file to load in. The type of this data may be determined by the file suffix. It is also possible to use the **TYPE** attribute to explicitly declare the MIME type for the data to use.

Using ActiveX Without Programming

Developers can access an abundance of available controls for various purposes. There are many repositories of free and commercial ActiveX controls, such as ActiveX.com (www.activex.com). Microsoft already includes a variety of controls built in to Internet Explorer; these include a variety of form-like elements, a timer, a preloader control that allows pages and objects to be prefetched, and many others. Microsoft also promotes controls for multimedia such as ActiveMovie and Netshow, and controls for database access such as ActiveX Data Objects (ADO), Remote Data Services, and Tabular Data Control (TDC). Microsoft even provides a control called the Agent control, which can be used to add an animated agent to a Web page that the user can interact with (shown in Figure 14-12).

As with Java applets, page designers can use prebuilt controls for most functions. Many Web page development tools, like Microsoft Control Pad, provide an easy way to string together ActiveX controls.

Page designers can also write their own ActiveX controls, though in some cases this may be like reinventing the wheel. Controls can be created using a variety of languages such as Visual Basic, C++, and Java. It is also possible to convert existing Windows programs to controls. The ActiveX model is not limited to client-side controls. It is part of a larger framework known as the Active Platform, with server-side and distributed aspects, which is beyond the scope of this book. However, one important aspect of the Active Platform is that client-side controls expose their interfaces through the Component Object Model, which can be accessed and controlled easily through scripting languages.

ActiveX Controls and Scripting

As with Java applets, it is possible to control ActiveX controls using a scripting language like JavaScript or VBScript. One advantage to ActiveX controls is that there are many premade controls with exposed properties that can be easily manipulated by a scripting language. Before a control can be modified, however, it must be named using the **ID** attribute. After this, scripting code for a particular event can be set for the control so it can respond to events. As discussed in the last chapter, Microsoft supports a rich event model. However, many of these events (noted with an asterisk) are beyond the current HTML 4.0 specification. The **<OBJECT>** element supports the following events: **onafterupdate***, **onbeforeupdate***, **onblur***, **onclick**, **ondblclick**,

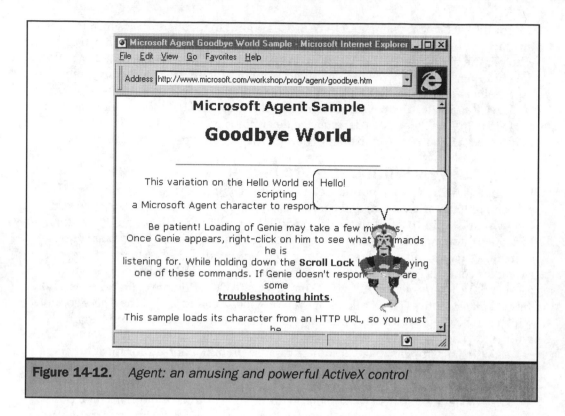

Figure 14-12.   *Agent: an amusing and powerful ActiveX control*

ondragstart*, **onfocus***, **onhelp***, **onkeydown**, **onkeypress**, **onkeyup**, **onmousedown**, **onmousemove**, **onmouseout**, **onmouseover**, **onmouseup**, **onreadystatechange***, **onresize***, **onrowenter***, **onrowexit***, and **onselectstart***. However, these are generally not used directly with JavaScript as attributes to the **<OBJECT>** element. VBScript access may be more appropriate. The following example was created with the Control Pad and shows how two ActiveX command buttons can be used to communicate with a label control to change its message.

```
<HTML>
<HEAD>
<TITLE>ActiveX Scripting Demo</TITLE>

<SCRIPT LANGUAGE="VBScript">
<!--

Sub CommandButton1_Click()
    Label1.Caption = "I've been clicked!"
end sub
```

```
Sub CommandButton2_Click()
    Label1.Caption = "Not Set"
end sub

-->

</SCRIPT>

</HEAD>
<BODY>

<H1 ALIGN="CENTER">ActiveX Scripting</H1>
<HR>

<B>Label:</B>

<OBJECT
     CLASSID="CLSID:978C9E23-D4B0-11CE-BF2D-00AA003F40D0"
     ALIGN="TOP" ID="Label1" HEIGHT="80" WIDTH="200">
    <PARAM NAME="BackColor" VALUE="8454143">
    <PARAM NAME="Caption" VALUE="Not set">
    <PARAM NAME="Size" VALUE="4233;1212">
    <PARAM NAME="BorderColor" VALUE="8421504">
    <PARAM NAME="BorderStyle" VALUE="1">
    <PARAM NAME="FontHeight" VALUE="200">
    <PARAM NAME="FontCharSet" VALUE="0">
    <PARAM NAME="FontPitchAndFamily" VALUE="2">
    <PARAM NAME="ParagraphAlign" VALUE="3">
</OBJECT>

<HR>

<OBJECT ALIGN="TOP" ID="CommandButton1" WIDTH="168" HEIGHT="52"
 CLASSID="CLSID:D7053240-CE69-11CD-A777-00DD01143C57">
    <PARAM NAME="ForeColor" VALUE="65535">
    <PARAM NAME="BackColor" VALUE="10485760">
    <PARAM NAME="Caption" VALUE="Update Label">
    <PARAM NAME="Size" VALUE="3577;1101">
    <PARAM NAME="FontHeight" VALUE="200">
    <PARAM NAME="FontCharSet" VALUE="0">
    <PARAM NAME="FontPitchAndFamily" VALUE="2">
```

```
         <PARAM NAME="ParagraphAlign" VALUE="3">
</OBJECT>

<OBJECT ALIGN="TOP" ID="CommandButton2" WIDTH="168" HEIGHT="52"
  CLASSID="CLSID:D7053240-CE69-11CD-A777-00DD01143C57">
         <PARAM NAME="ForeColor" VALUE="65535">
         <PARAM NAME="BackColor" VALUE="10485760">
         <PARAM NAME="Caption" VALUE="Reset Label">
         <PARAM NAME="Size" VALUE="3577;1101">
         <PARAM NAME="FontHeight" VALUE="200">
         <PARAM NAME="FontCharSet" VALUE="0">
         <PARAM NAME="FontPitchAndFamily" VALUE="2">
         <PARAM NAME="ParagraphAlign" VALUE="3">
</OBJECT>

</BODY>
</HTML>
```

Note that the event handlers are written in VBScript. This file will not work in anything other than Internet Explorer 3.0 or better running on a Windows-based system. While scripting is simple but powerful for ActiveX controls, the problem with controls (as with plug-ins) is that they tend to be too platform specific to be used for external Web sites unless pages are coded very carefully. On a Windows-centered intranet, however, the use of platform-dependent controls and VBScript might not be a problem.

Cross-Platform Support with Plug-ins and ActiveX Controls

While the whole point of Java applets is to deal with cross-platform compatibility issues, Microsoft ActiveX controls and Netscape plug-ins are extremely platform and browser dependent. It is possible, however, to provide limited support for both platforms. Netscape users interested in running ActiveX controls may want to look at the ScriptActive plug-in available from Ncompass Labs (www.ncompasslabs.com). This plug-in will provide general compatibility under Netscape for ActiveX controls, assuming the site using them pays attention to Ncompass conventions. The Ncompass approach is not terribly robust. A preferred method is to attempt to provide a plug-in solution in conjunction with an ActiveX solution. Consider the inclusion of Macromedia Flash media in a Web page. Internet Explorer will prefer the Flash control while Netscape will prefer a Flash plug-in. Both can be accommodated with the following code fragment:

```
<OBJECT CLASSID="CLSID:D27CDB6E-AE6D-11cf-96B8-444553540000"
        CODEBASE="swflash.cab#version=2,0,0,0"
        HEIGHT="100" WIDTH="100">

<PARAM NAME="Movie" VALUE="SplashLogo.swf">
<PARAM NAME="Play" Value="True">

<!-- Netscape syntax here -->
<EMBED SRC="SplashLogo.swf"
PLUGINSPAGE="http://www.macromedia.com/shockwave/
        download/index.cgi?P1_Prod_Version=ShockwaveFlash2"
PLUGINURL="http://www.bigcompany.com/flash.jar"
HEIGHT="100" WIDTH="100" PLAY="TRUE">

<!-- No plug-ins and no controls so go to GIF  -->

<NOEMBED>
<A HREF="corepage.htm">
<IMG SRC="SplashLogo.gif"
     HEIGHT="100" WIDTH="100"
     BORDER="0" ALT="Big Company, Inc."></A>
</NOEMBED>

</OBJECT>
```

In this example, the browser should try for an ActiveX control. If it can't handle it, it should go for a plug-in. In the last resort, it should end up with an animated GIF. Of course, the plug-in example does not provide an accurate reference to a JAR file for automatic download of the plug-in, but it gets the point across. Careful thought combined with some server- or client-side scripting should make it possible to deal with the various browser conditions that may occur. It isn't terribly pretty, but until the syntax for including objects is straightened out it is the only reasonable approach short of locking users out of a page or falling back to less interactive or motivating technology.

The Future of <OBJECT>

According to the HTML 4.0 specification, **<OBJECT>** will be the main way to add any form of object to a Web page, whether it's an image, image map, sound, video, ActiveX control, Java applet, or anything else. This seems the appropriate thing to do, but before rushing out to use **<OBJECT>**, understand the ramifications. Even though

<OBJECT> can be used in some browsers, the syntax is not consistent. **<OBJECT>** is still mostly used to include ActiveX controls in a page. Other meanings are not fully supported, if at all. According to the HTML 4.0 specification, it is possible to use the **<OBJECT>** element to include HTML from another file by using the **DATA** attribute. Any file included must not introduce elements that would ruin the syntax of the document. For example, including a file that already has a **<HEAD>** and **<BODY>** element may result in a ill-formed document with multiple **<HEAD>** and **<BODY>** elements. Imagine specifying a header file called header.htm with the contents shown here:

```
<H1 ALIGN="CENTER">Big Company, Inc.</H1>
<HR>
```

This file could then be included in a Web page using the **<OBJECT>** element like so:

```
<OBJECT DATA="header.htm">
Header not included
</OBJECT>
```

This example should pull in the contents of the file header.htm in browsers that support this feature and display "Header not included" in all others. No major browser appears to support this functionality for the **<OBJECT>** element, so this should be avoided in favor of technologies like server-side includes (Chapter 12) and dynamic documents generated with JavaScript.

Eventually the **<OBJECT>** element will be used in a generalized sense. For now, HTML page authors should use the **<APPLET>** , **<IMG>**, and **<EMBED>** elements to include binary forms beyond ActiveX controls in pages.

Summary

With the inclusion of programmed objects like ActiveX controls, Java applets, and Netscape plug-ins, Web pages can become complex living documents. Choosing the appropriate component technology is not very straightforward. While Netscape plug-ins are very popular for including media elements such as Shockwave movies, video, or sound files, they are platform specific and somewhat specific to Netscape browsers. While Microsoft supports the **<EMBED>** element syntax to include plug-ins in a page, the preferred solution in the Microsoft world is ActiveX controls. ActiveX controls are just as platform specific as Netscape plug-ins, and have some potential security issues. Solving the cross-platform problem requires complex page scripting or the use of Java applets that provide cross-platform object support, typically at the expense of performance. Either way, the page rendering should degrade gracefully if the user can't support the particular object technology. Eventually the syntax for all included media will be handled with the **<OBJECT>** element, but for now **<EMBED>** and **<APPLET>** should be used within **<OBJECT>** to provide backward compatibility for including plug-ins and Java applets in a Web page.

Chapter 15

Putting It All Together:
Delivering the Web Site

So far nothing has been said about how to deliver Web pages. Even if developers master the creation of Web pages using HTML, they can still fall flat on their faces if they don't pay careful consideration to how they deliver the pages to the user. As far as the viewer of a page is concerned, the Web is one big system. If a page is slow because of a server, the user still views the site in a negative light no matter how compelling the content or inspiring the design. Ignoring such site delivery issues as outsourcing, Web server choice, and protocol issues may doom a Web project to failure.

Publishing the Site

Even a modem user with a dial-up SLIP/PPP connection can run a Web server. This isn't a great idea, since the connection won't be up all the time, and will probably be very slow. On a more effective level, there are two basic choices for publishing your HTML documents on the Internet. One way involves having a dedicated connection to the Internet and running your own server. The other approach involves renting space or bandwidth from an outside vendor to place your server or pages outside your organization.

While running your own Web server and connection to the Internet seems like the way to go, it can be quite expensive. A common leased line like a T1 with Internet services may cost tens of thousands of dollars a year. When factoring in labor, server, facilities, and other expenses, the total cost starts to approach six figures. In many cases, many of these facilities are already available within the organization and should be used. Yet using someone else's server may be the only choice for people who want to publish Web documents but can't afford a huge fee. Even those firms that have capable staffs should consider outsourcing as it provides many benefits. Figure 15-1 provides a basic overview of the two hosting approaches.

Outsourcing Web Hosting

As Web sites become more critical to the information infrastructure of companies, there is a growing need to provide high-quality, high-availability solutions. However, it is expensive to develop the talents and facilities in-house to run a mission-critical Web site. Because of this fact, many firms have decided to outsource their Web facilities. In general, Web server outsourcing comes in two basic flavors: *hosting* and *co-location*.

Web hosting involves using the shared server facilities of a hosting vendor. This means that the site will share Web server resources and bandwidth with other hosted sites. Sharing can be problematic. Server responsiveness may be significantly affected because of other hosted Web sites, particularly if those sites become popular. Furthermore, many customers are wary of sharing a server with others, because security often cannot be guaranteed on these shared systems. Despite its drawbacks, hosting is still relatively inexpensive. Shared hosting prices are dependent on the extra

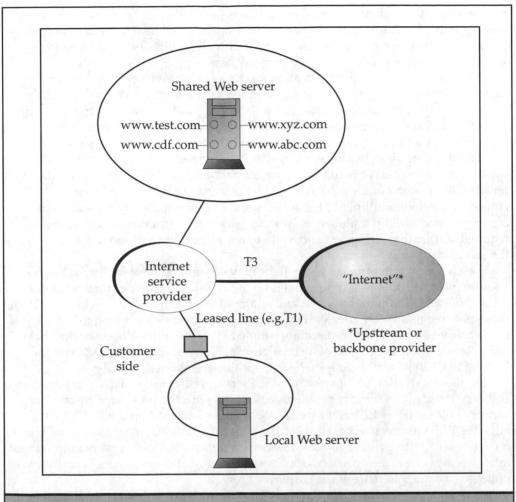

Figure 15-1.   *Shared hosting versus dedicated line hosting*

services offered and the traffic expected. Consumer-grade hosting can cost as little as $20 per month. High-availability, and possibly mirrored, hosting can run into thousands, if not tens of thousands, of dollars a month. Many Internet Service Providers and specialized hosting companies offer professional-quality shared Web hosting services.

The other Web server outsourcing option is often called co-location. This describes the use of a dedicated server, often owned by the organization purchasing the service. Co-location provides a greater degree of autonomy than shared Web services. In fact, the co-located machine typically only shares physical facilities, and possibly network bandwidth, with other customers. Co-location is generally more expensive than hosting; it may cost anywhere from around a thousand dollars to tens of thousands per month. Many of the large Internet service providers (ISPs) offer co-location services as well as specialized data center providers.

Price is often the essential motivation for outsourcing Web services. Research suggests that Web server outsourcing is as much as one-third the cost of providing an equivalent service in-house. Yet, the cost differences don't always add up, since a great deal of control and security will be lost. Looking beyond cost, there are major benefits for Web server outsourcing, including bandwidth, security, and facilities issues.

Having enough bandwidth available can be important for mission-critical Web sites. Regardless of server bottlenecks, a mere fractional-T1 or full-T1 leased line might not provide enough bandwidth to deal with the bursty nature of Web access. However, installing multiple T3 leased lines just to deal with the occasional flash crowd that may swamp a site seems wasteful given the significant investment required. Rather than bringing bandwidth to the server, why not move the server to the bandwidth?

Even if bandwidth is not an issue, there may be some issue of network closeness. Because there will always be a site that is far away, using a provider that can provide mirrors of the site around the world and automatically redirect the Web browser to the closest site seems appropriate. Many high-end providers are beginning to use products that are capable of redirecting people to the network's closest or least busy server to provide some degree of load balancing. Many of the popular sites on the Internet like Yahoo! already use such sophisticated techniques.

Another motivation for outsourcing Web services is security. Many companies are still very afraid of the security problems associated with the Internet. Firewalls and security policies can help, but if a public Web server is located on the firm's LAN, allowing Web viewers to access it is similar to asking potential robbers to come knock on your door. Putting public use information on outsourced Web servers keeps casual intruders away from a firm's network access point and allows stronger security policies to be put into place at the corporate firewall.

Facilities are often an overlooked benefit of outsourced Web services. With high-end data centers, co-location or hosting the facility provides benefits that would be expensive to replicate otherwise. These benefits may include around-the-clock live monitoring rather than automated monitoring, high-quality power services including backup generators, computer-sensitive fire suppression systems, disaster recovery–oriented construction, and sophisticated physical security.

Despite all the benefits of Web server outsourcing, there are some potentially significant drawbacks. Not all hosting vendors are created equal. Choosing the wrong vendor can lead to serious problems. While ISPs have more than enough bandwidth to host Web sites or co-locate machines, many providers are more knowledgeable about networks than servers. This shows when they are questioned about available development tools and server maintenance policies. Data center vendors may be more on top of the server aspect of the puzzle, but they often come at a significantly higher price. If the correct vendor can be isolated, the only sacrifices facing the outsourced site are security and control.

While outsourcing Web service can help separate a sensitive network from the Internet, it also begs the question of the security of the Web server. If the outsourced site contains sensitive information, there is always the possibility this information may be compromised. Hosting vendors generally do not provide complete guarantees of data integrity. Careful reading of the fine print of hosting contracts indicates, at most, a "best effort" to protect data. In some cases, there is no guarantee whatsoever. Even if the hosting vendors protect against outside intrusion internally, security is often very lax. Security itself is just an example of the general problem of Web server outsourcing—a lack of control.

The biggest problem with many outsourced Web services, particularly hosting, is control. Most hosting vendors do not necessarily allow customers to do what they want. The choice of Web server, server software, development tools such as database development tools, and statistics packages are often up to the discretion of the hosting vendor. Particularly with lower-priced hosting services, use of a particular database, operating system, and statistics package may be forced on the customer. While customization is still often available, it may come at a significantly higher price. The ramifications of control go far beyond choice of operating system. Don't be surprised if a hosting vendor decides to upgrade its Web server during the middle of the day. It is the vendor's server, after all, and, logically or not, the vendor decides how to run it. With co-location, control is generally more in the customer's hand, since the vendor only provides network access, power, and safe facilities.

Companies looking to save money on Web hosting find outsourcing very attractive, but some flexibility and security may have to be sacrificed. With less-experienced hosting companies, this lack of control can be disastrous, resulting in hidden costs in site redevelopment or problems with reliability. Those who want more control over their Web services should consider co-location or running their own servers locally. This is a more viable option than shared hosting, but it will certainly come at a higher cost.

Virtual Hosting

Hosting on a shared Web server often provides support for the feature known as *virtual hosting*. In essence, this feature enables multiple domain names to be hosted on the same server, yet appear as if each were running on its own server. Each machine on the Internet has an address such as www.bigcompany.com; this address maps to a particular (Internet Protocol) IP address, as explained in Chapter 5. In the case of virtual hosting, the operating system the Web server runs on has the capability of mapping multiple IP addresses to a single network interface card installed in the server hardware. In turn, multiple domain names can be mapped to these IP addresses.

Different types of virtual hosting are offered. Most hosting services offer a true virtual hosting service, where the URL for a customer's Web site is as would normally be expected: www.bigcompany.com automatically goes to the customer's home page. The address is mapped to a single IP address. However, in some implementations of virtual hosting, multiple domain names may be mapped to only a single IP address. In this case, customers are given an address with a notation like www.bigcompany.com/~*bigco*, where /~*bigco* indicates the actual user name of the customer on the Web server. The common ~ notation is a server setting that enables all users on a particular server to have Web pages in their home directory and have a URL based on their user names.

A step up from this, but still not true virtual hosting, comes in the form of having an address like www.bigcompany.com/*bigco*, where /*bigco* is a specific directory assigned to a customer for hosting a Web page. In selecting a shared Web server hosting provider, potential customers should be careful to ask hosting companies of the type of address provided in their virtual hosting services. The HTTP 1.1 protocol, as discussed in "How Web Servers Work" later in the chapter, supports virtual hosting using a single IP address, and will make managing virtual hosting services easier from the server administrator's point of view.

Running a Local Web Server

Besides outsourcing hosting, it is also possible to pull in a full-time connection to the Internet and run your own Web server. When doing this, consider what Web servers actually do. In some sense, a Web server is a glorified file server, and occasionally an application server. Browsers make requests to the Web server for files. These files are located on the disk drive and then copied out to the network. In the case of running Common Gateway Interface (CGI) programs or similar server-side technology, a request is made to the server to run a program. The program is then loaded from disk and run, and the result is sent out on to the network. To make the best Web server possible, you should pay careful attention to the disk and network interface. While many are quick to jump on the processor speed or amount of memory, the disk is often the greatest bottleneck for a Web server. The big question is how to pick the best possible hardware platform, operating system, and Web server software combination to serve pages. Of course, all these decisions must consider budget.

Selecting a Web Server

Price and performance are the basic issues for choosing a Web server. First, you need to understand what kind of activity to expect and what type of data you will serve. Then you need to set a budget for your server. A personal Web server might use freeware or shareware and run on a low-cost personal computer such as PC or Macintosh. A large corporate system might use a powerful UNIX workstation running commercial-grade Web server software. There is no single correct hardware/software combination for Web page serving. One of the main considerations for a Web server will be the operating system used. Each operating system popular for Web service has its own pros and cons summarized in Table 15-1.

Operating System	Pros	Cons
UNIX	*Tends to run on fast hardware such as UltraSparc and Alpha systems. *Very flexible. *High-end applications such as object databases are ported to major UNIX variants first.	*Can be complicated to use and difficult to maintain. *Labor costs may be high. *Buy-in costs for hardware and software are relatively high.
Windows NT	*Can run on both high-end and low-end systems, from Intel to Alpha systems. *Relatively robust. *Fairly easy to administer and may have lower maintenance costs. *Numerous high-end applications are being ported this operating system.	*May require more high-end hardware for adequate performance. *May not be as flexible as UNIX for some Internet-related tasks. *Some high-end business applications may not be available on this platform yet.
Windows 95	*Easy to run. *Equipment costs and labor costs are low. *Web server and development software is cheap.	*Not as robust as Windows NT or UNIX, prone to crashes. *May require a fast system for adequate performance. *Not as much server software is ported to Windows 95 as to Windows NT. *Not as flexible as UNIX or Windows NT.
Macintosh	*Easy to run. *Equipment and labor costs are very low. *Software is cheap.	*Operating system architecture may inhibit performance. *Relatively little Web software available. *Not as flexible as Windows NT or UNIX. *Not robust and prone to crashes, like Windows 95.

Table 15-1.   *Operating System Summary*

While Table 15-1 presents a good overview of the issues of choosing one operating system over another for a Web server, the decision may often be made due to familiarity or personal taste. There is nothing wrong with this. While one person may argue about the merits of UNIX, introducing a UNIX server into an environment with heavy Macintosh investment would be foolish. The bottom line is to always remember suitability. A small Web server for a school might do well on a Macintosh, while a Windows NT system might make a great departmental server, and a Sun server might be used for a high-performance Web site. Once the hardware and operating system are selected, you should consider which Web server software to use.

Only a few years ago, there were only two major Web servers available: NCSA's httpd server for UNIX and CERN's httpd server for UNIX. Both of these servers are free to use, but both require users to compile and install the software themselves. Today there are dozens of different Web servers available on a variety of machines. If you are interested in learning about all the servers, go to the Serverwatch home page, at www.serverwatch.com, which provides links and reviews of most of the Web servers currently available. Rather than considering all Web servers in your decision, it might be wise to look at the most common Web servers used. Based upon surveys and analysis of reachable servers on the Internet, these servers are well agreed upon, though their exact market percentage is a topic of hot debate.

These are the major Web servers:

Apache
Microsoft's IIS
NCSA
Netscape Web Servers
WebSite
Webstar

Each of the popular Web servers is discussed next. This should by no means be considered as approval of these products, just a synopsis of each product and some of its known issues.

Apache
http://www.apache.org/

A descendant of NCSA's httpd server, Apache is probably the first or second most popular Web server on the Internet. Apache's popularity stems from the fact that it is free and fast. It is also very powerful, supporting features like HTTP 1.1, extended server-side includes (SSIs), a module architecture similar to NSAPI/ISAPI, and numerous free modules that perform functions such as server-based Perl interpretation or interpretation of parsed HTML. However, Apache is not for everyone. The main issue with Apache is that it isn't a commercial package. While there is generally support available on the Internet, many firms may be hesitant to run their mission-critical systems on a user-supported product. However, as with operating systems like Linux, various third parties offer commercial support for Apache.

Another potential limiting factor for Apache is that the system currently is mainly for UNIX, although a port to Windows 95/Windows NT is in a prerelease stage. This may limit the use of Apache to high-use external and not-for-profit Web sites rather than intranets. Last, Apache might require modification of configuration files or even compilation in order to install. If you like to tinker, have a UNIX system, and don't have a lot of money, then Apache might just be for you. You'll be in good company: some of the largest Web sites on the Internet swear by this product.

 For Web trivia buffs, the name Apache is derived from the description of the software as a patched version of NCSA. Think "a patchy NCSA server."

Netscape Web Servers
http://home.netscape.com/

Netscape has a growing line of Web servers, ranging from its FastTrack system to its Enterprise server. Netscape Web servers run on most major variants of UNIX (Solaris, SunOS, AIX, HP-UX, Digital UNIX, and IRIX) as well as Windows 95/WindowsNT. The systems are advanced, supporting hooks with databases, content management, HTTP 1.1, and a variety of other features. Netscape has attempted to make the software more commercial grade, including Web-based installation and administration. The only gripes that people tend to make about Netscape servers is that they sometimes perform sluggishly. Otherwise, if you are in a cross-platform environment, then consider using Netscape servers. Netscape Web software is available for evaluation, but it is commercial and requires payment.

Microsoft Internet Information Server
http://www.microsoft.com/iis/

IIS is Microsoft's server for Windows NT. Windows 95 also supports a similar but much less powerful version of IIS called the Personal Web Server (PWS). While PWS is certainly popular, of the two, most organizations favor IIS. One very important aspect of IIS is that it is very tightly integrated with the Windows NT environment. Unfortunately, being so Windows NT specific is also considered one of the problems with IIS. Because of hardware and clustering issues, IIS hasn't proved quite as scalable as some UNIX-based servers. With new Microsoft clustering technologies and integration with a transaction processor, this scalability problem is likely to change. For an intranet environment, particularly one with heavy Microsoft investment, it is difficult to beat the services offered by IIS—particularly its integration with other Microsoft products such as the SQL-Server database system. The price for IIS is currently a big selling point for the software: it's free.

NCSA
http://hoohoo.ncsa.uiuc.edu/

Still one of the top Web servers on the Internet, NCSA continues to be popular with UNIX-based Web masters. This software was one of the original two Web servers used on the Internet. It is still widely used on UNIX systems. Though it is free, the software is not actively supported and is no longer being developed, and so it should be avoided if you are just starting out. Furthermore, many of the newer server features such as HTTP 1.1 are not supported by NCSA. People who want the power and the low price should move to Apache.

WebSite
http://website.ora.com/

A very easy-to-use Web server for Window 95/Windows NT, O'Reilly's WebSite is one of the only robust Web servers available for Windows 95. Though it lacks the performance of Netscape or Microsoft servers running on more powerful systems, WebSite is considered one of the easiest servers to install and administer. Furthermore, the system provides many nice development features such as integration with Cold Fusion, advanced SSI, and special APIs for server extensions. For intranets or sites that don't need the performance of Windows NT or UNIX, WebSite is a great choice.

WebStar
http://www.starnine.com/

The most popular Web server for the Macintosh was originally based on MacHTTPD. WebStar integrates well with the Macintosh. It supports AppleScript and other Macintosh-specific tools and ideas such as automatic binhexing of files. The system supports UNIX-style CGI programs, a Java virtual machine for server-side Java, and extended SSI. The performance of WebStar often leaves much to be desired, though claims have been made that this has been improved. WebStar is probably more than adequate for intranets or small Web sites.

In the Web server software discussion, people often don't consider that different packages will have different performance characteristics. Using the same hardware, one Web server software package may far outperform another. When planning to build a Web server, start either from the hardware and build up, or start from the particular software and build down picking the best possible hardware. If you make good software and hardware choices, the performance of the site can be significantly improved.

How Web Servers Work

When it comes to the physical process of publishing documents, the main issues are whether to run your own server, or to host elsewhere in conjunction with Web server software and hardware. An understanding of how Web servers do their job is important to understanding potential bottlenecks, and leads to an in-depth understanding of how the Web works. In some sense, all that a Web server does is listen for requests from browsers or, as they are called more generically, *user agents*. Once the server receives a request, typically to deliver a file, it determines if it should do it. If so, it copies the file from the disk out to the network. In some cases, the user agent may ask the server to execute a program, but the idea is the same: eventually, some data is transmitted back to the browser for display. This discussion between the user agent, typically a Web browser, and server takes place using the HTTP protocol.

HTTP

The Hypertext Transfer Protocol (HTTP) is the basic underlying application-level protocol used to facilitate the transmission of data to and from a Web server. HTTP provides a simple, fast way to specify the interaction between client and server. The protocol actually defines how a client must ask for data from the server and how the server returns it. HTTP does not specify how the data is actually transferred; this is up to lower-level network protocols such as TCP.

The first version of HTTP, known as version 0.9, was used as early as 1990. The current version of HTTP, 1.0 as defined by RFC 1945, is supported by most servers and clients (Web browsers). However, the 1.0 version of HTTP does not properly handle the effects of hierarchical proxies and caching, or provide features to facilitate virtual hosts. More important, the 1.0 version of HTTP has significant performance problems due to the opening and closing of many connections for a single Web page.

HTTP 1.1 solves many of these problems. It is currently supported by newer 4.0 generation Web browsers as well as servers. There are still many limitations to HTTP, however. HTTP is used increasingly in applications that need more sophisticated features, including distributed authoring, collaboration, and remote procedure calls. The Protocol Extension Protocol (PEP) is a proposed extension to HTTP designed to address the tension between browser, server, and proxy vendor enhancement agreements and public specifications. PEP allows the software to introduce new protocols during communication, negotiate protocols or content, or even switch between protocols on the fly. For now, such protocols are still in development. This discussion will deal with HTTP 1.0 and 1.1.

The process of a Web browser or other user agent such as Web spider or Robot requesting a document from a Web, or more correctly HTTP, server is simple, and has been discussed throughout the book. The overall process is diagrammed in Figure 15-2.

In Figure 15-2, the user first requests a document from a Web server by specifying the URL of the document desired.

Note *During this step, a domain name lookup may occur, which translates a machine name like www.bigcompany.com to an underlying IP address such as 192.102.249.3. If the domain name lookup fails, an error message such as "No Such Host" or "The server does not have a DNS entry" will be returned. Certain assumptions, such as the default service port to access for HTTP requests (80), may also be made. This is transparent to the user, who simply uses a URL to access a page.*

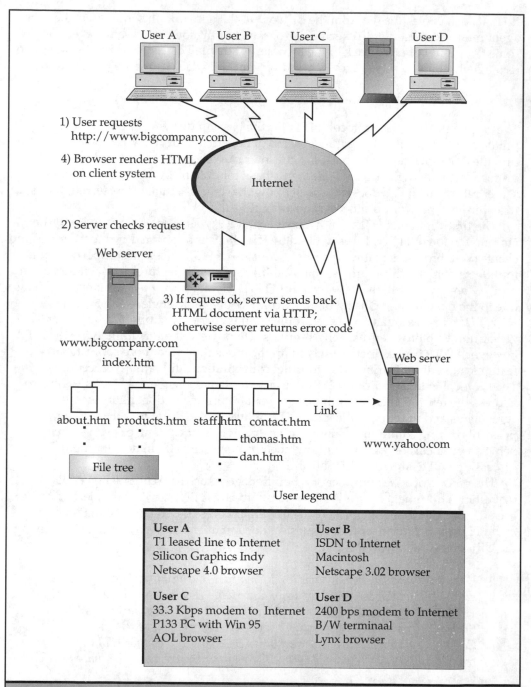

1) User requests
   http://www.bigcompany.com

4) Browser renders HTML
   on client system

2) Server checks request

Web server

3) If request ok, server sends back
   HTML document via HTTP;
   otherwise server returns error code

www.bigcompany.com

index.htm

about.htm products.htm staff.htm contact.htm — — Link — →

thomas.htm

dan.htm

File tree

Web server

www.yahoo.com

User legend

User A	User B
T1 leased line to Internet	ISDN to Internet
Silicon Graphics Indy	Macintosh
Netscape 4.0 browser	Netscape 3.02 browser

User C	User D
33.3 Kbps modem to Internet	2400 bps modem to Internet
P133 PC with Win 95	B/W terminaal
AOL browser	Lynx browser

Figure 15-2.   *Overview of Web client/server relationship*

The browser then forms the proper HTTP request and sends the request to the server residing at the address specified by the URL. A typical HTTP request consists of

```
HTTP-Method Identifier HTTP-version
<Optional additional request headers>
```

In this example, the HTTP-Method would be **GET** or **POST**. An identifier might correspond to the file desired (for example, /reports/latest.html) and the HTTP-version indicates the dialect of HTTP being used, such as HTTP/1.0.

If a user requests a document with the URL http://www.bigcompany.com/reports/lastest.html, the browser might generate a request like the one shown here to retrieve the object from the server:

```
GET /reports/latest.html HTTP/1.0
If-Modified-Since: Tuesday, 12-Aug-97 01:39:39 GMT; Referer:
http://www.bigcompany.com/reports/index.html
Connection: Keep-Alive
User-Agent: Mozilla/4.02 [en] (X11; I; SunOS 5.4 sun4m)
Accept: image/gif, image/x-xbitmap, image/jpeg, image/pjpeg, */*
Accept-Language: en
Accept-Charset: iso-8859-1,*,utf-8
```

People often ask why the complete URL is not shown in the request. It isn't necessary in most cases, except when using a proxy server. The use of a relative URL in the header is adequate. The server knows where it is; it just needs to know what document to get from its own file tree. In the case of using a proxy server, which requests a document on behalf of a browser, a full URL is passed to it that is later made relative by the proxy. Besides the simple **GET** method, there are various other methods specified in HTTP. Not all are commonly used. Table 15-2 provides a summary of the HTTP 1.1 request methods.

Within an HTTP request, there is a variety of optional fields for creating a complete request. The common fields and an example for each is shown in Table 15-3.

Note that the request headers seem very familiar. They constitute the same environment variables that you can access from within a CGI program. Now it should be clear how this information is obtained.

After receiving a request, the Web server attempts to process the request. The result of the request is indicated by a server status line that contains a response code; for example, the ever-popular "404 Not Found." The server response status line takes this form:

```
HTTP-version Status-code Reason-String
```

Method	Description
GET	Returns the object specified by the identifier.
HEAD	Returns information about the object specified by the identifier, such as last modification data, but does not return the actual object.
OPTIONS	Returns information about the capabilities supported by a server if no location is specified, or the possible methods that can be applied to the specified object.
POST	Send information to the address indicated by the identifier. Generally this method is used to transmit information from a form using the METHOD="POST" attribute of the <FORM> element to a server-based CGI program.
PUT	Sends data to the server and writes it to the address specified by the identifier overwriting previous content. In the basic form, PUT can be used for file upload.
DELETE	Removes the file specified by the identifier. This method is generally disallowed.
TRACE	This method is used to provide diagnostic information by allowing the client to see what is being received on the server.

Table 15-2.   *Summary of HTTP 1.1 Request Methods*

For a successful query, a status line might read as follows:

```
HTTP/1.0   200   OK
```

while in case of error the status line might read

```
HTTP/1.0   404   Not Found
```

The status codes for the emerging HTTP 1.1 standard are shown in Table 15-4.

After the status line, the server responds with information about itself and the data being returned. There are various selected response headers, but the most important indicates the type of data in the form of a MIME-type and subtype that will be returned. Like request headers, many of these codes are optional and depend on the status of the request.

Client Request Field	Description	Example
Accept: MIME-type/ MIME-subtype	Used to indicate the data types accepted by the browser. An entry of */* indicates anything is accepted; however, it is possible to indicate particular content types like image/jpeg so the server can make a decision on what to return. This facility could be used to introduce a form of content negotiation so that a browser could be served only data it understands or prefers, although this approach is not widely understood nor implemented.	Accept: image/gif, image/x-xbitmap, image/jpeg, image/pjpeg, */*
Accept-Charset: charset	Used to indicate the character set that is accepted by the browser, such as ASCII or foreign character encodings.	Accept-Charset: iso-8859-1,*,utf-8
Accept-Encoding: encoding-type	Used to instruct the server what type of encoding the browser understands. Typically this field is used to indicate to the server that compressed data can be handled.	Accept-Encoding: x-compress

Table 15-3.   *Common Request Headers*

Client Request Field	Description	Example
Accept-language: language	Lists the languages preferred by the browser and could be used by the server to pass back the appropriate language data.	Accept-Language: en
Authorization: authorization-scheme authorization-data	Typically used to indicate the userid and "encrypted" password if the user is returning authorization information.	Authorization: user joeblow:testpass
Content-length: bytes	Gives the length in bytes of the message being sent to the server, if any. Remember that the browser may upload or pass data using the PUT or POST methods.	Content-length: 1805
Content-type: MIME-type/MIME-subtype	Indicates the MIME type of a message being sent to a server, if any. The value of this field would be particularly important in the case of file upload.	Content-type: text/plain
Date: date-time	Indicates the date and time in Greenwich Mean Time (GMT) that a request was made. GMT time is mandatory for time consistency, given the world wide nature of the Web.	Date: Thursday, 15-Jan-98 01:39:39 GMT

Table 15-3. *Common Request Headers (continued)*

Client Request Field	Description	Example
From: e-mail address	If given, may contain an e-mail address for the requesting browser. For privacy reasons this request header is often not sent.	From: joe@bigcompany.com
Host	Indicates the host and port of the server that the request is being made to.	Host: www.bigcompany.com
If-Modified-Since: date-time	Used to indicate file freshness to improve the efficiency of the GET method. When used in conjunction with a GET request for a particular file, the requested file is checked to see if it has been modified since the time specified in the field. If the file has not been modified, a "not modified code" (304) is sent to the client so a cached version of the document can be used; otherwise, the file is returned normally.	If-Modified-Since: Thursday, 15-Jan-98 01:39:39 GMT
If-Match: selector-string	Used to make a request conditionally only if the items match some selector value passed in. Imagine only using POST to add data once it has been moved to a file called "olddata."	If-Match: "olddata"

Table 15-3.   *Common Request Headers* (continued)

Client Request Field	Description	Example
If-None-Match: selector-string	Does the opposite of If-Match. The method is conditional only if the selector does not match anything. This might be useful to keep from overwriting existing files.	If-None-Match: "newfile"
If-Range: selector	If a client has a partial copy of an object in its cache, and wishes to have an up-to-date copy of the entire object in its cache, it could use the Range request-header with this conditional If-Range modifier to update the file. Modification selection can take place on time as well.	If-Range: Thursday, 15-Jan-98 01:39:39 GMT;
If-Unmodified-Since	Used to make a conditional method. If the requested file has not been modified since the specified time, the server should perform the requested method, otherwise the method should fail.	If-Unmodified-Since: Thursday, 15-Jan-98 01:39:39 GMT
Max-Forwards: integer	Used with the TRACE method to limit the number of proxies or gateways that can forward the request. This would be useful to determine failures if a request moves through many proxies before reaching the final server.	Max-Forwards: 6

Table 15-3. *Common Request Headers* (continued)

Client Request Field	Description	Example
MIME-version: version-number	Used to indicate the MIME protocol version, understood by the browser, that the server should use when fulfilling requests.	MIME-Version: 1.0
Proxy-Authorization: Authorization Information	Used so the client can identify itself or the user to a proxy that requires authentication.	Proxy-Authorization: joeblow: testpass; Realm: All
Pragma: Server-directive	Used to pass information to a server; for example, this field can be used to inform a caching proxy server to fetch a fresh copy of a page.	Pragma: no-cache
Range: Byte-range	Used to request a particular range of a file such as a certain number of bytes. The example shows a request for the last 500 bytes of a file.	Range: bytes=-500
Referer: URL	Indicates the URL of the document from which the request originates, in other words, the linking document. This value may be empty if the user has entered the URL directly rather than following a link.	Referer: http://www.bigcompany.com/reports/index.html
User-Agent: Agent-code	Indicates the type of browser making the request.	User-Agent: Mozilla/3.0 (Windows 95; Internet Explorer)

Table 15-3.   *Common Request Headers* (continued)

Status-Code	Reason-String	Description
Informational Codes (process continues after this)		
100	Continue	An interim response issued by the server that indicates the request is in progress but has not been rejected or accepted. This status code is in support of the persistent connection idea introduced in HTTP 1.1
101	Switching Protocols	Can be returned by the server to indicate that a different protocol should be used to improve communication. This could be used to initiate a real-time protocol.
Success Codes (request understood and accepted)		
200	OK	Indicates the successful completion of a request.
201	Created	Indicates the successful completion of a PUT request and the creation of the file specified.
202	Accepted	This code indicates that the request has been accepted for processing, but that the processing has not been completed and the request may or may not actually finish properly.
203	Non-Authoritative Information	Indicates a successful request, except that returned information, particularly meta information about a document, comes from a third source and is unverifiable.
204	No Content	Indicates a successful request, but there is no new data to send to the client.
205	Reset Content	Indicates that the client should reset the page that sent the request (potentially for more input). This could be used on a form page that needs consistent refreshing, rather than reloading as might be used in a chat system.
206	Partial Content	Indicates a successful request for a piece of a larger document or set of documents. This response typically is encountered when media is sent out in a particular order, or byte-served, as with streaming Acrobat files.

Table 15-4.   *HTTP 1.1 Status Codes*

Status-Code	Reason-String	Description
Redirection Codes (further action necessary to complete request)		
300	Multiple Choices	Indicates that there are many possible representations for the requested information so the client should use the preferred representation, which may be in the form of a closer server or different data format.
301	Moved Permanently	Requested resource has been assigned a new permanent address and any future references to this resource should be done using one of the returned addresses.
302	Moved Temporarily	Requested resource temporarily resides at a different address. For future requests, the original address should still be used.
303	See Other	Indicates that the requested object can be found at a different address and should be retrieved using a GET method on that resource.
304	Not Modified	Issued in response to a conditional GET; indicates to the agent to use a local copy from cache or similar action as the request object has not changed.
305	Use Proxy	Indicates that the requested resource must be accessed through the proxy given by the URL in the Location field.
Client Error Codes (syntax error or other problem causing failure)		
400	Bad Request	Indicates that the request could not be understood by the server due to malformed syntax.
401	Unauthorized	Request requires user authentication. The authorization has failed for some reason, so this code is returned.
402	Payment Required	Obviously in support of commerce, this code is currently not well defined.

Table 15-4.   *HTTP 1.1 Status Codes* (continued)

Status-Code	Reason-String	Description
\multicolumn{3}{l}{Client Error Codes (syntax error or other problem causing failure) *(continued)*}		
403	Forbidden	Request is understood but disallowed and should not be reattempted, compared to the 401 code, which may suggest a reauthentication. A typical response code in response to a query for a directory listing when directory listings are disallowed.
404	Not Found	Usually issued in response to a typo by the user or a moved resource, as the server can't find anything that matches the request nor any indication that the requested item has been moved.
405	Method Not Allowed	Issued response to a method request like GET, POST, or PUT on an object where such a method is not supported. Generally an indication of what methods are supported will be returned.
406	Not Acceptable	Indicates that the response to the request will not be in one of the content types acceptable by the browser, so why bother doing the request? This is an unlikely response given the */* acceptance issued by most if not all browsers.
407	Proxy Authentication Required	Indicates that the proxy server requires some form of authentication to continue. This code is similar to the 401 code.
408	Request Time-out	Indicates that the client did not produce or finish a request within the time that the server was prepared to wait.
409	Conflict	The request could not be completed because of a conflict with the requested resource; for example, the file might be locked.

Table 15-4. *HTTP 1.1 Status Codes* (continued)

Status-Code	Reason-String	Description
Client Error Codes (syntax error or other problem causing failure) (*continued*)		
410	Gone	Indicates that the requested object is no longer available at the server and no forwarding address is known. Search engines may want to add remote references to objects that return this value since it is a permanent condition.
411	Length Required	Indicates that the server refuses to accept the request without a defined Content-Length. This may happen when a file is posted without a length.
412	Precondition Failed	Indicates that a precondition given in one or more of the request-header fields, such as If-Unmodified-Since, evaluated to false.
413	Request Entity Too Large	Indicates that the server is refusing to return data because the object may be too large or the server may be too loaded to handle the request. The server may also provide information indicating when to try again if possible, but just as well may terminate any open connections.
414	Request-URI Too Large	Indicates that the Uniform Resource Identifier (URI), generally a URL, in the request field is too long for the server to handle. This is unlikely to occur since browsers will probably not allow such transmissions.
415	Unsupported Media Type	Indicates the server will not perform the request because the media type specified in the message is not supported. This code might be returned when a server receives a file it is not configured to accept via the PUT method.

Table 15-4.   *HTTP 1.1 Status Codes* (continued)

Status-Code	Reason-String	Description
Server Error Codes (server can't fulfill a potentially valid request)		
500	Internal Server Error	A serious error message indicating that the server encountered an internal error that keeps it from fulfilling the request.
501	Not Implemented	This response is to a request that the server does not support or may be understood but not implemented.
502	Bad Gateway	Indicates that the server acting as a proxy encountered an error from some other gateway and is passing the message along.
503	Service Unavailable	Indicates the server is currently overloaded or is undergoing maintenance. Headers may be sent to indicate when the server will be available.
504	Gateway Time-out	Indicates that the server, when acting as a gateway or proxy, encountered too long a delay from an upstream proxy and decided to time out.
505	HTTP Version not supported	Indicates that the server does not support the HTTP version specified in the request.

Table 15-4.   *HTTP 1.1 Status Codes* (continued)

An example server response for the request shown earlier in the chapter is shown here:

```
HTTP/1.0 200 OK
Server: Netscape-Commerce/1.12
Date: Thursday, 01-Aug-96 13:05:08 GMT
Content-type: text/html
Last-modified: Thursday, 01-Aug-96 10:09:00 GMT
Content-length: 205

<HTML>
<HEAD>
<TITLE>Report 1</TITLE>
```

```
</HEAD>
<BODY>
<H1>Report About Important Things</H1>
<HR>
<P>Here is some information about important things. </P>
</BODY>
</HTML>
```

A list of the common server response headers for HTTP 1.1, as well as examples of each, can be found in Table 15-5.

The most important header response field is the Content-type field. The MIME type indicated by this field is a device by which the browser is able to figure out what to do with the data being returned.

Response Header	Description	Example
Age	Shows the sender's estimate of the amount of time since the response was generated at the origin server. Age values are nonnegative decimal integers, representing time in seconds.	Age: 10
Content-Encoding	Indicates the encoding the data returned is in.	Content-Encoding: x-compress
Content-Language	Indicates the language used for the data returned by the server.	Content-Language: en
Content-Length	Indicates the number of bytes returned by the server.	Content-length: 205
Content-Range	Indicates the range of the data being sent back by the server.	Content-Range: -500

Table 15-5. *Common HTTP 1.1 Server Response Headers*

Response Header	Description	Example
Content-Type	This is probably the most important field and indicates what type of content is being returned by the server in the form of a MIME type.	Content-type: text/html
Expires	Gives the date/time after which the returned data should be considered stale and should not be returned from a cache.	Expires: Thu, 04 Dec 1997 16:00:00 GMT
Last-Modified	The Last-Modified response-header field is used to indicate the date the content returned was last modified. This can be used by caches to decide to keep local copies of objects.	Last-modified: Thursday, 01-Aug-96 10:09:00 GMT
Location	Used to redirect the browser to another page. Occasionally scripts will use this method for browser redirection based on capability.	Location: http://www.bigcompany. com/netscapehome.htm
Proxy-Authenticate	Included with a 407 (Proxy Authentication Required) response. The value of the field consists of a challenge that indicates the authentication scheme and parameters applicable to the proxy for the request.	Proxy-Authenticate: GreenDecoderRing: 0124.

Table 15-5. *Common HTTP 1.1 Server Response Headers* (continued)

Response Header	Description	Example
Public	Lists the set of methods supported by the server. The purpose of this field is strictly to inform the browser of the capabilities of the server when new or unusual methods are encountered.	Public: OPTIONS, MGET, MHEAD, GET, HEAD
Retry-After	Can be used in conjunction with a 503 (Service Unavailable) response to indicate how long the service is expected to be unavailable to the requesting client. The value of this field can be either an HTTP-date or an integer number of seconds after which to retry.	Retry-After: Fri, 31 Dec 1999 23:59:59 GMT Retry-After: 60
Server	Contains information about the Web software used.	Server: Netscape-Commerce/ 1.12
Warning	Used to carry additional information about the status of a response that may not be found in the status code.	Warning: 10 Response is stale
WWW-Authenticate	Included with a 401 (Unauthorized) response message. The field consists of at least one challenge that indicates the authentication scheme and parameters applicable to the request made by the client.	WWW-Authenticate: Magic-Key-Challenge= 555121, DecoderRing= Green

Table 15-5.   *Common HTTP 1.1 Server Response Headers* (continued)

MIME

MIME (Multipurpose Internet Mail Extensions) was originally developed as an extension to the Internet mail protocol that allows for the communication of multimedia. The basic idea of MIME is transmission of text files with headers that indicate binary data that will follow. Each MIME header is composed of two parts that indicate the data type and subtype in the following format:

Content-type: *type/subtype*

where *type* can be image, audio, text, video, application, multipart, message, or extension-token. *subtype* gives the specifics of the content. Some samples are listed here:

text/html
application/x-director
application/x-pdf
video/quicktime
video/x-msvideo
image/gif
audio/x-wav

Beyond these basic headers, you may also include information such as the character encoding language. For more information about MIME, look at RFC 1521 at ds.internic.net or the list of registered MIME types at ftp://ftp.isi.edu/in-notes/iana/assignments/media-types/.

When a Web server delivers a file, the header information is intercepted by the browser and questioned. The MIME type, as mentioned earlier, is specified by the Content-type server response field. For example, if a browser receives a basic HTML file, the text/html header indicates what to do and typically renders the file in the browser window. If the browser receives a type it does not understand, for example application/x-director, it may ask the user to pick a helper, save it, or delete it, as shown by the familiar dialog box shown here:

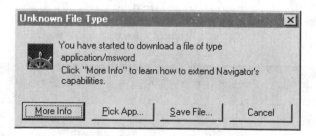

Normally, users hope that helper applications or plug-ins will intercept any MIME typed data that their browser doesn't understand and deal with it. It is interesting to note how little is said about MIME, but how important it is in the discussion between the browser and the server.

Speed and State Problems with HTTP

HTTP is a very simple protocol. That is, in a sense, its problem: it may be too simple. As a simple request-response protocol, HTTP can sometimes be very inefficient. Consider a Web page with five images on it. In order to fetch this Web page, it may take six or seven individual requests to pull down all the files. These may include one request for the HTML text, five for the images, and perhaps even a redirect request for a partially formed URL. Each HTTP request has a little overhead with it. Do you see a potential problem? HTTP 1.0 suffered from this performance problem. HTTP 1.1, however, attempts to get around this problem by keeping connections open and pipelining responses. Browser vendors are also worried about performance issues and enable their browsers to request multiple objects at once to get around performance drags.

The other problem with HTTP is that it is stateless. After a Web server has finished fulfilling a client request, the server retains no "memory" of the request that just took place, except in the form of an entry in a log file, which records the request. An example of this "lack of memory" is how a user may partially fill in a form on a Web page, leave the site, and then come back and find the form cleared. As discussed in Chapters 11 and 12, the state problem is one of the biggest challenges to building complex applications on the Web. Not having to preserve state is what keeps HTTP relatively simple and fast.

The Realities of Publishing and Maintaining a Web Site

While understanding how Web servers work and the issues in choosing an in-house or outsourced server appears easy enough, it does not hint at the challenges of actually running a Web site. Far too often, Web professionals are quick to start a Web project, but slow to continue it. The fun is often in the development of the site, setting the structure, designing the navigation, setting the look and feel, and then coding the page. But what happens next? The site is now released to its intended audience, but you can't abandon it now. Web sites need care and feeding. Depending on the site, there may be daily, weekly, or monthly maintenance to perform. Adding new information, checking for broken links, continually testing under new browsers, upgrading HTML or script code to modern standards, running statistics and performing various server-related activities such as upgrading software or running backups, are all vital tasks. The real work of the site comes after it is released. The site was built for some purpose, and now it is time to fulfill it.

Summary

Site development should address the need of hosting pages on a Web server. Developers can choose to host sites on servers within companies; obtain the necessary hardware, software, Internet connection and labor required to do hosting themselves; or elect to outsource hosting to an ISP or Web hosting company. Because of the costs and complications involved in trying to provide sufficient resources to do your own hosting, it often makes sense to outsource. This approach presents the options of renting space on a shared server or the co-location of a dedicated server at a hosting facility. There is more flexibility in running your own server, rather than being at the mercy of what a shared hosting provider makes available. Running your own server requires selection and evaluation of server software and hosting platform as well as consideration of performance requirements. In addition to server and hosting choices, an understanding of how Web servers work using the HTTP and MIME protocols can be essential to monitoring and improving server performance for better Web page delivery.

Chapter 16

XML: Beyond HTML

With much fanfare, Extensible Markup Language (XML) has emerged rapidly as a new approach to delivering structured data over the Web. Why XML? Simply put, XML will allow authors to define their own elements using this Web-efficient version of Standard Generalized Markup Language (SGML), the mother language used to define HTML. While much of the full XML vision is still in a discussion phase and the core language hasn't been finalized, the effects of XML can already be felt. Microsoft, Sun, and Netscape are furiously working to make XML real under the aegis of the World Wide Web Consortium (W3C). And as usual, browser vendors are attempting to support XML documents or ideas even before standards are put in place. For example, Microsoft's push-technology Channel Definition Format (CDF), as well as Open Software Description (OSD) format, are both based on an XML data format. But what's so wrong with HTML? Quite simply, it is not flexible enough to meet the document-structuring requirements of specific industries or new viewing environments.

Relationship Between HTML, SGML, and XML

To understand what all the excitement is about, it is necessary to understand the connection between HTML, SGML, and XML. XML is defined as an application profile of SGML designed to support the efficient use of SGML documents over the Web. Informally, an *application profile* means a subset of a standard that's given a little twist to accommodate real-world use. To understand the twist XML gives to SGML, it is necessary to understand the strengths and weaknesses of the language and its most famous application, HTML. However, the goal of XML is not to replace either technology but to complement and augment them as appropriate.

Let's start with HTML. What could be wrong with HTML? Any technology globally used by tens of millions of people must be doing something right. As a general-purpose technology, HTML meets an extraordinarily broad set of user needs. It does not, however, fit very well with applications that rely upon specialized information, either as data files or complex structured documents. Imagine trying to format a complex mathematical formula in HTML. The only choice is to make an image out of the formula, embed a special math technology, or even use another document-formatting technology like Adobe's Acrobat. The HTML language cannot realistically accommodate the formatting needs of documents that need more than paragraphs, sections, and simple structure. What keeps the language from dealing with such application-specific problems is that the elements of HTML are fixed; the language contains no provision for extending itself, namely, for defining new elements. While browser vendors used to add new elements all the time, any proposed extension entails lengthy advocacy before the W3C. But in reality, adding more element types to HTML doesn't make sense. The language is already large enough. It is meant to be a general-purpose language capable of handling a large variety of documents. HTML needs some mechanism so that its general-purpose framework can be augmented to accommodate specialized content.

SGML seems like a reasonable candidate to increase HTML's flexibility. SGML is a *meta-language,* a language used to define other languages. While HTML is the best known SGML-defined language, SGML has successfully been used to define special document types ranging from aviation maintenance manuals to scholarly texts. SGML can represent very complex information structures, and it scales well to accommodate enormous volumes of information. However, SGML is extremely complex and was not built with today's online applications in mind. The language first appeared in the 1970s, the golden age of batch processing, and was not designed to be used in networked interactive applications. Without resolving these issues, the full SGML language cannot be efficiently used over the Web.

XML is an attempt to define a subset of SGML that is specifically designed for use in a Web context. As such, it will be influenced not just by its SGML parent but by HTML as well. The exact way that XML will fit into Web documents is still hazy, but the general role of the language is clear. Initially, it will be used to represent specialized data to augment HTML documents. It is already being used to do this. For example, the Channel Definition Format (CDF) from Microsoft specifies documents for "push" delivery on the Internet and is actually an application of XML. (*Push* is a technology in which data, such as news, is sent to users on a scheduled basis, saving them the trouble of hunting for it.)

Purpose-specific extensions to Web documents will be the first use of XML, but at some point XML will be used in its own right for Web documents instead of HTML. At present, XML is already being used to add data to HTML documents, such as forms of meta-data that describe the document. What's unusual about these specific examples of XML use is that the core language syntax has not yet been finalized. It is still in the working-draft stage. Leave it to the browser vendors to implement first and ask questions later. The features that will make XML a document platform in its own right are even more tentative. For example, linking models are at the draft stage, and style sheet use and Document Object Model relationships are still at the discussion stage.

So is XML just a work in progress? Yes, as much as HTML is. XML is already arriving in various forms such as CDF, OSD, Mathematical Markup Language (MathML), and Chemical Markup Language (CML). Other possible XML-based languages are being discussed in the world at large as well. These include such languages as Hand-held Device Markup Language (HDML), Resource Description Framework (RDF), and Platform for Internet Content Selection-Next Generation (PICS-NG). Given the overwhelming interest in XML, it would be wise to look at the current state of its syntax, as well as its likely future directions.

Basic XML

Because XML is a subset of SGML, it should be somewhat familiar, as HTML itself is an application of SGML. However, to support efficient Web usage, XML does not allow the use of many SGML constructs used to define documents. The eliminated constructs are either infrequently used or add a performance penalty to document parsing. Writing XML sounds like a daunting task, requiring esoteric knowledge of SGML generally beyond the capabilities of most HTML authors. Actually, writing simple XML documents is fairly easy. Suppose that you had a compelling need to define some elements to represent parrots in a rain forest, and each parrot needed a name and a color. How would you do this in XML? You would simply write something like this:

```
<RAINFOREST>

    <PARROT     NAME="BILLIE"     COLOR="RED" />

    <PARROT     NAME="SUZIE"     COLOR="GREEN" />

    <PARROT     NAME="FIONA"    COLOR="MAUVE" />

</RAINFOREST>
```

How do you know to name the element **<RAINFOREST>** instead of **<FOREST>** or **<ECOSYSTEM>**? It's completely up to you. Choose any element and attribute names that meaningfully represent the domain you wish to model. Does this mean that there are no rules? There are rules, but they are few, simple, and only related to syntax.

■ **First rule:** Just like well-written HTML, all elements must be properly nested.

```
This is correct: <OUTER><INNER>ground zero</INNER></OUTER>
This is not: <OUTER><INNER>ground zero</OUTER></INNER>
```

■ **Second rule:** All attribute values must be quoted. In HTML, quoting is good authoring practice, but it is only required for values that contain characters other than letters (A–Z, a–z), numbers (0–9), hyphens (-), or periods (.), so under XML,

```
<BLASTOFF COUNT="10">
```

is correct, while

```
<BLASTOFF COUNT=10>
```

is not.

These last two rules should be familiar to HTML writers who practice good authoring style. However, the final rule may seem a bit odd. In XML, all elements with empty content must be self-identifying by ending in "/>" instead of the familiar ">". An empty element is one like the HTML **
, **<HR>, or **<IMG>** elements. In XML these would be represented, respectively, as **
, **<HR/> and **<IMG SRC="test.gif" />**.

Why is this necessary? Because unlike HTML and traditional SGML, XML documents may not have a formal document type definition (DTD) associated with them. Lacking a DTD, there is no way for a parser to know if a tag like **
** is empty or contains a matching **</BR>** tag much later in the document. For parsing efficiency, XML needs a syntactic signal to identify empty elements.

A document constructed according to the previous simple rules is known as a *well-formed document*. SGML purists may find this notion eccentric and somewhat troubling. Although SGML itself is currently being revised, traditional SGML had no notion of well-formed documents—documents that are in some sense okay because they conform to some basic syntax guidelines. Instead, conventional SGML uses the notion of *valid* documents—documents that adhere to a formally defined DTD. We know that while this concept is also part of HTML, it is often lost on many page authors; but for anything beyond casual applications, there are real benefits to having a DTD and validating documents against it. XML supports both well-formed and valid documents. The well-formed model should encourage those not schooled in the intricacies of SGML to begin authoring XML documents, thus making it as accessible as HTML has been. The valid model is available for applications where a document's logical structure needs to be verified.

Valid Documents

While nearly all HTML authors are familiar with basic elements and attributes, due to the rising complexity of pages they are becoming more familiar with the importance of making an HTML document conform to the rules of a document type definition such as HTML 4.0. As noted in the previous paragraph, a document that conforms to a DTD is said to be valid. Unlike most HTML authors, SGML authors normally concern themselves with producing valid documents. Many also concern themselves with writing the DTDs that HTML authors can take for granted. With the appearance of XML, HTML authors can look forward to mastering a new skill: writing DTDs. The following example illustrates how XML might be used to track student performance in an instructional management system. A definition of the sample language to accomplish this task can be found within the document, though it is possible to keep this definition outside the file as well.

```
<?XML VERSION="1.0"?>
<!DOCTYPE PERFORMANCE  [
<!ELEMENT  STUDENT (COURSE+)>
<!ATTLIST  STUDENT  NAME  CDATA  #REQUIRED
        SEX  (M|F)  #REQUIRED
        LEVEL  (6|7|8) #REQUIRED>

<!ELEMENT  COURSE EMPTY>
<!ATTLIST  COURSE TITLE  CDATA  #REQUIRED
```

```
         GRADE   (PASS|FAIL) #REQUIRED>
]>
<!- -the document instance - ->

<STUDENT NAME="BILLIE" SEX="M" LEVEL="7">
    <COURSE TITLE="MATH" GRADE="PASS" />
    <COURSE TITLE="ENGLISH"  GRADE="FAIL" />
</STUDENT>

<STUDENT NAME="FIONA" SEX="F"  LEVEL="7">
    <COURSE TITLE="MATH"  GRADE="PASS" />
    <COURSE TITLE="ART" GRADE="PASS" />
</STUDENT>
```

The meaning of this language is straightforward. A document is made of **<STUDENT>** elements that have **NAME**, **SEX**, and **GRADE** attributes. The **NAME** attribute can be any character data (**CDATA**), the **SEX** attribute can be **M** or **F**, and the **LEVEL** can be **6, 7,** or **8.** The **<STUDENT>** element may contain one or more **<COURSE>** elements. The **<COURSE>** element is an empty element. However, each **<COURSE>** element has a **TITLE** attribute, which can contain character data, and a **GRADE** attribute, which can be either **PASS** or **FAIL**. The example document shows the use of these new elements.

Although not apparent from the DTD rules in this brief example, XML significantly reduces the complexity of full SGML. A couple of metrics may help you appreciate the extent of this reduction. First, the full SGML standard is about 500 pages long. On the other hand, the working-draft XML specification is less than 30 pages long. Second, XML removes about 30 constructs that SGML uses to define DTDs. The constructs are either infrequently used or introduce ambiguities that would make it difficult to efficiently parse the document. The following valid SGML declaration for an HTML 4.0 **<BODY>** element can be used to illustrate some of the features removed from SGML:

```
<!ELEMENT BODY O O (%block) -BODY +(INS|DELS) - - the body tag - ->
```

The first syntax difference is that XML does not allow omitted tags. The "O O" following the **BODY** identifier indicates that the start and end tags are optional and can be omitted. Their presence can be contextually inferred. Next, notice the **-BODY**. This kind of identifier is known as an *exclusion*. It modifies the basic content model for the **<BODY>** element by saying that it cannot include another **<BODY>** element. XML does not support exclusions. Following this segment is **+(INS | DELS)** which specifies an *inclusion*. It modifies the basic content model of the **<BODY>** element by saying that it can additionally use the <INS> or <DELS> elements anywhere inside its content. XML does not support inclusions. **(INS|DELS)** is also known as a *name group*—a construct, not supported by XML, used to indicate that a declaration applies to multiple elements. Last, the **- - the body tag - -** is an embedded comment. XML supports comments but not inside declarations.

While XML will not support some SGML capabilities, it will retain powerful capabilities not found in standard HTML. One example is XML general entities. These are essentially macros that associate an identifier with replacement text defined either inside the declaration or in an external file. HTML authors may be familiar with character entities like **"** used to insert special characters. XML general entities are used in the same way, except that the replacement text can be arbitrarily long. Anyone who has ever needed to modify something repeated many times in a document will appreciate entities. By using the entity name throughout the document, the replacement text can be modified in a single place, the entity declaration. Entities can also refer to an external file, very useful when many documents need to update a common header or footer. The following example defines two entities, **FifthGrade** and **Grammar**. The **FifthGrade** entity is used to include an external file that contains all the information about the fifth-grade students, while the **Grammar** entity acts as a shorthand notation for a longer course name.

```
<?XML VERSION="1.0"?>
<!DOCTYPE PERFORMANCE  [

<!-- An entity whose replacement text exists in an
  external file -->
<!ENTITY  FifthGrade    SYSTEM "fifthgrade.xml">
<!-- An entity whose replacement text is immediately defined -->
<!ENTITY  GRAMMAR    "Language Studies: Introduction to English Grammar">

<!ELEMENT   STUDENT (COURSE+)>
<!ATTLIST  STUDENT  NAME     CDATA  #REQUIRED
        SEX     (M|F)  #REQUIRED
        LEVEL  (6|7|8)    #REQUIRED>

<!ELEMENT   COURSE EMPTY>
<!ATTLIST  COURSE TITLE       CDATA    #REQUIRED
        GRADE      (PASS|FAIL)   #REQUIRED>
]>
<!- -the document instance - ->

&FifthGrade;
```

```
<STUDENT    NAME="BILLIE"  SEX="M" LEVEL="7">
   <COURSE TITLE ="MATH" GRADE="PASS" />
   <COURSE TITLE =&GRAMMAR;  GRADE="FAIL" />
</STUDENT>

<STUDENT    NAME="FIONA"   SEX="F"  LEVEL="7">
   <COURSE TITLE ="MATH"  GRADE="PASS" />
   <COURSE TITLE =&GRAMMAR; GRADE="PASS" />
</STUDENT>
```

XML Uncertainties

Despite its simplicity, XML inherits from SGML a problem-solving approach that differs radically from common HTML usage. As XML evolves, it is not clear whether it will move toward HTML usage or preserve its SGML heritage. As an example, consider the problem of incorporating a GIF or JPEG media file into a document. Doing this in HTML is simple. An appropriate element refers to the file using a reference like **<IMG SRC="http://mypic.gif">**. At this point, the browser takes over. It checks the file's MIME type. If the browser understands the MIME type, it renders the file. If not, it asks the user what to do. The SGML approach is much more complicated. This approach requires a **NOTATION** declaration to declare GIF as a special data format and indicate where that format is defined. It requires an **ENTITY** declaration to assign an entity name to the .gif file and indicate where it can be found. It requires the element type that will refer to the file to declare an appropriate attribute whose value will be an entity. Finally, it requires an actual element instance that will refer to the file indirectly using its entity name. If this sounds complex, it is. Let's take a look at the example for importing a GIF file into a document.

First, inside the DTD we would have to define what GIF is, as follows:

```
<!NOTATION   GIF   PUBLIC
"+//ISBN 0-7923-9432-1::Graphic Notation//NOTATION
CompuServe Graphic Interchange Format//EN">
```

Next, we would have to define an external entity in the proper notation and relate it to the actual image we want to use:

```
<!ENTITY   MYPICT   SYSTEM   "mypict.gif"   NDATA GIF>
```

Now we have to define a special attribute in the element we want to associate an image with—in this case, an **<IMAGE>** element:

```
<!ELEMENT    IMAGE EMPTY>
<!ATTLITST   IMAGE SOURCE ENTITY #REQUIRED>
```

Finally, we can use the **<IMAGE>** element. If we did things this way in XML, it might look something like this:

```
<IMAGE SOURCE="MYPICT" />
```

From an HTML perspective, this seems a convoluted, roundabout way to get the job done. From an SGML perspective, however, it makes good sense. When managing complex, interrelated sets of documents, it is important that all relationships be explicitly defined in a way that can be easily changed. In this area as in others, XML faces the challenge of finding common ground between two technologies whose pieces don't always fit neatly together. It is probably safe to bet that XML will become more like HTML in the sense of dealing with external files.

Application Models

Once an XML document is defined, either with or without a DTD, how does it get used? At least three distinct application models are on the horizon:

- Using XML for special data files that support HTML applications
- Embedding XML elements into HTML documents
- Using XML by itself as the basis for interactive documents

XML for Data Files

The first pervasive use of XML is to define special data files that support HTML applications. This use is already in place in newer browser releases. The Microsoft Internet Explorer 4.0 browser relies upon an XML-based language to support *push functionality*, the ability of viewers to subscribe to Web sites that are automatically updated on a scheduled basis. The language, known as Channel Definition Format (CDF), is the most publicized of several other "helper" languages to suddenly appear. A related language is Open Software Description (OSD), used to support the automatic downloading of software. The slogan that Microsoft uses to describe the HTML/XML relationship is that HTML is for presentation, while XML is for data.

Operationally, these XML-based language documents are identified by a special file extension like .cdf that is analogous to the special extensions used for .gif and .jpeg files. XML files are retrieved like files for HTML media inserts but processed in a special way. Instead of being handled by a browser extension for visual rendering, they are handled by an extension that parses the document and uses the information it contains to control the browser's behavior. This use only requires those few XML features needed to define data and does not approach the full XML vision. Because these documents are not directly viewed, they can function quite well without those XML capabilities that are still under active discussion: hyperlinking, style sheets, and the Document Object Model.

The CDF language illustrates the characteristics of the "XML as data model." It contains no linking information beyond the common **HREF** attribute used in HTML. It contains no style information for rendering CDF elements in an HTML browser. It only contains the information-building blocks needed to define a channel. The small CDF document shown next presents an example of some of the more common CDF elements. The **<CHANNEL>** element defines the channel and points to an initial HTML document. It contains a **<SCHEDULE>** for updating the channel. It contains several **<ITEM>** elements defining viewable items such as pages and even a screen saver. Viewable pages have an **<ABSTRACT>** to summarize their content and may have both a large and a small graphic logo associated with them, as specified by the empty **<LOGO/>** element:

```
<?XML VERSION="1.0"?>
<CHANNEL HREF="http://www.bigcompany.com/">
  <TITLE>Big Company Channel</TITLE>
  <ABSTRACT>
  Welcome to the Big Company channel, a comprehensive
  guide to the latest book examples.
  </ABSTRACT>
<LOGO HREF="http://www.bigcompany.com/imageslogo.ico"
      STYLE="ICON"/>
<LOGO HREF="http://www.bigcompany.com/images/logo.gif"
      STYLE="IMAGE"/>

<SCHEDULE ENDDATE="1998.12.31">
    <INTERVALTIME DAY="1"/>
</SCHEDULE>

<ITEM HREF="http://www.bigcompany.com/p1.html">

<LOGO HREF="http://www.bigcompany.com/images/pagelogo.ico"
 STYLE="ICON"/>
<LOG VALUE="document:view"/>
<TITLE>Page 1</TITLE>
<ABSTRACT>Abstract for Page 1</ABSTRACT>
</ITEM>
```

```
<ITEM HREF="http://www.bigcompany.com/page2.html">
<LOGO HREF="http://www.bigcompany.com/images/pagelogo.ico"
STYLE="ICON"/>
      <LOG VALUE="document:view"/>
      <TITLE>Page 2</TITLE>
      <ABSTRACT>Abstract for Page 2</ABSTRACT>
  </ITEM>

<ITEM HREF="http://www.bigcompany.com/scrnsave.html">
    <USAGE VALUE="ScreenSaver"></USAGE>
</ITEM>
</CHANNEL>
```

The point of the last example is not to explain the CDF syntax, but to show how XML represents data in a real application. Readers interested in making a CDF channel should visit Microsoft's Sitebuilder network (www.microsoft.com/sitebuilder/) for the latest CDF syntax. Here's one other point about CDF to consider: this file format is external to HTML files. Like any other media type (fractal images, Shockwave, and so on), it could be handled by an external helper application or even a plug-in. But is it possible to think about putting a language like CDF right into an HTML document?

Embedding XML into HTML documents

While the syntax mechanism remains unclear, the expectation exists for a means to embed XML elements into HTML documents. One approach would be to directly intermix XML-defined elements with HTML elements. Another approach is to use a special element like **<XML>** to indicate sections of XML content. This approach was suggested in Microsoft's "Web Collections using XML" submission to the W3C. This element could be used anywhere within an HTML document to enclose XML content, which might work as shown here:

```
<HTML>
<HEAD>
<TITLE>New XML Approach</TITLE>
</HEAD>
<BODY>
<H1>Regular HTML Here</H1>
<XML>
    <SPECIAL>New XML Here</SPECIAL>
</XML>
</BODY>
</HTML>
```

Proposing to use XML inside HTML documents creates the expectation that XML elements will integrate into the HTML application environment. Placing XML elements inside an HTML document's **<HEAD>** element is consistent with the "XML as data" model. After all, the purpose of the head of the document is to house the document's meta data. However, placing XML elements inside the **<BODY>** element introduces an additional complication. Since the elements are in the body of the document, most browsers will want to view the contents of the elements. Unlike HTML, XML elements have no default appearance; they must be assigned one. Cascading Style Sheet (CSS) rules seem a logical candidate for this activity, although there are few problems. For example, the CSS display property supports simple block, inline, or list-item content. It does not support tables. How, then, would one use CSS to display a table defined in XML? The answers to the questions raised by embedding XML inside HTML documents cannot be answered yet, beyond saying this: The W3C's Document Object Model (DOM) group's working requirements say that HTML, XML, and CSS will share a core DOM. Convergence of these technologies is in the cards, but the details are not yet clear.

XML-Based Interactive Documents

The discussion thus far has treated XML as a technology to augment HTML with specialized data. The full XML vision implies that XML can be used in a more ambitious way: as a self-sufficient platform for interactive documents. Some complex enterprise applications rely upon specialized SGML documents that cannot be translated effectively into HTML. Many enterprise applications require hypermedia capabilities beyond those supported by HTML. These applications are candidates for what is currently the least understood emerging XML application: applications using XML rather than HTML as the framework for interactive documents.

There are two areas where existing SGML practice and potentially XML points beyond the capabilities of HTML: linking and style sheets. HyTime is an ISO standard that uses SGML to represent sophisticated hypermedia capabilities such as linking and spatial or temporal events. The Text Encoding Initiative (TEI) is an international collaboration to define SGML guidelines for encoding scholarly documents. Collectively, HyTime and TEI define a richer model for hyperlinking than the simple, unidirectional model found in HTML. The SGML tradition also has its own ISO standard style language: the Document Style Semantics and Specification Language (DSSSL). DSSSL is a full-featured programming language that allows document content to be selected, reordered, or generated, and then formatted using a rich palette of visual containers. HyTime and DSSSL both rely upon the grove data structure, a graph representation of documents that corresponds roughly to HTML's DOM.

To satisfy the SGML community's usage expectations, XML will need to support linking and style functionality beyond that found in HTML. Indeed, the XML discussion documents regarding linking and style sheets show heavy influence from HyTime, TEI, and DSSSL. They also show a need to accommodate the constraints of

Web delivery in an environment ubiquitously shaped by HTML. At this time, the form this accommodation will take is by no means clear.

The core XML language is intentionally very small. How can functionality such as linking and style be added to XML? If it is not possible to address these issues, it is unlikely that XML will become anything more than a data description language. The HTML approach of defining special-purpose elements is clearly not an option. At present, the only published clues occur in the draft documents for linking under XML, which follow a convention modeled after HyTime architectural forms.

XML Linking Preview

Of the proposed extensions to XML, linking capabilities are the most evolved of the language's extended architecture. While the documents describing this currently exist only as working drafts, they are clear enough to understand XML's probable linking capabilities.

Intuitively, HTML users think of a hyperlink as a piece of underlined text or a hot spot on a graphic that they click on to go somewhere else. Actually, a rich vocabulary exists to describe the types of hyperlinks that can occur in hypermedia systems. HTML supports only the simplest forms of these. The proposed XML linking model builds upon the capabilities supported by HTML but can considerably exceed them.

A linking element describes a link relationship between two or more information resources. An example is the HTML **<A>** element that describes a link relationship between a source and a target resource, typically two Web pages. A linking element identifies an information resource by using an addressing scheme known as a *locator*. Locators in HTML use the uniform resource locator (URL) addressing scheme.

Theoretically in hypertext, links can be *inline* or *out of line*. In an inline link, the linking element and one resource connected by the link are tightly bound together: the resource contains the linking element. In the HTML **<A>** element, for example, the element describing the link is the source of the link. In other words, the link element refers to itself as the start of the link. In HTML, all links are inline. By comparison, out-of-line links exist in a different location from any of the resources they refer to as links, often in a different file. Another difference between rich linking models and HTML is that links can be unidirectional or multidirectional. A unidirectional link can only be traversed by starting from one of the resources it connects. All links in HTML are unidirectional: they take you from one resource to another. Whether you return to the original resource by a different link of a browser command, you do not use the original link. By comparison, multidirectional links can be traversed starting from more than one of the resources they connect. Multidirectional links are necessarily out-of-line links.

The link model under development for XML supports the capabilities found in HTML, but extends them in important ways to consider the ideas of richer linking models. Borrowing HyTime's division of links into two basic types, XML supports the definition of simple and extended links. *Simple links* are inline and unidirectional. They are comparable to the links found in HTML and HyTime's *clinks* (contextual links). Extended links can be out of line and multidirectional. This means they may exist in another file and even reference many objects at once. Extended links are comparable to HyTime's *ilinks* (independent links). XML adopts the basic URL locator model found in HTML. It adds an addressing mechanism to locate document elements by referring to a document's parse tree. This mechanism is adopted from the Text Encoding Initiative's Extended Pointer and can be used interchangeably where HTML uses fragment identifiers set using the **NAME** or **ID** attribute for elements.

Looking in depth at the capabilities of simple XML links as defined in the June 30, 1997 W3C working draft shows how XML linking may be different from HTML linking. The following definition for the **<SIMPLE>** element contains the attributes used to define a simple XML link:

```
<!ELEMENT   SIMPLE ANY>
<!ATTLIST   SIMPLE
XML-LINK   CDATA   #FIXED "SIMPLE"
   ROLE      CDATA #IMPLIED
   HREF      CDATA #REQUIRED
   TITLE   CDATA #IMPLIED
   INLINE   (TRUE|FALSE)   "TRUE"
   CONTENT-ROLE   CDATA   #IMPLIED
   CONTENT-TITLE CDATA   #IMPLIED
   SHOW     (EMBED|REPLACE|NEW) "REPLACE"
   ACTUATE  (AUTO|USER) "USER"
   BEHAVIOR  CDATA #IMPLIED>
```

The first thing to notice about this declaration is the name of the element. Authors defining a simple XML link are not required to name their element **SIMPLE**. This is a meta-element declaration. It illustrates a usage pattern for defining elements that contain the attributes that make an element an XML link. The way that an element becomes an XML link is that it contains the attribute **XML-LINK** with an appropriate value. The template just shown says that an XML simple link will have an **XML-LINK** attribute whose value is **simple**. It is also required to have an **HREF** attribute to refer to a link location. The other attributes are optional with **REPLACE** being the default value for the attribute **SHOW** if none other is specified. Element declarations that use **XML-LINK** can define other attributes as well, just as they can use other content models than **ANY**. Given the previous definition, let's go ahead and define a new link element called **RATEDLINK**, as shown here.

```
<!ELEMENT RATEDLINK (#PCDATA)>
<!ATTLIST  RATEDLINK  XML-LINK  CDATA #FIXED SIMPLE
       ROLE      CDATA #IMPLIED
       HREF      CDATA #REQUIRED
       TITLE   CDATA #IMPLIED
```

```
INLINE (TRUE|FALSE)  "TRUE"
CONTENT-ROLE  CDATA  #IMPLIED
CONTENT-TITLE CDATA  #IMPLIED
SHOW   (EMBED|REPLACE|NEW) "REPLACE"
ACTUATE (AUTO|USER) "USER"
BEHAVIOR  CDATA #IMPLIED
QUALITY (POOR|OKAY|GREAT)

"OKAY">
```

Let's look at what a few of the XML link attributes do. The **XML-LINK** attribute identifies the element as a hyperlink. The value indicates the hyperlink type: **SIMPLE** or one of several other values used to implement extended links. Normally the value for **XML-LINK** will be fixed for a particular element declaration. Declaring it as such has the benefit that it is assumed as the default for the element type and does not need to be specified for each element instance. That is why, in the previous example, it is not necessary to include **XML-LINK="SIMPLE"** in the **<RATEDLINK>** element instance.

This optional **ROLE** attribute indicates the logical role performed by an element that is part of a hyperlink. While it can be used with simple links, its major importance is in extended links made up of multiple elements, each defining a different hyperlink anchor. The **ROLE** attribute can assign semantic roles to these anchors appropriate for a particular hyperlink architecture. Possible values for the **ROLE** attribute are **previous**, **next**, and **parent**. This should suggest the improved structuring that might be possible with XML links.

The mandatory **HREF** attribute contains a locator: the address of a hyperlink anchor. A simple link contains only one locator and makes XML links roughly equivalent to HTML links. However, an extended link can contain multiple locators, each part of a locator element.

The values for the **SHOW** attribute indicate how the target anchor for a hyperlink should be displayed. The **EMBED** value indicates that linked content should be directly embedded in the current document. This could be used to embed objects such as images into an XML document. A value of **REPLACE** indicates that the current document should be replaced by the linked content. This default is how most Web pages work. A value of **NEW** indicates that the linked content should be displayed in a new window. It is interesting to note how the functionality of the **TARGET** attribute for HTML links can be described with this.

The **ACTUATE** attribute indicates how a hyperlink should be activated. The default value, **USER**, indicates that some action on the user's part activates the link. A value of **AUTO** indicates that the hyperlink should be automatically activated when the link reference is encountered in the source document. At first glance, this may seem like an odd notion. The **AUTO** value has a practical use, in conjunction with a **SHOW** value of **EMBED**, that allows XML to implement media inserts analogous to the **<IMG>** or **<OBJECT>** tags in HTML. It also allows XML to perform client-pull style page loads, in which a document automatically loads another document after a specified delay.

Given even the most basic XML link attributes, it should be evident that XML could be used to mimic the functionality of HTML's **<A>** element. Giving the **SHOW** attribute the value of **REPLACE** causes the linked resource to replace the current document. It is necessary to add the **ID** attribute so that the element can be the named target of a hyperlink. What's even more interesting, as alluded to earlier, is that XML's simple link also allows element types to be defined that are analogous to HTML's media insertion elements. The declaration shown in the following code example is analogous to HTML's **<IMG>** element.

```
<!ELEMENT IMG  EMPTY>
<!ATTLIST  IMG  XML-LINK  CDATA  #FIXED  "SIMPLE"
    HREF    CDATA   #REQUIRED
    SHOW    (EMBED|REPLACE|NEW) "EMBED"
    ACTUATE  (AUTO|USER) "AUTO"
    other required attribute declarations>
```

Giving the **SHOW** attribute the **EMBED** value causes the linked resource to be embedded in the current document. Giving the **ACTUATE** attribute the value **AUTO** causes the link to be automatically activated when it is encountered. For HTML authors, it may be counterintuitive to think of links in this way. In XML, media inserts are links that are automatically activated and embedded in the current document. At the time of this writing, it is unclear how XML documents will indicate support for particular media types.

The usage of the **<IMG>** element defined here for XML would look almost the same as HTML, except for the trailing (/) character:

```
<IMG HREF="URL" />
```

While it is interesting to see that XML could provide the same functionality as HTML and even provide some semblance of backward compatibility, it can provide much more. In addition to simple links, XML supports extended links. Extended links use two elements, a link element to name and define, and the actual link itself. This encloses multiple locator elements (addresses), one for each anchor contained by the link. The meta-element template for these two element types is shown here:

```
<!ELEMENT  EXTENDED   ANY>
<!ATTLIST  EXTENDED
```

```
XML-LINK   CDATA   #FIXED "EXTENDED"
    ROLE      CDATA   #IMPLIED
    TITLE   CDATA   #IMPLIED
    INLINE    (TRUE|FALSE)   "TRUE"
    CONTENT-ROLE   CDATA   #IMPLIED
    CONTENT-TITLE CDATA   #IMPLIED
    SHOW      (EMBED|REPLACE|NEW) "REPLACE"
    ACTUATE    (AUTO|USER)   "USER"
    BEHAVIOR   CDATA   #IMPLIED>


<!ELEMENT LOCATOR ANY>
<!ATTLIST   LOCATOR
    XML-LINK   CDATA   #FIXED "LOCATOR"
    ROLE      CDATA   #IMPLIED
    HREF      CDATA   #REQUIRED
    TITLE   CDATA   #IMPLIED
    SHOW      (EMBED|REPLACE|NEW) "REPLACE"
    ACTUATE    (AUTO|USER)   "USER"
    BEHAVIOR   CDATA   #>
```

A few observations about these two meta-element templates: As with simple links, the element identifiers **EXTENDED** and **LOCATOR** can be replaced with whatever identifiers make sense to an XML author. Remember, what makes an element an XML link is not its name, but the presence of the **XML-LINK** attribute with an appropriate value. Notice that in an extended link, an extended element contains a locator element. It can, and usually will, contain multiple locator elements. It can also contain parsed character data (**#PCDATA**). This means an extended link element can contain text and entities like **"** that expand to text, but not markup tags. Remember how this was used in a previous part of the chapter as a macro expansion to bring in many elements at once? Finally, notice that the attributes used by the **EXTENDED** and **LOCATOR** link types are identical to the attributes used by the **SIMPLE** link type, but some attributes are distributed. Only the **EXTENDED** element type contains the **INLINE**, **CONTENT-ROLE**, and **CONTENT-TYPE** attributes. Only the **LOCATOR** element type contains the **HREF** attribute.

What does it mean to have an extended link? It can serve as a more sophisticated version of an inline link that may, for example, have multiple target locations associated with it. The following example defines an external file that specifies a few extended links that may be included in documents and processed by a special link engine:

```
<!ENTITY  START  CDATA "http://www.bigcompany.com/start.xml">
<!ENTITY  GLOSSARY  CDATA "http://www.bigcompany.com/glossary.xml">

<PAGELINK XML-LINK=EXTENDED  ID="PAGE1">
<LOCATOR ROLE="START" HREF=&START;>
<LOCATOR ROLE="PREV" HREF="http://www.bigcompany.com/start.xml">
<LOCATOR ROLE="NEXT" HREF="http://www.bigcompany.com/page2.xml">
<LOCATOR ROLE="GLOSSARY" HREF=&GLOSSARY;>
</PAGELINK>

<PAGELINK XML-LINK=EXTENDED  ID="PAGE2">
<LOCATOR ROLE="START" HREF=&START;>
<LOCATOR ROLE="PREV" HREF="http://www.bigcompany.com/page1.xml">
<LOCATOR ROLE="NEXT" HREF="http://www.bigcompany.com/page3.xml">
<LOCATOR ROLE="GLOSSARY" HREF=&GLOSSARY;>
</PAGELINK>

<PAGELINK XML-LINK=EXTENDED ID="PAGE3">
<LOCATOR ROLE="START" HREF=&START;>
<LOCATOR ROLE="PREV"  HREF="http://www.bigcompany.com/page2.xml">
<LOCATOR ROLE="NEXT"  HREF="http://www.company.org/page4.xml">
<LOCATOR ROLE="GLOSSARY" HREF=&GLOSSARY;>
</PAGELINK>
```

In this example, all the links needed to navigate between pages in a document are contained in an external file. If different documents are used, rather than needing to update the locations in different documents as is currently done in HTML, only the file containing the links needs to be modified. The benefit of this approach becomes clear when the location of an anchor referred to by many links needs to be modified. In the preceding example, the **START** and **GLOSSARY** anchors fit this problem. In a conventional HTML approach to this problem, the extended link format used in this example would be replaced by a set of inline links in every document, as shown here:

```
<A HREF="http://www.company.org/start.xml">Start</A>
<A HREF="http://www.company.org/page1.xml">Previous</A>
<A HREF="http://www.company.org/page3.xml">Next</A>
<A HREF="http://www.company.org/glossary.xml">Glossary</A>
```

Using the conventional HTML approach, deciding to use a different Start or Glossary document presents a maintenance problem. The corresponding **HREF** values need to be updated in every document containing a source hyperlink. Using XML out-of-line extended links, all the links can be stored in a single file that is the only document that needs to be modified. A capability that XML inherits from SGML makes updating a value shared by multiple elements even easier. In the preceding example, the Start and Glossary entities are defined to associate a symbolic entity name with the related URLs. These entity names are used instead of explicit **HREF** values and the associated values are substituted when the document is parsed. Changing the value for the Start or Glossary URLs in the associated entities results in that single change being replicated throughout the document.

XML linking introduces some powerful addressing capabilities to the locator model used in HTML. XML introduces some new options. It replaces the hash symbol (#) used in HTML to signal a fragment identifier with the more general concept of a connector. A connector can take one of three values (#, **XML-XPTR?**, and |) that can occur anywhere the # symbol is currently used in HTML.

The # symbol used in HTML locators has the same syntax in XML. However, its meaning has been made clearer. This has the meaning of "locate the fragment in the document that has been requested but retrieve the entire document." Using a fragment identifier of **XML-XPTR?** has the semantic meaning of "locate the fragment in the document that has been requested and only retrieve that part of the document—forget the rest." Obviously, this might be nice for saving bandwidth. The pipe symbol (|) has the semantic meaning of "locate the fragment in the document that has been requested, but it doesn't matter if the whole document or just the fragment is retrieved."

This introduction of new connector types may seem a little arcane. Why are connector types important? The issue motivating this introduction is that XML documents, drawing from their SGML heritage, can be expected to occasionally be much larger than the norm for HTML documents. The **XML-XPTR?=** construct allows XML to only request the part of a document it is interested in and can tractably handle. For example, it allows XML to request "Chapter 5, Section 3" from a large industrial maintenance document that in its entirety might be hundreds of pages: too long for efficient transmission over the Web. The "|" construct leaves it up to the server software to decide whether to send a document in its entirety. Essentially, it signals permission for the server to optionally improve performance by transmitting a smaller document.

Even beyond the improved fragment linking structure, XML may support an alternate and more powerful way of referring to locations inside the document by utilizing the document's structure. This is referred to as an *Xpointer*. It is based on the TEI pointer model defined by the Text Encoding Initiative, the differences being largely syntactic to make the TEI model compatible with URL syntax.

Xpointers are composed of one or more terms that refer to element locations in a document's parse tree. The terms can refer to a location using an absolute identifier: for example, the element whose **ID** attribute equals **start**. The terms can also refer to an element relationally: for example, the third **<P>** element inside the contents of the current element. A position inside a document is located by following a sequence of terms, the address specified by each term being relative to the previous term. Xpointers expose the structure of documents allowing document fragments to be referenced using structural concepts like parent, child, and sibling.

SUMMARIZING XML LINKS   This concludes an overview of XML's linking capabilities as they are currently described in public documents. It should be apparent that they go far beyond what is possible within the current HTML framework. Resources like HyTime from the SGML tradition suggest some future possibilities. For the present, a reasonable question to ask is which of these linking capabilities are likely to be found soon in commercial browsers? A case can be made that extended linking capabilities are not important when XML is used as a data format supporting HTML documents. They become important when XML is used as a platform for documents in its own right and not as a supporting technology. Technically, a good part of the functionality required for simple XML links already exists in HTML browsers. Dynamic HTML's ability to access any document element goes a long way toward the tree-based addressing. Extended links can be implemented in so many ways that it is questionable if an attempt at a general solution will be a built-in feature of browsers. Specialized link engines are likely to arise for those vertical applications adopting XML as a document platform.

Style in XML

For most of its history, HTML had no concept of style sheets. All elements inside the document had a default presentation style without any action on the HTML author's part. The problem was that HTML's presentation behavior was browser dependent, platform dependent, and could not be precisely specified. The CSS style language was added to HTML to remedy these shortcomings.

The way that HTML handles presentation is unusual for an SGML-based language. One of the guiding motivations behind SGML is to clearly separate content from presentation. Content then becomes easily reused for many different applications and presentation media. This capability is especially important in the enterprise applications that motivated the development of SGML in the first place. It allows content to exist in a neutral, archival format that is not dependent on the rapid changes in access technology, thus improving document lifetime. HTML sacrificed this benefit by combining content with presentation. Given this mixture of structure and style, it will be interesting to see the maintainability of HTML content over the next five years.

XML returns to the mainstream SGML practice of separating content from presentation. Aside from the technical benefits from doing this, there is simply no practical way to assign default presentation to the many element types that XML authors will invent. For XML content to be visible, the XML author must associate it with presentation semantics. This task, which the HTML author optionally performs with CSS, is mandatory with XML. How will this be accomplished?

Assuming the use of XML inside an HTML document, one possibility is element mapping. This will work by using a special attribute inside an XML tag to associate it with an HTML tag for presentation purposes. This is saying, "I may be called **<LEADPARAGRAPH>**, but just display me as a **<P>** tag, which may in turn reference a style rule."

While the previous approach may occur, the most common way to define the presentation of XML content is to directly use a style sheet language. The question is, which one? There are two leading choices; each has its own strengths and weaknesses. From the HTML tradition, the obvious choice is CSS, as discussed in Chapter 10. The SGML tradition has its own style sheet language, an ISO standard known as Document Style Semantics and Specification Language (DSSSL). The W3C has plans to develop a style language for XML known as XSL. Since discussion began about this language, the intention has been to use DSSSL as the point of departure. Balanced against this is the reality that DSSSL is an emerging technology, while CSS is built into newer Microsoft and Netscape browsers. For XML applications, it is not clear whether CSS and DSSSL/XSL will be competing technologies, converging technologies, or distinct technologies targeted at applications of different complexity. At this point, the most that can be done here is to articulate the issues that an XML style language will need to solve and to contrast how CSS and DSSSL/XSL address those issues.

CSS Versus DSSSL

For simple style rule declarations, the CSS and DSSSL languages seem to be equally complex. The style examples compared side by side in Table 16-1 define equivalent styles for the HTML **<H2>** element.

CSS Syntax	DSSSL Syntax
H2　{display:block; 　　　font-size: 133%; 　　　margin-top: 1.5em; 　　　margin-bottom: 1em; 　　　font-weight: bold}	H2 (element H2 　　(make-paragraph 　　　font-size: (* 1.3 (inherited-font-size)) 　　　space-before: 1.5em 　　　space-after: 1em 　　　font-weight: bold))

Table 16-1.　*CSS and DSSSL Syntax Comparison*

The differences between these two languages are not apparent from this simple example, except for the slightly heavier emphasis on parentheses that hints at DSSSL's Lisp programming language background. This example illustrates most of the capabilities of CSS while illustrating only the most basic aspects of DSSSL functionality.

DSSSL is more powerful than CSS because it supports style programming, and CSS does not. All CSS statements are simple and declarative. A CSS style rule is just a list of one or more property/value pairs associated by a selector with some document content. The simplicity of the CSS language is intentional. It was designed for wide use by many Web authors without requiring any special training. The DSSSL style language, on the other hand, is a full-featured programming language. It is based on Scheme, an ISO-standard programming language belonging to the Lisp language family. What can you do with this programming capability? It allows content to be retrieved from different parts of the source document and incorporated into a style. For example, a page footer could include a document's title, not by including the literal title inside a footer tag but by having a footer style programmatically retrieve the content from the document's title. It also allows an element's style to depend on where the element occurs in the document. For example, it would be straightforward to define different formatting for odd- or even-numbered paragraphs. Finally, programming makes the DSSSL style language extensible. DSSSL can define new presentation templates—*flow objects* in its terminology. By analogy to CSS, if the basic **block** display property were not adequate for some reason DSSSL could programmatically define a new display property.

While CSS is simple and declarative, this may not be as limiting as it sounds. It is true that CSS is not extensible in the way that DSSSL is. There is no way to programmatically define the equivalent of new flow object classes. This is an important limitation. On the other hand, CSS evolved to fit into an interactive environment supporting scripting languages and the Document Object Model. The interactive behavior of CSS properties can be programmed in a straightforward way using client-side scripts, Java applets, and ActiveX controls. While DSSSL uses an ISO-standard language, Scheme is not supported by current Web browsers and is esoteric for most Web authors. While academics will certainly tout the elegance of a Scheme-like language, the likelihood of the public embracing the Lisp-like syntax is slim at best. The most common language used to program CSS properties is JavaScript, which recently, as ECMA Script, also became a standard. Indeed, a proposed draft for the XSL implementation of DSSSL that replaces Scheme with ECMA Script for procedural functionality is already in circulation.

Another dimension, in which DSSSL goes beyond CSS, this time unambiguously, is in the presentation templates it supports. In CSS, a style's presentation template is treated as just one among its many properties—its **display** property. CSS supports just four values for the display property: **block**, **inline**, **list-item**, and **none**. These values do not fully cover the visual objects found in HTML. Tables, for example, are an important omission. The DSSSL standard defines a comprehensive set of several dozen flow objects. The XSL implementation of DSSSL will use only a tractable subset of these, sufficient to address some glaring omissions in CSS, such as support for tables.

A point-for-point comparison between DSSSL and CSS may be disingenuous, because these languages have evolved to solve different problems. Thus far, DSSSL has been presented as if it were a style language roughly comparable to CSS. In fact, the full DSSSL project is much more ambitious. The DSSSL standard defines two independent languages: a transformation language and a style language. The discussion thus far has only touched on the style language because that is the part of DSSSL under consideration for the base of XSL. The transformation language has a radically different purpose: to transform content from one or more SGML documents into a new SGML document by processes of selection, reordering, and content generation. The transformation and style languages can be combined in a two-step process. Step one is using the transformation language to massage SGML resources into an SGML output document ready for formatting. Step two is using the style language to combine content with formatting information. The result is a document in an appropriate format, such as RTF or PostScript, ready to be rendered. Thus, the full DSSSL model was originally conceived as a linear batch process to transform SGML resources into files that can be rendered. The initial emphasis was on printed output, with considerations of interactive media coming later. The objective of this process was to support institutionalized, enterprise-scale information management.

Contrast the DSSSL model with that of CSS. In CSS, there is no overarching consideration of a linear information management process. CSS was designed to support an interactive client in a client-server system. The initial emphasis was on interactive hypermedia with considerations for printing coming later. CSS already has market acceptance in the form of support from the two major browser vendors. Already, extensions are being made such as cursor, media filters, and transitions, making CSS even more Web oriented. While DSSSL clearly has the edge in templates intended for print media, the evolution of CSS is more in line with the movement of Web applications toward the rich media experience of CD-ROMs.

As style languages for XML, whether CSS and DSSSL/XSL will complement or compete with each other remains to be seen. Industry discourse suggests that CSS is sufficient for simple XML documents but inadequate for the more complex documents found in enterprise applications. Those documents require some of the style language features that XSL intends to bring from DSSSL. Will XSL become accepted as the language supporting those features or will market forces cause them to appear in CSS first? Only time will tell.

Summary

This discussion of XML's core syntax and extension only scratches the surface of what remains an emerging technology. The best way to track XML's rapid evolution is to closely monitor the XML activity at the World Wide Web Consortium, http://www.w3.org. The implications of XML are enormous. Just as a meta-data definition language, XML has some wonderful uses for extending the Web. CDF shows how XML was used to define a push language. Other languages are certainly possible, including markup to help search engines more accurately index Web pages. However, eventually there will be a desire to include XML directly into HTML pages to augment the functionality of the page, or maybe even replace the page outright.

As it stands, XML is still missing well-defined linking and style definitions. As a middle-ground language, XML attempts to provide much of the power of SGML and related technologies like HyTime and DSSSL, while keeping the application oriented to the Web and within the easy-to-use spirit of HTML. What XML will eventually bring, if it can be used directly within Web pages, is the power to make data more regular and more specific to particular applications or industries. With improved structure, migrating Web data to and from databases, exchanging documents with other parties, and navigating large collections of documents could get significantly easier.

Like many new hot technologies, XML will go through a hype phase that suggests it is good for everything. However, at least in the short term, XML will augment HTML and address its weaknesses rather than replace it outright. Just as Windows relied on DOS and did not quickly supplant it, the market-driven nature of Web technologies in conjunction with the existing heavy investment in HTML-based information will probably spur an XML evolution rather than XML revolution.

The Complete Reference

HTML

Chapter 17

Future Directions

Where HTML is heading isn't always easy to predict. The Web has been rocked by rapid commercialization and the introduction of numerous new technologies. However, the evolution of Web technology is far from finished. Only a few years ago it was hard to imagine the types of multimedia and programmed sites that are common on the Web today. Current trends in presentation, programming, page structure, and the Web in general suggest what might happen to HTML and the Web in the near future.

Presentation Issues

Getting pages to look a particular way is one of the chief goals of Web page designers. With the rise of Cascading Style Sheets (CSS1) and the CSS positioning extensions (CSS-P), style sheets provide many of the layout features that page designers want. However, the CSS language is far from perfect; it is particularly lacking in adequate support for tables, multimedia, and fonts. One approach to dealing with tables is not to have CSS address them, and leave that for HTML. HTML 4.0 already provides a rich table model, so this may be adequate. However, other style sheet technologies such as DSSSL show that it is possible to address table support at the style sheet level. It is unclear in which direction table support will go. For now, as style sheets grow in acceptance, tables will probably continue to serve double duty both as traditional tables and as positioning devices to create well-laid-out Web pages.

Another aspect of presentation that isn't perfectly clear yet is fonts. It is critical that downloadable fonts come to the Web. Having page designers rely on certain fonts being installed on the end user's computer or attempting to embed fonts as pictures is not reasonable. Microsoft and Netscape have already demonstrated that Web fonts are possible. Even so, the issue of fonts isn't solved. As the difference between the desktop and the Web shrinks, an issue of font compatibility arises. On the desktop, we use TrueType and PostScript fonts. On the Web, we use TrueDoc or OpenType fonts. There is a conflict here when moving documents back and forth. Microsoft's OpenType is intended to format for both the Web and the desktop. This seems logical. Netscape however, is looking to create a Web-specific font technology. Despite logic, which font format will win is still far from clear. The World Wide Web Consortium (W3C) is working hard on font-embedding specifications, including defining a way to create fonts from font objects so that it is possible to avoid downloading complete font sets for very similar fonts.

A great deal of the discussion about Web presentation is based on the desire to reach print standards, but are we really looking to mimic print? The Web is more about multimedia than about paper. Things like multiple windows, or frames, animated buttons, and page transitions are inevitable additions to Web pages. How should these features be added? In some cases, new HTML elements have been introduced to support these features, such as the **<MARQUEE>** element. Experts feel that this isn't the best way to introduce these technologies. Small embedded binaries should probably be used to add new multimedia features, but how will they be referenced from HTML and style sheets? Microsoft has shown that it is possible to add numerous multimedia features, in the form of filters, to style sheets. Many more features for multimedia will undoubtedly be added. The **<OBJECT>** element may serve as the generic way to add new binary forms. Which binary forms will dominate the Web is hard to predict, but it is unlikely that more than two formats will be viable in sound, animation, video, and 3-D. Even binary forms such as Adobe Acrobat will continue to thrive online in areas where style sheets and HTML come up short, such as electronics specifications.

Programming Issues

The Web isn't just about print. A transition is already underway from a page-oriented view of the Web to a more program-oriented view of Web sites. Think of a complex system like a job postings Web site. The site must be able to provide dynamic listings of various jobs, support keyword searches, accept résumés, schedule interviews, and perform a variety of other tasks. It should do this within the constraints of the different browsers that might access the site. Described this way, Web sites sound more like software. The truth is, many sites *are* like software.

Adding interactivity to Web sites is now commonplace. There are various new technologies to choose from. Some of these, such as CGI, NSAPI/ISAPI, and server-side scripting, are server side. Others, such as plug-ins, are client side. And still others, such as JavaScript, VBScript, and Java are used on both ends of the transaction. Choosing which technology to use, and when, is a challenge. Too much emphasis on the server can slow the site down and keep it from scaling. Placing too much responsibility on the client side can also be problematic, since it is often difficult to ensure that all clients support the technology properly. Because the client is beyond the page designer's control, it may be hard to ensure that things don't go wrong, even with careful design and rigorous testing. There is a balance between what should be done on the client side and what should be done on the server.

The chief problems with programming facilities being added to Web sites include standardization, scalability, and methodology. Web programming technologies like Java and JavaScript are far from standardized. There seems to be a growing rift between one browser's idea of Java and another's. Netscape's JavaScript and Microsoft's JScript have major differences despite conformance to the ECMAScript standard. These issues will have to be sorted out soon if there is to be any hope for a true cross-platform programming environment. Otherwise, it may be necessary to use platform-specific technologies like ActiveX controls or Netscape plug-ins in conjunction with server-side technologies, regardless of what makes sense in theory.

As more and more users get on the Internet, some programmed sites are going to face a critical problem of scalability. Imagine an airline reservation system on the Web. How is it going to handle tens or hundreds of thousands of people who use it nearly at the same time to order cheap tickets for the holidays? Another example of the problem of scalability was when, in the fall of 1997, trading and related news sites were quicky swamped after the stock market took a plunge. The need to build large, robust systems will increase as electronic commerce develops. Today, however, most systems simply won't scale. The applications aren't distributed across many servers, and it is difficult to create distributed systems. Many industry pundits like to discuss how programming objects will be flung far over the Internet, and how corporate networks will be served out from various application servers to help solve scalability problems. These objects should help when you think of many application servers distributing ordering objects to airline ticket buyers. In this sense, the Web turns into a giant distributed system. The question arises of how well these objects are going to interact. Even on a single user's computer, the idea of having objects communicate with each other has been less than straightforward. Doing this over a network only makes things worse. The battle for the object world, already in progress, pits a loose alliance of Common Object Request Broker Architecture (CORBA) and Java against Microsoft's Distributed Component Object Model (DCOM). Which of these particular object technologies will dominate the Internet is unclear. One may be popular on intranets, while the other is popular outside the corporation.

With the rise of complexity in programming systems, particularly those that must be built to scale, rigorous development methodologies must be adopted. The current state of affairs on the Web overemphasizes the look and feel of a site. Back-end work on databases and programming often take a backseat to visuals. Testing is poorly considered. Sites are often built without solid plans, in a mad rush to get on the Web or outdo the competition. This has to change. To build complex systems, the ideas of software engineering will have to be applied to Web pages. The ad hoc approaches used to date won't work; tools won't save the developer.

The idea of using simple what-you-see-is-what-you-get (WYSIWYG) development tools to link together components in a Rapid Application Development (RAD) style is a tempting idea, but it doesn't work. RAD is widely practiced on the Web, but in a form that often causes more harm than benefit. The key to RAD is the idea of prototype-driven design. On the Web, this would mean creating a Web site and then working over the site in numerous iterations with user input, including design meetings, until the final design falls out. In this sense, RAD means building the wrong site multiple times until the right site falls out of the process. How far is the rapidly developed Web site from what the users actually want? Will there be repercussions if a subpar site is launched for public use? Looking at all the sites with "under construction" signs on them, it seems that RAD is very popular on the Web. It is not, however, a safe approach to building Web sites, least of all complex ones.

RAD grew from the maturity of the software engineering discipline. Before RAD came a variety of structured design paradigms that helped developers understand the systems they were developing. How can one create a RAD-based tool or philosophy for an environment that is still in its infancy? RAD will work, and it will certainly have its place on the Web, but it is too soon for Web RAD. Many Web page developers are hardly schooled in software development, let alone structured software development. Ask yourself if the HTML code, let alone the scripts, of many Web site files exhibits strict coding standards. Naming conventions, organization, and coding rules are not widely promoted on the Web.

No more evidence of the Web's lack of software development maturity is required than the state of testing. Vague references to "test your site under other browsers" are the typical depth of this discussion, which invariably omits test plans and matrices, test types, regression testing, and so on. Even if browser testing were the only aspect to Web testing, just how many versions of browsers are there? There are literally hundreds. The payoff of making a site work under the Commodore 64 browser (there is one) is generally minor. How many versions of Netscape are there? A quick survey shows ports to Macintosh, Windows 3.1, Windows 95/NT, OS/2, and numerous flavors of Unix. The browser itself has gone through four major releases at the time of this writing (1.x, 2.x, 3.x, 4.x), and there are various beta versions still floating around. So what? you might ask. The problem is that these browsers act differently when it comes to programming facilities. Serious bugs exist, programming wise, under different versions of the browser, such as JavaScript support. Ad hoc "looks right so it must be right" testing by example could spell disaster for complex programmed Web sites. This is not a proclamation of doom and gloom for Web development, simply a wakeup call to the requirements of programmed sites.

There should be no doubt that, when appropriate, the programming paradigm of Web sites is here. Many of the more interesting sites that do something have sophisticated backend systems, and often tie in with databases. Scripting and objects have made it to the client. The idea of Dynamic HTML (DHTML) makes the page a dynamic document rather than a print-oriented one. However, these changes come with a potential price. Remember how mixing the structure of a Web page with presentation by forcing layout with HTML was considered a bad idea? Now add in a heavy amount of scripting. Without careful decomposition in pages to keep content separate in a structured fashion from presentation and logic, can pages live on past the current state?

Structure

One of a Web designer's chief roles is bringing order to the chaos, simply to provide structure. As mentioned throughout this book, the original intent of HTML was as a structuring language, but its purpose was often misunderstood. The structure that HTML provides for documents is not enough, particularly when considering the site as a whole. While it is easy enough to collect documents, how do they relate, and how will the documents be managed? Many Web sites manage their information as a collection of files in directories. This won't work as the site scales unless very strict rules are followed. The key to solving many of the problems of document management and site structure is databases. A database can be used to hold content that is pulled out of a database and flowed into HTML templates. The HTML templates are then combined with style sheets, binary objects, and programming logic to form a complex Web-based application. An overview of this separation is shown in Figure 17-1.

The benefits of such harsh borders are not always obvious. Using a database as a centralized repository for information can provide significant benefits. Imagine the knowledge of a company stored in a document repository that can be mined to pull data out and flowed into various different presentation formats like PageMaker files, HTML files, and so on. These files can then be distributed in a variety of fashions: paper, Web, or even CD-ROM. Figure 17-2 provides an overview of this idea.

While all this makes sense, few people are really doing it. In many cases, HTML is the primary form of the data; the structure and the content of the document are tightly bound. Is this such a wise idea? Think back to just one year ago. Are last year's HTML facilities considered passé? How easy is it to retrofit these documents and bring them up to the latest features? In some cases, certain HTML elements have been depreciated. The way HTML is being used today does not promote long document

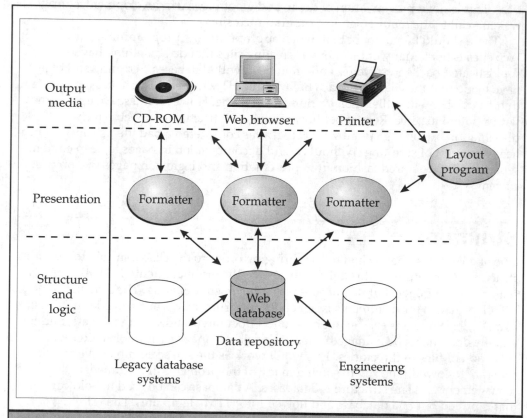

Figure 17-1. *Separation of style, structure, and logic*

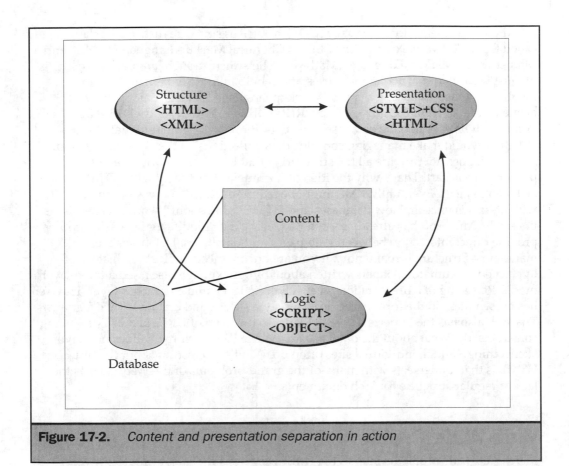

Figure 17-2.   *Content and presentation separation in action*

life. While this may keep Web professionals in business, it really isn't the best approach. Document form should be dependent on the purpose and life expectancy of the information. Certain documents might not work well in HTML. Adobe Acrobat, which allows the display of more complicated documents in a Web browser, might be a great solution, particularly as it also permits easier printing of those documents. Translating certain low-priority documents from Microsoft Word to the Web might be totally wasteful given the possibility of using word processing files on the Web. HTML does bring structure, but there are other ways to do things.

XML may provide the structure that HTML does not, particularly for industry-specific applications. HTML is a generalized markup language that provides structures like headings, lists, and paragraphs. However, data often has a much richer meaning than simply being a paragraph. Imagine a summary paragraph for a technical paper. Perhaps you would want to indicate such a structure with a **<SUMMARY>** tag. In XML, it would be possible to deploy such specific markup. XML already has been used to develop a special push-technology markup language called Channel Definition Language (CDF), as well as software distribution language called Open Software Description (OSD), a Chemical Markup Language (CML), and a Mathematical Markup Language (MathML). The structure such languages provide is not just helpful for particular industries; it can help migrate data in and out of databases. Imagine creating a special markup language for electronics parts with elements like **<PRODUCTID>**, **<DESCRIPTION>**, **<PRICE>**, and **<DIESIZE>**. Wouldn't it be easy to have database table definitions with similar names? Such structure would make managing complex data collections on the Web much easier.

HTML does not provide all the structuring that is necessary, but when used properly, it's a start. That's why the idea of document structuring with HTML should be taken to heart. Eventually, XML might be required. Exactly how XML and HTML will interact is unclear. How databases and HTML/XML should work together is also uncertain. Microsoft has already shown that, using data binding, it is possible to provide direct interaction between Web pages and databases. Databases are mandatory. Structure is mandatory. If you are unconvinced, look at the history of hypermedia. Numerous papers written about hypertext have discussed a three-layer model consisting of a presentation layer, a linking layer, and a database layer. The Web has presentation in the form of the browser, style sheets, and certain HTML features. The Web also has the hypertext abstract layer in the form of URLs and HTML linking constructs. But what about the database layer? The Web itself really does not have such a thing, though individual sites often do. What's interesting about the future of HTML is that it intersects with many of the grand problems of the Web, such as the lack of regular structure for Web documents.

Web-Wide Problems

Many Web-wide problems intersect HTML every day. One major problem involves searching the Web. It is very difficult to find things on the Internet using a search engine. Why this is a problem is obvious if you consider how search engines work. A search engine looks at a Web page and indexes the words it sees there. The engine determines what the page is about based upon a heuristic that combines how many times a particular word occurs, the value of the keywords specified by the **<META>** elements in the document, and the title of the document. This is terribly imprecise, as anyone who has searched the Web knows. A Web page that contains the word "Intel" in it may have nothing to do with the Intel Corporation. Typing this word in a search engine might return hundreds of thousands of responses. You should hope to see a site like www.intel.com listed first, but this rarely happens. The robots or spiders that index Web pages really have no idea what they are indexing. They can provide no value to the indexing that a human might. For the search engines to understand the information they are looking at, wouldn't they have to possess artificial intelligence? Yes, if data is unstructured. If structure can be added to data, then it is very easy to index information. HTML elements like **<META>** and new meta-data formats written in XML should bring such order. However, this is actually more difficult than it sounds. Getting people to agree on the structure of more complex meta-data, the allowable words in the data, and the organizations that will certify the correctness of the meta-data will be very difficult.

As searching suggests, navigating around the Web is less than straightforward. People are perpetually lost in cyberspace; the back button is their only way to safety. The linking mechanisms of the Web will certainly be improved. Eventually, even some type of uniform naming scheme, like a uniform resource name (URN), will arise. HTML will have to be extended to deal with a richer linking structure, because the <A> element provides only limited functionality as it stands. The <META> element provides some relief; but after looking at complex timing and linking technologies used with SGML, such as HyTime, there are many other extensions that may have to be made to HTML.

Another Web-wide problem is that of accessibility. Accessibility comes in many forms: an international user dealing with an English-only environment, a visually impaired user dealing with a site that has too much visual emphasis, or a technology-poor user unable to run Netscape to enter the latest and greatest site. The bottom line is that the Web and HTML should not intentionally lock people out. There may be cases where the designers of the site want to limit access based upon their own views, but the technology itself should not be designed to do such a thing.

The first example of accessibility is internationalization. The Web is supposed to be the World Wide Web, but it seems as if a U.S.-centric viewpoint often dominates the landscape. The Web needs to be improved to support other languages' character sets and reading directions. HTML 4.0 is already moving toward a more international approach, but there is still a long way to go. English will probably serve as the dominant language, but Web documents in French, Spanish, German, Japanese, Chinese, Korean, and Russian are already commonplace. Undoubtedly, more languages will be used online. There will need to be facilities to provide friendly help to those with a less-than-perfect mastery of a given language.

Much can also be said about how unfriendly the Web can be for those who have handicaps. Many Web sites completely lock out those users who are sight impaired because such sites provide no meaningful **ALT** text and rely heavily on graphics. (You may recall that the **ALT** attribute provides alternative text for user agents that do not display images, or for graphical browsers where the user has turned image rendering off.) While the Web will continue to be a medium rich in visuals, the W3C is making sure that many users are not left out of the experience by extending HTML to help make pages more accessible via keyboard, voice, and Braille.

Last, there are those users who, because of limited bandwidth or computing technology, don't often receive the complete picture. HTML does not always degrade gracefully when older or less common browsers view pages. More work, both in standards and development techniques, will be required to keep the Web open to those people who don't always use the latest and greatest gadgets or applications.

Despite all the problems with accessibility, the biggest gripe with the Web is performance. The Internet is growing at such a wild pace that traffic snarls are an everyday occurrence. New protocols like HTTP 1.1, image formats with better compression schemes like Portable Network Graphics (PNG), and new technologies like xDSL and cable modems will help speed the delivery of Web pages in the future. However, the amount of data that users want is quickly increasing. Bandwidth-hungry media forms like video don't work reliably on the Internet. Delivering reasonable quality video over today's Web is impossible. Even still images can seem to take an eternity. HTML has been extended to help improve the usability of multimedia-laden pages. Remember the **HEIGHT**, **WIDTH**, and **LOWSRC** attributes for the **<IMG>** element? Other approaches that have been considered are the ideas of suggesting which pages will be visited next so that they can be prefetched for the user. WebTV shows one way HTML can be used to provide such functionality.

Other approaches that will help speed the Web experience include caches, alternative transport protocols like WebNFS, and page-level compression. However, delivery always breaks down because of the idea of point sources. With single Web servers delivering data, eventually there is going to be a bottleneck. Content must be replicated around caches and delivered from mirror sites, or even broadcast. One technique is the use of intelligent hardware devices to balance distribution of pages among different Web servers based on how busy the servers are or by determining which server is closest to the user requesting pages. Another approach is with the proposed Distribution and Replication Protocol (DRP) protocol. DRP distributes updates to content such as Web pages in a differential fashion, meaning that if only part of a file has been changed, just that part will be sent, instead of the whole file. These and other approaches to better content distribution models are just now being determined, but many sites (including Yahoo!) already use some of these techniques to provide a high level of performance. While the Web may be slow, the problems are being addressed at the network level with improvements in the Internet infrastructure and better protocols such as IP Multicast and IPv6. These address inefficiencies in the current TCP/IP protocol, and protocols based on it like HTTP. The idea of multicast, for example, enables the broadcast delivery of a single file to multiple destinations, instead of sending the same file many times to multiple destinations. Some of these solutions will certainly affect HTML. Remember that the network is the medium of the Web; its effect is significant. How people access the Web will certainly affect the direction HTML takes.

Application-Specific Presentation

As the Internet and the Web become more mainstream, the way they are used will certainly change. In just a few years, the Web has gone from being an environment of engineers and academics to being a very commercial environment with many consumers. The major change is still to come. Many people are not on the Web, and the potential uses of the medium have not been fully explored.

The Web is very computer centered, but this may change somewhat. Many people do not have computers, but many want to get one just to get on the Web. Because of such interest, consumer-oriented devices such as WebTV, RCA Electronics' nc-1000, the

Teknema set-top box, and the Sega Saturn Netlink have been developed. While none of these devices is as common as VCRs or CD players, the adoption rate of WebTV is higher than the initial adoption rate of VCRs. People often forget that consumer electronics may take five or ten years to become mainstream. The CD player was initially considered a status symbol in the early 80s before it finally caught on and all but replaced cassettes and LPs in the consumer market. It is obvious that consumer Web devices will not be the way that most people will access the Internet for the near term. However, their development and initial acceptance points to an interesting trend toward nontraditional, computer-based Web use. This has some interesting ramifications for HTML.

HTML may have to become more of an application specification. At the very least, new languages will be developed to deal with such applications. This book has mentioned numerous WebTV extensions. Regardless of your particular slant on whether vendors should make such extensions to HTML, television-based Web viewing is very different from computer-based browsing. People tend to browse Web sites by themselves, close up to a computer with a high-resolution monitor. They may not read information onscreen; they may print it instead. Now think of using a WebTV. The WebTV uses a large screen with relatively low resolution. People, often many of them at once, tend to sit far away from the screen they are viewing. People probably will not read large amounts of text on a TV screen. They may use a remote or a wireless keyboard to interact with information. A traditional mouse pointer is out of the question when you are sitting on the couch. Given WebTV's unique environment, it seems obvious that less text in bigger size would probably work better. The dimensions of the screen are different as well. Other considerations arise. Won't people have to consume the information onscreen? How much information can be positioned onscreen? How should the navigation work? Many of the HTML extensions made by WebTV address some of these problems, though in subtle ways. These extensions make it easier to fill out forms, and constrain pages not to scroll left to right, among other things. WebTV shows that applications will influence what features will have to be included.

Other application-specific environments that may need special extensions or HTML-like languages include voice browsing and cellular phone browsing. Devices that allow you to view a Web page with a telephone or pocket organizer, such as a Windows-CE hand-held device, are already available. These systems are very different from traditional computer screens; they often have tiny screens with only four shades of gray. Furthermore, many hand-held devices have slower access rates to the Internet, even as low as 4800 bps via a wireless network. Traditional HTML may not be well suited to these low-speed, small-screen environments. A language called HDML (Hand-held Device Markup Language) has already been submitted to the W3C as a proposed standard. Whether special languages are implemented as new languages, subsets of HTML, supersets of HTML, or as new languages written as applications of XML remains unclear. With the rise of network computers, hand-held personal information managers, sophisticated digital cellular phones, and consumer-oriented network device, the ideas of HTML may have to be modified to fit a radically different application environment.

What Is the Future of HTML?

After all this discussion, one might wonder what can be said for sure about the future of HTML. One thing is certain: page designers won't do things the way they do now. Hacking around in HTML is a throwback to the days of page-setting languages like .troff or LaTeX. With the rise of PostScript and the tools that could output it, document designers stopped editing files directly in most cases. While older page-setting technologies are still used, and some people even program directly in PostScript, most do not. Using a tool to output PostScript, whether a word processor or a page layout program tool, is the way most designers create documents. As HTML settles down and becomes more standardized, tools will certainly be developed that can output pages appropriately. Right now, with standards and browsers in flux, tool vendors have a nearly impossible time creating such tools. For the moment, HTML designers often have to resort to doing tweaks, if not the whole page, by hand. This won't last long. Within five years, HTML hackers will be in about as much demand as typesetting machine operators. With the rise of electronic and improved mechanical printing technologies, the demand for these skills quickly went away. However, HTML as a print formatting language is not the point. The migration to a dynamic program-like environment should already be clear. Dynamic HTML, databases, and embedded objects all point the way to the Web of tomorrow. Knowledge of HTML will serve as a backbone for accessing these technologies. The benefit of short-term mastery of HTML will be early access to these ideas.

Summary

While standards and the open philosophy of the Web are important, there is one big lesson to be learned from the past, present, and future of HTML: there is no single correct solution to the Web puzzle. What is cutting edge today will be trivial tomorrow. Tools will eventually make intimate knowledge of HTML obsolete. So why did you even read this book? Because today you have to build Web pages, and HTML is one of the primary tools for this task. Don't lose perspective: HTML and the other technologies are just tools to help people accomplish goals for disseminating information and providing services. Not everybody has the same goals. This book has discussed how things can be done and provided some information on why, but the real answer to the why question is up to you. Many of the ideas and the syntax presented here will undoubtedly be passé in a few years, but that doesn't matter. Implementing a site today and reaching your goals is the main point of the Web. Most people will not judge a site by its conformance to the document type definition, but by whether it was useful or enjoyable. This is often forgotten when talking about HTML.

Knowing the particular syntax of an HTML element or the correct structure for HTML documents is very important, just as the rules and standards are important. But they are just rules. Now that you have mastered what is common HTML today, you are ready to decide for yourself what should be done in order to reach your Web site goals.

Appendix A

HTML Element Reference

This appendix provides a complete reference of the HTML 4.0 specification elements and the elements commonly supported by Netscape, Internet Explorer, and WebTV. Many of the elements presented in this appendix may be nonstandard or depreciated, but are included because browser vendors continue to support them or they are still in common use. Since this reference section is based on information that changes rapidly, you can make sure you are up to date by regularly visiting the HTML support site at http://www.htmlref.com or the World Wide Web Consortium (W3C) site at http://www.w3.org.

Core Attributes Reference

The HTML 4.0 specification provides four main attributes that are common to nearly all elements and have the same meaning for all elements. These elements are **ID**, **CLASS**, **STYLE**, and **TITLE**.

ID

This attribute is used to specify a unique alphanumeric identifier to be associated with an element. Naming an element is important to being able to access it with a style sheet, a link, or a scripting language. Names should be unique to a document and should be meaningful, so while **ID="x1"** is perfectly valid, **ID="Paragraph1"** might be better. Values for the **ID** attribute must begin with a letter (A–Z and a–z) and may be followed by any number of letters, digits, hyphens, and periods.

One potential problem with the **ID** attribute is that for some elements, particularly form controls and images, the **NAME** attribute already is serving its function. Values for **NAME** should collide with values for **ID**, as they share the same naming space. The example

```
<B ID="element1">This is a test</B>
<IMG NAME="element1" SRC="logo.gif">
```

would not be allowed. There is some uncertainty about what to do to ensure backward compatibility with browsers that understand **NAME** but not **ID**. Some people may suggest that

```
<IMG NAME="corplogo" ID="corplogo" SRC="logo.gif">
```

is invalid. Since **NAME** and **ID** are naming the same item, there should be no problem and the common browsers do not have an issue with such markup. Complex scripting necessary to deal with two different names for the image, like

```
<IMG NAME="corplogoname" ID="corplogoid" SRC="logo.gif">
```

is possible, but may not be necessary.

Page designers are encouraged to pick a naming strategy and use it consistently. Once elements are named, they should be easy to manipulate with a scripting language and allow migration to Dynamic HTML (DHTML). For more information on DHTML, see Chapter 13.

Like the **CLASS** attribute, the **ID** attribute is also used by style sheets for accessing a particular element.

For example, an element named Paragraph1 can be referenced by a style rule in a document-wide style using a fragment identifier:

```
#Paragraph1    {color: green}
```

For more information on how style sheets reference objects with the **ID** attribute, see Chapter 10.

Once an element is named using **ID**, it is also a potential destination for an anchor. In the past, an **<A>** element was used to set a destination; now any element may be a destination. For example:

```
<B ID="firstbolditem">This is important</B>

<A HREF="#firstbolditem">Go to first bold element</A>
```

CLASS

This attribute is used to indicate the class or classes that a particular element belongs to. A class name is used by a style sheet to associate style rules to multiple elements at once. For example, it may be desirable to associate a special class name called "important" with all elements that should be rendered with a yellow background. Since class values are not unique to a particular element, **<B CLASS="important">** could be used as well as **<P CLASS="important">** in the same document. It is also possible to have multiple values for the **CLASS** attribute separated by white space; **<STRONG CLASS="important special-font">** would define two classes with the particular **<STRONG>** element. Currently, most browsers recognize only one class name for this attribute. For more information on how to use the **CLASS** attribute with style sheets, see Chapter 10.

STYLE

This attribute is used to specify an inline style associated with the element. The style information is used to determine the rendering of the affected element. Because the **STYLE** attribute allows style rules to be used directly with the element, it gives up much of the benefit of style sheets that divide the presentation of an HTML document from its structure. An example of this attribute's use is shown here:

```
<STRONG STYLE="font-family: Impact; font-size: 24pt">Very
Important</STRONG>
```

For more information on how the **STYLE** attribute is used, see Chapter 10.

TITLE

This attribute is used to supply advisory text for the element that may be rendered as a tool tip when the mouse is over the element. A title may also simply provide information that alerts future document maintainers to the meaning of the element and its enclosed content. In some cases, such as the **<A>** element, the **TITLE** attribute may provide additional help in bookmarking. Like the title for the document itself, as advisory information **TITLE** attribute values should be short, yet useful. For example, **<P TITLE="paragraph1">** provides little information of value, while **<P TITLE="HTML: The Complete Reference: Chapter 1, Paragraph 10">** provides much more detail; and when combined with scripting, it may provide facilities for automatic index generation.

Language Reference

One of the main goals of the HTML 4.0 specification is better support for languages other than English. The use of other languages in a Web page may require that text direction be changed from left to right or right to left. Furthermore, once supporting non-ASCII languages becomes easier, it may be more common to see documents in mixed languages. Thus, there must be a way to indicate the language in use.

LANG

This attribute indicates the language being used for the enclosed content. The language is identified using the ISO-standard language abbreviation, such as fr for French, en for English, and so on. RFC 1766 (ftp://ds.internic.net/rfc/rfc1766.txt) describes these codes and their formats.

DIR

This attribute sets the text direction as related to the **LANG** attribute. The accepted values under the HTML 4.0 specification are **RTL** (right to left) and **LTR** (left to right). It is possible to override whatever direction a user agent sets by using the **<BDO>** element.

Events Reference

In preparation for a more dynamic Web, the W3C has defined a set of core events that are associated with nearly every HTML element. Most of these events cover simple user interaction such as the click of a mouse button or a key being pressed. A few elements, such as form controls, have some special events associated with them, signaling that the field has received focus from the user or the form was submitted. Last, intrinsic events like a document loading and unloading are also described. The core events are summarized in Table A-1.

"Most display elements" means all elements except <APPLET>, <BASE>, <BASEFONT>, <BDO>, <BR>, <FONT>, <FRAME>, <FRAMESET>, <HEAD>, <HTML>, <IFRAME>, <ISINDEX>, <META>, <PARAM>, <SCRIPT>, <STYLE>, and <TITLE>.

This event model is far from complete, and it is still not fully supported by browsers. The event model should be considered a work in progress. It will certainly change as the Document Object Model (DOM) is more carefully defined. Further information about the core events and the extended events described next can be found in Chapter 13.

Extended Events

Browsers may support other events than those defined in the preliminary HTML 4.0 specification. Microsoft in particular has introduced a variety of events to capture more complex

Event Attribute	Event Description	Allowed Elements Under HTML 4.0
onblur	Occurs when an element loses focus, meaning that the user has moved focus to another element, typically either by clicking the mouse on it or tabbing to it.	<A>, <AREA>, <BUTTON>, <INPUT>, <LABEL>, <SELECT>, <TEXTAREA> Also <APPLET>, <AREA>, <DIV>, <EMBED>, <HR>, <IMG>, <MARQUEE>, <OBJECT>, <SPAN>, <TABLE>, <TD>, <TR> (Internet Explorer 4.0); <BODY>(window) (Internet Explorer 4.0 and Netscape 4.0); <FRAMESET>, <ILAYER>, <LAYER>(Netscape 4.0)
onchange	Signals that the form control has lost user focus and its value has been modified during its last access.	<INPUT>, <SELECT>, <TEXTAREA>
onclick	Indicates that the element has been clicked.	Most display elements Also <APPLET>, <FONT> (Internet Explorer 4.0)
ondblclick	Indicates that the element has been double clicked, which is two clicks quickly.	Most display elements Also <APPLET>, <FONT> (Internet Explorer 4.0)
onfocus	The focus event describes when an element has received focus, namely, it has been selected for manipulation or data entry.	<A>, <AREA>, <BUTTON>, <INPUT>, <LABEL>, <SELECT>, <TEXTAREA> Also <APPLET>, <DIV>, <EMBED>, <HR>, <IMG>, <MARQUEE>, <OBJECT>, <SPAN>, <TABLE>, <TD>, <TR> (Internet Explorer 4.0); <BODY>(window) (Netscape 4.0, Internet Explorer 4.0); <FRAMESET>, <ILAYER>, <LAYER> (Netscape 4.0)
onkeydown	Indicates that a key is being pressed down with focus on the element.	Most display elements Also <APPLET>, <FONT> (Internet Explorer 4.0)
onkeypress	Describes the event of a key being pressed and released with focus on the element.	Most display elements Also <APPLET>, <FONT> (Internet Explorer 4.0)
onkeyup	Indicates that a key is being released with focus on the element.	Most display elements Also <APPLET>, <FONT> (Internet Explorer 4.0)

Table A-1. *Core Events*

Event Attribute	Event Description	Allowed Elements Under HTML 4.0
onload	Indicates the event of a window or frame set finishing loading a document.	\<BODY>, \<FRAMESET> Also \<APPLET>, \<EMBED>, \<LINK>, \<SCRIPT>, \<STYLE> (Internet Explorer 4.0); \<ILAYER>, \<IMG>, \<LAYER> (Netscape 4.0, Internet Explorer 4.0)
onmousedown	Indicates the press of a mouse button with focus on the element.	Most display elements Also \<APPLET>, \<FONT> (Internet Explorer 4.0)
onmousemove	Indicates that the mouse has moved while over the element.	Most display elements. Also \<APPLET> and \<FONT> (Internet Explorer 4.0).
onmouseout	Indicates that the mouse has moved away from an element.	Most display elements Also \<APPLET>, \<FONT> (Internet Explorer 4.0); \<ILAYER>, \<LAYER> (Netscape 4.0)
onmouseover	Indicates that the mouse has moved over an element.	Most display elements Also \<APPLET>, \<FONT> (Internet Explorer 4.0); \<ILAYER>, \<LAYER> (Netscape 4.0)
onmouseup	Indicates the release of a mouse button with focus on the element.	Most display elements Also \<APPLET>, \<FONT> (Internet Explorer 4.0)
onreset	Indicates that the form is being reset, possibly by the press of a reset button.	\<FORM>
onselect	Indicates the selection of text by the user, typically by highlighting the desired text.	\<INPUT>, \<TEXTAREA>
onsubmit	Indicates a form submission, generally by pressing a submit button.	\<FORM>
onunload	Indicates that the browser is leaving the current document and unloading it from the window or frame.	\<BODY>, \<FRAMESET>

Table A-1. *Core Events* (continued)

mouse actions like dragging, element events like the bouncing of **<MARQUEE>** text, and data binding events signaling the loading of data. The events are described in more detail in Table A-2.

 Documentation errors may exist. Microsoft currently documents events in the object model, not in the HTML reference. On inspection, some events are obviously not supported or may have been omitted. Events were tested by the author for accuracy, but for an accurate, up-to-date event model for these browsers, visit http://developer.netscape.com or http://www.microsoft.com/sitebuilder.

Event Attribute	Event Description	Associated Elements	Compatibility
onabort	Triggered by the user aborting the image load with a stop button or similar effect.	<IMG>	Netscape 3.0, 4.0 Internet Explorer 4.0
onafterupdate	Fires after the transfer of data from the element to a data provider, namely a data update.	<APPLET>, <BODY>, <BUTTON>, <CAPTION>, <DIV>, <EMBED>, <IMG>, <INPUT>, <MARQUEE>, <OBJECT>, <SELECT>, <TABLE>, <TD>, <TEXTAREA>, <TR>	Internet Explorer 4.0
onbeforeunload	Fires just prior to a document being unloaded from a window.	<BODY>, <FRAMESET>	Internet Explorer 4.0
onbeforeupdate	Is triggered before the transfer of data from the element to the data provider. May be triggered explicitly or by a loss of focus or a page unload forcing a data update.	<APPLET>, <BODY>, <BUTTON>, <CAPTION>, <DIV>, <EMBED>, <HR>, <IMG>, <INPUT>, <OBJECT>, <SELECT>, <TABLE>, <TD>, <TEXTAREA>, <TR>	Internet Explorer 4.0
onbounce	Triggered when the bouncing contents of a marquee touch one side or another.	<MARQUEE>	Internet Explorer 4.0

Table A-2.   *Extended Event Model*

Event Attribute	Event Description	Associated Elements	Compatibility
ondataavailable	Fires when data arrives from data sources that transmit information asynchronously.	<APPLET>, <OBJECT>	Internet Explorer 4.0
ondatasetchanged	Triggered when the initial data is made available from the data source or when the data changes.	<APPLET>, <OBJECT>	Internet Explorer 4.0
ondatasetcomplete	Indicates that all the data is available from the data source.	<APPLET>, <OBJECT>	Internet Explorer 4.0
ondragstart	Fires when the user begins to drag a highlighted selection.	<A>, <ACRONYM>, <ADDRESS>, <APPLET>, <AREA>, <B>, <BIG>, <BLOCKQUOTE>, <BODY> (document), <BUTTON>, <CAPTION>, <CENTER>, <CITE>, <CODE>, <DD>, <DEL>, <DFN>, <DIR>, <DIV>, <DL>, <DT>, <EM>, <FONT>, <FORM>, <FRAMESET> (document), <H1>, <H2>, <H3>, <H4>, <H5>, <H6>, <HR>, <I>, <IMG>, <INPUT>, <KBD>, <LABEL>, <LI>, <LISTING>, <MAP>, <MARQUEE>, <MENU>, <OBJECT>, <OL>, <OPTION>, <P>, <PLAINTEXT>, <PRE>, <Q>, <S>, <SAMP>, <SELECT>, <SMALL>, <SPAN>, <STRIKE>, <STRONG>, <SUB>, <SUP>, <TABLE>, <TBODY>, <TD>, <TEXTAREA>, <TFOOT>, <TH>, <THEAD>, <TR>, <TT>, <U>, <UL>, <VAR>, <XMP>	Internet Explorer 4.0

Table A-2. *Extended Event Model* (continued)

Event Attribute	Event Description	Associated Elements	Compatibility
ondragdrop	Triggered when the user drags an object onto the browser window to attempt to load it.	<BODY>, <FRAMESET> (window)	Netscape 4.0
onerror	Fires when the loading of a document, particularly the execution of a script, causes an error. Used to trap syntax errors.	<BODY>, <FRAMESET> (window), <IMG> (<LINK>, <OBJECT>, <SCRIPT>, <STYLE>, in Internet Explorer 4.0)	Netscape 3.0, 4.0, Internet Explorer 4.0
onerrorupdate	Fires if a data transfer has been canceled by the onbeforeupdate event handler.	<A>, <APPLET>, <OBJECT>, <SELECT>, <TEXTAREA>	Internet Explorer 4.0
onfilterchange	Fires when a page filter changes state or finishes.	Nearly all elements	Internet Explorer 4.0
onfinish	Triggered when a looping marquee finishes.	<MARQUEE>	Internet Explorer 4.0
onhelp	Triggered when the user presses the F1 key or similar help button in the user agent.	Nearly all elements under Internet Explorer 4.0 only	Internet Explorer 4.0
onmove	Triggered when the user moves a window.	<BODY>, <FRAMESET>	Netscape 4.0
onreadystatechange	Similar to onload. Fires whenever the ready state for an object has changed.	<APPLET>, <BODY>, <EMBED>, <FRAME>, <FRAMESET>, <IFRAME>, <IMG>, <LINK>, <OBJECT>, <SCRIPT>, <STYLE>	Internet Explorer 4.0
onresize	Triggered whenever an object is resized. Can only be bound to the window under Netscape as set via the <BODY> element.	<BODY>*, <APPLET>, <BUTTON>, <CAPTION>, <DIV>, <EMBED>, <FRAMESET>, <HR>, <IMG>, <MARQUEE>, <OBJECT>, <SELECT>, <TABLE>, <TD>, <TEXTAREA>, <TR>	Netscape 4.0*, Internet Explorer 4.0

Table A-2. *Extended Event Model* (continued)

Event Attribute	Event Description	Associated Elements	Compatibility
onrowenter	Indicates that a bound data row has changed and new data values are available.	<APPLET>, <BODY>, <BUTTON>, <CAPTION>, <DIV>, <EMBED>, <HR>, <IMG>, <MARQUEE>, <OBJECT>, <SELECT>, <TABLE>, <TD>, <TEXTAREA>, <TR>	Internet Explorer 4.0
onrowexit	Fires just prior to a bound data source control changing the current row.	<APPLET>, <BODY>, <BUTTON>, <CAPTION>, <DIV>, <EMBED>, <HR>, <IMG>, <MARQUEE>, <OBJECT>, <SELECT>, <TABLE>, <TD>, <TEXTAREA>, <TR>	Internet Explorer 4.0
onscroll	Fires when a scrolling element is repositioned.	<BODY>, <DIV>, <FIELDSET>, <IMG>, <MARQUEE>, <SPAN>, <TEXTAREA>	Internet Explorer 4.0
onselectstart	Fires when the user begins to select information by highlighting.	Nearly all elements	Internet Explorer 4.0
onstart	Fires when a looped marquee begins or starts over.	<MARQUEE>	Internet Explorer 4.0

Table A-2. *Extended Event Model* (continued)

HTML Element Reference

<!-- ... --> (Comment)

DESCRIPTION This construct is used to include text comments that will not be displayed by the browser.

Syntax

```
<!-- ... -->
```

Attributes
None.

EVENT HANDLERS   None.

Example

```
<!-- This is an informational comment that can occur
     anywhere in an HTML document -->
```

COMPATIBILITY   W3C 2.0, 3.2, 4.0; Netscape 1.x, 2.x, 3.x, 4.x; Internet Explorer 2.x, 3.x, 4.x; and WebTV

Notes
The comment element should be used to enclose the content of **<SCRIPT>** and **<STYLE>** tags to prevent processing by nonsupporting browsers. The string "--" (two hyphens in a row) is generally disallowed within an HTML comment.

<!DOCTYPE>

DESCRIPTION   This SGML construct specifies the Document Type Definition corresponding to the document.

Syntax

```
<!DOCTYPE "DTD Identifier">
```

Attributes
None.

EVENT HANDLERS   None.

Example

```
<!DOCTYPE HTML PUBLIC "-//W3C/DTD HTML 4.0//EN"
"http://www.w3.org/DTD/HTML4-strict.dtd">
```

COMPATIBILITY   W3C 2.0, 3.2, 4.0; Netscape 1.x, 2.x, 3.x, 4.x; Internet Explorer 2.x, 3.x, 4.x; and WebTV

Notes

The **<!DOCTYPE>** element should be used as the first line of all HTML documents. Validation programs may use this construct when determining the correctness of an HTML document. Always use the DOCTYPE that is proper for the elements used in the document.

<A> (Anchor)

DESCRIPTION   This element is used to indicate the portion of the document that is a hyperlink or the named target destination for a hyperlink.

Syntax

```
<A
     ACCESSKEY=key
     CHARSET=character code for language of linked resource
     CLASS=class name(s)
     COORDS=comma-separated list of numbers
     DATAFLD=name of column supplying bound data    (IE 4.0)
     DATASRC=id of data source object supplying data   (IE 4.0)
     DIR=LTR | RTL
     HREF=URL
     HREFLANG=language code
     ID=unique alphanumeric identifier
     LANG=language code
     LANGUAGE=JAVASCRIPT | JSCRIPT | VBSCRIPT | VBS    (IE 4.0)
     METHODS=http-method    (IE 4.0)
     NAME=name of target location
     NOCOLOR    (WebTV)
     REL=comma-separated list of relationship values
     REV=comma-separated list of relationship values
     SELECTED    (WebTV)
     SHAPE=DEFAULT | CIRCLE |RECT | POLY
     STYLE=style information
     TABINDEX=number
     TARGET=_blank | _parent | _self | _top | frame-name
     TITLE=advisory text
     TYPE=content type of linked data
     URN=urn (IE 4.0)

     onblur="script"
     onclick="script"
     ondblclick="script"
     ondragstart="script"    (IE 4.0)
     onerrorupdate="script" (IE 4.0)
     onfocus="script"
     onhelp="script"    (IE 4.0)
     onkeydown="script"
     onkeypress="script"
```

```
onkeyup="script"
onmousedown="script"
onmousemove="script"
onmouseout="script"
onmouseover="script"
onmouseup="script"
onselectstart="script">    (IE 4.0)

Linked content

</A>
```

Attributes

ACCESSKEY   This attribute specifies a keyboard navigation accelerator for the element. Pressing ALT or a similar key (depending on the browser and operating system) in association with the specified key selects the anchor element correlated with that key.

CHARSET   This attribute defines the character encoding of the linked resource. The value is a space- and/or comma-delimited list of character sets as defined in RFC 2045. The default value is ISO-8859-1.

CLASS   See "Core Attributes Reference" earlier in this appendix.

COORDS   For use with object shapes, this attribute uses a comma-separated list of numbers to define the coordinates of the object on the page.

DATAFLD   This attribute specifies the column name from the data source object that supplies the bound data. This attribute is specific to Microsoft's Data Binding in Internet Explorer 4.0.

DATASRC   This attribute indicates the **ID** of the data source object that supplies the data that is bound to this element. This attribute is specific to Microsoft's Data Binding in Internet Explorer 4.0.

DIR   See "Language Reference" earlier in this appendix.

HREF   This is the single required attribute for anchors defining a hypertext source link. It indicates the link target, either a URL or a URL fragment, that is a name preceded by a hash mark (#), which specifies an internal target location within the current document. As discussed in Chapter 5, URLs are not restricted to Web (http)-based documents. URLs may use any protocol supported by the browser. For example, file ftp and mailto work in most user agents.

HREFLANG   This attribute is used to indicate the language of the linked resource. See "Language Reference" earlier in this appendix for information on allowed values.

ID   See "Core Attributes Reference" earlier in this appendix.

LANG   See "Language Reference" earlier in this appendix.

LANGUAGE   This attribute specifies the language the current script is written in and invokes the proper scripting engine. The default value is **JAVASCRIPT**. **JAVASCRIPT** and **JSCRIPT** represent that the scripting language is written in JavaScript. **VBS** and **VBSCRIPT** represent that the scripting language is written in VBScript. It may also be possible to use extended names such as JavaScript 1.1 to hide code from JavaScript-aware browsers that don't conform to a particular version of the language.

METHODS   The value of this attribute provides information about the functions that may be performed on an object. The values are generally given by the HTTP protocol when it is used, but it may, for similar reasons as for the **TITLE** attribute, be useful to include advisory information, in advance, in the link. For example, the browser may choose a different rendering of a link as a function of the methods specified; something that is searchable may get a different icon, or an outside link may render with an indication of leaving the current site. This element is not well understood, nor supported even by the defining browser, Internet Explorer 4.0.

NAME   This attribute is required in an anchor defining a target location within a page. A value for **NAME** is similar to a value for the **ID** core attribute and should be an alphanumeric identifier unique to the document.

NOCOLOR   Supported only by WebTV, this attribute overrides the **LINK** color set in the **BODY** element and prevents the link from changing color.

REL   For anchors containing the **HREF** attribute, this attribute specifies the relationship of the target object to the link object. The value is a comma-separated list of relationship values. The values and their semantics will be registered by some authority that may have meaning to the document author. The default relationship, if no other is given, is **void**. The **REL** attribute should be used only when the **HREF** attribute is present.

REV   This attribute specifies a reverse link, the inverse relationship of the **REL** attribute. It is useful for indicating where an object came from, such as the author of a document.

SELECTED   Supported only in WebTV, this attribute selects the anchor with a yellow highlight box.

SHAPE   This attribute is used to define a selectable region for hypertext source links associated with a figure to create an image map. The values for the attribute are **DEFAULT**, **CIRCLE**, **RECT**, and **POLYGON**. The format of the **COORDS** attribute depends on the value of **SHAPE**. For **CIRCLE**, the value is **x,y,r** where **x** and **y** are the pixel coordinates for the center of the circle and **r** is the radius value in pixels. For **RECT**, the **COORDS** attribute should be **x,y,w,h**. The **x,y** values define the upper left-hand corner of the rectangle, while **w** and **h** define the width and height, respectively. A value of **POLYGON** for **SHAPE** requires **x1,y1,x2,y2,...** values for **COORDS**. Each of the x,y pairs define a point in the polygon, with successive points being joined by straight lines and the last point joined to the first. The value **DEFAULT** for **SHAPE** defines that the entire enclosed area, typically an image, be used.

STYLE   See "Core Attributes Reference" earlier in this appendix.

TABINDEX   This attribute uses a number to identify the object's position in the tabbing order for keyboard navigation using the TAB key.

TARGET   This attribute specifies the target window for a hypertext source link referencing frames. The information linked to will be displayed in the named window. Frames must be named to be targeted. There are, however, special name values, including **_blank**, which indicates a new window; **_parent**, which indicates the parent frame set containing the source link; **_self**, which indicates the frame containing the source link; and **_top**, which indicates the full browser window.

TITLE   See "Core Attributes Reference" earlier in this appendix.

TYPE   This attribute specifies the media type in the form of a MIME type of the link target. Generally this is provided strictly as advisory information; however, in the future a browser may add a small icon for multimedia types. For example, a browser might add a small speaker icon when **TYPE** was set to audio/wav.

EVENT HANDLERS   See "Events Reference" earlier in this appendix.

Examples

```
<!-- anchor linking to external file -->
<A HREF="http://www.pint.com/">External Link</A>


<!-- anchor linking to file on local filesystem -->
<A HREF="file:/c:\html\index.htm">local file link</A>


<!-- anchor invoking anonymous FTP -->
<A HREF="ftp://pint.com/workshop/freestuff">Anonymous FTP link</A>


<!-- anchor invoking FTP with password -->
<A HREF="ftp://user:password@company.com/path/file">
FTP with password</A>


<!-- anchor invoking mail -->
<A HREF="mailto:fakeid@bigcompany.com">Send mail</A>


<!-- anchor used to define target destination within document -->
<A NAME="jump">Jump target</A>


<!-- anchor linking internally to previous target anchor-->
<A HREF="#jump">Local jump within document</A>


<!-- anchor linking externally to previous target anchor -->
<A HREF="http://www.company.com/document#jump">
Remote jump within document</A>
```

COMPATIBILITY   W3C 2.0, 3.2, 4.0; Netscape 1.x, 2.x, 3.x, 4.x; Internet Explorer 2.x, 3.x, 4.x; and WebTV

Notes

The following are reserved browser key bindings for the two major browsers and should not be used as values to **ACCESSKEY: F, E, C, V, G, A, H**, left arrow, and right arrow.

Internet Explorer 4.0 does not support the following attributes: **CHARSET, COORDS, HREFLANG, SHAPE, TABINDEX**, and **TYPE**.

Netscape 4.0 does not support the following attributes: **ACCESSKEY, CHARSET, COORDS, HREFLANG, REL, REV, SHAPE, TABINDEX, TITLE, TYPE, ondblclick, onkeydown, onkeypress, onkeyup, onmousedown, onmousemove**, and **onmouseup**.

Note that WebTV supports only the **onclick, onmouseout**, and **onmouseover** attributes for this element. WebTV does not support the following attributes: **ACCESSKEY, CLASS, CHARSET, COORDS, HREFLANG, REV, SHAPE, STYLE, TABINDEX, TARGET, TITLE, TYPE**, and other event handler attributes such as onkeyup.

The **URN** attribute was defined in HTML 2.0. Although Internet Explorer 4.0 supports it, its use is unclear, particularly since URNs are not yet well defined.

HTML 3.2 defines only **NAME, HREF, REL, REV**, and **TITLE**.

HTML 2.0 defines only **NAME, HREF, METHODS, REL, REV, TITLE**, and **URN**.

The **TARGET** attribute is not defined in browsers that do not support frames, such as Netscape 1.x-generation browsers.

<ABBR>

DESCRIPTION   This element allows authors to clearly indicate a sequence of characters that compose an acronym or abbreviation for a word (XML, WWW, and so on). The content of the **ABBR** element specifies the abbreviation itself.

Syntax

```
<ABBR
    CLASS=class name(s)
    DIR=LTR | RTL
    ID=unique alphanumeric identifier
    LANG=language code
    LANGUAGE=JAVASCRIPT | JSCRIPT | VBSCRIPT | VBS    (IE 4.0)
    STYLE=style information
    TITLE=advisory text

    onclick="script"
    ondblclick="script"
    ondragstart="script"   (IE 4.0)
    onhelp="script"    (IE 4.0)
    onkeydown="script"
    onkeypress="script"
    onkeyup="script"
    onmousedown="script"
    onmousemove="script"
    onmouseout="script"
    onmouseover="script"
```

```
        onmouseup="script"
        onselectstart="script">   (IE 4.0)

</ABBR>
```

Attributes

CLASS   See "Core Attributes Reference" earlier in this appendix.

DIR   See "Language Reference" earlier in this appendix.

ID   See "Core Attributes Reference" earlier in this appendix.

LANG   See "Language Reference" earlier in this appendix.

LANGUAGE   This attribute specifies the language the current script is written in and invokes the proper scripting engine. The default value is **JAVASCRIPT**. **JAVASCRIPT** and **JSCRIPT** represent that the scripting language is written in JavaScript. **VBS** and **VBSCRIPT** represent that the scripting language is written in VBScript. It may also be possible to use extended names such as JavaScript 1.1 to hide code from JavaScript-aware browsers that don't conform to a particular version of the language.

TITLE   See "Core Attributes Reference" earlier in this appendix.

STYLE   See "Core Attributes Reference" earlier in this appendix.

EVENT HANDLERS   See "Events Reference" earlier in this appendix.

Examples

```
<ABBR TITLE="Extensible Markup Language">XML</ACRONYM>

<ABBR LANG="fr" TITLE="Soci&eacute;t&eacute; Nationale de
Chemins de Fer">SNCF</ACRONYM>
```

COMPATIBILITY   W3C 4.0; Internet Explorer 4.0

Notes

Support for this element is unclear. Netscape does not document it, though Internet Explorer 4.0 supports **<ACRONYM>**, which was the old name of this element before it was changed to **<ABBR>** in the final draft. At this point there is no rendering difference for this element in either of the popular browsers.

<ABBR> is a relatively new element and is not defined under HTML 2.0 or HTML 3.2.

<ADDRESS>

DESCRIPTION   This element marks up text indicating authorship or ownership of information. It typically occurs at the beginning or end of a document.

Syntax

```
<ADDRESS
    CLASS=class name(s)
    DIR=LTR | RTL
    ID=unique alphanumeric identifier
    LANG=language code
    LANGUAGE=JAVASCRIPT | JSCRIPT | VBSCRIPT | VBS   (IE 4.0)
    STYLE=style information
    TITLE=advisory text

    onclick="script"
    ondblclick="script"
    ondragstart="script"   (IE 4.0)
    onhelp="script"   (IE 4.0)
    onkeydown="script"
    onkeypress="script"
    onkeyup="script"
    onmousedown="script"
    onmousemove="script"
    onmouseout="script"
    onmouseover="script"
    onmouseup="script"
    onselectstart="script"> (IE 4.0)

</ADDRESS>
```

Attributes

CLASS   See "Core Attributes Reference" earlier in this appendix.

DIR   See "Language Reference" earlier in this appendix.

ID   See "Core Attributes Reference" earlier in this appendix.

LANG   See "Language Reference" earlier in this appendix.

LANGUAGE   This attribute specifies the language the current script is written in and invokes the proper scripting engine. The default value is **JAVASCRIPT**. **JAVASCRIPT** and **JSCRIPT** represent that the scripting language is written in JavaScript. **VBS** and **VBSCRIPT** represent that the scripting language is written in VBScript. It may also be possible to use extended names such as JavaScript 1.1 to hide code from JavaScript-aware browsers that don't conform to a particular version of the language.

STYLE   See "Core Attributes Reference" earlier in this appendix.

TITLE   See "Core Attributes Reference" earlier in this appendix.

EVENT HANDLERS   See "Events Reference" earlier in this appendix.

Example

```
<ADDRESS>Big Company, Inc.<BR>2105 Demo Street<BR>
San Diego, CA U.S.A.</ADDRESS>
```

COMPATIBILITY   W3C 2.0, 3.2, 4.0; Netscape 1.x, 2.x, 3.x, 4.x; Internet Explorer 2.x, 3.x, 4.x; and WebTV

Notes

Internet Explorer 4.0 does not support the **DIR** attribute.
Netscape 4.0 does not support the following attributes: **DIR, TITLE, onclick, ondblclick, onkeydown, onkeypress, onkeyup, onmousedown, onmousemove, onmouseover, onmouseout,** and **onmouseup**.
Under HTML 3.2, 2.0 and WebTV there are no attributes for **<ADDRESS>**.

<APPLET>   (Java Applet)

DESCRIPTION   This element identifies the inclusion of a Java applet.

Syntax

```
<APPLET
      ALIGN=TOP | MIDDLE | BOTTOM | LEFT | RIGHT |
      ABSBOTTOM* | ABSMIDDLE*| BASELINE* |
      CENTER* |  TEXTTOP*      *(IE 4.0, N4.0)
      ALT=alternative text
      ARCHIVE=URL of archive file
      CLASS=class name(s)
      CODE=URL of Java class file
      CODEBASE=URL for base referencing
      DATAFLD=name of column supplying bound data   (IE 4.0)
      DATASRC=id of data source object supplying data   (IE 4.0)
      HEIGHT=pixels
      HSPACE=pixels
      ID=unique alphanumeric identifier
      MAYSCRIPT    (N 3.0, N 4.0)
      NAME=unique name for scripting reference
      OBJECT=file name
      SRC=URL   (IE 4.0)
      STYLE=style information
```

```
        TITLE=advisory text
        VSPACE=pixels
        WIDTH=pixels

        onafterupdate="script"    (IE 4.0)
        onbeforeupdate="script"    (IE 4.0)
        onblur="script"   (IE 4.0)
        onclick="script"    (IE 4.0)
        ondataavailable="script"    (IE 4.0)
        ondatasetchanged="script"    (IE 4.0)
        ondatasetcomplete="script"    (IE 4.0)
        ondblclick="script"    (IE 4.0)
        onerrorupdate="script"    (IE 4.0)
        ondragstart="script"    (IE 4.0)
        onfocus="script"    (IE 4.0)
        onhelp="script"    (IE 4.0)
        onkeydown="script"    (IE 4.0)
        onkeypress="script"    (IE 4.0)
        onkeyup="script"    (IE 4.0)
        onmousedown="script"    (IE 4.0)
        onmousemove="script"    (IE 4.0)
        onmouseout="script"    (IE 4.0)
        onmouseover="script"    (IE 4.0)
        onmouseup="script"    (IE 4.0)
        onreadystatechange="script"    (IE 4.0)
        onresize="script"    (IE 4.0)
        onrowenter="script"    (IE 4.0)
        onrowexit="script">    (IE 4.0)

        <PARAM> elements
        Alternative content

    </APPLET>
```

Attributes

ALIGN   This attribute is used to position the applet on the page relative to content that may flow around it. The W3C 4.0 HTML specification defines values of **TOP**, **MIDDLE**, **BOTTOM**, **LEFT**, and **RIGHT**, while Microsoft and Netscape may also support **ABSBOTTOM**, **ABSMIDDLE**, **BASELINE**, **CENTER**, and **TEXTTOP**.

ALT   This attribute causes a descriptive text alternate to be displayed on browsers that do not support Java. Page designers should also remember that content enclosed within the **<APPLET>** element may also be rendered as alternative text.

ARCHIVE   This attribute refers to an archived or compressed version of the applet and its associated class files, which may help reduce download time.

CLASS   See "Core Attributes Reference" earlier in this appendix.

CODE   This attribute specifies the URL of the applet's class file to be loaded and executed. Applet filenames are identified by a .class filename extension. The URL specified by **CODE** may be relative to the **CODEBASE** attribute.

CODEBASE   This attribute gives the absolute or relative URL of the directory where applets .class files referenced by the **CODE** attribute are stored.

DATAFLD   This attribute, supported by Internet Explorer 4.0, specifies the column name from the data source object that supplies the bound data. This attribute may be used to specify the various **<PARAM>** elements passed to the Java applet.

DATASRC   Like **DATAFLD**, this attribute is used for data binding under Internet Explorer 4.0. It indicates the **ID** of the data source object that supplies the data that is bound to the **<PARAM>** elements associated with the applet.

HEIGHT   This attribute specifies the height, in pixels, that the applet needs.

HSPACE   This attribute specifies additional horizontal space, in pixels, to be reserved on either side of the applet.

ID   See "Core Attributes Reference" earlier in this appendix.

NAME   This attribute assigns a name to the applet so that it can be identified by other resources, particularly scripts.

MAYSCRIPT   In the Netscape implementation, this attribute allows access to an applet by programs in a scripting language embedded in the document.

OBJECT   This attribute specifies the URL of a serialized representation of an applet.

SRC   As defined for Internet Explorer 4.0, this attribute specifies a URL for an associated file for the applet. The meaning and use is unclear and not part of the HTML standard.

STYLE   See "Core Attributes Reference" earlier in this appendix.

TITLE   See "Core Attributes Reference" earlier in this appendix.

VSPACE   This attribute specifies additional vertical space, in pixels, to be reserved above and below the applet.

WIDTH   This attribute specifies in pixels the width that the applet needs.

EVENT HANDLERS   None.

Example

```
<APPLET CODE="game.class"
     ALIGN="LEFT"
```

```
        ARCHIVE="game.zip"
        HEIGHT="250" WIDTH="350">

<PARAM NAME="DIFFICULTY" VALUE="EASY">

<B>Sorry, you need Java to play this game.</B>

</APPLET>
```

COMPATIBILITY   W3C 3.2, 4.0; Netscape 2.x, 3.x, 4.x; and Internet Explorer 3.x, 4.x

Notes

The **<APPLET>** element replaces the original **<APP>** element. Parameter values can be passed to applets using the **<PARAM>** element in the applet's content area.

Internet Explorer 4.0 does not support the following attributes: **ARCHIVE** and **OBJECT**.

Netscape 4.0 does not support the **TITLE** attribute.

The W3C's HTML 4.0 specification does not encourage the use of **<APPLET>** and prefers the use of the **<OBJECT>** element. Under the strict definition of HTML 4.0, this element is not defined.

WebTV's current implementation does not support Java applets.

Java applets were first supported under Netscape 2.0-level browsers and Internet Explorer 3.0-level browsers.

<AREA>

DESCRIPTION   **<AREA>** is an empty element used within the content model of the **<MAP>** element to implement client-side image maps. It defines a hot spot region on the map and associates it with a hypertext link.

Syntax

```
<AREA
    ACCESSKEY=character
    ALT=alternative text
    CLASS=class name(s)
    COORDS=comma separated list of values
    DIR=LTR | RTL
    HREF=URL
    ID=unique alphanumeric identifier
    LANG=language code
    LANGUAGE=JAVASCRIPT | JSCRIPT | VBSCRIPT | VBS    (IE 4.0)
    NAME=file name    (N 4.0, WebTV)
    NOHREF
    NOTAB    (WebTV)
    SHAPE=RECT | RECTANGLE* | CIRCLE | CIRC* | POLY | POLYGON*
    DEFAULT    (*IE 4.0)
```

```
STYLE=style information
TABINDEX=number
TARGET=_blank | _parent | _self | _top | frame-name
TITLE=advisory text

onblur="script"
onclick="script"
ondblclick="script"
ondragstart="script"    (IE 4.0)
onfocus="script"
onhelp="script"    (IE 4.0)
onkeydown="script"
onkeypress="script"
onkeyup="script"
onmousedown="script"
onmousemove="script"
onmouseout="script"
onmouseover="script"
onmouseup="script"
onselectstart="script">    (IE 4.0)
```

Attributes

ALT   This attribute contains a text string alternative to display on browsers than cannot display images.

CLASS   See "Core Attributes Reference" earlier in this appendix.

COORDS   This attribute contains a set of values specifying the coordinates of the hot spot region. The number and meaning of the values depend upon the value specified for the **SHAPE** attribute. For a **RECT** or **RECTANGLE** shape, the **COORDS** value are two x,y pairs: **left**, **top**, **right**, and **bottom**. For a **CIRC** or **CIRCLE** shape, the **COORDS** value is **x,y,r** where **x,y** is a pair specifying the center of the circle and **r** is a value for the radius. For a **POLY** or **POLYGON** shape, the **COORDS** value is a set of x,y pairs for each point in the polygon: **x1,y1,x2,y2,x3,y3** and so on.

DIR   See "Language Reference" earlier in this appendix.

HREF   This attribute specifies the hyperlink target for the area. Its value is a valid URL. Either this attribute or the **NOHREF** attribute must be present in the element.

ID   See "Core Attributes Reference" earlier in this appendix.

LANG   See "Language Reference" earlier in this appendix.

LANGUAGE   This attribute specifies the language the current script is written in and invokes the proper scripting engine. The default value is **JAVASCRIPT**. **JAVASCRIPT** and **JSCRIPT** represent that the scripting language is written in JavaScript. **VBS** and **VBSCRIPT** represent that the scripting language is written in VBScript. It may also be possible to use extended names, such as JavaScript 1.1, to hide code from JavaScript-aware browsers that don't conform to a particular version of the language.

NAME   This attribute is used to define a name for the clickable area so that it can be scripted by older browsers.

NOHREF   This attribute indicates that no hyperlink exists for the associated area. Either this attribute or the **HREF** attribute must be present in the element.

NOTAB   Supported by WebTV, this attribute keeps the element from appearing in the tabbing order.

SHAPE   This attribute defines the shape of the associated hot spot. HTML 4.0 defines the values **RECT**, which defines a rectangular region; **CIRCLE**, which defines a circular region; **POLY**, which defines a polygon; and **DEFAULT**, which indicates the entire region beyond any defined shapes. Many browsers, notably Internet Explorer 4.0, support **RECTANGLE**, **CIRC**, and **POLYGON** as valid values for **SHAPE**.

STYLE   See "Core Attributes Reference" earlier in this appendix.

TABINDEX   This attribute represents a numeric value specifying the position of the defined area in the browser tabbing order.

TARGET   This attribute specifies the target window for hyperlink referencing frames. The value is a frame name or one of several special names. A value of **_blank** indicates a new window. A value of **_parent** indicates the parent frame set containing the source link. A value of **_self** indicates the frame containing the source link. A value of **_top** indicates the full browser window.

TITLE   See "Core Attributes Reference" earlier in this appendix.

EVENT HANDLERS   See "Events Reference" earlier in this appendix.

Example

```
<MAP NAME="main">
<AREA SHAPE="CIRCLE" COORDS="200,250,25"  HREF="interesting.html">
<AREA SHAPE="DEFAULT" NOHREF>
</MAP>
```

COMPATIBILITY   W3C 3.2, 4.0; Netscape 1.x, 2.x, 3.x, 4.x; Internet Explorer 2.x, 3.x, 4.x; and WebTV

Notes

Internet Explorer 4.0 does not support the **TABINDEX** attribute.
Netscape 4.0 does not support the following attributes: **ALT** and **TABINDEX**.
WebTV does not support the following attributes: **ALT** and **TABINDEX**.
By the HTML 3.2 and 4.0 specifications, the end tag **</AREA>** is forbidden.

The **ID**, **CLASS**, and **STYLE** attributes have the same meaning as the core attributes defined in the HTML 4.0 specification, but only Netscape and Microsoft define them. Netscape 1.x-level browsers do not understand the **TARGET** attribute as it relates to frames. HTML 3.2 defines only **ALT**, **COORDS**, **HREF**, **NOHREF**, and **SHAPE**.

<AUDIOSCOPE>

DESCRIPTION   This WebTV-specific element displays an audioscope for a sound resource that displays a dynamic, graphical display of a sound's amplitude.

Syntax

```
<AUDIOSCOPE
     ALIGN=ABSBOTTOM | ABSMIDDLE | BASELINE | BOTTOM |
          LEFT | MIDDLE | RIGHT | TEXTTOP | TOP
     BORDER=pixels
     GAIN=number
     HEIGHT=pixels
     LEFTCOLOR=#RRGGBB | color name
     LEFTOFFSET=number
     MAXLEVEL=TRUE | FALSE
     RIGHTCOLOR=#RRGGBB | name
     RIGHTOFFSET=number
     WIDTH=pixels>
```

Attributes

ALIGN   This attribute positions the audioscope object on the page relative to text or other content that may flow around it.

BORDER   This attribute sets the width of the audioscope border in pixels. The default value is **1**.

GAIN   This attribute takes a numeric value, which is a multiplier for the amplitude display. The default value is **1**.

HEIGHT   This attribute sets the height of the audioscope in pixels. The default value is **80** pixels.

LEFTCOLOR   This attribute sets the color of the line displaying the left audio channel in the audioscope. Values can be given either as named colors or in the numeric #*RRGGBB* format. The default value is **#8ECE10**.

LEFTOFFSET   This attribute sets the vertical offset for the display of the left audio channel relative with positive and negative values relative to the center of the audioscope. The default value is **0**.

MAXLEVEL   This Boolean attribute specifies whether the audioscope should clip sound according to the specified gain. The default value is **FALSE**.

RIGHTCOLOR   This attribute sets the color of the line displaying the right audio channel in the audioscope. Values can either be given as named colors or in the numeric #*RRGGBB* format. The default value is **#8ECE10**.

RIGHTOFFSET   This attribute sets the vertical offset for the display of the right audio channel relative with positive and negative values relative to the center of the audioscope. The default value is **1**.

WIDTH   This attribute sets the width of the audioscope in pixels. The default width is **100** pixels.

EVENT HANDLERS   None.

Example

```
<AUDIOSCOPE  HEIGHT="120" WIDTH="240" GAIN="2">
```

COMPATIBILITY   WebTV

Notes

This is an empty element that requires no closing tag.

<B>   (Bold)

DESCRIPTION   This element indicates that the enclosed text should be displayed in boldface.

Syntax

```
<B
     CLASS=class name(s)
     DIR=LTR | RTL
     ID=unique alphanumeric identifier
     LANG=language code
     LANGUAGE=JAVASCRIPT | JSCRIPT | VBSCRIPT | VBS    (IE 4.0)
     STYLE=style information
     TITLE=advisory text

     onclick="script"
     ondblclick="script"
     ondragstart="script"  (IE 4.0)
     onhelp="script"   (IE 4.0)
     onkeydown="script"
     onkeypress="script"
     onkeyup="script"
     onmousedown="script"
     onmousemove="script"
     onmouseout="script"
```

```
        onmouseover="script"
        onmouseup="script"
        onselectstart="script">   (IE 4.0)
</B>
```

Attributes

CLASS   See "Core Attributes Reference" earlier in this appendix.

DIR   See "Language Reference" earlier in this appendix.

ID   See "Core Attributes Reference" earlier in this appendix.

LANG   See "Language Reference" earlier in this appendix.

LANGUAGE   This attribute specifies the language the current script is written in and invokes the proper scripting engine. The default value is **JAVASCRIPT**. **JAVASCRIPT** and **JSCRIPT** represent that the scripting language is written in JavaScript. **VBS** and **VBSCRIPT** represent that the scripting language is written in VBScript. It may also be possible to use extended names, such as JavaScript 1.1, to hide code from JavaScript-aware browsers that don't conform to a particular version of the language.

STYLE   See "Core Attributes Reference" earlier in this appendix.

TITLE   See "Core Attributes Reference" earlier in this appendix.

EVENT HANDLERS   See "Events Reference" earlier in this appendix.

Example

Here is some **<B>**bold text**</B>**.

COMPATIBILITY   W3C 2.0, 3.2, 4.0; Netscape 1.x, 2.x, 3.x; Internet Explorer 2.x, 3.x, 4.x; and WebTV

Notes
Internet Explorer 4.0 does not support the **DIR** attribute.
Netscape 4.0 does not support the following attributes: **DIR**, **TITLE**, **onclick**, **ondblclick**, **onkeydown**, **onkeypress**, **onkeyup**, **onmousedown**, **onmousemove**, **onmouseover**, **onmouseout**, and **onmouseup**.
WebTV, HTML 2.0, and HTML 3.2 do not support any attributes for this element.

<BASE>

DESCRIPTION   This element specifies the base URL to use for all relative URLs contained within a document. It occurs only in the scope of a **<HEAD>** element.

Syntax

```
<BASE
    HREF=URL
    TARGET=frame-name | _blank | _parent | _self |  _top>
```

Attributes

HREF   This attribute specifies the base URL to be used throughout the document for relative URL addresses.

TARGET   For documents containing frames, this attribute specifies the default target window for every link that does not have an explicit target reference. Besides named frames, several special values exist. A value of **_blank** indicates a new window. A value of **_parent** indicates the parent frame set containing the source link. A value of **_self** indicates the frame containing the source link. A value of **_top** indicates the full browser window.

EVENT HANDLERS   None.

Example

```
<BASE HREF="http://www.bigcompany.com/">
```

COMPATIBILITY   W3C 2.0, 3.2, 4.0; Netscape 1.x, 2.x, 3.x, 4.x; Internet Explorer 2.x, 3.x, 4.x; and WebTV

Notes

HTML 2.0 and 3.2 support only the **HREF** attribute.

\<BASEFONT>

DESCRIPTION   This element establishes a default font size for a document. Font size can then be varied relative to the base font size using the **\<FONT>** element. The **\<BASEFONT>** element must be placed near the beginning of the body part of the page.

Syntax

```
<BASEFONT
    CLASS=class name(s)    (IE 4.0)
    COLOR=color name | #RRGGBB
    FACE=font name(s)
    ID=unique alphanumeric identifier
    LANG=language code    (IE 4.0)
    SIZE=1-7 | +/-int>
```

Attributes

CLASS Internet Explorer 4.0 documentation indicates that the **CLASS** can be set for the <BASEFONT> element; however, this has no presentation value, and is probably a mistake in the documentation.

COLOR This attribute sets the text color using either a named color or a color specified in the hexadecimal *#RRGGBB* format.

FACE This attribute contains a list of one or more font names. The document text in the default style is rendered in the first font face that the client's browser supports.

ID See "Core Attributes Reference" earlier in this appendix.

LANG Internet Explorer 4.0 documentation also mentions use of the **LANG** attribute to indicate the language used. Meaning with this element is not well defined.

SIZE This attribute specifies the font size as either a numeric or relative value. Numeric values range from **1** to **7** with **1** the smallest and **3** the default.

EVENT HANDLERS None.

Example

```
<BASEFONT COLOR="Red" FACE="Helvetica, Times Roman" SIZE="5">
```

COMPATIBILITY W3C 3.2, 4.0 (transitional); Netscape 1.1, 2.x, 3.x, 4.x; Internet Explorer 2.x, 3.x, 4.x; and WebTV

Notes

Internet Explorer 4.0 does not support the **DIR** attribute.
Netscape 4.0 does not support the following attributes: **COLOR** and **FACE**.
WebTV does not support the following attributes: **COLOR** and **FACE**.
HTML 3.2 supports the <BASEFONT> element and the **SIZE** attribute. HTML 4.0 transitional specification adds support for **COLOR** and **FACE** as well.
HTML 4.0 strict specification does not support this element.
The font sizes indicated by numeric values are browser dependent and not absolute.

<BDO> (Bidirectional Override)

DESCRIPTION This element is used to override the current directionality of text.

Syntax

```
<BDO
    CLASS=class name(s)
    DIR=LTR | RTL
```

```
      ID=unique alphanumeric identifier
      LANG=language code
      STYLE=style information
      TITLE=advisory text>

</BDO>
```

Attributes

CLASS   See "Core Attributes Reference" earlier in this appendix.

DIR   This attribute is required for the **<BDO>** element. It sets the text direction either to left to right (**LTR**) or right to left (**RTL**).

ID   See "Core Attributes Reference" earlier in this appendix.

LANG   See "Language Reference" earlier in this appendix.

STYLE   See "Core Attributes Reference" earlier in this appendix.

TITLE   See "Core Attributes Reference" earlier in this appendix.

EVENT HANDLERS   None.

Example

```
<!-- Switch text direction -->

<BDO ID="switch1" DIR="RTL">

Text that should go right to left

</BDO>
```

COMPATIBILITY   W3C 4.0

Notes

Neither of the main browsers (Netscape, Internet Explorer) appear to support this element yet. It is possible to set text direction with Unicode characters as well as with the **DIR** attribute of many HTML elements. Problems may occur if multiple directionality methods are used and are in conflict.

<BGSOUND>   (Background Sound)

DESCRIPTION   This Internet Explorer and WebTV element associates a background sound with a page.

Syntax

```
<BGSOUND
    BALANCE=number    (IE 4.0)
    CLASS=class name(s)    (IE 4.0)
    ID=unique alphanumeric identifier    (IE 4.0)
    LANG=language code    (IE 4.0)
    LOOP=number    (IE 4.0, WebTV)
    SRC=URL of sound file    (IE 4.0, WebTV)
    TITLE=advisory text    (IE 4.0)
    VOLUME=number>    (IE 4.0)
```

Attributes

BALANCE   A number between –10,000 and +10,000 that determines how the volume will be divided between the speakers.

CLASS   See "Core Attributes Reference" earlier in this appendix.

ID   See "Core Attributes Reference" earlier in this appendix.

LANG   See "Language Reference" earlier in this appendix.

LOOP   This attribute indicates the number of times a sound is to be played and either has a numeric value or the keyword **infinite**.

SRC   This attribute specifies the URL of the sound file to be played, which must be one of the following types: .wav, .au, or .mid.

TITLE   See "Core Attributes Reference" earlier in this appendix.

VOLUME   A number between -10,000 and 0 that determines the loudness of a page's background sound.

Examples

```
<BGSOUND SRC="sound1.mid">

<BGSOUND SRC="sound2.au" LOOP="INFINITE">
```

EVENT HANDLERS   None.

COMPATIBILITY   Internet Explorer 2.x, 3.x, 4.x; WebTV

Notes

Similar functionality can be achieved in Netscape using the **<EMBED>** element to invoke LiveAudio, as discussed in Chapter 7.

<BIG>

DESCRIPTION   This element indicates that the enclosed text should be displayed in a larger font relative to the current font.

Syntax

```
<BIG
    CLASS=class name(s)
    DIR=LTR | RTL
    ID=unique alphanumeric identifier
    LANG=language code
    LANGUAGE=JAVASCRIPT | JSCRIPT | VBSCRIPT | VBS    (IE 4.0)
    STYLE=style information
    TITLE=advisory text

    onclick="script"
    ondblclick="script"
    ondragstart="script"    (IE 4.0)
    onhelp="script"    (IE 4.0)
    onkeydown="script"
    onkeypress="script"
    onkeyup="script"
    onmousedown="script"
    onmousemove="script"
    onmouseout="script"
    onmouseover="script"
    onmouseup="script"
    onselectstart="script">    (IE 4.0)

</BIG>
```

Attributes

CLASS   See "Core Attributes Reference" earlier in this appendix.

DIR   See "Language Reference" earlier in this appendix.

ID   See "Core Attributes Reference" earlier in this appendix.

LANG   See "Language Reference" earlier in this appendix.

LANGUAGE   This attribute specifies the language the current script is written in and invokes the proper scripting engine. The default value is **JAVASCRIPT**. **JAVASCRIPT** and **JSCRIPT** represent that the scripting language is written in JavaScript. **VBS** and **VBSCRIPT** represent that the scripting language is written in VBScript.

STYLE   See "Core Attributes Reference" earlier in this appendix.

TITLE   See "Core Attributes Reference" earlier in this appendix.

EVENT HANDLERS   See "Events Reference" earlier in this appendix.

Example

```
This text is regular size. <BIG>This text is larger</BIG>.
```

COMPATIBILITY   W3C 3.2, 4.0; Netscape 2.x, 3.x, 4.x; Internet Explorer 2.x, 3.x, 4.x; and WebTV

Notes

Internet Explorer 4.0 does not support the **DIR** attribute.
Netscape 4.0 does not support the following attributes: **DIR, TITLE, onclick, ondblclick, onkeydown, onkeypress, onkeyup, onmousedown, onmousemove, onmouseover, onmouseout,** and **onmouseup**.
WebTV does not support any attributes for this element.
HTML 3.2 does not support any attributes for this element.

<BLACKFACE>

DESCRIPTION   This WebTV element renders the enclosed text in a double-weight boldface font. It is used for headings and other terms needing special emphasis.

Syntax

```
<BLACKFACE> text </BLACKFACE>
```

Attributes

None.

Example

```
<BLACKFACE>Special !!!</BLACKFACE> This week only!
```

EVENT HANDLERS   None.

COMPATIBILITY   WebTV

Notes

This element is used as part of the style conventions followed by WebTV pages.

<BLINK>

DESCRIPTION   This Netscape-specific element causes the enclosed text to flash slowly.

Syntax

```
<BLINK
    CLASS=class name(s)    (N 4.0)
    ID=unique alphanumeric identifier    (N 4.0)
    LANG=language code    (N 4.0)
    STYLE=style information>    (N 4.0)

</BLINK>
```

Attributes

CLASS   See "Core Attributes Reference" earlier in this appendix.

ID   See "Core Attributes Reference" earlier in this appendix.

LANG   See "Language Reference" earlier in this appendix.

STYLE   See "Core Attributes Reference" earlier in this appendix.

Example

```
<BLINK>Buy me now!!!</BLINK>
```

EVENT HANDLERS   None.

COMPATIBILITY   Netscape 1.x, 2.x, 3.x, 4.x

Notes

While not defined explicitly in Netscape documentation, the **CLASS**, **ID**, **LANG**, and **STYLE** attributes are mentioned to be universal to all elements under Netscape 4.x and may have meaning here.

Many Web design professionals recommend against using this element because it is considered annoying.

<BLOCKQUOTE>

DESCRIPTION   This block element indicates that the enclosed text is an extended quotation. Usually this is rendered visually by indentation.

Syntax

```
<BLOCKQUOTE
    CITE=URL of source information
    CLASS=class name(s)
```

```
DIR=LTR | RTL
ID=unique alphanumeric identifier
LANG=language code
LANGUAGE=JAVASCRIPT | JSCRIPT | VBSCRIPT | VBS    (IE 4.0)
STYLE=style information
TITLE=advisory text

onclick="script"
ondblclick="script"
ondragstart="script"   (IE 4.0)
onhelp="script"   (IE 4.0)
onkeydown="script"
onkeypress="script"
onkeyup="script"
onmousedown="script"
onmousemove="script"
onmouseout="script"
onmouseover="script"
onmouseup="script"
onselectstart="script">   (IE 4.0)
```

```
</BLOCKQUOTE>
```

Attributes

CITE   The value of this attribute should be a URL of the document in which the information cited can be found.

CLASS   See "Core Attributes Reference" earlier in this appendix.

DIR   See "Language Reference" earlier in this appendix.

ID   See "Core Attributes Reference" earlier in this appendix.

LANG   See "Language Reference" earlier in this appendix.

LANGUAGE   This attribute specifies the language the current script is written in and invokes the proper scripting engine. The default value is **JAVASCRIPT**. **JAVASCRIPT** and **JSCRIPT** represent that the scripting language is written in JavaScript. **VBS** and **VBSCRIPT** represent that the scripting language is written in VBScript.

STYLE   See "Core Attributes Reference" earlier in this appendix.

TITLE   See "Core Attributes Reference" earlier in this appendix.

EVENT HANDLERS   See "Events Reference" earlier in this appendix.

Example

The following paragraph is taken from the mentioned report:
`<BLOCKQUOTE CITE="thereport.htm">` ... text ... `</BLOCKQUOTE>`

COMPATIBILITY   W3C 2.0, 3.2, 4.0; Netscape 1.x, 2.x, 3.x, 4.x; Internet Explorer 2.x, 3.x, 4.x; and WebTV

Notes

Internet Explorer 4.0 does not support the **CITE** and **DIR** attributes.

Netscape 4.0 does not support the following attributes: **CITE, DIR, TITLE, onclick, ondblclick, onkeydown, onkeypress, onkeyup, onmousedown, onmousemove, onmouseover, onmouseout,** and **onmouseup.**

WebTV does not support any attributes for this element.

HTML 2.0 and 3.2 do not support any attributes for this element.

Some browsers understand the **<BQ>** shorthand notation.

<BODY>

DESCRIPTION   This element encloses a document's displayable content, in contrast to the descriptive and informational content contained in the **<HEAD>** element.

Syntax

```
<BODY
    ALINK=color name | #RRGGBB
    BACKGROUND=URL of background image
    BGCOLOR=color name | #RRGGBB
    BGPROPERTIES=FIXED    (IE 4.0)
    BOTTOMMARGIN=pixels    (IE 4.0)
    CLASS=class name(s)
    CREDITS=URL    (WebTV)
    DIR=LTR | RTL
    FONTSIZE=SMALL |MEDIUM | LARGE    (WebTV)
    HSPACE=pixels    (WebTV)
    ID=unique alphanumeric identifier
    INSTRUCTIONS=URL    (WebTV)
    LANG=language code
    LANGUAGE=JAVASCRIPT | JSCRIPT | VBSCRIPT | VBS    (IE 4.0)
    LEFTMARGIN=pixels    (IE 4.0)
    LINK=color name | #RRGGBB
    LOGO=URL    (WebTV)
    NOHTILEBG    (WebTV)
    NOVTILEBG    (WebTV)
    RIGHTMARGIN=pixels    (IE 4.0)
    SCROLL=YES | NO    (IE 4.0)
```

```
          STYLE=style information
          TEXT=color name | #RRGGBB
          TITLE=advisory text
          TOPMARGIN=pixels   (IE 4.0)
          VLINK=#RRGGBB | color name
          VSPACE=pixels   (WebTV)
          XSPEED=0|1|2|3|4   (WebTV)
          YSPEED=0|1|2|3|4   (WebTV)

          onafterupdate="script"   (IE 4.0)
          onbeforeunload="script"   (IE 4.0)
          onbeforeupdate="script"   (IE 4.0)
          onblur="script"   (IE 4.0, N 4.0)
          onclick="script"
          ondblclick="script"
          ondragstart="script"   (IE 4.0)
          onfocus="script"   (IE 4.0, N 4.0)
          onhelp="script"   (IE 4.0)
          onkeydown="script"
          onkeypress="script"
          onkeyup="script"
          onload="script"
          onmousedown="script"
          onmousemove="script"
          onmouseout="script"
          onmouseover="script"
          onmouseup="script"
          onrowenter="script"   (IE 4.0)
          onrowexit="script"   (IE 4.0)
          onscroll="script"   (IE 4.0)
          onselect="script"   (IE 4.0)
          onselectstart="script"   (IE 4.0)
          onunload="script">

</BODY>
```

Attributes

ALINK   This attribute sets the color for active links within the document. Active links represent the state of a link as it is being pressed. The value of the attribute can either be a browser-dependent named color or a color specified in the hexadecimal #*RRGGBB* format.

BACKGROUND   This attribute contains a URL for an image file, which will be tiled to provide the document background.

BGCOLOR   This attribute sets the background color for the document. Its value can be either a browser-dependent named color or color specified using the hexadecimal #*RRGGBB* format.

BGPROPERTIES   This attribute, first introduced in Internet Explorer 2.x, has one value, **FIXED**, which causes the background image to not scroll and act as a fixed watermark.

BOTTOMMARGIN   This attribute specifies the bottom margin for the entire body of the page and overrides the default margin. When set to **0** or **""**, the bottom margin is the bottom edge of the window or frame the content is displayed in.

CLASS   See "Core Attributes Reference" earlier in this appendix.

CREDITS   In the WebTV implementation, this attribute contains the URL of the document to retrieve when the viewer presses the credits button on the Info Panel.

DIR   See "Language Reference" earlier in this appendix.

FONTSIZE   In the WebTV implementation, this attribute sets the font size for the document and overrides viewer preferences. The default value is **MEDIUM**.

HSPACE   In the WebTV implementation, this attribute sets the fixed horizontal space surrounding body content. The default value is **8** pixels.

ID   See "Core Attributes Reference" earlier in this appendix.

INSTRUCTIONS   In the WebTV implementation, this attribute contains the URL of the document to retrieve when the viewer presses the instructions button on the Info Panel.

LANG   See "Language Reference" earlier in this appendix.

LANGUAGE   This attribute specifies the language the current script is written in and invokes the proper scripting engine. The default value is **JAVASCRIPT**. **JAVASCRIPT** and **JSCRIPT** represent that the scripting language is written in JavaScript. **VBS** and **VBSCRIPT** represent that the scripting language is written in VBScript.

LEFTMARGIN   This Internet Explorer-specific attribute sets the left margin for the page in pixels, overriding the default margin. When set to **0** or **""**, the left margin is the left edge of the window or the frame.

LINK   This attribute sets the color for hyperlinks within the document that have not yet been visited. Its value can be either a browser-dependent named color or a color specified using the hexadecimal *#RRGGBB* format.

LOGO   In the WebTV implementation, this attribute contains the URL of a 70×52-pixel thumbnail image for the page that is used in the history and bookmarks for WebTV.

NOHTILEBG   In the WebTV implementation, this prevents a background image from tiling horizontally. When this attribute is set, the background image does not scroll.

NOVTILEBG   In the WebTV implementation, this prevents a background image from tiling vertically. When this attribute is set , the background image does not scroll.

RIGHTMARGIN   This Internet Explorer-specific attribute sets the right margin for page in pixels, overriding the default margin. When set to **0** or **""**, the right margin is the right edge of the window or the frame.

SCROLL   This attribute turns the scroll bars on or off. The default value is **YES**.

STYLE   See "Core Attributes Reference" earlier in this appendix.

TEXT   This attribute sets the text color for the document. Its value can be either a browser-dependent named color or a color specified using the hexadecimal *#RRGGBB* format.

TITLE   See "Core Attributes Reference" earlier in this appendix.

TOPMARGIN   This Internet Explorer-specific attribute sets the top margin for the document in pixels. If set to **0** or **""**, the top margin will be exactly on the top edge of the window or frame.

VLINK   This attribute sets the color for links within the document that have already been visited. Its value can be either a browser-dependent named color or a color specified using the hexadecimal *#RRGGBB* format.

VSPACE   In the WebTV implementation, this attribute sets the fixed vertical space surrounding body content. The default value is **6** pixels.

XSPEED   In the WebTV implementation, this attribute sets the horizontal scrolling speed for background images. Integer values range from **0**, stationary, to **4**, fast scrolling. The default is **0**. Body content does not scroll.

YSPEED   In the WebTV implementation, this attribute sets the vertical scrolling speed for background images. Integer values range from **0**, stationary, to **4**, fast scrolling. The default is **0**. Body content does not scroll.

EVENT HANDLERS   See "Events Reference" earlier in this appendix.

Example

```
<BODY BACKGROUND="pattern.gif"
   BGCOLOR="White"
   ALINK="Red"
   LINK="Blue"
   VLINK="Red"
   TEXT="Black"> ... </BODY>

<!-- myLoadFunction defined in document head in
     <SCRIPT> element -->
<BODY onload="myLoadFunction()"> ... </BODY>
```

COMPATIBILITY   W3C 2.0, 3.2, 4.0; Netscape 1.x, 2.x, 3.x, 4.x; Internet Explorer 2.x, 3.x, 4.x; and WebTV

Notes

When defining text colors, it is important to be careful to specify both foreground and background explicitly so that they are not masked out by browser defaults set by the user. Under the HTML 4.0 strict definition, all color-setting attributes and background attributes are not allowed. This includes the **ALINK, BACKGROUND, BGCOLOR, LINK, TEXT**, and **VLINK** attributes.

Internet Explorer 4.0 does not support the **DIR** attribute. Internet Explorer 4.0 documentation suggests that **onblur** and **onfocus** are not supported for the window; however they are supported.

Netscape 4.0 does not support the following attributes: **DIR, TITLE, onclick, ondblclick, onkeydown, onkeypress, onkeyup, onmousedown, onmousemove, onmouseover, onmouseout**, and **onmouseup**.

WebTV does not support the following attributes: **ALINK, CLASS, DIR, ID, LANG, STYLE, TITLE, onclick, ondblclick, onkeydown, onkeypress, onkeyup, onmousedown, onmousemove, onmouseover, onmouseout**, and **onmouseup**.

This element must be present in all documents except those declaring a frame set.

<BQ>   (Block Quote)

DESCRIPTION   This element signifies that the enclosed text is an extended quotation. Though it has been defined in early HTML specifications, it is currently supported only by the WebTV browser as an alias for the **<BLOCKQUOTE>** element.

Syntax

```
<BQ>
</BQ>
```

Attributes

None.

EVENT HANDLERS   None.

Example

```
<BQ>HTML: The Complete Reference says "Don't use this element."</BQ>
```

COMPATIBILITY   WebTV

Notes

This element originated in the early days of HTML and is considered obsolete. It should not be used.

   (Line Break)

DESCRIPTION   This empty element forces a line break.

Syntax

```
<BR
    CLASS=class name(s)
    CLEAR=ALL | LEFT | NONE | RIGHT
    ID=unique alphanumeric identifier
    LANGUAGE=JAVASCRIPT | JSCRIPT | VBSCRIPT | VBS    (IE 4.0)
    STYLE=style information
    TITLE=advisory text>
```

Attributes

CLASS   See "Core Attributes Reference" earlier in this appendix.

CLEAR   This attribute forces the insertion of vertical space so that the tagged text may be positioned with respect to images. A value of **LEFT** clears text that flows around left-aligned images to the next full left margin, a value of **RIGHT** clears text that flows around right-aligned images to the next full right margin, and a value of **ALL** clears text until it can reach both full margins. The default value according to the HTML 4.0 transitional specification is **NONE**, but its meaning is generally supported as just introducing a return and nothing more.

ID   See "Core Attributes Reference" earlier in this appendix.

LANGUAGE   This attribute specifies the language the current script is written in and invokes the proper scripting engine. The default value is **JAVASCRIPT**. **JAVASCRIPT** and **JSCRIPT** represent that the scripting language is written in JavaScript. **VBS** and **VBSCRIPT** represent that the scripting language is written in VBScript.

STYLE   See "Core Attributes Reference" earlier in this appendix.

TITLE   See "Core Attributes Reference" earlier in this appendix.

EVENT HANDLERS   None.

Examples

```
This text will be continued <BR> on the next line

<IMG SRC="test.gif" ALIGN="RIGHT">
This is the image caption.<BR CLEAR="RIGHT">
```

COMPATIBILITY   W3C 3.2, 4.0; Netscape 1.x, 2.x, 3.x, 4.x; Internet Explorer 2.x, 3.x, 4.x; and WebTV

Notes
WebTV does not support the following attributes: **CLASS**, **ID**, **STYLE**, and **TITLE**.
This is an empty element. A closing tag is invalid.

Under the HTML 4.0 strict specification, the **CLEAR** attribute is not valid. Style sheet rules provide the functionality of the **CLEAR** attribute.

<BUTTON>

DESCRIPTION   This element defines a nameable region known as a button, which may be used together with scripts.

Syntax

```
<BUTTON
     ACCESSKEY=key
     CLASS=class name(s)
     DATAFLD=name of column supplying bound data    (IE 4.0)
     DATAFORMATAS=HTML | TEXT    (IE 4.0)
     DATASRC=id of data source object supplying data    (IE 4.0)
     DIR=LTR | RTL
     DISABLED
     ID=unique alphanumeric identifier
     LANG=language code
     LANGUAGE=JAVASCRIPT | JSCRIPT | VBSCRIPT | VBS    (IE 4.0)
     NAME=button name
     STYLE=style information
     TABINDEX=number
     TITLE=advisory text
     TYPE=BUTTON | SUBMIT | RESET
     VALUE=button value

     onafterupdate="script"    (IE 4.0)
     onbeforeupdate="script"    (IE 4.0)
     onblur="script"
     onclick="script"
     ondblclick="script"
     ondragstart="script"    (IE 4.0)
     onfocus="script"
     onhelp="script"    (IE 4.0)
     onkeydown="script"
     onkeypress="script"
     onkeyup="script"
     onmousedown="script"
     onmousemove="script"
     onmouseout="script"
     onmouseover="script"
     onmouseup="script"
     onresize="script"    (IE 4.0)
     onrowenter="script"    (IE 4.0)
     onrowexit="script"    (IE 4.0)
     onscroll="script"    (IE 4.0)
```

```
        onselectstart="script">    (IE 4.0)

</BUTTON>
```

Attributes

ACCESSKEY   This attribute specifies a keyboard navigation accelerator for the element. Pressing ALT or a similar key in association with the specified key selects the anchor element correlated with that key.

CLASS   See "Core Attributes Reference" earlier in this appendix.

DATAFLD   This attribute specifies the column name from the data source object that supplies the bound data that defines the information for the **<BUTTON>** element's content.

DATAFORMATAS   This attribute indicates if the bound data is plain text or HTML.

DATASRC   This attribute indicates the **ID** of the data source object that supplies the data that is bound to the **<BUTTON>** element.

DIR   See "Language Reference" earlier in this appendix.

DISABLED   Used to disable the button.

ID   See "Core Attributes Reference" earlier in this appendix.

LANG   See "Language Reference" earlier in this appendix.

LANGUAGE   This attribute specifies the language that the current script associated with the event handlers is written in and invokes the proper scripting engine. The default value is **JAVASCRIPT**. **JAVASCRIPT** and **JSCRIPT** represent that the scripting language is written in JavaScript. **VBS** and **VBSCRIPT** represent that the scripting language is written in VBScript.

NAME   This attribute is used to define a name for the button so that it can be scripted by older browsers or used to provide a name for submit buttons when there is more than one in a page.

STYLE   See "Core Attributes Reference" earlier in this appendix.

TABINDEX   This attribute uses a number to identify the object's position in the tabbing order.

TITLE   See "Core Attributes Reference" earlier in this appendix.

TYPE   Defines the type of button. According to the HTML 4.0 specification, by default the button is undefined. Possible values include **BUTTON**, **SUBMIT**, and **RESET**, which are used to indicate the button is a plain button, submit button, or reset button, respectively.

VALUE   Defines the value that is sent to the server when the button is pressed. As mentioned in Chapter 11, this may be useful when using multiple **SUBMIT** buttons that perform different actions to indicate which button was pressed to the handling CGI program.

EVENT HANDLERS   See "Events Reference" earlier in this appendix.

Examples

```
<BUTTON NAME="Submit" VALUE="Submit" TYPE="Submit">Submit</BUTTON>

<BUTTON TYPE="BUTTON" onClick="doSomething()">Click Me</BUTTON>

<BUTTON TYPE="BUTTON"><IMG SRC="pretty.gif" ALT="Pretty"></BUTTON>
```

COMPATIBILITY   W3C 4.0; Internet Explorer 4.0

Notes

According to documentation, Internet Explorer 4.0 does not support the following attributes: **DIR, NAME, TABINDEX,** and **VALUE.** It is most likely that these are simply oversights, particularly **NAME** and **VALUE.**

It is invalid to associate an image map with an **<IMG>** that appears as the contents of a **BUTTON** element.

The HTML 4.0 specification reserves the data binding attributes **DATASRC, DATAFLD,** and **DATAFORMATS** for future use.

<CAPTION>   (Figure or Table Caption)

DESCRIPTION   This element is used within both the figure and table elements to define a caption.

Syntax

```
<CAPTION
    ALIGN=BOTTOM | LEFT | RIGHT |
        TOP | CENTER*    (*IE 4.0, *WebTV)
    CLASS=class name(s)
    DIR=LTR | RTL
    ID=unique alphanumeric identifier
    LANG=language code
    LANGUAGE=JAVASCRIPT | JSCRIPT | VBSCRIPT | VBS    (IE 4.0)
    STYLE=style information
    TITLE=advisory text
    VALIGN=TOP | BOTTOM    (IE 4.0)

    onafterupdate="script"    (IE 4.0)
    onbeforeupdate="script"    (IE 4.0)
    onblur="script"    (IE 4.0)
    onchange="script"    (IE 4.0)
    onclick="script"
    ondblclick="script"
```

```
ondragstart="script"   (IE 4.0)
onfocus="script"   (IE 4.0)
onhelp="script"   (IE 4.0)
onkeydown="script"
onkeypress="script"
onkeyup="script"
onmousedown="script"
onmousemove="script"
onmouseout="script"
onmouseover="script"
onmouseup="script"
onresize="script"   (IE 4.0)
onrowenter="script"   (IE 4.0)
onrowexit="script"   (IE 4.0)
onselectstart="script">   (IE 4.0)
```

```
</CAPTION>
```

Attributes

ALIGN   This attribute specifies the alignment of the caption. HTML 4.0 defines **TOP**, **BOTTOM**, **LEFT**, and **RIGHT** as valid values. Internet Explorer and WebTV also support **CENTER**. Because this does not provide the possibility to put a caption on the top left or bottom right, Microsoft has introduced the **VALIGN** attribute for the **<CAPTION>** element.

CLASS   See "Core Attributes Reference" earlier in this appendix.

DIR   See "Language Reference" earlier in this appendix.

ID   See "Core Attributes Reference" earlier in this appendix.

LANG   See "Language Reference" earlier in this appendix.

LANGUAGE   This attribute specifies the language the current script is written in and invokes the proper scripting engine. The default value is **JAVASCRIPT**. **JAVASCRIPT** and **JSCRIPT** represent that the scripting language is written in JavaScript. **VBS** and **VBSCRIPT** represent that the scripting language is written in VBScript.

STYLE   See "Core Attributes Reference" earlier in this appendix.

TITLE   See "Core Attributes Reference" earlier in this appendix.

VALIGN   This Internet Explorer-specific attribute is used to specify whether the table caption appears at the top or bottom.

EVENT HANDLERS   See "Events Reference" earlier in this appendix.

Example

```
<TABLE>
   <CAPTION ALIGN="TOP">Fancy Food Table</CAPTION>
</TABLE>
```

COMPATIBILITY   W3C 3.2, 4.0; Netscape 1.1, 2.x, 3.x, 4.x; Internet Explorer 2.x, 3.x, 4.x; and WebTV

Notes

Internet Explorer 4.0 does not support the **DIR** attribute.

There should be only one caption per table.

Netscape 4.0 does not support the attributes: **DIR, TITLE, onclick, ondblclick, onkeydown, onkeypress, onkeyup, onmousedown, onmousemove, onmouseover, onmouseout,** and **onmouseup.** It also does not support values of **LEFT, RIGHT,** and **CENTER** for the **ALIGN** attribute.

WebTV does not support the following attributes: **CLASS, DIR, ID, LANG, STYLE, TITLE, onclick, ondblclick, onkeydown, onkeypress, onkeyup, onmousedown, onmousemove, onmouseover, onmouseout,** and **onmouseup.**

HTML 3.2 only defines the **ALIGN** attribute with values of **TOP** and **BOTTOM**. No other attributes are defined prior to HTML 4.0.

<CENTER>

DESCRIPTION   This element causes the enclosed content to be centered within the margins currently in effect. Margins are either the default page margins or those imposed by overriding elements such as tables.

Syntax

```
<CENTER
    CLASS=class name(s)
    DIR=LTR | RTL
    ID=unique alphanumeric identifier
    LANG=language code
    LANGUAGE=JAVASCRIPT | JSCRIPT | VBSCRIPT | VBS    (IE 4.0)
    STYLE=style information
    TITLE=advisory text

    onclick="script"
    ondblclick="script"
    ondragstart="script"   (IE 4.0)
    onhelp="script"    (IE 4.0)
    onkeydown="script"
    onkeypress="script"
    onkeyup="script"
```

```
        onmousedown="script"
        onmousemove="script"
        onmouseout="script"
        onmouseover="script"
        onmouseup="script"
        onselectstart="script">    (IE 4.0)

    </CENTER>
```

Attributes

CLASS   See "Core Attributes Reference" earlier in this appendix.

DIR   See "Language Reference" earlier in this appendix.

ID   See "Core Attributes Reference" earlier in this appendix.

LANG   See "Language Reference" earlier in this appendix.

LANGUAGE   This attribute specifies the language the current script is written in and invokes the proper scripting engine. The default value is **JAVASCRIPT**. **JAVASCRIPT** and **JSCRIPT** represent that the scripting language is written in JavaScript. **VBS** and **VBSCRIPT** represent that the scripting language is written in VBScript.

STYLE   See "Core Attributes Reference" earlier in this appendix.

TITLE   See "Core Attributes Reference" earlier in this appendix.

EVENT HANDLERS   See "Events Reference" earlier in this appendix.

Example

`<CENTER>I am in the center of the page.</CENTER>`

COMPATIBILITY   W3C 3.2, 4.0 (transitional); Netscape 1.1, 2.x, 3.x, 4.x; Internet Explorer 2.x, 3.x, 4.x; and WebTV

Notes
The **<CENTER>** element defined by the W3C is a shorthand notation for **<DIV ALIGN=CENTER>**. The strict version of HTML 4.0 does not include the **<CENTER>** element. Internet Explorer 4.0 does not support the **DIR** attribute.
Netscape 4.0 does not support the following attributes: **DIR, TITLE, onclick, ondblclick, onkeydown, onkeypress, onkeyup, onmousedown, onmousemove, onmouseover, onmouseout,** and **onmouseup**.
Netscape 3.0 and 4.0 documentation indicates support for the **CLASS, ID, LANG,** and **STYLE** attributes but does not explicitly define them.

WebTV does not support any attributes for this element.

HTML 3.2 does not support any attributes for this element.

<CITE> (Citation)

DESCRIPTION This element indicates a citation from a book or other published source and is usually rendered in italics by a browser.

Syntax

```
<CITE
    CLASS=class name(s)
    DIR=LTR | RTL
    ID=unique alphanumeric identifier
    LANG=language code
    LANGUAGE=JAVASCRIPT | JSCRIPT | VBSCRIPT | VBS    (IE 4.0)
    STYLE=style information
    TITLE=advisory text

    onclick="script"
    ondblclick="script"
    ondragstart="script"    (IE 4.0)
    onhelp="script"    (IE 4.0)
    onkeydown="script"
    onkeypress="script"
    onkeyup="script"
    onmousedown="script"
    onmousemove="script"
    onmouseout="script"
    onmouseover="script"
    onmouseup="script"
    onselectstart="script">    (IE 4.0)

</CITE>
```

Attributes

CLASS See "Core Attributes Reference" earlier in this appendix.

DIR See "Language Reference" earlier in this appendix.

ID See "Core Attributes Reference" earlier in this appendix.

LANG See "Language Reference" earlier in this appendix.

LANGUAGE This attribute specifies the language the current script is written in and invokes the proper scripting engine. The default value is **JAVASCRIPT**. **JAVASCRIPT** and **JSCRIPT**

represent that the scripting language is written in JavaScript. **VBS** and **VBSCRIPT** represent
that the scripting language is written in VBScript.

STYLE   See "Core Attributes Reference" earlier in this appendix.

TITLE   See "Core Attributes Reference" earlier in this appendix.

EVENT HANDLERS   See "Events Reference" earlier in this appendix.

Example

```
This example is taken from
<CITE>HTML: The Complete Reference</CITE>.
```

COMPATIBILITY   W3C 2.0, 3.2, 4.0; Netscape 1.x, 2.x, 3.x, 4.x; Internet Explorer 2.x, 3.x, 4.x;
and WebTV

Notes

Internet Explorer 4.0 does not support the **DIR** attribute.
Netscape 4.0 does not support the following attributes: **DIR, TITLE, onclick, ondblclick,
onkeydown, onkeypress, onkeyup, onmousedown, onmousemove, onmouseover,
onmouseout,** and **onmouseup.**
Netscape documentation only implies the use of **CLASS, ID, LANG,** and **STYLE** in Netscape
4.0 browsers and does not explicitly define it for this element.
WebTV does not support any attributes for this element.
HTML 2.0 and 3.2 do not indicate any attributes for this element.

<CODE>

DESCRIPTION   This element indicates that the enclosed text is source code in a programming
language. Usually it is rendered in a monospaced font.

Syntax

```
<CODE
    CLASS=class name(s)
    DIR=LTR | RTL
    ID=unique alphanumeric identifier
    LANG=language code
    LANGUAGE=JAVASCRIPT | JSCRIPT | VBSCRIPT | VBS   (IE 4.0)
    STYLE=style information
    TITLE=advisory text

    onclick="script"
    ondblclick="script"
    ondragstart="script"   (IE 4.0)
```

```
      onhelp="script"    (IE 4.0)
      onkeydown="script"
      onkeypress="script"
      onkeyup="script"
      onmousedown="script"
      onmousemove="script"
      onmouseout="script"
      onmouseover="script"
      onmouseup="script"
      onselectstart="script">    (IE 4.0)

</CODE>
```

Attributes

CLASS   See "Core Attributes Reference" earlier in this appendix.

DIR   See "Language Reference" earlier in this appendix.

ID   See "Core Attributes Reference" earlier in this appendix.

LANG   See "Language Reference" earlier in this appendix.

LANGUAGE   This attribute specifies the language the current script is written in and invokes the proper scripting engine. The default value is **JAVASCRIPT**. **JAVASCRIPT** and **JSCRIPT** represent that the scripting language is written in JavaScript. **VBS** and **VBSCRIPT** represent that the scripting language is written in VBScript.

STYLE   See "Core Attributes Reference" earlier in this appendix.

TITLE   See "Core Attributes Reference" earlier in this appendix.

EVENT HANDLERS   See "Events Reference" earlier in this appendix.

Example

To increment a variable called "count," use

```
<CODE> count++ </CODE>
```

COMPATIBILITY   W3C 2.0, 3.2, 4.0; Netscape 1.x, 2.x., 3.x, 4.x; Internet Explorer 2.x, 3.x, 4.x; and WebTV

Notes

This element is best for short code fragments because it does not preserve special indentation. For multiline code fragments, page authors tend to use the **<PRE>** element.
Internet Explorer 4.0 does not support the **DIR** attribute.

Netscape 4.0 does not support the following attributes: **DIR, TITLE, onclick, ondblclick, onkeydown, onkeypress, onkeyup, onmousedown, onmousemove, onmouseover, onmouseout,** and **onmouseup**.
WebTV does not support any attributes for this element.
HTML 2.0 and 3.2 do not support any attributes for this element.

<COL> (Column)

DESCRIPTION   This element defines a column within a table and is used for grouping and alignment purposes. It is generally found within a **<COLGROUP>** element.

Syntax

```
<COL
     ALIGN=LEFT | CENTER | RIGHT | JUSTIFY | CHAR
     CHAR=character
     CHAROFF=number
     CLASS=class name(s)
     DIR=LTR | RTL
     ID=unique alphanumeric identifier
     LANG=language code
     REPEAT=number
     STYLE=style information
     TITLE=advisory text
     VALIGN=BASELINE | BOTTOM | MIDDLE | TOP
     WIDTH=column width specification

     onclick="script"
     ondblclick="script"
     onkeydown="script"
     onkeypress="script"
     onkeyup="script"
     onmousedown="script"
     onmousemove="script"
     onmouseout="script"
     onmouseover="script"
     onmouseup="script">
```

Attributes

ALIGN   This attribute specifies horizontal alignment of cell's contents.

CHAR   This attribute is used to set the character to align the cells in a column on. Typical values for this include a period "." when attempting to align numbers or monetary values.

CHAROFF   This attribute is used to indicate the number of characters to offset the column data from the alignment characters specified by the **CHAR** value.

CLASS See "Core Attributes Reference" earlier in this appendix.

DIR See "Language Reference" earlier in this appendix.

ID See "Core Attributes Reference" earlier in this appendix.

LANG See "Language Reference" earlier in this appendix.

REPEAT When present, this attribute specifies the default number of columns in this group. User agents should ignore this attribute if the current column group contains one or more **COL** elements. The default value of this attribute is **1**.

STYLE See "Core Attributes Reference" earlier in this appendix.

TITLE See "Core Attributes Reference" earlier in this appendix.

VALIGN This attribute specifies the vertical alignment of the text within the cell. Possible values for this attribute are **BASELINE**, **BOTTOM**, **MIDDLE**, and **TOP**.

WIDTH This attribute specifies a default width for each column in the current column group. In addition to the standard pixel and percentage values, this attribute may take the special form **0***, which means that the width of each column in the group should be the minimum width necessary to hold the column's contents. Relative widths like **0.5*** can also be used.

EVENT HANDLERS See "Events Reference" earlier in this appendix.

Examples

```
<COL ALIGN="RIGHT" COL="30" >

<COL ALIGN="CHAR" CHAR=":">
```

COMPATIBILITY W3C 4.0; Internet Explorer 4.0

Notes

According to documentation, Internet Explorer 4.0 does not support the following attributes: **CHAR**, **CHAROFF**, **DIR**, **LANG**, **onclick**, **ondblclick**, **onkeydown**, **onkeypress**, **onkeyup**, **onmousedown**, **onmousemove**, **onmouseover**, **onmouseout**, and **onmouseup**. On the **ALIGN** attribute, Internet Explorer 4.0 does not support the **JUSTIFY** or **CHAR** values.
As an empty element, **<COL>** does not require a closing tag.
This element generally appears within a **<COLGROUP>** element and like that element is somewhat of a convenience feature used to set attributes with one or more table columns.

<COLGROUP> (Column Group)

DESCRIPTION This element creates an explicit column group to access a group of table columns for scripting or formatting.

Syntax

```
<COLGROUP
    ALIGN=CENTER | CHAR | JUSTIFY | LEFT | RIGHT
    CHAR=character
    CHAROFF=number
    CLASS=class name(s)
    DIR=LTR | RTL
    ID=unique alphanumeric identifier
    LANG=language code
    SPAN=number
    STYLE=style information
    TITLE=advisory text
    VALIGN=BASELINE | BOTTOM | MIDDLE | TOP
    WIDTH=column width specification

    onclick="script"
    ondblclick="script"
    onkeydown="script"
    onkeypress="script"
    onkeyup="script"
    onmousedown="script"
    onmousemove="script"
    onmouseout="script"
    onmouseover="script"
    onmouseup="script">

    <COL> elements
</COLGROUP>
```

Attributes

ALIGN   This attribute specifies horizontal alignment of contents of the cells in the column group. The values of **CENTER**, **LEFT**, and **RIGHT** have obvious meanings. A value of **JUSTIFY** for the attribute should attempt to justify all the column's contents. A value of **CHAR** attempts to align the contents based on the value of the **CHAR** attribute in conjunction with **CHAROFF**.

CHAR   This attribute is used to set the character to align the cells in a column on. Typical values for this include a period "." when attempting to align numbers or monetary values.

CHAROFF   This attribute is used to indicate the number of characters to offset the column data from the alignment characters specified by the **CHAR** value.

CLASS   See "Core Attributes Reference" earlier in this appendix.

DIR   See "Language Reference" earlier in this appendix.

ID   See "Core Attributes Reference" earlier in this appendix.

LANG   See "Language Reference" earlier in this appendix.

SPAN   When present, this attribute specifies the default number of columns in this group. Browsers should ignore this attribute if the current column group contains one or more **<COL>** elements. The default value of this attribute is **1**.

STYLE   See "Core Attributes Reference" earlier in this appendix.

TITLE   See "Core Attributes Reference" earlier in this appendix.

VALIGN   This attribute specifies the vertical alignment of the contents of the cells within the column group.

WIDTH   This attribute specifies a default width for each column and its cells in the current column group. In addition to the standard pixel and percentage values, this attribute may take the special form **0***, which means that the width of each column in the group should be the minimum width necessary to hold the column's contents.

EVENT HANDLERS   See "Events Reference" earlier in this appendix.

Examples

```
<COLGROUP SPAN="10" ALIGN="CHAR" CHAR=":" VALIGN="CENTER">


<COLGROUP STYLE="{background: yellow}">
<COL ALIGN="LEFT">
<COL ALIGN="CENTER">
</COLGROUP>
```

COMPATIBILITY   W3C 4.0; Internet Explorer 4.0

Notes

According to documentation, Internet Explorer 4.0 does not support the following attributes: **CHAR, CHAROFF, DIR, LANG, onclick, ondblclick, onkeydown, onkeypress, onkeyup, onmousedown, onmousemove, onmouseover, onmouseout,** and **onmouseup**. It does not support the **JUSTIFY** and **CHAR** values for **ALIGN**.

Each column group defined by a **<COLGROUP>** may contain zero or more **<COL>** elements.

<COMMENT>

DESCRIPTION   This nonstandard element treats enclosed text as nondisplaying comments while processing enclosed HTML. This element should not be used.

Syntax

```
<COMMENT
     ID=unique alphanumeric identifier  (IE 4.0)
     LANG=language code  (IE 4.0)
     TITLE=advisory text>  (IE 4.0)

     Commented information

</COMMENT>
```

Attributes

ID   See "Core Attributes Reference" earlier in this appendix.

LANG   See "Language Reference" earlier in this appendix.

TITLE   See "Core Attributes Reference" earlier in this appendix.

EVENT HANDLERS   None.

Example

```
<COMMENT>This is not the proper way to form comments.</COMMENT>
```

COMPATIBILITY   Internet Explorer 4.0; WebTV

Notes

It is better to use the **<!-- -->** element, an alternate comment element that does not process enclosed HTML in all specification-conforming browsers.

Because the **<COMMENT>** element is not supported by all browsers, commented text done in this fashion will appear in Netscape browsers.

While some notes indicate that the **<COMMENT>** element will render HTML included within it, in practice this does not seem to be the case.

<DD>   (Definition in a Definition List)

DESCRIPTION   This element indicates the definition of a term within a list of defined terms **<DT>** enclosed by a definition list **<DL>**.

Syntax

```
<DD
     CLASS=class name(s)
     DIR=LTR | RTL
```

```
ID=unique alphanumeric identifier
LANG=language code
LANGUAGE=JAVASCRIPT | JSCRIPT | VBSCRIPT | VBS    (IE 4.0)
STYLE=style information
TITLE=advisory text

onclick="script"
ondblclick="script"
ondragstart="script"   (IE 4.0)
onhelp="script"    (IE 4.0)
onkeydown="script"
onkeypress="script"
onkeyup="script"
onmousedown="script"
onmousemove="script"
onmouseout="script"
onmouseover="script"
onmouseup="script"
onselectstart="script">    (IE 4.0)
```

`</DD>`

Attributes

CLASS   See "Core Attributes Reference" earlier in this appendix.

DIR   See "Language Reference" earlier in this appendix.

ID   See "Core Attributes Reference" earlier in this appendix.

LANG   See "Language Reference" earlier in this appendix.

LANGUAGE   This attribute specifies the language the current script is written in and invokes the proper scripting engine. The default value is **JAVASCRIPT**. **JAVASCRIPT** and **JSCRIPT** represent that the scripting language is written in JavaScript. **VBS** and **VBSCRIPT** represent that the scripting language is written in VBScript.

STYLE   See "Core Attributes Reference" earlier in this appendix.

TITLE   See "Core Attributes Reference" earlier in this appendix.

EVENT HANDLERS   See "Events Reference" earlier in this appendix.

Examples

```
<DL>
    <DT>HOE
```

```
<DD>A garden tool used to remove weeds and till the soil.
    <DT>RAKE
<DD>A garden tool used to gather leaves and rubbish.
</DL>
```

COMPATIBILITY   W3C 2.0, 3.2, 4.0; Netscape 1.x, 2.x, 3.x, 4.x; Internet Explorer 2.x, 3.x, 4.x; and WebTV

Notes

The close tag for this element is optional, though encouraged when it will help make the list more understandable.

This element occurs within a list of defined terms enclosed by the **<DL>** element. Typically associated with it is the term it defines, indicated by the **<DT>** element that just precedes it.

According to documentation, Internet Explorer 4.0 does not support the **DIR** attribute.

Netscape 4.0 does not support the following attributes: **DIR**, **TITLE**, **onclick**, **ondblclick**, **onkeydown**, **onkeypress**, **onkeyup**, **onmousedown**, **onmousemove**, **onmouseover**, **onmouseout**, and **onmouseup**.

WebTV does not support any attributes for this element.

HTML 3.2 and 2.0 define no attributes for this element.

<DEL>   (Deleted Text)

DESCRIPTION   This element is used to indicate that text has been deleted from a document. A browser may render deleted text as strikethrough text.

Syntax

```
<DEL>
    CITE=URL
    CLASS=class name(s)
    DATETIME=date
    DIR=LTR | RTL
    ID=unique alphanumeric identifier
    LANG=language code
    LANGUAGE=JAVASCRIPT | JSCRIPT | VBSCRIPT | VBS    (IE 4.0)
    STYLE=style information
    TITLE=advisory text

    onclick="script"
    ondblclick="script"
    ondragstart="script"    (IE 4.0)
    onhelp="script"    (IE 4.0)
    onkeydown="script"
    onkeypress="script"
    onkeyup="script"
    onmousedown="script"
```

```
        onmousemove="script"
        onmouseout="script"
        onmouseover="script"
        onmouseup="script">

</DEL>
```

Attributes

CITE   The value of this attribute is a URL that designates a source document or message that may give a reason why the information was deleted.

CLASS   See "Core Attributes Reference" earlier in this appendix.

DATETIME   This attribute is used to indicate the date and time the deletion was made. The value of the attribute is a date in a special format as defined by ISO 8601. The basic date format is

```
YYYY-MM-DDThh:mm:ssTZD
```

where the following is true:

```
YYYY=four-digit year such as 1997
 MM=two-digit month (01=January, 02=February, and so on.)
 DD=two-digit day of the month (01 through 31)
 hh=two digit hour (00 to 23) (24 hour clock, not AM or PM)
 mm=two digit minute (00 through 59)
 ss=two digit second (00 through 59)
TZD=time zone designator
```

The time zone designator is either **Z**, which indicates UTC (Coordinated Universal Time), or **+hh:mm**, which indicates that the time is a local time that is *hh* hours and *mm* minutes ahead of UTC. Alternatively, the format for the time zone designator could be **-hh:mm**, which indicates that the local time is behind UTC. Note that the letter T actually appears in the string, all digits must be used, and **00** values for minutes and seconds may be required. An example value for the **DATETIME** attribute might be **1997-10-6T09:15:00-05:00**, which corresponds to October 6, 1997, 9:15 A.M., U.S. Eastern Standard Time.

DIR   See "Language Reference" earlier in this appendix.

ID   See "Core Attributes Reference" earlier in this appendix.

LANG   See "Language Reference" earlier in this appendix.

LANGUAGE   In the Microsoft implementation, this attribute specifies the scripting language to be used with an associated script bound to the element, typically through an event handler

attribute. Possible values may include **JAVASCRIPT, JSCRIPT, VBSCRIPT,** and **VBS**. Other values that include the version of the language used, such as JavaScript 1.1, may also be possible.

STYLE   See "Core Attributes Reference" earlier in this appendix.

TITLE   See "Core Attributes Reference" earlier in this appendix.

EVENT HANDLERS   See "Events Reference" earlier in this appendix.

Example

```
<DEL CITE="http://www.bigcompany.com/changes/oct97.htm"
    DATETIME="1997-10-06T09:15:00-05:00">
    The penalty clause applies to client lateness as well.
</DEL>
```

COMPATIBILITY   W3C 4.0; Internet Explorer 4.x

Notes

Browsers may render deleted **<DEL>** text in a different style to show the changes that have been made to the document. Internet Explorer 4.0 renders the text as strikethrough text. Eventually a browser may have a way to show a revision history on a document. User agents that do not understand **<INS>** or **<DEL>** will show the information anyway, so there is no harm in adding information—only in deleting it. Because of the fact that **<DEL>** enclosed text may show up, it may be wise to comment it out within the element as shown here:

```
<DEL>
<!-- This is old information -->
</DEL>
```

The **<DEL>** element is not supported under HTML 3.2 and HTML 2.0 specifications.

<DFN>   (Defining Instance of a Term)

DESCRIPTION   This element encloses the defining instance of a term. It is usually rendered as bold or bold italic text.

Syntax

```
<DFN
    CLASS=class name(s)
    DIR=LTR | RTL
    ID=unique alphanumeric identifier
    LANG=language code
    LANGUAGE=JAVASCRIPT | JSCRIPT | VBSCRIPT | VBS    (IE 4.0)
    STYLE=style information
```

```
TITLE=advisory text

onclick="script"
ondblclick="script"
ondragstart="script"   (IE 4.0)
onhelp="script"   (IE 4.0)
onkeydown="script"
onkeypress="script"
onkeyup="script"
onmousedown="script"
onmousemove="script"
onmouseout="script"
onmouseover="script"
onmouseup="script"
onselectstart="script">   (IE 4.0)

</DFN>
```

Attributes

CLASS   See "Core Attributes Reference" earlier in this appendix.

DIR   See "Language Reference" earlier in this appendix.

ID   See "Core Attributes Reference" earlier in this appendix.

LANG   See "Language Reference" earlier in this appendix.

LANGUAGE   This attribute specifies the language the current script is written in and invokes the proper scripting engine. The default value is **JAVASCRIPT**. **JAVASCRIPT** and **JSCRIPT** represent that the scripting language is written in JavaScript. **VBS** and **VBSCRIPT** represent that the scripting language is written in VBScript.

STYLE   See "Core Attributes Reference" earlier in this appendix.

TITLE   See "Core Attributes Reference" earlier in this appendix.

EVENT HANDLERS   See "Events Reference" earlier in this appendix.

Example

```
A <DFN>microsite</DFN> is a small Web site generally built for a specific purpose.
```

COMPATIBILITY   W3C 2.0, 3.2, 4.0; Netscape 1.x, 2.x, 3.x, 4.x; Internet Explorer 2.x, 3.x, 4.x; and WebTV

Notes

According to documentation, Internet Explorer 4.0 does not support the **DIR** attribute.
Netscape 4.0 does not support the following attributes: **DIR, TITLE, onclick, ondblclick,
onkeydown, onkeypress, onkeyup, onmousedown, onmousemove, onmouseover,
onmouseout,** and **onmouseup.**
WebTV does not support any attributes for this element.
HTML 3.2 and 2.0 define no attributes for this element.

<DIR> (Directory List)

DESCRIPTION   This element encloses a list of brief, unordered items, such as might occur in
a menu or directory. The individual items are indicated by the **<LI>** element. Use of this element
is not encouraged, as it is not part of the HTML 4.0 strict specification and provides little extra
benefit over the **<UL>** element.

Syntax

```
<DIR
     CLASS=class name(s)
     COMPACT
     DIR=LTR | RTL
     ID=unique alphanumeric identifier
     LANG=language code
     LANGUAGE=JAVASCRIPT | JSCRIPT | VBSCRIPT | VBS    (IE 4.0)
     STYLE=style information
     TITLE=advisory text

     onclick="script"
     ondblclick="script"
     ondragstart="script"    (IE 4.0)
     onhelp="script"    (IE 4.0)
     onkeydown="script"
     onkeypress="script"
     onkeyup="script"
     onmousedown="script"
     onmousemove="script"
     onmouseout="script"
     onmouseover="script"
     onmouseup="script"
     onselectstart="script">    (IE 4.0)

</DIR>
```

Attributes

COMPACT   This attribute reduces the white space between list items.

CLASS   See "Core Attributes Reference" earlier in this appendix.

DIR   See "Language Reference" earlier in this appendix.

ID   See "Core Attributes Reference" earlier in this appendix.

LANG   See "Language Reference" earlier in this appendix.

LANGUAGE   This attribute specifies the language the current script is written in and invokes the proper scripting engine. The default value is **JAVASCRIPT**. **JAVASCRIPT** and **JSCRIPT** represent that the scripting language is written in JavaScript. **VBS** and **VBSCRIPT** represent that the scripting language is written in VBScript.

STYLE   See "Core Attributes Reference" earlier in this appendix.

TITLE   See "Core Attributes Reference" earlier in this appendix.

EVENT HANDLERS   See "Events Reference" earlier in this appendix.

Example

```
<DIR>
<LI>Header Files
<LI>Code Files
<LI>Comment Files
</DIR>
```

COMPATIBILITY   W3C 2.0, 3.2, 4.0 (transitional); Netscape 1.x, 2.x, 3.x, 4.x; Internet Explorer 2.x, 3.x, 4.x; and WebTV

Notes

Because the **<DIR>** element is supposed to be used with short lists, the items in the list should have a maximum width of 20 characters.

The HTML 4.0 strict specification does not support this element.

Many browsers will not render the **<DIR>** element any differently than the **<UL>** element.

Many browsers will not render the **COMPACT** list style.

According to Microsoft documentation, Internet Explorer 4.0 does not support the **COMPACT** and **DIR** attributes.

Netscape 4.0 does not support the following attributes: **COMPACT, DIR, TITLE, onclick, ondblclick, onkeydown, onkeypress, onkeyup, onmousedown, onmousemove, onmouseover, onmouseout,** and **onmouseup**.

WebTV does not support any attributes for this element.

HTML 3.2 and 2.0 support only the **COMPACT** attribute.

<DIV>   (Division)

DESCRIPTION   This element indicates a block of document content that should be treated as a logical unit.

Syntax

```
<DIV
      ALIGN=LEFT | CENTER | RIGHT | JUSTIFY
      CHARSET= character set
      CLASS=class name(s)
      DATAFLD=name of column supplying bound data    (IE 4.0)*
      DATAFORMATAS=HTML | text    (IE 4.0)*
      DATASRC=id of data source object supplying data    (IE 4.0)*
      DIR=LTR | RTL
      HREF= URL of linked content
      HREFLANG= Language code for linked content
      ID=unique alphanumeric identifier
      LANG=language code
      LANGUAGE=JAVASCRIPT | JSCRIPT | VBSCRIPT | VBS    (IE 4.0)
      MEDIA= Media descriptor
      REL=comma-separated list of relationship values
      REV=comma-separated list of relationship values
      STYLE=style information
      TARGET=_blank | _parent | _self | _top | frame-name
      TITLE=advisory text
      TYPE= MIME type

      onafterupdate="script"    (IE 4.0)
      onbeforeupdate="script"    (IE 4.0)
      onblur="script"    (IE 4.0)
      onclick="script"
      ondblclick="script"
      ondragstart="script"    (IE 4.0)
      onfocus="script"    (IE 4.0)
      onhelp="script"    (IE 4.0)
      onkeydown="script"
      onkeypress="script"
      onkeyup="script"
      onmousedown="script"
      onmousemove="script"
      onmouseout="script"
      onmouseover="script"
      onmouseup="script"
      onresize="script"    (IE 4.0)
      onrowenter="script"    (IE 4.0)
      onrowexit="script"    (IE 4.0)
      onscroll="script"    (IE 4.0)
      onselectstart="script">    (IE 4.0)

</DIV>
```

*These attributes are reserved under the HTML 4.0 specification and may become part of the standard.

Attributes

ALIGN   This attribute indicates how the tagged text should be horizontally aligned on the page. The default value is **LEFT**. The **JUSTIFY** value is supported only by the Microsoft implementation.

CHARSET   This attribute defines the character encoding of the linked resource specified by the **HREF** attribute. The value is a space- and/or comma-delimited list of character sets as defined in RFC 2045. The default value is ISO-8859-1.

CLASS   See "Core Attributes Reference" earlier in this appendix.

DATAFLD   This attribute specifies the column name from the data source object that supplies the bound data.

DATAFORMATS   This attribute indicates whether the bound data is plain text or HTML.

DATASRC   This attribute indicates the **ID** of the data source object that supplies the data that is bound to this element.

DIR   See "Language Reference" earlier in this appendix.

HREF   This attribute is used to specify the URL of a resource that provides more information about the content enclosed by the **<DIV>** element.

HREFLANG   This attribute is used to indicate the language of the linked resource. See "Language Reference" earlier in this appendix for information on allowed values.

ID   See "Core Attributes Reference" earlier in this appendix.

LANG   See "Language Reference" earlier in this appendix.

LANGUAGE   This attribute specifies the language the current script is written in and invokes the proper scripting engine. The default value is **JAVASCRIPT**. **JAVASCRIPT** and **JSCRIPT** represent that the scripting language is written in JavaScript. **VBS** and **VBSCRIPT** represent that the scripting language is written in VBScript.

MEDIA   This attribute is used to specify the destination medium for any linked information, particularly when the **REL** attribute is set to **STYLESHEET**. The value of the attribute may be a single media descriptor like **SCREEN**, or a comma-separated list. Possible values for this attribute include **SCREEN, PRINT, PROJECTION, BRAILLE, AURAL**, and **ALL**. Other values may also be defined, depending on the browser. This attribute was added very late to the HTML 4.0 specification, and its meaning with the **<DIV>** element is far from clear. Furthermore, this attribute is not yet supported by any browser.

REL   For anchors containing the **HREF** attribute, this attribute specifies the relationship of the target object to the link object. The value is a comma-separated list of relationship values. The values and their semantics will be registered by some authority, which may have meaning to the document author. The default relationship, if no other is given, is **void**. The **REL** attribute should be used only when the **HREF** attribute is present.

REV   This attribute specifies a reverse link, the inverse relationship of the **REL** attribute. It is useful for indicating where an object came from, such as the author or a document.

STYLE   See "Core Attributes Reference" earlier in this appendix.

TARGET   This attribute specifies the target window for a hypertext source link referencing frames. The information linked to will be displayed in the named window. Frames must be named to be targeted. There are, however, special name values, including **_blank**, which indicates a new window; **_parent**, which indicates the parent frame set containing the source link; **_self**, which indicates the frame containing the source link; and **_top**, which indicates the full browser window. This attribute was added very late to the HTML 4.0 specification; its meaning is unclear, and the attribute is not supported by any known browser.

TITLE   See "Core Attributes Reference" earlier in this appendix.

TYPE   This attribute specifies the media type in the form of a MIME type of the linked content. Generally this is provided strictly as advisory information; however, in the future a browser may add a small icon for multimedia types. For example, a browser might add a small speaker icon when **TYPE** is set to audio/wav.

EVENT HANDLERS   See "Events Reference" earlier in this appendix.

Examples

```
<DIV ALIGN="JUSTIFY">
  All text within this division will be justified
</DIV>


<DIV CLASS="special" ID="div1" STYLE="{background: yellow}">
Get ready to animate and stylize this.
</DIV>
```

COMPATIBILITY   W3C 3.2, 4.0; Netscape 2.x, 3.x, 4.x; Internet Explorer 2.x, 3.x, 4.x; and WebTV

Notes
Many users are confused by the proper use of the **<DIV>** element, since all it does is create a block element. It is very useful for binding scripts or styles to an arbitrary section of a document. In this sense, **<DIV>** complements **<SPAN>**, which is used inline.
The attributes **CHARSET**, **HREF**, **HREFLANG**, **MEDIA**, **REL**, **REV**, **TARGET**, and **TYPE** for **<DIV>** were added to the HTML 4.0 specification just before the final draft was released. The meaning of these attributes is not well documented. Since no browsers support them at the time of this writing, it is difficult to determine how or even if they will be used.
The HTML 4.0 specification specifies that **DATASRC**, **DATAFLD**, and **DATAFORMATS** are reserved attributes for **<DIV>** and may be supported in the future.
Under the strict specification of HTML 4.0, the **ALIGN** attribute is not supported.
Internet Explorer 4.0 does not support the **DIR** attribute.

Netscape 4.0 does not support the following attributes: **DIR, TITLE, onclick, ondblclick, onkeydown, onkeypress, onkeyup, onmousedown, onmousemove, onmouseover, onmouseout,** and **onmouseup.**

WebTV does not support the following attributes: **CLASS, DIR, ID, LANG, STYLE, TITLE, onclick, ondblclick, onkeydown, onkeypress, onkeyup, onmousedown, onmousemove, onmouseover, onmouseout,** and **onmouseup.**

HTML 3.2 supports only the **ALIGN** attribute.

<DL>   (Definition List)

DESCRIPTION   This element encloses a list of terms and definition pairs. A common use for this element is to implement a glossary.

Syntax

```
<DL
     CLASS=class name(s)
     COMPACT
     DIR=LTR | RTL
     ID=unique alphanumeric identifier
     LANG=language code
     LANGUAGE=JAVASCRIPT | JSCRIPT | VBSCRIPT | VBS    (IE 4.0)
     STYLE=style information
     TITLE=advisory text

     onclick="script"
     ondblclick="script"
     ondragstart="script" (IE 4.0)
     onhelp="script"    (IE 4.0)
     onkeydown="script"
     onkeypress="script"
     onkeyup="script"
     onmousedown="script"
     onmousemove="script"
     onmouseout="script"
     onmouseover="script"
     onmouseup="script"
     onselectstart="script">    (IE 4.0)

</DL>
```

Attributes

CLASS   See "Core Attributes Reference" earlier in this appendix.

COMPACT   This attribute reduces the white space between list items.

DIR   See "Language Reference" earlier in this appendix.

ID   See "Core Attributes Reference" earlier in this appendix.

LANG   See "Language Reference" earlier in this appendix.

LANGUAGE   This attribute specifies the language the current script is written in and invokes the proper scripting engine. The default value is **JAVASCRIPT**. **JAVASCRIPT** and **JSCRIPT** represent that the scripting language is written in JavaScript. **VBS** and **VBSCRIPT** represent that the scripting language is written in VBScript.

STYLE   See "Core Attributes Reference" earlier in this appendix.

TITLE   See "Core Attributes Reference" earlier in this appendix.

EVENT HANDLERS   See "Events Reference" earlier in this appendix.

Example

```
<DL>
<DT>Rake</DT>
<DD>A garden tool used to gather leaves and rubbish.</DD>
<DT>Trowel</DT>
<DD>A small garden tool used to shovel earth.</DD>
</DL>
```

COMPATIBILITY   W3C 2.0, 3.2, 4.0; Netscape 1.x, 2.x, 3.x, 4.x; Internet Explorer 2.x, 3.x, 4.x; and WebTV

Notes

The items in the list comprise two parts: the term, indicated by the **<DT>** element, and its definition, indicated by the **<DD>** element.

Some page designers may use the **<DL>** element or **<UL>** element to help create text indent. While this is a common practice on the Web, it is not advisable because it confuses the meaning of the element by making it a physical layout device rather than a list.

Under the strict HTML 4.0 definition, the **COMPACT** attribute is not allowed.

According to documentation, Internet Explorer 4.0 does not support the following attributes: **DIR**, **onkeydown**, **onkeypress**, and **onkeyup**. The lack of events is probably an oversight and the browser may support the event attributes.

Netscape 4.0 does not support the following attributes: **DIR**, **TITLE**, **onclick**, **ondblclick**, **onkeydown**, **onkeypress**, **onkeyup**, **onmousedown**, **onmousemove**, **onmouseover**, **onmouseout**, and **onmouseup**.

WebTV does not support any attributes for this element.

HTML 2.0 and 3.2 support only the **COMPACT** attribute for this element.

<DT>   (Term in a Definition List)

DESCRIPTION   This element indicates the term associated with a definition in a definition list term-definition pair.

Syntax

```
<DT
    CLASS=class name(s)
    DIR=LTR | RTL
    ID=unique alphanumeric identifier
    LANG=language code
    LANGUAGE=JAVASCRIPT | JSCRIPT | VBSCRIPT | VBS    (IE 4.0)
    STYLE=style information
    TITLE=advisory text

    onclick="script"
    ondblclick="script"
    ondragstart="script"   (IE 4.0)
    onhelp="script"    (IE 4.0)
    onkeydown="script"
    onkeypress="script"
    onkeyup="script"
    onmousedown="script"
    onmousemove="script"
    onmouseout="script"
    onmouseover="script"
    onmouseup="script"
    onselectstart="script">   (IE 4.0)
```

Attributes

CLASS   See "Core Attributes Reference" earlier in this appendix.

DIR   See "Language Reference" earlier in this appendix.

ID   See "Core Attributes Reference" earlier in this appendix.

LANG   See "Language Reference" earlier in this appendix.

LANGUAGE   This attribute specifies the language the current script is written in and invokes the proper scripting engine. The default value is **JAVASCRIPT**. **JAVASCRIPT** and **JSCRIPT** represent that the scripting language is written in JavaScript. **VBS** and **VBSCRIPT** represent that the scripting language is written in VBScript.

STYLE   See "Core Attributes Reference" earlier in this appendix.

TITLE   See "Core Attributes Reference" earlier in this appendix.

EVENT HANDLERS   See "Events Reference" earlier in this appendix.

Examples

```
<DL>

<DT>Rake</DT>
<DD>A garden tool used to gather leaves and rubbish.</DD>

<DT>Trowel</DT>
<DD>A small garden tool used to shovel earth.</DD>

</DL>
```

COMPATIBILITY   W3C 2.0, 3.2, 4.0; Netscape 1.x, 2.x, 3.x, 4.x; Internet Explorer 2.x, 3.x, 4.x; and WebTV

Notes

This element occurs within a list of defined terms enclosed by the **<DL>** element. It is generally used in conjunction with the **<DD>** element, which indicates its definition. However, **<DT>** elements do not require a one-to-one correspondence with **<DD>** elements.

The close tag for the element is optional but suggested when it will make things more clear, particularly with multiple-line definitions.

According to documentation, Internet Explorer 4.0 does not support the **DIR** attribute.

Netscape 4.0 does not support the following attributes: **DIR**, **TITLE**, **onclick**, **ondblclick**, **onkeydown**, **onkeypress**, **onkeyup**, **onmousedown**, **onmousemove**, **onmouseover**, **onmouseout**, and **onmouseup**.

WebTV does not support any attributes for **<DT>**.

HTML 2.0 and 3.2 support no attributes for this element.

<EM>   (Emphasis)

DESCRIPTION   This element indicates emphasized text, which many browsers will display as italic text.

Syntax

```
<EM
     CLASS=class name(s)
     DIR=LTR | RTL
     ID=unique alphanumeric identifier
     LANG=language code
     LANGUAGE=JAVASCRIPT | JSCRIPT | VBSCRIPT | VBS    (IE 4.0)
     STYLE=style information
     TITLE=advisory text

     onclick="script"
     ondblclick="script"
```

```
        ondragstart="script"   (IE 4.0)
        onhelp="script"   (IE 4.0)
        onkeydown="script"
        onkeypress="script"
        onkeyup="script"
        onmousedown="script"
        onmousemove="script"
        onmouseout="script"
        onmouseover="script"
        onmouseup="script"
        onselectstart="script">   (IE 4.0)

</EM>
```

Attributes

CLASS   See "Core Attributes Reference" earlier in this appendix.

DIR   See "Language Reference" earlier in this appendix.

ID   See "Core Attributes Reference" earlier in this appendix.

LANG   See "Language Reference" earlier in this appendix.

LANGUAGE   This attribute specifies the language the current script is written in and invokes the proper scripting engine. The default value is **JAVASCRIPT**. **JAVASCRIPT** and **JSCRIPT** represent that the scripting language is written in JavaScript. **VBS** and **VBSCRIPT** represent that the scripting language is written in VBScript.

STYLE   See "Core Attributes Reference" earlier in this appendix.

TITLE   See "Core Attributes Reference" earlier in this appendix.

EVENT HANDLERS   See "Events Reference" earlier in this appendix.

Example

```
Here is an <EM>important point</EM> to consider.
```

COMPATIBILITY   W3C 2.0, 3.2, 4.0; Netscape 1.x, 2.x, 3.x, 4.x; Internet Explorer 2.x, 3.x, 4.x; and WebTV

Notes

As a logical element, **<EM>** is a prime candidate to bind style information to. For example, to define emphasis to mean a larger font in Impact, you might use a CSS rule like

```
EM{font-size: larger; font-family: Impact;}
```

in a document-wide style sheet.

According to documentation, Internet Explorer 4.0 does not support the **DIR** attribute. Netscape 4.0 does not support the following attributes: **DIR, TITLE, onclick, ondblclick, onkeydown, onkeypress, onkeyup, onmousedown, onmousemove, onmouseover, onmouseout,** and **onmouseup**.

WebTV does not support any attributes for this element.

HTML 2.0 and 3.2 support no attributes for this element.

<EMBED>   (Embedded Object)

DESCRIPTION   This widely supported but nonstandard element specifies an object, typically a multimedia element, to be embedded in an HTML document.

Syntax

```
<EMBED
      ALIGN=ABSBOTTOM | ABSMIDDLE | BASELINE | BOTTOM | LEFT |
            MIDDLE | RIGHT | TEXTTOP | TOP
      ALT=alternative text   (IE 4.0)
      BORDER=pixels    (N 4.0, WebTV)
      CLASS=class name(s)    (IE 4.0, N 4.0)
      CODE=file name    (IE 4.0)
      CODEBASE=URL    (IE 4.0)
      HEIGHT=pixels    (IE 4.0, N 4.0, WebTV)
      HIDDEN=TRUE|FALSE    (N 4.0, WebTV)
      HSPACE=pixels    (IE 4.0, N 4.0, WebTV)
      ID=unique alphanumeric identifier   (IE 4.0, N 4.0)
      NAME=string    (IE 4.0, N 4.0, WebTV)
      PALETTE=BACKGROUND|FOREGROUND    (N 4.0)
      PLUGINSPAGE=URL    (N 4.0)
      SRC=URL    (IE 4.0, N 4.0,     (WebTV))
      STYLE=style information   (IE 4.0, N 4.0)
      TITLE=advisory text    (IE 4.0)
      TYPE=MIME Type    (N 4.0)
      UNITS=en | pixels    (IE 4.0, N 4.0)
      VSPACE=pixels    (IE 4.0, N 4.0, WebTV)
      WIDTH=pixels>    (IE 4.0, N 4.0, WebTV)

</EMBED>
```

Attributes

ALIGN   This attribute controls the alignment of adjacent text with respect to the embedded object. The default value is **LEFT**.

ALT   This attribute indicates the text to be displayed if the applet cannot be executed.

BORDER   This attribute specifies the size in pixels of the border around the embedded object.

CLASS   See "Core Attributes Reference" earlier in this appendix.

CODE   The name of the file containing the compiled Java class if the **<EMBED>** element is used to include a Java applet. This is a strange alternate form of Java inclusion documented by Microsoft.

CODEBASE   This specifies the base URL for the plug-in or potential applet in the case of the alternative form under Internet Explorer.

HEIGHT   The attribute sets the height in pixels of the embedded object.

HIDDEN   If this attribute is set to the value **TRUE**, the embedded object is not visible on the page and implicitly has a size of zero.

HSPACE   This attribute specifies in pixels the size of the left and right margin between the embedded object and surrounding text.

ID   See "Core Attributes Reference" earlier in this appendix.

NAME   This attribute specifies a name for the embedded object, which can be referenced by client-side programs in an embedded scripting language.

PALETTE   This attribute is used only on Windows systems to select the color palette used for the plug-in and may be set to **FOREGROUND** or **BACKGROUND**. The default is **BACKGROUND**.

PLUGINSPAGE   This attribute contains the URL of instructions for installing the plug-in required to render the embedded object.

SRC   This attribute specifies the URL of source content for embedded object.

STYLE   See "Core Attributes Reference" earlier in this appendix.

TITLE   See "Core Attributes Reference" earlier in this appendix.

TYPE   This attribute specifies the MIME type of the embedded object. It is used by the browser to determine an appropriate plug-in for rendering the object. It can be used instead of the **SRC** attribute for plug-ins that have no content or that fetch it dynamically.

UNITS   This Netscape-specific attribute is used to set the units for measurement for the embedded object either in **EM** or in the default, **PIXELS**.

VSPACE   This attribute specifies in pixels the size of the top and bottom margin between the embedded object and surrounding text.

WIDTH   This attribute sets the width in pixels of the embedded attribute.

EVENT HANDLERS   See "Events Reference" earlier in this appendix.

HTML ELEMENT
REFERENCE

Examples

```
<!-- EMBED without a close tag -->
<EMBED SRC="testmovie.mov" HEIGHT="150" WIDTH="150">
<NOEMBED>
<IMG SRC="testgif.gif" HEIGHT="150" WIDTH="150" ALT="Test Image">
</NOEMBED>


<!-- EMBED with a close tag -->
<EMBED SRC="testmovie.mov" HEIGHT="150" WIDTH="150">
<NOEMBED>
<IMG SRC="testgif.gif" HEIGHT="150" WIDTH="150" ALT="Test Image">
</NOEMBED>
</EMBED>
```

COMPATIBILITY   Netscape 2.x, 3.x, 4.x; Internet Explorer 3.x, 4.x; and WebTV

Notes

It is unclear whether or not the close tag for **<EMBED>** is required. Many sites tend not to use it, and documentation is not consistent. Some people claim that a close tag is required and should surround any alternative content in a **<NOEMBED>** element; others do not use a close tag. Since this element should eventually be phased out in favor of **<OBJECT>**, this may be a moot issue. While WebTV may support the **<EMBED>** element, it can deal only with media types the equipment knows how to handle, such as Macromedia Flash or certain standard audio files. Other plug-ins cannot be added to the system.

The **<EMBED>** element is not favored by the W3C and is not part of any official HTML specification; however, it is very common. The HTML specification says to use the **<OBJECT>** element, which can be used in conjunction with the **<EMBED>** element to provide backward compatibility.

Embedded objects are multimedia content files of arbitrary type, which are rendered by browser plug-ins. The **TYPE** attribute uses a file's MIME type to determine an appropriate browser plug-in. Any attributes not defined are treated as object-specific parameters and passed through to the embedded object. Consult the plug-in or object documentation to determine these. The standard parameters supported by the Microsoft implementation are **HEIGHT**, **NAME**, **PALETTE**, **SRC**, **UNITS**, and **WIDTH**.

<FIELDSET>   (Form Field Set)

DESCRIPTION   This element allows form designers to group thematically related controls together.

Syntax

```
<FIELDSET
    ALIGN=CENTER | LEFT | RIGHT    (IE 4.0)
    CLASS=class name(s)
```

```
DIR=LTR | RTL
ID=unique alphanumeric identifier
LANG=language code
LANGUAGE=JAVASCRIPT | JSCRIPT | VBSCRIPT | VBS    (IE 4.0)
STYLE=style information
TITLE=advisory text

onblur="script"    (IE 4.0)
onchange="script"    (IE 4.0)
onclick="script"
ondblclick="script"
ondragstart="script"    (IE 4.0)
onhelp="script"    (IE 4.0)
onkeydown="script"
onkeypress="script"
onkeyup="script"
onmousedown="script"
onmousemove="script"
onmouseout="script"
onmouseover="script"
onmouseup="script"
onresize="script"    (IE 4.0)
onscroll="script"    (IE 4.0)
onselect="script"    (IE 4.0)
onselectstart="script">    (IE 4.0)

</FIELDSET>
```

Attributes

ALIGN   Internet Explorer defines the **ALIGN** attribute, which sets how the element and its contents are positioned in a table or the window.

CLASS   See "Core Attributes Reference" earlier in this appendix.

DIR   See "Language Reference" earlier in this appendix.

ID   See "Core Attributes Reference" earlier in this appendix.

LANG   See "Language Reference" earlier in this appendix.

LANGUAGE   This attribute specifies the language the current script is written in and invokes the proper scripting engine. The default value is **JAVASCRIPT**. **JAVASCRIPT** and **JSCRIPT** represent that the scripting language is written in JavaScript. **VBS** and **VBSCRIPT** represent that the scripting language is written in VBScript.

STYLE   See "Core Attributes Reference" earlier in this appendix.

TITLE   See "Core Attributes Reference" earlier in this appendix.

EVENT HANDLERS   See "Events Reference" earlier in this appendix.

Example

```
<FIELDSET>
<LEGEND>Customer Identification</LEGEND>
<BR>
<LABEL>Customer Name:
<INPUT TYPE="TEXT" ID="CustName" SIZE="25">
</FIELDSET>
```

COMPATIBILITY   W3C 4.0; Internet Explorer 4.0

Notes

Grouping controls makes it easier for users to understand controls' purposes, while simultaneously facilitating tabbing navigation for visual user agents and speech navigation for speech-oriented user agents. The proper use of this element makes documents more accessible to people with disabilities.

The caption for this element is defined by the **<LEGEND>** element within the **<FIELDSET>** element.

Internet Explorer 4.0 does not support the **DIR** attribute.

<FN>   (Footnote)

DESCRIPTION   This WebTV-specific element indicates either a reference to a footnote or the footnote itself.

Syntax

```
<FN
    HREF=URL      (WebTV)
    ID=unique alphanumeric identifier>   (WebTV)
</FN>
```

Attributes

HREF   This attribute contains a URL that references the footnote. Typically the URL is a fragment in the form of the # symbol followed by the name of the footnote anchor. It indicates that the tagged text is a reference to a footnote.

ID   This attribute contains the name of the footnote anchor. It indicates that the tagged text is a footnote.

EVENT HANDLERS   None.

Examples

```
This wonderful idea came from <FN HREF="#smith">Smith</FN>

<FN ID="smith">Smith, Fred, Journal of Really Good Ideas</FN>
```

COMPATIBILITY   WebTV

Notes

Footnotes are implemented as internal links within a document. Use the **HREF** attribute to indicate a reference to a footnote. Use the **ID** attribute to indicate the footnote itself. Footnotes are not to be used outside the WebTV environment. They are a leftover of the failed HTML 3.0 proposal.

<FONT>

DESCRIPTION   This element allows specification of the size, color, and font of the text it encloses. Use of this element is not encouraged as it is not part of the HTML 4.0 strict specification, and style sheets provide a cleaner way of providing the same functionality when they are supported.

Syntax

```
<FONT
    CLASS=class name(s)
    COLOR=#RRGGBB | color name
    DIR=LTR | RTL
    EFFECT=RELIEF | EMBOSS | SHADOW    (WebTV)
    FACE=font name
    ID=unique alphanumeric identifier
    LANG=language code
    LANGUAGE=JAVASCRIPT | JSCRIPT | VBSCRIPT | VBS    (IE 4.0)
    POINT-SIZE=point size for font    (N 4.0)
    SIZE=1 to 7 |  +1 to +6 | -1 to -6
    STYLE=style information
    TITLE=advisory text
    TRANSPARENCY=0 to 100    (WebTV)
    WEIGHT=100 | 200 | 300 | 400 | 500 | 600 | 700 |
           800 | 900 (N 4.0)

    onclick="script"    (IE 4.0)
    ondblclick="script"    (IE 4.0)
    ondragstart="script"    (IE 4.0)


    onhelp="script"    (IE 4.0)
    onkeydown="script"    (IE 4.0)
```

```
        onkeypress="script"   (IE 4.0)
        onmousedown="script"   (IE 4.0)
        onmousemove="script"   (IE 4.0)
        onmouseout="script"  (IE 4.0)
        onmouseover="script"   (IE 4.0)
        onmouseup="script"   (IE 4.0)
        onselectstart="script">  (IE 4.0)
  </FONT>
```

Attributes

CLASS   See "Core Attributes Reference" earlier in this appendix.

COLOR   This attribute sets the text color using either a browser-dependent named color or a color specified in the hexadecimal #*RRGGBB* format.

DIR   See "Language Reference" earlier in this appendix.

EFFECT   In the WebTV implementation, this attribute renders the tagged text in a special way. The **RELIEF** value causes the text to appear raised off the page. The **EMBOSS** value causes the text to appear embossed into the page.

FACE   This attribute contains a list of one or more font names separated by commas. The user agent looks through the specified font names and renders the text in the first font that is supported.

ID   See "Core Attributes Reference" earlier in this appendix.

LANG   See "Language Reference" earlier in this appendix.

LANGUAGE   This attribute specifies the language the current script is written in and invokes the proper scripting engine. The default value is **JAVASCRIPT**. **JAVASCRIPT** and **JSCRIPT** represent that the scripting language is written in JavaScript. **VBS** and **VBSCRIPT** represent that the scripting language is written in VBScript.

POINT SIZE   This Netscape 4.0-specific attribute is used to specify the point size of text and is used with downloadable fonts.

SIZE   This attribute specifies the font size as either a numeric or relative value. Numeric values range from **1** to **7** with **1** the smallest and **3** the default. The relative values, **+** and **-**, increment or decrement the font size relative to the current size. The value for increment or decrement should range only from **+1** to **+6** or **-1** to **-6**.

STYLE   See "Core Attributes Reference" earlier in this appendix.

TITLE   See "Core Attributes Reference" earlier in this appendix.

   WebTV's proprietary **TRANSPARENCY** attribute is used to set the transparency level of the text. A value of **0** indicates the text is opaque; a value of 100 indicates text is fully transparent, allowing the background to show through. The default value for this attribute is **0**.

WEIGHT   Under Netscape 4.0, this attribute specifies the weight of the font, with a value of **100** being lightest and **900** being heaviest.

EVENT HANDLERS   See "Events Reference" earlier in this appendix.

Example

```
<FONT COLOR="RED" FACE="Helvetica, Times Roman" SIZE="+1">
Relatively large red text in Helvetica or Times
</FONT>
```

COMPATIBILITY   W3C 3.2, 4.0; Netscape 1.1, 2.x, 3.x, 4.x; Internet Explorer 2.x, 3.x, 4.x; and WebTV

Notes

The default text size for a document can be set using the **SIZE** attribute of the **<BASEFONT>** element.

WebTV does not support the **FACE** attribute.

The HTML 3.2 specification supports only the **SIZE** and **COLOR** attributes for this element.

The HTML 4.0 transitional specification supports the **SIZE**, **COLOR**, **FACE**, **ID**, **CLASS**, **LANG**, **DIR**, **STYLE**, and **TITLE** attributes.

The HTML 4.0 strict specification does not support the **<FONT>** element at all.

<FORM>

DESCRIPTION   The element defines a fill-in form to contain labels and form controls, such as menus, and text entry boxes that may be filled in by a user.

Syntax

```
<FORM
     ACCEPT-CHARSET=list of supported character sets
     ACTION=URL
     CLASS=class name(s)
     DIR=LTR | RTL
     ENCTYPE=application/x-www-form-urlencoded |
             multipart/form-data | text/plain |
         Media Type as per RFC2045
     ID=unique alphanumeric identifier
     LANG=language code
     LANGUAGE=JAVASCRIPT | JSCRIPT | VBSCRIPT | VBS   (IE 4.0)
     METHOD=GET | POST

     NAME=string   (IE 4.0, N4.0)
     STYLE=style information
     TARGET=frame name | _blank | _parent | _self | _top
```

```
TITLE=advisory text

onclick="script"
ondblclick="script"
ondragstart="script"    (IE 4.0)
onhelp="script"    (IE 4.0)
onkeydown="script"
onkeypress="script"
onkeyup="script"
onmousedown="script"
onmousemove="script"
onmouseout="script"
onmouseover="script"
onmouseup="script"
onreset="script"
onselectstart="script"    (IE 4.0)
onsubmit="script">
```

```
</FORM>
```

Attributes

ACCEPT CHARSET   This attribute specifies the list of character encodings for input data that must be accepted by the server processing form. The value is a space- or comma-delimited list of character sets as defined in RFC 2045. The default value for this attribute is the reserved value **UNKNOWN**.

ACTION   This attribute contains the URL of the server program, which will process the contents of the form. Some browsers may also support a mailto URL, which may mail the results to the specified address.

CLASS   See "Core Attributes Reference" earlier in this appendix.

DIR   See "Language Reference" earlier in this appendix.

ENCTYPE   This attribute indicates how form data should be encoded before being sent to the server. The default is **application/x-www-form-urlencoded**. This encoding replaces blank characters in the data with a + and all other nonprinting characters with a % followed by the character's ASCII HEX representation. The multipart/form-data option does not perform character conversion and transfers the information as a compound MIME document. This must be used when using **<INPUT TYPE="FILE">**. It may also be possible to use another encoding like text/plain to avoid any form of hex encoding, which may be useful with mailed forms.

ID   See "Core Attributes Reference" earlier in this appendix.

LANG   See "Language Reference" earlier in this appendix.

LANGUAGE   This attribute specifies the language the current script is written in and invokes the proper scripting engine. The default value is **JAVASCRIPT**. **JAVASCRIPT** and **JSCRIPT**

represent that the scripting language is written in JavaScript. **VBS** and **VBSCRIPT** represent that the scripting language is written in VBScript.

METHOD   This attribute indicates how form information should be transferred to the server. The **GET** option appends data to the URL specified by the **ACTION** attribute. This approach gives best performance, but imposes a size limitation determined by the command-line length supported by the server. The **POST** option transfers using an HTTP post transaction. This approach is more secure and imposes no data size limitation.

NAME   This attribute specifies a name for the form and can be used by client-side programs to reference form data.

STYLE   See "Core Attributes Reference" earlier in this appendix.

TARGET   In documents containing frames, this attribute specifies the target frame to display the results of a form submission. In addition to named frames, several special values exist. The **_blank** value indicates a new window. The **_parent** value indicates the parent frame set containing the source link. The **_self** value indicates the frame containing the source link. The **_top** value indicates the full browser window.

TITLE   See "Core Attributes Reference" earlier in this appendix.

EVENT HANDLERS   See "Events Reference" earlier in this appendix.

Example

```
<FORM ACTION="http://www.bigcompany.com/cgi-bin/processit.exe"
METHOD="POST" NAME="testform" onsubmit="validate()">
Enter your comments:<BR>
<TEXTAREA NAME="comments" COLS="30" ROWS="8"></TEXTAREA>
<BR>
<INPUT TYPE="SUBMIT">
<INPUT TYPE="RESET">
</FORM>
```

COMPATIBILITY   W3C 2.0, 3.2, 4.0; Netscape 1.x, 2.x, 3.x, 4.x; Internet Explorer 2.x, 3.x, 4.x; and WebTV

Notes

Form content is defined using the **<BUTTON>**, **<INPUT>**, **<SELECT>** and **<TEXTAREA>** elements, as well as other HTML formatting and structuring elements. Special grouping elements like **<LABEL>**, **<LEGEND>**, and **<FIELDSET>** have been introduced to provide better structuring for forms, but other HTML elements such as **<DIV>** and **<TABLE>** may also be used to improve form layout.

Internet Explorer 4.0 does not support the following attributes: **ACCEPT-CHARSET**, **DIR**, and **onkeyup**.

Netscape 4.0 does not support the following attributes: **ACCEPT-CHARSET, DIR, TITLE, onclick, ondblclick, onkeydown, onkeypress, onkeyup, onmousedown, onmousemove, onmouseover, onmouseout,** and **onmouseup.**

WebTV does not support the following attributes: **ACCEPT-CHARSET, CLASS, DIR, ENCTYPE, ID, LANG, STYLE, TITLE, onclick, ondblclick, onkeydown, onkeypress, onkeyup, onmousedown, onmousemove, onmouseover, onmouseout,** and **onmouseup.**

HTML 2.0 and 3.2 support only the **ACTION, METHOD,** and **ENCTYPE** attributes for the **<FORM>** element.

<FRAME>

DESCRIPTION   This element defines a nameable window region, known as a frame, that can independently display its own content.

Syntax

```
<FRAME
     BORDERCOLOR=#RRGGBB | color name     (IE 4.0, N 4.0)
     CLASS=class name(s)
     DATAFLD=name of column supplying bound data    (IE 4.0)
     DATASRC=id of data source object supplying data   (IE 4.0)
     FRAMEBORDER=YES* | NO* | 1 | 0  *(IE 4.0, N 4.0)
     ID=unique alphanumeric identifier
     LANG=language code   (IE 4.0, N 4.0)
     LANGUAGE=JAVASCRIPT | JSCRIPT | VBSCRIPT | VBS   (IE 4.0)
     LONGDESC=URL of description
     MARGINHEIGHT=pixels
     MARGINWIDTH=pixels
     NAME=string
     NORESIZE
     SCROLLING=YES | NO | AUTO
     SRC=URL of frame contents
     STYLE=style information
     TITLE=advisory text

     onreadystatechange="script">   (IE 4.0)
```

Attributes

BORDERCOLOR   This attribute sets the color of the frame's border using either a named color or a color specified in the hexadecimal *#RRGGBB* format.

CLASS   See "Core Attributes Reference" earlier in this appendix.

DATAFLD   This Internet Explorer attribute specifies the column name from the data source object that supplies the bound data.

DATASRC   This Internet Explorer attribute indicates the **ID** of the data source object that supplies the data that is bound to this element.

FRAMEBORDER   This attribute determines whether the frame is surrounded by an outlined three-dimensional border. The HTML specification prefers the use of **1** for the frame border on and **0** for off; most browsers also acknowledge the use of **YES** and **NO**.

ID   See "Core Attributes Reference" earlier in this appendix.

LANG   See "Language Reference" earlier in this appendix.

LANGUAGE   This attribute specifies the language the current script is written in and invokes the proper scripting engine. The default value is **JAVASCRIPT**. **JAVASCRIPT** and **JSCRIPT** represent that the scripting language is written in JavaScript. **VBS** and **VBSCRIPT** represent that the scripting language is written in VBScript.

LONGDESC   This attribute is used to specify a URL of a document that contains a long description of the frame's content. This attribute should be used in conjunction with the <TITLE> element.

MARGINHEIGHT   This attribute sets the height in pixels between the frame's content and its top and bottom borders.

MARGINWIDTH   This attribute sets the width in pixels between the frame's content and its left and right borders.

NAME   This attribute assigns the frame a name so that it can be the target destination of hyperlinks, as well as be a possible candidate for manipulation via a script.

NORESIZE   This attribute overrides the default ability to resize frames and gives the frame a fixed size.

SCROLLING   This attribute determines if the frame has scroll bars. A **YES** value forces scroll bars, a **NO** value prohibits them, and an **AUTO** value lets the browser decide. When not specified, the default value of **AUTO** is used. Authors are recommended to leave the value as **AUTO**. If you turn off scrolling and the content ends up being too large for the frame (due to rendering differences, window size, etc) the user will not be able to scroll to see the rest of the content. If you turn scrolling on and the content all fits in the frame, the scroll bars will needlessly consume screen space. With **AUTO** scroll bars appear only when needed.

SRC   This attribute contains the URL of the content to be displayed in the frame. If absent nothing will be loaded in the frame.

STYLE   See "Core Attributes Reference" earlier in this appendix.

TITLE   See "Core Attributes Reference" earlier in this appendix.

EVENT HANDLERS   See "Events Reference" earlier in this appendix.

Examples

```
<FRAMESET ROWS=20%,80%>
<FRAME SRC="controls.htm" NAME="controls"
NORESIZE SCROLLING="NO">
<FRAME SRC="content.htm">
</FRAMESET>
```

COMPATIBILITY   W3C 4.0; Netscape 2.x, 3.x, 4.x; Internet Explorer 2.x, 3.x, 4.x; and WebTV

Notes

A frame must be declared as part of a frame set as set by the **<FRAMESET>** element, which specifies the frame's relationship to other frames on a page. A frame set occurs in a special HTML document in which the **<FRAMESET>** element replaces the **<BODY>** element. Another form of frames called independent frames, or *floating frames*, is also supported by Microsoft as well as the HTML 4.0 transitional specification, which supports floating frames. Floating frames can be directly embedded in a document without belonging to a frameset. These are defined with the **<IFRAME>** element.

WebTV does not support the following attributes: **NORESIZE** and **SCROLLING**. Numerous browsers do not support frames and require the use of the **<NOFRAMES>** element. Frames introduce potential navigation difficulties; their use should be limited to instances where they can be shown to help navigation rather than hinder it.

<FRAMESET>

DESCRIPTION   This element is used to define the organization of a set of independent window regions known as frames as defined by the **<FRAME>** element. This element replaces the **<BODY>** element in framing documents.

Syntax

```
<FRAMESET
     BORDER=pixels    (IE 4.0, N 4.0, WebTV)
     BORDERCOLOR=#RRGGBB | color name   (IE 4.0, N 4.0)
     CLASS=class name(s)
     COLS=list of columns
     FRAMEBORDER=0 | 1| YES | NO   (IE 4.0, N 4.0, WebTV)
     FRAMESPACING=pixels   (IE 4.0, WebTV)
     ID=unique alphanumeric identifier
     LANG=language code   (IE 4.0, N 4.0)
     LANGAUGE=JAVASCRIPT | JSCRIPT | VBSCRIPT | VBS   (IE 4.0)
     ROWS=list or rows
     STYLE=style information
     TITLE=advisory text

     onblur="script"   (N 4.0)
```

```
        onfocus="script"    (N 4.0)
        onload="script"
        onunload="script">

    <FRAME> elements and <NOFRAMES>

</FRAMESET>
```

Attributes

BORDER   This attribute sets the width in pixels of frame borders within the frame set. Setting **BORDER=0** eliminates all frame borders. This attribute is not defined in the HTML specification but is widely supported.

BORDERCOLOR   This attribute sets the color for frame borders within the frame set using either a named color or a color specified in the hexadecimal #*RRGGBB* format.

CLASS   See "Core Attributes Reference" earlier in this appendix.

COLS   This attribute contains a comma-delimited list, which specifies the number and size of columns contained within a set of frames. List items indicate columns, left to right. Column size is specified in three formats, which may be mixed. A column can be assigned a fixed width in pixels. It can also be assigned a percentage of the available width, such as 50 percent. Last, a column can be set to expand to fill the available space by setting the value to *****, which acts as a wildcard.

FRAMEBORDER   This attribute controls whether or not frame borders should be displayed. Netscape supports **YES** and **NO** values. Microsoft uses **1** and **0** as well as **YES** and **NO**.

FRAMESPACING   This attribute indicates the space between frames in pixels.

ID   See "Core Attributes Reference" earlier in this appendix.

LANG   See "Language Reference" earlier in this appendix.

LANGUAGE   This attribute specifies the language the current script is written in and invokes the proper scripting engine. The default value is **JAVASCRIPT**. **JAVASCRIPT** and **JSCRIPT** represent that the scripting language is written in JavaScript. **VBS** and **VBSCRIPT** represent that the scripting language is written in VBScript.

ROWS   This attribute contains a comma-delimited list that specifies the number and size of rows contained within a set of frames. The number of entries in the list indicates the number of rows. Row size is specified with the same formats used for columns.

STYLE   See "Core Attributes Reference" earlier in this appendix.

TITLE   See "Core Attributes Reference" earlier in this appendix.

EVENT HANDLERS   See "Events Reference" earlier in this appendix.

Example

```
<!--
defines a frame set of three columns
the middle column is 50 pixels wide
the first and last columns fill the remaining space
the last column takes twice as much space as the first
-->

<FRAMESET COLS="*,50,*">
<FRAME SRC="column1.htm">
<FRAME SRC="column2.htm">
<FRAME SRC="column3.htm">
</FRAMESET>
```

COMPATIBILITY   WC3 4.0; Netscape 2.x, 3.x, 4.x; Internet Explorer 2.x, 3.x, 4.x; and WebTV

Notes

The **<FRAMESET>** element contains one or more **<FRAME>** elements, which are used to indicate the framed contents. The **<FRAMESET>** element may also contain a **<NOFRAMES>** element whose content will be displayed on browsers that do not support frames.
The **<FRAMESET>** element replaces the **<BODY>** element in a framing document as shown here:

```
<HTML>
<HEAD>
<TITLE>Collection of Frames</TITLE>
</HEAD>
<FRAMESET COLS="*,50,*">
<FRAME SRC="column1.htm">
<FRAME SRC="column2.htm">
<FRAME SRC="column3.htm">
<NOFRAMES>
Please visit our < A HREF="noframes.htm">no frames</A> site.
</FRAMESET>
</HTML>
```

Netscape 4.0 does not support the **TITLE** attribute.

<H1> Through <H6>   (Headings)

DESCRIPTION   These tags implement six levels of document headings; **<H1>** is the most prominent, and **<H6>** is the least prominent.

Syntax

```
<H1
      ALIGN=LEFT | RIGHT | CENTER | JUSTIFY
      CLASS=class name(s)
      DIR=LTR | RTL
      ID=unique alphanumeric identifier
      LANG=language code
      LANGUAGE=JAVASCRIPT | JSCRIPT | VBSCRIPT | VBS    (IE 4.0)
      STYLE=style information
      TITLE=advisory text

      onclick="script"
      ondblclick="script"
      ondragstart="script"   (IE 4.0)
      onhelp="script"   (IE 4.0)
      onkeydown="script"
      onkeypress="script"
      onkeyup="script"
      onmousedown="script"
      onmousemove="script"
      onmouseout="script"
      onmouseover="script"
      onmouseup="script"
      onselectstart="script">   (IE 4.0)

</H1>
```

Attributes

ALIGN   This attribute controls the horizontal alignment of the heading with respect to the page. The default value is **LEFT**.

CLASS   See "Core Attributes Reference" earlier in this appendix.

DIR   See "Language Reference" earlier in this appendix.

ID   See "Core Attributes Reference" earlier in this appendix.

LANG   See "Language Reference" earlier in this appendix.

LANGUAGE   This attribute specifies the language the current script is written in and invokes the proper scripting engine. The default value is **JAVASCRIPT**. **JAVASCRIPT** and **JSCRIPT** represent that the scripting language is written in JavaScript. **VBS** and **VBSCRIPT** represent that the scripting language is written in VBScript.

STYLE   See "Core Attributes Reference" earlier in this appendix.

TITLE   See "Core Attributes Reference" earlier in this appendix.

EVENT HANDLERS   See "Events Reference" earlier in this appendix.

Examples

```
<H1>This is a Major Document Heading</H1>
<H2 ALIGN="CENTER">Second heading, aligned to the center</H2>
<H3 ALIGN="RIGHT">Third heading, aligned to the right</H3>
<H4>Fourth heading</H4>
<H5 STYLE="{font-size: 20pt}">
   Fifth heading with style information</H5>
<H6>The smallest heading</H6>
```

COMPATIBILITY   W3C 2.0, 3.2, 4.0; Netscape 1.x, 2.x, 3.x, 4.x; Internet Explorer 2.x, 3.x, 4.x; and WebTV

Notes

In most implementations, heading numbers correspond inversely with the six font sizes supported by the **<FONT>** element. For example, **<H1>** corresponds to **<FONT SIZE=6>**. The default font size is **3**. However, this approach to layout is not encouraged and page designers should consider using styles to set even relative sizes.

Internet Explorer 4.0 does not support the **DIR** attribute. Documentation suggests that the **JUSTIFY** value for **ALIGN** is not supported for headings.

Netscape 4.0 does not support the following attributes: **TITLE, onclick, ondblclick, onkeydown, onkeypress, onkeyup, onmousedown, onmousemove, onmouseover, onmouseout,** and **onmouseup**.

WebTV supports only the **ALIGN** attribute for this element.

HTML 3.2 supports only the **ALIGN** attribute. HTML 2.0 does not support any attributes for headings.

The strict definition of HTML 4.0 does not include support for the **ALIGN** attribute. Style sheets should be used instead.

<HEAD>   (Document Head)

DESCRIPTION   This element indicates the document head that contains descriptive information about the HTML document, as well as other supplementary information like style rules or scripts.

Syntax

```
<HEAD
    CLASS=class name(s)    (IE 4.0, N 4.0)
    DIR=LTR | RTL
    ID=unique alphanumeric identifier    (IE 4.0, N 4.0)
    LANG=language code
```

```
        PROFILE=URL
        TITLE=advisory text>    (IE 4.0)

</HEAD>
```

Attributes

CLASS   See "Core Attributes Reference" earlier in this appendix.

DIR   See "Language Reference" earlier in this appendix.

ID   See "Core Attributes Reference" earlier in this appendix.

LANG   See "Language Reference" earlier in this appendix.

PROFILE   This attribute specifies a URL for a meta-information dictionary. The specified profile should indicate the format of allowed meta-data and the potential meaning of the data.

STYLE   See "Core Attributes Reference" earlier in this appendix.

TITLE   See "Core Attributes Reference" earlier in this appendix.

Event Handlers
None.

Example

```
<HEAD>
<TITLE>Big Company Home Page</TITLE>
<BASE HREF="http://www.bigcompany.com">
<META NAME="Keywords"  CONTENT="BigCompany, SuperWidget">
</HEAD>
```

COMPATIBILITY   W3C 2.0, 3.2, 4.0; Netscape 1.x, 2.x, 3.x, 4.x; Internet Explorer 2.x, 3.x, 4.x; and WebTV

Notes
The **<HEAD>** element must contain a **<TITLE>** element. It may also contain the **<ISINDEX>**, **<BASE>**, **<META>**, **<SCRIPT>**, **<STYLE>**, and **<LINK>** elements.
While the HTML 4.0 specification shows support for the **PROFILE** attribute, no browsers appear to support it.
Internet Explorer 4.0 does not support the **DIR**, **LANG**, and **PROFILE** attributes.
Internet Explorer 4.0 defines the **<BGSOUND>** element as another valid element within **<HEAD>**.
Netscape 4.0 does not support the **DIR** and **PROFILE** attributes.

WebTV supports no attributes for this element.
HTML 2.0 and 3.2 support no attributes for this element.

<HR>   (Horizontal Rule)

DESCRIPTION   This element is used to insert a horizontal rule to visually separate document sections. Rules are usually rendered as raised or etched lines.

Syntax

```
<HR
    ALIGN=CENTER | LEFT | RIGHT
    CLASS=class name(s)
    COLOR=#RRGGBB | color name    (IE 4.0)
    ID=unique alphanumeric identifier
    INVERTBORDER    (WebTV)
    LANG=language code    (IE 4.0)
    LANGUAGE=JAVASCRIPT | JSCRIPT | VBSCRIPT | VBS    (IE 4.0)
    NOSHADE
    SIZE=pixels
    STYLE=style information
    TITLE=advisory information
    WIDTH=pixels | percentage

    onbeforeupdate="script"    (IE 4.0)
    onblur="script"    (IE 4.0)
    onclick="script"
    ondblclick="script"
    ondragstart="script"    (IE 4.0)
    onfocus="script"    (IE 4.0)
    onhelp="script"    (IE 4.0)
    onkeydown="script"
    onkeypress="script"
    onkeyup="script"
    onmousedown="script"
    onmousemove="script"
    onmouseout="script"
    onmouseover="script"
    onmouseup="script"
    onresize="script"    (IE 4.0)
    onrowenter="script"    (IE 4.0)
    onrowexit="script"    (IE 4.0)
    onselectstart="script">    (IE 4.0)
```

Attributes

ALIGN   This attribute controls the horizontal alignment of the rule with respect to the page. The default value is **LEFT**.

CLASS   See "Core Attributes Reference" earlier in this appendix.

COLOR   This attribute sets the rule color using either a named color or a color specified in the hexadecimal *#RRGGBB* format. This attribute is currently supported only by Internet Explorer.

ID   See "Core Attributes Reference" earlier in this appendix.

INVERTBORDER   This WebTV-specific attribute creates a horizontal rule that appears raised, as opposed to embossed, on the surface of the page.

LANG   See "Language Reference" earlier in this appendix.

LANGUAGE   This attribute specifies the language the current script is written in and invokes the proper scripting engine. The default value is **JAVASCRIPT**. **JAVASCRIPT** and **JSCRIPT** represent that the scripting language is written in JavaScript. **VBS** and **VBSCRIPT** represent that the scripting language is written in VBScript.

NOSHADE   This attribute causes the rule to be rendered as a solid bar without shading.

SIZE   This attribute indicates the height in pixels of the rule.

SRC   This attribute specifies a URL for an associated file.

STYLE   See "Core Attributes Reference" earlier in this appendix.

TITLE   See "Core Attributes Reference" earlier in this appendix.

WIDTH   This attribute indicates how wide the rule should be specified either in pixels or as a percent of screen width, such as 80 percent.

EVENT HANDLERS   See "Events Reference" earlier in this appendix.

Example

```
<HR ALIGN="LEFT" NOSHADE SIZE="4" WIDTH="30%">
```

COMPATIBILITY   W3C 2.0, 3.2, 4.0; Netscape 1.x, 2.x, 3.x, 4.x; Internet Explorer 2.x, 3.x, 4.x; and WebTV

Notes

It is considered poor design to include an excessive number of rules in a page. A safe number of rules is three or less. If a page has too many rules in your opinion, it may indicate that the page may need to be broken up.

Netscape 4.0 does not support the following attributes: **TITLE, onclick, ondblclick, onkeydown, onkeypress, onkeyup, onmousedown, onmousemove, onmouseover, onmouseout,** and **onmouseup.**

WebTV does not support the following attributes: **CLASS, ID, STYLE, TITLE, onclick, ondblclick, onkeydown, onkeypress, onkeyup, onmousedown, onmousemove, onmouseover, onmouseout,** and **onmouseup.**

HTML 3.2 supports only the **ALIGN**, **NOSHADE**, **SIZE**, and **WIDTH** attributes. The strict definition of HTML 4.0 removes support for the **ALIGN**, **NOSHADE**, **SIZE**, and **WIDTH** attributes for horizontal rules. These effects are possible using style sheets.

<HTML> (HTML Document)

DESCRIPTION   This element identifies a document as containing HTML-tagged content.

Syntax

```
<HTML
    DIR=LTR | RTL
    LANG=language code
    TITLE=advisory text    (IE 4.0)
    VERSION=URL>

</HTML>
```

Attributes

DIR   See "Language Reference" earlier in this appendix.

LANG   See "Language Reference" earlier in this appendix.

TITLE   See "Core Attributes Reference" earlier in this appendix.

VERSION   The version attribute is used to set the URL of the location of the document type definition (DTD) that the current document conforms to. The DTD is also specified by the **<!DOCTYPE>** comment. Since few if any browsers support the **VERSION** attribute, it should be used only in conjunction with a **<!DOCTYPE>** and not instead of one.

EVENT HANDLERS   None.

Example

```
<!-- Minimal HTML document -->
<HTML>
<HEAD><TITLE></TITLE></HEAD>
<BODY></BODY>
</HTML>
```

COMPATIBILITY   W3C 4.0; Netscape 4.0; Internet Explorer 4.0; and WebTV

Notes

The **<HTML>** element is the first element in an **<HTML>** document. Except for comments, the only tags it directly contains are the **<HEAD>** element followed by either a **<BODY>** element or a **<FRAMESET>** element.

Internet Explorer 4.0 doesn't support the **VERSION** and **DIR** attributes.
Netscape 4.0 does not support the following attributes: **DIR, LANG,** and **VERSION**.
WebTV does not support any attributes for this element.

<I>   (Italic)

DESCRIPTION   This element indicates that the enclosed text should be displayed in an italic typeface.

Syntax

```
<I
    CLASS=class name(s)
    DIR=LTR | RTL
    ID=unique alphanumeric identifier
    LANG=language code
    LANGUAGE=JAVASCRIPT | JSCRIPT | VBSCRIPT | VBS   (IE 4.0)
    STYLE=style information
    TITLE=advisory text

    onclick="script"
    ondblclick="script"
    ondragstart="script"   (IE 4.0)
    onhelp="script"   (IE 4.0)
    onkeydown="script"
    onkeypress="script"
    onkeyup="script"
    onmousedown="script"
    onmousemove="script"
    onmouseout="script"
    onmouseover="script"
    onmouseup="script"
    onselectstart="script">   (IE 4.0)

</I>
```

Attributes

CLASS   See "Core Attributes Reference" earlier in this appendix.

DIR   See "Language Reference" earlier in this appendix.

ID   See "Core Attributes Reference" earlier in this appendix.

LANG   See "Language Reference" earlier in this appendix.

LANGUAGE   This attribute specifies the language the current script is written in and invokes the proper scripting engine. The default value is **JAVASCRIPT**. **JAVASCRIPT** and **JSCRIPT**

represent that the scripting language is written in JavaScript. **VBS** and **VBSCRIPT** represent that the scripting language is written in VBScript.

STYLE   See "Core Attributes Reference" earlier in this appendix.

TITLE   See "Core Attributes Reference" earlier in this appendix.

EVENT HANDLERS   See "Events Reference" earlier in this appendix.

Example

```
Here is some <I>italic</I> text.
```

COMPATIBILITY   W3C 4.0; Netscape 4.0; Internet Explorer 4.0; and WebTV

Notes

Internet Explorer 4.0 does not support the **DIR** attribute.
Netscape 4.0 does not support the following attributes: **DIR**, **TITLE**, **onclick**, **ondblclick**, **onkeydown**, **onkeypress**, **onkeyup**, **onmousedown**, **onmousemove**, **onmouseover**, **onmouseout**, and **onmouseup**.
WebTV does not support any attributes for this element.

<IFRAME>   (Floating Frame)

DESCRIPTION   This element indicates a floating frame, an independently controllable content region that can be embedded in a page.

Syntax

```
<IFRAME
     ALIGN=TOP | MIDDLE | BOTTOM | LEFT | RIGHT
     ABSBOTTOM* | ABSMIDDLE* | BASELINE* | TEXTTOP*    *(IE 4.0)
     BORDER=pixels    (IE 4.0)
     BORDERCOLOR=color name | #RRGGBB    (IE 4.0)
     CLASS=class name(s)
     DATAFLD=name of column supplying bound data    (IE 4.0)
     DATASRC=id of data source object supplying data    (IE 4.0)
     FRAMEBORDER=NO* | YES* | 0 | 1    *(IE 4.0)
     FRAMESPACING=pixels    (IE 4.0)
     HEIGHT=pixels | percentage
     HSPACE=pixels    (IE 4.0)
     ID=unique alphanumeric identifier
     LANG=language code    (IE 4.0)
     LANGUAGE=JAVASCRIPT | JSCRIPT | VBSCRIPT | VBS    (IE 4.0)
     LONGDESC=URL of description
     MARGINHEIGHT=pixels
```

```
    MARGINWIDTH=pixels
    NAME=string
    NORESIZE (IE 4.0)
    SCROLLING=AUTO | YES | NO
    SRC=URL of frame contents
    STYLE=style information
    TITLE=advisory text
    VSPACE=pixels    (IE 4.0)
    WIDTH=pixels | percentage>

</IFRAME>
```

Attributes

ALIGN   This attribute controls the horizontal alignment of the floating frame with respect to the page. The default is **LEFT**.

BORDER   This attribute specifies the thickness of the border in pixels.

BORDERCOLOR   This attribute specifies the color of the border.

CLASS   See "Core Attributes Reference" earlier in this appendix.

DATAFLD   This attribute specifies the column name from the data source object that supplies the bound data.

DATASRC   This attribute indicates the **ID** of the data source object that supplies the data that is bound to this element.

FRAMEBORDER   This attribute determines whether the frame is surrounded by a border. The HTML 4.0 specification defines **0** to be off and **1** to be on. The default value is **1**. Internet Explorer also defines the values **YES** and **NO**.

FRAMESPACING   This attribute creates additional space between the frames.

HEIGHT   The attribute sets the floating frame's height in pixels.

HSPACE   This attribute specifies margins for the frame.

ID   See "Core Attributes Reference" earlier in this appendix.

LANG   See "Language Reference" earlier in this appendix.

LANGUAGE   This attribute specifies the language the current script is written in and invokes the proper scripting engine. The default value is **JAVASCRIPT**. **JAVASCRIPT** and **JSCRIPT** represent that the scripting language is written in JavaScript. **VBS** and **VBSCRIPT** represent that the scripting language is written in VBScript.

LONGDESC   This attribute is used to specify a URL of a document that contains a long description of the frame's contents. Particularly, this may be as a complement to the <TITLE> element.

MARGINHEIGHT   This attribute sets the height in pixels between the floating frame's content and its top and bottom borders.

MARGINWIDTH   This attribute sets the width in pixels between the floating frame's content and its left and right borders.

NAME   This attribute assigns the floating frame a name so that it can be the target destination of hyperlinks.

NORESIZE   When **NORESIZE** is included, the frame cannot be resized by the user.

SCROLLING   This attribute determines if the frame has scroll bars. A **YES** value forces scroll bars; a **NO** value prohibits them.

SRC   This attribute contains the URL of the content to be displayed in the floating frame. If absent, the frame is blank.

STYLE   See "Core Attributes Reference" earlier in this appendix.

TITLE   See "Core Attributes Reference" earlier in this appendix.

VSPACE   This attribute specifies margins for the frame.

WIDTH   This attribute sets the floating frame's width in pixels.

EVENT HANDLERS   See "Events Reference" earlier in this appendix.

Example

```
<IFRAME SRC="http://www.bigcompany.com" HEIGHT="150"
        WIDTH="200" NAME="FloatingFrame1">
   Sorry, your browser doesn't support inlined frames.
</IFRAME>
```

COMPATIBILITY   W3C 4.0; Internet Explorer 3.x, 4.x

Notes

A floating frame does not need to be declared by the **<FRAMESET>** element as part of a frame set. WebTV and Netscape 4.0 do not support floating frames.

Under HTML 4.0's strict definition, the **<IFRAME>** element is not defined. Floating frames may be imitated using the **<DIV>** element and CSS positioning facilities.

<ILAYER> (Inflow Layer)

DESCRIPTION   This Netscape-specific element allows the definition of overlapping content layers that can be positioned, hidden or shown, rendered transparent or opaque, reordered front to back, and nested. An *inflow layer* is a layer with a relative position that appears where it would naturally occur in the document, in contrast to a *general layer*, which may be positioned absolutely regardless of its location in a document. The functionality of layers is available using CSS positioning, and page developers are advised not to use this element.

Syntax

```
<ILAYER
    ABOVE=layer    (N 4.0)
    BACKGROUND=URL of image    (N 4.0)
    BELOW=layer    (N 4.0)
    BGCOLOR=#RRGGBB | color name    (N 4.0)
    CLASS=class name(s)        (N 4.0)
    CLIP=x1, y1, x2, y2        (N 4.0)
    HEIGHT=pixels | percentage      (N 4.0)
    ID=unique alphanumeric identifier    (N 4.0)
    LEFT=pixels        (N 4.0)
    NAME=string        (N 4.0)
    PAGEX=pixels        (N 4.0)
    PAGEY=pixels        (N 4.0)
    SRC=URL of layer contents        (N 4.0)
    STYLE=style information        (N 4.0)
    TOP=pixels        (N 4.0)
    VISIBILITY=HIDE | INHERIT | SHOW    (N 4.0)
    WIDTH=pixels | percentage        (N 4.0)
    Z-INDEX=number        (N 4.0)
    onblur="script"    (N 4.0)
    onfocus="script"      (N 4.0)
    onload="script"      (N 4.0)
    onmouseout="script"      (N 4.0)
    onmouseover="script">    (N 4.0)

</ILAYER>
```

Attributes

ABOVE   This attribute contains the name of the layer to be rendered above the current layer.

BACKGROUND   This attribute contains the URL of a background image for the layer.

BELOW   This attribute contains the name of the layer to be rendered below the current layer.

BGCOLOR   This attribute specifies a layer's background color. Its value can be either a named color or a color specified in the hexadecimal *#RRGGBB* format.

CLASS   This attribute specifies the class name(s) for access via a style sheet.

CLIP   This attribute specifies the clipping region or viewable area of the layer. All layer content outside that rectangle will be rendered as transparent. The clip rectangle is defined by two x,y pairs: top x, left y, bottom x, and right y. Coordinates are relative to the layer's origin point, 0,0 in its top left corner.

HEIGHT   This attribute specifies the height of a layer in pixel or percentage values.

ID   See "Core Attributes Reference" earlier in this appendix.

LEFT   This attribute specifies in pixels the horizontal offset of the layer. The offset is relative to its parent layer if it has one or to the left page margin if it does not.

PAGEX   This attribute specifies the horizontal position of the layer relative to the browser window.

PAGEY   This attribute specifies the vertical position of the layer relative to the browser window.

SRC   This attribute is used to set the URL of a file that contains the content to load into the layer.

STYLE   This attribute is used to specify an inline style for the layer.

TOP   This attribute specifies in pixels the top offset of the layer. The offset is relative to its parent layer if it has one or the top page margin if it does not.

VISIBILITY   This attribute specifies whether a layer is hidden, shown, or inherits its visibility from the layer that includes it.

WIDTH   This attribute specifies a layer's width in pixels.

Z INDEX   This attribute specifies a layer's stacking order relative to other layers. Position is specified with positive integers, with **1** indicating the bottommost layer.

EVENT HANDLERS   None.

Example

```
<P>Content comes before</P>
<ILAYER NAME="background" BGCOLOR="green">
   <P>Layered information goes here</P>
</ILAYER>
<P>Content comes after</P>
```

COMPATIBILITY   Netscape 4.0

Notes

This element will likely fall out of fashion because of its lack of cross-browser compatibility. The functionality of **<ILAYER>** is possible using the positioning features in CSS, and page developers are encouraged not to use this element.

Applets, plug-ins, and other embedded media forms generically called objects may be included in a layer; however, they will float to the top of all other layers even if their containing layer is obscured.

\<IMG\>   (Image)

DESCRIPTION   This element indicates a media object to include in an HTML document. Usually the object is a graphic image, but some implementations support movies and animations.

Syntax

```
<IMG
     ALIGN=TOP | MIDDLE | BOTTOM | LEFT | RIGHT
     ABSBOTTOM* | ABSMIDDLE*| BASELINE* |
     TEXTTOP*    *(IE 4.0, N 4.0)
     ALT=alternative text
     BORDER=pixels
     CLASS=class name(s)
     CONTROLS      (IE 3.0, WebTV)
     DATAFLD=name of column supplying bound data   (IE 4.0)
     DATASRC=id of data source object supplying data   (IE 4.0)
     DIR=LTR | RTL
     DYNSRC=URL of movie   (IE 4.0)
     HEIGHT=pixels
     HSPACE=pixels
     ID=unique alphanumeric identifier
     ISMAP
     LANG=language code
     LANGUAGE=JAVASCRIPT | JSCRIPT | VBSCRIPT | VBS   (IE 4.0)
     LONGDESC=URL of description file
     LOOP=number | INFINITE   (IE 4.0)
     LOWSRC=URL of low resolution image   (IE 4.0, N 4.0)
     NAME=unique alphanumeric identifier   (IE 4.0, N 4.0, WebTV)
     RELOAD=seconds   (WebTV)
     SELECTED=x,ypair   (WebTV)
     SRC=URL of image to include
     START=FILEOPEN | MOUSEOVER
     STYLE=style information
     TITLE=advisory text
     TRANSPARENCY=1 - 100   (WebTV)
     USEMAP=URL of map file
     VSPACE=pixels
     WIDTH=pixels

     onabort="script"   (IE 4.0, N 4.0, WebTV)
     onafterupdate="script"   (IE 4.0)
     onbeforeupdate="script"   (IE 4.0)
     onblur="script"   (IE 4.0)
     onclick="script"
     ondblclick="script"
     ondragstart="script"   (IE 4.0)
```

```
onerror="script"   (IE 4.0, N 4.0, WebTV)
onfocus="script"   (IE 4.0)
onhelp="script"    (IE 4.0)
onkeydown="script"
onkeypress="script"
onkeyup="script"
onload="script"    (IE 4.0, N 4.0, WebTV)
onmousedown="script"
onmousemove="script"
onmouseout="script"
onmouseover="script"
onmouseup="script"
onresize="script"   (IE 4.0)
onrowenter="script"   (IE 4.0)
onrowexit="script"   (IE 4.0)
onselectstart="script">   (IE 4.0)
```

Attributes

ALIGN   This attribute controls the horizontal alignment of the image with respect to the page. The default value is **LEFT**. Only the Netscape, Internet Explorer 4.0, and WebTV implementations support the **ABSBOTTOM, ABSMIDDLE, BASELINE,** and **TEXTTOP** values.

ALT   This attribute contains a string to display instead of the image, for browsers that cannot display images.

BORDER   This attribute indicates the width in pixels of the border surrounding the image.

CLASS   See "Core Attributes Reference" earlier in this appendix.

CONTROLS   Under Internet Explorer 3.0 and WebTV, it is possible to set the controls to show by placing this attribute in the **<IMG>** element. This attribute does not appear to be supported under Internet Explorer 4.0, and users are encouraged to use the **<OBJECT>** element to embed video for Internet Explorer.

DATAFLD   This attribute specifies the column name from the data source object that supplies the bound data to set the **SRC** of the **<IMG>** element.

DATASRC   This attribute indicates the **ID** of the data source object that supplies the data that is bound to this **<IMG>** element.

DIR   See "Language Reference" earlier in this appendix.

DYNSRC   In the Microsoft and WebTV implementations, this attribute indicates the URL of a movie file and is used instead of the **SRC** attribute.

HEIGHT   This attribute indicates the height in pixels of the image.

HSPACE   This attribute indicates the horizontal space in pixels between the image and surrounding text.

ID   See "Core Attributes Reference" earlier in this appendix.

ISMAP   This attribute indicates that the image is a server-side image map. User mouse actions over the image are sent to the server for processing.

LANG   See "Language Reference" earlier in this appendix.

LANGUAGE   This attribute specifies the language the current script is written in and invokes the proper scripting engine. The default value is **JAVASCRIPT**. **JAVASCRIPT** and **JSCRIPT** represent that the scripting language is written in JavaScript. **VBS** and **VBSCRIPT** represent that the scripting language is written in VBScript.

LONGDESC   This attribute is used to specify a URL of a document that contains a long description of the image. This attribute is used as a complement for the **ALT** attribute.

LOOP   In the Microsoft implementation, this attribute is used with the **DYNSRC** attribute to cause a movie to loop. Its value is either a numeric loop count or the keyword **INFINITE**.

LOWSRC   In the Netscape implementation, this attribute contains the URL of an image to be initially loaded. Typically the **LOWSRC** image is a low-resolution or black-and-white image that provides a quick preview of the image to follow. Once the primary image is loaded, it replaces the **LOWSRC** image.

NAME   This common attribute is used to bind a name to the image. Older browsers understand the **NAME** field, and in conjunction with scripting languages it is possible to manipulate images by their defined names to create effects like "rollover" buttons. The **ID** attribute under HTML 4.0 is used to specify element identifiers; for backward compatibility, **NAME** may still be used.

RELOAD   In the WebTV implementation, this attribute indicates in seconds how frequently an image should be reloaded.

SELECTED   In the WebTV implementation, this attribute indicates the initial x,y coordinate location on the image. The cursor is placed at that location when the image is loaded. It requires either the **ISMAP** or **USEMAP** attribute.

SRC   This attribute indicates the URL of an image file to be displayed.

START   In the Microsoft implementation, this attribute indicates how a movie should begin playing. The default, **FILEOPEN**, starts playing a movie as its file is opened. The **MOUSEOVER** option starts playing a movie when the viewer moves the mouse cursor over it.

STYLE   See "Core Attributes Reference" earlier in this appendix.

TITLE   See "Core Attributes Reference" earlier in this appendix.

TRANSPARENCY   In the WebTV implementation, this attribute allows the background to show through the image. It takes a numeric argument indicating the degree of transparency, from fully opaque (**0**) to fully transparent (**100**).

USEMAP   This attribute makes the image support client-side image mapping. Its argument is a URL specifying the map file, which associates image regions with hyperlinks.

VSPACE   This attribute indicates the vertical space in pixels between the image and surrounding text.

WIDTH   This attribute indicates the width in pixels of the image.

EVENT HANDLERS   See "Events Reference" earlier in this appendix.

Examples

```
<IMG SRC="padres.gif" LOWSRC="padresbw.gif"
ALT="San Diego Padres" HEIGHT="100" WIDTH="300">

<IMG SRC="hugeimagemap.gif" USEMAP="mainmap" BORDER="0"
    HEIGHT="200" WIDTH="200" ALT="Image Map Here">
```

COMPATIBILITY   WC3 2.0, 3.2, 4.0; Netscape 1.x, 2.x, 3.x, 4.x; Internet Explorer 2.x, 3.x, 4.x; and WebTV

Notes

No browser currently appears to support **LONGDESC**.

Typically, when you use the **USEMAP** attribute the URL is a fragment, like #map1, rather than a full URL. Some browsers do not support external client-side map files.

Internet Explorer 4.0 does not support the **DIR** and **LONGDESC** attributes.

Netscape 4.0 does not support the following attributes: **DIR, LONGDESC, TITLE, onclick, ondblclick, onkeydown, onkeypress, onkeyup, onmousedown, onmousemove, onmouseover, onmouseout,** and **onmouseup.**

WebTV does not support the following attributes: **ALT, CLASS, DIR, LANG, LONGDESC, STYLE, TITLE, onclick, ondblclick, onkeydown, onkeypress, onkeyup,** and **onmousedown.**

Under the HTML 4.0 strict definition, the **<IMG>** element does not support **ALIGN, BORDER, HEIGHT, HSPACE, VSPACE,** and **WIDTH.** The functionality of these attributes should be possible using style sheet rules.

While the HTML 4.0 specification reserves data binding attributes like **DATASRC** or **DATAFLD,** it is not specified for **<IMG>,** although Internet Explorer provides support for these attributes.

<INPUT>   (Input Form Control)

DESCRIPTION   This element is used to specify an input control for a form. The type of input is set by the **TYPE** attribute and may be a variety of different types, including single-line text field, multiline text field, password style, checkbox, radio button, or push button.

Syntax

```
<INPUT

   ACCEPT=MIME TYPES
    ACCESSKEY=character
    ACTION=URL    (WebTV)
    ALIGN=ABSBOTTOM* | ABSMIDDLE* | BASELINE* | BOTTOM |
          CENTER** | LEFT | MIDDLE | RIGHT | TEXTTOP* | TOP
           (*N 4.0, ** IE 4.0)
    ALLCAPS    (WebTV)
    ALT=text
    AUTOACTIVATE    (WebTV)
    AUTOCAPS    (WebTV)
    AUTOSUBMIT    (WebTV)
    BGCOLOR="#RRGGBB" | "color name"    (WebTV)
    BORDERIMAGE=URL    (WebTV)
    CHECKED
    CLASS=class name(s)
    CURSOR="#RRGGBB" | "color name"    (WebTV)
    DIR=LTR|RTL
    DISABLED
    ID=unique alphanumeric identifier
    LANG=language code
    LANGUAGE=JAVASCRIPT | JSCRIPT | VBSCRIPT | VBS    (IE 4.0)
    MAXLENGTH=maximum field size
    NAME=field name
    NOARGS    (WebTV)
    NOCURSOR    (WebTV)
    NOHIGHLIGHT    (WebTV)
    NOSUBMIT    (WebTV)
    NUMBERS    (WebTV)
    READONLY
    SIZE=field size
    SRC=URL of image file
    STYLE=style information
    SUBMITFORM    (WebTV)
    TABINDEX=number
    TITLE=advisory text
    TYPE=TEXT | PASSWORD | CHECKBOX | RADIO | SUBMIT |
         RESET | BUTTON | FILE | HIDDEN | IMAGE
    USEFORM=name of form    (WebTV)
    USEMAP=URL of map file
    USESTYLE (WebTV)
    VALUE="field value"
    WIDTH=pixels (WebTV)

    onafterupdate="script"    (IE 4.0)
```

```
onbeforeupdate="script"   (IE 4.0)
onblur="script"
onchange="script"
onclick="script"
ondblclick="script"
ondragstart="script"   (IE 4.0)
onfocus="script"
onhelp="script"   (IE 4.0)
onkeydown="script"
onkeypress="script"
onkeyup="script"
onmousedown="script"
onmousemove="script"
onmouseout="script"
onmouseover="script"
onmouseup="script"
onselect="script"
onselectstart="script">   (IE 4.0)
```

Attributes

ACCEPT   This attribute is used to list the MIME types accepted for file uploads when **TYPE="FILE"**.

ACCESSKEY   This attribute specifies a keyboard navigation accelerator for the element. Pressing ALT or a similar key in association with the specified character selects the form control correlated with that key sequence. Page designers are forewarned to avoid key sequences already bound to browsers.

ACTION   In the WebTV implementation, this attribute contains the URL of a server program to immediately execute whenever the associated control is selected. This action overrides the action specified by the **<FORM>** element containing the control.

ALIGN   With image form controls (**TYPE=IMAGE**), this attribute aligns the image with respect to surrounding text. The HTML 4.0 transitional specification defines **TOP, MIDDLE, BOTTOM, LEFT**, and **RIGHT** as allowable values. Netscape and Microsoft browsers may also allow the use of attribute values like **ABSBOTTOM** or **ABSMIDDLE**. Like other presentation-specific aspects of HTML, the **ALIGN** attribute is dropped under the strict HTML 4.0 specification.

ALLCAPS   In the WebTV implementation, this attribute is used with text form controls (**TYPE=TEXT**) to render all user-entered text in capital letters. This is a user interface improvement, which may help users entering in data via a slow television environment.

ALT   Used to display an alternative description of image buttons for text-only browsers. The meaning of **ALT** for forms of **<INPUT>** beyond **TYPE=INPUT** is unclear.

AUTOACTIVATE In the WebTV implementation, this attribute causes a text form control (**TYPE=TEXT**) to immediately activate for text input when the user selects it. This attribute requires no value.

AUTOCAPS In the WebTV implementation, the presence of this attribute causes the first letter of each word to automatically be capitalized. The attribute should be used only with text form controls; it requires no value.

AUTOSUBMIT In the WebTV implementation, this attribute is used with a **HIDDEN** control. It causes a form to be automatically submitted whenever the viewer leaves the page. This attribute requires no value.

BGCOLOR In the WebTV implementation, this attribute specifies the background color of a text form control (**TYPE=TEXT**). The value of the attribute can be either a named color or a color specified in the hexadecimal *#RRGGBB* format.

BORDERIMAGE In the WebTV implementation, this attribute allows specification of a graphical border for **RESET**, **SUBMIT**, and **TEXT** controls. Its value is the URL of a .bif (Border Image File) graphics file that specifies the border. Border image files tend to reside in WebTV ROM; the common values are **file://ROM/Border/ButtonBorder2.bif** and **file://ROM/Border/ButtonBorder3.bif**, though other values may be present under later versions of WebTV.

CHECKED This attribute should be used only for checkbox (**TYPE="CHECKBOX"**) and radio (**TYPE="RADIO"**) form controls. The presence of this attribute indicates that the control should be displayed in its checked state.

CLASS See "Core Attributes Reference" earlier in this appendix.

CURSOR In the WebTV implementation, this attribute sets the cursor color for a text form control (**TYPE=TEXT**). The attribute's value is either a named color or a color specified in the hexadecimal *#RRGGBB* format.

DIR See "Language Reference" earlier in this appendix.

DISABLED This attribute is used to turn off a form control. Elements will not be submitted, nor may they receive any focus from the keyboard or mouse. Disabled form controls will not be part of the tabbing order. The browser may also gray out the form that is disabled, in order to indicate to the user that the form control is inactive. This attribute requires no value.

ID See "Core Attributes Reference" earlier in this appendix.

LANG See "Language Reference" earlier in this appendix.

LANGUAGE In the Microsoft implementation, this attribute specifies the scripting language to be used with an associated script bound to the element typically through an event handler attribute. Possible values may include **JAVASCRIPT**, **JSCRIPT**, **VBSCRIPT**, and **VBS**. Other values that include the version of the language used, such as JavaScript 1.1, may also be possible.

MAXLENGTH   This attribute indicates the maximum content length that can be entered in a text form control (**TYPE="TEXT"**). The maximum number of characters allowed differs from the visible dimension of the form control, which is set with the **SIZE** attribute.

NAME   This attribute allows a form control to be assigned a name so that it can be referenced by a scripting language. **NAME** is supported by older browsers such as Netscape 2.x-generation browsers, but the W3C encourages the use of the **ID** attribute. For compatibility purposes, both may have to be used.

NOARGS   In the WebTV implementation, this attribute is used with the **ACTION** attribute to prevent form control-specific arguments from being appended to an action request. This may be useful with button form controls. This attribute requires no value.

NOCURSOR   In the WebTV implementation, this attribute makes selecting an image a single-step interaction. The default WebTV interaction is a two-step process: the viewer clicks an image to activate it, then moves and eventually clicks again with a special cursor to select a hot spot. In the **NOCURSOR** option, the viewer clicks only once. The hot spot is assumed to be the x,y coordinate at the center of the image. This attribute requires no value.

NOHIGHLIGHT   In the WebTV implementation, this attribute suppresses display of the yellow "highlight" rectangle when the user selects a control. This attribute requires no value.

NOSUBMIT   In the WebTV implementation, this attribute is used with a text form control (**TYPE="TEXT"**) to indicate that a viewer entering "return" in the text area should not cause the associated form to be submitted. This attribute requires no value.

NUMBERS   In the WebTV implementation, this attribute causes the number "1" to be selected in the onscreen keyboard in anticipation of the viewer entering a numeric value. This attribute requires no value.

READONLY   This attribute prevents the form control's value from being changed. Form controls with this attribute set may receive focus from the user but may not be modified. Since it receives focus, a **READONLY** form control will be part of the form's tabbing order. Last, the control's value will be sent on form submission. This attribute can only be used with <INPUT> when **TYPE** is **TEXT** or **PASSWORD**. The attribute is also used with the <TEXTAREA> element.

SIZE   This attribute indicates the visible dimension, in characters, of a text form control (**TYPE="TEXT"**). This differs from the maximum length of content, which can be entered in a form control set by the **MAXLENGTH** attribute.

SRC   This attribute is used with image form controls (**TYPE="IMAGE"**) to specify the URL of the image file to load.

STYLE   See "Core Attributes Reference" earlier in this appendix.

SUBMITFORM   In the WebTV implementation, this attribute causes a form to be immediately submitted when the value of the associated form control is changed. This attribute requires no value.

TABINDEX   This attribute takes a numeric value that indicates the position of the form control in the tabbing index for the form. Tabbing proceeds from the lowest positive **TABINDEX** value to the highest. Negative values for **TABINDEX** will leave the form control out of the tabbing order. When tabbing is not explicitly set, the browser may tab through items in the order they are encountered. Form controls that are disabled due to the presence of the **DISABLED** attribute will not be part of the tabbing index, though read-only controls will be.

TITLE   See "Core Attributes Reference" earlier in this appendix.

TYPE   This attribute specifies the type of the form control. A value of **BUTTON** indicates a general-purpose button with no well-defined meaning. However, an action can be associated with the button using an event handler attribute, such as onclick. A value of **CHECKBOX** indicates a checkbox control. Checkbox form controls have a checked and nonchecked set, but even if these controls are grouped together, they allow a user to select multiple checkboxes at once. In contrast, a value of RADIO indicates a radio button control. When grouped, radio buttons allow only one of the many choices to be selected at a given time.

A form control type of **HIDDEN** indicates a field that is not visible to the viewer but is used to store information. A hidden form control is often used to preserve state information between pages. A value of **FILE** for the **TYPE** attribute indicates a control that allows the viewer to upload a file to a server. The filename can be entered in a displayed field, or a user agent may provide a special browse button allowing the user to locate the file. A value of **IMAGE** indicates a graphic image form control that a user can click on to invoke an associated action. A value of **PASSWORD** for the **TYPE** attribute indicates a password entry field. A password field will not display text entered as it is typed; it may instead show a series of dots. Note that password-entered data is not transferred to the server in any secure fashion. A value of **RESET** for the **TYPE** attribute is used to insert a button that resets all controls within a form to their default values. A value of **SUBMIT** inserts a special submission button that, when pressed, sends the contents of the form to the location indicated by the **ACTION** attribute of the enclosing **<FORM>** element. Last, a value of **TEXT** (the default) for the **TYPE** attribute indicates a single-line text input field.

USEFORM   In the WebTV implementation, this attribute can be used with the **SUBMIT** button to cause it to submit a different form on the page when the button is pressed. The value for this attribute is the name of the form to submit, which must be indicated in that form using either the **ID** or **NAME** attribute for the **<FORM>** element. If no value is specified, the enclosing form is always assumed.

USEMAP   This HTML 4.0 attribute is used to indicate the map file to be associated with an image when the form control is set with **TYPE=IMAGE**. The value of the attribute should be a URL of a map file, but will generally be in the form of a URL fragment that references a map file within the current file.

USESTYLE   In the WebTV implementation, the presence of this attribute causes control text to be rendered in the default text style for the page. This attribute requires no value.

VALUE   This attribute has two different uses, depending on the value for the **TYPE** attribute. With data entry controls (**TYPE="TEXT"** and **TYPE="PASSWORD"**), this attribute is used to set the default value for the control. When used with checkbox or radio form controls, this attribute is used to specify the return value for the control when it is turned on, rather than the default Boolean value submitted.

WIDTH   This WebTV attribute is used to set the size of the form control in pixels.

EVENT HANDLERS   See "Events Reference" earlier in this appendix.

Examples

```
<FORM>
    Which is your favorite food ?
    <INPUT TYPE="RADIO" NAME="favorite" VALUE="Mexican">Mexican
    <INPUT TYPE="RADIO" NAME="favorite" VALUE="Italian">Italian
    <INPUT TYPE="RADIO" NAME="favorite" VALUE="Japanese">Japanese
    <INPUT TYPE="RADIO" CHECKED NAME="favorite" VALUE="Other">Other
</FORM>


<FORM>
    Enter your name: <INPUT TYPE="TEXT" MAXLENGTH="35" SIZE="20"><BR>
    Enter your password: <INPUT TYPE="PASSWORD" MAXLENGTH="35"
SIZE="20"><BR>
    <BR>
    <INPUT TYPE="SUBMIT" VALUE="Submit">
    <INPUT TYPE="RESET" VALUE="Reset">
</FORM>
```

COMPATIBILITY   W3C 2.0, 3.2, 4.0; Netscape 1.x, 2.x, 3.x, 4.x; Internet Explorer 2.x, 3.x, 4.x; and WebTV

Notes
The <INPUT> element is an empty element and requires no closing tag.
Some documents suggest the use of **TYPE="TEXTAREA"**. Even if this style is supported, it should be avoided in favor of the <TEXTAREA> element, which is common to all browsers.
The HTML 3.2 and 2.0 specifications support only the **ALIGN, CHECKED, MAXLENGTH, NAME, SIZE, SRC, TYPE,** and **VALUE** attributes for the <INPUT> element.
WebTV supports only the **onblur, onchange, onfocus,** and **onselect** events.
The HTML 4.0 specification also reserves the use of the **DATASRC, DATAFLD,** and **DATAFORMATAS** data binding attributes. While Microsoft initially supported these attributes for the <INPUT> element, the current support is unclear in the documentation.
Under the strict HTML 4.0 specification, the **ALIGN** attribute is not allowed.

<INS>   (Inserted Text)

DESCRIPTION   This element is used to indicate that text has been added to the document.

Syntax

```
<INS
    CITE=URL
    CLASS=class name(s)
    DATETIME=date
```

```
            ID=unique alphanumeric identifier
            LANG=language code
            LANGUAGE=JAVASCRIPT | JSCRIPT | VBSCRIPT | VBS    (IE 4.0)
            STYLE=style information
            TITLE=advisory text

            onclick="script"
            ondblclick="script"
            ondragstart="script"   (IE 4.0)
            onhelp="script"   (IE 4.0)
            onkeydown="script"
            onkeypress="script"
            onkeyup="script"
            onmousedown="script"
            onmousemove="script"
            onmouseout="script"
            onmouseover="script"
            onmouseup="script">

    </INS>
```

Attributes

CITE   The value of this attribute is a URL that designates a source document or message for the information inserted. This attribute is intended to point to information explaining why the text was changed.

CLASS   See "Core Attributes Reference" earlier in this appendix.

DATETIME   This attribute is used to indicate the date and time the insertion was made. The value of the attribute is a date in a special format as defined by ISO 8601. The basic date format is

```
YYYY-MM-DDThh:mm:ssTZD
```

where:

```
YYYY=four-digit year such as 1997
     MM=two-digit month (01=January, 02=February, and so on.)
     DD=two-digit day of the month (01 through 31)
     hh=two digit hour (00 through 23) (24 hour clock not AM or PM)
     mm=two digit minute (00 through 59)
     ss=two digit second (00 through 59)
     TZD=time zone designator
```

The time zone designator is either **Z**, which indicates UTC (Coordinated Universal Time), or **+hh:mm**, which indicates that the time is a local time that is *hh* hours and *mm* minutes ahead of UTC. Alternatively, the format for the time zone designator could be **-hh:mm**, which indicates that the local time is behind UTC. Note that the letter T actually appears in the string, all digits must be used, and **00** values for minutes and seconds may be required. An example value for the **DATETIME** attribute might be **1997-10-6T09:15:00-05:00**, which corresponds to October 6, 1997, 9:15 A.M., U.S. Eastern Standard Time.

ID   See "Core Attributes Reference" earlier in this appendix.

LANG   See "Language Reference" earlier in this appendix.

LANGUAGE   In the Microsoft implementation, this attribute specifies the scripting language to be used with an associated script bound to the element, typically through an event handler attribute. Possible values may include **JAVASCRIPT**, **JSCRIPT**, **VBSCRIPT**, and **VBS**. Other values that include the version of the language used, such as JavaScript 1.1, may also be possible.

STYLE   See "Core Attributes Reference" earlier in this appendix.

TITLE   See "Core Attributes Reference" earlier in this appendix.

EVENT HANDLERS   See "Events Reference" earlier in this appendix.

Example

```
<INS CITE="http://www.bigcompany.com/changes/oct97.htm"
     DATE="1997-10-06T09:15:00-05:00">
   The penalty clause applies to client lateness as well.
</INS>
```

COMPATIBILITY   W3C 4.0; Internet Explorer 4.x

Notes

Browsers may render inserted **<INS>** or deleted **<DEL>** text in a different style to show the changes that have been made the document. Eventually a browser may have a way to show a revision history on a document. User agents that do not understand **<INS>** or **<DEL>** will show the information anyway, so there is no harm in adding information, only in deleting it. The **<INS>** element is not supported under HTML 3.2 and HTML 2.0 specifications.

<ISINDEX>   (Index Prompt)

DESCRIPTION   This element indicates that a document has an associated searchable keyword index. When a browser encounters this element, it inserts query entry field at that point in the document. The viewer can enter query terms to perform a search. This element is depreciated under the strict HTML 4.0 specification and should not be used.

Syntax

```
<ISINDEX
       ACTION=URL    (IE 3.0)
       CLASS=class name(s)
       DIR=LTR | RTL
       HREF=URL    (Nonstandard but common)
       ID=unique alphanumeric identifier
       LANG=language code
       LANGUAGE=JAVASCRIPT | JSCRIPT | VBSCRIPT | VBS    (IE 4.0)
       PROMPT=string
       STYLE=style information
       TITLE=advisory text>
```

Attributes

ACTION   This attribute specifies the URL of the query action to be executed when the viewer hits the RETURN key. While this attribute is not specified under specification, it is common to many browsers, particularly Internet Explorer 3.0.

CLASS   See "Core Attributes Reference" earlier in this appendix.

DIR   See "Language Reference" earlier in this appendix.

HREF   The **HREF** attribute is used with the **<ISINDEX>** element as a way to indicate what the search document is. Another approach is to use the **<BASE>** element for the document. The HTML 2.0 documentation suggests that this is a valid approach, and browsers appear to support it; however, it is poorly documented at best.

ID   See "Core Attributes Reference" earlier in this appendix.

LANG   See "Language Reference" earlier in this appendix.

LANGUAGE   In the Microsoft implementation, this attribute specifies the scripting language to be used with an associated script bound to the element typically through an event handler attribute. Possible values may include **JAVASCRIPT**, **JSCRIPT**, **VBSCRIPT**, and **VBS**. Other values that include the version of the language used, such as JavaScript 1.1, may also be possible.

PROMPT   This attribute allows a custom query prompt to be defined. The default prompt is "This is a searchable index. Enter search keywords." WebTV does not implement this attribute

TITLE   See "Core Attributes Reference" earlier in this appendix.

EVENT HANDLERS   None.

Examples

```
<ISINDEX ACTION="cgi-bin/search" PROMPT="Enter search terms">

<ISINDEX HREF="cgi-bin/search" PROMPT="Keywords:">

<BASE HREF="cgi-bin/search">
<ISINDEX PROMPT="Enter search terms">
```

COMPATIBILITY W3C 2.0, 3.2, 4.0 (transitional); Netscape 1.x, 2.x, 3.x, 4.x; Internet Explorer 2.x, 3.x, 4.x; and WebTV

Notes

As an empty element, **<ISINDEX>** requires no closing tag.

The HTML 3.2 specification only allows the **PROMPT** attribute, while HTML 2.0 expected a text description to accompany the search field.

Netscape 1.1 originated the use of the **PROMPT** attribute. WebTV does not support this attribute. Originally, the W3C intended this element to be used in a document's header. Browser vendors have relaxed this usage to allow the element in a document's body. Early implementations did not support the **ACTION** attribute and used the **<BASE>** element or an **HREF** attribute to specify an search functions URL.

Older versions of Internet Explorer also support the **ACTION** attribute, which is used to specify the URL to use for the query rather than relying on the URL set in the **<BASE>** element.

<KBD>   (Keyboard Input)

DESCRIPTION This element logically indicates text as keyboard input. A browser generally renders text enclosed by this element in a monospaced font.

Syntax

```
<KBD
     CLASS=class name(s)
     DIR=LTR | RTL
     ID=unique alphanumeric identifier
     LANG=language code
     LANGUAGE=JAVASCRIPT | JSCRIPT | VBSCRIPT | VBS    (IE 4.0)
     STYLE=style information
     TITLE=advisory text

     onclick="script"
     ondblclick="script"
     ondragstart="script"   (IE 4.0)
     onhelp="script"    (IE 4.0)
     onkeydown="script"
     onkeypress="script"
```

```
      onkeyup="script"
      onmousedown="script"
      onmousemove="script"
      onmouseout="script"
      onmouseover="script"
      onmouseup="script"
      onselectstart="script">   (IE 4.0)
  </KBD>
```

Attributes

CLASS   See "Core Attributes Reference" earlier in this appendix.

DIR   See "Language Reference" earlier in this appendix.

ID   See "Core Attributes Reference" earlier in this appendix.

LANG   See "Language Reference" earlier in this appendix.

LANGUAGE   In the Microsoft implementation, this attribute specifies the scripting language to be used with an associated script bound to the element, typically through an event handler attribute. Possible values may include **JAVASCRIPT**, **JSCRIPT**, **VBSCRIPT**, and **VBS**. Other values that include the version of the language used, such as JavaScript 1.1, may also be possible.

STYLE   See "Core Attributes Reference" earlier in this appendix.

TITLE   See "Core Attributes Reference" earlier in this appendix.

EVENT HANDLERS   See "Events Reference" earlier in this appendix.

Example

```
Enter the change directory command at the prompt as shown below<BR>
    <BR>
<KBD>CD .. </KBD>
```

COMPATIBILITY   W3C 2.0, 3.2, 4.0; Netscape 1.x, 2.x, 3.x, 4.x; Internet Explorer 2.x, 3.x, 4.x; and WebTV

Notes
The HTML 2.0 and 3.2 specifications support no attributes for this element.

<LABEL>   (Form Control Label)

DESCRIPTION   This HTML 4.0 element is used to relate descriptions to form controls.

Syntax

```
<LABEL
    ACCESSKEY=key
    CLASS=class name(s)
    DATAFLD=name of column supplying bound data (IE 4.0)
    DATAFORMATAS=HTML | TEXT    (IE 4.0)
    DATASRC=ID of data source object supplying data (IE 4.0)
    DIR=LTR | RTL
    FOR=ID of control
    ID=unique alphanumeric identifier
    LANG=language code
    LANGUAGE=JAVASCRIPT | JSCRIPT | VBSCRIPT | VBS    (IE 4.0)
    STYLE=style information
    TITLE=advisory text

    onblur="script"
    onclick="script"
    ondblclick="script"
    ondragstart="script"    (IE 4.0)
    onfocus="script"
    onhelp="script"    (IE 4.0)
    onkeydown="script"
    onkeypress="script"
    onkeyup="script"
    onmousedown="script"
    onmousemove="script"
    onmouseout="script"
    onmouseover="script"
    onmouseup="script"
    onselectstart="script">    (IE 4.0)

</LABEL>
```

Attributes

ACCESKEY   This attribute specifies a keyboard navigation accelerator for the element. Pressing ALT or a similar key in association with the specified key selects the anchor element correlated with that key.

CLASS   See "Core Attributes Reference" earlier in this appendix.

DATAFLD   This attribute is used to indicate the column name in the data source that is bound to the content of the **<LABEL>** element.

DATAFORMATAS   This attribute indicates if the bound data is plain text (**TEXT**) or HTML (**HTML**). The data bound with **<LABEL>** is used to set the content of the label.

DATASRC   The value of this attribute is an identifier indicating the data source to pull data from.

DIR   See "Language Reference" earlier in this appendix.

FOR   This attribute specifies the **ID** for the form control element the label references. This is optional when the label encloses the form control it is bound to. In many cases, particularly when a table is used to structure the form, the **<LABEL>** element will not be able to enclose the associated form control, so the **FOR** attribute should be used. This attribute allows more than one label to be associated with the same control by creating multiple references.

ID   See "Core Attributes Reference" earlier in this appendix.

LANG   See "Language Reference" earlier in this appendix.

LANGUAGE   In the Microsoft implementation, this attribute specifies the scripting language to be used with an associated script bound to the element, typically through an event handler attribute. Possible values may include **JAVASCRIPT**, **JSCRIPT**, **VBSCRIPT**, and **VBS**. Other values that include the version of the language used, such as JavaScript 1.1, may also be possible.

STYLE   See "Core Attributes Reference" earlier in this appendix.

TITLE   See "Core Attributes Reference" earlier in this appendix.

EVENT HANDLERS   See "Events Reference" earlier in this appendix.

Example

```
<FORM>
    <LABEL ID="usernamelabel">
    Name
    <INPUT TYPE="TEXT" ID="username">
    </LABEL>
</FORM>

<FORM>
  <TABLE>
   <TR>
     <TD><LABEL FOR="username">Name</LABEL></TD>
     <TD><INPUT TYPE="TEXT" ID="username"></TD>
   </TR>
  </TABLE>
</FORM>
```

COMPATIBILITY   W3C 4.0; Internet Explorer 4.x

Notes

To associate a label with another control implicitly, make the control the contents of the **LABEL**. In this case, a **<LABEL>** element may only contain one other control element. The label itself may be positioned before or after the associated control. If it is impossible to enclose the associated form control, the **FOR** attribute may be used.

The HTML 4.0 specification specifies the **onfocus** and **onblur** events for **<LABEL>**. However, Internet Explorer 4.0 does not document their use.

<LAYER>

DESCRIPTION   This Netscape-specific element allows the definition of overlapping content layers that can be exactly positioned, hidden or shown, rendered transparent or opaque, reordered front to back, and nested. The functionality of layers is available using CSS positioning facilities; page developers are advised not to use the **<LAYER>** element.

Syntax

```
<LAYER
      ABOVE=layer name    (N 4.0)
      BACKGROUND=URL of background image    (N 4.0)
      BELOW=layer name    (N 4.0)
      BGCOLOR=color value    (N 4.0)
      CLASS=class name(s)    (N 4.0)
      CLIP=clip region coordinates in x1, y1, x2, y2 form (N 4.0)
      HEIGHT=pixels | percentage    (N 4.0)
      ID=unique alphanumeric identifier    (N 4.0)
      LEFT=pixels    (N 4.0)
      NAME=string    (N 4.0)
      PAGEX=horizontal pixel position of layer    (N 4.0)
      PAGEY=vertical pixel position of layer    (N 4.0)
      SRC=URL of layer's contents    (N 4.0)
      STYLE=style information    (N 4.0)
      TITLE=advisory text    (N 4.0)
      TOP=pixels    (N 4.0)
      VISIBILITY=HIDE | INHERIT | SHOW    (N 4.0)
      WIDTH=pixels | percentage    (N 4.0)
      Z-INDEX=number    (N 4.0)

      onblur="script"    (N 4.0)
      onfocus="script"    (N 4.0)
      onload="script"    (N 4.0)
      onmouseout="script"    (N 4.0)
      onmouseover="script">    (N 4.0)

</LAYER>
```

Attributes

ABOVE   This attribute contains the name of the layer (as set with the **NAME** attribute) to be rendered directly above the current layer.

BACKGROUND   This attribute contains the URL of a background pattern for the layer. Like backgrounds for the document as a whole, the image may tile.

BELOW   This value of this attribute is the name of the layer to be rendered below the current layer.

BGCOLOR   This attribute specifies a layer's background color. The attribute's value can be either a named color, such as **red**, or a color specified in the hexadecimal *#RRGGBB* format, such as **#FF0000**.

CLASS   See "Core Attributes Reference" earlier in this appendix.

CLIP   This attribute clips a layer's content to a specified rectangle. All layer content outside that rectangle will be rendered transparent. The clip rectangle is defined by two x,y pairs that correspond to the top x, left y, bottom x, and right y coordinate of the rectangle. The coordinates are relative to the layer's origin point, 0,0 in its top left corner, and may have nothing to do with the pixel coordinates of the screen.

DIR   See "Language Reference" earlier in this appendix.

HEIGHT   This attribute is used to set the height of the layer in either pixels or as a percentage of the screen or region the layer is contained within.

ID   See "Core Attributes Reference" earlier in this appendix.

LEFT   This attribute specifies in pixels the left offset of the layer. The offset is relative to its parent layer, if it has one, or to the left browser margin if it does not.

NAME   This attribute assigns the layer a name that can be referenced by programs in a client-side scripting language. The **ID** attribute can also be used.

PAGEX   This attribute is used to set the horizontal pixel position of the layer relative to the document window rather than any enclosing layer.

PAGEY   This attribute is used to set the vertical pixel position of the layer relative to the document window rather than any enclosing layer.

SRC   This attribute is used to specify the URL that contains the content to include in the layer. Using this attribute with an empty element is a good way to preserve layouts under older browsers.

STYLE   See "Core Attributes Reference" earlier in this appendix.

TITLE   See "Core Attributes Reference" earlier in this appendix.

TOP   This attribute specifies in pixels the top offset of the layer. The offset is relative to its parent layer if it has one, or the top browser margin if it is not enclosed in another layer.

VISIBILITY   This attribute specifies whether a layer is hidden (**HIDDEN**), shown (**SHOW**), or inherits (**INHERITS**) its visibility from the layer enclosing it.

WIDTH This attribute specifies a layer's width in pixels or as a percentage value of the enclosing layer or browser width.

Z INDEX This attribute specifies a layer's stacking order relative to other layers. Position is specified with positive integers, with "1" indicating the bottommost layer.

EVENT HANDLERS See "Events Reference" earlier in this appendix.

Examples

```
<LAYER NAME="scene" BGCOLOR="GREEN">
  <LAYER NAME="George" LEFT="100" TOP="100">
    <IMG SRC="georgejungle.gif">
  </LAYER>
  <LAYER NAME="Ape" LEFT="200" TOP="100" VISIBLITY="HIDDEN">
    <IMG SRC="ApeNamedApe.gif">
  </LAYER>
</LAYER>

<!--The better way to do layers -->
<LAYER SRC="contents.htm" LEFT="20" TOP="20"
    HEIGHT="80%" WIDTH="80%">
</LAYER>
```

COMPATIBILITY Netscape 4.x

Notes

This element will likely fall out of fashion because it lacks cross-browser compatibility. The functionality of **<LAYER>** is possible using the positioning features in CSS; page developers are encouraged not to use the **<LAYER>** element.
Applets, plug-ins, and other embedded media forms, generically called objects, may be included in a layer. However, they will float to the top of all other layers even if their containing layer is obscured.

<LEGEND> (Field Legend)

DESCRIPTION This HTML 4.0 element is used to assign a caption to a set of form fields as defined by the **<FIELDSET>** element.

Syntax

```
<LEGEND
    ACCESSKEY=character
    ALIGN=BOTTOM | CENTER* | LEFT | RIGHT | TOP    (* IE 4.0)
    CLASS=class name(s)
    DIR=LTR | RTL
```

```
          ID=unique alphanumeric identifier
          LANG=language code
          LANGUAGE=JAVASCRIPT | JSCRIPT | VBSCRIPT | VBS    (IE 4.0)
          STYLE=style information
          TITLE=advisory text
          VALIGN=BOTTOM | TOP    (IE 4.0)

          onclick="script"
          ondblclick="script"
          ondragstart="script"    (IE 4.0)
          onhelp="script"    (IE 4.0)
          onkeydown="script"
          onkeypress="script"
          onkeyup="script"
          onmousedown="script"
          onmousemove="script"
          onmouseout="script"
          onmouseover="script"
          onmouseup="script">


    </LEGEND>
```

Attributes

ACCESKEY   This attribute specifies a keyboard navigation accelerator for the element. Pressing ALT or a similar key in association with the specified key selects the form section or the legend itself.

ALIGN   This attribute indicates where the legend value should be positioned within the border created by a **<FIELDSET>** element. The default position for the legend is the upper left corner. It is also possible to position the legend to the right by setting the attribute to **RIGHT**. The specification defines **BOTTOM** and **TOP** as well. Microsoft defines the use of the **CENTER** and also defines another attribute, **VALIGN**, to set the vertical alignment separately. Future support for **VALIGN** is unclear; page designers are encouraged to use only the **ALIGN** attribute and to eventually rely on style sheets for legend positioning.

CLASS   See "Core Attributes Reference" earlier in this appendix.

DIR   See "Language Reference" earlier in this appendix.

ID   See "Core Attributes Reference" earlier in this appendix.

LANG   See "Language Reference" earlier in this appendix.

LANGUAGE   In the Microsoft implementation, this attribute specifies the scripting language to be used with an associated script bound to the element, typically through an event handler

attribute. Possible values may include **JAVASCRIPT, JSCRIPT, VBSCRIPT,** and **VBS.** Other values that include the version of the language used, such as JavaScript 1.1, may also be possible.

STYLE   See "Core Attributes Reference" earlier in this appendix.

TITLE   See "Core Attributes Reference" earlier in this appendix.

VALIGN   This Microsoft-specific attribute is used to set whether the legend appears on the **TOP** or the **BOTTOM** of the border defined by the enclosing **<FIELDSET>** element. The attribute will probably be dropped, as it is nonstandard.

EVENT HANDLERS   See "Events Reference" earlier in this appendix.

Example

```
<FORM>
 <FIELDSET>
   <LEGEND ALIGN="TOP">User Information</LEGEND>
   First Name: <INPUT TYPE="TEXT" ID="firstname" SIZE="20"><BR>
   Last Name: <INPUT TYPE="TEXT" ID="lastname" SIZE="20"><BR>
 </FIELDSET>
</FORM>
```

COMPATIBILITY   W3C 4.0; Internet Explorer 4.0

Notes

The **<LEGEND>** element should occur only within the **<FIELDSET>** element. There should be only one **<LEGEND>** per **<FIELDSET>** element.

The legend improves accessibility when the **FIELDSET** is rendered nonvisually.

The Microsoft implementation can use the **CENTER** option in the **ALIGN** attribute. Microsoft also defines the **VALIGN** attribute for legend positioning. However, the **VALIGN** attribute does not to appear to work consistently.

WebTV and Netscape do not yet support this element.

<LI>   (List Item)

DESCRIPTION   This element is used to indicate a list item as contained in an ordered list (**<OL>**), unordered list (**<UL>**), or older list styles like **<DIR>** and **<MENU>**.

Syntax

```
<LI
    CLASS=class name(s)
    DIR=LTR | RTL
    ID=unique alphanumeric identifier
    LANG=language code
```

```
LANGUAGE=JAVASCRIPT | JSCRIPT | VBSCRIPT | VBS    (IE 4.0)
STYLE=style information
TITLE=advisory text
TYPE=CIRCLE | DISC | SQUARE | a | A | i | I | 1
VALUE=number

onclick="script"
ondblclick="script"
ondragstart="script"    (IE 4.0)
onhelp="script"    (IE 4.0)
onkeydown="script"
onkeypress="script"
onkeyup="script"
onmousedown="script"
onmousemove="script"
onmouseout="script"
onmouseover="script"
onmouseup="script"
onselectstart="script">    (IE 4.0)

</LI>
```

Attributes

CLASS   See "Core Attributes Reference" earlier in this appendix.

DIR   See "Language Reference" earlier in this appendix.

ID   See "Core Attributes Reference" earlier in this appendix.

LANG   See "Language Reference" earlier in this appendix.

LANGUAGE   In the Microsoft implementation, this attribute specifies the scripting language to be used with an associated script bound to the element, typically through an event handler attribute. Possible values may include **JAVASCRIPT**, **JSCRIPT**, **VBSCRIPT**, and **VBS**. Other values that include the version of the language used, such as JavaScript 1.1, may also be possible.

STYLE   See "Core Attributes Reference" earlier in this appendix.

TITLE   See "Core Attributes Reference" earlier in this appendix.

TYPE   This attribute indicates the bullet type used in unordered lists or the numbering type used in ordered lists. For ordered lists, a value of **a** indicates lowercase letters, **A** indicates uppercase letters, **i** indicates lowercase Roman numerals, **I** indicates uppercase Roman numerals, and **1** indicates numbers. For unordered lists, values are used to specify bullet types. While the browser is free to set bullet styles, a value of **DISC** generally specifies a filled circle, a value of **CIRCLE** specifies an empty circle, and a value of **b** specifies a filled square. Browsers like WebTV may include other bullet shapes like triangles.

VALUE This attribute indicates the current number of items in an ordered list as defined by the **<OL>** element. Regardless of the value of **TYPE** being used to set Roman numerals or letters, the only allowed value for this attribute is a number. List items that follow will continue numbering from the value set. The **VALUE** attribute has no meaning for unordered lists.

EVENT HANDLERS See "Events Reference" earlier in this appendix.

Examples

```
<UL>
   <LI TYPE="CIRCLE">First list item is a circle
   <LI TYPE="SQUARE">Second list item is a square
   <LI TYPE="DISC">Third list item is a square
</UL>

<OL>
   <LI TYPE="I">Roman Numerals
   <LI TYPE="A" VALUE="3">Second list item is letter C
   <LI TYPE="a">Continue on in lower case letters
</OL>
```

COMPATIBILITY W3C 2.0, 3.2, 4.0; Netscape 1.x, 2.x, 3.x, 4.x; Internet Explorer 2.x, 3.x, 4.x; and WebTV

Notes

Under the strict HTML 4.0 definition, the **<LI>** element loses the **TYPE** and **VALUE** attributes, as these functions can be performed with style sheets.
While bullet style can be set explicitly, browsers tend to change styles for bullets when **<UL>** lists are nested. However, ordered lists generally do not change style automatically nor do they support outline style number (1.1, 1.1.1, and so on).

<LIMITTEXT>

DESCRIPTION This WebTV-specific element is used to set the width of an area to display text within.

Syntax

```
<LIMITTEXT

    SIZE="number"    (WebTV)

    VALUE="url"    (WebTV)

    WIDTH=pixels or # of characters>    (WebTV)
```

Attributes

SIZE   This attribute indicates the maximum width, in characters, of displayed text. There is no limit to the value of this attribute.

VALUE   This attribute sets the text string that will be limited. In general this attribute is set to specially encoded text of some dynamic form, since it provides little benefit for hard coded text.

WIDTH   This attribute indicates the maximum width of the text region in pixels.

EVENT HANDLERS   None.

Example

```
<LIMITTEXT SIZE="25" VALUE="&url; a crazy expanding encoded string
with a bunch of stuff in it">
```

COMPATIBILITY   WebTV

Notes

This element is an empty element and requires no closing tag.
If both **SIZE** and **WIDTH** are used, the browser will use the smaller of the two values specified.
Since the content of the **<LIMITTEXT>** element is contained with the attribute **VALUE**, nothing will be displayed in browsers that do not understand this element.

<LINK>

DESCRIPTION   This empty element specifies relationships between the current document and other documents. Possible uses for this element include defining a relational framework for navigation and linking the document to a style sheet.

Syntax

```
<LINK
    CHARSET=charset list from RFC 2045
    CLASS=class name(s)
    DIR=LTR | RTL
    DISABLED    (IE 4.0)
    HREF=URL
    HREFLANG=language code
    ID=unique alphanumeric identifier
    LANG=language code
    MEDIA=ALL | SCREEN | PRINT | PROJECTION |  BRAILLE | AURAL | other
    REL=relationship value
    REV=relationship value
    STYLE=style information
```

```
TARGET=frame name
TITLE=advisory information
TYPE=content type

onclick="script"
ondblclick="script"
onkeydown="script"
onkeypress="script"
onkeyup="script"
onmousedown="script"
onmousemove="script"
onmouseout="script"
onmouseover="script"
onmouseup="script">
```

Attributes

CHARSET   This attributes specifies the character set used by the linked document. Allowed values for this attribute are character set names, such as EUC-JP, as defined in RFC 2045.

CLASS   See "Core Attributes Reference" earlier in this appendix.

DIR   See "Language Reference" earlier in this appendix.

DISABLED   This Microsoft-defined attribute is used to disable a link relationship. The presence of the attribute is all that is required to remove a linking relationship. In conjunction with scripting, this attribute could be used to turn on and off various style sheet relationships.

HREF   This attribute is used to specify the URL of the linked resource. A URL may be absolute or relative.

HREFLANG   This attribute is used to indicate the language of the linked resource. See "Language Reference" earlier in this appendix for information on allowed values.

ID   See "Core Attributes Reference" earlier in this appendix.

LANG   See "Language Reference" earlier in this appendix.

MEDIA   This attribute is used to specify the destination medium for any linked style information, as indicated when the **REL** attribute is set to **STYLESHEET**. The value of the attribute may be a single media descriptor like **SCREEN**, or a comma-separated list. Possible values for this attribute include **SCREEN, PRINT, PROJECTION, BRAILLE, AURAL**, and **ALL**. Other values may also be defined, depending on the browser. Internet Explorer supports **SCREEN, PRINT**, and **ALL** as values for this attribute.

REL   This attribute names a relationship between the linked document and the current document. Possible values for this attribute include **ALTERNATE, STYLESHEET, START**,

NEXT, PREV, CONTENTS, INDEX, GLOSSARY, COPYRIGHT, CHAPTER, SECTION, SUBSECTION, APPENDIX, HELP, and **BOOKMARK.** The most common use of this attribute is to specify a link to an external style sheet. The **REL** attribute is set to **STYLESHEET,** and the **HREF** attribute is set to the URL of an external style sheet to format the page. WebTV also supports the use of the value **NEXT** for **REL** to preload the next page in a document series.

REV   The value of the **REV** attribute shows the relationship of the current document to the linked document, as defined by the **HREF** attribute. The attribute thus defines the reverse relationship compared to the value of the **REL** attribute. Values for the **REV** attribute are similar to the possible values for **REL**. They may include **ALTERNATE, STYLESHEET, START, NEXT, PREV, CONTENTS, INDEX, GLOSSARY, COPYRIGHT, CHAPTER, SECTION, SUBSECTION, APPENDIX, HELP,** and **BOOKMARK.**

STYLE   See "Core Attributes Reference" earlier in this appendix.

TARGET   The value of the **TARGET** attribute is used to define the frame or window name that has the defined linking relationship or that will show the rendering of any linked resource.

TITLE   See "Core Attributes Reference" earlier in this appendix.

TYPE   This attribute is used to define the type of the content linked to. The value of the attribute should be a MIME type such as **text/html, text/css,** and so on. The common use of this attribute is to define the type of style sheet linked and the most common current value is **text/css,** which indicates a Cascading Style Sheet format.

EVENT HANDLERS   See "Event Reference" earlier in this appendix.

Examples

```
<LINK HREF="products.htm" REL="parent">

<LINK HREF="corpstyle.css" REL="stylesheet" TYPE="text/css" MEDIA="ALL">

<LINK HREF="nextpagetoload.htm" REL="next">
```

COMPATIBILITY   W3C 2.0, 3.2, 4.0; Netscape 4.x; Internet Explorer 3.x, 4.x; and WebTV

Notes

As an empty element **<LINK>** has no closing tag.
The **<LINK>** element can occur only in the **<HEAD>** element; there may be multiple occurrences of the element.
HTML 3.2 defines only the **HREF, REL, REV,** and **TITLE** attributes for the **<LINK>** element.
HTML 2.0 defines the **HREF, URN, REL, REV, TITLE,** and **METHODS** attributes for the **<LINK>** element. The **URN** and **METHODS** attributes were later removed from specifications.
The WebTV implementation supports only the **HREF** and **REL** attributes for this element.
The HTML 4.0 specification defines event handlers for the **<LINK>** element, but it is unclear how they would be used.

<LISTING>

DESCRIPTION   This depreciated element from HTML 2.0 is used to indicate a code listing; it is no longer part of the HTML standard. Text tends to be rendered in a smaller size within this element. Otherwise, the **<PRE>** element should be used instead of **<LISTING>** to indicate preformatted text.

Syntax

```
<LISTING
     CLASS=class name(s)    (IE 4.0)
     ID=unique alphanumeric string    (IE 4.0)
     LANG=language code    (IE 4.0)
     LANGUAGE=JAVASCRIPT | JSCRIPT | VBSCRIPT | VBS    (IE 4.0)
     STYLE=style information    (IE 4.0)
     TITLE=advisory text    (IE 4.0)

     onclick="script"    (IE 4.0)
     ondblclick="script"    (IE 4.0)
     ondragstart="script"    (IE 4.0)
     onhelp="script"    (IE 4.0)
     onkeydown="script"    (IE 4.0)
     onkeypress="script"    (IE 4.0)
     onkeyup="script"    (IE 4.0)
     onmousedown="script"    (IE 4.0)
     onmousemove="script"    (IE 4.0)
     onmouseout="script"    (IE 4.0)
     onmouseover="script"    (IE 4.0)
     onmouseup="script"    (IE 4.0)
     onselectstart="script">    (IE 4.0)

</LISTING>
```

Attributes

CLASS   See "Core Attributes Reference" earlier in this appendix.

ID   See "Core Attributes Reference" earlier in this appendix.

LANG   See "Language Reference" earlier in this appendix.

LANGUAGE   In the Microsoft implementation, this attribute specifies the scripting language to be used with an associated script bound to the element, typically through an event handler attribute. Possible values may include **JAVASCRIPT**, **JSCRIPT**, **VBS**, and **VBSCRIPT**. Other values that include the version of the language used, such as JavaScript 1.1, may also be possible.

STYLE   See "Core Attributes Reference" earlier in this appendix.

TITLE   See "Core Attributes Reference" earlier in this appendix.

EVENT HANDLERS   See "Events Reference" earlier in this appendix.

Example

```
<LISTING>
   This is a code listing. The preformatted text
   element &lt;PRE&gt; should be used instead
   of this depreciated element.
</LISTING
```

COMPATIBILITY   W3C 2.0; Netscape 1.x, 2.x, 3.x, 4.x; Internet Explorer 2.x, 3.x, 4.x; and WebTV

Notes

As a depreciated element, this element should not be used. This element is not supported by HTML 4.0. It is still documented by many browser vendors, however, and does creep into some pages. The **<PRE>** element should be used instead of **<LISTING>**.

It appears that Netscape and Internet Explorer browsers also make text within **<LISTING>** one size smaller than normal text, probably because the HTML 2.0 specification suggested that 132 characters fit to a typical line rather than 80.

WebTV supports no attributes for this element.

Netscape does not document support for this element, though it is still supported.

<MAP>

DESCRIPTION   This element is used to implement client-side image maps. The element is used to define a map to associate locations on an image with a destination URL. Each hot region or hyperlink mapping is defined by an enclosed **<AREA>** element. A map is bound to a particular image through the use of the **USEMAP** attribute in the **<IMG>** element, which is set to the name of the map.

Syntax

```
<MAP
    CLASS=class name(s)
    DIR=LTR | RTL
    ID=unique alphanumeric identifier
    LANG=language code
    NAME=unique alphanumeric identifier
    STYLE=style information
    TITLE=advisory text

    onclick="script"
    ondblclick="script"
```

```
        ondragstart="script"    (IE 4.0)
        onhelp="script"   (IE 4.0)
        onkeydown="script"
        onkeypress="script"
        onkeyup="script"
        onmousedown="script"
        onmousemove="script"
        onmouseout="script"
        onmouseover="script"
        onmouseover="script"
        onmouseup="script"
        onselectstart="script">    (IE 4.0)

  <AREA> elements

</MAP>
```

Attributes

CLASS   See "Core Attributes Reference" earlier in this appendix.

DIR   See "Language Reference" earlier in this appendix.

ID   See "Core Attributes Reference" earlier in this appendix.

LANG   See "Language Reference" earlier in this appendix.

NAME   Like **ID**, this attribute is used to define a name associated with the element. In the case of the **<MAP>** element, the **NAME** attribute is the common way to define the name of the image map to be referenced by the **USEMAP** attribute within the **<IMG>** element.

STYLE   See "Core Attributes Reference" earlier in this appendix.

TITLE   See "Core Attributes Reference" earlier in this appendix.

EVENT HANDLERS   See "Events Reference" earlier in this appendix.

Example

```
<MAP NAME="mainmap">
  <AREA SHAPE="CIRCLE" COORDS="200,250,25" HREF="file1.htm">
  <AREA SHAPE="RECTANGLE" COORDS="50,50,100,100"
    HREF="file2.htm#important">
  <AREA SHAPE="DEFAULT" NOHREF>
</MAP>
```

COMPATIBILITY   W3C 3.2, 4.0; Netscape 1.x, 2.x, 3.x, 4.x; Internet Explorer 2.x, 3.x, 4.x; and WebTV

Notes

HTML 3.2 supports only the **NAME** attribute for the **<MAP>** element.
Client-side image maps are not supported under HTML 2.0. They were first suggested by Spyglass and later incorporated in Netscape and other browsers.

<MARQUEE>

DESCRIPTION   This proprietary element is used to specify a scrolling, sliding, or bouncing text marquee. This is primarily a Microsoft-specific element, though a few other browsers, notably WebTV, support it as well.

Syntax

```
<MARQUEE
     ALIGN=LEFT | CENTER | RIGHT | TOP | BOTTOM    (WebTV)
     BEHAVIOR=ALTERNATE | SCROLL | SLIDE    (IE 4.0, WebTV)
     BGCOLOR=color name | #RRGGBB    (IE 4.0, WebTV)
     CLASS=class name(s)    (IE 4.0)
     DATAFLD=column name    (IE 4.0)
     DATAFORMATAS=HTML | TEXT    (IE 4.0)
     DATASRC=data source ID    (IE 4.0)
     DIRECTION=DOWN* | LEFT | RIGHT | UP*    (*IE 4.0 only, WebTV)
     HEIGHT=pixels or percentage    (IE 4.0, WebTV)
     HSPACE=pixels    (IE 4.0, WebTV)
     ID=unique alphanumeric identifier    (IE 4.0)
     LANG=language code    (IE 4.0)
     LANGUAGE=JAVASCRIPT | JSCRIPT | VBSCRIPT | VBS    (IE 4.0)
     LOOP=number | INFINITE    (IE 4.0, WebTV)
     SCROLLAMOUNT=pixels    (IE 4.0, WebTV)
     SCROLLDELAY=milliseconds    (IE 4.0)
     STYLE=style information    (IE 4.0)
     TITLE=advisory text    (IE 4.0)
     TRUESPEED    (IE 4.0)
     TRANSPARENCY=0 - 100    (WebTV)
     VSPACE=pixels    (IE 4.0, WebTV)
     WIDTH=pixels or percentage    (IE 4.0, WebTV)

     onafterupdate="script"    (IE 4.0)
     onblur="script"    (IE 4.0)
     onbounce="script"    (IE 4.0)
     onclick="script"    (IE 4.0)
     ondblclick="script"    (IE 4.0)
     ondragstart="script"    (IE 4.0)
     onfinish="script"    (IE 4.0)
     onfocus="script"    (IE 4.0)
```

```
        onhelp="script"   (IE 4.0)
        onkeydown="script"   (IE 4.0)
        onkeypress="script"   (IE 4.0)
        onkeyup="script"   (IE 4.0)
        onmousedown="script"  ·(IE 4.0)
        onmousemove="script"   (IE 4.0)
        onmouseout="script"   (IE 4.0)
        onmouseover="script"   (IE 4.0)
        onmouseup="script"   (IE 4.0)
        onresize="script"   (IE 4.0)
        onrowenter="script"   (IE 4.0)
        onrowexit="script"   (IE 4.0)
        onselectstart="script"   (IE 4.0)
        onstart="script">   (IE 4.0)

    Marquee text

</MARQUEE>
```

Attributes

ALIGN   This WebTV-specific attribute is used to indicate how the marquee should be aligned with surrounding text. The alignment values and rendering are similar to other embedded objects, like images. The default value for this attribute under WebTV is **LEFT**. Microsoft Internet Explorer no longer supports this attribute.

BEHAVIOR   This attribute controls the movement of marquee text across the marquee. The **ALTERNATE** option causes text to completely cross the marquee field in one direction and then cross in the opposite direction. A value of **SCROLL** for the attribute causes text to wrap around and start over again. This is the default value for a marquee. A value of **SLIDE** for this attribute causes text to cross the marquee field and stop when its leading character reaches the opposite side.

BGCOLOR   This attribute is used to specify the marquee's background color. The value for the attribute can either be a color name or a color value defined in the hexadecimal *#RRGGBB* format.

CLASS   See "Core Attributes Reference" earlier in this appendix.

DATAFLD   This attribute is used to indicate the column name in the data source that is bound to the **<MARQUEE>** element.

DATAFORMATAS   This attribute indicates if the bound data is plain text (**TEXT**) or HTML (**HTML**). The data bound with **<MARQUEE>** is used to set the message that is scrolled.

DATASRC   The value of this attribute is set to an identifier indicating the data source to pull data from. Bound data is used to set the message that is scrolled in the **<MARQUEE>**.

DIRECTION   This attribute specifies the direction in which the marquee should scroll. The default is **LEFT**. Other possible values for **DIRECTION** include **RIGHT**, **TOP**, and **DOWN**. WebTV does not support the **UP** and **DOWN** values.

HEIGHT   This attribute specifies the height of the marquee in pixels or as a percentage of the window.

HSPACE   This attribute indicates the horizontal space in pixels between the marquee and surrounding content.

ID   See "Core Attributes Reference" earlier in this appendix.

LANG   See "Language Reference" earlier in this appendix.

LANGUAGE   In the Microsoft implementation, this attribute specifies the scripting language to be used with an associated script bound to the element, typically through an event handler attribute. Possible values may include **JAVASCRIPT**, **JSCRIPT**, **VBSCRIPT**, and **VBS**. Other values that include the version of the language used, such as JavaScript 1.1, may also be possible.

LOOP   This attribute indicates the number of times the marquee content should loop. By default, a marquee loops infinitely unless the **BEHAVIOR** attribute is set to **SLIDE**. It is also possible to use a value of **INFINITE** or **-1** to set the text to loop indefinitely.

SCROLLAMOUNT   This attribute specifies the width in pixels between successive displays of the scrolling text in the marquee.

SCROLLDELAY   This attribute specifies the delay in milliseconds between success displays of the text in the marquee.

STYLE   See "Core Attributes Reference" earlier in this appendix.

TITLE   See "Core Attributes Reference" earlier in this appendix.

TRANSPARENCY   In the WebTV implementation, this attribute specifies the marquee's degree of transparency. Values range from **0**, totally opaque, to **100**, totally transparent. A value of **50** is optimized for fast rendering.

TRUESPEED   When this attribute is present, it indicates that the **SCROLLDELAY** value should be honored for its exact value. If the attribute is not present, any values less than 60 are rounded up to 60 milliseconds.

VSPACE   This attribute indicates the vertical space in pixels between the marquee and surrounding content.

WIDTH   This attribute specifies the width of the marquee in pixels or as a percentage of the enclosing window.

EVENT HANDLERS   The <MARQUEE> element has a few unique events. For examples, an event is triggered when the text bounces off one side on the marquee or another. This can be caught with the **onbounce** event handler attribute. When the text first starts scrolling, the start event fires, which can be caught with **onstart**; when the marquee is done, a finish event fires,

which can be caught with **onfinish**. The other events are common to HTML 4.0 elements with
Microsoft extensions.

Examples

```
<MARQUEE BEHAVIOR="ALTERNATE">
  SPECIAL VALUE !!! This week only !!!
</MARQUEE>

<MARQUEE ID="marquee1" BGCOLOR="RED" DIRECTION="RIGHT"
      HEIGHT="30" WIDTH="80%" HSPACE="10" VSPACE="10">
    The super scroller scrolls again!!
    More fun than a barrel of &lt;BLINK&gt; elements.
</MARQUEE>
```

Notes

The **<MARQUEE>** element is supported only by Microsoft and WebTV.

<MENU>

DESCRIPTION   This element is used to indicate a short list of items that might occur in a
menu of choices. Like the ordered and unordered lists, the individual items in the list are
indicated by the **<LI>** element. Most browsers render the **<MENU>** exactly the same as the
unordered list, so there is little reason to use it. Under the HTML 4.0 strict specification,
<MENU> is no longer supported.

Syntax

```
<MENU
     CLASS=class name(s)
     COMPACT
     DIR=LTR | RTL
     ID=unique alphanumeric string
     LANG=language code
     LANGUAGE=JAVASCRIPT | JSCRIPT | VBSCRIPT | VBS    (IE 4.0)
     STYLE=style information
     TITLE=advisory text

     onclick="script"
     ondblclick="script"
     ondragstart="script"    (IE 4.0)
     onhelp="script"    (IE 4.0)
     onkeydown="script"
     onkeypress="script"
     onkeyup="script"
     onmousedown="script"
```

```
onmouseout="script"
onmouseover="script"
onmouseup="script"
onselectstart="script">   (IE 4.0)

</MENU>
```

Attributes

CLASS   See "Core Attributes Reference" earlier in this appendix.

COMPACT   This attribute indicates that the list should be rendered in a compact style. Few browsers actually change the rendering of the list regardless of the presence of this attribute. The **COMPACT** attribute requires no value.

DIR   See "Language Reference" earlier in this appendix.

ID   See "Core Attributes Reference" earlier in this appendix.

LANG   See "Language Reference" earlier in this appendix.

LANGUAGE   In the Microsoft implementation, this attribute specifies the scripting language to be used with an associated script bound to the element, typically through an event handler attribute. Possible values may include **JAVASCRIPT**, **JSCRIPT**, **VBSCRIPT**, and **VBS**. Other values that include the version of the language used, such as JavaScript 1.1, may also be possible.

STYLE   See "Core Attributes Reference" earlier in this appendix.

TITLE   See "Core Attributes Reference" earlier in this appendix.

EVENT HANDLERS   See "Events Reference" earlier in this appendix.

Example

```
<H2>Taco List</H2>
  <MENU>
    <LI>Fish
    <LI>Pastor
    <LI>Beef
    <LI>Chicken
  </MENU>
```

COMPATIBILITY   W3C 2.0, 3.2, 4.0 (transitional); Netscape 1.x, 2.x, 3.x, 4.x; Internet Explorer 2.x, 3.x, 4.x; and WebTV

Notes

Under the HTML 4.0 strict specification, this element is not defined. Since most browsers simply render this style of list as an unordered list, using **<UL>** element instead is preferable.

Most browsers tend not to support the **COMPACT** attribute.

The HTML 3.2 and 2.0 specifications support only the **COMPACT** attribute.

<META> (Meta-Information)

DESCRIPTION   This element specifies general information about a document, which can be used in document indexing. It also allows a document to define fields in the HTTP response header when it is sent from the server. A common use of this element is for *client-pull* page loads, which allows a document automatically to load another document after a specified delay.

Syntax

```
<META
     CONTENT=string
     DIR=LTR | RTL
     HTTP-EQUIV=http header string
     LANG=language code
     NAME=name of meta information
     SCHEME=scheme type>
```

Attributes

CONTENT   This attribute contains the actual meta-information. The form of the actual meta-information varies greatly, depending on the value set for **NAME**.

DIR   Text direction of the content of the **<META>** element as defined by the **CONTENT** attribute.

HTTP-EQUIV   This attribute binds the meta-information in the **CONTENT** attribute to an HTTP response header. If this attribute is present, the **NAME** attribute should not be used. The **HTTP-EQUIV** attribute is often used to create a document that automatically loads another document after a set time. This is called *client-pull*. The form of a client-pull **<META>** element is

```
<META HTTP-EQUIV="REFRESH" CONTENT="10;URL='nextpage.htm'">
```

Note that the **CONTENT** attribute contains two values. The first is the number of seconds to wait, and the second is the identifier URL and the URL to load after the specified time.

LANG   This attribute is the language code associated with the language used in the **CONTENT** attribute.

NAME   This attribute associates a name with the meta-information contained in the **CONTENT** attribute. If present, the **HTTP-EQUIV** attribute should not be used.

SCHEME   The scheme attribute is used to indicate the expected format of the value of the **CONTENT** attribute. The particular scheme may also be used in conjunction with the meta-data profile as indicated by the **PROFILE** attribute for the **<HEAD>** element.

EVENT HANDLERS   None.

Examples

```
<!-- Use of the META element to assist document indexing -->
<META NAME="KEYWORDS" CONTENT="HTML, SCRIPTING" SCHEME="Lycos">

<!-- Use of the META element to implement client-pull to
     automatically load a page -->
<META HTTP-EQUIV="REFRESH" CONTENT="3;URL='http://www.pint.com/'">

<!-- Use of the META element to add rating information -->
<META HTTP-EQUIV="PICS-Label" CONTENT='(PICS-1.1
     "http://www.rsac.org/ratingsv01.html"
     1 gen true comment "RSACi North America Server"
     by "webmaster@bigcompany.com" for
     http://www.bigcompany.com" on
     "1997.05.26T13:05-0500" r (n 0 s 0 v 0 1 1))'>
```

COMPATIBILITY   W3C 2.0, 3.2, 4.0; Netscape 1.1, 2.x, 3.x, 4.x; and Internet Explorer 2.x, 3.x, 4.x

Notes

The **<META>** element can occur only in the **<HEAD>** element. It may be defined multiple times. The **<META>** element is an empty element and does not have a closing tag nor contain any content.

A common use of the **<META>** element is to set information for indexing tools such as search engines. The common values for the **NAME** attribute when performing this function include **AUTHOR, DESCRIPTION**, and **KEYWORDS**; other attributes may also be possible.

Along the same line as indexing, meta-information is also used for rating pages.

Microsoft documentation describes a URL attribute for the **<META>** element but appears to have to confused the use of the keyword URL within the **CONTENT** attribute when creating a client-pull page. The URL attribute does not exist.

The HTML 3.2 and 2.0 specifications define only the **CONTENT, HTTP-EQUIV**, and **NAME** attributes.

<MULTICOL>   (Multiple Column Text)

DESCRIPTION   This Netscape-specific element renders the enclosed content in multiple columns. This element should not be used in favor of a table, which is a more standard way to render multiple columns of text across browsers. It is likely that style sheets will provide for multicolumn rendering in the future.

HTML ELEMENT
REFERENCE

Syntax

```
<MULTICOL
    CLASS=class name(s)    (N 4.0)
    COLS=number of columns    (N 3.0, N 4.0)
    GUTTER=pixels    (N 3.0, N 4.0)
      ID=unique alphanumeric identifier    (N 4.0)
    STYLE=style information    (N 4.0)
    TITLE=advisory text    (N 4.0)
    WIDTH=pixels>    (N 3.0, 4.0)

</MULTICOL>
```

Attributes

CLASS   See "Core Attributes Reference" earlier in this appendix.

COLS   This attribute indicates the number of columns in which to display the text. The browser attempts to fill the columns evenly.

GUTTER   This attribute indicates the width in pixels between the columns. The default value for this attribute is **10** pixels.

ID   See "Core Attributes Reference" earlier in this appendix.

STYLE   See "Core Attributes Reference" earlier in this appendix.

TITLE   See "Core Attributes Reference" earlier in this appendix.

WIDTH   This attribute indicates the column width for all columns. The width of the each column is set in pixels and is equivalent for all columns in the group. If the attribute is not specified, the width of columns will be determined by taking the available window size, subtracting the number of pixels for the gutter between the columns as specified by the **GUTTER** attribute, and evenly dividing the result by the number of columns in the group as set by the **COLS** attribute.

EVENT HANDLERS   None.

Example

```
<MULTICOL COLS="3" GUTTER="20">
   Put a long piece of ... text ... here
</MULTICOL>
```

COMPATIBILITY   Netscape 3.x, 4.x

Notes

Do not attempt to use images or other embedded media within a multicolumn layout as defined by **<MULTICOL>**.

Do not set the number of columns to high or resize the browser very small, as text will overwrite other lines.

<NOBR> (No Breaks)

DESCRIPTION This proprietary element renders enclosed text without line breaks. Break points for where text may wrap can be inserted using the **<WBR>** element.

Syntax

```
<NOBR

    CLASS=class name(s)
      (Netscape, Internet Explorer, WebTV)
    ID=unique alphanumeric identifier
      (Netscape, Internet Explorer, WebTV)
    STYLE=style information
      (Netscape, Internet Explorer, WebTV)
    TITLE=advisory text>
      (Netscape, Internet Explorer, WebTV)

</NOBR>
```

Attributes

CLASS See "Core Attributes Reference" earlier in this appendix.

ID See "Core Attributes Reference" earlier in this appendix.

STYLE See "Core Attributes Reference" earlier in this appendix.

TITLE See "Core Attributes Reference" earlier in this appendix.

EVENT HANDLERS None.

Examples

```
<NOBR> This really long ... text ... will not be broken </NOBR>

<NOBR>With this element it is often important to hint where a line
may be broken using <WBR>. This element acts as a soft return.</NOBR>
```

COMPATIBILITY Netscape 1.1, 2.x, 3.x, 4.x; Internet Explorer 2.x, 3.x, 4.x; and WebTV

Notes

While many browsers support this attribute, it is not part of any W3C standard.
WebTV supports no attributes for this element.

<NOEMBED>   (No Embedded Media Support)

DESCRIPTION   This Netscape-specific element is used indicates alternate content to display
on browsers that cannot support an embedded media object. It should occur in conjunction with
the **<EMBED>** element.

Syntax

```
<NOEMBED>
    Alternative content here
</NOEMBED>
```

Attributes

Netscape does not specifically define attributes for this element; however, documentation
suggests that **CLASS, ID, STYLE,** and **TITLE** may be supported for this element.

EVENT HANDLERS   None.

Example

```
<EMBED SRC="trailer.mov" HEIGHT="150" WIDTH="150">
   <NOEMBED>
     <IMG SRC="trailer.gif">
     <BR>
   Sorry, this browser is not configured to display video.
   </NOEMBED>
</EMBED>
```

COMPATIBILITY   Netscape 2.x, 3.x, 4.x

Notes

This element will disappear as the **<OBJECT>** style of inserting media into a page becomes
more common.

<NOFRAMES>   (No Frame Support Content)

DESCRIPTION   This element is used to indicate alternate content to display on browsers that
do not support frames.

Syntax

```
<NOFRAMES
    CLASS=class name(s)
    DIR=LTR | RTL
    ID=unique alphanumeric identifier
    LANG=language code
    STYLE=style information
    TITLE=advisory text

    onclick="script"
    ondblclick="script"
    onkeydown="script"
    onkeypress="script"
    onkeyup="script"
    onmousedown="script"
    onmouseout="script"
    onmouseover="script"
    onmouseup="script">

   alternative content for non-frame supporting browsers

</NOFRAMES>
```

Attributes

CLASS   See "Core Attributes Reference" earlier in this appendix.

DIR   See "Language Reference" earlier in this appendix.

ID   See "Core Attributes Reference" earlier in this appendix.

LANG   See "Language Reference" earlier in this appendix.

STYLE   See "Core Attributes Reference" earlier in this appendix.

TITLE   See "Core Attributes Reference" earlier in this appendix.

EVENT HANDLERS   It is interesting to note that while the **<NOFRAMES>** element does support the common events for nearly all HTML 4.0 elements, their value seems unclear. The only time that content within a **<NOFRAMES>** could be rendered is on a browser that does not support frames; however, browsers that do not support frames are unlikely to support an event model or similar features. There might be some possibility with clever scripting to access framed and nonframed content, but for now the benefit of the events seems unclear. For more information, see "Events Reference" earlier in this appendix.

Example

```
<FRAMESET ROWS="100,*">
   <FRAME SRC="controls.htm">
   <FRAME SRC="content.htm
      <NOFRAMES>
  Sorry this browser does not support frames
      </NOFRAMES>
</FRAMESET>
```

COMPATIBILITY   W3C 4.0; Netscape 2.x, 3.x, 4.x; Internet Explorer 2.x, 3.x, 4.x; and WebTV

Notes

This element should be used within the scope of the **<FRAMESET>** element.
The benefit of events and sophisticated attributes like **STYLE** is unclear for browsers that would use content within **<NOFRAMES>**, given that older browsers that don't support frames would probably not support these features.

<NOSCRIPT>   (No Script Support Content)

DESCRIPTION   This element is used to enclose content that should be rendered on browsers that do not support scripting or that have scripting turned off.

Syntax

```
<NOSCRIPT
      CLASS=class name(s)
      DIR=LTR | RTL
      ID=unique alphanumeric identifier
      LANG=language code
      STYLE=style information
      TITLE=advisory text

      onclick="script"
      ondblclick="script"
      onkeydown="script"
      onkeypress="script"
      onkeyup="script"
      onmousedown="script"
      onmouseout="script"
      onmouseover="script"
      onmouseup="script">

   alternative content for non-script supporting browsers

</NOSCRIPT>
```

Attributes

CLASS   See "Core Attributes Reference" earlier in this appendix.

DIR   See "Language Reference" earlier in this appendix.

ID   See "Core Attributes Reference" earlier in this appendix.

LANG   See "Language Reference" earlier in this appendix.

STYLE   See "Core Attributes Reference" earlier in this appendix.

TITLE   See "Core Attributes Reference" earlier in this appendix.

EVENT HANDLERS   As defined in the preliminary specification of HTML 4.0, the benefits of event handlers are not very obvious, considering that content within the **<NOSCRIPT>** element assumes the browser does not support scripting, while the script handlers themselves are for browsers that support scripting. These are standard events for nearly all HTML 4.0 elements. For definitions, see "Events Reference" earlier in this appendix.

Example

```
Last Updated:
 <SCRIPT LANGUAGE="JAVASCRIPT">
   <!-- document.writeln(document.lastModified); //-->
 </SCRIPT>
 <NOSCRIPT>
    1997
 </NOSCRIPT>
```

COMPATIBILITY   W3C 4.0; Netscape 2.x, 3.x, 4.x; Internet Explorer 3.x, 4.x; and WebTV

Notes

Improved functionality for the **<NOSCRIPT>** element may come if it is extended to deal with the lack of support for one scripting language or another. Currently the element is used only to indicate if any scripting is supported or not.

<NOSMARTQUOTES>   (No Smart Quotes)

DESCRIPTION   This WebTV-specific element indicates that quote marks should not be rendered as "smart" quotes as defined by the character entities **“** and **&#148**. Instead, the normal quote characters " and " should be used.

Syntax

```
<NOSMARTQUOTES>
   &#147;quoted text goes here&#148;
</NOSMARTQUOTES>
```

Attributes

None.

EVENT HANDLERS None.

Example

```
This is &#147;smart quotes.&#148;
<NOSMARTQUOTES>This is "regular quotes"</NOSMARTQUOTES>
```

COMPATIBILITY WebTV

<OBJECT>

DESCRIPTION This element specifies an arbitrary object to be included into an HTML document. Initially, this element was used to insert ActiveX controls, but according to the HTML 4.0 specification, an object may be any media object, document, applet ActiveX control, or even image.

Syntax

```
<OBJECT
    ACCESSKEY=character    (IE 4.0)
    ALIGN=ABSBOTTOM* | ABSMIDDLE* | BASELINE* | BOTTOM |
    LEFT | MIDDLE | RIGHT | TEXTOP* | TOP    (* IE 4.0)
    ARCHIVE=URL
    BORDER=pixels | percentage
    CLASS=class name(s)
    CLASSID=ID
    CODE=URL    (IE 3.0)
    CODEBASE=URL
    CODETYPE=MIME Type
    DATA=URL of data
    DATAFLD=column name    (IE 4.0)
    DATAFORMATAS=HTML | TEXT    (IE 4.0)
    DATASRC=ID for bound data    (IE 4.0)
    DECLARE
    DIR=LTR  | RTL
    EXPORT
    HEIGHT=pixels | percentage
    HSPACE=pixels | percentage
    ID=unique alphanumeric identifier
    LANG=language code
    LANGUAGE=JAVASCRIPT | JSCRIPT | VBSCRIPT | VBS    (IE 4.0)
    NAME=unique alphanumeric name
    SHAPES
```

```
        STANDBY=standby text string
        STYLE=style information
        TABINDEX=number
        TITLE=advisory text
        TYPE=MIME Type
        USEMAP=URL
        VSPACE=pixels | percentage
        WIDTH=pixels | percentage

        onafterupdate="script"    (IE 4.0)
        onbeforeupdate="script"    (IE 4.0)
        onblur="script"  (IE 4.0)
        onclick="script"
        ondblclick="script"
        ondragstart="script"    (IE 4.0)
        onfocus="script"  (IE 4.0)
        onhelp="script"    (IE 4.0)
        onkeydown="script"
        onkeypress="script"
        onkeyup="script"
        onmousedown="script"
        onmousemove="script"
        onmouseout="script"
        onmouseover="script"
        onmouseup="script"
        onreadystatechange="script"    (IE 4.0)
        onresize="script"    (IE 4.0)
        onrowenter="script"    (IE 4.0)
        onrowexit="script"    (IE 4.0)
        onselectstart="script">    (IE 4.0)

</OBJECT>
```

Attributes

ACCESSKEY   This Microsoft attribute specifies a keyboard navigation accelerator for the element. Pressing ALT or a similar key in association with the specified character selects the form control correlated with that key sequence. Page designers are forewarned to avoid key sequences already bound to browsers.

ALIGN   This attribute aligns the object with respect to the surrounding text. The default is **LEFT**. The HTML specification defines **RIGHT**, **TOP**, **BOTTOM**, and **MIDDLE** as well. Browsers may provide an even richer set of alignment values. The behavior of alignment for objects is similar to images. Under the strict HTML 4.0 specification, the **<OBJECT>** element does not support this attribute.

ARCHIVE   This attribute contains a URL for the location of an archive file. An archive file is typically used to contain multiple object files to improve the efficiency of access.

BORDER   This attribute specifies the width in pixels or percentages of the object's borders.

CLASSID   This attribute contains a URL for an object's implementation. The URL syntax depends upon the object's type. With ActiveX controls, the value of this attribute does not appear to be a URL but something of the form *CLSID: object-id*; for example, **CLSID: 99B42120-6EC7-11CF-A6C7-00AA00A47DD2**.

CLASS   See "Core Attributes Reference" earlier in this appendix.

CODE   Under the old Microsoft implementation, this attribute contains the URL referencing a Java applet class file. The way to access a Java applet under the HTML 4.0 specification is to use **<OBJECT CLASSID="java: classname.class">** the pseudo-URL java: is used to indicate a Java applet. Microsoft Internet Explorer 4.0 and beyond support this style so **CODE** should not be used.

CODEBASE   This attribute contains a URL to use as a relative base to access the object specified by the **CLASSID** attribute.

CODETYPE   This attribute specifies an object's MIME type. Do not confuse this attribute with **TYPE**, which specifies the MIME type of the data the object may used as defined by the **DATA** attribute.

DATA   This attribute contains a URL for data required by an object.

DATAFLD   This attribute is used to indicate the column name in the data source that is bound to the **<OBJECT>** element.

DATAFORMATAS   This attribute indicates if the bound data is plain text (**TEXT**) or HTML (**HTML**).

DATASRC   The value of this attribute is set to an identifier indicating the data source to pull data from.

DECLARE   This attribute declares an object without instantiating it. This is useful when the object will be a parameter to another object.

DIR   See "Language Reference" earlier in this appendix.

EXPORT   Presence of this attribute indicates that an image map defined within this particular **<OBJECT>** can be exported to any enclosing **<OBJECT>** element.

HEIGHT   This attribute specifies the height of the object in pixels or as a percentage of the enclosing window.

HSPACE   This attribute indicates the horizontal space in pixels or percentages between the object and surrounding content.

ID   See "Core Attributes Reference" earlier in this appendix.

LANG   See "Language Reference" earlier in this appendix.

LANGUAGE In the Microsoft implementation, this attribute specifies the scripting language to be used with an associated script bound to the element, typically through an event handler attribute. Possible values may include **JAVASCRIPT**, **JSCRIPT**, **VBSCRIPT**, and **VBS**. Other values that include the version of the language used, such as JavaScript 1.1, may also be possible.

NAME This attribute under the Microsoft definition defines the name of the control so scripting can access it. The HTML specification suggests that it is a name for form submission, but this meaning is unclear and not supported by browsers.

SHAPES This attribute indicates that the object contains hot spot hyperlinks. This attribute requires no value and simply indicates that the **<OBJECT>** element references a client-side image map. The actual shapes that define the active regions of the image are found with the **<OBJECT>** element.

STANDBY This attribute contains a text message to be displayed while the object is loading.

STYLE See "Core Attributes Reference" earlier in this appendix.

TABINDEX This attribute takes a numeric value indicating the position of the object in the tabbing index for the document. Tabbing proceeds from the lowest positive **TABINDEX** value to the highest. Negative values for **TABINDEX** will leave the object out of the tabbing order. When tabbing is not explicitly set, the browser may tab through items in the order they are encountered.

TITLE See "Core Attributes Reference" earlier in this appendix.

TYPE This attribute specifies the MIME type for the object's data. This is different from the **CODETYPE**, which is the MIME type of the object and not the data it uses.

USEMAP This attribute contains the URL of the image map to be used with the object. Typically the URL will be a fragment identifier references a **<MAP>** element somewhere else within the file. The presence of this attribute indicates that the type of object being includes is an image.

VSPACE This attribute indicates the vertical space in pixels or percentages between the object and surrounding text.

WIDTH This attribute specifies the width of the object in pixels or as a percentage of the enclosing window.

EVENT HANDLERS See "Events Reference" earlier in this appendix.

Examples

```
<OBJECT ID="IeLabel1" WIDTH=325 HEIGHT=65
    CLASSID="CLSID:99B42120-6EC7-11CF-A6C7-00AA00A47DD2">
    <PARAM NAME="_ExtentX" VALUE="6879">
    <PARAM NAME="_ExtentY" VALUE="1376">
    <PARAM NAME="Caption" VALUE="Hello World">
    <PARAM NAME="Alignment" VALUE="4">
```

```
    <PARAM NAME="Mode" VALUE="1">
    <PARAM NAME="ForeColor" VALUE="#FF0000">
    <PARAM NAME="FontName" VALUE="Arial">
    <PARAM NAME="FontSize" VALUE="36">
     <B>Hello World for non-ActiveX users!</B>
</OBJECT>


<OBJECT CLASSID="java:Blink.class"    STANDBY="Here it comes"
    HEIGHT="100" WIDTH="300">
    <PARAM NAME=LBL VALUE="Java, is, fun, exciting, and new.">
    <PARAM NAME=SPEED VALUE="2">
   This will display in non-Java aware or enabled browsers.
</OBJECT>


<OBJECT DATA="pullinthisfile.html">
   Data not included!
</OBJECT>


<OBJECT DATA="bigimage.gif" SHAPES>
 <A HREF="page1.htm" SHAPE="RECT" COORDS="10,10,40,40">Page 1</A>
 <A HREF="page2.htm" SHAPE="CIRCLE" COORDS="100,90,20 ">Page 2</A>
</OBJECT>
```

COMPATIBILITY   W3C 4.0; Netscape 4.x; and Internet Explorer 3.x, 4.x

Notes
Under the strict HTML 4.0 specification the **<OBJECT>** element loses most of its presentation attributes including **ALIGN**, **BORDER**, **HEIGHT**, **HSPACE**, **VSPACE**, and **WIDTH**. These attributes are replaced by style sheet rules.

The HTML 4.0 specification reserves the **DATAFORMATAS**, **DATASRC**, and **DATAFLD** attributes for future use.

Alternative content should be defined within the **<OBJECT>** element after the **<PARAM>** elements.

The **<OBJECT>** element is still mainly used to include binaries in pages. While the specification defines that it can load in HTML files and create image maps few, if any, browsers support this.

<OL>   (Ordered List)

DESCRIPTION   This element is used to define an ordered or numbered list of items. The numbering style comes in many forms including letters, Roman numerals, and regular numerals. The individual items within the list are specified by **<LI>** elements included with the **<OL>** element.

Syntax

```
<OL
     CLASS=class name(s)
     COMPACT
     DIR=LTR | RTL
     ID=unique alphanumeric identifier
     LANG=language code
     LANGUAGE=JAVASCRIPT | JSCRIPT | VBSCRIPT | VBS    (IE 4.0)
     START=number
     STYLE=style information
     TITLE=advisory text
     TYPE=a | A | i | I | 1

     onclick="script"
     ondblclick="script"
     ondragstart="script"   (IE 4.0)
     onhelp="script"   (IE 4.0)
     onkeydown="script"
     onkeypress="script"
     onkeyup="script"
     onmousedown="script"
     onmouseout="script"
     onmouseover="script"
     onmouseup="script"
     onselectstart="script">   (IE 4.0)

</OL>
```

Attributes

CLASS   See "Core Attributes Reference" earlier in this appendix.

COMPACT   This attribute indicates that the list should be rendered in a compact style. Few browsers actually change the rendering of the list regardless of the presence of this attribute. The **COMPACT** attribute requires no value.

DIR   See "Language Reference" earlier in this appendix.

ID   See "Core Attributes Reference" earlier in this appendix.

LANG   See "Language Reference" earlier in this appendix.

LANGUAGE   In the Microsoft implementation, this attribute specifies the scripting language to be used with an associated script bound to the element, typically through an event handler attribute. Possible values may include **JAVASCRIPT**, **JSCRIPT**, **VBSCRIPT**, and **VBS**. Other values that include the version of the language used, such as JavaScript 1.1, may also be possible.

START This attribute is used to indicate the value to start numbering the individual list items from. While the ordering type of list elements may be Roman numerals like XXXI or letters the value of **START** is always represented as number. To start numbering elements from the letter 'C' use <OL TYPE="A" START="3">

STYLE See "Core Attributes Reference" earlier in this appendix.

TITLE See "Core Attributes Reference" earlier in this appendix.

TYPE This attribute indicates the numbering type: "a" indicates lowercase letters, "A" indicates uppercase letters, "i" indicates lowercase Roman numerals, "I" indicates uppercase Roman numerals, "1" indicates numbers. Type set in the <OL> element is used for the entire list unless a **TYPE** attribute is used within an enclosed <LI> element.

EVENT HANDLERS See "Events Reference" earlier in this appendix.

Examples

```
<OL TYPE="1">
   <LI>First step
   <LI>Second step
   <LI>Third step
</OL>

<OL COMPACT TYPE="I" START="30">
   <LI> Clause 30
   <LI> Clause 31
   <LI> Clause 32
</OL>
```

COMPATIBILITY W3C 2.0, 3.2, 4.0; Netscape 1.x, 2.x, 3.x, 4.x; Internet Explorer 2.x, 3.x, 4.x; and WebTV

Notes

Under the strict HTML 4.0 specification, the <OL> element no longer supports the **COMPACT**, **START**, and **TYPE** attributes. These aspects of lists can be controlled with style sheet rules. The HTML 3.2 specification supports only the **COMPACT**, **START**, and **TYPE** attributes. The HTML 2.0 specification supports only the **COMPACT** attribute.
WebTV supports only the **START** and **TYPE** attributes.

<OPTGROUP> (Option Grouping)

DESCRIPTION This element is used to specify a grouping of items in a selection list defined by <OPTION> elements so that the menu choices may be presented in a hierarchical menu or similar alternative fashion to improve access via nonvisual browsers.

Syntax

```
<OPTGROUP
     CLASS=class name(s)
     DIR=LTR | RTL
     DISABLED
     ID=unique alphanumeric identifier
     LABEL=text description
     LANG=language code
     STYLE=style information
     TITLE=advisory text

     onclick="script"
     ondblclick="script"
     onkeydown="script"
     onkeypress="script"
     onkeyup="script"
     onmousedown="script"
     onmouseout="script"
     onmouseover="script"
     onmouseup="script">

<OPTION> Elements

</OPTGROUP>
```

Attributes

CLASS   See "Core Attributes Reference" earlier in this appendix.

DISABLED   Occurrence of this attribute indicates that the enclosed set of options should be disabled.

DIR   See "Language Reference" earlier in this appendix.

ID   See "Core Attributes Reference" earlier in this appendix.

LABEL   This attribute contains a short label that may be more appealing to use when the selection list is rendered as items in a hierarchy.

LANG   See "Language Reference" earlier in this appendix.

STYLE   See "Core Attributes Reference" earlier in this appendix.

TITLE   See "Core Attributes Reference" earlier in this appendix.

EVENT HANDLERS   See "Events Reference" earlier in this appendix.

Example

```
Where would you like to go for your vacation ?<BR>
<SELECT>
   <OPTION ID="ch1" VALUE="China">The Great Wall

<OPTGROUP LABEL="Mexico">
      <OPTION ID="ch2" LABEL="Los Cabos" VALUE="Los Cabos">Los Cabos,
Mexico

  <OPTION ID="ch3" LABEL="Leon" VALUE="Leon">Leon, Mexico
      <OPTION ID="ch4" VALUE="MXC">Mexico City

</OPTGROUP>
   <OPTION ID="ch5" VALUE="home" SELECTED>Your backyard
</SELECT>
```

COMPATIBILITY   W3C 4.0

Notes

This element was proposed for inclusion in the HTML 4.0 specification by MegaZone, the
technical reviewer of this book.
This element should only occur within the context of a **<SELECT>** element.

<OPTION>   (Option in Selection List)

DESCRIPTION   This element is used to specify an item in a selection list defined by the
<SELECT> element.

Syntax

```
<OPTION
      CLASS=class name(s)
      DIR=LTR | RTL
      DISABLED
      ID=unique alphanumeric identifier
      LABEL=text description
      LANG=language code
      LANGUAGE=JAVASCRIPT | JSCRIPT | VBSCRIPT | VBS    (IE 4.0)
      SELECTED
      STYLE=style information
      TITLE=advisory text
      VALUE=option value

      onclick="script"
      ondblclick="script"
```

```
        ondragstart="script"    (IE 4.0)
        onhelp="script"    (IE 4.0)
        onkeydown="script"
        onkeypress="script"
        onkeyup="script"
        onmousedown="script"
        onmouseout="script"
        onmouseover="script"
        onmouseup="script"
        onselectstart="script">    (IE 4.0)

</OPTION>
```

Attributes

CLASS   See "Core Attributes Reference" earlier in this appendix.

DISABLED   Presence of this attribute indicates that the particular item is not selectable.

DIR   See "Language Reference" earlier in this appendix.

ID   See "Core Attributes Reference" earlier in this appendix.

LABEL   This attribute contains a short label that may be more appealing to use when the selection list is rendered as a hierarchy due to the presence of an **<OPTGROUP>** element.

LANG   See "Language Reference" earlier in this appendix.

LANGUAGE   In the Microsoft implementation, this attribute specifies the scripting language to be used with an associated script bound to the element, typically through an event handler attribute. Possible values may include **JAVASCRIPT**, **JSCRIPT**, **VBSCRIPT**, and **VBS**. Other values that include the version of the language used, such as JavaScript 1.1, may also be possible.

SELECTED   This attribute indicates that the associated item is the default selection. If not included, the first item in the selection list is the default. If the **<SELECT>** element enclosing the **<OPTION>** elements has the **MULTIPLE** attribute, the **SELECTED** attribute may occur in multiple entries. Otherwise, it should occur only in one entry.

STYLE   See "Core Attributes Reference" earlier in this appendix.

TITLE   See "Core Attributes Reference" earlier in this appendix.

VALUE   This attribute indicates the value to include with the form result when the item is selected.

EVENT HANDLERS   See "Events Reference" earlier in this appendix.

Examples

```
Where would you like to go for your vacation ?<BR>
<SELECT>
    <OPTION ID="choice1" VALUE="China">The Great Wall
    <OPTION ID="choice2" VALUE="Mexico">Los Cabos
    <OPTION ID="choice3" VALUE="Home" SELECTED>Your backyard
</SELECT>
```

COMPATIBILITY   W3C 2.0, 3.2. 4.0; Netscape 1.x, 2.x, 3.x, 4.x; Internet Explorer 2.x, 3.x, 4.x; and WebTV

Notes

The closing tag for **<OPTION>** is optional.
This element should only occur within the context of a **<SELECT>** element.
The W3C HTML 3.2 and 2.0 specifications only define the **SELECTED** and **VALUE** attributes for this element.

<P>   (Paragraph)

DESCRIPTION   This element is used to define a paragraph of text. Browsers typically insert a blank line before and after a paragraph of text.

Syntax

```
<P
    ALIGN=CENTER | JUSTIFY |  LEFT | RIGHT
    CLASS=class name(s)
    DIR=LTR | RTL
    ID=unique alphanumeric identifier
    LANG=language code
    LANGUAGE=JAVASCRIPT | JSCRIPT | VBSCRIPT | VBS   (IE 4.0)
    STYLE=style information
    TITLE=advisory text

    onclick="script"
    ondblclick="script"
    ondragstart="script"   (IE 4.0)
    onhelp="script"   (IE 4.0)
    onkeydown="script"
    onkeypress="script"
    onkeyup="script"
    onmousedown="script"
    onmouseout="script"
    onmouseover="script"
    onmouseup="script"
```

```
    onselectstart="script">   (IE 4.0)

</P>
```

Attributes

ALIGN   This attribute is used to specify the alignment of text within a paragraph. The default value is **LEFT**. The transitional specification for HTML also defines **RIGHT**, **CENTER**, and **JUSTIFY**. However, under the strict specification of HTML 4.0 text alignment can be handled through a style sheet rule.

CLASS   See "Core Attributes Reference" earlier in this appendix.

DIR   See "Language Reference" earlier in this appendix.

ID   See "Core Attributes Reference" earlier in this appendix.

LANG   See "Language Reference" earlier in this appendix.

LANGUAGE   In the Microsoft implementation, this attribute specifies the scripting language to be used with an associated script bound to the element, typically through an event handler attribute. Possible values may include **JAVASCRIPT**, **JSCRIPT**, **VBSCRIPT**, and **VBS**. Other values that include the version of the language used, such as JavaScript 1.1, may also be possible.

STYLE   See "Core Attributes Reference" earlier in this appendix.

TITLE   See "Core Attributes Reference" earlier in this appendix.

EVENT HANDLERS   See "Events Reference" earlier in this appendix.

Examples

```
<P ALIGN="RIGHT">A right aligned paragraph</P>

<P ID="Para1" CLASS="defaultParagraph"
   TITLE="Introduction Paragraph">
This is the introduction paragraph for the very
long paper about nothing.
</P>
```

COMPATIBILITY   W3C 2.0, 3.2, 4.0; Netscape 1.x, 2.x, 3.x, 4.x; Internet Explorer 2.x, 3.x, 4.x; and Web TV

Notes

Under the strict HTML 4.0 specification the **ALIGN** attribute is not supported. Alignment of text can be accomplished using style sheets.

The closing tag for the **<P>** element is optional.

As a logical element, empty paragraphs are ignored by browsers, so do not try to use multiple **<P>** elements in a row like **<P><P><P><P>** to add blank lines to a Web page. This will not work; use the **
** element instead.

The HTML 3.2 specification supports only the **ALIGN** attribute with values of **LEFT**, **RIGHT**, and **CENTER**.

The HTML 2.0 specification supports no attributes for the **<P>** element.

<PARAM>   (Object Parameter)

DESCRIPTION   This element is used to specify a parameter to pass to an embedded object using the **<OBJECT>** or **<APPLET>** element. This element should occur only within the scope of one of these elements.

Syntax

```
<PARAM
     DATAFLD=column name    (IE 4.0)
     DATAFORMATAS=HTML | TEXT    (IE 4.0)
     DATASRC=data source ID   (IE 4.0)
     ID=unique alphanumeric identifier
     NAME=parameter name
     TYPE=MIME Type
     VALUE=parameter value
     VALUETYPE=DATA | REF | OBJECT>

</PARAM>
```

Attributes

DATAFLD   This Internet Explorer-specific attribute is used to indicate the column name in the data source that is bound to the **<PARAM>** element's value.

DATAFORMATAS   This Internet Explorer-specific attribute indicates if the bound data is plain text (**TEXT**) or HTML (**HTML**).

DATASRC   The value of this attribute is set to an identifier indicating the data source to pull data from. Bound data is used to set the value of the parameters passed to the object or applet with which this **<PARAM>** element is associated.

ID   See "Core Attributes Reference" earlier in this appendix.

NAME   This attribute contains the parameter's name. The name of the parameter depends on the particular object being inserted into the page, and it is assumed that the object knows how to handle the passed data. Do not confuse the **NAME** attribute with the **NAME** attribute used for form elements. In the latter case, the **NAME** attribute does not have a similar meaning as **ID**, but rather is used to specify the name of the data to be passed to an enclosing **<OBJECT>** element.

TYPE   When the **VALUETYPE** attribute is set to **REF**, the **TYPE** attribute can be used to indicate the type of the information to be retrieved. Valid values for this attribute are in the form of MIME types like text/html.

VALUE   This attribute contains the parameter's value. The actual contents of this attribute depends on the object and the particular parameter being passed in, as determined by the **NAME** attribute.

VALUETYPE   This HTML 4.0-specific attribute is used to specify the type of the **VALUE** attribute being passed in. Possible values for this attribute include **DATA**, **REF**, and **OBJECT**. A value of **DATA** specifies that the information passed in through the **VALUE** parameter should be treated just as data. A value of **REF** indicates that the information being passed in is a URL that indicates where the data to use is located. The information is not retrieved, but the URL is passed to the object which may then retrieve the information if necessary. The last value of **OBJECT** indicates that the value being passed in is the name of an object as set by its **ID** attribute. In practice, the **DATA** attribute is used by default.

EVENT HANDLERS   None.

Examples

```
<APPLET CODE="plot.class">
    <PARAM NAME="min" VALUE="5">
    <PARAM NAME="max" VALUE="30">
    <PARAM NAME="ticks" VALUE=".5">
    <PARAM NAME="line-style" VALUE="dotted">
</APPLET>


<OBJECT CLASSID="clsid:D27CDB6E-AE6D-11cf-96B8-444553540000"
    CODEBASE="swflash.cab#version=2,0,0,0"
    HEIGHT="100" WIDTH="100">
    <PARAM ID="param1" NAME="Movie" VALUE="SplashLogo.swf">
    <PARAM ID="param2" NAME="Play" Value="True">
</OBJECT>
```

COMPATIBILITY   W3C 3.2, 4.0; Netscape 2.x, 3.x, 4.x; and Internet Explorer 3.x, 4.x

Notes
The closing tag for this element is forbidden.
The HTML 3.2 specification supports only the **NAME** and **VALUE** attributes for this element.

<PLAINTEXT>

DESCRIPTION   This depreciated element from the HTML 2.0 specification renders the enclosed text as plain text and forces the browser to ignore any enclosed HTML. Typically, information affected by the **<PLAINTEXT>** element is rendered in monospaced font. This element is no longer part of the HTML standard.

Syntax

```
<PLAINTEXT
    CLASS=class name(s)   (IE 4.0)
    ID=unique alphanumeric identifier   (IE 4.0)
    LANG=language code   (IE 4.0)
    LANGUAGE=JAVASCRIPT | JSCRIPT | VBSCRIPT | VBS   (IE 4.0)
    STYLE=style information   (IE 4.0)
    TITLE=advisory text   (IE 4.0)

    onclick="script"   (IE 4.0)
    ondblclick="script"   (IE 4.0)
    ondragstart="script"   (IE 4.0)
    onhelp="script"   (IE 4.0)
    onkeydown="script"   (IE 4.0)
    onkeypress="script"   (IE 4.0)
    onkeyup="script"   (IE 4.0)
    onmousedown="script"   (IE 4.0)
    onmouseout="script"   (IE 4.0)
    onmouseover="script"   (IE 4.0)
    onmouseup="script"   (IE 4.0)
    onselectstart="script">   (IE 4.0)
```

Attributes

CLASS   See "Core Attributes Reference" earlier in this appendix.

DIR   See "Language Reference" earlier in this appendix.

ID   See "Core Attributes Reference" earlier in this appendix.

LANG   See "Language Reference" earlier in this appendix.

LANGUAGE   In the Microsoft implementation, this attribute specifies the scripting language to be used with an associated script bound to the element, typically through an event handler attribute. Possible values may include **JAVASCRIPT**, **JSCRIPT**, **VBSCRIPT**, and **VBS**. Other values that include the version of the language used, such as JavaScript 1.1, may also be possible.

STYLE   See "Core Attributes Reference" earlier in this appendix.

TITLE   See "Core Attributes Reference" earlier in this appendix.

EVENT HANDLERS   See "Events Reference" earlier in this appendix.

Example

```
I am tired of HTML. The rest of the file is in plain text.
    <PLAINTEXT>
  Even though this is supposed to be <B>bold</B>, the tags
```

```
still show.  There is no way to turn plain text off once
it is on.Even
</BODY>
</HTML>  will show up.
```

COMPATIBILITY   W3C 2.0; Netscape 1.x, 2.x, 3.x, 4.x; and Internet Explorer 2.x, 3.x, 4.x

Notes

No closing tag for this element is necessary, since the browser will ignore all tags after the start tag. This element should not be used. Plain text information can be indicated by a file type and information can be inserted in a preformatted fashion using the **<PRE>** element.

<PRE>   (Preformatted Text)

DESCRIPTION   This element is used to indicate that the enclosed text is preformatted, meaning that spaces, returns, tabs, and other formatting characters are preserved. Browsers will, however, acknowledge most HTML elements that are found with the **<PRE>** element. Preformatted text will generally be rendered by the browsers in a monospaced font.

Syntax

```
<PRE
    CLASS=class name(s)
    DIR=LTR | RTL
    ID=unique alphanumeric value
    LANG=language code
    LANGUAGE=JAVASCRIPT | JSCRIPT | VBSCRIPT | VBS   (IE 4.0)
    STYLE=style information
    TITLE=advisory text
    WIDTH=number

    onclick="script"
    ondblclick="script"
    ondragstart="script"   (IE 4.0)
    onhelp="script"   (IE 4.0)
    onkeydown="script"
    onkeypress="script"
    onkeyup="script"
    onmousedown="script"
    onmouseout="script"
    onmouseover="script"
    onmouseup="script"
    onselectstart="script">   (IE 4.0)

</PRE>
```

Attributes

CLASS   See "Core Attributes Reference" earlier in this appendix.

DIR   See "Language Reference" earlier in this appendix.

ID   See "Core Attributes Reference" earlier in this appendix.

LANG   See "Language Reference" earlier in this appendix.

LANGUAGE   In the Microsoft implementation, this attribute specifies the scripting language to be used with an associated script bound to the element, typically through an event handler attribute. Possible values may include **JAVASCRIPT**, **JSCRIPT**, **VBSCRIPT**, and **VBS**. Other values that include the version of the language used, such as JavaScript 1.1, may also be possible.

STYLE   See "Core Attributes Reference" earlier in this appendix.

TITLE   See "Core Attributes Reference" earlier in this appendix.

WIDTH   This attribute should be set to the **WIDTH** of the preformatted region. The value of the attribute should be the number of characters to display. In practice, this attribute is not supported and is dropped under the strict HTML 4.0 specification.

EVENT HANDLERS   See "Events Reference" earlier in this appendix.

Example

```
<PRE>
    Within PREFORMATTED text     A L L     formatting
     IS      PRESERVED
        NO     m     a     t     e     r
    how wild it is.  Remember that some <B>HTML</B> markup is
    allowed within the &lt;PRE&gt; element.
</PRE>
```

COMPATIBILITY   W3C 2.0, 3.2, 4.0; Netscape 1.x, 2.x, 3.x, 4.x; Internet Explorer 2.x, 3.x, 4.x; and WebTV

Notes

The HTML 4.0 transitional specification states that the **<IMG>**, **<OBJECT>**, **<APPLET>**, **<BIG>**, **<SMALL>**, **<SUB>**, **<SUP>**, **<FONT>**, and **<BASEFONT>** elements should not be used within the **<PRE>** element. The strict HTML 4.0 specification states that only the **<IMG>**, **<OBJECT>**, **<BIG>**, **<SMALL>**, **<SUB>**, and **<SUP>** elements should not be used within the **<PRE>** element. The other excluded elements are missing, as they are depreciated from the strict specification. While these attributes should not be used, it appears that the two most popular browsers will render them anyway.

The strict HTML 4.0 specification drops support for the **WIDTH** attribute, which was not generally supported anyway.

The HTML 3.2 and 2.0 specifications supports only the **WIDTH** attribute for **<PRE>**, which was not widely supported.

<Q> (Quote)

DESCRIPTION   This element indicates that the enclosed text is a short inline quotation.

Syntax

```
<Q
      CITE=URL of source
      CLASS=class name(s)
      DIR=LTR | RTL
      ID=unique alphanumeric string
      LANG=language code
      LANGUAGE=JAVASCRIPT | JSCRIPT | VBSCRIPT | VBS    (IE 4.0)
      STYLE=style information
      TITLE=advisory text

      onclick="script"
      ondblclick="script"
      ondragstart="script"   (IE 4.0)
      onhelp="script"   (IE 4.0)
      onkeydown="script"
      onkeypress="script"
      onkeyup="script"
      onmousedown="script"
      onmouseout="script"
      onmouseover="script"
      onmouseup="script"
      onselectstart="script">   (IE 4.0)

</Q>
```

Attributes

CITE   The value of this attribute is a URL that designates a source document or message for the information quoted. This attribute is intended to point to information explaining the context or the reference for the quote.

CLASS   See "Core Attributes Reference" earlier in this appendix.

DIR   See "Language Reference" earlier in this appendix.

ID   See "Core Attributes Reference" earlier in this appendix.

LANG   See "Language Reference" earlier in this appendix.

LANGUAGE   In the Microsoft implementation, this attribute specifies the scripting language to be used with an associated script bound to the element, typically through an event handler attribute. Possible values may include **JAVASCRIPT**, **JSCRIPT**, **VBSCRIPT**, and **VBS**. Other values that include the version of the language used, such as JavaScript 1.1, may also be possible.

STYLE   See "Core Attributes Reference" earlier in this appendix.

TITLE   See "Core Attributes Reference" earlier in this appendix.

EVENT HANDLERS   See "Events Reference" earlier in this appendix.

Examples

```
Tarbash said, <Q>"I do one magic act."</Q>

<Q STYLE="color: green">"A few green balls and a rainbow bar
and you have yourself a Web page Christmas Tree!"</Q>
```

COMPATIBILITY   W3C 4.0; Internet Explorer 4.x

Notes

This element is intended for short quotations that don't require paragraph breaks, as compared to text that would be contained within **<BLOCKQUOTE>**. Microsoft documentation continues to indicate this is a block element, when it is not.

Internet Explorer does not make any sort of style change for quotations, but it is possible to apply a style rule.

<S>   (Strikethrough)

DESCRIPTION   This element renders the enclosed text with a line drawn through it.

Syntax

```
<S
    CLASS=class name(s)
    DIR=LTR | RTL
    ID=unique alphanumeric identifier
    LANG=language code
    LANGUAGE=JAVASCRIPT | JSCRIPT | VBSCRIPT | VBS   (IE 4.0)
    STYLE=style information
    TITLE=advisory text

    onclick="script"
    ondblclick="script"
    ondragstart="script"  (IE 4.0)
    onhelp="script"  (IE 4.0)
```

```
    onkeydown="script"
    onkeypress="script"
    onkeyup="script"
    onmousedown="script"
    onmouseout="script"
    onmouseover="script"
    onmouseup="script"
    onselectstart="script"  (IE 4.0)>

</S>
```

Attributes

CLASS   See "Core Attributes Reference" earlier in this appendix.

DIR   See "Language Reference" earlier in this appendix.

ID   See "Core Attributes Reference" earlier in this appendix.

LANG   See "Language Reference" earlier in this appendix.

LANGUAGE   In the Microsoft implementation, this attribute specifies the scripting language to be used with an associated script bound to the element, typically through an event handler attribute. Possible values may include **JAVASCRIPT**, **JSCRIPT**, **VBSCRIPT**, and **VBS**. Other values that include the version of the language used, such as JavaScript 1.1, may also be possible.

STYLE   See "Core Attributes Reference" earlier in this appendix.

TITLE   See "Core Attributes Reference" earlier in this appendix.

EVENT HANDLERS   See "Events Reference" earlier in this appendix.

Examples

```
This line contains a <S>misstake</S> error

<S ID="strike1" onmouseover='this.style.color="red"'
onmouseout='this.style.color="black"'>Fastball</S>
```

COMPATIBILITY   W3C 4.0 (transitional); Netscape 3.x; Internet Explorer 2.x, 3.x, 4.x; and WebTV

Notes

This element should act the same as the **<STRIKE>** element.

This HTML 3.0 element was eventually adopted by Netscape and Microsoft and was later incorporated into the HTML 4.0 transitional specification.

The strict HTML 4.0 specification does not include the **<S>** element or the **<STRIKE>** element. It is possible to indicate strikethrough text using a style sheet.

<SAMP> (Sample Text)

DESCRIPTION This element is used to indicate sample text. Enclosed text is generally rendered in a monospaced font.

Syntax

```
<SAMP
    CLASS=class name(s)
    DIR=LTR | RTL
    ID=unique alphanumeric string
    LANG=language code
    LANGUAGE=JAVASCRIPT | JSCRIPT | VBSCRIPT | VBS   (IE 4.0)
    STYLE=style information
    TITLE=advisory text

    onclick="script"
    ondblclick="script"
    ondragstart="script"   (IE 4.0)
    onhelp="script"   (IE 4.0)
    onkeydown="script"
    onkeypress="script"
    onkeyup="script"
    onmousedown="script"
    onmouseout="script"
    onmouseover="script"
    onmouseup="script"
    onselectstart="script">   (IE 4.0)

</SAMP>
```

Attributes

CLASS See "Core Attributes Reference" earlier in this appendix.

DIR See "Language Reference" earlier in this appendix.

ID See "Core Attributes Reference" earlier in this appendix.

LANG See "Language Reference" earlier in this appendix.

LANGUAGE In the Microsoft implementation, this attribute specifies the scripting language to be used with an associated script bound to the element, typically through an event handler attribute. Possible values may include **JAVASCRIPT**, **JSCRIPT**, **VBSCRIPT**, and **VBS**. Other values that include the version of the language used, such as JavaScript 1.1, may also be possible.

STYLE   See "Core Attributes Reference" earlier in this appendix.

TITLE   See "Core Attributes Reference" earlier in this appendix.

EVENT HANDLERS   See "Events Reference" earlier in this appendix.

Example

```
Use the following salutations in all e-mail messages to the boss:
<SAMP>Please excuse the interruption, oh exalted manager.</SAMP>
```

COMPATIBILITY   W3C 2.0, 3.2, 4.0; Netscape 1.x, 2.x, 3.x, 4.x; Internet Explorer 2.x, 3.x, 4.x; and WebTV

Notes

As a logical element. **<SAMP>** is useful to bind style rules to.
WebTV, HTML 3.2 and 2.0 specifications supported no attributes for this element.

<SCRIPT>   (Scripting)

DESCRIPTION   This element encloses statements in a scripting language for client-side processing. Scripting statements can either be included inline or loaded from an external file and may be commented out to avoid execution by non-script-aware browsers.

Syntax

```
<SCRIPT
    CHARSET=character set
    CLASS=class name(s)    (IE 4.0)
    DEFER
    EVENT=event name    (IE 4.0)
    FOR=element ID    (IE 4.0)
    ID=unique alphanumeric identifier    (IE 4.0)
    LANGUAGE=scripting language name
    SRC=URL of script code
    TITLE=advisory text    (IE 4.0)
    TYPE=MIME type>

</SCRIPT>
```

Attributes

CHARSET   This attribute defines the character encoding of the script. The value is a space- and/or comma-delimited list of character sets as defined in RFC 2045. The default value is ISO-8859-1.

CLASS   This Microsoft-defined attribute does not make much sense given that scripting code would not be bound by style sheet rules. Its meaning as defined in the "Core Attributes Reference" in this appendix is unclear within the context of the **<SCRIPT>** element.

DEFER   Presensce of this attribute indicates that the browser may defer execution of the script enclosed by the **<SCRIPT>** element. In practice deferring code may be more up to the position of the **<SCRIPT>** element or the contents. This attribute was added very late to the HTML 4.0 specification, and its support is currently minimal.

EVENT   This Microsoft attribute is used to define a particular event that the script should react to. It must be used in conjunction with the **FOR** attribute. Event names are the same as event handler attributes, for example **onclick**, **ondblclick**, and so on.

ID   See "Core Attributes Reference" earlier in this appendix.

FOR   The **FOR** attribute is used to define the **NAME** or **ID** of the element to which an event defined by the **EVENT** attribute is related. For example, **<SCRIPT EVENT="onclick" FOR="button1" LANGUAGE="VBSCRIPT">** defines a VBScript that will execute when a click event is issued for an element named "button1."

LANGUAGE   This attribute specifies the scripting language being used. The Netscape implementation supports JavaScript. The Microsoft implementation supports JScript (a JavaScript clone) as well as VBScript, which can be indicated by either **VBSCRIPT** or **VBS**. Other values that include the version of the language used, such as JavaScript 1.1 and JavaScript 1.2, may also be possible and are useful to exclude browsers from executing script code that is not supported.

SRC   This attribute is used to specify the URL of a file containing scripting code. Typically files containing JavaScript code will have a .js extension, and a server will attach the appropriate MIME type; if not, the **TYPE** attribute may be used to explicitly set the content type of the external script file. The **LANGUAGE** attribute may also be helpful in determining this.

TITLE   See "Core Attributes Reference" earlier in this appendix.

TYPE   This attribute should be set to the MIME type corresponding to the scripting language used. For JavaScript, for example, this would be **text/javascript**. In practice, the **LANGUAGE** attribute is the more common way to indicate which scripting language is in effect.

EVENT HANDLERS   There are no events directly associated with the **<SCRIPT>** element. However, the Microsoft implementation does allow the **EVENT** attribute to be used to indicate what event a particular script may be associated with.

Examples

```
<SCRIPT LANGUAGE="JavaScript">
<!-- alert("Hello World !!!"); //-->
</SCRIPT>

<!-- code in external file -->
```

```
<SCRIPT LANGUAGE="JavaScript1.2" SRC="superrollover.js"></SCRIPT>

<SCRIPT FOR="myButton" EVENT="onclick" LANGUAGE="JavaScript">
  <!-- alert("I've been clicked!"); //-->
</SCRIPT>
<FORM>
<INPUT TYPE="BUTTON" NAME="myButton" VALUE="Click me">
</FORM>
```

COMPATIBILITY   W3C 4.0; Netscape 2.x, 3.x, 4.x; and Internet Explorer 3.x, 4.x

Notes

It is common practice to "comment out" statements enclosed by the <SCRIPT> element. Without commenting, scripts are displayed as page content by browsers that do not support scripting. The particular comment style may be dependent on the language be used. For example, in JavaScript use the following:

```
<SCRIPT LANGUAGE="JavaScript">
   <!-- JavaScript code here // -->
</SCRIPT>
```

For VBScript, use the following:

```
<SCRIPT LANGUAGE="VBSCRIPT">
   <!-- VBScript code here ' -->
</SCRIPT>
```

The HTML 3.2 defined a placeholder <SCRIPT> element, but otherwise the element is new to HTML 4.0.
Refer to the <NOSCRIPT> element reference in this appendix to see how content may be identified for non-script-aware browsers.

<SELECT>   (Selection List)

DESCRIPTION   This element defines a selection list within a form. Depending on the form of the selection list, the control allows the user to select one or more list options.

Syntax

```
<SELECT
    ACCESSKEY=character    (IE 4.0)
    ALIGN=ABSBOTTOM | ABSMIDDLE | BASELINE | BOTTOM |
          LEFT | MIDDLE | RIGHT | TEXTTOP | TOP    (IE 4.0)
```

```
    AUTOACTIVATE    (WebTV)
    BGCOLOR=color name | #RRGGBB    (WebTV)
    CLASS=class name(s)
    DATAFLD=column name    (IE 4.0)
    DATAFORMATAS=TEXT | HTML    (IE 4.0)
    DATASRC=data source ID    (IE 4.0)
    DIR=LTR | RTL
    DISABLED
    EXCLUSIVE    (WebTV)
    ID=unique alphanumeric identifier
    LANG=language code
    LANGUAGE=JAVASCRIPT | JSCRIPT | VBSCRIPT | VBS    (IE 4.0)
    MULTIPLE
    NAME=unique alphanumeric name
    SELCOLOR=color name | #RRGGBB    (WebTV)
    SHOWEMPTY    (WebTV)
    SIZE=number
    STYLE=style information
    TABINDEX=number
    TEXT=color name | #RRGGBB    (WebTV)
    TITLE=advisory text
    USESTYLE    (WebTV)

    onafterupdate="script"    (IE 4.0)
    onbeforeupdate="script"    (IE 4.0)
    onblur="script"
    onchange="script"
    onfocus="script"
    onclick="script"
    ondblclick="script"
    ondragstart="script"    (IE 4.0)
    onhelp="script"    (IE 4.0)
    onkeydown="script"
    onkeypress="script"
    onkeyup="script"
    onmousedown="script"
    onmousemove="script"
    onmouseout="script"
    onmouseover="script"
    onmouseup="script"
    onresize="script"    (IE 4.0)
    onrowenter="script"    (IE 4.0)
    onrowexit="script"    (IE 4.0)
    onselectstart="script">    (IE 4.0)

    <OPTION> elements

</SELECT>
```

Attributes

ACCESSKEY   This Microsoft attribute specifies a keyboard navigation accelerator for the element. Pressing ALT or a similar key in association with the specified character selects the form control correlated with that key sequence. Page designers are forewarned to avoid key sequences already bound to browsers.

ALIGN   This Microsoft-specific attribute controls the alignment of the image with respect to the content on the page. The default value is **LEFT**, but other values like **ABSBOTTOM**, **ABSMIDDLE**, **BASELINE**, **BOTTOM**, **MIDDLE**, **RIGHT**, **TEXTTOP**, and **TOP** may also be supported. The meaning of these values should be similar to inserted objects like images.

AUTOACTIVATE   In the WebTV implementation, this attribute causes the selection list control to activate immediately when the user selects it, allowing the user to quickly use the arrow keys to move up and down. Without this attribute, the process is a two-step procedure to select the control and then move around.

BGCOLOR   In the WebTV implementation, this attribute specifies the background color the selection list. The value for this attribute can be either a named color, such as **red**, or a color specified in the hexadecimal *#RRGGBB* format, such as **#FF0000**.

CLASS   See "Core Attributes Reference" earlier in this appendix.

DATAFLD   This attribute is used to indicate the column name in the data source that is bound to the options in the **<SELECT>** element.

DATAFORMATAS   This attribute indicates if the bound data is plain text (**TEXT**) or HTML (**HTML**). The data bound with **<SELECT>** should be used to set the potential options to choice from and will probably be in HTML format.

DATASRC   The value of this attribute is set to an identifier indicating the data source to pull data from.

DIR   See "Language Reference" earlier in this appendix.

DISABLED   This attribute is used to turn off a form control. Elements will not be submitted nor may they receive any focus from the keyboard or mouse. Disabled form controls will not be part of the tabbing order. The browser may also gray out the form that is disabled, in order to indicate to the user that the form control is inactive. This attribute requires no value.

EXCLUSIVE   In the WebTV implementation, this attribute prevents duplicate entries in the selection list. The attribute requires no value.

ID   See "Core Attributes Reference" earlier in this appendix.

LANG   See "Language Reference" earlier in this appendix.

LANGUAGE   In the Microsoft implementation, this attribute specifies the scripting language to be used with an associated script bound to the element, typically through an event handler

attribute. Possible values may include **JAVASCRIPT**, **JSCRIPT**, **VBSCRIPT**, and **VBS**. Other values that include the version of the language used, such as JavaScript 1.1, may also be possible.

MULTIPLE   This attribute allows the selection of multiple items in the selection list. The default is single-item selection.

NAME   This attribute allows a form control to be assigned a name so that it can be referenced by a scripting language. **NAME** is supported by older browsers such as Netscape 2.x-generation browsers, but the W3C encourages the use of the **ID** attribute. For compatibility purposes both may have to be used.

SELCOLOR   In the WebTV implementation, this attribute specifies the background color for selected items. Its value can be either a named color, such as **green**, or a color specified in the hexadecimal *#RRGGBB* format, such as **#00FF00**. The default for this attribute in WebTV is **#EAEAEA**.

SHOWEMPTY   In the WebTV implementation, this attribute forces empty lists to display the string "empty" rather than a line or blank entry.

SIZE   This attribute sets the number of visible items in the selection list. When the **MULTIPLE** attribute is not present, only one entry should show; however, when **MULTIPLE** is present, this attribute is useful to set the size of the scrolling list box.

STYLE   See "Core Attributes Reference" earlier in this appendix.

TABINDEX   This attribute takes a numeric value indicating the position of the form control in the tabbing index for the form. Tabbing proceeds from the lowest positive **TABINDEX** value to the highest. Negative values for **TABINDEX** will leave the form control out of the tabbing order. When tabbing is not explicitly set the browser may tab through items in the order they are encountered. Form controls that are disabled due to the presence of the **DISABLED** attribute will not be part of the tabbing index, though read-only controls will be.

TEXT   In the WebTV implementation, this attribute specifies the text color for items in the list. Its value can be either a named color, such as **blue**, or a color specified in the hexadecimal *#RRGGBB* format, such as **#0000FF**.

TITLE   See "Core Attributes Reference" earlier in this appendix.

USESTYLE   This WebTV-specific attribute causes text to be rendered in the style in effect for the page. The attribute requires no value.

EVENT HANDLERS   See "Events Reference" earlier in this appendix.

Examples

```
Choose your favorite colors
<SELECT MULTIPLE SIZE="2">
   <OPTION>Red
   <OPTION>Blue
```

HTML ELEMENT
REFERENCE

```
    <OPTION>Green
    <OPTION>Yellow
</SELECT>

Taco Choices
<SELECT NAME="tacomenu">
    <OPTION VALUE="SuperChicken">Chicken
    <OPTION VALUE="Baja">Fish
    <OPTION VALUE="RX-Needed">Carnitas
</SELECT>
```

COMPATIBILITY   W3C 2.0, 3.2, 4.0; Netscape 1.x, 2.x, 3.x, 4.x; Internet Explorer 2.x, 3.x, 4.x; and WebTV

Notes

The HTML 4.0 specification reserves the attributes **DATASRC**, **DATAFORMATAS**, and **DATAFLD** for future use.

The HTML 3.2 and 2.0 specifications defines only **MULTIPLE**, **NAME**, and **SIZE** attributes. Netscape supports only the **onblur**, **onchange**, **onclick**, and **onfocus** events for this element.

<SHADOW>   (Shadow Text)

DESCRIPTION   This WebTV-specific element renders the enclosed text with a thin, black shadow projected down and to the right.

Syntax

```
<SHADOW>
    text goes here
</SHADOW>
```

Attributes

None.

EVENT HANDLERS   None.

Example

```
The<SHADOW>Shadow</SHADOW>knows.
```

COMPATIBILITY   WebTV

<SIDEBAR>   (Sidebar)

DESCRIPTION   This WebTV-specific element is used to specify a nonscrolling area on the left side of the screen, which is useful for navigation controls and other constant information. This element is supposed to provide functionality somewhat similar to frames.

Syntax

```
<SIDEBAR
     ALIGN=LEFT | CENTER | RIGHT    (WebTV)
     WIDTH=pixels or percentage>    (WebTV)
</SIDEBAR>
```

Attributes

ALIGN   This attribute specifies the alignment of text within the sidebar. The default value is **LEFT**; other values include **RIGHT** and **CENTER**.

WIDTH   This attribute specifies the width of the sidebar either as an absolute width in pixels or as a percent of the screen width. The default value is **0**.

EVENT HANDLERS   None.

Example

```
<SIDEBAR ALIGN="CENTER" WIDTH="20%">

<B>The Sidebar</B>
<BR>
   <A HREF="page1.htm">Page1 </A><BR>
   <A HREF="page2.htm">Page2 </A><BR>

</SIDEBAR>
```

COMPATIBILITY   WebTV

Notes

To create a colored sidebar, use a borderless table the same size as the sidebar and set the background color for the table.

<SMALL>   (Small Text)

DESCRIPTION   This element renders the enclosed text one font size smaller than a document's base font size unless it is already set to the smallest size.

Syntax

```
<SMALL
     CLASS=class name(s)
     DIR=LTR | RTL
     ID=unique alphanumeric string
     LANG=language code
     LANGUAGE=JAVASCRIPT | JSCRIPT | VBSCRIPT | VBS    (IE 4.0)
     STYLE=style information
     TITLE=advisory text

     onclick="script"
     ondblclick="script"
     ondragstart="script"    (IE 4.0)
     onhelp="script"    (IE 4.0)
     onkeydown="script"
     onkeypress="script"
     onkeyup="script"
     onmousedown="script"
     onmouseout="script"
     onmouseover="script"
     onmouseup="script"
     onselectstart="script">    (IE 4.0)

</SMALL>
```

Attributes

CLASS   See "Core Attributes Reference" earlier in this appendix.

DIR   See "Language Reference" earlier in this appendix.

ID   See "Core Attributes Reference" earlier in this appendix.

LANG   See "Language Reference" earlier in this appendix.

LANGUAGE   In the Microsoft implementation, this attribute specifies the scripting language to be used with an associated script bound to the element, typically through an event handler attribute. Possible values may include **JAVASCRIPT**, **JSCRIPT**, **VBSCRIPT**, and **VBS**. Other values that include the version of the language used, such as JavaScript 1.1, may also be possible.

STYLE   See "Core Attributes Reference" earlier in this appendix.

TITLE   See "Core Attributes Reference" earlier in this appendix.

EVENT HANDLERS   See "Events Reference" earlier in this appendix.

Examples

```
Here is some <SMALL>small text</SMALL>.

This element can be applied <SMALL><SMALL><SMALL>multiple
times</SMALL></SMALL></SMALL> to make things even smaller.
```

COMPATIBILITY   W3C 3.2, 4.0; Netscape 2.x, 3.x, 4.x; Internet Explorer 2.x, 3.x, 4.x; and WebTV

Notes

The **<SMALL>** element can be used multiple times to decrease the size of text to a greater degree. Using more than six **<SMALL>** elements together doesn't make sense, since browsers currently only support relative font sizes from 1 to 7. As style sheets become more common, this element may fall out of favor.

The default base font size for a document is typically **3** though it can be changed with the **<BASEFONT>** element.

<SPACER>

DESCRIPTION   This proprietary element is used to specify an invisible region for pushing content around a page.

Syntax

```
<SPACER
    ALIGN=ABSMIDDLE | ABSBOTTOM | BASELINE | BOTTOM | LEFT |
    MIDDLE | RIGHT | TEXTTOP | TOP    (N 3.0, N 4.0, WebTV)
    HEIGHT=pixels    (N 3.0, N 4.0, WebTV)
    SIZE=pixels    (N 3.0, N 4.0, WebTV)
    TYPE=BLOCK | HORIZONTAL | VERTICAL    (N 3.0, N 4.0, WebTV)
    WIDTH=pixels>
```

Attributes

ALIGN   This attribute specifies the alignment of the spacer with respect to surrounding text. It is only used with spacers with **TYPE=BLOCK**. The default value for the **ALIGN** attribute is **BOTTOM**. The meaning of the **ALIGN** values are similar to the **<IMG>** element.

HEIGHT   This attribute is used to specify the height of the invisible region in pixels. It is only used with spacers with **TYPE=BLOCK**.

SIZE   Used with **TYPE=BLOCK** and **TYPE=HORIZONTAL** spacers, this attribute sets the spacer's width in pixels. Used with a **TYPE=VERTICAL** spacer, this attribute is used to set the spacer's height.

TYPE This attribute indicates the type of invisible region. A **HORIZONTAL** spacer adds horizontal space between words and objects. A **VERTICAL** spacer is used to add space between lines. A **BLOCK** spacer defines a general-purpose positioning rectangle like an invisible image that text may flow around.

WIDTH This attribute is used only with the **TYPE=BLOCK** spacer and is used to set the width of the region in pixels.

EVENT HANDLERS None.

Examples

```
A line of text with two<SPACER TYPE="HORIZONTAL" SIZE="20">words
separated by 20 pixels. Here is a line of text.<BR>
<SPACER TYPE="VERTICAL" SIZE="50">
Here is another line of text with a large space between the two
lines.<SPACER ALIGN="LEFT" TYPE="BLOCK" HEIGHT="100" WIDTH="100">
This is a bunch of text which flows around an invisible block
region. You could have easily performed this layout with a table.
```

COMPATIBILITY Netscape 3.x, 4.x; WebTV

Notes

This element should not be used. If the effect of this element is required and style sheets cannot be used, an invisible pixel trick may be a more appropriate choice. The invisible pixel trick requires a transparent image, which is then resized with the **HEIGHT** and **WIDTH** attributes of the **<IMG>** element:

```
<IMG SRC="pixel.gif" HEIGHT="100" WIDTH="100">
```

This is an empty element; no closing tag is allowed.

<SPAN> (Text Span)

DESCRIPTION This element is used to group inline text, typically so scripting or style rules can be applied to the content. As it has no preset or rendering meaning, this is the most useful inline element for associating style and script with content.

SYNTAX

```
<SPAN
    CHARSET= character set
    CLASS=class name(s)
    DATAFLD=column name    (IE 4.0)
    DATAFORMATAS=HTML | TEXT    (IE 4.0)
```

```
DATASRC=data source ID    (IE 4.0)
DIR=LTR | RTL
HREF= URL of linked resource
HREFLANG= language code
ID=unique alphanumeric string
LANG=language code
LANGUAGE=JAVASCRIPT | JSCRIPT | VBSCRIPT | VBS    (IE 4.0)
MEDIA= Media description
REL=comma-separated list of relationship values
REV=comma-separated list of relationship values
STYLE=style information
TARGET=_blank | _parent | _self | _top | frame-name
TITLE=advisory text
TYPE= MIME type

onclick="script"
ondblclick="script"
ondragstart="script"    (IE 4.0)
onhelp="script"    (IE 4.0)
onkeydown="script"
onkeypress="script"
onkeyup="script"
onmousedown="script"
onmousemove="script"
onmouseout="script"
onmouseover="script"
onmouseup="script"
onselectstart="script">    (IE 4.0)

</SPAN>
```

Attributes

CHARSET   This attribute defines the character encoding of the linked resource. The value is a space- and/or comma-delimited list of character sets as defined in RFC 2045. The default value is ISO-8859-1.

CLASS   See "Core Attributes Reference" earlier in this appendix.

DATAFLD   This attribute is used to indicate the column name in the data source that is bound to the contents of the **<SPAN>** element.

DATAFORMATAS   This attribute indicates if the bound data is plain text (**TEXT**) or HTML (**HTML**). The data bound with **<SPAN>** should be used to set the content of the element and may include HTML markup.

DATASRC   The value of this attribute is set to an identifier indicating the data source to pull data from.

DIR   See "Language Reference" earlier in this appendix.

HREF   This attribute is used to specify the URL of a resource that provides more information about the content enclosed by the <SPAN> element.

HREFLANG   This attribute is used to indicate the language of the linked resource. See "Language Reference" earlier in this appendix for information on allowed values.

ID   See "Core Attributes Reference" earlier in this appendix.

LANG   See "Language Reference" earlier in this appendix.

LANGUAGE   In the Microsoft implementation, this attribute specifies the scripting language to be used with an associated script bound to the element, typically through an event handler attribute. Possible values may include **JAVASCRIPT**, **JSCRIPT**, **VBSCRIPT**, and **VBS**. Other values that include the version of the language used, such as JavaScript 1.1, may also be possible.

MEDIA   This attribute is used to specify the destination medium for any linked information, particularly when the **REL** attribute is set to **STYLESHEET**. The value of the attribute may be a single media descriptor like **SCREEN**, or a comma-separated list. Possible values for this attribute might include **SCREEN**, **PRINT**, **PROJECTION**, **BRAILLE**, **AURAL**, and **ALL**. Other values may also be defined, depending on the browser. This attribute was added very late to the HTML 4.0 specification, and its meaning with the <SPAN> element is far from clear. Furthermore, this attribute is not yet supported by any browser.

REL   For elements containing the **HREF** attribute, this attribute specifies the relationship of the target object to the link object. The value is a comma-separated list of relationship values. The values and their semantics will be registered by some authority, which may have meaning to the document author. The default relationship, if no other is given, is **void**. The **REL** attribute should be used only when the **HREF** attribute is present.

REV   This attribute specifies a reverse link, the inverse relationship of the **REL** attribute. It is useful for indicating where an object came from, such as the author of a document.

STYLE   See "Core Attributes Reference" earlier in this appendix.

TARGET   This attribute specifies the target window for a hypertext source link referencing frames. The information linked to will be displayed in the named window. Frames must be named to be targeted. There are, however, special name values, including **_blank**, which indicates a new window; **_parent**, which indicates the parent frame set containing the source link; **_self**, which indicates the frame containing the source link; and **_top**, which indicates the full browser window. This attribute was added very late to the HTML 4.0 specification and its meaning is unclear. Furthermore, the attribute is not supported by any known browser.

TITLE   See "Core Attributes Reference" earlier in this appendix.

TYPE   This attribute specifies the media type in the form of a MIME type of the linked content. Generally this is provided strictly as advisory information; however, in the future a browser may add a small icon for multimedia types. For example, a browser might add a small speaker icon when **TYPE** was set to audio/wav.

EVENT HANDLERS   See "Events Reference" earlier in this appendix.

Examples

```
Here is some<SPAN STYLE="font: 14pt; color: purple">
very strange
</SPAN>text.
<SPAN ID="toggletext" onclick="this.style.color='red'"
ondblclick="this.style.color='black'">
Click and Double Click Me
</SPAN>
```

COMPATIBILITY   W3C 4.0; Netscape 4.x; and Internet Explorer 3.x, 4.x

Notes

The HTML 4.0 specification reserves the **DATAFLD, DATASRC,** and **DATAFORMATAS**
attributes for future use.

The attributes **CHARSET, HREF, HREFLANG, MEDIA, REL, REV, TARGET,** and **TYPE** were
added to the HTML 4.0 specification just before the final draft was released. The meaning of
these attributes is not well documented; since no browsers support them at the time of the
writing, is difficult to determine how or even if they will be used.

Unlike **<DIV>,** as an inline element **<SPAN>** does not cause any line breaks.

Netscape currently does not support any events for the **<SPAN>** element; thus it can only be
used for style-sheet application.

<STRIKE>   (Strikeout Text)

DESCRIPTION   This element is used to indicate strikethrough text, namely text with a line
drawn through it. The **<S>** element provides shorthand notation for this element.

Syntax

```
<STRIKE
    CLASS=class name(s)
    DIR=LTR | RTL
    ID=unique alphanumeric string
    LANG=language code
    LANGUAGE=JAVASCRIPT | JSCRIPT | VBSCRIPT | VBS   (IE 4.0)
    STYLE=style information
    TITLE=advisory text

    onclick="script"
    ondblclick="script"
    ondragstart="script"   (IE 4.0)
    onhelp="script"   (IE 4.0)
    onkeydown="script"
```

```
    onkeypress="script"
    onkeyup="script"
    onmousedown="script"
    onmouseout="script"
    onmouseover="script"
    onmouseup="script"
    onselectstart="script">   (IE 4.0)

</STRIKE>
```

Attributes

CLASS   See "Core Attributes Reference" earlier in this appendix.

DIR   See "Language Reference" earlier in this appendix.

ID   See "Core Attributes Reference" earlier in this appendix.

LANG   See "Language Reference" earlier in this appendix.

LANGUAGE   In the Microsoft implementation, this attribute specifies the scripting language to be used with an associated script bound to the element, typically through an event handler attribute. Possible values may include **JAVASCRIPT**, **JSCRIPT**, **VBSCRIPT**, and **VBS**. Other values that include the version of the language used, such as JavaScript 1.1, may also be possible.

STYLE   See "Core Attributes Reference" earlier in this appendix.

TITLE   See "Core Attributes Reference" earlier in this appendix.

EVENT HANDLERS   See "Events Reference" earlier in this appendix.

Example

```
This line contains a spelling <STRIKE>misstake</STRIKE> mistake
```

COMPATIBILITY   W3C 3.2, 4.0 (transitional); Netscape 3.x; Internet Explorer 2.x, 3.x, 4.x; and WebTV

Notes
This element should act the same as the **<S>** element.
The strict HTML 4.0 specification does not include the **<STRIKE>** element nor the **<S>** element. It is possible to indicate strikethrough text using a style sheet.

<STRONG>

DESCRIPTION   This element indicates strongly emphasized text. It is usually rendered in a bold typeface, but is a logical element rather than a physical one.

Syntax

```
<STRONG
     CLASS=class name(s)
     DIR=LTR | RTL
     ID=unique alphanumeric string
     LANG=language code
     LANGUAGE=JAVASCRIPT | JSCRIPT | VBSCRIPT | VBS    (IE 4.0)
     STYLE=style information
     TITLE=advisory text

     onclick="script"
     ondblclick="script"
     ondragstart="script"   (IE 4.0)
     onhelp="script"   (IE 4.0)
     onkeydown="script"
     onkeypress="script"
     onkeyup="script"
     onmousedown="script"
     onmouseout="script"
     onmouseover="script"
     onmouseup="script"
     onselectstart="script">   (IE 4.0)

</STRONG>
```

Attributes

CLASS   See "Core Attributes Reference" earlier in this appendix.

DIR   See "Language Reference" earlier in this appendix.

ID   See "Core Attributes Reference" earlier in this appendix.

LANG   See "Language Reference" earlier in this appendix.

LANGUAGE   In the Microsoft implementation, this attribute specifies the scripting language to be used with an associated script bound to the element, typically through an event handler attribute. Possible values may include **JAVASCRIPT**, **JSCRIPT**, **VBSCRIPT**, and **VBS**. Other values that include the version of the language used, such as JavaScript 1.1, may also be possible.

STYLE   See "Core Attributes Reference" earlier in this appendix.

TITLE   See "Core Attributes Reference" earlier in this appendix.

EVENT HANDLERS   See "Events Reference" earlier in this appendix.

Examples

```
It is really <STRONG>important</STRONG> to pay attention.

<STRONG STYLE="font-family: impact; font-size: 28pt">
Important Info
</STRONG>
```

COMPATIBILITY W3C 2.0, 3.2, 4.0; Netscape 1.x, 2.x, 3.x, 4.x; Internet Explorer 2.x, 3.x, 4.x; and WebTV

Notes

This element generally renders as bold text. As a logical element, however, **<STRONG>** is useful to bind style rules to.

As compared to **<B>**, this element does have meaning and voice browsers may state **<STRONG>** enclosed text in a different voice than text that is enclosed by **<B>**.

<STYLE> (Style Information)

DESCRIPTION This element is used to surround style sheet rules for a document. This element should be found only in the **<HEAD>** of a document. Style rules within a document's **<BODY>** element should be set with the **STYLE** attribute for a particular element.

Syntax

```
<STYLE
    DIR=LTR | RTL
    DISABLED  (IE 4.0)
    LANG=language code
    MEDIA=SCREEN | PRINT | ALL | others
    TITLE=advisory text
    TYPE=MIME Type>

</STYLE>
```

Attributes

DIR This attribute is used to set the text direction of the title for the style sheet, either right to left (**RTL**) or left to right (**LTR**).

DISABLED This Microsoft-defined attribute is used to disable a style sheet. The presence of the attribute is all that is required to disable the style sheet. In conjunction with scripting, this attribute could be used to turn on and off various style sheets in a document.

LANG The value of this attribute is a language code, like all other **LANG** attributes; however, this attribute defines the language of the **TITLE** attribute rather than the content of the element.

MEDIA   This attribute is used to specify the destination medium for the style information. The value of the attribute may be a single media descriptor like **SCREEN** or a comma-separated list. Possible values for this attribute include **SCREEN, PRINT, PROJECTION, BRAILLE, AURAL,** and **ALL**. Other values may also be defined, depending on the browser. Internet Explorer supports **SCREEN, PRINT,** and **ALL** as values for this attribute.

TITLE   This attribute associates an informational title with the style sheet.

TYPE   This attribute is used to define the type of style sheet. The value of the attribute should be the MIME type of the style sheet language used. The most common current value for this attribute is **text/css**, which indicates a Cascading Style Sheet format.

EVENT HANDLERS   None.

Example

```
<HTML>
<HEAD>
<TITLE>Style Sheet Example</TITLE>
<STYLE TYPE="text/css">
<!--
BODY {background: black; color: white; font: 12pt Helvetica}
H1 {color: red; font: 14pt Impact}
-->
</STYLE >
</HEAD>
<BODY>
<H1>A 14 point red Impact heading on a black background.</H1>
Regular body text, which is 12 point white Helvetica.
</BODY>
</HTML>
```

COMPATIBILITY   W3C 4.0; Netscape 4.x; and Internet Explorer 3.x, 4.x

Notes

Style information can also be specified in external style sheets as defined by the **<LINK>** element. Style information can also be associated with a particular element using the **STYLE** attribute. Style rules are generally commented out within the **<STYLE>** element to avoid interpretation by nonconforming browsers.

<SUB>   (Subscript)

DESCRIPTION   This element renders its content as subscripted text.

Syntax

```
<SUB
    CLASS=class name(s)
    DIR=LTR | RTL
    ID=unique alphanumeric string
    LANG=language code
    LANGUAGE=JAVASCRIPT | JSCRIPT | VBSCRIPT | VBS    (IE 4.0)
    STYLE=style information
    TITLE=advisory text

    onclick="script"
    ondblclick="script"
    ondragstart="script"   (IE 4.0)
    onhelp="script"    (IE 4.0)
    onkeydown="script"
    onkeypress="script"
    onkeyup="script"
    onmousedown="script"
    onmouseout="script"
    onmouseover="script"
    onmouseup="script"
    onselectstart="script">    (IE 4.0)

</SUB>
```

Attributes

CLASS   See "Core Attributes Reference" earlier in this appendix.

DIR   See "Language Reference" earlier in this appendix.

ID   See "Core Attributes Reference" earlier in this appendix.

LANG   See "Language Reference" earlier in this appendix.

LANGUAGE   In the Microsoft implementation, this attribute specifies the scripting language to be used with an associated script bound to the element, typically through an event handler attribute. Possible values may include **JAVASCRIPT**, **JSCRIPT**, **VBSCRIPT**, and **VBS**. Other values that include the version of the language used, such as JavaScript 1.1, may also be possible.

STYLE   See "Core Attributes Reference" earlier in this appendix.

TITLE   See "Core Attributes Reference" earlier in this appendix.

EVENT HANDLERS   See "Events Reference" earlier in this appendix.

Example

```
Here is some <SUB>subscripted</SUB> text
```

COMPATIBILITY   W3C 3.2, 4.0; Netscape 2.x, 3.x, 4.x; Internet Explorer 2.x, 3.x, 4.x; and WebTV

Notes

The HTML 3.2 specification supports no attributes for the **<SUP>** element. WebTV supports no attributes for this element.

<SUP>   (Superscript)

DESCRIPTION   This element renders its content as superscripted text.

Syntax

```
<SUP
    CLASS=class name(s)
    DIR=LTR | RTL
    ID=unique alphanumeric string
    LANG=language code
    LANGUAGE=JAVASCRIPT | JSCRIPT | VBSCRIPT | VBS   (IE 4.0)
    STYLE=style information
    TITLE=advisory text

    onclick="script"
    ondblclick="script"
    ondragstart="script"   (IE 4.0)
    onhelp="script"   (IE 4.0)
    onkeydown="script"
    onkeypress="script"
    onkeyup="script"
    onmousedown="script"
    onmouseout="script"
    onmouseover="script"
    onmouseup="script"
    onselectstart="script">   (IE 4.0)

</SUP>
```

Attributes

CLASS   See "Core Attributes Reference" earlier in this appendix.

DIR   See "Language Reference" earlier in this appendix.

ID   See "Core Attributes Reference" earlier in this appendix.

LANG   See "Language Reference" earlier in this appendix.

LANGUAGE   In the Microsoft implementation, this attribute specifies the scripting language to be used with an associated script bound to the element, typically through an event handler attribute. Possible values may include **JAVASCRIPT**, **JSCRIPT**, **VBSCRIPT**, and **VBS**. Other values that include the version of the language used, such as JavaScript 1.1, may also be possible.

STYLE   See "Core Attributes Reference" earlier in this appendix.

TITLE   See "Core Attributes Reference" earlier in this appendix.

EVENT HANDLERS   See "Events Reference" earlier in this appendix.

Example

```
Here is some <SUP>superscripted</SUP> text
```

COMPATIBILITY   W3C 3.2, 4.0; Netscape 2.x, 3.x, 4.x; Internet Explorer 2.x, 3.x, 4.x; and WebTV

Notes
The HTML 3.2 specification defines no attributes for this element.
WebTV supports no attributes for this element.

<TABLE>

DESCRIPTION   This element is used to define a table. Tables are used to organize data as well as structuring devices to lay pages out nicely.

Syntax

```
<TABLE
    ALIGN=LEFT | CENTER  | RIGHT | BLEEDLEFT* |
        BLEEDRIGHT* | JUSTIFY*   (*WebTV)
    BACKGROUND=URL of image file   (IE 4.0, N 4.0, WebTV)
    BGCOLOR=color name | #RRGGBB
    BORDER=pixels
    BORDERCOLOR=color name | #RRGGBB   (IE 4.0, N 4.0)
    BORDERCOLORDARK=color name | #RRGGBB   (IE 4.0)
    BORDERCOLORLIGHT=color name | #RRGGBB   (IE 4.0)
    CELLBORDER=pixels   (WebTV)
    CELLPADDING=pixels
    CELLSPACING=pixels
    CLASS=class name(s)
    COLS=number of columns   (N 4.0)
    DATAPAGESIZE=number of records to display   (IE 4.0)
```

```
DATASRC=data source ID    (IE 4.0)
DIR=LTR | RTL
FRAME=ABOVE | BELOW | BORDER | BOX | HSIDES |
LHS | RHS | VOID | VSIDES
HREF=URL    (WebTV)
HEIGHT=pixels | percentages*  (IE 4.0, N 4.0) *(IE 4.0)
HSPACE=pixels    (N 4.0, WebTV)
ID=unique alphanumeric identifier
LANG=language code
LANGUAGE=JAVASCRIPT | JSCRIPT | VBSCRIPT | VBS    (IE 4.0)
NAME=string    (WebTV)
NOWRAP    (WebTV)
RULES=ALL | COLS | GROUPS | NONE | ROWS
STYLE=style information
SUMMARY=summary information
TITLE=advisory text
TRANSPARENCY=0 to 100    (WebTV)
VALIGN=BASELINE | BOTTOM | MIDDLE | TOP
VSPACE=pixels    (N 4.0, WebTV)
WIDTH=pixels | percentage

onafterupdate="script"    (IE 4.0)
onbeforeupdate="script"    (IE 4.0)
onblur="script"  (IE 4.0)
onclick="script"
ondblclick="script"
ondragstart="script"    (IE 4.0)
onfocus="script"    (IE 4.0)
onhelp="script"    (IE 4.0)
onkeydown="script"
onkeypress="script"
onkeyup="script"
onmousedown="script"
onmosuemove="script"
onmouseover="script"
onmouseout="script"
onmouseup="script"
onresize="script"    (IE 4.0)
onrowenter="script"    (IE 4.0)
onrowexit="script"    (IE 4.0)
onselectstart="script">    (IE 4.0)
```

```
</TABLE>
```

Attributes

ALIGN   This attribute specifies the alignment of the table with respect to surrounding text. The HTML 4.0 specification defines **LEFT**, **RIGHT**, and **CENTER**. WebTV also defines

BLEEDRIGHT and **BLEEDLEFT**, which cause the table to bleed over the right and left margins of the page, and **JUSTIFY**, which is used to justify the table within the browser window. Some browsers may also support alignment values, like **ABSMIDDLE**, that are common to block objects.

BACKGROUND   This nonstandard attribute, which is supported by Internet Explorer, Netscape, and WebTV, is used to specify the URL of a background image for the table. The image is tiled if it is smaller than the table dimensions.

BGCOLOR   This attribute specifies a background color for a table. Its value can be either a named color, such as **red**, or a color specified in the hexadecimal #*RRGGBB* format, such as **#FF0000**.

BORDER   This attribute specifies in pixels the width of a table's borders. A value of **0** makes a borderless table, which is useful for graphic layout.

BORDERCOLOR   This attribute supported by Internet Explorer and Netscape is used to set the border color for a table. The attribute should only be used with a positive value for the **BORDER** attribute. The value of the attribute can be either be a named color, such as **green**, or a color specified in the hexadecimal #*RRGGBB* format, such as **#00FF00**.

BORDERCOLORDARK   This Internet Explorer-specific attribute specifies the darker of two border colors used to create a three-dimensional effect for cell borders. It must be used with the **BORDER** attribute set to a positive value. The attribute value can be either a named color, such as **blue**, or a color specified in the hexadecimal #*RRGGBB* format, such as **#00FF00**.

BORDERCOLORLIGHT   This Internet Explorer-specific attribute specifies the lighter of two border colors used to create a three-dimensional effect for cell borders. It must be used with the **BORDER** attribute set to a positive value. The attribute value can be either a named color, such as **red**, or a color specified in the hexadecimal #*RRGGBB* format, such as **#FF0000**.

CELLBORDER   In the WebTV implementation, this attribute sets the width in pixels of the border between table cells. If this value is not present, the default border as specified by the **BORDER** attribute is used.

CELLPADDING   This attribute sets the width in pixels between the edge of a cell and its content.

CELLSPACING   This attribute sets the width in pixels between individual cells.

CLASS   See "Core Attributes Reference" earlier in this appendix.

COLS   This attribute specifies the number of columns in the table as is used to help quickly calculate the size of the table. This attribute was part of the preliminary HTML 4.0 specification but was later dropped. A few browsers, notably Netscape 4.0, already support it.

DATAPAGESIZE   The value of this Microsoft-specific attribute is the number of records that can be displayed in the table when data binding is used.

DATASRC   The value of this Microsoft-specific attribute is an identifier indicating the data source to pull data from.

DIR   See "Language Reference" earlier in this appendix.

FRAME   This attribute specifies which edges of a table are to display a border frame. A value of **ABOVE** indicates only the top edge; **BELOW** indicates only the bottom edge; and **BORDER** and **BOX** indicate all edges, which is the default when the **BORDER** attribute is a positive integer. A value of **HSIDES** indicates only the top and bottom edges should be displayed; **LHS** indicates the left-hand edge should be displayed; **RHS** indicates the right-hand edge is displayed; **VSIDES** indicates the left and right edges should both be displayed; and **VOID** indicates no border should be displayed.

HEIGHT   For Netscape 4.0, this attribute allows the author to specify the height of the table in pixels. Internet Explorer 4.0 allows both pixels and percentages.

HREF   This WebTV-specific attribute is used to make the entire table function as a hyperlink anchor to the specified URL.

HSPACE   This Netscape-specified attribute indicates the horizontal space in pixels between the table and surrounding content. This attribute is also supported by WebTV but, oddly, not by Internet Explorer.

ID   See "Core Attributes Reference" earlier in this appendix.

LANG   See "Language Reference" earlier in this appendix.

LANGUAGE   In the Microsoft implementation, this attribute specifies the scripting language to be used with an associated script bound to the element, typically through an event handler attribute. Possible values may include **JAVASCRIPT**, **JSCRIPT**, **VBSCRIPT**, and **VBS**. Other values that include the version of the language used, such as JavaScript 1.1, may also be possible.

NAME   This WebTV attribute is used to assign the table a unique name. It is synonymous with the **ID** attribute.

NOWRAP   This WebTV-specific attribute keeps table rows from wrapping if they extend beyond the right margin. The attribute requires no value.

RULES   This attribute controls the display of dividing rules within a table. A value of **ALL** specifies dividing rules for rows and columns. A value of **COLS** specifies dividing rules for columns only. A value of **GROUPS** specifies horizontal dividing rules between groups of table cells defined by the <THEAD>, <TBODY>, <TFOOT>, or <COLGROUP> elements. A value of **ROWS** specifies dividing rules for rows only. A value of **NONE** indicates no dividing rules and is the default.

STYLE   See "Core Attributes Reference" earlier in this appendix.

SUMMARY   This attribute is used to provide a text summary of the table's purpose and structure. This element is used for accessibility, and its presence is important for nonvisual user agents.

TITLE   See "Core Attributes Reference" earlier in this appendix.

TRANSPARENCY   This WebTV-specific attribute specifies the degree of transparency of the table. Values range from **0**, totally opaque, to **100**, totally transparent. A value of **50** is optimized for fast rendering.

VSPACE   This Netscape attribute indicates the vertical space in pixels between the table and surrounding content. This attribute is also supported by WebTV but, oddly, not by Internet Explorer.

WIDTH   This attribute specifies the width of the table either in pixels or as a percentage value of the enclosing window.

EVENT HANDLERS   See "Events Reference" earlier in this appendix.

Examples

```
<TABLE BGCOLOR="WHITE" BORDER="4">
    <TR>
      <TD>Cell 1</TD>
      <TD>Cell 2</TD>
      <TD>Cell 3</TD>
      <TD>Cell 4</TD>
    </TR>
    <TR>
      <TD>Cell 5</TD>
      <TD>Cell 6</TD>
    </TR>
</TABLE>


<TABLE RULES="ALL" BGCOLOR="YELLOW">
 <CAPTION>Widgets by Area</CAPTION>
   <THEAD ALIGN="CENTER" BGCOLOR="GREEN" VALIGN="CENTER">
     <TD>This is a header</TD>
   </THEAD>
   <TFOOT ALIGN="RIGHT" BGCOLOR="RED" VALIGN="BOTTOM">
     <TD>This is part of the footer</TD>
     <TD>This is also part of the footer</TD>
   </TFOOT>

<TBODY>
   <TR>
     <TD></TD>
     <TH>Regular Widget</TD>
     <TH>Super Widget</TD>
   </TR>
   <TR>
     <TH>West Coast</TH>
     <TD>10</TD>
     <TD>12</TD>
```

```
    </TR>
    <TR>
      <TH>East Coast</TH>
      <TD>1</TD>
      <TD>20</TD>
    </TR>

  </TBODY>
</TABLE>
```

COMPATIBILITY   W3C 3.2, 4.0; Netscape 1.1, 2.x, 3.x, 4.x; Internet Explorer 2.x, 3.x, 4.x; and WebTV

Notes

In addition to displaying tabular data, tables are used to support graphic layout and design.
The HTML 4.0 specification reserves the future use of the **DATASRC**, **DATAFLD**, and **DATAFORMATAS** attributes for the **<TABLE>** element.
The HTML 3.2 specification defines only the **ALIGN**, **BORDER**, **CELLSPACING**, **CELLPADDING**, and **WIDTH** attributes for the **<TABLE>** element.
Currently only Internet Explorer 4.0 supports a majority of the HTML 4.0 table extensions.
The **COLS** attribute may provide an undesirable result under Netscape, which assumes the size of each column in the table is exactly the same.

<TBODY>   (Table Body)

DESCRIPTION   This element is used to group the rows within the body of a table so that common alignment and style defaults can be set easily for numerous cells.

Syntax

```
<TBODY
     ALIGN=CENTER | CHAR | JUSTIFY | LEFT | RIGHT
     BGCOLOR=color name | #RRGGBB    (IE 4.0)
     CHAR=character
     CHAROFF=offset
     CLASS=class name(s)
     DIR=LTR | RTL
     ID=unique alphanumeric identifier
     LANG=language code
     LANGUAGE=JAVASCRIPT | JSCRIPT | VBSCRIPT | VBS    (IE 4.0)
     STYLE=style information
     TITLE=advisory text
     VALIGN=BASELINE | BOTTOM | CENTER* | MIDDLE | TOP   (*IE 4.0)

     onclick="script"
     ondblclick="script"
```

```
      ondragstart="script"   (IE 4.0)
      onhelp="script"   (IE 4.0)
      onkeydown="script"
      onkeypress="script"
      onkeyup="script"
      onmousemove="script"
      onmouseout="script"
      onmouseover="script"
      onselectstart="script">   (IE 4.0)

</TBODY>
```

Attributes

ALIGN   This attribute is used to align the contents of the cells within the **<TBODY>** element. Common values are **LEFT**, **RIGHT**, **CENTER**, and **JUSTIFY**. The HTML 4.0 specification also defines a value of **CHAR**. When **ALIGN** is set to **CHAR**, the attribute **CHAR** must be present and set to the character to which cells should be aligned. A common use of this approach would be to set cells to align on a decimal point.

BGCOLOR   This attribute specifies a background color for the cells within the **<TBODY>** element. Its value can be either a named color, such as **red**, or a color specified in the hexadecimal *#RRGGBB* format, such as **#FF0000**.

CHAR   This attribute is used to define the character to which element contents are aligned when the **ALIGN** attribute is set to the **CHAR** value.

CHAROFF   This attribute contains an offset as a positive or negative integer to align characters as related to the **CHAR** value. A value of **2**, for example, would align characters in a cell two characters to the right of the character defined by the **CHAR** attribute.

CLASS   See "Core Attributes Reference" earlier in this appendix.

DIR   See "Language Reference" earlier in this appendix.

ID   See "Core Attributes Reference" earlier in this appendix.

LANG   See "Language Reference" earlier in this appendix.

LANGUAGE   In the Microsoft implementation, this attribute specifies the scripting language to be used with an associated script bound to the element, typically through an event handler attribute. Possible values may include **JAVASCRIPT**, **JSCRIPT**, **VBSCRIPT**, and **VBS**. Other values that include the version of the language used, such as JavaScript 1.1, may also be possible.

STYLE   See "Core Attributes Reference" earlier in this appendix.

TITLE   See "Core Attributes Reference" earlier in this appendix.

VALIGN   This attribute is used to set the vertical element for the table cells with the **<TBODY>** element. HTML 4.0 defines **BASELINE, BOTTOM, MIDDLE,** and **TOP.** Internet Explorer further defines **CENTER,** which should act just like **MIDDLE.**

EVENT HANDLERS   See "Events Reference" earlier in this appendix.

Example

```
<TABLE RULES="ALL" BGCOLOR="YELLOW">

  <TBODY ALIGN="CENTER" BGCOLOR="RED" STYLE="bodystyle"
VALIGN="BASELINE" >
    <TR>
     <TD></TD>
     <TH>Regular Widget</TH>
     <TH>Super Widget</TH>
    </TR>
<TR>
   <TH>West Coast</TH>
   <TD>10</TD>
   <TD>12</TD>
</TR>
<TR>
   <TH>East Coast</TH>
   <TD>1</TD>
   <TD>20</TD>
</TR>

</TBODY>
</TABLE>
```

COMPATIBILITY   W3C 4.0; Internet Explorer 4.x

Notes

This element is contained by the **<TABLE>** and contains one or more table rows as indicated by the **<TR>** element.

<TD>   (Table Data)

DESCRIPTION   This element is used to specify a data cell in a table. The element should occur within a table row as defined by the **<TR>** element.

Syntax

```
<TD
    ABBR=abbreviation
    ABSHEIGHT=pixels    (WebTV)
```

```
ABSWIDTH=pixels    (WebTV)
ALIGN=CENTER | JUSTIFY | LEFT | RIGHT
AXIS=group name
BACKGROUND=URL of image file    (IE 4.0, N 4.0, WebTV)
BGCOLOR=color name | #RRGGBB
BORDERCOLOR=color name | #RRGGBB    (IE 4.0, N 4.0)
BORDERCOLORDARK=color name | #RRGGBB    (IE 4.0)
BORDERCOLORLIGHT=color name | #RRGGBB    (IE 4.0)
CHAR=character
CHAROFF=offset
CLASS=class name
COLSPAN=number
DIR=LTR | RTL
HEADERS=space separated list of associated header
        cell's ID values
HEIGHT=pixels
ID=unique alphanumeric identifier
LANG=language code
LANGUAGE=JAVASCRIPT | JSCRIPT | VBSCRIPT | VBS    (IE 4.0)
MAXLINES=number    (WebTV)
NOWRAP
ROWSPAN=number
STYLE=style information
TITLE=advisory text
TRANSPARENCY=0 to 100    (WebTV)
VALIGN=BASELINE | BOTTOM | CENTER* |  MIDDLE | TOP (* IE 4.0)
WIDTH=pixels

onafterupdate="script"    (IE 4.0)
onbeforeupdate="script"    (IE 4.0)
onblur="script"   (IE 4.0)
onclick="script"
ondblclick="script"
ondragstart="script"    (IE 4.0)
onfocus="script"    (IE 4.0)
onhelp="script"    (IE 4.0)
onkeydown="script"
onkeypress="script"
onkeyup="script"
onmousedown="script"
onmousemove="script"
onmouseout="script"
onmouseover="script"
onmouseup="script"
onresize="script"    (IE 4.0)
onrowenter="script"    (IE 4.0)
onrowexit="script"    (IE 4.0)
onscroll="script"    (IE 4.0)
```

```
        onselectstart="script">  (IE 4.0)

</TD>
```

Attributes

ABBR   The value of this attribute is an abbreviated name for a header cell. This may be useful when attempting to display large tables on small screens.

ABSHEIGHT   This WebTV-specific attribute sets the absolute height of a cell in pixels. Content that does not fit within this height is clipped.

ABSWIDTH   This WebTV-specific attribute sets the absolute width of a cell in pixels. Content that does not fit within this width is clipped.

ALIGN   This attribute is used to align the contents of the cells within the **<TBODY>** element. Common values are **LEFT**, **RIGHT**, **CENTER**, and **JUSTIFY**.

AXIS   This attribute is used to provide a name for a group of related headers.

BACKGROUND   This nonstandard attribute, which is supported by Internet Explorer, Netscape and WebTV, is used to specify the URL of a background image for the table cell. The image is tiled if it is smaller than the cell's dimensions.

BGCOLOR   This attribute specifies a background color for a table cell. Its value can be either a named color, such as **red**, or a color specified in the hexadecimal *#RRGGBB* format, such as **#FF0000**.

BORDERCOLOR   This attribute supported by Internet Explorer and Netscape is used to set the border color for a table cell. The attribute should only be used with a positive value for the **BORDER** attribute. The value of the attribute can be either be a named color, such as **green**, or a color specified in the hexadecimal *#RRGGBB* format, such as **#00FF00**.

BORDERCOLORDARK   This Internet Explorer-specific attribute specifies the darker of two border colors used to create a three-dimensional effect for a cell's borders. It must be used with the **BORDER** attribute set to a positive value. The attribute value can be either a named color, such as **blue**, or a color specified in the hexadecimal *#RRGGBB* format, such as **#00FF00**.

BORDERCOLORLIGHT   This Internet Explorer-specific attribute specifies the lighter of two border colors used to create a three-dimensional effect for a cell's borders. It must be used with the **BORDER** attribute set to a positive value. The attribute value can be either a named color, such as **red**, or a color specified in the hexadecimal *#RRGGBB* format, such as **#FF0000**.

CHAR   This attribute is used to define the character to which element contents are aligned when the **ALIGN** attribute is set to the **CHAR** value.

CHAROFF   This attribute contains an offset as a positive or negative integer to align characters as related to the **CHAR** value. A value of **2**, for example, would align characters in a cell two characters to the right of the character defined by the **CHAR** attribute.

CLASS   See "Core Attributes Reference" earlier in this appendix.

COLSPAN   This attribute takes a numeric value that indicates how many columns wide a cell should be. This is useful to create tables with cells of different widths.

DIR   See "Language Reference" earlier in this appendix.

HEADERS   This attribute takes a space-separated list of **ID** values that correspond to the header cells related to this cell.

HEIGHT   This attribute indicates the height in pixels of the cell.

ID   See "Core Attributes Reference" earlier in this appendix.

LANG   See "Language Reference" earlier in this appendix.

LANGUAGE   In the Microsoft implementation, this attribute specifies the scripting language to be used with an associated script bound to the element, typically through an event handler attribute. Possible values may include **JAVASCRIPT**, **JSCRIPT**, **VBSCRIPT**, and **VBS**. Other values that include the version of the language used, such as JavaScript 1.1, may also be possible.

MAXLINES   This WebTV-specific attribute takes a numeric argument indicating the maximum number of content lines to display. Content beyond these lines is clipped.

NOWRAP   This attribute keeps the content within a table cell from automatically wrapping.

ROWSPAN   This attribute takes a numeric value that indicates how many rows high a table cell should span. This is attribute is useful in defining tables with cells of different heights.

SCOPE   This attribute is used to specify the table cells that the current cell provides header information for. A value of **COL** indicates that the cell is a header for the the rest of the column below it. A value of **COLGROUP** indicates that the cell is a header for its current column group. A value of **ROW** indicates that that the cell contains header information for the rest of the row it is in. A value of **ROWGROUP** indicates that the cell is a header for its row group. This attribute may be used in place of the **HEADER** attribute and is useful for rendering assistance by nonvisual browsers. This attribute was added very late to the HTML 4.0 specification, so support for it is minimal.

STYLE   See "Core Attributes Reference" earlier in this appendix.

TITLE   See "Core Attributes Reference" earlier in this appendix.

TRANSPARENCY   This WebTV-specific attribute specifies the degree of transparency of the table cell. Values range from **0**, totally opaque, to **100**, totally transparent. A value of **50** is optimized for fast rendering.

VALIGN   This attribute is used to set the vertical element for the table cell. HTML 4.0 defines **BASELINE**, **BOTTOM**, **MIDDLE**, and **TOP**. Internet Explorer further defines **CENTER**, which should act just like **MIDDLE**.

WIDTH   This attribute specifies the width of a cell in pixels.

EVENT HANDLERS   See "Events Reference" earlier in this appendix.

Examples

```
<TD ALIGN="LEFT" VALIGN="TOP">
Put me in the top left corner.
</TD>

<TD ALIGN="BOTTOM" BGCOLOR="RED" VALIGN="RIGHT">
Put me in the bottom right corner.
</TD>

<TABLE BORDER="1" WIDTH="80%">
  <TR>
    <TD COLSPAN="3">
    A pretty wide cell
    </TD>
  <TR>
    <TD>Item 2</TD>
    <TD>Item 3</TD>
    <TD>Item 4</TD>
  </TR>
</TABLE>
```

COMPATIBILITY   W3C 3.2, 4.0; Netscape 1.1, 2.x, 3.x, 4.x; Internet Explorer 2.x, 3.x, 4.x; and WebTV

Notes

The HTML 3.2 specification defines only **ALIGN**, **COLSPAN**, **HEIGHT**, **NOWRAP**, **ROWSPAN**, **VALIGN**, and **WIDTH** attributes.
This element should always be within the **<TR>** element.

<TEXTAREA>   (Multiline Text Input)

DESCRIPTION   This element is used to specify a multiline text input field contained within a form.

Syntax

```
<TEXTAREA
     ACCESSKEY=character    (IE 4.0)
     ALLCAPS    (WebTV)
     ALIGN=ABSBOTTOM | ABSMIDDLE |  BASELINE | BOTTOM |
          LEFT | MIDDLE | RIGHT | TEXTTOP | TOP    (IE 4.0)
     AUTOACTIVATE    (WebTV)
     AUTOCAPS    (WebTV)
     BGCOLOR=color name |  #RRGGBB    (WebTV)
```

```
CLASS=class name
COLS=number
DATAFLD=column name    (IE 4.0)
DATAFORMATAS=TEXT | HTML    (IE 4.0)
DATASRC=data source id    (IE 4.0)
DIR=LTR | RTL
DISABLED
CURSOR=color name | #RRGGBB    (WebTV)
GROWABLE    (WebTV)
ID=unique alphanumeric identifier
LANG=language code
LANGUAGE=JAVASCRIPT | JSCRIPT | VBSCRIPT | VBS    (IE 4.0)
NAME=unique alphanumeric identifier
NOHARDBREAKS    (WebTV)
NOSOFTBREAKS    (WebTV)
NUMBERS    (WebTV)
READONLY
ROWS=number
SHOWKEYBOARD    (WebTV)
STYLE=style information
TABINDEX=number
TITLE=advisory text
USESTYLE    (WebTV)
WRAP=OFF | HARD* | SOFT* | PHYSICAL** | VIRTUAL**
                ( *N 4.0   **IE 4.0)

onafterupdate="script"    (IE 4.0)
onbeforeupdate="script"    (IE 4.0)
onblur="script"
onchange="script"
onclick="script"
ondblclick="script"
ondragstart="script"    (IE 4.0)
onfocus="script"    (IE 4.0)
onhelp="script"    (IE 4.0)
onkeydown="script"
onkeypress="script"
onkeyup="script"
onmousedown="script"
onmousemove="script"
onmouseout="script"
onmouseover="script"
onmouseup="script"
onresize="script"    (IE 4.0)
onrowenter="script"    (IE 4.0)
onrowexit="script"    (IE 4.0)
onscroll="script"    (IE 4.0)
onselect="script"
onselectstart="script">    (IE 4.0)


</TEXTAREA>
```

Attributes

ACCESSKEY   This Microsoft-specific attribute specifies a keyboard navigation accelerator for the element. Pressing ALT or a similar key in association with the specified character selects the form control correlated with that key sequence. Page designers are forewarned to avoid key sequences already bound to browsers.

ALIGN   Microsoft defines alignment values for this element. The values for this attribute should behave similar to any included object or image.

ALLCAPS   This WebTV-specific attribute renders all viewer entered text in capital letters. This attribute requires no value.

AUTOACTIVATE   This WebTV-specific attribute causes the text input control to immediately activate. This attribute requires no value.

AUTOCAPS   This WebTV-specific attribute renders the first letter of all viewer-entered words in a capital letter. This attribute requires no value.

BGCOLOR   This WebTV-specific attribute specifies the background color for the text input area. Its value can be either a named color, such as **red**, or a color specified in the hexadecimal *#RRGGBB* format, such as **#FF0000**. The default color for the **<TEXTAREA>** element under WebTV is **#EAEAEA**.

CLASS   See "Core Attributes Reference" earlier in this appendix.

COLS   This attribute sets the width in characters of the text area. The typical default values for the size of a **<TEXTAREA>** element when this attribute is not set is **20** characters.

CURSOR   This WebTV-specific attribute is used to indicate the cursor color for the text input area. Its value can be either a named color, such as **red**, or a color specified in the hexadecimal *#RRGGBB* format, such as **#FF0000**. The default value for the cursor color in the WebTV browser is **darkblue (#3333AA)**.

DATAFLD   This attribute is used to indicate the column name in the data source that is bound to the content enclosed by the **<TEXTAREA>** element.

DATAFORMATAS   This attribute indicates if the bound data is plain text (**TEXT**) or HTML (**HTML**). The data bound with **<TEXTAREA>** should be used to set the potential options to choice from and will probably be in HTML format.

DATASRC   The value of this attribute is an identifier indicating the data source to pull data from.

DIR   See "Language Reference" earlier in this appendix.

DISABLED   This attribute is used to turn off a form control. Elements will not be submitted nor may they receive any focus from the keyboard or mouse. Disabled form controls will not be part of the tabbing order. The browser may also gray out the form that is disabled, in order to indicate to the user that the form control is inactive. This attribute requires no value.

GROWABLE   When present, this WebTV-specific attribute allows the text input area to expand vertically to accommodate extra text entered by the user. This attribute requires no value.

ID   See "Core Attributes Reference" earlier in this appendix.

LANG   See "Language Reference" earlier in this appendix.

LANGUAGE   In the Microsoft implementation, this attribute specifies the scripting language to be used with an associated script bound to the element, typically through an event handler attribute. Possible values may include **JAVASCRIPT**, **JSCRIPT**, **VBSCRIPT**, and **VBS**. Other values that include the version of the language used, such as JavaScript 1.1, may also be possible.

NAME   This attribute allows a form control to be assigned a name so that it can be referenced by a scripting language. **NAME** is supported by older browsers, such as Netscape 2.x-generation browsers, but the W3C encourages the use of the **ID** attribute. For compatibility purposes, boeth attributes may have to be used.

NOHARDBREAKS   This WebTV-specific attribute causes a press of the RETURN key to select the next form element rather than causing a line break in the text input area. The attribute requires no value.

NOSOFTBREAKS   This attribute removes breaks automatically inserted into the text by line wrapping when the form is submitted. The attribute requires no value.

NUMBERS   This WebTV-specific attribute causes the number "1" to be selected in the onscreen keyboard in anticipation of the viewer entering a numeric value.

READONLY   This attribute prevents the form control's value from being changed. Form controls with this attribute set may receive focus from the user but may not be modified. Since they receive focus, a **READONLY** form control will be part of the form's tabbing order. Last, the control's value will be sent on form submission. The attribute can only be used with **<INPUT>** when **TYPE** is **TEXT** or **PASSWORD**. The attribute is also used with the **<TEXTAREA>** element.

ROWS   This attribute sets the number of rows in the text area. The value of the attribute should be a positive integer.

SHOWKEYBOARD   In the WebTV implementation, this attribute causes the on-screen keyboard to be displayed when the **<TEXTAREA>** element is selected.

STYLE   See "Core Attributes Reference" earlier in this appendix.

TABINDEX   This attribute takes a numeric value indicating the position of the form control in the tabbing index for the form. Tabbing proceeds from the lowest positive **TABINDEX** value to the highest. Negative values for **TABINDEX** will leave the form control out of the tabbing order. When tabbing is not explicitly set, the browser may tab through items in the order they are encountered. Form controls that are disabled due to the presence of the **DISABLED** attribute will not be part of the tabbing index, though read-only controls will be.

TITLE   See "Core Attributes Reference" earlier in this appendix.

USESTYLE This WebTV-specific attribute causes text to be rendered in the style in effect for the page. The attribute requires no value.

WRAP In Netscape and Microsoft browsers, this attribute controls word wrap behavior. A value of **OFF** for the attribute forces the **<TEXTAREA>** not to wrap text, so the viewer must manually enter line breaks. A value of **HARD** causes word wrap and includes line breaks in text submitted to the server. A value of **SOFT** causes word wrap but removes line breaks from text submitted to the server. Internet Explorer supports a value of **PHYSICAL**, which indicates that text should be wrapped both on screen and when it is submitted. Internet Explorer interprets a value of **VIRTUAL** to mean that text should be displayed as word wrapped but submitted as typed.

EVENT HANDLERS See "Events Reference" earlier in this appendix.

Example

```
<TEXTAREA NAME="CommentBox" COLS="40" ROWS="8">
Default text in field
</TEXTAREA>
```

COMPATIBILITY W3C 2.0, 3.2, 4.0; Netscape 1.x, 2.x, 3.x, 4.x; Internet Explorer 2.x, 3.x, 4.x; and WebTV

Notes

Any text between the **<TEXTAREA>** and **</TEXTAREA>** tags is rendered as the default entry for the form control.
The HTML 3.2 and 2.0 specifications define only the **COLS**, **NAME**, and **ROWS** attribute for this element.
WebTV and Netscape support only the **onblur**, **onchange**, **onfocus**, and **onselect** event attributes for this element.
The HTML 4.0 specification reserves the **DATAFLD**, **DATAFORMATAS**, and **DATASRC** attributes for future use with the **<TEXTAREA>** element.

<TFOOT> (Table Footer)

DESCRIPTION This element is used to group the rows within the footer of a table so that common alignment and style defaults can be set easily for numerous cells. This element may be particularly useful when setting a common footer for tables that are dynamically generated.

Syntax

```
<TFOOT
    ALIGN=CENTER | CHAR | JUSTIFY | LEFT | RIGHT
    BGCOLOR=color name | #RRGGBB    (IE 4.0)
    CHAR=character
    CHAROFF=offset
```

```
CLASS=class name(s)
DIR=LTR | RTL
ID=unique alphanumeric identifier
LANG=language code
LANGUAGE=JAVASCRIPT | JSCRIPT | VBSCRIPT | VBS   (IE 4.0)
STYLE=style information
TITLE=advisory text
VALIGN=BASELINE | BOTTOM | CENTER* | MIDDLE | TOP   (*IE 4.0)

onclick="script"
ondblclick="script"
ondragstart="script"   (IE 4.0)
onhelp="script"   (IE 4.0)
onkeydown="script"
onkeypress="script"
onkeyup="script"
onmousemove="script"
onmouseout="script"
onmouseover="script"
onselectstart="script">   (IE 4.0)
```

```
</TFOOT>
```

Attributes

ALIGN   This attribute is used to align the contents of the cells within the **<TFOOT>** element. Common values are **LEFT**, **RIGHT**, **CENTER**, and **JUSTIFY**. The HTML 4.0 specification also defines a value of **CHAR**. When **ALIGN** is set to **CHAR**, the attribute **CHAR** must be present and set to the character to which cells should be aligned. A common use of this approach would be to set cells to align on a decimal point.

BGCOLOR   This attribute specifies a background color for the cells within the **<TFOOT>** element. Its value can be either a named color, such as **red**, or a color specified in the hexadecimal #*RRGGBB* format, such as **#FF0000**.

CHAR   This attribute is used to define the character to which element contents are aligned when the **ALIGN** attribute is set to the **CHAR** value.

CHAROFF   This attribute contains an offset as a positive or negative integer to align characters as related to the **CHAR** value. A value of **2**, for example, would align characters in a cell two characters to the right of the character defined by the **CHAR** attribute.

CLASS   See "Core Attributes Reference" earlier in this appendix.

DIR   See "Language Reference" earlier in this appendix.

ID   See "Core Attributes Reference" earlier in this appendix.

LANG   See "Language Reference" earlier in this appendix.

LANGUAGE   In the Microsoft implementation, this attribute specifies the scripting language to be used with an associated script bound to the element, typically through an event handler attribute. Possible values may include **JAVASCRIPT**, **JSCRIPT**, **VBSCRIPT**, and **VBS**. Other values that include the version of the language used, such as JavaScript 1.1, may also be possible.

STYLE   See "Core Attributes Reference" earlier in this appendix.

TITLE   See "Core Attributes Reference" earlier in this appendix.

VALIGN   This attribute is used to set the vertical element for the table cells with the **<TFOOT>** element. HTML 4.0 defines **BASELINE**, **BOTTOM**, **MIDDLE**, and **TOP**. Internet Explorer further defines **CENTER**, which should act just like **MIDDLE**.

EVENT HANDLERS   None.

Example

```
<TABLE BORDER="1" BGCOLOR="YELLOW" WIDTH="80%">
    <TBODY CLASS="tablebody">
     <TR>
<TD>The contents of the table!</TR>
    </TBODY>
    <TFOOT ALIGN="CENTER" BGCOLOR="RED" CLASS="footer"
VALIGN="BOTTOM">
<TD>This is part of the footer</TD>
<TD> Part of the footer</TD>
    </TFOOT>
</TABLE>
```

COMPATIBILITY   W3C 4.0; Internet Explorer 4.x

Notes

This element is only contained by the **<TABLE>** element and contains table rows as delimited by **<TR>** elements.

<TH>   (Table Header)

DESCRIPTION   This element is used to specify a header cell in a table. The element should occur within a table row as defined by a **<TR>** element. The main difference between this element and **<TD>** is that browsers may render table headers slightly differently.

Syntax

```
<TH
    ABBR=abbreviation
    ABSHEIGHT=pixels    (WebTV)
    ABSWIDTH=pixels     (WebTV)
    ALIGN=CENTER | JUSTIFY | LEFT | RIGHT
    AXIS=group name
    BACKGROUND=URL of image file    (IE 4.0, N 4.0, WebTV)
    BGCOLOR=color name | #RRGGBB
    BORDERCOLOR=color name | #RRGGBB    (IE 4.0, N 4.0)
    BORDERCOLORDARK=color name | #RRGGBB    (IE 4.0)
    BORDERCOLORLIGHT=color name | #RRGGBB    (IE 4.0)
    CHAR=character
    CHAROFF=offset
    CLASS=class name
    COLSPAN=number
    DIR=LTR | RTL
    HEADERS=space-separated list of associated header
            cell's ID values
    HEIGHT=pixels
    ID=unique alphanumeric identifier
    LANG=language code
    LANGUAGE=JAVASCRIPT | JSCRIPT | VBSCRIPT | VBS    (IE 4.0)
    MAXLINES=number    (WebTV)
    NOWRAP
    ROWSPAN=number
    SCOPE=COL | COLGROUP | ROW | ROWGROUP
    STYLE=style information
    TITLE=advisory text
    TRANSPARENCY=0 to 100    (WebTV)
    VALIGN=BASELINE | BOTTOM | CENTER* | MIDDLE | TOP    (* IE 4.0)
    WIDTH=pixels

    onafterupdate="script"    (IE 4.0)
    onbeforeupdate="script"    (IE 4.0)
    onclick="script"
    ondblclick="script"
    ondragstart="script"    (IE 4.0)
    onfocus="script"    (IE 4.0)
    onhelp="script"    (IE 4.0)
    onkeydown="script"
    onkeypress="script"
    onkeyup="script"
    onmousedown="script"
    onmousemove="script"
    onmouseout="script"
    onmouseover="script"
    onmouseup="script"
```

```
        onresize="script"   (IE 4.0)
        onrowenter="script"   (IE 4.0)
        onrowexit="script"   (IE 4.0)
        onscroll="script"   (IE 4.0)
        onselectstart="script">  (IE 4.0)

 </TH>
```

Attributes

ABBR   The value of this attribute is an abbreviated name for a header cell. This may be useful when attempting to display large tables on small screens.

ABSHEIGHT   This WebTV-specific attribute sets the absolute height of a cell in pixels. Content that does not fit within this height is clipped.

ABSWIDTH   This WebTV-specific attribute sets the absolute width of a cell in pixels. Content that does not fit within this width is clipped.

ALIGN   This attribute is used to align the contents of the cells within the **<TBODY>** element. Common values are **LEFT**, **RIGHT**, **CENTER**, and **JUSTIFY**.

AXIS   This attribute is used to provide a name for a group of related headers.

BACKGROUND   This nonstandard attribute, which is supported by Internet Explorer, Netscape and WebTV, is used to specify the URL of a background image for the table cell. The image is tiled if it is smaller than the cell's dimensions.

BGCOLOR   This attribute specifies a background color for a table cell. Its value can be either a named color, such as red, or a color specified in the hexadecimal *#RRGGBB* format, such as **#FF0000**.

BORDERCOLOR   This attribute supported by Internet Explorer and Netscape is used to set the border color for a table cell. The attribute should only be used with a positive value for the **BORDER** attribute. The value of the attribute can be either be a named color, such as **green**, or a color specified in the hexadecimal *#RRGGBB* format, such as **#00FF00**.

BORDERCOLORDARK   This Internet Explorer-specific attribute specifies the darker of two border colors used to create a three-dimensional effect for a cell's borders. It must be used with the **BORDER** attribute set to a positive value. The attribute value can be either a named color, such as **blue**, or a color specified in the hexadecimal *#RRGGBB* format, such as **#00FF00**).

BORDERCOLORLIGHT   This Internet Explorer-specific attribute specifies the lighter of two border colors used to create a three-dimensional effect for a cell's borders. It must be used with the **BORDER** attribute set to a positive value. The attribute value can be either a named color, such as **red**, or a color specified in the hexadecimal *#RRGGBB* format, such as **#FF0000**.

CHAR This attribute is used to define the character to which element contents are aligned when the **ALIGN** attribute is set to the **CHAR** value.

CHAROFF This attribute contains an offset as a positive or negative integer to align characters as related to the **CHAR** value. A value of **2**, for example would align characters in a cell two characters to the right of the character defined by the **CHAR** attribute.

CLASS See "Core Attributes Reference" earlier in this appendix.

COLSPAN This attribute takes a numeric value that indicates how many columns wide a cell should be. This is useful to create tables with cells of different widths.

DIR See "Language Reference" earlier in this appendix.

HEADERS This attribute takes a space separated list of **ID** values that correspond to the header cells related to this cell.

HEIGHT This attribute indicates the height in pixels of the header cell.

ID See "Core Attributes Reference" earlier in this appendix.

LANG See "Language Reference" earlier in this appendix.

LANGUAGE In the Microsoft implementation, this attribute specifies the scripting language to be used with an associated script bound to the element, typically through an event handler attribute. Possible values may include **JAVASCRIPT**, **JSCRIPT**, **VBSCRIPT**, and **VBS**. Other values that include the version of the language used, such as JavaScript 1.1, may also be possible.

MAXLINES This WebTV-specific attribute takes a numeric argument indicating the maximum number of content lines to display. Content beyond these lines is clipped.

NOWRAP This attribute keeps the content within a table header cell from automatically wrapping.

ROWSPAN This attribute takes a numeric value that indicates how many rows high a table cell should span. This is attribute is useful in defining tables with cells of different heights.

SCOPE This attribute is used to specify the table cells that the current cell provides header information for. A value of **COL** indicates that the cell is a header for the the rest of the column below it. A value of **COLGROUP** indicates that the cell is a header for its current column group. A value of **ROW** indicates that that the cell contains header information for the rest of the row it is in. A value of **ROWGROUP** indicates that the cell is a header for its row group. This attribute may be used in place of the **HEADER** attribute and is useful for rendering assistance by nonvisual browsers. This attribute was added very late to the HTML 4.0 specification, so support for it is minimal.

STYLE See "Core Attributes Reference" earlier in this appendix.

TITLE See "Core Attributes Reference" earlier in this appendix.

HTML ELEMENT REFERENCE

TRANSPARENCY   This WebTV-specific attribute specifies the degree of transparency of the table header. Values range from **0**, totally opaque, to **100**, totally transparent. A value of **50** is optimized for fast rendering.

VALIGN   This attribute is used to set the vertical element for the table cell. HTML 4.0 defines **BASELINE**, **BOTTOM**, **MIDDLE**, and **TOP**. Internet Explorer further defines **CENTER**, which should act just like **MIDDLE**.

WIDTH   This attribute specifies the width of a header cell in pixels.

EVENT HANDLERS   See "Events Reference" earlier in this appendix.

Examples

```
<TABLE BORDER="1">
    <TR>
        <TH>Names</TH>
        <TH>Apples</TH>
        <TH>Oranges</TH>
    </TR>
    <TR>
        <TD>Boby</TD>
        <TD>10</TD>
        <TD>5</TD>
    </TR>
    <TR>
        <TD>Ruby Sue</TD>
        <TD>20</TD>
        <TD>3</TD>
    </TR>
</TABLE>
```

COMPATIBILITY   W3C 3.2, 4.0; Netscape 1.1, 2.x, 3.x, 4.x; Internet Explorer 2.x, 3.x, 4.x; and WebTV

Notes
The HTML 3.2 specification defines only **ALIGN**, **COLSPAN**, **HEIGHT**, **NOWRAP**, **ROWSPAN**, **VALIGN**, and **WIDTH** attributes.
This element should always be within the **<TR>** element.

<THEAD>   (Table Header)

DESCRIPTION   This element is used to group the rows within the header of a table so that common alignment and style defaults can be set easily for numerous cells. This element may be particularly useful when setting a common head for tables that are dynamically generated.

Syntax

```
<THEAD
     ALIGN=CENTER | CHAR | JUSTIFY | LEFT | RIGHT
     BGCOLOR=color name | #RRGGBB    (IE 4.0)
     CHAR=character
     CHAROFF=offset
     CLASS=class name(s)
     DIR=LTR | RTL
     ID=unique alphanumeric identifier
     LANG=language code
     LANGUAGE=JAVASCRIPT | JSCRIPT | VBSCRIPT | VBS    (IE 4.0)
     STYLE=style information
     TITLE=advisory text
     VALIGN=BASELINE | BOTTOM | CENTER* | MIDDLE | TOP    (*IE 4.0)

     onclick="script"
     ondblclick="script"
     ondragstart="script"    (IE 4.0)
     onhelp="script"    (IE 4.0)
     onkeydown="script"
     onkeypress="script"
     onkeyup="script"
     onmousedown="script"
     onmousemove="script"
     onmouseout="script"
     onmouseover="script"
     onmouseup="script"
     onselectstart="script">    (IE 4.0)

</THEAD>
```

Attributes

ALIGN   This attribute is used to align the contents of the cells within the **<THEAD>** element. Common values are **LEFT**, **RIGHT**, **CENTER**, and **JUSTIFY**. The HTML 4.0 specification also defines a value of **CHAR**. When **ALIGN** is set to **CHAR**, the attribute **CHAR** must be present and set to the character to which cells should be aligned. A common use of this approach would be to set cells to align on a decimal point.

BGCOLOR   This attribute specifies a background color for the cells within the **<THEAD>** element. Its value can be either a named color, such as **red**, or a color specified in the hexadecimal *#RRGGBB* format, such as **#FF0000**.

CHAR   This attribute is used to define the character to which element contents are aligned when the **ALIGN** attribute is set to the **CHAR** value.

CHAROFF   This attribute contains an offset as a positive or negative integer to align characters as related to the **CHAR** value. A value of 2, for example would align characters in a cell two characters to the right of character defined by the **CHAR** attribute.

CLASS   See "Core Attributes Reference" earlier in this appendix.

DIR   See "Language Reference" earlier in this appendix.

ID   See "Core Attributes Reference" earlier in this appendix.

LANG   See "Language Reference" earlier in this appendix.

LANGUAGE   In the Microsoft implementation, this attribute specifies the scripting language to be used with an associated script bound to the element, typically through an event handler attribute. Possible values may include **JAVASCRIPT**, **JSCRIPT**, **VBSCRIPT**, and **VBS**. Other values that include the version of the language used, such as JavaScript 1.1, may also be possible.

STYLE   See "Core Attributes Reference" earlier in this appendix.

TITLE   See "Core Attributes Reference" earlier in this appendix.

VALIGN   This attribute is used to set the vertical element for the table cells with the <THEAD> element. HTML 4.0 defines **BASELINE**, **BOTTOM**, **MIDDLE**, and **TOP**. Internet Explorer further defines **CENTER**, which should act just like **MIDDLE**.

EVENT HANDLERS   See "Events Reference" earlier in this appendix.

Example

```
<TABLE BORDER="1" BGCOLOR="YELLOW" WIDTH="80%">
   <THEAD ALIGN="CENTER" BGCOLOR="RED" CLASS="footer"
VALIGN="BOTTOM">
      <TD>This is the important table headline</TD>
   </THEAD>
 <TBODY CLASS="tablebody">
   <TR>
      <TD>The contents of the table!</TR>
   </TBODY>
 </TABLE>
```

COMPATIBILITY   W3C 4.0; Internet Explorer 3.0, 4.0

Notes

This element is only contained by the <TABLE> element and contains table rows as delimited by <TR> elements.

<TITLE>   (Document Title)

DESCRIPTION   This element encloses the title of an HTML document. It must occur within a document's **<HEAD>** element and must be present in all valid documents. Meaningful titles are very important since they are used for bookmarking a page and may be used by search engines attempting to index the document.

Syntax

```
<TITLE
    DIR=LTR | RTL
    ID=unique alphanumeric identifier  (IE 4.0)
    LANG=language code
    TITLE=advisory text>   (IE 4.0)

</TITLE>
```

Attributes

DIR   See "Language Reference" earlier in this appendix.

ID   See "Core Attributes Reference" earlier in this appendix.

LANG   See "Language Reference" earlier in this appendix.

TITLE   See "Core Attributes Reference" earlier in this appendix.

EVENT HANDLERS   None.

Example

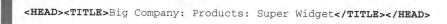

<HEAD><TITLE>Big Company: Products: Super Widget**</TITLE></HEAD>**

COMPATIBILITY   W3C 2.0, 3.2, 4.0; Netscape 1.x, 2.x, 3.x, 4.x; Internet Explorer 2.x, 3.x, 4.x; and WebTV

Notes

Meaningful names should provide description about the document. A poor title would be something like "My Home Page," while a better title would be "Joe Smith Home."

Older versions of Netscape allowed for multiple occurrences of the <TITLE> element. When multiple <TITLE> elements were encountered, they could be used to simulate an animated title bar. This was a bug with the Netscape browser, however, and the effect of multiple **<TITLE>** elements no longer works.

Browsers may be extremely sensitive with the <TITLE> element. If the title element is malformed or not closed, the page may not even render in the browser.

The HTML 2.0 and 3.2 specification define no attributes for the **<TITLE>** element.

<TR>   (Table Row)

DESCRIPTION   This element is used to specify a row in a table. The individual cells of the row are defined by the **<TH>** and **<TD>** elements.

Syntax

```
<TR
     ALIGN=CENTER | JUSTIFY | LEFT | RIGHT
     BGCOLOR=color name | #RRGGBB
     BORDERCOLOR=color name | #RRGGBB    (IE 4.0)
     BORDERCOLORDARK=color name | #RRGGBB    (IE 4.0)
     BORDERCOLORLIGHT=color name | #RRGGBB    (IE 4.0)
     CHAR=character
     CHAROFF=offset
     CLASS=class name(s)
     DIR=LTR | RTL
     ID=unique alphanumeric identifier
     LANG=language code
     LANGUAGE=JAVASCRIPT | JSCRIPT | VBSCRIPT | VBS    (IE 4.0)
     NOWRAP    (WebTV)
     STYLE=style information
     TITLE=advisory text
     TRANSPARENCY=0 to 100    (WebTV)
     VALIGN=BASELINE | BOTTOM | CENTER* | MIDDLE | TOP    (*IE 4.0)

     onafterupdate="script"    (IE 4.0)
     onbeforeupdate="script"    (IE 4.0)
     onblur="script"    (IE 4.0)
     onclick="script"
     ondblclick="script"
     ondragstart="script"    (IE 4.0)
     onfocus="script"    (IE 4.0)
     onhelp="script"    (IE 4.0)
     onkeydown="script"
     onkeypress="script"
     onkeyup="script"
     onmousedown="script"
     onmousemove="script"
     onmouseout="script"
     onmouseover="script"
     onmouseup="script"
     onresize="script"    (IE 4.0)
     onrowenter="script"    (IE 4.0)
     onrowexit="script"    (IE 4.0)
     onselectstart="script">    (IE 4.0)

</TR>
```

Attributes

ALIGN   This attribute is used to align the contents of the cells within the **<THEAD>** element. Common values are **LEFT**, **RIGHT**, **CENTER**, and **JUSTIFY**.

BGCOLOR   This attribute specifies a background color for all the cells in a row. Its value can be either a named color, such as **red**, or a color specified in the hexadecimal *#RRGGBB* format, such as **#FF0000**.

BORDERCOLOR   This attribute supported by Internet Explorer and Netscape is used to set the border color for a table cells in the row. The attribute should only be used with a positive value for the **BORDER** attribute. The value of the attribute can be either be a named color, such as **green**, or a color specified in the hexadecimal *#RRGGBB* format, such as **#00FF00**.

BORDERCOLORDARK   This Internet Explorer-specific attribute specifies the darker of two border colors used to create a three-dimensional effect for the cell's borders. It must be used with the **BORDER** attribute set to a positive value. The attribute value can be either a named color, such as **blue**, or a color specified in the hexadecimal *#RRGGBB* format, such as **#00FF00**.

BORDERCOLORLIGHT   This Internet Explorer-specific attribute specifies the lighter of two border colors used to create a three-dimensional effect for a cell's borders. It must be used with the **BORDER** attribute set to a positive value. The attribute value can be either a named color, such as **red**, or a color specified in the hexadecimal *#RRGGBB* format, such as **#FF0000**.

CHAR   This attribute is used to define the character to which element contents are aligned when the **ALIGN** attribute is set to the **CHAR** value.

CHAROFF   This attribute contains an offset as a positive or negative integer to align characters as related to the **CHAR** value. A value of **2**, for example, would align characters in a cell two characters to the right of the character defined by the **CHAR** attribute.

CLASS   See "Core Attributes Reference" earlier in this appendix.

DIR   See "Language Reference" earlier in this appendix.

ID   See "Core Attributes Reference" earlier in this appendix.

LANG   See "Language Reference" earlier in this appendix.

LANGUAGE   In the Microsoft implementation, this attribute specifies the scripting language to be used with an associated script bound to the element, typically through an event handler attribute. Possible values may include **JAVASCRIPT**, **JSCRIPT**, **VBSCRIPT**, and **VBS**. Other values that include the version of the language used, such as JavaScript 1.1, may also be possible.

NOWRAP   This WebTV-specific attribute keeps table rows from wrapping if they extend beyond the right margin.

STYLE   See "Core Attributes Reference" earlier in this appendix.

TITLE   See "Core Attributes Reference" earlier in this appendix.

TRANSPARENCY   This WebTV-specific attribute specifies the degree of transparency of the table. Values range from **0**, totally opaque, to **100**, totally transparent. A value of **50** is optimized for fast rendering.

VALIGN   This attribute is used to set the vertical element for the table cells with the **<TR>** element. HTML 4.0 defines **BASELINE**, **BOTTOM**, **MIDDLE**, and **TOP**. Internet Explorer further defines **CENTER**, which should act just like **MIDDLE**.

EVENT HANDLERS   See "Events Reference" earlier in this appendix.

Example

```
<TABLE WIDTH="300" BORDER="1">
   <TR BGCOLOR="RED" ALIGN="CENTER" VALIGN="CENTER">
     <TD>3</TD>
     <TD>5.6</TD>
     <TD>7.9</TD>
   </TR>
</TABLE>
```

COMPATIBILITY   W3C 3.2, 4.0; Netscape 1.1, 2.x, 3.x, 4.x; Internet Explorer 2.x, 3.x, 4.x; and WebTV

Notes
This element is contained by the **<TABLE>**, **<THEAD>**, **<TBODY>**, and **<TFOOT>** element. It contains the **<TH>** and **<TD>** elements.
The HTML 3.2 specification defines only the **ALIGN** and **VALIGN** attributes for this element.

<TT>   (Teletype Text)

DESCRIPTION   This element is used to indicate that text should be rendered in a monospaced font similar to teletype text.

Syntax

```
<TT
    CLASS=class name(s)
    DIR=LTR | RTL
    ID=unique alphanumeric identifier
    LANG=language code
    LANGUAGE=JAVASCRIPT | JSCRIPT | VBSCRIPT | VBS   (IE 4.0)
    STYLE=style information
    TITLE=advisory text

    onclick="script"
```

```
        ondblclick="script"
        ondragstart="script"   (IE 4.0)
        onhelp="script"   (IE 4.0)
        onkeydown="script"
        onkeypress="script"
        onkeyup="script"
        onmousedown="script"
        onmousemove="script"
        onmouseout="script"
        onmouseover="script"
        onmouseup="script"
        onselectstart="script">   (IE 4.0)

</TT>
```

Attributes

CLASS   See "Core Attributes Reference" earlier in this appendix.

DIR   See "Language Reference" earlier in this appendix.

ID   See "Core Attributes Reference" earlier in this appendix.

LANG   See "Language Reference" earlier in this appendix.

LANGUAGE   In the Microsoft implementation, this attribute specifies the scripting language to be used with an associated script bound to the element, typically through an event handler attribute. Possible values may include **JAVASCRIPT**, **JSCRIPT**, **VBSCRIPT**, and **VBS**. Other values that include the version of the language used, such as JavaScript 1.1, may also be possible.

STYLE   See "Core Attributes Reference" earlier in this appendix.

TITLE   See "Core Attributes Reference" earlier in this appendix.

EVENT HANDLERS   See "Events Reference" earlier in this appendix.

Example

```
Here is some <TT>monospaced text</TT>.
```

COMPATIBILITY   W3C 2.0, 3.2, 4.0; Netscape 1.x, 2.x, 3.x, 4.x; Internet Explorer 2.x, 3.x, 4.x; and WebTV

<U>   (Underline)

DESCRIPTION   This element is used to indicate that the enclosed text should be displayed underlined.

Syntax

```
<U
    CLASS=class name(s)
    DIR=LTR | RTL
    ID=unique alphanumeric string
    LANG=language code
    LANGUAGE=JAVASCRIPT | JSCRIPT | VBSCRIPT | VBS    (IE 4.0)
    STYLE=style information
    TITLE=advisory text

    onclick="script"
    ondblclick="script"
    ondragstart="script"   (IE 4.0)
    onhelp="script"   (IE 4.0)
    onkeydown="script"
    onkeypress="script"
    onkeyup="script"
    onmousedown="script"
    onmousemove="script"
    onmouseout="script"
    onmouseover="script"
    onmouseup="script"
    onselectstart="script">   (IE 4.0)

</U>
```

Attributes

CLASS   See "Core Attributes Reference" earlier in this appendix.

DIR   See "Language Reference" earlier in this appendix.

ID   See "Core Attributes Reference" earlier in this appendix.

LANG   See "Language Reference" earlier in this appendix.

LANGUAGE   In the Microsoft implementation, this attribute specifies the scripting language to be used with an associated script bound to the element, typically through an event handler attribute. Possible values may include **JAVASCRIPT**, **JSCRIPT**, **VBSCRIPT**, and **VBS**. Other values that include the version of the language used, such as JavaScript 1.1, may also be possible.

STYLE   See "Core Attributes Reference" earlier in this appendix.

TITLE   See "Core Attributes Reference" earlier in this appendix.

EVENT HANDLERS   See "Events Reference" earlier in this appendix.

Examples

```
Here is some <U>underlined text</U>.

Be careful with <U>underlined</U> text, it looks like
<A HREF="http://www.yahoo.com/">links</A>.
```

COMPATIBILITY   W3C 3.2, 4.0 (transitional); Netscape 3.x, 4.x; Internet Explorer 2.x, 3.x, 4.x; and WebTV

Notes

Under the strict HTML 4.0 specification, the **<U>** element is not defined. The capabilities of this element are possible using style sheets.
Underlining text can be problematic because it looks similar to a link, especially in a black-and-white environment.

<UL>   (Unordered List)

DESCRIPTION   This element is used to indicate an unordered list, namely a collection of items that do not have a numerical ordering. The individual items in the list are defined by the **<LI>** element, which is the only allowed element within **<UL>**.

Syntax

```
<UL
    CLASS=class name(s)
    COMPACT
    DIR=LTR | RTL
    ID=unique alphanumeric identifier
    LANG=language code
    LANGUAGE=JAVASCRIPT | JSCRIPT | VBSCRIPT | VBS   (IE 4.0)
    STYLE=style information
    TITLE=advisory text
    TYPE=CIRCLE | DISC | SQUARE

    onclick="script"
    ondblclick="script"
    ondragstart="script"  (IE 4.0)
    onhelp="script"    (IE 4.0)
    onkeypress="script"
    onkeydown="script"
    onkeyup="script"
    onmousedown="script"
    onmousemove="script"
    onmouseout="script"
    onmouseover="script"
```

```
     onmosueup="script"
     onselectstart="script">   (IE 4.0)
     list items specified by <LI> elements
</UL>
```

Attributes

CLASS   See "Core Attributes Reference" earlier in this appendix.

COMPACT   This attribute indicates that the list should be rendered in a compact style. Few browsers actually change the rendering of the list regardless of the presence of this attribute. The **COMPACT** attribute requires no value.

DIR   See "Language Reference" earlier in this appendix.

ID   See "Core Attributes Reference" earlier in this appendix.

LANG   See "Language Reference" earlier in this appendix.

LANGUAGE   In the Microsoft implementation, this attribute specifies the scripting language to be used with an associated script bound to the element, typically through an event handler attribute. Possible values may include **JAVASCRIPT**, **JSCRIPT**, **VBSCRIPT**, and **VBS**. Other values that include the version of the language used, such as JavaScript 1.1, may also be possible.

STYLE   See "Core Attributes Reference" earlier in this appendix.

TITLE   See "Core Attributes Reference" earlier in this appendix.

TYPE   The **TYPE** attribute is used to set bullet style for the list. The values defined under HTML 3.2 and the transitional version of HTML 4.0 are **DISC**, **SQUARE**, and **CIRCLE**. A user agent may decide to use a different bullet depending on the nesting level of the list unless the **TYPE** attribute is used. The WebTV interface also supports a **TRIANGLE** bullet. The **TYPE** attribute is dropped under the strict version of HTML 4.0, since style sheets can provide richer bullet control.

EVENT HANDLERS   See "Events Reference" earlier in this appendix.

Examples

```
<UL COMPACT TITLE="Sushi Short List" TYPE="CIRCLE">
    <LI>Maguro
    <LI>Ebi
    <LI>Hamachi
</UL>

<!-- Common but bad example -->
```

```
<UL>
    Indenting using lists should not be used, though it is common.
    Many Web editors generate code laden with non-breaking
    spaces and unordered lists.
</UL>
```

COMPATIBILITY   W3C 2.0, 3.2, 4.0; Netscape 1.x, 2.x, 3.x, 4.x; Internet Explorer 2.x, 3.x, 4.x; and WebTV

Notes

HTML 2.0 supports only the **COMPACT** attribute.
The HTML 3.2 specification supports **TYPE** and **COMPACT**.
Under the strict HTML 4.0 specification, the **<UL>** element does not support the **COMPACT** attribute nor the **TYPE** attribute. Both of these attributes can be safely replaced with style rules. Many Web page designers and page development tools use the **<UL>** element to indent text. Be aware that the only element that should occur within a **<UL>** element is **<LI>**, according to HTML standards, so such HTML markup does not conform to standards. However, this common practice is likely to continue.

<VAR>   (Variable)

DESCRIPTION   This element is used to indicate a variable. Variables are identifiers that occur in a programming language or a mathematical expression. The element is logical, though enclosed text is often rendered in italics.

Syntax

```
<VAR
    CLASS=class name(s)
    DIR=LTR | RTL
    ID=unique alphanumeric value
    LANG=language code
    LANGUAGE=JAVASCRIPT | JSCRIPT | VBSCRIPT | VBS    (IE 4.0)
    STYLE=style information
    TITLE=advisory text

    onclick="script"
    ondblclick="script"
    ondragstart="script"   (IE 4.0)
    onhelp="script"    (IE 4.0)
    onkeydown="script"
    onkeypress="script"
    onkeyup="script"
    onmousedown="script"
    onmousemove="script"
```

```
        onmouseout="script"
        onmouseover="script"
        onmouseup="script"
        onselectstart="script">    (IE 4.0)

    </VAR>
```

Attributes

CLASS   See "Core Attributes Reference" earlier in this appendix.

DIR   See "Language Reference" earlier in this appendix.

ID   See "Core Attributes Reference" earlier in this appendix.

LANG   See "Language Reference" earlier in this appendix.

LANGUAGE   In the Microsoft implementation, this attribute specifies the scripting language to be used with an associated script bound to the element, typically through an event handler attribute. Possible values may include **JAVASCRIPT**, **JSCRIPT**, **VBSCRIPT**, and **VBS**. Other values that include the version of the language used, such as JavaScript 1.1, may also be possible.

STYLE   See "Core Attributes Reference" earlier in this appendix.

TITLE   See "Core Attributes Reference" earlier in this appendix.

EVENT HANDLERS   See "Events Reference" earlier in this appendix.

Example

```
Assign the value 5 to the variable <VAR>x</VAR>.
```

COMPATIBILITY   W3C 2.0, 3.2, 4.0; Netscape 1.x, 2.x, 3.x, 4.x; Internet Explorer 2.x, 3.x, 4.x; and WebTV

Notes
As a logical element, **<VAR>** is a perfect candidate for style sheet binding.
The HTML 2.0 and 3.2 specifications support no attributes for this element.

<WBR>   (Word Break)

DESCRIPTION   This nonstandard element is used to indicate a place where a line break can occur if necessary. This element is used in conjunction with the **<NOBR>** element, which is used to keep text from wrapping. When used this way, **<WBR>** can be thought of as a soft line break in comparison to the **
** element. This element is common to both Netscape and Microsoft implementations, though it is not part of any HTML standard.

Syntax

```
<WBR
    CLASS=class name(s)    (N 4.0, IE 4.0)
    ID=unique alphanumeric value   (N 4.0, IE 4.0)
    LANGUAGE=JAVASCRIPT | JSCRIPT | VBSCRIPT | VBS   (IE 4.0)
    STYLE=style information   (N 4.0, IE 4.0)
    TITLE=advisory text>   (N 4.0, IE 4.0)
```

Attributes

CLASS   See "Core Attributes Reference" earlier in this appendix.

DIR   See "Language Reference" earlier in this appendix.

ID   See "Core Attributes Reference" earlier in this appendix.

LANG   See "Language Reference" earlier in this appendix.

LANGUAGE   In the Microsoft implementation, this attribute specifies the scripting language to be used with an associated script bound to the element, typically through an event handler attribute. Possible values may include **JAVASCRIPT**, **JSCRIPT**, **VBSCRIPT**, and **VBS**. Other values that include the version of the language used, such as JavaScript 1.1, may also be possible.

STYLE   See "Core Attributes Reference" earlier in this appendix.

TITLE   See "Core Attributes Reference" earlier in this appendix.

EVENT HANDLERS   See "Events Reference" earlier in this appendix.

Example

```
<NOBR>A line break can occur here<WBR>but not
elsewhere, even if the line is really long.</NOBR>
```

COMPATIBILITY   Netscape 1.1, 2.x, 3.x, 4.x; Internet Explorer 2.x, 3.x, 4.x

Notes

This element was introduced in Netscape 1.1. It is an empty element, so no closing tag is required.

<XMP>   (Example)

DESCRIPTION   This depreciated element indicates that the enclosed text is an example. Example text is generally rendered in a monospaced font, and the spaces, tabs, and returns are preserved, as with the **<PRE>** element. As the **<XMP>** element is no longer standard, the **<PRE>** or **<SAMP>** elements should be used instead.

Syntax

```
<XMP
     CLASS=class name(s)    (N 4.0, IE 4.0)
     ID=unique alphanumeric value    (N 4.0, IE 4.0)
     LANG=language code    (IE 4.0)
     LANGUAGE=JAVASCRIPT | JSCRIPT | VBSCRIPT | VBS    (IE 4.0)
     STYLE=style information    (N 4.0, IE 4.0)
     TITLE=advisory text    (N 4.0, IE 4.0)

     onclick="script"    (IE 4.0)
     ondblclick="script"    (IE 4.0)
     ondragstart="script"    (IE 4.0)
     onhelp="script"    (IE 4.0)
     onkeydown="script"    (IE 4.0)
     onkeypress="script"    (IE 4.0)
     onkeyup="script"    (IE 4.0)
     onmousedown="script"    (IE 4.0)
     onmousemove="script"    (IE 4.0)
     onmouseout="script"    (IE 4.0)
     onmouseover="script"    (IE 4.0)
     onmouseup="script"    (IE 4.0)
     onselectstart="script">    (IE 4.0)

</XMP>
```

Attributes

CLASS See "Core Attributes Reference" earlier in this appendix.

DIR See "Language Reference" earlier in this appendix.

ID See "Core Attributes Reference" earlier in this appendix.

LANG See "Language Reference" earlier in this appendix.

LANGUAGE In the Microsoft implementation, this attribute specifies the scripting language to be used with an associated script bound to the element, typically through an event handler attribute. Possible values may include **JAVASCRIPT**, **JSCRIPT**, **VBSCRIPT**, and **VBS**. Other values that include the version of the language used, such as JavaScript 1.1, may also be possible.

STYLE See "Core Attributes Reference" earlier in this appendix.

TITLE See "Core Attributes Reference" earlier in this appendix.

EVENT HANDLERS See "Events Reference" earlier in this appendix.

Example

```
<XMP>This is a large block of text used as an example.
Note that returns as well as    S P A C E S are preserved.</XMP>
```

COMPATIBILITY W3C 2.0; Netscape 1.x, 2.x, 3.x, 4.x; Internet Explorer 2.x, 3.x, 4.x; and WebTV

Notes

This element is very old, though it continues to be documented. It was first depreciated under HTML 3.2 and continues to be unsupported under HTML 4.0. Page designers should not use this element.

Appendix B

Style Sheet Reference

C ascading Style Sheets (CSS1), covered in Chapter 10, offer a powerful new tool for Web page layout. When used properly, style sheets also separate style from document structure as originally intended in HTML. Many of the style properties defined by the CSS1 specification are supported by major browsers, including Internet Explorer 3.0, Internet Explorer 4.0, and Netscape Navigator 4.0. This appendix provides a concise look at style sheet rules, a complete listing of style properties and their values, as well as their current compatibility with the major browsers.

Style Sheet Terms

This section defines some basic terms used when working with style sheets.

Embedded Styles

Document-wide styles can be embedded in a document's **<HEAD>** element, using the **<STYLE>** element. Note that styles should be commented out to avoid interpretation by non-style-aware browsers.

EXAMPLE

```
<HEAD>
<STYLE>
<!--
P {font-size: 14pt; font-face: Times; color: blue; backgroundcolor: yellow}
EM {font-size: 16pt; color: green}
-- >
</STYLE>
<TITLE> . . . </TITLE></HEAD>
```

BROWSER SUPPORT   Internet Explorer 3.0 and 4.0, Netscape 4.0.

Linked Styles

Style can be contained in an external style sheet linked to a document or set of documents (see Chapter 10), as shown in the following example. Linking information should be placed inside the **<HEAD>** element.

EXAMPLE

```
<LINK REL="stylesheet" TYPE="text/css" HREF="newstyle.css">
```

BROWSER SUPPORT   Internet Explorer 3.0 and 4.0, Netscape 4.

Imported Styles

Styles can be imported from an external file and expanded in place, much like a macro. Importing can be used to include multiple style sheets. An imported style is defined with the **<STYLE>** element and the **TYPE** attribute, followed by the URL for the style sheet, as shown here:

EXAMPLE

```
<HEAD>
<STYLE TYPE="text/css">
@import url(newstyle.css)
<TITLE> . . . </TITLE></HEAD>
```

BROWSER SUPPORT   Not supported.

Inline Styles

Styles can be applied directly to elements in the body of a document. Rather than set document-wide values for the **<H1>** element, it is possible to set the style for an individual header, as shown here:

EXAMPLE

```
<H1 STYLE="font-size: 48pt; font-family: Arial;
color: green">CSS1 Test</H1>
```

An **<H1>** header elsewhere in the document could be assigned a completely different style.

BROWSER SUPPORT   Internet Explorer 3.0 and 4.0, Netscape 4.0.

Selectors

A selector is an HTML element, identifier, or class name associated with a style rule. In the following examples, **P** and **DIV** are the selectors.

EXAMPLES

```
P {font-size: 12pt}

DIV {font-family: Courier}
```

BROWSER SUPPORT   Internet Explorer 3.0 and 4.0, Netscape 4.0.

Rules

Style rules determine the styles to be associated with a selector. Style rules are enclosed within braces. A rule must include a property (**font-face**, in the following example) and a value (the font name **Impact**, in this case).

EXAMPLE

```
P {font-face: Impact}
```

Multiple rules may be included within a single style specification, but they must be separated by semicolons.

EXAMPLE

```
P {font-face: Impact; font-size: 12pt; line-height: 16pt}
```

BROWSER SUPPORT   Internet Explorer 3.0 and 4.0, Netscape 4.0.

Grouping

Selectors and declarations can be grouped together so that all the selectors are associated with a particular rule. Note that the listed selectors are separated by commas.
EXAMPLE

```
P, DIV, SPAN {background-color: yellow; font-face: Arial;
color: black; font-size: 14pt}
```

BROWSER SUPPORT   Internet Explorer 3.0 and 4.0, Netscape 4.0.

Inheritance

In most cases, elements contained within another element inherit the property values specified for the parent element unless those properties are defined differently for the nested elements. In the following example, the **<P>** element retains the background color and font color defined for the **<BODY>** element; only the font face changes.
EXAMPLE

```
BODY {background-color: blue; font-face: Courier; color: white}
P {font-face: Arial}
```

BROWSER SUPPORT   Internet Explorer 3.0 and 4.0, Netscape 4.0.

Class Selectors

Multiple classes may be defined for individual elements (selectors). To create a class selector, attach a class name to a selector; separate the selector from the class name with a period. Repeat this with the same selector, but give it a different name.
EXAMPLE

```
P.one {font-face: Arial; font-size: 12pt}
P.two {font-face: Verdana; font-size: 14pt}
```

There are now two different paragraph styles to choose from. Use the **CLASS** attribute with the **<P>** element to distinguish between them in the body of the document.
EXAMPLE

```
<P CLASS="one">This is paragraph style one.</P>
<P CLASS="two">This is paragraph style two.</P>
```

It is also possible to create stand-alone class selectors by omitting element names.
EXAMPLE

```
.one {font-face: Arial; font-size: 12pt}
.two {font-face: Verdana; font-size: 14pt}

<P CLASS=one>This is paragraph style one.</P>
<P CLASS=two>This is paragraph style two.</P>
<H1 CLASS=two>This header will also be style two.</P>
```

BROWSER SUPPORT   Internet Explorer 3.0 and 4.0, Netscape 4.0.

ID Selectors

Styles may be assigned independent of elements by creating ID selectors. Create an ID selector by creating a name preceded by the character # and following it with the style to be associated with that ID.
EXAMPLE

```
#style43 {font-size: 6pt; font-face: Verdana; font-variant: small-caps}
```

In the body of the document, use the **ID** attribute to assign the style to an element or elements.
EXAMPLE

```
<P ID=style43>This text is hard to read.</P>
<H1 ID=style43>So is the text in this header.</H1>
```

ID must be unique. Each value must appear only once in a given document.

BROWSER SUPPORT   Internet Explorer 3.0 and 4.0, Netscape 4.0.

Contextual Selectors

Contextual selectors define the display of elements within other specific elements. In the following example, **<STRONG>** text within a **<DIV>** element displays as green; however, **<STRONG>** text outside the context of the **<DIV>** element is not affected by this style. Note that the contextual selectors **DIV** and **STRONG** are separated by white space, not by commas. Another way to state this is that a **<STRONG>** element with a **<DIV>** ancestor will match this style.
EXAMPLE

```
DIV STRONG {color: green}
```

BROWSER SUPPORT   Internet Explorer 3.0 and 4.0, Netscape 4.0.

Pseudo-Classes

Elements can be assigned pseudo-classes to affect their display. There are three pseudo-classes: **A:link**, **A:visited**, and **A:active**.

A:link

Sets properties for text in unvisited links.
EXAMPLE

```
A:link {text-decoration: underline}
```

BROWSER SUPPORT   Internet Explorer 3.0 and 4.0, Netscape 4.0.

A:visited

Sets properties for text in visited links.
EXAMPLE

```
A:visited {text-decoration: line-through}
```

BROWSER SUPPORT   Internet Explorer 4.0; Netscape 4.0 (incomplete).

A:active

Sets properties for display of text in active links.
EXAMPLE

```
A:active {text-decoration: none}
```

BROWSER SUPPORT   Not supported.

Pseudo-Elements

This section discusses pseudo-elements, which affect typographical items, such as the first line of a paragraph, rather than structural elements, such as the paragraph (**<P>**) itself.

first-letter

Specifies the display of the first letter of text in a block-level element.
EXAMPLE

```
P:first-letter {font-face: Arial Black; font-size: 25pt}
```

BROWSER SUPPORT   Not supported.

first-line

Specifies the display of the first line of text in a block-level element.

EXAMPLE

```
P:first-line {font-face: Arial Black; font-size: 150%; font-weight: bold}
```

BROWSER SUPPORT   Not supported.

Miscellaneous

This section discusses some miscellaneous terms associated with style sheets.

/* comments */

Comments can be placed within style sheets. HTML comment syntax (**<!-- comment -->**) does not apply. Style sheets use the comment syntax used in C programming (**/*comment*/**).

EXAMPLE

```
<STYLE>
P {font-face: Courier; font-size: 14pt; font-weight: bold; background-color: yellow}
/*This style sheet was created at Big Company, Inc. All rights reserved.*/
</STYLE>
```

BROWSER SUPPORT   Internet Explorer 3.0 and 4.0, Netscape 4.0.

! important

Specifies that a style takes precedence over any different, conflicting styles. A style specified as important by an author takes precedence over a rule set by an end user.

EXAMPLE

```
DIV {font-size: 14pt; line-height: 150%; font-family: Arial ! important}
```

BROWSER SUPPORT   Not supported.

Fonts

The font properties are **font-family**, **font-size**, **font-style**, **font-weight**, **font-variant**, **text-transform**, and **text-decoration**. An additional property, **font**, can be used as a shorthand notation of font values.

EXAMPLE

```
{font-family: Arial, sans-serif; font-size: 18pt; font-style: italic;
font-weight: bold: font-variant: normal; text-transform: capitalize;
text-decoration: underline}
```

font-family

Sets the font face for text. Equivalent to the **FACE** attribute of the HTML element **<FONT>**.
EXAMPLE

```
{font-family: "Arial, Helvetica, sans-serif"}
```

Fonts are read in descending order. They must be separated by commas. In the preceding example, Arial is the primary font and will be displayed by browsers and systems with that font. If Arial is not available, Helvetica will be displayed. The final option, the generic font name **sans-serif**, will be used when no other listed font is available.

BROWSER SUPPORT   Internet Explorer 3.0 and 4.0, Netscape 4.0.

Font Family: Name Values

Defines a specific font family or families.
EXAMPLES

```
{font-family: "Times New Roman"}

{font-family: "Courier"}

{font-family: "Times New Roman, Courier"}
```

BROWSER SUPPORT   Internet Explorer 3.0 and 4.0, Netscape 4.0.

Font Family: Generic Font Names

Generic font names provide a final option, generally to the default generic font on a user's system. For instance, serif commonly defaults to Courier on many systems. There are five generic font names currently available: **serif**, **sans-serif**, **cursive**, **fantasy**, and **monospace**.

serif   Specifies a default serif font.
EXAMPLES

```
{font-family: "serif"}

{font-family: "Times New Roman, serif"}
```

BROWSER SUPPORT   Internet Explorer 3.0 (Windows only) and 4.0, Netscape 4.0.

sans-serif   Specifies a default sans serif font.
EXAMPLES

```
{font-family: sans-serif}

{font-family: "Arial, sans-serif"}
```

BROWSER SUPPORT   Internet Explorer 3.0 (Windows only) and 4.0, Netscape 4.0.

cursive   Specifies a default cursive font.
EXAMPLE

```
{font-family: cursive}
```

BROWSER SUPPORT   Internet Explorer 3.0 (Windows only) and 4.0.

fantasy   Specifies a default fantasy font.
EXAMPLE

```
{font-family: fantasy}
```

BROWSER SUPPORT   Internet Explorer 3.0 (Windows only) and 4.0.

monospace   Specifies a default monospace font.
EXAMPLE

```
{font-family: monospace}
```

BROWSER SUPPORT   Internet Explorer 3.0 and 4.0, Netscape 4.0.

font-size

Sets the font size of text. Options include exact size (point, pixel, or other values), absolute font sizes, relative font sizes, or percentages.
EXAMPLE

```
{font-face: Arial; font-size: 18pt}
```

BROWSER SUPPORT   Internet Explorer 3.0 and 4.0, Netscape 4.0.

Exact Font Size

Sets font size in points (pt) or pixels (px).

EXAMPLES

```
{font-size: 12pt}

{font-size: 30px}
```

BROWSER SUPPORT   Internet Explorer 3.0 and 4.0, Netscape 4.0.

Absolute Font Size

Sets font size to one of seven absolute font sizes: **xx-small**, **x-small**, **small**, **medium**, **large**, **x-large**, and **xx-larg**.
EXAMPLE

```
{font-size: xx-small}
```

BROWSER SUPPORT   Internet Explorer 3.0 and 4.0, Netscape 4.0.

xx-small   The smallest absolute font size, **xx-small** is usually equivalent to one point size smaller than the HTML code **<FONT SIZE="1">**.
EXAMPLE

```
{font-size: xx-small}
```

BROWSER SUPPORT   Internet Explorer 3.0 and 4.0, Netscape 4.0.

x-small   The second smallest absolute font size, **x-small** is equivalent to the HTML code **<FONT SIZE="1">**.
EXAMPLE

```
{font-size: x-small}
```

BROWSER SUPPORT   Internet Explorer 3.0 and 4.0, Netscape 4.0.

small   The third smallest absolute font size, **small** is equivalent to the HTML code **<FONT SIZE="2">**.
EXAMPLE

```
{font-size: small}
```

BROWSER SUPPORT   Internet Explorer 3.0 and 4.0, Netscape 4.0.

medium   The middle absolute font size, **medium** is equivalent to the HTML code **<FONT SIZE="3">**.

EXAMPLE

```
{font-size: medium}
```

BROWSER SUPPORT   Internet Explorer 3.0 and 4.0, Netscape 4.0.

large   The third largest absolute font size, **large** is equivalent to the HTML code
<FONT SIZE="4">.
EXAMPLE

```
{font-size: large}
```

BROWSER SUPPORT   Internet Explorer 3.0 and 4.0, Netscape 4.0.

x-large   The second largest absolute font size, **x-large** is equivalent to the HTML code
<FONT SIZE="5">.
EXAMPLE

```
{font-size: x-large}
```

BROWSER SUPPORT   Internet Explorer 3.0 and 4.0, Netscape 4.0.

xx-large   The largest absolute font size, **xx-large** is equivalent to the HTML code
<FONT SIZE="6">.
EXAMPLE

```
{font-size: xx-large}
```

BROWSER SUPPORT   Internet Explorer 3.0 and 4.0, Netscape 4.0.

Percentage Font Size Values

Sets font size to a percentage of the primary font size of a section or document. For instance, if
font size for the **<BODY>** element were set to 12 points, and font size for a **<P>** element inside
the body were set to 200 percent, the text inside the **<P>** element would display as 24 points.
This could be cleared on inheritance.
EXAMPLE

```
{font-size: 75%}
```

BROWSER SUPPORT   Internet Explorer 3.0 (incomplete), Internet Explorer 4.0, Netscape 4.0.

Relative Font Size Values

These values define font size relative to the primary font size of a document or section.

smaller   Sets font size one point smaller than the primary font size of a section or document. Equivalent to the HTML code **<FONT SIZE=-1>**.
EXAMPLE

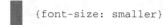

```
{font-size: smaller}
```

BROWSER SUPPORT   Internet Explorer 4.0, Netscape 4.0.

larger   Sets font size one point larger than the primary font size of a section or document. Equivalent to the HTML code **<FONT SIZE=+1>**.
EXAMPLE

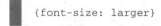

```
{font-size: larger}
```

BROWSER SUPPORT   Not supported, Internet Explorer 4.0, Netscape 4.0.

font-style

Sets the style of a font to normal, oblique, or italic. This can also be done by using a specific font (for example, Times New Roman Italic). Also allows control of style across font families.
EXAMPLES

```
{font-style: normal}

{font-style: oblique}

{font-style: italic}
```

BROWSER SUPPORT   Internet Explorer 3.0 (incomplete) and 4.0, Netscape 4.0.

normal

Sets the style of a font to a Roman style.
EXAMPLE

```
{font-style: normal}
```

BROWSER SUPPORT   Internet Explorer 4.0, Netscape 4.0.

italic

Sets the style of a font to an italic style.
EXAMPLE

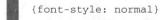

```
{font-style: normal}
```

BROWSER SUPPORT   Internet Explorer 3.0 and 4.0, Netscape 4.0.

oblique
Sets the style of a font to an oblique style.
EXAMPLE

```
{font-style: normal}
```

BROWSER SUPPORT   Internet Explorer 4.0, Netscape 4.0.

font-weight

Sets the weight, or relative boldness, of a font. Values can be set with named values (**normal**, **bold**, **bolder**, or **lighter**) or with numbered values (**100** through **900**).
EXAMPLES

```
{font-weight: bold}

{font-weight: 300}
```

BROWSER SUPPORT   Internet Explorer 3.0 (incomplete) and 4.0, Netscape 4.0 (incomplete).

normal
Sets the weight of the font to normal.
EXAMPLE

```
{font-weight: normal}
```

BROWSER SUPPORT   Internet Explorer 4.0, Netscape 4.0.

bold
Sets the weight of the font to bold.
EXAMPLE

```
{font-weight: bold}
```

BROWSER SUPPORT   Internet Explorer 3.0 and 4.0, Netscape 4.0.

bolder
Sets the weight of the font to a bolder font.
EXAMPLE

```
{font-weight: bolder}
```

BROWSER SUPPORT   Internet Explorer 4.0.

lighter

Sets the weight of the font to a bolder font.
EXAMPLE

```
{font-weight: lighter}
```

BROWSER SUPPORT   Internet Explorer 4.0.

100–900

Sets the weight of the font from lightest (**100**) to boldest (**900**) in increments of 100. In practice, under Internet Explorer 4.0 and Netscape 4.0 the values **100** through **500** display as normal text, **600** through **800** display as bold, and **900** displays as extra bold; browser support for other values is inconsistent at best.
EXAMPLE

```
{font-weight: 600}
```

BROWSER SUPPORT   Internet Explorer 4.0 (Windows only, incomplete), Netscape 4.0 (incomplete for Macs).

font-variant

Sets a variation of the specified or default font family. Values currently supported are **normal** and **small-caps**.
EXAMPLE

```
{font-family: Courier; font-size: 14pt; font-variant: small-caps}
```

BROWSER SUPPORT   Internet Explorer 4.0.

normal

Default, or "off" value for **font-variant**. Sets display to font's normal appearance.
EXAMPLE

```
{font-family: Arial; font-size: 12pt; font-variant: normal}
```

BROWSER SUPPORT   Internet Explorer 4.0.

small-caps

Sets text to all small capitals.
EXAMPLE

```
{font-family: Times New Roman; font-size: 20pt; font-variant: small-caps}
```

BROWSER SUPPORT   Internet Explorer 4.0.

text-transform

Transforms the case of affected text. Values: **capitalize**, **uppercase**, **lowercase**, and **none**.
EXAMPLE

```
{text-transform: capitalize}
```

BROWSER SUPPORT   Internet Explorer 4.0, Netscape 4.0 (incomplete for Macs).

capitalize

Capitalizes the initial letter of each word in the affected text.
EXAMPLE

```
{font-family: Times New Roman; font-size: 20pt; text-transform: capitalize}
```

BROWSER SUPPORT   Internet Explorer 4.0, Netscape 4.0.

uppercase

Capitalizes all the letters of each word in the affected text.
EXAMPLE

```
{font-family: Helvetica; font-size: 10pt; text-transform: uppercase}
```

BROWSER SUPPORT   Internet Explorer 4.0, Netscape 4.0.

lowercase

Sets the letters of each word in the affected text to lowercase.
EXAMPLE

```
{font-family: Verdana; font-size: 14pt; text-transform: lowercase}
```

BROWSER SUPPORT   Internet Explorer 4.0, Netscape 4.0.

none

Leaves text unaffected or overrides another established value.
EXAMPLE

```
{font-family: Arial; font-size: 12pt; text-transform: none}
```

BROWSER SUPPORT   Internet Explorer 4.0, Netscape 4.0.

text-decoration

Defines specific text effects. Values: **blink**, **line-through**, **overline**, **underline**, and **none**.
EXAMPLE

```
{text-decoration: underline}
```

This property is often used with the **<A>** element and its associated pseudoclasses (**A:link**, **A:active**, and **A:visited**). The next example draws a line through visited links in a page.
EXAMPLE

```
A:visited {text-decoration: line-through}
```

BROWSER SUPPORT   Internet Explorer 3.0 (incomplete) and 4.0, Netscape 4.0 (incomplete).

blink

Causes text to blink.
EXAMPLE

```
{text-decoration: blink}
```

BROWSER SUPPORT   Netscape 4.0.

line-through

Draws a line through text.
EXAMPLE

```
{text-decoration: line-through}
```

BROWSER SUPPORT   Internet Explorer 3.0 and 4.0, Netscape 4.0.

overline

Draws a line over text.
EXAMPLE

```
{text-decoration: overline}
```

BROWSER SUPPORT   Internet Explorer 4.0.

underline

Draws a line under text.
EXAMPLE

```
{text-decoration: underline}
```

BROWSER SUPPORT   Internet Explorer 3.0 and 4.0, Netscape 4.0.

none

Displays plain text. Can be used with **A:link**, **A:active**, and **A:visited** to turn off underlining of links.
EXAMPLE

```
{text-decoration: none}
```

BROWSER SUPPORT   Internet Explorer 3.0 and 4.0, Netscape 4.0.

font

Provides a shorthand way to specify all font properties with one style rule. Properties:
font-style, **font-variant**, **font-weight**, **font-size/line-height**, and **font-family**. It is not necessary
to include all properties. The **line-height** attribute is discussed in the following text section.
Font names with more than one word in them should be placed in quotation marks. Lists of
variant fonts should be separated by commas and also placed in quotations.
EXAMPLE

```
{font: normal small-caps bold 12pt/18pt "Times New Roman, Courier, serif"}
```

BROWSER SUPPORT   Internet Explorer 3.0 (incomplete), Internet Explorer 4.0, Netscape 4.0
(incomplete for Macs).

Text

This section discusses style attributes that affect text-level elements.

word-spacing

Sets the spacing between words. Values can be set in inches (**in**), centimeters (**cm**), millimeters
(**mm**), points (**pt**), pica (**pc**), em (**em**), and pixels (**px**), or to the default value **normal**.
EXAMPLES

```
{font-family: Arial; font-size: 16pt; word-spacing: 3pt}
```

```
{font-family: Helvetica; font-size: 12pt; word-spacing: normal}
```

BROWSER SUPPORT   Not supported.

normal

Defaults to the browser's word-spacing settings.
EXAMPLE

```
{font-family: Arial; font-size: 10pt; word-spacing: normal}
```

BROWSER SUPPORT   Not supported.

letter-spacing

Sets the spacing between letters. Values can be set in various units or to the default value normal.

EXAMPLE

```
{font-family: Arial; font-size: 14pt; letter-spacing: 2pt}
```

BROWSER SUPPORT   Internet Explorer 4.0.

Unit Values

Sets **letter-spacing** to a certain number of units: inches (**in**), centimeters (**cm**), millimeters (**mm**), points (**pt**), pica, (**pc**), em (**em**), and or (**px**).

EXAMPLE

```
{font-family: Arial; font-size: 14pt; letter-spacing: 2pt}
```

BROWSER SUPPORT   Internet Explorer 4.0.

normal

Sets **letter-spacing** to the browser's default settings.

EXAMPLE

```
{font-family: Arial; font-size: 14pt; letter-spacing: normal }
```

BROWSER SUPPORT   Internet Explorer 4.0.

line-height

Sets the height (leading) between lines of text in a block-level element like a paragraph. Values can be set as the number of lines, a number of units (pixels, points, and so on), or as a percentage of the font size. This is generally used in conjunction with **font-size**.

EXAMPLES

```
{font-family: Arial; font-size: 14pt; line-height: 2}

{font-family: Arial; font-size: 14pt; line-height: 16px}

{font-family: Arial; font-size: 14pt; line-height: normal}

{font-family: Arial; font-size: 14pt; line-height: 125%}
```

BROWSER SUPPORT   Internet Explorer 3.0 and 4.0, Netscape 4.0.

text-align

Sets the horizontal alignment of text block-level elements. Values: **left**, **right**, **center**, and **justify**. The default value is **left**. Similar to the **ALIGN** attribute available with block-level elements like **<P>** in HTML.

BROWSER SUPPORT   Internet Explorer 3.0 (incomplete) and 4.0 (Windows only, incomplete), Netscape 4.0.

left

Sets the horizontal alignment of text in block-level elements to the left.
EXAMPLE

```
P {text-align: left}
```

BROWSER SUPPORT   Internet Explorer 3.0 and 4.0, Netscape 4.0.

right

Sets the horizontal alignment of text in block-level elements to the right.
EXAMPLE

```
P {text-align: right}
```

BROWSER SUPPORT   Internet Explorer 3.0 and 4.0, Netscape 4.0.

center

Sets the horizontal alignment of text in block-level elements to the center.
EXAMPLE

```
P {text-align: center}
```

BROWSER SUPPORT   Internet Explorer 3.0 and 4.0, Netscape 4.0.

justify

Sets the horizontal alignment of text block-level elements flush to the left and the right.
EXAMPLE

```
P {text-align: justify}
```

BROWSER SUPPORT   Netscape 4.0.

vertical-align

Sets the vertical positioning of text and images with respect to the baseline setting. Values: **baseline**, **sub**, **super**, **top**, **text-top**, **middle**, **bottom**, **text-bottom**, and **percentage**. The default value is **baseline**.

EXAMPLE

```
P {vertical-align: baseline}
```

BROWSER SUPPORT   Internet Explorer 4.0 (incomplete).

baseline

Aligns text or images to the baseline setting. This is the default value for **vertical-align**.
EXAMPLE

```
P {vertical-align: baseline}
```

BROWSER SUPPORT   Not supported.

sub

Positions text or images as a subscript of the baseline setting.
EXAMPLE

```
P {vertical-align: sub}
```

BROWSER SUPPORT   Internet Explorer 4.0.

super

Positions text or images as a superscript of the baseline setting.
EXAMPLE

```
P {vertical-align: super}
```

BROWSER SUPPORT   Internet Explorer 4.0.

top

Aligns the top of text or images with the top of the tallest element relative to the baseline.
EXAMPLE

```
P {vertical-align: top}
```

BROWSER SUPPORT   Not supported.

text-top

Aligns the top of text or images with the top of the font in the containing element.
EXAMPLE

```
P {vertical-align: text-top}
```

BROWSER SUPPORT   Not supported.

middle

Aligns the middle of text or images to the middle of the x-height of the containing element.
EXAMPLE

```
P {vertical-align: middle}
```

BROWSER SUPPORT   Not supported.

bottom

Aligns the bottom of text or images with the bottom of the lowest element relative to the baseline.
EXAMPLE

```
P {vertical-align: bottom}
```

BROWSER SUPPORT   Not supported.

text-bottom

Align the bottom of text or images with the bottom of the font in the containing element.
EXAMPLE

```
P {vertical-align: text-bottom}
```

BROWSER SUPPORT   Not supported.

text-indent

Indents the text in the first line of a block-level element. Values can be defined as length values (.5cm, 15px, 12pt, and so on) or as a percentage of the width of the block element. The default value is **0**, which indicates no indentation.
EXAMPLES

```
{text-indent: 5pt}

{text-indent: 15%}
```

BROWSER SUPPORT   Internet Explorer 3.0 and 4.0, Netscape 4.0.

Colors and Backgrounds

This section discusses style attributes that affect the color of text, as well as backgrounds and various concerns (such as color, images, and scrolling) associated with backgrounds.

color

Sets the color of text. Values can be set as color names, hex values in three- or six-digit format, or red-green-blue (RGB) values (numbers or percentages). See "Style Sheet Color Values" at the end of this appendix for browser support of color values.

EXAMPLES

```
{color: yellow}

{color: #FFFF00}

{color: #FF0}

{color: rgb(255,255,0)}

{color: rgb(100%,100%,0%)}
```

BROWSER SUPPORT   Internet Explorer 3.0 and 4.0, Netscape 4.0.

background-color

Sets an element's background color. Often used in conjunction with the color property that sets text color (preceding example). Used with block elements, **background-color** colors content and padding, but not margins. The default value is **transparent**, which allows any underlying content to show through. See "Style Sheet Color Values" at the end of this appendix for browser support of color values.

EXAMPLES

```
{background-color: #00CCFF}

{background-color: orange}

{background-color: rgb(255, 0, 255}
```

BROWSER SUPPORT   Internet Explorer 4.0, Netscape 4.0.

transparent

The default value for **background-color**.

EXAMPLE

```
{background-color: transparent}
```

BROWSER SUPPORT   Internet Explorer 4.0, Netscape 4.0.

background-image

Associates a background image with an element. Underlying content shows through transparent regions in the source image. The background image requires a URL (complete or relative) linking it to the source image (GIF or JPEG). The default value is **none**.

BROWSER SUPPORT   Internet Explorer 4.0, Netscape 4.0.

Background Image URL

Provides a URL link to a source image for the background image.
EXAMPLE

```
{background-image: url(yellowpattern.gif)}
```

BROWSER SUPPORT   Internet Explorer 4.0, Netscape 4.0.

none

Default value for **background-image**. No background image displays if this value is set. Underlying content will show through.
EXAMPLE

```
{background-image: none}
```

BROWSER SUPPORT   Internet Explorer 4.0, Netscape 4.0.

background-repeat

Determines how background images tile when they are smaller than the canvas space used by their associated elements. Used in conjunction with **background-image**. Values: **repeat**, **repeat-x**, **repeat-y**, and **no-repeat**.

BROWSER SUPPORT   Internet Explorer 4.0, Netscape 4.0.

repeat

The default value for **background-repeat**. Sets the background image to repeat horizontally and vertically.
EXAMPLE

```
{background-image: url(yellowpattern.gif) background-repeat: repeat}
```

BROWSER SUPPORT   Internet Explorer 4.0, Netscape 4.0.

repeat-x

Sets the background image to repeat horizontally only.

EXAMPLE

```
{background-image: url(yellowpattern.gif); background-repeat: repeat-x}
```

BROWSER SUPPORT   Internet Explorer 4.0, Netscape 4.0.

repeat-y
Sets the background image to repeat vertically only.
EXAMPLE

```
{background-image: url(yellowpattern.gif); background-repeat: repeat-y}
```

BROWSER SUPPORT   Internet Explorer 4.0, Netscape 4.0.

no-repeat
Prevents the background image from repeating.
EXAMPLE

```
{background-image: url(yellowpattern.gif);
 background-repeat: no-repeat}
```

BROWSER SUPPORT   Internet Explorer 4.0, Netscape 4.0.

background-attachment

Sets the background image to scroll or not scroll with its associated element's content. The default value is **scroll**. The alternate value, **fixed**, is intended to create a watermark effect similar to the proprietary attribute **BGPROPERTIES** of the **<BODY>** element introduced by Microsoft.
EXAMPLE

```
{background-image: url(yellowpattern.gif);
 background-attachment: scroll}
```

BROWSER SUPPORT   Not supported.

scroll
Sets the background image to scroll with associated content, such as text.
EXAMPLE

```
{background-image: url(yellowpattern.gif);
 background-attachment: scroll}
```

BROWSER SUPPORT   Not supported.

fixed

Sets the background image to remain static while associated content, such as text, scrolls.
EXAMPLE

```
{background-image: url(yellowpattern.gif);
 background-attachment: fixed}
```

BROWSER SUPPORT   Not supported.

background-position

Sets how a background image is positioned within the canvas space used by its associated element. The position of the image's upper-left corner of the image can be specified as an absolute distance in pixels. It can also be specified as a percentage along the horizontal and vertical dimensions. Finally, the position can be specified with named values that describe the horizontal and vertical dimensions. The named values for the horizontal axis are **left**, **center**, and **right**; those for the vertical axis are **top**, **center**, and **bottom**. The default keyword for an unspecified dimension is assumed to be **center**.
EXAMPLES

```
{background-image: url(yellowpattern.gif);
 background-position: 50px 100px}
```

```
{background-image: url(yellowpattern.gif);
 background-position: 10% 45%}
```

```
{background-image: url(yellowpattern.gif);
 background-position: top center}
```

BROWSER SUPPORT   Internet Explorer 4.0.

Background Position Length Values

Sets the position of the background image by specifying a specific pixel position for the upper-left corner of the image.
EXAMPLE

```
{background-image: url(picture.gif);
 background-position: 10px 10px}
```

BROWSER SUPPORT   Internet Explorer 4.0.

Background Position Percentage Values

These values define a background's position as a percentage of its parent element's horizontal and vertical axes.

EXAMPLE

```
{background-image: url(picture.gif);
 background-position: 20% 40%}
```

BROWSER SUPPORT   Internet Explorer 4.0.

Background Position Named Values

These named values (**top**, **center**, **bottom**, **left**, and **right**) define the position of a background image relative to its parent element.

top   Sets the position of the background image to the top of its associated element. May be used in combination with a horizontal value (**left**, **right**) or **center**.
EXAMPLES

```
{background-image: url(picture.gif);
 background-position: top}

{background-image: url(picture.gif);
 background-position: top left}
```

BROWSER SUPPORT   Internet Explorer 4.0.

center   Sets the position of the background image to the center of its associated element. May be used in combination with a vertical value (**top**, **bottom**).
EXAMPLES

```
{background-image: url(picture.gif);
 background-position: center}

{background-image: url(picture.gif);
 background-position: center bottom}
```

BROWSER SUPPORT   Internet Explorer 4.0.

bottom   Sets the position of the background image to the bottom of its associated element. May be used in combination with a horizontal value (**left**, **right**) or **center**.
EXAMPLES

```
{background-image: url(picture.gif);
 background-position: bottom}

{background-image: url(picture.gif);
 background-position: bottom left}
```

BROWSER SUPPORT   Internet Explorer 4.0.

left   Sets the position of the background image to the left side of its associated element. May be used in combination with a vertical value (**top, bottom**) or center.
EXAMPLES

```
{background-image: url(picture.gif);
 background-position: left}
```

```
{background-image: url(picture.gif);
 background-position: left center}
```

BROWSER SUPPORT   Internet Explorer 4.0.

right   Sets the position of the background image to the left side of its associated element. May be used in combination with a vertical value (**top, bottom**) or **center**.
EXAMPLES

```
{background-image: url(picture.gif);
 background-position: right}
```

```
{background-image: url(picture.gif);
 background-position: right top}
```

BROWSER SUPPORT   Internet Explorer 4.0.

background

Sets any or all background properties, including images. Properties not specified use their default values. Property order does not matter. Semicolons are not required.
EXAMPLE

```
{background: white url(picture.gif) repeat-y center}
```

BROWSER SUPPORT   Internet Explorer 3.0 and 4.0, Netscape 4.0 (incomplete).

transparent
As with **background-color**, this value sets the background color to a transparent setting.
EXAMPLE

```
{background: transparent}
```

BROWSER SUPPORT   Internet Explorer 3.0 and 4.0, Netscape 4.0.

Background URL Values
Sets a background image using the same syntax as **background-image**.

EXAMPLE

```
{background: url(yellowpattern.gif)}
```

BROWSER SUPPORT   Internet Explorer 3.0 and 4.0, Netscape 4.0.

none
Specifies that there will be no background image. This is the default value for **background**.
EXAMPLE

```
{background: none}
```

BROWSER SUPPORT   Internet Explorer 3.0 and 4.0, Netscape 4.0.

repeat
Sets the background image to repeat horizontally and vertically. If this is not specified, **repeat** is the default value.
EXAMPLE

```
{background: url(yellowpattern.gif) repeat}
```

BROWSER SUPPORT   Internet Explorer 3.0 and 4.0, Netscape 4.0.

repeat-x
Sets the background image to repeat horizontally only.
EXAMPLE

```
{background: url(yellowpattern.gif) repeat-x}
```

BROWSER SUPPORT   Internet Explorer 3.0 and 4.0, Netscape 4.0.

repeat-y
Sets the background image to repeat vertically only.
EXAMPLE

```
{background: url(yellowpattern.gif) repeat-y}
```

BROWSER SUPPORT   Internet Explorer 3.0 and 4.0, Netscape 4.0.

no-repeat
Specifies that the background image does not repeat.

EXAMPLE

```
{background: url(yellowpattern.gif) no-repeat}
```

BROWSER SUPPORT   Internet Explorer 3.0 and 4.0, Netscape 4.0.

scroll

Specifies that the background image scrolls with its associated content. Under Internet Explorer 3.0, setting the scroll value does not work; if this value is not specified, however, the background scrolls with its associated content.

EXAMPLE

```
{background: url(yellowpattern.gif) repeat scroll}
```

BROWSER SUPPORT   Internet Explorer 4.0.

fixed

Specifies that the background image remains stationary while its associated content scrolls.

EXAMPLE

```
{background: url(yellowpattern.gif) fixed}
```

BROWSER SUPPORT   Internet Explorer 3.0 and 4.0.

Background Positioning: Percentage Values

Sets the position of the background image as a percentage along the horizontal and vertical dimensions. The first percentage value sets horizontal placement; the second sets vertical placement. If only one value is specified, the vertical placement value will default to **50%**. Use of these values in a page with no content can lead to problems under Internet Explorer 3.0. (For example, a value of **bottom** aligns the bottom of the image with the top of the browser window, thus placing it completely out of view. This has been corrected in Internet Explorer 4.0, which displays the image properly at the bottom of the browser window.) If no values are set, placement defaults to the upper-left corner of the browser window.

EXAMPLE

```
{background url(picture.gif) no-repeat 20% 50%}
```

BROWSER SUPPORT   Internet Explorer 3.0 and 4.0.

Background Positioning: Named Values

Sets the position of the background image. The values **top**, **bottom**, and **middle** assign vertical positions; **left**, **right**, and **center** assign horizontal positions. Values can be combined as common sense suggests. If no values are set, placement defaults to the upper-left corner of the browser window.

EXAMPLES

```
{background url(picture.gif) no-repeat top center}
```

```
{background url(picture.gif) no-repeat right bottom}
```

BROWSER SUPPORT   Internet Explorer 3.0 and 4.0.

top   Sets the position of the background image to the top of its associated element. If no other value is set, the top-aligned image defaults to the left.
EXAMPLE

```
{background url(picture.gif) no-repeat top}
```

BROWSER SUPPORT   Internet Explorer 3.0 and 4.0.

center   Sets the position of the background image to the horizontal center of its associated element. If no other value is set, the center-aligned image defaults to the vertical middle.
EXAMPLE

```
{background url(picture.gif) no-repeat center}
```

BROWSER SUPPORT   Internet Explorer 3.0 and 4.0.

middle   Sets the position of the background image to the vertical middle of its associated element. If no other value is set, the middle-aligned image defaults to the left. Under Internet Explorer 4.0, **middle** works only when assigned a horizontal value; otherwise, the background image defaults to the upper left.
EXAMPLE

```
{background url(picture.gif) no-repeat middle}
```

BROWSER SUPPORT   Internet Explorer 3.0; Internet Explorer 4.0 (incomplete).

bottom   Sets the position of the background image to the bottom of its associated element. If no other value is set, the bottom-aligned image defaults to the left.
EXAMPLE

```
{background url(picture.gif) no-repeat bottom}
```

BROWSER SUPPORT   Internet Explorer 3.0 and 4.0.

left   Sets the position of the background image to the left of its associated element. Left is the default horizontal position.

EXAMPLE

```
{background url(picture.gif) no-repeat left}
```

BROWSER SUPPORT   Internet Explorer 3.0 and 4.0.

right   Sets the position of the background image to the right of its associated element.
EXAMPLE

```
{background url(picture.gif) no-repeat right}
```

BROWSER SUPPORT   Internet Explorer 3.0 and 4.0.

Layout

This section discusses style attributes that affect the layout of HTML documents.

Margins

Style sheets can be used to set margins around an element with the margin property. Margin values can be set to a specific length (15pt, 2em, and so on) or a percentage value of the block element's width. Another value, **auto**, attempts to calculate the margin automatically . The **auto** value is not supported. Four distinct margins may be set separately from one another: **top-margin**, **bottom-margin**, **left-margin**, and **right-margin**. By itself, **margin** sets a consistent margin on all four sides of the affected element. Margins may be set to negative values.

BROWSER SUPPORT   Internet Explorer 3.0 (Windows only), Internet Explorer 4.0, Netscape 4.0.

margin-top

Sets an element's top margin.
EXAMPLE

```
{margin-top: 15pt}
```

BROWSER SUPPORT   Internet Explorer 3.0 (Windows only) and 4.0, Netscape 4.0.

margin-bottom

Sets an element's bottom margin.
EXAMPLE

```
{margin-bottom: 10pt}
```

BROWSER SUPPORT   Internet Explorer 3.0 (Windows only) and 4.0, Netscape 4.0.

margin-right

Sets an element's right margin.
EXAMPLE

```
{margin-right: 15pt}
```

BROWSER SUPPORT   Internet Explorer 3.0 and 4.0, Netscape 4.0.

margin-left

Sets an element's left margin.
EXAMPLE

```
{margin-left: 12pt}
```

BROWSER SUPPORT   Internet Explorer 3.0 and 4.0, Netscape 4.0.

margin

Sets all margins for an element. Up to four values can be defined, in this order: top, right, bottom, and left. Values are the same as for the margin properties discussed above; **auto** is not currently supported. A single value defines the same margin for all four sides.
EXAMPLE

```
{margin: 25pt}
```

If two values are specified, the first defines the top and bottom margins, while the second value defines the left and right margins.
EXAMPLE

```
{margin: 15pt, 25pt}
```

If three values are specified, the first defines the top margin, the second value defines the left and right margins, and the third value defines the bottom margin. Note that the unspecified margin is inferred from the value defined for its opposite side.
EXAMPLE

```
{margin: 25pt, 50pt, 25pt}
```

Finally, all four margins can be set to different values if desired (top, right, bottom, and left).
EXAMPLE

```
{margin: 15pt, 25pt, 50pt, 10pt}
```

BROWSER SUPPORT   Internet Explorer 3.0 (incomplete) and 4.0, Netscape 4.0.

Borders

There are five properties to set the width of borders: **border-top-width**, **border-right-width**, **border-bottom-width**, **border-left-width**, and **border-width**. The first four set the width of specific borders; **border-width** is used to set all four. Values can be set in numeric measurements or with the named values **thin**, **medium**, and **thick**.

border-top-width

Sets the width of an element's top border. Values: keywords (**thin**, **medium**, and **thick**) and numerical lengths.

EXAMPLES

```
{border-top-width: thin}

{border-top-width: 25px}
```

BROWSER SUPPORT   Internet Explorer 4.0, Netscape 4.0.

border-bottom-width

Sets the width of an element's bottom border. Values: keywords (**thin**, **medium**, and **thick**) and numerical lengths.

EXAMPLES

```
{border-bottom-width: medium}

{border-bottom-width: 15px}
```

BROWSER SUPPORT   Internet Explorer 4.0, Netscape 4.0.

border-right-width

Sets the width of an element's right border. Values: keywords (**thin**, **medium**, and **thick**) and numerical lengths.

EXAMPLES

```
{border-right-width: thick}

{border-right-width: 40px}
```

BROWSER SUPPORT   Internet Explorer 4.0, Netscape 4.0.

border-left-width

Sets the width of an element's left border. Values: keywords (**thin**, **medium**, and **thick**) and numerical lengths.

STYLE SHEET REFERENCE

EXAMPLES

```
{border-left-width: thin}

{border-left-width: 5px}
```

BROWSER SUPPORT   Internet Explorer 4.0, Netscape 4.0.

border-width

Sets the width of an element's complete border. Values: keywords (**thin**, **medium**, and **thick**) and numerical lengths.

EXAMPLES

```
{border-width: thin}

{border-width: 5px}
```

BROWSER SUPPORT   Internet Explorer 4.0, Netscape 4.0.

thin

Sets the width of an element's border to thin.

EXAMPLE

```
{border-right-width: thin}
```

BROWSER SUPPORT   Internet Explorer 4.0, Netscape 4.0.

medium

Sets the width of an element's border to medium.

EXAMPLE

```
{border-top-width: medium}
```

BROWSER SUPPORT   Internet Explorer 4.0, Netscape 4.0.

thick

Sets the width of an element's border to thick.

EXAMPLE

```
{border-width: thick}
```

BROWSER SUPPORT   Internet Explorer 4.0, Netscape 4.0.

border-color

Defines the color of an element's border. See "Style Sheet Color Values" at the end of this appendix for browser support of color values.
EXAMPLES

```
{border-color: blue}

{border-color: #0000EE}
```

BROWSER SUPPORT   Internet Explorer 4.0, Netscape 4.0.

border-style

Defines an element's border style.
EXAMPLE

```
{border-style: solid}
```

The border-style property may take up to four values: **top**, **right**, **bottom**, and **left**, in that order. Missing values are inferred from the value defined for the opposite side.
EXAMPLE

```
{border-style: solid, thin, medium, solid}
```

Netscape 4.0 supports only one value for border-style. Use of multiple values will create erratic display under that browser.

BROWSER SUPPORT   Internet Explorer 4.0; Netscape 4.0 (incomplete).

none

"Turns off" the border, even if other border properties have been set.
EXAMPLE

```
{border-style: none}
```

BROWSER SUPPORT   Internet Explorer 4.0, Netscape 4.0.

dotted

Defines a dotted border style.
EXAMPLE

```
{border-style: dotted}
```

BROWSER SUPPORT   None.

dashed

Defines a dashed border style.
EXAMPLE

```
{border-style: dashed}
```

BROWSER SUPPORT   None.

solid

Sets the border to a solid line; this is the default value and need not be set.
EXAMPLE

```
{border-style: solid}
```

BROWSER SUPPORT   Internet Explorer 4.0, Netscape 4.0.

double

Sets the border to two solid lines.
EXAMPLE

```
{border-style: double}
```

BROWSER SUPPORT   Internet Explorer 4.0, Netscape 4.0.

groove

Sets the border to resemble a grooved line.
EXAMPLE

```
{border-style: grooved}
```

BROWSER SUPPORT   Internet Explorer 4.0, Netscape 4.0.

ridge

Sets the border to resemble a raised ridge by reversing the shading of the grooved rendering.
EXAMPLE

```
{border-style: ridge}
```

BROWSER SUPPORT   Internet Explorer 4.0, Netscape 4.0.

inset

Sets the border to display a lighter shade of the border color on its right and bottom sides.
EXAMPLE

```
{border-style: inset}
```

BROWSER SUPPORT   Internet Explorer 4.0, Netscape 4.0.

outset

Sets the border to display a lighter shade of the border color on its top and left sides.
EXAMPLE

```
{border-style: outset}
```

BROWSER SUPPORT   Internet Explorer 4.0, Netscape 4.0.

border-top

Defines the width, style, and color for the top border of an element.
EXAMPLE

```
{border-top: thin solid blue}
```

BROWSER SUPPORT   Internet Explorer 4.0.

border-bottom

Defines the width, style, and color for the bottom border of an element.
EXAMPLE

```
{border-bottom: thick double #CCFFCC}
```

BROWSER SUPPORT   Internet Explorer 4.0.

border-right

Defines the width, style, and color for the right border of an element.
EXAMPLE

```
{border-right: thick solid black}
```

BROWSER SUPPORT   Internet Explorer 4.0.

border-left

Defines the width, style, and color for the left border of an element.
EXAMPLE

```
{border-left: normal inset green}
```

BROWSER SUPPORT   Internet Explorer 4.0.

border

Defines the width, style, and color for all four sides of an element's border.
EXAMPLE

```
{border: normal inset green}
```

BROWSER SUPPORT   Internet Explorer 4.0, Netscape 4.0.

Padding

The padding properties set the space between an element's border and its content. There are five properties: **padding-top**, **padding-right**, **padding-bottom**, **padding-left**, and **padding**. The first four set the padding for specific sides; **padding** sets all four. Values can be set as specific values (pixels, points, and so on) or as a percentage of the element's overall width. Unlike the margin property, the **padding** property cannot take negative values.

padding-top

Sets the distance between an element's top border and the top of its content.
EXAMPLE

```
{padding-top: 25px}
```

BROWSER SUPPORT   Internet Explorer 4.0, Netscape 4.0.

padding-bottom

Sets the distance between an element's bottom border and the bottom of its content.
EXAMPLE

```
{padding-bottom: 15px}
```

BROWSER SUPPORT   Internet Explorer 4.0, Netscape 4.0.

padding-right

Sets the distance between an element's right border and the right side of its content.

EXAMPLE

```
{padding-right: 5px}
```

BROWSER SUPPORT   Internet Explorer 4.0, Netscape 4.0.

padding-left

Sets the distance between an element's left border and the left side of its content.
EXAMPLE

```
{padding-left: 25px}
```

BROWSER SUPPORT   Internet Explorer 4.0, Netscape 4.0.

padding

Sets the distance between an element's border and its contents. A single value creates equal padding on all sides.
EXAMPLE

```
{border-style: solid; padding: 10px}
```

Up to four values can be used, in the following clockwise order: **top**, **right**, **bottom**, and **left**.
EXAMPLE

```
{border-style: solid; padding: 10px 20px 10px 50px}
```

Any missing value defaults to the value defined for the side opposite to it.
EXAMPLE

```
{border-style: solid; padding: 10px 20px 10px}
```

BROWSER SUPPORT   Internet Explorer 4.0, Netscape 4.0.

width

The width property sets the width of an element's content region (excluding padding, border, or margin). The next example sets a paragraph with a width of 400 pixels.
EXAMPLE

```
P {width: 400px; padding: 10px; border: solid 5px }
```

Percentage values, based on the width of the containing element, may also be used.
EXAMPLE

```
P {width: 80%; padding: 10px; border: solid 5px }
```

The **auto** value automatically calculates the width of an element, based on the width of the containing element and the size of the content.
EXAMPLE

```
P {width: auto; padding: 10px; border: solid 5px }
```

BROWSER SUPPORT   Netscape 4.0.

height

The **width** property sets the height of an element's content region (excluding padding, border, or margin). The next example sets a paragraph with a height of 200 pixels.
EXAMPLE

```
P {height: 200px; padding: 10px; border: solid 5px}
```

Percentage values, based on the height of the containing element, may also be used.
EXAMPLE

```
P {height: 80%; padding: 10px; border: solid 5px}
```

The **auto** value automatically calculates the height of an element, based on the height of the containing element and the size of the content.
EXAMPLE

```
P { height: auto; padding: 10px; border: solid 5px }
```

BROWSER SUPPORT   Not supported.

float

Influences the horizontal alignment of an element, making it "float" towards the left or right margin of its containing element. Three values are available: **left**, **right**, and **none**.
EXAMPLE

```
IMG {float: right}
```

BROWSER SUPPORT   Internet Explorer 4.0, Netscape 4.0.

left

Causes an element to float towards the left margin of its containing element.

EXAMPLE

```
IMG {float: left}
```

BROWSER SUPPORT   Internet Explorer 4.0, Netscape 4.0.

right

Causes an element to float towards the right margin of its containing element.

EXAMPLE

```
IMG {float: right}
```

BROWSER SUPPORT   Internet Explorer 4.0, Netscape 4.0.

none

Prevents an element from floating.

EXAMPLE

```
IMG {float: none}
```

EXAMPLE

```
IMG {float: none}
```

The default value for **float**. Prevents an element from floating

BROWSER SUPPORT   Internet Explorer 4.0, Netscape 4.0.

clear

Specifies the placement of an element in relation to floating objects. Available values: **left**, **right**, **both**, and **none**.

EXAMPLE

```
{clear: right}
```

BROWSER SUPPORT   Netscape 4.0 (incomplete).

left

Clears floating objects to the left of the element.

EXAMPLE

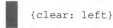
```
{clear: left}
```

BROWSER SUPPORT   Netscape 4.0 (incomplete).

right

Clears floating objects to the right of the element.
EXAMPLE

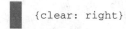
```
{clear: right}
```

BROWSER SUPPORT   Netscape 4.0 (incomplete).

both

Clears floating objects to both side of the element.
EXAMPLE

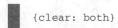
```
{clear: both}
```

BROWSER SUPPORT   Netscape 4.0 (incomplete).

none

The default value for **clear**.
EXAMPLE

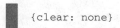
```
{clear: none}
```

BROWSER SUPPORT   Netscape 4.0.

Layers and Positioning

This section discusses style attributes that affect layering and positioning of elements.

position

Defines how an element is positioned relative to other elements, using the values **static**, **absolute**, and **relative**. The **left** and **top** properties define the element's precise location, using the affected element's upper-left corner ("0,0") as reference. Because elements may contain other elements, "0,0" is not necessarily the upper-left corner of the browser.
EXAMPLE

```
{position: relative; right: 190px; top: 30px}
```

BROWSER SUPPORT   Internet Explorer 4.0.

static

Places elements according to the natural order they occur in a document. This is the default value for **position**.

EXAMPLE

```
{position: static; left: 120px; top: 50px}
```

BROWSER SUPPORT   Internet Explorer 4.0.

absolute

Defines a coordinate system independent from other block and inline element placement. An element whose position is absolute acts as a visual container for any elements enclosed in its content. All elements defined inside it move with it. Contained elements assigned coordinates outside their container's dimensions will disappear.

EXAMPLE

```
{position: absolute; left: 120px; top: 50px}
```

BROWSER SUPPORT   Internet Explorer 4.0.

relative

Positions elements relative to their natural position in document flow.

EXAMPLE

```
{position: relative; left: 120px; top: 50px}
```

BROWSER SUPPORT   Internet Explorer 4.0.

left

Defines the x (horizontal) coordinates for a positioned element, relative to the upper-left corner. Values may be specified as a length (pixels, and so on), as a percentage of the containing object's dimensions, or as **auto**.

EXAMPLES

```
{position: absolute; left: 120px; top: 50px}

{position: absolute; left: 30%; top: 50%}

{position: absolute; left: auto; top: auto}
```

BROWSER SUPPORT   Internet Explorer 4.0, Netscape 4.0.

STYLE SHEET
REFERENCE

top

Defines the y (vertical) coordinates for a positioned element, relative to the upper-left corner. Values may be specified as a length (pixels, and so on), as a percentage of the containing object's dimensions, or as **auto**.

EXAMPLES

```
{position: absolute; left: 100px; top: 150px}

{position: absolute; left: 50%; top: 30%}

{position: absolute; left: auto; top: auto}
```

BROWSER SUPPORT   Internet Explorer 4.0, Netscape 4.0.

width

Defines the width of an element. Values can be set as lengths (positive values only), percentage (relative to the containing element's width), or **auto** (default to the element's natural width).

EXAMPLE

```
IMG {position: absolute; left: 120px; top: 50px; height: 200px; width:
400px }
```

BROWSER SUPPORT   Internet Explorer 4.0.

height

Defines the height of an element. Values can be set as lengths (positive values only), percentage (relative to the containing element's width), or **auto** (default to the element's natural width).

EXAMPLE

```
IMG {position: absolute; left: 120px; top: 50px; height: 100px; width:
150px }
```

BROWSER SUPPORT   Internet Explorer 4.0.

clip

Sets the coordinates of the clipping rectangle that houses the content of elements set to a position value of absolute. Coordinate values are **top**, **right**, **bottom**, and **left**, and **auto**.

EXAMPLE

```
{position: absolute; left: 20; top: 20; width:100; height:100; clip:
rect(10 90 90 10)}
```

BROWSER SUPPORT   Not supported.

overflow

Determines an element's behavior when its content doesn't fit into the space defined by the element's other properties. Available values: **clip**, **scroll**, and **none**.
EXAMPLE

```
{position: absolute; left: 20; top: 20; width: 100; height: 100; clip:
rect(10 90 90 10); overflow: scroll}
```

BROWSER SUPPORT   Not supported.

clip

Clips content to the size defined for the container.
EXAMPLE

```
{position: absolute; left: 20; top: 20; width: 100; height: 100; clip:
rect(10 90 90 10); overflow: clip}
```

BROWSER SUPPORT   Not supported.

scroll

Allows content to scroll using scroll bars or another browser-dependent mechanism.
EXAMPLE

```
{position: absolute; left: 20; top: 20; width: 100; height: 100; clip:
rect(10 90 90 10); overflow: scroll}
```

BROWSER SUPPORT   Not supported.

none

This value does nothing, but may allow clipping of the content.
EXAMPLE

```
{position: absolute; left: 20; top: 20; width: 100; height: 100; clip:
rect(10 90 90 10); overflow: none}
```

BROWSER SUPPORT   Not supported.

z-index

Defines a layering context for elements containing inside elements with relative or absolute positioning. By default, overlapping elements stack in the order they are defined in an HTML document. The **z-index** property can override default layering by assigning numeric layering values to an element; higher numbers layer above lower numbers. The **auto** value tries to determine the z-placement of an element automatically.

EXAMPLE

```
{position: absolute; top:20;left:20; height: 50; width: 50;
background-color: blue; z-index: 2}
```

BROWSER SUPPORT   Netscape 4.0.

visibility

Determines if an element is visible or not. Available values: **hidden**, **visible**, and **inherit**.
EXAMPLE

```
{visibility: inherit}
```

BROWSER SUPPORT   Internet Explorer 4.0.

hidden

Specifies that an element is hidden from view. A hidden element still occupies its full canvas space.
EXAMPLE

```
{visibility: hidden}
```

BROWSER SUPPORT   Internet Explorer 4.0.

visible

Specifies that an element is visible.
EXAMPLE

```
{visibility: visible}
```

BROWSER SUPPORT   Internet Explorer 4.0.

inherit

Specifies that an element inherits its visibility state from the element that contains it.
EXAMPLE

```
{visibility: inherit}
```

BROWSER SUPPORT   Internet Explorer 4.0.

Classification

This section discusses style attributes that affect the display type of elements (block-level, inline, and so on) and the display of white space and lists.

display

Specifies an element's display type. This property can override an element's defined display type. For instance, block elements can be redefined as inline elements, so that extra lines will not be placed between them.

EXAMPLE

```
P {display: inline}
```

BROWSER SUPPORT   Internet Explorer 4.0 (incomplete), Netscape 4.0 (incomplete).

block

Sets an element to display as a block element.

EXAMPLE

```
{display: block}
```

BROWSER SUPPORT   Netscape 4.0.

inline

Sets an element to display as an inline element.

EXAMPLE

```
P {display: inline}
```

BROWSER SUPPORT   None.

list-item

Sets an element to display as a list-item element.

EXAMPLE

```
P {display: list-item}
```

BROWSER SUPPORT   Netscape 4.0.

none

Turns off the display of an element. Unlike the hidden value of the **visibility** property, **none** does not preserve an element's canvas space.

EXAMPLE

```
P {display: none}
```

BROWSER SUPPORT   Internet Explorer 4.0, Netscape 4.0.

white-space

Controls how spaces, tabs, and new line characters are handled in an element. Values: **normal**, **pre**, and **nowrap**.
EXAMPLE

```
{white-space: pre}
```

BROWSER SUPPORT   Internet Explorer 4.0, Netscape 4.0 (incomplete).

normal

Collapses white space characters into a single space and automatically wraps lines, as in normal HTML.
EXAMPLE

```
{white-space: normal}
```

BROWSER SUPPORT   Netscape 4.0.

pre

Preserves white space formatting; similar to the **<PRE>** element in HTML.
EXAMPLE

```
{white-space: pre}
```

BROWSER SUPPORT   Netscape 4.0.

nowrap

Prevents lines from wrapping if they exceed the element's content width.
EXAMPLE

```
{white-space: nowrap}
```

BROWSER SUPPORT   Internet Explorer 4.0, Netscape 4.0.

list-style-type

Defines labels for ordered and unordered lists. There are five values for ordered lists: **decimal**, **lower-roman**, **upper-roman**, **lower-alpha**, and **upper-alpha**. There are three values for unordered lists: **disc**, **circle**, and **square**. The value none prevents a label from displaying.
EXAMPLES

```
OL {list-style-type: upper-roman}

UL {list-style-type: disc}
```

BROWSER SUPPORT   Internet Explorer 4.0, Netscape 4.0.

decimal

Specifies Arabic numerals (1, 2, 3, 4…) for the labeling of items in an ordered list.
EXAMPLE

```
OL {list-style-type: decimal}
```

BROWSER SUPPORT   Internet Explorer 4.0, Netscape 4.0.

lower-roman

Specifies lowercase Roman numerals (i, ii, iii, iv…) for the labeling of items in an ordered list.
EXAMPLE

```
OL {list-style-type: lower-roman}
```

BROWSER SUPPORT   Internet Explorer 4.0, Netscape 4.0.

upper-roman

Specifies uppercase Roman numerals (I, II, III, IV…) for the labeling of items in an ordered list.
EXAMPLE

```
OL {list-style-type: upper-roman}
```

BROWSER SUPPORT   Internet Explorer 4.0, Netscape 4.0.

lower-alpha

Specifies lowercase letters (a, b, c, d…) for the labeling of items in an ordered list.
EXAMPLE

```
OL {list-style-type: lower-alpha}
```

BROWSER SUPPORT   Internet Explorer 4.0, Netscape 4.0.

upper-alpha

Specifies uppercase letters (A, B, C, D…) for the labeling of items in an ordered list.
EXAMPLE

```
OL {list-style-type: upper-alpha}
```

BROWSER SUPPORT   Internet Explorer 4.0, Netscape 4.0.

disc

Specifies a black dot bullet for items in an unordered list.
EXAMPLE

```
UL {list-style-type: disc}
```

BROWSER SUPPORT   Internet Explorer 4.0, Netscape 4.0.

circle

Specifies a circular bullet for items in an unordered list.
EXAMPLE

```
UL {list-style-type: circle}
```

BROWSER SUPPORT   Internet Explorer 4.0, Netscape 4.0.

square

Specifies a square bullet for items in an unordered list.
EXAMPLE

```
UL {list-style-type: square}
```

BROWSER SUPPORT   Internet Explorer 4.0, Netscape 4.0.

none

Specifies that no label will be displayed for items in ordered or unordered lists.
EXAMPLES

```
OL {list-style-type: none}
```

```
UL {list-style-type: none}
```

BROWSER SUPPORT   Internet Explorer 4.0.

list-style-image

Assigns a graphic image to a list label, using the URL of the image. The only other value for
list-style-image is **none**.
EXAMPLE

```
UL {list-style-image: url(ball.gif)}
```

BROWSER SUPPORT   Internet Explorer 4.0.

list-style-position

Specifies that the labels for an element's list items are positioned inside or outside the "box" defined by the area. By default, labels appear outside the "box."

EXAMPLE

```
OL {list-style-type: upper-roman; list-style-position: outside;
background: yellow}
```

The **inside** value places the bullets inside the "box."

EXAMPLE

```
UL {list-style-type: square; list-style-position: inside; background:
yellow}
```

BROWSER SUPPORT   Not supported.

list-style

A more concise property that sets type, image, or position properties for ordered and unordered lists. The properties may appear in any order. "Inside" and "outside" values are not supported.

EXAMPLES

```
UL {list-style: inside url("bullet.gif")}

UL {list-style: outside square}

OL {list-style: lower-roman inside}
```

BROWSER SUPPORT   Internet Explorer 4.0, Netscape 4.0 (both incomplete).

Style Sheet Measurement Values

This section discusses measurement values used in association with style sheets.

in

Defines a measurement in inches.

EXAMPLE

```
P {word-spacing: .25in}
```

BROWSER SUPPORT   Internet Explorer 3.0 and 4.0, Netscape 4.0.

cm

Defines a measurement in centimeters.
EXAMPLE

```
DIV {margin-bottom: 1cm}
```

BROWSER SUPPORT   Internet Explorer 3.0 and 4.0, Netscape 4.0.

mm

Defines a measurement in millimeters.
EXAMPLE

```
P {word-spacing: 12mm}
```

BROWSER SUPPORT   Internet Explorer 3.0 and 4.0, Netscape 4.0.

pt

Defines a measurement in points.
EXAMPLE

```
BODY {font-size: 14pt}
```

BROWSER SUPPORT   Internet Explorer 3.0 and 4.0, Netscape 4.0.

pc

Defines a measurement in picas.
EXAMPLE

```
P {font-size: 10pc}
```

BROWSER SUPPORT   Internet Explorer 3.0 and 4.0, Netscape 4.0.

em

Defines a measurement in ems (the height of the font).
EXAMPLE

```
P {letter-spacing: 5em}
```

BROWSER SUPPORT   Internet Explorer 3.0 (Mac only), Netscape 4.0 (incomplete).

ex (x-height)

Defines a measurement relative to a font's x-height. X-height is determined by the height of the font's lowercase "x."

EXAMPLE

```
P {font-size: 14pt; line-height: 2ex}
```

BROWSER SUPPORT   Internet Explorer 3.0 (Mac only), Netscape 4.0 (incomplete).

px

Defines a measurement in pixels.

EXAMPLE

```
P {padding: 15px}
```

BROWSER SUPPORT   Internet Explorer 3.0 and 4.0, Netscape 4.0.

%

Defines a measurement as a percentage relative to another value.

EXAMPLE

```
P {font-size: 14pt; line-height: 150%}
```

BROWSER SUPPORT   Internet Explorer 3.0 and 4.0, Netscape 4.0.

Style Sheet Color Values

This section discusses color values used in association with style sheets.

Named Color Values

Color values can be defined using sixteen color names: Aqua, Black, Blue, Fuchsia, Gray, Green, Lime, Maroon, Navy, Olive, Purple, Red, Silver, Teal, White, and Yellow. (An extended list of color names was introduced by Netscape, but it is safer to use their hexadecimal equivalents; see Appendix E.)

EXAMPLE

```
BODY {font-family: Arial; font-size: 12pt; color: red}
```

BROWSER SUPPORT   Internet Explorer 3.0 and 4.0, Netscape 4.0.

Six-Digit Hexadecimal Color Values

Color values can be defined using the six-digit hexadecimal color values commonly used on the Web.

EXAMPLE

```
DIV {font-family: Courier; font-size: 10pt; color: #00CCFF}
```

BROWSER SUPPORT   Internet Explorer 3.0 and 4.0, Netscape 4.0.

Three-Digit Hexadecimal Color Values

Color values can be defined using three-digit hexadecimal color values, a concise version of the six-digit values just noted.

EXAMPLE

```
SPAN {font-family: Helvetica; font-size: 14pt; color: #0CF}
```

BROWSER SUPPORT   Internet Explorer 3.0 and 4.0, Netscape 4.0.

RGB Color Values

Color values can be defined using RGB values. Colors are defined by the letters rgb, followed by three numbers between 0 and 255, in containing parentheses, separated by commas, with no spaces between them.

EXAMPLE

```
P {color: rgb(204,0,51)}
```

BROWSER SUPPORT   Internet Explorer 4.0, Netscape 4.0.

RGB Color Values (Percentage)

RGB color values can also be defined using percentages. The format is the same, except that the numbers are replaced by percentage values between **0%** and **100%**.

EXAMPLE

```
P {color: rgb(75%,10%,50%)}
```

BROWSER SUPPORT   Internet Explorer 4.0, Netscape 4.0.

The Complete Reference

HTML

Appendix C

Special Characters

This appendix lists the special characters available in standard HTML and HTML 4.0. Note that browser support of elements in Appendix C is based on testing in the following browser versions: Netscape 1.22, Netscape 2.02, Netscape 3.01, Netscape Communicator 4.0, Internet Explorer 3.02, Internet Explorer 4.0, and WebTV. In the tables in this appendix, the following abbreviations are used for the different Netscape and Internet Explorer versions:

N1 = Netscape 1.22
N2 = Netscape 2.02
N3 = Netscape 3.01
N4 = Netscape Communicator 4.0
IE3 = Internet Explorer 3.02
IE4 = Internet Explorer 4.0

"Standard" HTML Character Entities

As discussed in Chapter 4, Web browsers do not read certain characters if they appear in an HTML document. To get around this limitation, codes have been assigned to certain characters. These codes consist of numbered entities, and some, but not all, of these numbered entities have corresponding named entities. For example, the numbered entity Ë produces the character Ë. The named entity Ë produces the same character. Note that the named entity suggests the intended rendering of the character, which provides a handy mnemonic device for dedicated HTML codes. While Ë is widely supported, not all character entities work in all browsers. Theoretically, a browser vendor could even create arbitrary interpretations of these codes. For instance, WebTV has assigned its own unique renderings for the entities numbered 128 and 129. Under the HTML specifications, 128 and 129 are not assigned a character. The codes numbered 32 through 255 (with some gaps) were assigned standard keyboard characters. Some of these codes duplicate characters that Web browsers can already interpret. The entity 5 represents the numeral five, while ¥ represents "A." Character entities become more practical when it is necessary to employ characters used in foreign languages, such as "Œ" or "Å," or special characters such as "¶." The following chart lists these "standard" entities and their intended renderings, and identifies which browsers support each.

Named Entity	Browser Support	Numbered Entity	Browser Support	Intended Rendering	Description
		&#32;	N1, N2, N3, N4, IE3, IE4, WebTV		Space
		&#33;	N1, N2, N3, N4, IE3, IE4, WebTV	!	Exclamation point
&quot;	N1, N2, N3, N4, IE3, IE4, WebTV	&#34;	N1, N2, N3, N4, IE3, IE4, WebTV	"	Double quotes
		&#35;	N1, N2, N3, N4, IE3, IE4, WebTV	#	Number symbol
		&#36;	N1, N2, N3, N4, IE3, IE4, WebTV	$	Dollar symbol
		&#37;	N1, N2, N3, N4, IE3, IE4, WebTV	%	Percent symbol
&amp;	N1, N2, N3, N4, IE3, IE4, WebTV	&#38;	N1, N2, N3, N4, IE3, IE4, WebTV	&	Ampersand
		&#39;	N1, N2, N3, N4, IE3, IE4, WebTV	'	Single quote
		&#40;	N1, N2, N3, N4, IE3, IE4, WebTV	(	Opening parenthesis
		&#41;	N1, N2, N3, N4, IE3, IE4, WebTV	)	Closing parenthesis
		&#42;	N1, N2, N3, N4, IE3, IE4, WebTV	*	Asterisk
		&#43;	N1, N2, N3, N4, IE3, IE4, WebTV	+	Plus sign

Named Entity	Browser Support	Numbered Entity	Browser Support	Intended Rendering	Description
		&#44;	N1, N2, N3, N4, IE3, IE4, WebTV	,	Comma
		&#45;	N1, N2, N3, N4, IE3, IE4, WebTV	-	Minus sign (hyphen)
		&#46;	N1, N2, N3, N4, IE3, IE4, WebTV	.	Period
		&#47;	N1, N2, N3, N4, IE3, IE4, WebTV	/	Slash/virgule/bar
		&#48;	N1, N2, N3, N4, IE3, IE4, WebTV	0	Zero
		&#49;	N1, N2, N3, N4, IE3, IE4, WebTV	1	One
		&#50;	N1, N2, N3, N4, IE3, IE4, WebTV	2	Two
		&#51;	N1, N2, N3, N4, IE3, IE4, WebTV	3	Three
		&#52;	N1, N2, N3, N4, IE3, IE4, WebTV	4	Four
		&#53;	N1, N2, N3, N4, IE3, IE4, WebTV	5	Five
		&#54;	N1, N2, N3, N4, IE3, IE4, WebTV	6	Six
		&#55;	N1, N2, N3, N4, IE3, IE4, WebTV	7	Seven

Named Entity	Browser Support	Numbered Entity	Browser Support	Intended Rendering	Description
		&#56;	N1, N2, N3, N4, IE3, IE4, WebTV	8	Eight
		&#57;	N1, N2, N3, N4, IE3, IE4, WebTV	9	Nine
		&#58;	N1, N2, N3, N4, IE3, IE4, WebTV	:	Colon
		&#59;	N1, N2, N3, N4, IE3, IE4, WebTV	;	Semicolon
&lt;	N1, N2, N3, N4, IE3, IE4, WebTV	&#60;	N1, N2, N3, N4, IE3, IE4, WebTV	<	Less than symbol
		&#61;	N1, N2, N3, N4, IE3, IE4, WebTV	=	Equal sign
&gt;	N1, N2, N3, N4, IE3, IE4, WebTV	&#62;	N1, N2, N3, N4, IE3, IE4, WebTV	>	Greater than symbol
		&#63;	N1, N2, N3, N4, IE3, IE4, WebTV	?	Question mark
		&#64;	N1, N2, N3, N4, IE3, IE4, WebTV	@	At symbol
		&#65;	N1, N2, N3, N4, IE3, IE4, WebTV	A	
		&#66;	N1, N2, N3, N4, IE3, IE4, WebTV	B	
		&#67;	N1, N2, N3, N4, IE3, IE4, WebTV	C	

Named Entity	Browser Support	Numbered Entity	Browser Support	Intended Rendering	Description
		&#68;	N1, N2, N3, N4, IE3, IE4, WebTV	D	
		&#69;	N1, N2, N3, N4, IE3, IE4, WebTV	E	
		&#70;	N1, N2, N3, N4, IE3, IE4, WebTV	F	
		&#71;	N1, N2, N3, N4, IE3, IE4, WebTV	G	
		&#72;	N1, N2, N3, N4, IE3, IE4, WebTV	H	
		&#73;	N1, N2, N3, N4, IE3, IE4, WebTV	I	
		&#74;	N1, N2, N3, N4, IE3, IE4, WebTV	J	
		&#75;	N1, N2, N3, N4, IE3, IE4, WebTV	K	
		&#76;	N1, N2, N3, N4, IE3, IE4, WebTV	L	
		&#77;	N1, N2, N3, N4, IE3, IE4, WebTV	M	
		&#78;	N1, N2, N3, N4, IE3, IE4, WebTV	N	
		&#79;	N1, N2, N3, N4, IE3, IE4, WebTV	O	

Named Entity	Browser Support	Numbered Entity	Browser Support	Intended Rendering	Description
		&#80;	N1, N2, N3, N4, IE3, IE4, WebTV	P	
		&#81;	N1, N2, N3, N4, IE3, IE4, WebTV	Q	
		&#82;	N1, N2, N3, N4, IE3, IE4, WebTV	R	
		&#83;	N1, N2, N3, N4, IE3, IE4, WebTV	S	
		&#84;	N1, N2, N3, N4, IE3, IE4, WebTV	T	
		&#85;	N1, N2, N3, N4, IE3, IE4, WebTV	U	
		&#86;	N1, N2, N3, N4, IE3, IE4, WebTV	V	
		&#87;	N1, N2, N3, N4, IE3, IE4, WebTV	W	
		&#88;	N1, N2, N3, N4, IE3, IE4, WebTV	X	
		&#89;	N1, N2, N3, N4, IE3, IE4, WebTV	Y	
		&#90;	N1, N2, N3, N4, IE3, IE4, WebTV	Z	
		&#91;	N1, N2, N3, N4, IE3, IE4, WebTV	[	Opening bracket

Named Entity	Browser Support	Numbered Entity	Browser Support	Intended Rendering	Description
		&#92;	N1, N2, N3, N4, IE3, IE4, WebTV	\	Backslash
		&#93;	N1, N2, N3, N4, IE3, IE4, WebTV	]	Closing bracket
		&#94;	N1, N3, N4, IE3, IE4, WebTV	^	Caret
		&#95;	N1, N2, N3, N4, IE3, IE4, WebTV	_	Underscore
		&#96;	N1, N2, N3, N4, IE3, IE4, WebTV	'	Grave accent, no letter
		&#97;	N1, N2, N3, N4, IE3, IE4, WebTV	a	
		&#98;	N1, N2, N3, N4, IE3, IE4, WebTV	b	
		&#99;	N1, N2, N3, N4, IE3, IE4, WebTV	c	
		&#100;	N1, N2, N3, N4, IE3, IE4, WebTV	d	
		&#101;	N1, N2, N3, N4, IE3, IE4, WebTV	e	
		&#102;	N1, N2, N3, N4, IE3, IE4, WebTV	f	
		&#103;	N1, N2, N3, N4, IE3, IE4, WebTV	g	

Named Entity	Browser Support	Numbered Entity	Browser Support	Intended Rendering	Description
		&#104;	N1, N2, N3, N4, IE3, IE4, WebTV	h	
		&#105;	N1, N2, N3, N4, IE3, IE4, WebTV	i	
		&#106;	N1, N2, N3, N4, IE3, IE4, WebTV	j	
		&#107;	N1, N2, N3, N4, IE3, IE4, WebTV	k	
		&#108;	N1, N2, N3, N4, IE3, IE4, WebTV	l	
		&#109;	N1, N2, N3, N4, IE3, IE4, WebTV	m	
		&#110;	N1, N2, N3, N4, IE3, IE4, WebTV	n	
		&#111;	N1, N2, N3, N4, IE3, IE4, WebTV	o	
		&#112;	N1, N2, N3, N4, IE3, IE4, WebTV	p	
		&#113;	N1, N2, N3, N4, IE3, IE4, WebTV	q	
		&#114;	N1, N2, N3, N4, IE3, IE4, WebTV	r	
		&#115;	N1, N2, N3, N4, IE3, IE4, WebTV	s	

SPECIAL CHARACTERS

Named Entity	Browser Support	Numbered Entity	Browser Support	Intended Rendering	Description
		&#116;	N1, N2, N3, N4, IE3, IE4, WebTV	t	
		&#117;	N1, N2, N3, N4, IE3, IE4, WebTV	u	
		&#118;	N1, N2, N3, N4, IE3, IE4, WebTV	v	
		&#119;	N1, N2, N3, N4, IE3, IE4, WebTV	w	
		&#120;	N1, N2, N3, N4, IE3, IE4, WebTV	x	
		&#121;	N1, N2, N3, N4, IE3, IE4, WebTV	y	
		&#122;	N1, N2, N3, N4, IE3, IE4, WebTV	z	
		&#123;	N1, N2, N3, N4, IE3, IE4, WebTV	{	Opening brace
		|	N1, N2, N3, N4, IE3, IE4, WebTV	|	Vertical bar
		&#125;	N1, N2, N3, N4, IE3, IE4, WebTV	}	Closing brace
		&#126;	N1, N2, N3, N4, IE3, IE4, WebTV	~	Equivalency symbol (tilde)

Named Entity	Browser Support	Numbered Entity	Browser Support	Intended Rendering	Description
		&#127;	n/a		No character (Note: In the standard, the values from 127 to 159 are not assigned. Authors are advised not to use them. Many of them only work under Windows or produce different characters on other operating systems or with different default font sets.)
		&#128;	WebTV (nonstandard)*		No character defined
&trade;	IE3, IE4	&#129;	WebTV (nonstandard)†	™	Trademark symbol (Nonstandard numeric value; use ™ or ™ instead.)
		&#130;	N3, N2, N4, IE3, IE4, WebTV	‚	Low-9 quote (nonstandard)
		&#131;	N3, N4, IE3, IE4, WebTV	ƒ	Small "f" with hook (nonstandard)

Named Entity	Browser Support	Numbered Entity	Browser Support	Intended Rendering	Description
		&#132;	N2, N3, N4, IE3, IE4, WebTV	„	Low-9 double quotes (nonstandard)
		&#133;	N2, N3, N4, IE3, IE4, WebTV	…	Ellipsis (nonstandard)
		&#134;	N2, N3, N4, IE3, IE4, WebTV	†	Dagger (nonstandard)
		&#135;	N2, N3, N4, IE3, IE4, WebTV	‡	Double dagger (nonstandard)
		&#136;	N3, N4, IE3, IE4, WebTV	^	Circumflex accent, no letter (nonstandard)
		&#137;	N2, N3, N4, IE3, IE4, WebTV	‰	Per thousand (nonstandard)
		&#138;	N3, N4, IE3, IE4, WebTV	Š	Uppercase S with caron (nonstandard)
		&#139;	N2, N3, N4, IE3, IE4, WebTV	<	Opening single angle quote (nonstandard)
		&#140;	N3, N4, IE3, IE4, WebTV	Œ	Uppercase "OE" ligature (nonstandard)
		&#141;	None	Ÿ	Uppercase "Y" with umlaut (nonstandard)
		&#142;	n/a		No character
		&#143;	n/a		No character

Named Entity	Browser Support	Numbered Entity	Browser Support	Intended Rendering	Description
		&#144;	n/a		No character
		&#145;	N1, N2, N3, N4, IE3, IE4, WebTV	'	Opening "smart" single quote (nonstandard)
		&#146;	N1, N2, N3, N4, IE3, IE4, WebTV	'	Closing "smart" single quote (nonstandard)
		&#147;	N2, N3, N4, IE3, IE4, WebTV	"	Opening "smart" double quote (nonstandard)
		&#148;	N2, N3, N4, IE3, IE4, WebTV	"	Closing "smart" double quote (nonstandard)
		&#149;	N2, N3, N4, IE3, IE4, WebTV	•	Bullet (nonstandard)
		&#150;	N2, N3, N4, IE3, IE4, WebTV	–	En dash (nonstandard)
		&#151;	N2, N3, N4, IE3, IE4, WebTV	—	Em dash (nonstandard)
		&#152;	N3, N4, IE3, IE4, WebTV	~	Tilde (nonstandard)
&trade;	IE3, IE4	&#153;	N2, N3, N4, IE3, IE4, WebTV	™	Trademark symbol ‡ (nonstandard numeric value; use ™ or ™ instead)

Named Entity	Browser Support	Numbered Entity	Browser Support	Intended Rendering	Description
		&#154;	N3, N4, IE3, IE4, WebTV	š	Lowercase S with caron (nonstandard)
		&#155;	N2, N3, N4, IE3, IE4, WebTV	>	Closing single angle quote (nonstandard)
		&#156;	N3, N4, IE3, IE4, WebTV	œ	Lowercase "oe" ligature (nonstandard)
		&#157;	n/a		No character
		&#158;	n/a		No character
		&#159;	N3, N4, IE3	Ÿ	Uppercase "Y" with umlaut (nonstandard)
	N1, N3, N4, IE3		N1, N2, N3, N4, IE3, IE4		Nonbreaking space
&iexcl;	N3, N4, IE3, IE4, WebTV	&#161;	N1, N3, N4, IE3, IE4, WebTV	¡	Inverted exclamation point
&cent;	N3, N4, IE3, IE4, WebTV	&#162;	N1, N3, N4, IE3, IE4, WebTV	¢	Cent symbol
&pound;	N3, N4, IE3, IE4, WebTV	&#163;	N1, N3, N4, IE3, IE4, WebTV	£	Pound sterling symbol
&curren;	N3, N4, IE3, IE4, WebTV	&#164;	N1, N2, N3, N4, IE3, IE4, WebTV	¤	Currency symbol
&yen;	N3, N4, IE3, IE4, WebTV	&#165;	N1, N3, N4, IE3, IE4, WebTV	¥	Japanese Yen

Named Entity	Browser Support	Numbered Entity	Browser Support	Intended Rendering	Description
&brvbar;	N3, N4, IE3, IE4, WebTV	&#166;	N2, N3, N4, IE3, IE4, WebTV	¦	Broken vertical bar
&sect;	N3, N4, IE3, IE4, WebTV	&#167;	N1, N2, N3, N4, IE3, IE4, WebTV	§	Section symbol
&uml;	N3, N4, IE3, IE4, WebTV	&#168;	N1, N3, N4, IE3, IE4, WebTV	¨	Umlaut, no letter
&copy;	N1, N2, N3, N4, IE3, IE4, WebTV	&#169;	N1, N2, N3, N4, IE3, IE4, WebTV	©	Copyright symbol
&ordf;	N3, N4, IE3, IE4, WebTV	&#170;	N1, N3, N4, IE3, IE4, WebTV	ª	Feminine ordinal indicator
&laquo;	N3, N4, IE3, IE4, WebTV	&#171;	N1, N2, N3, N4, IE3, IE4, WebTV	«	Opening double angle quote
&not;	N3, N4, IE3, IE4, WcbTV	&#172;	N1, N2, N3, N4, IE3, IE4, WebTV	¬	Logical "not" symbol
&shy;	N3, N4, IE3, IE4, WebTV	&#173;	N1, N2, N3, N4, IE3, IE4, WebTV	-	Soft hyphen
&reg;	N1, N2, N3, N4, IE3, IE4, WebTV	&#174;	N1, N2, N3, N4, IE3, IE4, WebTV	®	Registration mark
&macr;	N3, N4, IE3, IE4, WebTV	&#175;	N1, N3, N4, IE3, IE4, WebTV	¯	Macron
&deg;	N3, N4, IE3, IE4, WebTV	&#176;	N1, N2, N3, N4, IE3, IE4, WebTV	°	Degree symbol
&plusmn;	N3, N4, IE3, IE4, WebTV	&#177;	N1, N2, N3, N4, IE3, IE4, WebTV	±	Plus/minus symbol

Named Entity	Browser Support	Numbered Entity	Browser Support	Intended Rendering	Description
&sup2;	N3, N4, IE3, IE4, WebTV	&#178;	N1, N3, N4, IE3, IE4, WebTV	2	Superscript 2
&sup3;	N3, N4, IE3, IE4, WebTV	&#179;	N1, N3, N4, IE3, IE4, WebTV	3	Superscript 3
&acute;	N3, N4, IE3, IE4, WebTV	&#180;	N1, N3, N4, IE3, IE4, WebTV	´	Acute accent, no letter
&micro;	N3, N4, IE3, IE4, WebTV	&#181;	N1, N2, N3, N4, IE3, IE4, WebTV	µ	Micron
&para;	N3, N4, IE3, IE4, WebTV	&#182;	N1, N2, N3, N4, IE3, IE4, WebTV	¶	Paragraph symbol
&middot;	N3, N4, IE3, IE4, WebTV	&#183;	N1, N3, N4, IE3, IE4, WebTV	•	Middle dot
&cedil;	N3, N4, IE3, IE4, WebTV	&#184;	N1, N3, N4, IE3, IE4, WebTV	¸	Cedilla
&sup1;	N3, N4, IE3, IE4, WebTV	&#185;	N1, N3, N4, IE3, IE4, WebTV	1	Superscript 1
&ordm;	N3, N4, IE3, IE4, WebTV	&#186;	N1, N3, N4, IE3, IE4, WebTV	º	Masculine ordinal indicator
&raquo;	N3, N4, IE3, IE4, WebTV	&#187;	N1, N2, N3, N4, IE3, IE4, WebTV	»	Closing double angle quotes
&frac14;	N3, N4, IE3, IE4, WebTV	&#188;	N1, N3, N4, IE3, IE4, WebTV	¼	One-quarter fraction
&frac12;	N3, N4, IE3, IE4, WebTV	&#189;	N1, N3, N4, IE3, IE4, WebTV	½	One-half fraction

Named Entity	Browser Support	Numbered Entity	Browser Support	Intended Rendering	Description
&frac34;	N3, N4, IE3, IE4, WebTV	&#190;	N1, N3, N4, IE3, IE4, WebTV	¾	Three-fourths fraction
&iquest;	N3, N4, IE3, IE4, WebTV	&#191;	N1, N3, N4, IE3, IE4, WebTV	¿	Inverted question mark
&Agrave;	N1, N3, N4, IE3, IE4, WebTV	&#192;	N1, N3, N4, IE3, IE4, WebTV	À	Uppercase "A" with grave accent
&Aacute;	N1, N3, N4, IE3, IE4, WebTV	&#193;	N1, N3, N4, IE3, IE4, WebTV	Á	Uppercase "A" with acute accent
&Acirc;	N1, N3, N4, IE3, IE4, WebTV	&#194;	N1, N3, N4, IE3, IE4, WebTV	Â	Uppercase "A" with circumflex
&Atilde;	N1, N3, N4, IE3, IE4, WebTV	&#195;	N1, N3, N4, IE3, IE4, WebTV	Ã	Uppercase "A" with tilde
&Auml;	N1, N3, N4, IE3, IE4, WebTV	&#196;	N1, N3, N4, IE3, IE4, WebTV	Ä	Uppercase "A" with umlaut
&Aring;	N1, N3, N4, IE3, IE4, WebTV	&#197;	N1, N3, N4, IE3, IE4, WebTV	Å	Uppercase "A" with ring
&AElig;	N1, N3, N4, IE3, IE4, WebTV	&#198;	N1, N3, N4, IE3, IE4, WebTV	Æ	Uppercase "AE" ligature
&Ccedil;	N1, N3, N4, IE3, IE4, WebTV	&#199;	N1, N3, N4, IE3, IE4, WebTV	Ç	Uppercase "C" with cedilla
&Egrave;	N1, N3, N4, IE3, IE4, WebTV	&#200;	N1, N3, N4, IE3, IE4, WebTV	È	Uppercase "E" with grave accent
&Eacute;	N1, N3, N4, IE3, IE4, WebTV	&#201;	N1, N3, N4, IE3, IE4, WebTV	É	Uppercase "E" with acute accent

SPECIAL CHARACTERS

Named Entity	Browser Support	Numbered Entity	Browser Support	Intended Rendering	Description
&Ecirc;	N1, N3, N4, IE3, IE4, WebTV	&#202;	N1, N3, N4, IE3, IE4, WebTV	Ê	Uppercase "E" with circumflex
&Euml;	N1, N3, N4, IE3, IE4, WebTV	&#203;	N1, N3, N4, IE3, IE4, WebTV	Ë	Uppercase "E" with umlaut
&Igrave;	N1, N3, N4, IE3, IE4, WebTV	&#204;	N1, N3, N4, IE3, IE4, WebTV	Ì	Uppercase "I" with grave accent
&Iacute;	N1, N3, N4, IE3, IE4, WebTV	&#205;	N1, N3, N4, IE3, IE4, WebTV	Í	Uppercase "I" with acute accent
&Icirc;	N1, N3, N4, IE3, IE4, WebTV	&#206;	N1, N3, N4, IE3, IE4, WebTV	Î	Uppercase "I" with circumflex
&Iuml;	N1, N3, N4, IE3, IE4, WebTV	&#207;	N1, N3, N4, IE3, IE4, WebTV	Ï	Uppercase "I" with umlaut
&ETH;	N1, N3, N4, IE3, IE4, WebTV	&#208;	N1, N3, N4, IE3, IE4, WebTV	Ð	Capital "ETH"
&Ntilde;	N1, N3, N4, IE3, IE4, WebTV	&#209;	N1, N3, N4, IE3, IE4, WebTV	Ñ	Uppercase "N" with tilde
&Ograve;	N1, N3, N4, IE3, IE4, WebTV	&#210;	N1, N3, N4, IE3, IE4, WebTV	Ò	Uppercase "O" with grave accent
&Oacute;	N1, N3, N4, IE3, IE4, WebTV	&#211;	N1, N3, N4, IE3, IE4, WebTV	Ó	Uppercase "O" with acute accent
&Ocirc;	N1, N3, N4, IE3, IE4, WebTV	&#212;	N1, N3, N4, IE3, IE4, WebTV	Ô	Uppercase "O" with circumflex
&Otilde;	N1, N3, N4, IE3, IE4, WebTV	&#213;	N1, N3, N4, IE3, IE4, WebTV	Õ	Uppercase "O" with tilde

Named Entity	Browser Support	Numbered Entity	Browser Support	Intended Rendering	Description
&Ouml;	N1, N3, N4, IE3, IE4, WebTV	&#214;	N1, N3, N4, IE3, IE4, WebTV	Ö	Uppercase "O" with umlaut
&times;	N3, N4, IE3, IE4, WebTV	&#215;	N1, N3, N4, IE3, IE4, WebTV	×	Multiplication symbol
&Oslash;	N1, N3, N4, IE3, IE4, WebTV	&#216;	N1, N3, N4, IE3, IE4, WebTV	Ø	Uppercase "O" with slash
&Ugrave;	N1, N3, N4, IE3, IE4, WebTV	&#217;	N1, N3, N4, IE3, IE4, WebTV	Ù	Uppercase "U" with grave accent
&Uacute;	N1, N3, N4, IE3, IE4, WebTV	&#218;	N1, N3, N4, IE3, IE4, WebTV	Ú	Uppercase "U" with acute accent
&Ucirc;	N1, N3, N4, IE3, IE4, WebTV	&#219;	N1, N3, N4, IE3, IE4, WebTV	Û	Uppercase "U" with circumflex accent
&Uuml;	N1, N3, N4, IE3, IE4, WebTV	&#220;	N1, N3, N4, IE3, IE4, WebTV	Ü	Uppercase "U" with umlaut
&Yacute;	N1, N3, N4, IE3, IE4, WebTV	&#221;	N1, N3, N4, IE3, IE4, WebTV	Ý	Uppercase "Y" with acute accent
&THORN;	N1, N3, N4, IE3, IE4, WebTV	&#222;	N1, N3, N4, IE3, IE4, WebTV	Þ	Capital "thorn"
&szlig;	N1, N3, N4, IE3, IE4, WebTV	&#223;	N1, N3, N4, IE3, IE4, WebTV	ß	"SZ" ligature
&agrave;	N1, N3, N4, IE3, IE4, WebTV	&#224;	N1, N3, N4, IE3, IE4, WebTV	à	Lowercase "a" with grave accent

SPECIAL CHARACTERS

Named Entity	Browser Support	Numbered Entity	Browser Support	Intended Rendering	Description
&aacute;	N1, N3, N4, IE3, IE4, WebTV	&#225;	N1, N3, N4, IE3, IE4, WebTV	á	Lowercase "a" with acute accent
&acirc;	N1, N3, N4, IE3, IE4, WebTV	&#226;	N1, N3, N4, IE3, IE4, WebTV	â	Lowercase "a" with circumflex
&atilde;	N1, N3, N4, IE3, IE4, WebTV	&#227;	N1, N3, N4, IE3, IE4, WebTV	ã	Lowercase "a" with tilde
&auml;	N1, N3, N4, IE3, IE4, WebTV	&#228;	N1, N3, N4, IE3, IE4, WebTV	ä	Lowercase "a" with umlaut
&aring;	N1, N3, N4, IE3, IE4, WebTV	&#229;	N1, N3, N4, IE3, IE4, WebTV	å	Lowercase "a" with ring
&aelig;	N1, N3, N4, IE3, IE4, WebTV	&#230;	N1, N3, N4, IE3, IE4, WebTV	æ	Lowercase "ae" ligature
&ccedil;	N1, N3, N4, IE3, IE4, WebTV	&#231;	N1, N3, N4, IE3, IE4, WebTV	ç	Lowercase "c" with cedilla
&egrave;	N1, N3, N4, IE3, IE4, WebTV	&#232;	N1, N3, N4, IE3, IE4, WebTV	è	Lowercase "e" with grave accent
&eacute;	N1, N3, N4, IE3, IE4, WebTV	&#233;	N1, N3, N4, IE3, IE4, WebTV	é	Lowercase "e" with acute accent
&ecirc;	N1, N3, N4, IE3, IE4, WebTV	&#234;	N1, N3, N4, IE3, IE4, WebTV	ê	Lowercase "e" with circumflex
&euml;	N1, N3, N4, IE3, IE4, WebTV	&#235;	N1, N3, N4, IE3, IE4, WebTV	ë	Lowercase "e" with umlaut
&igrave;	N1, N3, N4, IE3, IE4, WebTV	&#236;	N1, N3, N4, IE3, IE4, WebTV	ì	Lowercase "i" with grave accent

Named Entity	Browser Support	Numbered Entity	Browser Support	Intended Rendering	Description
&iacute;	N1, N3, N4, IE3, IE4, WebTV	&#237;	N1, N3, N4, IE3, IE4, WebTV	í	Lowercase "i" with acute accent
&icirc;	N1, N3, N4, IE3, IE4, WebTV	&#238;	N1, N3, N4, IE3, IE4, WebTV	î	Lowercase "i" with circumflex
&iuml;	N1, N3, N4, IE3, IE4, WebTV	&#239;	N1, N3, N4, IE3, IE4, WebTV	ï	Lowercase "i" with umlaut
&eth;	N1, N3, N4, IE3, IE4, WebTV	&#240;	N1, N3, N4, IE3, IE4, WebTV	ð	Lowercase "eth"
&ntilde;	N1, N3, N4, IE3, IE4, WebTV	&#241;	N1, N3, N4, IE3, IE4, WebTV	ñ	Lowercase "n" with tilde
&ograve;	N1, N3, N4, IE3, IE4, WebTV	&#242;	N1, N3, N4, IE3, IE4, WebTV	ò	Lowercase "o" with grave accent
&oacute;	N1, N3, N4, IE3, IE4, WebTV	&#243;	N1, N3, N4, IE3, IE4, WebTV	ó	Lowercase "o" with acute accent
&ocirc;	N1, N3, N4, IE3, IE4, WebTV	&#244;	N1, N3, N4, IE3, IE4, WebTV	ô	Lowercase "o" with circumflex accent
&otilde;	N1, N3, N4, IE3, IE4, WebTV	&#245;	N1, N3, N4, IE3, IE4, WebTV	õ	Lowercase "o" with tilde
&ouml;	N1, N3, N4, IE3, IE4, WebTV	&#246;	N1, N3, N4, IE3, IE4, WebTV	ö	Lowercase "o" with umlaut
&divide;	N3, N4, IE3, IE4, WebTV	&#247;	N1, N3, N4, IE3, IE4, WebTV	÷	Division symbol

SPECIAL CHARACTERS

Named Entity	Browser Support	Numbered Entity	Browser Support	Intended Rendering	Description
&oslash;	N1, N3, N4, IE3, IE4, WebTV	&#248;	N1, N3, N4, IE3, IE4, WebTV	ø	Lowercase "o" with slash
&ugrave;	N1, N3, N4, IE3, IE4, WebTV	&#249;	N1, N3, N4, IE3, IE4, WebTV	ù	Lowercase "u" with grave accent
&uacute;	N1, N3, N4, IE3, IE4, WebTV	&#250;	N1, N3, N4, IE3, IE4, WebTV	ú	Lowercase "u" with acute accent
&ucirc;	N1, N3, N4, IE3, IE4, WebTV	&#251;	N1, N3, N4, IE3, IE4, WebTV	û	Lowercase "u" with circumflex
&uuml;	N1, N3, N4, IE3, IE4, WebTV	&#252;	N1, N3, N4, IE3, IE4, WebTV	ü	Lowercase "u" with umlaut
&yacute;	N1, N3, N4, IE3, IE4, WebTV	&#253;	N1, N3, N4, IE3, IE4, WebTV	ý	Lowercase "y" with acute accent
&thorn;	N1, N3, N4, IE3, IE4, WebTV	&#254;	N1, N3, N4, IE3, IE4, WebTV	þ	Lowercase "thorn"
&yuml;	N1, N3, N4, IE3, IE4, WebTV	&#255;	N1, N3, N4, IE3, IE4, WebTV	ÿ	Lowercase "y" with umlaut

* WebTV renders € as a right-pointing arrowhead.

† WebTV renders  as a left-pointing arrowhead.

‡ Support for ™ (™) is inconsistent across platforms. Alternative tagging such as ^{<SMALL>TM</SMALL>} is recommended, at least until there is wider support for &trade (™) as standardized under HTML 4.0. (see Chapter 4).

HTML 4.0 Character Entities

The HTML 4.0 specification introduces a wide array of new character entities. These include additional Latin characters, the Greek alphabet, special spacing characters, arrows, technical symbols, and various shapes. Some of these entities have yet to be supported by browser vendors. Netscape 4.0 supports only a few of the extended

Latin characters and some entities that duplicate characters already available in the "standard" list (34 through 255). Microsoft has taken the lead in this area; Internet Explorer 4.0 supports many of these entities, including the Greek alphabet and mathematical symbols. These character entities expand the presentation possibilities of HTML, particularly in the presentation of foreign languages. Netscape's neglect of these tags is an unfortunate oversight that should be corrected as soon as possible.

Latin Extended-A

Named Entity	Browser Support	Numbered Entity	Browser Support	Intended Rendering	Description
&Oelig;	IE4	&#338;	IE4, N4	Œ	Uppercase ligature "OE"
&oelig;	IE4	&#339;	IE4, N4	œ	Lowercase ligature "oe"
&Scaron;	IE4	&#352;	IE4, N4	Š	Uppercase "S" with caron
&scaron;	IE4	&#353;	IE4, N4	š	Lowercase "s" with caron
&Yuml;	IE4	&#376;	IE4, N4	Ÿ	Uppercase "Y" with umlaut

Latin Extended-B

Named Entity	Browser Support	Numbered Entity	Browser Support	Intended Rendering	Description
&fnof;	IE4	&#402;	IE4, N4	ƒ	Latin small "f" with hook

Spacing Modifier Letters

Named Entity	Browser Support	Numbered Entity	Browser Support	Intended Rendering	Description
&circ;	IE4	&#710;	IE4, N4	^	Circumflex accent
&tilde;	IE4	&#732;	IE4, N4	~	Small tilde

General Punctuation

Named Entity	Browser Support	Numbered Entity	Browser Support	Intended Rendering	Description
	None		None		En space
	None		None		Em space
	None		None		Thin space
&zwnj;	IE4	&#8204;	IE4 (NT)	|	Zero width nonjoiner
&zwj;	IE4	&#8205;	IE4 (NT)	ⱦ	Zero width joiner
&lrm;	None	&#8206;	None	Unknown	Left-to-right mark
&rlm;	None	&#8207;	None	Unknown	Right-to-left mark
&ndash;	IE4	&#8211;	IE4, N4	–	En dash
&mdash;	IE4	&#8212;	IE4, N4	—	Em dash
&lsquo;	IE4	&#8216;	IE4, N4	'	Left single quotation mark
&rsquo;	IE4	&#8217;	IE4, N4	'	Right single quotation mark
&sbquo;	IE4	&#8218;	IE4, N4	,	Single low-9 quotation mark
&ldquo;	IE4	&#8220;	IE4, N4	"	Left double quotation mark
&rdquo;	IE4	&#8221;	IE4, N4	"	Right double quotation mark
&bdquo;	IE4	&#8222;	IE4, N4	„	Double low-9 quotation mark
&dagger;	IE4	&#8224;	IE4, N4	†	Dagger

Named Entity	Browser Support	Numbered Entity	Browser Support	Intended Rendering	Description
&Dagger;	IE4	&#8225;	IE4, N4	‡	Double dagger
&bull;	IE4	&#8226;	IE4, N4	•	Bullet
&hellip;	IE4	&#8230;	IE4, N4	…	Horizontal ellipsis
&permil;	IE4	&#8240;	IE4, N4	‰	Per thousand sign
&prime;	IE4 (NT)	&#8242;	IE4 (NT)	'	Prime, minutes, or feet
&Prime;	IE4 (NT)	&#8243;	IE4 (NT)	"	Double prime, seconds, or inches
&lsaquo;	IE4	&#8249;	IE4, N4	<	Single left-pointing angle quotation mark
&rsaquo;	IE4	&#8250;	IE4, N4	>	Single right-pointing angle quotation mark
&oline;	IE4 (NT)	&#8254;	IE4 (NT)	‾	Overline
&frasl;	IE4 (NT)	&#8260;	IE4 (NT)	/	Fraction slash

Greek

Note *Testing suggests that Internet Explorer support for this set of characters only works under Windows NT, not under Windows 95.*

Named Entity	Browser Support	Numbered Entity	Browser Support	Intended Rendering	Description
&Alpha;	IE4 (NT)	&#913;	IE4 (NT)	A	Greek capital letter alpha
&Beta;	IE4 (NT)	&#914;	IE4 (NT)	B	Greek capital letter beta
&Gamma;	IE4 (NT)	&#915;	IE4 (NT)	Γ	Greek capital letter gamma
&Delta;	IE4 (NT)	&#916;	IE4 (NT)	Δ	Greek capital letter delta
&Epsilon;	IE4 (NT)	&#917;	IE4 (NT)	E	Greek capital letter epsilon
&Zeta;	IE4 (NT)	&#918;	IE4 (NT)	Z	Greek capital letter zeta
&Eta;	IE4 (NT)	&#919;	IE4 (NT)	H	Greek capital letter eta
&Theta;	IE4 (NT)	&#920;	IE4 (NT)	Θ	Greek capital letter theta
&Iota;	IE4 (NT)	&#921;	IE4 (NT)	I	Greek capital letter iota
&Kappa;	IE4 (NT)	&#922;	IE4 (NT)	K	Greek capital letter kappa
&Lambda;	IE4 (NT)	&#923;	IE4 (NT)	Λ	Greek capital letter lambda
&Mu;	IE4 (NT)	&#924;	IE4 (NT)	M	Greek capital letter mu
&Nu;	IE4 (NT)	&#925;	IE4 (NT)	N	Greek capital letter nu
&Xi;	IE4 (NT)	&#926;	IE4 (NT)	Ξ	Greek capital letter xi

Named Entity	Browser Support	Numbered Entity	Browser Support	Intended Rendering	Description
&Omicron;	IE4 (NT)	&#927;	IE4 (NT)	O	Greek capital letter omicron
&Pi;	IE4 (NT)	&#928;	IE4 (NT)	Π	Greek capital letter pi
&Rho;	IE4 (NT)	&#929;	IE4 (NT)	P	Greek capital letter rho
&Sigma;	IE4 (NT)	&#931;	IE4 (NT)	Σ	Greek capital letter sigma
&Tau;	IE4 (NT)	&#932;	IE4 (NT)	T	Greek capital letter tau
&Upsilon;	IE4 (NT)	&#933;	IE4 (NT)	Y	Greek capital letter upsilon
&Phi;	IE4 (NT)	&#934;	IE4 (NT)	Φ	Greek capital letter phi
&Chi;	IE4 (NT)	&#935;	IE4 (NT)	X	Greek capital letter chi
&Psi;	IE4 (NT)	&#936;	IE4 (NT)	Ψ	Greek capital letter psi
&Omega;	IE4 (NT)	&#937;	IE4 (NT)	Ω	Greek capital letter omega
&alpha;	IE4 (NT)	&#945;	IE4 (NT)	α	Greek small letter alpha
&beta;	IE4 (NT)	&#946;	IE4 (NT)	β	Greek small letter beta
&gamma;	IE4 (NT)	&#947;	IE4 (NT)	γ	Greek small letter gamma
&delta;	IE4 (NT)	&#948;	IE4 (NT)	δ	Greek small letter delta
&epsilon;	IE4 (NT)	&#949;	IE4 (NT)	ε	Greek small letter epsilon
&zeta;	IE4 (NT)	&#950;	IE4 (NT)	ζ	Greek small letter zeta

SPECIAL CHARACTERS

Named Entity	Browser Support	Numbered Entity	Browser Support	Intended Rendering	Description
&eta;	IE4 (NT)	&#951;	IE4 (NT)	η	Greek small letter eta
&theta;	IE4 (NT)	&#952;	IE4 (NT)	θ	Greek small letter theta
&iota;	IE4 (NT)	&#953;	IE4 (NT)	ι	Greek small letter iota
&kappa;	IE4 (NT)	&#954;	IE4 (NT)	κ	Greek small letter kappa
&lambda;	IE4 (NT)	&#955;	IE4 (NT)	λ	Greek small letter lambda
&mu;	IE4 (NT)	&#956;	IE4 (NT)	μ	Greek small letter mu
&nu;	IE4 (NT)	&#957;	IE4 (NT)	ν	Greek small letter nu
&xi;	IE4 (NT)	&#958;	IE4 (NT)	ξ	Greek small letter xi
&omicron;	IE4 (NT)	&#959;	IE4 (NT)	o	Greek small letter omicron
&pi;	IE4 (NT)	&#960;	IE4 (NT)	π	Greek small letter pi
&rho;	IE4 (NT)	&#961;	IE4 (NT)	ρ	Greek small letter rho
&sigmaf;	IE4 (NT)	&#962;	IE4 (NT)	ς	Greek small letter final sigma
&sigma;	IE4 (NT)	&#963;	IE4 (NT)	σ	Greek small letter sigma
&tau;	IE4 (NT)	&#964;	IE4 (NT)	τ	Greek small letter tau
&upsilon;	IE4 (NT)	&#965;	IE4 (NT)	υ	Greek small letter upsilon
&phi;	IE4 (NT)	&#966;	IE4 (NT)	φ	Greek small letter phi

Named Entity	Browser Support	Numbered Entity	Browser Support	Intended Rendering	Description
&chi;	IE4 (NT)	&#967;	IE4 (NT)	χ	Greek small letter chi
&psi;	IE4 (NT)	&#968;	IE4 (NT)	ψ	Greek small letter psi
&omega;	IE4 (NT)	&#969;	IE4 (NT)	ω	Greek small letter omega
&thetasym;	None	&#977;	None	θ	Greek small letter theta symbol
&upsih;	None	&#978;	None	Not available	Greek upsilon with hook symbol
&piv	None	&#982;	None	Π	Greek pi symbol

Letter-like Symbols

Named Entity	Browser Support	Numbered Entity	Browser Support	Intended Rendering	Description
&weierp;	None	&#8472;	None	℘	Script capital P, power set
&image;	None	&#8465;	None	ℑ	Blackletter capital I, or imaginary part symbol
&real;	None	&#8476;	None	ℜ	Blackletter capital R, or real part symbol
&trade;	IE3, IE4	&#8482;	IE4, N4	™	Trademark symbol
&alefsym;	None	&#8501;	None	ℵ	Alef symbol, or first transfinite cardinal

Arrows

| Note | *Testing suggests that Internet Explorer support for this set of characters only works under Windows NT, not under Windows 95.* |

Named Entity	Browser Support	Numbered Entity	Browser Support	Intended Rendering	Description
&larr;	IE4 (NT)	&#8592;	IE4 (NT)	←	Leftward arrow
&uarr;	IE4 (NT)	&#8593;	IE4 (NT)	↑	Upward arrow
&rarr;	IE4 (NT)	&#8594;	IE4 (NT)	→	Rightward arrow
&darr;	IE4 (NT)	&#8595;	IE4 (NT)	↓	Downward arrow
&harr;	IE4 (NT)	&#8596;	IE4 (NT)	↔	Left-right arrow
&crarr;	None	&#8629;	None	↵	Downward arrow with corner leftward
&lArr;	None	&#8656;	None	⇐	Leftward double arrow
&uArr;	None	&#8657;	None	⇑	Upward double arrow
&rArr;	IE4 (NT)	&#8658;	IE4 (NT)	⇒	Rightward double arrow
&dArr;	None	&#8659;	None	⇓	Downward double arrow
&hArr;	IE4 (NT)	&#8660;	IE4 (NT)	⇔	Left-right double arrow

Mathematical Operators

Named Entity	Browser Support	Numbered Entity	Browser Support	Intended Rendering	Description
&forall;	IE4 (NT)	&#8704;	IE4 (NT)	∀	For all
&part;	IE4 (NT)	&#8706;	IE4 (NT)	∂	Partial differential

Named Entity	Browser Support	Numbered Entity	Browser Support	Intended Rendering	Description
&exist;	IE4 (NT)	&#8707;	IE4 (NT)	∃	There exists
&empty;	None	&#8709;	None	∅	Empty set, null set, diameter
&nabla;	IE4 (NT)	&#8711;	IE4 (NT)	∇	Nabla, or backward difference
&isin;	IE4 (NT)	&#8712;	IE4 (NT)	∈	Element of
&notin;	None	&#8713;	None	∉	Not an element of
&ni;	IE4 (NT)	&#8715;	IE4 (NT)	∋	Contains as member
&prod;	IE4 (NT)	&#8719;	IE4 (NT)	∏	N-ary product, or product sign
&sum;	IE4 (NT)	&#8721;	IE4 (NT)	Σ	N-ary summation
&minus;	IE4 (NT)	&#8722;	IE4 (NT)	−	Minus sign
&lowast;	None	&#8727;	None	∗	Asterisk operator
&radic;	IE4 (NT)	&#8730;	IE4 (NT)	√	Square root, radical sign
&prop;	IE4 (NT)	&#8733;	IE4 (NT)	∼	Proportional to
&infin;	IE4 (NT)	&#8734;	IE4 (NT)	∞	Infinity
&ang;	IE4 (NT)	&#8736;	IE4 (NT)	∠	Angle
&and;	IE4 (NT)	&#8869;	IE4 (NT)	∧	Logical and
&or;	IE4 (NT)	&#8870;	IE4 (NT)	∨	Logical or
&cap;	IE4 (NT)	&#8745;	IE4 (NT)	∩	Intersection, cap
&cup;	IE4 (NT)	&#8746;	IE4 (NT)	∪	Union, cup
&int;	IE4 (NT)	&#8747;	IE4 (NT)	∫	Integral

Named Entity	Browser Support	Numbered Entity	Browser Support	Intended Rendering	Description
&there4;	IE4 (NT)	&#8756;	IE4 (NT)	∴	Therefore
&sim;	None	&#8764;	None	~	Tilde operator
&cong;	None	&#8773;	None	≅	Approximately equal to
&asymp;	IE4 (NT)	&#8776;	IE4 (NT)	~	Almost equal to, asymptotic to
&ne;	IE4 (NT)	&#8800;	IE4 (NT)	≠	Not equal to
&equiv;	IE4 (NT)	&#8801;	IE4 (NT)	≡	Identical to
&le;	IE4 (NT)	&#8804;	IE4 (NT)	≤	Less than or equal to
&ge;	IE4 (NT)	&#8805;	IE4 (NT)	≥	Greater than or equal to
&sub;	IE4 (NT)	&#8834;	IE4 (NT)	⊂	Subset of
&sup;	IE4 (NT)	&#8835;	IE4 (NT)	⊃	Superset of
&nsub;	None	&#8836;	None	⊄	Not a subset of
&sube;	IE4 (NT)	&#8838;	IE4 (NT)	⊆	Subset of or equal to
&supe;	IE4 (NT)	&#8839;	IE4 (NT)	⊇	Superset of or equal to
&oplus;	None	&#8853;	None	⊕	Circled plus, direct sum
&otimes;	None	&#8855;	None	⊗	Circled times, vector product
&perp;	IE4 (NT)	&#8869;	IE4 (NT)	⊥	Perpendicular
&sdot;	None	&#8901;	None	⋅	Dot operator

Technical Symbols

Named Entity	Browser Support	Numbered Entity	Browser Support	Intended Rendering	Description
&lceil;	None	&#8968;	None	⌈	Left ceiling, apl upstile
&rceil;	None	&#8969;	None	⌉	Right ceiling

Named Entity	Browser Support	Numbered Entity	Browser Support	Intended Rendering	Description
&lfloor;	None	&#8970;	None	⌊	Left floor, apl downstile
&rfloor;	None	&#8971;	None	⌋	Right floor
&lang;	None	&#9001;	None	⟨	Left-pointing angle bracket
&rang;	None	&#9002;	None	⟩	Right-pointing angle bracket

Geometric Shapes

Named Entity	Browser Support	Numbered Entity	Browser Support	Intended Rendering	Description
&loz;	IE4 (NT)	&#9674;	IE4 (NT)	◊	Lozenge

Miscellaneous Symbols

Named Entity	Browser Support	Numbered Entity	Browser Support	Intended Rendering	Description
&spades;	IE4 (NT)	&#9824;	IE4 (NT)	♠	Black spade suit
&clubs;	IE4 (NT)	&#9827;	IE4 (NT)	♣	Black club suit
&hearts;	IE4 (NT)	&#9829;	IE4 (NT)	♥	Black heart suit
&diams;	IE4 (NT)	&#9830;	IE4 (NT)	♦	Black diamond suit

SPECIAL CHARACTERS

Appendix D

Fonts

This appendix lists fonts commonly available on most systems, as well as those that come with Internet Explorer. While other fonts may be available on users' systems, it is advisable to limit font choices to those most likely to be in use, or to provide these as alternative fonts (as discussed in Chapter 8) in case a preferred but uncommon font is not available.

Fonts for Microsoft Platforms and Browsers

The following fonts are available for Microsoft browsers and systems, and they are displayed in Figure D-1.

Font	Systems
Arial	Windows 95, Windows 3.1x, Windows NT 3.x
Arial Black	Internet Explorer 3
Arial Bold	Windows 95, Windows 3.1x, Windows NT 3.x
Arial Italic	Windows 95, Windows 3.1x, Windows NT 3.x
Arial Bold Italic	Windows 95, Windows 3.1x, Windows NT 3.x
Comic Sans MS	Internet Explorer 3, Internet Explorer 4
Comic Sans MS Bold	Internet Explorer 3
Courier New	Windows 95, Windows 3.1x, Windows NT 3.x
Courier New Bold	Windows 95, Windows 3.1x, Windows NT 3.x
Courier New Italic	Windows 95, Windows 3.1x, Windows NT 3.x
Courier New Bold Italic	Windows 95, Windows 3.1x, Windows NT 3.x
Impact	Internet Explorer 3
Lucida Sans Unicode	Windows NT 3.x (except NT 3.0)
Lucida Console	Windows NT 3.x (except NT 3.0)
Marlett	Windows 95
Symbol	Windows 95, Windows 3.1x, Windows NT 3.x
Times New Roman	Windows 95, Windows 3.1x, Windows NT 3.x
Times New Roman Bold	Windows 95, Windows 3.1x, Windows NT 3.x
Times New Roman Italic	Windows 95, Windows 3.1x, Windows NT 3.x
Times New Roman Bold Italic	Windows 95, Windows 3.1x, Windows NT 3.x
Verdana	Internet Explorer 3, Internet Explorer 4

Font	Systems
Verdana Bold	Internet Explorer 3, Internet Explorer 4
Verdana Italic	Internet Explorer 3, Internet Explorer 4
Verdana Bold Italic	Internet Explorer 3, Internet Explorer 4
Webdings	Internet Explorer 4.0
Wingdings	Windows 95, Windows 3.1x, Windows NT 3.x

Figure D-1. *Font families available for Microsoft browsers and systems*

Fonts for Apple Macintosh System 7

The following fonts are available for Macintosh System 7, and they are displayed in
Figure D-2.

Chicago
Courier Regular
Geneva
Helvetica
Monaco
New York
Palatino
Symbol
Times

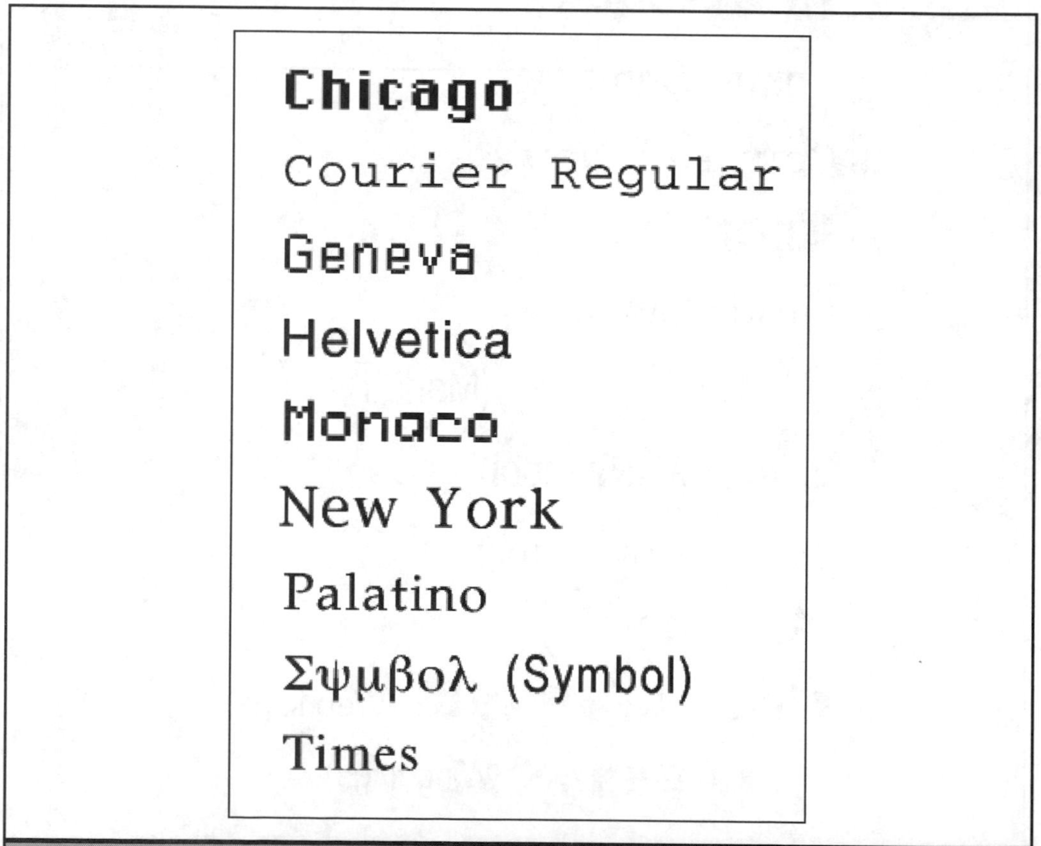

Figure D-2. *Font families available with Macintosh System 7*

Fonts for Unix Systems

The following fonts are available for Unix systems, and they are displayed in Figure D-3.

Charter
Clean
Courier
Fixed
Helvetica
Lucida
Lucida Bright
Lucidatypewriter
New Century Schoolbook
Symbol
Terminal
Times
Utopia

Charter
Clean
Courier
Fixed
Helvetica
Lucida
Lucidabright
New Century Schoolbook
Σψμβολ (Symbol)
Terminal
Times
Utopia

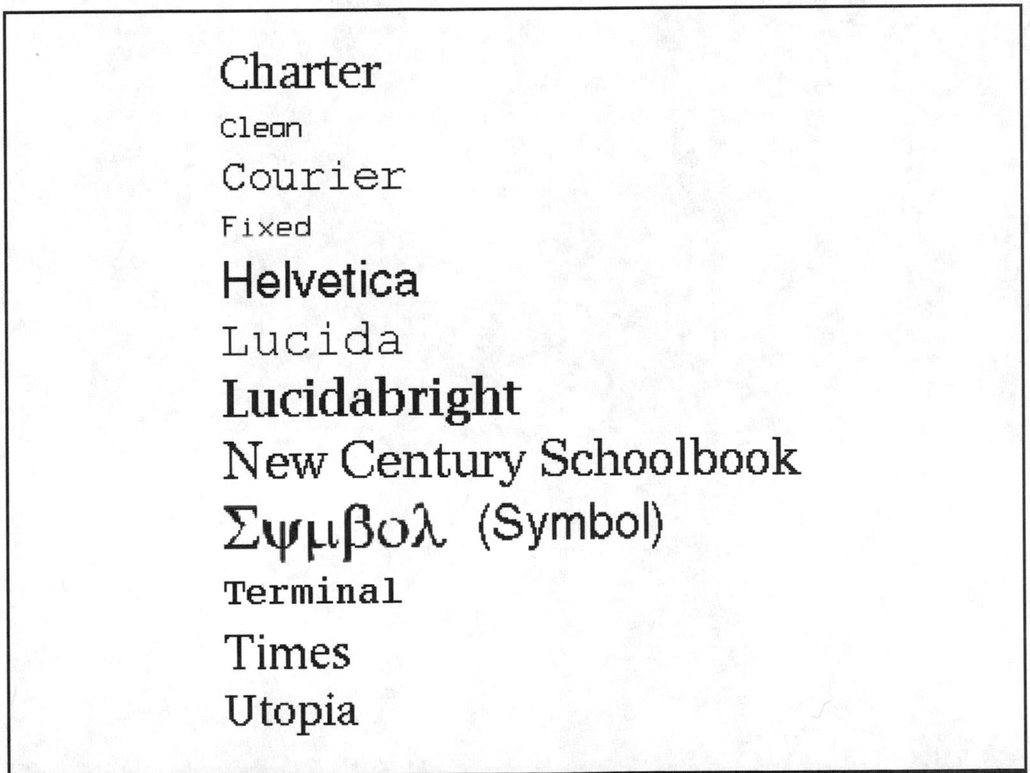

Figure D-3.   *Font families available on Unix systems*

The Complete Reference

Appendix E

Color Names and
Hexadecimal Codes

The following table lists all the color names commonly supported by the major browsers (Netscape 3.0 and better, Internet Explorer 3.0 and better, and WebTV). Sixteen colors (aqua, black, blue, fuchsia, gray, green, lime, maroon, navy, olive, purple, red, silver, teal, white, and yellow) were introduced by Microsoft; the rest were introduced by Netscape. The corresponding hexadecimal code is shown next to each color name. Thus, the code **<BODY BGCOLOR=lightsteelblue>** would produce the same result as **<BODY BGCOLOR="#B0C4DE">** under any browser that supported these color names. Color names are easier to remember than numerical codes, but may cause trouble when viewed under old or uncommon browsers. It is advisable to stick with the hexadecimal approach to colors, as it is generally safer. WebTV supports the color names but displays several colors (noted below) differently. General WebTV color support may also vary due to the differences between computer monitors and television screens.

Hexadecimal Code	Name	Notes
F0F8FF	aliceblue	The name "aliceblue" is not supported by Netscape.
FAEBD7	antiquewhite	
00FFFF	aqua	
7FFFD4	aquamarine	
F0FFFF	azure	
F5F5DC	beige	
FFE4C4	bisque	
000000	black	
FFEBCD	blanchedalmond	
0000FF	blue	
8A2BE2	blueviolet	WebTV displays "blueviolet" the same as "blue" (0000EE).
A52A2A	brown	
DEB887	burlywood	
5F9EA0	cadetblue	
7FFF00	chartreuse	
D2691E	chocolate	
FF7F50	coral	

Hexadecimal Code	Name	Notes
6495ED	cornflowerblue	
FFF8DC	cornsilk	
DC143C	crimson	
00FFFF	cyan	
00008B	darkblue	
008B8B	darkcyan	
B8860B	darkgoldenrod	
A9A9A9	darkgray	
006400	darkgreen	
BDB76B	darkkhaki	
8B008B	darkmagenta	
556B2F	darkolivegreen	
FF8C00	darkorange	
9932CC	darkorchid	
8B0000	darkred	
E9967A	darksalmon	
8FBC8F	darkseagreen	
483D8B	darkslateblue	
2F4F4F	darkslategray	
00CED1	darkturquoise	
9400D3	darkviolet	
FF1493	deeppink	
00BFFF	deepskyblue	
696969	dimgray	
1E90FF	dodgerblue	
B22222	firebrick	
FFFAF0	floralwhite	
228B22	forestgreen	
FF00FF	fuchsia	

Hexadecimal Code	Name	Notes
DCDCDC	gainsboro	
F8F8FF	ghostwhite	
FFD700	gold	
DAA520	goldenrod	WebTV displays "goldenrod" the same as "gold" (FFD700).
808080	gray	
008000	green	
ADFF2F	greenyellow	WebTV displays "greenyellow" the same as "green" (008000).
F0FFF0	honeydew	
FF69B4	hotpink	
CD5C5C	indianred	
4B0082	indigo	
FFFFF0	ivory	
F0E68C	khaki	
E6E6FA	lavender	
FFF0F5	lavenderblush	
7CFC00	lawngreen	
FFFACD	lemonchiffon	
ADD8E6	lightblue	
F08080	lightcoral	
E0FFFF	lightcyan	
FAFAD2	lightgoldenrodyellow	
90EE90	lightgreen	
D3D3D3	lightgrey	
FFB6C1	lightpink	
FFA07A	lightsalmon	
20B2AA	lightseagreen	

Hexadecimal Code	Name	Notes
87CEFA	lightskyblue	
778899	lightslategray	
B0C4DE	lightsteelblue	
FFFFE0	lightyellow	
00FF00	lime	
32CD32	limegreen	WebTV displays "limegreen" the same as "lime" (00FF00).
FAF0E6	linen	
FF00FF	magenta	
800000	maroon	
66CDAA	mediumaquamarine	
0000CD	mediumblue	
BA55D3	mediumorchid	
9370DB	mediumpurple	
3CB371	mediumseagreen	
7B68EE	mediumslateblue	
00FA9A	mediumspringgreen	According to the WebTV specification, WebTV supports "mediumspringgreen," but the name display does not match the numerical code display.
48D1CC	mediumturquoise	
C71585	mediumvioletred	
191970	midnightblue	
F5FFFA	mintcream	
FFE4E1	mistyrose	
FFE4B5	moccasin	
FFDEAD	navajowhite	

COLOR NAMES AND
HEXADECIMAL CODES

Hexadecimal Code	Name	Notes
000080	navy	
9FAFDF	navyblue	WebTV displays "navyblue" the same as "navy" (000080).
FDF5E6	oldlace	
808000	olive	
6B8E23	olivedrab	WebTV displays "olivedrab" the same as "olive" (808000).
FFA500	orange	
FF4500	orangered	WebTV displays "orangered" the same as "orange" (FFA500).
DA70D6	orchid	
EEE8AA	palegoldenrod	
98FB98	palegreen	
AFEEEE	paleturquoise	
DB7093	palevioletred	
FFEFD5	papayawhip	
FFDAB9	peachpuff	
CD853F	peru	
FFC0CB	pink	
DDA0DD	plum	
B0E0E6	powderblue	
800080	purple	
FF0000	red	
BC8F8F	rosybrown	
4169E1	royalblue	
8B4513	saddlebrown	
FA8072	salmon	
F4A460	sandybrown	

Hexadecimal Code	Name	Notes
2E8B57	seagreen	
FFF5EE	seashell	
A0522D	sienna	
C0C0C0	silver	
87CEEB	skyblue	
6A5ACD	slateblue	
708090	slategray	
FFFAFA	snow	
00FF7F	springgreen	
4682B4	steelblue	
D2B48C	tan	
008080	teal	
D8BFD8	thistle	
FF6347	tomato	
40E0D0	turquoise	
EE82EE	violet	
F5DEB3	wheat	
FFFFFF	white	
F5F5F5	whitesmoke	
FFFF00	yellow	
9ACD32	yellowgreen	WebTV displays "yellowgreen" the same as "yellow" (FFFF00).

Note *Many online color references claim that further color variations can be introduced by adding the numbers 1 through 4 to color names. If this were correct, cadetblue1, cadetblue2, cadetblue3, and cadetblue4 would display as different shades of the same color, with 1 being the lightest and 4 the darkest. Some of these references also claim that gray supports up to 100 color variations (gray10, gray 50, gray90, etc.). Testing reveals that this does not work under Netcape, Internet Explorer, or WebTV.*

Appendix F

Reading a Document Type Definition

HTML dialects are defined using SGML, a complex language with many nuances. This appendix presents the Document Type Definitions (DTDs) for HTML 4.0. Fortunately, only a small amount of SGML needs to be understood to read the HTML DTDs. Before turning to the DTDs, this appendix examines how to read them.

Element Type Declarations

Two common types of declarations should be familiar to HTML authors: element type declarations and attribute list declarations. Beyond these, the less familiar declarations for general and parameter entities are not very complicated.

An *element type declaration* defines three characteristics:

- The element type's name, also known as its *generic identifier*

- Whether or not start and end tags are required, forbidden (end tags on empty elements), or may be omitted

- The element type's *content model,* or what content it can enclose

All element type declarations begin with the keyword **ELEMENT** and have the following form.

```
<!ELEMENT name minimization content_model >
```

The declaration for the HTML 2.0 **
** element type gives a simple example:

```
<!ELEMENT BR - O EMPTY>
```

Tag minimization is declared by two parameters that indicate the start and end tags. These parameters may take one of two values. A hyphen indicates the tag is required. An uppercase "O" indicates it may be omitted. The combination of "O" for the end tag and the content model EMPTY means the end tag is forbidden. Thus, the **
** tag requires a start tag but not an end tag. Since the **
** tag does not contain any content, its content model is defined by the keyword **EMPTY**.

Most HTML elements enclose content. If a content model is declared, it is enclosed within parentheses and known as a *model group*. The HTML 4.0 declaration for a selection list option gives an example:

```
<!ELEMENT OPTION - O (#PCDATA)*>
```

Note that the model group contains the keyword **#PCDATA**. This stands for *parsed character data,* character content that contains no element markup but that may contain entity symbols for special characters.

Occurrence Indicators

In the previous example, also note the asterisk appended to the model group. This is an *occurrence indicator,* a special symbol that qualifies the element type or model group to which it is appended, indicating how many times it may occur. There are three occurrence indicators:

- **?** means optional and at most one occurrence (zero or one occurrence)
- ***** means optional and any number of occurrences (zero or more occurrences)
- **+** means at least one occurrence required (one or more occurrences)

Thus, the content model in the previous declaration says that the **<OPTION>** element may contain any amount of character content, including none.

Content models can also define an element type as containing element content, illustrated by the HTML 2.0 declaration for a definition list (**<DL>**):

```
<!ELEMENT DL - - (DT | DL)+>
```

Logical Connectors

Note that the model group contains **DT** and **DL**, the names of element types that a **<DL>** element may enclose. Note also the vertical bar separating **DT** and **DL**. This is a *logical connector,* a special symbol indicating how the content units it connects relate to each other. There are three logical connectors:

- **|** means "or" (one and only one of the connected content units must occur)
- **&** means "and" (all of the connected content units must occur)
- **,** means "sequence" (the connected content units must occur in the specified order)

Thus, the content model in the previous declaration says that the **<DL>** element must contain either a **<DT>** or **<DL>** element and may contain any additional number of **<DT>** or **<DL>** elements.

Model groups can be nested inside other model groups. Very flexible content models can be declared by combining this with the ability to qualify content units with

occurrence indicators and logical operators. The HTML 4.0 declaration for the
<TABLE> element type illustrates this point:

```
<!ELEMENT TABLE - - (CAPTION?, ((COL*|COLGROUP*),
        THEAD?, TFOOT?, TBODY+), CAPTION?)>
```

The content model for the **<TABLE>** element type reads as follows:

1. Table content begins with zero or one **<CAPTION>** element.
2. This must be followed by a content group.
3. The content group must contain zero or more **<COL>** elements or zero or more **<COLGROUP>** elements.
4. This must be followed by zero or one **<THEAD>** element.
5. This must be followed by zero or one **<TFOOT>** element.
6. This must be followed by one or more **<TBODY>** elements.
7. The content ends with zero or one **<CAPTION>** element.

Content Exclusion

Occasionally the need arises to declare that an element type cannot contain certain
other element types. This is known as a *content exclusion*. The excluded tags follow the
model group, enclosed by parentheses and preceded by the minus sign:

```
(model group) -(excluded tags)
```

Content Inclusion

A related special need is the ability to declare that an element type can occur anywhere
inside a content model. This is known as a *content inclusion*. The included tags follow
the model group, enclosed by parentheses and preceded by the plus sign:

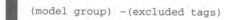

```
(model group) +(included tags)
```

The HTML 4.0 declaration for the **<BODY>** element type illustrates both excluded
and included elements:

```
<!ELEMENT BODY O O (%block;) -(BODY) +(INS|DEL)>
```

Why are insertions and deletions used in this declaration? The content inclusion says that the **<INS>** and **<DEL>** elements can occur anywhere in **<BODY>** content. Pragmatically, **<INS>** and **<DEL>** are used to indicate modifications, any inserted or deleted **<BODY>** content. They need to be freed from the normal structural constraints imposed on other **<BODY>** elements.

The content exclusion says that a **<BODY>** element cannot contain another **<BODY>** element. This is necessary because of the curious "**%block**" declaration used in the model group. The leading % character identifies this as a *parameter entity*, essentially a macro symbol that refers to a longer character string declared elsewhere in the DTD. Parameter entities, which commonly occur in HTML DTDs, will be discussed shortly (see "Parameter Entities"). The "**%block**" entity reference is a shorthand way of referring to all block element types that happen to include **<BODY>**. It is easier to exclude **<BODY>** from the list of block elements than to define a special purpose declaration.

Attribute Declarations

All attribute declarations begin with the keyword **ATTLIST** followed by name of the element type they are associated with. Following this are declarations for one or more individual attributes. Each of these has three parts:

- The attribute's name
- The attribute's value type
- The attribute's default

```
<!ATTLIST  element-type
    name1  type1  default1
    ...
    nameN  typeN  defaultN
>
```

The HTML 4.0 **<BDO>** element type illustrates a small attribute declaration:

```
<!ATTLIST   BDO
    lang  NAME     #IMPLIED
    dir   (ltr|rtl) #REQUIRED
>
```

SGML Keywords

This example declares the **lang** attribute as having values of type **NAME**, an alphabetic string. **NAME** is one of several SGML keywords occurring in HTML declarations to declare an attribute's type:

- **CDATA** Unparsed character data
- **ID** A document-wide unique identifier
- **IDREF** A reference to a document-wide identifier
- **NAME** An alphabetic character string plus a hyphen and a period
- **NMTOKEN** An alphanumeric character string plus a hypen and a period
- **NUMBER** A character string containing decimal numbers

The **dir** attribute does not declare its type using a keyword. Instead, the type is specified using an enumerated list containing two possible values, **ltr** and **rtl**.

In the example, the attribute's default behavior is specified with a keyword. A default value may be specified using a quoted string.

- **#REQUIRED** A value must be supplied for the attribute.
- **#IMPLIED** The attribute is optional.
- **#FIXED** The attribute has a fixed value that is declared in quotes using an additional parameter. Because the attribute/value pair is assumed to be constant, it does not need to be used in the document instance.

Parameter Entities

An entity is essentially a macro that allows a short name to be associated with replacement text. Parameter entities define replacement text used in DTD declarations. Syntactically, a parameter entity is distinguished by using the percent (%) symbol. Its general form is shown here:

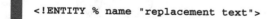

```
<!ENTITY % name "replacement text">
```

It is used in DTDs as follows:

```
%name;
```

Parameter entities are a convenient way to define commonly occurring pieces of a DTD so that changes only need to be made in one place. HTML 4.0 uses a parameter entity to define the core attributes common to most elements.

```
<!ENTITY % coreattrs
   "id           ID           #IMPLIED
    class        CDATA        #IMPLIED
    style        CDATA        #IMPLIED
    title        CDATA        #IMPLIED "
 >
```

These attributes could be added to an attribute list declaration as follows:

```
<!ATTLIST some-element  %coreattrs;>
```

In fact, HTML 4.0 also uses the **coreattrs** parameter entity in a different way. Parameter entities can be used inside other parameter entity declarations. The **coreattrs** parameter entity is used with the i18n and events parameter entities to define the expansion text for an aggregate entity called **attrs**.

```
<!ENTITY % attrs "%coreattrs %i18n %events">
```

General Entities

While parameter entities are used to manipulate syntax in DTD declarations, general entities are used to associate symbols with replacement text for use in actual documents. General entities have a versatile syntax. One type is familiar to many HTML authors: the character entity used for special symbols. For example, HTML authors needing to use the ampersand character (&) use the **&** entity. It is declared as follows:

```
<!ENTITY amp CDATA "&#38;">
```

The **ENTITY** keyword without the % character identifies this as a general entity. The name of the entity is **amp**. The entity type is indicated by the **CDATA** keyword, for *character data*. This is followed by the replacement text.

Comments

DTDs contain the type of comments familiar to HTML authors:

```
<!- - this is a comment - ->
```

Comments may also be embedded inside HTML declarations for explanatory purposes. Embedded comments are delimited by two dashes, and a single declaration may contain many embedded comments:

```
<!ATTLIST PARAM
  name      CDATA              #REQUIRED -- property name --
  value     CDATA              #IMPLIED  -- property value --
  valuetype (DATA|REF|OBJECT) DATA -- How to interpret value --
  type      CDATA              #IMPLIED  -- Internet media type --
  >
```

Marked Section Declaration

Some HTML DTDs use a special SGML construct to allow them to optionally include or exclude certain declarations from a DTD, such as those supporting deprecated tags. An SGML *marked section declaration* uses keywords to indicate that the content it encloses should be treated in a special way. HTML DTDs use parameter entities to assign the **INCLUDE** and **IGNORE** keywords to marked section declarations. This causes the declarations enclosed by the sections to be included or ignored, respectively.

```
<! [keyword [
affected declarations
]]>

<!ENTITY % HTML.Deprecated "IGNORE">

<! [ %HTML.Deprecated [
affected declarations
]]>
```

The rest of this appendix presents the Document Type Definitions for HTML 4.0, starting with the transitional DTD, which is recommended. This is followed by the strict definition, which removes the presentational elements from HTML. The latest versions of these DTDs can be retrieved from the W3C (www.w3.org), as can the DTDs for HTML 2.0 (www.w3.org/MarkUp/html-spec/html.dtd) and HTML 3.2 (www.w3.org/TR/REC-html32#dtd).

HTML 4.0 Transitional DTD

```
<!--
    This is an EXPERIMENTAL version of the HTML 4.0 "transitional"
    DTD which includes presentation attributes and elements that
    W3C expects to phase out as support for style sheets matures.
    HTML 4.0 includes mechanisms for style sheets, scripting,
    embedding objects, improved support for right to left and mixed
    direction text, and enhancements to forms for improved
    accessibility for people with disabilities.

        Draft: $Date: 1997/11/07 15:32:37 $

        Authors:
            Dave Raggett <dsr@w3.org>
            Arnaud Le Hors <lehors@w3.org>

    This is work in progress, subject to change at any time.
    It does not imply endorsement by, or the consensus of,
    either W3C or members of the HTML working group. Further
    information about HTML 4.0 is available at:

        http://www.w3.org/TR/PR-html40
-->
<!ENTITY % HTML.Version "-//W3C//DTD HTML 4.0 Transitional//EN"
    -- Typical usage:

    <!DOCTYPE HTML PUBLIC "-//W3C//DTD HTML 4.0 Transitional//EN"
            "http://www.w3.org/TR/PR-html40/loose.dtd">
    <html>
    <head>
    ...
    </head>
    <body>
    ...
    </body>
    </html>

    The URL used as a system identifier with the public identifier allows
    the user agent to download the DTD and entity sets as needed.

    The FPI for the strict HTML 4.0 DTD is:

        "-//W3C//DTD HTML 4.0//EN"

    and its URL is:
```

```
       http://www.w3.org/TR/PR-html40/strict.dtd
```

Authors should use the strict DTD unless they need the
presentation control for user agents that don't (adequately)
support style sheets.

If you are writing a frameset document you should use the
following FPI:

```
    "-//W3C//DTD HTML 4.0 Frameset//EN"
```

with the URL:

```
       http://www.w3.org/TR/PR-html40/frameset.dtd
```

The following URLs are supported in relation to HTML 4.0

```
"http://www.w3.org/TR/PR-html40/strict.dtd" (Strict DTD)
"http://www.w3.org/TR/PR-html40/loose.dtd" (Loose DTD)
"http://www.w3.org/TR/PR-html40/frameset.dtd" (Frameset DTD)
"http://www.w3.org/TR/PR-html40/HTMLlat1.ent" (Latin-1 entities)
"http://www.w3.org/TR/PR-html40/HTMLsymbol.ent" (Symbol entities)
"http://www.w3.org/TR/PR-html40/HTMLspecial.ent" (Special entities)
```

These URLs point to the latest version of each file. To reference
this specific revision use the following URLs:

```
"http://www.w3.org/TR/PR-html40-971107/strict.dtd"
"http://www.w3.org/TR/PR-html40-971107/loose.dtd"
"http://www.w3.org/TR/PR-html40-971107/frameset.dtd"
"http://www.w3.org/TR/PR-html40-971107/HTMLlat1.ent"
"http://www.w3.org/TR/PR-html40-971107/HTMLsymbol.ent"
"http://www.w3.org/TR/PR-html40-971107/HTMLspecial.ent"
```

```
-->

<!--=================== Imported Names =====================================-->

<!ENTITY % ContentType "CDATA"
    -- media type, as per [RFC2045]
    -->

<!ENTITY % ContentTypes "CDATA"
    -- comma-separated list of media types, as per [RFC2045]
    -->
```

```
<!ENTITY % Charset "CDATA"
    -- a character encoding, as per [RFC2045]
    -->

<!ENTITY % Charsets "CDATA"
    -- a space separated list of character encodings, as per [RFC2045]
    -->

<!ENTITY % LanguageCode "NAME"
    -- a language code, as per [RFC1766]
    -->

<!ENTITY % Character "CDATA"
    -- a single character from [ISO10646]
    -->

<!ENTITY % LinkTypes "CDATA"
    -- space-separated list of link types
    -->

<!ENTITY % MediaDesc "CDATA"
    -- single or comma-separated list of media descriptors
    -->

<!ENTITY % URL "CDATA"
    -- a Uniform Resource Locator,
       see [RFC1808] and [RFC1738]
    -->

<!ENTITY % Datetime "CDATA" -- date and time information. ISO date format -->


<!ENTITY % Script "CDATA" -- script expression -->

<!ENTITY % FrameTarget "CDATA" -- render in this frame -->


<!ENTITY % Text "CDATA" -- render in this frame -->


<!-- Parameter Entities -->

<!ENTITY % head.misc "SCRIPT|STYLE|META|LINK" -- repeatable head elements -->

<!ENTITY % heading "H1|H2|H3|H4|H5|H6">
```

```
<!ENTITY % list "UL | OL | DIR | MENU">

<!ENTITY % preformatted "PRE">

<!ENTITY % Color "CDATA" -- a color using sRGB: #RRGGBB as Hex values -->

<!-- There are also 16 widely known color names with their sRGB values:

    Black   = #000000    Green  = #008000
    Silver  = #C0C0C0    Lime   = #00FF00
    Gray    = #808080    Olive  = #808000
    White   = #FFFFFF    Yellow = #FFFF00
    Maroon  = #800000    Navy   = #000080
    Red     = #FF0000    Blue   = #0000FF
    Purple  = #800080    Teal   = #008080
    Fuchsia= #FF00FF    Aqua   = #00FFFF
 -->


<!ENTITY % bodycolors "
  bgcolor %Color;    #IMPLIED      -- document background color --
  text    %Color;    #IMPLIED      -- document text color --
  link    %Color;    #IMPLIED      -- color of links --
  vlink   %Color;    #IMPLIED      -- color of visited links --
  alink   %Color;    #IMPLIED      -- color of selected links --
  ">

<!--=============== Character mnemonic entities =========================-->

<!ENTITY % HTMLlat1 PUBLIC
   "-//W3C//ENTITIES Latin1//EN//HTML"
   "http://www.w3.org/TR/PR-html40/HTMLlat1.ent">
%HTMLlat1;


<!ENTITY % HTMLsymbol PUBLIC
   "-//W3C//ENTITIES Symbols//EN//HTML"
   "http://www.w3.org/TR/PR-html40/HTMLsymbol.ent">
%HTMLsymbol;


<!ENTITY % HTMLspecial PUBLIC
   "-//W3C//ENTITIES Special//EN//HTML"
   "http://www.w3.org/TR/PR-html40/HTMLspecial.ent">
%HTMLspecial;
<!--=================== Generic Attributes ===============================-->

<!ENTITY % coreattrs
 "id          ID         #IMPLIED  -- document-wide unique id --
  class       CDATA      #IMPLIED  -- space separated list of classes --
```

```
    style        CDATA        #IMPLIED   -- associated style info --
    title        %Text;       #IMPLIED   -- advisory title/amplification --"
    >

<!ENTITY % i18n
  "lang       %LanguageCode; #IMPLIED   -- language code --
   dir          (ltr|rtl)    #IMPLIED   -- direction for weak/neutral text --"
   >

<!ENTITY % events
  "onclick       %Script;     #IMPLIED   -- a pointer button was clicked --
   ondblclick    %Script;      #IMPLIED   -- a pointer button was double clicked
--
   onmousedown  %Script;     #IMPLIED   -- a pointer button was pressed down --
   onmouseup    %Script;     #IMPLIED   -- a pointer button was released --
   onmouseover  %Script;     #IMPLIED   -- a pointer was moved onto --
   onmousemove  %Script;     #IMPLIED   -- a pointer was moved within --
   onmouseout   %Script;     #IMPLIED   -- a pointer was moved away --
   onkeypress   %Script;     #IMPLIED   -- a key was pressed and released --
   onkeydown    %Script;     #IMPLIED   -- a key was pressed down --
   onkeyup      %Script;     #IMPLIED   -- a key was released --"
   >

<!-- Reserved Feature Switch -->
<!ENTITY % HTML.Reserved "IGNORE">

<!-- The following attributes are reserved for possible future use -->
<![ %HTML.Reserved; [
<!ENTITY % reserved
  "datasrc       %URL;        #IMPLIED   -- a single or tabular Data Source --
   datafld       CDATA        #IMPLIED   -- the property or column name --
   dataformatas (plaintext|html) plaintext -- text or html --"
   >
]]>

<!ENTITY % reserved "">

<!ENTITY % attrs "%coreattrs; %i18n; %events;">

<!ENTITY % align "align (left|center|right|justify)  #IMPLIED"
                 -- default is left for ltr paragraphs, right for rtl --
   >
```

```
<!--==================== Text Markup =======================================-->

<!ENTITY % fontstyle
 "TT | I | B | U | S | STRIKE | BIG | SMALL">

<!ENTITY % phrase "EM | STRONG | DFN | CODE |
                   SAMP | KBD | VAR | CITE | ABBR">

<!ENTITY % special
   "A | IMG | APPLET | OBJECT | FONT | BASEFONT | BR | SCRIPT |
    MAP | Q | SUB | SUP | SPAN | BDO | IFRAME">

<!ENTITY % formctrl "INPUT | SELECT | TEXTAREA | LABEL | BUTTON">

<!-- %inline; covers inline or "text-level" elements -->
<!ENTITY % inline "#PCDATA | %fontstyle; | %phrase; | %special; |
%formctrl;">

<!ELEMENT (%fontstyle;|%phrase;) - - (%inline;)*>
<!ATTLIST (%fontstyle;|%phrase;)
  %attrs;                          -- %coreattrs, %i18n, %events --
  >

<!ELEMENT (SUB|SUP) - - (%inline;)* -- subscript, superscript -->
<!ATTLIST (SUB|SUP)
  %attrs;                          -- %coreattrs, %i18n, %events --
  >

<!ELEMENT SPAN - - (%inline;)*     -- generic language/style container -->
<!ATTLIST SPAN
  %attrs;                          -- %coreattrs, %i18n, %events --
  charset     %Charset;   #IMPLIED -- char encoding of linked resource --
  type        %ContentType; #IMPLIED -- advisory content type --
  href        %URL;       #IMPLIED -- URL for linked resource --
  hreflang %LanguageCode; #IMPLIED -- language code --
  target      %FrameTarget; #IMPLIED -- render in this frame --
  rel         %LinkTypes; #IMPLIED -- forward link types --
  rev         %LinkTypes; #IMPLIED -- reverse link types --
  media       %MediaDesc; #IMPLIED -- for rendering on these media --
  %reserved;                       -- reserved for possible future use --
  >

<!ELEMENT BDO - - (%inline;)*     -- I18N BiDi over-ride -->
<!ATTLIST BDO
  %coreattrs;                       -- id, class, style, title --
  lang        %LanguageCode; #IMPLIED  -- language code --
```

```
    dir          (ltr|rtl)  #REQUIRED -- directionality --
    >

<!ELEMENT BASEFONT - O EMPTY -- base font size -->
<!ATTLIST BASEFONT
    id           ID          #IMPLIED  -- document-wide unique id --
    size         CDATA       #REQUIRED -- base font size for FONT elements --
    color        %Color;     #IMPLIED  -- "#RRGGBB" in hex, e.g. red: "#FF0000"
--
    face         CDATA       #IMPLIED  -- comma separated list of font names --
    >

<!ELEMENT FONT - - (%inline;)*  -- local change to font -->
<!ATTLIST FONT
    %coreattrs;                         -- id, class, style, title --
    %i18n;                              -- lang, dir --
    size         CDATA       #IMPLIED  -- [+|-]nn e.g. size="+1", size="4" --
    color        %Color;     #IMPLIED  -- "#RRGGBB" in hex, e.g. red: "#FF0000" --
    face         CDATA       #IMPLIED  -- comma separated list of font names --
    >

<!ELEMENT BR - O EMPTY          -- forced line break -->
<!ATTLIST BR
    %coreattrs;                         -- id, class, style, title --
    clear (left|all|right|none) none -- control of text flow --
    >

<!--================= HTML content models =================================-->

<!--
    HTML has two basic content models:

        %inline;    character level elements and text strings
        %block;     block-like elements e.g. paragraphs and lists
-->

<!ENTITY % block
    "P | %heading; | %list; | %preformatted; | DL | DIV | CENTER |
     NOSCRIPT | NOFRAMES | BLOCKQUOTE | FORM | ISINDEX | HR |
     TABLE | FIELDSET | ADDRESS">

<!ENTITY % flow "%block; | %inline;">

<!--================= Document Body =======================================-->

<!ELEMENT BODY O O (%flow;)* +(INS|DEL) -- document body -->
<!ATTLIST BODY
```

```
   %attrs;                              -- %coreattrs, %i18n, %events --
   background  %URL;       #IMPLIED  -- texture tile for document background
--
   %bodycolors;                         -- bgcolor, text, link, vlink, alink --
   onload      %Script;   #IMPLIED  -- the document has been loaded --
   onunload    %Script;   #IMPLIED  -- the document has been removed --
   >

<!ELEMENT ADDRESS - - ((%inline;) | P)* -- information on author -->
<!ATTLIST ADDRESS
   %attrs;                              -- %coreattrs, %i18n, %events --
   >

<!ELEMENT DIV - - (%flow;)* -- generic language/style container -->
<!ATTLIST DIV
   %attrs;                              -- %coreattrs, %i18n, %events --
   charset     %Charset;   #IMPLIED -- char encoding of linked resource --
   type        %ContentType; #IMPLIED -- advisory content type --
   href        %URL;       #IMPLIED -- URL for linked resource --
   hreflang %LanguageCode; #IMPLIED -- language code --
   target      %FrameTarget; #IMPLIED -- render in this frame --
   rel         %LinkTypes; #IMPLIED -- forward link types --
   rev         %LinkTypes; #IMPLIED -- reverse link types --
   media       %MediaDesc; #IMPLIED -- for rendering on these media --
   %align;                              -- align, text alignment --

   %reserved;                           -- reserved for possible future use --
   >

<!ELEMENT CENTER - - (%flow;)* -- shorthand for DIV with align=center -->
<!ATTLIST CENTER
   %attrs;                              -- %coreattrs, %i18n, %events --
   >

<!--================== The Anchor Element ==================================-->

<!ENTITY % Shape "(rect|circle|poly|default)">
<!ENTITY % Coords "CDATA" -- comma separated list of numbers -->

<!ELEMENT A - - (%inline;)* -(A) -- anchor -->
<!ATTLIST A
   %attrs;                              -- %coreattrs, %i18n, %events --
   charset     %Charset;   #IMPLIED -- char encoding of linked resource --
   type        %ContentType; #IMPLIED -- advisory content type --
   name        CDATA       #IMPLIED -- named link end --
   href        %URL;       #IMPLIED -- URL for linked resource --
   hreflang %LanguageCode; #IMPLIED -- language code --
```

```
    target    %FrameTarget;  #IMPLIED -- render in this frame --
    rel          %LinkTypes;  #IMPLIED -- forward link types --
    rev          %LinkTypes;  #IMPLIED -- reverse link types --
    accesskey    %Character;  #IMPLIED -- accessibility key character --
    shape        %Shape;      rect     -- for use with OBJECT SHAPES --
    coords       %Coords;     #IMPLIED -- for use with OBJECT SHAPES --
    tabindex     NUMBER       #IMPLIED -- position in tabbing order --
    onfocus      %Script;     #IMPLIED -- the element got the focus --
    onblur       %Script;     #IMPLIED -- the element lost the focus --
    >

<!--================= Client-side image maps =============================-->

<!-- These can be placed in the same document or grouped in a
     separate document although this isn't yet widely supported -->

<!ELEMENT MAP - - (AREA)+ -- client-side image map -->
<!ATTLIST MAP
    %attrs;                              -- %coreattrs, %i18n, %events --
    name        CDATA      #REQUIRED  -- name of image map for refs by usemap
--
    >

<!ELEMENT AREA - O EMPTY -- client-side image map area -->
<!ATTLIST AREA
    %attrs;                              -- %coreattrs, %i18n, %events --
    shape        %Shape;     rect      -- controls interpretation of coords --
    coords       %Coords;    #IMPLIED  -- comma separated list of lengths --
    href         %URL;       #IMPLIED  -- URL for linked resource --
    target    %FrameTarget;   #IMPLIED -- render in this frame --
    nohref       (nohref)    #IMPLIED  -- this region has no action --
    alt          %Text;      #REQUIRED -- short description --
    tabindex     NUMBER      #IMPLIED  -- position in tabbing order --
    accesskey    %Character; #IMPLIED  -- accessibility key character --
    onfocus      %Script;    #IMPLIED  -- the element got the focus --
    onblur       %Script;    #IMPLIED  -- the element lost the focus --
    >

<!--================= The LINK Element ===================================-->

<!--
  Relationship values can be used in principle:

     a) for document specific toolbars/menus when used
        with the LINK element in document head e.g.
          start, contents, previous, next, index, end, help
     b) to link to a separate style sheet (rel=stylesheet)
```

```
    c) to make a link to a script (rel=script)
    d) by stylesheets to control how collections of
       html nodes are rendered into printed documents
    e) to make a link to a printable version of this document
       e.g. a postscript or pdf version (rel=alternate media=print)
-->

<!ELEMENT LINK - O EMPTY -- a media-independent link -->
<!ATTLIST LINK
  %attrs;                          -- %coreattrs, %i18n, %events --
  charset    %Charset;    #IMPLIED -- char encoding of linked resource --
  href       %URL;        #IMPLIED -- URL for linked resource --
  hreflang   %LanguageCode; #IMPLIED -- language code --
  type       %ContentType; #IMPLIED -- advisory content type --
  rel        %LinkTypes;  #IMPLIED -- forward link types --
  rev        %LinkTypes;  #IMPLIED -- reverse link types --
  media      %MediaDesc;  #IMPLIED -- for rendering on these media --
  target     %FrameTarget; #IMPLIED -- render in this frame --
  >


<!--==================== Images ====================================-->

<!-- Length defined in strict DTD for cellpadding/cellspacing -->
<!ENTITY % Length "CDATA" -- nn for pixels or nn% for percentage length -->
<!ENTITY % MultiLength "CDATA" -- pixel, percentage, or relative -->

<!ENTITY % MultiLengths "CDATA" -- comma-separated list of MultiLength -->

<!ENTITY % Pixels "CDATA" -- integer representing length in pixels -->

<!ENTITY % IAlign "(top|middle|bottom|left|right)"  -- center? -->

<!-- To avoid problems with text-only UAs as well as
     to make image content understandable and navigable
     to users of non-visual UAs, you need to provide
     a description with ALT, and avoid server-side image maps -->
<!ELEMENT IMG - O EMPTY          -- Embedded image -->
<!ATTLIST IMG
  %attrs;                          -- %coreattrs, %i18n, %events --
  src        %URL;        #REQUIRED -- URL of image to embed --
  alt        %Text;       #REQUIRED -- short description --
  longdesc   %URL;        #IMPLIED -- link to long description (complements alt) --
  height     %Length;     #IMPLIED -- override height --
  width      %Length;     #IMPLIED -- override width --
  align      %IAlign;     #IMPLIED -- vertical or horizontal alignment --
  border     %Length;     #IMPLIED -- link border width --
```

```
    hspace      %Pixels;    #IMPLIED  -- horizontal gutter --
    vspace      %Pixels;    #IMPLIED  -- vertical gutter --
    usemap      %URL;       #IMPLIED  -- use client-side image map --
    ismap       (ismap)     #IMPLIED  -- use server-side image map --
    >

<!-- USEMAP points to a MAP element which may be in this document
  or an external document, although the latter is not widely supported -->


<!--==================== OBJECT =======================================-->
<!--
  OBJECT is used to embed objects as part of HTML pages
  PARAM elements should precede other content. SGML mixed content
  model technicality precludes specifying this formally ...
-->

<!ELEMENT OBJECT - - (PARAM | %flow;)*
  -- generic embedded object -->
<!ATTLIST OBJECT
  %attrs;                              -- %coreattrs, %i18n, %events --
  declare     (declare) #IMPLIED  -- declare but don't instantiate flag --
  classid     %URL;     #IMPLIED  -- identifies an implementation --
  codebase    %URL;     #IMPLIED  -- base URL for classid, data, archive --
  data        %URL;     #IMPLIED  -- reference to object's data --
  type        %ContentType; #IMPLIED  -- content type for data --
  codetype    %ContentType; #IMPLIED  -- content type for code --
  archive     %URL;     #IMPLIED  -- space separated archive list --
  standby     %Text;    #IMPLIED  -- message to show while loading --
  height      %Length;  #IMPLIED  -- override height --
  width       %Length;  #IMPLIED  -- override width --
  align       %IAlign;  #IMPLIED  -- vertical or horizontal alignment --
  border      %Length;  #IMPLIED  -- link border width --
  hspace      %Pixels;  #IMPLIED  -- horizontal gutter --
  vspace      %Pixels;  #IMPLIED  -- vertical gutter --
  usemap      %URL;     #IMPLIED  -- use client-side image map --
  shapes      (shapes)  #IMPLIED  -- object has shaped hypertext links --
  export      (export)  #IMPLIED  -- export shapes to parent  --
  name        CDATA     #IMPLIED  -- submit as part of form --
  tabindex    NUMBER    #IMPLIED  -- position in tabbing order --
  %reserved;                       -- reserved for possible future use --
    >

<!ELEMENT PARAM - O EMPTY            -- named property value -->
<!ATTLIST PARAM
  id          ID        #IMPLIED  -- document-wide unique id --
  name        CDATA     #REQUIRED -- property name --
  value       CDATA     #IMPLIED  -- property value --
```

```
    valuetype (DATA|REF|OBJECT) DATA -- How to interpret value --
    type      %ContentType; #IMPLIED -- content type for value
                                         when valuetype=ref --
    >


<!--==================== Java APPLET ====================================-->
<!--
    One of code or object attributes must be present.
    Place PARAM elements before other content.
-->
<!ELEMENT APPLET - - (PARAM | %flow;)* -- Java applet -->
<!ATTLIST APPLET
    %coreattrs;                         -- id, class, style, title --
    codebase    %URL;      #IMPLIED  -- optional base URL for applet --
    archive     CDATA      #IMPLIED  -- comma separated archive list --
    code        CDATA      #IMPLIED  -- applet class file --
    object      CDATA      #IMPLIED  -- serialized applet file --
    alt         %Text;     #IMPLIED  -- short description --
    name        CDATA      #IMPLIED  -- allows applets to find each other --
    width       %Length;   #REQUIRED -- initial width --
    height      %Length;   #REQUIRED -- initial height --
    align       %IAlign;   #IMPLIED  -- vertical or horizontal alignment --
    hspace      %Pixels;   #IMPLIED  -- horizontal gutter --
    vspace      %Pixels;   #IMPLIED  -- vertical gutter --
    >
<!--==================== Horizontal Rule ================================-->

<!ELEMENT HR - O EMPTY -- horizontal rule -->
<!ATTLIST HR
    %coreattrs;                         -- id, class, style, title --
    %events;
    align (left|center|right) #IMPLIED
    noshade     (noshade)  #IMPLIED
    size        %Pixels;   #IMPLIED
    width       %Length;   #IMPLIED
    >


<!--================== Paragraphs =======================================-->

<!ELEMENT P - O (%inline;)* -- paragraph -->
<!ATTLIST P
    %attrs;                             -- %coreattrs, %i18n, %events --
    %align;                             -- align, text alignment --
    >
```

```
<!--=================== Headings =========================================-->

<!--
  There are six levels of headings from H1 (the most important)
  to H6 (the least important).
-->

<!ELEMENT (%heading;)  - - (%inline;)* -- heading -->
<!ATTLIST (%heading;)
  %attrs;                           -- %coreattrs, %i18n, %events --
  %align;                           -- align, text alignment --
  >


<!--=================== Preformatted Text ================================-->

<!-- excludes markup for images and changes in font size -->
<!ENTITY % pre.exclusion "IMG|OBJECT|APPLET|BIG|SMALL|SUB|SUP|FONT|BASEFONT">

<!ELEMENT PRE - - (%inline;)* -(%pre.exclusion;) -- preformatted text -->
<!ATTLIST PRE
  %attrs;                           -- %coreattrs, %i18n, %events --
  width         NUMBER    #IMPLIED
  >


<!--==================== Inline Quotes ===================================-->

<!ELEMENT Q - - (%inline;)* -- short inline quotation -->
<!ATTLIST Q
  %attrs;                           -- %coreattrs, %i18n, %events --
  cite          %URL;     #IMPLIED  -- URL for source document or msg --
  >


<!--=================== Block-like Quotes ================================-->

<!ELEMENT BLOCKQUOTE - - (%flow;)* -- long quotation -->
<!ATTLIST BLOCKQUOTE
  %attrs;                           -- %coreattrs, %i18n, %events --
  cite          %URL;     #IMPLIED  -- URL for source document or msg --
  >


<!--=================== Inserted/Deleted Text ============================-->


<!-- INS/DEL are handled by inclusion on BODY -->
<!ELEMENT (INS|DEL) - - (%flow;)* -- inserted text, deleted text -->
<!ATTLIST (INS|DEL)
  %attrs;                           -- %coreattrs, %i18n, %events --
```

```
      cite        %URL;       #IMPLIED   -- info on reason for change --
      datetime    %Datetime; #IMPLIED   -- date and time of change --
      >


<!--=================== Lists =========================================-->

<!-- definition lists - DT for term, DD for its definition -->

<!ELEMENT DL - - (DT|DD)+ -- definition list -->
<!ATTLIST DL
      %attrs;                           -- %coreattrs, %i18n, %events --
      compact     (compact) #IMPLIED  -- reduced interitem spacing --
      >

<!ELEMENT DT - O (%inline;)* -- definition term -->
<!ELEMENT DD - O (%flow;)*    -- definition description -->
<!ATTLIST (DT|DD)
      %attrs;                           -- %coreattrs, %i18n, %events --
      >

<!-- Ordered lists (OL) Numbering style

      1    arablic numbers    1, 2, 3, ...
      a    lower alpha        a, b, c, ...
      A    upper alpha        A, B, C, ...
      i    lower roman        i, ii, iii, ...
      I    upper roman        I, II, III, ...

    The style is applied to the sequence number which by default
    is reset to 1 for the first list item in an ordered list.

    This can't be expressed directly in SGML due to case folding.
-->

<!ENTITY % OLStyle "CDATA"      -- constrained to: "(1|a|A|i|I)" -->

<!ELEMENT OL - - (LI)+ -- ordered list -->
<!ATTLIST OL
      %attrs;                           -- %coreattrs, %i18n, %events --
      type        %OLStyle; #IMPLIED  -- numbering style --
      compact     (compact) #IMPLIED  -- reduced interitem spacing --
      start       NUMBER    #IMPLIED  -- starting sequence number --
      >

<!-- Unordered Lists (UL) bullet styles -->
<!ENTITY % ULStyle "(disc|square|circle)">
```

```
<!ELEMENT UL - - (LI)+ -- unordered list -->
<!ATTLIST UL
  %attrs;                             -- %coreattrs, %i18n, %events --
  type          %ULStyle;  #IMPLIED -- bullet style --
  compact       (compact)  #IMPLIED -- reduced interitem spacing --
  >


<!ELEMENT (DIR|MENU) - - (LI)+ -(%block;) -- directory list, menu list -->
<!ATTLIST DIR
  %attrs;                             -- %coreattrs, %i18n, %events --
  compact       (compact)  #IMPLIED
  >
<!ATTLIST MENU
  %attrs;                             -- %coreattrs, %i18n, %events --
  compact       (compact)  #IMPLIED
  >


<!-- <DIR>              Directory list              -->
<!-- <DIR COMPACT>      Compact list style          -->
<!-- <MENU>             Menu list                   -->
<!-- <MENU COMPACT>     Compact list style          -->

<!ENTITY % LIStyle "CDATA" -- constrained to: "(%ULStyle;|%OLStyle;)" -->

<!ELEMENT LI - O (%flow;)* -- list item -->
<!ATTLIST LI
  %attrs;                             -- %coreattrs, %i18n, %events --
  type          %LIStyle;  #IMPLIED -- list item style --
  value         NUMBER     #IMPLIED -- reset sequence number --
  >


<!--================ Forms ===================================================-->
<!ELEMENT FORM - - (%flow;)* -(FORM) -- interactive form -->
<!ATTLIST FORM
  %attrs;                             -- %coreattrs, %i18n, %events --
  action        %URL;      #REQUIRED -- server-side form handler --
  method        (GET|POST) GET        -- HTTP method used to submit the form
--
  enctype %ContentType; "application/x-www-form-urlencoded"
  onsubmit      %Script;   #IMPLIED  -- the form was submitted --
  onreset       %Script;   #IMPLIED  -- the form was reset --
  target  %FrameTarget;    #IMPLIED -- render in this frame --
  accept-charset %Charsets; #IMPLIED -- list of supported charsets --
  >

<!-- Each label must not contain more than ONE field -->
<!ELEMENT LABEL - - (%inline;)* -(LABEL) -- form field label text -->
```

```
<!ATTLIST LABEL
  %attrs;                              -- %coreattrs, %i18n, %events --
  for          IDREF       #IMPLIED   -- matches field ID value --
  accesskey    %Character; #IMPLIED   -- accessibility key character --
  onfocus      %Script;    #IMPLIED   -- the element got the focus --
  onblur       %Script;    #IMPLIED   -- the element lost the focus --
  >

<!ENTITY % InputType
  "(TEXT | PASSWORD | CHECKBOX |
    RADIO | SUBMIT | RESET |
    FILE | HIDDEN | IMAGE | BUTTON)"
    >

<!-- attribute name required for all but submit & reset -->
<!ELEMENT INPUT - O EMPTY -- form control -->
<!ATTLIST INPUT
  %attrs;                              -- %coreattrs, %i18n, %events --
  type         %InputType; TEXT       -- what kind of widget is needed --
  name         CDATA       #IMPLIED   -- submit as part of form --
  value        CDATA       #IMPLIED   -- required for radio and checkboxes --
  checked      (checked)   #IMPLIED   -- for radio buttons and check boxes --
   disabled    (disabled)    #IMPLIED   -- control is unavailable in this
context --
  readonly     (readonly)  #IMPLIED   -- for text and passwd --
  size         CDATA       #IMPLIED   -- specific to each type of field --
  maxlength    NUMBER      #IMPLIED   -- max chars for text fields --
  src          %URL;       #IMPLIED   -- for fields with images --
  alt          CDATA       #IMPLIED   -- short description --
  usemap       %URL;       #IMPLIED   -- use client-side image map --
  align        %IAlign;    #IMPLIED   -- vertical or horizontal alignment --
  tabindex     NUMBER      #IMPLIED   -- position in tabbing order --
  accesskey    %Character; #IMPLIED   -- accessibility key character --
  onfocus      %Script;    #IMPLIED   -- the element got the focus --
  onblur       %Script;    #IMPLIED   -- the element lost the focus --
  onselect     %Script;    #IMPLIED   -- some text was selected --
  onchange     %Script;    #IMPLIED   -- the element value was changed --
  accept  %ContentTypes;   #IMPLIED   -- list of MIME types for file upload --
  %reserved;                          -- reserved for possible future use --
  >

<!ELEMENT SELECT - - (OPTGROUP|OPTION)+ -- option selector -->
<!ATTLIST SELECT
  %attrs;                              -- %coreattrs, %i18n, %events --
  name         CDATA       #IMPLIED   -- field name --
  size         NUMBER      #IMPLIED   -- rows visible --
  multiple     (multiple)  #IMPLIED   -- default is single selection --
```

```
    disabled    (disabled) #IMPLIED  -- control is unavailable in this context --
    tabindex    NUMBER     #IMPLIED  -- position in tabbing order --
    onfocus     %Script;   #IMPLIED  -- the element got the focus --
    onblur      %Script;   #IMPLIED  -- the element lost the focus --
    onchange    %Script;   #IMPLIED  -- the element value was changed --
    %reserved;                       -- reserved for possible future use --
    >

<!ELEMENT OPTGROUP - - (OPTGROUP|OPTION)+ -- option group -->
<!ATTLIST OPTGROUP
    %attrs;                          -- %coreattrs, %i18n, %events --
    disabled    (disabled) #IMPLIED  -- control is unavailable in this context --
    label       %Text;     #REQUIRED -- for use in hierarchical menus --
    >

<!ELEMENT OPTION - O (#PCDATA) -- selectable choice -->
<!ATTLIST OPTION
    %attrs;                          -- %coreattrs, %i18n, %events --
    selected    (selected) #IMPLIED
    disabled    (disabled) #IMPLIED  -- control is unavailable in this context --
    label       %Text;     #IMPLIED  -- for use in hierarchical menus --
    value       CDATA      #IMPLIED  -- defaults to element content --
    >

<!ELEMENT TEXTAREA - - (#PCDATA) -- multi-line text field -->
<!ATTLIST TEXTAREA
    %attrs;                          -- %coreattrs, %i18n, %events --
    name        CDATA      #IMPLIED
    rows        NUMBER     #REQUIRED
    cols        NUMBER     #REQUIRED
    disabled        (disabled) #IMPLIED   -- control is unavailable in this
context --
    readonly    (readonly) #IMPLIED
    tabindex    NUMBER     #IMPLIED  -- position in tabbing order --
    onfocus     %Script;   #IMPLIED  -- the element got the focus --
    onblur      %Script;   #IMPLIED  -- the element lost the focus --
    onselect    %Script;   #IMPLIED  -- some text was selected --
    onchange    %Script;   #IMPLIED  -- the element value was changed --
    %reserved;                       -- reserved for possible future use --
    >

<!--
  #PCDATA is to solve the mixed content problem,
  per specification only whitespace is allowed there!
  -->
<!ELEMENT FIELDSET - - (#PCDATA,LEGEND,(%flow;)*) -- form control group -->
<!ATTLIST FIELDSET
```

```
    %attrs;                              -- %coreattrs, %i18n, %events --
    >


<!ELEMENT LEGEND - - (%inline;)* -- fieldset legend -->
<!ENTITY % LAlign "(top|bottom|left|right)">

<!ATTLIST LEGEND
    %attrs;                              -- %coreattrs, %i18n, %events --
    align        %LAlign;   #IMPLIED  -- relative to fieldset --
    accesskey    %Character; #IMPLIED  -- accessibility key character --
    >

<!ELEMENT BUTTON - -
      (%flow;)* -(A|%formctrl;|FORM|ISINDEX|FIELDSET|IFRAME)
      -- push button -->
<!ATTLIST BUTTON
    %attrs;                              -- %coreattrs, %i18n, %events --
    name         CDATA      #IMPLIED  -- for scripting/forms as submit button --
    value        CDATA      #IMPLIED  -- gets passed to server when submitted --
    type (button|submit|reset) submit -- for use as form submit/reset button --
    disabled     (disabled) #IMPLIED  -- control is unavailable in this context --
    tabindex     NUMBER     #IMPLIED  -- position in tabbing order --
    accesskey    %Character; #IMPLIED  -- accessibility key character --
    onfocus      %Script;   #IMPLIED  -- the element got the focus --
    onblur       %Script;   #IMPLIED  -- the element lost the focus --
    %reserved;                         -- reserved for possible future use --
    >


<!--======================= Tables ========================================-->

<!-- IETF HTML table standard, see [RFC1942] -->

<!--
 The BORDER attribute sets the thickness of the frame around the
 table. The default units are screen pixels.

 The FRAME attribute specifies which parts of the frame around
 the table should be rendered. The values are not the same as
 CALS to avoid a name clash with the VALIGN attribute.

 The value "border" is included for backwards compatibility with
 <TABLE BORDER> which yields frame=border and border=implied
 For <TABLE BORDER=1> you get border=1 and frame=implied. In this
 case, it is appropriate to treat this as frame=border for backwards
 compatibility with deployed browsers.
-->
<!ENTITY % TFrame "(void|above|below|hsides|lhs|rhs|vsides|box|border)">
```

```
<!--
The RULES attribute defines which rules to draw between cells:

If RULES is absent then assume:
    "none" if BORDER is absent or BORDER=0 otherwise "all"
-->

<!ENTITY % TRules "(none | groups | rows | cols | all)">

<!-- horizontal placement of table relative to document -->
<!ENTITY % TAlign "(left|center|right)">

<!-- horizontal alignment attributes for cell contents -->
<!ENTITY % cellhalign
  "align (left|center|right|justify|char) #IMPLIED
   char       %Character;   #IMPLIED  -- alignment char, e.g. char=':' --
   charoff    %Length;      #IMPLIED  -- offset for alignment char --"
  >

<!-- vertical alignment attributes for cell contents -->
<!ENTITY % cellvalign
  "valign (top|middle|bottom|baseline) #IMPLIED"
  >

<!ELEMENT TABLE - -
    (CAPTION?, (COL*|COLGROUP*), THEAD?, TFOOT?, TBODY+)>
<!ELEMENT CAPTION  - - (%inline;)* -- table caption -->
<!ELEMENT THEAD    - O (TR)+       -- table header -->
<!ELEMENT TFOOT    - O (TR)+       -- table footer -->
<!ELEMENT TBODY    O O (TR)+       -- table body -->
<!ELEMENT COLGROUP - O (col)*      -- table column group -->
<!ELEMENT COL      - O EMPTY       -- table column -->
<!ELEMENT TR       - O (TH|TD)+    -- table row -->
<!ELEMENT (TH|TD)  - O (%flow;)*   -- table header cell, table data cell -->

<!ATTLIST TABLE                    -- table element --
  %attrs;                          -- %coreattrs, %i18n, %events --
  summary     %Text;    #IMPLIED  -- purpose/structure for speech output --
  align       %TAlign;  #IMPLIED  -- table position relative to window --
  bgcolor     %Color;   #IMPLIED  -- background color for cells --
  width       %Pixels;  #IMPLIED  -- table width relative to window --
  border      CDATA     #IMPLIED  -- controls frame width around table --
  frame       %TFrame;  #IMPLIED  -- which parts of table frame to include --
  rules       %TRules;  #IMPLIED  -- rulings between rows and cols --
  cellspacing %Length;  #IMPLIED  -- spacing between cells --
  cellpadding %Length;  #IMPLIED  -- spacing within cells --
```

```
        %reserved;                          -- reserved for possible future use --
        >


<!ENTITY % CAlign "(top|bottom|left|right)">

<!ATTLIST CAPTION
    %attrs;                                 -- %coreattrs, %i18n, %events --
    align       %CAlign;    #IMPLIED -- relative to table --
        >


<!--
COLGROUP groups a set of COL elements. It allows you to group
several semantically related columns together.
-->
<!ATTLIST COLGROUP
    %attrs;                                 -- %coreattrs, %i18n, %events --
    span        NUMBER      1       -- default number of columns in group --
    width    %MultiLength; #IMPLIED  -- default width for enclosed COLs --
    %cellhalign;                            -- horizontal alignment in cells --
    %cellvalign;                            -- vertical alignment in cells --
        >


<!--


COL elements define the alignment properties for cells in
one or more columns.

The WIDTH attribute specifies the width of the columns, e.g.

    width=64            width in screen pixels
    width=0.5*          relative width of 0.5


The REPEAT attribute allows you to repeat the effects of
a COL element as if the same element was repeated n times.
There are no grouping semantics for repeated columns.
-->
<!ATTLIST COL                   -- column groups and properties --
    %attrs;                             -- %coreattrs, %i18n, %events --
    repeat          NUMBER      1       -- repeat count for COL --
    width    %MultiLength; #IMPLIED  -- column width specification --
    %cellhalign;                            -- horizontal alignment in cells --
    %cellvalign;                            -- vertical alignment in cells --
        >


<!--
    Use THEAD to duplicate headers when breaking table
    across page boundaries, or for static headers when
```

```
        TBODY sections are rendered in scrolling panel.

        Use TFOOT to duplicate footers when breaking table
        across page boundaries, or for static footers when
        TBODY sections are rendered in scrolling panel.

        Use multiple TBODY sections when rules are needed
        between groups of table rows.
-->
<!ATTLIST (THEAD|TBODY|TFOOT)     -- table section --
  %attrs;                           -- %coreattrs, %i18n, %events --
  %cellhalign;                      -- horizontal alignment in cells --
  %cellvalign;                      -- vertical alignment in cells --
  >


<!ATTLIST TR                      -- table row --
  %attrs;                           -- %coreattrs, %i18n, %events --
  %cellhalign;                      -- horizontal alignment in cells --
  %cellvalign;                      -- vertical alignment in cells --
  bgcolor      %Color;    #IMPLIED -- background color for row --
  >



<!-- Scope is simpler than axes attribute for common tables -->
<!ENTITY % Scope "(row|col|rowgroup|colgroup)">

<!-- TH is for headers, TD for data, but for cells acting as both use TD -->
<!ATTLIST (TH|TD)                     -- header or data cell --
  %attrs;                             -- %coreattrs, %i18n, %events --
  abbr         %Text;    #IMPLIED -- abbreviation for header cell --
  axis         CDATA     #IMPLIED -- names groups of related headers--
  headers      IDREFS    #IMPLIED -- list of id's for header cells --
  scope        %Scope;   #IMPLIED -- scope covered by header cells --
  nowrap       (nowrap)  #IMPLIED -- suppress word wrap --
  bgcolor      %Color;   #IMPLIED -- cell background color --
  rowspan      NUMBER    1        -- number of rows spanned by cell --
  colspan      NUMBER    1        -- number of cols spanned by cell --
  %cellhalign;                    -- horizontal alignment in cells --
  %cellvalign;                    -- vertical alignment in cells --
  width        %Pixels;  #IMPLIED -- width for cell --
  height       %Pixels;  #IMPLIED -- height for cell --
  >

<!--================== Document Frames =====================================-->


<!--
  The content model for HTML documents depends on whether the HEAD is
```

```
followed by a FRAMESET or BODY element. The widespread omission of
the BODY start tag makes it impractical to define the content model
without the use of a marked section.
-->

<!-- Feature Switch for frameset documents -->
<!ENTITY % HTML.Frameset "IGNORE">

<![ %HTML.Frameset; [
<!ELEMENT FRAMESET - - ((FRAMESET|FRAME)+ & NOFRAMES?)
    -- window subdivision -->
<!ATTLIST FRAMESET
  %coreattrs;                         -- id, class, style, title --
  rows    %MultiLengths; #IMPLIED  -- list of lengths. Default: 100% (1 row) --
  cols    %MultiLengths; #IMPLIED  -- list of lengths. Default: 100% (1 col) --
  onload      %Script;   #IMPLIED  -- all the frames have been loaded  --
  onunload    %Script;   #IMPLIED  -- all the frames have been removed --
  >
]]>

<![ %HTML.Frameset; [
<!-- reserved frame names start with "_" otherwise starts with letter -->
<!ELEMENT FRAME - O EMPTY -- subwindow -->
<!ATTLIST FRAME
  %coreattrs;                         -- id, class, style, title --
  longdesc    %URL;      #IMPLIED  -- link to long description (complements title) --
  name        CDATA      #IMPLIED  -- name of frame for targetting --
  src         %URL;      #IMPLIED  -- source of frame content --
  frameborder (1|0)      1         -- request frame borders? --
  marginwidth %Pixels;   #IMPLIED  -- margin widths in pixels --
  marginheight %Pixels;  #IMPLIED  -- margin height in pixels --
  noresize    (noresize) #IMPLIED  -- allow users to resize frames? --
  scrolling (yes|no|auto) auto     -- scrollbar or none --
  >
]]>

<!ELEMENT IFRAME - - (%flow;)* -- inline subwindow -->
<!ATTLIST IFRAME
  %coreattrs;                         -- id, class, style, title --
  longdesc    %URL;      #IMPLIED  -- link to long description (complements title) --
  name        CDATA      #IMPLIED  -- name of frame for targetting --
  src         %URL;      #IMPLIED  -- source of frame content --
  frameborder (1|0)      1         -- request frame borders? --
  marginwidth %Pixels;   #IMPLIED  -- margin widths in pixels --
  marginheight %Pixels;  #IMPLIED  -- margin height in pixels --
  scrolling (yes|no|auto) auto     -- scrollbar or none --
  align       %IAlign;   #IMPLIED  -- vertical or horizontal alignment --
```

```
   height         %Length;     #IMPLIED  -- frame height --
   width          %Length;     #IMPLIED  -- frame width --
   >

<![ %HTML.Frameset; [
<!ENTITY % noframes.content "(BODY) -(NOFRAMES)">
]]>

<!ENTITY % noframes.content "(%flow;)*">

<!ELEMENT NOFRAMES - - %noframes.content;
 -- alternate content container for non frame-based rendering -->
<!ATTLIST NOFRAMES
  %attrs;                          -- %coreattrs, %i18n, %events --
  >

<!--=============== Document Head =========================================-->
<!-- %head.misc; defined earlier on as "SCRIPT | STYLE | META | LINK" -->
<!ENTITY % head.content "TITLE & ISINDEX? & BASE?">

<!ELEMENT HEAD O O (%head.content;) +(%head.misc;) -- document head -->
<!ATTLIST HEAD
  %i18n;                          -- lang, dir --
  profile     %URL;      #IMPLIED  -- named dictionary of meta info --
  >

<!-- The TITLE element is not considered part of the flow of text.
       It should be displayed, for example as the page header or
       window title. Exactly one title is required per document.
     -->
<!ELEMENT TITLE - - (#PCDATA) -(%head.misc;) -- document title -->
<!ATTLIST TITLE %i18n>

<!ELEMENT ISINDEX - O EMPTY -- single line prompt -->
<!ATTLIST ISINDEX
  %coreattrs;                     -- id, class, style, title --
  %i18n;                          -- lang, dir --
  prompt      %Text;    #IMPLIED  -- prompt message -->

<!ELEMENT BASE - O EMPTY -- document base URL -->
<!ATTLIST BASE
  href        %URL;      #IMPLIED  -- URL that acts as base URL --
  target      %FrameTarget;   #IMPLIED -- render in this frame --
  >

<!ELEMENT META - O EMPTY          -- generic metainformation -->
<!ATTLIST META
```

```
  %i18n;                                -- lang, dir, for use with content string --
  http-equiv   NAME       #IMPLIED   -- HTTP response header name    --
  name         NAME       #IMPLIED   -- metainformation name --
  content      CDATA      #REQUIRED  -- associated information --
  scheme       CDATA      #IMPLIED   -- select form of content --
  >

<!ELEMENT STYLE - - CDATA        -- style info -->
<!ATTLIST STYLE
  %i18n;                                -- lang, dir, for use with title --
  type      %ContentType; #REQUIRED  -- content type of style language --
  media     %MediaDesc;   #IMPLIED   -- designed for use with these media --
  title     %Text;        #IMPLIED   -- advisory title --
  >

<!ELEMENT SCRIPT - - CDATA       -- script statements -->
<!ATTLIST SCRIPT
  charset   %Charset;     #IMPLIED -- char encoding of linked resource --
  type      %ContentType; #REQUIRED -- content type of script language --
  language  CDATA         #IMPLIED -- predefined script language name --
  src       %URL;         #IMPLIED -- URL for an external script --
  defer     (defer)       #IMPLIED -- UA may defer execution of script --
  >

<!ELEMENT NOSCRIPT - - (%flow;)*
  -- alternate content container for non script-based rendering -->
<!ATTLIST NOSCRIPT
  %attrs;                           -- %coreattrs, %i18n, %events --
  >


<!--=============== Document Structure ===================================-->
<!ENTITY % version "version CDATA #FIXED '%HTML.Version;'">

<![ %HTML.Frameset; [
<!ENTITY % html.content "HEAD, FRAMESET">
]]>


<!ENTITY % html.content "HEAD, BODY">

<!ELEMENT HTML O O (%html.content;) -- document root element -->
<!ATTLIST HTML
  %version;
  %i18n;                            -- lang, dir --
  >
```

HTML 4.0 Strict DTD

```
<!--
    This is an EXPERIMENTAL version of the HTML 4.0 DTD which
    excludes presentation attributes and elements that W3C expects
    to phase out as support for style sheets matures. If you need
    these features please use the transitional DTD. HTML 4.0
    includes mechanisms for style sheets, scripting, embedding
    objects, improved support for right to left and mixed direction
    text, and enhancements to forms for improved accessibility for
    people with disabilities.

        Draft: $Date: 1997/11/07 15:32:37 $

        Authors:
            Dave Raggett <dsr@w3.org>
            Arnaud Le Hors <lehors@w3.org>

    This is work in progress, subject to change at any time.
    It does not imply endorsement by, or the consensus of,
    either W3C or members of the HTML working group. Further
    information about HTML 4.0 is available at:

        http://www.w3.org/TR/PR-html40
-->
<!ENTITY % HTML.Version "-//W3C//DTD HTML 4.0//EN"
    -- Typical usage:

    <!DOCTYPE HTML PUBLIC "-//W3C//DTD HTML 4.0//EN"
            "http://www.w3.org/TR/PR-html40/strict.dtd">
    <html>
    <head>
    ...
    </head>
    <body>
    ...
    </body>
    </html>

    The URL used as a system identifier with the public identifier allows
    the user agent to download the DTD and entity sets as needed.

    The FPI for the transitional HTML 4.0 DTD is:

        "-//W3C//DTD HTML 4.0 Transitional//EN"
```

and its URL is:

http://www.w3.org/TR/PR-html40/loose.dtd

If you are writing a frameset document you should use the following FPI:

"-//W3C//DTD HTML 4.0 Frameset//EN"

with the URL:

http://www.w3.org/TR/PR-html40/frameset.dtd

The following URLs are supported in relation to HTML 4.0

"http://www.w3.org/TR/PR-html40/strict.dtd" (Strict DTD)
"http://www.w3.org/TR/PR-html40/loose.dtd" (Loose DTD)
"http://www.w3.org/TR/PR-html40/frameset.dtd" (Frameset DTD)
"http://www.w3.org/TR/PR-html40/HTMLlat1.ent" (Latin-1 entities)
"http://www.w3.org/TR/PR-html40/HTMLsymbol.ent" (Symbol entities)
"http://www.w3.org/TR/PR-html40/HTMLspecial.ent" (Special entities)

These URLs point to the latest version of each file. To reference this specific revision use the following URLs:

"http://www.w3.org/TR/PR-html40-971107/strict.dtd"
"http://www.w3.org/TR/PR-html40-971107/loose.dtd"
"http://www.w3.org/TR/PR-html40-971107/frameset.dtd"
"http://www.w3.org/TR/PR-html40-971107/HTMLlat1.ent"
"http://www.w3.org/TR/PR-html40-971107/HTMLsymbol.ent"
"http://www.w3.org/TR/PR-html40-971107/HTMLspecial.ent"

```
<!--================= Imported Names ======================================-->

<!ENTITY % ContentType "CDATA"
    -- media type, as per [RFC2045]
    -->


<!ENTITY % ContentTypes "CDATA"
    -- comma-separated list of media types, as per [RFC2045]
    -->


<!ENTITY % Charset "CDATA"
    -- a character encoding, as per [RFC2045]
    -->
```

```
<!ENTITY % Charsets "CDATA"
    -- a space separated list of character encodings, as per [RFC2045]
    -->

<!ENTITY % LanguageCode "NAME"
    -- a language code, as per [RFC1766]
    -->

<!ENTITY % Character "CDATA"
    -- a single character from [ISO10646]
    -->

<!ENTITY % LinkTypes "CDATA"
    -- space-separated list of link types
    -->

<!ENTITY % MediaDesc "CDATA"
    -- single or comma-separated list of media descriptors
    -->

<!ENTITY % URL "CDATA"
    -- a Uniform Resource Locator,
       see [RFC1808] and [RFC1738]
    -->

<!ENTITY % Datetime "CDATA" -- date and time information. ISO date format -->

<!ENTITY % Script "CDATA" -- script expression -->

<!ENTITY % FrameTarget "CDATA" -- render in this frame -->


<!ENTITY % Text "CDATA" -- render in this frame -->


<!-- Parameter Entities -->

<!ENTITY % head.misc "SCRIPT|STYLE|META|LINK" -- repeatable head elements
-->

<!ENTITY % heading "H1|H2|H3|H4|H5|H6">

<!ENTITY % list "UL | OL">

<!ENTITY % preformatted "PRE">
```

```
<!--================ Character mnemonic entities ========================-->

<!ENTITY % HTMLlat1 PUBLIC
    "-//W3C//ENTITIES Latin1//EN//HTML"
    "http://www.w3.org/TR/PR-html40/HTMLlat1.ent">
%HTMLlat1;

<!ENTITY % HTMLsymbol PUBLIC
    "-//W3C//ENTITIES Symbols//EN//HTML"
    "http://www.w3.org/TR/PR-html40/HTMLsymbol.ent">
%HTMLsymbol;

<!ENTITY % HTMLspecial PUBLIC
    "-//W3C//ENTITIES Special//EN//HTML"
    "http://www.w3.org/TR/PR-html40/HTMLspecial.ent">
%HTMLspecial;
<!--=================== Generic Attributes ==============================-->

<!ENTITY % coreattrs
 "id            ID          #IMPLIED  -- document-wide unique id --
  class         CDATA       #IMPLIED  -- space separated list of classes --
  style         CDATA       #IMPLIED  -- associated style info --
  title         %Text;      #IMPLIED  -- advisory title/amplification --"
  >

<!ENTITY % i18n
 "lang      %LanguageCode; #IMPLIED  -- language code --
  dir            (ltr|rtl)  #IMPLIED  -- direction for weak/neutral text --"
  >

<!ENTITY % events
 "onclick       %Script;    #IMPLIED  -- a pointer button was clicked --
  ondblclick    %Script;    #IMPLIED  -- a pointer button was double clicked --
  onmousedown   %Script;    #IMPLIED  -- a pointer button was pressed down --
  onmouseup     %Script;    #IMPLIED  -- a pointer button was released --
  onmouseover   %Script;    #IMPLIED  -- a pointer was moved onto --
  onmousemove   %Script;    #IMPLIED  -- a pointer was moved within --
  onmouseout    %Script;    #IMPLIED  -- a pointer was moved away --
  onkeypress    %Script;    #IMPLIED  -- a key was pressed and released --
  onkeydown     %Script;    #IMPLIED  -- a key was pressed down --
  onkeyup       %Script;    #IMPLIED  -- a key was released --"
  >


<!-- Reserved Feature Switch -->
<!ENTITY % HTML.Reserved "IGNORE">
```

```
<!-- The following attributes are reserved for possible future use -->
<![ %HTML.Reserved; [
<!ENTITY % reserved
 "datasrc      %URL;      #IMPLIED  -- a single or tabular Data Source --
  datafld      CDATA      #IMPLIED  -- the property or column name --
  dataformatas (plaintext|html) plaintext -- text or html --"
  >
]]>


<!ENTITY % reserved "">

<!ENTITY % attrs "%coreattrs; %i18n; %events;">



<!--=================== Text Markup =====================================-->

<!ENTITY % fontstyle
 "TT | I | B | BIG | SMALL">

<!ENTITY % phrase "EM | STRONG | DFN | CODE |
                   SAMP | KBD | VAR | CITE | ABBR">

<!ENTITY % special
   "A | IMG | OBJECT | BR | SCRIPT | MAP | Q | SUB | SUP | SPAN | BDO">

<!ENTITY % formctrl "INPUT | SELECT | TEXTAREA | LABEL | BUTTON">

<!-- %inline; covers inline or "text-level" elements -->
<!ENTITY % inline "#PCDATA | %fontstyle; | %phrase; | %special; | %formctrl;">

<!ELEMENT (%fontstyle;|%phrase;) - - (%inline;)*>
<!ATTLIST (%fontstyle;|%phrase;)
  %attrs;                         -- %coreattrs, %i18n, %events --
  >

<!ELEMENT (SUB|SUP) - - (%inline;)* -- subscript, superscript -->
<!ATTLIST (SUB|SUP)
  %attrs;                         -- %coreattrs, %i18n, %events --
  >

<!ELEMENT SPAN - - (%inline;)*       -- generic language/style container -->
<!ATTLIST SPAN
  %attrs;                         -- %coreattrs, %i18n, %events --
  charset     %Charset;   #IMPLIED -- char encoding of linked resource --
  type        %ContentType; #IMPLIED -- advisory content type --
  href        %URL;       #IMPLIED -- URL for linked resource --
  hreflang %LanguageCode; #IMPLIED -- language code --
```

```
  target    %FrameTarget;  #IMPLIED -- render in this frame --
  rel       %LinkTypes; #IMPLIED -- forward link types --
  rev       %LinkTypes; #IMPLIED -- reverse link types --
  media     %MediaDesc; #IMPLIED -- for rendering on these media --
  %reserved;                      -- reserved for possible future use --
  >


<!ELEMENT BDO - - (%inline;)*     -- I18N BiDi over-ride -->
<!ATTLIST BDO
  %coreattrs;                      -- id, class, style, title --
  lang    %LanguageCode; #IMPLIED -- language code --
  dir       (ltr|rtl)  #REQUIRED -- directionality --
  >



<!ELEMENT BR - O EMPTY             -- forced line break -->
<!ATTLIST BR
  %coreattrs;                      -- id, class, style, title --
  >


<!--================== HTML content models ===============================-->

<!--
    HTML has two basic content models:

        %inline;     character level elements and text strings
        %block;      block-like elements e.g. paragraphs and lists
-->

<!ENTITY % block
     "P | %heading; | %list; | %preformatted; | DL | DIV | NOSCRIPT |
      BLOCKQUOTE | FORM | HR | TABLE | FIELDSET | ADDRESS">

<!ENTITY % flow "%block; | %inline;">

<!--================== Document Body =====================================-->

<!ELEMENT BODY O O (%block;|SCRIPT)+ +(INS|DEL) -- document body -->
<!ATTLIST BODY
  %attrs;                          -- %coreattrs, %i18n, %events --
  onload    %Script;   #IMPLIED -- the document has been loaded --
  onunload  %Script;   #IMPLIED -- the document has been removed --
  >


<!ELEMENT ADDRESS - - (%inline;)* -- information on author -->
<!ATTLIST ADDRESS
```

```
    %attrs;                                  -- %coreattrs, %i18n, %events --
    >

<!ELEMENT DIV - - (%block;|SCRIPT)+ -- generic language/style container -->
<!ATTLIST DIV
    %attrs;                                  -- %coreattrs, %i18n, %events --
    charset     %Charset;    #IMPLIED -- char encoding of linked resource --
    type        %ContentType; #IMPLIED -- advisory content type --
    href        %URL;        #IMPLIED -- URL for linked resource --
    hreflang %LanguageCode; #IMPLIED -- language code --
    target      %FrameTarget; #IMPLIED -- render in this frame --
    rel         %LinkTypes;  #IMPLIED -- forward link types --
    rev         %LinkTypes;  #IMPLIED -- reverse link types --
    media       %MediaDesc;  #IMPLIED -- for rendering on these media --

    %reserved;                               -- reserved for possible future use --
    >


<!--================= The Anchor Element ===================================-->

<!ENTITY % Shape "(rect|circle|poly|default)">
<!ENTITY % Coords "CDATA" -- comma separated list of numbers -->

<!ELEMENT A - - (%inline;)* -(A) -- anchor -->
<!ATTLIST A
    %attrs;                                  -- %coreattrs, %i18n, %events --
    charset     %Charset;    #IMPLIED -- char encoding of linked resource --
    type        %ContentType; #IMPLIED -- advisory content type --
    name        CDATA        #IMPLIED -- named link end --
    href        %URL;        #IMPLIED -- URL for linked resource --
    hreflang %LanguageCode; #IMPLIED -- language code --
    target      %FrameTarget; #IMPLIED -- render in this frame --
    rel         %LinkTypes;  #IMPLIED -- forward link types --
    rev         %LinkTypes;  #IMPLIED -- reverse link types --
    accesskey   %Character;  #IMPLIED -- accessibility key character --
    shape       %Shape;      rect     -- for use with OBJECT SHAPES --
    coords      %Coords;     #IMPLIED -- for use with OBJECT SHAPES --
    tabindex    NUMBER       #IMPLIED -- position in tabbing order --
    onfocus     %Script;     #IMPLIED -- the element got the focus --
    onblur      %Script;     #IMPLIED -- the element lost the focus --
    >

<!--================= Client-side image maps ============================-->

<!-- These can be placed in the same document or grouped in a
      separate document although this isn't yet widely supported -->
```

```
<!ELEMENT MAP - - (AREA)+ -- client-side image map -->
<!ATTLIST MAP
  %attrs;                          -- %coreattrs, %i18n, %events --
  name          CDATA      #REQUIRED  -- name of image map for refs by usemap --
  >


<!ELEMENT AREA - O EMPTY -- client-side image map area -->
<!ATTLIST AREA
  %attrs;                          -- %coreattrs, %i18n, %events --
  shape        %Shape;     rect      -- controls interpretation of coords --
  coords       %Coords;    #IMPLIED  -- comma separated list of lengths --
  href         %URL;       #IMPLIED  -- URL for linked resource --
  target       %FrameTarget;  #IMPLIED -- render in this frame --
  nohref       (nohref)    #IMPLIED  -- this region has no action --
  alt          %Text;      #REQUIRED -- short description --
  tabindex     NUMBER      #IMPLIED  -- position in tabbing order --
  accesskey    %Character; #IMPLIED  -- accessibility key character --
  onfocus      %Script;    #IMPLIED  -- the element got the focus --
  onblur       %Script;    #IMPLIED  -- the element lost the focus --
  >


<!--================= The LINK Element ===================================-->

<!--
  Relationship values can be used in principle:

  a) for document specific toolbars/menus when used
     with the LINK element in document head e.g.
        start, contents, previous, next, index, end, help
  b) to link to a separate style sheet (rel=stylesheet)
  c) to make a link to a script (rel=script)
  d) by stylesheets to control how collections of
     html nodes are rendered into printed documents
  e) to make a link to a printable version of this document
     e.g. a postscript or pdf version (rel=alternate media=print)
-->


<!ELEMENT LINK - O EMPTY -- a media-independent link -->
<!ATTLIST LINK
  %attrs;                          -- %coreattrs, %i18n, %events --
  charset      %Charset;   #IMPLIED -- char encoding of linked resource --
  href         %URL;       #IMPLIED -- URL for linked resource --
  hreflang %LanguageCode; #IMPLIED -- language code --
  type         %ContentType; #IMPLIED -- advisory content type --
  rel          %LinkTypes; #IMPLIED -- forward link types --
  rev          %LinkTypes; #IMPLIED -- reverse link types --
  media        %MediaDesc; #IMPLIED -- for rendering on these media --
```

```
    target    %FrameTarget;      #IMPLIED -- render in this frame --
    >


<!--================== Images =====================================-->

<!-- Length defined in strict DTD for cellpadding/cellspacing -->
<!ENTITY % Length "CDATA" -- nn for pixels or nn% for percentage length -->
<!ENTITY % MultiLength "CDATA" -- pixel, percentage, or relative -->

<!ENTITY % MultiLengths "CDATA" -- comma-separated list of MultiLength -->

<!ENTITY % Pixels "CDATA" -- integer representing length in pixels -->


<!-- To avoid problems with text-only UAs as well as
     to make image content understandable and navigable
     to users of non-visual UAs, you need to provide
     a description with ALT, and avoid server-side image maps -->
<!ELEMENT IMG - O EMPTY            -- Embedded image -->
<!ATTLIST IMG
    %attrs;                              -- %coreattrs, %i18n, %events --
    src         %URL;       #REQUIRED -- URL of image to embed --
    alt         %Text;      #REQUIRED -- short description --
    longdesc    %URL;       #IMPLIED  -- link to long description (complements alt) --
    height      %Length;    #IMPLIED  -- override height --
    width       %Length;    #IMPLIED  -- override width --
    usemap      %URL;       #IMPLIED  -- use client-side image map --
    ismap       (ismap)     #IMPLIED  -- use server-side image map --
    >

<!-- USEMAP points to a MAP element which may be in this document
     or an external document, although the latter is not widely supported -->

<!--==================== OBJECT =======================================-->
<!--
    OBJECT is used to embed objects as part of HTML pages
    PARAM elements should precede other content. SGML mixed content
    model technicality precludes specifying this formally ...
-->

<!ELEMENT OBJECT - - (PARAM | %flow;)*
 -- generic embedded object -->
<!ATTLIST OBJECT
    %attrs;                              -- %coreattrs, %i18n, %events --
    declare     (declare)   #IMPLIED  -- declare but don't instantiate flag --
    classid     %URL;       #IMPLIED  -- identifies an implementation --
    codebase    %URL;       #IMPLIED  -- base URL for classid, data, archive --
```

```
data        %URL;        #IMPLIED   -- reference to object's data --
type        %ContentType; #IMPLIED  -- content type for data --
codetype    %ContentType; #IMPLIED  -- content type for code --
archive     %URL;        #IMPLIED   -- space separated archive list --
standby     %Text;       #IMPLIED   -- message to show while loading --
height      %Length;     #IMPLIED   -- override height --
width       %Length;     #IMPLIED   -- override width --
usemap      %URL;        #IMPLIED   -- use client-side image map --
shapes      (shapes)     #IMPLIED   -- object has shaped hypertext links --
export      (export)     #IMPLIED   -- export shapes to parent  --
name        CDATA        #IMPLIED   -- submit as part of form --
tabindex    NUMBER       #IMPLIED   -- position in tabbing order --
%reserved;                          -- reserved for possible future use --
>

<!ELEMENT PARAM - O EMPTY           -- named property value -->
<!ATTLIST PARAM
id           ID          #IMPLIED   -- document-wide unique id --
name         CDATA       #REQUIRED  -- property name --
value        CDATA       #IMPLIED   -- property value --
valuetype (DATA|REF|OBJECT) DATA    -- How to interpret value --
type        %ContentType; #IMPLIED  -- content type for value
                                       when valuetype=ref --
>


<!--==================== Horizontal Rule =====================================-->

<!ELEMENT HR - O EMPTY -- horizontal rule -->
<!ATTLIST HR
%coreattrs;                         -- id, class, style, title --
%events;
>


<!--=================== Paragraphs ===========================================-->

<!ELEMENT P - O (%inline;)* -- paragraph -->
<!ATTLIST P
%attrs;                             -- %coreattrs, %i18n, %events --
>


<!--=================== Headings =============================================-->

<!--
There are six levels of headings from H1 (the most important)
to H6 (the least important).
```

```
-->

<!ELEMENT (%heading;)  - - (%inline;)* -- heading -->
<!ATTLIST (%heading;)
  %attrs;                          -- %coreattrs, %i18n, %events --
  >


<!--=================== Preformatted Text ================================-->

<!-- excludes markup for images and changes in font size -->
<!ENTITY % pre.exclusion "IMG|OBJECT|BIG|SMALL|SUB|SUP">

<!ELEMENT PRE - - (%inline;)* -(%pre.exclusion;) -- preformatted text -->
<!ATTLIST PRE
  %attrs;                          -- %coreattrs, %i18n, %events --
  >


<!--=================== Inline Quotes ===================================-->

<!ELEMENT Q - - (%inline;)* -- short inline quotation -->
<!ATTLIST Q
  %attrs;                          -- %coreattrs, %i18n, %events --
  cite         %URL;      #IMPLIED -- URL for source document or msg --
  >


<!--=================== Block-like Quotes ===============================-->

<!ELEMENT BLOCKQUOTE - - (%block;|SCRIPT)+ -- long quotation -->
<!ATTLIST BLOCKQUOTE
  %attrs;                          -- %coreattrs, %i18n, %events --
  cite         %URL;      #IMPLIED -- URL for source document or msg --
  >


<!--=================== Inserted/Deleted Text ===========================-->


<!-- INS/DEL are handled by inclusion on BODY -->
<!ELEMENT (INS|DEL) - - (%flow;)* -- inserted text, deleted text -->
<!ATTLIST (INS|DEL)
  %attrs;                          -- %coreattrs, %i18n, %events --
  cite         %URL;      #IMPLIED -- info on reason for change --
  datetime     %Datetime; #IMPLIED -- date and time of change --
  >


<!--=================== Lists ===========================================-->

<!-- definition lists - DT for term, DD for its definition -->
```

```
<!ELEMENT DL - - (DT|DD)+ -- definition list -->
<!ATTLIST DL
  %attrs;                          -- %coreattrs, %i18n, %events --
  >


<!ELEMENT DT - O (%inline;)* -- definition term -->
<!ELEMENT DD - O (%flow;)*   -- definition description -->
<!ATTLIST (DT|DD)
  %attrs;                          -- %coreattrs, %i18n, %events --
  >



<!ELEMENT OL - - (LI)+ -- ordered list -->
<!ATTLIST OL
  %attrs;                          -- %coreattrs, %i18n, %events --
  >

<!-- Unordered Lists (UL) bullet styles -->

<!ELEMENT UL - - (LI)+ -- unordered list -->
<!ATTLIST UL
  %attrs;                          -- %coreattrs, %i18n, %events --
  >



<!ELEMENT LI - O (%flow;)* -- list item -->
<!ATTLIST LI
  %attrs;                          -- %coreattrs, %i18n, %events --
  >


<!--=============== Forms ===================================================-->
<!ELEMENT FORM - - (%block;|SCRIPT)+ -(FORM) -- interactive form -->
<!ATTLIST FORM
  %attrs;                          -- %coreattrs, %i18n, %events --
  action       %URL;       #REQUIRED -- server-side form handler --
  method       (GET|POST) GET        -- HTTP method used to submit the form --
  enctype      %ContentType; "application/x-www-form-urlencoded"
  onsubmit     %Script;    #IMPLIED  -- the form was submitted --
  onreset      %Script;    #IMPLIED  -- the form was reset --
  target     %FrameTarget;   #IMPLIED -- render in this frame --
  accept-charset %Charsets; #IMPLIED -- list of supported charsets --
  >

<!-- Each label must not contain more than ONE field -->
<!ELEMENT LABEL - - (%inline;)* -(LABEL) -- form field label text -->
<!ATTLIST LABEL
```

```
    %attrs;                           -- %coreattrs, %i18n, %events --
    for         IDREF      #IMPLIED   -- matches field ID value --
    accesskey   %Character; #IMPLIED  -- accessibility key character --
    onfocus     %Script;   #IMPLIED   -- the element got the focus --
    onblur      %Script;   #IMPLIED   -- the element lost the focus --
    >


<!ENTITY % InputType
  "(TEXT | PASSWORD | CHECKBOX |
    RADIO | SUBMIT | RESET |
    FILE | HIDDEN | IMAGE | BUTTON)"
    >


<!-- attribute name required for all but submit & reset -->
<!ELEMENT INPUT - O EMPTY -- form control -->
<!ATTLIST INPUT
    %attrs;                           -- %coreattrs, %i18n, %events --
    type        %InputType; TEXT      -- what kind of widget is needed --
    name        CDATA      #IMPLIED   -- submit as part of form --
    value       CDATA      #IMPLIED   -- required for radio and checkboxes --
    checked     (checked)  #IMPLIED   -- for radio buttons and check boxes --
    disabled    (disabled) #IMPLIED   -- control is unavailable in this context --
    readonly    (readonly) #IMPLIED   -- for text and passwd --
    size        CDATA      #IMPLIED   -- specific to each type of field --
    maxlength   NUMBER     #IMPLIED   -- max chars for text fields --
    src         %URL;      #IMPLIED   -- for fields with images --
    alt         CDATA      #IMPLIED   -- short description --
    usemap      %URL;      #IMPLIED   -- use client-side image map --
    tabindex    NUMBER     #IMPLIED   -- position in tabbing order --
    accesskey   %Character; #IMPLIED  -- accessibility key character --
    onfocus     %Script;   #IMPLIED   -- the element got the focus --
    onblur      %Script;   #IMPLIED   -- the element lost the focus --
    onselect    %Script;   #IMPLIED   -- some text was selected --
    onchange    %Script;   #IMPLIED   -- the element value was changed --
    accept  %ContentTypes; #IMPLIED   -- list of MIME types for file upload --
    %reserved;                        -- reserved for possible future use --
    >

<!ELEMENT SELECT - - (OPTGROUP|OPTION)+ -- option selector -->
<!ATTLIST SELECT
    %attrs;                           -- %coreattrs, %i18n, %events --
    name        CDATA      #IMPLIED   -- field name --
    size        NUMBER     #IMPLIED   -- rows visible --
    multiple    (multiple) #IMPLIED   -- default is single selection --
    disabled       (disabled) #IMPLIED   -- control is unavailable in this
context --
    tabindex    NUMBER     #IMPLIED   -- position in tabbing order --
```

```
  onfocus     %Script;    #IMPLIED   -- the element got the focus --
  onblur      %Script;    #IMPLIED   -- the element lost the focus --
  onchange    %Script;    #IMPLIED   -- the element value was changed --
  %reserved;                         -- reserved for possible future use --
  >


<!ELEMENT OPTGROUP - - (OPTGROUP|OPTION)+ -- option group -->
<!ATTLIST OPTGROUP
  %attrs;                            -- %coreattrs, %i18n, %events --
  disabled    (disabled) #IMPLIED   -- control is unavailable in this context --
  label       %Text;     #REQUIRED  -- for use in hierarchical menus --
  >


<!ELEMENT OPTION - O (#PCDATA) -- selectable choice -->
<!ATTLIST OPTION
  %attrs;                            -- %coreattrs, %i18n, %events --
  selected    (selected) #IMPLIED
  disabled    (disabled) #IMPLIED   -- control is unavailable in this context --
  label       %Text;     #IMPLIED   -- for use in hierarchical menus --
  value       CDATA      #IMPLIED   -- defaults to element content --
  >


<!ELEMENT TEXTAREA - - (#PCDATA) -- multi-line text field -->
<!ATTLIST TEXTAREA
  %attrs;                            -- %coreattrs, %i18n, %events --
  name        CDATA      #IMPLIED
  rows        NUMBER     #REQUIRED
  cols        NUMBER     #REQUIRED
  disabled    (disabled) #IMPLIED   -- control is unavailable in this context --
  readonly    (readonly) #IMPLIED
  tabindex    NUMBER     #IMPLIED   -- position in tabbing order --
  onfocus     %Script;   #IMPLIED   -- the element got the focus --
  onblur      %Script;   #IMPLIED   -- the element lost the focus --
  onselect    %Script;   #IMPLIED   -- some text was selected --
  onchange    %Script;   #IMPLIED   -- the element value was changed --
  %reserved;                        -- reserved for possible future use --
  >


<!--
  #PCDATA is to solve the mixed content problem,
  per specification only whitespace is allowed there!
  -->
<!ELEMENT FIELDSET - - (#PCDATA,LEGEND,(%flow;)*) -- form control group -->
<!ATTLIST FIELDSET
  %attrs;                            -- %coreattrs, %i18n, %events --
  >
```

```
<!ELEMENT LEGEND - - (%inline;)* -- fieldset legend -->
<!ENTITY % LAlign "(top|bottom|left|right)">

<!ATTLIST LEGEND
  %attrs;                            -- %coreattrs, %i18n, %events --
  accesskey  %Character; #IMPLIED  -- accessibility key character --
  >


<!ELEMENT BUTTON - -
     (%flow;)* -(A|%formctrl;|FORM|FIELDSET)
     -- push button -->
<!ATTLIST BUTTON
  %attrs;                            -- %coreattrs, %i18n, %events --
  name       CDATA       #IMPLIED  -- for scripting/forms as submit button --
  value      CDATA       #IMPLIED  -- gets passed to server when submitted --
  type (button|submit|reset) submit -- for use as form submit/reset button --
  disabled    (disabled) #IMPLIED  -- control is unavailable in this context --
  tabindex   NUMBER      #IMPLIED  -- position in tabbing order --
  accesskey  %Character; #IMPLIED  -- accessibility key character --
  onfocus    %Script;    #IMPLIED  -- the element got the focus --
  onblur     %Script;    #IMPLIED  -- the element lost the focus --
  %reserved;                        -- reserved for possible future use --
  >


<!--======================= Tables ========================================-->

<!-- IETF HTML table standard, see [RFC1942] -->

<!--
 The BORDER attribute sets the thickness of the frame around the
 table. The default units are screen pixels.

 The FRAME attribute specifies which parts of the frame around
 the table should be rendered. The values are not the same as
 CALS to avoid a name clash with the VALIGN attribute.

 The value "border" is included for backwards compatibility with
 <TABLE BORDER> which yields frame=border and border=implied
 For <TABLE BORDER=1> you get border=1 and frame=implied. In this
 case, it is appropriate to treat this as frame=border for backwards
 compatibility with deployed browsers.
-->
<!ENTITY % TFrame "(void|above|below|hsides|lhs|rhs|vsides|box|border)">

<!--
 The RULES attribute defines which rules to draw between cells:
```

```
  If RULES is absent then assume:
      "none" if BORDER is absent or BORDER=0 otherwise "all"


-->


<!ENTITY % TRules "(none | groups | rows | cols | all)">


<!-- horizontal placement of table relative to document -->
<!ENTITY % TAlign "(left|center|right)">


<!-- horizontal alignment attributes for cell contents -->
<!ENTITY % cellhalign
  "align (left|center|right|justify|char) #IMPLIED
   char        %Character;   #IMPLIED -- alignment char, e.g. char=':' --
   charoff     %Length;      #IMPLIED -- offset for alignment char --"
  >


<!-- vertical alignment attributes for cell contents -->
<!ENTITY % cellvalign
  "valign (top|middle|bottom|baseline) #IMPLIED"
  >


<!ELEMENT TABLE - -
      (CAPTION?, (COL*|COLGROUP*), THEAD?, TFOOT?, TBODY+)>
<!ELEMENT CAPTION  - - (%inline;)* -- table caption -->
<!ELEMENT THEAD    - O (TR)+       -- table header -->
<!ELEMENT TFOOT    - O (TR)+       -- table footer -->
<!ELEMENT TBODY    O O (TR)+       -- table body -->
<!ELEMENT COLGROUP - O (col)*      -- table column group -->
<!ELEMENT COL      - O EMPTY       -- table column -->
<!ELEMENT TR       - O (TH|TD)+    -- table row -->
<!ELEMENT (TH|TD)  - O (%flow;)*   -- table header cell, table data cell -->


<!ATTLIST TABLE                    -- table element --
  %attrs;                          -- %coreattrs, %i18n, %events --
  summary     %Text;      #IMPLIED -- purpose/structure for speech output --
  width       %Pixels;    #IMPLIED -- table width relative to window --
  border      CDATA       #IMPLIED -- controls frame width around table --
  frame       %TFrame;    #IMPLIED -- which parts of table frame to include --
  rules       %TRules;    #IMPLIED -- rulings between rows and cols --
  cellspacing %Length;    #IMPLIED -- spacing between cells --
  cellpadding %Length;    #IMPLIED -- spacing within cells --
  %reserved;                       -- reserved for possible future use --
  >


<!ENTITY % CAlign "(top|bottom|left|right)">
```

```
<!ATTLIST CAPTION
  %attrs;                              -- %coreattrs, %i18n, %events --
  >


<!--
COLGROUP groups a set of COL elements. It allows you to group
several semantically related columns together.
-->
<!ATTLIST COLGROUP
  %attrs;                              -- %coreattrs, %i18n, %events --
  span         NUMBER     1            -- default number of columns in group --
  width        %MultiLength; #IMPLIED  -- default width for enclosed COLs --
  %cellhalign;                         -- horizontal alignment in cells --
  %cellvalign;                         -- vertical alignment in cells --
  >


<!--
COL elements define the alignment properties for cells in
one or more columns.

The WIDTH attribute specifies the width of the columns, e.g.

    width=64        width in screen pixels
    width=0.5*      relative width of 0.5

The REPEAT attribute allows you to repeat the effects of
a COL element as if the same element was repeated n times.
There are no grouping semantics for repeated columns.

-->
<!ATTLIST COL                   -- column groups and properties --
  %attrs;                              -- %coreattrs, %i18n, %events --
  repeat       NUMBER     1            -- repeat count for COL --
  width        %MultiLength; #IMPLIED  -- column width specification --
  %cellhalign;                         -- horizontal alignment in cells --
  %cellvalign;                         -- vertical alignment in cells --
  >


<!--
   Use THEAD to duplicate headers when breaking table
   across page boundaries, or for static headers when
   TBODY sections are rendered in scrolling panel.

   Use TFOOT to duplicate footers when breaking table
   across page boundaries, or for static footers when
   TBODY sections are rendered in scrolling panel.
```

```
      Use multiple TBODY sections when rules are needed
      between groups of table rows.

-->
<!ATTLIST (THEAD|TBODY|TFOOT)    -- table section --
  %attrs;                          -- %coreattrs, %i18n, %events --
  %cellhalign;                     -- horizontal alignment in cells --
  %cellvalign;                     -- vertical alignment in cells --
  >

<!ATTLIST TR                     -- table row --
  %attrs;                          -- %coreattrs, %i18n, %events --
  %cellhalign;                     -- horizontal alignment in cells --
  %cellvalign;                     -- vertical alignment in cells --
  >


<!-- Scope is simpler than axes attribute for common tables -->
<!ENTITY % Scope "(row|col|rowgroup|colgroup)">

<!-- TH is for headers, TD for data, but for cells acting as both use TD
-->
<!ATTLIST (TH|TD)                -- header or data cell --
  %attrs;                          -- %coreattrs, %i18n, %events --
  abbr       %Text;    #IMPLIED -- abbreviation for header cell --
  axis       CDATA     #IMPLIED -- names groups of related headers--
  headers    IDREFS    #IMPLIED -- list of id's for header cells --
  scope      %Scope;   #IMPLIED -- scope covered by header cells --
  rowspan    NUMBER    1        -- number of rows spanned by cell --
  colspan    NUMBER    1        -- number of cols spanned by cell --
  %cellhalign;                     -- horizontal alignment in cells --
  %cellvalign;                     -- vertical alignment in cells --
  >


<!--================= Document Head =========================================-->
<!-- %head.misc; defined earlier on as "SCRIPT | STYLE | META | LINK" -->
<!ENTITY % head.content "TITLE & BASE?">

<!ELEMENT HEAD O O (%head.content;) +(%head.misc;) -- document head -->
<!ATTLIST HEAD
  %i18n;                           -- lang, dir --
  profile    %URL;     #IMPLIED -- named dictionary of meta info --
  >

<!-- The TITLE element is not considered part of the flow of text.
     It should be displayed, for example as the page header or
```

```
        window title. Exactly one title is required per document.
   -->
<!ELEMENT TITLE - - (#PCDATA) -(%head.misc;) -- document title -->
<!ATTLIST TITLE %i18n>


<!ELEMENT BASE - O EMPTY -- document base URL -->
<!ATTLIST BASE
  href         %URL;       #IMPLIED  -- URL that acts as base URL --
  target    %FrameTarget;    #IMPLIED -- render in this frame --
  >

<!ELEMENT META - O EMPTY          -- generic metainformation -->
<!ATTLIST META
  %i18n;                           -- lang, dir, for use with content string --
  http-equiv  NAME       #IMPLIED  -- HTTP response header name   --
  name        NAME       #IMPLIED  -- metainformation name --
  content     CDATA      #REQUIRED -- associated information --
  scheme      CDATA      #IMPLIED  -- select form of content --
  >

<!ELEMENT STYLE - - CDATA       -- style info -->
<!ATTLIST STYLE
  %i18n;                           -- lang, dir, for use with title --
  type     %ContentType; #REQUIRED -- content type of style language --
  media     %MediaDesc;  #IMPLIED  -- designed for use with these media --
  title     %Text;       #IMPLIED  -- advisory title --
  >

<!ELEMENT SCRIPT - - CDATA       -- script statements -->
<!ATTLIST SCRIPT
  charset   %Charset;    #IMPLIED -- char encoding of linked resource --
  type      %ContentType; #REQUIRED -- content type of script language --
  language    CDATA      #IMPLIED -- predefined script language name --
  src        %URL;       #IMPLIED -- URL for an external script --
  defer      (defer)     #IMPLIED -- UA may defer execution of script --
  >

<!ELEMENT NOSCRIPT - - (%block;)+
  -- alternate content container for non script-based rendering -->
<!ATTLIST NOSCRIPT
  %attrs;                          -- %coreattrs, %i18n, %events --
  >
```

```
<!--=============== Document Structure ===================================-->
<!ENTITY % version "version CDATA #FIXED '%HTML.Version;'">


<!ENTITY % html.content "HEAD, BODY">

<!ELEMENT HTML O O (%html.content;) -- document root element -->
<!ATTLIST HTML
  %i18n;                             -- lang, dir --
  >
```

HTML 4.0 Frameset DTD

```
<!-->
    This is an EXPERIMENTAL version of the HTML 4.0 "frameset" DTD
    which differs from the normal DTD by the content of the HTML
    element. For frameset documents the FRAMESET element is used
    in place of the BODY element.

        Draft: $Date: 1997/09/16 12:26:34 $

        Authors:
            Dave Raggett <dsr@w3.org>
            Arnaud Le Hors <lehors@w3.org>

    This is work in progress, subject to change at any time.
    It does not imply endorsement by, or the consensus of,
    either W3C or members of the HTML working group. Further
    information about HTML 4.0 is available at:

        http://www.w3.org/TR/WD-html40/.

--
<!ENTITY % HTML.Version "-//W3C//DTD HTML 4.0 Frameset//EN"
  -- Typical usage:

    <!DOCTYPE HTML PUBLIC "-//W3C//DTD HTML 4.0 Frameset//EN">
    <html>
    <head>
    ...
    </head>
    <frameset>
    ...
    </frameset>
    </html>
```

```
--

<!ENTITY % HTML.Frameset "INCLUDE">
<!ENTITY % HTML4.dtd PUBLIC "-//W3C//DTD HTML 4.0 Transitional//EN">
%HTML4.dtd;
```

Index